1940–1990
Fifty Years of Scholarship

The JOURNAL of ECONOMIC HISTORY

VOLUME L MARCH 1990 NUMBER 1

PUBLISHED FOR
THE ECONOMIC HISTORY ASSOCIATION
IN COOPERATION WITH
RENSSELAER POLYTECHNIC INSTITUTE

CARTER AND SAVOCA
Labor Mobility and Lengthy Jobs in Nineteenth-Century America
HUMPHRIES
Enclosures, Common Rights, and Women
WHATLEY
Getting a Foot in the Door: the Racial Integration of Firms
GROSS
Israeli Economic Policies, 1948–1951
ROSENBLOOM
Labor Market Integration in the Late Nineteenth-Century United States
BLACK AND GILMORE
Crowding Out during Britain's Industrial Revolution
DAVIS AND PECQUET
Interest Rates in the Civil War South
HUNT
A New Look at the Dealings of the Bardi and Peruzzi with Edward III
NOTES AND DISCUSSION: PATTERSON AND REIFFEN
REVIEW ARTICLE: MOKYR AND NYE

CAMBRIDGE UNIVERSITY PRESS

THE JOURNAL OF ECONOMIC HISTORY

ISSN 0022-0507

Published for the Economic History Association in cooperation with Rensselaer Polytechnic Institute by Cambridge University Press

Aims and Scope: *The Journal of Economic History* seeks to promote the scholarly study of economic aspects of the human past from a diversity of perspectives, notably those of economists and historians. By encouraging careful formulation of issues and clear exposition of methods, the JOURNAL hopes to stimulate discourse among scholars with varied interests and modes of inquiry.

The JOURNAL is abstracted in *The Journal of Economic Literature,* which is part of the DIALOG on-line data service.

Instructions for Contributors: Articles on economic history and related aspects of history or economics will be considered for publication by the Editors on the understanding that the articles have not previously been published and are not under consideration elsewhere. Papers should indicate the wider significance of detailed original research findings as well as the logic and limitations of specialized techniques of analysis. Comments and shorter notes are also welcome. The JOURNAL does not accept unsolicited book reviews, nor can it honor requests to review particular works. Contributions should be typed double-spaced. Footnotes, also double-spaced, should be grouped at the end of the paper, along with figures and tables. Four copies of each manuscript should be submitted. Prospective contributors may obtain a copy of the Style Sheet for the JOURNAL from the Editorial Office. A submission fee of $20.00 or a year's membership (fee schedule below) is required from nonmembers of the Association.

Editorial Office Address: The Editors, *The Journal of Economic History,* Folsom Library, Rensselaer Polytechnic Institute, Troy, NY 12180-3590, U.S.A. Telephone: (518) 276-2784.

Association Office Address and Membership Information: Individuals who are members of the Economic History Association receive the JOURNAL as part of their annual dues. Membership rates (in U.S. dollars) are: $30.00 for those with income above $30,000 a year; $25.00 for those with income below $30,000; $15.00 for students and professors emeriti who have been members of the Association for 10 years; $600.00 for life membership. Payment of an *additional* $20.00 permits joint membership with the Economic History Society (UK). Applications and inquiries concerning membership should be addressed to the Economic History Association, Dept. of History, George Washington University, Washington, DC 20052, U.S.A.

Subscription, Publishing and Advertising Office Address: Cambridge University Press, 40 West 20th Street, New York, NY 10011, U.S.A.; or Cambridge University Press, The Edinburgh Building, Shaftesbury Road, Cambridge CB2 2RU, England.

Subscription Information: *The Journal of Economic History* is published quarterly in March, June, September, and December. Annual institutional subscription rate (1990) US $50.00 in the United States and Canada; UK £31.00 elsewhere. Individuals may subscribe by becoming a member of the Economic History Association (see above). Prices include surface postage and insurance.

The Journal of Economic History (USPS 279-580) is published quarterly by Cambridge University Press. Second-class postage paid at New York, NY and additional mailing offices. Postmaster: Send address changes to *The Journal of Economic History*, Cambridge University Press, 110 Midland Avenue, Port Chester, NY 10573.

Printed in the United States of America.

THE JOURNAL
OF ECONOMIC HISTORY

Volume L *March 1990* *Number 1*

ARTICLES

SUSAN B. CARTER AND ELIZABETH SAVOCA
Labor Mobility and Lengthy Jobs in Nineteenth-Century America 1

JANE HUMPHRIES
Enclosures, Common Rights, and Women: The Proletarianization of Families in the Late Eighteenth and Early Nineteenth Centuries 17

WARREN C. WHATLEY
Getting a Foot in the Door: "Learning," State Dependence, and the Racial Integration of Firms 43

NACHUM T. GROSS
Israeli Economic Policies, 1948–1951: Problems of Evaluation 67

JOSHUA L. ROSENBLOOM
One Market or Many? Labor Market Integration in the Late Nineteenth-Century United States 85

ROBERT A. BLACK AND CLAIRE G. GILMORE
Crowding Out during Britain's Industrial Revolution 109

GEORGE K. DAVIS AND GARY M. PECQUET
Interest Rates in the Civil War South 133

EDWIN S. HUNT
A New Look at the Dealings of the Bardi and Peruzzi with Edward III 149

NOTES AND DISCUSSION

MARGARET PATTERSON AND DAVID REIFFEN
The Effect of the Bubble Act on the Market for Joint Stock Shares 163

REVIEW ARTICLE

JOEL MOKYR AND JOHN V. C. NYE
La Grande Quantification 172

EDITORS' NOTES 177

REVIEWS OF BOOKS

ANCIENT, MEDIEVAL, AND EARLY MODERN

GIBSON AND GESELOWITZ, Eds. *Tribe and Polity in Late Prehistoric Europe: Demography, Production and Exchange in the Evolution of Complex Social Systems*	A. H. Goodman	182
WALTER AND SCHOFIELD, Eds. *Famine, Disease and the Social Order in Early Modern Society*	M. K. Matossian	183
BIDDICK. *The Other Economy: Pastoral Husbandry on a Medieval Estate*	R. C. Stacey	184
PRYOR. *Geography, Technology, and War: Studies in the Maritime History of the Mediterranean, 649–1571*	J. E. Dotson	186
KELLENBENZ AND PRODI, Eds. *Fisco religione Stato nell'età confessionale*	A. Molho	187
SWAIN. *Industry before the Industrial Revolution: North-East Lancashire, c. 1500–1640*	J. S. Lyons	189
COLLINS. *Fiscal Limits of Absolutism: Direct Taxation in Early Seventeenth-Century France*	M. P. Holt	191
ISRAEL. *European Jewry in the Age of Mercantilism, 1550–1750*	C. R. Friedrichs	192

MODERN EUROPE

GOODMAN AND HONEYMAN. *Gainful Pursuits: The Making of Industrial Europe, 1600–1914*	H. Freudenberger	194
BRULAND. *British Technology and European Industrialization: The Norwegian Textile Industry in the Mid Nineteenth Century*	J. V. Nye	194
WOOD. *West Cumberland Coal, 1600–1982/3*	D. Levine	196
BERESFORD. *East End, West End: The Face of Leeds During Urbanisation, 1684–1842*	R. Fishman	197
JONES. *Trade and Shipping, Lord Inchcape, 1852–1932*	M. Huberman	198
ACCAMPO. *Industrialization, Family Life, and Class Relations: Saint Chamond, 1815–1914*	J. R. Lehning	199
L'Electricité et ses consommateurs	R. L. Frost	200
ALTER. *Family and the Female Life Course: The Women of Verviers, Belgium, 1849–1880*	N. Fitch	202
KINDLEBERGER. *The German Economy, 1945–1947: Charles P. Kindleberger's Letters From the Field*	A. S. Milward	203

AFRICA, ASIA, AUSTRALIA

ILIFFE. *The African Poor: A History*	P. Manning	204
LAL. *The Hindu Equilibrium*. Vol. 1: *Cultural Stability and Economic Stagnation*. Vol. 2: *Aspects of Indian Labour*	G. Rosen	206
FITZGERALD. *Rising Damp: Sydney, 1870–90*	J. C. Brown	208
BUCKLEY AND WHEELWRIGHT. *No Paradise for Workers: Capitalism and the Common People in Australia, 1788–1914*	F. D. Lewis	209

LATIN AMERICA

GUTIÉRREZ BROCKINGTON. *The Leverage of Labor: Managing the Cortés Haciendas in Tehuantepec, 1588–1688*	J. F. Schwaller	211
SOLOW AND ENGERMAN, Eds. *British Capitalism and Caribbean Slavery: The Legacy of Eric Williams*	R. R. Menard	212
HABER. *Industry and Underdevelopment: The Industrialization of Mexico, 1890–1940*	S. Topik	213

UNITED STATES AND CANADA

TRUXES. *Irish-American Trade, 1660–1783*	E. J. Perkins	214
WILSON AND FERRIS, Eds. *Encyclopedia of Southern Culture*	G. Wright	215
SPANN. *Brotherly Tomorrows: Movements for a Cooperative Society in America, 1820–1920*	M. S. Snow	217
ORSER. *The Material Basis of the Postbellum Tenant Plantation: Historical Archaeology in the South Carolina Piedmont*	L. J. Alston	219
RASMUSSEN. *Taking the University to the People: Seventy-five Years of Cooperative Extension*	R. C. Graham	220
STEEL, Ed. *The Speeches and Writings of Mother Jones*	A. Schofield	221
BRYANT, Ed. *Encyclopedia of American Business History and Biography: Railroads in the Age of Regulation, 1900–1980*	T. S. Ulen	222
HOUNSHELL AND SMITH. *Science and Corporate Strategy: Du Pont Research and Development, 1902–1980*	J. A. Heitmann	223
GOLDBERG. *A Tale of Three Cities: Labor Organization and Protest in Paterson, Passaic, and Lawrence, 1916–1921*	H. M. Gitelman	225
LUTTRELL. *The High Cost of Farm Welfare*	F. M. Howland	226
DARITY, Ed. *Race, Radicalism, and Reform: Selected Papers of Abram L. Harris*	M. E. Cookingham	227
FELTON AND ANDERSON, Eds. *Regulation and Deregulation of the Motor Carrier Industry*	W. R. Childs	228
PHELAN. *William Green: A Biography of a Labor Leader*	B. A. Rubin	229
KIMELDORF. *Reds or Rackets? The Making of Radical and Conservative Unions on the Waterfront*	M. Isserman	231
CLINGERMAN. *Field Man: The Chronicle of a Bank Farm Manager in the 1940s*	R. Lambert	232
FINK AND GREENBERG. *Upheaval in the Quiet Zone: A History of Hospital Workers' Union, Local 1199*	E. P. Duggan	233
MORONE AND WOODHOUSE. *The Demise of Nuclear Power? Lessons for Democratic Control of Technology*	R. Cowan	234
LITAN, LAWRENCE, AND SCHULTZE, Eds. *American Living Standards: Threats and Challenges*	E. Smolensky	236
FABRITIUS AND BORGES. *Saving the Savings and Loan: The U.S. Thrift Industry and the Texas Experience, 1950–1988*	D. Graddy	237
EICHLER. *The Thrift Debacle*	D. Graddy	237

ECONOMIC THOUGHT

DEANE. *The State and the Economic System: An Introduction to the History of Political Economy*	A. J. Cohen	240

Backhouse. *Economists and the Economy: The Evolution of Economic Ideas, 1600 to the Present Day* — D. Colander 241
Neufeldt. *The Economist: Henry Thoreau and Enterprise* — L. Buell 242
Clarke. *The Keynesian Revolution in the Making, 1924–1936* — D. Dillard 243
Meltzer. *Keynes's Monetary Theory: A Different Interpretation* — R. C. Schiming 244
Schumpeter. *Essays and Entrepreneurs: Innovations, Business Cycles and the Evolution of Capitalism* — M. I. Kamien 246
Mirowski. *Against Mechanism: Protecting Economics from Science* — A. J. Field 247
McCraw, Ed. *The Essential Alfred Chandler: Essays toward a Historical Theory of Big Business* — M. Yeager 250

GENERAL AND MISCELLANEOUS

Mayntz and Hughes, Eds. *The Development of Large Technical Systems* — K. Lipartito 252
Brown. *Egalitarianism and the Generation of Inequality* — S. Lebergott 254
Tarr and Dupuy, Eds. *Technology and the Rise of the Networked City in Europe and America* — J. C. Brown 255
Pohl and Treue, Eds. *The Concentration Process in the Entrepreneurial Economy Since the Late Nineteenth Century* — J. M. MacDonald 257
Brown. *The Flight of International Capital: A Contemporary History* — F. Capie 258
Bordo, Ed. *Money, History and International Finance: Essays in Honor of Anna J. Schwartz* — B. Eichengreen 259
Currie and Vines, Eds. *Macroeconomic Interactions between North and South* — J. R. Hanson 260
Rosen, Ed. *Fiscal Federalism: Quantitative Studies* — J. B. Legler 261
A Note of Technical Correction — I. Adelman and C. T. Morris 262

THE JOURNAL OF ECONOMIC HISTORY

VOLUME L MARCH 1990 NUMBER 1

Labor Mobility and Lengthy Jobs in Nineteenth-Century America

SUSAN B. CARTER AND ELIZABETH SAVOCA

Extensive amounts of geographic mobility and high rates of labor turnover before World War I gave rise to the notion that the industrial labor force was "casual" and "impermanent." But data from firms' payrolls and from nineteenth-century surveys conducted by state labor statistics bureaus show that male workers averaged about four years of experience in their current jobs. Data from an 1892 survey of San Francisco workers show that the average non-union male could expect to remain with his current employer almost 13 years.

The American labor market's provision of "stable, near-lifetime employment to an important fraction of the labor force" is thought to be a post-World War I development.[1] Prior to that time, the "drive system" of labor management, workers' allegiance to nonindustrial

The Journal of Economic History, Vol. L, No. 1 (Mar. 1990). ISSN 0022-0507.

Susan B. Carter is Associate Professor of Economics, Smith College, Northampton, MA 01063. Elizabeth Savoca is Assistant Professor of Economics, Smith College, Northampton, MA 01063 and Fellow, Institution for Social and Policy Studies, Yale University, New Haven, CT 06520.

Participants in economic history workshops at the University of Massachusetts at Amherst; Harvard University; the University of California at Berkeley, Davis, Riverside, and Santa Cruz; Stanford University; and the California Institute of Technology and at the Econometrics Society meeting made valuable comments on early drafts. The research was funded, in part, by the National Science Foundation and by the Picker Fellowship Fund at Smith College. The data in this project were made available by the University of California's History of Saving Project. The processing of the original published data into a computerized format was supervised by Roger L. Ransom, Richard Sutch, and Charles Wetherell. Financial support for this work has been provided by the National Science Foundation and the University of California. The data are archived at the Laboratory for Historical Research at the University of California at Riverside. We gratefully acknowledge the support of Ransom and Sutch, who made these data available to us. Errors are our responsibility.

[1] The quotation is from Robert E. Hall, "The Importance of Lifetime Jobs in the U.S. Economy," *American Economic Review*, 72 (Sept. 1982), p. 716. On dating the transition to stable, lengthy employment spells, see Arthur M. Ross, "Do We Have a New Industrial Feudalism?" *American Economic Review*, 48 (Dec. 1958), pp. 903–20; Jeffrey Sachs, "The Changing Cyclical Behavior of Wages and Prices: 1890–1976," *American Economic Review*, 70 (Mar. 1980), pp. 78–90; Sanford M. Jacoby, *Employing Bureaucracy: Managers, Unions, and the Transformation of Work in American Industry, 1900–1945* (New York, 1985); and J. Bradford De Long and Lawrence H. Summers, "The Changing Cyclical Variability of Economic Activity in the United States," in Robert J. Gordon, ed., *The American Business Cycle: Continuity and Change* (Chicago, 1986), pp. 679–734.

work cultures, the limited power of unions, and rapid shifts in the geographic locus of opportunity are thought to have meant brief job spells for most workers.[2]

The brevity of jobs has been inferred, in part, from apparently high rates of geographic mobility. Stephan Thernstrom's calculations that in the mid-nineteenth century as few as 35 percent of unskilled laborers remained in Newburyport, MA, for as long as a decade led him to conclude:

> Contemporary observers were correct in characterizing the new working class as floating. For a majority of these permanent transients, Newburyport provided no soil in which to sink roots. It was only one more place in which to carry on the struggle for existence for a few years, until driven onward again.[3]

The seemingly sensitive responsiveness of the American labor force to interregional wage differentials is consistent with this view. As Richard Easterlin shows, the magnitude and direction of labor mobility was "such as to significantly alter the relative rates of growth of labor supply in the various regions in a direction that, other things being equal, would have made for convergence of relative income levels."[4] Adjustments were not instantaneous, of course, and industrialization, land augmentation, and foreign immigration were constantly shifting the locus of relative opportunity. What seems to have been special about the American case is that disequilibrium appears to have been due to rapid shifts in opportunity rather than to workers' reluctance to respond.[5] Worker responsiveness seemed so obvious that, except for native-born females in the Northeast and for the special case of the

[2] See Daniel Nelson, *Managers and Workers: Origins of the New Factory System in the United States, 1880–1920* (Madison, 1975); Jacoby, *Employing Bureaucracy*; Alexander Keyssar, *Out of Work: The First Century of Unemployment in Massachusetts* (Cambridge, MA, 1986); Herbert G. Gutman, *Work, Culture and Society in Industrializing America* (New York, 1977); and Eric H. Monkkonen, ed., *Walking to Work* (Lincoln, NE, 1984).

[3] Stephan Thernstrom, *Poverty and Progress: Social Mobility in a Nineteenth Century City* (Cambridge, MA, 1975), p. 85.

[4] Richard Easterlin, "Regional Growth of Income: Long Term Tendencies," in *Population Redistribution and Economic Growth: United States, 1870–1950*, vol. 2 (Philadelphia, 1960), pp. 141–204. For other evidence of labor market integration, see Stanley Lebergott, *Manpower in Economic Growth* (New York, 1964); Robert A. Margo and Georgia C. Villaflor, "The Growth of Wages in Antebellum America: New Evidence," this JOURNAL, 47 (Dec. 1987), pp. 873–95; Winifred B. Rothenberg, "The Emergence of Farm Labor Markets and the Transformation of the Rural Economy: Massachusetts, 1750–1855," this JOURNAL, 48 (Sept. 1988), pp. 537–66; and Joshua L. Rosenbloom, "Labor Market Institutions and the Geographic Integration of Labor Markets in the Late Nineteenth Century United States" (Ph.D. diss., Stanford University, 1988).

[5] See Jeffrey G. Williamson, "Did British Labor Markets Fail During the Industrial Revolution?" (Harvard Institute for Economic Research, Discussion Paper No. 1209, Feb. 1986), for a discussion of the literature on labor market failure.

South, no literature on American labor market failure has appeared.[6] The apparent willingness of workers to respond to better opportunities, even when it meant moving to another part of the country, prompted Sanford Jacoby to write: "Extensive mobility during these years [1830 through 1920] was an indicator of the tenuousness of the employment relationship and the fluidity of the labor market."[7]

Data on quit rates and job tenure seem to support this view. An annual series on average monthly quit rates assembled by Arthur Ross shows quit rates in excess of 100 percent per year in the 1910s. The dramatic drop in this series in the mid-1920s has been widely interpreted as indicating the appearance of stability in the employment relation, the appearance of a "New Industrial Feudalism."[8] Measures of average work experience at a point in time have also been interpreted as evidence of tenuous job attachment.[9] Caroline Ware, for example, concluded that the mid-nineteenth-century cotton textile labor force "was at best a very impermanent working group." Her evidence is "statistics compiled from eight Lowell mills in 1845 [which] showed that twenty-five per cent of the girls had been in the mills for less than one year, fifty per cent less than three years."[10]

This article, a re-evaluation of the evidence on job tenure in nineteenth-century America, is motivated by the recent interest of macroeconomists in the nature of employment relations prior to World War I. New evidence of striking differences in the cyclical behavior of the economy over time have sparked investigations of long-term changes in the employment relation, to which job tenure provides an important clue. Brief jobs suggest a perfectly competitive market which clears rapidly as workers respond readily to wage disparities. Lengthy jobs suggest explicit or implicit contracts which lead to relatively sluggish wage responses to varying market conditions. Long-term jobs are also consistent with models which stress the importance of community

[6] See Gavin Wright, *Old South, New South: Revolutions in the Southern Economy Since the Civil War* (New York, 1986), on the failure of the southern labor market. See Alexander James Field, "Sectoral Shift in Antebellum Massachusetts: A Reconsideration," *Explorations in Economic History*, 15 (Apr. 1978), pp. 146–71, on the female labor market in the antebellum Northeast.

[7] Jacoby, *Employing Bureaucracy*, pp. 36–37.

[8] Ross, "New Industrial Feudalism," p. 911.

[9] Jacoby, *Employing Bureaucracy*, provides a good summary of this evidence. Susan B. Carter, "The Changing Importance of Lifetime Jobs, 1892–1978," *Industrial Relations*, 27 (Fall 1988), pp. 287–300, shows that lengthy employment spells were more common in the 1890s than case study evidence seems to indicate. Michael J. Carter and Susan B. Carter, "Internal Labor Markets in Retailing: The Early Years," *Industrial and Labor Relations Review*, 38 (July 1985), pp. 586–98; and William A. Sundstrom, "Internal Labor Markets before World War I: On-the-Job Training and Employee Promotion," *Explorations in Economic History*, 25 (Oct. 1988), pp. 424–45, present evidence of internal labor markets prior to the 1920s.

[10] Caroline Ware, *The Early New England Cotton Manufacture: A Study of Industrial Beginnings* (Boston, 1931), p. 224.

notions of "fairness" or reputation in limiting the downward movement of wages, thus leading to involuntary unemployment.[11]

MOBILITY VERSUS JOB TENURE

In their seminal piece on the nature of unemployment in the 1970s, Kim Clark and Lawrence Summers found that while the average unemployment spell is short, most unemployment is concentrated in lengthy spells. Similarly, Robert Hall finds that while the "typical job is extremely brief," most employment is concentrated in near-lifetime jobs.[12] This seemingly contradictory finding can be explained by reference to demographers' distinction between life expectancy at birth and life expectancy of the average person. Although turnover among newly hired workers (infant mortality) is high and the average job (life expectancy at birth) may be brief, the job of the average worker (life expectancy of the population) is lengthy.

This point was recognized when twentieth-century quit rate data were first analyzed. Writing in 1919 Sumner Slichter noted: "A turnover rate of 100 percent may be caused by every position in the establishment being vacated once a year, or by one-tenth of the positions being vacated ten times a year, . . ." For the second decade of the twentieth century Slichter felt that "the high turnover rate in most plants is due to a few men changing rapidly while the great majority of the force is stable."[13]

Gavin Wright also found a stable labor force in the southern textile mills in this era:

> Employers complained endlessly about 'the moving disposition of mill people,'. . . . [and] [e]xtremely high turnover rates are often quoted for the southern textile industry, with the implication that the labor force was highly unstable and migratory. But most of this turnover was concentrated in a minority of families

[11] Sachs, "The Changing Cyclical Behavior of Wages and Prices," pp. 78–90; Robert J. Gordon, "A Century of Evidence on Wage and Price Stickiness in the United States, the United Kingdom, and Japan," in James Tobin, ed., *Macroeconomics, Prices, and Quantities* (Washington, DC, 1983), pp. 85–120; and De Long and Summers, "Changing Cyclical Variability," pp. 679–734. For a model of the effect of community standards of "fairness" on wage flexibility, see George A. Akerlof, "A Theory of Social Custom, of Which Unemployment May Be One Consequence," *The Quarterly Journal of Economics*, 94 (June 1980), pp. 749–75.

[12] Kim Clark and Lawrence Summers, "Labor Market Dynamics and Unemployment: A Reconsideration," *Brookings Papers on Economic Activity*, 1 (1979), pp. 13–60; and Hall, "The Importance of Lifetime Jobs," p. 716. See also George A. Akerlof and Brian G. M. Main, "An Experience-Weighted Measure of Employment and Unemployment Durations," *American Economic Review*, 71 (Dec. 1981), p. 1003.

[13] Sumner Slichter, *The Turnover of Factory Labor* (New York, 1919), p. 43.

and unattached individuals who moved often, while the core of the labor force for a typical mill came from a group of families who were more-or-less permanent.[14]

Recognition of the distinction between the length of the average job and the average length of job spells currently in progress suggests that Thernstrom's low geographic persistence estimates may not necessarily indicate unstable job attachment. His lowest decadal persistence rate of 35 percent implies that the average resident remained for roughly 10 years.[15] Since recent work argues that persistence rates were considerably greater than Thernstrom's estimates, the geographic mobility of nineteenth-century American workers need not imply that their job spells were brief.[16] For example, a 50 percent persistence rate would imply average residence of 15 years.

Job tenure statistics from nineteenth-century payrolls and surveys provide more direct evidence that the average duration of completed employment spells was lengthy. Table 1 reports evidence on tenure with a firm from a variety of industry studies and from surveys conducted by state bureaus of labor statistics in the late nineteenth century. The average job tenure of manufacturing, mining, professional, technical, clerical, and service workers from the earliest years of the industrial revolution to the eve of World War I are included among the surveys. Except for cotton textile workers at the Hamilton and Alamance mills in the years just after these mills commenced operations, the evidence indicates average job tenure of three or more years.

Moreover, these data on the average length of the current job spell underestimate the length of a completed tenure. In a steady state, where a survey is equally likely to occur at any point during a job in progress, tenure to date is on average half as long as a completed spell. Thus the

[14] Wright, *Old South, New South*, p. 140.

[15] The estimate of average length of residence of 10 years was computed by assuming that the average residence of the 65 percent of unskilled laborers who had left Newburyport by the end of the decade was five years; assuming that the remaining 35 percent of laborers would leave in the following decade after an average residence of 15 years and so forth. This exercise implies that the average resident stayed 10.38 years.

[16] A number of recent investigations suggest that Thernstrom's estimates overstate the extent of geographic mobility. Donald Parkerson concludes that "the record-linkage process itself has been responsible for a significant underestimation of nineteenth-century persistence." See Donald H. Parkerson, "How Mobile Were Nineteenth-Century Americans?" *Historical Methods*, 15 (Summer 1982), p. 105. Morgan Kousser, Gary Cox, and David Galenson find, not a "floating proletariat," but rather a "youthful mobility, comparatively settled middle age, and the accumulation of human and physical capital over the lifecycle." See J. Morgan Kousser, Gary W. Cox, and David W. Galenson, "Log-Linear Analysis of Contingency Tables," *Historical Methods*, 15 (Fall 1982), p. 164. See also David W. Galenson and Daniel S. Levy, "A Note on Biases in the Measurement of Geographic Persistence Rates," *Historical Methods*, 19 (Fall 1986), pp. 171–79; and Avery M. Guest, "Notes from the National Panel Study: Linkage and Migration in the Late Nineteenth Century," *Historical Methods*, 20 (Spring 1987), p. 76.

TABLE 1
EVIDENCE ON YEARS WITH PRESENT EMPLOYER:
NINETEENTH- AND TWENTIETH-CENTURY SOURCES

Year	Employees	Number of Years Tenure with Firm to Date
1836	Textile workers, Hamilton Mill (1825)	
	Native-born males[1]	2.2
	Native-born females[1]	1.8
1845	Textile mill operatives, females, eight Lowell mills[2]	3.7
1860	Textile workers, Hamilton Mill	
	Native-born males[3]	6.9
	Native-born females[3]	3.7
1878	Ohio, 182 male wage earners, various occupations[4]	5.7
1879	Teachers, San Francisco public school system: males[5]	6.9
	females[5]	6.6
1888	Fire clay industry, Michigan, males[6]	4.6
1888	Gypsum industry, Michigan, males[6]	3.7
1888	Grindstone industry, Michigan, males[6]	3.9
1889	Furniture workers, Michigan, males[7]	3.0
1892	San Francisco: males[8]	3.9
	females[8]	2.4
1893	New Hampshire, males[9]	3.7
1890–1912	Cotton textile operatives, Alamance Mill, Alamance County, NC[10]	
	1890	2.7
	1900	7.0
	1910	9.7
	1912	10.3

Sources: [1] Thomas Dublin, *Women at Work: The Transformation of Work and Community in Lowell, Massachusetts, 1826–1860* (New York, 1979), p. 189. [2] Henry A. Miles, *Lowell as It Was and as It Is* (2nd edn., Lowell, 1847), pp. 162–94, cited in Caroline Ware, *Early New England Cotton Manufacture* (Boston, 1931), p. 224. [3] Dublin, *Women at Work*, p. 189. [4] Ohio Bureau of Labor Statistics, *Third Annual Report 1879* (Columbus, 1880). [5] San Francisco Superintendent of Public Schools, *Report of the Superintendent of Common Schools 1879*, cited in Myra H. Strober and Laura Best, "The Female/Male Salary Differential in Public Schools: Some Lessons from San Francisco, 1879," *Economic Inquiry*, 17 (Apr. 1979), pp. 218–36. [6] Michigan Bureau of Labor and Industrial Statistics, *Sixth Annual Report* (Lansing, 1888). [7] Michigan Bureau of Labor and Industrial Statistics, *Seventh Annual Report* (Lansing, 1890). Means from Roger L. Ransom and Richard Sutch, "Codebook: A Sample of Male Workers from the Furniture Industry in Michigan, 1889" (University of California Project on the History of Saving, Mar. 14, 1989). [8] California Bureau of Labor Statistics, *Fifth Biennial Report* (Sacramento, 1893). [9] New Hampshire Bureau of Labor, *Second Annual Report 1894,* "Wage-Earners' Statistics" (Concord, 1894). [10] Cathy L. McHugh, *Mill Family: The Labor System in the Southern Cotton Textile Industry, 1880–1915* (New York, 1988), p. 23.

figures in Table 1 suggest that the average job in the nineteenth century lasted about eight years. Ware's data imply that the female cotton textile operatives were employed for an average of 7.5 years. Female school teachers, whose brief job tenure is legendary, are shown to have stayed with their employers for over 13 years.[17] While these spells are less than the 18 years estimated for male workers in the modern labor force, they are far lengthier than the terms "casual" and "impermanent" lead one to expect.[18]

We are able to present a more systematic account of job duration and make more explicit comparisons between the nineteenth-century experience and that in the modern labor market. Using job tenure data from a sample of non-union male workers employed in San Francisco in 1892, we estimate a continuous time model of job duration. This approach allows us to weigh the effects of personal and industry characteristics on job duration and to calculate the effects of these variables on the expected length of time a worker will remain on his current job. A comparison of our estimates with those found in modern data sets gives us some insights into behavioral changes in turnover which may have occurred over time.

Our data comes from a survey of workers conducted by the California Bureau of Labor Statistics in San Francisco in 1892.[19] For each worker in the sample, information on a range of personal characteristics including gender, age, nativity, union membership, industry and occupation, work experience, and wage was reported. Interviewed workers were drawn largely from the manufacturing sector of the San Francisco economy although, as entrepôt for the Pacific Coast and as the center for the coastal trade from Alaska to Panama, over a fourth of the San Francisco labor force was employed in trade and transportation and over a third in the professional, domestic, and service sectors.[20] The distribution of the manufacturing sample across industries is too heavily weighted toward light manufacturing when compared with manufacturing in San Francisco and in the United States as a whole, although the relatively capital-intensive breweries, iron works, and shoe factories are represented. Because descriptive literature suggests that in this period the conditions which generated the tenure patterns of females and of union members differed substantially from those of non-union males, we exclude females and union members from this analysis.[21]

[17] For discussions of turnover and careers of nineteenth-century female school teachers, see Willard S. Elsbree, *The American Teacher: Evolution of a Profession in a Democracy* (New York, 1939), pp. 293–95; Richard M. Bernard and Maris A. Vinovskis, "The Female School Teacher in Antebellum America," *Journal of Social History*, 10 (Mar. 1977), pp. 332–45; and Susan B. Carter and Elizabeth Savoca, "Teacher Turnover, Teacher Tenure: Tales Out of Iowa School Data, 1884" (paper presented at the Social Science History Association Meetings, Nov. 1989).

[18] The 18-year estimate for the modern era is from Akerlof and Main, "An Experience-Weighted Measure." It is an average across all sectors.

[19] California Bureau of Labor Statistics, *Fifth Biennial Report* (Sacramento, 1893). The report contains no explicit discussion of how the data were collected.

[20] William Issel and Robert W. Cherney, *San Francisco, 1865–1932: Politics, Power and Urban Development* (Berkeley, 1986), p. 54.

[21] See Monkkonen, ed., *Walking to Work*; and Claudia Goldin, "Monitoring Costs and Occupational Segregation by Gender," *Journal of Labor Economics*, 1 (Jan. 1986), pp. 1–27. The

TABLE 2
NON-UNION MALES, SAN FRANCISCO 1892:
MEANS AND STANDARD DEVIATIONS OF VARIABLES

	Mean	Standard Deviation
Worker Characteristics		
TENURE WITH FIRM	4.411	5.044
SCHOOL	8.554	2.319
SINGLE	0.624	0.484
DEPENDENTS	1.124	1.742
HOME OWNER	0.104	0.306
AGE	29.551	11.750
PROPORTION TAILORS	0.018	0.133
PROPORTION IN BREWERIES	0.046	0.021
Industry Characteristics		
CAPITAL-LABOR RATIO	2.739	1.881
EMPLOYMENT GROWTH	1.044	0.475

Notes: *N* is equal to 1,158. The capital-labor ratio is measured in thousands of dollars per worker. The employment growth is the ratio of employment in 1900 to that in 1890.
Sources: California Bureau of Labor Statistics, *Fifth Biennial Report* (Sacramento, 1893); and U.S. Department of the Interior, Bureau of the Census, *Report on Manufacturing Industries in the United States at the Eleventh Census: 1890* (Washington, DC, 1895), vol. 6, part 2, "Statistics of Cities."

Means and standard deviations of the variables used in our analysis are reported in Table 2 for non-union men. The variable "Years Engaged, Present Employer," which we label *TENURE WITH FIRM*, provides the information on job tenure.[22] These sample data have been supplemented by evidence on the average firm characteristics for the industry in which each worker is employed.[23] Thus we know, for instance, the average capital-labor ratio of firms in the industry but not the capital-labor ratio in the firm in which the worker was actually employed.

THE MODEL AND FINDINGS

We use these data to estimate a continuous time model of job duration. In this model the population distribution of completed job

exclusion of union males only marginally affects the representativeness of our sample since unionized males comprised less than 5 percent of the labor force. See Gerald Friedman, "Politics and Union Growth: Unions and the Labor Movement in France and the United States" (Ph.D. diss., Harvard University, 1985). Analysis of women's job tenure awaits further research.

[22] Workers in this era experienced substantial periods of seasonal unemployment. We do not know if they deducted these from the length of job tenure to date which they report. In any case the point is irrelevant, as our interest is in the elapsed time since the initiation of the employment relation. Some of the other variables in Table 2 also require discussion. What we label *SCHOOL* is computed in the standard way, subtracting from "Age began Work" the number six to reflect the typical school entry age. We excluded workers for which this procedure yielded implausibly high levels of schooling, in the range of 15 to 20 years.

[23] Susan B. Carter, et al., "Codebook and User's Manual: A Survey of 3,493 Workers in California, 1892" (Historical Labor Statistics Project, University of California, 1989).

spells is completely characterized by the hazard rate, $h(t)$, which represents the probability that a worker will leave his job in time, $t + dt$, given that he has remained on the job for t periods.

We assume a proportional hazard function of the form:

$$h(t) = \tau \alpha t^{\alpha - 1} \tag{1}$$

where $\tau = \exp(Z\beta)$, Z is a vector of exogenous variables that influence the worker's and firm's decisions to terminate employment, and α and β are unknown parameters. This specification allows the probability of leaving the job to vary with time on the job. If $\alpha > 1$, then the model exhibits positive duration dependence, that is, the probability of leaving rises with time employed; if $\alpha < 1$, then the probability of leaving declines with time employed; while $\alpha = 1$ implies no duration dependence. Details on the estimation of the model are contained in the Appendix.[24]

Table 3 presents estimates of the hazard rate for the non-unionized male work force.[25] *SINGLE*, *HOME OWNER*, and *DEPENDENTS* refer to the worker's situation at the time of the survey while *AGE* and *SCHOOL* are measured as of the start of the current job.

Some historians argue that job separation was far less predictable in the nineteenth century than today. On the labor supply side, nonindustrial work cultures emanating from the artisanal activity and home production to which wage work was subordinate are thought to have set such a high value on independence that they discouraged some individuals from pursuing monetary goals. Phyllis Williams found that some immigrants simply "never adjusted to factory labor. After 'years' of 'excellent' factory work, some 'began . . . to have minor accidents' and others 'suddenly give up and are found in their homes complaining of a vague indisposition with no apparent physical basis.' " On the labor demand side, the absence of union work rules and the foreman's control over hiring and firing are thought to have encouraged arbitrary dismiss-

[24] While these data allow us to estimate job duration, they do not give us any insight into why jobs come to an end when they do. We suspect that most jobs in our sample were ended by a voluntary quit since, with the exception of trough years of business cycles, voluntary quits were the proximate cause of most job separations in the turnover data collected after 1909. See Slichter, *The Turnover of Factory Labor*, p. 85; Paul Brissenden and Emil Frankel, *Labor Turnover in Industry: A Statistical Analysis* (New York, 1922), p. 79; and W. S. Woytinsky, *Three Aspects of Labor Dynamics* (Washington, DC, 1942), p. 2. The California survey was taken at the peak of a business cycle. Wesley Mitchell estimated that Jan. 1892 marked the eighth month of an expansion that peaked in Jan. 1893. See Wesley Mitchell, *What Happens During Business Cycles? A Progress Report* (Cambridge, MA, 1951), p. 12. While it is likely that quits were the cause of most of the separations of workers in our sample, variables were included in our specification to represent factors expected to influence all types of job terminations—layoffs, firings, retirements, and deaths, as well as voluntary quits.

[25] Preliminary analysis which stratified the sample by nativity found no statistically significant difference in coefficients between native- and foreign-born workers. Hence, the full sample estimates are reported in Table 3.

TABLE 3
ESTIMATES OF THE PROPORTIONAL HAZARD MODEL

Variable	Coefficient	Standard Error
CONSTANT	−2.090*	0.281
SCHOOL	0.009	0.012
SINGLE	0.446*	0.083
DEPENDENTS	−0.086*	0.024
HOME OWNER	−0.676*	0.121
AGE	0.276	0.149
*AGE*²	−0.028	0.024
TAILOR	0.212	0.264
BREWERY WORKER	0.878*	0.251
CAPITAL-LABOR RATIO	−0.064*	0.028
GROWTH IN INDUSTRY EMPLOYMENT	0.219*	0.063
ALPHA	0.982**	0.052

* Significantly different from 0 at the 5 percent level.
** Significantly different from 0 at the 5 percent level, not significantly different from 1 at the 5 percent level.
Notes: *N* is equal to 1,158. The log of the likelihood function is −2,745.489. The capital-labor ratio is measured in thousands of dollars per worker. *AGE* is measured in years divided by 10, and AGE^2 is measured in years divided by 100.
Sources: The coefficients were obtained by maximum likelihood estimation of a proportional hazard model of job leaving for a sample of non-union male workers from San Francisco in 1892. See text and the Appendix for greater details.

als.[26] This is not what we find. Our results suggest that the quantitative effects of key personal and industry characteristics were remarkably similar to their effects today.

Marital status, number of dependents, and home ownership have a large impact on the job-exit rate. The probability of job leaving is 36 percent lower for married men; home owners are roughly one-half as likely to leave their jobs; and the job-exit rate for a worker with two dependents is 84 percent of the rate for a worker with no dependents.[27] These responses are comparable to those observed in modern labor markets. For example, Christopher Flinn and James Heckman find that the transition rate from employment to nonemployment for married white males with spouses present is between one-third and one-half the

[26] Gutman, *Work, Culture and Society*, p. 24; Nelson, *Managers and Workers*; and Jacoby, *Employing Bureaucracy*.

[27] In a proportional hazard model individuals with different background characteristics have hazards which are proportional to each other at any given level of tenure, *t*. In a proportional hazard of the form:

$$\exp(\beta_0 + \beta_1 Z_1 + \beta_2 Z_2 + \ldots + \beta_k Z_k)\alpha\, t^{\alpha-1}$$

the impact of a 0–1 dummy variable, say Z_1, can be measured as the ratio of the hazard for an individual for whom $Z_1 = 1$ to the hazard for a person for whom $Z_1 = 0$:

$$\frac{\exp(\beta_0 + \beta_1 + \beta_2 Z_2 + \ldots + \beta_k Z_k)\alpha t^{\alpha-1}}{\exp(\beta_0 + \beta_2 Z_2 + \ldots + \beta_k Z_k)\alpha t^{\alpha-1}} = \exp(\beta_1)$$

Similarly, the impact of a change in a continuous variable, say Z_2, can be expressed as $\exp(\beta_2 \Delta Z_2)$.

rate for unmarried males.[28] Katherine Abraham and Henry Farber estimate that the job-leaving rate of married males is 40 percent lower than single males among non-unionized blue-collar workers.[29] Stuart Weiner estimates effects of similar magnitude for white-male transition rates from employment to unemployment.[30]

The estimated effect of schooling on the hazards of non-union male workers is small and statistically insignificant. Age at the start of the current job initially raises and then lowers the job-exit rate, although the effect is also statistically insignificant. Similar ambiguities exist in the estimated impact of schooling and age on the labor market transitions of post-World War II males. Weiner finds that age has statistically insignificant effects on male transitions out of employment. Mark Meitzen finds that male quit rates are unrelated to age and level of schooling. Kenneth Burdett, Nicholas Kiefer, and Sunil Sharma find that the probability of becoming unemployed falls and then rises with age. Abraham and Farber measure a positive schooling effect for nonprofessional workers.[31]

Capital-intensive production processes are associated with lower job-leaving probabilities in our sample. An individual working in the production of reed and rattan products, in which firms averaged $933 of capital per worker, is 1.7 times more likely to leave his job than one working in the breweries, which averaged $9,157 worth of capital per worker in 1890. This result is consistent with Donald Parsons's finding that manufacturing layoff rates in the late 1950s and early 1960s are negatively related to capital per worker.[32] This result is generally

[28] Christopher J. Flinn and James J. Heckman, "Models for the Analysis of Labor Force Dynamics," in Robert L. Basmann and George F. Rhodes, eds., *Advances in Econometrics* (Greenwich, 1982).

[29] Katherine B. Abraham and Henry S. Farber, "Job Duration, Seniority, and Earnings," *American Economic Review*, 77 (June 1987), pp. 278–97.

[30] Stuart E. Weiner, "Labor Market Flows and Nested Survival Models" (Research Working Paper No. 85-05, Federal Reserve Bank of Kansas City, July 1985).

[31] Weiner, "Labor Market Flows"; Mark E. Meitzen, "Differences in Male and Female Job-Quitting Behavior," *Journal of Labor Economics*, 4 (Apr. 1986), pp. 151–67; Kenneth Burdett, Nicholas Kiefer, and Sunil Sharma, "Layoffs and Duration Dependence: A Model of Turnover," *Journal of Econometrics*, 28 (Apr. 1985), pp. 51–69; and Abraham and Farber, "Job Duration." These ambiguous effects of schooling and age may be due to the fact that in our specification these variables capture offsetting effects. While the more educated may have greater alternative opportunities and hence a higher probability of quitting, they may also be of greater value to the firm and therefore less likely to be laid off. The coefficient on *AGE* may also reflect several counteracting forces. On the one hand, youths may enter the job with less knowledge of their labor market opportunities and engage in more job switching. As workers age, the number of years over which returns to job mobility can be captured decline. These factors make the probability of job leaving fall with age. On the other hand, older workers who have acquired a greater stock of general skills may have greater job opportunities and thus be more likely to switch jobs if this tendency is not offset by firm efforts to retain more experienced workers. Older workers are also more likely to leave jobs through retirement and death. These factors cause job leaving to rise with age.

[32] See Donald O. Parsons, "Specific Human Capital: An Application to Quit Rates and Lay Off Rates," *Journal of Political Economy*, 80 (Nov./Dec. 1972), pp. 1120–43; and John H. Pencavel,

attributed to a correlation between the capital-labor ratio of an industry and its level of required firm-specific skills. The firm-specific skills raise hiring and training costs, leading firms to adopt personnel policies designed to reduce turnover.[33]

For two industries in our sample, the breweries and men's clothing, we felt that average capital-labor ratios did not accurately reflect the set of factors, such as above-market wages and nonwage benefits, which generally raise the costs of job separations and increase the length of completed jobs for workers in more capital-intensive industries. In the case of breweries the capital-intensive methods had just been implemented.[34] Descriptive evidence suggests that the labor policies which promote the efficient operation of these methods had not yet been devised.[35] In the case of men's clothing the fact that the census reported information for firms with $500 or more in sales excludes a large proportion of small custom shops. Thus the capital-labor ratio reported by the census overstated the average for the industry. We believe that this bias is more serious in the case of men's clothing than in the case of other industries in our sample. Our parameter estimates indicate that job-leaving rates are higher for tailors and brewery workers, all else being equal.

We include the ratio of employment in 1900 to employment in 1890 for the worker's industry of employment to account for differences across industries in the strength of labor demand. In industries where employment is growing we expect exit rates to be high, reflecting the response of quits to the availability of jobs. Our results indicate that, indeed, exit rates are highly sensitive to labor market tightness.

The one apparent difference between our results and those derived from analyses of modern labor markets is the relationship between job tenure and the hazard rate, duration dependence. Our duration dependence parameter, α, is not significantly different from one, indicating no relationship between job tenure and job-leaving probabilities. This result stands in contrast to the relationship between job tenure and turnover in post-World War II labor markets. As Boyan Jovanovic wrote of the empirical studies of turnover conducted in the seventies:

"Wages, Specific Training, and Labor Turnover in U.S. Manufacturing Industries," *International Economic Review*, 13 (Feb. 1972), pp. 53–64.

[33] Alternatively, the above-market wages offered by firms in capital-intensive industries, which in turn lead to low quit rates, may result from efforts to discourage shirking and/or to share risks or rents. For a survey of these models, see George A. Akerlof and Janet L. Yellen, eds., *Efficiency Wage Models of the Labor Market* (Cambridge, 1986), pp. 1–21; and Daniel M. G. Raff, "Wage Determination Theory and the Five-Dollar Day at Ford," this JOURNAL, 48 (June 1988), pp. 387–99. These explanations are consistent with our findings as well.

[34] See Thomas C. Cochran, *The Pabst Brewing Company: The History of an American Business* (New York, 1948).

[35] See testimony of brewers reported in California Bureau of Labor Statistics, *Third Biennial Report* (Sacramento, 1888).

TABLE 4
THE DISTRIBUTION OF COMPLETED JOB SPELLS, 1892, FOR NON-UNION MALES

Percentage of Spells Ending in the Specified Length	
Less than 1 year	0.00%
1–3 years	6.44
3–5 years	26.89
5–7 years	21.32
7–10 years	18.45
10–15 years	14.10
15–20 years	5.92
20 or more years	6.88

Note: The estimates of the length of completed jobs are conditional upon tenure with firm at the time of the survey.
Sources: The estimated completed job spells are inferred from the estimated hazard model reported in Table 3. See text and the Appendix for greater detail.

"The strongest and most consistent finding in all these studies is a negative relationship between quits and layoffs, on the one hand, and job tenure, on the other. This finding is equally strong for quits and layoffs."[36] More recent studies which use methodologies similar to the one used in this article find evidence of negative duration dependence in hazards for job leaving.[37] However, these studies fail to account for unobserved heterogeneity in the sample. As first noted by Tony Lancaster, unobserved heterogeneity introduces a downward bias into the estimated duration dependence parameter.[38] In fact, after accounting for unobserved heterogeneity, Flinn and Heckman find no evidence of duration dependence among young males in the early 1970s.[39]

The overall importance of lengthy jobs in the 1890s is revealed in Table 4, which reports the sample distribution of completed job spells implied by our estimates. This distribution is derived by computing for each individual in the sample the expected job length conditional on

[36] Boyan Jovanovic, "Firm-Specific Capital and Turnover," *Journal of Political Economy*, 87 (Dec. 1979), p. 1246.

[37] See Burdett, Kiefer, and Sharma, "Layoffs and Duration Dependence"; Abraham and Farber, "Job Duration"; Weiner, "Labor Market Flows"; and Meitzen, "Differences in Male and Female Job-Quitting Behavior."

[38] Tony Lancaster, "Econometric Methods for the Duration of Unemployment," *Econometrica*, 47 (July 1979), pp. 939–56.

[39] See Flinn and Heckman, "Models for the Analysis of Labor Force Dynamics." There are further econometric reasons for questioning the reliability of the estimates of duration dependence. Heckman and Burton Singer find that estimates of duration dependence are highly sensitive to the manner in which covariates that vary across the course of the job, such as age, are introduced into the hazard. They also point out that in single spell duration models it may be impossible to separate the effects of time-varying regressors from true duration dependence, particularly in the case of a regressor such as age which has no independent variation from time on the job. See James Heckman and Burton Singer, "Econometric Analysis of Longitudinal Data," in Zvi Griliches and Michael Intriligator, eds., *Handbook of Econometrics*, vol. 3 (New York, 1986).

tenure to date with his current firm.[40] The proportion of jobs which are brief is negligible, with the bulk of spells estimated to last between 5 and 15 years and averaging to 8.5 years.[41] These figures most likely understate job length among the manufacturing labor force as a whole in 1890 since the nationwide manufacturing labor force contained a significantly larger proportion of married, homeowning workers. To obtain a measure of average job length which would reflect the greater maturity of the nationwide manufacturing labor force we evaluated the average duration of completed spells in progress at the mean characteristics of the sample but with the 1890 mean values of marital status, homeownership, and number of dependents in place of their sample averages. This calculation implies an average job length of 13 years.[42]

IMPLICATIONS

We have found that brief job attachment does not describe the typical employment experience of workers in the late nineteenth century. Rather, most employment was concentrated in lengthy spells. While this result appears to be at variance with the widely cited evidence on job tenure prior to the mid-1920s, most of that evidence is based on turnover statistics that do not accurately reflect the experiences of employed individuals.

We do find differences in the job tenure of the average nineteenth- and twentieth-century male worker. While employment spells were lengthy in the nineteenth century, there were far fewer lifetime jobs. Bradford De Long and Lawrence Summers attribute the growing importance of lifetime jobs to increases in the capital intensity of production and to the growing importance of "something that might be called job-specific

[40] In our computation we assume that workers do not work beyond age 65. For evidence on the timing and extent of retirement in the late nineteenth century, see Roger L. Ransom and Richard Sutch, "The Labor of Older Americans: Retirement of Men On and Off the Job, 1870–1937," this JOURNAL, 46 (Mar. 1986), pp. 1–30.

[41] The absence of spells of less than one year arises from the fact that short spells have a low probability of being sampled at any point in time. Abraham and Farber also find that short spells are virtually nonexistent among the sample of workers whose spells were in progress at the time the survey used in their analysis was taken. Only 0.6 percent of these workers were predicted to have completed employment spells of less than a year. See Abraham and Farber, "Job Duration."

[42] In 1890, 39.2 percent of males engaged in gainful, nonagricultural occupations were single. See U.S. Department of the Interior, Bureau of the Census, *Report on the Population of the United States at the Eleventh Census: 1890* (Washington, DC, 1897), vol. 1, part 2, p. 744, table 119. Average "family" size was 4.9, where "family" is defined as "not only the normal family, as generally understood, but also all persons living alone, and all larger aggregations of people having only the tie of a common roof and table, as the inmates of hotels, hospitals, prisons, and asylums." The census goes on to express the opinion that "considered as regards great bodies of population, the presence of these large 'census' families does not probably have any very appreciable effect on the average size of the family." See *Eleventh Census: 1890*, vol. 1, part 1, p. clxxxviii. We took 3.9 as the average number of dependents per male wage earner. Thirty-seven percent of nonfarm families owned their own homes. See *Eleventh Census: 1890*, vol. 13, p. 27.

human capital, and therefore in implicit long-term contracts.''[43] Indeed, our estimates suggest that the difference between our 13-year estimate and George Akerlof and Brian Main's 18-year estimate can be accounted for by growth in the capital-labor ratio. Replacing the sample value of the capital-labor ratio in our calculation of average job duration in 1890 with its 1980 value produces an estimated job length of over 19 years.[44] To the extent that the capital-labor ratio reflects the firm-specific skills associated with the job, this statistic supports De Long and Summers's claim.

But the important result is that despite low capital-labor ratios, jobs were not ''brief'' in the nineteenth century. Indeed, our finding of 13-year jobs in the 1890s calls into question the ''spot market'' characterization of labor markets in that era. As Akerlof and Main note with regard to contemporary labor markets: ''If an 'I quit' was induced at each opportunity of a job paying a few dollars more; or a 'you're fired' was forthcoming at every deviation from required productivity, currently employed males would hardly be expected to average an eighteen-year job tenure on their current jobs!''[45] One would hardly expect 13 years either.

Appendix

AN ECONOMETRIC MODEL OF JOB DURATION

In order to obtain consistent estimates of the parameters of the hazard rate we need to derive the likelihood function of the job spells in our sample. It is well known that, given the form of the hazard rate in equation 1, the density of a completed job spell, $f(t)$, follows a Weibull density:

$$f(t) = \tau\alpha\, t^{\alpha-1} \exp(-\tau\, t^{\alpha}) \qquad (2)$$

with parameters τ and α.

In our sample, a worker is observed in the midst of his job spell. The length of the spell up to the time of the survey is measured. As measures of completed spell lengths, these observed durations suffer from two well-known sources of censoring bias.[46] First is the downward ''interruption'' bias which results from the fact that the duration is measured before the spell ends (that is, the spell is right-censored). The second is the upward ''length'' bias which results from the fact that longer spells are more likely to be sampled by the survey (the spells are left-censored).

[43] De Long and Summers, ''Changing Cyclical Variability,'' p. 41.

[44] Akerlof and Main's estimated mean completed tenure of 18 years refers to all industries. For manufacturing, the relevant comparison to our calculations, their estimates are 18.3 and 19.5 for durable and nondurable manufacturing, respectively. See Akerlof and Main, ''Experience-Weighted Measures,'' p. 1007.

[45] Ibid., p. 1008.

[46] Stephen W. Salant, ''Search Theory and Duration Data: A Theory of Sorts,'' *Quarterly Journal of Economics*, 91 (Feb. 1977), pp. 39–57.

Takeshi Amemiya shows that, given the population distribution F and density f of completed spells, the density of our surveyed spell length $g(s)$ can be expressed as:

$$g(s) = \frac{1 - F(s)}{ES} \tag{3}$$

where ES equals the mean duration of completed spells in the population, that is, $ES = \int_0^\infty xf(x)dx$.[47]

Given our functional form assumptions, $g(s)$ can be written as:

$$g(s) = \frac{\exp(-\tau s^{\alpha})}{\tau^{-1/\alpha}\Gamma(1 + \alpha^{-1})} \tag{4}$$

where Γ denotes the gamma function. Assuming independence across individuals the log of the likelihood function of our sample is:

$$L = \sum_{i=1}^{N} g_i(s) \tag{5}$$

This log-likelihood function is maximized with respect to β and α using the algorithm developed by Ernst Berndt and others.[48]

[47] Takeshi Amemiya, *Advanced Econometrics* (Cambridge, MA, 1985). Note that this result relies on the assumption of a constant entry rate. That is, the probability of beginning a job is unrelated to calendar time.

[48] Ernst K. Berndt, et al., "Estimation and Inference in Nonlinear Structural Models," *Annals of Economic and Social Measurement*, 3/4 (1974), pp. 653–65.

Enclosures, Common Rights, and Women: The Proletarianization of Families in the Late Eighteenth and Early Nineteenth Centuries

JANE HUMPHRIES

This article argues against the mainstream view that eighteenth-century common rights were of little significance to working people. Markets in common rights and in their products provide an index of value, and when neither common rights nor derived products were bought and sold, values are imputed from the market prices of similar goods. Since women and children were the primary exploiters of common rights, their loss led to changes in women's economic position within the family and more generally to increased dependence of whole families on wages and wage earners.

In his classic "Enclosure and the Labour Supply in the Industrial Revolution," J. D. Chambers disputed Marx's claim that parliamentary enclosure was instrumental in the creation of an English proletariat.[1] A critical element in Chambers's argument was his belittlement of cottagers' and squatters' common rights and therefore their ability to mitigate wage dependence. Common rights were but "a thin and squalid curtain" between the "growing army of labourers" and "utter proletarianization."[2] Although other aspects of Chambers's influential anti-Marxist tract have undergone substantive revision, his verdict on the significance of common rights has remained largely unchallenged.[3]

The Journal of Economic History, Vol. L, No. 1 (Mar. 1990). ISSN 0022-0507.

The author is a member of the Faculty of Economics and Politics, Cambridge University, Sidgwick Avenue, Cambridge CB3 9DD, United Kingdom.

I would like to thank Carol Heim, William Lazonick, Robin Matthews, N. E. Savin, the editors, and the referees for comments on earlier drafts of this article. The article also benefited from criticism and discussion at the Washington DC and Columbia Economic History Seminars.

[1] J. D. Chambers, "Enclosure and the Labour Supply in the Industrial Revolution," *Economic History Review*, 5 (No. 3, 1953), pp. 319–43.

[2] Ibid., p. 117.

[3] N. F. R. Crafts, "Enclosure and the Labour Supply Revisited," *Explorations in Economic History*, 15 (Apr. 1978), pp. 172–83; W. Lazonick, "Karl Marx and Enclosures in England," *Review of Radical Political Economics*, 6, pt. 2 (Summer 1974), pp. 1–59; M. E. Turner, "Parliamentary Enclosure and Landownership Change in Buckinghamshire," *Economic History Review*, 28 (Nov. 1975), pp. 563–79; J. A. Yelling, *Common Field and Enclosure in England, 1450–1850* (London, 1977); K. D. M. Snell, *Annals of the Labouring Poor: Social Change and Agrarian England, 1660–1900* (Cambridge, 1985); Robert C. Allen, "The Growth of Labor Productivity in Early Modern English Agriculture," *Explorations in Economic History*, 25 (June 1988), pp. 117–46; Robert C. Allen, "Agrarian Fundamentalism and English Agricultural Development," paper presented at the Harvard Economic Workshop, October 6, 1989.

Scholarly neglect of common rights derives from two sources. First, both Chambers and J. H. Clapham, another distinguished critic of Marx, argued that as wage labor predated and was not significantly enlarged by enclosure, the two could not be causally related: enclosure was irrelevant to proletarianization. Second, where commons and wastes were exploited on sufferance, that is, where consent had been implied by lack of interference, and not as a legal right, their alienation left no legal trace, making it impossible, according to Chambers and Clapham, to gauge the proportion of the rural population affected.[4] Researchers turned with relief to more amenable aspects of the debate.

Undoubtedly wage labor was of relatively long standing in the English context. Prior to parliamentary enclosure families in receipt of wages comprised a significant proportion of the rural population.[5] What these figures do not capture is the extent to which families were *dependent* on wages, for, as Charles Tilly suggests, "it is possible to be a little bit proletarian." Rather than pushing families out of one category (propertied/peasant) into another (proletarian), parliamentary enclosure eroded nonwage sources of subsistence available to semi-proletarian families and left them increasingly dependent on wages. In this sense it affected some of the 60 percent of families already in receipt of wages by the end of the seventeenth century, as well as the additional 15 percent earning wages by 1830.[6]

As in many parts of the Third World today, semi-proletarianization took the form of the husband/father working for wages while the wife/mother and the children added to family subsistence by exploiting traditional rights to rural resources.[7] Misled by ahistoric stereotypes of male breadwinners and appurtenant wives and children, economic historians have overlooked the commons' value in facilitating contributions to family subsistence from wives and children, contributions which were not insubstantial compared with the male wage or with what

[4] "Since they [cottage labourers with customary useage of the commons] had no proprietary rights they do not appear in the enclosure award or land tax returns . . ." (Chambers, "Enclosure," p. 104); see also J. H. Clapham, *An Economic History of Modern Britain*, vol. 1: *The Early Railway Age* (Cambridge, 1967).

[5] Clapham, *Economic History*, p. 113; C. Tilly, "Demographic Origins of the European Proletariat," in David Levine, ed., *Proletarianization and Family History* (London, 1984), pp. 1–85; D. Levine, "Production, Reproduction and the Proletarian Family in England, 1500–1851," in Levine, ed., *Proletarianization*, pp. 87–128.

[6] These estimates and the quotation are from Tilly, "Demographic Origins," p. 8; see also Snell, *Annals*, p. 168; Lazonick, "Karl Marx," p. 87.

[7] Sometimes even sympathetic authorities choose to emphasize the ideological or sociological implications of the loss of the commons. The Orwins' emphasis on the erosion of collective responsibility, Thirsk's on the boost given to individualism, and Mill's on the reduced sense of independence, although raising important points, obscure evidence that working people suffered specific economic injuries. See C. S. and C. S. Orwin, *The Open Fields* (Oxford, 1967); Joan Thirsk, ed., *The Agrarian History of England and Wales* (Cambridge, 1967); Dennis R. Mills, "The Nineteenth Century Peasant at Melbourn, Cambridgeshire," in Richard M. Smith, ed., *Land, Kinship and Life Cycle* (Cambridge, 1984).

women and children themselves could earn in wages. By eliminating the basis of such contributions in common rights, enclosure increased families' dependence on wages and wage earners, pressures which can be understood only in the context of the importance of family participation in securing an eighteenth-century livelihood. If proletarianization is seen as a process of gradual elimination of sources of family subsistence other than wages, a causal link between the loss of common rights and wage dependence is reestablished. Its analysis must involve the valuation of common rights and the effects of their alienation.

Nor is the failure of enclosure awards to record the expurgation of customarily enjoyed but nonlegal rights an insuperable obstacle to rigorous analysis of cottagers' and squatters' losses. On the basis of contemporary testimony, culled from government reports, agricultural surveys, and village autobiographies, as well as evidence from manorial court rolls and probate records, modern scholars have constructed a picture of widespread access to agricultural resources by way of customary and common rights, surviving well into the eighteenth century. Thus R. W. Malcolmson writes: "In areas of wide expanse—the fens of East Anglia, Dartmoor and other Moorland districts, the open field countryside of central England, forests throughout the country—cottagers and smallholders sustained a viable, if often tenuous, economy because of their ability to keep stock; and in many individual parishes in regions of intensive arable husbandry villagers enjoyed similar advantages from a local marsh, waste or other uncultivated piece of land, or from rights of access to unenclosed fields at times when no crops were growing."[8]

Although legally demonstrable entitlements were compensated, enclosure awards probably did not benefit the smallholders to the same extent as had traditional landholding arrangements. The considerable expenses of enclosure, their disproportionate allocation, and the inability of smallholders to mobilize their land award in the same way that common rights had been utilized, often made smallholders' posi-

[8] R. W. Malcolmson, "Ways of Getting a Living in Eighteenth Century England," in R. E. Pahl, ed., *On Work* (Oxford, 1988), p. 51. Similarly, J. M. Martin emphasizes the prevalence of common rights among cottagers and small-scale landowners in the Feldon of Warwickshire, and June Sheppard stresses the universality of access to the wastes for all established households in the Yorkshire townships which she surveyed. See J. M. Martin, "Village Traders and the Emergence of a Proletariat in South Warwickshire," *Agricultural History Review*, 32, pt. 2 (1984), pp. 179–88; and June A. Sheppard, "Field Systems of Yorkshire," in A. R. H. Baker and R. A. Butlin, eds., *Studies of Field Systems in the British Isles* (Cambridge, 1973), pp. 145–87. For the classic view of a pre-enclosure democratic pattern of ownership, see G. E. Slater, *The English Peasantry and the Enclosure of Common Fields* (New York, 1968). And for a qualified view, which still includes beneficiaries whose common rights were legally insecure, "the cottager with little or no land who none the less kept a cow remained as an important figure in the late eighteenth century common field community," see Yelling, *Common Field*, p. 229.

tions untenable. The reaction was, all too often, a hasty sale to cover costs.[9]

On the fate of the second category of commoner, those without legal rights, there is even more general agreement: rights of custom were simply disregarded by the vast majority of enclosure commissions.[10] In the rare cases where such rights were acknowledged, the beneficiaries were subject to the same kinds of pressures as were smallholders with legal claims. Thus at St. Neots, where a very small plot of land was given in lieu of a cowkeep, results were tragic: ". . . the enclosure of which land costing more than they could afford, they sold the lots at £5. The money was drank at the ale house, and the men spoiled by the habit came with their families to the parish."[11] More usual forms of compensation were the creation of small commons for use by the poor, or the sale of land to establish funds which the guardians could distribute at their discretion to those considered deserving.[12]

So although strict quantification of the extent to which common rights and privileges were exploited is impossible, the issue seems uncontroversial: if beneficiaries from custom are included alongside those with legal entitlement, the commons appear to have been employed by a significant portion of the rural population, and in the unenclosed villages of the midland counties, perhaps the majority, until the era of parliamentary enclosure.

Although heaths and commons did not entirely disappear with enclosure, their size was drastically curtailed. Those who had hitherto exploited these resources, although initially differentiated according to

[9] Confutation of this view has been based on the stability of size distributions of farms before and after enclosure; see J. D. Chambers, "Enclosures and the Small Landowner," *Economic History Review*, 10 (Nov. 1940), pp. 118–27; G. E. Mingay, *Enclosure and the Small Farmer in the Age of the Industrial Revolution: Studies in Economic History* (London, 1968); K. Collins, "Marx on the English Agricultural Revolution: Theory and Evidence," *History and Theory: Studies in the Philosophy of History*, 6 (No. 3, 1967), pp. 351–81. But Michael Turner's investigation of several Buckinghamshire villages suggests that after enclosure many independent smallholders were replaced by tradespeople, professionals, and petty rentiers from the towns. Their influx left the distribution of holdings unchanged, but "on the other hand the personal constitution of landownership was sometimes restructured completely"; see Turner, "Parliamentary Enclosure," p. 569. J. M. Martin's documentation of extensive traffic in common rights before enclosure and in allotments after enclosure provides supporting evidence from Warwickshire; see Martin, "The Small Landowner and Parliamentary Enclosure in Warwickshire," *Economic History Review*, 32 (Aug. 1979), pp. 328–43.

[10] E. C. K. Gonner, *Common Land and Enclosures* (London, 1912), p. 365; Yelling, *Common Field*, p. 230.

[11] *Annals of Agriculture*, 16 (1791), p. 483; for other examples see Snell, *Annals*, pp. 190–91; Martin detects "a distinct decline in generosity over time" in the compensation meted out to the village poor by enclosure commissioners, see "Village Traders," p. 185.

[12] Gonner, *Common Land*, p. 367; P. M. Giles, "The Enclosure of Common Lands in Stockport," *Transactions of the Lancashire and Cheshire Antiquarian Society*, 62 (1950–1), pp. 73–110, details how apparently unusually disinterested burghers enclosed and sold local commons allegedly to finance the construction of a prison and workhouse, but then belies this picture of public-spirited generosity with evidence of subsequent misappropriation of the proceeds.

their legal status, often came ultimately to the same dependence on wages. The question then becomes: what kind of a barrier against total wage dependence did the commons and wastes afford? Were the products of the commons, as the proponents of enclosure allege, "the trifling fruits of overstocked and ill-kempt lands?"[13] This article argues they were more, concentrating on the specific advantages that poor people derived from rural resources. Markets in common rights and in their products provide an index of value, and when neither common rights nor their fruits were bought and sold, values are imputed from the market prices of similar goods. Since women and children were the primary exploiters of common rights, their loss led to changes in women's economic position within the family and more generally to increased dependence of whole families on wages and wage earners.

THE VALUE OF COMMON RIGHTS: "THE TRIFLING FRUITS OF OVERSTOCKED AND ILL-KEMPT LANDS"

Widespread opposition to enclosure, even in the face of severe legal, economic, and social sanctions, suggests that cottagers and squatters felt aggrieved by the associated changes in agrarian organization.[14] Migrants' attraction to areas of extensive commons is further testimony to their worth.[15] Moreover, it is hard to reconcile the disparagement of the commons with the assiduity with which laborers sought to exploit them. As Arthur Young observed, claims that enclosure benefited the poor were "directly in the teeth of their own feelings and positive assertions, as well as those of many other respectable eye witnesses."[16]

Unlike orthodox economists, who ascribe a low probability to false consciousness and irrational expectations, contemporary proponents of enclosure (and ironically their modern counterparts) dismissed opposition as wrongheaded even when sympathetic to the motives of opponents. Thus the "anxiety in the customary tenants to have their little patrimony descend to their children," although thought "laudable," did nothing to check J. Bailey and G. Culley's enthusiasm for enclosure in Northumberland.[17] In a less compassionate mood, Arthur Young wrote

[13] R. Parkinson, *A General View of the Agriculture of the County of Huntingdon* (London, 1813), p. 256; J. Bailey and G. Culley, *A General View of the Agriculture of the County of Northumberland* (London, 1813), p. 36.

[14] J. L. and B. Hammond, *The Village Labourer, 1760–1832* (London, 1919); E. J. Hobsbawm and G. Rude, *Captain Swing* (London, 1969); E. P. Thompson, *The Making of the English Working Class* (New York, 1963); Snell, *Annals*; J. M. Neeson, "The Opponents of Enclosure in Eighteenth Century Northamptonshire," *Past and Present*, 105 (Nov. 1984), pp. 114–39.

[15] Thirsk, *The Agrarian History of England and Wales*, pp. 10–13, 204, 403; K. Wrightson, *English Society, 1580–1680* (London, 1982), pp. 126–27.

[16] A. Young, *General Report on Enclosures* (London, 1808), p. 12.

[17] Bailey and Culley, *Northumberland*, p. 263.

of enclosure in Northamptonshire: "The advantages of inclosing to every class of the people are now so well understood and combated at present but by a few old women who dislike it for no other reason but a love of singularity and a hatred of novelty."[18] He was, of course, subsequently to admit the harmful effects of enclosure on the poor although always maintaining that they could have been obviated by the wise use of waste land, on which cottages could have been built, the poor then moving bodily from commons to wastes.[19]

Debate on the merits of enclosure anticipated philosophical issues covered in modern welfare economics. Joseph Plymley struck a modern note in arguing that a net gain, and therefore the possibility of compensation, even if it was never actually paid, justified economic change: "Without looking minutely where the principal benefit of enclosure rests there is certainly a sufficient balance of advantage upon the whole to warrant the strenuous endeavours of every friend to mankind in forwarding them."[20] He noted the external ecological cost of enclosing a beautiful area like Clun Forest, but was unmoved: ". . . when it is considered how little profit is produced to those who have a legal right in these wastes or to the public at large; what a scope is given to industry by their enclosure; and that the population of this country seems to require an extended cultivation, the latter motives must predominate."[21] Similarly, A. Pringle argued that "the interests of a few individuals ought to give way to those of the community," and Arthur Young that possibly adverse effects on the poor could "never prove a reason against inclosing . . . [as] . . . the national benefits are much too great . . . but at most, call merely for a more tender attention to their interests."[22]

Contributors to the Board of Agriculture's county surveys acknowledged the skewed distribution of the benefits from enclosure. Thomas Davis, for example, reported from Wiltshire, that "the advantages to be derived from a removal of these impediments to good husbandry, need not be enumerated . . . but it must be remarked, that, in many parts of this district, these advantages apply more forcefully to the case of the great farmer than the little one."[23] Similarly, the 1844 *Report from the Committee on Commons Inclosure* affirmed the optimality of enclosure by reference to the increased rental value of enclosed

[18] *Annals of Agriculture*, 16 (1791), p. 502.

[19] A. Young, "An Inquiry into the Propriety of Applying Wastes to the Better Maintenance and Support of the Poor," *Annals of Agriculture*, 36 (1801), p. 515; E. P. Hunt, *Arthur Young on Industry and Economics* (Bryn Mawr, 1926).

[20] J. Plymley, *A General View of the Agriculture of Shropshire* (London, 1813), p. 145.

[21] Ibid.

[22] A. Pringle, *A General View of the Agriculture of the County of Westmoreland* (London, 1813), p. 354; Young, *General Report*, p. 12.

[23] Thomas Davis, *A General View of the Agriculture of the County of Wiltshire* (London, 1813), p. 40.

land, resulting from its improved productivity, independently of any change in the distribution of agricultural resources and income from them.[24]

Modern welfare economics requires that the distributional implications of social change figure explicitly in any cost-benefit analysis. Some contemporaries were disturbed by the asymmetric distribution of the costs and benefits of enclosure, which they regarded as unnecessary, even seeing enclosure as a lost opportunity to reverse the trend towards landlessness. Arthur Young regretted that "instead of giving property to the poor, or preserving it, or enabling them to acquire it, the very contrary effect has taken place . . . and as this evil was by no means necessarily connected with the measure of enclosing, it was a mischief that might easily have been avoided."[25]

Clearly a cost-benefit analysis of enclosure ultimately involves a complex counterfactual. The issue explored here has more modest dimensions, though perhaps its investigation is a necessary input into the grander calculus: how valuable were common rights to the village poor, and how extensive were their losses on enclosure compared with other sources of family income? Valuation can be based on the rents charged for common rights when such rights were marketed, or by imputing values to the produce of common rights from the market prices of similar goods.

Let us begin with grazing rights. Common rights could be hired cheaply, especially in areas of poor pasture. Ten sheep could be kept for a whole year for sixpence in Westmoreland, and even in Wales, where the commons were better, fourpence per head per year was the going rate in 1808.[26] According to Young the privilege of stocking a common, worth only 10s to 12s if hired out, could provide claim to land which after enclosure had an annual value of £3 to £20.[27] But such comparisons, as Young himself acknowledged, missed the point as far as cottagers' gains and losses are concerned. If a poor family was unable to stock the commons, the price at which the right was let need not indicate its value; and, second, as discussed above, rights legally or customarily enjoyed prior to enclosure were not necessarily effectively

[24] *Parliamentary Papers*, 5 (1844); for an excellent summary of the modern treatment of rent increases as a motive to enclose, see Michael Turner, *English Parliamentary Enclosure: Its Historical Geography and Economic History* (London, 1980), p. 98 ff. and references cited therein.

[25] Young, "An Inquiry," p. 515; here Young anticipates the framework and conclusions, if not the method, of a recent comment on the welfare implications of enclosure. Nick von Tunzelmann's use of dynamic optimization to evaluate actual and feasible time paths of consumption per head for industrializing Britain suggests that a less brutal pace of enclosure would not have retarded growth significantly, see his "The Standard of Living Debate and Optimal Economic Growth," in Joel Mokyr, ed., *The Economics of the Industrial Revolution* (London, 1985).

[26] Young, *General Report*, pp. 3–4.

[27] Ibid., pp. 6–7.

confirmed in enclosed villages.[28] Consequently here the emphasis is on the value of the products of cowkeeping.

Poor people themselves allegedly valued their cows at around 5s or 6s each per week, which compares favorably with the 7s to 8s that late eighteenth-century agricultural laborers could hope to earn, an order of magnitude confirmed by David Levine's recent description of a laborer's cow as "worth almost as much as his wages."[29] Participants in the debate on the efficiency of cottager cowkeeping, conducted by the Board of Agriculture in the 1790s and 1800s, provided detailed analyses of the costs and benefits of different systems, including direct comparisons of schemes dependent on the preservation of commons with schemes which employed enclosed cowkeeps. These assessments, summarized in Table 1, facilitate more detailed accounts.

Arthur Young's eulogy to the cow seems clearly vindicated. According to Mr. Kent's figures, with a decent cow producing six quarts of milk per day worth around a penny a quart in 1800, the revenue from sales of milk or butter, or from suckling calves, amounted to 3s 6d per week or £9 2s per year. The other estimates of receipts from sales of dairy produce are in the same range and although they fall short of the valuations quoted above, they remain significant compared with laborers' wages. On an annual basis the comparison would probably be even more favorable to cowkeeping: the agricultural laborer could expect disruptions to earnings from underemployment and unemployment in the winter months that were only partly offset by harvest overtime, whereas Mr. Kent's figures include an allowance for the cow's dry periods and variable milk yields.[30]

Moreover these figures underestimate revenues because they do not include the many by-products of cowkeeping, which had considerable value within the cottager economy. Where possible these by-products have been valued. Their importance in raising the revenue from cowkeeping is shown in the third column of Table 1.

One important by-product was the skim milk left over from making butter. Milk was rarely available at prices affordable by the poor, especially during the high price years from 1795 to 1820, which might perhaps itself indicate that cowkeeping had declined.[31] Milk provided a gratifying addition to the monotonous diet of the adult farm worker, but more importantly, it was crucial to the healthy development of laborers' children. No wonder that in their cost-benefit analyses of cowkeeping

[28] Ibid., pp. 12–13.

[29] Young, "An Inquiry," p. 510; D. Levine, *Reproducing Families: The Political Economy of English Population History* (London, 1987), p. 67.

[30] " . . . setting the profit of the calf against the loss sustained when the cow is dry"; Mr. Kent's estimate appears as a footnote in Sir John Sinclair, "Observations on the Means of Enabling a Cottager to Keep A Cow," *Communications to the Board of Agriculture*, 4 (1805), pp. 358–69.

[31] Clapham, *An Economic History*, p. 496.

Lord Winchilsea, Mr. Crutchley, Sir John Sinclair, and Thomas Babington all mention the importance of milk for cottagers' children and its unavailability unless produced domestically. David Davies and Frederic Eden make the same point in their seminal accounts of working-class budgets at the end of the eighteenth century.[32] John Burnett and J. C. Drummond and Anne Wilbraham, historians of the English diet, cite declining access to land as a factor in the deterioration of the diets of southern agricultural laborers.[33] Milk also provided the dressing needed to make potatoes palatable, and its greater availability in the north, perhaps linked to the lesser impact of enclosures, facilitated the use of oatmeal.[34]

Milk, along with the means to keep a cow, was also important within the cottage smallholder's productive system. Skim milk could be fed to the pigs along with supernumerary potatoes, garden produce, and cow fodder. In winter sheep could be kept on the cow pasture and the dung from cows and sheep could be used to manure the arable or garden, or sold to the farmers for 15s a wagon load. Conservation and recycling made the cottager economy pay.[35]

If we turn to costs, we find that cows themselves cost between £7 and £10 in the 1790s according to the Board of Agriculture. Neglecting feed and labor costs, a cow could pay for itself in about a year. As far as rents were concerned, common rights had been enjoyed gratis, whereas land allotted to the cottagers on enclosure figured in the determination of their rent and rates. Even if their common rights provided only a summer keep, with several neighboring open-field parishes it was possible to buy hay to feed the cows in winter. But with enclosure, particularly if this reduced grassland, hay became much more expensive and difficult to procure.[36] In the schemes discussed by the Board of Agriculture the laborers rented land, either for grazing or for arable on which to grow fodder, and so it is possible, given prevailing rents and the requisite volume of hay, turnips, and greenfeed, to estimate the extent to which having to rent land and buy hay reduced profits. As columns four and five in Table 1 show, paying for both summer and winter feed approximately halved profits.

[32] David Davies, *The Case of Laborers in Husbandry* (New Brunswick, 1977); Frederic Morton Eden, *The State of the Poor* (London, 1928). See also the historians of diet: J. C. Drummond and A. Wilbraham, *The Englishman's Food: A History of Five Centuries of English Diet* (London, 1950); D. J. Oddy and D. S. Miller, eds., *The Making of the British Diet* (London, 1976); John Burnett, *Plenty and Want: A Social History of Diet in England from 1815 to the Present Day* (London, 1966).

[33] Burnett, *Plenty*, pp. 254–55; Drummond and Wilbraham, *The Englishman's Food*, p. 245.

[34] Burnett, *Plenty*, pp. 254–55; Drummond and Wilbraham, *The Englishman's Food*, pp. 247–48.

[35] Davis, *Wiltshire*, p. 41; "An Account of the Produce of Milk and Butter from a Cow, the Property of William Cramp of Lewes in the County of Sussex," *Communications to the Board of Agriculture*, 5 (1801), pp. 122–25.

[36] Mr. Barker (to Lord Winchilsea), reported in Lord Winchilsea, "Cottages," *Communications to the Board of Agriculture*, 1 (1797), p. 80.

TABLE 1
THE VALUE OF A COW

Author (date, location)	Annual Revenue from Butter and Milk or Suckling Calves	Other Gains	Rent and Other Costs	Net Profit per Cow
Winchilsea (1797, Rutland)	£8 6s 8d	Sheep in winter kept on cow pastures; skim milk for their children[a]	£4 0s 0d	£4 6s 8d
Brownlow (1796, Welton)	£7 0s 0d	Pig adds £2 to net profit; keep lambs[b]	£1 17s 6d plus 2½ tons of hay[c]	£7 2s 6d
Crutchley (1796, Burleigh)	£7 10s 0d from butter or £5 from suckling calves	Pigs kept on skim milk worth 18d per week; milk, butter, cheese, and bacon consumed at home; 2 sheep kept on summer pasture at 5s[d]	£3 15s 0d plus £1 0s od marketing cost[e]	£3 0s 0d
Babington (1795, na)[f]	na	Vegetables and pigs add £1 to £3 to net profit; milk consumed at home	na	£4 0s 0d to £8 0s 0d
Sinclair (1801, na)	£7	Hogs add at least another £3 to net profit[g]	£4 10s, plus labor costs, seeds, and so forth	£5 10s 0d
Kent (1801, na)[h]	£9 2s 0d	na	na	na
Vavasour (1801, Yorkshire)	na	See[i]	£9[j] plus labor costs, seeds, and so forth	£4 10s 0d

[a] Sheep kept in winter on cow pasture at 2s 6d per sheep and the value of the skim milk used in the family is included in revenue here, but other dairy produce consumed at home is not. Thus Winchilsea believed that the figure for net profit per cow underestimated the real benefit to the family: ". . . those who manage well will clear about twenty-pence a week or £4 6s 8d per ann. by each cow . . . Certainly those who have a cow appear to be (in comparison with those who have none) much more than twenty-pence per week richer," Lord Winchilsea, "Cottages," *Communications to the Board of Agriculture*, 1 (1797), pp. 77–78.

[b] "Cottagers who keep a cow always keep a pig or two . . . the profit from thence is very considerable as a pig is maintained . . . by what else be thrown away; and a pig bought for 20s at midsummer will be worth £3 at Christmas," Lord Brownlow, "Queries Concerning Cottagers," *Communications to the Board of Agriculture*, 1 (1797), p. 88.

[c] Net profit here would be very sensitive to the price of hay.

[d] The skim milk is assumed to be sold and included in the revenue figure in column 2, so to include the pigs too would involve an element of double counting; the 5s from pasturing sheep is all additional revenue. The family's domestic consumption of bacon and dairy produce is not counted. See Mr. Crutchley, "Answers to the Queries Respecting Cottagers Renting Land," *Communications to the Board of Agriculture*, 1 (1797), pp. 93–96.

[e] Crutchley includes £1 to cover the "trouble and expense" of marketing; this plus the relatively high rent reduces his net profit. See Crutchley, "Answers," p. 94.

[f] See Thomas Babington, "Account of Some Cottagers," *Communications to the Board of Agriculture*, 4 (1805), pp. 392–98.

TABLE 1—continued

[g] The cow is maintained on the basis of three acres of arable land divided into four plots of three roods each and cultivated so as to feed and litter the cow year round and provide potatoes and grain for the family or for sale, milk for the children, some orchard produce, some food for the pigs, and some poultry and eggs. Sinclair estimates that his system of management would yield produce valued at £21 2s 0d. I have artificially separated the cow from the interrelated system of farming for purposes of comparison. Note that the value of the produce is only slightly less than the cottager's earnings from wage labor after deducting the 20 days' work which Sinclair estimated would be required in addition to the laborer's and his family's "by hours," Sir John Sinclair, "Observations on the Means of Enabling a Cottager to Keep a Cow," *Communications to the Board of Agriculture*, 4 (1805), pp. 358–69.

[h] Mr. Kent's estimate is reported by Sinclair, "Observations," pp. 362–63.

[i] Vavasour's cottager scheme in Yorkshire was also at least partially based on the arable cultivation of a small plot of land; cowkeeping was an integral part. Again I have tried to isolate the profit on a cow and set it against some relevant rental charges. Excluding the sales of butter, the profit on the land net of rent, seeds, and labor cost (ploughing) was estimated at £31 10s 0d and the family allegedly "made the rent in butter besides a little used in the family." But note that some of the produce undoubtedly went to feed the two cows and two pigs and so the value of the butter sales cannot just be added to the value of output without double counting, see Sir Henry Vavasour, "Case of a Cottager," *Communications to the Board of Agriculture*, 4 (1805), pp. 632–63.

[j] Includes house rent. The net return on hogs as joint products with butter production is included in net profit, but the accounts do not include the benefits derived from combining cowkeeping with some arable, for example, the availability of manure, Vavasour, "Case of a Cottager."

Source: *Communications to the Board of Agriculture* (London, select years, 1797–1805).

The obvious counterargument is that although the cowkeep in these schemes cost more than the maintenance associated with the open fields, it was a superior provision: a cow would fare better and be more productive. But the keep had to be much richer to compensate laborers newly required to pay rents. In many cases access to common grazing retained its edge, as reflected in several proposals for cottager cowkeeping. For example, Lord Winchilsea ranked various ways in which cottagers could find both summer and winter keep for a cow according to their efficiency. His most preferred option involved the possession of a sufficient quantity of enclosed grassland to enable one or more cows to be kept throughout the year. His second choice was enclosed summer pasture and some arable land on which to grow winter fodder. The third possibility entailed a "right of common for the summer keep and a meadow or arable or a meadow in common for the winter."[37] This possibility was held to be "nearly so advantageous as small enclosures," except that "nine commons out of ten are so much overstocked that the summer keep is bad," a disadvantage that was compounded if the meadow was also held in common.[38]

Advocates of enclosure, ancient and modern, have depicted overstocking as an inevitable problem when land is held in common.[39] But there are many references to grazing where the number of animals to be

[37] Lord Winchilsea, "Cottages," p. 81.

[38] Ibid.

[39] Bailey and Cully, *Northumberland*, p. 236; Plymley, *Shropshire*, pp. 224–25.

kept at different times of the year was clearly specified, and once specified these "stints" were carefully policed. References also occur to clearly defined and well-regulated turbary (rights to dig turf or peat) and estover (rights to cut wood).[40] Lord Brownlow's description of actual cottager cowkeeping schemes contains one primarily based on common pasture which was carefully stinted.[41] Here 13 out of 25 cottagers stocked the commons themselves, but the value of this well-regulated common is underlined by the other dozen's ability to let their rights to the farmers "who are ready to hire them at a price equal at least to what they pay for houses and commons" (35s per year).[42] Contrast these arrangements with those Brownlow (relatively) generously made available when newly enclosing, as summarized in Table 1. Here the 2.5 acres needed to keep a cow cost 15s per acre and the cottage with its less than one rood of garden another £2 10s per year.

The imposition of rent, rates, and higher prices for hay must have made some previously profitable cowkeeping uneconomic. But for many cottagers these calculations were irrelevant: cowkeeps were not made available on any terms. Even when legislation in 1819 and 1831 allowed parishes to obtain land for letting to the poor, and in 1832 enabled allotments to be set aside at enclosure, opposition from the farmers, high rents, and the use of unsuitable land limited the impact of such schemes.

What labor costs, here principally the opportunity cost in terms of wages forgone, did the cowkeeping cottager incur? Substantial underemployment and unemployment in many southern and southeastern agricultural districts might be thought to imply little real tension between the exploitation of the commons and the performance of locally available waged work, especially as laborers and their families were likely to minimize the opportunity costs of such self-employment by working in the evenings or on Sundays or by using the labor time of family members who were not working for wages: this latter response gave the commons labor force its characteristic age/sex composition, as discussed below. But wage-earning opportunities were sometimes sacrificed, much to the farmer's chagrin: "If you give them work, they will tell you that they must go to look up their sheep, cut furzes, get their cow out of the pound, and perhaps say that they must take their horse to be shod that he might carry them to a horse race or a cricket

[40] Pringle, *Westmoreland*, p. 322; Giles, "Enclosure in Stockport," pp. 87–88; this is not to deny that population growth put pressure on stint agreements, see Turner, *English Parliamentary Enclosure*, chap. 6.

[41] Lord Brownlow, "Queries Concerning Cottagers," *Communications to the Board of Agriculture*, 1 (1797), p. 85.

[42] Ibid.; for other evidence of the lucrative hiring out of common rights, see Pringle, *Westmoreland*, p. 321.

match."[43] Perhaps the laborers preferred to spend time "sauntering after their cattle," because the return to such activities exceeded the wage. Brownlow opposed laborers' possession of arable land because "it takes up so much of their time that they will not go to labourers' work at the times the farmers most want them; being, as I have often heard them say, better employed about their own business which if they neglected they lost more than their earnings as labourers."[44]

Before mechanization, at haymaking and harvest the farmers' requirements could not be met from the local pool of day labor, and the wives and children of the laborers constituted an essential labor reserve, whose availability was often an implicit condition of hiring.[45] But the independence conferred by common rights had disruptive implications for agricultural relations of production and threatened the cereal farmers with inadequate labor reserves at key times in the seasonal cycle. The threat posed by an insufficiently elastic labor supply, which had long provided an incentive to the capitalist farmers of southern and southeastern districts to retain a pool of underemployed men and unemployed women, became more deadly as the cereal belt widened.[46] Crops ripening simultaneously over a wide area could disrupt interregional flows of labor and throw additional pressure on local labor markets. Under these circumstances farmers became increasingly intolerant of distractions from waged work. Laborers with livestock, with gardens, and with rights of turbary and estover were not always at the farmers' beck and call. Nor were their wives and children only a seasonal labor reserve readily mobilized out of want and worklessness.

The farmers castigated the commons for obstructing agricultural progress, but also for promoting indiscipline and indolence among the workers.[47] Captured by the farmers and their perspective, the Board of Agriculture set hopelessly incompatible objectives: to enable laborers to be independent when old or unemployed, without lessening their commitment to wage labor.

Sir John Sinclair's principles for guiding the design of cowkeeping schemes illustrate the incompatibilities involved. The first principle,

[43] Arbuthnot, quoted in Ann Kussmaul, *Servants in Husbandry in Early Modern England* (Cambridge, 1981), pp. 22–23.

[44] Brownlow, "Queries," p. 86.

[45] E. J. T. Collins, "Labour Supply and Demand in European Agriculture, 1800–1880," in E. L. Jones and S. J. Woolf, eds., *Agrarian Change and Economic Development: The Historical Problems* (London, 1969), pp. 61–94; *Parliamentary Papers*, 21–22 (1861).

[46] Levine, *Reproducing Families*, p. 67.

[47] For a modern orthodox perspective on the efficiency of open field agriculture, see D. N. McCloskey, "The Enclosure of Open Fields: Preface to a Study of its Impact on the Efficiency of English Agriculture in the Eighteenth Century," this JOURNAL, 32 (Mar. 1972), pp. 15–35; but M. A. Havinden, "Agricultural Progress in Open Field Oxfordshire," *Agricultural History Review*, 4 (1961), pp. 73–83, demonstrates that enclosure was not a necessary condition for progressive farming; the link between the commons and the discipline of agricultural labor is a major theme in Snell, *Annals*, p. 170 ff.

"that the cottager shall raise by his own labour some of the most material articles of subsistence for himself and his family," and the second, "that he shall be enabled to supply the adjoining markets with the smaller agricultural productions," surely clashed with the third, "that both he and his family shall have it in their power to assist the neighbouring farmers, at all seasons of the year, almost equally as well as if they had no land in their occupation."[48] Significantly the Board reserved its accolades for schemes which minimized the disruptions to wage labor. Winchilsea preferred the possession of enclosed grassland because "except the haymaking, the rest of the business is done by his [the laborer's] wife and his labour is not interrupted."[49] But in many counties where the soil was not suited to grazing or where cereal production was replacing pasture, cowkeeping schemes had to involve some stall feeding with hay and vegetables. Basically there was not enough land to satisfy the demands of the farmers and leave enough over to enclose grassland for the cottagers. But the alternative of growing enough food for a cow was much more labor-intensive and in particular required both more male labor, as land had to be dug and ploughed, and more attention from other family members at harvest time coincident with the peak demands of the capitalist farmers.[50]

Sinclair's arable scheme required 558 hours, many of which were expected to come from the laborer's free time, but as an extreme case he assumed that the digging, manuring, and harvesting required 20 entire days in addition to by-hours and the labor of unemployed family members. Allowing 60 days for Sundays and holidays, this still left 285 days for the ordinary hand labor of the cottager. To reduce further the potential interference with wage labor, digging was to be "diversified as much as possible so as not to interfere materially with the other occupations of the cottager," and if even then "a cottager . . . could not work as a common daily labourer, he might at least answer, as a useful labourer by the piece," an ominous conclusion from the farmers' viewpoint.[51] Henry Vavasour admired his Yorkshire cottager Mr. Rook primarily because he and his family cultivated their three acres "in their *spare* hours from their daily hired work with seldom a whole day off except in harvest."[52] But even here the mention of distractions at the

[48] Sinclair, "Observations," pp. 358–59.

[49] Winchilsea, "Cottages," p. 80.

[50] In Sir John Sinclair's scheme the cow was maintained by arable farming, which "requires unquestionably more labour on the part of the cottager, and of his family: at the same time, the occupation of so great an extent of ground is not so necessary . . .," "Observations," p. 358.

[51] Ibid., p. 367.

[52] Winchilsea, "Cottages," p. 80; Henry Vavasour, "Reference to the Flemish Manner," *Communications to the Board of Agriculture*, 4 (1805), p. 308.

busiest time of the agricultural year would suffice to make many employers blench.[53]

Thus the growth of wage dependence which accompanied enclosure was not universally perceived as a drawback. The farmers actively welcomed it.[54] Disliking common rights precisely (if not solely) for the independence that they bestowed on laboring families, the farmers opposed the transfer of any functional equivalents into the post-enclosure relations of agricultural production.[55]

Summarizing, then, for a family in the fortunate position of being able to keep a cow, by and large on common land, and assuming the opportunity cost of the labor involved, though not negligible, was minimized by the employment of underemployed family members and offset by the value of by-products such as skim milk and manure, then the annual income from the cow was often more than half the adult male laborer's wage and an average-priced cow would pay for itself in about a year. If after enclosure the family retained some access to a cowkeep, their rent was adjusted accordingly, and if food had to be grown on an enclosed plot of arable, the opportunity cost in terms of wages forgone was undoubtedly raised. This cut profits in half. But for the majority of families even this reduced rate of return was unavailable, as all possibility of cowkeeping was eliminated with enclosure.

Although the cow was often the lynchpin of the cottager system of management, families that did not have a cow could still benefit from common grazing. Horses, for example, were crucial to the participation of J. M. Martin's village traders in the extensive carrying trade between the Feldon and the nearby Warwickshire coalfield.[56] The tenement garden, though strictly speaking not a common right, often disappeared with enclosure and certainly had an enhanced value when combined with access to pasture. Winchilsea ranked possession of a right of common and a garden as the fourth most comfortable state for a laborer: "This is certainly very beneficial to them: geese and pigs can be kept upon the common and the latter fed with the produce of the garden and a small quantity of purchased food."[57] In the late 1790s a pig, bought for 20s at Michaelmas, would be worth £3 by Christmas, much of the difference being net profit because the pig was fed mainly on "what else

[53] See also D. C. Barnett, "Allotments and the Problem of Rural Poverty, 1780–1840," in E. L. Jones and G. E. Mingay, eds., *Land, Labour and Population in the Industrial Revolution* (London, 1967), pp. 162–86.

[54] Yelling, *Common Field*; Snell, *Annals*.

[55] Snell, *Annals*; Barnett, "Allotments." Note here too the farmers' apparent reluctance to encourage cowkeeping by selling hay to their laborers, a stance which Mr. Barclay argued against on the grounds that a laborer who was dependent on a farmer for hay would "keep more closely by his work." See Robert Barclay, "On Labourers in Husbandry Renting Land," *Communications to the Board of Agriculture*, 1 (1797), pp. 91–92.

[56] Martin, "Village Traders."

[57] Winchilsea, "Cottages," p. 81.

be thrown away."[58] In the northwest the commoners' sheep could be sold for 9s to 13s per head and geese to the Yorkshire drovers at 1s 4d per head.[59] Their wool and their eggs could also be used domestically or sold on the local market.

Common rights other than pasture were also important. Laborers retained privileges in "the shrubs, woods, undergrowth, stone quarries and gravel pits, thereby obtaining fuel for cooking and wood for repairing houses, useful dietary supplements from the wild bird and animal life, crab apples and cob nuts from the hedgerows, brambles, whortles and juniper berries from the heaths, and mint, thyme, balm, tansy and other wild herbs from any other little patch of waste. . . . Almost every living thing in the parish however insignificant could be turned to some good use."[60]

Taxonomies of the products that could be hunted and gathered for consumption, or sale, or as the raw materials for some handicraft production, usually receive a condescending sneer. William Stevenson, in his survey of Surrey, observed the employment of women in cutting long heath to make besom brooms, from the sale of which they made 3s per week. Other women in the neighborhood gathered blueberries and whortleberries. He despised these activities as "miserable productions and trifling employments which the heaths in general afford."[61] Three shillings per week would amount to £7 16s per year, but assuming four weeks were lost in sickness and holidays, yearly earnings would be just over £7, which compares not unfavorably with what women could make in other employment.[62] Self-employment was an *economic* option and its relative attractions increased with the probability of unemployment and irregular earnings. Moreover, children, who were a burden for women attempting wage labor, were a help in freelance gathering activities.

One product of the commons and wastes escaped the usual scorn: free fuel or its availability at opportunity cost was universally recognized as making a major difference in the poor family's budget.[63] Sir John Sinclair's cottager accounts, which conclude with a nominal surplus, carried the ominous caveat that fuel costs would "greatly affect" any

[58] Brownlow, "Queries," p. 90.

[59] Pringle, *Westmoreland*.

[60] Alan Everitt, "Farm Labourers," in Thirsk, ed., *Agrarian History*, pp. 396–465.

[61] William Stevenson, *A General View of the Agriculture of the County of Surrey* (London, 1813), p. 459.

[62] In his *Annals*, Keith Snell gives £5.20, £6.87, and £7.87 as average female earnings in Surrey, Kent, Essex, and Hertfordshire in 1801–5, 1806–10, and 1811–15. Of course, any one gathering activity would be unlikely to provide year-round employment, but different kinds of self-employment, often including cottage industry, could be patched together and integrated with domestic work and childcare.

[63] Pamela Horn, *Labouring Life in the Victorian Countryside* (Dublin, 1976).

actual surplus.[64] Cobbett believed that abundance of fuel gave woodlanders significant advantage over laboring families elsewhere. But even in open country whatever could be scavenged rather than purchased was gratefully exploited. The main fuels were peat and wood, but those who could do no better burned sticks collected from hedgerows and copses, supplemented with large quantities of cow and horse dung. On islands and along the coast seaweed was burned; inland, depending on the local vegetation, they would cut heather, broom, furze, and gorse.[65] More or less anything that women and children could gather was burned.

A Mr. Keen, in testimony to the 1844 Committee on Commons' Inclosure, reported fuel costs in Godalming in Surrey, enclosed some 35 years previously.[66] Keen figured that the annual fuel consumption of a town cottager with four rooms was about two tons of coal and 100 faggots, which, in Godalming, cost £3 4s and £1 0s 10d respectively, or £4 4s 10d altogether. As the cottager could sell the ashes back to the farmer for 12s 6d, annual net fuel costs were about £3 12s 4d. As Godalming stood at the extreme point of coal supply lines, this probably represented a maximum cost. More generally coal was available at around 20s a ton, and faggots at 12s a hundred, so that 50s per annum was nearer the average cost to a laborer "not having the advantage of cutting his fuel."[67]

According to Keen, the laborer who did exercise rights of turbary seldom cut the fuel himself but "hired those who are not fortunate enough to be in constant work" to do it at 2s per 1,000 turfs. Given a requirement of 5,000 to 8,000 turfs per year, fuel cost at most 20s, plus the cost of faggots and the carting, which the laborer often obtained free in return for the ashes.

Generally the difference between buying coal and cutting turf worked out at about £1 per year, but the saving was more where coal was especially expensive or where family members cut the fuel in their spare time. Even the conservatively estimated saving of 20s per year was not insubstantial compared with laborers' wages.

The Hammonds arrived at a similar evaluation of common rights to fuel based on David Davies's working-class budgets. They assumed that a man could cut enough fuel in a week to provide for his family for about a year and that the week's wages forgone were 10s. The value of the fuel, as imputed from market equivalents in southern counties, averaged £2 8s. So the net gain from the week's work was around £1 18s, a princely reward by agricultural laborers' standards in the late eighteenth century. The Hammonds noted that "it must be remembered that the

64 Sinclair, "Observations," p. 364.

65 William Cobbett, *Rural Rides* (London, 1922); Caroline Davidson, *A Woman's Work is Never Done: A History of Housework in the British Isles, 1650–1950* (London, 1982).

66 *Parliamentary Papers, Commons Inclosure*, p. 55ff.

67 Ibid., p. 71.

10s opportunity cost is calculated on the assumption that the man would otherwise be working whereas in reality he could cut his turf in slack times and in odd hours when there was no money to be made by working for someone else."[68] Alternatively women and children could cut the turf when they had no waged work.

Suggestions that the land on which common rights of turbary were exercised should be sold to establish a "coal fund" to which the needy might apply were popular with the farmers, partly because they transformed a right into a charitable donation, available only at the discretion of the fund's administrators and undoubtedly conditional on the applicants' "characters" and "behavior."[69] In his testimony before the Committee on Commons Inclosure Mr. Keen resisted this idea, arguing that, if regulated, turf cutting was an efficient system. The chairman's intervention to the effect that cottagers would be better off with less fuel, as their "immoderate grates" were the cause of frequent accidents, typifies the class-biased casuistry of this committee.[70]

One final benefit that the poor commonly enjoyed in rural England was the right to glean. Gleaning was not strictly linked to common rights, and could operate over enclosed fields, but with more difficulty than over open ones, and it meant nothing if the land was converted to pasture. So it too was threatened by enclosure. The agricultural laborers themselves, and those commentators who appreciated the cottager economy, testified that particularly at times of scarcity and high prices, "in its small way [gleaning] . . . contributed much to the benefit of the poor."[71]

Working people's defense of the right to glean confirms that significant returns were involved, while the farmers' opposition illustrates again the hostility and suspicion of class relations in the countryside. In wheat, gleaning constituted a cleaning operation and was beneficial to the farmers. Consequently prosecutions were rare, although farmers opposed gleaning until the fields were cleared completely in case the temptation to rob the stooks proved too great. With barley and beans the situation was different and almost all court cases refer to them.

Barley and beans were used as livestock feed and access to their waste encouraged laborers to keep animals. Apart from the anxiety that if workers owned animals they would be distracted and undisciplined, farmers also worried that when the stock of harvest gleanings was

[68] Hammond and Hammond, *Village Labourer*, p. 107.

[69] Ibid., p. 129; Wrightson, *English Society*, p. 175.

[70] *Parliamentary Papers, Commons Inclosure*, p. 77.

[71] Yelling, *Common Field*, p. 227; Martin, "Village Traders," p. 183, quotes Homer to the effect that gleaning rights were a "special boon" to the cottagers precisely because the product did not vary with good or bad harvests and so was "most advantageous when most wanted to be so."

exhausted, laborers would pilfer from their barns and granaries.[72] Barley was also often undersown with grass to provide grazing for sheep or cattle in the few short weeks between harvest and autumn frosts. Animals could not be let into fields where gleaning was in process and the farmers chafed at such constraints.

Again it is possible to impute fairly precise values to gleaning. Witness the circumstances of a laboring family reported in 1795. The father earned only 7s or 8s a week plus his food during the harvest month. The family grew its own potatoes and was allowed a ton of coal from the parish. With wheat costing 13s 6d per bushel and the family's minimal consumption reduced to half a bushel, the wife's gleaning of three of four bushels, though it might not prevent her children from going hungry, was an important contribution. Even if it took her the whole harvest month to salvage the three or four bushels, her imputed weekly earnings were almost twice as high as the normal earnings of her husband.[73]

In some places gleaning was even more rewarding. At Rode in Northamptonshire, for example, several families allegedly gathered enough wheat to keep themselves in bread for the whole year and as many beans as they needed to keep a pig.[74] Ivy Pinchbeck gives five or six bushels as the amount that a women herself could usually glean.[75] Including the contribution of other family members, when a bushel of wheat costs almost double the weekly wages of a farm laborer, the gains were vital within the family economy.

WOMEN AND ENCLOSURE: USING HOURS THAT WOULD "BE OTHERWISE WORSE THAN LOST"

Women have figured frequently in these descriptions of the mobilization of common resources. It is now more than fifty years since Ivy Pinchbeck first suggested that enclosures limited the opportunities available to working women and increased their dependence on husbands, fathers, and the poor rates.[76] Since then a more general debate about the effects of industrialization and the transition to capitalism on the welfare and status of women has rumbled on, usually in the pages of feminist or radical journals, but occasionally erupting into the main-

[72] David H. Morgan notes that on some farms, laborers, particularly those with access to stocks, were prohibited from keeping pigs and poultry; see "The Place of Harvesters in Nineteenth-Century Village Life," in Raphael Samuel, ed., *Village Life and Labour* (London, 1975), pp. 27–72.

[73] E. Harries, "Letter," *Annals of Agriculture*, 25 (1796), p. 488; Jennie Kitteringham, "Country Work Girls in Nineteenth-Century England," in Samuel, ed., *Village Life*, pp. 73–139, also suggests that, with hard work, it was possible to glean enough to supply bread for a family during the winter months.

[74] Eden, *State of the Poor*, p. 547.

[75] Ivy Pinchbeck, *Women Workers and the Industrial Revolution* (New York, 1969).

[76] Ibid.

stream.[77] One school of thought, the optimists, have emphasized alleged employment gains and derived improvements in women's status within the family. They contrast this with the harsh conditions of life for women and patriarchal culture of precapitalism.[78] The opposing school of thought, the pessimists, have argued that the transition to capitalism in Britain limited women's economic options, crystallized the division of labor between paid and unpaid work, exaggerated sex segmentation in the former, and reduced women's participation in wage labor, trends only reversed in the twentieth century.[79] In contrast they emphasize the rude egalitarianism implicit in the shared work and tough conditions of the feudal era. Much (too much) of this debate has focused on the experiences of women in the early factories of the industrial revolution, particularly in textiles and pottery.

More recently women workers in other sectors have received attention.[80] But despite the revived interest of historians, until K. D. M. Snell's recent monograph the particular links between enclosure and these trends have been neglected.[81] Instead, changes in technology and the organization of production or, more convincingly, women's historically specific biological responsibilities for children were cited as shaping women's economic roles. Early modern mothering did not readily combine with capitalist wage labor.[82]

In precapitalist production the domestic and production units were partially fused, allegedly facilitating the combination of pregnancy and nursing with women's work in a wide variety of agricultural and industrial tasks. Capitalist development eroded the imbrication of domestic and production activities. Labor was intensified, effort was concentrated, and the workday and workplace were formalized. There were no spontaneous pauses in which to nurse and babies were banished

[77] For an excellent survey of this debate, see Janet Thomas, "Women and Capitalism: Oppression or Emancipation? A Review Article," *Comparative Studies in Society and History*, 30 (1988), pp. 534–49.

[78] For the important references, see ibid.

[79] Eric Richards, "Women in the British Economy since about 1700: An Interpretation," *History*, 59 (Oct. 1974), pp. 337–57; Louise A. Tilly and Joan W. Scott, *Women, Work and Family* (New York, 1978); D. C. Baines, "The Labour Supply and the Labour Market, 1860–1914," in Roderick Floud and Donald McCloskey, eds., *The Economic History of Britain Since 1700* (Cambridge, 1981); K. D. M. Snell, "Agricultural Seasonal Unemployment, the Standard of Living and Women's Work in the South and East, 1690–1860," *Economic History Review*, 34 (Aug. 1981), pp. 407–37; George Joseph, *Women at Work* (Oxford, 1983).

[80] For example, Kitteringham, "Country Work Girls"; Kussmaul, *Servants*.

[81] Snell, *Annals*.

[82] Modern research confirms fragmentary historical evidence suggesting that in the absence of facilities for bottle-feeding, sterilization equipment, appropriate food, and pure water, breastfeeding was essential for infant survival, see UNICEF, *The World's Children* (Paris, 1978); Joanna Brenner and Maria Ramas, "Rethinking Women's Oppression," *New Left Review*, 144 (Mar.-Apr. 1981), pp. 33–71; Jane Humphries, "The Sexual Division of Labour and Social Control: An Interpretation," *Review of Radical Political Economics* (forthcoming).

from workshops and factories. Wives and mothers found it increasingly difficult to participate in the ascendant mode of work.

Changes in the organization of agricultural production produced analogous tensions. In eighteenth-century England the daughters of agricultural laborers hired themselves out annually as servants in husbandry, or more rarely, sought wage labor. After marriage, with the critical exceptions of haymaking and harvest, waged work was infrequent. Thus in a sample of 120 laboring families, the mother/wife on average contributed only 7 percent of family income, mainly from harvest earnings.[83] Similarly, responses to the Poor Law Authorities' investigation of the availability and remuneration of employment for women and children in 1834 suggest, first, that there was little continuous agricultural work available, and, second, that married women with children were not thought (at least by the responding officials) to be in a position to undertake regular wage labor. If such attitudes influenced the distribution of relief, they may have played a role in laboring families' ability not to send wives/mothers out to work as day laborers.[84]

But this does not mean that these women did not work. As Pinchbeck argued, the commons, along with cottage industry (the two often being combined in the cottager economy), allowed wives and mothers to augment their families' resources without recourse to regular wage labor. Women could more easily combine self-employment than early capitalist wage labor with the care and nourishment of their children. C. T. Haden, a contemporary expert on childhood diseases, emphasized that poor mothers organized their work so as not to interfere with their nursing, and their nursing so as not to interfere with their work.[85] In contrast, agricultural wage labor often required work far from home, for specific hours, and without interruption. Working at or from home, women could also utilize the labor of their children, transmit skills, and keep a watchful eye on the chance encounters of their growing daughters.

In this context, many gathering, scavenging, and processing activities, as well as the care of livestock and the cultivation of a garden, were relatively rewarding. Remember that women's wages in agriculture

[83] Eden, *The State of the Poor*; Davies, *The Case of Labourers*. Data for a group of families in Lincolnshire in 1868 also suggests that the harvest earnings of women represented about 7 percent of annual income. But these women were able to work for additional wages in the spring, increasing their yearly contribution to 12 to 14 percent. Inclusion of the harvest earnings of children boosted the contribution of autumnal wages to around one-seventh of the whole livelihood: see Horn, *Labouring Life in the Victorian Countryside*. Recasting David Morgan's judgment in terms of rural families, not individual workers, such earnings could indeed be the key to survival, "The Place of Harvesters," p. 38.

[84] "Report from his Majesty's Commissioners for Inquiring into the Operation of the Poor Laws in England and Wales: Appendix B 1," *Parliamentary Papers*, 30 (1834).

[85] C. T. Haden, *Practical Observations on the Management and Disease of Children* (London, 1827), pp. 24, 124.

were only one-half to two-thirds the male wage and sometimes even lower. Moreover, despite the comments of many contemporaries, eking out a livelihood on the commons was no more risky than wage labor. Diversity and flexibility could be built into self-employment, whereas the eighteenth century saw a long-term reduction in women's work in the southeastern counties and a decline in yearly hiring as employers responded to the settlement laws by shortening tenures and increasing turnover. The long-term reduction in women's work in the southeastern counties made their wage labor more uncertain.[86]

So, as in many parts of the Third World today, proletarianization took the form of the husband/father working for wages, while the wife/mother and the children added, often significantly, to family subsistence by exploiting traditional rights to rural resources. The husband/father sometimes also made nonwage contributions to the family's livelihood, and the wife/mother and the children frequently also contributed wages earned at harvest and haymaking, or more regularly if the age-sex composition of the family facilitated their employment and work was available. What evidence is there to support this hypothesis?

If women, in particular, gained from the commons and wastes, they would surely have figured in the popular opposition to enclosure. The evidence suggests that they did.[87] Remember it was a few old *women* whom Arthur Young identified as implacably opposed to enclosure in Sussex. Perhaps their opposition had less to do with "singularity" than self-interest. Women also appeared frequently in court proceedings against gleaners.[88]

There is also direct evidence that it was women specifically who exploited the opportunities of the commons. Women exploited common grazing as an alternative to charity, the poor law, or burdening their children.[89] The widow and her cow were probably as common in reality as they are in fairy tales. Z, the son of a stable-helper and laborer, who appears in Briscoe Eyre's accounts of life in the New Forest, derived a double advantage from the local common. It provided both a summer keep for his own three cows and enabled his widowed mother to remain independent by keeping a cow and a pig, "almost entirely on the common."[90]

Widows' traditional recourse to cowkeeping was even institutionalized as a public panacea for feminized poverty. The guardians often

[86] Pinchbeck, *Women*; Kussmaul, *Servants*; Snell, *Annals*.

[87] Hammond and Hammond, *The Village Labourer*; Hobsbawm and Rude, *Captain Swing*; Wrightson, *English Society*.

[88] Morgan, "The Place of Harvesters," p. 58.

[89] Pinchbeck, *Women*.

[90] G. E. Briscoe Eyre, *The New Forest, Its Common Rights and Cottage Stock-Keepers* (Lyndhurst, 1883), pp. 54–55.

purchased cows for older women to try to keep them off the rates.[91] But for the cow to be a functional equivalent for social security, continued access to land was required: hence the significance of the commons to this section of the rural population.

The tradition of using the underemployed or low-paid labor of women in milking and buttermaking characterized the Board of Agriculture's schemes for cowkeeping by the rural poor. It was emphasized by proponents as reducing the labor demands on husbands and fathers, and so less likely to interfere with the supply of day labor to capitalist farms. "The wives and daughters milk and manage the cows, with occasional assistance from their husbands; but the latter are not prevented from working for their masters the farmers, or pursuing their trades, with great regularity through the year, except for about a week in hay harvest; and a few days at other times, when the carrying of their manure or some other work that the women cannot perform demands their attention."[92]

Such arrangements were touted as ideal. The employer gained because cow or allotment-keeping cottagers ate better and so worked harder for the same wages. The husband would "think himself extremely happy if, while he was working for his rich neighbor . . . his wife could be employed at home in managing a cow and a pig."[93] Society at large benefited by usefully filling the spare time of the laborers: "they are still more benefitted by the improvement of their habits, than they are by the increase of their comforts. When they have a little spare time the men go off to their land and their stock, rather than to the alehouse; and the women employ many hours in the care of their cows and dairies, which would be otherwise worse than lost in idleness and gossip."[94]

Women's readiness to mobilize rural resources is also reflected in their primary responsibility for cottage gardens.[95] Jane Millward, a collier's wife, developed a prizewinning scheme for cultivating about 1.5 acres, and she did so in the course of bearing and rearing 11 chil-

[91] Winchilsea, "Cottages," p. 78; Pinchbeck, *Women.*

[92] Mr. Crutchley, "Answers to the Queries Respecting Cottagers Renting Land," *Communications to the Board of Agriculture*, 1 (1797), p. 94.

[93] Thomas Thompson, "Reasons for Giving Lands to Cottagers to Enable them to Keep Cows," *Communications to the Board of Agriculture*, 4 (1805), p. 427.

[94] Thomas Babington, "Account of Some Cottagers," *Communications to the Board of Agriculture*, 4 (1805), p. 394. Social benefits significantly collapsed into benefits to ratepayers. The Board of Agriculture's schemes were intended to reduce applications for relief, and similarly Arthur Young's calculations of the costs and benefits were in terms of the impact on poor law expenditures. The logic was impeccable: if families' incomes were not to be supplemented from the rates, and if wages were not to increase, underemployed women and children had to be found work.

[95] Pinchbeck, *Women.*

dren![96] Nor were women's efforts directed only to raising food for family consumption. They often grew cash crops and projects could expand into the cultivation of common land. For example, hemp growing in allotments on the commons took "the place of poultry rearing as a recognised source of income for women" in parts of Dorset in the late 1700s.[97]

Women also predominate in accounts of gathering and scavenging activities associated with the commons and wastes. The berry gatherers and besom makers of Surrey were women. Women and girls, in gangs and independently, cockled and musselled around the Lancashire coast and along the shores of the Wash. Although all family members took pride in their pig, mothers and children were particularly creative in their use of humble resources in its fattening. Reflecting on her Norfolk childhood, one woman remembered going with her mother to gather "all the food that was for free: watercress from running streams, rabbits, pigeons, wild raspberries, wild plums and blackberries, crabapples, hazel nuts, chestnuts, walnuts. No squirrels hoarded these more carefully than we did . . . ."[98]

Women were also the principal gatherers of fuel: in Cornwall they would cut furze in early summer from thickets up to ten feet high, in the Midlands collect straw and stubble, and in Surrey bring home prodigious loads of wood or sacks of fir cones picked up in the woods a mile or more away.[99] And they combined this with other responsibilities: George Sturt remembered meeting women bent nearly double under loads of fire wood, "toiling painfully along, with hats or bonnets pushed awry . . . occasionally tiny urchins, too small to be left at home alone, would be clinging to their mothers' frocks."[100] The preparation of peat, which was burned in many counties, was a family enterprise, but women and children usually performed the drying and stacking operations, and in some districts peat was transported home on women's backs.

Gleaning was also women's work. In reality a far from picturesque activity, it must have been exhausting coming immediately after women's harvest work. As with harvesting and other gathering activities, women could combine gleaning with childcare. Indeed the assistance provided by older children was essential if the opportunities in the harvest waste were to be exhausted. Flora Thompson's description of

[96] Sir William Pulteney, "Account of a Cottager," *Communications to the Board of Agriculture*, 4 (1805), p. 344.

[97] Barbara Kerr, *Bound to the Soil: A Social History of Dorset, 1750–1918* (London, 1968), pp. 80–81.

[98] Norfolk Federation of Women's Institutes, *Within Living Memory*, quoted in Horn, *Labouring Life*, p. 30.

[99] See Davidson, *Woman's Work*.

[100] George Sturt, *Change in the Village* (London, 1912), p. 23.

the back-breaking work, the need for "well-disciplined" children, the suckling of babies in the rest hour, and the pride in women and children's "little bit o' leazings," vividly captures the conditions and importance of this almost forgotten female labor.[101]

But if commons and wastes were mainly exploited by women and children, whose labor was not regularly required by or supplied to the capitalist farms, how can the loss of common rights be causally linked to proletarianization? First, the elimination of nonwage sources of survival increased dependence on wages and wage-earners. The implications for labor discipline and intrafamily relationships were far-reaching. Second, the closure of options other than wage labor ensured women's availability for employment, if and when they were needed. Here the emphasis has been on large seasonal fluctuations in demand for agricultural labor in the context of an unmechanized harvest, but the loss of common rights also made women more readily available for domestic, proto-industrial, and industrial work.[102] Without access to rural resources, children too could contribute only through waged work, and were more likely to be "put out to labor *early*."[103]

In contrast, by providing some members of the laborer's family with alternatives to wage labor, the commons liberated them from the beck and call of the farmers. Access to other sources of subsistence meant that, in the short term at least, a wageless laborer would not starve. Nor would his family. In the terms of the times these were not paltry degrees of freedom.

CONCLUSION

Proletarianization has been interpreted ahistorically as the transformation of self-sufficient peasants into breadwinning wage laborers. The overwhelming emphasis has been on the male experience. But in reality survival seldom depends on a single breadwinner: a family's subsistence derived from the productive contributions of all its members. Proletarianization was a gradual process whereby access to resources other than wages was slowly eliminated. Employers' interests in the development of proletarianization, directly motivated by seasonal and sectoral variations in the demand for labor, necessarily spilled over into interests in intrafamily patterns of dependence and support. The dependence of whole families on wages ensured a sufficiently elastic labor supply to cope with an unmechanized harvest. The dependence of whole families

[101] Flora Thompson, *Lark Rise to Candleford* (London, 1954), p. 14.

[102] Plymley's views are typical: "the commons operates upon their minds as a sort of independence: this idea leads the man to lose many days work by which he gets a habit of indolence: a daughter kept at home to milk a poor half-starved cow, who being open to temptation soon turns harlot, and becomes a distressed ignorant mother instead of making a useful servant." *Shropshire*, p. 225.

[103] Ibid., p. 225, his emphasis.

on wage earners strengthened discipline and commitment: to be a good husband or father it became necessary to be a good wage earner.

Not surprisingly then, proletarianization was uneven and particularized in its impact on different family members. Here I have emphasized the specific implications for women of the loss of certain rural resources. I have shown hitherto despised activities and denigrated resources to have had historical significance. In the light of the experience of wives and mothers, historians should revise their view of the value of the commons, and, incidentally, the role of enclosures in the genesis of wage labor. But there is more at stake than a partial rehabilitation of Marx. An analysis of the links among enclosure, common rights, and wage dependence which attends to the experience of women is not just more complete and more conceptually sophisticated. It is better history.

Getting a Foot in the Door: "Learning," State Dependence, and the Racial Integration of Firms

WARREN C. WHATLEY

Economists have emphasized supply-side learning when explaining long-term trends in racial income differences. This article demonstrates that learning also occurred on the demand side. Estimation of a state-dependence model of the sequence of racial employment outcomes of firms in Cincinnati, Ohio, during World War I shows that the introduction of black workers into a previously all-white firm generated new experiences within the firm, altering its future racial employment decisions. This suggests that more research should be done on how firms and labor markets processed information about workers and how that influenced worker opportunities.

Recent treatments of long-term black economic gain, including the works of James Smith, Finis Welch, and Robert Margo, place heavy emphasis on supply-side factors.[1] In particular they stress the low level of black educational attainment caused by racial inequalities in the "separate-but-equal" educational systems in the South and emphasize how these poorly educated cohorts dominated the black male labor force for the first half of the twentieth century. Following improved education after World War II relative black economic well-being advanced.

Without denying the importance of supply-side learning in explaining long-term trends, there is reason to believe that learning occurred on the

The Journal of Economic History, Vol. L, No. 1 (Mar. 1990). ISSN 0022-0507.

The author is Associate Professor of Economics at the University of Michigan, Ann Arbor, MI 48109.

The research reported here was funded by National Science Foundation Grant no. 8300696 and a research grant from the Rackham Graduate School, University of Michigan. For helpful comments I would like to thank Lee Alston, Charlie Brown, William Darity, Paul David, Price Fishback, Sherrie Kossoudji, Robert Margo, Gary Solon, Gavin Wright, and several anonymous referees. I am grateful to Thomas Weiss, whose editorial suggestions substantially improved the final draft. I also want to thank Mary Kosnick and especially Tom Maloney for excellent research assistance.

[1] James Smith, "Race and Human Capital," *American Economic Review*, 74 (Sept. 1984); James Smith and Finis Welch, *Closing the Gap: Forty Years of Economic Progress for Blacks* (Santa Monica, 1986); James Smith and Finis Welch, "Black Economic Progress After Myrdal," *Journal of Economic Literature*, 27 (June 1989), pp. 519–64; Finis Welch, "Education and Racial Discrimination," in Orley Ashenfelter, ed., *Discrimination in Labor Markets* (Princeton, 1973); Robert Margo, "Race and Human Capital: Comment," *American Economic Review*, 76 (Dec. 1986), pp. 1221–24; Robert Margo, "Race, Educational Attainment and the 1940 Census," this JOURNAL, 46 (Mar. 1986), pp. 189–98; and Robert Margo, "Educational Achievement in Segregated School Systems: The Effects of 'Separate-but-Equal,' " *American Economic Review*, 76 (Sept. 1986), pp. 794–801.

demand side as well and is an important part of the story. When events during World War I cut off the supply of unskilled immigrant workers from Europe, many northern employers were forced to learn how to integrate black workers into their work environments for the first time. Gunnar Myrdal placed great faith in what he called the "American Creed" and believed northern firms would learn through increased contact between blacks and whites that many of the popularly held views of the time on racial prejudices and stereotypes were unfounded:

> Employers who do employ Negroes . . . often get a greater appreciation of them than employers who do not. The same is true of white workers. If they actually work together with Negro workers, they come to like them better, or to dislike them less, than they expected.[2]

But Myrdal was too optimistic. More recent empirical studies show that race remained an explicit criterion for job assignments and promotions for long periods of time, even in firms, industries, and regions where black workers were substantial in number.[3] According to labor historians, firms of the late nineteenth century came to rely increasingly on "internal labor market" systems, so that worker progress came to depend more on the opportunities made available in their firm.[4] Perhaps firms learned that it was profitable to devise race-specific criteria for job assignments and promotions that reflected the prevailing state of thinking about race at the time.

Under the assumptions of perfect competition the learning is usually taken to be a straightforward and simple process. Conventional economic models have shown that rational employers will learn to segregate workers who do not share a common outlook, language, or any other characteristics that make integration costly.[5] Competition in labor

[2] Gunnar Myrdal, *An American Dilemma* (New York, 1944), p. 392.

[3] See, for example, Richard Rowan, *The Negro in the Textile Industry* (Philadelphia, 1970), pp. 65–68; Bernard Anderson, *The Negro in the Public Utilities Industries* (Philadelphia, 1970), pp. 162–71; Dennis C. Dickerson, *Out of the Crucible: Black Steel Workers in Western Pennsylvania, 1875–1980* (Albany, 1986), pp. 240–62; Walter Fogel, *The Negro in the Meat Packing Industry* (Philadelphia, 1970), pp. 101–10; Herbert Northrup, *The Negro in the Tobacco Industry* (Philadelphia, 1970), pp. 2–5, 60–84; Lester Rubin, *The Negro in the Shipbuilding Industry* (Philadelphia, 1970), pp. 112–19; Carol King and Howard W. Risher Jr., *The Negro in the Petroleum Industry* (Philadelphia, 1969), pp. 26–29; and Herbert Northrup, *The Negro in the Rubber Tire Industry* (Philadelphia, 1969), pp. 30–39.

[4] See Sanford M. Jacoby, *Employing Bureaucracy: Managers, Unions, and the Transformation of Work in American Industry, 1900–1945* (New York, 1985); and William Sundstrom, "Internal Labor Markets Before World War I: On the Job Training and Employment Promotion," *Explorations in Economic History*, 25 (Oct. 1988), pp. 425–45.

[5] See Kenneth Arrow, "The Theory of Discrimination," in Orley Ashenfelter and Albert Rees, eds., *Discrimination in Labor Markets* (Princeton, 1973); Kenneth Arrow, "Some Mathematical Models of Racial Discrimination in the Labor Market," in Anthony Pascal, ed., *Racial Discrimination in Economic Life* (Lexington, 1972); and Kevin Lang, "A Language Theory of Discrimination," *Quarterly Journal of Economics*, 101 (May 1986), pp. 363–82.

markets tends to limit the resulting segregation patterns to innocuous forms that have little appreciable long-term effect on wages.

But at least two historical conditions make the learning and adjustment processes more complex. First, employers seldom had perfect information about the productive abilities of new hires, especially northern employers of black migrants during World War I. Models of statistical discrimination have shown that firms using unreliable indicators of workers' abilities tend to treat individuals according to group characteristics and undervalue talented members of disadvantaged groups hired on the open market.[6] These imperfect beginnings can have lasting consequences, for even if employers subsequently learn the true abilities of these workers, a rational employer may still discriminate against them in promotion so that their true ability is not revealed to other employers.[7] Since these workers' job skills are less fully rewarded than those of other workers, they will have less incentive to invest in their own human capital.[8]

Second, what employers, managers, and workers learned about the meaning of race in the work place and in the labor market may have had adverse feedback effects on the structure of opportunities offered to black workers because the learning occurred when racialistic and nativistic modes of thinking were popular in American culture and undoubtedly influenced how economic agents interpreted information and economic outcomes.[9] As Charles Johnson succinctly put it when commenting on the generally held belief that black workers were "specially useful" in certain occupations:

> There is probably no more actual truth in the belief that they (black workers) are better adapted than most races to work in the presence of heat than that they cannot do skilled work; rather the probability is that having been permitted "heat" jobs on this assumption, a normal success has provided support for the assumption.[10]

One can think of this type of equilibrium as the result of a complex path-dependent adjustment process where historically contingent events influence the final outcome by influencing both the probability that certain states of the world occur and how those states are interpreted. Such an adjustment path need not converge on an innocu-

[6] See Dennis J. Aigner and Glen Cain, "Statistical Theories of Discrimination in the Labor Market," *Industrial and Labor Relations Review*, 30 (Apr. 1977), pp. 175–87.

[7] Paul Milgrom and Sharon Oster, "Job Discrimination, Market Forces, and the Invisibility Hypothesis," *Quarterly Journal of Economics*, 102 (Aug. 1987), pp. 453–76.

[8] Shelly J. Lundberg and Richard Startz, "Private Discrimination and Social Intervention in Competitive Labor Markets," *American Economic Review*, 73 (June 1983), pp. 340–47.

[9] On these modes of thought, see Stephen J. Gould, *The Mismeasure of Man* (New York, 1981); George M. Fredrickson, *The Black Image in the White Mind* (Middletown, CT, 1971); and George M. Fredrickson, *The Arrogance of Race* (Middletown, CT, 1988).

[10] Charles S. Johnson, *The Negro in American Civilization* (New York, 1930), p. 81.

ous pattern of racial segregation. Start, for example, with the simplest initial condition: economic discrimination against black workers during the initial period of racial integration when agents were learning how to segregate workers. One of the many forms of discrimination economists expect to occur during this period is in the quality of jobs. Black workers will not only be offered the most dangerous, disagreeable, and difficult jobs, but they will accept them without the compensating wage differential required to attract white workers whose opportunities are not circumscribed by discrimination. Starting with racialist priors, northerners may then come to believe that black workers are better adapted for these jobs "because of their nature," not because of their economic condition—"a normal success provides support for the assumption." Employers continue offering these types of jobs to black workers because they have "learned" about their "comparative advantage." They tend not to offer them other types of jobs, thereby reducing the probability of observing other possible states of the world.

Learning on the demand side is then an important but neglected area of research in the study of race and economics. The World War I North is an ideal site to use in examining this type of learning, but our existing knowledge of this period is chiefly aggregate or anecdotal. Aggregate occupational and industry data by race have been gathered and analyzed by Smith, Dale Hienstand, Dean Dutcher, Herbert Northrup, Richard Rowan, and others.[11] But no study has analyzed the process by which northern firms racially integrated their work forces. Consequently, we do not know which firms integrated, how they did so, or why. More important, we do not know if the lessons learned from the initial experiences with race had any impact on the future employment prospects for blacks.

This article is the initial step in my attempt to address these questions. Here I report results from a newly developed data set that allows, among other things, a test for state dependence in the racial employment outcomes of firms.

It is important to distinguish state-dependent outcomes from path-dependent adjustment processes. In both schemes the occurrence of a particular outcome in one period influences the probability of the occurrence of a particular outcome in the next period. If an outcome is state dependent, then past events influence the probability structure of future outcomes, making some more likely and others less likely.[12] An

[11] Smith, *Race and Human Capital*; Dale Hienstand, *Economic Growth and Employment Opportunities for Minorities* (New York, 1964); Dean Dutcher, *The Negro in Modern Industrial Society* (New York, 1931); Herbert Northrup, et al., *Negro Employment in Basic Industry* (Philadelphia, 1970); and Herbert Northrup and Richard Rowan, *Negro Employment in Southern Industry* (Philadelphia, 1970).

[12] See James Heckman, "Heterogeneity and State-Dependence," in Sherwin Rosen, ed., *Studies in Labor Markets* (Chicago, 1981), pp. 91–139; and David T. Ellwood, "Teenage

outcome is path dependent when a complex sequence of state-dependent outcomes converges on a particular equilibrium which is "selected" from a set of possible equilibria by the stochastic (or historically contingent) elements of the world.[13] One should therefore interpret the results reported in the last section of this article as a necessary but not sufficient test for path dependence in the racial integration of northern firms. Better data are needed to test for path dependence.

The data used here are panel data on employment for 151 firms in Atlanta and 324 in Cincinnati, most of which give employment information for 1914 through late 1918.[14] For 1918 the survey also collected information on the number of workers by race in 14 wage classes ranging from \$6 to \$10 up to \$65 and over per week. These data permit the calculation of average firmwide wages for 1918. Information was also collected on the nature of work done in the plant and the amount of work done under government contract.

These data were supplemented by two additional sources of information. First, occupation data were collected from the 1910 population census, where information on employment by occupation was given for 85 separate industry classifications. Workers fell into over 500 occupations and the percentages skilled, semiskilled, and common were calculated for each industry. The skill breakdown by industry was used to proxy the occupational structure of the firms in the sample.[15] Second, ward-level information about each firm's location was collected from the 1910 and 1920 population censuses.[16] Community characteristics were then used to control for racial labor supply differences across firms

---

Unemployment: Permanent Scars or Temporary Blemishes," in Richard Freeman and David Wise, eds., *The Youth Labor Market Problem* (Chicago, 1982).

[13] See Paul David, "Clio and the Economics of QWERTY," *American Economic Review*, 75 (May 1985), pp. 332–37; Paul David, "Why and When Does History Matter?" this JOURNAL, 50 (June 1990), forthcoming; W. Brian Arthur, Yuri M. Ermoliev, and Yuri M. Kaniovski, "On Generalized Urn Schemes of the Polya Kind," *Cybernetics*, 19 (March 1983); and W. Brian Arthur, Yuri M. Ermoliev and Yuri M. Kaniovski, "Path-Dependent Processes and the Emergence of Macro-Structure," *European Journal of Operational Research*, 30 (March 1987).

[14] The sample of firms is drawn from the U.S. Housing Corporation survey of firms in late 1918. The manuscripts are housed in the National Archives. These data are unique because the survey collected firm-level information on the racial composition of work forces for the last weeks of 1913, 1916, 1917, and "last payroll" (late 1918—usually Oct. 1918). The dates are actually the first weeks of 1914, 1917, 1918, and "last payroll," but it is best to think of the observation as the results of the previous year's employment experiences. This is the interpretation used throughout this article and is the reason why the dating convention mentioned in the text is adopted.

[15] Firms were then placed into two-digit Standard Industrial Classification categories. All are two-digit level except Fertilizer and Cottonseed Oil. These two are singled out because they are such large employers of blacks in the South.

[16] Firms' addresses were used to locate them on ward maps for 1920, and ward-level data on the racial composition of population were gathered from the U.S. Bureau of the Census, *14th Census of the United States, 1920*, vol. 3: *Population-Composition and Characteristics of the Population By States* (Washington, DC, 1920), pp. 226, 447.

that emanated from locations in the city's transportation system and racial residential patterns.

INCREASED RACIAL CONTACT

At the turn of the century most northerners had little, if any, direct experience with black workers. As late as 1910 the vast majority of black Americans still resided and worked in the Black Belt counties of the Deep South created during the days of slavery, while industrialists to the north relied primarily on native-white and immigrant workers from Europe. The isolation of southern blacks from northern industrial labor markets was remarkable.[17] Beginning with World War I changes in these racial segregation patterns began to accelerate. It has been estimated that 400,000 to 500,000 southern blacks migrated north during the war, most settling in cities along the industrial belt stretching from New York to Chicago.[18] Between 1910 and 1920 the black share of industrial employment in most of these cities more than doubled. In Cincinnati it increased by 98 percent. In Detroit the increase was tenfold. During this decade foreign immigration slowed considerably, especially during the war, when it dropped to one-fourth of its 1914 level. Initially unemployment remained high and in fact increased during 1915. Starting in 1916 labor markets began to tighten, and this is when the northern migration of blacks accelerated.[19]

A greater proportion of these migrants came from the more racially

[17] Even within the rural South the degree of geographic concentration by race was high. In 1910, 45 percent of southern blacks lived in counties where they were the majority of the population. Only 4.6 percent lived in counties with less than 12.5 percent black, while 12.1 percent lived in counties that were more than 75 percent black. See Robert Higgs, *Competition and Coercion: Blacks in the American Economy, 1865–1914* (Chicago, 1980), pp. 24–32. Typically, blacks were concentrated in rural southern counties growing cotton with a mule and plow on small plots of land rented annually from landlords. See Warren Whatley, "Southern Agrarian Labor Contracts as Impediments to Cotton Mechanization," this JOURNAL, 42 (Mar. 1987), pp. 45–70. Some of the voluminous literature on the isolation of southern blacks from northern industrial labor markets includes Gavin Wright, *Old South, New South: Revolutions in the Southern Economy since the Civil War* (New York, 1986); Robert Higgs, *Competition and Coercion*, pp. 24–32; Jay Mandle, *The Roots of Black Poverty* (Durham, 1978); Myrdal, *An American Dilemma*, pp. 182–201; and Brinley Thomas, "Negro Migration and The American Urban Dilemma," *Migration and Urban Development* (London, 1972), pp. 140–69.

[18] U.S. Department of Labor, *The Negro at Work during the World War and Reconstruction* (Washington, DC, 1921), p. 68. Also see U.S. Department of Labor, *Negro Migration in 1916–1917* (Washington, DC, 1919); Emmett J. Scott, *Negro Migration during the War* (New York, 1969); Louise Kennedy, *The Negro Peasant Turns Cityward* (New York, 1930); and Florette Henri, *Black Migration: Movement North 1900–1920* (New York, 1976).

[19] U.S. Dept. of Labor, *Negro Migration in 1916–1917*, pp. 68, 88, 105. In 1910 total black employment in Detroit was only 3,310. The labor department estimates that Detroit received more than 25,000 new black inhabitants during 1916. New Jersey also received over 25,000, and Ohio received more than 37,000. During 1917 Detroit received another 30,000 and Chicago added approximately 50,000. The Housing Corporation sample shows that between 1914 and 1916 the black share of employment in Cincinnati increased by 20 percent and most of this probably occurred during 1916. During 1917 alone the increase was 34.6 percent.

segregated and rural Deep South than had been the case prior to the war, primarily because of the disruptive effects of the boll weevil on the southern cotton economy. Robert Higgs argues that the pull of new opportunities in the North was enough to precipitate the migration because blacks left border states with prosperous agriculture (Virginia, Kentucky, and the Carolinas) as readily as they left Deep South states plagued by the boll weevil (like Alabama and Mississippi).[20] But the border states had high decennial rates of outmigration before 1910, while outmigration from Deep South states like Alabama and Mississippi, meager by comparison before 1910, exploded during the war.[21]

Labor market institutions adapted to facilitate the longer-distance migration. In Alabama, for example, rural migrants moved first to small towns around railroad depots.[22] From there they purchased tickets to the coal and iron district of Birmingham and Bessemer. The district became an important entrepôt because of its railway connections, and various travel arrangements could be secured there from northern labor recruiters. "Justice tickets" allowed migrants to offer their belongings as collateral in exchange for the fare north and a percentage of their first year's wages.[23] Special cars were dispatched by northern mines to carry the "boll weevil Negro" directly to work camps in the North.[24]

Many firms in the North received their first direct experience with black workers after 1916. On the eve of the war 33.2 percent of the sampled firms in Cincinnati hired black workers. By the end of 1916, 39.0 percent employed blacks, and by the end of 1917, 45.8 percent had done so. The percentage was 50.1 by late 1918. The Westinghouse Electric and Manufacturing Corporation began employing blacks in considerable number in 1916 because of the shortage of native-white

[20] See Robert Higgs, "The Boll Weevil, the Cotton Economy, and Black Migration, 1910–1930," *Agricultural History*, 50 (Apr. 1976), p. 491.

[21] Between 1900 and 1910 the outmigration rates for blacks in Virginia, Kentucky, and North Carolina were 14.8, 13.8, and 8.3 percent. Between 1910 and 1920 they were 16.1, 18.5, and 9.8 percent. In Alabama and Mississippi the rates increased from 6.3 and 5.7 percent in the 1900s to 11.9 and 12.7 percent in the 1910s. See William Vickery, "The Economics of the Negro Migration, 1900–1960" (Ph.D. diss., University of Chicago, 1969), p. 26. The fact that unemployed southerners displaced by the boll weevil tended to migrate first may explain why the migration left the north-south gap in unskilled wages virtually unaffected. See Gavin Wright, *Old South, New South*, pp. 64–69.

[22] The following account is taken from U.S. Dept. of Labor, *Negro Migration in 1916–1917*.

[23] Flora Gill found that migration was a response to economic incentives, but the financial constraint caused by poverty and imperfect capital markets bore heavily on the decision to move. See Flora Gill, "The Economics of the Black Exodus" (Ph.D. diss., Stanford University, 1974).

[24] Between Nov. 1, 1916, and May 1, 1917, one railroad is reported to have carried 12,731 black workers to the North. A labor recruiting firm founded in Bessemer, AL, in Feb. 1917 purchased a recruiter's license (which had risen to $1,050 to deter such a practice) and by June 1917 had shipped 4,456 blacks to northern and eastern states. See U.S. Dept. of Labor, *Negro Migration in 1916–1917*.

and immigrant labor.[25] For the same reasons the Bethlehem Steel Corporation and many other large and small enterprises started employing blacks heavily in 1916.[26]

Increased racial contact in the North precipitated major race riots in East St. Louis in 1917, and Washington, DC, and Chicago in 1919. In Detroit and Chicago major studies of the race issue were commissioned by their respective city halls, and in May 1918 the Department of Labor established the Division of Negro Economics to organize interracial committees designed to ease adjustments in areas of large recent influx.[27] When the dust settled, black workers had become a permanent and identifiable feature of many northern industrial labor markets.

WAGES AND JOBS

How did black workers fare in the North as compared to the South? According to the Housing Corporation survey black workers fared better in Cincinnati than in Atlanta, but their wages still lagged far behind those of whites (see Table 1). In Atlanta the weekly black wage was 66 percent of the weekly white wage. In Cincinnati it was 78 percent. Much of the greater racial wage parity in Cincinnati is explained by the black wage being $1.97 or 13 percent above that in Atlanta, but some is explained by the curious fact that the white wage in Cincinnati was $1.11 or 5 percent below that in Atlanta.

A glance at the wage distribution reported in Table 2 reveals even more. All the distributions peak at the $16 to $20 range with exactly 44 percent of the white workers in both cities making less than $20 a week. In Cincinnati, however, a larger portion of whites fell in the upper range of the under $20 category (31 percent versus 23 in Atlanta), and a smaller percentage of workers in Atlanta were in the $21 to $30 range. These low-wage categories seem to reflect the lower entry-level wages in the South and work to pull down the average white wage in Atlanta. Overall the white wage in Atlanta is higher because a larger share of white workers in Atlanta made more than $30 per week (20.5 percent versus 15.1 in Cincinnati).[28] Regardless of whether the larger proportion

[25] Edward S. McClelland, personnel director, "The Negro in the Westinghouse Electric and Manufacturing Corporation," *Opportunity*, 1 (Jan. 1923), pp. 22–23.

[26] J. W. Knapp, personnel director, Bethlehem Steel Corporation, "An Experiment with Negro Labor," *Opportunity*, 1 (Feb. 1923), pp. 19–20. For reports on other similar episodes, see The Chicago Race Commission, *The Negro in Chicago* (Chicago, 1922); The Detroit Bureau of Government Research, *The Negro in Detroit* (Detroit, 1926); Dwight Farnham, "Negroes as a Source of Industrial Labor," *Industrial Management*, 56 (Aug. 1918), pp. 123–29; and Johnson, *The Negro in American Civilization*.

[27] Detroit Bureau of Government Research, *The Negro in Detroit*; Chicago Race Commission, *The Negro in Chicago*; and U.S. Dept. of Labor, *The Negro at Work during the World War*, p. 10.

[28] A lower cost of living in the South may explain the lower entry-level wage in Atlanta, but it would only exacerbate any wage premium skilled white workers in Atlanta might have enjoyed over skilled whites in Cincinnati. This finding becomes more puzzling when we note that whites in

TABLE 1
AVERAGE WEEKLY WAGES, LATE 1918

Industry	Cincinnati				Atlanta			
	Firms	White	Black	Ratio of Black to White	Firms	White	Black	Ratio of Black to White
Apparel	29	$15.76	$11.35	0.720	10	$13.74	$ 9.84	0.716
Chemicals	24	20.55	18.89	0.919	6	19.20	15.78	0.822
Cottonseed	1	18.15	20.00	1.102	5	24.59	16.68	0.678
Electrical	6	19.84	16.56	0.835				
Fabricated Metal	37	20.40	19.77	0.969	8	22.72	17.25	0.759
Fertilizer	6	23.62	21.28	0.901	6	24.30	17.12	0.705
Food	33	18.66	16.37	0.877	9	17.83	13.84	0.776
Furniture	12	17.21	15.63	0.908	12	19.56	13.14	0.672
Glass	6	18.26	13.75	0.753	1	14.38	15.09	1.049
Leather	19	19.83	18.86	0.951	2	17.66	12.50	0.708
Machine	30	22.36	17.53	0.784	6	24.08	14.58	0.605
Paper	12	16.92	17.90	1.058	6	13.51	11.75	0.870
Petroleum	3	17.84			1	22.19	17.76	0.800
Primary Metal	16	26.68	18.86	0.707	3	27.90	18.29	0.655
Printing	30	18.87	13.43	0.712	8	20.28	11.72	0.577
Rubber	2	21.20	17.50	0.825				
Sawing and Woodworking	14	20.51	17.78	0.867	13	21.78	13.91	0.639
Textile	5	14.23	14.47	1.017	9	15.37	11.91	0.775
Tobacco	2	18.39	10.83	0.589				
Transportation	17	19.59	18.16	0.927	8	24.77	16.26	0.656
Citywide	304	21.54	16.87	0.783	113	22.65	14.90	0.658

Notes: The overall average wage in Cincinnati equals $19.35 and in Atlanta $17.66. The weekly wage is the weighted average of the midpoints of the wage classes, where the weights are the percentages of workers in each class.
Source: U.S. Housing Corporation sample. This sample comes from a collection of unpublished surveys of firms conducted in late 1918. The unpublished manuscript copies of the surveys are housed in the National Archives in Washington, DC.

of high-paying jobs in Atlanta reflected a skill premium or relatively more skilled jobs, blacks did not benefit. For them, northern cities like Cincinnati offered better opportunities.

How and where did black workers find jobs in Cincinnati? Table 3 shows that black workers tended to find jobs in industries with large percentages of unskilled jobs. They made little advance in such industries as apparel, printing, and rubber but found substantial employment in chemicals, fertilizer, petroleum, primary metals, and sawing and

Atlanta were not more educated than whites in Cincinnati. In 1920 the illiteracy rate in Atlanta was 1.2 percent for whites over the age of 10. In Cincinnati it was 0.4 percent. In 1910, 79.3 percent of whites in Atlanta between the ages of 6 and 14 were in school. In Cincinnati the figure was 90.9. See U.S. Bureau of the Census, *Thirteenth Census of the United States, Population* (Washington, DC, 1913), vol. 3, part 2, pp. 418–19, and vol. 2, p. 400; and U.S. Bureau of the Census, *Fourteenth Census of the United States, Population* (Washington, DC, 1914), vol. 3, pp. 222, 784.

TABLE 2
DISTRIBUTION OF WEEKLY WAGES, 1918

Wage	Cincinnati White	Cincinnati Black	Atlanta White	Atlanta Black
$ 1–10	2.52%	3.22%	4.71%	6.85%
11–15	10.13	8.43	15.71	22.79
16–20	31.37	48.81	23.86	53.44
21–25	26.66	28.64	21.25	13.85
26–30	14.21	6.95	13.97	2.15
31–35	8.17	3.22	9.64	0.81
36–40	3.06	0.47	4.34	0.12
41–45	1.67	0.16	2.94	0.00
46–50	0.83	0.08	2.15	0.00
51–55	0.43	0.00	0.52	0.00
56–60	0.18	0.00	0.49	0.00
61–65	0.28	0.00	0.18	0.00
65 and over	0.48	0.00	0.24	0.00

Source: U.S. Housing Corporation sample.

woodworking.[29] They also tended to find jobs in industries that had southern branches in which they may have gained productivity-related experience before moving north.

These employment patterns are consistent with a general tendency for labor markets to match skills and experiences to jobs, but they do not preclude the possibility that other mechanisms were at work. Some firms hired no blacks at all, and there was a substantial amount of variance in the racial employment experiences for firms in the same industry. For example, one fabricated metal firm hired 42 percent black, while another hired none.

One possible explanation for the variance is the effects of wartime government intervention. Although prices were never controlled directly, the War Industries Board, created by the federal government, established the Priority System, whereby firms in industries crucial to the war effort got priority claims on inputs.[30] The lower initial reservation wage of black migrants from the South must have made them attractive alternatives to more expensive northern whites, especially in the lower priority industries.[31] This seems evident from the data in Table 4 showing the changes in black and total employment in Cincin-

[29] In Atlanta a similar pattern prevailed: black workers found jobs in industries that employed large percentages of common, unskilled labor.

[30] Bernard M. Baruch, *American Industry During the War* (New York, 1941), chaps. 4, 6, and appendices 5–10; and Hugh Rockoff, *Drastic Measures: A History of Wage and Price Controls in the United States* (Cambridge, 1984), chap. 3.

[31] This regional wage gap is one way to interpret the split labor market hypothesis. See Edna Bonicich, "A Theory of Ethnic Antagonism: The Split Labor Market," *American Sociological Review*, 37 (Oct. 1973); and Edna Bonicich, "Advanced Capitalism and Black/White Race Relations in the United States: A Split Labor Market Interpretation," *American Sociological Review*, 41 (Feb. 1976).

TABLE 3
BLACK EMPLOYMENT PATTERNS IN CINCINNATI, 1913 AND 1918

Industry	Percentage Unskilled	Number of Firms	Percentage Black		Percentage of Black Employment	
			1913	1918	1913	1918
Apparel	1.5%	15	2.5%	2.7%	1.2%	1.0%
Chemicals	45.1	16	3.2	10.5	2.6	6.3
Cottonseed	27.0	1	7.9	11.4	0.3	0.2
Electrical	7.1	5	3.1	5.1	5.2	5.4
Fabricated Metal	18.5	16	5.3	7.4	24.1	20.4
Fertilizer	73.9	5	28.5	63.4	10.1	14.9
Food	27.9	26	1.1	2.9	1.7	2.1
Furniture	16.4	9	0.5	1.9	0.2	0.3
Glass	14.8	6	6.2	7.2	2.6	0.7
Leather	5.7	14	0.8	5.7	0.7	4.2
Machine	18.5	24	2.8	4.0	7.3	11.1
Paper	13.1	9	8.2	4.5	11.0	2.7
Petroleum	27.0	3	27.7	20.4	1.7	0.5
Primary Metal	26.6	12	8.8	8.0	14.0	14.0
Printing	1.5	27	1.1	1.9	1.5	1.3
Rubber	14.9	2	2.9	1.6	0.3	0.1
Sawing and Woodworking	57.2	13	4.4	11.5	1.9	2.4
Textile	14.8	4	20.9	30.9	12.6	7.6
Tobacco	26.3	1	0.0	6.1	0.0	0.2
Transportation	15.7	13	0.4	4.3	0.6	4.7

Source: U.S. Housing Corporation sample.

nati between 1913 and late 1918. In the several industries where it seemed most likely that blacks took jobs previously held by whites—cottonseed, fertilizer, food, furniture, printing, sawing and woodworking, textiles, and tobacco—all but food were in the lowest priority class. These cases represent a maximum of 190 new jobs for blacks, or 20.3 percent of additional black employment.

We cannot know for certain whether more cheaply paid blacks were displacing whites or simply replacing those who had moved on to better-paying jobs, but there is reason to believe the latter dominated. By 1918 the unemployment rate was down to 1.4 percent, and displacement was not a major concern for most workers. Most employment growth for blacks and whites occurred in the same industries, all of which were high-growth industries during the war and, except for primary metals, could not find enough whites to sustain the prewar racial mixture. More than two-thirds of the additional black employment in these industries represented an increase in the black percentage of employment.

All of this is corroborated by the reduced-form wage regressions reported in Table 5. A firm's average weekly wage is taken to be a function of the black percentage of the firm's labor force, the scale of employment, the percentage of work done for the government, and the

TABLE 4
CHANGES IN BLACK EMPLOYMENT IN CINCINNATI BETWEEN 1913 AND 1918

Industry	Change in Black Employment	Change in Total Employment	Change in the Percent Black
Apparel	7	224	0.19
Chemicals	91	232	7.38
Cottonseed	1	−3	3.54
Electrical	52	337	2.00
Fabricated Metal	152	714	2.11
Fertilizer	185	83	3.49
Food	24	−215	1.80
Furniture	4	−48	1.42
Glass	−13	−244	1.07
Leather	76	576	12.38
Machine	144	2,805	2.33
Paper	−60	−185	−3.73
Petroleum	−9	−21	−7.24
Primary Metal	131	1,788	−0.78
Printing	10	−131	0.84
Rubber	−1	24	−1.34
Sawing and Woodworking	27	−45	7.09
Textile	19	−139	9.98
Tobacco	3	−5	6.12
Transportation	86	699	3.88
Citywide	935	6,401	2.66

Source: U.S. Housing Corporation sample.

percentage of jobs in the firm's industry that are skilled, semiskilled, and unskilled.

The variables measuring the skill composition of jobs have the expected signs. A greater percentage of skilled jobs tended to increase a firm's average weekly wage, while unskilled jobs reduced it. The regressions also show that black workers in Cincinnati did not depress wages. If labor markets were split along racial lines because of the lower initial reservation wage of black migrants (or for any other reason), then the presence of black workers in a firm's labor force should have reduced its average weekly wage. There is no evidence of this in 1918 Cincinnati. The impact of race on the average weekly wage was negative, but it was very small and not significant statistically. In Atlanta, on the other hand, race had a statistically significant effect on a firm's average weekly wage. The average firm in Atlanta saved $1.42 per worker per week by using black workers instead of white, amounting to 8 percent of the average weekly wage.

In Cincinnati firms working on government contracts tended to have higher average weekly wages, but this was an industry effect. When industry dummies are entered, the coefficient on government contracts becomes small, negative, and statistically insignificant. The industries

TABLE 5
1918 WAGE ESTIMATES FOR CINCINNATI AND ATLANTA

Variable	Cincinnati		Atlanta	
BLACK	−0.183	−0.153	−4.012	−3.749
	(−0.08)	(−0.08)	(−2.54)	(−2.10)
EMPLOYMENT	0.003	0.003	0.004	0.001
	(2.29)	(2.23)	(1.27)	(0.43)
GOVERNMENT	1.250	−0.589	0.702	−1.453
	(1.86)	(−0.73)	(0.63)	(−1.27)
SKILLED	2.089		1.507	
	(0.82)		(0.39)	
SEMISKILLED	−5.731		−4.456	
	(−1.98)		(−0.90)	
UNSKILLED	−6.352		−4.293	
	(−1.83)		(−0.93)	
Constant	16.337	18.984	23.269	17.964
	(7.38)	(12.03)	(6.57)	(9.11)
Industry Dummies				
Primary Metal		6.839		7.409
		(3.40)		(2.44)
Machinery		3.342		5.333
		(1.86)		(2.54)
Printing				6.526
				(2.93)
Metal Fabrication				6.963
				(2.74)
Transportation				4.603
				(2.20)
R^2	0.0754	0.1900	0.1693	0.3738
N	218	218	101	101

Notes: The dependent variable is average weekly wage. Employment is measured as the number of workers. The *BLACK* variable and the three skill category variables are measured as percentage shares of the firm's labor force. The omitted skill category is clerical and office workers. The *GOVERNMENT* variable represents the share of the firm's business (measured in dollars) that is done for the government. Student *t*-ratios are in parentheses. Only those industry dummies significant at the 90 percent level or above are listed.
Source: U.S. Housing Corporation sample.

with significant coefficients are primary metals and machinery—two industries providing the bulk of additional employment during the war.

Other surveys of industrial workers available for this period suggest that the racial wage patterns found in Cincinnati and Atlanta were not uncommon. In 1918 and 1919 the U.S. Department of Labor conducted a unique survey of 23 firms in six different industries scattered throughout Illinois, Ohio, and Pennsylvania. The survey covered 4,260 white and 2,722 black men in 195 skilled, semiskilled, and common labor occupations. The comparison of hourly wages of white and black workers holding the same occupation in the same firm showed no discernible pattern of job-specific racial wage differences. Blacks' wages exceeded whites' as often as whites' wages exceeded blacks', regardless of skill category.[32] Late in the interwar period southern employers paid beginning white workers a premium of more than 25 percent, while in the North there was no racial wage differential. In fact, beginning black workers in the North averaged slightly higher wages than did whites.[33]

The lack of evidence on job-specific racial wage differentials does not mean there were no racial barriers in the North. None of these surveys report information on individual characteristics of workers and jobs. Discrimination may have forced some black workers to take the more difficult and dangerous jobs without receiving the compensating wage differential needed to attract comparable whites. In Cincinnati the black percentage of employment tended to be highest in what one might call the "dirty" industries—chemicals, cottonseed, metals, fertilizers, petroleum, and sawing and woodworking (see Table 3). Even in the auto industry, usually considered a high-wage assembly industry, blacks were confined primarily to the foundry. In rubber it was the compound room.[34]

Discrimination may have also excluded blacks from better-paying jobs through one barrier or another. Craft unions were notoriously discriminatory, but other barriers existed as well.[35] Black workers were often excluded from supervisory positions because whites refused to take orders from them.[36] Donald Dewey called this form of discrimination a "law" in the South.[37] But it was not confined to the South. In a postwar survey in Chicago not one black worker complained of unequal pay for equal work, but about 10 percent of those surveyed complained

[32] The comparison, by skill category, shows the following:

	Number of Occupations		
	Skilled	Semiskilled	Unskilled
Black Wage greater than White Wage	2	8	18
Black Wage less than White Wage	4	5	22
Black Wage equal to White Wage	2	12	12

The figures are from U.S. Department of Labor, *The Negro at Work during the World War*, pp. 40–49.

[33] See Jacob Perlman and Edward K. Frazier, "Entrance Rates of Common Laborers in 20 Industries, July 1937," *Monthly Labor Review*, 45 (Dec. 1937), pp. 1494, 1497. In the North the average white wage for entry-level workers in 20 industries was 55.8 cents, that for blacks was 56.6 cents. In the South the figures were 43.4 and 34.5 cents.

[34] See Lloyd C. Bailer, "The Negro Automobile Worker," *Journal of Political Economy*, 51 (Oct. 1943), pp. 415–29; and Northrup, *The Negro in the Rubber Tire Industry*, pp. 30–39.

[35] See Phillip S. Foner, *Organized Labor and the Black Worker: 1619–1973* (New York, 1974); Herbert Northrup, *Organized Labor and the Negro* (New York, 1944); and W. E. B. Du Bois, *The Negro Artisan* (Atlanta, 1902).

[36] Price Fishback, "Segregation in Job Hierarchies: West Virginia Coal Mining, 1906–1932," this Journal, 44 (Sept. 1984), pp. 755–74.

[37] See Donald Dewey, "Negro Employment in Southern Industry," *Journal of Political Economy*, 60 (Aug. 1952).

TABLE 6
THE RANDOM PROBABILITY OF RACIAL SEGREGATION OF FIRMS IN CINCINNATI

Year	Number of All-White Firms	Average Size of All-White Firms	Average Size of Integrated Firms	White Share of City Labor Force	Probability of Hiring Only Whites	Percent of Average Size Firms that are All White
1913	157	67.8	130.5	0.9552	4.47	72.0%
1916	144	75.4	124.6	0.9470	1.65	57.1
1917	127	66.2	131.2	0.9277	0.69	52.9
1918	116	58.6	124.0	0.9286	1.30	51.7

Notes: The probability of hiring only whites is equal to $W^n \cdot 100$, where W is the white share of the city's labor force and n is the average size of all-white firms.
Source: U.S. Housing Corporation sample.

of promotion discrimination, where promotion ceilings were often reached within six months of employment, and often because whites refused to work beneath blacks.[38]

Still another racial barrier was the simple refusal by some firms to hire black workers. In late 1918, 50 percent of the firms in Cincinnati were still without a black worker. Some of this firm-level segregation was generated randomly, but not much. Given the white proportion of a city's labor force the probability that a firm would hire an all-white labor force of size n can be calculated.[39] Table 6 shows that the probability of having randomly hired the average size all-white firm was very low in Cincinnati, ranging from 0.69 percent in 1917 to 4.47 percent in 1913. Yet more than 50 percent of the firms of that size were all white for each year of the sample. Surely some of the firm-level segregation was the outcome of conscious employment decisions made by firms.

We can characterize the demand for black workers as a function of their wage, total employment, the percentage of work done on government contract, and the skill composition of jobs. The black wage is endogenous and is a function of the productivity-related characteristics of black workers and the black percentage of population in the firm's ward, the idea being that firms can attract workers with a lower wage if they live nearby.[40] The survey did not collect information on produc-

[38] Chicago Race Commission, *The Negro in Chicago*, pp. 365–66, 385–91.

[39] The probability is equal to W^n. Robert Higgs uses this formula to explain the variation in integration by scale in 1909 Virginia. See Robert Higgs, "Firm Specific Evidence on Racial Wage Differentials and Workforce Segregation," *American Economic Review*, 67 (Mar. 1977).

[40] Both cities had racially segregated residential patterns. In Cincinnati blacks were concentrated along the waterfront, and in Atlanta they were concentrated in the western-middle section of the city. As one study of workers in Cincinnati found, "less than one-third were in walking distance of their jobs," and "when going to their jobs and returning home . . . the street cars are crowded, jammed, loaded-down, and decorated like bequilled porcupines with tools." Some paid up to 10 percent of their wages on transportation. See Zane Miller, *Boss Cox's Cincinnati* (New York, 1968), p. 32. For Atlanta, see Howard Preston, *Automobile Age Atlanta* (Athens, 1981). The Housing Corporation data show statistically significant cross-sectional variation in racial wage ratios for firms in both cities. Of the 12 wards in Atlanta with firms that employed blacks, four had

TABLE 7
RACIAL EMPLOYMENT REGRESSIONS, 1918

	Probit Estimates		Ordinary Least Squares Estimates	
Variables	Cincinnati	Atlanta	Cincinnati	Atlanta
LABOR FORCE	1.27	−1.08	15.82	0.456
	(1.79)	(−1.28)	(0.92)	(0.04)
GOVERNMENT	0.461	−0.578	18.39	−4.54
	(1.90)	(−0.961)	(3.00)	(−0.556)
EMPLOYMENT	0.003	0.053	0.054	0.265
	(4.01)	(2.86)	(6.51)	(17.27)
SKILLED	−2.27	−6.83	−6.45	−2.81
	(−2.53)	(−2.32)	(−0.26)	(−0.10)
SEMISKILLED	0.217	−5.00	12.69	8.26
	(0.22)	(−1.32)	(0.51)	(0.24)
UNSKILLED	0.514	−3.18	61.41	59.63
	(0.48)	(−0.96)	(2.21)	(1.83)
Constant	−0.335	4.61	−16.01	−8.36
	(−0.45)	(1.72)	(−0.85)	(−0.34)
$N = 0$	129	12	0	0
$N = 1$	134	117	134	117
Log-Likehood	−182.2	−39.92		
R^2			0.4397	0.7612
		Elasticities at Means		
LABOR FORCE	0.0787	−0.5156	0.0881	0.0049
GOVERNMENT	0.0815	−0.0150	0.3425	−0.0364
EMPLOYMENT	0.1428	0.0892	0.5002	0.7189
SKILLED	−0.2200	−0.1483	−0.0465	−0.0129
SEMISKILLED	0.0636	−0.2429	0.3076	0.1026
UNSKILLED	0.0696	−0.0656	0.6755	0.4838

Notes: Columns 1 and 2 are Probit values. The dependent variable is black employment and equals one if the firm hired blacks and zero if it did not. The dependent variable in columns 3 and 4 is the number of blacks in the firm. The sample data for this equation include only firms that hired some blacks in 1918. *EMPLOYMENT* measures the number of workers employed. The skill variables are percentage shares of employment; *GOVERNMENT* measures the share of business, measured in dollars, done for the government; *LABOR FORCE* measures the black share of the population residing in the firm's neighborhood. Student *t*-statistics are in parentheses.

tivity-related characteristics of workers, so I estimated the reduced-form employment equations reported in Table 7. Columns 1 and 2 report racial integration probit values for firms in Cincinnati and Atlanta. Columns 3 and 4 report ordinary least square regression coefficients explaining black employment for firms hiring blacks in 1918. The bottom panel reports elasticities calculated at the mean values.

As expected, larger firms had a greater probability of employing at

average firm-level racial wage ratios that were significantly different from the city average and represented 46 percent of the firms in the sample that employed blacks. In Cincinnati, 9 of the 20 wards had average racial wage ratios significantly different from the city average and covered 35 percent of the firms that employed blacks.

least one black worker than did smaller firms. Also, blacks were less likely to get a foot in the door of firms that had a large percentage of skilled jobs. The percentage of work done for the government improved the probability of racial integration in Cincinnati but not Atlanta, probably because most firms in Atlanta were already integrated before the war. Similarly, the extent to which the community where the firm was located was black improved the probability of racial integration in Cincinnati but not Atlanta, again probably because blacks were such a large share of Atlanta's population. According to the elasticities, the skill content of jobs was the most important deterrent to blacks getting a foot in the door of firms in both cities.

Once in the door, black employment tended to grow with total employment, but again the elasticities reveal the importance of the skill composition of jobs. In Cincinnati a 1 percent increase in the percentage of jobs classified as unskilled increased the number of black workers by 0.68 percent. A 1 percent increase in employment increased black employment by 0.50 percent. In Atlanta as well the skill composition of jobs was a major determinant of the number of blacks hired.

LEARNING TO INTEGRATE

Another determinant of the number of blacks hired, one not captured by these regressions, is the new information generated within the firm by the concrete experience with black workers in the work place. Commenting on this, Myrdal observed that "[t]here are tremendous elements of inertia which resist the introduction of Negro labor where there had previously been none. . . . If they get in, however, they will have a better chance of staying." Why?

> Negro labor is often superior to the white man's expectation, partly because the thinking in averages and stereotypes makes him underestimate the individual Negro. Moreover, the fact that Negroes have greater difficulties than whites in securing any kind of employment renders it probable that there is a greater proportion of capable workers in the Negro than there is in the white unemployed labor reserve. Employers who do employ Negroes, therefore, often get a higher appreciation of them as workers than employers who do not. The same seems to be true of white workers. If they actually work together with Negro workers, they come to like them better, or to dislike them less, than they expected.[41]

[41] Myrdal, *An American Dilemma*, pp. 392–93. Others had similarly optimistic views. In 1906 W. L. Bulkley described the situation in New York City: "The northern employer is too prone to turn off the colored applicant with the bland assurance that he himself would have no objection, but his white workmen would disrupt the business if a black competitor were forced upon them. . . . This intolerant attitude against the Negro workman is largely a matter of fad and fancy. Upon the show of firmness on the part of the employer it would soon vanish away." W. L. Bulkley, "The Industrial Conditions of the Negro in New York City," *Annals of the American Academy*, 27 (1906), p. 87.

This was not always the case. Management was not always willing to risk disrupting the labor peace by forcing black workers on a resistant white labor force, and they often found a compromise that in many cases reinforced racial stereotypes. After 13 years as a "supervising engineer" and after establishing a successful consulting firm, Dwight Farnham recommended to his fellow managers in the trade journal *Industrial Management* that "a certain amount of segregation is necessary at times to preserve the peace. This is especially true when Negroes are first introduced into a plant."[42] Some kind of social distinction between the races—like partitions, walls, isolation, or separate bathrooms—existed in more than 20 percent of the firms surveyed in postwar Chicago. In each case the separation was made to reduce the expected disruptions from mixing races. Sometimes management tried to change its policy when it became clear that black resentment of segregation caused problems as well. But once the racial segregation patterns were established whites often insisted they remain.[43] It was a short step from those patterns to the belief among workers that occupations held by blacks were low grade or, as Myrdal put it, "declasse," effectively constraining management in the promotions and job assignments given black and white workers.[44]

Firms with little or no previous experience with black workers also had to learn how to evaluate their productive abilities. "Proper" management is often mentioned as a prerequisite for using black workers efficiently, and what was to become the standard of treatment had to be learned as well.[45] To some managers proper management meant black workers were different and had to be treated accordingly, while to others it meant black workers were not different and had to be treated accordingly. Either assumption was plausible for a firm that had no previous experience with black workers, but once blacks got a foot

[42] Farnham, "Negroes as a Source of Industrial Labor," p. 128.

[43] Chicago Race Commission, *The Negro in Chicago*, pp. 393–98.

[44] Milgrom and Oster generate an equilibrium where workers who are undervalued initially are discriminated against in promotion because promotion reveals their true abilities to potential "raider" firms. The resulting allocation of labor in the firm is inefficient but profitable because firms are able to reap rents from their invisible workers. See Milgrom and Oster, "Job Discrimination, Market Forces, and the Invisibility Hypothesis." One way to reap those rents without revealing this to the workers responsible is to segregate high-quality invisible workers and low-quality visible workers into different low-level jobs so that comparisons between them are never made.

[45] Economists working in both the Marxian and Coasian traditions have long emphasized how worker management influences labor performance, making a priori and independent measure of worker ability problematic. See Herbert Gintis, "The Nature of Labor Exchange and the Theory of Capitalist Production," *Review of Radical Political Economics*, 8 (Summer 1976), pp. 36–54; Samuel Bowles, "The Production Process in a Competitive Economy: Walrasian, Neo-Hobbesian, and Marxian Models," *American Economic Review*, 75 (Mar. 1985), pp. 16–36; Ronald Coase, "The Nature of the Firm," *Economica*, 4 (Nov. 1937), pp. 387–405; and Oliver Williamson, "The Organization of Work," *Journal of Economic Behavior and Organization*, 1 (Mar. 1980).

in the door, learning-by-doing would have occurred and would have influenced future hiring decisions.

Here the managers' views on race are decisive, and their words, such as those of the personnel manager of the National Malleable Casting Company of Cleveland, Ohio, express it best:

> We have used Negroes in our shop for many years. . . . But it has only been within the last few years that we have successfully used them in any class of work except common labor. Why? Because we did not know how to handle the colored man. He is constituted temperamentally quite different from the other classes of help that work in our shops. . . . I have found that with proper supervision the colored man could not only do the skilled work, but would also maintain the standard of quality and production as established in the shop.[46]

At some plants the management office learned it had to hire special welfare workers and personnel managers to get access to and interpret useful information. Developments at the Bethlehem Steel Corporation were typical:

> Southern Negro [workers] . . . coming as they did from rural agricultural sections of the South, bringing with them their old traditions and superstitions, they presented to us many new community problems . . . we felt it necessary in the early part of 1918 to put on a colored Welfare Worker, as we were of the opinion that through him, in conjunction with the Employment Manager, we could gain better results from our colored workmen, which has proven true beyond any doubt. . . . The Welfare Worker has given us insights into what we term the peculiarities of their race, that perhaps otherwise, could never have been understood.[47]

And Farnham stated his view in uncompromising terms:

> The difference is all in the management. . . . Once the plant executives, the foremen who come in contact with the workmen, realize that the negro is different physically, temperamentally and psychologically from any of the white races, the battle is half won.[48]

He also advised, without explaining why, that Irish foremen were the most effective supervisors of black workers, and "as in dealing with a child, firmness is absolutely necessary."

STATE DEPENDENCE

Was this type of learning effect widespread? Did the introduction of black workers into a firm's labor force generate experiences that altered

[46] J. O. Houze, personnel manager, The National Malleable Casting Company, "Negro Labor in the Industries," *Opportunity*, 1 (Jan. 1923), pp. 20–22.

[47] Knapp, "An Experiment with Negro Labor," p. 19. For similar accounts, see McClelland, "Negro Labor in the Westinghouse Electric and Manufacturing Corporation"; August Meier and Elliott Rudwick, *Black Detroit and the Rise of the UAW* (New York, 1979), pp. 10–12; and Dickerson, *Out of the Crucible*, chap. 5.

[48] Farnham, "Negroes as a Source of Industrial Labor," pp. 124–25.

its future racial hiring practices? In other words, was the extent of racial integration of firms in one year, say 1918, dependent on a state of the world created by previous experience with black workers?[49]

To answer this question we must isolate the effects of experience from the effects of other factors that influence racial employment. We must separate employment practices related to previous experience with black workers (state-dependent effects) from those that are related to other characteristics of firms that are correlated with previous and current employment of blacks (heterogeneity effects). Myrdal acknowledged this problem when he noted that "in addition, of course, the fact that some employers hire Negroes may indicate by itself that they have a higher appreciation of them from the start."[50] Some of the characteristics of firms that tended to hire blacks are observable—size, industry, skill composition of jobs, racial composition of population, and so forth. Some, however, are unobservable—such as the degree of white resistance to the initial employment of blacks, for whatever reason.

To capture the effects of experience on racial employment I estimate the following equation, which is an amended version of the reduced-form employment equation used in Table 7.

$$BLACK_{it} = \beta_{1t}\,(EMP_{it}) + \beta_{2t}\,(GOVT_{it}) + \gamma_{1t}\,(SK_i) + \gamma_{2t}\,(SSK_i) + \gamma_{3t}\,(UNSK_i) + \gamma_{4t}\,(INDUSTRY_i) + \Omega_t\,(LF_{it}) + \theta_{it}\,(BLACK_{it-1}) + \Psi_t\,(d_{it}) + \delta_{it} + \eta_{it}$$

Most of the variables have been defined above. The term δ_{it} is an individual constant and controls for firm-level heterogeneity such as the attitude of management or white workers toward blacks not captured by the other variables. The error term, η_{it}, is assumed to be normally and independently distributed. $BLACK_{it}$ measures the number of blacks employed in firm i at time t. The coefficient on $BLACK_{it-1}$ measures the extent of state dependence in the employment of blacks because it measures how changes in the firm's racial employment behavior that emanate from past experience with blacks alters the firm's current racial employment decisions. If past experience had no influence on current behavior, θ_{it} will equal zero.

Before we can interpret θ_{it} as a measure of the impact of experience we must purge $BLACK_{it-1}$ of any spurious correlation with $BLACK_{it}$. A firm with black workers on January 1, 1918, is likely to have black workers in October 1918 because it takes time to make adjustments to

[49] To demonstrate the probability structure of state dependence in outcomes, think of all firms having identical urns of balls at time t, each ball having a value y_t (say, the number of black workers hired at time t). A firm randomly chooses a ball from the urn which happens to have the value y_t^*. It then adds to the urn more balls with values greater than y_t^*. In the next period the firm randomly chooses a ball which happens to have the value y_{t+1}^{**}. The outcome in period $t + 1$ is state dependent because the outcome in period t increased the probability that y_{t+1}^{**} is greater than y_t^*.

[50] Myrdal, *An American Dilemma*, p. 392, fn. 6.

a labor force. While turnover was probably high during the war, we still want to make sure we minimize the effect of inertia picked up by θ_{it}. This is handled in two ways. First, a dummy variable is included that captures the state of the firm at the beginning of period *t*. The dummy variable (d_{it}) equals one if the firm started the period with black workers and zero if it did not. Second, the observations are distanced in time. $BLACK_{it}$ is the number of black workers employed in late 1918 and $BLACK_{it-1}$ is the number employed at the end of 1916. This two-year lag provided ample time for firms to make desired adjustments, and 1916 coincided with the accelerated migration north, when many firms hired blacks for the first time.[51]

For a number of reasons we cannot estimate this equation directly and instead estimate one in which the variables are expressed as first differences. This specification, however, still controls for observable and time-invariant unobservable characteristics of firms:[52]

$$BLACKS\ (16-18) = \beta_1\ [EMP\ (16-18)] + \beta_2\ [GOVT\ (16-18)] + \Omega\ [LF\ (16-18)] + \theta\ [BLACK\ (13-16)] + \Psi\ [d\ (16-18)] + \eta\ (16-18)$$

The parenthetical term represents the change in each variable between 1916 and 1918 (or 1913 to 1916 in the case of the lag *BLACK* variable).[53] The Tobit procedure is used to estimate the equation so as to take account of firms that did not employ blacks. The results are reported in Table 8.

In Cincinnati state dependence in the racial employment outcomes of firms, as evidenced by the coefficient of *BLACK* (13 − 16), is large, positive, and significant. Not all firms hired black workers, but those that did before the end of 1916 experienced something that compelled them on average to double the size of their black labor force by the end

[51] It is best to think of $BLACK_{it}$ as the result of the previous period's employment activity. $BLACK_{18}$ is the result of decisions made between Jan. 1, 1916, and Oct. 1918. $BLACK_{16}$ is the result for the period Jan. 1, 1914, to Dec. 31, 1916, and so forth. Ideally we would want continuous-state, continuous-time data so we could estimate instantaneous state dependence. Given our data limitations, the best we can do is measure the average state dependence emanating from the average experience of the previous period. The dates are chosen to make the periods approximately equal in length.

[52] Cross-sectional data cannot estimate this equation because each firm has its own intercept, producing more coefficients than observations. On the other hand, estimation of the equation without the inclusion of δ_{it} will create an upward bias in the estimated state-dependence coefficient unless that part of δ_{it} that is correlated with $BLACK_{it-1}$ is fully captured by a linear combination of the other independent variables. One way to handle this is to fix the individual component and coefficients over time and assume $Cov(n_{it}, n_{it-1}) = 0$. Now simple differencing eliminates δ_i. Time-invariant variables drop out of the equation, but here we are interested in θ as a measure of state dependence and θ is still identified.

[53] Moreover, the *LF* variable now measures the black percentage of population in the city, not the firm's ward, so as to pick up the effect wartime changes in the supply of black workers may have had on changes in black employment.

TABLE 8
STATE-DEPENDENCE REGRESSIONS

	All Firms		Firms with Blacks Before the War	
	Cincinnati	Atlanta	Cincinnati	Atlanta
BLACK(13–16)	1.06	−0.210	0.149	−0.202
	(4.30)	(−2.12)	(0.90)	(−1.90)
d(16–18)	1.71	1.70	−8.75	−2.85
	(0.46)	(0.23)	(−0.95)	(−0.29)
EMPLOYMENT(16–18)	0.037	0.462	0.020	0.470
	(3.99)	(10.17)	(2.83)	(9.57)
GOVERNMENT(16–18)	1.89	1.91	−2.68	2.55
	(0.76)	(0.35)	(−0.71)	(0.42)
Constant	0.071	1.19	1.55	0.820
	(0.05)	(0.49)	(0.76)	(0.28)
N	229	93	77	81
R^2	0.1552	0.5526	0.1132	0.5544

Notes: The dependent variable is the change in the number of black workers between 1916 and 1918. *BLACK*(13–16) is the change in the number of blacks between 1913 and 1916. All other time-variant independent variables measure changes between 1916 and 1918. *d*(16–18) measures changes in the dummy variable that captures the integration status of a firm at the beginning of the period. *d*16 equals one if the firm hired blacks at the beginning of 1916 and zero if it did not. The same applies to *d*18. See Tables 5 and 7 for other definitions. The *LF* variable now measures the black percentage of population in the city, not the firm's ward, and so picks up the effect wartime changes in the supply of black workers may have had on changes in black employment. *BLACK*16 is estimated using instrumental variables. The instruments are *BLACK*13, *SKILLED, SEMI-SKILLED, UNSKILLED, EMPLOYMENT*16, and industry dummies. Student *t*-statistics are reported in parentheses.

of 1918. Furthermore, it was integration as such—the *initial introduction* of black workers into firms—that was the source of the experience that changed racial hiring practices. As the third column of Table 8 shows, firms that had experiences with black workers before the war learned nothing new during the war that changed their racial hiring practices.

When black workers were introduced into previously all-white work forces, new experiences were bound to generate new information. The intensity and nature of racial prejudice among white workers was revealed; the productivity of black workers became known; the general manner in which the race issue would be managed had to be decided, and, if necessary, race-specific job hierarchies devised; and the firms acquired information on black workers' opportunity wages. These are but a few of the new concerns and problems that integration brought into a firm's management equation. Firms that integrated before the war probably had solved these problems by 1916, but those integrating during the war were still learning, experimenting, testing, and groping toward a solution. As they learned, black employment increased.

It is important to note that the state-dependence firms in Cincinnati was not caused by the wartime increase in the supply of black workers.[54] The shortage of white workers during the war and the increased availability of blacks forced many firms to consider integrating their work forces, but the estimated state dependence captures the effect on future hiring decisions of the firm's experience *after* blacks were brought in. Likewise, state dependence in Cincinnati was not due to firms' learning about changes in the characteristics of the black labor force caused by the rapid influx of new workers. That was something all firms had to learn. Yet state dependence was not present for those firms that hired blacks before the war.

Since the estimated regressions are in reduced form it is possible that some of the state dependence comes from the supply side. Black workers may have been more inclined to apply for employment at firms known to hire blacks. This would have increased the black percentage of job applicants and likely the number of blacks hired. But if this were the source of the state dependence, we would expect to observe it for all firms hiring blacks, not just recently integrated firms. We do not.

In Atlanta the situation was different. State dependence was smaller, negative, and less significant than in Cincinnati. Experience gained from the past induced firms to reduce the size of their black labor force by 21 percent on average. This is found for all firms regardless of when they integrated, so recent integration was not the source of the state dependence. The fact that the estimated state dependence is negative also eliminates integration as the experience picked up by the lagged dependent variable. Perhaps the opening up of employment opportunities in the North disrupted southern labor relations, making black workers less willing to accept their traditional place in southern labor markets. Firms may have experienced this as higher rates of turnover among black workers, greater demands for promotion, and other changes that made blacks less attractive employment prospects than they had been before the war. Some contemporary observers thought the new opportunities in the North and the outmigration of southern blacks during the war would change southern race relations forever. Emmett Scott, for example, argued that the wartime scarcity of workers would force southerners to offer black workers employment opportunities that had previously been reserved for whites.[55] But the regressions reported in Table 8 suggest that many firms simply let blacks go rather than challenge the status quo.

[54] *LF*(16 − 18) captures this. Since it is the same for all firms in the city it enters the regression as a constant, and the constant is never significant statistically.

[55] See Scott, *Negro Migration during the War*, chap. 8.

CONCLUSION

This study demonstrates that learning indeed occurred on the demand side. Some firms in Cincinnati learned how to integrate their work forces racially but only after having some concrete experience with black workers. Firms that refused to hire black workers reinforced racial barriers in employment, while those that employed blacks changed the future employment opportunities for other blacks as well.

Exactly what those opportunities were remains to be discovered. There is reason to doubt that integrated northern firms became color-blind. As late as 1948 a survey of black and white workers in three meat-packing centers (Fort Worth, Kansas City, and Omaha) found that 60 percent of them believed black workers were excluded from one or more departments, most frequently the mechanical departments, "as a matter of custom."[56] Race-specific job assignment and promotion systems in the tobacco industry are well known. They were not confined to southern plants. Branches operating in New Jersey followed policies similar to those found in the South.[57] In the rubber tire industry, which was concentrated in Ohio, black workers were almost always found in the nonmechanized compound room, known in some plants as the Black Department.[58]

The challenge is to understand how these job assignments and promotions systems came to crystalize around and reinforce racial attitudes and modes of processing information in ways that shaped the opportunities for black worker progress over long periods of time. Finding state dependence in racial employment is encouraging and suggests that a complex path-dependent adjustment process might best characterize the evolution of these systems. In order to understand these systems we must understand how they got that way, not as epiphenomenal "noise" between equilibrium states of the world, but as the complex unfolding of the historical drama. The experiences with black workers during World War I can be seen as the initial episode in this drama for a large number of northern firms and cities.

[56] Fogel, *The Negro in the Meat Packing Industry*, p. 105.
[57] Northrup, *The Negro in the Tobacco Industry*, pp. 73–74.
[58] Northrup, *The Negro in the Rubber Tire Industry*, p. 30.

Israeli Economic Policies, 1948–1951: Problems of Evaluation

NACHUM T. GROSS

The State of Israel was established in the midst of a war for its survival, and its population doubled within three years by mass immigration. The Israeli governments opted for a system of far-reaching and direct intervention in the economy as a means of winning the war, meeting basic consumption needs, and sustaining a high investment ratio. The circumstances and ideological premises of this policy are discussed, and the major problems of evaluation spelled out.

The establishment of the State of Israel in May 1948, following the UN resolution for the partition of Palestine in November 1947, created *the* great opportunity for achieving the Zionist movement's goals. These had been, in essence, to construct a Jewish commonwealth, growing rapidly by absorbing immigrants, based on its own (that is, Jewish) labor and a "normal" occupational structure; to develop a vital Hebrew culture; and to establish a "just" society. Much progress had been made during the interwar years under British Mandatory rule. Developments in Palestine politics after 1936, however, and even more so the wartime fate of European Jewry and the resettlement needs of its survivors, had convinced the Zionist leadership that only full formal sovereignty would enable it to make further satisfactory progress toward its objectives.

But the great opportunity also created ominous difficulties and a tremendous challenge. From the economic point of view, the new state needed, first, to set up its own currency system and foreign exchange regime, as well as a general fiscal and monetary administration. Second, since mass immigration doubled the Jewish population of the country within three years, the newcomers had to be fed, provided with at least temporary shelter, and—as soon as possible—gainfully employed. Third, all this had to be done while defending the state against violent Arab opposition to its creation and existence, and the war required both local and foreign resources. Lastly, the partition of Palestine disrupted and separated two sectors that had formerly been politically and

The Journal of Economic History, Vol. L, No. 1 (Mar. 1990). ISSN 0022-0507.

The author is Professor of Economics, The Hebrew University of Jerusalem, 91905 Jerusalem, Israel.

An earlier version of this article was presented at the 26th Atlantic Economic Conference, October 1988, in Philadelphia. For valuable and helpful criticism I wish to thank Richard T. Geruson and Joseph Prinziger, who discussed the paper at the Conference, my colleagues Haim Barkai, Ruth Klinov and Jacob Metzer, and the editor and anonymous referees of this JOURNAL.

economically components of one country. The war and the partition thus combined to destroy or dislocate much productive capacity.

BACKGROUND AND FOUNDATIONS

An economic historian, like all historians, is concerned with the past from the viewpoint of the present, but this concern has two distinctly different aspects. In the case discussed here, the interest lies first in revealing the foundations of the Israeli socioeconomic system as laid down forty years ago and in part still influencing current conditions and policies. The second task is to evaluate the economic policies of the first years of statehood. This can be done by investigating the conceptions, beliefs, and objectives on which those policies were based, and by assessing intentions and results in view of our current knowledge and in light of present theory and theoretical trends. This article attempts to reconstruct the circumstances and atmosphere in which Israeli decision-makers formulated their views and policies and to discuss explicitly whether the strong preference for a managed economy and an equitable distribution of hardship not only was understandable under the conditions of the period, but also perhaps represented a "correct" choice under these conditions—even if one distasteful to many of us today.

The new state inherited a body of economic legislation and administrative machinery and experience from the Mandatory government. Much of this was geared to the needs of a wartime economy, even though during the twenty interwar years the country had been under a practically laissez-faire regimen. Moreover, the Palestine government emulated the British policy of continuing controls—and in particular foreign currency and consumer goods rationing—into the postwar period. This was necessary in view of the dollar shortage prevailing in the sterling bloc, to which Palestine belonged; it was also part of the worldwide determination to avoid the gross mistakes of economic policy committed during the First World War and afterwards. Since the existing legislation was adopted by the new state to provide stability and continuity, and because large numbers of officials from the previous government, who embodied its experience, were now serving the new administration, the system of controls remained in effect.

At the time, however, the idea of a managed or planned economy had much broader appeal than merely as a set of emergency measures. The world in general, and the industrialized countries in particular, were still under the overwhelming influence of the Great Depression, of the mass unemployment that even in the wealthy United States had lasted a whole decade. The Depression was considered a failure of the free market system, even by those who did remain faithful to parliamentary democracy. The widespread sympathy for government economic intervention was also supported by what was generally considered the success of planned economies in Germany and the USSR, and by the great admiration for the heroic stand of Soviet Russia against the Nazi invasion. An additional factor was the positive experience with wartime controls in Britain and the United States. One well-known result was the commitment by all "western" governments, in one form or another, to preserve full employment in the postwar era. Moreover, both in Europe and in the colonies, soon to become independent and be labeled "underdeveloped" countries, the belief in the need for development planning was spreading rapidly.

This legacy and these dominant opinions were exceedingly well suited to the political culture of the Israeli leadership. Not only were its majority socialists of various shadings, but most of the rest also believed in some form of economic statism. Indeed, throughout the Mandate period Zionist politicians had aspired to "plan" the development of the Jewish economy and to direct private enterprise investments according to national priorities. Adherence to "old-time" economic liberalism was extremely rare among members of the newly established Israeli parliament. Only a few would have subscribed to statements such as Keynes's, that "the abolition of consumer's choice in favor of universal rationing is a typical product of that onslaught, sometimes called bolshevism, on differences between one man and another by which existence is enriched."[1] And even Keynes had to admit, in spite of his derogatory use of the term bolshevism, that direct intervention such as "price fixing and propaganda against price raising are . . . à la mode today."[2] Rather, the Zionist majority position (and its ambitions) was expressed, for instance in 1942 by the Fabian socialist economist Rita Hinden:

> The problem of developing the backward lands of the empire . . . is stimulating much serious thought and discussion at the present time. . . . [If] there is a lesson the opening up of Palestine can teach to other colonies, that lesson must be taught, and the political issues ignored in the teaching. Jewish colonization in Palestine has achieved its economic success, precisely because it has possessed the two elements which are essential for all colonial development—a free capital supply, and a planned economic policy based on the expansion and supply of the home market.[3]

Consistent with this approach, the Zionist establishment began quite early in the war to prepare plans for postwar economic needs and challenges. Prominent among these efforts was the activity of an "American Palestine Institute, a nonpartisan research organization," which began investigations in 1941 and in 1943 retained the services of Robert Nathan, who had been Director of the National Income Division

[1] J. M. Keynes, *How To Pay for the War* (London, 1940), p. 53.

[2] Ibid., p. 52.

[3] Rita Hinden, "Palestine and Colonial Economic Development," *The Quarterly Review*, 13 (Jan-Mar. 1942), p. 91.

of the U.S. Department of Commerce and chairman of the Central Planning Division of the War Production Board. Nathan was later joined by two additional economists, Oscar Gass and Daniel Creamer, and their joint product was a capacious volume titled *Palestine: Problem and Promise*.[4] Its first part was the most professional and comprehensive survey of the country's economy done until then (it is still referred to), while its second and larger part laid out plans for future mass immigration and development. It is intriguing to note the generally interventionist tenor of the book, expressed in the second part, as well as in criticism of the Palestine government's policies. The authors were obviously neither European social democrats nor members of the Palestine Zionist leadership. A number of quotes both illustrate the postwar views of Western economists and reveal the source of several specific measures undertaken by the Israeli government immediately after independence:

> Manufacturers and workers are not the only ones who learned how to do things during the war years. Government officials also learned much, particularly that the Government can play a constructive role in developing industry (p. 494).

> Ultimately the public monetary authority should become a central bank, extending credit to Government, assuring any necessary concentration of the country's foreign exchange holdings, and acting as the final source of credit for the whole economy (p. 633).

> [It should] in pursuance of its responsibility for exchange stability and an expansionist monetary policy . . . be transformed gradually, as needed, into a development-minded Central Bank, acting as a major instrument of public development policy (p. 605).

> Savers need to be encouraged. . . [But] failing an adequate flow of funds (and their use) in these private channels, only public and quasi-public institutions will be in a position to finance economic development (p. 606).

> More recently the range of banking risks has been greatly narrowed. Banks have shifted the risk-bearing function largely to government. . . . Where the Government is not lender it is often guarantor. . . . This trend for Government risk-bearing to become increasingly more important as compared to private banking risk-bearing seems to us to be irreversible. . . . Only Government can afford to unbalance its own accounts in an effort to balance the economy's accounts (p. 607).

> Several British and American economists have concluded that the appropriate measure to bring about a readjustment of the Palestine price level—after taking advantage of all other deflationary factors—is a controlled devaluation of . . . the Palestinian currency. . . . The general case for devaluation as an instrument of international price level readjustment is, however, of less force in Palestine under present circumstances than it

[4] Robert R. Nathan, Oscar Gass, and Daniel Creamer, *Palestine: Problem and Promise* (Washington, D.C., 1946), p. v. Years later, in 1953, Creamer with Simon Kuznets founded the Falk Project (later Institute) for Economic Research in Israel and was its director during 1954/55. At about the same time Gass was director of an Economic Advisory Staff for the government of Israel.

would normally be . . . [chiefly because] the Palestinian system of cost-of-living allowances negates [the] common relationship. Due to [it], a reduction in real wages cannot be brought about by indirect means (p. 599–600).

Probably some of these ideas were suggested by local experts, but it is nonetheless significant that they were adopted by the American advisory team. Many assumptions projected by that team into the postwar era were justified by the facts. In addition to developments already mentioned, two elements of the international scene after 1945 were particularly relevant to Israel's problems and policies: the Bretton Woods 1944 agreements concerning the international monetary regime, which *in effect* established fixed (dollar-pegged) exchange rates, supported—as long as necessary—by controls; and the emerging view that a "modest" inflation was conducive to full employment and growth, and in any case preferable to deflation-with-unemployment. Obviously, it was the forgoing of free convertibility which made such inflation, and at different individual rates, possible, but inflation in its turn precluded an easy return to convertibility.

Lastly, I must mention several components unique to ruling Zionist ideology. First and foremost it viewed Jewish immigration as the predominant national priority; in fact, one can say that this was the dominant argument for independence. Second, it preferred public and semipublic (such as Histadrut) enterprises, because private capital was suspected of seeking profit to the detriment of the national interest. An interrelated element of this tradition was the belief that the laws of economics did not apply to the Zionist endeavor; this was based on the fact that Jewish settlement in Palestine had been successful in the face of dire predictions by economic experts. Third, a high priority was assigned to agricultural settlement, for a whole set of reasons.[5]

It is against the background of this complex set of political tenets and external circumstances that we have to view the great opportunity provided the Zionist movement by the achievement of sovereignty: the State could permit free immigration, utilize public lands and water for settlement, impose protective tariffs, borrow funds abroad to supplement private transfers and contributions, and even print money for planned economic development. But it also faced the awesome challenge of how to live up to all the demands of both reality and ideology. Table 1 presents useful dates on the sequence of events in Israel at this time.

[5] See Jacob Metzer, "Economic Structure and National Goals: The Jewish National Home in Interwar Palestine," this JOURNAL, 38 (Mar. 1978), pp. 101–19.

TABLE 1
SOME USEFUL DATES

Date	Event
Nov. 29, 1947	The UN resolution to partition Palestine.
Feb. 22, 1948	Expulsion of Palestine from the sterling bloc.
May 15, 1948	End of the British Mandate (unilaterally); State of Israel declared and established.
Aug. 17, 1948	Establishment of the Israeli lira (pound).
Jan. 1949	Last battles; armistice negotiations started; first general elections.
Mar. 1949	First regular (coalition) government installed.
Apr. 26, 1949	The Austerity policy formally presented to parliament.
May 11, 1949	Israel admitted to the UNO.
Feb. 1952	New Economic Policy formally announced.

POLICIES

Popular Reactions

We may start by asking how the ordinary citizen lived up to those challenges in the first three years of Israeli independence.[6] Indications for an answer can be found, first of all, in the statistics of army mobilization and production. The approximately 20,000 volunteers in early 1948 rose, by conscription that included able immigrants, to some 100,000 soldiers at the year's end, about 15 percent of the Jewish population and at least one-third of its labor force.[7] Nevertheless, domestic product in 1948 as a whole was probably about equal to that of the Jewish sector in 1947, as far as can be gauged from admittedly deficient estimates for that year. This was in part the result of successfully maintaining Jewish citrus exports, through the ports of Haifa and Tel Aviv, and of the military demand for food and manufactures. With the gradual transition to a non-war economy, product grew by at least 70 to 80 percent in 1949 and by 25 to 35 percent more in both 1950 and 1951.[8] The intense production effort, in response to inflationary demand pressure, relied on high rates of investment and rapid growth of employment, but also on considerable enthusiasm. The latter was, of

[6] The following section relies heavily on Haim Barkai, *The Beginnings of the Israeli Economy* (Jerusalem 1983) (in Hebrew), and on the quantitative data there. He is, however, not responsible for any errors contained here or my interpretations and opinions, which are in part quite different from his.

[7] The numbers are from Ben-Gurion's *War Diaries* as quoted by Yitzhak Greenberg, "Financing the War of Independence," *Studies in Zionism* (Tel Aviv), 9 (1988), pp. 63–80; Barkai, *The Beginnings*, p. 37, cites an even larger number for "the second half of 1948."

[8] National Product estimates for these first years (especially 1948, omitted in most sources) entail—besides problems of data availability—methodological problems, not the least of which stem from distorted import prices. See discussions of these in the literature, particularly by A. L. Gaathon in Oscar Gass and A. L. Gaathon, "Memorandum: Israel's Economic Performance, 1949–1953" (mimeograph, Jerusalem, 1954). The lower figures in the text are close to Gaathon's estimates, while the higher ones are close to data cited by Barkai, *The Beginnings*.

course, the result first of independence and later of the military success in sustaining the State in the face of overwhelming odds.

This enthusiasm also caused the *initial* favorable and disciplined reaction to price controls and rationing required by the Austerity policy (see below). Combined with the preoccupation with survival, it explains the almost complete indifference towards the expulsion of Palestine from the sterling bloc in February 1948. This measure was part of Britain's policy of disengagement from all responsibility for Palestine. Its outcome was a textbook demonstration of the fact that a currency can continue to serve as the domestic means of payment even after losing its "backing" (sterling convertibility), and even after losing its legal status (with the end of the Mandate on May 15). With the social convention to accept the Palestine pound intact, there was no run on the banks, and—more important—no flight from money. Lastly, one is tempted to speculate that in this atmosphere the public would also have cooperated with a policy of absorbing purchasing power by higher taxation and attractive bond issues, if they had been initiated vigorously in 1949.

Fiscal Policy

The major question facing the newly established Israeli government was how to pay for the war, and it chose the route of a monetized deficit. A recently published estimate puts the domestic defense expenditure in the State's first year at 60 million Israeli lira (IL), or perhaps 40 percent of domestic product.[9] Of this sum, only 37 percent was financed by transfers from the published budget, sales of property, and loans from the public.[10] The rest was obtained by credits from commercial banks, chiefly in exchange for treasury bonds (which were viewed as reserve assets), and by some conversion of foreign exchange.[11] Even after armistice agreements put an end to hostilities in February 1949, defense expenditure remained a heavy fiscal burden.

Immigration had brought in about 350,000 people during 1948/49, and was to bring in the same number during 1950/1951—on a base of about 630,000 Jewish inhabitants at the end of 1947 (see Table 2). Moreover, most of the newcomers had no capital of their own. Thus the total government budget remained at about 50 percent of domestic product in 1949, and decreased only to around 45 percent and 36 percent in 1950

[9] Greenberg, "Financing the War," p. 69.

[10] As a matter of fact, "development" expenditures in the published budgets (the defense budget was kept secret) were also covered by borrowing.

[11] The bulk of foreign monies mobilized for the war effort from world Jewry was spent on purchasing equipment abroad. As a result, these sums were not included in fiscal reports or in the national product estimates. On domestic monetary demand and supply they had, of course, no effect.

TABLE 2
EARLY ISRAELI GROWTH

	1946	1948	1949	1950	1951
Population (average in thousands)	579[a]	850	1,059	1,267	1,494
Immigration (net in thousands)	19[a]	102	240	170	175
Gainfully employed (thousands)	243[a]	na	310	420	512
GNP (1950 = 100)	39[a]	na	79	100	129

[a] Jewish population of Palestine.
Source: Haim Barkai, *The Beginnings of the Israeli Economy* (in Hebrew) (Jerusalem, 1983), pp. 131–32.

and 1951 respectively.[12] Continuation of the monetized deficit appeared as the only practical solution, or as the easiest way out of a dilemma—depending on the historian's viewpoint. In any case, the nominal money supply (M1) grew at an annual rate of 36 percent from December 1948 to September 1951, including the increase in bank credits to the private sector. That was made possible by the method of government borrowing, and by the lack of any effective control over the banks' liquidity ratio.[13] Emanuel Levy, in his 1955 analysis, described the fiscal pressures in these words:

> The funds received from abroad were not capable by themselves, however, of sustaining and developing the economy. Large additional sums had to be raised in local currency in order to maintain essential social and defense services, finance the development and public works projects on which thousands of immigrants were employed, and to facilitate the completion of investments initiated in foreign currency. Government income from internal taxation and loans failed to keep pace with expenditure, and the choice had to be taken between acquiescing in the collapse of the development and defense programs or creating new means of payment.[14]

To be fair, expenditure was in fact gradually restrained and the effectiveness of taxation increased, so that by the fall of 1951 the printing of money—though not borrowing from the commercial banks—could be discontinued. The criticism of contemporary and especially of later observers, however, was not directed only at the lateness of these measures, but at the conception underlying this fiscal policy.

In effect, the concept assigned to a balanced budget and the balance of payments much lower priority than to winning the war, which was indeed a fight for survival, and to sheltering and employing the newcomers. As national product grew less rapidly than population despite the high investment ratio, and as foreign exchange for civilian uses was exceedingly scarce, primacy was assigned to an egalitarian distribution of essential consumer goods, that is, to nonfiscal means. This appeared

[12] For immigration data, see Moshe Sicron, *Immigration to Israel: 1948–1953. Statistical Supplement* (Jerusalem, 1957); for budget data and GNP shares, see Barkai, *The Beginnings*.

[13] Don Patinkin, *The Israel Economy: The First Decade* (Jerusalem, 1960), p. 108.

[14] Emanuel Levy, *Israel Economic Survey, 1953–54* (Jerusalem, 1955), p. 14.

the most natural approach both in view of the existing legal and administrative machinery for rationing and price controls, and because it followed from the ideological premises of the Israeli leadership. David Ben-Gurion, the charismatic premier and defense minister, definitely preferred a managed to a market economy, and this was much more weighty than his professed low opinion of the principles of economics. As to details—for which Ben-Gurion really did not seem to care as regards economic matters—he was persuaded to judge inflation by price changes only, so that he subscribed to the idea of "fighting inflation" by controlling prices.

"Austerity": Suppressed Inflation

The result of these priorities was the Austerity policy, officially initiated in March 1949 but in part implemented by the middle of 1948.[15] The system attempted to ration not only essential consumption goods but also raw materials, and generally to direct the allocation of resources. Its linchpin was the allocation of foreign exchange, which in an economy with such an exceedingly high import component was *the* strategic resource. The declared priorities were defense, immigration and absorption, and—to use a later term—a welfare-state regime.[16] Fighting inflation by preventing any further rise in the price level—which during the war had gotten out of hand and risen, according to the cost-of-living index, by 33 percent in 1948—was declared a major means to attain these ends.[17]

Significantly, the policy declarations of early 1949 used the two expressions, "inflation" and "the high cost of living," interchangeably. The idea was to improve the international competitiveness of Israeli products, whether for exports or for import substitution, and also to lower costs—particularly of construction and of public services—not only by preventing any further price rises but also by actually lowering prices and thus forcing the price-wage-price spiral downward. The first round of price decreases was to be achieved by auditing and revising producer calculations, cutting profit margins, and by some subsidizing of imported commodities. The process was then to continue under its own steam, thanks to the linkage of cost-of-living allowances to the

[15] This was part of the program presented by the first government, after the general elections of January 1949, and approved by the first Knesset. The title Austerity was taken from the British model, as were slogans and other details.

[16] The economic parts of the program are discussed by Nachum T. Gross, "Inflation and Economic Policy in Israel: The First Stage, 1949–1950" (in Hebrew) (M. A. thesis, The Hebrew University of Jerusalem, 1953), pp. 9–12; the expression used for absorption and growth was "intensive development of the country, based on a planned economy"; social welfare services were promised in several sections and aimed at "gradually and persistently raising the standard of living . . . of the entire population." See also in *Government Yearbook 1949/50* (Tel Aviv, 1949).

[17] Monthly index data cited by Gross, "Inflation and Economic Policy"; the wholesale price index rose 43 percent from November 1947 to November 1948.

cost-of-living index. Although this part of the Austerity policy did succeed in lowering the consumer price index 13.5 percent between April and December 1949, it lost momentum in 1950, and the index actually started to rise again in August of that year. The immediate causes for this reversal were the growing opposition of firms and trade unions to the policy and the turnaround in the trend of world prices.[18] The underlying factors, however, for the eventual breakdown of all components of the Austerity system were fundamental fallacies in its assumptions.

At this point it will be useful to remember that the first set of Israeli economic policies was largely based on plans formulated between 1944 and 1947, such as the Nathan-Gass-Creamer recommendations of which excerpts were cited above. Conditions had changed drastically, however, particularly with respect to the readjustment of prices. For one thing, inflation in Palestine continued after World War II, since none of the recommended measures for a smooth transition to peacetime conditions were implemented. Moreover, during the war for Israeli independence the remaining price controls became ineffective. Thus the gap between domestic and foreign price levels that was to be corrected by "readjustment" was now at least 50 percent larger, and the prospects of a downward-spiral policy became much dimmer.

Second, the massive creation of money by credits to the government and to the private sector, if we view the issue from the monetary side, or the massive excess demand stemming from the government budgets and from private investment (chiefly residential construction), if we look at the aggregate demand side, resulted in new inflationary pressures of unprecedented dimensions. Under these conditions, the lowering of prices added fuel to the inflationary fire by increasing the real value of liquid balances.[19] Instead of being, among other things, a policy of disinflation, the set of Austerity measures was in fact a policy of suppressed demand-pull inflation.

The trouble was that such a policy inevitably created cumulative pressures through forced consumer saving that diverted production and even imports to nonessentials—whose prices remained uncontrolled—that is, to "luxury" commodities, services, and housing. In addition, black markets in controlled commodities and materials developed, as public discipline and sympathy for the policy faltered. No less important was the fact that the overriding priority assigned to "fighting inflation" by means of controls prevented the introduction of other types of

[18] Due to the structure of the cost-of-living allowances, most real wages actually rose during the lowering of prices. Nevertheless, unions demanded a rise in "basic" wage rates at every renewal of the yearly collective contracts, just as they had done when prices were rising and the nominal wage was lagging. See David Horowitz, *In the Heart of Events* (in Hebrew) (Ramat Gan, 1975), for scathing criticism of this line of action.

[19] Patinkin, *The First Decade*, pp. 108–11.

anti-inflationary measures, such as raising indirect taxation and floating loans linked to the dollar or to the cost-of-living index.[20] The latter were avoided for fear that they would undermine public confidence in the price-control policy or in the fixed exchange rate. Indeed, the concern for the price level was a major argument against devaluation.

The Rate of Exchange

This is, of course, an issue of dominant importance. I have already referred to the establishment of an Israeli currency and of a foreign exchange regime, and also to the post-1945 world system of fixed exchange rates (maintained by rationing, if necessary). There was therefore no doubt that the Israeli lira (IL), established in August 1948, would have a fixed and controlled international value, and the only question was the specific rate to be chosen. Under the circumstances of a new state, however, at war with its much larger neighbors, and only partly recognized internationally, a country whose currency had until February 1948 been freely convertible to sterling *at par*, this seemed to be no genuine question either: the safest way to create and preserve public confidence in the new legal tender was a one-to-one exchange of Israeli lira for Palestine pounds. This preserved sterling parity, even though convertibility was no longer free. *But*, as part of the distortions and paradoxes of controlled prices, the previous Palestine government had allowed a nonconsistent exchange rate of only $3 per Palestinian pound, and this was continued for the Israeli lira.

At first sight, the system as a whole was consistent: the economy continued to be subject to a wartime regime of direct controls and rationing and of partial isolation from the world market. Foreign exchange was the major constraint, at first used almost exclusively for foodstuffs and fuel. Most production was directed to the rapidly growing home market, isolated from foreign competition by the controls except for the traditional exports of oranges and polished diamonds. Essential consumption, much of it rationed, was ensured to the entire population at controlled (and in effect highly subsidized) prices. A large share of resources was devoted to investment, and output—especially of food—increased very rapidly. The pegged exchange rate supported the policy of holding the price level constant and even lowering it, while the major share of foreign currency was obtained from sources that were insensitive to the exchange rate: contributions and other unilateral transfers, politically motivated loans, and the depletion of sterling balances accumulated during World War II and now "unblocked" by agreements with the British government. The fact that the currency was officially

[20] As a matter of fact, subsidies were raised from time to time, so that net indirect taxation decreased. Direct taxation was rising slowly, thanks to administrative improvements and public adjustment to the income tax.

TABLE 3
BALANCE OF PAYMENTS ESTIMATES
($ millions)

	(1946)[a]	1949	1950	1951
Imports	$(282)	$263	$328	$426
Exports	(110)	43	46	67
World Jewry, transfers		118	90	123
World Jewry, investments		25	21	97[b]
U.S. official loans		18	44	28
U.S. grants				14
Sales of foreign balances and securities		24	51	32
Short-term loans and errors and omissions		35	76	65

[a] Palestine, goods only.
[b] Includes $55M for Israel State Bonds.
Source: Nadav Halevi and Ruth Klinov-Malul, *The Economic Development of Israel* (New York, 1968), pp. 141, 294–99.

overvalued by a large margin was therefore considered a necessary and tolerable evil.

Along with the progressive erosion of the system on the domestic front, however, foreign exchange balances were also being exhausted. These included private foreign securities, whose owners were forced to sell them to the government. Moreover, the Israeli government's credit with suppliers and banks abroad had reached its limit. Thus the balance-of-payments problem was rapidly becoming the most urgent issue on the government's agenda (see Table 3). By mid-1951 at the latest the introduction of a new type of economic policy had become necessary, but it also became feasible: balancing the budget could be considered; the prospects for attracting tourism and foreign capital were improving; and the economy's capacity for domestic supply and increased exports alike had increased greatly. During 1951 several partial policy changes were introduced; most notably, borrowing from the central bank was discontinued, and a diversity of effective exchange rates was introduced by subsidizing exports and granting higher rates to selected imports and investors. Only the necessity to hold general elections in July 1951, and the ensuing political maneuvering among the prospective partners in a new coalition, delayed the declaration of a New Economic Policy until February 1952. Its cornerstone was a devaluation of the Israeli lira.

EVALUATION

With respect to several aspects of the economic policy which laid the foundations of Israel's political-economic system, a rather broad consensus seems to prevail. Thus, few would disagree that

The basic objects . . . were to a large extent achieved: for most of this period minimum consumption standards were provided for everyone, no one was without some kind of shelter, at no other time was such a relatively large share of resources devoted to investment, and output increased rapidly while unemployment declined. . . . [Yet,] several major problems remained unsolved: unemployment was still very high, about a fifth of the population lived in inadequate temporary housing, and foreign exchange reserves were very low. These undoubtedly reflect the sheer magnitude of the problems faced. But in addition, several other problems arose from the policy system itself. . . . Many mistakes were certainly made, but not all of them could have been avoided given the state of administrative organization at that time and the magnitude of the problems involved.[21]

Also

Viewed in retrospect, a certain degree of inflationary financing, at least as a temporary expedient, was probably unavoidable. The stupendous task of mass immigration and absorption had given rise to a situation resembling, in effect, a total war economy. And war financing, even in highly developed countries, has almost invariably proved inflationary.[22]

I have already noted that some of the "many mistakes" resulted from a fallacious identification of "inflation" as purely a price phenomenon, and from too little concern for the effects of massive money creation and excess aggregate demand. Few students of the period will disagree that these effects, and the distortions resulting from the suppressed inflation, could and should have been recognized much sooner by policymakers; the more so as critical views were being expressed in both public and closed discussions.[23] Specifically, the upturn of world prices in the summer of 1950 should have generated a thorough revision of Austerity policies rather than a hastily and ill-prepared extension of rationing to clothing and footwear, which set off a chain reaction of disillusionment with controls.[24] Although the cabinet was reshuffled in October 1950, this resulted only in minor policy changes.[25] It seems very clear that about a year was wasted from the point of view of economic policy. Nonetheless we must recognize that the main reason for the recurrent cabinet crises and the general elections of 1951 was precisely the lack of agreement between the major parties regarding economic policy. From this perspective the "wasted" year was required for Ben-Gurion and his leading supporters to come around to a partly new conception of economic policies.

In any case, on at least three issues—two of them matters of principle—opinions did differ and will continue to do so.

[21] Nadav Halevi and Ruth Klinov-Malul, *The Economic Development of Israel* (New York, 1968), pp. 6–7.

[22] Levy, *Survey, 1953–54*, p. 14.

[23] See Gross, "The First Stage," and Horowitz, *Heart of Events*, passim.

[24] This was conceded by Michael Kalecki, "Report on Main Current Economic Problems of Israel. Confidential" (mimeograph, Tel Aviv, September 1950), para. 65.

[25] Several of these followed Kalecki's September 1950 recommendations.

The lesser issue concerns the *timing of devaluation*. In the preceding sections I noted that the Palestine pound was overvalued relative to sterling and to the U.S. dollar at the end of World War II because of differences in inflation rates. That was even more the case at the end of 1947, and the gap increased still further during 1948. Although with respect to the dollar there had been a de facto devaluation of almost 30 percent, the Israeli lira was probably still doubly overvalued in the fall of 1949.[26] The British decision to devalue the pound sterling by 44 percent relative to the dollar in September 1949 provided the Israeli government with an excellent opportunity to correct the distortion. Indeed, the cabinet convened in special session to discuss the question. All the cabinet ministers except the Minister of Finance, however, and the heads of the largest bank (a special department of which fulfilled the function of an interim central bank) insisted on preserving the sterling parity, and so the effective devaluation vis à vis the dollar was only a minor correction of 8 percent.[27]

David Horowitz, the Director General of Finance and later the chief architect of the 1951/52 New Policy, severely criticizes this decision in his memoirs, and claims to have opposed it strongly at the time.[28] Haim Barkai fully supports this retrospective criticism, even though he reserves judgment with respect to the details of the debate.[29] Both also argue that the opposition of the bankers to a substantive devaluation was based on an overestimation of the danger to the Israeli lira's public standing at that point in time as well as on a lack of macroeconomic perspective. I disagree. We know very well from theory as well as from the experience of subsequent Israeli devaluations that the genuinely *inflationary* effects of devaluation have to be counteracted by adequate fiscal and monetary means.[30] In their absence, especially in an economy with an automatic (even if incomplete) price-wage linkage, devaluation leads to an acceleration of inflation and its benefits are sooner or later eroded in real terms. The bankers not only remembered what Nathan et al. and other experts had written on the subject in the past, but were also familiar with the state of Israeli fiscal and monetary policies *at that time*. Thus their opinion was not based mainly on micro versus macroeconomics.

The fact that a substantive devaluation was the most visible component of the 1952 New Policy supports my view, if full account of the

[26] According to Barkai, *Beginnings*, p. 65, the dollar rate in September 1949 should have been IL0.70 instead of the official IL0.33 *before* the correction; Gaathon, in Gass and Gaathon, "Memorandum," estimated the yearly average 1949 purchasing power parity at IL 0.593.

[27] The dollar/lira rate had already been only $3.00; in any case, the distortion of inconsistent dollar and sterling prices, with the opportunity for illegal arbitrage profits, was abolished.

[28] Horowitz, *Heart of Events*, pp. 42–43.

[29] Barkai, *Beginnings*, pp. 57–58 and fn. 21.

[30] Such inflationary effects would have been particularly strong in 1949/50, when the economy was operating practically at maximum potential and imports were about one-third of GNP.

preceding fiscal and monetary measures is taken. Significantly, in a semi-public lecture for students of economics at the Hebrew University in June 1950, Horowitz himself argued that devaluation should be a one-time measure, because of its effect on expectations, and therefore had to wait until it could, with a reasonable degree of certainty, "stabilize" the balance of payments. In a similar lecture, in June 1951, he repeated the argument and added that balancing the government budget and accumulating a certain reserve of foreign currency were prerequisites of such stabilization.[31]

The most fundamental question, perhaps, relates to the *philosophy or political culture* underlying the policies described. No doubt "this period combined the most severe problems with the greatest amount of government intervention in the economy," but is it certain that this situation could not be handled "without resort to massive controls"?[32] Ultimately, this is a question of political "worldview" that can be settled neither by economic theory nor by empirical study. It was no coincidence that the Israeli leadership preferred certain assumptions and recommendations, such as Michael Kalecki's *Report* of September 1950, while papers by other experts were shelved; nor that it took such a long time, even after two rounds of elections, which showed a severe erosion of public support for the leading social-democratic party, before the policy of direct controls was largely abandoned.[33] On the other hand, many who argue that devaluation should have been carried out much earlier most probably also sympathize with the "liberal" opposition of the period, which demanded a much larger role for market forces in the allocation of resources, including foreign currency.

But under what conditions would private capital—and how much of it—have found it advantageous to come to Israel? Would this not have perpetuated the low levels of skills and incomes of the majority of "mass" immigrants, due to a strong preference for labor-intensive techniques? Would free enterprise have developed agriculture, and later also manufacturing, to the same extent, and with such regional dispersion of the population? And would free competition, under the conditions of such a small market, not have led to even a higher degree of monopolistic concentration?

These hypothetical questions are also not questions of fact but of opinion (or of speculation), and even our experience in recent years can provide only ideological arguments for either side. Still, I would like to quote on this issue from Kalecki:

[31] Gross, "The First Stage," p. 19, based on notes taken at those lectures. It is, of course, quite possible that Horowitz argued differently in closed deliberations.

[32] Quoting Halevi and Klinov, *Development*, p. 7.

[33] Elections for local authorities were held in November 1950, and for parliament (the second Knesset) in July 1951.

> [It] is useful to consider briefly a theory which is often propounded in Israel. It is frequently maintained that all problems could be solved at one stroke by abolishing foreign exchange restrictions and [by] full decontrol at home. . . . This view point is, I think, entirely unrealistic (para. 7).
>
> There exists, I believe, in Israel a tendency to exaggerate the possibilities of foreign direct investment (para. 43).[34]

Lastly on this point, the Austerity policy has been severely criticized, for instance by Barkai, as a static "distribution of the available." One line of action by Ben-Gurion's government, however, implemented in part by Horowitz himself, was to search for new sources of long-term capital, that is, to *increase* the resources available, on terms conducive to development. In 1951 several of these efforts began to bear fruit—the Independence Bonds drive and U.S. foreign aid—while a new one had just begun—negotiations with West Germany about reparations. These were part of the new circumstances that prepared the way for the new policy.

The third issue is even more closely connected with politics, in this case with the question of how those in power at the time could most effectively remain in power. When in September 1948 Finance Minister E. Kaplan presented for the first time a half-yearly budget to the new Israeli parliament, he spoke of Austerity as a temporary lowering of the standard of living. This appeals to any economist. If we think of the vast needs for defense and investment in the face of limited resources, consumption obviously had to be curtailed in the short run, and rationing was to ensure an equitable distribution of that burden. By the time the policy was presented as part of the government's program in March 1949, however, this aspect of Austerity had disappeared from the text. Instead, and against all economic sense, the program promised not only defense, development, and social welfare services, but also a generally *rising* standard of living. Moreover, both in the short and in the longer run much of this promise was indeed kept, not only at the expense of faster growth, but also at the expense of equity. In order to satisfy its electorate, the ruling party chose to give preferential treatment to skilled, veteran workers and white-collar employees.

The argument that living standards were too high for sound development and economic independence has been a recurring theme from the book by Nathan et al. in 1946, to Don Patinkin's critical analysis of Israel's first decade, to practically all of David Horowitz's writings. Yet we cannot be sure that the politicians were not right in their judgment of what was practically feasible, and in particular which standards of living were necessary in each subperiod to attract additional immigration and prevent large emigration. It seems that even from the purely economic

[34] Kalecki, "Report" (September 1950).

viewpoint there is no clear-cut answer to the question of what time path of consumption would have been optimal for the growth of the economy. Needless to say, there is also no answer to the question of the optimal degree of income inequality, assuming a close connection between income differentials and productivity incentives.

Thus, on all three counts it appears that our ability both to draw lessons from the past and to utilize present experience and opinions for a better understanding of economic history has its limitations. Similarly, comparison with other emerging states of the post-1945 era has only limited value, due to the peculiarities of the Israeli case, such as its high levels of education and of political sophistication and organization.

CONCLUSION

We have seen that Israeli economic policy in the formative years from 1948 to 1951 was determined by two sets of factors: on the one hand were the tremendous disruptions and challenges resulting from the war and from massive immigration; on the other hand were the ideological preferences for a managed economy and for an equitable distribution of the burdens. We also saw that these preferences, as well as specific policy measures such as exchange controls, were in accord with worldwide tendencies and opinions. Finally, a regime of controls and rationing was, in effect, a convenient extension of the system which had prevailed under British rule. But even if the argument in favor of the actual policy choices may seem compelling, what can we say about the long-term price paid for this decision? Let me suggest that the record of rapid economic growth and of long-run absorption of immigrants in the years from 1953 to about 1970 appears to vindicate the view that the regime (including its various adaptations during that period) was well suited to Israel's needs and circumstances.

True, the cumulative evils of bureaucracy and far-reaching government intervention, combined with the apparent end of the era of large immigration, have led in the 1980s to widespread demands for a turnover of the political-economic system and a "return" to market economics. Quite significantly, these demands in Israel are again part of the worldwide trend. They do *not*, however, necessarily lead to the conclusion that economic policies after 1948—and in the years from 1948 to 1951 in particular—were all one big mistake.

One Market or Many? Labor Market Integration in the Late Nineteenth-Century United States

JOSHUA L. ROSENBLOOM

This article examines the geographic integration of U.S. labor markets from 1870 to 1898, using previously unexploited wage and price data for 23 occupations in 12 major cities. In contrast to the increasing nationalization found in other markets at that time, the labor market was characterized by large and persistent real wage differentials both within and between regions, leaving little doubt that late nineteenth-century labor markets remained far from completely integrated. The differentials, however, owed as much to substantial variations in labor demand growth as to the lack of labor market integration.

The late nineteenth century has often been regarded as the era in which a national economy first emerged in the United States. By 1869 transcontinental telegraph and railroad lines had been completed, and the elaboration of national rail and telegraph networks over the next 30 years reduced the costs and increased the speed of transportation and communication. Responding to the opportunities that these technologies created, manufacturers in a wide range of industries consolidated markets for their products and introduced new, capital-intensive methods of production made possible by the larger geographic scope of markets. At the same time, various innovative financial institutions were promoting the interregional mobilization of both short- and long-term capital. While the proliferation of banks helped to break down local monopoly power, the advent of commercial paper houses, insurance companies, and national stock and bond exchanges promoted the mobilization of capital from surplus to deficit savings regions.[1]

In contrast to the attention that late nineteenth-century financial and product market integration has attracted, the emergence of a U.S.

The Journal of Economic History, Vol. L, No. 1 (Mar. 1990). ISSN 0022-0507.

The author is Assistant Professor of Economics, University of Kansas, Lawrence, KS 66045.

I am grateful to Paul David, Gavin Wright, and John Pencavel for their extensive comments. I would also like to thank Gregory Clark, Shane Greenstein, and two anonymous referees for many helpful suggestions.

[1] For a general discussion of the formation of a national economy, see Harvey S. Perloff, et al., *Regions, Resources and Economic Growth* (Lincoln, NE, 1965), pp. 191–221. The emergence of big business and its lasting impact on the American economy is traced in Alfred D. Chandler, Jr., *The Visible Hand: The Managerial Revolution in American Business* (Cambridge, MA, 1977); see also Richard B. Duboff, "The Telegraph and the Structure of Markets in the United States, 1845–1890," *Research in Economic History,* vol. 8 (Greenwich, CT, 1983), pp. 253–77. On the emergence of a national capital market, see, for example, John A. James, *Money and Capital Markets in Postbellum America* (Princeton, 1978).

national labor market in this period has been largely neglected by economic historians, and what work has been done on labor market integration presents a confusing picture. While several studies have found evidence of a long-run tendency toward increasing integration, others indicate that the advance toward more efficient labor markets has not proceeded smoothly at all times or in all places. Stanley Lebergott and Richard Easterlin have found evidence of a long-run convergence in wages and earnings since the mid-nineteenth century, and a number of recent articles have concluded that labor market integration was increasing in the antebellum period as well.[2] On the other hand, the persistence of a large North-South wage differential during much of the twentieth century has been interpreted as a lack of labor market integration between these regions.[3] Similarly, several studies of late nineteenth-century wage data reveal the presence of persistent interregional differentials.[4]

In this article I present further evidence of the persistence of large geographic differentials in wage rates during the late nineteenth century. I show that although real wage rates in San Francisco converged toward eastern levels, large wage differentials persisted within as well as between the other regions of the country, with no trend toward convergence. Midwestern wages remained 20 to 25 percent higher than eastern wages—or about three to five times the magnitude of interregional differentials in the twentieth century—and differentials of 10 to 20 percent persisted between cities within the two regions. Closer examination suggests that these differentials owed as much to the substantial variation in rates of labor demand growth as to the lack of labor market integration.

[2] Stanley Lebergott, *Manpower in Economic Growth: The American Record Since 1800* (New York, 1964), pp. 239–40; Richard A. Easterlin, "Interregional Differences in Per Capita Income, Population, and Total Income, 1840–1950," in *Trends in the American Economy in the Nineteenth Century*, National Bureau of Economic Research, Studies in Income and Wealth, vol. 24 (Princeton, 1960), pp. 91–92. The antebellum labor market is discussed in Robert A. Margo and Georgia C. Villaflor, "The Growth of Wages in Antebellum America: New Evidence," this JOURNAL, 47 (Dec. 1987), pp. 873–95; and Winifred B. Rothenberg, "The Emergence of Farm Labor Markets and the Transformation of the Rural Economy: Massachusetts, 1750–1855," this JOURNAL, 48 (Sept. 1988), pp. 537–66.

[3] Gavin Wright, "The Economic Revolution in the American South," *Journal of Economic Perspectives*, 1 (Summer 1987), pp. 161–78.

[4] Clarence D. Long, *Wages and Earnings in the United States, 1860–1890*, National Bureau of Economic Research, General Series, no. 67 (Princeton, 1960), finds large interregional differentials in nominal wages from 1860 to 1890 with wages highest in the Midwest, lowest in the South, and intermediate in the East. Philip R. P. Coelho and James F. Shepherd, "Regional Differences in Real Wages: The United States, 1851–1880," *Explorations in Economic History*, 13 (Apr. 1976), pp. 203–30; and Philip R. P. Coelho and James F. Shepherd, "The Impact of Regional Differences in Prices and Wages on Economic Growth: The United States in 1890," this JOURNAL, 39 (Mar. 1979), pp. 69–85, report that adjusting nominal wages for differences in the cost of living across regions increases, rather than decreases, these wage differentials.

I. LABOR MARKET INTEGRATION AND WAGE BEHAVIOR

As geographically distinct markets become increasingly integrated, there should be a narrowing of differences in price levels.[5] Within a completely integrated labor market, workers at every location are aware of all employment opportunities elsewhere and through migration can offer their services to employers anywhere. As a result, the labor force at each location will adjust to equate the level of utility which may be achieved by a representative worker. If there are no site-specific amenities or disamenities, this adjustment will also result in the equalization of real wages for workers of equal ability doing identical work. In the presence of amenities, however, migration will cease when real wage differences just compensate individuals in each location for the variations in these amenities.[6]

Complete integration is unlikely to be observed in most real markets, and the empirical problem is that of determining the relative divergence of the observed situation from complete integration. Because potential migrants must bear the cost of acquiring information about employment opportunities at distant locations as well as the expense of transportation to get there, they will migrate only if the real wage differential exceeds these combined "costs of movement." Consequently, real wages may vary between locations but by no more than the cost of movement faced by the marginal migrant. The size of the real wage

[5] This is the criterion that has been used most often in historical studies of capital market integration. See, for example, Lance E. Davis, "The Investment Market, 1870–1914: The Evolution of a National Market," this JOURNAL, 25 (Sept. 1965), pp. 355–99; Gene Smiley, "Interest Rate Movements in the United States, 1888–1913," this JOURNAL, 35 (Sept. 1975), pp. 590–620; and John A. James, "The Development of a National Money Market," this JOURNAL, 36 (Dec. 1976), pp. 878–97. Recently, several articles in the antitrust literature have proposed that the extent of the market be measured by the similarity of price movements. George J. Stigler and Robert A. Sherwin, "The Extent of the Market," *Journal of Law and Economics,* 28 (Oct. 1985), pp. 555–85; and Pablo T. Spiller and Cliff J. Huang, "On the Extent of the Market: Wholesale Gasoline in the Northeastern United States," *Journal of Industrial Economics,* 35 (Dec. 1986), pp. 131–45. Kerry A. Odell, "The Integration of Regional and Interregional Capital Markets: Evidence from the Pacific Coast, 1883–1913," this JOURNAL, 49 (June 1989), pp. 297–310, suggests a method for combining these two criteria. While it is not practical to extend Odell's method to an examination of 12 distinct locations, the correlation of wage movements across cities largely confirms conclusions drawn on the basis of the pattern of intercity variation in wage levels. Joshua L. Rosenbloom, "Labor Market Institutions and the Geographic Integration of Labor Markets in the Late Nineteenth Century United States" (Ph.D. diss., Stanford University, 1988).

[6] The preceding discussion assumes that the location of "employers"—or more properly the other factors of production—are fixed. If the relocation of these other factors of production is taken into account, then the effect on wages of any site-specific amenities will eventually be eliminated since, unlike owners of labor services, the owners of these other factors of production do not have to move with these factors, and their location decisions will not be affected by the presence of amenities. Complete spatial equilibrium will be achieved only when all factor prices and utility levels are equalized. In the case where there are site-specific amenities this can occur either through the concentration of all workers and "employers" in one place (the site with the most favorable amenities) or through the dissipation of these amenities as the result of increased congestion at physically constrained locations.

differential may thus be used to measure the information and transportation costs preventing complete integration.[7] While the direct costs of transportation at any point in time reflect the resource costs of transferring labor from one place to another, the remainder of the differential reflects the costs of communicating labor market information and is thus a measure of the institutionally determined transactions cost preventing greater arbitrage.

II. WAGE AND PRICE DATA

In this article I consider daily wage rates for 23 occupations in 12 cities from 1870 to 1898.[8] This major collection of wage data provides the only annual coverage of a consistent sample of occupations and locations from 1870 until the end of the century.[9] In each city the wage quotations for each occupation were collected by the U.S. Department of Labor from the payroll records of at least two establishments that had "existed and done business continuously since 1870. . . ." Wages were not collected for every occupation in each city, but, where collected, they were reported for each year from 1870 to 1898. Data were collected for each individual employed by these establishments, but only the average wage for all individuals in a given city and occupation was reported.[10] The department's purpose in collecting the data was comparative, and the occupations included in the study were chosen because they were "susceptible to accurate definition."

Although neither the occupational nor geographic coverage can be considered representative of the economy as a whole, a wide range of

[7] Two problems make it difficult to infer the extent of labor market integration from the behavior of wages. First, measurement problems make it difficult to detect integration where it does exist. Heterogeneity in the workers' ability, the kind of work they are doing, the other conditions of employment, or the presence of site-specific amenities will distort the measurement of labor market integration since we are no longer comparing the prices of identical commodities. As a result, observed wages may differ across locations even in a completely integrated labor market. Second, the integration of markets for finished products and/or other factors of production will tend to equalize wages even if labor is completely immobile, creating the appearance of labor market integration even where it does not exist. Paul A. Samuelson, "Prices of Factors and Goods in General Equilibrium," *Review of Economic Studies,* 21 (1953–1954), pp. 1–21; and Robert A. Mundell, "International Trade and Factor Mobility," *American Economic Review,* 47 (June 1957), pp. 321–35. While the similarity of wage differentials in industries in which product market arbitrage is possible, such as the metal-working trades, with those in local market industries, such as construction, indicates that product market integration was not a significant influence on local wage rates, problems of measurement are more difficult to rule out, and their possible effects on wages are considered in more detail in Section IV.

[8] The data come from U.S. Department of Labor, "Wages in the United States and Europe, 1870–1898," *Bulletin of the Department of Labor,* no. 18 (Sept. 1898), pp. 665–93.

[9] The principal sources of wage data in the late nineteenth century are discussed in Long, *Wages and Earnings,* pp. 13–17.

[10] U.S. Dept. of Labor, "Wages in the United States and Europe," pp. 665–66. Correspondence with the historian of the department and with the staff of the National Archives uncovered no other records relating to this study and no trace of the more than 400 pages of underlying individual wage quotations to which the study refers.

activities and skill levels were included, and there is at least one city from each major region. The greatest number of occupations is in the construction and metal-working trades.[11] The geographic coverage is concentrated in the Northeast and Midwest, with 9 of the 12 cities in these two regions.[12] Nonetheless, one western city—San Francisco—and two southern cities—New Orleans and Richmond—are also represented.

The wage data are in nominal terms and must be adjusted for the relatively large geographic variations in the cost of living that prevailed during the late nineteenth century.[13] In order to examine real wages I constructed retail price indices for each of the 12 cities. Because of the limited availability of the requisite geographically disaggregated price data, the coverage was restricted to retail food prices in three years: 1869, 1890, and 1898.[14] Despite this limited coverage the resulting indices are still quite useful. The proportion of family budgets devoted to food remained by far the largest component of expenditures in working-class budgets—accounting for 56 percent of expenditures in 1875 and 41 percent in 1890.[15] Moreover, because retail margins are

[11] The occupations covered by the data are blacksmiths, boilermakers, iron molders, machinists, pattern makers, blacksmiths' helpers, boilermakers' helpers, iron molders' helpers, machinists' helpers, bricklayers, carpenters, stone masons, house painters, plumbers, hod carriers, common laborers, street laborers, teamsters, cabinet makers, compositors, railroad firemen, joiners, and stone cutters. While the coverage of the data is tilted toward craft workers and away from industrial employees, the occupations included nonetheless represent a considerable fraction of the urban manufacturing labor force.

[12] The northeastern cities are Boston, New York, Philadelphia, Baltimore, and Pittsburgh. The midwestern cities are Cincinnati, Chicago, St. Louis, and St. Paul.

[13] Philip R. P. Coelho and James F. Shepherd, "Differences in Regional Prices: The United States, 1851–1880," this JOURNAL, 34 (Sept. 1974), pp. 551–91; Coelho and Shepherd, "The Impact of Regional Differences"; and Michael R. Haines, "A State and Local Consumer Price Index for the United States in 1890," *Historical Methods,* 22 (Summer 1989). Unfortunately, the regional price indices constructed by Coelho and Shepherd are not sufficiently geographically disaggregated to be of direct use in examining intercity variations in retail prices. Haines reports price indices for individual cities, but his work became available too late to be employed in this study. Although the price indices I report later are based on a more restricted set of items than are those constructed by Haines, they appear quite similar for the 12 cities considered here, and no substantive changes would result from using Haines's estimates of the cost of living.

[14] Even so, for the beginning of the period it is necessary to settle for data at the state level. The data for 1869 are reported in U.S. Treasury Department, Bureau of Statistics, *The Cost of Labor and Subsistence in the United States in the Year 1869,* by Edward Young (Washington, DC, 1870). Prices were collected in the "towns" in each state. Although there is some basis for concern about how accurately prices in these towns will reflect prices in the large cities being examined here, Coelho and Shepherd, "The Impact of Regional Differences," pp. 80–81, find that in 1890 there was no correlation between city size and the level of urban prices. Their price index does not include housing costs, but neither does the price index employed in this article. Prices for every year between 1890 and 1898 are reported in U.S. Department of Commerce and Labor, *Eighteenth Annual Report of the Commissioner of Labor, 1903: Cost of Living and Retail Prices of Food* (Washington, DC, 1904).

[15] The results of late nineteenth-century expenditure surveys are summarized in Coelho and Shepherd, "Differences in Regional Prices," pp. 563–64. Their work also provides some indication of how accurately variations in retail food prices are likely to reflect variations in the prices of other

likely to depend upon such costs of doing business as site rent, they will reflect, at least partially, variations in other components of expenditures.[16] Thus, retail food prices should be a good proxy for the overall cost of living. Meanwhile, in view of the stability of relative price differentials revealed in both the data employed here and that discussed by Philip Coelho and James Shepherd the chronological restrictions do not appear to be a significant obstacle to comparisons of relative real wage levels.

Table 1 reports my estimates of relative retail food prices in each city for 1869, 1890, and 1898. In each year prices are expressed relative to the average across all 12 cities. On the whole these estimates conform to the pattern of variation found in previous studies: prices were highest in New England and the Middle Atlantic regions and markedly lower in the Midwest. Prices on the West Coast were above average but not appreciably above those in eastern cities. The two southern cities present a somewhat divergent picture, but it would appear that prices were only slightly below average in Richmond and New Orleans.

III. INTERCITY VARIATION IN REAL WAGES

The wage rate for any occupation reflects a variety of different influences. While wages vary from occupation to occupation because of human capital requirements or other characteristics specific to the occupation, wages vary from place to place because of intercity differences in the relative supply of and demand for labor of a particular type. It is these latter, geographic differences, which reflect the extent of labor market integration.

To measure the effects of labor market conditions on wages in each city—and hence the extent of labor market integration—requires some assumption about the way in which occupation and location influence wages. Adopting a linear in logarithms specification, the natural logarithm of wages in occupation i and city j may be expressed as

$$\ln(W_{ij}) = \rho_i + \pi_j + \varepsilon_{ij} \tag{1}$$

---

components of expenditures. They calculated both an overall price index for each region and subindices for food, rent, clothing, and fuel and light. Some differences are apparent in the behavior of the subindices, but retail food prices do a fairly good job of measuring the overall level of retail prices.

[16] The role of retail margins seems particularly important in accounting for the fact that retail prices varied considerably more between cities than did wholesale prices. Data collected by the Department of Agriculture indicate that wholesale prices of pork and wheat varied by only 2 or 3 percentage points between Chicago, St. Louis, and Cincinnati, while wholesale prices in these cities generally remained within 5 to 10 percentage points of those in New York, a much smaller variation than is revealed by the retail price data discussed later. U.S. Department of Agriculture, *Report of the Commissioner of Agriculture, 1881 and 1882* (Washington, DC, 1882), pp. 654–61; and U.S. Department of Agriculture, *Report of the Secretary of Agriculture, 1890* (Washington, DC, 1890), pp. 322–323.

TABLE 1
RELATIVE RETAIL FOOD PRICES IN SELECTED CITIES

City	1869	1890	1898
Northeast			
Boston	119.3	105.9	115.1
New York	104.4	113.6	111.1
Philadelphia	101.3	114.6	109.3
Baltimore	110.5	99.2	102.0
Pittsburgh	101.3	100.6	99.0
Midwest			
Cincinnati	84.5	98.2	96.8
Chicago	86.8	92.5	84.8
St. Louis	89.8	86.7	91.2
St. Paul	81.8	87.3	85.2
West			
San Francisco	107.7	114.1	108.2
South			
Richmond	95.7	90.3	99.3
New Orleans	118.2	97.0	100.5

Note: Average across all cities equals 100 in each year.
Source: See the Appendix for a description of the construction of the price indices and their coverage.

where ρ_i represents the effects of factors common to occupation i in all cities, π_j represents the effects of factors common to all occupations in city j, and ε_{ij} is a residual representing the effects of factors specific to occupation i in city j.[17] Regressing the log of wages on a set of dummy variables for each city and occupation, ρ_i and π_j are measured by the coefficient on the relevant occupation and city dummy variables.[18] In effect this is an analysis of variance regression with no interaction. The parameter estimate π_j—hereafter called the "city effect"—measures the effect of general labor market conditions on wages, while the regression residual, ε_{ij}, measures the deviation of wages caused by local labor market conditions specific to the individual occupations.[19] Esti-

[17] The choice of a linear in logarithms decomposition is suggested by the a priori expectation that the costs of movement which the city effect is intended to measure are likely to be proportional to wages. Such a specification may be rationalized under the assumption that the primary costs of movement involve the expense of information gathering and hence will reflect the opportunity cost of time spent in other employment. If the true relationship takes some other form, then this specification may be regarded as a first order approximation to the true relationship. One alternative is the assumption that migrants in all occupations face an identical fixed cost of movement—such as would be the case if transportation costs were the major barriers to labor market integration. In this case an additive specification would make more sense. In practice the results reported below are insensitive to the choice between these two specifications.

[18] Alternatively, intercity wage differentials could be computed using the average wage in each city. However, because the occupational coverage of the data varies from city to city, average wages will confound the effects of these occupational differences with the spatial variations which we seek to measure. In contrast, the regression approach employed here corrects for these occupational differences.

[19] If ε_{ij} is assumed to be distributed normally, it is possible to test hypotheses about the statistical significance of differences in the magnitude of the coefficients estimated by the regression. It may

mates of regional effects on wages can be obtained in much the same manner by replacing individual city dummy variables with a set of regional dummy variables. In practice, the regression is most easily estimated by normalizing wages relative to a single city and occupation. The level of wages in this "excluded category" is estimated as the intercept in the regression, and the other parameter estimates constitute the incremental effect of being in any other city and/or occupation.[20]

Tables 2 and 3 report relative nominal and real wages by cities and regions for five-year intervals from 1870 to 1898.[21] The base for intercity comparisons is New York, that for interregional comparisons is the Northeast region. In all cases the excluded occupation is street laborers. Looking first at the behavior of nominal wages, with the exception of the precipitous decline of wages in San Francisco, relative wage levels were quite stable over time. In addition, a rough equalization of nominal wages prevailed across most of the cities. Richmond, in the South, and San Francisco, in the West, diverged appreciably from the levels in other cities, but wages elsewhere were closely grouped. After San Francisco, New York and Chicago had the highest wages. In three other cities—Boston, Cincinnati, and New Orleans—wages began in 1870 to 1874 at roughly the same level as New York but had fallen below by the mid-1880s. This decline resulted in the convergence of nominal wage rates in most of the cities at a level between 85 and 90 percent of those in New York. Only in Chicago were wages close to those in New York.

---

be, however, that disturbances are correlated across closely related occupations with a particular city. If so, then we would expect to find that the estimated city effects varied systematically between occupation groups. This possibility will be taken up later.

20 Defining the dummy variable δ_{ks} $(k = i, j)$ such that $\delta_{ks} = 1$ if $k = s$, and $\delta_{ks} = 0$ otherwise, the regression equation can be written as

$$\ln(W_{ijt}) = \alpha_t + \sum_{r=2}^{23} \rho_{rt}\delta_{irt} + \sum_{s=2}^{12} \pi_{st}\delta_{ist} + \varepsilon_{ijt},\ i = 1, \ldots, 23;\ j = 1, \ldots, 12$$

where i represents occupations, j represents cities, and t represents time periods. Parameter estimates can be obtained for each year separately, or data from a period of several years can be used to obtain long-run estimates of the parameters. The choice of a base city and occupation is arbitrary and will not affect the estimates of relative wage levels. The pattern of variation of the city effect over time for any one city will, however, depend on which city is chosen as the base.

21 Real wages are computed by deflating nominal wages by a linear interpolation of the relative retail price indices from Table 1. In the cities where no trend was apparent between 1869 and 1890–1898 (Pittsburgh, Chicago, Richmond, St. Louis, and San Francisco), I used the average of all three price level estimates. Where there was an apparent trend between 1869 and 1890–1898 (the other seven cities), I used the average of the estimates for 1890 and 1898 for these nine years and used a simple linear interpolation between this level and that for 1869 to compute the level in each of the intervening years. Initial estimates of intercity and interregional differentials indicated that coefficients varied only slightly from year to year and that comparisons could be simplified by estimating city and regional effects on data from five-year intervals. The use of a longer time period has the added advantage of smoothing out any short-run shocks to wages which might distort intercity comparisons in a single year.

Economic agents are concerned with real wages, not nominal ones. For employers the relevant price is the one they receive for their products. To employers operating in national markets and receiving a uniform price for their products, the equalization of nominal wages was equivalent to the equalization of real wages and would have made employers largely indifferent to the location of their production activities. The question of labor market integration, however, is primarily concerned with the responsiveness of labor supply. From this perspective the relevant price is the expenditure necessary for a representative worker to obtain a given level of utility, so it is necessary to evaluate the effect of differences in the cost of living on money wages.

Adjusting for differences in the cost of living substantially alters the pattern of geographic wage differentials, introducing a much greater degree of variation. As Table 3 shows, variations between regions are more pronounced in real than in nominal terms, and variations within regions remain quite large. Within the Midwest real wages in the two northern cities—Chicago and St. Paul—exceeded those in their southern neighbors—Cincinnati and St. Louis—by as much as 10 to 20 percent. The range of variation among the eastern cities is comparable, although wage differences outside of New York appear to have been somewhat smaller.[22] Despite intraregional differences, however, a clear pattern of variation is also apparent between regions. In Chicago, Cincinnati, St. Louis, and St. Paul the lower level of retail prices raised real wages, opening a substantial gap between these cities and those in the East. In Cincinnati rising prices and falling wages reduced this advantage appreciably, but there was no more generalized decline in midwestern real wages. The regional differential between midwestern and eastern wages fluctuated between 20 and 30 percent, with no indication of any significant convergence.

Even after adjusting for differences in the cost of living, Richmond remains the city with the lowest wages, although the gap between it and the eastern cities is reduced somewhat by the lower than average level of prices. In New Orleans the high but falling level of prices largely offset the decline in nominal wages, resulting in a persistent east-west wage gap within the South. Adjusting for differences in relative prices does not alter the convergence of wages in San Francisco toward eastern levels, leaving it almost as pronounced in real terms as it was in money terms.

Some sense of the significance of these magnitudes is provided by comparing them with interregional wage differentials at other dates.[23]

[22] There is some evidence discussed below to suggest that housing costs in New York were disproportionately large and that some of the variation in eastern wage levels may be attributable to the fact that this expense is not fully represented in the price index used in this section.

[23] An alternative comparison is provided by contemporaneous variations in the prices for other commodities. For example, wholesale prices for agricultural commodities, such as pork and wheat,

TABLE 2
RELATIVE NOMINAL WAGE LEVELS, 1870–1898

	1870–1874	1875–1879	1880–1884	1885–1889	1890–1894	1895–1898
CITIES						
Northeast						
New York	100.0	100.0	100.0	100.0	100.0	100.0
Boston	103.1	96.9	91.6	91.7	91.2	92.1
Baltimore	87.4	91.0	84.5	83.5	82.2	82.6
Philadelphia	92.3	90.2	83.3	85.5	85.6	85.9
Pittsburgh	89.6	83.0	84.4	85.7	88.3	87.2
Midwest						
Cincinnati	98.9	98.0	90.1	87.8	87.7	82.9
Chicago	102.7	97.2	94.6	95.0	96.3	99.4
St. Louis	85.3	93.7	90.0	87.7	89.2	89.4
St. Paul	86.1	95.1	93.4	91.9	90.4	90.4
West						
San Francisco	141.3	139.2	119.2	118.0	111.8	112.2
South						
Richmond	77.1	77.8	70.6	69.2	69.1	68.2
New Orleans	106.3	105.5	92.7	89.7	88.0	88.1
REGIONS						
Northeast	100.0	100.0	100.0	100.0	100.0	100.0
Midwest	98.5	104.2	104.2	101.8	102.0	101.5
West	149.9	151.3	135.2	133.0	125.9	126.2
South	98.8	101.0	93.8	90.7	89.5	89.0

Notes: City and regional effects are derived by exponentiating the city and regional effect estimated from a regression of the natural logarithm of wages in city j and occupation i (W_{ij}) on a series of dummy variables for each occupation and for each city or region. This regression expresses the log of wages as $\ln W_{ij} = \alpha + \rho_i + \pi_j + \varepsilon_{ij}$, where the intercept, α, is the log of wages of street laborers in the excluded city or region, and the occupation effect, ρ_i, and the city or region effect, π_j, measure the incremental effect on the log of wages from being in occupation i and city or region j.
Source: U.S. Department of Labor, "Wages in the United States and Europe, 1870–1898," *Bulletin of the Department of Labor*, no. 18 (Sept. 1898), pp. 665–93.

Although precisely comparable wage data are not available for later dates, other studies indicate that the differential between midwestern and eastern real wages persisted at least until 1909, but that a substantial convergence must have taken place some time before the late 1930s. In 1909 a survey of wages and prices in American cities conducted by the British Board of Trade found a pattern of wages and retail prices quite similar to that described above.[24] According to this report, a slight midwestern advantage in money wages was reinforced by the lower level of retail prices, resulting in real wage differentials of 5 to 15 percent for a group of occupations closely resembling those examined in this article. By the time of a National Industrial Conference Board survey

reveal interregional differentials that were typically less than 10 percent. U.S. Dept. of Agriculture, *Report of the Commissioner*, pp. 654–61; and U.S. Dept. of Agriculture, *Report of the Secretary*, pp. 322–33.

[24] Great Britain Board of Trade of London, *Cost of Living in American Towns*, reprinted by U.S. Senate, 62nd Congress, 2nd session, S. Doc. 22, vol. 4 (Washington, DC, 1911).

TABLE 3
RELATIVE REAL WAGE LEVELS, 1870–1898

	1870–1874	1875–1879	1880–1884	1885–1889	1890–1894	1895–1898
CITIES						
Northeast						
New York	100.0	100.0	100.0	100.0	100.0	100.0
Boston	92.2	89.8	88.0	91.3	92.8	93.7
Baltimore	84.6	91.6	88.5	91.1	91.9	92.3
Philadelphia	94.7	92.0	84.4	86.1	85.9	86.2
Pittsburgh	94.3	88.9	92.1	95.1	99.0	97.7
Midwest						
Cincinnati	120.8	117.7	106.5	102.1	101.1	95.6
Chicago	123.1	118.7	117.5	120.0	123.0	126.9
St. Louis	100.9	112.8	110.4	109.3	112.4	112.6
St. Paul	110.2	122.4	120.8	119.4	117.5	119.1
West						
San Francisco	135.6	136.0	118.5	119.4	114.3	114.7
South						
Richmond	85.6	87.9	81.2	81.0	81.7	80.6
New Orleans	97.2	102.4	95.5	98.2	100.1	100.3
REGIONS						
Northeast	100.0	100.0	100.0	100.0	100.0	100.0
Midwest	122.5	128.0	126.3	121.8	121.2	120.5
West	146.2	147.5	131.8	129.6	122.6	122.9
South	97.2	102.0	97.2	96.5	96.9	96.3

Notes: The method of computing the city effects in this table is identical to that described in the Table 2 notes with the exception that the wage data have been deflated by the cost-of-living estimates from Table 1.
Source: See Table 2.

based on payroll records from 1937, however, real wages in the Midwest were only about 3 to 5 percent above those in the East.[25] More recent work, employing data from the 1967 Census of Manufactures, found that the differential was between 4.6 and 8.4 percent, depending on the price index used to adjust for geographic differences in the cost of living.[26]

The relative real wage levels reported in Table 3 reflect only that portion of the intercity wage variation caused by factors common to all 23 occupations covered by the data. The actual relative wage levels will be distributed around this value, reflecting the effects of differences in the extent of product market integration, institutional differences in the operation of labor markets for various occupations, or differences in the magnitude of local market disturbances producing systematic variations in the level of relative wages. The extent of this variation around the overall city effect may be examined by adding interaction terms to the regression, allowing the city effects for certain occupations or groups of occupations to differ from the overall level.

[25] Margaret Ada Beney, *Differentials in Industrial Wages and Hours in the United States*, National Industrial Conference Board Studies, no. 238 (New York, 1938).

[26] Philip R. P. Coelho and Moheb A. Ghali, "The End of the North-South Wage Differential: Reply," *American Economic Review*, 63 (Sept. 1973), pp. 757–62.

Table 4 shows relative real wage rates calculated separately for the three most numerous groups of occupations in the sample—skilled construction workers and skilled and semiskilled metal workers—as well as for common laborers. Although relative real wage rates for each occupation group varied around the overall city levels (as shown in Table 3), their departures were not particularly striking. Within the eastern cities only relative wages for skilled construction workers in Boston were significantly different from those for all occupations in the city for an extended period of time. In the midwestern cities wages deviated more noticeably. With the exception of Cincinnati and the semiskilled metal workers in St. Louis, the relative level of wages in the metal-working trades was well above the overall city level, resulting in an even greater real wage differential between these cities and those in the East.[27]

Among the southern and western cities, only New Orleans reveals any marked variation across occupation groups. In San Francisco the relative wages of the different occupation groups were clustered closely around the overall level, departing significantly in only a few years. Similarly, in Richmond there was little variation in relative wages across the different occupation groups. In New Orleans, on the other hand, the wages of skilled construction workers were significantly below the overall city effect, while those for the two metal-working trades were appreciably above the overall city effect. While it is possible that the relatively high level of metal-working wages in New Orleans is a reflection of integration with the midwestern cities, the large divergence between relative wage levels in the construction and metal-working trades might also be interpreted as an indication of the general isolation of this city from the prevailing norms determining the relative wages of workers in different occupations.

IV. INTERPRETING INTERCITY VARIATION IN REAL WAGE LEVELS

The existence of large and persistent intercity real wage differentials, especially those between the East and Midwest, in the decades after the Civil War is in striking contrast to the general perception of the late nineteenth century as a period of increasing geographic integration.[28]

[27] The low relative wage level of the semiskilled metal workers in St. Louis appears, however, to be caused by one extremely low wage occupation, machinists' helpers. Dropping this series from the estimates results in only a minor adjustment of the overall level of wages but raises the relative wages of semiskilled metal workers substantially. Excluding machinists' helpers, relative wages of semiskilled metal workers in St. Louis were 101.5 in the 1870–1874 period, around 110 between the 1875–1879 and 1885–1889 periods, and reached 133.3 in the 1895–1898 period.

[28] Although the differentiation of northern and southern labor markets has long been a theme in U.S. economic history, the distinction between antebellum midwestern and northeastern labor markets has only recently been noted. See Alexander James Field, "Sectoral Shift in Antebellum Massachusetts: A Reconsideration," *Explorations in Economic History,* 15 (Apr. 1978), pp.

TABLE 4
RELATIVE REAL WAGE LEVELS FOR SPECIFIED GROUPS OF OCCUPATIONS, 1870–1898

	1870–1874	1875–1879	1880–1884	1885–1889	1890–1894	1895–1898
SKILLED CONSTRUCTION WORKERS						
Northeast						
New York	100.0	100.0	100.0	100.0	100.0	100.0
Boston	85.5	80.0[a]	76.8[a]	81.5[a]	83.2[a]	81.1[a]
Baltimore	88.2	97.7	91.3	91.1	90.9	82.2[a]
Philadelphia	95.9	94.0	76.5	79.5[a]	81.5	77.9[a]
Pittsburgh	89.5	85.8	88.4	94.5	97.1	89.2[a]
Midwest						
Cincinnati	114.3	113.0	98.0[a]	98.0	96.7	83.5[a]
Chicago	107.6[a]	107.3[a]	109.5[b]	113.2[b]	114.1[b]	114.3[a]
St. Louis	102.4	127.7[a]	120.3[a]	112.9	116.1	107.9
St. Paul	103.1	119.8	122.1	118.8	105.1[a]	100.0[a]
West						
San Francisco	135.5	137.6	113.0	110.1[a]	105.8[b]	101.2[a]
South						
Richmond	95.4[b]	96.2[a]	83.8	81.3	80.4	74.2
New Orleans	74.3[a]	83.6[a]	76.9[a]	77.5[a]	86.7[a]	80.7[a]
SKILLED METAL WORKERS						
Northeast						
New York	100.0	100.0	100.0	100.0	100.0	100.0
Boston	112.4[a]	93.9	93.4	92.7	94.0	100.1
Baltimore	87.5	88.2	89.9	90.6	89.3	96.4
Philadelphia	97.0	84.0	85.6	85.1	81.4	86.1
Pittsburgh	94.0	85.4	92.4	92.9	92.1[b]	97.4
Midwest						
Cincinnati	130.7	109.7	108.0	97.6	94.3[b]	95.7
Chicago	146.1[a]	126.2	127.3[b]	126.6	127.8	136.8[b]
St. Louis	124.1[a]	119.3	116.9	114.3	114.0	120.1
St. Paul	149.7[a]	141.2[a]	134.7[a]	130.6[a]	134.0[a]	139.1[a]
West						
San Francisco	141.7	128.6	120.1	121.8	115.2	122.5
South						
Richmond	100.4[a]	94.7	89.1	83.9	80.3	82.3
New Orleans	127.1[a]	111.6[b]	110.4[a]	110.5[a]	110.4[a]	119.8[a]
SEMISKILLED METAL WORKERS						
Northeast						
New York	100.0	100.0	100.0	100.0	100.0	100.0
Boston	84.8	92.3	89.2	98.0	102.7[a]	116.6[a]
Baltimore	73.6[a]	85.1	85.6	91.7	94.3	107.8[a]
Philadelphia	90.1	87.6	84.6	87.3	90.2	96.9[a]
Pittsburgh	86.6	85.9	88.2	92.1	97.6	105.8
Midwest						
Cincinnati	109.2[b]	120.9	108.5	101.4	101.3	107.7[a]
Chicago	129.0	129.6	122.7	129.7[b]	136.5[a]	153.3[a]
St. Louis	80.0[a]	90.2[a]	86.5[a]	90.9[a]	94.7[a]	108.9
St. Paul	125.8[b]	135.3[b]	132.6[b]	134.6[b]	142.3[a]	154.7[a]
West						
San Francisco	131.1	134.6	123.0	131.4[b]	127.2[a]	143.7[a]
South						
Richmond	66.3[a]	69.2[a]	66.2[a]	67.2[a]	68.1[a]	76.7
New Orleans	102.1	113.0[b]	102.6	109.4[a]	109.4[b]	122.7[a]

TABLE 4—Continued

	1870–1874	1875–1879	1880–1884	1885–1889	1890–1894	1895–1898
COMMON LABORERS						
Northeast						
New York	100.0	100.0	100.0	100.0	100.0	100.0
Boston	66.5[a]	87.5	88.8	89.5	87.6	91.7
Baltimore	66.3[b]	80.7	81.4	82.5	83.2	89.5
Philadelphia	77.1[b]	89.7	87.9	91.5	89.7	96.4
Pittsburgh						
Midwest						
Cincinnati	114.4	118.6	114.3	108.6	112.1	115.4
Chicago	111.2	122.4	120.0	114.9	114.6	122.7
St. Louis	88.1	115.9	114.3	113.3	112.6	121.1
St. Paul	79.4[a]	106.5	120.6	120.3	120.9	125.2
West						
San Francisco	107.5[b]	133.3	123.6	122.1	106.4	108.8
South						
Richmond						
New Orleans	68.1[a]	99.2	96.1	109.2	98.1	91.1

[a] Occupation-specific city effect is statistically significantly different from the city effect for all occupations at the 1 percent level.
[b] Occupation-specific city effect is statistically significantly different from the city effect for all occupations at the 5 percent level.
Notes: The relative real wages reported here are obtained by regressing the logarithm of real wages in city j and occupation i (W_{ij}) on a series of dummy variables for each city and occupation and a set of interactions between dummy variables for each group of occupations and the city dummies. The log of wages may then be expressed as $lnW_{ij} = \alpha + \rho_i + \pi_j + \psi_{nj} + \varepsilon_{ij}$, where the city effect, π_j, measures the incremental effect on wages for all occupations of being in city j, and the coefficient on the interaction term, ψ_{nj}, measures the difference between the city effect for all occupations and the city effect for the nth subset of occupations in city j.
Source: See Table 2.

These differentials suggest that significant variations in the relative scarcity of labor persisted over more than three decades and that potential opportunities for arbitrage went unexploited. This condition prevailed primarily because of the high costs of acquiring information. Direct costs of transportation would have been only a slight deterrent early in the period and would have posed no problem by the turn of the century. By the early 1870s a well-developed railroad network provided passenger connections throughout the East and Midwest, and a special system of "emigrant" trains offered reduced fares to the interior.[29] By 1870 it was possible to travel from New York to Chicago for just $13.00.[30]

146–71; and Paul A. David, "Industrial Labor Market Adjustment in a Region of Recent Settlement: Chicago, 1848–1868," in Peter Kilby, ed., *Quantity and Quiddity: Essays in U.S. Economic History* (Middletown, CT, 1987).

[29] Although this service was neither as comfortable nor as fast as first-class passenger service, fares were two-thirds the regular rate, and travel times to the major cities of the interior were only two or three days.

[30] Fares to St. Louis, $16.10, and St. Paul, $33.00, were somewhat higher than those to Chicago, but they fell more quickly in the succeeding years. Frank B. Goddard, *Where to Emigrate and Why*

While this sum represented about nine days' wages to a common laborer, it was small compared to the potential increase in real wages. As documented in the previous section, real daily wages in Chicago exceeded those in eastern cities by 20 percent, so it would have taken just 43 days to recoup the investment in such a ticket. The only city for which the cost of transportation was likely to have been a significant barrier was San Francisco. In 1870 the fare on the newly opened transcontinental railroad was $160.00, but fare reductions over the next 30 years were most pronounced on long-distance routes, and by the turn of the century the difference between fares to San Francisco and cities in the Midwest had been greatly reduced.[31]

The differentials do not arise from problems in measuring real wages for homogeneous labor services. The prediction that increased labor market integration would be reflected in increased equalization of real wage levels applies strictly only to "real wages for homogeneous labor services." Discrepancies between this theoretical construct and measured wages may arise either because of biases in the measurement of the cost of living or because the wage data do not refer to strictly homogeneous labor services, and either of these factors could produce the appearance of intercity wage differentials even in a completely integrated market. Although it is difficult to assess the importance of these sources of measurement error, the available data offer no evidence that they played an important role in explaining the persistence of intercity real wage variations.

In fact, it appears that any bias in the measured relative costs of living works to understate the real wage gap and narrow it over time. The chief deficiency in the cost-of-living index is that it relies entirely on food items, excluding other items of consumption. After food, housing was the single largest item of expenditure and the one that varied the most between regions.[32] Yet both the magnitude and nature of the variations in housing costs that would have been necessary to offset the pattern of real wage variation described above appear implausible. Taking the level of nominal wages and retail food prices as given, the level of housing costs in Chicago would have had to exceed those in New York by over 50 percent to equate real wages in the two cities.[33] Since real wages in the other eastern cities were lower than in New York, an even

(Philadelphia, 1869), pp. 583–84; and W. Hoff and F. Schwabach, *North American Railroads: Their Administration and Economic Policy* (New York, 1906), p. 244.

[31] Hoff and Schwabach, *North American Railroads*, p. 244.

[32] Coelho and Shepherd, "Differences in Regional Prices," pp. 573–76.

[33] This calculation assumes that the prices of other commodities varied with a weighted average of food and housing costs and assigns weights of 0.7 and 0.3 to food and housing, respectively. The differential in housing costs implied for St. Louis (8 percent) and St. Paul (23 percent) are smaller but appear unlikely in light of the limited evidence on spatial variations in housing costs that is reviewed below.

larger differential in housing costs would be required to bring midwestern wages into equality with those in the other eastern cities.

The possibility of large variations in housing quality within and between cities makes comparisons of actual housing costs in different locations tentative, but it appears they would have accentuated, not offset, differences in food costs. Coelho and Shepherd's regional price level estimates for 1870 to 1880 show that although rents in the East North Central region were approximately one-third higher than those in New England, they were from 8 to 14 percent below those in the Middle Atlantic region during most of the decade.[34] Table 5 presents data from two other studies of housing costs. Although the data for 1869 indicate that housing costs were higher in the Midwest than in the East, the data for 1909 are consistent with Coelho and Shepherd's estimates. The divergence between the 1869 state-level estimates and Coelho and Shepherd's regional estimates for the 1870s provides some indication of the potential variability of housing cost estimates. While little is known about the method used in collecting the data on which these earlier estimates rest, the British Board of Trade, which collected the data for 1909, went to great lengths in its efforts to control for quality variations. To that extent, its estimates showing lower housing costs in the Midwest would appear to be more reliable than either of the estimates based on earlier data. Thus, although inclusion of housing costs might have reduced real wage differentials at the beginning of the period, the subsequent decline in midwestern housing costs indicated by the data from 1909 would have contributed to interregional divergence of real wages.

Turning to the measurement of nominal wage levels, a variety of sources of heterogeneity are possible, but none were of any substance in the period in question. There are two broad categories of heterogeneity, the first arising because of variations in the character of the work or other nonwage aspects of the labor bargain and the second resulting from differences in the quality of workers performing otherwise identical jobs. Although the wage data are for narrowly defined occupations and were intended to be comparable, some degree of variation in job characteristics is still possible. This variation would not, however, affect overall geographic wage differentials unless job characteristics in the different occupations varied systematically across cities. There is no way to assess this possibility, but it would be difficult to reconcile the

[34] The precise magnitude of the interregional differentials fluctuated considerably over the course of the decade. While the differential between New England and the East North Central region remained fairly steady during these years, the rents in the Middle Atlantic region converged somewhat toward those in the East North Central region. Coelho and Shepherd, "Differences in Regional Prices," p. 591.

TABLE 5
RELATIVE RENTAL HOUSING COSTS, 1869–1909

	Average Across All Cities = 100	New York = 100	
	1869	1869	1909
Northeast			
Boston	98.9	116.1	82.0
New York	85.2	100.0	100.0
Philadelphia	57.0	67.7	79.0
Baltimore	68.1	80.4	54.0
Pittsburgh	57.0	67.7	94.1
Midwest			
Cincinnati	78.9	92.7	93.1
Chicago	111.8	131.4	70.1
St. Louis	122.2	143.5	101.1
St. Paul	107.1	125.7	77.0
West			
San Francisco	138.9	163.9	
South			
Richmond	95.8	112.1	
New Orleans	179.7	211.3	72.0

Notes and Sources: For 1869 housing costs are computed as an unweighted average of the rent for four- and six-room apartments as reported for the cities in each state in U.S. Treasury Department, Bureau of Statistics, *The Costs of Labor and Subsistence in the United States for the Year 1869,* by Edward Young (Washington, DC, 1870). The index for 1909 is taken from Great Britain Board of Trade of London, *Cost of Living in American Towns*, reprinted by U.S. Senate, 62nd Congress, 2nd session, S. Doc. 22, vol. 4 (Washington, DC, 1911), pp. xxxvii–xxxviii.

emergence of such systematic differences with the notion of an integrated market.[35]

Employment relationships involve a broad array of variables, and it is possible that intercity differences in nonwage aspects of the labor bargain were reflected in compensating variations in wages among workers performing otherwise identical tasks. Fringe benefits were unimportant for manual workers in the nineteenth century and so could not explain much wage variation, and the scattered facts available do not suggest that differences in the length of the work day, the extent of seasonality, or the risk of unemployment explain the intercity variation in real wages.

The Labor Department said nothing about these issues in reporting the wage data used here, and there are only fragments of information on spatial variation in these features of the employment relationship. The 1890 Census of Manufactures, for example, reports both average daily hours and the typical number of weeks in operation for selected industries in major cities. In foundries and machine shops, which

[35] If employers in various cities were in fact engaged in production requiring employees with different qualifications, then there would be in effect no basis for labor market arbitrage between different cities, and the question of labor market integration would be moot.

employed many of the metal workers included in the wage data, average daily hours in the high-wage midwestern cities exceeded those in most eastern cities by no more than 2 to 3 percent.[36] Seasonality in employment appears to have been equally invariant across locations: the typical number of weeks in operation ranged from 49.8 in St. Paul to 51.6 in New York. Seasonal work patterns were probably more important in the construction trades, but the binding constraint in extending the work year in construction arose not from inclement weather but from the organization of the industry. Summarizing the results of a number of studies from the early twentieth century, William Haber concluded that despite extreme variations in climate, the number of days worked in cities such as New York, St. Paul, and Montreal was "about the same" as in Los Angeles, San Francisco, and New Orleans.[37] Finally, although there were differences in the risks of unemployment, the census data for 1890 and 1900 reveal no systematic relationship with wages.[38]

The second possible source of intra-occupation variations in wage rates is variation in the quality of workers between cities. Since the wage data are averages over a number of employees, random variations in individual ability should not be a major source of geographic differentials, and there do not appear to be any systematic variations in population characteristics across cities. Although no data bearing directly on differences in productivity are available, it is possible to measure geographic variations in a number of observable characteristics—sex, race, age, and ethnicity—which are often treated as proxies

[36] For the summer months the greatest difference was about 6.5 percent between Chicago (9.94 hours) and Baltimore (9.33 hours). In the winter months hours in a number of the eastern cities actually exceeded those in midwestern cities. U.S. Department of the Interior, "Manufactures: Statistics of Cities," *Eleventh Census of the United States (1890)*, vol. 12 (Washington, DC, 1895), pp. 724–33. The impression that the length of the work day did not vary systematically across locations is confirmed by data presented in U.S. Department of Interior, "Report on the Statistics of Wages in Manufacturing Industries with Supplementary Reports," *Tenth Census of the United States (1880)*, vol. 20 (Washington, DC, 1886), pp. xxviii–xxxiii.

[37] William Haber, *Industrial Relations in the Building Industry*, Wertheim Fellowship Publications, no. 3 (Cambridge, MA, 1930), pp. 97–115.

[38] U.S. Department of the Interior, *Eleventh Census (1890)*, "Population," part 2 (Washington, DC, 1897), pp. 630–743; and U.S. Department of Commerce and Labor, Bureau of the Census, *Occupations at the Twelfth Census* (Washington, DC, 1904), pp. 480–743. The computation of unemployment rates is discussed in Rosenbloom, "Labor Market Institutions," pp. 116–17. Unemployment rates in the Midwest exceeded those in the East in 1900, but unemployment rates in the two regions were similar in 1890. It might be hypothesized that workers are primarily concerned about the risk of unemployment during cyclical downturns, making the 1900 figures the more relevant ones and suggesting that a portion of the higher real wage in the midwestern cities compensated workers for a narrower and hence more unstable employment base. It is difficult to believe, however, that the differences in unemployment rates were large enough to account for more than a small part of the 20 to 25 percent difference in real wages between eastern and midwestern cities in the 1890s. In addition, the growth of the midwestern cities seems likely to have increased rather than reduced the diversity of employment opportunities over time, thus reducing the risk of unemployment in these cities.

for labor quality. Because very few women were employed in the manual trades covered by the wage data, and blacks accounted for only a small proportion of the labor force in eastern and midwestern cities, we may concentrate on the effects of intercity variations in the age distribution and ethnic make-up of the labor force. Census data reveal that the proportion of the labor force in the 25 to 44 age group was highest in the midwestern cities and San Francisco, but that the extent of this difference was diminishing over time.[39] Since the 25 to 44 age group is likely to have the highest labor force participation rate and is less likely to have established strong geographic attachments than older workers, this is precisely the pattern of heterogeneity that we would expect to find in response to a geographic differential in real wages. Nonetheless, the pattern is not sharp enough to account for the wage differential. Although workers in the 25 to 44 age group were likely to be more productive than other workers, the small magnitude of the geographic variation in age distributions and their convergence over time indicate that this factor could not have contributed appreciably to explaining the real wage differential between the midwestern and eastern cities. Intercity differences in ethnic composition also look more like the consequence than the cause of real wage variation. In contrast to the expectation that the presence of less skilled immigrant workers would exert a downward pressure on wages, both the percentage of the population foreign born and the percentage of the foreign born from southern and eastern Europe are positively correlated with real wage levels.[40]

If, as the preceding evidence suggests, intercity real wage variations reflected genuine differences in the economic opportunities offered in various locations, we should find positive signs of this in aggregate migration rates. In particular, the conclusion that cities with the highest levels of real wages were in fact attracting the greatest volume of migration would confirm the impression that labor market conditions in those cities were more favorable than in cities with lower wage rates, but that the difficulty of acquiring and acting on information about these opportunities prevented more complete equalization of wages.

From 1870 to 1900 the population of the two midwestern cities with

[39] Rosenbloom, "Labor Market Institutions," pp. 118–19.

[40] Data on country of birth are available in each of the four decennial censuses from 1880 through 1900 for all 12 cities and in 1870 for all of the cities except St. Paul. U.S. Department of the Interior, *Compendium of the Ninth Census (1870)* (Washington, DC, 1872), table 20; U.S. Department of the Interior, *Compendium of the Tenth Census (1880),* part 1 (Washington, DC, 1883), table 33; U.S. Department of the Interior, *Eleventh Census (1890),* "Population," part 1 (Washington, DC, 1897), table 34; and U.S. Department of Commerce and Labor, *Abstract of the Twelfth Census (1900)* (Washington, DC, 1904), tables 81, 82. The correlation between the log of relative real wages and the fraction of the population foreign born in the four census years (using wages in 1898 for 1900) is 0.71, while the correlation between the fraction of the foreign born from countries other than Germany, Great Britain, and Ireland is 0.45.

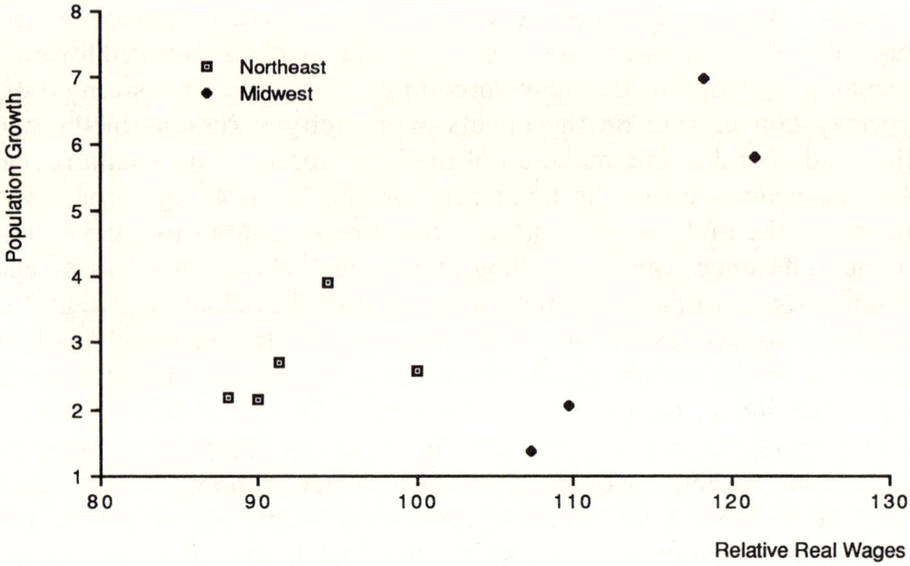

FIGURE 1

AVERAGE ANNUAL RATE OF POPULATION GROWTH AND AVERAGE RELATIVE REAL WAGE RATE, 1870–1900

the highest real wage levels—Chicago and St. Paul—grew by more than 5 percent per annum, a rate of growth which resulted in a more than fivefold increase in population over the period. Clearly such rapid growth could not have been achieved without a substantial influx of population.[41] Rates of growth in the other seven northeastern and midwestern cities were distinctly slower, but, as Figure 1 suggests, they were roughly correlated with variations in relative real wage levels, although it appears that midwestern cities required higher wage levels to maintain any given rate of population growth. Given the huge increase in labor supply that these data reveal for Chicago and St. Paul, it is certainly remarkable that there was no appreciable reduction in relative real wages in these cities. Such a situation can only be explained by a correspondingly rapid outward movement of the labor demand schedule in these cities.

V. CONCLUSIONS

Although the behavior of wages provides only an imperfect indication of the extent of labor market integration, the evidence examined in this

[41] Although the rate of net immigration into individual cities cannot be measured directly, variations in rates of population growth are likely to be a good proxy for this variable. According to estimates by Paul A. David, "Industrialization and the Changing Labor Supply in a Region of Recent Settlement," *Memorandum 25–26,* Research Center in Economic Growth (Stanford, 1963), migration accounted for between three-fourths and four-fifths of the growth in Chicago's population in the decades between 1870 and 1900.

article leaves little doubt that late nineteenth-century labor markets remained far from completely integrated. Where the barriers of distance were largest, improvements in transportation and communication did make a difference, as indicated by the convergence of real wages in San Francisco toward those in the rest of the country. Over shorter distances, however, there was no consistent reduction in geographic differentials. Most striking is the conclusion that real wages in midwestern cities were more than 20 percent higher than those in eastern cities. Although intraregional differentials were not as large, a considerable wage gap also persisted within the Northeast and Midwest. Measurements of real wage levels are subject to a variety of biases, of course, but neither these biases nor the direct costs of movement between locations seems capable of accounting for the observed pattern of real wage variation, at least within the eastern and midwestern cities. While it appears justified to interpret these differentials as an indication of the persistence of substantial intercity differences in labor scarcity, the rapid growth of population in the high wage cities of the Midwest suggests that these differentials reflect the interaction of large geographic variations in the rate of growth of labor demand with imperfections in the labor market. As a result, a complete account of labor market integration in the late nineteenth century will require disentangling the simultaneous effects of supply and demand factors in determining local wage rates.

Appendix

CONSTRUCTION OF COST-OF-LIVING INDICES

Ideally, comparison of the cost of living would be based on the minimum cost of obtaining an identical level of utility in each location.[42] In practice, however, comparisons of relative consumer price levels in different regions are usually made using a fixed weight Laspeyres index of retail prices, in which the cost of a fixed bundle of goods is computed in terms of the prices prevailing in the different regions. Historical data on expenditures are in the form of expenditure shares, however, and this has led previous researchers to construct estimates of the relative level of prices as weighted averages of price relatives.[43] Thus, the index for city j is computed as

$$P_j = \sum_k w_k(P_{jk}/P_k) \tag{2}$$

[42] John H. Pencavel, "Constant-Utility Index Numbers of Real Wages," *American Economic Review,* 67 (Mar. 1977), pp. 91–100.

[43] See, for example, Ethel D. Hoover, "Retail Prices After 1850," in *Trends in the American Economy in the Nineteenth Century,* National Bureau of Economic Research, Studies in Income and Wealth, vol. 24 (Princeton, 1960), pp. 140–90; and Coelho and Shepherd, "Differences in Regional Prices," pp. 551–91.

where w_k is the weight given to commodity k, P_{jk} is the price of commodity k in city j, and P_k is the price of commodity k in the base region. If these weights had been derived by computing the expenditure shares from the base region quantities and prices, so that

$$w_k = Q_k P_k / \sum_k Q_k P_k \quad (3)$$

then equation 2 would reduce to a Laspeyres price index. Since the expenditure weights were derived independently of the prices, however, this is not strictly true.

The estimates of relative retail food prices in this article were computed using equation 2, taking the average price of each commodity across all cities as the base. The commodities used in constructing the index and their weights are listed in Table 6. The list of commodities for which prices were available closely paralleled those used by Philip Coelho and James Shepherd in constructing their regional price level estimates for the years from 1851 to 1880. Rather than deriving a new set of weights I have adapted their commodity weights by redistributing the weights for missing commodities to other similar ones.[44] Although state and federal labor bureaus began conducting expenditure studies in the mid-1870s, it was not until the 1890s that these studies provided sufficient detail to allow the calculation of detailed commodity weights.[45] The weights calculated by Coelho and Shepherd are based on data from the 2,561 "normal" families studied by the U.S. Bureau of Labor in 1890 to 1891.[46]

For 1869 the price quotations are taken from a report by Edward Young which was published by the Treasury Department. This source provides only a single quotation for each commodity in each state.[47] For 1890 and 1898, data were taken from surveys of retail food prices conducted by the Department of Labor. These surveys report a number of quotations for each commodity in each city.[48] For these latter years the price in each city is taken to be the unweighted average of all of the price quotations for each commodity in that city.

As Table 6 shows, the food items included in the index have been subdivided into several major groups. Where prices were missing for any commodity, it has been assumed that its price varied with the other commodities in its group, and its weight has been redistributed evenly among those commodities.

[44] Coelho and Shepherd, "Differences in Regional Prices," pp. 585–86, appendix table 1.

[45] These studies are reviewed in Jeffrey G. Williamson, "Consumer Behavior in the Nineteenth Century: Carroll D. Wright's Massachusetts Workers in 1875," *Explorations in Entrepreneurial History,* 2nd series, 4 (Winter 1967), pp. 98–135.

[46] Coelho and Shepherd, "Differences in Regional Prices," pp. 562–64.

[47] U.S. Treasury Dept., *The Costs of Labor and Subsistence.*

[48] The results of these surveys are reported in U.S. Dept. of Commerce and Labor, *Eighteenth Annual Report,* pp. 664–845, table 1.

TABLE 6
COMMODITIES AND WEIGHTS USED IN CONSTRUCTING
RELATIVE RETAIL FOOD PRICE INDICES

Commodity and Major Group	Weights	
	1869	1890 and 1898
Cereals		
Flour, wheat (superfine)	7.083	17.669
Flour, wheat (extra family)	7.083	
Flour, rye	2.000	
Corn meal	2.000	2.004
Rice	0.364	0.364
Meat and Fish		
Beef, fresh roasting pieces	4.736	7.808[a]
Beef, fresh rump steaks	4.736	7.808
Beef, fresh soup pieces	1.093	
Beef, corned	1.093	1.615
Pork, fresh	2.368	3.500
Pork, corned and salted	0.547	
Pork, bacon	0.547	2.020
Pork, smoked ham	0.547	2.020
Pork, shoulders	0.547	
Pork, sausage	0.547	
Veal, forequarters	0.911	
Veal, hindquarters	0.911	
Veal, cutlets	0.911	
Mutton, forequarters	0.911	
Mutton, legs	0.911	
Mutton, chops	0.911	
Mackeral, pickled	1.275	
Codfish, dry	1.275	
Dairy Products		
Milk	5.465	5.465
Butter	10.747	10.747
Cheese	0.911	0.911
Vegetables		
Potatoes	8.379	8.379
Beans	4.372	4.372
Other Food		
Eggs	4.189	4.220
Tea	2.368	2.385
Coffee, green	3.643	
Coffee, roasted	3.643	7.339
Lard	2.732	2.752
Sugar		8.256
Yellow B	2.732	
Yellow C	2.732	
Good Brown	2.732	
Molasses		0.367
New Orleans	0.189	
Puerto Rico	0.189	
Syrup	0.189	

[a] Includes stewing pieces.
Source: See the Appendix.

Crowding Out during Britain's Industrial Revolution

ROBERT A. BLACK AND CLAIRE G. GILMORE

Contrary to earlier assertions, the historical data for Britain do confirm a (lagged) crowding-out effect during the Industrial Revolution. Heavy government borrowing after 1793 for the wars with France raised interest rates. These results are confirmed with nominal-interest-rate equations rather than with real-rate equations, which impose restrictive assumptions about the adjustment of nominal rates to inflation expectations. We see no reason to abandon the neoclassical, factor-allocation model of saving and investment in favor of a theory asserting that firms accumulate capital for investment independently of household saving decisions.

Recent interest in Britain's rate of economic growth during the "First Industrial Revolution" has led to a discussion of whether heavy borrowing to finance the French Wars of 1793 to 1815 crowded out private investment, limiting the country's capital formation and growth.[1] Using a neoclassical general-equilibrium model, Jeffrey Williamson concluded that "the rate of [capital] accumulation was suppressed by war well below what it would have been in peace."[2] But Carol Heim and

The Journal of Economic History, Vol. L, No. 1 (Mar. 1990). ISSN 0022-0507.

The authors are Associate Professor of Economics, King College, Bristol, TN 37620, and Instructor of Finance, Drexel University, Philadelphia, PA 19104.

The authors wish to thank Thomas Chiang, Roger McCain, Jeffrey Williamson, the editor, and two anonymous referees for numerous helpful suggestions on earlier drafts.

[1] Whether borrowing by Britain to finance war efforts in the late eighteenth and early nineteenth centuries affected interest rates and private investment is by no means a recent issue. Mill is among the nineteenth-century writers who suggested that war debts could, under certain circumstances, displace private capital accumulation. See John Stuart Mill, *Principles of Political Economy* (1862; New York, 1909 printing of 5th edn.), pp. 873–75. The recent interest in historical crowding out is related to U.S. experience with high budget deficits in the 1980s. A number of studies have examined the potential for deficits, or government expenditure, to crowd out private investment. See, for example: Paul Evans, "Do Deficits Raise Interest Rates?" *Journal of Monetary Economics,* 20 (Sept. 1987), pp. 281–300; Gerald P. Dwyer, Jr., "Federal Deficits, Interest Rates and Monetary Policy," *Journal of Money, Credit, and Banking,* 17 (Nov. 1985, Part 2), pp. 655–81; Robert J. Barro, "Government Spending, Interest Rates, Prices, and Budget Deficits in the United Kingdom, 1701–1918," *Journal of Monetary Economics,* 20 (Sept. 1987), pp. 221–47; John A. Tatom, "Two Views of the Effects of Government Budget Deficits in the 1980's," Federal Reserve Bank of St. Louis *Review,* 67 (Oct. 1985), pp. 5–16; and Michael D. Bradley, "Government Spending or Deficit Financing: Which Causes Crowding Out?" *Journal of Economics and Business,* 38 (Aug. 1986), pp. 203–14. Bradley includes a brief summary of the results from 14 earlier studies of the link between deficits and interest rates.

[2] Jeffrey G. Williamson, "Why Was British Growth So Slow During the Industrial Revolution?" this JOURNAL, 44 (Sept. 1984), pp. 687–712, see especially p. 712. It is wartime borrowing that is at the heart of the argument. For a study of crowding out during the Civil War, World War I, and World War II in the United States, see Paul Evans, "Do Large Deficits Produce High Interest Rates?" *American Economic Review,* 75 (Mar. 1985), pp. 69–87. An interesting classical view on why the "want of parsimony" among sovereigns during peace gives rise to wartime borrowing in

Philip Mirowski (hereafter referred to as HM) found no evidence of crowding out in this period.[3] They broke the crowding-out argument into two parts: first, large government debts produce higher real interest rates; second, higher rates negatively influence investment decisions by the private sector. Based on data for the period 1782 to 1816, their empirical work focused on the first link, the effect of government borrowing on real interest rates.[4] HM's results showed no relation between real interest rates and real net receipts from borrowing but a strong relation between real interest rates and the change in real debt. They accepted the first result as evidence against crowding out and rejected the second as due to simultaneity bias.[5] In reviewing their evidence, however, Williamson noted the "need to do more work on just how price expectations are formed."[6]

Beyond the crowding-out question, another issue is at stake in the Williamson and HM exchanges: the appropriateness of the neoclassical model of saving and investment. In this model the principal source of investment funds is households, whose savings allocations are based on their intertemporal utility-maximizing decisions. Firms do not generate their own investment funds internally but must compete with government and others in capital markets. Distribution of scarce investment funds among competing borrowers is accomplished through the allocative mechanism of the price of funds, measured as the market rate of interest. But in the event that increased borrowing does not lead to rising interest rates or crowding out, is it necessary to assume, as HM apparently did, that the neoclassical model is inappropriate? Should it be replaced by a model in which investment funds come primarily from the firm's own accumulation of capital rather than from household savings?[7]

In this article we reexamine the empirical evidence regarding the effect of government borrowing on interest rates during the early British Industrial Revolution. We also address the issue of the connection between the empirical results and the viability of the neoclassical model

---

the first place is in Adam Smith, *The Wealth of Nations* (1776; New York, 1937), pp. 861–62. Smith also noted that "in the war which began in 1688 . . . the foundation of the . . . enormous debt of Great Britain was first laid" (see pp. 873–74).

[3] Carol E. Heim and Philip Mirowski, "Interest Rates and Crowding-Out During Britain's Industrial Revolution," this JOURNAL, 47 (Mar. 1987), pp. 117–39.

[4] Ibid., p. 118.

[5] Ibid., pp. 121–22.

[6] Jeffrey G. Williamson, "Debating the Industrial Revolution," *Explorations in Economic History*, 24 (July 1987), p. 288; see also Williamson's response to HM in "Has Crowding Out Really Been Given a Fair Test? A Comment," this JOURNAL, 47 (Mar. 1987), pp. 214–16. The same point regarding the inadequacy of the expectations variable was also made to the present authors by Thomas Chiang.

[7] HM hold to this concept of business investment. See "Interest Rates and Crowding Out," p. 137–38.

of saving and investment. Our estimates provide information about inflation expectations and lags in borrowing effects which are material to a correct understanding of the impact of wartime borrowing on interest rates. The estimates confirm that wartime borrowing in Britain did raise the nominal rate of interest, but with a lag. We then show that even the absence of interest-rate effects would not invalidate a crowding-out argument or the neoclassical model; a variety of intervening historical factors could have offset the effects of wartime borrowing. We conclude with anecdotal evidence that borrowing by Britain for the earlier Seven Years War had also raised interest rates and that this affected the availability of funds for private investment. In short, we find evidence of both crowding out and the applicability of the neoclassical model during wartime in the early stages of Britain's Industrial Revolution.

I. GOVERNMENT BORROWING, INTEREST RATES, AND INFLATION: SPECIFICATION OF AN APPROPRIATE MODEL

To test the first link in the crowding-out argument, HM estimated the following equation:

$$RY_t = a_0 + a_1 \cdot RGB_t \tag{1}$$

where RY_t equals real yield on debt and RGB_t equals real government borrowing. They used both a long-term and a short-term interest rate and three different price deflators.[8] Two real-borrowing variables were employed: real net receipts from borrowing and the change in real debt. The regression failed to support a crowding-out hypothesis when real net receipts from borrowing was the independent variable; these results were accepted. However, a regression using the change in real debt did support a crowding-out hypothesis; these results were dismissed due to possible simultaneity bias from the discounting of bonds and from the use of nominal rates to calculate the value of annuities.[9] The estimates

[8] Ibid., p. 121. HM chose the rate on the popular and liquid East India Company bonds to "reflect conditions in the short-term private bond market" (p. 121). They chose the real consol yield as a measure of conditions in the long-term debt market. On this issue, see Sidney Homer, *A History of Interest Rates* (2nd edn., New Brunswick, 1977), pp. 159–60. Because the choice of price index did not affect HM's results in any crucial way, we use only the Schumpeter-Gilboy consumer price index. The data are reported in "Interest Rates and Crowding Out," table 1 (p. 120) and table 3 (p. 124). To accommodate long lags in estimating inflation expectations, we took additional Schumpeter-Gilboy price data from B. R. Mitchell and P. Deane, *Abstract of British Historical Statistics* (Cambridge, 1962), p. 469.

[9] HM, "Interest Rates and Crowding Out," p. 126, 127, fn. 16. HM also cited a potential complication in the data on real government debt due to debt-conversion operations beginning in 1808 (p. 126). The real net receipts from borrowing series corrects for these defects, limiting results to the years 1782 to 1816 (see also p. 123). Since the interpretation of HM's empirical results depends on the assumption of simultaneity bias, we tested for its presence when change in real debt is the debt variable, using the procedure outlined in James B. Ramsey and Peter Schmidt, "Some Further Results on the Use of OLS and BLUS Residuals in Specification Error Tests," *Journal of*

themselves are based on two restrictive assumptions: real yields were calculated using a perfect-foresight model of inflation expectations, and government borrowing was assumed to affect interest rates without lag. Furthermore, no other explanatory variables were considered. These assumptions are not warranted and they distort the evidence regarding crowding out.

Testing for Perfect-Foresight Inflation Expectations

HM recognized the importance of selecting an appropriate model of inflation expectations, but in the absence of "a canonical neoclassical model which can claim widespread allegiance in this area, [they chose] to adopt a simple version [of expected inflation] widely employed in the economics literature . . . the actual ex post observed rate."[10] This perfect-foresight model assumes that expected inflation (the inflation premium included in nominal yields) can be approximated by actual inflation, in other words, that market forecasts of inflation in the period were quite accurate.

A test of the perfect-foresight inflation-expectations mechanism becomes possible by means of a simple transformation of equation 1. First, express real yields as follows:

$$RY_t = NY_t - PP_t^e - NY_t \cdot PP_t^e \tag{2}$$

where RY_t equals real yield on debt, PP_t^e equals expected percentage change in price, based on information available at time t minus 1, and NY_t equals nominal yield on debt. Average inflation for the period is quite low (as discussed below), so we can ignore the interaction term.[11] Assuming perfect foresight, the real yield can be written as the nominal yield less actual current inflation:

$$RY_t = NY_t - PP_t \tag{3}$$

where PP_t equals actual percentage change in price at time t. Since the real yield in equation 1 assumes perfect foresight, it can be expressed in nominal terms by adding current inflation (PP_t) to both sides:

$$NY_t = a_0 + a_1 \cdot RGB_t + a_2 \cdot PP_t. \tag{4}$$

Equation 4 allows for a direct test of the perfect-foresight model of real yields. Perfect foresight implies that the coefficient of adjustment,

---

the American Statistical Association, 71 (1976), pp. 389–90. The results supported the hypothesis of simultaneity bias for change in real debt but not for real net receipts from borrowing.

[10] "Interest Rates and Crowding Out," p. 121.

[11] An anonymous referee noted a difficulty in estimating equation 2 with the interaction term: the nominal yield appears on both sides of the equation. Ignoring the interaction term could bias estimates of the coefficients, particularly a_2 in equation 4. Accounting for the interaction, however, introduces its own substantial bias. Furthermore, low coefficients on inflation expectations in the nominal-rate equations reported below suggest that, if bias is present, it is not very substantial.

TABLE 1
ESTIMATES OF EQUATION 4: 1782 TO 1816

	Nominal India Bond Yield		Nominal Consol Yield	
Dependent Variable	Real Net Receipts from Borrowing	Change in Real Debt	Real Net Receipts from Borrowing	Change in Real Debt
Constant Term	4.42**	4.54**	4.29**	4.53**
	(30.55)	(43.40)	(29.12)	(42.50)
Real Government Borrowing	0.03	0.003	0.05**	0.01**
	(1.66)	(1.39)	(3.40)	(3.25)
Current Inflation	−0.007	0.006	0.003	0.034**
	(−0.70)	(0.49)	(0.33)	(2.63)
Adjusted R^2	0.028	0.004	0.23	0.213
Durbin-Watson	0.72	0.70	1.31	1.56
$F_{regression}$	1.49	1.07	6.12	5.61
	(2,32)	(2,32)	(2,32)	(2,32)

* Significant at the 5 percent level, one-tailed test.
** Significant at the 1 percent level, one-tailed test.
Notes: Figures in parentheses below coefficients are *t*-statistics; figures in parentheses below *F*-statistics are degrees of freedom.

a_2, is significant and equal to one. Table 1 presents estimates of equation 4 and offers evidence that actual inflation is not an adequate representation of expected inflation or the inflation premium. The coefficient is significantly different from zero only for the equation which uses change in real debt and nominal consol yield. Furthermore, it is much closer to zero than to one, no matter which nominal yield or which real-debt variable is used. A test for whether the coefficients are equal to one is rejected in all cases.

Another interesting feature of the results in Table 1 is that the equations for the two debt variables, change in real debt and real net receipts from borrowing, now look quite similar. In fact, the significance of the effect of government borrowing now depends not on the choice of a debt variable, but on the choice of a yield variable. As a result a crowding-out hypothesis is supported for the nominal consol yield, even when real net receipts from borrowing is the debt variable; furthermore, the hypothesis only narrowly fails for nominal India bond yields (at 5 percent significance for a one-tailed test), using both debt variables.

The estimates reported for nominal yields in Table 1 show the difficulty in estimating crowding-out effects using ex post real yields as in equation 1. But it is also inappropriate to accept these results for nominal yields without question. First, since estimates in Table 1 reject the perfect-foresight hypothesis regarding expected inflation, other expectations models need to be investigated. Second, the Durbin-Watson statistics indicate potentially serious trouble with first-order autocorrelation of the errors. An improved specification or an estimation approach which accounts for the serial correlation is needed.[12] We respecify the equation below by introducing a different model of inflation expectations and also by including lagged borrowing terms as well as lagged nominal yields and lagged money growth.

The Inflation Premium and Models of Inflation Expectations

Henry Thornton wrote in 1811 that the inflation during the Napoleonic wars had caused an inflation premium to be incorporated into British interest rates.[13] Can the inflation premium during the period be adequately represented by current inflation, a perfect-foresight approach? Hardly. To understand why not, consider the requirements of a perfect-foresight approach: most of the variation in inflation must be forecastable and markets must have used optimal—that is, nonbiased and efficient—forecasts of inflation. If unforecastable shocks dominate variations in measured inflation, then current inflation and forecast inflation will not be closely related and perfect foresight will not be appropriate.

A negative rate of inflation, or deflation, creates another technical difficulty with the perfect-foresight approach. Since no one will lend at negative interest rates, preferring to hold money instead, the nominal rate of interest will never be less than zero. By implication, a negative inflation premium or expected rate of deflation can never be greater in absolute value than the real rate of interest.[14] When prices fall more than the usual real rate, say 3 to 5 percent, perfect foresight is not a meaningful assumption.

Available evidence indicates that the general level of British prices during the late eighteenth and early nineteenth centuries was indeed quite volatile, with numerous instances of deflation.[15] This is illustrated by Figure 1, which also suggests that average inflation tended to be quite low over most of the period; average prices rose about 0.7 percent annually.[16] As a result of volatile prices, using actual inflation for expected inflation results in equally volatile and sometimes negative real interest rates.[17] The real consol rate, for example, changes

[12] While it is possible to correct for autocorrelation using one of several econometric procedures, the preferred approach to autocorrelated errors is first to review the theoretical specification. The reason is that serially correlated omitted variables can induce serial correlation in the error term, which captures the effects of omitted variables along with random shocks.

[13] Thomas M. Humphrey, "The Early History of the Real/Nominal Interest Rate Relationship," *Essays on Inflation* (5th edn., Richmond, 1986), p. 151.

[14] See the discussion of Irving Fisher's *Appreciation and Interest* (1896) in ibid., pp. 156–57.

[15] T. S. Ashton, in *An Economic History of England: The 18th Century* (1955; London, 1972), p. 199, notes that it was primarily agricultural prices which were volatile. Phyllis Deane and W. A. Cole show that the period of 1790 to 1825 exhibited especially severe short-run reversals in price movements; see *British Economic Growth, 1688–1959* (Cambridge, 1967), p. 351, fig. 7.

[16] The price trend was calculated using a five-year moving average, including the current rate of inflation and four lagged values.

[17] See HM, "Interest Rates and Crowding Out," p. 120, table 1.

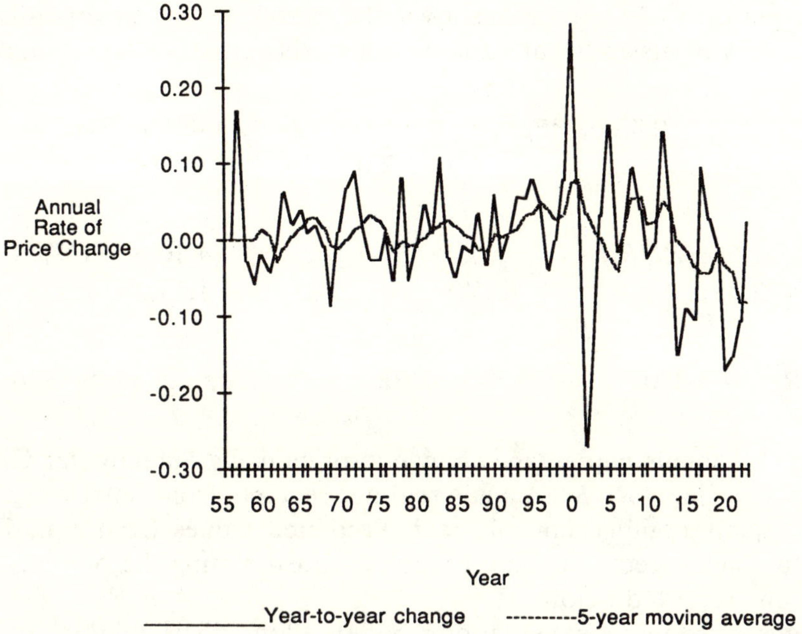

FIGURE 1

INFLATION AND ITS TREND IN BRITAIN, 1755 TO 1823: SCHUMPETER-GILBOY PRICE INDEX FOR CONSUMEER GOODS

Source: B. R. Mitchell and P. Deane, *Abstract of British Historical Statistics* (Cambridge, 1962), p. 469.

from about −28 percent to 27.5 percent between 1800 and 1802. The rate is back to −10 percent by 1805 and then up to 6.6 percent in the following year. When current inflation is so dominated by random shocks, an expectations mechanism based on perfect foresight is not adequate.

Two alternative approaches are used here. One is to duplicate the market's inflation forecasting model by estimating the best inflation equation given the available data and then incorporating the optimal forecasts as an explanatory variable in a nominal-yield equation. The second method is to assume that markets did not base risk premiums on the best forecast of inflation and that some other mechanism—such as adaptive expectations—served to calculate the premium.

We estimated an inflation equation which allowed for up to three lagged values of all the variables, including past inflation, past yields, and past government borrowing, to provide the best inflation equation possible. Separate equations were estimated for peacetime and wartime periods, but an F-test for the significance of a regime change showed that separate equations were not superior to a single equation for the entire period.[18] Equation 5 shows the result of fitting an inflation equation, with insignificant variables deleted (t-statistics less than one):

$$PP_t = \underset{(1.40)}{17.67} + \underset{(2.72)}{0.43} \cdot PP_{t-1} - \underset{(-3.23)^{**}}{0.50} \cdot PP_{t-2} + \underset{(1.30)}{0.56} \cdot RNRB_{t-1}$$

$$- \underset{(-2.53)}{1.58} \cdot RNRB_{t-2} + \underset{(2.59)}{1.45} \cdot RNRB_{t-3} - \underset{(-1.39)}{4.10} \cdot NCY_{t-3} \qquad (5)$$

$$R^2_{adj} = 0.370 \qquad DW = 2.38 \qquad \text{Sample: 1785–1816}$$

where PP_t equals percentage change in price using Schumpeter-Gilboy consumer prices, $RNRB_t$ equals real net receipts from borrowing, and NCY_t equals nominal consol yield. Predicted values from equation 5 serve as one expected-inflation variable in estimating the nominal-rate equations reported below.

Under an adaptive expectations model, a long distributed lag of past inflation values, rather than the best forecast of inflation, serves as the expectations variable. Such an approach to inflation expectations is by no means innovative, neither is the implied rejection of a perfect-foresight approach. In *The Theory of Interest,* Irving Fisher developed a model of real interest rates in which he tested and rejected the immediate adjustment of nominal interest rates to inflation.[19] He also found no statistical relation between nominal rates and *individual* values of lagged inflation; instead he found a strong relation between nominal rates and a distributed lag of inflation. Fisher concluded:

> By assuming a distribution of [the] effect of price changes over several years according to the form described above, the relationship between price changes and interest rates which was only faintly revealed by the first direct comparison is clearly revealed.[20]

[18] An anonymous referee suggested that inflation be explained using all the available information, including information on debt and nominal yields as well as information on past inflation. We also included the growth rate of money but this did not add to the significance of the regression, perhaps because debt and money are correlated. On the role of debt as money, see the discussion below in section 3. The same referee also suggested that the data on price included a possible regime change when the British economy went from peace to war in 1793. Estimating separate equations did show some changes in coefficients but an F-test for the significance of separate regressions showed that allowing for a regime change did not significantly increase the ability to explain inflation. In testing for crowding out, a peacetime/wartime inflation-expectations variable in unreported nominal-yield regressions did not change the results for the crucial borrowing variable.

[19] (New York, 1930), chap. 19. See especially pp. 416–25 for a study of the relation between inflation and nominal consol yields in Britain from 1820 to 1924. Fisher argued that realized, or ex post, real rates would be more volatile than nominal rates because "men are unable or unwilling to adjust at all accurately and promptly the money interest rates to changed price levels" (p. 415).

[20] Ibid., pp. 424–25.

Fisher's results imply that expectations about inflation adjust to actual inflation with a lag. If so, then some weighted average of past inflation rates may be appropriate for an expectations variable:

$$PP_t^e = \sum_{i=1}^{n} b_i \cdot PP_{t-i} \qquad (6)$$

Fisher's estimates suggested that the length of the lag ran as many as 20 or 30 years for Britain in the mid-nineteenth century; he used an arithmetic lag distribution for statistical simplicity. Another approach to estimating the long lag distribution in equation 6 is with polynomial smoothing constraints to conserve degrees of freedom. It is important to see that using a long polynomial lag will not necessarily give the best forecasting equation for inflation. It does not matter, however, if the distributed lag is not the best forecast of inflation as long as it captures the mechanism generating the inflation premium in nominal interest rates.

To understand this better, consider the following simple nominal-India-bond-yield equation without borrowing effects:

$$NIBY_t = n_0 + n_1 \cdot NIBY_{t-1} + n_2 \cdot PP_t^e \qquad (7)$$

In forecasting inflation, equation 5 outperforms a polynomial distributed lag.[21] But when one estimates equation 7 for the period from 1785 to 1816, first substituting the inflation forecast from equation 5 and then substituting a polynomial lag of inflation as alternative expected inflation variables, a reversal takes place. Now the lengthy distributed-lag variable gives more explanatory power and a higher adjusted R^2 than the optimal inflation forecast (0.587 compared with 0.514; equation 7 without *any* expectations variable has an adjusted R^2 of 0.529). In addition, the expectations coefficient for the distributed lag is larger and more significant than for the optimal forecast (n_2 equals 0.215 and t equals 2.02 compared with n_2 equals −0.003 and t equals −0.28). This result suggests quite clearly that the best inflation forecast may not be the best estimate of the inflation premium incorporated into nominal yields. Given the results, the nominal-rate equations were estimated using both the best forecast of inflation and a long distributed lag on inflation as the expectations variable. These estimates also accounted for the timing of borrowing effects on nominal yields.

[21] Estimating current inflation (PP_t rather than PP_t^e) as a 25-year distributed lag of past inflation for 1785 to 1816 will give an adjusted R^2 of only about 0.020. Comparing this result with equation 5 shows that the distributed lag approach is indeed inferior as an inflation forecasting equation. Even if information on government borrowing and nominal yields were not included in equation 5, its adjusted R^2 would only drop to 0.285, leaving it well above that for the distributed-lag equation.

TABLE 2
WARTIME REAL NET RECEIPTS FROM BORROWING AND NOMINAL CONSOL YIELDS: A SEARCH FOR LAGS

Year	Real Net Receipts from Borrowing (in £ millions)	Nominal Consol Yield (in percent)
1782 to 1792	£2.13[a]	4.29[b]%
1793	5.19	3.90
	(0.65)	(−0.61)
1794	9.12	4.44
	(1.49)	(1.49)
1795	15.51**	4.82
	(2.85)	(0.83)
1796	20.78**	4.34
	(3.97)	(0.08)
1797	19.12**	6.04*
	(3.62)	(2.73)
1798	10.34	6.09**
	(1.75)	(2.81)
1799	12.31*	5.55*
	(2.17)	(1.97)
1800	11.08*	4.72
	(1.91)	(0.67)

* Significant at the 5 percent level, one-tailed test.
** Significant at the 1 percent level, one-tailed test.
[a] Average borrowing for the period with n = 11. Standard deviation of real net receipts from borrowing is 4.69.
[b] Average yield for the period with n = 13. Standard deviation of the nominal consol yields is 0.64.

Lagged Borrowing and Nominal Yields

An important issue in any test for a "first link" between borrowing and interest rates is the potential for lagged effects of borrowing.[22] It is reasonable to assume that the full effects of borrowing on nominal interest rates may have developed over two or more years.[23]

A preliminary investigation of lagged borrowing effects supports, not a one-year lag, but a two-year lag between changes in government borrowing and changes in nominal yields. Wartime government borrowing and nominal interest rates were compared with their peacetime averages from before 1793. Table 2 provides evidence of a two-year lag in the statistical relation between real net receipts from borrowing and nominal consol yields. Obviously, this statistical relation does not prove

[22] HM's choice of the date on which to measure interest rates, the first Wednesday of April of each year, makes the issue of lags all the more important. Much of the government borrowing in 1782, for example, probably took place after the date in question, assuming a fairly even rate of borrowing. As a result one ought to allow not only for a contemporaneous effect but also for a one-year lagged effect of borrowing on interest rates. See HM, "Interest Rates and Crowding Out," p. 119.

[23] See, for example, the studies by Evans, "Do Large Deficits Produce High Interest Rates?" and "Do Deficits Raise Interest Rates?" which also assume lagged borrowing effects.

causality (nor for that matter does the regression analysis reported below), but it is consistent with a crowding-out theory.

The *t*-statistic for each observation in Table 2 tests the hypothesis that wartime values were drawn from the same distribution which generated the prewar averages. The *t*-statistics, therefore, show exactly when wartime borrowing and interest rates "broke out" of their prewar patterns. It appears that borrowing exceeded normal prewar limits two years before interest rates exceeded their prewar boundaries. This two-year lagged statistical relation seems to persist for all eight years considered in Table 2 (1793 to 1800).

The years covered in Table 2 contain one of the more notable highlights of British financial history, the suspension of specie payments in 1797. If the lagged effect of borrowing is ignored, it would seem that the suspension of specie payments early in that year might have had an immediate and clearly discernible impact on the nominal consol yield. If, however, one maintains a two-year lag in the effect of borrowing on nominal yields, then both the sharp increase in yields in 1797 and 1798 and the crisis which led to the suspension could possibly be attributed to the equally sharp rise in borrowing in 1795 and 1796.[24] Furthermore,

[24] An indication that borrowing could have a lagged effect on interest rates emerges from a report on the suspension of specie payment in 1797, an event that is closely related to the heavy wartime borrowing by the British government. In an anonymous tract, "Note on the Suspension of Cash Payments, at the Bank of England, in 1797," in John R. McCulloch, ed., *A Select Collection of Scarce and Valuable Tracts and Other Publications, on Paper Currency and Banking* (1857; New York, 1966), pp. 95–96, a contemporary writer highlighted the severity of the financial crisis leading to the suspension and outlined its probable causes, as well as the Bank of England's response:

By far the most important crisis in the history of the paper currency of Great Britain took place in 1797. Owing partly to events connected with the war in which we were then engaged, to loans to the Emperor of Germany, to bills drawn on the treasury by the British agents abroad, and partly and chiefly, perhaps, to the large advances made by the Bank of England to Government, the exchange became unfavorable in 1795, and in that and the following year large quantities of specie were demanded from the Bank. No doubt, however, the ultimate crisis was wholly owing to political causes. Alarms with respect to invasion, and reports of descents, said to have been made on the coast, became exceedingly prevalent in the latter part of 1796, and the beginning of 1797. This produced a strong desire among many individuals, but chiefly among the small farmers and retail dealers, to convert as much as possible of their property into cash. . . . Demands for supplies of cash poured in upon the Bank of England from all parts of the country; and the stock of coin and bullion in her coffers, which amounted to £7,940,000 in March, 1795, was reduced on Saturday, the 25th of February, 1797, to £1,272,000 with every prospect of a violent run taking place on the following Monday. In this emergency, a meeting of the Privy Council was held, when it was resolved to suspend payments in cash at the Bank until the sense of Parliament could be taken on the matter.

The important point to observe from this account is an implied lag in the effect of governmental borrowing. Borrowing for the war with France, which began in 1793 and became quite heavy by 1795, was one underlying cause of the financial crisis in late 1796 and the subsequent suspension of specie payment early in 1797. The clear suggestion here is that the effect of wartime borrowing may have operated on the financial community, in particular on the nominal rate of interest, with a lag.

the subsequent fall in the yield in 1800 could be attributed to substantially lower borrowing two years earlier.

The implication is that the nominal rate may have generally responded to borrowing with a lag. This evidence, though, requires further support from a multiple regression test of the lagged effect. Moreover, since a two-year lag in estimating a nominal-yield equation presents some theoretical difficulties, a distributed lag of zero to two or more years should be estimated instead.[25] In addition, several other factors should be included in a nominal-yield equation. First, changes in the money supply could lead to changes in the yield. An increase in the money supply, for example, could work through its direct effect on liquidity, leading to lower yields, or through its effects on prices, leading to higher inflation premiums. Second, yields may have adjusted slowly to these factors, meaning that lagged yields may be important in explaining current yields.

Equation 8 takes account of the hypothesized lagged effect of government borrowing on nominal yields; it also allows for an inflation-expectations variable and lagged effects of changes in the money supply and nominal yields themselves.

$$NY_t = a_0 + \sum_{i=1}^{m} b_j \cdot NY_{t-j} + \sum_{j=0}^{n} c_j \cdot RGB_{t-j} + \sum_{k=1}^{q} d_j \cdot PM_{t-j} + e \cdot PP^e_{t-i} \quad (8)$$

where NY_t equals nominal yield on debt, RGB_t equals real government borrowing, PM_t equals percentage change in stock of Bank of England notes, and PP^e_t equals expected percentage change in price based on equation 5 or on a 25-year polynominal distributed lag on inflation.

Equation 8 was estimated with all lags except the one for real government borrowing (and for the inflation-distributed lag) set to a maximum of two years; pretesting showed that a lag of three years was

[25] An anonymous referee suggested that a long delay of two years in the effect of borrowing on rates "is inconsistent with the simplest principles of asset pricing [which] require that predictable changes in asset prices be smooth. Large predictable changes in interest rates due to information about government activity last year would imply forecastable profits." To avoid this difficulty, estimates of the yield equation reported below were first run with a smooth lag distribution running from zero to three years. Nevertheless, the coefficient on borrowing at a two-year lag was, for the nominal India bond yields, the first consistently significant one. In estimates for nominal consol yields, however, the one- and two-year lags were both significant; this finding *would* be consistent with asset pricing theory, given the choice of date for measuring the interest rate (see the discussion of this point earlier in this section). More evidence on the institutional aspects of financial markets is needed to reconcile the empirical data with a reasonable theoretical proposition.

TABLE 3
ESTIMATES OF EQUATION 8 USING INFLATION FORECASTS FROM EQUATION 5 AS EXPECTED INFLATION: 1785 TO 1816

Dependent Variable	Nominal India Bond Yield	Nominal Consol Yield
Constant Term	1.53**	4.56**
	(2.70)	(34.68)
Nominal Yield$_{-1}$[a]	0.64**	
	(4.67)	
Real Net Receipts$_{-1}$[a]		0.03
		(1.44)
Real Net Receipts$_{-2}$[a]	0.08**	0.07**
	(2.88)	(3.42)
Real Net Receipts$_{-3}$[a]	−0.04**	
	(−2.51)	
Money Growth$_{-1}$[a]	−0.01**	−0.01
	(−2.77)	(−1.62)
Expected Inflation (from equation 5)	0.01	0.02**
	(1.30)	(2.33)
Adjusted R^2	0.726	0.683
Durbin-Watson	2.04	2.13
$F_{\text{regression}}$	17.40**	17.71**
	(5,26)	(4,27)

* Significant at the 5 percent level, one-tailed test.
** Significant at the 1 percent level, one-tailed test.
[a] Negative subscripts indicate lag length.
Notes: Figures in parentheses below coefficients are *t*-statistics; figures in parentheses below *F*-statistic are degrees of freedom.

needed for borrowing (only with nominal India bond yields) but not for any of the other variables.

Table 3 shows a final estimate of equation 8, where the expectations variable was formed using the earlier forecasts of inflation from equation 5; insignificant lags on variables were deleted and the regressions recalculated each time to arrive at the final equation reported in the table.[26] Table 4 shows estimates of equation 8 where the expectations variable was formed using a 25-year polynomial-distributed lag on inflation; insignificant lags on variables were again deleted and the regressions recalculated each time. These equations confirm a lagged relation between borrowing and nominal yields, no matter which expectations variable is used.[27] The results hold whether consol yields or nominal India bond yields are used as the dependent variable. The coefficients for borrowing lagged two years are significant in all equa-

[26] The rule for respecification was to keep a variable if its coefficient had a *t*-statistic greater than one. This is approximately the rule used in several recently developed statistical criteria for model selection. See George G. Judge, et al., *The Theory and Practice of Econometrics* (New York, 1980), pp. 420–22. Given the available data on real net receipts from borrowing (1782 to 1816), a lag of three years on government borrowing left 1785 as the starting year for the sample.

[27] The results do not differ when change in real debt is substituted for real net receipts, the variable preferred by HM.

TABLE 4
ESTIMATES OF EQUATION 8 USING ADAPTIVE INFLATION EXPECTATIONS: 1785 TO 1816

Dependent Variable	Nominal India Bond Yield	Nominal Consol Yield
Constant Term	1.93**	4.03**
	(3.14)	(34.68)
Nominal $Yield_{-1}$[a]	0.49**	
	(3.08)	
Real Net $Receipts_{-1}$[a]		0.03
		(1.44)
Real Net $Receipts_{-2}$[a]	0.05**	0.05**
	(3.06)	(3.42)
Real Net $Receipts_{-3}$[a]	−0.02	
	(−1.11)	
Money $Growth_{-1}$[a]	−0.02**	−0.01
	(−3.05)	(−1.62)
Money $Growth_{-2}$[a]		−0.01
		(−1.05)
Expected Inflation (sum of distributed lag effects)[b]	0.19*	0.08
	(2.35)	(0.71)
Adjusted R^2	0.756	0.616
Durbin-Watson	1.90	1.91
$F_{regression}$	17.00**	8.12**
	(6,25)	(7,24)

* Significant at the 5-percent level, one-tailed test.
** Significant at the 1-percent level, one-tailed test.
[a] Negative subscripts indicate lag length.
[b] Sum of distributed lag coefficients and its *t*-statistic are reported. Estimation used a second-degree polynomial for India bond yields and a third-degree polynomial for consol yields, both with lag lengths of 25 years.
Notes: Figures in parentheses below coefficients are *t*-statistics; figures in parentheses below *F*-statistic are degrees of freedom.

tions. Thus the assumption of a lag in the effect of government borrowing is supported by the data although a contemporaneous relation is not.

The low coefficients on inflation expectations in Table 3 are not at all surprising. The market would not necessarily have adjusted long-term nominal rates to estimates of current inflation because current inflation was volatile and perhaps quite impossible to predict. Since the average yearly rate of inflation between 1760 and 1790 was only about 0.7 percent, people may reasonably have ignored the wild swings in current inflation. As a result the very low coefficients of adjustment in Table 3 along with the poor performance of the perfect-foresight, real-yield equations in Table 1 are quite understandable. In Table 4 the India-bond-yield equation showed the highest coefficient of adjustment, using the adaptive-expectations mechanism; nonetheless its value was only about 0.2, showing much less than complete adjustment of nominal yields even to this expectations variable.

The relation between government borrowing and interest rates which has been established in Table 3 does not seem to depend on any particular assumption about inflation expectations.[28] Instead, the results depend on relaxing the assumption that the nominal rate adjusts fully to the current rate of inflation (or even to its forecasts) and on relaxing the assumption that the relation between borrowing and interest rates is purely contemporaneous.

Summary of Estimation Results

The empirical evidence confirms a lagged relation between British interest rates and government borrowing during the early Industrial Revolution. Taking an average of the estimates in Tables 3 and 4, with other things constant, a sustained increase in the net receipts from borrowing of £12 million would have increased the nominal consol yield by about 1 percent after two years. This is approximately what is implied by the data in Table 2; in the first five years of the French war, average borrowing increased £11.8 million over prewar levels while, allowing for a two-year lag, average nominal consol yields increased 1.1 percent.

To what extent is the evidence on nominal consol yields and nominal India bond yields representative of the general effects of wartime borrowing on interest rates and private borrowing? According to Ricardo, the effects were indeed widespread and substantial:

> During the present war, Exchequer and Navy Bills have been frequently at so high a discount, as to afford the purchasers of them 7, 8 per cent., or a greater rate of interest for their money. Loans have been raised by Government at an interest exceeding 6 per cent., and individuals have been frequently obliged, by indirect means, to pay more than 10 per cent. for the interest of money.[29]

Our empirical estimates explain why Ricardo found that interest on government loans was in excess of 6 percent. Net receipts from borrowing exceeded the prewar average by £13.4 million in 1795 and £18.6 million in 1796; according to estimates in Tables 3 and 4, this rise in borrowing largely explains why consol yields rose above 6 percent—almost 2 percent higher than their prewar average—in 1797 and 1798.

Our estimates also confirm Williamson's suggestion that the formation of price expectations is central to understanding the impact of government borrowing on interest rates.[30] The estimates reject a perfect-foresight assumption about inflation expectations and suggest

[28] The results for lagged borrowing held up in tests with alternative expectations assumptions: an autoregressive expectations variable which only considered two lagged values of inflation; a perfect-foresight approach; and Fisher's distributed-lag approach, using polynomial lags of 5, 10, 15, 20, and 30 years.

[29] David Ricardo, *Principles of Political Economy and Taxation* (3rd edn., 1821; reprinted London, 1908), p. 281.

[30] "Debating the Industrial Revolution," p. 288, and "Has Crowding Out," pp. 214–16.

that nominal rates did not include much information about current inflation; therefore, accurate forecasts of current inflation were not crucial in modeling expected inflation. Markets apparently used information on long-term averages of inflation, gearing the inflation premium to that longer view and ignoring the volatile short-run information about current inflation. As a result our test of a crowding-out hypothesis focused on estimating nominal-rate equations rather than using an inflation-expectations variable to first calculate a real rate and then estimate a real-rate equation. The choice of an expectations model was not as critical in establishing a crowding-out hypothesis as the refusal to impose a model on the estimation procedure by calculating real rates of interest.

The estimates help resolve an apparent contradiction between those who have concluded that heavy wartime borrowing by the British government between 1793 and 1815 did not cause increases in interest rates and those who have concluded that it did. While the *realized* real rate of interest during the period may not be "a scarcity index for capital conceived as a factor of production," the nominal rate would appear to be such an index.[31]

II. INTEREST RATES, CROWDING OUT, AND THE NEOCLASSICAL MODEL: SOME HISTORICAL CONSIDERATIONS

The results above show that British data from the early Industrial Revolution support a "first link" in the crowding-out argument: wartime government borrowing raised nominal interest rates. What remains is to clarify the connection between crowding out and the neoclassical model. The model is compatible with the existence of alternative sources of additional investment funds. Consequently, the absence of evidence establishing an interest-rate effect of government borrowing would not justify the conclusion that the neoclassical factor-allocation model should be replaced by one in which firms generate their own investment funds. A number of factors were present in Britain after 1792 which could have ameliorated the effects of borrowing on interest rates.[32] First, a changing money supply could have offset the effects of changing government borrowing. Next, increased borrowing could have affected private saving behavior. Third, the availability of foreign capital might have increased in response to the heavy borrowing. Finally, the usury ceiling in force at the time could have distorted the

[31] HM, "Interest Rates and Crowding Out," p. 127.

[32] Evans, "Do Large Deficits Produce High Interest Rates?" pp. 72–73, for example, found no empirical connection between government deficits and interest rates for the United States during the Civil War period. His explanation of this result lists arguments which are similar to some of those to be discussed below.

TABLE 5
BANK OF ENGLAND NOTES IN CIRCULATION: 1780 TO 1825
(£ millions)

Year	Bank Notes in Circulation	Percentage Change from Five Years Earlier
1780	£7.4	
1785	6.2	−17.6%
1790	10.7	53.3
1795	12.4	14.7
1800	15.9	24.7
1805	17.1	7.3
1810	22.9	29.0
1815	27.3	17.5
1820	23.9	−13.3
1825	20.1	−17.3

Source: B. R. Mitchell and Phyllis Deane, *Abstract of British Historical Statistics* (Cambridge, 1962), pp. 442–43.

link between borrowing and interest rates when market rates were above the ceiling.

Variations in the Supply of Money

Textbook models of crowding out normally assume a fixed money supply. This is an implausible assumption for the period under study, however, for several reasons. First, the suspension of specie payment was followed by an excessive issue of notes by the Bank of England, at least according to Ricardo and other bullionists of the day.[33] The quantity of Bank of England notes in circulation for the years 1780 to 1825 and the percentage change from five years earlier are presented in Table 5. It can be seen that the five-year rate of change is quite variable. In addition, the estimates of equation 8 in Tables 3 and 4 give evidence that changes in money growth did have a negative, lagged impact on nominal yields; increased money growth and the accompanying increase in liquidity drove nominal interest rates down, at least in the short run.

Second, bonds themselves may have circulated as currency of a sort. T. S. Ashton noted that a number of short-term, and to some extent long-term, instruments served as media of exchange during the eighteenth century:

> Shortly before the eighteenth century opened the creation of the national debt had brought into being a mass of securities bearing more or less fixed interest rates. Some

[33] See David Ricardo, "The High Price of Bullion a Proof of the Depreciation of Bank Notes," *The Works and Correspondence of David Ricardo,* Piero Sraffa and M. H. Dobb, eds. (Cambridge, 1962), vol. 3, pp. 47–98; see also William Blake, "Observations on the Principles which Regulate the Course of Exchange: and on the Present Depreciated State of the Currency" (1810), in McCulloch, ed., *A Select Collection of Scarce and Valuable Tracts and Other Publications, on Paper Currency and Banking*, pp. 523–24.

of these, including exchequer bills, navy bills, and lottery tickets (as also the short-term obligations of the East India Company, the Bank of England, and the South Sea Company) could be used to settle accounts between individuals, and may perhaps, therefore, be thought of as falling within the somewhat shadowy boundaries of "money." Even the long-dated securities had some effect on purchasing power.[34]

Significant liquidity of government securities would tend to alter the interpretation of a test of the first link in the crowding-out hypothesis. If the debt instruments served as money, any increase in government debt during the period would not necessarily have caused a one-for-one reduction in the purchasing power of the public and investment might not have been impeded.

Taken together, the liquidity of government securities and the over-issue of Bank of England notes make it unreasonable to assume that the money supply was held constant while new war debt was accumulating. This means that the increased wartime government expenditure and borrowing, when accompanied by an increase in the issue of bank notes, could have left interest rates unchanged. New money, rather than diverted saving, would have financed the new debt until prices and expectations adjusted fully.[35]

Changes in the Rate of Saving

The impact of government borrowing on interest rates depends partly on the effect of that borrowing on private saving. Ricardo suggested that increased government borrowing could stimulate additional private saving to pay for the anticipated future tax liabilities resulting from that borrowing.[36] If households responded to increased government borrowing by supplying extra funds in the capital markets, the increased saving could accommodate the borrowing without a rise in interest rates and without a drop in private borrowing. The effect of borrowing would then be to crowd out consumption rather than investment. It is not necessary that consumption be completely crowded out by this equivalence effect. In fact, Williamson pointed out that Ricardo believed that in practice taxes and borrowing would not be treated equivalently.[37] But even an

[34] *An Economic History of England*, pp. 177–78.

[35] This could be illustrated by a rightward shift of both the IS and the LM curves so as to leave the nominal interest rate unchanged. Until inflation expectations began to catch up, the nominal rate would not adjust.

[36] See Ricardo, "Funding System," in *Works and Correspondence*, vol. 4, pp. 185–88. Robert J. Barro, in "Are Government Bonds Net Wealth?" *Journal of Political Economy*, 82 (Nov./Dec. 1974), pp. 1095–117, labeled this the Ricardian equivalence principle, whereby increased taxes or debt to finance increased government expenditure would have the same effects on the economy. For a helpful account of this and other issues regarding classical thought on government debt, see C. K. Rowley, "Classical Political Economy and the Debt Issue," in J. M. Buchanan, C. K. Rowley, and R. D. Tollison, eds., *Deficits* (Oxford, 1986), pp. 49–74, esp. 65–69. For a critical discussion of Ricardian equivalence, see James Tobin, *Asset Accumulation and Economic Activity: Reflections on Contemporary Macroeconomic Theory* (Chicago, 1980), chap. 3.

[37] Williamson, "Why Was British Growth So Slow," pp. 100–1.

incomplete adjustment of saving to government borrowing could reduce the response of interest rates to government borrowing.

All this would be irrelevant, though, if households had been generally unable or unwilling to save before and during the French war. But the evidence is that even poor laborers had occasion to save by joining "friendly societies," which, among other things, promoted thrift among their members. The number and influence of these societies was substantial even in the eighteenth century: over a thousand societies served several million members.[38] An Act of 1793 further "encouraged . . . the already numerous" societies.[39] Thus, thrift was becoming a habit even in the laboring classes by the end of the eighteenth century, leaving at least the potential for increased saving and crowding out of consumption during the French war.

Evidence that consumption was reduced during the war has been found by Brian Murphy, who cited lower industrial rates of growth for consumer-oriented leather and beer production for the period from 1795 to 1805 as compared with the previous ten years: for leather the decline was from 1.5 to 0.25 percent growth per year while for beer the decline was from 1.75 to 0 percent growth per year; soap and glass production growth rates also declined.[40] Further evidence suggests that the wartime borrowing may also have changed the mix of production, since pig-iron production growth rates remained high due to wartime demand for arms.[41]

Neither evidence about crowding out of consumption rather than investment nor evidence of a shift in the mix of production invalidate the neoclassical model in any way. The model can incorporate crowding out of investment *or* consumption and was formulated specifically for analyzing problems of allocation of means among competing ends. In fact, crowding out of consumption and the Ricardian-equivalence effect can be derived in the context of the saving and consumption decisions of utility-maximizing households.[42]

[38] E. Lipson, *The Growth of English Society* (New York, 1950), p. 357. Clapham is more conservative; he puts the "recognized membership" in the "year of Waterloo" at nearly a million but notes that this did not include members of informal secret orders. See J. H. Clapham, *An Economic History of Modern Britain* (Cambridge, 1930), p. 211.

[39] Paul Mantoux, *The Industrial Revolution of the Eighteenth Century* (revised edn., New York, 1961), p. 450.

[40] Cotton production, however, was in the midst of a period of great innovation, and the rate of growth of output increased. See Brian Murphy, *A History of the British Economy: 1088–1970* (London, 1973), p. 416, table II.5.

[41] Ibid. Murphy's evidence on pig-iron production supports HM's ("Interest Rates and Crowding Out," pp. 136–37) contention that the mix of output may have been changed by wartime expenditures. For a contrary view, see Williamson, "Why Was British Growth So Slow," p. 188.

[42] Paul Evans, "Are Consumers Ricardian? Evidence for the United States," *Journal of Political Economy,* 96 (Oct. 1988), pp. 983–1004.

Increased Foreign Lending

Crafts has suggested that the supply of investment funds may have been quite elastic during Britain's early Industrial Revolution due to the availability of foreign capital.[43] The effect would have been to reduce the response of interest rates to increased wartime government borrowing. As soon as British rates rose above rates in other financial markets, funds would have moved to Britain, especially with the turmoil on the Continent. The importance of foreign lending to the British government during this period, especially by the Dutch, was recognized by Ashton.[44] As Williamson observes, "while domestic savings may have been unresponsive to British rates of return, total savings could have been responsive to the extent that foreign capital markets were fairly well integrated."[45]

While the availability of foreign lending is evidence against a closed-economy model of crowding out, it should not be taken as evidence against the neoclassical model in general. The main reason is that there were presumably some limits even to the availability of foreign lending. The fact that the supply of capital was not perfectly elastic during the period is illustrated by the evidence presented above showing that wartime borrowing did indeed raise rates.

The Usury Ceiling

An additional factor that had at least the potential to affect the response of interest rates to wartime borrowing was the law against usury. Ashton noted that a usury ceiling of 5 percent was in effect on all private debt after 1714 in Britain.[46] Such a ceiling would have enhanced the ability of the government to sell bonds whenever the market rate, represented by the yield on consols, was pushed above the ceiling of 5 percent. This could reduce the effect of government borrowing on interest rates; it could also increase the wartime crowding out of private investment by diverting even more funds to the government when private borrowers could not pay the higher rates even if they wanted to.

The evidence on the actual effect of the ceiling is mixed and needs to be considered carefully. Interpretation hinges on whether market rates rose above the legal limit due to a totally ineffective ceiling or to a partially effective ceiling which caused rationing among private borrow-

[43] N. F. R. Crafts, "British Economic Growth, 1700–1850: Some Difficulties of Interpretation," *Explorations in Economic History*, 24 (July 1987), p. 247.

[44] *An Economic History of England*, p. 193.

[45] "Why Was British Growth So Slow," p. 290. HM, "Interest Rates and Crowding Out," pp. 133–34, also noted the role of the Dutch and other Europeans in lending to Great Britain, but they cited this as evidence against the neoclassical model rather than consistent with it. For a further discussion of financial integration, see Larry Neal, "Integration of International Capital Markets: Quantitative Evidence from the Eighteenth to Twentieth Centuries," this JOURNAL, 45 (June 1985), pp. 219–26.

[46] *An Economic History of England*, p. 27.

ers due to higher lending costs. On the one hand, the ceiling was not totally effective and rates did rise above legal rates as markets found ways to circumvent its restrictions. Ricardo, for example, noted the ineffectiveness of the ceiling by remarking that, while wartime interest rates were high, "during this same period the legal rate of interest has been uniformly [less than the market rate] at 5 per cent."[47] On the other hand, circumventing the ceiling was costly. As a result, J. R. McCulloch contended, the usury ceiling was itself responsible for high interest rates on private debt:

> When the rate fixed by law is less than the market or customary rate, lenders and borrowers are obliged to resort to circuitous devices to evade the law; and as these devices are always attended with more or less trouble and risk, the rate of interest is proportionately enhanced. During the late war it was not uncommon for persons to pay ten or twelve per cent for loans, which, had there been no usury laws, they might have got for six or seven per cent.[48]

McCulloch's assertion suggests that the usury ceiling may have indirectly increased funds available to the government during the war; while driving private rates up and quantity demanded down, the ceiling would have diverted funds to the government and moderated the rate the government paid.

One point is clear from reviewing all these factors which could have affected interest rates: it is possible to find no strong link between government borrowing and interest rates while still maintaining the stylized truth of the neoclassical model. In sum, the neoclassical model is able to incorporate or explain circumstances under which one-for-one or partial crowding out do not occur. Thus, finding no relation between interest rates and government borrowing would not by itself invalidate the factor-allocation view embodied in the model. Given the number of potentially strong intervening factors, it is all the more remarkable that government borrowing did apparently lead to increases in the interest rate on government debt, as our empirical findings have suggested.

III. CONCLUSIONS

This article has presented new econometric evidence regarding crowding out during the Industrial Revolution in Britain. Using different

[47] Ricardo, *Principles of Political Economy*, p. 281. See the quote in the conclusions to section I.

[48] J. R. McCulloch, *Principles of Political Economy* (2nd edn., Edinburgh, 1843), p. 520. Henry Dunning Macleod, *History of Economics* (London, 1896), p. 470, gives further evidence of the ceiling leading to high rates on various occasions: "The experience of several commercial crises had demonstrated that in consequence of the law attempting to prevent persons paying more than 5 per cent. for a loan of money, they often had to pay 50, 60, and 70 percent by the methods they were forced to adopt." No doubt such high rates had a chilling effect on private borrowing.

assumptions about inflation expectations and the timing of the crowding-out effect, we have found evidence of a strong effect of government borrowing on nominal interest rates. We have also argued that failure to find such an effect would not necessarily constitute evidence against crowding out, nor would it be sufficient to invalidate the neoclassical model of the economy.

The finding of a link between British wartime borrowing and interest rates is not new; the same conclusion was announced by Mill as part of his discussion of conditions under which government borrowing encroaches on private employment:

> When they do raise the rate of interest, as they did in a most extraordinary degree during the French war, this is positive proof that the government is a competitor for capital with the ordinary channels of productive investment, and is carrying off, not merely funds which would not, but funds which would, have found productive employment within the country. To the full extent, therefore, to which the loans of government, during the war, caused the rate of interest to exceed what it was before, and what it has been since, those loans are chargeable with all the evils which have been described.[49]

HM have suggested that more remains to be done in the area of a detailed study of the records of individual firms operating during the Industrial Revolution.[50] Our results simply suggest that more information is also available from the aggregate data itself, through an investigation of the timing of government-borrowing effects and the assumptions about real interest rates and expected inflation. But if one chooses to study effects of wartime government borrowing on individual firms, then perhaps the anecdotal evidence cited by Ashton is also appropriate. He tells of Jedediah Strutt and his brother-in-law, William Woollatt, who in 1757 were hoping to patent their Derby-rib stocking frame and to borrow money to promote the invention.

> Strutt's wife, Elizabeth, had previously been in service with the Rev. Dr. Benson who was, at this time, living in London. In the hope of inducing him to finance the new enterprise, she travelled from Derby to his home in Goodman's Fields; but in a letter dated "3 May 1757 6 o'clock in the morning" she had to inform her husband that her mission had failed:
>
> > Ye Dr. is pritty well again and I have acquainted him with our scheme which, so far as he understands it may do very well and he will do all he can for us, and wou^{d} willingly supply us with ye money. Mr. William Cook at ye same time wanted to Borrow of him one thousand pound (and) in order to furnish boath of us he went to ye Bank to sell out but ye War makes ye Stocks run so very low y^{t} he will loose a Hundred pound if he sells out now, and they will rise as much in proportion if there comes a peace.

[49] Mill, *Principles*, p. 874.

[50] "Interest Rates and Crowding Out," pp. 138–39.

In May 1757 the 3 per cent. annuities stood at 90. Dr. Benson was unwilling to forgo the chance of a recovery in the capital value of his holding. But he may also have reflected that the yield on investment in the annuities was now 3.3 per cent. and that the difference between this and the 4 per cent. offered by Strutt was small compensation for the additional risk.[51]

This information supports the notion of government crowding out of private investment, particularly during heavy wartime borrowing. It also supports the neoclassical view of the economy as "primarily a mechanism for allocating scarce factors . . . in which utility-maximizing household decisions figure prominently in the supply of saving to the rest of the economy."[52] The case of the Strutts and Woollatt would also seem to suggest that capital markets were becoming "somewhat integrated" during the period and that funds were at least potentially mobile between uses.[53]

[51] *An Economic History of England,* pp. 28–29. Ashton cites this story from R. S. Fitton and A. P. Wadsworth, *The Strutts and the Arkwrights, 1758–1830* (New York, 1958), p. 30.

[52] HM, "Interest Rates and Crowding Out," p. 117. Their point, though, was that the evidence did *not* support this view.

[53] For the contrary view, see ibid., p. 129.

Interest Rates in the Civil War South

George K. Davis and Gary M. Pecquet

Interest rates in the Civil War South were quite stable and even declined a bit during the war. In this article we explain the mechanism that produced this puzzling result. The existence of a fixed-rate call certificate redeemable at par anchored interest rates expressed in terms of Confederate dollars. When expressed in terms of gold, they were volatile, high, and reflected war events.

The Confederate dollar price of southern bonds exhibited great stability throughout the Civil War. This is remarkable because standard economic theory predicts that in light of military defeats and rampant inflation the Confederate dollar value of long-term government securities should have fallen and nominal interest rates should have risen. In fact, interest rates had a modest downward trend. Eugene Lerner attributed the aberrant interest-rate behavior to nonmarket forces and suggested political or patriotic motives as possible explanations.[1]

The desire to control interest rates was not unique to the Confederacy. In effect the North issued greenbacks to peg the nominal interest rate to expected inflation.[2] Here we argue that the Confederate treasury authorities obtained the same result by providing a liquid, interest-bearing asset convertible into cash at par at the pleasure of the holder. The existence of such call certificates effectively fixed the nominal yields on Confederate securities by placing a floor on the dollar price of bonds. The method used to fix nominal rates made the money supply endogenous, with important implications for the behavior of prices in the South.

When the market yields of Confederate securities and the value of paper money are calculated on a gold basis, the impact of military events becomes apparent, resolving the paradox posed by Lerner. Our findings again are similar to those for the North. Interest rates on northern securities indicate little connection between military

The Journal of Economic History, Vol. L, No. 1 (Mar. 1990). ISSN 0022-0507.

George K. Davis is Assistant Professor of Economics, Miami University, Oxford, OH 45056. Gary M. Pecquet is Assistant Professor of Economics, Southwest Texas State University, San Marcos, TX 78666.

We would like to thank William Hutchinson, T. Windsor Fields, Loren Langan, Bob Holland, Dave MacPherson, Mark Toma, Dan Seiver, Claudia Goldin, Thomas Weiss, and four anonymous referees for their very helpful comments.

[1] Eugene Lerner, "The Monetary and Fiscal Programs of the Confederate Government, 1861–1865," *Journal of Political Economy*, 62 (Dec. 1954), pp. 506–22.

[2] Charles Calomiris, "Price and Exchange Rate Determination during the Greenback Suspension," *Oxford Economic Papers*, 40 (Dec. 1988), pp. 719–50.

events and the greenback prices of U.S. securities, but a very close relationship between military events and the gold prices of the same bonds.[3]

I. THE CONFEDERATE DEBT

Recent contributions by Charles Calomiris, Bruce Smith, and Elmus Wicker have emphasized the importance of tax backing in the determination of currency values.[4] The value of money depends upon the expectations about future fiscal policy in addition to the quantity of money and debt that is outstanding.[5] In particular, it depends on the government's willingness and ability to resume specie parity in the future. The Confederate government lost most of its revenues due to the Union naval blockade, which restricted foreign trade and tariff collections. The South also had trouble establishing direct taxing mechanisms, obtaining only 10.5 percent of its total funds from taxation.[6] A Confederate victory, however, would have reopened the southern ports and customs collections. The expectation of that victory "backed" the Confederate debt.[7]

The Confederate debt included a variety of notes, call certificates, and bonds. Non-interest-bearing treasury notes became the primary exchange medium.[8] Interest-bearing treasury notes issued in denomina-

[3] Richard Roll, "Interest Rates and Price Expectations During the Civil War," this JOURNAL, 32 (June 1972), pp. 476–98.

[4] See Charles W. Calomiris, "Institutional Failure, Monetary Scarcity, and the Depreciation of the Continental," this JOURNAL, 48 (Mar. 1988), pp. 47–68; Calomiris, "Price and Exchange Rate Determination"; Bruce Smith, "Some Colonial Evidence on Two Theories of Money: Maryland and the Carolinas," *Journal of Political Economy*, 93 (Dec. 1985), pp. 1178–1211; Bruce Smith, "American Colonial Monetary Regimes: The Failure of the Quantity Theory of Money and Some Evidence in Favor of an Alternative View," *Canadian Journal of Economics*, 18 (Aug. 1985), pp. 531–65; and Elmus Wicker, "Colonial Monetary Standards Contrasted: Evidence from the Seven Years' War," this JOURNAL, 45 (Dec. 1985), pp. 869–84.

[5] See the rational expectations literature for the theoretical underpinnings including Neil Wallace, "A Miller-Modigliani Theorem for Open Market Operations," *American Economic Review*, 71 (June 1981), pp. 267–74; and Robert J. Barro, "Are Government Bonds Net Wealth?" *Journal of Political Economy*, 82 (Nov. 1974), pp. 1095–1117.

[6] John Munro Godfrey, *Monetary Expansion in the Confederacy* (New York, 1978), p. 14. The absence of efficient tax collections also explains the South's reliance on the inflation tax to finance their war effort.

[7] Late in the war, when military defeat became almost certain, the currency could only be supported by the prospect of near-term tax payments. For an analysis of the use of taxes to support Confederate money late in the war, see Gary M. Pecquet, "Money in the Trans-Mississippi and the Confederate Currency Reform Act of 1864," *Explorations in Economic History*, 24 (Apr. 1987), pp. 218–43.

[8] The demand for Confederate treasury notes initially depended upon making them receivable for state dues and taxes and forcing banks to suspend specie payments and accept the new currency. In this way the treasury notes were placed into circulation. See Jefferson Davis Bragg, *Louisiana in the Confederacy* (Baton Rouge, 1941), pp. 67–72; James F. Morgan, *Graybacks and Gold: Confederate Monetary Policy* (Pensacola, 1985), pp. 23–25, Larry Schweikart, "Secession and Southern Banks," *Civil War History*, 31 (June 1985), pp. 111–25; and Larry L. Schweikart,

tions of $100 bore 3.65 and 7.3 percent interest annually.[9] Both types of notes were acceptable at par for most tax obligations of the central government except export duties.

Call certificates initially earned 6 percent interest, but the rate was lowered gradually and by the end of the war calls earned 4 percent. The 6 percent call certificates could be purchased in $500 denominations and "called" or reconverted into cash on demand at par.[10] This asset was provided in perfectly elastic supply, or nearly so, at the prevailing call rate of interest. This unique redemption feature implies that the Confederate dollar price of the call certificates would never have fallen below par. If it had, a certain profit could have been made by buying calls and immediately redeeming them at par. The price of calls would have risen until it returned to its face value.[11]

Confederate bonds authorized during 1861 bore 8 percent coupons payable semiannually in specie.[12] The treasury did not have sufficient amounts of coin to honor the coupons in gold and made payments in Confederate notes instead. Confederate dollar payments were substituted for gold payments on a one-to-one basis. No attempt was made to compensate bond holders for the depreciation (in terms of gold) of the Confederate dollar. Two separate classes of bonds may be distinguished: the $15 million loan and the $100 million loan.

The $15 million loan represented the senior debt of the Confederate government. It was the first security issued, and the Confederate Congress guaranteed it with the proceeds from a special export duty on

---

Banking in the American South: From the Age of Jackson to Reconstruction (Baton Rouge, 1987), pp. 293–95. For a listing of all Confederate securities, see Raphael P. Thian, compiler, *Register of the Confederate Debt* (Boston, 1972 [originally published in 1880]).

[9] The 7.3 percent interest note accrued interest at the rate of 2 percent per day on the $100 par value. At semiannual intervals the note could be brought to the treasury and stamped "paid." See Godfrey, *Monetary Expansion in the Confederacy*, p. 8. A similar class of 3.65 percent notes were also issued, but only in comparatively small quantities. The Currency Reform Act of 1864 provided that the 7.3 percent notes would no longer be tax receivable and would be payable two years after a successful peace treaty. See Pecquet, "Money in the Trans-Mississippi," p. 224. It is perhaps noteworthy that the North also experimented with 3.65 percent and 7.3 percent interest-bearing notes. See W. C. Mitchell, *A History of the Greenbacks* (Chicago, 1903), p. 16.

[10] See Richard C. Todd, *Confederate Finance* (Athens, 1954), pp. 245, 253; Godfrey, *Monetary Expansion in the Confederacy*, p. 9; and W. B. Yearns, *The Confederate Congress* (Athens, 1960), p. 195. The North also experimented with call certificates for a short time. See Mitchell, *A History of the Greenbacks*.

[11] Call certificates were issued and redeemed quite freely. Confederate treasury records indicate the exact totals between Oct. 13, 1862, and Jan. 1, 1863. See Raphael P. Thian, compiler, *Reports of the Secretary of the Confederate States of America 1861–1865,* Appendix Part 3 (Washington, DC, 1878 [on microfilm at the National Archives]), pp. 136–38. Quarterly estimates of the number of outstanding call certificates and other monetary aggregates can be found in Godfrey, *Monetary Expansion in the Confederacy*, pp. 40–46.

[12] Todd, *Confederate Finance*, p. 26.

cotton.[13] This duty easily could have raised sufficient funds to repay the loan, but the proceeds were quickly interrupted by the Union blockade. The coupons of this loan could have been used at their gold value to pay export or import duties that were otherwise payable only in specie.[14] This does not mean, however, that these bonds were as good as gold. The repayment of the principal in gold was uncertain, and there was the possibility that the privilege to use the coupons to pay import and export duties would be rescinded.

The other class of bonds issued during 1861—the $100 million loan—was a general obligation bond as were most of the bonds issued thereafter. These coupons were also pledged to be paid in gold, but payments were actually paid in cash. Again there was no attempt to compensate holders for the depreciation of the Confederate dollar. The coupons could have been used in lieu of specie to pay import duties levied by the central government but could not have been used to pay the special export duty on cotton. The maturity dates on the $100 million loan ranged from 1864 to 1892. The prices of these bonds did not stray far from par until 1863, when longer-term issues began to trade at market premiums.

Later bond series issued by the Confederacy included the funding loan of 1863 and 20-year, 4 percent bonds issued in 1864. The bonds from the funding loan had 8 and 7 percent coupon rates and were of a similar nature to the original $100 million loan. With the $100 million loan, the total volume of these loans outstanding at the end of the war was about $263 million.[15]

II. NOMINAL RATES OF INTEREST IN THE SOUTH

The actions of the Confederate Congress and treasury secretaries indicate their intention to restrain interest rates, presumably to minimize the postwar interest burden in the event of a Confederate victory.[16] Confederate policy makers were successful in restraining the effective nominal yields on government securities until the final months

[13] Ibid.

[14] Ibid.

[15] Ibid., pp. 74–75, 83. Of less significance for our purposes are certain special experimental classes of bonds including 6 percent cotton interest bonds, the Erlanger loan from Europe, 6 percent "income tax" bonds, and an 1864 issue of 6 percent nontaxable bonds. Ibid., pp. 25–85.

[16] As late as Sept. 1864 the second Confederate treasury secretary seriously contemplated and described how the Confederate debt could be retired following a successful peace treaty. See Raphael P. Thian, compiler, *Correspondence of the Treasury Department of the Confederate States of America* (Washington, DC, 1879 [on microfilm at the National Archives]), pp. 754–57. Also note that the attempt to minimize the postwar interest burden implies that, in the absence of an efficient tax collection system, money creation and the attendant changes in prices bear the brunt of government appropriations.

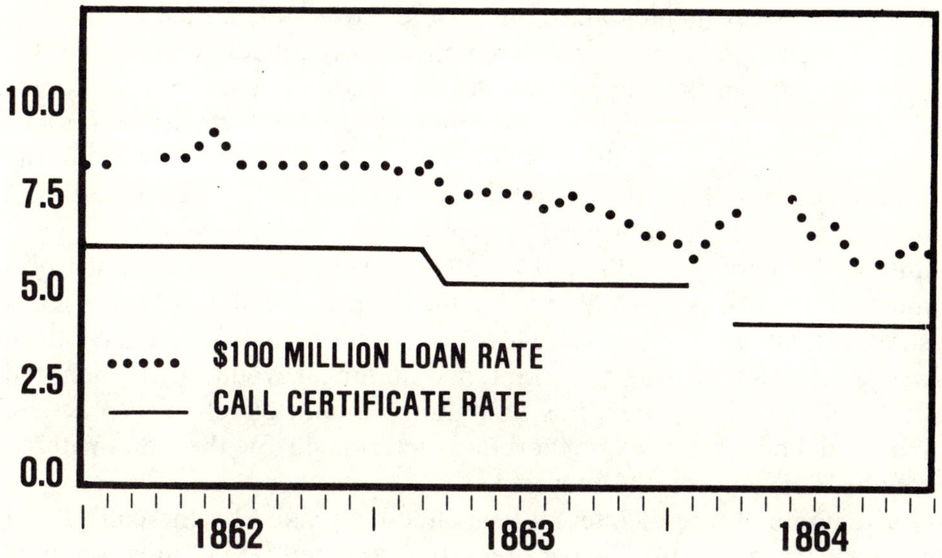

FIGURE 1

NOMINAL RATES OF INTEREST ON CALL CERTIFICATES AND THE ISSUE OF THE $100 MILLION LOAN

Source: See the Appendix.

of the conflict (see Figure 1).[17] This restraint was chiefly accomplished by the use of call certificates.

Call certificates and the 8 percent bonds of the $100 million class proved to be close substitutes. They had similar risk characteristics, sharing the same default risk since their fates rested solely on that of the Confederate government.[18] The liquidity risk of the two assets differed because of the absence of the call feature on Confederate bonds. Nevertheless, bonds were still highly liquid assets, owing to the existence of organized secondary auction markets. The absence of the call feature meant that bonds bore some capital risk, which calls did not, and this capital risk produced a liquidity premium of roughly 2 percent.[19]

[17] The equation used to calculate the nominal and gold bond yields is

$$P^B = \sum_{t=1}^{N}(c/2)/(1 + i)^{t/2} + F/(1 + i)^N$$

where P^B is the price of the bond, c is the coupon payment, N is the term to maturity, F is the face value, and i is the yield to maturity. For the calculation of the nominal (gold) yield P^B, c, and F are expressed in Confederate dollars (gold).

[18] Calls could be exchanged for Confederate currency, but in the event of a southern defeat the currency would also default.

[19] This premium is relatively small. Its magnitude reflects the degree of substitutability between bonds and calls.

Since call certificates and bonds were close substitutes, one would expect their rates to have remained close. Any tendency of bond rates to stray far from the call rate would have been cut short by a call. For example, anyone who held a 6 percent call certificate when bond prices began to fall would have cashed the call certificates and used the proceeds to purchase the now more attractive bonds. This substitution would have pushed bond prices up and their rates down until the yield differential between calls and bonds reflected only the liquidity premium. This process was limited by the supply of call certificates. At a sufficiently high expected price level all the certificates would have been converted, and the call rate of interest no longer would have anchored the bond rate. However, this limitation was not effective in practice. Nominal bond rates were therefore determined by the administered (nonmarket) call rate of interest.[20]

The nominal rate of interest was effectively fixed by the call rate of interest. In light of the Fisher effect, the expected rate of inflation must have been small and unresponsive to war news.[21] This means that the price level must have adjusted immediately to adverse war news. If the price level had adjusted only gradually to bad news, it would have implied a rising price of gold. This expectation of inflation would then have required an inflation premium for interest rates that would have been inconsistent with the call rate of interest. Thus, the price level must have discontinuously jumped in response to adverse war news.[22]

Call certificates provided the mechanism that brought about the discontinuous jump in the price level by making the supply of Confederate notes endogenous. As argued earlier, had bad news about the war put upward pressure on bond rates the exercise of calls would have checked the rise in bond rates. But in addition, this shift from calls to

[20] According to our argument, expected inflation is the difference between the pegged nominal rate of interest and the real rate of interest. If default risk on bonds raised the real rate of interest above the nominal rate, then deflation would be implied. It is possible that this would make the real return on bonds negative. However, this would not necessarily lead to a conversion of calls into money because the increase in risk on bonds is matched by an increase in the riskiness of holding currency. The relative risks, and hence the relative demands, for calls and money are essentially unaffected.

[21] The Fisher effect refers to the change in nominal rates of interest when expected inflation changes. See Irving Fisher, *Theory of Interest* (New York, 1930). In the present context a Fisher-type equation can be obtained with an argument similar to the reasoning that lies behind the interest-rate parity results of international finance. Specifically, the parity analogy leads to $i^G + \Delta p = i^D$, where i^G (i^D) is the gold (dollar) yield and Δp is the expected rate of change in the price of gold. There is, however, a complication with this analogy. If the Confederacy eventually paid its obligation in gold, then, ignoring coupon payments, Δp would equal zero. Also, since payment was uncertain there should also be a rather hefty risk premium.

[22] See Calomiris, "Price and Exchange Rates," for similar reasoning applied to the northern experience. We are grateful to an anonymous referee for this argument and the one that directly follows in the text.

TABLE 1
THE BEHAVIOR OF GOLD PRICES

Regression

$$P^G{}_t = 0.54 + 1.03P^G{}_{t-1} + e_t$$
$$(1.23)\,(24.1)$$

Random Walk Test

Lags	Q-Statistic	Significance Level
10	5.98	0.82
15	7.40	0.95
20	8.01	0.99

Notes: $P^G{}_t$ is the price of gold in month t. The t-statistics are in parentheses. R^2 is equal to 0.96. The sample period is March 1862 through April 1864. The t-statistic for the test that the coefficient on $P^G{}_{t-1}$ is different than unity is 0.71. We therefore cannot reject the null hypothesis that the coefficient equals one.
Source: See the Appendix.

bonds would have caused an increase in the money supply and produced the required jump in the price level.[23]

This explanation requires the price level to have followed a random walk. We present evidence in Table 1 that supports this hypothesis. The estimate of the lagged coefficient in a first-order autoregression is not significantly different from one. Moreover, the Q-statistic for innovations in the price of gold support the hypothesis that at 10, 15, and 20 lags the partial autocorrelation coefficients are all zero. This finding is similar to that of Richard Roll and Charles Calomiris, who find that the greenback value of gold in the North also followed a random walk.[24]

The above arguments also imply that changes in the price of gold should have been highly correlated with changes in gold rates of interest. A plot of innovations in gold yields and innovations in the price of gold is given in Figure 2. The innovations are normalized in order to reveal the close correlation between the two series.

Call certificates issued during 1861 and 1862 earned 6 percent interest per year. The rate remained at 6 percent until April 1863, when currency reform measures affected the call markets. In an obvious attempt to induce people to convert more treasury notes into long-term bonds, the Confederate Congress in October 1862 provided that by April outstanding treasury notes could be exchanged for 7 percent rather than 8 percent bonds.[25] During March 1863 it gave the holders of 6 percent call

[23] This implication could be tested if adequate money supply data were available. Godfrey presented quarterly data but some of his estimates were obtained by interpolation.
[24] See Roll, "Interest Rates"; and Calomiris, "Price and Exchange Rates."
[25] Thian, compiler, *Correspondence of the Treasury*, p. 370.

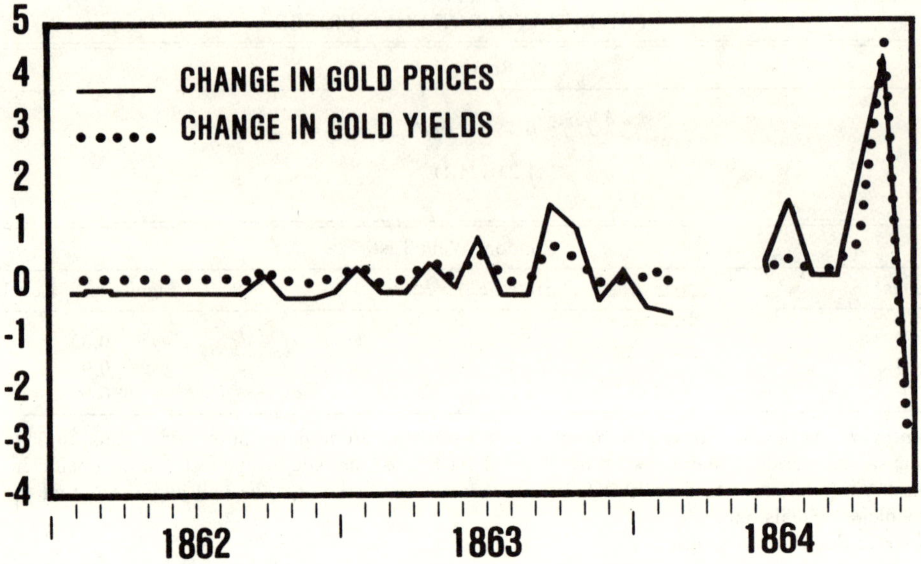

FIGURE 2

NORMALIZED DIFFERENCES IN GOLD PRICES AND YIELDS

Source: See the Appendix.

certificates until July 1, 1863, to convert them into cash. Those that remained outstanding would be considered as 6 percent, 30-year bonds. The same law provided for the issue of a new class of 5 percent call certificates which shared most of the features of the 6 percent certificates, except that the 5 percent calls could be held for only six months, after which they too would become long-term bonds.[26]

The impact of these measures reduced the entire yield structure of Confederate securities through the substitution process described earlier. The yields on 8 percent bonds soon fell to 7 percent, maintaining the 2 percent premium above the call rate during the summer of 1863. Moreover, nominal bond yields did not respond to the military disasters of Vicksburg and Gettysburg in July 1863. In fact, the nominal yields of 8 percent fell to about 6 percent by December—perhaps in light of a new debate in the Confederate Congress over a coming currency reform measure which promised even more forced bond sales to absorb outstanding treasury notes (that is, to further blur the distinction between currency and bonds and thus reduce the liquidity premium).[27]

[26] Ibid., pp. 432–33.

[27] In Dec. 1863 Treasury Secretary Christopher G. Memminger proposed sweeping monetary reform measures in order to curb inflation. Various currency reform measures were proposed and debated in the Confederate Congress from Dec. 1863 until Feb. 1864. Some of these would have wiped out most of the existing currency by forced conversion into bonds. See Yearns, *The Confederate Congress*, pp. 203–8; and Raphael P. Thian, compiler, *Extracts from the Journals of*

The Currency Reform Act of February 17, 1864, again disrupted the market yields on Confederate securities. This act provided that most of the outstanding currency and call certificates would be taxed at a rate of 33.33 percent on April 1, 1864. After that date old currency could be exchanged for a new issue at the rate of three old dollars for two new ones. The act had a number of complicating features such as the depreciation of $100 notes by an additional 10 percent each month following April, the 33 percent depreciation on $5 notes taking place on July 1, and the maintenance of all small bills under $5 at their full face values.[28] Furthermore, all old currency that remained outstanding after January 1, 1865, would become worthless. A new series of 4 percent, 20-year coupon bonds was also established. The old currency could be used to purchase these bonds at par before the April 1 funding date or at a 33 percent discount thereafter.[29]

This act produced two effects.[30] First, the liquidity premium on bonds increased and consequently a short and moderate lapse in the connection between call and bond yields occurred. Second, the stock of money balances fell by 43 percent and the supply of real money balances fell by about 35 percent between February 17 and April 1, 1864.[31] Given that

---

the Provisional Congress and of the First and Second Congresses of the Confederate States of America (Washington, DC, 1890 [on microfilm at the National Archives]), pp. 526–678.

[28] In April and May $5 bills circulated at a 15 to 20 percent discount in anticipation of a tax change in July. See Pecquet, "Money in the Trans-Mississippi," p. 228.

[29] Thian, compiler, *Correspondence of the Treasury*, pp. 588–92; and Todd, *Confederate Finance*, pp. 74–75. The similarities between northern and southern financial policies are interesting. A possible explanation for the similarities is that both shared the common goal of interest-rate controls and lacked a central bank to achieve their goal. This left the North and South with similar policy options.

[30] An additional impact of reform was felt in securities markets. The market for most Confederate securities became very thin between Apr. and Aug. 1864. The few bond price quotations during the summer months came from Wilmington, NC, rather than Richmond. The apparent reason for this "thinness" and the somewhat higher rates on 8 percent bonds is that people had been induced to buy so many 4 percent bonds that the total demand for bonds had virtually disappeared. Confederate treasury records indicate that many 8 percent bonds were shipped overseas during the summer of 1864. Perhaps this explains the presence of bond price quotations in Wilmington (a port city) during this period. See Thian, compiler, *Correspondence of the Treasury*, pp. 729–31.

[31] According to Godfrey, *Monetary Expansion of the Confederacy*, who included all treasury notes and call certificates in his definition of the money supply, these aggregates fell from $926 million to $632 million between Feb. 17 and Apr. 1. He also estimated net bank money, which similarly fell from $91 to $17 million Confederate dollars during the same period. If we are correct that bank notes were worth approximately three Confederate dollars (see Pecquet, "Money in the Trans-Mississippi," p. 222), then the decline in nominal money balances can be estimated by

$$1 - \frac{632 + (3)\,17}{926 + (3)\,91} = 0.43$$

The decline in real money balances can be estimated by adjusting for the decline in the price of the nominal supply of money was endogenous, the change in real money balances must have been driven by changes in money demand. The decline in money demand was presumably caused by the 33 percent tax on money that was to be paid on April 1.[32]

This discussion is summarized in Figure 1. It is clear, with the exception of the few months in late 1863 and early 1864, that the yield on 8 percent bonds maintained a 2 percent liquidity premium over the call rate. Call rates were lowered in two steps during the war, and this induced a substitution process that brought bond yields down in two steps. The downward drift in the nominal rate of interest is thus explained by the downward steps of the call rate.

III. YIELD CALCULATIONS FOR CONFEDERATE BONDS AND THE RESPONSE OF REAL RATES TO WAR EVENTS

The Confederacy pledged to pay its debt obligations in gold but was unable to honor the pledge. The default on gold payments was partial in the sense that there was some chance that a victorious peace would be secured and gold payments resumed. The yield to maturity on a Confederate bond can be calculated on the basis of resumed gold payments. This is the real yield.

By definition the yield to maturity on an asset is the discount rate that makes the present value of the stream of coupon and face value payments equal to the current price of the bond. Its calculation assumes that all current and future stated payments will be made. The riskiness of the asset is therefore reflected in the bond price and the yield to maturity. A risky bond will have a lower price and consequently a higher yield. The South set an effective ceiling on nominal yields by issuing fixed-rate call certificates. However, the price of gold was free to vary, and hence the yield on a gold basis could vary as well. There was not a ceiling on the real rate of interest.

Two series of real interest rates are plotted in Figure 3, and they reflect with considerable accuracy the course of the war. The real rate rose steadily from December 1861 through the spring of 1863 in response to the partial default, the realization that the war would be drawn out, and the uncertainty of victory. The siege and eventual fall of Vicksburg and General Robert E. Lee's defeat at Gettysburg correspond to a steep rise in the rate that began in the summer of 1863. The ascent of the real

---

gold, which fell from \$25 to \$22 during the same period. See Todd, *Confederate Finance*, p. 198. This becomes

$$1 - \frac{25}{22}(0.57) = 0.35$$

[32] An anonymous referee suggested that an additional decline in money demand may have been caused by a flight from an uncertain currency.

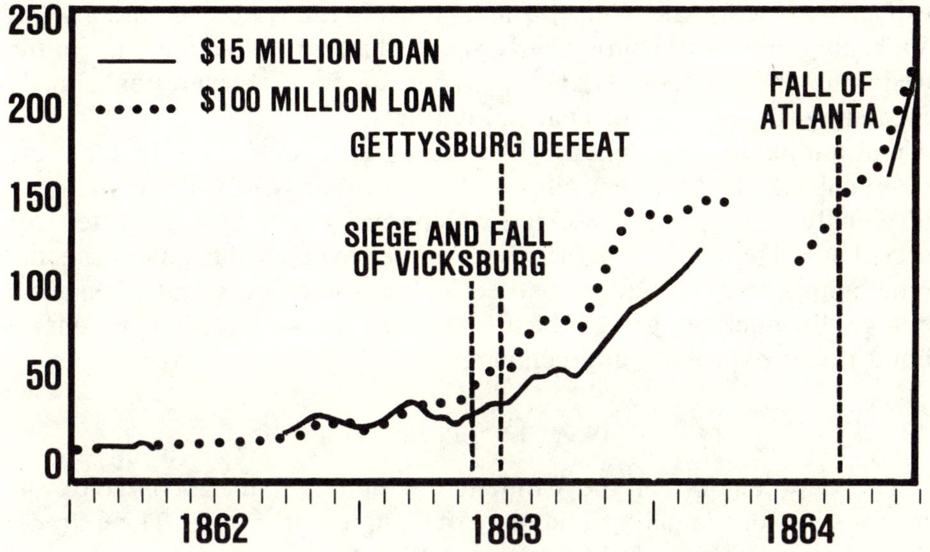

FIGURE 3

GOLD YIELDS ON THE ISSUES FROM THE $100 MILLION AND $15 MILLION LOANS

Source: See the Appendix.

rate was interrupted twice, once in the autumn of 1863 and again in the spring and summer of 1864. The autumn interruption coincides with the September 1863 Confederate victory at Chickamauga, while the second interruption corresponds to the implementation phase of the Currency Reform Act, when bond prices were not reported. In September, when data were again available, the rate was nearly at its March level. This stability reflects the effects of currency reform and perhaps also the stalemate at the Battle of the Wilderness in May and the hope for President Abraham Lincoln's defeat in the coming election. However, after the fall of Atlanta rates jumped sharply, and shortly thereafter price quotes were no longer available.

Lerner did not uncover this relationship because he looked only at the Confederate dollar price of bonds from the $15 million loan. The bond support program discussed earlier constrained the Confederate dollar price of bonds from reacting to unfavorable war news. Once we turn to gold yields the mystery disappears, and it is apparent that the market assessed a large real premium on Confederate bonds.

The movement in real yields was driven by changes in the risk of default. By fixing the Confederate dollar price of bonds, the South kept nominal and real yields close. Nevertheless, the real rate of interest did respond to war events as predicted by economic theory, and thus Lerner's puzzle is solved. Unfavorable war news increased the probability of Confederate defeat, and the increased risk of continued and complete default caused an increase in the real rate of interest. This was especially true for the major turning points in the war. The outcomes of Vicksburg and Gettysburg clearly signaled a more rapid advance in the real rate. The fall of Atlanta marked the final acceleration shortly preceding the collapse of financial markets.

Our findings are consistent with those of Roll, who did a similar study of greenbacks and interest rates in the Civil War North. His conclusion is equally appropriate here if Confederate dollar is substituted for greenback. He writes: "In fact, bond prices expressed in gold terms did react appropriately to major battles such as Gettysburg and Vicksburg; but gold's fluctuating greenback premium masked the movement of bond prices expressed in greenback terms."[33]

IV. YIELD DIFFERENTIALS

The depreciation of the Confederate dollar in terms of gold was responsible for the falling gold price of Confederate bonds. The extraordinary real yields on bonds reflected this deterioration. On the other hand, the yield differentials on bonds issued by various levels of government were due to differences in their risk characteristics, not to the course of the price of gold.

Normally, the lowest yields would be found on federal bonds, followed by the yields on state bonds, with the highest yields on bonds issued by cities.[34] This pattern reflects the structure of default risk, which for the most part reflects the differing sizes of each level's tax base. In the Civil War South this structure was turned on its head. City bonds earned the lowest yields, and the highest yields were found on Confederate bonds. This inversion of the rate structure reflects the reversal of the ordering of default risk caused by the war.

For most of the war we have monthly data on yields for bonds issued by the city of Richmond, the state of Virginia, and two distinct issues of the Confederacy. The gold yields on the Confederate bonds are plotted in Figure 3. The yields on Virginia and Richmond bonds and the differences between them are charted in Figure 4.

Early in the war the yield on the issue of the $15 million loan exceeded the yield on the bonds of the $100 million loan, even though the price of the former exceeded that of the latter. The higher gold yield on the bonds of the $15 million loan resulted from its shorter term to maturity. By March 1863 the price of the bonds from the $15 million loan had grown sufficiently large to offset the difference in maturity dates, and the bonds earned a lower real yield for the remainder of the war.

The differential reflected the preferential treatment given the coupons from the $15 million loan and the seniority of this issue. Coupons from

[33] See Roll, "Interest Rates," p. 480.

[34] This structure holds after correction for the preferential tax treatment given to state and local bonds.

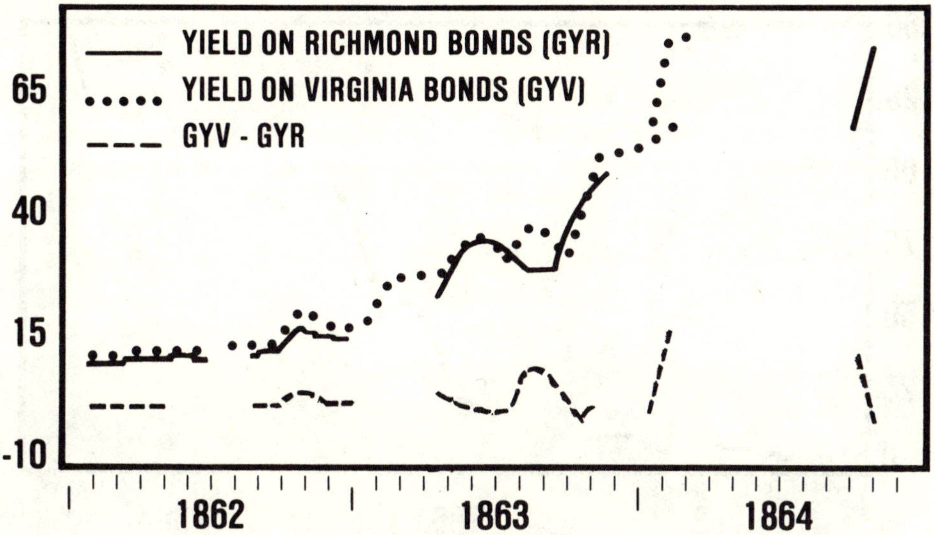

FIGURE 4

GOLD YIELDS AND DIFFERENCES ON RICHMOND AND VIRGINIA BONDS

Source: See the Appendix.

this issue were receivable at their gold value for payment of the export duty on cotton, which had been levied to fund this loan. The blockade of southern ports made it impossible for the South to carry out its plan to provide a sinking fund for the loan. However, plans were proposed for the defeat of the blockade. In this event the Confederacy may have paid coupons in gold, and as the senior debt the coupons of the $15 million loan likely would have received priority.

The yields on both types of Confederate bonds exceeded the yields on state and city bonds. It is also apparent from Figure 4 that with very few exceptions the real yield on Virginia bonds was greater than the real yield on Richmond bonds. The states were the political units in rebellion. It was, therefore, more likely that states would be dissolved or otherwise reconstituted in the event of defeat than it was that the cities would lose their political identity. As a result, the default risk on city bonds was lower than the default risk on state bonds, and the rate structure reflected this difference.

There was some chance that states and perhaps even cities would lose their political identity, but it was certain that the Confederacy would default in the face of defeat. In any event, it is reasonable to assume that changes in the yield structure reflected changes in relative default risk, and that changes in relative default risk were primarily caused by increases in the probability of a southern defeat. The yield differential between Richmond city bonds and the bonds of the $100 million loan is plotted in Figure 5. It clearly reflects war events and moves over the

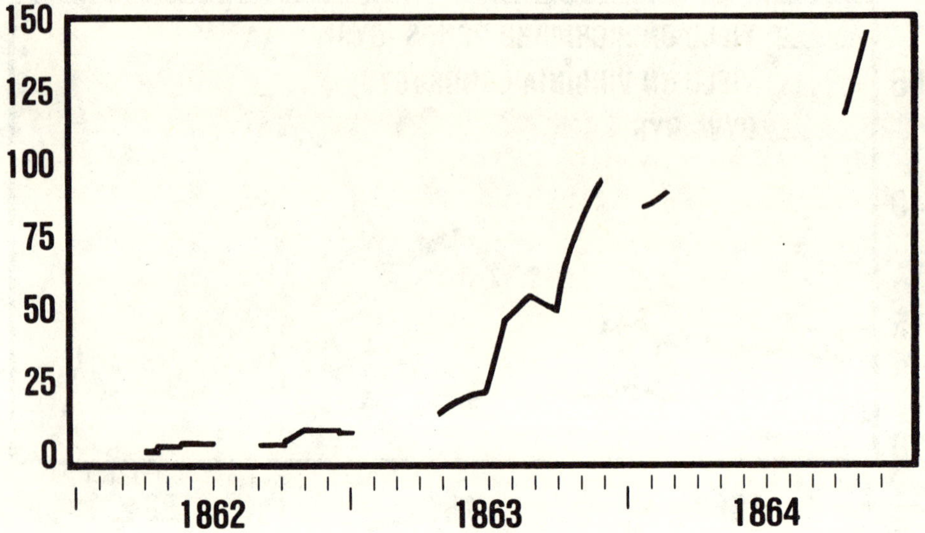

FIGURE 5

YIELD DIFFERENTIAL BETWEEN THE BONDS OF THE $100 MILLION LOAN AND RICHMOND BONDS

Source: See the Appendix.

course of the war in a way similar to the Confederate gold yields of Figure 3. Indeed, the effects of the siege and fall of Vicksburg and the defeat at Gettysburg in July 1863 are dramatically portrayed by the change in the yield differential.

It is likely that privately issued bonds carried the lowest yields, reflecting the higher probability that they would repay their debt even in the event of a southern defeat. The observations we have on Southland Railroad bonds confirm this expectation.[35] Since the yields on private railroad bonds may have risen above those on other private issues, because the companies suffered capital losses and their ability to operate was in constant jeopardy, this evidence of low yields is quite compelling.

V. CONCLUSION

Milton Friedman noted that war times provide excellent laboratories for economic experiments.[36] War brings dramatic events that can expose otherwise hidden or obscure relationships. The experience of the South provided the laboratory as we sought to solve the puzzle of interest-rate behavior during the Civil War.

[35] See the Appendix for the data sources.

[36] See Milton Friedman, "Prices, Income, and Monetary Changes in Three Wartime Periods," *American Economic Review*, 42 (May 1952), pp. 612–25, reprinted in *The Optimum Quantity of Money and Other Essays* (Chicago, 1969), pp. 157–97.

The stability of bond prices quoted in Confederate dollars is explained by the existence of call certificates. The failure of rates to respond to war events was more apparent than real. If the yield is calculated on a gold basis, war events are clearly reflected in yield movements. The relationship of the yields on bonds issued by various levels of government also shows the effects of the war. The nature of the conflict inverted the normal ranking of default risk and the normal yield structure. Moreover, the yield differential between Confederate and Richmond city bonds clearly reveals the changes in relative risk that occurred as the tide of war turned against the South and buttresses the earlier result that war events are reflected in the real rate of interest.

Appendix

Five price series form the basis for the calculations used in this article. The five series are the Confederate dollar prices of a gold dollar; bonds from the $100 million loan; bonds from the $15 million loan; Virginia state bonds; and Richmond city bonds. The data come from market reports in Richmond newspapers, including the *Richmond Whig*, the *Richmond Sentinel*, the *Richmond Enquirer*, and the *Richmond Dispatch*. We also have some quotations for railroad bonds from these papers. The data for the summer months of 1864 come from the *Wilmington Journal* of Wilmington, NC, due to a lack of bond price quotations in the Richmond market. The bond quotations were taken from reports as near as possible to mid-month. Gold price quotations were taken nearest the date of bond quotation from the $100 million loan. When a range was given we took the upper bound for the long-term rate, and when more than one quote was available on a particular maturity date or on gold an average was taken. The gold prices for two dates—August 1863 and October 1864—were obtained by interpolation using data from Richard Todd as a guide.

In order to calculate yields to maturity it is necessary to have a maturity date. The day and month of maturity were not known for any issue so we used mid-year, July 1. The $15 million loan matured in 1871. There were various maturity dates for the other issues. For the $100 million loan there were many maturity dates. When maturity dates were reported we used the issues that matured in 1881, or the year nearest to that date because it was the most often reported. For about the first year and a half of the period under study the maturity dates on bonds from the $100 million loan were unspecified. We took this to mean that the yield curve was flat and so used 1881 as the maturity date. The maturity date was seldom given for the Virginia state and Richmond city bonds, so we chose the year 1887. In that year some bonds did mature, and it was roughly the average maturity date for the dated long-term issues that we do have. Some experimentation with alternative dates revealed that the arguments and conclusions of the text are not sensitive to different maturity dates.

The actual market date was used in the calculation of the yield to maturity. All of the raw data are available on request from the authors. The data used to construct the diagrams are presented in Table 2.

TABLE 2
THE DATA

Date		Gold Yields					
		$100 Million Bonds	$15 Million Bonds	Richmond Bonds	Virginia Bonds	Interest Rate[a]	Gold Price
January	1862	12.71				8.000	
February	1862	12.71	14.65	9.90	11.04	8.050	1.500
March	1862		15.25	9.77	10.61		1.550
April	1862	14.09	18.00	10.72	11.52	8.276	1.775
May	1862	15.40		10.87	11.39	8.150	1.800
June	1862	17.02		11.31	11.80	8.819	1.875
July	1862	16.43	18.86	10.82		8.156	1.875
August	1862	17.22			12.93	7.999	2.050
September	1862	17.23		11.51	12.93	7.998	2.050
October	1862	18.43	22.14	12.37	13.76	7.998	2.200
November	1862	26.92	30.35	16.64	20.19	7.998	3.300
December	1862	25.78	28.91	15.54	17.57	7.999	3.125
January	1863	23.90	27.15	14.53	16.40	7.999	2.900
February	1863	25.96	29.67		18.28	7.895	3.200
March	1863	38.01	40.56	22.24	26.98	7.998	4.750
April	1863	36.52	30.69		26.89	7.017	5.000
May	1863	39.71	29.36	23.62	27.54	7.392	5.250
June	1863	54.35	37.10	32.29	33.39	7.344	7.250
July	1863	57.50	39.83	34.49	34.49	7.246	7.750
August	1863	80.01	54.11	31.74	32.24	6.917	11.250
September	1863	83.14	57.17	28.71	37.92	7.338	11.250
October	1863	79.40	55.06	28.38	32.79	6.866	11.250
November	1863	116.49	71.28	40.65	38.93	6.819	16.710
December	1863	140.31	88.96	46.45	51.13	6.291	21.000
January	1864	140.06	98.72		51.44	6.372	20.875
February	1864	138.91	109.23	53.17	53.19	5.673	22.500
March	1864	147.15	123.70	56.87	74.74	6.626	22.000
April	1864	145.49			75.26	6.990	21.000
May	1864						
June	1864					7.395	
July	1864	114.41				6.262	17.000
August	1864	128.82				6.522	19.000
September	1864	152.20	129.46	56.05	65.25	5.677	24.875
October	1864	159.11				5.665	26.375
November	1864	174.97	164.07	56.78	68.65	6.072	27.875
December	1864	218.68	209.12	73.15	68.97	5.899	34.625

[a] Interest Rate is the Confederate Dollar Yield on the $100 million loan.
Source: See the Appendix.

A New Look at the Dealings of the Bardi and Peruzzi with Edward III

EDWIN S. HUNT

The Bardi and Peruzzi of Florence became in the early fourteenth century the largest merchant-bankers ever seen in medieval Europe. Their collapse in the 1340s has been attributed by most historians to huge losses on loans to Edward III of England. This article explores some flaws in the conventional explanation and shows that the firms lacked the resources to have made loans on the generally accepted scale. It also suggests means by which the companies could have recovered at least part of their advances to the king without the results appearing in government ledgers.

The Bardi and Peruzzi are well known to medieval historians as the two largest Florentine merchant-banking companies of the fourteenth century. They were manufacturers, traders, and bankers with widespread operations throughout the Mediterranean and western Europe—in many ways an ancestral form of the modern multinational corporation. The collapse of these firms, the Peruzzi in 1343 and the Bardi in 1346, followed a run of severe reverses in virtually all of their businesses, resulting in a total combined loss calculated by the contemporary chronicler, Giovanni Villani, at over 1.75 million florins, a prodigious sum for the time.[1] Villani asserted that the greater part of this loss—900,000 Florentine gold florins for the Bardi and 600,000 for the Peruzzi—was incurred as a result of Edward III's failure to pay his debts to those organizations.[2]

Most historians accept Villani's figures at face value, and unquestioningly attribute the bankruptcies of these firms to the defalcations of Edward III. Yet the two scholars who have conducted the most detailed research on the Bardi and Peruzzi, Armando Sapori and E. B. Fryde,

The Journal of Economic History, Vol. L, No. 1 (Mar. 1990). ISSN 0022-0507.

The author is a doctoral student in the History Department of the University of Cincinnati, Cincinnati, Ohio 45221.

I would like to express my thanks to James Murray, John Brackett, and Ronald Pollitt, for their comments and encouragement.

[1] Giovanni Villani, *Storia de Giovanni Villani* (Florence, 1587), book 12, chap. 54, pp. 862–63. In addition to the English losses of 1.5 million florins for the two companies, Villani cites repudiations by the king of Sicily of 200,000 florins and severe property damage in Florence stemming from the uprising of September 1343.

[2] It should be noted that Edward III, unlike Philip of Spain in the sixteenth century, never specifically repudiated his debts to the Italian companies. His commissioners disputed the amounts and scaled them back sharply after a series of audits, but the final acknowledged debts were simply never paid. For a detailed account of these proceedings, see Ephraim Russell, "The Societies of the Bardi and Peruzzi and Their Dealings with Edward III, 1327–45," in G. Unwin, ed., *Finance and Trade under Edward III* (London, 1918), pp. 93–135.

have concluded that the companies' failure was caused primarily by financial and political difficulties in Florence. They maintain, nevertheless, that the losses suffered at the hands of Edward III were colossal and contributed greatly to the bankruptcies. Sapori started with the level of debt acknowledged by Edward III to the Bardi in March 1346, and added a series of royal promises recorded in the Calendars of Patent and Close Rolls but not included in the king's acknowledgment, to reach a total of nearly 600,000 florins. Despite this, Sapori was unwilling to repudiate Villani's calculations even though he could not confirm them, and accordingly assessed the Bardi losses in England at "somewhere between 594,000 and 900,000 florins" and those of the Peruzzi at two-thirds of that amount.[3] Fryde calculated the king's debt, including interest, to be a more modest but still enormous £103,000 (687,000 florins) to the Bardi and £71,000 (474,000 florins) to the Peruzzi as of 1345.[4]

Because Villani is regarded as a reputable and knowledgeable chronicler of commercial affairs, and because his estimates are at least partially supported by English records, historians, including Sapori and Fryde, have tended to overlook serious anomalies in the data. First, we are told that the Bardi and Peruzzi, acknowledged as Europe's most experienced and sophisticated companies in dealing with monarchs, let themselves become hopelessly and foolishly overcommitted to Edward III, while relative parvenus such as William de la Pole and various Flemish and German merchants limited their losses or even made profits on their loans to the king. Fryde's suggestion that the Bardi and Peruzzi failed because they placed "excessive trust in the king's promises" is an inadequate explanation.[5] Another unanswered question is where the companies obtained the huge sums to lend to the king. Historians have simply assumed that because these firms were very large, they had the resources to advance the indicated funds to Edward III. Yet available data on the companies demonstrate that their resources fell far short of the amounts purportedly loaned. A third mystery is how the firms were able to stay in business for so many years after their English advances, and hence much of their cash flow, had apparently become frozen. Finally, there is the unexplained coincidence that the third-largest Florentine company, the Acciaiuoli, failed at the same time as the Peruzzi, despite having made no loans to King Edward.

These anomalies need to be addressed in order to arrive at reliable

[3] A. Sapori, *La crisi delle compagnie mercantile dei Bardi e dei Peruzzi* (Florence, 1926). Sapori's calculations and conclusions from them appear on pp. 74–77, where he actually shows a total of 535,000 florins. Later he adjusted the figure to 594,000 florins after reconsidering the sterling-florin exchange rate (see fn. 6).

[4] E. B. Fryde, "Public Credit, with Special Reference to North-Western Europe," *The Cambridge Economic History of Europe* (Cambridge, 1963), vol. 3, p. 460.

[5] E. B. Fryde, *William de la Pole* (London, 1988), p. 88.

conclusions regarding the failure of the Bardi and Peruzzi. Their investigation will entail a brief summary of the Bardi and Peruzzi activities in England, an examination of the companies' ability to provide loans of the magnitude indicated, and finally, an evaluation of the records in the context of "normal" business practice of the time.[6]

The Bardi began business in England as early as 1267 and within a decade participated in wool exports, papal banking, and a loan to Edward I. Their operations were on a modest scale and grew slowly until the reign of Edward II. Loans to the monarchy totaled only £4,900 between 1290 and 1310, but increased after collapse of the rival Ricciardi and Frescobaldi companies to almost £68,000 between 1311 and 1326. Early in Edward III's reign the pace of lending accelerated, and by 1329 the Bardi effectively became banker to the Crown. The Peruzzi were much later in starting commercial activity in England and eschewed royal lending until 1336, the eve of the Hundred Years' War, when they allied with the Bardi in what today would be called a joint venture.[7]

The early business in England of both companies was in the wool trade, the main economic attraction of that country. English wools were the finest and were essential to the fabrication of luxury cloth. The Italian companies contracted growers for supplies which they sold to their client manufacturers in Flanders and Italy or converted into cloth in their own facilities in Florence. As the Bardi records indicate, the wool and cloth businesses were highly profitable, accounting for over half of that firm's earnings in the years 1330/31 and 1331/32.[8] To secure adequate quantities, the companies contracted for several years ahead, paying the growers a large lump-sum cash advance. The monasteries were important growers and invariably took advantage of this credit, but effectively paid heavy interest for it in the form of discounts in cash or kind from market prices.[9] The Bardi activities among the monasteries

[6] For the sake of simplicity, the data will be presented in only two currencies, the Florentine florin and the English pound. The commercial relationship between the florin and the English pound varied, but there was an "official" rate fixed at one florin equals three shillings, that is, £1 equals 6.67 florins, which was used in transactions between the companies and Edward III during the late 1330s and early 1340s. Some scholars have argued that the fixed rate created advantages for the companies while others contend that Edward benefited. Because the fixed rate applied to transactions in both directions, the net effect on any of the parties was probably small; in any case, because of its consistent use in the period under review, the fixed rate is appropriate for this study. See Michael Prestwich, "Early Fourteenth-Century Exchange Rates," *The Economic History Review*, 2nd series, 32 (Summer 1979), pp. 470–82.

[7] E. B. Fryde, "Deposits of Hugh Despenser the Younger with Italian Bankers," in his *Studies in Medieval Trade and Finance* (London, 1983), Item III, p. 347.

[8] R. S. Lopez and I. W. Raymond, *Medieval Trade in the Mediterranean World* (New York, 1955), pp. 370–71; Sapori, *La Crisi*, p. 218.

[9] E. Power, *The Wool Trade in Medieval English History* (Oxford, 1941), p. 43.

are particularly well documented by their well-known representative Francesco Pegolotti in his handbook *La Pratica della Mercatura.*[10]

A further advantage of dealing with the monasteries was that it complemented the companies' papal banking activity. When the papacy instructed the Bardi or Peruzzi to transfer funds accumulated in England to Avignon, the London branch would have the Florence headquarters provide the money from its resources. The papacy's cash would thus be available in England to lend to the monasteries, which, in turn, would likely use some of the credits to pay their papal dues. The money would then flow back to the company, completing a lucrative cycle. The very large asset figure (over £12,000) reported from the Bardi's London branch in 1318, a time of modest dealings with the English monarch, appears to confirm the substantial level of lending to wool growers.[11]

These attractive arrangements were possible only with the support of the monarchy, which exacted a price for its protection. Medieval rulers suffered from a perpetual cash-flow problem. Their expenses were always immediate and pressing, but their income was uneven and usually delayed. Tax revenues were especially slow to be collected in time of war, as the subsidies agreed by the monarch's subjects would trickle in long after the expenses of mobilization had to be met. Thus kings needed loans and looked to the wealthy merchants to provide them; on their side the merchants, especially foreign merchants, could not expect to do business without "the purchased favor of the prince."[12] The credits were made for a variety of purposes. Aside from the war loans, the companies made numerous advances of varying sizes to the king and members of the royal family to fund monthly household expenses, diplomatic efforts, and the acquisition of luxury goods.

The king promised repayment of such loans and, in addition, undertook to reward the merchants with concealed interest described as "gifts" or "damages" to avoid violating usury prohibitions. The prizes that the merchants really sought took the form of privileges, such as rights of monopoly or duty reliefs, which could be highly advantageous to the merchants' trading operations but are difficult to quantify. Merchant-bankers were primarily merchants who counted on trade for most of their profits. Banking for princes was thus mainly a means to this end. Reimbursements of loans were made from a variety of sources, but, for the most part, came from anticipated royal revenues.[13] The

[10] J. P. Bischoff, "Pegolotti: an Honest Merchant?" *The Journal of European Economic History*, 6 (Spring 1977), pp. 103–8.

[11] Sapori, *La crisi*, p. 216.

[12] R. L. Reynolds, "Origins of Modern Business Enterprise: Medieval Italy," this JOURNAL, 12 (Fall 1952), p. 365.

[13] E. B. Fryde, "Loans to the English Crown, 1328–31," *English Historical Review*, 70 (Spring 1955), p. 208, reprinted in *Studies in Medieval Trade*. Here Fryde cites many kinds of royal revenue

monthly household advances cited above, for example, were repaid by the assignment of customs revenues from certain ports. Some of the war loans were to be paid by the assignment of tax levies, others through the grant of wool export monopolies, and still others through grants of sacks of wool or of customs exemptions. The scale and importance of such exemptions in 1338/39 has prompted the observation that "only those who held them could hope to make appreciable profits."[14]

Some scholars have tried to calculate the total sums loaned by the Bardi and Peruzzi and the total reimbursements received by them. Unfortunately the only period for which complete information has been discovered is 1328 through 1331. Fryde, in a meticulous survey of that time span, determined that the Bardi advanced the Crown in cash and goods a total of £42,000 and were promised repayment of over £53,000, including interest equivalents.[15] By early 1332 the Bardi had obtained reimbursements adding up to £45,000, along with a note for the balance of "interest" due. This study confirms Fryde's observation that rulers usually contracted numerous short-term loans at fairly frequent intervals, with repayment proceeding "simultaneously with the contracting of new debts, often destined to be equally short-lived."[16] It also mirrors the companies' experience with the Angevin kings in southern Italy—frequent loans and constant repayments ensured by the companies' close follow-up.[17] Only payment of interest seems to have been stretched out.

From 1332 onward, however, gaps in the data have required scholars to resort to estimates. Moreover, even where information is available, it becomes less trustworthy, especially for the larger loans. Some of the loans recorded were not all paid over to the Crown at the time, and parts of them may never have been paid. Certainly many of the assignments made by the king to the merchant-bankers were deferred or never fulfilled. What the records tell us is that the size of the loans increased sharply during the mid 1330s to help finance the war with Scotland. After the declaration of war with France and the involvement of the Peruzzi, reported lending to the king by the two companies escalated to £82,400 between September 1336 and December 1337 and £71,700 in 1338, but then dropped to £28,400 from Michaelmas 1338 to February

---

used to pay the Bardi—sale of surplus royal victuals, land revenues, fines, fees, and a share of the indemnity paid by the king of Scotland under the peace treaty terms, as well as cash from the treasury.

[14] E. B. Fryde, "Parliament and the French War, 1336–40," in *Studies in Medieval Trade*, Item V, p. 265.

[15] Fryde, "Loans to the English Crown," p. 204.

[16] Fryde, "Public Credit," p. 436.

[17] G. Yver, *Le Commerce et les marchands dans l'Italie méridionale au xiiie et au xive siècle* (Paris, 1903); see especially chap. 6, "Les opérations des compagnies florentines."

1340.[18] According to Villani, the companies were driven into bankruptcy with the king owing them the equivalent of £230,000. Because lending by the companies after 1340 was relatively modest, we are forced by these figures to assume that virtually all of the advances made to the king from 1337 onward were never repaid.

Sapori and other historians seem to have been beguiled by a fragment of the Bardi 1318 accounts into believing that the Bardi and Peruzzi operations were large enough to embark upon and sustain new lending of this magnitude. These accounts show assets totaling nearly 874,000 florins, equivalent to about £130,000; however, only a small fraction of these assets would normally be available for new loans.[19]

Assets take a variety of forms. Some would have been property, buildings, and equipment in Florence and in the branches; other assets would have included inventories of raw materials, especially wool, in-process cloth, and finished merchandise in Florence, the branches, and in transit. Most of the remainder would have been in financial assets, such as accounts receivable from customers, the advances to English wool suppliers cited above, papal cash transfers, loans to third parties, and commercial bills of exchange. Finally, a large portion of the assets was widely dispersed geographically; over 300,000 florins, or 35 percent of the Bardi 1318 totals, were located in ten or more foreign branches. As a result of all these factors, the asset figures do not provide reliable indicators of the amount of free cash available for lending. Although specific breakdowns for the Bardi in 1318 are lacking, the surviving records from the Alberti of 1315 support this analysis and confirm that in a going concern, the level of free cash is usually very low.[20]

The financing of assets normally came from four main sources. The first was the shareholders' equity, that is, their capital and retained earnings, which formed a company's financial underpinning. This was not a major source because retained earnings were distributed to the shareholders after each closing of the books (typically every two to five years), and the capital subscriptions tended to be relatively modest, especially during the 1330s. Shareholder loans, called *sopraccorpo*, and third-party deposits, on which the companies paid interest at about 8 percent, contributed additional medium-term finance. As Sapori points out, however, the bulk of most companies' business was financed not by

[18] E. B. Fryde, "The Financial Resources of Edward III in the Netherlands, 1337–40," *Revue Belge de Philologie et d'Histoire*, 45 (1967), pp. 1146, 1153, 1159; reprinted in *Studies in Medieval Trade*.

[19] Sapori, *La crisi*, p. 216.

[20] R. de Roover, "The Story of the Alberti Company, 1302–1348, as Revealed in its Account Books," *The Business History Review*, 32 (Spring 1958), pp. 51–59. Cash on hand was insignificant in seven out of eight statements over a period of 25 years. The exception was a depressed year when cash equaled 10 percent of assets.

shareholders' equity and large deposits, but by funds provided by myriads of small investors. These investments were of two types; participations in specific commercial ventures, called *accomandigia*, and advances on merchandise ordered, called *depositi*.[21] Such financing was essentially short-term, earmarked for specific limited-risk commerce and not intended for lending to improvident monarchs. Finally, there would be some additional short-term financing from routine accounts payable to suppliers.

The surviving "Sixth Books" of the Peruzzi are especially helpful in giving a picture of the financing capability of that company before and during the period of its dealings with Edward III. They show that the Peruzzi Company suffered losses of over 40,000 florins for the years July 1, 1331 through June 30, 1335, wiping out two-thirds of the shareholders' capital. On July 1, 1335, its assets totaled over 500,000 florins, but well over half of them were scattered among thirteen foreign branches. With equity reduced to 21,000 florins and *sopraccorpo* standing at 14,000 florins, the Peruzzi business, including a portion of its foreign operations, was largely funded by means of approximately 220,000 florins in deposits and short-term advances from Florentine merchants.[22] The Bardi, being larger and apparently somewhat better financed, were in a stronger position, but their profits are believed to have declined sharply after 1332.[23]

In light of the above data, only a small part of the enormous advances recorded in 1337 and 1338 to Edward III—some £154,100, equivalent to over one million florins—could have been derived from company resources. Nor could the companies have obtained money on this scale from large depositors outside of Florence. Edward III was squeezing funds out of every possible source in England, Flanders, Germany, and Italy; the Bardi and Peruzzi were by no means Edward's only Italian lenders.[24] The Avignon Papacy restricted its dealings with the companies to transferring funds; the papal treasury neither placed deposits nor borrowed money at that time.[25] Southern Italy was a drain rather than a source of cash for both firms, as indicated by Georges Yver's analysis, and by the Naples branch totals in the 1335 Peruzzi accounts, which

[21] A. Sapori, *Studi di storia economica medievale* (Florence, 1947), p. 278.

[22] A. Sapori, *I libri di commercio dei Peruzzi* (Florence, 1934). This book is mainly a transcript of the remnants of the Peruzzi accounts for the period beginning in 1335, but provides balances and allocations of losses from the "old company" of 1331–35. Summaries of assets appear on pp. 1–12 and of liabilities on pp. 190–197, 318.

[23] Sapori, *La crisi*, p. 106.

[24] Fryde, "The Financial Resources of Edward III." Italian lenders to Edward III during the period from 1337 to 1340 included, among others, the Portinari and Bonaccorsi of Florence, Bartholomei of Lucca, Pisani of Venice, and Leopardi of Asti.

[25] Y. Renouard, *Les Relations des papes d'Avignon et des compagnies commerciales et bancaires de 1316 à 1378* (Paris, 1941).

show that the amount owed to the branch exceeded the amount owed by the branch by over 30,000 florins.[26]

Thus, by process of elimination, most of the new funds made available to the companies for lending to the English king perforce originated from Florentine depositors, but the amounts purportedly remitted exceed any reasonable estimate of the capacity or the willingness of such investors. First, during 1337/38 Florentines were already being pressed to raise 600,000 florins to finance the war they were waging against the Della Scala of Verona.[27] Second, according to the incomplete but voluminous records of the Peruzzi Company between 1335 and its collapse in 1343, deposit activity was unimpressive and the shareholders' *sopraccorpo* actually declined by at least 13,000 florins.[28] This evidence should not be surprising, given the fact that investors earned only 7 percent on Peruzzi deposits as opposed to an average of 15 percent obtainable on loans to the commune. Moreover, the Peruzzi accounts reveal a modest overall scale of operations that would have been dwarfed by the attributed English lending. To illustrate, the Peruzzi share of the million florins reportedly advanced to Edward III in 1337 and 1338 was 40 percent or 400,000 florins, equivalent to almost twice the total value of all the company's assets in Florence in 1335. Even at the low rate of 7 percent, the interest cost of these new funds would have exceeded two times the profit the company earned in all but its very best years.[29] The only direct evidence we have of significant deposits made by Florentines for lending to Edward III is found in a list of deductions made in 1348 from the amount Edward acknowledged owing the Bardi Company which he said he would satisfy independently. These deductions totaled £9,500 (63,000 florins), which the Bardi company had apparently borrowed from a number of Italian individuals, including Paul de Monte Florum and several members of the Bardi family.[30]

Sapori, unable to find the source of an extraordinary increase in deposits in the Peruzzi accounts, has, *faute de mieux,* attributed it to "the myriads of small investors" mentioned earlier, and historians have generally accepted this explanation. But there is no evidence whatsoever to support the claim, nor to suggest even the possibility that such

[26] G. Yver, *Le Commerce dans l'Italie méridionale*, chap. 6; Sapori, *Libri di commercio dei Peruzzi*, pp. 8, 193.

[27] Villani, *Storia*, book 11, chap. 89, p. 754.

[28] Sapori, *Libri di commercio*. My analysis of the Peruzzi *libro segreto sesto* shows that 19 of the 21 shareholders reduced their net loans to the company from 14,077 florins in July 1335 to 1,151 florins in July 1343. No opening balance appears for the two remaining shareholders, but their 1343 balances reflect *borrowing* from the company of 9,129 florins.

[29] A. Sapori, *Studi di storia economica* (Florence, 1955), vol 2, pp. 665–78. From the data presented, the annual profit of the Peruzzi between 1300 and 1324 can be calculated at an average of around 13,000 florins, with a peak of 18,000 florins in 1308/10.

[30] Sapori, *La crisi*, p. 78.

people could generate surplus long-term cash on the necessary scale. To put the figures into perspective, the extra 400,000 florins allegedly required by the Peruzzi alone in 1337/38 equal Villani's estimate of the payroll of the entire Florentine cloth industry in 1338, the livelihood of over 30,000 people at that time.[31] Finally, the source of financing cannot be found in the creation of credit, which in the fourteenth century was very restricted and largely in the hands of moneychangers, who operated almost entirely on a local basis.[32]

Since the companies had limited access to new money, they could have sustained the reported level of lending only by achieving reasonably rapid recoveries of their loans by one means or another. Had they not done so, they would have promptly defaulted on their regular bill-of-exchange and papal-transfer obligations and would have been forced into immediate bankruptcy. There are records of only a few temporary defaults on relatively minor transactions, reflecting troublesome, but not fatal, cash-flow difficulties.[33] The companies survived for several years and did not lose their valuable papal business until late 1341, after Florence had alienated Pope Benedict XII by making overtures to his arch enemy, Ludwig of Bavaria, and by revealing Florentine military weakness in its crushing defeat at the hands of Pisa.

This evidence strongly suggests that the English Crown's net indebtedness to the Bardi and Peruzzi could not have reached anything approaching the levels estimated by Fryde and Sapori, let alone those indicated by Villani. The best way to square such a position with the records of the English monarchy is to consider the means by which recoveries might have been made by the companies which would not necessarily have appeared in the English records.

Such recoveries would have taken three main forms. First, a portion of the advances made by the companies would have been used by the king to repay their previous loans, consistent with the short-term revolving-loan pattern applied routinely by the companies in southern Italy and England, as discussed earlier. This time-honored practice between banks and governments of using part of the proceeds of new loans to pay principal and interest on old ones is still utilized today and was certainly applied by the Bardi and Peruzzi.[34]

The second form of recovery would have been actual repayment. The Crown did make substantial reimbursements, either in cash through

[31] Villani, *Storia*, book 11, chap. 93, p. 758.

[32] F. C. Lane and R. C. Mueller, *Money and Banking in Medieval and Renaissance Venice* (Baltimore, 1985), vol. I, pp. 62–64, and R. A. Goldthwaite, "Local Banking in Renaissance Florence," *Journal of European Economic History*, 14 (Spring 1985), pp. 37–38, 48.

[33] Y. Renouard, *Les Relations des papes*, pp. 134, 138; Fryde, "The Financial Resources of Edward III," pp. 1169–70.

[34] On at least two occasions the king urged his collectors to repay the Bardi as promptly as possible because they had promised to re-lend the money to him (*Calendar of Close Rolls*, 1337–39, pp. 294 and 309).

assignments of taxes or in sacks of wool. These repayments, although often less than promised and usually seriously delayed, were significant. Fryde has been able to document repayments totaling £74,000, equivalent to almost 500,000 florins, during the period July 1338 to January 1340. Of this amount, £38,000 were paid in England out of tax proceeds, £18,800 in Flanders from customs revenue on the export of wool, and £17,200 in Flanders in the form of grants of wool. Fryde also demonstrates that the firms were awarded very large "gifts" of cash and wool, although he cannot establish how much was actually paid.[35] Most often it was such "gifts" that went unpaid; over half of the amount Sapori itemized as owed by the king to the Bardi was in the form of unfulfilled promises of "gifts" or "damages," not money actually borrowed by him.

The third form rested in the lucrative business advantages derived from royal grants. Shrewd Florentine businessmen with extensive first-hand experience of the unreliability of princes were not prepared to advance large sums merely on the strength of royal promises. What they received was something tangible and very valuable, the monopoly privilege to export wool to southern Europe. The Patent and Close Rolls contain references not only to numerous releases of wool to the companies at the onset of their joint venture in 1337, but also to the imprisonment and seizure of assets of all other foreign merchants.[36] Fryde estimates that the companies shipped to Italy alone a total of at least 7,365 sacks between 1338 and 1340.[37] Fryde has also computed that English merchants cleared a profit on sales to Flanders of between £2 and £3 per sack, after all expenses.[38] Having a monopoly position in southern Europe, especially while exports to Flanders were curtailed, must have resulted in an even higher profit per sack for the Florentines. The companies may very well have earned £20,000 (over 130,000 florins) or more on such sales, which would have helped finance a good deal of their lending to the king.

It is also very probable that the Bardi and Peruzzi, like all other merchants at the time, cheated, providing themselves with an illegitimate means of recovery. Being foreign, they may have had to be somewhat more circumspect than their English counterparts, but they were also more experienced and sophisticated, and well positioned to

[35] Fryde, "The Financial Resources of Edward III," pp. 1143–44, 1159, 1162. See also E. B. Fryde, "Materials for the Study of Edward III's Credit Operations, 1327–48," *Bulletin of the Institute of Historical Research*, 22 (1949), pp. 105–38.

[36] *Calendar of Patent Rolls*, 1334–38, p. 506, and 1338–40, p. 123. By these orders the king exonerated his sheriff from claims relating to the imprisonment and seizure of valuables of all foreign merchants, except the Bardi and Peruzzi.

[37] E. B. Fryde, "Italian Maritime Trade with Medieval England (c. 1270–c. 1530)," *Studies in Medieval Trade and Finance*, Item XIV, p. 301.

[38] E. B. Fryde, "The Wool Accounts of William de la Pole," *Studies in Medieval Trade and Finance*, Item IX, p. 14.

exploit the splendid opportunities created by the financial mismanagement of Edward's administration. In an old, but well-researched and documented study, Dorothy Hughes uncovered persuasive evidence that virtually everyone associated with raising funds for the monarchy—collectors, officers, customs officials, and above all merchants—were routinely cheating on a significant scale.[39] Collectors underpaid growers for purveyanced wool and underreported the amount collected. In 1340 the Easter Parliament found it necessary to order the removal and replacement of all customs collectors and wool controllers because they "permitted merchandise to be exported without custom, not only by negligence, but openly and by connivance."[40] Exporters found ways to avoid paying customs and to divert wool from government to private use after shipment abroad, leading to large disappearances. For example, in September 1338 a total of 5,532 sacks of wool was shipped to the king in Flanders, "but no more than 4,973 sacks are known for certain to have reached him," a discrepancy which would have been worth over £4,000 even at the depressed prices at the time.[41] Although most of the data relate to English operators, especially William de la Pole, there are references to the Bardi and Peruzzi, who appear to have been involved, directly or indirectly, in large-scale swindles, and who were frequently found guilty of commercial and legal abuses in Florence.[42]

The weakness of Edward III's administration is somewhat masked by the deceptively orderly presentation of its accounts. An example is provided by the Wardrobe Book of William de Norwell, who served as Edward III's Keeper of the Wardrobe from July 1338 to May 1340, a period when that office was located on the continent.[43] His accounts show total receipts from the Bardi and Peruzzi of £8,692, a curiously small amount compared with the £68,700 received from William de la Pole, given the Italians' superior continental connections. Repayments totaled £6,400, including £4,000 from recorded sales of wool. On closer scrutiny, the treatment of the wool receipts seems disturbingly loose. Norwell reports accepting 1,000 sacks of wool from the Bardi, but turning over the proceeds of sales of only 250 sacks to the Bardi. There is no record here of what happened to the remaining 750 sacks. On another occasion, Norwell reports the sale of 230 sacks of wool, but notes that no money changed hands because the Bardi and Peruzzi made the sale and kept the proceeds.[44] Under such circumstances it is

[39] D. Hughes, *A Study of Social and Constitutional Tendencies in the Early Years of Edward III* (London, 1915).

[40] Ibid., p. 94.

[41] Fryde, "The Financial Resources of Edward III," p. 1,162.

[42] M. Becker, *Florence in Transition* (Baltimore, 1989), vol. 1, pp. 202–7.

[43] M. Lyon, B. Lyon, and H. Lucas, *The Wardrobe Book of William de Norwell, 12 July 1338 to 27 May 1340* (Brussels, 1983).

[44] Ibid., pp. cix–cx.

possible, even probable, that the Bardi and Peruzzi were able to retrieve more of their advances than were recorded in the books.

Whatever the means employed by the Bardi and Peruzzi, the incontrovertible fact is that they managed to stay afloat for several years, maintaining sufficient cash flow to keep their multifarious businesses turning over and their Florentine creditors at bay. Moreover, their eventual failure appears to be more closely connected with their intimate involvement in the political and economic convulsions in Florence than with any specific events in England. They, along with most other merchant-bankers in Florence, had firmly supported the wars in northern Tuscany in the belief that acquisition of territories there would increase the security of their trade with northern Europe. The high cost and poor results of this policy, along with a severe economic downturn, motivated part of the Bardi clan to lead an abortive coup against the regime in November 1340. Despite the exile of sixteen family members, the Bardi remained powerful; they and the Peruzzi used their influence to help install Walter of Brienne, Duke of Athens, as tyrant of the city in 1342.

The Bardi and Peruzzi were very active in shaping Brienne's foreign policy, serving as ambassadors and counselors. Domestically, they helped persuade him to lift the exile of the Bardi and others, and to grant all near-bankrupt companies a three-year immunity against creditors. Unfortunately cash constraints forced him to take a number of measures, including repudiation of the commune's debt, which were unacceptable to the merchant-bankers, and in July 1343 they participated in deposing him.[45] Their triumph was short-lived, however, as an amalgamation of lower-order guildsmen and workers violently overturned the big merchants' regime in September 1343. Within a few weeks both the Peruzzi and the Acciaiuoli declared themselves bankrupt. The Bardi did not succumb until early 1346, shortly after the commune decided to restructure and effectively devalue its large public debt, of which the Bardi company was a major holder.[46]

In any case the end, when it came, was not totally disastrous for the creditors. Final settlements were agreed at 36.25 percent of the creditors' claims on the Peruzzi and 46.25 percent on the Bardi. Actual payments generated by company assets augmented by personal assets of shareholders reached 37 percent and 48 percent respectively.[47] These relatively high creditor recoveries are inconsistent with the monumental losses believed to have been sustained by the companies in their English lending. Moreover, they were only modestly lower than the recoveries

[45] Becker, *Florence*, vol. 1, pp. 150–72.

[46] Ibid. As early as the 1320s the Bardi held at least 30,000 florins, over 10 percent of the commune's public debt (pp. 78–79), and as late as 1344 were still lending "sizable sums" to the treasury (p. 158).

[47] Sapori, *La crisi*, p. 174.

of the creditors of the Acciaiuoli firm (50 percent), which was not involved in any lending to Edward III.[48]

Finally, there is little evidence to support the scale and scope of suffering that should have taken place in the Florentine business community if purported English losses had been incurred. The Bardi and Peruzzi remained among the wealthiest families in Florence in the 1350s. The other old families continued to be rich and powerful after the crash, and the new families that rose to prominence in the 1340s seem to have been untouched.[49] Specific evidence found in the accounts of one of the larger surviving firms, the Alberti, shows an unrecovered claim against the Bardi of approximately 1,000 florins, a serious but not overwhelming loss for a company with a capital of over 17,000 florins.[50]

The evidence I have presented leads to three conclusions. The first is that although the Bardi and Peruzzi were large, diversified, sophisticated organizations, they were not so large as to be able to cope with more than a fraction of the lending attributed to them by historians. The second is that the only source of significant funds on which the companies could have drawn for lending to the king was a Florentine business community which faced many other demands on its limited resources. The third is that there were many means by which the companies could recover or recycle at least part of their investments without the results necessarily appearing in any government ledgers. These conclusions do not dispute the notion that the companies suffered important losses in their dealings with the English king. Taken together, however, they indicate a much lower level of English lending than generally believed, and reinforce the intuitive contention of Fryde and Sapori that the collapse of the companies was due primarily to the political and economic convulsions in Florence.

In short, the traditional views about the extent of the Bardi and Peruzzi losses, and Edward's share in them, are not sustainable under close scrutiny. The image of a wily English king outwitting and callously disposing of greedy Italian bankers once they could no longer be of use to him may be an attractive piece of historical drama, but is far from historical fact. The reality is much more in keeping with what one would expect from a chivalric warrior-prince—a man with little talent for attracting, at reasonable cost, the vast sums of money needed to carry out his ambitious political ventures. Historians have tended to follow Ephraim Russell's lead in characterizing Edward's commission audits of the companies in the early 1340s as contrived, and his successive scaling-down of his acknowledged debt to them as flagrantly dishonest.

48 Ibid., p. 193.

49 G. Brucker, *Florentine Politics and Society* (Princeton, 1962), p. 18.

50 De Roover, "The Story of the Alberti Company," p. 29.

It is interesting to observe that in the final review of Edward's debt to the Bardi in 1348 the amount was set at a little over £13,000.[51] This figure is seen by Russell as derisory, but does not look unrealistic in the light of the actual losses reported by creditors and shareholders in Florence and the lack of evidence of significant losses elsewhere. From this it would seem that the warrior-king may have given a reasonably accurate acknowledgement of a just debt even though he never got around to paying it.

[51] Russell, "The Societies of the Bardi and Peruzzi," p. 127.

The Effect of the Bubble Act on the Market for Joint Stock Shares

MARGARET PATTERSON AND DAVID REIFFEN

In 1720 the Bubble Act was passed in the English Parliament.[1] There is a commonly held view that the Bubble Act was passed either as a result of the collapse of the bull market (the bursting of the speculative "bubble"), or as a result of the abuses to investors caused by the speculative frenzy.[2] While these explanations have surface plausibility, they are inconsistent with the actual timing of the Act. The Act was passed June 11, 1720; the "bubble" burst in September of that year. Indeed, the act may have played a role in causing the market collapse.[3]

If the Act was not intended to remedy excesses which led to a crash, why was it passed? We believe passage of the Bubble Act was a consequence of changes in the business environment during the early eighteenth century. As non-corporations began to assume many of the rights previously enjoyed only by chartered corporations, the ability of governmental authorities to raise revenue through the issuance of charters diminished. The Bubble Act was specifically intended to prevent non-chartered firms from using the formal market, and it succeeded in doing this.

The explanation also accounts for the observation of Philip Mirowski regarding activity in the market for joint-stock shares.[4] Mirowski finds that well-organized capital markets were already in existence at the outset of the eighteenth century, as were their institutional structures, including property transfer rules, widely dispersed price information, and professional arbitrageurs. Activity on these markets appears to have declined throughout the century. Some existing firms ceased using the formal share market, and the shares of few, if any, firms commenced trading there.

Mirowski uses his findings to cast doubt upon what he considers a central contention in neoclassical economic history, usefully expressed as follows. A market mechanism is the most efficient way of allocating resources and processing information. Hence, in the absence of legal constraints that prevent their use, markets must inevitably arise. According to Mirowski, imperfections and rigidities were being removed during the eighteenth century in England, and using the neoclassical paradigm, we would expect to see an increased use of the market mechanism for raising capital and exchanging shares in joint-stock companies. This leads him to conclude that the first premise of the

The Journal of Economic History, Vol. L, No. 1 (Mar. 1990). ISSN 0022-0507.

Margaret Patterson is a graduate student in the Department of Economics at University of California, Los Angeles, CA 90024. David Reiffen is an economist at Capital Economics, 1730 Pennsylvania Avenue, NW, Washington, D. C. 20006. The authors would like to thank David Glasner and Randy Kroszner for their insightful commentary.

[1] It was, more precisely, "An Act to Restrain the Extravagant and Unwarrantable Practice of Raising Money by Voluntary Subscription for Carrying on Projects Dangerous to the Trade and Subjects of the Kingdom." A. B. DuBois, *The English Business Company After the Bubble Act, 1720–1800* (New York, 1938), p. 2.

[2] See Christine E. Amsler, Robin L. Bartlett, and Craig J. Bolton, "Thoughts of some British economists on early limited liability and corporate legislation," *History of Political Economy*, 13 (Winter 1981), p. 776; Burton G. Malkiel, *A Random Walk Down Wall Street* (1st edn., 1973; 4th edn., New York, 1985), p. 37; H. A. Shannon, "The Coming of General Limited Liability," *Economic History*, 2 (Jan. 1931), p. 268.

[3] Henry N. Butler, "General Incorporation in Nineteenth Century England: Interaction of Common Law and Legislative Processes," *International Review of Law and Economics*, 6 (Dec. 1986), p. 172. Also see fn. 39 below.

[4] Philip Mirowski, "The Rise (and Retreat) of a Market: English Joint Stock Shares in the Eighteenth Century," this JOURNAL, 41 (Sept. 1981), pp. 559–77.

neoclassical contention must be invalid, or as Mirowski puts it, "The metaphor of the Rise of the Market is flawed."[5]

The premise of this note suggests that Mirowski subjects the metaphor of the "Rise of the Market" to an improper test. The second leg of the argument is factually incorrect: the very intention of the Bubble Act was to deny market access to unchartered firms.[6] It is these new constraints, and not necessarily any defect in the market mechanism, that most likely accounts for Mirowski's empirical observation.

CORPORATE STATUS IN THE LATE SEVENTEENTH AND EARLY EIGHTEENTH CENTURY

To understand the consequences of the Bubble Act, it is necessary to consider the nature of the seventeenth-century corporation. Incorporation was not freely available during the period, but rather was granted by Parliament or the Crown on a case-by-case basis. Typically, a quid pro quo was extracted for a royal charter or Parliamentary Act of Incorporation.[7] Successful petitioners had usually offered a direct profit interest or loans on favorable terms, or had assumed responsibility for government debt by persuading holders of this debt to surrender it in exchange for shares of the newly created corporation.[8]

Raising revenue through the granting of incorporation has a long history. From Elizabethan times through to the English civil war in the 1640s, the granting of charters was closely tied to Crown financing needs and foreign policy. By the early eighteenth century, however, the motives for granting corporate charters became distinctly more private than public. Members of both the House of Lords and the House of Commons profited considerably from bribes, gifts, and purchases of stock in the South Sea Company.[9] Outright bribery for legislative favors was apparently the "custom of the times."[10]

The greater the profitability of corporations, the more Parliament could charge for corporate status. Prior to 1623, Parliament could ensure the profitability of corporations by granting legal monopolies to corporations in specific industries.[11] This was altered, however, in 1623 by the Statute of Monopolies, under which "it was enacted that all monopolies, however granted, should be absolutely void."[12] Nonetheless,

[5] Ibid., p. 577.

[6] While Mirowski acknowledges that the decline in the market coincides with the duration of the Bubble Act, he contends that the Act was not responsible for it. He supports this view by citing the lack of enforcement of the Act and concludes, "One cannot have it both ways: an ineffectual Bubble Act cannot sabotage a dynamically expanding market." Ibid.

[7] For Acts of Parliament, see William Holdsworth, *A History of English Law* (New York, 1922–1926), vol. 8, pp. 211, 212, 218; and for royal charters, see ibid., p. 209.

[8] Examples of direct payments to the Crown and Parliament abound in W. R. Scott's *The Constitution and Finance of English, Scottish, and Irish Joint Stock Companies to 1720* (Cambridge, 1912), see vol. 1, pp. 242, 324, 366, 408; vol. 2, pp. 156–57; vol. 3, p. 315. In addition to initial payments and specified royalties, both Parliament and the Crown extracted loans from corporations (ibid., vol. 1, p. 237). The government also borrowed heavily during the protectorate (ibid., vol. 1, p. 258). Other examples of payments for charters are cited in Butler "General Incorporation in Nineteenth Century England," p. 171; and Holdsworth, *A History of English Law*, pp. 208–9.

[9] Scott, *Constitution and Finance of . . . Joint Stock Companies*, vol. 3, p. 332; see also fn. 7.

[10] Scott, *Constitution and Finance of . . . Joint Stock Companies*, vol. 3, p. 344.

[11] More generally, as discussed below, the grantor of corporate status could be the Crown or Parliament. At the loss of some accuracy but to avoid cumbersome language, we use the term Parliament to signify the grantor of corporate status.

[12] The exception to this was "Letters Patent and grants of privileges for terms not exceeding fourteen years, for the working or making of new manufactures within the realm, in favor of the true and first inventors thereof" (Edward Jenks, *A Short History of English Law* [Boston, 1913],

Parliament did endeavor to increase the value of chartered corporations through other means.

Many, if not most, of the firms receiving corporate charters in the seventeenth century were engaged in either trade and exploration or certain sorts of domestic construction.[13] The primary motivation for these firms in obtaining corporate status was different from that of modern corporations. Specific charters were required for exploration companies—those firms raising money and putting together ships and armaments for exploration of, and trading with, foreign countries. Similarly, firms establishing toll roads, water-supply systems, and other domestic activities required a corporate charter—because payment for these services was seen as a form of taxation—and hence had to be explicitly recognized by charter.

By restricting corporate status to relatively few firms and preventing competition between the firms, Parliament could increase the value of charters. The rights of early corporations were far more circumscribed than those of modern corporations. The initial act creating the corporation might specify the activities of the firm, its maximum capitalization, and even the lifespan of the charter.[14] By imposing these restrictions, Parliament in effect assigned rights to corporate status in different endeavors.

The choice of a limited life span for corporate charters is somewhat curious in that Parliament created an instrument with built-in obsolescence, rather than a perpetual charter at a correspondingly higher price. One explanation for the limited life span is that it complemented Parliament's allocation of rights by enabling Parliament to define more completely rights to corporate status in various industries as new opportunities became apparent. For example, if a charter were truly perpetual and a trade route became newly profitable, the question would arise whether this route was included in the original charter of some existing corporation. The costs of devising a charter with provisions to cover all such eventualities seem significant. Short-term charters were one solution; they enabled Parliament to define property rights to corporate status in new routes.[15]

---

p. 129). That is, the Act specifically made exceptions of new patents and nondomestic commerce. In both cases the exceptions encouraged innovation—either technological or geographical—but did not create monopolies in otherwise competitive industries.

[13] In *Selected Charters of Trading Companies* (London, 1913), Cecil Carr details 22 nonmonopoly charters granted between 1660 and 1707 (and 19 charters granted before 1660). Of the 22, 6 were trading companies, and 1 was involved in a domestic activity requiring a charter. Most of the remainder involved either new technology or mining. Carr notes that his study of 41 charters "omits many interesting charters that have already been printed" (p. i). These include the East India Company, some of the Levant charters, and many of the American plantation charters. It appears that most of the omitted charters involved overseas trade.

[14] DuBois, *The English Business Company*, p. 91, notes that 21 years was a common fixed life span for corporate charters. In *Selected Charters*, Carr states that "there are exceptions to the rule that a corporation is 'immortal' . . . there were cases where exclusive powers were conceded of such an unusual or experimental nature as to require periodic revision . . . where it was felt necessary to keep a tight hand over the company, charters which imposed no time limit often contained provisions for termination upon warning from the Crown" (p. 15).

[15] Another explanation for short-term charters relates to Parliament's ability to commit to a long-term charter. That is, once a payment is made for a charter that is thought to be exclusive, Parliament could turn around and issue additional charters to competing firms, at some lower price. This means that unless Parliament could credibly commit itself to limiting the number of charters, a rational petitioner would not pay a price reflecting the perpetual right to, for example, a particular trade route. It seems unlikely that Parliament, being an elected body, would be in a position to make such a commitment. For example, following the Glorious Revolution of 1688 Parliament ignored the charter of the East India Company and auctioned the rights to a monopoly of trade with East India to anyone who was willing to subscribe to a loan of £2,000,000 to the state; see Scott,

Limiting the number of charters also benefited existing corporations by reducing competition in capital markets. Partnerships were at an inherent disadvantage in using formal capital markets.

Under the partnership form a partner may at any time threaten to dissolve the firm, liquidate its assets, and claim his proportionate share of the proceeds. If the firm is capital-intensive, it may be costly to reestablish the firm and as a result the threat may be significant. Hence partnerships were less likely to be capital-intensive than firms adopting the corporate form. Unlike a partner, an equity owner of a corporation has no right to dissolve the business, and hence cannot extract a payment in excess of his proportional share from other equity owners. Partnerships were therefore unlikely to compete with corporations in loanable funds markets. Eliminating competition for loanable funds in formal capital markets permitted corporations to secure funds on more favorable terms than if all firms had unrestricted access to capital markets.

Thus through various restrictions Parliament was able to maintain corporate profitability and its own revenue. To the extent that the Crown and Parliament had similar powers to grant corporate status, they might have competed away the government's share of the rents associated with the granting of corporate status, but it appears that competition between the Crown and Parliament was minimized by specifying the areas in which each was the preeminent grantor. Parliament could grant charters with broader powers. It was recognized at least as early as 1610 that the king could neither give nor take away powers from a corporation that he could not give or take away from a natural man.[16] An Act of Parliament "can of course do anything; so that it can give a corporation powers which, without such a sanction, would infringe the principles of common law, or it can vary its powers."[17] Frequently Parliament would pass an act to "amplify the royal prerogative by . . . confer[ring] a charter of incorporation with privileges beyond those which the Crown could confer."[18] For example, the South Sea Company was formed by a charter preceded by a Parliamentary statute.[19] Included among the rights that only Parliament could confer was the right to limited liability.

On the other hand, prior to the Glorious Revolution of 1688 the Crown retained sole power to grant charters to firms involved in foreign trade. After 1688 Parliament became increasingly influential in the administration and regulation of foreign trade.[20] Parliament had by that time already achieved a position of influence in the administering of monopoly privileges in domestic trade.[21] Throughout the eighteenth century Parliament was the dominant provider of corporate status to business projectors, although until the latter part of the century it was common for Parliament to exercise this power by recommending to the Crown that a charter be granted. Between 1770 and 1800

The Constitution and Finance of . . . Joint Stock Companies, vol. 1, p. 324. Even the Crown could not make such a commitment, as it was not uncommon for one monarch to revise or ignore the promises made in a charter by a predecessor. Indeed, when faced with changed circumstances a monarch might reverse him- or herself. The experiences of the Civil War, the Protectorate, the Restoration, and the Glorious Revolution no doubt convinced companies that promises made in corporate charters were only as durable as the regimes that created them; see ibid., pp. 238, 247, 321–24; vol. 2, pp. 112–14. See also Ronald Coase, "Durability and Monopoly," *Journal of Law and Economics*, 15 (Apr. 1972), pp. 143–49; and J. I. Bulow, "An Economic Theory of Planned Obsolescence," *Quarterly Journal of Economics*, 10 (Nov. 1986), pp. 729–49, for analyses of the issue of the credibility of the commitment in the context of a durable-good monopolist.

[16] Holdsworth, *A History of English Law*, vol. 9, p. 55.

[17] Ibid., p. 48.

[18] L. C. B. Gower, *Principles of Modern Company Law* (London, 1979), p. 22.

[19] Ibid., p. 28, fn. 28.

[20] Butler, "General Incorporation in Nineteenth Century England," p. 171.

[21] Ibid.

applications to the Crown for charters of incorporation for business organizations were relatively infrequent and most corporations were created solely by acts of Parliament.[22] Over time Parliament became the prime source of corporate status.

The system by which corporate charters were granted increased the likelihood of corporate profits and made these charters valuable. Further, by limiting competition between Parliament and the Crown, the grantor of corporate status could extract a large share of the expected profitability of the corporation.

AN ALTERNATIVE INTERPRETATION OF THE GENESIS OF THE BUBBLE ACT

Against this institutional background, events that would curtail Parliament's ability to extract a share of corporate profitability began to unfold. In 1719 the South Sea Company, a chartered corporation, received an Act of Parliament amending its charter of 1711 to authorize an increase in its capital. The "aggressive marketing scheme" it pursued triggered a bull market, which benefited not only its own new issue of shares, but those of other incorporated and unincorporated joint-stock companies as well.[23] Some of the unincorporated companies were in the process of seeking corporate charters; some merely claimed to be seeking charters, and some were organized for the purely fraudulent purpose of cashing in on the bull market.[24] To the extent that investors did not distinguish between the shares of these companies and those of legitimate corporations, Parliament's ability to raise revenue through the issuance of corporate charters was undermined.

In the light of modern analysis that emphasizes the importance of limited liability for the operation of a formal, impersonal share market, it is perhaps surprising that the shares of unlimited liability firms were traded on such a market.[25] One reason they could be traded impersonally was that these companies were primarily (if not exclusively) equity-financed, so liability for the firm's debts was not an important issue.

Although records exist of the outstanding bonds of many corporations, these instruments bear little relationship to today's corporate debt. Generally, the bonds were short-term, nontransferable obligations, and certainly not used to finance capital

[22] DuBois, *The English Business Company*, p. 34.

[23] Butler, "General Incorporation in Nineteenth Century England," p. 171. DuBois, *The English Business Company*, p. 2, claims that in fact unincorporated joint-stock companies entering the bull market were more numerous than either incorporated companies or companies seeking corporate status. That unincorporated joint-stock companies found it to their liking to raise new issues in this bull market bears emphasis, as investors in such companies were subject to unlimited liability for the debts of their companies. C. A. Cooke, *Corporation, Trust and Company* (Cambridge, MA, 1951), notes that in the wake of the stock manipulations by the Board of the South Sea Company, "it seemed suddenly to become a widely held belief that to subscribe to a capital fund was to become rich. The belief was based more on the upward movement of the stock markets than on any thoughts of probable earning powers. When merely to hold shares was to become richer, money was available for any sort of scheme" (p. 18). The problems associated with the threat of dissolution inherent in partnership was apparently mitigated by the rise of the trustee device, under which ownership rights to the property of the partnership were vested in trustees.

[24] Some of the purposes for which capital funds were raised at that time were "to make salt water fresh," "for fatting of hogs," "for a wheel of perpetual motion," "for importing Jackasses from Spain," and "for an undertaking which shall in due time be revealed." Cooke, *Corporation, Trust*, p. 81.

[25] Limited liability could be acquired only by Special Act of Parliament, and hence not all corporations had limited liability. It was only later in the eighteenth century that legal opinions evolved to the point where corporations possessed limited liability unless Parliament specified unlimited liability.

investments.[26] Total outstanding debt was generally small compared to available callable equity financing, and hence default risk was low.[27] If default risk is minimal, then the identity of other shareholders is not an important investment consideration, and unlimited liability will not prevent unrestricted alienability. To the extent that there was some risk of default, unlimited liability companies may have offered a higher rate of return to equity holders than limited liability companies.[28]

During the late seventeenth and early eighteenth centuries a trade in "used" corporate charters began, apparently fostered by the idea that the activities of an incorporated society were limited neither by the terms of its charter, nor by the purposes for which the charter had been originally granted.[29] Business interests that chose not to seek a charter of their own, because they either feared they would not get one or did not want to spend the time and resources required to petition for one, bought up shares of moribund corporations, thereby obtaining a charter.[30] Parliament lost wealth that it might otherwise have captured because parties that could have successfully petitioned for corporate status chose instead to obtain used charters. Since Parliament had not anticipated a used-charter market, it had not extracted a payment for the "salvage value" of a charter when the charter was originally granted. Thus the sale of used charters both reduced the wealth Parliament derived from new charter sales and represented a wealth transfer from purchasers to sellers of used charters in which Parliament did not share.

The same belief that gave rise to the charter resale market—the belief that a corporation's activities were not constrained by the activities enumerated in the charter or enabling Act—had also encouraged many original recipients of corporate charters to engage in profitable enterprises not named in their charters. When a corporate charter was used more broadly than Parliament had expected when granting the charter, profits were earned from which Parliament was not able to extract a share.

The direct effect of the resale market was a one-time loss to Parliament. Several

[26] Scott, *The Constitution and Finance of . . . Joint Stock Companies*, vol. 1, p. 304. The government would be unlikely to permit the widespread issuance of debt instruments that could compete with their own bonds.

[27] Scott (ibid., pp. 305, 381, 477) notes the dearth of failures due to problems with debt financing. Usury laws offered one important constraint on the use of debt financing. If the legal maximum interest rate was below the risk-adjusted rate for a specific firm, it would be difficult to write contracts that did not violate the usury laws, yet were sophisticated enough to guarantee the right risk-adjusted rate. Not surprisingly, the development of debenture bonds for the financing of fixed capital has been traced to the quarter century after the 1855 introduction of general limited liability and the 1854 repeal of usury laws. See James B. Jeffrey, *Business Organization in Great Britain, 1856–1914* (New York, 1977), pp. 241, 251–52.

[28] During the seventeenth century the extent to which liability was truly limited for an incorporated, profit-making venture was at best uncertain. Shareholders typically invested in corporations "on subscription," with initial payments equal to as little as 1 percent of the nominal value of a share. Their subscription purchase obligated them to provide the balance upon the corporation's call and thus could be attached by creditors of the firm. This meant that the identity of other shareholders was important even for limited liability companies. While it seems curious that companies did not simply limit their liability by setting nominal value equal to their initial payment, such a strategy could be costly. If the company subsequently decided to increase capitalization, a new charter would be required. Hence the distinction between limited and unlimited liability in the seventeenth century was not the crisp one associated with modern companies.

[29] Holdsworth, *A History of English Law*, vol. 8, p. 215.

[30] Ibid. Holdsworth documents a variety of corporate charters appropriated in this manner: the York Buildings Company abandoned the business for which it had received a charter in 1691 and in 1719 began a different business; the charter of a company formed in 1691 was sold at least twice in the resale market; a mining company charter was sold to an insurance company.

indirect effects also reduced Parliament's ability to extract some of the profits from chartered corporations. That is, even after all current charters expired (abstracting from the fact that some charters were perpetual), Parliament would still not be able to raise as much revenue from the issuance of charters, in part because Parliament could no longer promise a petitioner exclusivity. Corporations would tend to compete against one another in profitable industries, so for any given number of charters the profitability of all corporations would be lowered. Moreover, Parliament could no longer price discriminate when awarding charters because the charter awarded in a relatively low-profit industry at a price reflecting that low profitability might be sold to a firm in some other industry.

These two events—a bull market that did not distinguish between corporate and noncorporate shares, and the rise of a resale market in corporate charters—reduced Parliament's ability to raise revenue through the issuance of charters. Wealth that Parliament or corporate companies would otherwise have captured was taken instead by unincorporated companies, by incorporated companies offering new issues not explicitly authorized in their charters, and by participants in the used-charter market. As a result, corporations seeking equity financing consistent with their charters wished to deny other entities access to formal capital markets in order to concentrate all buying interest, some of which was due to "bull-market hysteria," on their shares. At the same time Parliament wished to regain control of the uses made of corporate charters. The Bubble Act was a means to accomplish both objectives: excluding interlopers from formal capital markets and curtailing the use and resale of existing corporate charters.

The two objectives are evident in the wording of the Act, which begins by repeating a resolution the House of Commons had issued shortly before the passage of the Act. That resolution stated in part, "That for some time past several large subscriptions have been made by great numbers of persons *in the city of London* to carry on public undertakings" (emphasis added).[31]

Under the Act, organizations that "presumed to act as a corporation" were considered to be public nuisances, and were made unlawful.[32] The Act condemned as illegal

> subscriptions, assignments, transfers and other things for furthering such undertakings; the acting or presuming to act as a corporate body; *the raising of a transferable stock, or the assigning of such stock without authority* either by Act of Parliament or charter; *acting under any charter formerly granted by the crown for purposes other than those expressed in the charter*. It was provided that these acts should be deemed to be public nuisances, that the persons guilty thereof should incur the penalties provided by the statute of Praemunire, that merchants injured by them could sue for treble damages, *and that brokers dealing in the shares of such undertakings should be liable to a penalty of £500* (emphasis added).[33]

The italicized sections support our contention that the Act was designed to deny unincorporated companies access to formal capital markets (located in the City of London) and to tighten the Parliamentary control over the exercise of corporate privileges.

In one important provision the Act prohibited unrestricted or "free" transferability of shares. By free transferability, we refer to the right of equity owners to sell their interest to any prospective purchaser. Free transferability increases the liquidity of owning equity and, other things equal, increases the value of shares. If a firm's shares were not freely transferable, informal transfers within a firm would be possible, but these would require the approval of the other owners of the firm. While informal transfers did allow an individual owner to liquidate all or a portion of his interest without liquidating the

[31] Ibid., p. 220.
[32] DuBois, *The English Business Company*, p. 3.
[33] Holdsworth, *A History of English Law*, vol. 8, p. 220.

firm, prohibition of free transferability effectively eliminated a firm from the formal capital market.

Historical evidence indicates that the Bubble Act did not seek to discourage use of large partnerships with transferable (but not freely transferable) shares. For example, during the 1750s and 1760s it became quite common for the Crown, in declining petitions for incorporation, to suggest to petitioners that the same enterprise be carried out as a partnership.[34] A. B. DuBois has noted that

> It is perhaps going too far to say that the use of a transferable share was a time-honoured way of running a partnership. On the other hand, some partnerships were so operated, and if the more or less exceptional situation be included in a general statement, one can expect the exception to dominate in the norm. In any event, in the period (1750–1800) there was a nebulous haze over exactly what the Crown officers meant by their references to "partnership." The business man was obviously the last one who wanted to see this enigma resolved.[35]

Not surprisingly, when setting up unincorporated joint-stock companies business projectors of the time frequently sought the advice of counsel, since the Bubble Act "was a latent menace present in every board room . . . when problems of business organizations were deliberated."[36] Sergeant Thomas Pengelley, a leading commercial lawyer in London at the time, stressed repeatedly to clients that it was the creation of freely transferable shares, regardless of the method of share transfer, that was the dominating point in the prohibitions of the Act.[37]

That businessmen of the time were advised against the use of freely transferable shares is consistent with the enforcement record under the Act, despite the relative dearth of prosecutions. Immediately after its passage the Act was swiftly enforced against unincorporated companies that had come into existence after the deadline (June 24, 1718) established by the Bubble Act and that were operating in the new issues market.[38]

These cases were brought by serving writs of scire facias on unincorporated companies active on the new issues market. The writs ordered companies to produce corporate charters indicating that they were authorized to raise funds by selling transferable shares of stock. Being unincorporated, these firms obviously could not produce such charters, and as a result were forced out of business.[39] Considerable enforcement activities were also directed against firms that were operating under

[34] By this time it was understood that a charter or act of incorporation conveyed limited liability unless unlimited liability was explicitly stipulated; see ibid. and Dubois, *The English Business Company*, pp. 34, 236. Also, at p. 40, DuBois notes that at about this time, restraints in the articles of association of unincorporated joint-stock companies with regard to transfer of shares became less common. One interpretation of this is that the Crown recognized that large partnerships required increased alienability of shares to work effectively.

[35] DuBois, *The English Business Company*, p. 236. Although DuBois's work is limited to the period from 1720 to 1800, the conditions he described for the second half of the eighteenth century appear to have persisted until the repeal of the Bubble Act in 1825.

[36] Ibid., p. 11.

[37] Pengelley was consulted in relation to the Act's scope in connection with at least 27 organizations in the year immediately following the Act's passage. See ibid., p. 4.

[38] Even those undertakings established prior to June 24, 1718, were not safe from legal action; see Holdsworth, *A History of English Law*, vol. 3, p. 220. Corporations trading under obsolete charters, or those trading in a manner not allowed by their charters prior to that date, were still liable to legal proceedings under the common law. Indeed, in 1720 the South Seas Company instigated legal proceedings against some of those companies (ibid., p. 216).

[39] Cooke, *Corporation, Trust*, p. 83. Cooke notes that forcing certain firms out of business may have caused the collapse of the market which occurred subsequent to the Act's passage. As certain firms' stock became valueless, "in many cases . . . loans [were] raised on that stock. Other stocks came on the market to meet this indebtedness and a general wave of selling followed."

expired charters, or corporations that were overreaching the authority granted to them by Parliament.[40] This again supports our view that the Bubble Act was intended to ensure that only corporations operating within the scope of their charters had access to the formal share market.

CONCLUSION

The decline in the market for joint stock shares in eighteenth-century England can be traced to the enactment of the Bubble Act. The passage and enforcement of the Bubble Act were predictable consequences of the assumption by non-corporations of many of the rights associated exclusively with corporations. Parliament's ability to raise revenue by issuing charters was thereby impaired. The Bubble Act was calculated to, and in fact did, enhance the importance of charters. The enforcement record under the Act is consistent with an attempt to maintain Parliament's ability to extract a share of corporate profits.

[40] DuBois, *The English Business Company*, p. 4.

La Grande Quantification

L'économie française au XIXe siècle: Analyse macro-économique. By Maurice Lévy-Leboyer and François Bourguignon. Paris: Economica, 1985. Pp. 362. F 185.

For the quantitative historian of modern France the paucity of economic time series and cliometric analysis has always served as both a source of frustration and a spur to further research. Given the importance of France as the major continental economy in the early period of industrialization, it is all the more galling that detailed cliometric research of the sort available in abundance for Great Britain should be so lacking. It is therefore with much eagerness and gratitude that we examine this imposing work by Maurice Lévy-Leboyer and François Bourguignon, a macroeconomic analysis of nineteenth-century France based on the time-series data collected by Lévy-Leboyer.

If nothing else, the data collected by Lévy-Leboyer—the result of a lifetime's work—serve as a new benchmark for all future discussions of the French economy in the nineteenth century, to be placed alongside the pioneering efforts of Walther Hoffmann in Germany and Charles Feinstein and Brian Mitchell in Britain. The data appendix to this volume contains 67 annual series, most of which have not been available in print before. It contains annual series between 1820 and 1913 of GDP, agricultural and industrial output, investment, nominal and real wages, volumes of exports and imports, interest rates, price data, and much more.

The book at hand is more, however, than a retelling of nineteenth-century French history in the light of the newly available data. It is also an ambitious attempt to rethink and reevaluate the economy's evolution through the estimation of an elaborate macromodel of nineteenth-century France. Despite the authors' herculean efforts, the model and the conclusions drawn from it will give readers pause. Limitations in the available series are such that even with the abundance of material Lévy-Leboyer has given us, enormous constraints are imposed on the model that can be estimated from the series. Given the state of knowledge, such models go only so far toward settling the debates that have so exercised both traditional and quantitative historians.

The model is odd in two ways. First it is a declared macromodel, but it does not deal with the standard fare of macroeconomics, such as business cycles, price movements, balance-of-payments disequilibria, unemployment, or investment fluctuations. Instead, we find a long-term growth model with some short-run general equilibrium features. It is devoid of microfoundations, yet it is not a Keynesian macromodel because it has no unemployment or short-run national income determination. It seems difficult to explain long-term economic growth with a model of this type, because it contains nothing that relates output to inputs. There is no equation for the relation between capital stock and output; indeed there are no figures for the capital stock outside manufacturing and social overhead. Technological change is hardly mentioned, but is approximated, without so much as an apology, by patents. Nor is there a persuasive model for capital formation and savings.

The book consists of four parts: a historical analysis, which concentrates on aggregate demand more than on aggregate supply; an econometric analysis of the data, which presents the elasticities and relationships estimated between the variables; a set of simulations testing the importance of selected hypotheses concerning French economic

The Journal of Economic History, Vol. L, No. 1 (Mar. 1990). ISSN 0022-0507.

Joel Mokyr is Professor of Economics and History, Northwestern University, Evanston, IL 60201; John V. C. Nye is Assistant Professor of Economics, Washington University, St. Louis, MO 63130.

They are grateful to François Bourguignon for providing some of the material used to write this review and to Douglass North for comments and discussion. Of course the authors retain all responsibility for any errors in the essay.

development; and the data appendices. Insofar as the analysis consists of descriptions based on a straightforward perusal of the series there can be little dispute about what happened. For instance, as elsewhere in Europe, real wages show no sign of rising before the middle of the nineteenth century, and then rise more or less consistently from the mid-sixties until 1913.[1] The expansion of international trade accelerates after 1850 and remains brisk throughout the third quarter of the century. After a slowdown between 1875 and 1896, trade picks up again in the period from 1896 to 1913.

The econometric analysis of the findings for the long nineteenth century is carried out in three subperiods: early (1820 to 1859), middle (1860 to 1886), and late (1887 to 1913). This periodization dominates much of the analysis because a central finding of the book is that the economy behaved quite differently in the middle period than it did in the early and late periods. The authors argue that the middle period witnessed a slowing down in industrialization for two basic reasons: first, a rise in wages redistributed income to lower classes, thus increasing the demand for agricultural goods at the expense of manufactured goods; second, the opening up of the French economy to world markets reduced the competitiveness of the French economy. Many of the parameters estimated differ quite violently among the different periods. An extreme example is the elasticity of net nonagricultural investment with respect to its determinants. The elasticity with respect to interest is −0.97 for the first period, −4.04 in the second and −2.10 in the third. The elasticity with respect to wages is 0.68, 2.60 and −5.63 respectively (p. 182). All these elasticities are reported to be statistically significant, but what do they mean? Structural changes clearly explain part of the shifts, but the volatility of the parameters is indicative of deeper data and estimation difficulties.

The periodization will seem questionable to some. By choosing the midpoint of the Second Empire as the dividing line, the authors have rendered comparisons between the July Monarchy, the Second Empire, and the Third Republic hard to make. The authors justify choosing 1860 because it was the beginning of the era of free trade, but by their own assessment, trade restrictions and tariffs had only a minor effect on economic development. In fact, the data show that exports and imports grew twice as fast before 1860 than afterward; the Cobden-Chevalier treaty was the culmination, not the start, of the opening of the French economy. The trend in real wages is more difficult to discern, but an unambiguous rise does not start until the late 1860s. On the other hand, consumption per capita shows a steady growth rate averaging 1.2 percent per year, with a number of sharp but short-lived crises and a marked acceleration in the final quarter-century. Perhaps there is no natural way to use economic criteria to divide the long nineteenth century into subperiods. If so, it seems plausible to return to the political subperiods traditionally employed in the literature.

The Second Empire was bounded by two troughs, one in 1848 (going back to the Second Republic) and the other in 1871. An analysis of the data employing a different periodization from the one chosen by Lévy-Leboyer and Bourguignon shows clearly what the effects of the Empire were: it slowed down the rate of growth of industrial output (from 1.94 to 1.52 percent per year). At the same time it accelerated the rate of growth of GDP from 1.43 percent per year to 2.51 percent. The Third Republic reversed this once again. The annual rate of growth of industrial output under the Third Republic exceeded that of GDP growth (1.63 percent versus 1.23 percent respectively). This casts new light on the much-discussed policies of the Second Empire and the extent to which they redirected the economy toward agriculture, in which France apparently had a comparative advantage, an issue the econometric analysis in this book cannot address. By opening up the economy to foreign competition, industrialization was slowed down.

[1] This pattern of changing real wages seems to hold for a number of other countries as well. See Joel Mokyr, "Dear Labor, Cheap Labor, and the Industrial Revolution," in Patrice Higonnet and Henry Rosovsky, eds., *Economic Growth: Constraints and Responses* (forthcoming).

That, however, does not mean that these policies did not have a positive effect on technological progress and what we generally refer to as "modernization." What macromodels such as this one cannot discern is the positive effects of trade liberalization in forcing the adoption of efficient techniques and in weakening what Mancur Olson has called the "distributional coalitions" which would have been less open to technological progress.[2]

Furthermore, an analysis of the effects of trade liberalization does not ask whether growth in the period of free trade was higher than before. Rather, it tests whether, given existing trade conditions, lower tariffs and lowered trade barriers raised economic welfare over what it would have been in the absence of such measures. Finally, more open trade would have the—not easily observable—effect of eliminating industries in which France had no comparative advantage, thus increasing overall welfare and efficiency. It is probable that earlier protectionist policies unduly favored inefficient industries and biased total output composition in a manner unfavorable to the economy at large. Napoleon III's attempts to reform the economy most likely served to redress the balance by encouraging the segments of the economy where France stood to gain the most at the expense of more inefficient industries. This would be consistent with the observed slowing of industrial growth while GDP growth accelerated.

Thus, slow growth in the French textile industry after tariff reform, for example, does not need to be viewed as failure in any sense. Rather, it may be seen as evidence that protectionism in the earlier part of the century biased French development away from France's comparative advantage. The authors' claim that tariff reforms may have been unimportant because the tariffs prior to Napoleon III's liberalizations were not all that high misses the point of trade reforms. Protectionism before the 1860s mostly took the form of outright prohibitions and highly restrictive regulations, whereas trade reform meant the substitution of moderate tariffs for the varying prohibitions. Moreover, low average tariffs in the 1850s were partly the result of small but significant reforms begun before the advent of the Cobden-Chevalier treaty, for which Napoleon III's government should also receive credit.[3]

The question the book poses is why there was a lull in growth between 1860 and 1886. The authors' answer appears in two parts. One is that the middle period saw rising real wages which expanded demand for agricultural goods that in turn became a retardative factor. The other is that France lost its competitive position in world trade as a consequence of supply-side failures. Once again, the problem may be a result of the periodization. The periods chosen for the comparison affect such matters as the estimated value of the elasticity of world demand for French products—the most important determinant of the authors' notion of *competitivité*. Given the change in regime brought about by widespread trade liberalization in Western Europe, it is not surprising that measured demand elasticities should be higher in the period of free trade than before or after. Perhaps more interesting to find out is whether demand for French products was already changing prior to trade reform. This hypothesis needs further investigation.

The authors argue that growing demand for agricultural goods after 1860 hindered development. They do not discuss the role of agriculture in nineteenth-century French economic growth at great length, but the simulations and the data shed some light on this area. The simulations show that agriculture contributed a 1 percent growth rate of GDP

[2] Mancur Olson, *The Rise and Decline of Nations* (New Haven, 1982).

[3] It is worth noting, however, that the average level of French tariffs was rather low throughout the nineteenth century, particularly in comparison to Great Britain. Even so, there was a substantial drop in this level throughout the 1850s and 1860s. The issue of relative tariff levels is taken up in John V. C. Nye, "The Myth of Free-Trade Britain and Protectionist France: Tariffs and Trade in the Nineteenth Century," manuscript, Washington University, 1989.

before 1860, which is two-thirds of total GDP growth (p. 219). For the late period, this contribution is much reduced; unfortunately no estimate is provided for the middle period. Nonetheless some indication is given by the terms of trade between agriculture and industry, which rise gradually after 1848. As France was on balance an importer of agricultural goods (p. 45), its international terms of trade worsened steadily from 1850 to 1880. It is not easy, however, to distinguish between the hypotheses that this price change was caused by a rise in domestic demand, a decline in supply, or events in the world economy into which France was increasingly integrated. Since the terms of trade between agriculture and manufacturing in Britain moved roughly in the same direction, it seems worth considering whether the terms of trade were not largely determined by worldwide conditions. In an open economy, concepts like the "contribution" of agriculture to growth become nebulous.

Medium-term growth models should try to disentangle demand from supply factors. In doing so, the authors seem to adhere to two separate hypotheses. One asserts that the level of final demand (measured by consumption) was insufficient in some periods. Slow population growth and apparent difficulties in penetrating foreign markets limited aggregate demand. The other holds that the level of saving and investment constituted a binding constraint on growth. The two models imply very different mechanisms: the first must specify scale economies or learning-by-doing effects, while the latter is the more conventional view implicit in standard growth models. By advocating both views to some extent, the authors can make any change in the structure of aggregate demand consistent with slow growth. The absence of a clear-cut growth model makes it difficult to interpret the authors' findings concerning the causes of faster and slower growth. A similar problem attaches to the modeling of factor markets: data constraints dictated that no explicit modeling of the labor market could be incorporated despite the authors' explicit reference to dual labor market models in the tradition of W. A. Lewis. On the other hand, the capital market is explicitly modeled, with interest rates set in money markets, and in turn determining long-term investment. This uneven treatment of factor markets makes it difficult to analyze their role in the long run.

One of the most important findings of the simulation exercise is that capital exports in the period from 1887 to 1913 did in fact impose a serious cost on the French economy. The simulations indicate that a halving of capital exports would have increased output and consumption and increased nonagricultural investment by 36 percent. A similar debate has been raging for years now about the effects of British foreign investment, and some of the arguments used in that debate will doubtlessly resurface here. The absence of a production function makes it impossible to assess the counterfactual because the redirection of capital from foreign to domestic investors would have depressed domestic rates of return to some unknown degree. Moreover, the idea that investing at home is better than abroad only makes sense if investment is necessary to introduce new technologies, or if the economy is suffering from Keynesian unemployment. Unfortunately, the relation between capital formation and technological change is more easily asserted than measured, and Lévy-Leboyer and Bourguignon wisely do not attempt it. No evidence is presented to support the existence of underemployed resources that would have been activated by higher investment. For the time being, therefore, the question must still be regarded as open.

It seems to us that the data appendices will prove in the long term to be the most widely consulted and cited part of this book and it is refreshing to come across a quantitative work which makes its data so readily available to all readers. There are some difficulties, however, with using the data to evaluate the regressions that form the core of the analysis. For one thing, some of the series necessary to replicate many of the calculations are not listed in the appendix (such as disaggregated export volume). Furthermore, there is some uncertainty regarding the data series themselves. One of the authors of this review obtained a diskette from F. Bourguignon containing the data series apparently used to produce the regressions. Although these include numerous series not available in the book, some lacunae are still evident. More puzzling are the slight discrepancies in these series relative to the same series contained in the back of the book. Undoubtedly, some of these problems stem from various disaggregations made in the course of writing the book. Since the discrepancies we have found are small, there should not be major changes in the book's results, but we would all benefit from a revised version of the work that presented the statistical appendix in a manner permitting easy replication of the econometrics and a more clear-cut discussion of the data.

Economic historians—particularly in the English-speaking world—have witnessed in the past decade a revision of the customary interpretation of French economic growth in the nineteenth century, exemplified by Patrick O'Brien and Caglar Keyder's well-known *Economic Growth in Britain and France*.[4] The "new view" of French industrialization challenges the argument that the French experience was in any sense inferior to that of Britain and maintains that France's path to the twentieth century was simply different, not worse. This revisionism has not gone unchallenged, and the issue of "French backwardness" is still a lively issue in the periodical literature and in classrooms today. Lévy-Leboyer and Bourguignon's book does not address the issue directly; indeed, it hardly refers to this literature. Their verdict on the French performance is certainly far from smug, the period between 1860 and 1886 coming in for serious criticism in terms of its economic achievements. The authors accept many of the more traditional explanations for what they perceive as the slowdown in growth after the middle of the nineteenth century: entrepreneurial failure, a proclivity for family enterprise, a bias toward public employment, risk aversion, and a domination of small workshops (p. 8).[5] These explanations clearly place the authors in the Landes-Kindleberger camp and, given the impressive quantitative arsenal at their disposal, they might have produced results that would give the revisionists cause to rethink their position. Nonetheless, because they do not address the issues of comparative economic performance directly and accept the traditional explanations so automatically, with neither testing nor economic modeling, the work as it stands will have only limited impact on the debate. To be sure, Lévy-Leboyer and Bourguignon take a more sophisticated view in that they allow for the possibility that some of the supposed causes for the slowdown in growth were in part consequences of the low productivity growth, but they treat none of these issues directly in their econometrics. Still, enough questions remain that only a more thorough analysis will be sufficient to settle these debates in a manner convincing to bystanders committed to neither the traditional nor the revisionist position.

JOEL MOKYR, *Northwestern University*
JOHN V. C. NYE, *Washington University*

[4] The various pieces in the revisionist and anti-revisionist tradition are too numerous to mention by now, but important references relevant to the debate can be found in the following: Patrick O'Brien and Caglar Keyder, *Economic Growth in Britain and France 1780–1914* (London, 1978); Rondo Cameron and Charles E. Freedeman, "French Economic Growth: A Radical Revision," *Social Science History*, 7 (Winter 1983), pp. 3–30; N. F. R. Crafts, "Economic Growth in France and Britain, 1830–1910: A Review of the Evidence," this JOURNAL, 44 (Mar. 1984), pp. 49–67; Richard Roehl, "French Industrialization: A Reconsideration," *Explorations in Economic History*, 13 (July 1976), pp. 233–81; Patrick O'Brien, "Do We Have a Typology for the Study of European Industrialization in the XIXth Century?" *The Journal of European Economic History*, 15 (Fall 1986), pp. 291–333.

[5] Several papers have appeared that question some of the specific arguments relating to the alleged French failure. These include John Vincent Nye, "Firm Size and Economic Backwardness: A New Look at the French Industrialization Debate," this JOURNAL, 47 (Sept. 1987), pp. 649–69; and several articles in Patrick Fridenson and André Straus, eds., *Le Capitalisme français 19e–20e siècle: Blocages et dynamismes d'une croissance* (Paris, 1987).

Editors' Notes

EDITORS' REPORT, SEPTEMBER 1989

A quietly busy year is the best way to sum up the first half of the current regime, with the home office at Rensselaer in the care of Margaret Mirabelli, and Tom Weiss and Donna Gullett's "American" operation in full swing at the University of Kansas. We happily acknowledge the institutional support both offices enjoy. We also thank our editorial assistants: Zhang Jing, Christina White, and Stuart McCook in Troy, and Joshua Rosenbloom in Lawrence.

The JOURNAL is in the end what the contributors make it, and they have continued to produce diligently. The visible efforts of successful authors and of reviewers can be judged by each of you as readers; authors and would-be authors receive the fruits of referees' unseen labors, but only editors can truly appreciate them. To all for their promptness and patience, thanks.

For a change, we are able to report summary statistics for both editorial operations, with the usual label warnings good economic historians apply to any numerical data. Submissions were little changed from last year: 48 + 68 = 116 regular submissions (non-American office figure first) plus 24 for the "Tasks" (June) issue. Last year's total was four fewer. In Troy, the 48 papers included 14 acceptances—a marked improvement over last year—21 rejections, and 13 pending or back for revision. In Lawrence, the disposition was as follows: 8 acceptances, 47 rejections, 7 back for revision, and 6 pending. Dare one suggest that new editors, like new assistant professors, impose tough standards? As before, 12 papers were selected for the Tasks issue. Book reviews continue to occupy a substantial place in the JOURNAL, and any significant increase or decrease in that share is likely to elicit more criticism than praise. Eager readers can compile the numbers of articles, notes, and reviews and their respective share of pages; we will gladly pass their findings on in future reports.

Few things concern authors more than long delays in refereeing and publication. Editors, of course, can only threaten tardy readers with more work, which is hardly the road to faster turnaround. Nor are we free of blame; the temptation to use LIFO methods of work management leads to a few victimized authors bearing the brunt of our derelictions. In all seriousness, we believe the JOURNAL performs honorably, and give credit—repetition is warranted—to our generally prompt as well as thoughtful outside experts. The Kansas office averaged 80 days (104 for accepted articles) from submission to decision. The range is 26 to 250 days. Of course that is an FOB measure; authors wait two mail intervals more. For Troy, the data on time to a response are best shown as a frequency distribution:

Time (months)	1	2	3	4	5	6	7	11+
Number	10	8	11	8	5	1	2	3

Clearly, the fastest decisions involve submissions or resubmissions that do not, for whatever reason, require new external readers. As for the total time a paper may remain in the pipeline, few journals stay with authors as long as this one does or encourage revision as frequently. Opinions may differ as to whether we are patient or picky.

We close with the distribution of submissions by field. The category "political economy" proves a useful catch-all for otherwise hard-to-classify papers. The drought in international economics and public finance continues; apparently, "read my lips" applies to studying as well as to levying taxes.

Field	Non-American	American	Tasks	Total
Agriculture	7	3	3	13
Population	1	1	4	6
Growth	1	3		4
Industrial	3	5	7	15
Technology	1	6	2	9
Labor	6	17	1	24
Money/Banking/Macro	15	9	1	25
Public Finance	1	1		2
Thought	2	3		5
International Trade and Finance	2	1		3
Urban and Regional	2	5		7
Political Economy	7	14	6	27
Total	48	68	24	140

In addition to members of the editorial board, we are greatly indebted to the following outside referees for their generous assistance during the year:

Donald Adams, University of West Virginia
Robert Allen, University of British Columbia
Lee Alston, University of Illinois
Ben Baack, Ohio State University
Fred Bateman, Indiana University
Kathleen A. Biddick, University of Notre Dame
Jack Blicksilver, Georgia State University
Michael Bordo, Rutgers University
George Borts, Brown University
Malcolm Burns, University of Kansas
Charles Calomiris, Northwestern University
Ann Carlos, University of Western Ontario
Susan Carter, Smith College
Gregory Clark, University of Michigan
Sally Clarke, University of Texas, Austin
John Coatsworth, University of Chicago
David Crew, University of Texas, Austin
Lance Davis, California Institute of Technology
Stephen DeCanio, University of California, Santa Barbara
Trevor Dick, University of Lethbridge
Matthew D. Edel, Queens College
Martin Eisenberg, Knox College
Bernard Elbaum, University of California, Santa Cruz
Stanley Engerman, University of Rochester
David Feeny, McMaster University
Stefano Fenoaltea, Princeton University
Louis Ferleger, University of Massachusetts, Boston
Price V. Fishback, University of Georgia
Dennis Flynn, University of the Pacific
Gerald Friedman, University of Massachusetts
Henry Gemery, Colby College
Richard T. Gill
Claudia Goldin, University of Pennsylvania
George Grantham, McGill University

H. Peter Gray, Rensselaer Polytechnic Institute
Alan Green, Queen's University
C. Knick Harley, University of Western Ontario
William Hausman, College of William and Mary
Carol Heim, University of Massachusetts, Amherst
Alan Heston, University of Pennsylvania
Philip Hoffman, California Institute of Technology
Glenn R. Hueckel, Purdue University
Kris Inwood, University of Guelph
Charles Issawi, Princeton University
Harold James, Princeton University
John James, University of Virginia
Peter Kilby, Wesleyan University
Charles Kindleberger, Massachusetts Institute of Technology
Ann Kussmaul, York University
Richard Langlois, University of Connecticut
William Lazonick, Bernard College
Wayne Lewchuk, McMaster University
Donald Lien, University of Kansas
Peter Lindert, University of California, Davis
Diane Lindstrom, University of Wisconsin
John S. Lyons, Miami University
James MacDonald, Rensselaer Polytechnic Institute
Mary MacKinnon, McGill University
Anthony Marino, University of Southern California
Roderick McDonald, Rider College
Robert McGuire, University of California, Davis
David Meyer, Brown University
Joel Mokyr, Northwestern University
Anthony Molho, Brown University
Douglass C. North, Washington University
Anthony P. O'Brien, Lehigh University
Kerry Odell, Scripps College
Avner Offer, York University (UK)
Lawrence H. Officer, University of Illinois, Chicago
Cormac Ó'Gráda, University College, Dublin
Martha Olney, University of Massachusetts, Amherst
Hugh T. Patrick, Columbia University
Dwight Perkins, Harvard University
Edwin Perkins, University of Southern California
Joseph Pratt, Texas A&M University
Daniel Raff, Harvard Business School
Roger L. Ransom, University of California, Riverside
Thomas Rawski, University of Pittsburgh
James C. Riley, Indiana University
David R. Ringrose, University of California, San Diego
Hugh Rockoff, Rutgers University
Richard Roehl, University of Michigan, Dearborn
Joshua L. Rosenbloom, University of Kansas
Henry Rosovsky, Harvard University
Elyce J. Rotella, Indiana University
Winifred Rothenberg, Tufts University
Kazuo Sato, Rutgers University

Anna J. Schwartz, National Bureau of Economic Research
Larry Schweikart, University of Dayton
Gene Smiley, Marquette University
Kenneth Sokoloff, University of California, Los Angeles
Barbara Solow, Harvard University
Martin C. Spechler, Indiana University-Purdue University
Robert C. Stacey, University of Washington
Stanley J. Stein, Princeton University
William Sundstrom, Santa Clara University
Richard Sylla, North Carolina State University
Mark Thomas, University of Virginia
Robert Tollison, George Mason University
Elias Tuma, University of California, Davis
Thomas S. Ulen, University of Illinois
Maris Vinovskis, University of Michigan
Donald Vitaliano, Rensselaer Polytechnic Institute
John J. Wallis, University of Maryland
Lori Warner
James L. A. Webb, Colby College
David Weiman, Yale University
Michael Weinstein, Haverford College
Warren Whatley, University of Michigan
David Wheelock, University of Texas, Austin
Peter Wiles, London School of Economics
Jeffrey G. Williamson, Harvard University
Dan Wildcat, Haskell Indian Junior College
Martin Wolfe, University of Pennsylvania
Gavin Wright, Stanford University

CONFERENCES

The Third Textile History Conference will be held on September 21–23, 1990, at the Holiday Inn in Tewksbury, MA. Persons interested in attending can obtain a registration form and a copy of the program by writing to Textile Bicentennial Conference, c/o Museum of American Textile History, 800 Massachusetts Avenue, North Andover, MA 01845; telephone (508) 686-0191.

The Design History Society of the United Kingdom is holding an International Design History Conference at the Victoria and Albert Museum, London, on December 7–9, 1990. The theme of the conference is industry and anti-industry; papers will focus on the effect of industry upon the populations it services. For further information, please contact Elizabeth Farrelly, V&A/RCA Course Rooms, Victoria and Albert Museum, South Kensington, London SW7 2RL, Great Britain.

NATIONAL INSTITUTE ON GENEALOGICAL RESEARCH

The National Institute of Genealogical Research will be held June 11–16, 1990, at the National Archives in Washington, DC. The Institute is a one-of-a-kind educational program for experienced genealogists, historians, librarians, and archivists. The program will focus on federal records of genealogical value located in the National Archives. The faculty includes professional genealogists and specialists from the Archives staff. Enrollment is limited. For more information or an application, write the National Institute on Genealogical Research, P. O. Box 14274, Washington, DC 20044-4274.

CALLS FOR PAPERS

The International Association for the Study of Common Property will hold its first annual meeting on September 27–30, 1990, at Duke University in Durham, NC. The Association takes an interdisciplinary approach to understanding and improving the management of environmental resources held or used collectively by communities, whether in developing or developed countries. It seeks to bring together scholars, government officials, development consultants, and resource managers. The theme of the conference is "Designing Sustainability on the Commons." The Association welcomes proposals for papers and entire panels. For further information about joining the Association or participating in the conference, please write Margaret McKean, Program Chair, Department of Political Science, Duke University, Durham, NC 27706.

The North American Labor History Conference will hold its 12th annual meeting October 18–20, 1990, at Wayne State University, Detroit, MI. The program committee is soliciting papers dealing with the history of labor and related social and economic reforms movements, especially the relationship of labor to gender, race, or ethnicity. Please submit proposals by May 1, 1990, to Professor Stanley D. Solvick, Program Chair, Department of History, Wayne State University, Detroit, MI 48202; telephone (313) 577-6145 or 577-2525.

The 17th Conference on the Application of Quantitative Methods in Canadian Economic History will be held on November 9–10, 1990, at Queen's University in Kingston. Those wishing to participate—and graduate students are encouraged to do so—should submit an abstract by June 1, 1990 to Professor Mary MacKinnon, Department of Economics, McGill University, 855 Sherbrooke St. W., Montreal, Quebec, H3A 2T7, Canada.

FELLOWSHIPS

Doctoral candidates and recent PhDs are invited to apply for Sullivan Fellowships for the calendar year 1991. Research topics should be related to the study of the role of the textile industry in the United States between c. 1750 and c. 1980. For information write: Editorial and Research Committee, Museum of American Textile History, 800 Massachusetts Avenue, North Andover, MA 01845.

HANDBOOK OF AMERICAN BUSINESS HISTORY

Volume 1 of The Handbook of American Business History will be published in September 1990 under the title *Manufacturing: A Historigraphical and Bibliographical Guide*. Volumes 2 and 3 are in progress, but the editor will consider new contributions for these and other volumes. Scholars interested in participating should contact Professor David O. Whitten, Editor, The Handbook of American Business History, Department of Economics, Auburn University, Auburn, AL 36849-5242; telephone (205) 844-2928.

Reviews of Books

ANCIENT, MEDIEVAL, AND EARLY MODERN

Tribe and Polity in Late Prehistoric Europe: Demography, Production and Exchange in the Evolution of Complex Social Systems. Edited by D. Blair Gibson and Michael N. Geselowitz. New York: Plenum Press, 1988. Pp. 234. $42.50.

Later European prehistory and protohistory is defined by the editors of this monograph as roughly including the first millenniums A.D. and B.C. This time in Europe, on the border between prehistory and history, has long fascinated archaeologists such as V. G. Childe and others interested in the development of European societies and cultures. During the period one begins to witness the formation of European feudalism and Europeans increasingly come in contact with peoples from other continents. The period provides the background to the development of European capitalism and world systems, as outlined by Immanuel Wallerstein and others. The rich data base of European protohistory allows the testing of a variety of theories about the relationship between local level phenomena and broader historical events, how production and social formation intersect with exchange, and regional dynamics.

The monograph grew out of a symposium, part of the May 1977 Society for American Archaeology meetings, designed to bring together researchers and archaeologists from both Europe and North America with interests in later European history and protohistory. Divided essentially into three main parts, the book begins with a rather lengthy theoretical overview by the editors. Following this are eight chapters, revised from symposium presentations and organized by region: agro-pastoralism and social organization in Ireland (D. Blair Gibson), coinage and sociopolitical change in Britain (Colin Haselgrove), settlement in Sweden (Thomas Larsson), Hallstatt period of east central Europe demography (Janusz Ostoja-Zagorski), ironworking (Michael Geselowitz), dietary reconstruction (Matthew Murray and Margaret Schoeninger), and evidence for slavery in Germany (Bettina Arnold) and complexity in Italy (Stephen Dyson). The regional papers are followed by two discussion-and-review chapters: Peter Wells focuses on industry and production and Bernard Wailes on method and interpretation.

The first half of the introduction provides a highly readable overview of recent theoretical trends in archaeology. The second half is somewhat less satisfactory because the authors attempt a new paradigmatic approach that focuses on the development of institutions within a substantivist framework. While interesting, the material comes too early in the volume. It does little to help explain or put in context the chapters that follow.

Most disappointing are the central chapters. The limited data are not presented in a very rigorous way. Many chapters contain a substantial theoretical overview, but most of this discussion is too narrowly focused on the particular time and place of the chapter. Ostoja-Zagorski rightly characterizes his demographic data as "preliminary and, undoubtedly, highly debatable" (p. 123). Arnold's discussion of slavery is provocative but based on little evidence. Murray and Schoeninger, lamenting on their small sample size and poor provenance, suggest that their methods, stable carbon and nitrogen analysis of bone collagen, might be more fruitfully applied to other sites where faunal and floral remains have been recovered and can provide a basis for the analysis of diet (p. 169). Most of these papers are really only marginally acceptable journal articles.

The two final chapters are interesting, short critical reviews. While the discussions sound a bit too much like unedited comments—most glaringly apparent when Wailes comments on Crumley's paper, which was not made part of the final book—both chapters have something to say, and both make strong attempt to pull issues out of the prior chapters.

The monograph maintains the strengths and weaknesses of a symposium. While the introduction and discussion essays provide some integration, the central articles are too disparate and fail to address the time period in a satisfying way. Only in the most limited fashion does the collection deal with the development of European society as a general, historical process. After the foreword no mention can be found of world systems, and outside of Dyson's chapter there is little information on the relationship between Europe and the rest of the world.

In summary, the book has a lot of promise, but much of it remains unfulfilled. It is an interesting and varied compilation of articles, perhaps strongest on issues of exchange, social class, and regional social change. The editors, authors, and publisher should be commended for producing the book so quickly, for it will surely be of interest to specialists. I doubt, however, it will attract a wider readership.

ALAN H. GOODMAN, *Hampshire College*

Famine, Disease and the Social Order in Early Modern Society. Edited by John Walter and Roger Schofield. New York: Cambridge University Press, 1989. Pp. xiv, 355. $49.50.

The title of this book is misleading, because the contents do not cover Europe, but mainly England, with an occasional sideways glance at France and Ireland. The book does not address a clearly stated problem, such as what factors caused mortality crises in early modern Europe. Rather it is a collection of papers dedicated to the memory of the late Andrew Appleby. Nevertheless, demographic historians and historical demographers will find much that is interesting here: the latest thinking of E. A. Wrigley, Roger Schofield, and Peter Laslett; a preview sketch of the thinking of Jacques Dupâquier, who does not believe that the theories of the Cambridge group can be applied to the case of France; and papers by younger scholars.

The most valuable aspect of the book is that it points out puzzling facts about mortality crises which any successful theory must explain. These include the following. Subsistence crises (as exemplified in high cereal prices) predict only a small part of the variance in mortality. When commerce developed, and people were exposed more to contagious diseases, mortality declined. Mortality crises did not affect all parishes in a region suffering from a climatic shock—England's worst crisis (in 1557–1558) affected only about one-third of all parishes observed. Mortality crises did not always occur at the end of spring when the grain supply was lowest. After 1665 bubonic plague ceased to be a major health problem in Europe, but so far no explanation has won wide support.

From the beginning the editors concede that the belief in a causal link between insufficient food intake and death is simplistic. Naturally some people starved outright, but rising food prices in the late sixteenth century did not cause a rise in mortality rates. In years of high food prices mortality crises were localized and scattered. By the middle of the seventeenth century England had escaped the bonds of famine. Curiously, food prices were negatively correlated with fertility and predicted as much as 64 percent of the variance in fertility.

Four contributers (Dupâquier, David Weir, P. R. Galloway, and J. Landers) find evidence that variation in food prices affected mortality indirectly by causing migrations of the poor, who spread epidemic diseases.

Galloway finds that the greater the level of economic development, the lower the response of mortality rates to food price fluctuations. The patterns of mortality as a whole, the editors believe, were profoundly mediated by the social and economic order.

John Walter's discussion of public and private activities to feed the hungry in bad years loses its focus. Were these activities more important in England than elsewhere? Were they more important in relieving hunger than increases in agricultural productivity and improvements in food transport? The case is not made.

Keith Wrightson and David Levine limit their study to one community (Whickham), and they try to bring the subject of death to life by a discussion of death rituals and the content of wills. But they also lose their bearings in a forest of details.

Paul Slack discusses government responses to plague epidemics but does not explain how putting human beings in quarantine could restrict the movements of rats and fleas.

The best contribution comes from Jacques Dupâquier, who shows the discrepancies in the timing of mortality crises in England and France. No one has explained this. Did pathogens have trouble crossing the English Channel? Dupâquier thinks "fungal infections" were an important independent variable, but does not elaborate or cite any sources.

David Weir points out that after 1750 in northern France wheat price fluctuations no longer influenced the timing of deaths or long-run population growth. He suggests that improvement in the weather from 1600 to 1789 might have been responsible. But he has not studied the weather, so does not realize that it deteriorated between 1768 and 1789.

E. A. Wrigley develops the concept of net versus gross cereal yields and speculates as to its usefulness in future research.

Roger Schofield concedes the importance of greater agricultural productivity in population growth. Modifying an earlier position, he acknowledges that in relation to real wages the proportion ever marrying is more important than age at marriage. He does not believe that "proletarianization" caused the fall in the age of marriage during the eighteenth-century because industrial wage work was not new. Pointing out that the age at marriage increased during the early nineteenth century, he says he believes that the eighteenth-century pattern of early marriage was a temporary aberration.

Jacques Dupâquier's new *Histoire de la population française* was not cited, probably because it was not ready when this book went to press. Another notable bibliographic omission is *The Europe Crisis of the 1590s*, edited by Peter Clark (London, 1985). The book offers no consideration of Christiaan Vandenbroeke's studies of Flemish diet and demography, such as *Agriculture et alimentation* (Ghent, 1975). I was disappointed that none of the contributors cited my suggestion concerning mold poisoning and population growth that appeared in this JOURNAL in 1984. Now that it is available in book form (*Poisons of the Past* [New Haven, 1989]), they will no longer find it so easy to ignore.

MARY KILBOURNE MATOSSIAN, *University of Maryland*

The Other Economy: Pastoral Husbandry on a Medieval Estate. By Kathleen Biddick. Berkeley: University of California Press, 1989. Pp. xvii, 230. $30.00.

Studies of medieval English agriculture have traditionally concentrated on the production of grain and wool, the two chief cash crops of the thirteenth- and fourteenth-century era of high farming. Implicit in this focus has been the assumption that the agricultural economies of great monastic estates were dictated principally by the demands of the market, and only secondarily by the consumption demands of their lords. And since wheat and wool clearly were market-oriented products, the circularity of this approach has rarely been remarked.

No longer. In this important book Kathleen Biddick challenges such over-simple models of monastic agricultural production. Analyzing the management of livestock by Peterborough Abbey, she shows how the consumption requirements of the Abbey influenced almost every aspect of its arable and pastoral husbandry. By 1300 the Abbey's manors constituted a highly integrated system of production and consumption that bred nearly all the Abbey's plough beasts and riding horses, supplied its meat requirements, and consumed almost 60 percent of its total cereal production annually. Wool was the only pure cash crop on the estate; otherwise, consumption and marketing were coordinate strategies, determined by the domestic requirements of the Abbey household and by logistical factors of distance, transport, and market exposure.

Nor were arable and pastoral husbandry at Peterborough locked in the stark opposition surmised by M. M. Postan, in which rising population forced an expansion of arable acreage, reducing the pasturage for animals and thus the supply of fertilizer necessary to maintain arable fertility. Rather, Biddick shows that much of Peterborough's expanding arable acreage was in fact devoted to fodder crops, such as oats and legumes, which the Abbey fed exclusively to animals.

Cattle herds were maintained primarily to breed oxen for the ploughs, and although the relative importance of cattle to dairying rose during the thirteenth century as the sheep flock became a specialized unit for wool production and sheep milking ceased, the Abbey continued to sell off its surplus fodder and pasturage rather than increase its dairy herd. It simply did not conceive of the cattle herd as an enterprise oriented towards the market. Instead it organized all its herds toward producing the single output for which each was intended: cattle for breeding oxen, oxen for ploughing, horses for transport and some ploughing, sheep for wool, and pigs for meat.

Within these categories, however, the balance of the herds changed markedly. In 1125 cattle and oxen represented two-thirds of the livestock on the manors, sheep and horses one-third; by 1300 sheep and horses had risen to two-thirds, and cattle and oxen declined to one-third. This shift resulted mainly from greatly increased numbers of horses, both for carting and riding. John Langdon's work has shown clearly the economic importance of this shift towards horses for hauling, and its connection with marketing. But at Peterborough, transport costs were further increased by the herd of riding horses maintained by the Abbey as an aspect of lordly display. So costly had its horses become by 1300 that had the Abbey not grown its own oats, it would have spent more in a year on transport costs than it made from its wool sales.

The book's interest extends beyond agricultural history. Biddick does a fine job of reconstructing the early history of the Abbey from the scrappy evidence of texts and archeology; she demolishes claims that the Abbey exploited its demesne directly prior to the twelfth century; and she offers a bold hypothesis to explain why English landlords took their demesnes in hand from the end of the twelfth century to manage them directly, rather than continuing to lease them out. Her suggestion, that this shift resulted from the structural indebtedness of English landlords to wool merchants and financiers like William Cade, will certainly be controversial. It seems to me to go beyond the evidence, and may also overestimate the importance of Flemings versus Jews in late twelfth-century lending. In either event, it is hard to see how Biddick's claim that such loans were "really instruments of trade" which "drew the agrarian producer into vertical links with financiers who monopolized the exchange of agricultural products . . . to the . . . industrializing sectors they represented" (p. 51) can apply to loans from Jews like Aaron of Lincoln, whose debts on the 1191 Pipe Roll dwarf those owing to Cade, yet still represent only a fraction of those owed him at his death in 1186. Biddick's handling of these debts is the only misstep in an otherwise surefooted performance.

It would be misleading, however, to end on this minor note. This is a challenging, intelligent, and important book. It wastes no words, and makes few concessions to its readers. But it is a book which anyone interested in medieval economic history will want to read.

ROBERT C. STACEY, *University of Washington*

Geography, Technology, and War: Studies in the Maritime History of the Mediterranean, 649–1571. By John H. Pryor. New York: Cambridge University Press, 1988. Pp. xviii, 238. $39.50.

The interplay between geography, technology, and war is masterfully handled in this work, which promises to become a classic in Mediterranean maritime history. Maritime historians have long understood—as did sailors long before them—that in the age of sail and oar, wind and current set hard limits to the possible. Pryor's great contributions have been to provide a detailed analysis of the geographic, oceanographic, and climatologic factors that affected seaborne traffic in the medieval Mediterranean as well as of the means available for transport and combat in that arena, and then to produce a rounded picture of the interaction between these two elements, the environmental and the technological.

In the first three chapters Pryor describes "The Sea," "The Ships," and "Navigation." This foundation, on which the rest of the study is erected, is the book's most estimable part. These chapters will be valuable not only to those interested in medieval naval history, but to anyone interested in travel on the sea, whether for commerce or war, in the Mediterranean before the age of steam. The description of currents and winds, illuminated by clear maps and tables, makes evident why certain routes and seasons were favored for navigation. The discussion of the ships provides an intelligent overview of the vessels available for crossing the sea in the Middle Ages. Pryor has based his summary on recent marine archeology as well as the longer tradition of documentary analysis and iconographic studies. In addition to offering physical descriptions of the ships, he is willing to make informed guesses about the performance capabilities of medieval sailing ships and galleys. In doing so he treads in an area where a neverending debate rages, but his estimates are based on a generous and extensive survey of the work of other scholars and provide a reasonable and reasoned estimation of just what the different kinds of vessels could accomplish. The analysis takes into account the balance between the capabilities of the lateen rig and the limitations of tubby medieval hulls in considering the abilities of medieval sailors to beat to windward. Medieval galleys were restricted not only by the stamina of their crews, but by their limited capacity for carrying fresh water, which was as important to the performance of those sweating hordes as to the steam engines of a later age.

In his discussion of "Navigation: the routes and their implications" Pryor brings together geographical and technological information to explain the rhythms and routes of Mediterranean navigation. He makes it plain that while the sailing season was gradually extended during the late Middle Ages later into the autumn and begun earlier in the spring until there was no longer a distinct "closing of the seas," it still took pressing reasons and superior equipment to undertake a voyage in winter. He describes the various main sea lanes, the "trunk routes," and why maritime traffic was forced into these few, predictable patterns. He explains why certain areas where trunk routes intersected, or passed through straits, acted as "focal sectors" where, because shipping could reliably be found there, pirate, corsair, and naval campaigns tended to concentrate. The nature of the coastlines, currents, and prevailing winds combined to channel most of the Mediterranean's major sea lanes in such a way that a strategic advantage accrued to powers that could control the sea's northern coast.

It is the greatest weakness of Pryor's book that he conceives of the naval history of the Mediterranean in the Middle Ages as a long, two-sided war between "Muslims" and "Christians," a viewpoint summed up in a sentence: "The history of the maritime security of the Crusader states in these two centuries [the twelfth and thirteenth] in fact provides a classic illustration of the ways in which geographical factors and contemporary naval technology formed a nexus which favoured *one of the two belligerents* in the struggle at sea" (p. 113, reviewer's emphasis). This is a naval analysis of the Crusades, not a maritime history of the medieval Mediterranean, and even as that it tends to underplay the complex mosaic of independent powers, ambitions, and conflicts that composed each of his two simple blocs. The choice to present the naval history of the Mediterranean as an ideological conflict between two great power blocs skirts perilously close to viewing the Middle Ages through the lens of the twentieth century.

The analysis of the campaigns of the Crusades is nonetheless thought-provoking and carefully worked out. The Crusading situation, especially that between the Crusading states and Egypt in the twelfth century, provides an abundance of situations to test Pryor's thesis that the forces of nature so dominated the available technology that certain patterns of behavior were virtually forced on the mariners of the medieval Mediterranean. The rise of Ottoman power shows how, by holding strategic coasts and islands along the major sea lanes, the Turks were able to succeed where the Egyptians had failed. By providing a contrary case, it also acts as a test of Pryor's earlier discussion of the importance of control of the Mediterranean's northern coastlines to western European maritime dominance of the sea.

The index of this otherwise carefully detailed book is disappointing. Yet in sum, this important book makes clear the interactions between environment and technology which affected not only the military situation between the Muslim and Christian worlds, which is its chief focus, but also many of the economic patterns of the medieval Mediterranean. It is sure to provoke discussion, and perhaps even controversy. That may be its most valuable contribution to scholarship.

JOHN E. DOTSON, *Southern Illinois University, Carbondale*

Fisco religione Stato nell'età confessionale. Edited by Hermann Kellenbenz and Paolo Prodi. Bologna: II Mulino, 1989. Pp. 530.

In his introduction to this volume, which reproduces the proceedings of a seminar sponsored by the Istituto storico italo-germanico in the autumn of 1987, Paolo Prodi states that the object of the enterprise was to trace the phenomenon of the "secularization of the Church and the "ecclesiologization" (*ecclesiasticizzazione*) of the State (p. 20). This topic raises a set of themes which are not entirely novel.

In 1901 Maitland ironically referred to the parsonification of the king's figure in medieval political theory. More recently, in *The King's Two Bodies* (Princeton, 1957) Ernst Kantorowicz brilliantly examined the "parallel" processes of the "imperialization of the Papacy and [the] sanctification of the secular state and its institutions" (p. 185). In a chapter entitled "Christus Fiscus," he analyzed a set of ideas which bear directly on questions Prodi and a team of Italian and German historians set out to investigate in this seminar, on the relationship between public finances, religion, and the state in the "confessional age," from the fifteenth to the mid-seventeenth centuries. The great German-American historian argued that in the thirteenth century, first in Sicily and subsequently in other European regions, there emerged an "antithesis or parallelism of Christus and Fiscus," a concept which was to become a "central problem of political thought in the period of transition from mediaeval to modern times" (p. 173). Even outside the realm of political theory, the point made by Prodi is not entirely new. Historians have for decades touched upon the implications of the parallel emergence of territorial states and territorial churches in late medieval and early modern Europe. Much work has been done, in England, parts of Germany, and the Scandinavian states, on the consequences of the confiscations of church lands which followed the adoption of Protestantism. The economic benefits to the states of these expropriations and more generally of the taxation of church properties, the fate of the ecclesiastical institutions, particularly the economic bases of their subsequent existence, and the state's assumption of responsibilities once largely monopolized by the Church (above all, education and welfare) have been examined with varying degrees of attention by historians, many of whose works are noted in the pages of this book, although one could perhaps suggest that insufficient attention has been paid to the historiography of comparable English developments. The complex of these phenomena were discussed in their general outlines and from an overall European perspective by H. J. Cohn as long ago as 1971.

Prodi declares that in this seminar he and his colleagues aspired to "go beyond" (*andare oltre*) this previous work. His aim was to explore the idea that the State did not merely expropriate ecclesiatical goods, but that increasingly it assumed characteristics of a confessional body. The State "does not limit itself to an external relationship of the expropriation and exploitation of goods. In some ways it assumes a new character in political theory and practice. Contrarily and contemporaneously, the Church becomes increasingly secularized through a process of osmosis which absorbs the most directly internal functions of the State's economic and political life" (p. 9). In his introduction Prodi identifies some of the themes which it would be necessary to address in order to pursue these ideas. One might quibble that he does not acknowledge as explicitly as he might the degree to which other scholars have explored these same topics. More importantly, the agenda of the seminar, held two years ago, and the contents of this book would most probably have been considerably clearer and more important had some effort been exerted at the outset to take careful stock of the state of the question. The decision to publish a group of substantially unrevised talks and, crucially, not to add a concluding, synthetic essay greatly undermines the value of a book which could have contributed substantially to our understanding of early modern European state-building both in its theoretical and practical aspects.

As it is, the volume contains a series of interesting, but only loosely connected essays. Two, written by Marco Bianchini and by Aldo Mazzacane, address questions belonging more to the realm of political theory. The rest investigate the histories of individual regions in Germany and Italy and seek to trace the relationships between local churches and local states. One essay, by Kersten Krüger, on public finance in Denmark and Sweden, raises only tangentially the issues which, according to Prodi, were central to the seminar's enterprise. Perhaps quite predictably, in the largest group of essays two themes predominate over the rest: the strengthening of the State and the roles assumed by Church and State as a consequence of the expropriation of ecclesiastical properties.

Hermann Kellenbenz dwells upon the expansion of "princely fiscalism" (p. 42) in the German states, both reformed and catholic. Karlheinz Blaschke, focusing on Saxony, repeats this theme and asserts that in the course of the Reformation "the patrimonial relationships between Church and State" were noticeably shifted toward the State (p. 74). Meinrab Schaab, in a comparison of the history of the Palatinate with those of Baden and Würtenberg, remarks upon the "extraordinary consolidation and concentration experienced by the territorial State thanks to its power to dispose of ecclesiastical goods" (p. 112). Gerhard Immler, in his study of fiscal relations between Church and State in Bavaria concludes that the Thirty Years' War allowed the State to penetrate into the affairs of the Church (passim, but especially pp. 223–24). This theme is repeated as a refrain through most of the other essays. It may, nonetheless, be appropriate to point out that this emphasis on the importance of the State (always spelled with a capital S) appears much more evident among students of German history. Their counterparts who in this volume write on Italian history seem to me to have a more complex and nuanced view of the history of late medieval and early modern states. The tone here is set by Roberto Bizzocchi who, repeating themes he first presented in his recent book on the Tuscan territorial church in the fifteenth and sixteenth centuries, seeks to specify with some precision the social realities and power relationships masked by the term "state." Bizzocchi concludes that in Tuscany the "interpenetration" (*compenetrazione*) between Church and State was mediated by the role of the local, Florentine aristocracy, whose material interests, in the end, were protected by both state and church fiscal policies. Giuseppe delle Torre, writing on Venice (particularly pp. 411, 417), and Aurelio Musi, writing on the Italian South (p. 457), seem to share fully Bizzocchi's view.

Perhaps most compelling among the other themes which emerge in these essays is the assumption of new socioeconomic and ideological roles by Church and State. Schaab (p. 113), Othmar Pickl, who writes on Habsburg Austria (p. 121), and Schubert (p. 151) point to the development in the region which each investigates of an incipient local patriotic sentiment, by-product of fiscal policies and overlapping responsibilities of ecclesiastical and state authorities. Having either been deprived of much of their previous wealth, or forced to accommodate themselves to harsher fiscal regimes than those prevalent before the Reformation, churches were drawn more directly into the social and economic lives of their local societies. Although he does not himself argue this point, it would appear that Blaschke's conclusion (p. 78) also points in that direction, for he argues that the Saxon Church, as a result of its poverty following the loss of its lands, financed itself by assessing a tax of four *pfennig* on every member of the congregation. As a result, there emerged a much keener sense of community among members of the church. Conversely, Gauro Coppola, writing on the archdiocese of Milan during the episcopacy of Carlo Borromeo, concludes (p. 340 ff.) that the more intense sense of community between church and society was based upon Borromeo's prior elevation of the moral and ethical standards of the ecclesiastical orders and the archbishop's consequent freedom to intervene in the ethical and practical problems of secular society.

In conclusion, one can find much food for thought in this volume. It is a pity that the principal points of these often rich and empirically deeply grounded essays could not have been teased out and systematically presented by the volume's editor so that they could have been made more easily accessible to a general reader.

ANTHONY MOLHO, *Brown University*

Industry before the Industrial Revolution: North-East Lancashire, c. 1500–1640. By John T. Swain. Manchester: Manchester University Press for the Chetham Society, 1986. Pp. 235. $43.00.

A few years ago I had occasion to travel in Lancashire on the Colne Valley Line of British Rail, from Chorley through Blackburn, into the Pennine uplands through Accrington, Burnley, and Nelson (formerly Marsden), to Colne, now the end of the line. As we made our leisurely climb, I could see the remnants of industrial north-east Lancashire of a century and more ago. I was being carried into what had been the last bastion of handloom weaving in the 1840s and 1850s, and what was shortly afterward to become a major center of small-scale powerloom weaving firms. Then, as now, industrial Colne was bounded by pasture, and the cows could graze virtually to the factory walls. Two and three centuries earlier the town, with the neighboring Forests of Trawden and Pendle, and the remainder of Colne Manor, was similarly bucolic, but, as John Swain's study, *Industry before the Industrial Revolution*, tells us, it was also nearly as "industrial."

Swain's objectives are to illuminate "the extent to which industrial and craft activities were practiced well before the Industrial Revolution," as well as "the important contribution that this early experience was to have in helping to shape later industrial developments" (p. 1). The author virtually attains his first goal, but I doubt many will agree he arrives at the second.

In the mid-sixteenth century this sector of north-east Lancashire contained about 1,800 people; a century later there were perhaps 3,900 inhabitants, reflecting growth somewhat more rapid than the intrinsic population growth rate estimated by A. E. Wrigley and R. Schofield for England over the same period. As Swain demonstrates, economic activity in the region was not only heavily agricultural (pastoral, mostly), but also became progressively more devoted to "industrial" activity in clothmaking, largely of kerseys, at least until the crisis of the 1620s. The bulk of the book is devoted to chapters on agriculture, lordship, landholding, wealth and poverty, and to a single extensive chapter on cloth manufacture. A small amount of space is given to relatively minor activities such as coal mining, quarrying, and various services and crafts, all introduced by a discussion of what little can be ascertained about population change. That is, Swain attempts to provide a view of the entire local economy over the course of a century and more, based on intensive work with a wide range of documents from the period.

Although it may be obscured from time to time in the details of herd sizes, tillage patterns, probate inventories, and inheritance practices, there is a broader agenda: to test, in some sense, a model of rural "industrialization" built on the pioneering work of Joan Thirsk, E. L. Jones, Franklin Mendels, and others. Swain accepts the general proposition that links low agricultural productivity with manufacturing by-employments, but questions some elements of the model emphasized elsewhere. For example, from examination of surviving wills, Swain argues that there is no necessary relationship between landholding fragmentation and partible inheritance practices: in north-east Lancashire primogeniture was the rule, but egalitarian distribution of personalty often left the landed heir cash-poor and liable to sell or mortgage the patrimony. This, in combination with squatting and other forms of tolerated encroachment on the lands of gentry, nobility, and the king, yields the parcellized, unviable upland agricultural holdings so dear to some generalizers, and central to Swain's view of the rise of industry in Colne and environs.

Population growth and a trend to smaller landholdings led to worsening poverty, which then led to "considerable demand for supplementary income" (p. 98). This phrase, which appears in similar guises elsewhere in the book, may simply be Swain's way of referring to growing availability of a low-cost supply of labor, but it jars in the economist's ear, and suggests that the causal model being employed is not fully articulated. The demographic data are by no means adequate to answer sophisticated questions, but Swain plausibly suggests that there was immigration to the region in the late sixteenth century (while England as a whole was sending abroad a small but significant fraction of its people), and that the commercial crisis of the 1620s led to an important emigration as employment in clothmaking became less remunerative. Swain does not examine thoroughly enough the obverse of his proposition, however, that the higher-than-average population growth of the region did not cause the influx of enterprise in making kerseys, but may indeed have been caused by it.

While the implicit model may not be thoroughly grounded, by and large the facts are well demonstrated, albeit within the narrow limits set by the data extant. By the turn of the seventeenth century clothmaking was widespread among the region's households, and was usually combined with one or more additional forms of endeavor. Occupational designations (for example in court records) and probate inventories strongly suggest this was the case, but for those people crucial to the model, the poor or landless, the available evidence is either defective or mute. Just as "everyone" in the modern First World is "middle class," whether this is true or not, so "all" were then "yeomen," no matter how they earned their livelihoods. Further, virtually all of the probate inventories Swain was able to examine were in the *supra* category, with estates valued at £40 or more, representing merchants, millers, gentry, true yeomen, clothiers, and the like. There were 253 inventories available for the period, accounting for perhaps one-sixth to one-fifth of the deaths of household heads, most of those at or near the top of the wealth and income distribution. It is a reasonable guess, but no more, that those at the bottom of the distribution were equally as or more likely to have possessed clothmaking implements, and that the agrarian and rural economy of the time was infused with manufacture.

Further, the reader (at least this one) is left uncertain about the relative importance of agriculture, the cloth industry, and other activities in the local economy. Much of the quantitative data derive from the wills and inventories, but nowhere in the book can one find a comprehensive tabulation of occupation, status, or assets derived from these data. From the many partial tabulations actually published, it appears that it might have been possible to make at least a rough estimate of shares of local income originating from the various activities otherwise thoroughly discussed in the book, and thus to measure the impact of "proto-industrialization" on the economy of the region.

My objections and reservations are more than mere quibbles, but I emphasize that the structure and presentation of the book reflect scholarly care, mastery of sources, and due caution; Swain has given us an excellent study of a time and period unduly neglected for most of this century. That he does not demonstrate any necessary link between the "overwhelming importance of industry, particularly cloth manufacture, in the local economy" (p. 207) in the "preindustrial" period, and the fact of factories two to three centuries later, is not all that significant. What he has shown us is more than adequate.

JOHN S. LYONS, *Miami University*

Fiscal Limits of Absolutism: Direct Taxation in Early Seventeenth-Century France. By James B. Collins. Berkeley: University of California Press, 1988. Pp. xii, 256. $34.00.

The author of this fine study begins by quoting Richelieu to the effect that finances were the sinews of the state in the early seventeenth century. Collins is trying to show that the revenues collected and expended by the crown determined to a large degree the success or failure of its political program; in the period from the end of the wars of religion to the Fronde the fiscal system was both the French crown's greatest strength and its greatest weakness. Because direct taxation affected all levels of French society to one degree or another, the author contents that an analysis of the financial system has much to offer in understanding the body politic and the body social of early modern France.

The most striking aspect of the French fiscal system in the reigns of Henry IV and Louis XIII is the heavy burden of deficit financing, necessary largely because of heavy military spending during the two periods of open warfare—1589 to 1598 and 1627 to 1659—and because of the growing royal debt. So much of the revenue from direct taxation had already become alienated by the early seventeenth century that Louis XIII was forced to spend 30 million *livres tournois*, or half his total annual income, just to service the debt. As the costs of current wars ate heavily into the remainder, it is little wonder that these monarchs were hardly able to force their will arbitrarily on the state. They did have other sources of funds at their disposal, as Collins takes pains to point out. Sales of new offices and *droits*, just two examples, resembled direct taxation in that they raised short-term sums from those who were most able to contribute to the crown's coffers and who were otherwise exempt from the *taille*. And monarchs could also declare partial bankruptcies, as they did in 1604 and 1634, in order to reduce the pressure of royal debts on annual revenues. While such remedies went a long way toward keeping the state afloat in the seventeenth century, Collins is right to emphasize that in the long run the innate flaws in the system would not permit it to survive indefinitely. When in the 1630s the peasants reached the limit of their ability to contribute any further through taxation, they revolted or simply stopped paying. Moreover, the bureaucratic officers who were squeezed the hardest for *rentes*, *droits*, and other forced "loans" were precisely the officials designated to collect those same revenues. Combined with a foreign policy in the 1630s and 1640s which required significant new revenues to finance French involvement in the Thirty Years' War, the rickety structure could not hold up to the multiple pressures of Old Regime spending and "in the long run this fundamental flaw in the structure of the French monarchy led to its collapse" (p. 17).

Despite its title, the book covers a greater span of time than the first half of the seventeenth century. The book begins by summarizing the history of French taxation from the fourteenth century up to the reign of Henry IV. It makes much clearer the murky waters of the French financial system during the wars of religion and goes a long way toward substantiating the claims made by Scott Van Doren and others that the fiscal innovations of the early seventeenth century—the crown's attempt to introduce *élections* into the *pays d'états* being the most notable example—were really following (albeit more successfully) the example of Henry III. Collins demonstrates, however, that the monarchy was never able to effect the financial independence it sought, even though Henry IV and Louis XIII were more successful than Henry III had been. Thus, the fiscal system itself and how it operated—always forced to compromise itself in order to stay in operation at all—severely limited the power of the so-called absolute monarchy. The author's conclusions fit nicely with the work of William Beik and others, who have demonstrated that the concept of absolute monarchy itself is in need of an overhaul. The real paradox is whether it was despite or because of these compromises and limitations that the monarchy managed to survive so well far into the eighteenth century.

MACK P. HOLT, *George Mason University*

European Jewry in the Age of Mercantilism, 1550–1750. By Jonathan I. Israel. 2nd Edition. Oxford: Clarendon Press, 1989. Pp. xv, 312. £10.95.

The early modern era is not normally regarded as a glamorous era in the history of European Jewry. The epoch began with the brutal expulsion of the Jews from the Iberian peninsula in the 1490s. It ended in the late eighteenth century when, under the influence of Enlightenment ideas, European governments slowly began to grant the Jews the civil rights that made possible their eventual absorption into the dominant society. The intervening years, from the sixteenth to the mid-eighteenth century, are generally described as an era of persecution, ghettoization, and cultural stagnation among the Jews of Europe. To be sure, the seventeenth century did see the emergence of "court Jews" whose financial acumen proved valuable to many of the princes of central Europe—but the loyalties of these financiers were often directed towards their princely patrons rather than the Jewish people as a whole.

This is, of course, a simplification of the traditional view. Jewish history is a richly studied topic, and historians have added countless nuances and modifications to the conventional picture. But Jonathan Israel, the eminent specialist in seventeenth-century Dutch history at the University of London, does not simply continue to modify the customary view. He attacks it head on. The period from 1550 to 1750, he argues, was the "age of maximum cohesion in the history of Jewish culture" (p. 33), and at the high point of this era, in the second half of the seventeenth century, the Jews had "the most profound and pervasive impact on the west which they were ever to exert whilst still retaining a large measure of social and cultural cohesion" (p. 1). By contrast, the eighteenth century—an era generally seen in positive terms as ushering in the eventual emancipation of the Jews—is described by Israel as an epoch of economic malaise, social degradation, and "cultural impoverishment" (p. 252).

These views are presented in a book which offers a brief but admirably comprehensive survey of the Jewish experience in Europe during the early modern period. No reader could fail to benefit from the breadth and scope of the author's treatment, which gives equal attention to the economic, political, spiritual, and cultural dimensions of Jewish life in this richly documented era. But the author never loses sight of the central arguments he hopes to advance. For most of the sixteenth century, Israel maintains, the economic and social position of the Jews continued to deteriorate in Western Europe, leading many Jews to migrate eastward. But dramatic changes set in towards the end of the century. One factor was the growing influence of some Christian thinkers who reacted to the religious conflicts of the Reformation by adopting a more sceptical, and thus more tolerant, attitude towards all religions. An equally important factor was the growth of "philosemitic mercantilism"—the attitude that the economic needs of the state could legitimately be promoted by taking advantage of what the Jews had to offer. The increased dispersion of Jewish populations meant in turn that Jews had something new to offer to the ambitious rulers of seventeenth-century Europe: an international network of merchants and financiers strategically positioned across the entire continent. Christian elites now tolerated the Jews sufficiently to be able to work comfortably with them. But traditional forms of discrimination were still so prevalent that most Jews were discouraged from assimilating into the dominant society. Jewish culture thus retained its coherent and close-knit character, providing a social and economic base for the court Jews who helped to finance not only German princelings but also the Anglo-Dutch-Habsburg coalition which waged war after war against Louis XIV in the late seventeenth century.

All this ended, Israel argues, in the early eighteenth century. Not only did the peace of 1713 bring to end the special conditions in which the Jewish network had prospered, but Christian attitudes made it difficult for Jews to enter new forms of enterprise. Manufacturing came increasingly to stand beside commerce as a source of wealth in the eighteenth century, but this was a sphere of activity which Jews found it much more difficult to penetrate. Meanwhile the pan-European unity of Jewish cultural and religious values began to disintegrate, permitting more and more individual Jews to adopt the norms of Christian society but diminishing the cohesion and impact of Jewish society as a whole.

This book was first published in 1985. The volume under review is already a second, revised edition. The author has updated the bibliography, added a helpful map, revised a few passages in the earlier part of the book, and, most importantly, substantially rewritten the last two chapters. Israel's arguments about Jewish "decline" in the eighteenth century have apparently generated the greatest amount of criticism, and the author felt compelled to clarify his treatment of this era. But he has not retreated. While he has added some passages about the spiritual "renewal" of Judaism in the later eighteenth century, especially in Eastern Europe, most of the new material is intended to bolster the author's original argument about the inability of Jewish merchants to hold their own in the changing economic environment of the eighteenth century. The Rothschilds, an apparent counter-example, are never mentioned—for they emerged just outside the chronological scope of this work.

Readers of this JOURNAL will, of course, be particularly interested in Israel's treatment of the pivotal role of Jews in the economy of seventeenth-century Europe. Some may be disappointed that the author did not attempt to bolster his description of the Jewish "network" with any statistical or quantitative data. But this would have been inconsistent with the author's approach, which argues for the "rise" and "decline" of Jewish influence as much in cultural and social terms as in strictly economic ones. The author certainly has provided a tightly argued case for a new chronology of Jewish history in the early modern era. It would be easy enough to nibble away at the edges of his argument by challenging some of his specific statements about particular merchants, princes, rabbis, or scholars. It would be much harder, however, to disprove his central thesis—for that would require an entirely new conceptual model of Jewish history in the early modern era.

CHRISTOPHER R. FRIEDRICHS, *University of British Columbia*

MODERN EUROPE

Gainful Pursuits: The Making of Industrial Europe, 1600–1914. By Jordan Goodman and Katrina Honeyman. London: Edward Arnold, 1988. Pp. 262. £10.95.

It is difficult to classify this book. It is not a textbook nor is it a monograph with original research. Instead, it uses the recent research of others to provide revisions of some standard themes. Nevertheless, it is quite ambitious in scope and does what one often misses in English books; it approaches Britain and the continent as one whole. In one way it is traditional in that it places major emphasis on Britain, France, and Germany and largely ignores the industrialization of other countries. Russia and the Habsburg monarchy, major countries between 1600 and 1914, are left out.

All the chapters, which encompass individual topics, purport to start with 1600 and end with 1914. Needless to say, on some subjects there is substantially less evidence for the earlier period than the latter. The organization at times becomes burdensome, and it is not always clear how a particular chapter is relevant to the main topic. The chapter on Europe and the integration of the world economy deserves a better rationalization, for example.

One chapter focuses on the gender division of labor. While claiming that other writers have ignored this subject is probably too strong, it is still useful to bring out the contribution of women to industry. The chapter on the development of consumer durables is without question useful and suggests an area for further research. Why the automobile industry is included in this chapter, or in the book at all, is not completely clear. It was certainly not of great importance by 1914. Similarly, the bicycle and sewing-machine industries had had a rather short history by 1914 although probably a more important one. With increasing prosperity in the nineteenth century households could purchase more durables, which in earlier years could be used as a form of saving to be pawned when times were bad. If the authors wished to discuss transportation over the entire period from 1600 to 1914, they should have considered horse-drawn and ox-drawn wagons and the construction and maintenance of roads and railroads. That railways are left out of discussion seems odd, given their importance in the nineteenth century. The authors seem to have some reservations about the concept of the Industrial Revolution. They point out that for a long time artisans produced the bulk of industrial production. Others before them have, of course, objected to the term but no one, including the authors, has come up with a better term. Nevertheless, they assert that by the middle of the nineteenth century, the European economic system was characterized by a boundless industrial dynamic, which could be interpreted to mean than an industrial revolution had in fact taken place. So it may be more the timing with which the authors quarrel.

HERMAN FREUDENBERGER, *Tulane University*

British Technology and European Industrialization: The Norwegian Textile Industry in the Mid Nineteenth Century. By Kristine Bruland. New York: Cambridge University Press, 1989. Pp. xi, 193. $39.50.

In surveying the literature on European industrialization and technological change, Kristine Bruland notes that "the principal weakness of this literature lies in its treatment of the technological level itself. What we have are histories of technological change and industrialization in Europe in which the process of technological change is conspicuous by its absence'' (p. 15). Her book attempts to fill that gap a little with a case study of British technology transfer to the Norwegian textile industry from about 1840 to 1870. Thus, this is not as general a work as the title leads one to expect; it is nonetheless a competent and interesting descriptive history of how British textile engineering companies exported their techniques to Norway.

The limited focus of the study is fortunate because it is the empirical description that contributes most to our knowledge. Despite the author's vigorous efforts to survey the literature and locate her research in the wider debates on industrialization and technological change, there is just not enough analysis—economic or otherwise—to make a fully convincing case for the generality of this study. Moreover, the stories we are told about Norwegian textiles are not used to show us how they might significantly change our analysis of industrialization and economic growth. The fact that standard histories of industrialization tend to shortchange the description of the actual technology transfers stems from the fact that most histories tend to be predominantly *economic* histories concerned with the analysis of development patterns in Western Europe. To the extent that recent work has tended to weaken the often unspoken identity between industrialization seen as the growth of mechanized industries and industrialization as the process of economic growth and development, economic historians have come to focus more on growth itself—its measurement and its sources.

Still, Bruland is correct to note that since what growth was about often involved continental emulation of British practice there is much to be learned from the study of that process itself. In particular, she shows us that technology-exporting firms as well as the importing nations had incentives to make sure that technology transfers did take place. This contrasts with traditional accounts that have stressed the problems of follower nations in importing British technology. Of course British machine exporters stood to profit from marketing their products abroad and therefore worked to overcome entrenched local resistance or skepticism.

Bruland's account of the relationship between Norwegian textile manufacturers and the British firms selling the latest technology demonstrates how detailed and thorough the arrangements were, with a whole ''package'' of goods and services being sold, including training, service, and the export of British workers as well as British equipment. Moreover, the package was then modified to suit specific market conditions of Norwegian industry. It was this fit or the lack of it that determined whether individual firms eventually adopted British technology.

This seems to suggest several important implications which might have been discussed and expanded upon. The first is that follower reluctance to imitate figured less in adoption or nonadoption of new technology than some have argued. The second is that where the new markets did *not* absorb new technologies, it is likely that existing techniques did not suit these nations, given the incentives to British firms to market as fully as possible. The latter point obviously could not be dealt with in studying the successful Norwegian case of technological adoption, but seems a logical offshoot of Bruland's line or reasoning. Finally, and perversely, the demonstration of British success in marketing new inventions *weakens* the importance of diffusion as a concept and supports Nathan Rosenberg's contention that technology adoption was simply a matter of profitability. It should therefore shift the focus of economic historical research away from the technologies themselves and back to differences in institutional features, factor prices, property rights, or political considerations as the explanatory variables of divergent growth patterns.

Finally I should note that while the book offers numerous illuminating discussions of theoretical issues, it also contains a number of analytical lapses that I simply find baffling. To cite but one instance, the author speaks of technical choice not in terms of "the economically efficient choice of technique in terms of capital/labour ratio—which is how technical choice is usually understood in the economics literature—so much as choice among the range of available machine configurations" (p. 80). There then follows a disquisition on the inappropriateness of the Habakkuk thesis to Norway. I had always thought that the choice of machine configuration was subsumed in the economist's definition of economic efficiency and that the use of the term capital/labor ratio involved an attempt to reduce the infinity of possible inputs to a couple of simplified aggregates. Moreover, Habakkuk's thesis did not deny the role of individual-firm problems in the matching of appropriate technologies to each industry but was an attempt to use macro differences in factor prices to account for large-scale differences of technical choice in cross-country comparisons. This problem of making economy-wide judgments based on studying narrowly firm-specific decisions recurs in a number of places.

Despite these reservations, I think the book is a much-needed and welcome study that should find its way onto the shelves of all scholars interested in the history of technological adoption and technological change in modern enterprise.

JOHN VINCENT NYE, *Washington University*

West Cumberland Coal, 1600–1982/3. By Oliver Wood. Kendall, England: Titus Wilson and Son, Ltd., 1988. Cumberland & Westmoreland Antiquarian & Archaelogical Society: Extra Series 24. Pp. 377.

At the end of the nineteenth century about 1 percent of the coal mined in Britain came from West Cumberland; these mines have now been closed in the postwar rationalizations of the National Coal Board. One might want to argue that the experience of West Cumberland provides a miniature of the British coal industry, but that is not Wood's purpose. Wood's book sticks so close to local sources that it rarely ventures into the larger, national framework; it is a work of local history with all the weaknesses of that genre and only some of its strengths.

The Victorian mines in West Cumberland were among the most inefficient in the country; they had the lowest output per worker/shift and were the last to be mechanized. Five generations earlier, in the middle years of the eighteenth century, the mines around Whitehaven were for a while the most productive in the realm and the Lowther family had become rich as Croesus through its careful husbanding of this cash-cow. But the geographical limitations of the coalfield and its restricted stocks of the black stuff could not last forever; in the second half of the nineteenth century the phenomenon of retardation set in rather earlier than in most other regions. Losing their hold over the Irish market in the middle years of the Victorian age was the key turning point; thereafter the mines became grazing grounds for the local ironworking companies. In the long view propounded by Wood, we see quite clearly how the retardation of the first industrial economy was part of its very successful origins. There is an interesting addendum to this theme in the experience of the West Cumberland coal mines, but it is not addressed here.

The economic historian with broader, more catholic interests will find this work a hard slog. Moreover, several disconcerting weaknesses mar its presentation. While acknowledging the inherent difficulties in estimating profitability in early industrial activity, I can find no excuse for determining the profit to be the difference between working costs and sale price without allowing for either capital costs or deferred income on that capital. Over the long run we are told about different wage levels, but only very rarely are we given any other information to determine if such wages were high or low in relation to the earnings of other workers. Similarly, we are given lots of incidental detail about mining catastrophes, but only occasionally sense of the total mining population at risk. This insensitivity to the representativeness of the data is a real pity since it would appear that the materials Wood used are very rich and could have been more profitably mined by a more skilled researcher. The present work simply feels like a shower of the author's index cards.

DAVID LEVINE, *The Ontario Institute for Studies in Education*

East End, West End: The Face of Leeds During Urbanisation, 1684–1842. By Maurice Beresford. Leeds: The Thoresby Society, 1988. Pp. xxi, 562.

This book is a remarkable demonstration of the value of "microtopography" to urban history. For more than thirty years Maurice Beresford has been patiently researching the building process that transformed Leeds between 1684 and 1842 into an industrial center. Best known for his *New Towns of the Middle Ages* (New York, 1965), Beresford brings a medievalist's passion for documents to his study. He has amassed information from rate books, deeds, insurance registries, maps, directories, photographs, and every other conceivable source. In addition, he has personally explored virtually every structure that survives from his period, often just ahead of the bulldozers.

Professor emeritus at the University of Leeds and Patron of the Thoresby Society, Beresford is a loyal son of Leeds. The story he tells, however, is a sad and frightening one of a society systematically degrading and poisoning its own environment. In telling this important story Beresford perhaps lacks Martin Daunton's gift for reconstructing working-class life from topographical details; nor does he offer the brilliant social history of the middle class that David Cannadine and Leonore Davidoff provide in their researches on Birmingham. Nevertheless, no other study offers so vivid and detailed an account of the whole range of the urban environment during these years of explosive growth.

As Beresford shows, Leeds in the late seventeenth century could still accommodate new building within its old central streets. There even the wealthiest merchants were content to occupy houses that combined residence and warehouse and whose "backsides" faced courtyards crowded with the cottages of the poor. In the second half of the eighteenth century, however, "gentlemen merchants" of the town attempted to create an elegant "West End" for themselves, founded on social segregation and modeled on the London squares or the Bath crescents. Yet by the 1840s the Leeds West End had been engulfed in the "noisome, unwholesome and offensive smells, stenches, smokes, and vapors" (p. 289), as one lawsuit put it, from the factories that those gentlemen owned.

The working class, of course, fared much worse. Workers in the new mills overflowed the old central courts and moved east toward speculative developments of high-density "back-to-back" houses. In the cholera years of the 1830s and 1840s this newly formed "East End" became the prime site for the disease, and the crowding, filth, and death recorded in Robert Baker's sanitary reports shocked the nation.

Beresford enriches this basic narrative with a wealth of microtopographical details that demonstrate how piecemeal and unexpected development appeared to contemporaries. For example, he shows that, although the West End was based on class segregation, the merchants who occupied the grand terraced houses or villas were not too proud to put their warehouses and even finishing shops in their backyards. These backyard shops helped to undermine the West End when some of them were transformed into full-scale factories.

But Beresford's emphasis on the inadvertent goes too far, in my view, when he argues for "the inadvertency of much slumdom" (p. xxix). By this he means that the back-to-backs merely copied and generalized the typical cottage in the old central courtyards; moreover, developers could not anticipate the baleful results of their back-to-backs until the whole East End was filled with them. The book, however, provides ample evidence that the worst features of the back-to-backs were the inevitable outcome of a high-profit system dominated by the land speculator and the absentee landlord.

As Beresford acknowledges, the inhuman crowding in the East End could not be blamed on the spatial constraints of a walking city. During the worst decades of cholera and overcrowding there were extensive open fields within easy walking distance of Leeds' mills. Nor could the high density be blamed entirely on the incapacity of working-class families to afford any but the lowest rents, for these low rents provided handsome yields to the landlord: 9.3 percent on the average working-class cottage in Beresford's calculation, compared to 6.25 percent for a middle class house or 3.5 percent for government bonds.

Beresford's own findings confirm Robert Baker's 1842 judgment that the inhumanity of the back-to-back was "part of the economy of buildings that are to pay a good percentage" (p. 430). To maintain that good percentage, wealthy landowners kept undeveloped land vitally needed for housing off the market until they got their price, and developers then carefully and cunningly laid out houses to maximize density and profit.

Alternatives to this system were virtually nonexistent for the Leeds working class. The few building societies that existed were in fact vehicles for lower-middle-class speculators seeking to be absentee landlords. The back-to-backs these societies constructed were virtually identical to those of the larger speculators. Nor did Leeds workers have the option, as North American workers often did, of building their own homes on cheap, unregulated land at the urban fringes. As a result, Beresford finds districts in the East End where only one house in forty was owner-occupied. There was nothing "inadvertent" about the consequences of a housing market structured to extract the largest profits from the poorest people.

ROBERT FISHMAN, *Rutgers University, Camden*

Trade and Shipping, Lord Inchcape, 1852–1932. By Stephanie Jones. Manchester: Manchester University Press, 1989. Pp. xiii, 222. $59.95.

In this slim volume Stephanie Jones accomplishes the large task of recording the business and public activities of the Napoleon of British commerce, James Lyle Mackay, the first Earl Inchcape. The growth of the Inchcape empire in the third quarter of the nineteenth century and its stagnation during the interwar period mirrored the course of the British economy. At its peak, the Inchcape group of related businesses, known as the Mackinnon/Inchcape group, spanned the globe with shipping and merchant interests in Australia, Africa, and Asia. In 1914 the combined fleet of the Pacific and Orient (P&O) and British India (BI) lines, two of Inchcape's concerns, accounted for about 10 percent of the world's shipping tonnage.

Drawing upon, among other sources, personal papers, business archives, and government records in Britain, India, and Australia, Jones explores the private and public personae of Inchcape. The book combines both chronological and thematic approaches. After a brief chapter which describes the Inchcape family's shipping and merchant background in Scotland and Canada, Jones divides Inchcape's career into two episodes, his experience in India between 1874 and 1894 working for the merchant house of Mackinnon Mackenzie and his rise through the firm, and the period after his return to England as chairman of the Mackinnon/Inchcape group of businesses. The recurrent theme throughout is Jones's assessment of Inchcape's role in shaping his own destiny.

Inchcape was born in Arbroath, Scotland, into a family which had long involvement in shipping; nonetheless it could hardly be said that this background paved the way to his later success. Jones attributes Inchcape's rise to his ability through hard work to capitalize on good fortune. When he joined Mackinnon Mackenzie in 1874 as a shipping clerk the company enjoyed great prominence in British India; Inchcape also faced little competition in his climb to the top of the organization. He returned to England in 1894 at a time when both BI and P&O needed new blood at the top. The high profits of the conglomerate in the early years under his control were largely associated with the demand for shipping services during World War I and not with any significant new changes in organization or technology. After the war, faced with increasing foreign competition, Inchcape's fortune changed along with the rest of the British shipping industry. Jones criticizes Inchcape's conservative financing practices during this period, and his failure to adopt new techniques and to delegate authority. Like other businessmen of the time, Inchcape believed that the dislocation of the interwar years could only be redressed by a return to the conditions and institutions of the prewar period. By the mid 1920s, Jones concludes, Inchcape was irreversibly out of touch.

Throughout his life Inchcape was as heavily involved in public institutions as he was in private business. Jones parallels his rise in official circles and his climb to the top of the Mackinnon/Inchcape group. In India he spoke for the British business community, and during the interwar period he played an important part in formulating British economic policy. He was a member of the Geddes Committee on public spending and the Cunliffe Committee on currency and foreign exchanges. His philosophy mirrored his belief that the government had not assisted his own rise; his proposed policies, like his business dealings, harked back to the practices of the golden age before the Great War.

Jones has achieved a business history which should have a wide audience. She discusses Inchcape's early years in the context of the part Scottish merchants played in British industry. Inchcape's experiences in India are related to the larger debate over British net investment and the Indian balance of payments. Those searching for entrepreneurial failure will also find the book rewarding. Finally, the author's account of Inchcape's committee work presents historians of policy formation with a new body of research.

The volume is part of a series, edited by Alex J. Robertson, which examines the role of business leaders in shaping modern British industrial society. Jones's contribution sets a high standard for the remaining volumes.

MICHAEL HUBERMAN, *Trent University*

Industrialization, Family Life, and Class Relations: Saint-Chamond, 1815–1914. By Elinor Accampo. Berkeley: University of California Press, 1989. Pp. xvii, 301. $35.00.

Elinor Accampo's case study of the French city of Saint-Chamond during the nineteenth century suggests the potential of a merger of family and labor history, as well as the difficulties that arise in such a project. Accampo's book focuses on two different aspects of the history of nineteenth-century Saint-Chamond, demographic behavior and class relations. Primarily using data from the reconstitution of marriages from 1816 to 1825 and 1861 to 1866, she argues that demographic behavior was linked to the organization of work. In the earlier period, proletarian families served as "a natural basis for work organization" (p. 45) in the artisanal nailmaking and ribbonweaving trades of the city. The most significant demographic characteristic of this population is the evidence of family limitation within marriage. Accampo suggests that this family limitation took the form of spacing as well as stopping behavior. This behavior, Accampo argues, was related to the pervasiveness of death in the city and to different responses to death arising from different family strategies, themselves linked to the organization of work. Ribbonweaver families needed the work of the wife and mother and therefore had children quickly, at the beginning of their marriage, then stopped. Nailmakers, on the other hand, had less use for the labor of their wives; their fertility remained close to natural limits.

In the second half of the century factory organization of work came to Saint-Chamond, making productive and reproductive activities difficult for women to coordinate. Low wages made the income of married women vital to their families' well-being, and so married women left home for the factories. Along with other changes, fertility within marriage declined, the result of attempts by factory workers to "regain some control over their lives" (p. 136) and of the ill health brought on by the appalling conditions in which these families lived.

The hostile environment in industrial Saint-Chamond also defined class relations within the city. Employers responded to these conditions by paternalistic attempts to alleviate the worst aspects of industrialism. But in the second half of the century republicanism and socialism gave workers a new perception of their relationship to their employers, and by the 1890s there is evidence of a rejection of the "moral and material hegemony" that the elite tried to exercise over the working class. In spite of the quiescent reputation of the Saint-Chamond working class, Accampo shows clearly that this was only in comparison with its more active neighbors in Saint-Etienne and Rive-de-Gier.

The book's argument is in most respects convincing, and Accampo breaks new ground in her analysis of the components of reduced marital fertility, the prevalence of abortion, and the role of various aspects of employer hegemony in the lives of the working class. But one might contest some aspects of her analysis of family formation and class relations in Saint-Chamond. Migration receives relatively short shrift, given its importance in the growth of the city's population. She seems to me to overestimate both differences in behavior between the countryside and Saint-Chamond—the decline of fertility, for example, occurred at the same time in both areas, except for a few pockets of very late decline in the countryside—and the extent to which the move to the city meant a cultural break with the countryside. Literacy is cited in one place as an agent of cultural change (pp. 70–71), while education is mentioned as a means by which conservative values were inculcated in children (p. 148). But the principal disappointment of this book lies in the structure of the argument. Family formation and class relations are presented as two outcomes of the same factors, the proletarianization and impoverishment of the Saint-Chamonnais working class, but are never brought together. Accampo does not connect workers' assertion of independence in labor relations, voting, and religion with their attempts to control family formation. The book is, then, an incomplete promise of the ways in which family history and labor history might interact to produce a more complete account of the societal transformations associated with industrialization.

JAMES R. LEHNING, *University of Utah*

L'Électricité et ses consommateurs. Actes du quatrième colloque de l'Association pour l'histoire de l'électricité en France, Paris, 19–21 mai 1987. Paris: Association pour l'histoire de l'électricité en France, 1987. Pp. 312.

The quality of this volume far surpasses its predecessors in the series, and it demonstrates that the efforts of the Association pour l'histoire de l'électricité en France (with the support of Electricité de France, EDF) are finally bearing rich fruit. Now that a significant body of scholars peoples the Association's conferences, the resulting volumes have fewer of the once-obligatory papers by retired industry spokesmen. Nonetheless, these papers indicate that the study of electrical history in France is concentrated at two centers, one at the Université de Paris-IV (under the directorship of François Caron), the other at the Ecole des Mines' Centre Sociologique de l'Innovation (CSI—under the directorship of Michel Callon). Despite Caron's presidency of the Association, the work in this volume from the latter group represents by far the more innovative scholarship.

Economic historians will be pleased to find a number of pieces on the issue of implanting electrical services, and these articles contribute fruitfully to debates over the character of demand, the costs of supply, and the concerns of utilities and governmental regulators. With the exception of a flat piece by Jean-Claude Ménégoz on power supply and demand in the Dauphiné up to World War I, these papers go far beyond the facile notion that the intrinsic advantages of electrical supply "created" a demand. Indeed, as a whole they show that the French state was justified in considering domestic electrical energy a luxury good and that cultural and institutional factors weighed as much as costs and prices in pacing system development. Among the nonacademic participants, Bernard Legrand and Georges Yelnick, officials of Péchiney, France's mammoth aluminum producer, give for the first time a concise history of that firm's endless search for cheap electricity. Their business perspective should give historians and policymakers pause since they demonstrate the firm's indifference toward its French roots as it pursued its quest from the Columbia basin to West Africa—no crude nationalism there.

Outstanding articles by Madeleine Akrich and Cécile Méadel (both of the CSI) show how a loose network of power companies, consulting firms, public agencies, and electrical device manufacturers had to invent the electrical power consumers that their institutions and systems seemed to require. The Akrich article in particular, which addresses West Africa, shows how the ostensibly simple task of connecting domestic consumers to power supplies entailed a transformation of housing (thatched huts couldn't support meters), property relations (collective ownership of land made right-of-way concessions and meter responsibility impossible), and social relations (electricity became a new emblem of social status). Both authors take us far from a simple economistic notion of demand and supply elasticities. Méadel shows how the success of the French radio industry hinged upon the invention of modern listeners through the development of radio program material and the consequent elbowing aside of hobbyists with their dual transmitter-receiver units. Philippe Mustar (also of the CSI) similarly analyzes the strategies of gas companies as they vacillated between seeking new consumers or increasing demand among existing users when demand stagnated in the 1880s. He argues that each approach implied the imposition of presumptions about the meanings of gas consumption upon customers, and his discussion directly parallels those within electrical utilities a century later.

Aside from an interesting yet unconvincing article by Bernard Barraqué on the link between Taylorism and the emergence of illuminating engineering, most of the articles in this volume concerning the actual activities of consumption deal with agricultural and domestic consumption. A superb piece of Thierry Nadau elegantly portrays the often bizarre (by today's standards) efforts to make electrical power replace oil products on the farm for such tasks as plowing, in order to increase consumption on high-cost, sparse rural networks. Papers by Fabienne Cardot, Jean Boin, and Jean Dubois examine the relationship between utilities and the housewife, though she remained to be invented in the period Cardot addresses. Cardot's article conceptually serves as a useful bridge between the CSI approaches and the strict reportage of Boin and Dubois, who are both EDF employees. As a group, these articles represent the first systematic foray into examining the transformation of domestic and family life and relations with the onset of electricity. Topically, they lay the foundation for work which can span economic, social, and technological history.

Other articles in the volume cover topics ranging from the development of meters and telegraphy devices to the military uses of electrochemistry. Other pieces discuss electrical rate-making, but they contribute little to the already voluminous literature on the subject. An oddly out-of-place article by W. Bernard Carlson elegantly discusses the complex inventive process of Elihu Thomson.

This volume should be of considerable interest and use not only to the readers of this JOURNAL who are concerned with electricity per se, but also to those who seek theoretical frameworks which allow us to understand the points of contact between supply and demand in new ways. This worthy collection is a credit to the Association and it charts a fascinating new set of directions which research in economic history could take.

ROBERT L. FROST, *State University of New York, Albany*

Family and the Female Life Course: The Women of Verviers, Belgium, 1849–1880. By George Alter. Madison: University of Wisconsin Press, 1988. Pp. xiv, 226. $39.50, cloth; $24.25, paper.

George Alter has written a methodologically sophisticated yet very readable history of the women who lived in Verviers, a textile town in Belgium, during the second half of the nineteenth century. Alter's use of proportional-hazard models and increment-decrement life tables will be unfamiliar to all but the most sophisticated demographic historians. Nonetheless, the state-of-the-art methodology should not repel less quantitatively oriented historians. Alter is unusually clear in his methodological explanations. He carefully lays out the assumptions behind his work and explains them in readable English. His chapter on methods and data can stand alone as an introduction to the methods of historical demography.

Based on a relatively unique source—-Belgium's late nineteenth-century population registers—Alter's book is able to shed new light on some of the most vexing questions in the history of women and work. The population registers—in principle—kept track of people from the time they were opened until they were closed. They recorded the births, deaths, marriages, and migrations pertaining to everyone included. Thus, they are like having running censuses combined with vital registers. The complete nature of the records allowed Alter to analyze the case histories of many people—primarily those whose marriages were disrupted or who migrated—usually discarded in traditional census or family reconstitution analysis. More important, the methodology and data permitted him to ask questions about sequences of events and transitions from one event to another. Moreover, although the occupational data were not particularly good, Alter was able to analyze women's career patterns in a limited way. Not content to allow his analysis to rest exclusively on the registers, Alter also linked the registers to tax records and censuses. He gathered data on wages for men and women in various occupations and made use of literary studies. In short, his book delivers much more than it promises. It is more than a study of the family and the female life course; it is a fairly complete picture of women, work, and working-class courtship in this interesting Belgian town.

Specialists will find his chapter on the fertility transition most interesting. Here Alter best exhibits his skills as a demographer and statistician in grappling with the most interesting questions in demographic history. Alter confirms recent work that points toward cultural rather than economic interpretations of fertility decline. Although family ties remained strong, Alter posits a shift in attitude from one wherein children were viewed in terms of the contributions they could make to their parents toward one wherein parents were responsible for their children. Significantly, he finds that older women migrants were much less likely to show signs of family limitation that women born or raised in the city.

Nonspecialists and those interested in women's history will find much of interest in his chapters on women's work and working-class courtship. Alter discovered that the life histories of women revealed a strong attachment to family life. Regardless of social and marital status, women remained closely tied to either their families of origin or their families of procreation. He also shows that women's occupations depended upon marital status and social class. He demonstrates that daughters of elite women very rarely worked. When they did, they pursued sewing and other occupations which would leave them in an exclusively female world. Most non-elite unmarried women reported a job; most poorer married women indicated that they did not work. Widowed women usually went back into the workforce, although this was a more common characteristic of poorer women. Whenever possible, women tried to move out of the workforce altogether. One reason for this was that whatever work women did, they were paid much less than men, and there was very little difference in what women earned for different jobs. At any given date they earned only slightly more than children. Although the wage differential between men's and women's work narrowed during the nineteenth century, the salient fact is that women were paid much less than men. Thus, especially given the atrocious conditions under which many women worked, it is not surprising that they aspired to domesticity. Domesticity, however, depended upon finding the right spouse. In one of Alter's most original chapters, he presents a refined analysis of the double standard to explain Verviers' high bridal-pregnancy and illegitimacy rates as the unwanted outcomes of complicated working-class courtship strategies.

As in every book, some conclusions seem less persuasive than others. One of Alter's most interesting findings is that very few women migrated to Verviers without their families. The few who came alone seem to have come to work as domestic servants. These women were often older. Alter wants to interpret this as a "career choice," although clearly these women could have come out of desperation and gotten stuck in undesirable positions. His data on occupational mobility in fact indicate that almost no one went into service after having another occupation. But this is a minor argument with an otherwise well-written methodological tour-de-force.

Alter is to be congratulated on producing a fine monograph which will set the standard for family and demographic history in the years to come.

NANCY FITCH, *California State University, Fullerton*

The German Economy, 1945–1947: Charles P. Kindleberger's Letters From the Field. By Charles P. Kindleberger. Westport, CT: Meckler, 1989. Pp. lvi, 230. $30.00.

Charles Kindleberger has published so many books and kept up such an uninterrupted barrage of lively perceptive comment on all aspects of modern economic history that it was surely inevitable that he would eventually commit a really grand literary eccentricity. This is an item of genuine bibliographical exotica, the kind of volume beloved of slightly deranged bibliophiles and one destined to appear for a long time in the smudgy catalogues of slightly deranged second-hand book dealers. It has three parts. One consists of facsimiles of letters which he wrote from Germany and Austria to colleagues and acquaintances back in Washington in August 1946 when he was head of the Division of German and Austrian Economic Affairs in the Department of State, interspersed with typeset paragraphs excerpted from letters to his wife. He wrote (and retained copies of) 46 long and detailed letters in that one month alone, not counting those to his wife. They are written in that breathlessly hasty and allusive style which will be familiar to readers of his recent works. It is no doubt a tribute to the power of academic conformism that this style did not invade his earlier work on economics. The second part is the same mixture as before but for mid-March to mid-April 1947, when he was a middle-rank official in the U.S. delegation to the Council of Foreign Ministers in Moscow. There are only 21 of these, plus the snippets from more intimate correspondence. There was perhaps more work to do, or the accommodation in Moscow was warmer. Finally come 5 miscellaneous letters written from Germany in April and May 1945.

I can not think of any other volume which deliberately contains so many pages of crossings-out and misprints and for the connoisseur of mistakes made by men in a hurry the facsimiles should be a source of boundless delight. But for the historian trying to use them as documentary sources they will more probably be the cause of "lots of rustration and beefs everywhere" (p. 149). This is because Kindleberger, although not important enough to be involved in high-level policy making, was deeply involved in the fine bureaucratic detail of trying to make sense of the policies of those who were. For the reader to make sense of his daily activities and comments so inconsequentially offered, an equally detailed exegesis of these texts was needed, explaining who all the people referred to were (especially because if they were foreigners their names are usually misspelled), of what the disputes over policy consisted, and what the position of the United States as opposed to that of the other occupying powers was. Instead we have a short general essay by Günter Bischof on Germany and Austria under the occupation which does not go into the detailed economic questions, such as coal allocation, food rationing, trade permits, and currency control with which the letters deal. Even the knowledgeable reader finds it difficult to follow the policy disputes with the other occupying powers with which much of the material is concerned, with "Koroschskin (if that is his name)" (p. 3), for example, or with "Kopalhov (???)" (p. 10), for example. Repelled by these interpretational difficulties the only recourse is to glean from the more general observations that Kindleberger saved for posterity, like the fact that on 16 August 1946 he saw a woman in Vienna carrying potatoes in a shopping bag. As in most Allied books on the occupation the Germans are only dimly to be discerned scurrying about in the background looking for a job, or just a cigarette. Thus in an addendum to one of the August letters we glimpse the distinguished economic statistician on whose work so many scholars have come to rely, Rolf Wagenführ, "Wagenfels (not sure of name but not Wagemann)" (p. 168), scraping a job off the British because the United States did not want him after the Russians had finished with him. Secretary Marshall is too remote to be discerned at all, except that the lower ranks in his delegation to Moscow thought that he made a poor start there. Even the great central figure General Lucius Clay "not a little scary for us State Department types" (p. 19) is obscured by the detail. What wonderful energy and creativity Kindleberger has. But not much time went to the preparation of this oddity, more's the pity, like the "property memo which I dashed off between 4 PM Sunday and 11 AM Monday morning with a certain amount of time out for food and sleep." Still, "Something of a tour de force, eh?" (p. 163).

ALAN S. MILWARD, *London School of Economics*

AFRICA, ASIA, AUSTRALIA

The African Poor: A History. By John Iliffe. New York: Cambridge University Press, 1987. Pp. ix, 387. $49.50, cloth; $14.95, paper.

This erudite work of synthesis and analysis defines the characteristics and limits of African poverty, sets forth the continuity and the transformation of poverty, and provides a rich background and implicit critique of current policies intended to ameliorate poverty. It reads with remarkable clarity and interest, especially given the wide range of regions and time the author encompasses.

Iliffe's analytical apparatus is simple, at base. He distinguishes land-rich poverty (where the poor are those unable to labor) from land-scarce poverty (where the poor are unable to sell their labor power). Then he distinguishes structural or long-term poverty from conjunctural poverty. The African poor, he argues, have been overwhelmingly structurally poor in land-rich societies. That is, they were incapacitated and unable to work—the lame, the leprous, and the old and young left without families. The very poor were dominantly female and dominantly young. Only recently, and particularly in southern Africa, have the poor begun to be dominated by able-bodied persons without access to land or to work. The strength of the apparatus comes in the persistence with which the author applies it and draws out results.

At the same time Iliffe devotes considerable effort to dispelling the myth that Africa had no poor. Europeans, who wrote most of the sources, tended to believe the myth of the omnipresent African family and its social safety net. African societies, in some cases, helped propagate the myth. It is in contrast to this myth that Iliffe asserts that "nothing illustrates the continuity of the African past more vividly than the study of poverty" (p. 81). For society after society Iliffe is able to demonstrate the existence of significant numbers of "the very poor,"as he calls them, to distinguish the destitute who were failing to survive from the much larger number ("the poor") who had to struggle to subsist. Iliffe begins with Christian Ethiopia, where an unusual development of charitable institutions made poverty more visible but probably not more common than in other parts of Africa. Elsewhere on the continent, even in Muslim Africa, charitable institutions were generally lacking, and the poor had mostly to fend for themselves. For precolonial Africa—the subject of about half the book—the reader is led through a fascinating range of social situations. Outstanding among them are such cases as the creation of a landless class through political manipulation in the kingdoms of Rwanda and Burundi, and the servile poverty of groups held in subjection by the desert-edge Tswana, reflected in a "rich vocabulary of poverty."

The book is also a history of European welfare ideas and activities in Africa. The significance of European perceptions is made clear in the case of missionary work among the Igbo. Anglicans, not trained in work with the poor, saw little poverty. Catholic missionaries (especially sisters), who sought out occasions for performing acts of mercy, were soon inundated by poor people, and saw Igbo society as in misery. Igbo society had many poor, but effectively hid them. The story of colonial welfare is brought up through the twentieth century, including the irony that South Africa, beginning in the 1940s, set up a welfare system for the indigent, structural poor just as poverty itself began to be dominated by those who were able-bodied but unable to find work.

The story has two endings. First, in independent Africa, mass famine returned in the 1980s after a half century of absence. The famines brought poverty to the attention of governments and international agencies. Yet as Iliffe argues, both the political left and right mistakenly saw poverty as recent, resulting either from colonial exploitation or African governmental incompetence, rather than as the reassertion of a historic pattern of land-rich poverty. The second ending is the transformation of poverty in southern Africa, and the spread of land-scarce poverty to other industrializing areas of the continent.

Iliffe's wide reading and determined synthesis have united disparate studies and documents into a field of study—the history of the African poor—and have demonstrated the relevance of this history to the current crisis of African poverty. For Iliffe, "the heroism of African history is to be found not in the deeds of kings but in the struggles of ordinary people" (p. 1). He suggests that his approach to reconstructing that past, through comparative social history, is an antidote to the limits of previous approaches: the parochial national histories of the past generation, and the elitist colonial studies of the preceding period. Whether this book represents a turning point in the literature remains to be seen, but it unquestionably sets a high standard for the continental synthesis of African history.

Patrick Manning, *Northeastern University*

The Hindu Equilibrium. Vol. 1: *Cultural Stability and Economic Stagnation*. Vol. 2: *Aspects of Indian Labour*. By Deepak Lal. New York: Oxford University Press, 1989. Vol. 1: Pp. xxvii, 345. $69.00. Vol. 2: Pp. xii, 197. $45.00.

Deepak Lal's two-volume book combines both an economic and social history of India with an analysis of the current economic situation that applies the history to today's issues. It is an unorthodox and provocative book with a breadth of approach well beyond formal economics, encompassing historical, anthropological, and political approaches to India's economic development. In its breadth the book is more in the older European tradition of the work of Albert Hirschman, Arthur Lewis, and Gunnar Myrdal among development economists than of today's narrower econometricians. The economic analysis is rigorous, but the author recognizes the limitations of his models in terms of assumptions and data, especially in the historical sections of his work. But while these strong positive elements in the book's two volumes make it well worth reading, the book is weakened—especially in some of the author's generalizations and his look at today's issues—by leaps in reasoning and by ideological biases that lead the author into what I feel are exaggerations and errors. In my review I will first summarize the book's arguments and then briefly point out the disagreements I have.

The summary is made easier by the author's introductory presentation and his summary chapter of Volume 1. His underlying economic argument, which disagrees with the conventional wisdom, is that India, for most of its history, has *not* been a labor surplus economy but rather a labor scarce and land surplus economy. The caste system evolved, and maintained itself successfully, as an institutional structure that strongly discouraged labor mobility in such a land-abundant environment. Economically the system led to "an average standard of living for the populace which, though stagnant and low by current standards, was for millenia not surpassed by most other countries of the world . . . [The] mass of Hindus (until fairly recently) had little incentive to alter a system which . . . has more than proved its worth" (p. 3). On the political and administrative level the system resulted in a local structure which made it possible for India's successive rulers, including the Moslem and British, to extract a revenue from the land, to support their higher administrations and empires, without disrupting the village economy. Thus foreign rulers as well, even though they did not sympathize with the caste system, had little incentive to change it.

After independence, however, the system became economically dysfunctional. In the face of rapidly accelerating population growth and resulting pressure upon the land, it became essential for India to speed up its industrialization. But the caste system, by giving highest status to religious, intellectual, and warrior groups within the Hindu population, slows up his process. It is the major social reason for the denigration of private profit—making business and entrepreneurial activities undesirable—and of the role of the market in general. This denigration has led to an emphasis upon the government as the controlling agency of the economy, with reliance upon such means as central planning carried out by intellectuals, an elaborate network of controls over industry enforced by a superior bureaucracy, and the direct government ownership of major sectors of industry. These industrial policies were laid down in the 1950s under the political and intellectual influence of Prime Minister Nehru, and were formulated by such intellectuals as P. C. Mahalanobis, whose ideas underlay the Second and Third Five Year Plans. The caste bias against business was reinforced by various experiences of and ideas from the later years of British rule. These included the protective tariff policy for Indian industry after World War I, the Fabian socialism imbibed by Indian leaders educated in England, and the contempt that the British rulers in India had for businessmen. These supported the inherent caste-induced bias against the market. "This intellectual or ideological parameter . . . prevents that movement from a traditional agricultural revenue economy to a market-based industrial economy, so essential for ending India's economic stagnation'' (p. 311). Instead it leads to the low ''Hindu rate of growth'' immortalized in Raj Krishna's famous phrase.

Volume I presents this broad thesis and applies it to the current scene. Volume II is, in effect, a lengthy technical economic appendix to Chapter 9, on labor markets, in Volume I. It examines in detail the argument of the surplus labor theory as it applies to India, by analyzing the functioning of rural and urban labor markets. Since historical data on this are very weak, most of the treatment is of the recent and current situation. The author concludes that the neoclassical theory of labor markets provides a satisfactory framework to explain the functioning of both rural and urban labor markets, and of movement of labor within and between those markets. Labor supply is not unlimited at a given wage; wages are responsive to changes in demand for labor at any given time, and labor in turn moves in response to changes in wages. A more rapid rate of industrialization would have a strong positive effect on the total demand for labor, thereby raising incomes of both urban and rural workers and reducing overall poverty. The ''trickle-down effect'' would work. It is the policy constraints to industrial growth that have led to India's economic stagnation. These in turn, coming back to Volume I, are the product of a social system that denigrates the role of the market and private profit-making entrepreneurship.

As I stated at the beginning, this is an imaginative and insightful book. Its hypothesis of the caste system as an effective and successful economic response to India's geopolitical environment is innovative and persuasive. It is even more persuasive in the light of the parallel hypothesis of a somewhat similar high-level equilibrium trap in the Chinese economy prior to the nineteenth century. That hypothesis also argues that the very success of the Chinese economy before the nineteenth century slowed the pace of the Chinese response to the subsequent Western intruders. That ingrained caste attitudes in India toward business may have subconsciously influenced leadership attitudes toward business, especially in combination with other rationales for the actual policies, is also somewhat persuasive.

But while the author recognizes that he cannot *prove* a close relationship between the caste system and government economic policy, he in my opinion overstresses the relationship. He bases his argument in large part on quotations from Nehru. Other national policymakers of the 1950s in the fields of political and economic policy, such as Sardar Patel and T. T. Krishnamachari had different attitudes toward business, and argued for other policies. The argument is further weakened by the fact that while the caste system is nationwide, rates of industrial growth in some of the states, such as Gujarat and Maharashtra, which have large business communities, have been high, although in other states, such as Bihar and Orissa, those rates have been low. The Hindu rate of growth is, of course, a national average that includes all the states. Were the effects of the caste system different in the different states? Economic policies have clearly been influenced by factors other than caste. In my opinion the original post-independence policies toward industry in India can better be explained by other more direct reasons than caste; the continuance of those policies reflects the political weight of influential economic groups, including private business ones, which have benefited from them. The recent work of Pranab Bardhan, Stanley Kochanek and Lloyd and Susanne Rudolph on political economy deal with this in depth. On the caste influence too, I think the author would have benefited by referring to Milton Singer's anthropological classic, *When A Great Tradition Modernizes* (Chicago, 1980), which looks specifically at the adaptation of high-caste groups in Madras to private business activity.

While the author's review of India's positive economic performance under British rule is both very useful and convenient and corrects various errors, it is marred, in my opinion, by his own misinterpretations. He argues that the introduction of a protective tariff by the British in the 1920s contributed to the subsequent decline in the rate of growth of industry in British India, and served as an inspiration and model for India's industrial protection and import-substitution policies following independence. He nowhere mentions the impact of the Great Depression of the 1930s on world trade and industry and its inevitable effects upon India's industrial growth, which must have far outweighed any effects of the protective tariffs. With respect to the reasons for post-independence protective policies, he ignores India's own nationalism and the strong Swadeshi movement before independence. He does not mention the export pessimism that reflected the experience of the 1930s, and which characterized the thinking of many Indian policymakers and economists. Possibly even more important, and unmentioned by the author in explaining the development of the complex system of control over industrial production and trade that characterizes India today, was the experience of World War II. This saw the establishment by the British of an elaborate control system, which India inherited at independence, and subsequently strengthened.

With respect to current issues, there are several other points on which I disagree with the author. He strongly overemphasizes the role of the Planning Commission in contemporary India. While its role was very important under Nehru, its importance has greatly diminished relative to the formal central government's economic ministries and the Prime Minister's office, as well as the state governments. Today the Planning Commission's role is marginal rather than central.

Lal also speaks, in a half-serious fashion, of the "immiserization" of the top 15 percent of India's population. I think he is wrong on this, especially if the underground economy is included. I think further that this top 15 percent of the population—or 100 million people—would provide a large internal market for Indian industry if industrial policy were changed to allow firms to produce industrial products to meet that potential demand. Foreign trade might then serve as a "handmaiden" of India's industrial growth, rather than as the "engine" that Lal advocates.

A final criticism I have is his tendency to lump together Marx and W. Arthur Lewis as the intellectual forebearers of India's post-independence economic policies, characterized by suspicion of "markets, merchants and the profit motive." I think Lal is incorrect in his interpretation of Arthur Lewis's ideology and economics, as well as of Lewis's influence in India; his remarks may reflect his own ideological bias.

But despite these caveats I would like to end this review by repeating that I consider the two volumes very interesting, clearly provocative, and well worth reading. All the same, Volume I, in its treatment of current issues other than the labor market, should be read with a grain of salt, and if possible together with other interpretations of India's current economic problems and policies.

George Rosen, *University of Illinois, Chicago*

Rising Damp: Sydney, 1870–90. By Shirley Fitzgerald. New York: Oxford University Press, 1987. Pp. xvi, 264. $42.50.

Although Friedrich Engels's Manchester may be the most infamous example of a city caught in the contradictory currents of rapid urbanization, Shirley Fitzgerald's Sydney during the years 1870 to 1890 offers the smoky cottonopolis stiff competition. Written in the tradition of the *Condition of the Working Class*, her spirited social history of Sydney during a long-running boom that ended in the downturn of the early 1890s contends that "there was a large and widening gap between myth and reality concerning standards of living in Sydney" (p. 201). The myth is the claim of the colony's promoters that labor scarcity in Australia ensured most workers a high and rising standard of living. The reality is that "just as rising damp was showing through the attractive facades of the boom-built houses, so living and working conditions were being slowly eroded" (p. 226).

The case for deterioration focuses on growth both in the city and in the burgeoning suburbs. Fitzgerald argues that the dominance of the provincial legislature by rural-based "pastoral" interests and their urban merchant allies blocked measures that would have curbed crowding and problems of sanitation. The high densities of the inner suburbs of Sydney by 1890 would have been absent if the responsible government authorities had opted to build commuter railways instead of the lower-cost (and slower) trams. Regulation of the noxious trades—the tanners, meat processors, and wool-washers crucial to Sydney's hinterland—likewise ran afoul of rural opposition. The municipal government is also taken to task, despite carrying out construction of a sewer system that was near completion in 1890 and installation of a new water supply by the mid-1890s. Rising mortality through the late 1870s in Sydney and the early 1880s in the suburbs is the primary quantitative evidence offered to support a case for deteriorating conditions, although the discussion fails to note that the urban-rural mortality differential showed continual—if modest—narrowing throughout the period (p. 99).

Fitzgerald argues further that improved working conditions or opportunities for upward mobility did not offset the impact of deterioration in living standards. Eschewing any serious discussion of real earnings, she suggests that the growth of casual labor in building, clothing manufacture, and the docks, along with seasonal rural-urban migration, led to rising insecurity. In any event the real way to test whether Sydney offered the opportunities promised by its boosters is to assess the chances for economic improvement. In the most substantial empirical contribution of the book, Fitzgerald presents the results of a study of occupational mobility using samples drawn from marriage registers for the early 1870s and late 1880s. In general, she concludes that young men tended to have the same or a lower occupational ranking than their fathers, with prospects for mobility worsening slightly over the period. Sydney's economy was not immune from the incursion of factory production methods and their potential for increased alienation and a "closing in" of real options (p. 143).

The major exception to this pattern are the Irish, who on the average experienced a substantial improvement relative to their fathers. This exception highlights a major concern with this path of analysis. The author agrees with contemporaries that relative to Britain, pay differentials between the unskilled and the skilled were compressed in Australia. She also notes that the bulk of immigrants were relatively skilled workers (pp. 219–20). For these newcomers the new life in Sydney may have implied a move downward in occupational status but a move up in income (and living standards), depending upon the relationship between real wages in Australia and the source country (mostly the United Kingdom). Unfortunately the author's disavowal of attempting "a serious comparison of living standards . . . between England and Australia" (p. 201) leaves this issue and most others critical to evaluating living standards in Sydney to others with more of a taste for dispassionate analysis and a careful weighing of the evidence.

JOHN C. BROWN, *Clark University*

No Paradise for Workers: Capitalism and the Common People in Australia, 1788–1914. By Ken Buckley and Ted Wheelwright. New York: Oxford University Press, 1988. Pp. vii, 296. $42.50.

The dustjacket describes *No Paradise for Workers* as "the first radical history of capitalism in Australia." Ken Buckley and Ted Wheelwright establish their radical perspective early on, introducing among their major themes: "the seizure of the means of production . . . imperialism and racism . . . the rape of the environment . . . the fetishism of commodities . . . neo-fascism.'' They describe capitalism as a system with two distinct classes, one which owns the means of production and the other which supplies only labor; they also claim that if agriculture is to function under the system, ''people must be driven off the land, so that capitalists can own it'' (p. 2). But despite the tone of the introduction, much of the book, which is drawn almost entirely from secondary sources, is quite conventional in its analysis.

The early chapters deal with the expropriation of land from the Aborigines and the use of convict labor. In these chapters, and indeed throughout, Buckley and Wheelwright try to relate their history to problems in current Australian society in an apparent effort to appeal to a wider readership. For a student or researcher, however, the result is more irritating than helpful. For example, they devote much of their short chapter on the Aborigines to the negotiations of Aboriginal land rights after 1960. Also diverting is an unrelated section on the actions of the Colonial Sugar Refining Company in Fiji. As a result, we learn little of the early land expropriation. The authors' discussion of the organization of the convict colony is better, but their chapter ''The Convict Basis of the Proletariat'' is too anecdotal to provide much insight into the nature of convict society. Much of it is devoted to accounts of floggings and other forms of punishment.

No Paradise for Workers is based on a series of studies edited by Buckley and Wheelwright over the past decade, and it sometimes has more the appearance of a patchwork quilt than an organized history. The presentation is by topic rather than chronological, and even the chapter titles often serve as little more than points of departure for discussion of a wide range of issues. Chapter 7, for example, ''Class War on the Land: Farmers and Squatters,'' begins with an admission that there really was no war, just ''problems'' between farmers and squatters that resulted in ''grim guerrilla skirmishes,'' that are not described (p. 116). The authors continue by giving a few selective estimates of land alienation from 1788 to 1891 and then discuss Premier John Robertson's Land Acts of 1861, which required that squatters purchase their land and which also made land available to selectors (the rough equivalent of North American homesteaders). The authors then discuss the use of ''dummies,'' employees and children, as selectors and relate this practice, in an obscure way, to the abolition of university fees in the 1970s. Various groups are said to have participated in the class war for land: farmers, squatters, selectors who were capitalists, ordinary selectors, and graziers. But because Buckley and Wheelwright do not distinguish the combatants clearly, the source and nature of the conflict among them is hard to discern. The authors then relate the activities of bushrangers such as the Kelly gang to the squatter-farmer conflict, pointing out that Ned Kelly struck a ''sympathetic chord'' with poor farmers. They continue with a discussion of Henry George's land tax, claiming its popularity was due to hostility towards ''land monopoly'' and squatters, but the source of the monopoly is unclear. Land nationalization was another policy that had support in some quarters. In 1888, for example, the Intercolonial Trades Union Congress not only supported land nationalization but also resolved ''to abolish all taxation save that on land values,'' two clearly inconsistent policies, which the authors fail to point out. Buckley and Wheelwright conclude with an anecdote told by Keynes of how Alfred Marshall received financial support to go to Cambridge from his uncle Charles, who had returned from Australia after having made a fortune as a pastoralist.

No Paradise for Workers is clearly not intended to break new ground, but rather to provide an entertaining overview of Australian development using an unconventional perspective. Unfortunately, the lack of a well-defined framework, radical or otherwise, the failure to organize the material, chronologically or otherwise, and the inappropriate use of anecdotes make this neither good entertainment nor good history.

FRANK D. LEWIS, *Queen's University*

LATIN AMERICA

The Leverage of Labor: Managing the Cortés Haciendas in Tehuantepec, 1588–1688. By Lolita Gutiérrez Brockington. Durham: Duke University Press, 1989. Pp. xxv, 245. $42.00.

The estates of the Marqueses del Valle, Fernando Cortés and his heirs, have been only slightly studied by historians. Aside from some work on the sugar estates of the Cuernavaca Valley and other preliminary work on the very early years in Tehuantepec, Mexico, very little analytical study has been made of these important holdings. Lolita Gutiérrez Brockington seeks to redress this in her work. Her study began not so much as an analysis of estate management but as an investigation into the labor system of the Tehuantepec estates and an attempt to explain the role of African slaves on the estates and in the region.

The book is divided into two large sections, each with four chapters. The first section deals with the overview and examination of the hacienda in Tehuantepec. The first chapter discusses the region, while the subsequent chapters focus in on the estate itself, its development, and role. The second section deals more specifically with questions of labor and management. After a general consideration of the patterns of labor usage on the estate, Gutiérrez Brockington then considers first nonslave labor followed by the slave component. Last, there is a look at the role of the interplay between labor and management in the operation of the hacienda. The work ends with a finely crafted chapter of conclusions. The text is supplemented by tables, maps, figures, and appendices which the author uses to present the vital information of the study.

The work focuses on the years 1588 to 1688 for rather practical reasons. The documentation is far superior for this time period than for the earlier or later periods. In spite of the Cortés hacienda papers being in a single location (the *ramo Hospital de Jesús* in the Archivo General de la Nación in Mexico), scholars have only recently begun to mine this rich vein. Beyond the practical considerations of the time frame, the period is important because it spans the critical last decades of the sixteenth century and yet takes the reader beyond the middle of the seventeenth century. In the late sixteenth century the economy of New Spain fought against the depredations of pestilence which devastated the Indian population, yet by the mid-1600s most scholars believe the native population had rebounded. The study then concentrates on the critical "lost years" of New Spain's economic history.

The author points out that there are some important similarities between the Cortés estates and other haciendas that have been studied, notably the Jesuit estates and, to a lesser degree, the cattle ranches of the northern and western regions. The Tehuantepec estates offer important insights into the paradigm because they relied largely on a resident labor population, nearly evenly split between slave and nonslave. This contrasts in proportion to the sugar estates and to the labor force seen in mining districts. Interestingly, the estate did not rely heavily on debt peonage, a similarity to the Jesuit estates.

The Cortés estates of Tehuantepec figured as part of an international commercial network administered by the Marqueses del Valle. The importance of the estates was related to their ability to produce a profit. Gutiérrez Brockington has found that they were profitable; yet for the estate, labor was one of the principal costs. As the native population declined, the cost of labor increased and was continually a drain on the hacienda's profits. Additionally, the author notes that the use of African slaves on the estate created mixed populations in the region. The free mulattoes could be used as wage laborers on the estates. While the on-site manager of the estate was white, the free mulattoes and estate slaves virtually ran the hacienda. But of greatest importance was that the estate produced for a market economy and was expected to product a profit. It was not an idle experiment in agribusiness. From beginning to end it was market oriented, and it had to compete in an economy which stretched far beyond the limits of the Isthmus of Tehuantepec, New Spain, or even Spain.

This is an important and well-written book. It provides yet another important piece to the picture of the management of the rural estate in colonial Mexico. The book compares very well with Herman Konrad's fine study of the Jesuit hacienda of Santa Lucia, and in fact many comparisons are made between the Cortés estates and Jesuit operations. In short, this is an excellent book on an important topic.

JOHN FREDERICK SCHWALLER, *Florida Atlantic University*

British Capitalism and Caribbean Slavery: The Legacy of Eric Williams. Edited by Barbara L. Solow and Stanley L. Engerman. New York: Cambridge University Press, 1987. Pp. x, 345. $29.95.

Eric Williams's *Capitalism and Slavery* (Chapel Hill, 1944) has shaped debate on several of the central themes in the history of the North Atlantic world for nearly half a century. As Barbara Solow and Stanley Engerman note in their introduction to this important collection of essays, Williams's major contribution was to advance four compelling and controversial arguments on the relationships between slavery, racism, abolition, the British West Indies, and England's industrial revolution. First, slavery was a way of exploiting workers and racism was thus "a consequence, not the cause, of slavery"; second, profits earned in the slave trade and on the sugar islands helped finance British industrialization; third, the profitability of slavery, the slave trade, and the Caribbean colonies declined in the aftermath of the American Revolution and their importance to England's economy waned; and, fourth, the "abolition of the slave trade and emancipation of the slaves in the British West Indies were driven not by philanthropy or humanitarianism but by economic motives within England" (p. 1). The 14 essays in this book, prepared for a 1984 conference on Williams's legacy (six of which were later published in the *Journal of Interdisciplinary History* [Spring 1987]), explore these four themes and provide a useful historiographic perspective on *Capitalism and Slavery*.

Although often sharply critical of Williams, these essays testify to the persistent influence of his work. However, as William Green notes, if *Capitalism and Slavery* has been "vindicated in the 1980s it was the direction of his thinking," his identification of central themes and insistence on new perspectives, and "not the credibility of his argument, that gained scholarly endorsement" (p. 35). Thus Green, in the sole essay on Williams's first theme, applauds the contention that slavery "was not born of racism" and his insistence that slavery was an economic phenomenon, but finds his dictim "that racism was a consequence of slavery" and his technological determinism evidence of monumental oversimplification (p. 49). Three essays, by Solow, Joseph Inikori, and David Richardson, explore the second theme of Williams's familiar thesis concerning the relationship between slavery and industrialization. Again, the essays applaud Williams's insight that slavery aided England's economic development, but Solow and Richardson reject his more excessive claims and shift the argument away from the emphasis on high profits and capital accumulation and toward the impact of colonial demand on the growth of British industry.

The third and fourth themes are explored by Selwyn Carrington, Seymour Drescher, David Brion Davis, and Howard Temperly. Here Williams fares less well, although he continues to define the terms of the debate. Carrington summarizes the evidence for the decline of the sugar colonies, emphasizing the impact of the American Revolution on England's North Atlantic trading system, but Drescher and Temperly make a persuasive case that the islands made as central a contribution to the British economy in 1830 as in 1750 and that abolition of the slave trade and emancipation of the slaves were legislative acts passed in contradiction to England's true economic interests. Even Davis, whose work might be read as a sophisticated reformulation of Williams's thesis concerning the impact of capitalism on slavery, has little patience with his "cynical reductionism" that makes it impossible to understand how the British abolition movement helped "to reinforce the hegemony of capitalist values" (pp. 209–10).

British Capitalism and Caribbean Slavery also delineates the limits of Williams's legacy, for several of the most interesting essays—Richard Dunn on slave work and slave demography, Michael Craton on slave resistance, and Gavin Wright on the economic development of Caribbean and North American slave societies—treat themes of major concern to current scholarship that received little attention in *Capitalism and Slavery*. If Williams did not anticipate all of the themes of present concern to historians, his work has had a continuing impact on several generations of scholars, as the historiographical essays by Hilary Beckles and Richard Sheridan ably demonstrate. Williams was a historian of power and originality whose work must still be reckoned with. *British Capitalism and Caribbean Slavery* will prove an indispensible aid in that task.

RUSSELL R. MENARD, *University of Minnesota*

Industry and Underdevelopment: The Industrialization of Mexico, 1890–1940. By Stephen H. Haber. Stanford: Stanford University Press, 1989. Pp. xiv, 238. $35.00.

With this book Stephen Haber joins the small group of historians who have applied cliometric techniques successfully to Latin America's past. Using a rich assortment of company reports and records, statistical yearbooks, and government and consular reports, he charts the birth and development of a dozen of the most important manufacturing concerns in Mexico over a half century.

Haber turns to the beginning of intense industrialization to explain why Mexican industry in the 1980s has stagnated after four decades of rapid expansion. He suggests that the blame lies with the structure of the manufacturing sector, which is oligopolistic and uncompetitive, employs inappropriate technology, and lacks a sophisticated capital-goods industry. Haber revises the conventional view when he suggests that Mexico's "peculiar industrial structure" was a product of its origins under Porfirio Díaz (1876–1911), not of the developmental regimes that emerged after the Mexican Revolution.

In a closely reasoned argument Haber clearly demonstrates the factors that led to a manufacturing sector dominated by a few large companies in its most dynamic sectors: steel, cement, beer, glass, dynamite, soap, paper, textiles, and cigarettes. The size and depth of the Mexican market was small. Moreover, the author suggests, the Mexican workers were relatively inefficient, so the export option was foreclosed. In important areas that comprised half of all manufacturing, firms had to import expensive and indivisible capital goods from countries where labor costs were high, causing excess capacity and inappropriate technology. Hence only a few large firms could survive. Before capitalists would invest under these rather unappealing conditions, they wanted government protection. The state complied, entrenching oligopolies by granting concessions and privileges.

Although Haber's analysis focuses on economics, paying little attention to factors whose importance he acknowledges—such as state policy, cultural proclivities, and the working class, he is sensitive to extra-market factors. By constructing for the first time a history of Mexican industry at the firm level, Haber provides a rich collective biography of key entrepreneurs which reveals that Mexico's most dynamic factories were founded not by tinkerers or mechanics, but by financiers and merchants, who were predisposed to assure profits by manipulating the market and the state rather than by improving the production process. They wanted to restrict competition rather than compete, so they created cartels, controlled credit and raw materials, and influenced the state. Indeed, says Haber, "it was not so much a case of the state representing the interests of these financiers, as it was that these financiers were the state." (p. 69).

Surprisingly, the companies that financiers founded did not usually show large returns. Because of the demands of technology and the hope of commanding the market, financiers created factories much larger than needed for the Mexican market. Haber maintains these financiers were counting on future growth creating further demand; therefore they invested even though dividends were small and stock prices flat. Such far-sighted planning was quite unusual in Latin America, especially for men who usually profited by using their influence to create favorable conditions rather than simply hoping for them to occur. Perhaps rather than putting their faith in the future, the organizers of the big businesses reaped their returns through special founders' allotments of stock or other privileges at the front end, while the small investor who put his faith and pesos in the financiers had to suffer the cost of the long incubation period.

Whatever the reason for the creation of excess capacity, the ills of Porfirian industry were inherited and exacerbated by the regimes that came to power after the Revolution. Although the same industrialists remained in control, the sector suffered a crisis of confidence. Stock prices fell. Industry recovered only two decades after the outbreak of the Revolution. Even then it was still dominated by the oligarchic firms which had grown up under Díaz. Some of the companies have continued until recently.

Although this study does not entirely explain why the structure of Mexican industry in 1940 allowed it to prosper for forty years before running into great difficulties, it is an excellent analysis of the forces and people that shaped industry during its formative first decades. The picture of large oligopolistic corporations created by financiers and directed by professionally trained managers in this early period clashes with the received wisdom of the Latin American industrialization experience. Was this in fact the case elsewhere as well? I hope that Haber or someone else answers the challenge and compares the Mexican experience with that of other Latin American countries or perhaps with the Asian "tigers."

STEVEN TOPIK, *University of California, Irvine*

UNITED STATES AND CANADA

Irish-American Trade, 1660–1783. By Thomas M. Truxes. New York: Cambridge University Press, 1989. Pp. xiv, 448. $39.50.

For years I never fully understood why the middle and New England colonies exported barrels of flaxseed to Ireland. Now I know—thanks to this recent study which closes another of those lingering gaps in historical knowledge: the trade between Ireland and various British colonies in the western hemisphere during the seventeenth and eighteenth centuries. Thomas Truxes describes these commercial patterns and analyzes the rationale for their development. Although he discusses events on both sides of the Atlantic, the author focuses more attention on the Irish economy than its American counterparts. Truxes argues that there was substantial economic integration within Britain's North Atlantic empire and that Ireland played an important but to date largely unappreciated role in the overall scheme of things.

Ireland had two major trading networks tied to the western hemisphere. The first pattern involved the exchange of Irish provisions—mainly preserved beef and pork plus butter—for sugar and rum from Barbados, Jamaica, and the lesser British outposts in the Caribbean. Most of these food exports were in the luxury class and intended for the consumption of Europeans living overseas, not the slave populations. Cork, along Ireland's southeastern coast, was the main port linked to the tropics. The second pattern consisted of the importation of tobacco from the Chesapeake region and the seed of flax plants harvested from Maryland to Connecticut in exchange primarily for cheap linens, supplemented by a steady stream of indentured servants. Ireland imported flaxseed for two reasons: flax cut before it ripened in the field produced higher quality cloth, while experience had shown that foreign seeds consistently spouted heartier crops on Irish soil. Truxes's chapter on the emigrant trade is excellent and reinforces the conclusions of David Galenson and Farley Grubb about the market orientation of the indentured servant trade.

Ireland was likewise enveloped within the British empire, and the author reveals how often special interest groups were able to exert sufficient influence in Parliament to shape legislation affecting the economy of the Emerald Isle. As a result, much of Ireland's overseas commerce was indirect since navigation regulations or economic incentives, such as bounties, caused goods to flow through England as an intermediary stopover. London merchants were also crucial in providing financial services for a huge share of Irish foreign trade. Truxes asserts the American colonies "remained relatively less developed than Ireland until after the American revolution" (p. 4), but that contention is hard to accept given the low wages prevailing in the island's linen industry and its emigration patterns to the New World.

Despite undeniable contributions to the advancement of knowledge, this volume has appalling shortcomings in terms of basic production values. If there was ever a publication that appeared untouched from its dissertation origins, this one surely qualifies. Redundancies abound; the text could easily have been cut by a third, and there are over 100 pages of padded endnotes. The text would have been enhanced by legible maps, but the three maps included are so small and the placenames so obscure that they are totally useless. Some paragraphs are confusing and even contradictory. Inexplicably, this sorry production came forth from the presses of one of the world's leading scholarly publishers.

If readers can avoid these irritating organizational and stylistic distractions, they will discover a cache of fresh information about another sphere of transatlantic commerce heretofore largely unexplored. The second appendix includes nearly 40 pages of tables on Irish imports and exports from 1698 to 1784. This study has its rough spots, but its claims to originality carry the day in the end.

EDWIN J. PERKINS, *University of Southern California*

Encyclopedia of Southern Culture. Edited by Charles Reagan Wilson and William Ferris. Chapel Hill: The University of North Carolina Press, 1989. Pp. xxi, 1634. $59.95.

This bulky new encyclopedia is something of a milestone in the evolution of the modern South. Sponsored by the Center for the Study of Southern Culture at the University of Mississippi, the book is a collaborative effort to define and display a culture which is distinctively southern and yet biracial. There are over 800 contributors, with entries divided into 24 major sections, each of which has its own primary consultant. Each section contains an overview essay by the consultant and two alphabetical sequences, first by thematic topic, next by proper noun. As the reviewer for the *New York Times Book Review* noted (Sept. 17, 1989), the interpretations strive to be modern in outlook, but the preponderance of contributors is still white, male, and academic (history being the largest discipline). Curiously, of the 24 major consultants, the three with nonsouthern addresses cover Black Life (Thomas Holt), Women's Life (Carol Ruth Berkin), and Violence (Raymond Gastil).

The first question that comes to mind for readers of this JOURNAL would be the usefulness of the encyclopedia for researchers in southern history and particularly southern economic history. Almost everyone will find this a valuable reference work, especially for those out-of-the-ordinary southern practices and institutions that you keep running across but cannot quite put your finger on. Here you can find well-informed entries with bibliographies on such topics as Juneteenth, Kudzu, Gumbo, Conch, Foxfire, Boll Weevil, Grits, Collard Greens, Shape-Note Singing Schools, Snake Handlers, and any number of other listings for names, places, and organizations. The book is a browser's delight, but it will also be a great help to serious scholars.

If, however, you turn to the encyclopedia for a weightier sort of help, for definitive essays on major aspects of southern history and culture, your reward will be more limited. For one thing you will find it awkward to look up any particular topic because the thematic entries are often given eccentric titles you are unlikely to think of: in the section on education, for example, you will find such topics as "Innovations in Education," "Classical Tradition," "Quality of Education," and "Politics of Education." (There are many cross-listings to help you, however, so you are bound to find something interesting.) More seriously, the substantive entries tend to be textbook-like summaries of conclusions rather than solid original analyses and syntheses. Despite the length of the volume as a whole, the individual entries have a packed-in quality, where no one contributor is ever given enough space to develop an argument. This is particularly true for economic history, which was evidently not high on the editors' priority list. The best material on economics is found in the section on Industry (edited by James Cobb), but the major southern industries (Textiles, Railroads, Tobacco, Furniture, and Mining) get no more than a half-page summary each. There is little quantitative material overall, and no attempt was made to develop the volume into a statistical reference work.

Perhaps an economic historian has no right to expect specialized attention to economic issues in an encyclopedia of culture, which plainly states at the outset that it approaches the South mainly as a cultural entity. The best and most novel sections are indeed those which concentrate on culture: art and architecture, folklife, language, music, recreation, religion, and others. Yet my uneasiness runs deeper than the mere question of specialization, to the matter of history itself. Though the volume is full of historical discussions, and though the majority of contributors are historians, the organization of the subject matter is not historical at all, and the very conception of "southern culture" which is implicitly represented by the project seems positively unhistorical. If you thumb through the pages randomly (probably not the best approach, to be sure), you find yourself jolted forward and backward by centuries at a page, losing a sense of context and of culture as an evolutionary phenomenon. Even if you organize your reading more prudently, you still frequently find wrenching historical leaps within single essays, because contributors were assigned culturally defined topics and asked to cover them for all of history. The effect is to exaggerate the distinctiveness and especially the changelessness of the highly abstract construction, "southern culture." Certainly no one here grapples seriously with analyzing the historical process by which highly variegated geographical, linguistic, ethnic, economic, and cultural groups came to be notionally amalgamated under the heading "southern." In "Rural Worlds Lost," Jack Temple Kirby has written: "*Southerner* is a rather pernicious abstraction when closely examined" (p. 223), but one will not find that proposition closely examined here.

As dramatically changed as the present-day South is (and this volume is a noteworthy indication of that change), perhaps it is not yet ready to ask that sort of question.

GAVIN WRIGHT, *Stanford University*

Brotherly Tomorrows: Movements for a Cooperative Society in America, 1820–1920. By Edward K. Spann. New York: Columbia University Press, 1989. Pp. xv, 354. $37.50.

Edward Spann assembles rich and insightful detail into the ideological underpinnings, practical operation, and eventual failure of communitarian experiments and non-Marxian socialist movements in the United States during the century commencing in 1820. His work thus begins in the period following the great religious awakenings in New York and New England and ends with the final collapse of the kind of naive, communitarian, often utopian and millenarian socialism characteristic of American thought and practice until the demoralizing years after World War I, when Marxism and Soviet communism captured the field.

As its author emphasizes, this book treats movements and experiments inspired by "radical social idealism," which he sees as embracing a "culture of dissent" from individualism, capitalism, competition, and industrialization in nineteenth-century America. In particular, he consciously omits those systems and experiments he categorizes as "sectarian," those informed primarily by a particular institutional variety of religious faith and practice. Those movements employing sufficiently diffuse invocations of ethical Christianity, including occasional appeals to millenarianism and the establishment of God's kingdom on earth, are not similarly excluded, since a measure of religious motivation was present in almost all American experiments in social and economic cooperation.

Chapters are organized around the actual experiments inspired and carried out by seminal thinkers and organizers; their ideas and literary-journalistic activities are also sketched. The coverge begins with the Harmonist theories and colonies of George Rapp, a German thinker. Next comes Robert Owen, the Englishman who organized New Harmony on the Wabash River. Emanuel Swedenborg makes a cameo appearance; apparently Johnny Appleseed sowed this Swedish mystic's religious notions along with his fruit trees. The ideas of Charles Fourier, the complex French utopian, are set forth in considerable detail, as well as their resonance in thought and practice on American soil. Brook Farm in Massachusetts, for example, abandoned its Transcendentalist roots for Fourierist ideas in 1844. Spann is clearly sympathetic with Fourier's young American disciples, whom he regards as "part of a culture fascinated with romantic heroes and with the idea of inspiring, redeeming genius. . . ." They were "Yankees . . . bearing the conscience of their Puritan forefathers" who "sought heroic achievement in the redemption of society" (p. 81). Among these disciples were Albert Brisbane, Charles Sears, and, for a time, Horace Greeley.

Native-born thinkers predominate after the demise of Fourierism in America. One is impressed by the force of ideas and personalities in launching vast, often inchoate schemes and movements. Henry George's *Progress and Poverty* (New York, 1985), for example, was one of the most widely read works in the century and laid the intellectual foundation for the single-tax movement. Edward Bellamy's *Looking Backward* (New York, 1982), a utopian novel set in the year 2000, prepared the way for social Nationalism; and Laurence Gronlund's *The Cooperative Commonwealth* (New York, 1890) presented a sanitized Marxism without class conflict or revolution.

Typically American traits of communitarianism and socialism emerge: political naiveté or perhaps cynicism about the political system; the absence of class conflict or violent revolution as a means to progress; and a retreat to remote tracts of land on or near the frontier to reduce physical and psychic contiguity with the emerging system of industrial capitalism. Perhaps the greatest merit of Spann's book is that its rich detail allows the reader to detect certain recurrent causes of the monotonously regular demise of virtually all the movements and experiments he documents. These causes include financial panics (particularly those of 1837 and 1893); wars (principally the Civil War and World War I); the physical absence of thinkers from the communities they inspired; conflagrations (the main building at Brook Farm, for example); the lack of steady financial backing, thereby obliging movement leaders to employ "booster" techniques to induce participants to buy land; non-Victorian views and practices of sex and marriage; the selection of remote sites subject to the ravages of disease; failure to provide for succession of leadership; a stubbornly nostalgic, agrarian refusal to adopt and exploit the new technologies of the Industrial Revolution; and a kind of critical-mass phenomenon whereby each small, beleaguered "island" or "oasis" of communitarian socialism was swamped by the vast and intractable "ocean" or "desert" of industrial capitalism surrounding it. For the most part, however, such experiments in "radical social idealism" carried out by "cultural dissenters" failed because of defects in human nature. These shortcomings were evidenced in class consciousness and conflict within individual communities and movements; struggles for leadership and succession; and the inability to instill in the younger generation a desire to stay on and resist the fleshpots of the host civilization.

After a brief treatment of the cooperative movement, Spann depicts in admiring detail the tragic-heroic figure of Eugene Debs, who presided over the apotheosis of non-Marxian socialism in the United States. His five unsuccessful bids for the presidency, his opposition to American involvement in World War I, his disillusionment with the political process and with many of those in his own movement, and his imprisonment for sedition during the 1920s foreshadowed the ultimate defeat of American-style socialism, cooperationism, and communitarianism. One feels that the story ends a bit too abruptly in the mid-1920s with the death of Debs. Where did all the doctrinaire American communists of the 1930s come from? Spann sees few links between the old and new socialists, although the same traditions of "cultural dissent" and "radical social idealism" that had fueled socialist thought and action for a century must certainly have underlain the attractiveness of communism and the Bolshevik Revolution to the generation of the 1930s.

Two points bear mention in evaluating the focus and treatment of this volume. First, the European intellectual antecedents of American communitarianism, with the exception of Fourierism, could have been dealt with more intensively. On the continent, for example, German philosophers, religious thinkers, economists, and historians such as Franz von Baader, Johann Gottlieb Fichte, Ludwig Gall, Heinrich Justi, Friedrich List, Karl Marlo, Emil Sax, Albert Schaffle, Wilhelm Weitling, and Adolf Wagner contributed to a theory of state involvement in the economy known as social economy or *Gemeinwirtschaftslehre* that still forms the intellectual undergirding of non-Marxian socialism in much of western Europe today. In addition, the links between the first cooperatives in England and early American cooperatives deserve to be more amply explored.

A more striking omission results from Spann's decision to exclude from scrutiny any thought or practice informed by "sectarian" religion. One infers that he favors heterodoxy to orthodoxy in pursuing social goals. In this way, perhaps, greater freedom of thought and action is preserved when a given result is obtained. Nevertheless, many communitarian and cooperative experiments in nineteenth-century America were derived from explicit religious beliefs and institutions that were translated into social action.

The Shakers, to be sure, are mentioned briefly, while the Hutterites and Amish are not. The omission of the Mormon experience, however, is more conspicuous. In Ohio,

Missouri, Illinois, and the Great Basin this group practiced and preached communitarian and cooperative approaches to organizing their social and economic affairs on a scale greatly exceeding any example offered by Spann. One searches his 18-page bibliography in vain, for example, for Leonard Arrington's seminal *Great Basin Kingdom* (Lincoln, NE, 1966), a magisterial treatment of Mormon economic history unexcelled since its publication. In it, and in the more specialized treatments it has inspired, one can read about vast and protracted programs of communitarianism, cooperation, economic autarky, and communal settlement and colonization involving hundreds of communities and hundreds of thousands of people over a 70-year period. Spann, for example, mentions Greeley, CO, and its eponymous founder, to which 442 eastern farmers repaired in 1869 to apply the "principles of cooperation" to agriculture in the "Great American Desert" (p. 135), something the Mormons had been doing on a much greater scale and with at least equal success for a quarter of a century. To omit the latter effort because it is "sectarian" rather than based on "radical social idealism" and "cultural dissent" seems arbitrary at best.

Quibbles about the scope of any work, however, are inevitable and occur in the eye of the beholder. Spann's work is a fresh, bracing, thoroughly researched, and valuable contribution to understanding America's early fascination with forms of economic and social organization outside the mainstream of the nineteenth-century market system.

MARCELLUS S. SNOW, *University of Hawaii, Manoa*

The Material Basis of the Postbellum Tenant Plantation: Historical Archaeology in the South Carolina Piedmont. By Charles E. Orser, Jr. Athens: The University of Georgia Press, 1988. Pp. xvii, 322. $35.00.

Charles Orser is an anthropologist whose purpose is to bring insights from archaeology to bear on historical issues. As the title suggests, Orser is concerned with the standard of living of plantation inhabitants—wage workers, tenants, managers, servants, and owners. His research is based on the excavation of the Millwood plantation in the South Carolina Piedmont. The Millwood plantation was composed of approximately 10,000 acres bordering on both sides of the Savannah River (hence located in both South Carolina and Georgia). The plantation was in use from 1834 until the mid-1920s, and throughout the period cotton was the principal cash crop. The plantation was owned and run by James Edward Calhoun from 1834 until his death in 1889. After his death the plantation was absentee-owned and run by a manager.

Orser begins by discussing the limits and benefits of historical archaeology. Like economic historians, historical archaeologists must please two masters. The archaeological findings need to be placed in a historical context. If done right, always the catch, the results will be of interest to scholars in many disciplines. Historical archaeology is most akin to social history. Both shed light on the daily lives of common folk, the humdrum not documented by contemporary chroniclers. For example, historical archaeology can definitively determine the square footage of tenant dwellings or the types of dinnerware used by wage laborers. Findings on material well-being can then be used as evidence in various debates about tenancy and race. For example, did the quality of housing vary more by race or by tenure status?

Historical context is important and Orser does a good job in setting the stage on which he places his findings. He first describes the physical setting of the Millwood plantation and how it compares to other areas in the Piedmont and South Carolina. Next, Orser has a lengthy discussion, approximately one-half of the book, about tenancy in the postbellum South, in South Carolina, and on the Millwood plantation. His survey of the issues is excellent, and because Orser focuses on the neglected Piedmont, he provides insights even for scholars knowledgeable about tenancy. We learn that blacks tended to reside on the same farm for a longer time than did their white counterparts of the same tenure status. Nevertheless, tenure status was more important than race in explaining job mobility.

The account of tenancy on the Millwood plantation is rich with historical detail. After the Civil War the plantation experimented with squad contracts, and Orser provides interesting detail about the early contractual arrangements. Labor arrangements changed over time to the more familiar share and cash rent variety.

After laying out the history, Orser presents the archaeological findings. He discusses housing in one chapter and personal possessions in another. We learn that wage hands most likely lived in ex-slave quarters close to the owner's house, while tenant quarters were scattered over the plantation. More importantly, Orser's findings suggest that there was a correlation between "one's place on the agricultural ladder and the size of one's house" (p. 229).

The dig resulted in 62,119 artifacts being collected, including such curiosities as a medallion from the St. Paul Winter Carnival found in a former tenant's house; however, the artifacts were predominantly pieces of plates, glasses, or other food wares. Orser conducted various tests to determine to what extent the type and quantity of artifacts are related to the owner's position on the agricultural ladder. Unfortunately, but not surprisingly, the tests are not conclusive. People at all tenure levels owned the sorts of things, like broken plates, that get left behind.

Although the evidence from the excavation about the standard of living of tenants is not voluminous, by using it in conjunction with the extant historical evidence, Orser succeeds in giving us a deep understanding of the material basis of tenants. If Orser's work is typical of historical archaeology, we will all benefit from seeing more of it.

LEE J. ALSTON, *University of Illinois*

Taking the University to the People: Seventy-five Years of Cooperative Extension. By Wayne D. Rasmussen. Ames: Iowa State University Press, 1989. Pp. x, 300. $24.95.

Information dissemination in a timely fashion was a crucial component in the growth of agricultural productivity in the United States. In this book Wayne Rasmussen describes the history of one component of that information dissemination network, the Cooperative Extension System.

In the first half of the nineteenth century, information dissemination in agriculture occurred in haphazard fashion. The establishment of a system of land-grant universities under the Morrill Act of 1862 represented a major step in improving the common farmer's access to information. However, the information available was, for the most part, limited to the practical details of farm operation. The Hatch Act of 1887, which established a national system of agricultural experiment stations, resulted in a rapid increase in research findings which exceeded the capacity of the information dissemination network then available. As a consequence, tentative efforts were made in states such as New York, Pennsylvania, and Texas to improve this network. These efforts were to provide the foundation for the establishment of the Cooperative Extension System.

The establishment of the Cooperative Extension System with the passage of the Smith-Lever Act of 1914 had as its stated purpose: "To aid in diffusing among the people of the United States useful and practical information on subjects relating to agriculture and home economics and to encourage application of the same" (p. 49). In terms of the practical fulfillment of this purpose, however, Seaman Knapp, the "father of Extension," perhaps stated it best: "What a man hears, he may doubt; what he sees, he may possibly doubt; but what he does, he cannot doubt" (p. 35). Through its organization around the county agent, Extension has emphasized the active participation of the individual in the application of new information.

In the first three decades of its existence the Cooperative Extension System responded to a number of critical situations, from the need to increase production during World Wars I and II to addressing financial weaknesses and overproduction during the 1920s and 1930s. Following World War II Extension continued to focus attention on increasing agricultural productivity while increasing the commitment to programs in home economics and 4-H. Today, Extension, in response to new priorities, is re-evaluating its mission while maintaining its central purpose "to bring the university to the people."

The Extension Committee on Organization and Policy commissioned Wayne Rasmussen to provide a historical perspective on Extension which would aid in the Committee's re-evaluation of Extension's mission. The resulting book can be subdivided into three sections. The first five chapters comprise the initial section which provides a historical overview of Extension and its mission. The second section, consisting of the next four chapters, provides a description of a number of Extension programs, including home economics, 4-H, and community resource development. The last chapter of the book comprises its final section. This chapter examines the evolution of Extension which is likely to occur in the future. As such, this chapter reflects the use of this book in providing a historical perspective on the future development of Extension.

Rasmussen has written a book which has substantial breadth in coverage. Any one of the three sections could have easily resulted in a volume of its own. This breadth of coverage, however, is achieved at the expense of a loss in the depth in that coverage. For example, in his consideration of the passage of the Smith-Lever Act, Rasmussen gives very little attention to the political aspects of its passage. Similarly, Extension's role in the implementation of New Deal legislation, summarizes rather than describes. For example, in considering AAA acreage allotments and payments, Rasmussen writes: "The county agent often was involved in acreage allotments and in resolving questions about division of payments between landowners and tenants on farms operated by tenants. This latter issue arose with frequency in the South, and its resolution was particularly difficult" (p. 99). However, Rasmussen then fails to describe in sufficient detail this resolution or the manner in which it was reached. Similar lack of detail applies to Rasmussen's descriptions of various Extension programs.

Rasmussen has written on a crucial yet often ignored component of the agricultural information dissemination network, the Cooperative Extension System. The substantial breadth of coverage makes this book an important starting point for future research on this institution. The lack of depth in coverage, however, fails to do justice to the soul of Extension.

ROBERT CHARLES GRAHAM, *University of North Carolina, Charlotte*

The Speeches and Writings of Mother Jones. Edited by Edward M. Steel. Pittsburgh: University of Pittsburgh Press, 1988. Pp. xvii, 333. $32.95.

Mary Harris "Mother" Jones delivered her first recorded speech to a United Mine Workers (UMW) convention in 1901 when she was almost 70 years old. It marked the beginning of a remarkable 20 years of activism during which she could be found at every site of the class struggle from mining camps to Mexico to Washington. Edward Steel has collected 30 speeches, 17 essays, and selected letters that introduce readers to the rhetoric and ideas of the "avenging nemesis of the coal miners."

Born in Ireland, Jones emigrated to the United States as a child. She married an iron molder in 1861, but six years later her husband and four children fell victim to a yellow fever epidemic. She worked as a nurse, teacher, and dressmaker, and in 1880 became an organizer and agitator for the labor movement. By the turn of the century she was identified principally with the United Mine Workers of America and spent much of the rest of her life speaking, organizing, and agitating for that union. She died seven months after her hundredth birthday.

"Mother" was an apt sobriquet for this tiny, always black-clad woman, for she was doting, uncritical, and laudatory in her support of miners and their families. They were quite literally her children and no one understood so intimately nor described so eloquently the unique circumstances of mining communities. She reserved the rough side of her tongue for enemies of the working class—mill owners ("vampires" who exploited child labor); society women ("parlor parasites"); and politicians ("the big gun of this nation, his royal nibs, Taft").

Mother Jones dignified the struggles of workers on strike in West Virginia, Pennsylvania, and Kentucky with her reminder they were in "the mightiest conflict of the age." She acted as liaison between class communities of workers and as ambassador of the working class to high-placed officials and industrialists. Her effectiveness can be gauged, as Steel tells us, by the "lengths to which her opponents were willing to go to prevent her speaking—injunctions, threats, deportation, quarantine, imprisonment" (p. xiii).

What did Mother Jones have to say that was so dangerous? Certainly she cast the class struggle in highly polarized terms and consistently proposed socialism as a solution. For her, socialism was part of an American political tradition that extended back to the Revolutionary Fathers and President Abraham Lincoln, whom she frequently invoked. Socialism was an international movement as well, for she called for support for Japanese and Mexican revolutionaries. And it should try to bring all workers, even police and militia, into the struggle. More fearful than Mother's message, though, was the response of her audiences, for she was a symbol, muse, and inspiration who could rejuvenate a flagging strike and galvanize a union convention. Her critics undoubtedly shared her opinion that "the whole machine of capitalism realize[s] for the first time in history that there is an intellectual awakening of the dog below, and he is barking" (p. 58).

This book will find an audience among rhetoricians and other students of language as well as among historians interested in labor, the left, and women. Unfortunately, Steel's introduction does not provide a comprehensive biography of Mother Jones (although there are headnotes at the beginning of each speech or essay and biographical notes at the end of the volume), so it should be read in tandem with Mother Jones's *Autobiography of Mother Jones* (Chicago, 1925), Dale Fetherling's biography, or Pricilla Long's recent study of Colorado miners.

ANN SCHOFIELD, *University of Kansas*

Encyclopedia of American Business History and Biography: Railroads in the Age of Regulation, 1900–1980. Edited by Keith L. Bryant, Jr. New York: Bruccoli Clark Layman, Inc. and Facts On File Publications, 1988. Pp. xxix, 518. $75.00.

This is a volume in a greater work, *The Encyclopedia of American Business History and Biography*, that will almost certainly become one of the most valuable and accessible scholarly resources on the growth and breadth of business enterprises. The current volume on railroads and federal regulation in the twentieth century is an excellent addition to the series. The encyclopedia has short entries, arranged alphabetically, on a single theme. The entries are written by experts in the topic of the volume and consist of short biographies of prominent business and governmental persons and of descriptions of such topics as companies, inventions, legal decisions, marketing innovations, and the like. Each biographical entry places the subject in its social, political, and economic context. Maps, photographs, and other graphic material are included in almost every entry. To help the reader place the material in context, the volume editor has written an introductory essay.

This volume ably illustrates all the virtues of the encyclopedia series. The introductory essay by Keith Bryant, the general editor of the volume, is a wonderful short history (approximately 20 pages) of railroads in the United States. The topics covered in the subsequent individual entries are extraordinarily far-ranging. For instance, there are short (about two pages) descriptions of every railroad (including Amtrak and the Consolidated Rail Corporation) that operated during the period covered. Each description contains a map of the principal routes and a copy of the road's logo. The biographical entries cover prominent railroad men both living and dead. Among the leading railroad scholars represented are Ari Hoogenboom, who wrote most of the entries on railroad regulation, including those on the Interstate Commerce Act and the Mann-Elkins Act; George Hilton, who contributed the entries on the Monon Railroad and on the Staggers Rail Act of 1980 (although the technical name and U.S. Code citation of that act are strangely omitted); John Stover and Maury Klein, who wrote several biographical entries; and George Drury (author of *The Historical Guide to North American Railroads* [Milwaukee, 1985]), who wrote the entry on dieselization and other technological matters. While most of the authors are academics, several are railroad men. Thus, the entry on the Association of American Railroads was written by Wallace Abbey of that association, and Arthur Lloyd of Amtrak wrote the entry on that road.

Both biographical and subject entries conclude with a short list of references. In some cases the authors also indicate which archives they have consulted in preparing their entry or in which interested readers will find additional information. When a biographical subject has himself been an author, all that person's publications are also listed at the end of an entry. (See, for example, William Doezema's excellent entry on Walker Hines.)

There are several shortcomings in this volume that make it more difficult to use than it should be. There is, curiously, no table of contents. Thus, the only way to find out the range of topics covered or whether a particular entry is included is to thumb through the volume. (I hasten to add that this is a delightful volume in which to browse.) Another curious omission is a set of cross-references at the end of each entry. Finally, the index is somewhat utilitarian. There ought to be more complete cross-referencing. And given the fact that the authors of the entries are so prominent, there ought to be an entry for those authors. These are things that would make this fine volume even easier to use and of even greater value to scholars.

THOMAS S. ULEN, *University of Illinois, Urbana-Champaign*

Science and Corporate Strategy: Du Pont Research and Development, 1902–1980. By David A. Hounshell and John Kenly Smith Jr. New York: Cambridge University Press, 1988. Pp. xx, 756. $39.50.

Knowledge is power, but, as Francis Bacon so aptly foresaw in his seventeenth-century fable *The New Atlantis*, without organization scientific knowledge has little chance of substantially improving the quality of life. For Bacon, the secret of surmounting the inherent stumbling blocks that separate theory and practice lay in the coordinated activities associated with his imaginary Solomon's House, a laboratory where a community of managers, thinkers, doers, and conceptual synthesizers worked together to create a new mechanical and material world. Although Bacon's vision of institutionalized research took several centuries to fully realize, the twentieth-century

Du Pont Company corporate research facilities, located on the banks of the Brandywine in Delaware, perhaps epitomize Bacon's "dream." For out of Du Pont's laboratories have emerged a host of genuinely new products, including Nylon, Neoprene, Orlon, Dacron, and Kevlar, thereby ushering in the synthetic age that is so characteristic of contemporary modern civilization. And according to David Hounshell and John Kenley Smith Jr., the authors of *Science and Corporate Strategy*, if we are to more fully comprehend our modern world then we must understand the dynamics of industrial research at key institutions like Du Pont, where for decades scientists and engineers have worked in a Solomon's House-like setting.

Hounshell and Smith have studied in a powerful fashion the complex internal and external forces that shaped the pursuit of science and technology at Du Pont. As a result of their painstaking efforts, a most detailed history has been producted that will stand for some time as a benchmark in the history of science and technology and business history. The authors trace the increasingly prominent role of science in the formulation of corporate strategy, explore the symbiotic yet at times tense relationship between management and professional scientists, and characterize the federal government's increasingly significant influence upon the course of scientific investigations. From Du Pont's inception of true scientific work in 1902 to the present, successive generations of Du Pont employees have confronted a recurrent set of similar questions concerning science's place within the corporate context. These questions include how to recruit and retain scientific talent? How much money should be allocated to support research activities and where should these funds be concentrated? How should short- and long-term objectives be balanced? When should a disappointing venture be terminated? For the Du Pont Executive Committee and upper-level management scientific research was akin to high-stakes gambling, where the decisions of when to raise and when to pass, when to draw, and when to fold ultimately led to either prosperity or financial ruin.

Whatever the outcome—and research at Du Pont resulted in both striking success (Nylon) and stunning reversal (Corfam)—the game was played within a corporate structure that the authors interpret largely from ideas first articulated by Alfred Chandler in *Strategy and Structure* (Cambridge, MA, 1962). Indeed, corporate decentralization led to numerous tensions and conflicts, as centralized research efforts were frequently undermined by dominant divisions like Textile Fibers during the post-World War II period. And, with the proliferation of competitors and rising complexity of modern technology during the 1950s and 1960s, a rather rigid organization creaked and groaned under pressures that demanded quick responses to rapidly changing and largely unforeseen external circumstances.

For Hounshell and Smith, managerial control and the unexpected "nylon drama" are the pivotal points about which the history of scientific research at Du Pont turns. And perhaps it is the managerial focus of this book that is its greatest weakness. Despite all the scientists mentioned, their hopes, aspirations, and laboratory culture are at best infrequently discussed. Second-level workers and technicians seem to have no place here, and yet in a complex environment that demands teamwork their contributions are obviously crucial. Although the authors gained complete academic freedom, this work, in my opinion, remains one endorsed by management and to a large degree about management. Thus an incomplete picture results.

On the whole, however, this work remains one of the most significant historical studies of the 1980s. Yet like many other seminal works it should not be viewed as the final word in the area of the history of industrial research, but rather the beginning of new thrusts into this largely unexplored window into the past.

JOHN A. HEITMANN, *University of Dayton*

A Tale of Three Cities: Labor Organization and Protest in Paterson, Passaic, and Lawrence, 1916–1921. By David J. Goldberg. New Brunswick: Rutgers University Press, 1989. Pp. xiv, 276. $38.00, cloth; $15.00, paper.

1919. Was it the best of times—when millions of workers in this and other industrial countries rose up to demand fulfillment of wartime promises of industrial democracy and a better life? Or was it the worst of times—when, wracked by influenza, inflation, industrial unrest, and fears of Bolshevism, the industrial world went mad and revanche became the order of the day? *A Tale of Three Cities* affords a glimpse into that tumultuous year as it attempts to explicate the causes of a failed organizing drive among textile workers in Lawrence, MA, Paterson, NJ, and Passaic, NJ.

By way of setting the stage, a brief chapter on wartime developments affecting textile workers is followed by sketches of each of the cities. The industry and enterprise characteristics, work force composition and allegiances, recent industrial relations history, and community infrastructure of each place is deftly outlined. Then the creation of the Amalgamated Textile Workers of America (ATWA) under the aegis of the Amalgamated Clothing Workers, and the character of the fledgling union's leadership are explored. The conduct and consequences of strikes in each town—all of which began on the same day in Feb. 1919 and all of which, though formally uncoordinated, were directed toward the same wage and hour objectives—are related in individual chapters, highlighting similarities and differences. A brief concluding chapter attempts to pinpoint why the ATWA, once it assumed the leadership of the strikes, could not win them even at the cost of its own existence.

This ambitious effort makes effective use of a wide array of primary and secondary sources. The records of the Justice Department's Bureau of Investigation (today's FBI) in particular are deployed in a way that reveals the surprisingly wide reach of government strike surveillance at the time—an effort that seems out of all proportion to any real threat to internal security and probably reflects the bureau's ignorance and fear of the immigrant ethnic populations involved.

The profiles of ethnic communities within each of the cities are the strong points of the work. Drawn primarily to address the role of population heterogeneity as a barrier to worker solidarity, they lead the author to conclude that the degree of religious skepticism evident within each group proved a more reliable indicator of behavior than date of arrival or ethnicity per se. Groups most strongly wedded to religious orthodoxy were least likely to form alliances that cut across ethnic and religious boundaries.

The reader is expected to carry forward a growing store of information about each city as the narrative progresses. Given the number of relevant variables and their variants in each place, plus comparisons and contrasts drawn backward and forward in time, the load at times becomes too heavy to bear. One wonders whether the end results would have been much different had a two-city strategy been employed.

As it is, the three-city design does not appear to increase explanatory power appreciably. The list of pertinent variables is reduced in the concluding chapter, but the weights to be attached to those that remain are still unknown. In addition, I came away with the feeling that the author sensed in the very end that something was missing from his analysis.

The conclusion that the intellectual character of the ATWA leadership did not much matter to the outcome is likely to prove controversial only to those who believe that leadership is *all* that matters. However, it is dismaying to encounter a discussion of the role of intellectuals that is uninformed by Selig Perlman's classic treatment of the subject.

As to the missing variable, perhaps Morris Hillguit's observation that it took almost 20 years to educate immigrant Jewish workers to the understanding that unions were more than strike vehicles is relevant. By consistently overestimating the speed of immigrant assimilation, the author may have blocked his view of this factor. And if, among populations new to industrialism, the propensity to organize lags behind the propensity to strike, then 1919 was the worst of times—a time when high hopes were destined to fail.

H. M. GITELMAN, *Adelphi University*

The High Cost of Farm Welfare. By Clifton B. Luttrell. Washington, DC: Cato Institute, 1989. Pp. xiii, 149. $19.95, cloth; $9.95, paper.

This brief work is a useful introduction to the history and current operation of U.S. agricultural price support policies and focuses on the economic effects of these programs. Clifton Luttrell has wisely chosen to provide a historical context for his strong criticism of current farm policies. He recognizes that present-day policies make little sense without an understanding of the forces that shaped them.

Anyone who tries to chronicle American agricultural policy runs the risk of losing the reader in a morass of legislation, dates, and arcane abbreviations. Luttrell's procedure is to chart the main currents of agricultural policy. He begins by tracing the origins of present-day farm policy in legislative initiatives in the 1920s and the massive programs of the New Deal. He then divides major developments in price supports since the New Deal into three phases: supply management (early 1930s to early 1950s), surplus problems and export subsidies (mid-1950s to early 1960s), and direct payments (mid-1960s to the present). Descriptions of two adjunct programs—food stamps and credit policy—follow, breaking the chronological scheme. Next, Luttrell considers the dairy and sugar programs—two programs he regards as especially egregious—in more detail. These case studies illustrate the variety of policies the government has undertaken and the dilemmas faced by current policy makers. The concluding chapter is a sweeping criticism of U.S. farm policy, arguing that current programs hurt developing countries, have very high net social costs, and help the well-off farmers much more than poorer farmers.

Luttrell's approach will save many readers from drowning in a swamp of detail. However, those readers who need to know the historical details are best advised to consult Murray Benedict's *Farm Policies of the United States, 1790–1950* (New York, 1953) and Willard Cochrane and Mary Ryan's *American Farm Policy, 1948–1973* (Minneapolis, 1976). Readers who have absorbed the broad historical picture from Luttrell and who wish to delve deeper into an economic analysis of farm policies might turn to Bruce Gardner's highly readable book, *The Governing of Agriculture* (Lawrence, KS, 1981), or his more advanced *The Economics of Agricultural Policies* (New York, 1987).

Luttrell could go further in two directions. First, he could incorporate more of the historical literature to give his account greater depth. For example, he omits a fascinating episode in the history of cotton price supports, namely, the impetus that the New Deal gave to the breakup of the sharecropping system and the mechanization of preharvest operations. As another example, Luttrell fails to convey adequately the magnitude of the agricultural depression of the 1920s and the accompanying tide of discontent among farmers. Second, his analysis of the politics of farm policies—which is largely confined to describing the vote trading between urban legislators who supported food stamps and rural legislators who supported price supports—would benefit from a more historical and comparative approach. While the New Deal contained the single greatest expansion of farm programs in U.S. history, many programs originated before 1933. Did the New Deal represent a radical departure in, or simply an acceleration of, farm policy? Furthermore, price supports are found in virtually all developed nations.

Following these suggestions would make for a much longer book, detracting from the forcefulness of its argument. However, Luttrell is sometimes too forceful. For example, on the basis of a series of arbitrary estimates and some debatable economic logic, he concludes that the 1985 programs, which cost the taxpayers $32 billion, had a net social cost of $31 billion. This heavy-handed approach detracts from Luttrell's more carefully grounded criticism of the incidence of farm program benefits: laborers and tenants gain very little, while people who bought land a long time ago gain a great deal, from current subsidies.

FRANK M. HOWLAND, *Wabash College*

Race, Radicalism, and Reform: Selected Papers of Abram L. Harris. Edited by William Darity Jr. New Brunswick, NJ: Transaction Publishers, 1989. Pp. viii, 521. $49.95.

Abram Lincoln Harris (1899–1963) was an economist at Howard and Chicago universities, a student of Wesley Mitchell, and member of the American Economic Association's executive committee between 1959 and 1962. Yet, like economists Jessica Peixotto and Sadie Miller, Harris did not share the dominant demographic characteristics of the profession in its first half century: male and white. One of the pioneer black Ph.D.s (Columbia, 1930), he died before the Civil Rights Act of 1964 was enacted—before Title IX executive orders, the presidential campaign of Jesse Jackson, recent events in South Africa, and the use of the terms black and African-American. Although this volume contains 29 of his essays, published between 1923 and 1964 in a wide variety of periodicals, the most intriguing are those that deal with race.

In a 1923 review article on South Africa, Harris expressed his opposition to segregationist policies. He argued that such programs would only intensify racial conflict; he felt increased familiarity and contact between races was the preferred route to black economic and social advancement. Harris felt that separate black economies, such as those promoted by Marcus Garvey, were unlikely to benefit black communities since they were inefficient and amounted to racial tariffs. In 1989 it is clear that apartheid, enacted in 1948, has *not* resolved South Africa racial problems, as Harris would have predicted.

In his article on slavery and reconstruction, Harris disagreed with W. E. B. DuBois's thesis that the South's defeat in the Civil War depended upon the withdrawal of black labor. Harris contended: "That the Negro soldiers and laborers played a really important role in the Civil War no unbiased historian would deny, but that they won the war by a general strike, or by any other means, cannot be established scientifically" (p. 211). Since Harris's comments were presented in a book review of *Black Reconstruction*, Harris did not provide new evidence or make a detailed argument of his own.

Harris also analyzed the role of blacks in the U.S. labor movement but rejected the assumption that the formation of unions would automatically improve the economic condition of blacks. Rather, he describes the poor treatment of blacks by some unions and the obstacles to the creation of a class consciousness that would unite white and black workers: many unions excluded blacks as members, only seeking their support when they thought it might strengthen their strike. The American Federation of Labor viewed a compromise on the creation of separate, black local unions as a victory (p. 196). Employers, on the other hand, used blacks to divide the labor movement, hiring them as strikebreakers and paying them low wages. Racial and ethnic conflict was frequently used to demoralize both black and white workers.

By 1963 Harris sounds cautiously optimistic about the economic position of blacks (p. 122). However, since most of his remarks about the need to improve the level of education among blacks are still applicable in 1989, Harris might be very skeptical about the United States's commitment to the achievement of racial equality if he were still alive today.

Harris's research at Chicago consisted mostly of analyses of Marx, Sombart, Mill, and Veblen—of interest to scholars in the history of economic thought, surely—but it is his earlier works that deserve note by historians interested in the South, slavery, reconstruction, migration, labor history, and the intellectual history of black Americans. A well-written introduction by William Darity Jr. summarizes Harris's two books, *The Black Worker: The Negro and the Labor Movement* (co-authored with Spero Sterling, New York, 1931) and *The Negro as Capitalist* (Philadelphia, 1936). Harris backed his arguments with statistics, analyzed hypotheses, but used neither formal statistical tests nor theoretical models in his writings. His work in economic history would be characterized as "the Old Economic History," institutional in the tradition of his dissertation director, and frequently presented in the form of book reviews.

In the book's introduction, Darity wonders why Chicago never made Harris a full member of the economics department. Instead he was given the title of professor in the College and limited to the teaching of undergraduates. Darity diplomatically suggests that race may have been a relevant factor, since he rules out political philosophy, citing Frank Knight and Paul Douglas. However, anyone who has studied the history of the academic profession knows that being black or female in the 1950s limited one's opportunities in most fields. Chicago was (and is) a profoundly segregated city, and the university has been embroiled in several celebrated disputes concerning the economics department, the university, and the city. (See William J. Barber, *Breaking the Academic Mould* [Middletown, CT, 1988], pp. 241–65.) Therefore, the university may have consciously tried to avoid further public relations difficulties by treating Harris differently. Before the advent of civil rights laws and regulations in the 1960s, a candidate's race and sex were openly discussed in university hiring decisions. So too, professors frequently had joint or specific appointments: Hazel Kyrk, for instance, was never a professor of economics, always a professor of economics and home economics.

I suspect Harris would be pleased that authors and reviewers today are conscious of the constraints that race and sex may impose on the professional achievement of workers and scholars. My university, Michigan State, was unusual in having two black members in the economics department in the late 1950s, but the University of Chicago, a predominantly white institution, hired Harris as its first black professor in *1945*. President Harry Truman did not desegregate the U.S. armed forces until 1948. Unfortunately, the reader learns little about Harris's reaction to the Chicago economics department—either as a black man or as an economist—through this collection. (Darity quotes only a very few letters from Harris to Knight and DuBois.) If additional letters by Harris emerge from the catacombs of university archives, we will have an even richer sense of what it was to be black in this part of white America.

MARY E. COOKINGHAM, *Michigan State University*

Regulation and Deregulation of the Motor Carrier Industry. Edited by John Richard Felton and Dale G. Anderson. Ames: Iowa State University Press, 1989. Pp. x, 210. $24.95.

As a historian of the early decades of the motor carrier industry and as a former truck driver, I was disappointed by this book. Supposedly a collection of essays "authored by faculty members and former graduate students of the University of Nebraska-Lincoln . . . [to furnish] a coherent body of literature on the evolution of trucking regulation and the evaluation of its economic consequences" (p. x), this book is really a rehash of John Felton's contributions to the study of motor carrier regulation. Of the 11 essays in this collection, Felton wrote seven and co-authored two others. Dale Anderson co-authored two of the essays. In all, seven of the essays had been published previously (pp. x, 42, 53, 66, 82, 99, 113, 121), and of those only two appeared as early as 1978; the rest appeared in the 1980s, which marks them as rather late contributions to the economists' crusade to deregulate the American economy. The result is not a "coherent body of literature" on the subject but rather an uneven overview of the kinds of new economic studies which underlay the movement toward deregulation of the motor carrier industry.

Focused on the economics of trucking, the essays mostly ignore the political and administrative forces that propelled the story of regulation in the 1920s and 1930s and later in the 1970s. One essay, "Trucking Regulation, 1935–1980," written by Anderson and Ray Huttsell, Jr., has some value for it offers the future historians of truck regulation a long list of sources essential to understanding the story after the enactment of the Motor Carrier Act of 1935. The authors, alas, do not analyze the facts from the sources they list. Chapters 8 and 9 (the former by Felton, the latter by Anderson and Elmo Falcon) offer some intriguing, though not definitive, evidence that questions the pro-regulation assertions that rural areas would lose truck service if deregulation occurred. Other than these essays, however, the book offers little in the way of new material or arguments. The editors do not furnish a coherent story of the evolution of regulation; instead, they reproduce essays on the economic consequences of some of the regulatory strategies followed by the Interstate Commerce Commission and by one state commission (Nebraska).

Felton concludes that the Motor Carrier Act of 1980, though not establishing complete deregulation of the industry, nonetheless has created a "deregulatory tide" which "even a pronounced proregulation commission in the future might not be able to reverse" (pp. 161–62). He may be correct; but without a more carefully constructed argument preceding the conclusion, it reads more like the pronouncement of a winner who is not quite sure his side won, much less why.

WILLIAM R. CHILDS, *Ohio State University*

William Green: A Biography of a Labor Leader. By Craig Phelan. Albany: State University of New York Press, 1989. Pp. x, 223. $39.50, cloth; $12.95, paper.

William Green has a place in labor history that few leaders would want; he presided over one of labor history's weakest periods. Craig Phelan's biography, a useful account of Green's life, provides an explanation for Green's leadership style (or lack thereof).

The story begins when Green's parents left England for Ohio in 1869 and ends with Green's death in 1952. Though Green had wanted a career in the ministry, economic reality drove him into the mines instead. Nevertheless, his commitment to religious ideals shaped his leadership strategies both in the United Mine Workers (UMW) and as president of the American Federation of Labor (AFL). This insight into Green's motivations is the major contribution of this biography.

The account of Green's life is divided into topics that overlap historically: the 1920s, the Depression, the efforts to organize under Section 7a (1933–1935), the conflict between Green and John Lewis in leadership styles (1932–1935), Green's crusade against insurgency (1935–1941), and the final years of Green's life (1941–1952). This format, while reasonable, creates a certain amount of confusion and redundancy; a chronological presentation would have been more straightforward since the major theme is consistent throughout. That theme is Green's Christianity and his unshakable belief in the necessity of a cooperative relationship between capital and labor. Equally important was Green's conviction that militancy was immoral and destructive to labor and his blindness to militancy on the part of capital.

As early as 1897, when the UMW struck to prevent wage reduction and won, Green internalized a vision of both well-organized labor and well-organized capital that could work "together for mutual benefit" (p. 11). What Green missed was the crucial role of labor militancy in creating the possibility of union victory. Green adopted a role of policing, rather than facilitating rank-and-file militancy.

Thus, during the capitalist offensive of the 1920s (the virulence of which Phelan minimizes), while the business community was crushing the growing union movement, Green was "selling" ideals of Christian accommodation between labor and management to business. Then, and throughout his presidency, Green was shocked when the business community ignored his vision. The combination of disbelief and reluctance to challenge capital continued to exemplify his style of "leading" throughout the 1920s and into the 1930s.

Consequently, Green ignored the seriousness of the stock market crash, criticized capital for being "immoral" in laying workers off, and, finally, in 1932 exhorted unions to use whatever weapon necessary although he hated doing so. Despite a growing understanding that capital would not hand labor organizational security on a silver platter, Green continued to miss organizational opportunities that the early 1930s provided. Even worse, he worked to prevent militancy rather than to mobilize workers. Despite an interest in organizing industrial workers, Green's moralism and reluctance to defy the conservative craft-dominated majority on the Executive Council of the AFL led him to lose the organizing opportunities that the first three years of the New Deal presented.

Thus he was unable to stop Lewis's increasing power and appeal as a champion of the working class. Lewis effectively channeled rank-and-file militancy and organized industrial workers. In response to the emergence of the Congress of Industrial Organizations (CIO), Green put his energy into crusading against dual unionism rather than mobilizing industrial labor.

World War II provided Green another opportunity to preach his gospel of class compromise. As they had done earlier, capitalists and President Franklin Roosevelt turned a deaf ear. Though Green supported the no-strike pledge and saw it as an opportunity to demonstrate the validity of his views, he was outraged when Roosevelt imposed wartime wage controls. Again, Phelan paints a picture of a man sorely out of touch with the economic and political realities with which he was dealing.

Labor emerged from the war a potentially powerful economic force with the potential to form institutional ties to the Democratic Party. While the CIO recognized the value of such ties, Green was unwilling to consider them. Again, Green's narrow vision obscured an important opportunity and weakened labor on a long-term basis. So did Green's ongoing concern with expunging communists from unions. While Green was red-baiting, capital was mobilizing and the Taft-Hartley Act was passed. No matter that most of organized labor viewed Taft-Hartley as a slave labor bill; Green urged compliance.

Green went to his death without changing his perspectives on labor strategies. Those strategies were, as Phelan notes, responsible in the long run for union weakness today, and, in fact, there are many parallels between unions now and unions under Green's presidency. Still, I think Phelan treads too softly. He paints a picture of a class collaborator who played an important role in disorganizing the working class as a class in a period in which capital was well organized. He leaves out of this account sufficient discussion of race, immigrant labor, and Green's reaction to both. Both blacks and immigrants played important parts in this history and warrant more discussion. More than that, why did Green stay in so powerful a position for so long?

BETH A. RUBIN, *Tulane University*

Reds or Rackets? The Making of Radical and Conservative Unions on the Waterfront. By Howard Kimeldorf. Berkeley: University of California Press, 1989. Pp. xii, 242. $27.50.

The history of longshore unionism has attracted more than its share of excellent scholarship, given the relatively small number of longshoremen in the work force. It may have something to do with the romance of the sea or the fact that the longshoremen do not seem to fit in with conventional assumptions about the nature and outlook of American workers. Howard Kimeldorf's *Reds or Rackets?* is, despite the lurid title, a worthy addition to the literature, which also includes Charles Larrowe's *Harry Bridges: The Rise and Fall of Radical Labor in the United States* (New York, 1977) and Bruce Nelson's *Workers on the Waterfront: Seamen, Longshoremen, and Unionism in the 1930s* (Champaign, 1988). Kimeldorf examines the question of why the radical left, which played a key role in the organization of the International Longshoremen's and Warehousemen's Union (ILWU) during the turbulent 1930s, was able to retain its leadership during the inhospitable years of antiradicalism that followed.

Kimeldorf's intention is to bring together "an attention to culture within an overall analytic focus on the world of production . . ." through a comparison of the background and experience of longshoremen on the East and West Coasts. He contends that the Pacific longshoremen owed much of their militance to their "Wobbly" heritage. Indeed, in his telling, the ILWU emerges as the Industrial Workers of the World's most lasting success: "the Wobblies bequeathed an enduring legacy of militant industrial unionism that profoundly shaped the political contours of longshore unionism in the West." This legacy included an emphasis on direct action, rank-and-file involvement, and responsive union leadership. The experience of eastern longshoremen was quite different. Ethnic tensions divided a work force already subject to the quietistic influence of the Catholic church on Irish longshoremen and the padrone system of labor recruitment on Italian longshoremen.

Kimeldorf also pays attention to the influence of maritime employers on the state of labor relations. A greater degree of economic concentration on the West Coast bred a combative attitude on the part of employers toward all unions, regardless of ideological complexion. The more competitive eastern shippers were unable to sustain a common strategy in dealing with their labor force, leading them to seek accommodation with conservative unionism. "Shipowner intransigence in the West," Kimeldorf concludes, "nourished the rich Wobbly legacy on the docks." It is an interesting argument, though it does not explain why those same eastern shipowners failed to reach any accommodation with their sailors, leading to the emergence of the militant, Communist-influenced National Maritime Union in the 1930s.

One of the best chapters in Kimeldorf's book describes the formative experience of the 1934 strike on West Coast longshoremen. During what is still referred to on Pacific docks as the "Big Strike," six strikers and strike sympathizers were killed by police. The memory of that bloodshed marked a generation: "Violence in the West unified its many victims, creating a cohort of battle-hardened militants whose deepening radicalization after the strike was grounded in a set of politically relevant historical experiences unique to their generation." Kimeldorf scores sociologists for their "intellectual predilection for stable routines and structures," which often causes them to ignore the importance of "abnormal occurrences" like the 1934 strike, which continue to have an impact long after they have faded from the headlines.

Reds or Rackets? is based on a thorough mining of the relevant primary and secondary literature, as well as extensive interviewing. It asks good questions and leaves us with an interesting counterfactual proposition to consider. Referring to the expulsion of 11 Communist-influenced unions, including the ILWU by the Congress of Industrial Organizations in 1949, Kimeldorf writes: "Looking back, we can only ponder how different labor's postwar trajectory might have been had a majority of the expelled unions been anything like the ILWU—tough, politically committed, and above all, resilient."

MAURICE ISSERMAN, *Williams College*

Field Man: The Chronicle of a Bank Farm Manager in the 1940s. By Harold Bennett Clingerman. Ames: Iowa State University Press, 1989. Pp. xii, 183. $19.95.

Books about economic depression, farm foreclosures, wartime rationing, and bank farm managers do not present an immediate appeal. *Field Man*, however, is a most enjoyable and even delightful book. Harold Clingerman spent eight years managing foreclosed farms for a bank in Omaha, NE, and provides a vivid and at times detailed narrative of that experience. The book is more than a memoir of those eight years, it is also a wise and thoughtful commentary on the social and economic life of the region.

Clingerman was one of a number of agents hired to protect the investors' interest and to manage and liquidate the many farms taken over by banks during the Great Depression. The author tries to show the "human side of the farm-mortgage story" (p. xi), as he believes that bankers have been wrongfully portrayed as heartless, greedy villians by history. Instead, he declares the banks did everything possible to avoid foreclosure and, with field men leading the way, "put the pieces of a shattered Nebraska agriculture back together" (p. x). Clingerman provides considerable evidence to support his argument. He recounts for farm after farm and family after family the role he played in helping the farmer to produce the best crops possible. He further sought to encourage and assist farm families to repurchase their old farms or to keep a new one.

Clingerman gives the reader real insight into the economic and social life of the farmer during depression and wartime. *Field Man* further provides considerable information about the interests and wishes of the investors who owned the farms, the strange middleman role that the banking personnel played, and the operation of the sharecrop rental system. Clingerman mentions but gives very limited information about the transformation of agriculture that was coming through New Deal measures as well as the wartime technological revolution. As he describes his function—visiting up to eight farms per day, keeping hammer, shovels, wrecking tools, fencing pincers, and so forth in the car to help with any emergency—Clingerman gives a clear picture of the state of agriculture in the 1940s in Nebraska and perhaps much of the country. His tenants were poor, none of them owned such "modern" farm machinery as combine harvesters. They still used the horse or, in some instances, tractor-drawn binders for cutting grain. They still held "threshing parties," where a number of neighbors would come in to help the farmer while the women prepared food for the entire group. All of Clingerman's tenants still kept horses even though some used tractors for most of the work. The manpower shortage of World War II forced some of his tenants to move into mechanized agriculture.

Clingerman gives considerable coverage to the impact of World War II on the social and economic life of Nebraska. He discusses issues ranging from the shortage of manpower through the necessity of reducing his car mileage by half to the replacement of sugar with honey (and his learning to like it) on his cereal. Clingerman describes the efforts of some young men to avoid the military by hiding "behind an old red cow," an attempt to become a farmer in order to avoid the draft.

Field Man is not a great work of history, but the book has considerable value for the historian. It is a personal tale about a limited geographical region and covers a short time period, but the attitudes and conditions that Clingerman describes in Nebraska in the 1940s probably applied to all the Midwest if not the entire country. So much of the material written on the 1930s and 1940s is centered on the government and new government programs, that this is a refreshing departure, reminding us that much of life was not yet under the direct control of the federal government. Clingerman's life prepared him to serve as a field man and to write this delightful book. His farming, newspaper, and real estate experiences all helped to prepare him for his duties with the bank. Those experiences also helped him to understand what he encountered, and perhaps his newspaper experience enabled him to remember it in such vivid detail for the recounting. A special value of this book, beyond its readability, is that "out of Washington" detail about social and economic life that has been largely ignored by too many of us.

ROGER LAMBERT, *Arkansas State University*

Upheaval in the Quiet Zone: A History of Hospital Workers' Union, Local 1199. By Leon Fink and Brian Greenberg. Champaign: University of Illinois Press, 1989. Pp. xvii, 298. $24.95, cloth; $9.95, paper.

This is a story about the power of history. Local 1199 flourished when it flowed with history, stumbled when it misread the currents.

In the 1950s Local 1199 of the Retail Drug Employees Union in New York City started to chafe at its all-too-stable membership of 6,000. The union began to organize support staffs at New York City's voluntary hospitals. These were the people who swept the floors, washed and pressed the laundry, collected the bedpans, maintained the equipment, cooked and delivered the meals, and generally enabled the hospitals to function. By the 1950s they were Hispanic and African-American and overwhelmingly female. In society's eyes they were not seen and, until Local 1199, neither did they speak.

Hospital managements paid them little attention. Work force control was feudal; divisions were ruled by satraps who made work assignments and scheduled work days without consultation. In retrospect, the voluntary hospitals were begging to be unionized. Local 1199 obliged.

Both Leon Davis, who had been president since 1934, and Elliott Godoff, the chief hospital organizer, were Russian Jews, once Communists. Their commitment to civil rights was unyielding and far ahead of their time. They performed masterfully in communities that they understood, such as New York City. Unfortunately, they were inflexible outside those communities and authoritarian within the union itself.

The union was first recognized as a bargaining agent by a warmly sympathetic Montefiore hospital in New York in 1958. The next year the union took on six other hospitals and struck for the first time. The settlement did not recognize the union as the bargaining agent, but the union acted as though it did and so convinced the newspapers. The union got strong support from the New York City AFL-CIO Central Labor Council, specific unions, the city's press, and civil rights groups.

Politics and economics flowed the right way for Local 1199 in the 1960s. For example, New York state labor law had not covered voluntary hospitals, which gave the hospitals a legal basis for ignoring the union. Local 1199 mustered political forces under the banner of civil rights, which encouraged Governor Nelson Rockefeller to sign a bill to change the law (though only for the City) in 1963.

Further, governments and insurers, not patients and philanthropists, were starting to pay the hospital bills. Indeed, the League of Voluntary Hospitals and Homes of New York considered its members merely "custodians of public funds." Settling a strike between a hospital and the union often meant figuring how much the government would be willing to pay.

This tactic worked well until the 1970s. New York City, whose political and financial intercession had served the union well, almost went bankrupt in 1975. Soaring health care costs unnerved both governments and insurers. Local 1199 had managed to boost the minimum hospital salary by 150 percent from 1958 to 1968, but could only gain 81 percent from 1968 to 1974, and even less (40 percent) from 1974 to 1980.

Further, the union did not know how to adapt to unfamiliar terrain. In Charleston, SC, 1199 hit a wall of resistance from a community which the union did not know how to convert. In Pittsburgh a year later the union started its organizing by nuzzling up to the black community, a tactic that worked in New York City, but which put off the white ethnic groups that made up three-fourths of the Pittsburgh hospital work force. The union's techniques worked in Philadelphia and Baltimore because work forces and communities there were more similar to those in New York City.

The union leadership roared for civil democracy in the country but bleated when pinched for more democracy in the union. There were plenty of elected delegates—roughly one for every 25 members—but they had no say in decision making. Hospital organizers and business agents were all appointed. Leon Davis, who was president for nearly 50 years (1934–1982), flat-out said that union members were not qualified to make decisions. He embraced a paternalistic pride: "We took backward people and elevated them." The presidency turned over several times after Davis's retirement, largely because he did not train a generation of managers beyond his own. He just didn't trust members to run the union the way he thought it should be run.

This book is a good read. Its pages throb with people who lived through the languor between contracts and the turmoil of negotiations. The authors use their plentiful interviews for more than the clever quote. They often write a paragraph or two, with accompanying photograph, about a laundress or a housekeeping aide, and let the person say why he or she took such risks.

This book is a fine labor history of a traditional kind. As in many labor histories, employers are one-dimensional and, though not devils, have no obvious redeeming features. However, the authors do not pull their punches when they discuss union failures. Still, we get little sense of a system of labor relations. The book is about the drama of struggle. It is about strikes, rallies, and political shoves and pulls, which, of course, might be just how things still are.

EDWARD P. DUGGAN, *Goucher College*

The Demise of Nuclear Power? Lessons for Democratic Control of Technology. By Joseph G. Morone and Edward J. Woodhouse. New Haven: Yale University Press, 1989. Pp. xii, 172. $22.50, cloth; $6.95, paper.

This very good book examines the history of nuclear power, focusing on the decision-making process and, in particular, on the critical decisions within the U.S. political process. The history of nuclear power is one of the evolution of a technology from a position of enormous promise and optimism to one in which no major participant (with the exception of the U.S. Navy) has received a benefit. The authors' goal is to discover how and why the U.S. political system failed to modify a technological system as it became more and more politically unacceptable. Is it simply the case that democracy is inconsistent with the rational management of complex technologies?

The decision-making process worked well in the forties and fifties. Many technologies were being explored, and there were extensive discussions about the relative merits of each. The safety philosophy was appropriate: containment combined with remote siting. In the event of an accident, harmful materials would be contained and minor breeches of containment would not be fatal, as reactors were located far from heavily populated areas. In the mid-sixties several bad decisions were made, the critical one being to scale up the size of reactors very rapidly. This was done on the basis of very little operating experience. With large reactors, however, containment ceased to be feasible, and so the safety philosophy changed from the mitigation of the effects of accidents to the total prevention of accidents. This shift must surely have given impetus to the growing antinuclear movement. "If an accident occurs we can contain it" is a much more believable claim than is "an accident can never happen."

The authors argue that what made these decisions crucial was the emergence of what they refer to as technological inertia. If there were alternative technologies available, it might be possible, given the dissatisfaction with the current one, to switch to another, but dynamic increasing returns, of the type frequently cited in the competing technologies literature, have acted to make it extremely difficult to produce an alternative to the current technology. Thus, in the United States, "nuclear power" has come to mean "light water reactor," and technological inertia has produced a situation in which only technologically minor variations are possible. The nuclear power decision has become a "this or nothing" decision, in which the safety philosophy has become crucial.

What the authors see in this history is that two unfortunate decisions in the mid-sixties (to scale up and the consequent shift in safety philosophy) led nuclear power onto a bad path. As the path became less and less acceptable, though, technological inertia made it more and more difficult to move to another one. Thus we find ourselves in the situation in which the current technology is unacceptable but that other potentially acceptable nuclear power technologies are unavailable.

Finally, the authors discuss the nature of the failures in crucial decisions and make prescriptions for the handling of large technology projects. They conclude that the democratic decision-making process failed to live up to its own standards. Making decisions about large, risky technologies involves five strategies: protecting against foreseeable hazards; erring on the side of caution; systematically attempting to reduce uncertainty; learning from experience; and setting priorities. In the mid-sixties "virtually every [strategy] was violated" (p. 136). The prescription is for "more democracy rather than less" (p. 140). More debate, the authors claim, would probably have led to more sensible decision making.

This is very likely true. The problem, however, would have been finding people to take "the other side" in the debate. At the time, when the crucial decisions were being made, there was considerable consensus about the virtues of nuclear power. The decisions were in fact very democratic in the sense that they were perfectly in tune with general opinions. The main source of dissent came from the experts—scientists at the national laboratories for example, who had doubts about the safety and economics of light water reactors. But taking decisions out of the hands of the experts is, to some extent at least, what the authors mean by democratic decision making. It is true that more debate would have been a good thing. It is also true that those making decisions thought that there had been enough debate. Surely they did not think they were being reckless, nor did they think they had failed to set priorities.

Throughout the book the authors are concerned with the question of whether democracy is capable of managing complex technologies. They conclude that it is and that the problem in the U.S. experience was not the presence of democracy but rather its presence in insufficient quantities. I have suggested that there could not have been more democracy in the U.S. experience, and I suspect that part of the reason the authors come to the conclusions they do has to do with the book's exclusive focus on U.S. history. Canada, France, and Japan all have had very different experiences. The authors acknowledge this but explain away France and Japan as relatively nonrepresentative democracies. Another possible explanation (and I emphasize that this is conjecture) is that these countries did not experience the same degree of optimism about nuclear power that occurred in the United States. Following the Soviet bomb in 1949 and Sputnik in 1957, the United States was very eager to demonstrate its technological abilities. There was considerable concern in the 1950s that the United States be first in the race for nuclear power. This concern and early successes with the technology soon generated a belief that nuclear power was under control. While the United States was being carried away on a wave of publicity about its technological invincibility, other countries were being more cautious and developed their nuclear power strategies more carefully. (The Canadian CANDU reactor is considered by many to be safer than the light water reactors; the French have standardized their reactor design, whereas in the United States every reactor is a new design.) What this suggests is that the problem is not democracy and technology but rather unbridled optimism and technology. The time at which we are most likely to make mistakes in the management of technology is precisely the time when we think we have it licked.

In spite of misgivings about some of its conclusions, I recommend this book. It is a very careful study of the decisions and forces that led to the current difficulties of nuclear power. It will be of interest to anyone concerned with the history of technology and efforts to manage or control that history.

ROBIN COWAN, *New York University*

American Living Standards: Threats and Challenges. Edited by Robert E. Litan, Robert Z. Lawrence, and Charles L. Schultze. Washington, DC: The Brookings Institution, 1988. Pp. xvi, 250. $29.95, cloth; $10.95, paper.

This book is not of much current interest for economic historians. However, a far-sighted young doctoral student might want to start collecting this type of book—those intended to influence the economic policies of a new president—for the year 2020 when they could be the basic sources for a fascinating book on the interplay of ideology, scholarship, and the practice of policy. Today, macrodata is a Rorschach blot on the escutcheon of economists in which analysts reveal much more about their intellectual origins than about the correctness of policy interventions. This Brookings Institution contribution is an example from the Paul Revere School of contemporary commentary. "The tragedy of national overspending and the budget deficit is that there has been no visible crises. Had there been, the nation might already have done something about it" (p. 5).

Here is the world as seen by Brookings in mid-1988. Things may look good on the surface, but tragedy is everywhere on the horizon unless we balance the federal budget soon—but not too soon. (It is the "not too soon" that distinguishes contemporary liberals from pre-Keynesian conservatives.) Each article in the book is complex, competent, and has a clear story line. The book is admirably tied together for a collection of essays by references back to the first, which sets the tone and provides parameters used throughout. It is an orderly tale, but as Levy himself says midway through the book, "the fact that a theory is plausible does not make it true" (p. 118). Which is not to say that I know it not to be true—we need to wait until 2020 for that.

There are six substantive chapters and an introductory one, which is a complete summary. Each chapter itself has a good summary so there is no missing the point here. In order, Robert Lawrence writes on the "International Dimension," Robert Litan on the "Risks of Recession," Frank Levy on inequality and the vanishing middle class, Robert Crandall on regional shifts, Martin Baily and Margaret Blair on "Productivity and American Management," and finally Richard Murnane on education.

The basic story is this: American living standards have been at high levels that are not sustainable. Consumption is so high and savings are so low because of the deficits in the government and trade sector. But foreign governments will not sustain our improvident ways forever and women's labor force participation rates cannot rise much more. Eventually the piper will have to be paid. We need to get the savings rate up now while a soft landing is still possible. And all of this was set in motion by the oil shock of 1973, when inexplicably productivity growth stopped. (Except, of course, that productivity growth slowed dramatically in 1968, not 1973.) Six years of boom do not shake these authors' conviction about all this at all. Nor do they ask how it is that real gross private investment keeps chugging right along whether savings or government spending is high or low. Nor, it turns out, do they know where the productivity gains are going to come from. Baily and Blair just know that the market will almost do it for us even though their references to Japan lead them time and again to the brink of saying quite the opposite. Their advice is that governments should do something since the social return to research and development exceeds the private return, but not quite as much as Adam Smith would have the government do. Murnane does not offer the prospect of solving the productivity decline through human capital either. In his view, education did not get us into this problem and so it will not get us out either. (Abandoning the central thesis of the book does make it possible for him to write a subtle chapter summarizing what has been recently learned about education and labor market productivity, however.)

So maybe Brookings has it backwards; other stories are also consistent with the facts. Maybe we do not save because business does not demand it? Maybe the Japanese want our assets, and that is why they pursue a surplus so ferociously. Maybe mergers are the only place for capital to go.

Maybe macro policy just does not matter much at all. Maybe it is all demography. Maybe when there is a plentiful labor supply, profit maximizing leads to investing in capital widening rather than capital deepening, and maybe labor-using non-traded sectors grow most rapidly, and kids in the bottom half of the academic skill distribution do not take school any more seriously than the market will, and maybe they would rather fix cars in San Jose than Detroit, and maybe their older, smaller cohort is complementary in production with them and their relative position deteriorates even further? And maybe when cohort size, and rates of change in capital-labor ratios, and industry mix and region, and school years completed all get entered linearly and separately into one regression we get current history as the product—that it is 60 percent random and nothing much matters a lot, though all the signs are right, so it must be the aligning of the heavens in 1973.

These are thoughtful essays. On their own merit, they deserve better treatment than this review has given them. Given the state of macro today, though, a book that argues its own position and does not confront the contending arguments cannot be compelling. Lawrence breaks new ground. Litan is gracious. Levy is richly textured and subtle. Yet this is a book for 2020 and not for today.

EUGENE SMOLENSKY, *University of California, Berkeley*

Saving the Savings and Loan: The U.S. Thrift Industry and the Texas Experience, 1950–1988. By M. Manfred Fabritius and William Borges. New York: Praeger Publishers, 1989. Pp. xii, 161. $37.95.

The Thrift Debacle. By Ned Eichler. Berkeley: University of California Press, 1989. Pp. x, 163. $15.95.

On Aug. 9, 1989, President George Bush signed into law sweeping legislation designed to rescue a U.S. thrift industry beleaguered by years of mismanagement, regulatory ineptness, prolonged regional distresses, massive restructurings in the financial services sector, and fundamental changes in central bank operating procedures. The legislation directs regulators to spend billions of dollars to close or sell hundreds of insolvent savings and loan associations (S & Ls) that were kept alive by creative accounting rules known as RAP (Regulatory Accounting Principles). In fact, the scale of liquidations promulgated by the new law has not been witnessed since the industry's debacle during the Great Depression. The long-term economic and political forces that culminated in the current maelstrom are the focus of the books examined in this review.

Both volumes begin by briefly tracing the history of S & Ls in the United States from their roots as terminating savings plans in the 1830s to the massive federal intervention and restructuring of the industry during the 1930s. Regulation of early S & Ls rested strictly in the hands of state governments, which exercised mild oversight through banking commissions or departments. However, as Manfred Fabritius and William Borges observe, the seeds for later federal policies were sown as early as 1894 when, in the Wilson Tariff Act, Congress recognized (or created) the special role of S & Ls as conduits for mortgage funds to moderate-income families. The perceived need to maintain or assure this special status of S & Ls as part of a national housing goal has dominated congressional thinking for most of the twentieth century.

Strong economic forces reshaped the financial landscape of the 1920s and redefined the traditional roles of depository institutions. While neither book emphasizes the point, market forces during this period were instigating a functional convergence among depository firms; an important trend that re-emerged during the 1970s. When the curtain of despair fell in the 1930s, depository institutions retrenched to their core products which for S & Ls were residential mortgages and time deposits. Subsequent federal legislation virtually sealed this functional segmentation until the deregulation acts of the 1980s. The inability of S & Ls to implement institutional innovations as a result of New Deal legislation explains much, but not all, of the industry's current dilemma. In fact, the recurring theme of the Fabritius and Borges's volume is Texas's success in allowing portfolio diversification among state-chartered S & Ls in the face of stiff federal resistance and how the Texas practices were eventually incorporated into the Depository Institutions Deregulation and Monetary Control Act of 1980 (DIDMCA). For Ned Eichler the eventual loosening of portfolio restrictions (particularly allowing direct real estate investment) on S & Ls was a prelude to further industry demise.

The New Deal reforms created a dual system for chartering, supervising, and insuring S & Ls and set the stage for the jurisdictional rivalries and regulatory innovations that were to arise in later years. The two books reviewed here examine the dynamics of the regulatory innovation process and its interaction with the federal deposit insurance system from the perspective of Texas and California, the two states that perhaps were most aggressive in their quest for jurisdictional dominance and where the impact of the current thrift debacle was greatest. For S & Ls, the World War II years were spent supporting the massive Treasury funding and refunding operations. After the war, their vast accumulation of government securities provided a springboard for meeting the pent-up demand for mortgage funds.

The 1950s were prosperous times for the S & L industry. Several factors converged to produce this result: a housing boom of historical proportions was underway; monetary policy was generally accommodative; inflation was low; ascending yield curves persisted; and federal housing policy emphasized the need for a healthy S & L industry.

As both books stress, however, even during the robust years of the 1950s disturbing undercurrents began to arise. First, tax laws and government regulations aimed at achieving national housing goals made asset diversification almost impossible. Second, competition with commercial banks for time deposits pushed the liabilities structure of S & Ls into shorter maturities. Funds gap positions became decidedly liability sensitive, making the net interest margin of most S & Ls highly vulnerable to rising market yields. Third, S & Ls became inherently illiquid as the bulk of their assets were invested in long-term mortgages for which no active secondary market existed at the time. When disintermediation occurred, S & Ls were put in an extremely precarious position. Advances from the Federal Home Loan Banks (FHLBs) were available; however, the funding of these advances through the issuance of FHLB bonds put further pressure on market yields, exacerbating the S & Ls' own problems. Finally, regulatory policy showed little flexibility even when confronted with these problems.

The first real crisis for S & Ls came in the "credit crunch" of 1966, when the Federal Reserve sharply reduced the growth rate of the money supply to curb the accelerating tendency toward inflation. Short-term interest rates ratcheted upward, causing massive declines in withdrawable shares. Fearing the impact of rate competition on its constituents, the Federal Home Loan Bank Board (FHLBB) pressed for rate ceilings on savings deposits and successfully lobbied Congress for temporary authority to implement them. With the support of industry trade groups, the FHLBB also convinced Congress that national housing policy mandated a positive ceiling differential in favor of S & Ls.

Serious credit crunches came again in 1969 and 1973 with their concomitant episodes of disintermediation. S & Ls stayed afloat through these storms, but like ships bashed against their moorings, many were structurally weakened. Increasing inflation and an array of new financial instruments, like NOW accounts and money market mutual fund shares, put continuous upward pressure on S & L funding costs. The severe squeeze on net interest margins prompted some states, most notably Texas and California, to allow their state-chartered institutions to issue variable rate mortgages and to make direct real estate investments. Federal restrictions on variable rate mortgages were not lifted until the early 1980s.

Neither book gives enough emphasis to the impact of the change in the Federal Reserve's operating procedure in Oct. 1979. By 1979 S & Ls were extremely vulnerable to rising interest rates. When the Federal Reserve shifted its focus from interest rates to monetary aggregates, the level and volatility of short-term yields increased dramatically. In fact, for S & Ls as a whole, the marginal cost of funds exceeded the average return on their mortgage portfolios. Both books see the passage of DIDMCA as easing the gap management problems for S & Ls. However, while deregulation was a necessary condition for cushioning the impact of higher interest rates, it was not a sufficient one. Thrifts needed time to alter their cost structures and portfolio mixes. Portfolio diversification required entry into new markets, and moving up the learning curve takes time.

But time was not on the side of S & Ls and the severe recession in 1981–1982 sounded the death knell for many of them. Regulators tried to rescue the struggling firms by further deregulation and by relaxing safety and soundness controls (forbearance). Nevertheless, keeping these failed associations open greatly exacerbated the industry's problems. Viewed realistically, however, it was probably impossible for the Federal Savings and Loan Insurance Corporation (FSLIC) to liquidate or merge all of the failed institutions, and Congress was unwilling to appropriate the money to do so.

To compete for deposits the failed firms paid substantial rate premiums, which tended to increase costs for solvent institutions as well. In addition, the moral hazard problem inherent in the deposit insurance system had pervasive risk effects throughout the industry. The deposit insurance premium established by the FSLIC did not reflect the unique risk structure of the S & Ls being insured. Thus, a strong incentive existed for S & Ls facing imminent failure to take exorbitant credit risk. For instance, Eichler describes how California thrifts generated high fee income by making acquisition, development, and construction (ADC) loans that were extremely risky in terms of the borrowers' willingness and ability to fulfill the provisions of the loan agreement. However, since the S & Ls were already in effect bankrupt, the risk fell on the FSLIC and ultimately on the taxpayer through treasury guarantees.

Interest rates declined precipitously after 1982, easing the gap management problem of S & Ls somewhat. But the recession that brought down rates, devastated the earnings of S & Ls, and encouraged them to restructure their portfolios by acquiring ADC loans and making direct real estate investments. By 1984 loan defaults began to eclipse the issue of gap management, and the S & L industry was faced with yet another crisis.

On the question of who is to blame for the S & L debacle Eichler is clearest. In his view, the industry's problems are attributable to a confluence of ideology, personality, and circumstance. The ideology was deregulation. Deregulation coupled with the mispricing of deposit insurance produced highly perverse results. The personalities were those of avid deregulators, bent on success and fearful of reregulation. Their zeal was directed at quick implementation of the provisions of the deregulation acts. Congressional procrastination, regulatory indecision, managerial incompetence and dishonesty, and economic dislocations of national and regional scope formed the circumstances in which deregulation was to occur. While Fabritius and Borges would probably agree with all of these factors, they placed little emphasis on the personalities of the players in the deregulation process.

Both books do a fine job in tracing the historical underpinnings of the current S & L crisis. Moreover, though they cover the same events, the books are complementary. Not only do they examine the impact of the S & L crisis in different states, but they also approach the issues from different perspectives.

DUANE GRADDY, *Middle Tennessee State University*

ECONOMIC THOUGHT

The State and the Economic System: An Introduction to the History of Political Economy. By Phyllis Deane. New York: Oxford University Press, 1989. Pp. xii, 205. $36.00, cloth; $11.95, paper.

This slim volume "on the interface between what seventeenth-century writers . . . would have called the polity (the civil order of society) and the economy" (p. v) sketches admirably "the ways in which the broader context of moral, scientific, and political ideas or events have influenced successive economists' vision of the operations of the changing economic system and their views of the scope for purposive State action to shape the process of change" (p. vi). While others often explain the interface between economic history and theory simplistically in terms of the historical or ideological determination of theories, Deane provides a exceptionally balanced descriptive narrative which reveals the richness and complexity of the interface.

After a brief introduction, Chapter 2 describes the emergence of a scientific attitude in the works of Galileo, Bacon, and Descartes, and its application to political economy by Petty. Common to all were the rejection of authority and the affirmation of the potential of observing and reasoning for understanding the natural and social universe. Chapter 3 examines the theories of Law, Cantillon, and Steuart, and the articulation of principles of causation, interdependence, and structural change for understanding the natural laws of trade and value. The application of these principles by the Physiocrats and Adam Smith to systematic theories of political economy is taken up in Chapter 4. Smith's use of systematic economic theory to evaluate and prescribe state policies for the growth of national wealth promoted a long-standing tradition in the discipline which provides the justification for the title of this book. Smith's reputation is linked to the resonance of his work with Enlightenment thinking and to the practical policy success of his advice.

The ways in which changing historical conditions led to changing policy concerns is the theme of Chapter 5. A demographic surge is linked to Malthus's work. The need for monetary policy to manage the financing of the Napoleonic Wars is seen as a stimulus for the monetary theories of Thornton and Ricardo. Accelerated industrialization in Britain and associated changes in income distribution are used to explain Ricardo's concern for distribution and its impact upon growth.

Chapter 6 describes the existence in England by the 1830s of a self-conscious discipline of political economy with a reasonable consensus on the existence of objective economic laws. There is an excellent discussion of the importance of Bentham's utility calculus both for providing the ideology to guide social policy and for allowing the Ricardian growth model—with its antagonistic class interests—to yield a morally defensible policy of distribution. The resonance of Mill's work with the conditions and ideas of the mid-nineteenth century is brilliantly described and then contrasted with Marx's exception to the English consensus. There is a concise and cogent exposition of Marx's intellectual influences and his theoretical framework. Marx's focus on "the dynamic characteristics of large-scale industry [and] the causes and consequences of continuous technological change" (p. 115) is contrasted with the more static ceteris paribus approach of other theorists. The incompatibility of Marxian and orthodox analysis is explained well by Marx's social determinism (as opposed to atomistic individualism) and his treatment of "social aspects of economic change as endogenous" (p. 116), as opposed to being impounded in ceteris paribus assumptions.

Further changes in historical conditions (mechanization, nondiminishing returns, the importance of fixed rather than circulating capital) made the classical model seem anachronistic and inapplicable, leading to an openness to new theories. Chapter 7, which covers the contributions of Jevons, Menger, Walras, and Marshall, develops this refreshing theme of the demand for the marginal revolution, instead of the typical supply-side explanation of simultaneous discovery. Keynes's contributions in response to the need for new macroeconomic policies are the subject of Chapter 8, and Chapter 9 provides the briefest sketch of macroeconomic developments from Keynes to the present.

The book is clearly written and provides much useful information and a remarkably tangible sense of place, particularly for the nineteenth-century material. Its most important strength lies in the objective exploration of the consistency or inconsistency of theorists with the ideas of their times. No judgments are passed from a modern conception of economic truth, and there is no name-calling of theories as mere ideologies. This strength has, unfortunately, a concomitant weakness. Because the book is (purposefully) descriptive, it has no thesis to explain the interface between history and theory. The introduction is, therefore, weak; there is no conclusion, and the details of the narrative are sometimes difficult to put into context. Despite these shortcomings, and the almost exclusive British focus, the book provides marvelous supplementary reading material for students of either British economic history or the history of thought.

AVI J. COHEN, *York University*

Economists and the Economy: The Evolution of Economic Ideas, 1600 to the Present Day. By Roger Backhouse. New York: Basil Blackwell, 1988. Pp. x, 224. $49.95.

When I was doing background reading for my history of thought book, essential works included Mark Blaug's *Economic Theory in Retrospect* (Homewood, IL, 1962) and Roger Backhouse's *A History of Modern Economic Analysis* (New York, 1985). With his new book, *Economists and the Economy*, Roger Backhouse is establishing himself as an even more important interpreter of modern economics.

Economists and the Economy is a nice blend of history of economic thought and economic history. Instead of presenting economic ideas chronologically, as almost all history of thought books do, Backhouse organizes the presentation by topic, tying the developments in economic ideas with the historical happenings in the economy. He considers five topics: "Growth and Development," "The Regulation of Trade and Industry," "Money and Inflation," "Employment and Economic Fluctuations," and "The Theory of a Market Economy." The five chapters devoted to these topics make up the core of the book. To these he adds an introductory and a concluding chapter which talk about the discipline of economics.

The task he sets for himself is monumental, and when he is successful, the book is a delight to read. He is especially successful in his discussions of growth, the regulation of trade, and money and inflation. These chapters nicely integrate economic history—the events that the economists were thinking about—and the economic theory that developed at that time and shows how theory reflected the reasoning economists used as they attempted to understand the events. His discussion highlights the work of some lesser-known economists, emphasizing that earlier economists were much more multidimensional and insightful than they are often given credit for having been. For example, he points out how, in the 1820s, J. R. McCulloch stressed invention and technical progress as the basis of growth and how Thomas Mun, in 1664, argued for the importance of trade in goods, not bullion flows. In his chapter on money and inflation, Backhouse strengthened my respect for Henry Thornton's insights into financial markets and made me think that perhaps Thornton's 1802 book on paper credit should replace most current money and banking books.

In each of these chapters Backhouse's approach works. Reading them gives one a deeper appreciation for the diversity of economic thought throughout history, how that history relates to events, and the problems with reducing that diversity of opinion into a school of thought.

I found the discussion on employment and economic fluctuations less satisfying, perhaps because I knew the literature better. Still, Backhouse's conclusions—that earlier writers were much more insightful than they are often presented today and that we can better understand their work if we know the economic events they were facing—are ones I can readily endorse.

I had a couple of minor complaints about the book. The chapter "The Theory of a Market Economy" seemed out of place; it lost much of the life and insight of the earlier chapters, in part because the topic was not amenable to the combined history of thought/economic history treatment the earlier chapters received. The concluding chapter, on the discipline of economics, similarly seems somewhat out of sorts with the earlier chapters. In it Backhouse spends a lot of time discussing recent developments in economic methodology, such as Donald McCloskey's work on rhetoric in economics. While I am in almost total agreement with Backhouse's assessment of recent theory and methodology, I found myself unhappy with this chapter because it did not tie in enough with the earlier chapters, or at least the connection was not clear to me.

My quibbles aside, the book is a scholarly contribution to economic literature and is definitely worth reading.

David Colander, *Middlebury College*

The Economist: Henry Thoreau and Enterprise. By Leonard N. Neufeldt. New York: Oxford University Press, 1989. Pp. xiii, 210. $29.95.

The Economist is a significant contribution to Henry Thoreau scholarship that ought to interest a number of this Journal's readers. Leonard Neufeldt's argument, focused especially on Thoreau's masterpiece *Walden* and his undervalued late essay "Life Without Principle," is that Thoreau both resisted and internalized the economic thought of his day. Thoreau's work, Neufeldt holds, constitutes a more sophisticated barometer of and response to the age of emerging industrial capitalism in which he lived than previous commentators have realized.

Neufeldt's intervention in Thoreau studies is part of a larger revisionary movement in scholarship on the so-called American literary renaissance, a movement that seeks to offset the main tendency of scholarship since the 1940s to focus on the formal properties of literary works qua verbal artifacts and to appraise their participation in contemporary social history much more cursorily. With respect to Thoreau's command of nineteenth-century economics, Neufeldt is especially concerned to demonstrate Thoreau's awareness of the available lexicon of terminology and its rapid changes in connotation (such as "commerce," "enterprise," and "finance"), to establish Thoreau's participation in what Neufeldt calls the rising "culture of enterprise," and to show how Thoreau used his work as a critique of and countermodel for the highly profitable vocational self-help manuals of his day. The first half of *The Economist* discusses in relatively general terms Thoreau's relation to the culture of enterprise as reflected in his statements and his literary professionalism. The book's second half discusses more specifically the economic themes of *Walden* and "Life Without Principle," ending with a detailed analysis of *Walden* as a serious parody of the generic success manual for young men.

For economic historians, this book henceforth will be the court of first resort for information about Thoreau's views. Even one not greatly interested in Thoreau may nonetheless find sections of considerable interest, such as Neufeldt's account of the conventions of success literature, his extensive discussions of the changes during the nineteenth century in the usage of key economic terms (and how Thoreau reflected this linguistic fluidity in the liberties he himself took with them), his depiction of how an astute and original mind played with the concept of "enterprise" in irreverently invigorating ways, and how, by the same token, the discourse of American capitalism managed very quickly to permeate the thinking of even an obdurate, standoffish anticapitalist. Neufeldt is himself more a literary critic and theorist than an economic historian (he relies on what appear to be standard monographs for his generalizations about American economic development and institutions), and his book seems less concerned with historical data and more preoccupied with discussion of texts than the average social scientist will expect. But the care and thoughtfulness with which *The Economist* reflects upon the interpenetration of these two domains seems to this reviewer exemplary.

LAWRENCE BUELL, *Oberlin College*

The Keynesian Revolution in the Making, 1924–1936. By Peter Clarke. Oxford: Clarendon Press, 1989. Pp. xii, 348. $64.00.

Peter Clarke has produced a scholarly book about the *historical* John Maynard Keynes during the dozen years in which he was making the Keynesian Revolution. The book is not a biography or a systematic exposition of Keynes's theoretical system. Instead it is a historical account of Keynes's arguments at several levels of discourse: politics, policy, and theory. He addresses his book to fellow historians. For historians of economic thought it is an important book that needed to be written because of the careful attention it gives to the relation of arguments in economic policy to arguments in economic theory.

In addition to a useful introduction and a disappointing conclusion. Clarke's book consists of three intermediate parts. Part 2 on "Sound Finance" describes the conventional wisdom, known as the "Treasury View," prevailing in the late 1920s. According to this view, attempts to reduce unemployment by programs such as public works would do no good because the funds needed to finance them would "crowd out" funds needed in the private sector of the economy. Keynes was the leading critic of this view.

Part 3 is on "A Revolution in Economic Policy?" and contains six of the thirteen chapters of the book. It is the book's most valuable section. Clarke adroitly blends Keynes's arguments about politics, economic policy, and economic theory. At a time when Keynes was completing his *Treatise on Money* (London, 1930), he was a member of the Macmillan Committee on Finance and Industry, which had been appointed to recommend measures to combat the Great Depression. Keynes utilized meetings of the committee to conduct seminars on the *Treatise* by way of arguing his case for interventionist policies.

Part 4 is titled "A Revolution in Economic Theory?" and describes Keynes's transition from the relatively orthodox theorist of the *Treatise* to a revolutionary dissenter in *The General Theory of Employment, Interest, and Money* (London, 1936). Clarke views effective demand as the centerpiece of Keynes's revolutionary new theory, with emphasis on his change (from the *Treatise*) in the relation of investment to savings, the fallacy of composition, and adjustment to equilibrium through changes in total output rather than price flexibility. The role of uncertainty and the monetary theory of production are briefly mentioned but not highlighted.

The great virtue of Clarke's work is that it traces the history of an argument, which in its most basic aspect is the far-reaching argument about the appropriate role of government in economic policy. Clarke approaches this issue in microcosm by skillfully interweaving Keynes's arguments about politics, policy, and theory. At one point Clarke writes that Keynes's "initiatives in policy dragged along a justifying body of theory in their wake—sometimes improvised on the spot" (p. 73). The evolution of intuitive insights in policy into formal theoretical constructs is illustrated by the multiplier. The concept is adumbrated in a political pamphlet Keynes wrote in defense of Lloyd George's platform for public works in Great Britain's general election of 1929. By 1936 this bit of campaign rhetoric had become an integral part of the theoretical explanation of fluctuations in employment and output.

As the sequence of the table of contents suggests, Clarke argues that Keynes's revolution in economic policy preceded his revolution in economic theory. In view of this, the reader might expect Clarke to carry through and interpret the *General Theory*, the revolution in economic theory, as an argument for Keynes's program of reform, including loan finance and the "socialisation of investment." Instead he shifts ground to write that the *General Theory* "must be understood as . . . the unfolding of an immanent logic of discovery" (p. 281). He points out that the *General Theory* is addressed to professional economists, has "almost nothing" about economic policies, and was written at a time when Keynes was politically inactive (pp. 305, 286). One may grant these facts about the *General Theory* and its author and still interpret the theory as an argument for Keynes's economic policies. Clarke is, of course, under no obligation to give this interpretation even though it would seem consistent with the general theme of his book as a whole. A little epistemological sophistication and a somewhat less literal-mindedness about side-by-side theory and policy could have resulted in a major contribution to the interpretation of the most vital figure in twentieth-century economic theory. It remains an important book, full of rich documentation on the relation between arguments in economic policy and arguments in economic theory, but it falls short of being a great book.

DUDLEY DILLARD, *University of Maryland*

Keynes's Monetary Theory: A Different Interpretation. By Allan H. Meltzer. New York: Cambridge University Press, 1989. Pp. xv, 336. $39.50.

Somewhere between Milton Friedman's famous assertion that "we are all Keynesians now" and Keynes's own cryptic confession that "I am not a Keynesian" lies the real message of the works of John Maynard Keynes. Today it is generally accepted that much of what passes as Keynesian thought is not so much the work of Keynes himself as that of his popularizers. Other economists tend to see their own reflection in the works of Keynes. *The General Theory of Employment, Interest, and Money* (London, 1936) has become a Procrustean bed whereby authors trim or stretch Keynes to suit their own purposes. Many authors have attempted either to restate Keynes's ideas in a more manageable form, rearrange his ideas, or fill in perceived gaps in his theory.

In this book Allan Meltzer wishes to come closer to the true legacy of Keynes and to offer an interpretation of Keynes that will revive interest in some of Keynes's ideas. In seven chapters Meltzer explores the Keynes of the 1920s, reviews two of Keynes's earlier works (*A Tract on Monetary Reform* [London, 1923] and *A Treatise on Money* [London, 1930]), links these writings to *The General Theory*, explores Keynes's view on international finance, and concludes by examining other significant interpretations of *The General Theory*.

It is Meltzer's "different interpretation" that Keynes has a consistent intellectual framework that can contain all his wide ranging policy recommendations and often seemingly contradictory theories. Keynes's work is seen here as evolutionary, with *The General Theory* growing logically out of his work of the 1920s. The nascent ideas in the *Tract* and the *Treatise* provide both the motivation for and the themes of *The General Theory*. Readers will be surprised at the number of ideas in the *Treatise* that have become part of the conventional Keynesian model supposedly found in *The General Theory*.

The major themes that weave their way through this interpretation of Keynes are opposition to strict laissez-faire capitalism, the overriding importance of the state in investment and economic planning, a concern for economic progress, and the critical role of investment in assuring that progress. Meltzer makes his most important assertion in finding that the core belief of Keynes is none of the above but rather Keynes's confidence that a proper set of rules and institutions could be established that would reduce uncertainty, thus stabilizing the economy at or near the full employment level of output.

Convincing support for this assertion is found when Meltzer focuses on the one area where Keynes spent much of his professional life—international monetary arrangements. Meltzer believes that this is where one gets closest to the fundamental Keynes, where one can find his unexploited legacy, and even where one may find the way in which *The General Theory* might have been revised. It certainly is true that here one can see the importance that Keynes attached to the correct institutional arrangements as he painstakingly tried to find a path between the rigid discipline of the international gold standard and the laxity of freely flexible exchange rates. His elaborate and detailed plans in international finance speak dramatically of his concern about the role of rules.

By the end of his book Meltzer has built a strong case for this reinterpretation and reinvigoration of Keynes. By returning to the writings of Keynes and citing from those voluminous works, Meltzer succeeds in constructing a more organic view of Keynes, where policy flows naturally from theory. Unfortunately, this type of argument can never be fully convincing as other authors can also cite chapter and verse from Keynes to support their particular view of Keynes.

By and large, Meltzer does a fine job in delineating the novelty of Keynes and his contributions. The book is extensively footnoted and contains a comprehensive bibliography. The comparison of Keynes's views with those of his contemporaries about the effectiveness of monetary and fiscal policy is drawn well. However, in the area of international finance, where Meltzer believes much of the true Keynes can be found, the comparisons with other economists could have been strengthened by providing more historical context and more discussion of the relevant alternatives, such as Harry Dexter White's plan at Bretton Woods.

In sum, this book is an important contribution to the continuing debate about Keynes and the Keynesians. With a relevance broader than its title indicates, the book will force each reader to re-examine his or her own attitude toward Keynes and to re-evaluate Keynes's contribution to economic thought.

RICHARD C. SCHIMING, *Mankato State University*

Essays and Entrepreneurs: Innovations, Business Cycles and the Evolution of Capitalism. By Joseph A. Schumpeter. Edited by Richard V. Clemence. New Brunswick: Transaction Publishers, 1989. Pp. xxxix, 341. $19.95.

When I go to a magic show I never think about how the tricks are done. I enjoy them even though I know I am being fooled. Of course, there must have been a rabbit in the hat before it was pulled out and the lady really does not float in midair—there are strings somewhere. But it is so much fun just to relax, suspend disbelief for a little while, and be entertained!

And that is how I feel about reading Schumpeter. The writing is great—that of a learned man—with references to historical events, to various economists, and even to theoretical physics. It is much more fun than wading through a heavy-duty modern theoretical article with endless assumptions and definitions, followed by theorems and their complicated proofs. But, alas, when I have to think precisely about what Schumpeter said I wish that he had included some of those definitions and assumptions explicitly, and maybe proved a theorem or two.

This book reprints 25 of Schumpeter's articles which appeared in a variety of journals and books. They cover his major themes on business cycles, entrepreneurs, and the evolution of capitalism. According to Schumpeter, business cycles are driven by the clustering of innovations, which he defines as "changes in production functions which cannot be decomposed into infinitesimal steps. Add as many mail-coaches as you please, you will never get a railroad by doing so" (p. 138). As to why innovation tends to cluster, Schumpeter asserts, "as soon as the various kinds of social resistance to something that is fundamentally new and untried have been overcome, it is much easier not only to do the same thing again but also to do *similar* things in different directions" (p. 141). The agent of change is the entrepreneur. "The mechanisms of economic change in capitalist society pivot on entrepreneurial activity" (p. 222). Moreover, "the entrepreneur and his function are not difficult to conceptualize: the defining characteristic is simply the doing of new things or the doing of things that are already being done in a new way (innovation). It is natural, and in fact it is an advantage, that such a definition does not draw any sharp line between what is and what is not 'enterprise' " (p. 223). That Schumpeter's desire to keep the definition of entrepreneurship vague has succeeded is evidence by a recent exchange in *The New York Times* (July 9, 1989), between advocates and opponents of a government-sponsored research joint venture for the development of HDTV. Richard Schaffer, arguing against, wrote: "Instead of busying ourselves with imitating the Japanese, we need to exhibit the self-confidence to rely on our traditional strengths—organizing entrepreneurial start-ups to exploit new technology." Robert Noyce, arguing in favor, wrote: "The national entrepreneurship spirit that spawned the agricultural and aerospace programs and similar efforts remain alive and well in America—as exhibited today by Sematech . . . ." Will the real entrepreneur stand up?

Then there is Schumpeter's bleak prognosis for the future of capitalism. "We observe that, as the capitalist epoch wears on, the individual leadership of the entrepreneur tends to lose its importance and to be increasingly replaced by the mechanized teamwork of specialized employees within large corporations; that the institutions and traditions that sheltered the structure of capitalism tend to wear away; that the capitalist process by its very success tends to raise the economic and political position of groups that are hostile to it; and the capitalist stratum itself, mainly owing to the decay of the bonds of family life that in turn may be traced to the 'rationalizing' influence of the capitalist process, tends to lose some of the grip and part of the scheme of motivation which it formerly had'' (p. 208). From this, together with what he saw as an ever-increasing role of government in the form of projects such as the TVA, the reliance on fiscal policy to maintain aggregate demand, and regulation of the capital markets would come ''*guided capitalism*'' or socialism. As he put it, ''Such a system will no doubt still be called capitalism. But it is capitalism in the oxygen tent—kept alive by artificial devices and paralyzed in all those functions that produced the successes of the past'' (p. 185). I wonder how he would have reacted to current developments in Russia and Eastern Europe.

There is, in addition, an introduction by Richard Swedberg that alone is worth the price of the book. Swedberg provides the intellectual antecedents to Schumpeter's thinking on the subjects covered along with interesting insights regarding Schumpeter the man. He suggests that Schumpeter might have been jealous of Keynes because Keynes threatened his ambition to be regarded as the world's greatest economist, a suspicion bolstered by Schumpeter's review of Keynes's *General Theory*. Here is Schumpeter, aspirant to being the world's greatest lover and greatest horseman—as well as the world's greatest economist, Harvard's then senior economic theorist, sharp dresser with the pocket handkerchief—writing on the *General Theory*: ''Those who had the opportunity to witness the expectations of the best of our students, the impatience they displayed at the delay in getting hold of their copies, the eagerness with which they devoured them, and the interest manifested by all sectors of Anglo-American communities that are up to this kind of reading . . . must first of all congratulate the author on a signal success, [and now the swift jab to the kidneys] a success not in the least smaller in the cases of negative reaction than in those in which the book elicited fervent admiration.'' Schumpeter's objection to the *General Theory* was not based on monetarism; he slaps down the monetarists too in his essay ''The Decade of the Twenties,'' but on its being founded on only one, albeit drastic, episode in the overall history of business cycles. That is surely a sensible objection, yet what Schumpeter fails to see is that what is general about the *General Theory* from a purely theoretical standpoint is the introduction of the possibility of an alternative to the classical full-employment equilibrium, namely, a less-than-full-employment equilibrium. The assumptions required to support a less-than-full employment equilibrium may be challenged as being unrealistic, but are the assumptions required for a full-employment equilibrium so realistic? Moreover, didn't Schumpeter himself advocate the unimportance of the classic, perfectly competitive system and the assumptions on which it was based? As for extrapolating from the particular to the general, Schumpeter's prognosis of the fate of capitalism was certainly influenced by the economic and political responses to the Great Depression.

Schumpeter appears to have held the view that ''Jews were 'early bloomers' who would unfairly receive more rewards than they deserved in free competition''—an opinion also held by the mathematician G. Birkhoff. This view seems not to have affected his personal relationships—perhaps some of his best friends were Jewish. We learn as well of his falling in love with a twelve-year-old girl, asking her father's permission to see to her education and to marry her when she came of age. He certainly had an eye for early bloomers!

Morton I. Kamien, *Northwestern University*

Against Mechanism: Protecting Economics from Science. By Philip Mirowski. Totowa, NJ: Rowman and Littlefield Publishers, 1988. Pp. ix, 250. $34.95.

In this book Philip Mirowski has assembled 10 of his previously published essays, included two new essays and a preface, and has sent the ensemble forth to do battle with neoclassical economics. Mirowski claims there are unifying themes and to a large extent he is right: disdain and scorn for orthodoxy permeate almost every page. But there is more than tilting at windmills here. The antagonism toward the conventional has fueled a powerful search for the origins of what irritates him so and, in the process, has generated some provocative, novel, and I think ultimately important hypotheses.

The most significant of these (Chapters 1–3, 6) is the claim that the defining feature of neoclassical economics is its mathematical methodology, combined with the proposition that this methodology was simply lifted from nineteenth-century physics, with a few changes of variable names, and without much consideration for the limitations of these methods in a discipline, economics, which is ultimately a social and human rather than a physical science. Mirowski aims first to demonstrate that the theoretical innovations of the progenitors of the marginal revolution, particularly Léon Walras and Stanley Jevons, had their origins in the new theoretical formulations of nineteenth-century physics and engineering, and that Karl Menger's role in the marginal revolution was small, as was his understanding of the mathematics of the new methods. Alfred Marshall is viewed as a packager and salesperson of the new methods, a softpedaler who, in spite of his ambivalent remarks on the value of mathematics in economic analysis, failed to confront the main problems entailed by this approach (pp. 27–29).

According to Mirowski, the first neoclassical economists simply redefined potential energy as utility: a field defined over commodity space, and relabeled kinetic energy as expenditure: the sum of prices times displacements (changes) in quantities; the budget constraint captured (although not entirely coherently in the economics context) the nineteenth-century notion that the sum of kinetic and potential energy had to be conserved (p. 150). Apply techniques of constrained maximization and voilà, the fundamental methodology of neoclassical economics with which, he argues, we are still saddled.

Mirowski's critique of this enterprise proceeds on a number of levels: the borrowing was done imperfectly because the pioneers didn't fully understand the subtleties of the mathematics; economics now remains wedded to a nineteenth-century methodology which has been superceded by developments in the discipline from which it was originally drawn; and the resulting models do not do a good job of capturing essential features of the process under study—particularly the historical character of economic phenomena.

The first two lines of criticism score points against his often long-dead adversaries but also run the danger of undermining his basic argument. After all, if economists are to be faulted for borrowing the methodology of nineteenth-century physics "lock, stock and barrel," is it not perhaps overkill to criticize them for neglecting or being unable to import several key parts and having to improvise others? That the borrowing was only partial is clear; Mirowski emphasizes the interpretation of utility as a force field capable of generating displacements of commodities in neoclassical models, but so too in such models are changes in technologies, factor endowments, and (if one is complete) rules, and not all of these have analogs in the physical model. If there was something wrong or scandalous about the borrowing Walras, Jevons, and Vilfredo Pareto did from nineteenth-century physics, then it seems beside the point to argue that they did it poorly or incompletely. Similarly, of what relevance are contemporary developments in the methods of physics? If it was inherently wrong to try and import the techniques of nineteenth-century physics, would it be right to try and mimic twentieth-century physics, and are economists to be faulted for not doing so?

Ultimately it is the third critique that should carry the most weight and here the argument is advanced that the importation of physical metaphors gave to neoclassical economics an ahistorical aspect. The basic nineteenth-century physical model lacked provisions for hysteresis effects: frictions or viscosity which in the economics context might delay or otherwise influence the response of endogenous variables (prices and quantities) to changes in the forces affecting them. Consequently, in pure neoclassical models, the (unique?) equilibrium values of endogenous variables are determined only by current values of exogenous variables; past values of such variables, or for that matter those of the endogenous variables, are irrelevant.

Certainly it can be valuable to study the way the economic analogs of friction and viscosity influence the evolution of an economy, and introduce such effects in economic models as they have been in physics, for example, in the study of magnetism. But even if these frictions are ruled out by assumption, partial, or general equilibrium analysis will still have a historical dimension unless the values of exogenous variables are eternally immutable. This Mirowski seems to deny, by implying that the introduction of hysteresis is the only route through which the study of economics can be rendered historical.

One of the challenges for economic historians has in fact been to chronicle (not necessarily explain) changes in these variables with an eye to their consequences. Economic theorists (and historians) have, however, sometimes been ambivalent about recognizing institutions or rules as a fourth category of exogenous variables, an ambivalence from which Mirowski has not entirely escaped. This is evident in Chapter 5, which focuses on game-theoretic approaches to institutions in the work of Martin Shubik and Andrew Schotter. Shubik's position has been more or less systematically to recognize the rules of the game as givens in game-theoretic (or economic) analysis (as did Walras; see pp. 14, 58). This position is intellectually coherent and defensible in a way that, for example, Schotter's often is not. Yet Mirowski is critical of Shubik's posture (p. 79), although the search for an axiomatically based filter with which to separate endogenous from exogenous components of institutions leads in the direction of a blind alley down which Schotter, Douglass North and Robert Thomas, and a host of others have at times trooped. Mirowski realizes this, of course, but although he bravely announces a typology of institutions at the conclusion of Chapter 5 and has kind words for evolutionary approaches, his own position on this most difficult of methodological issues is ambiguous. Mirowski is not happy with arbitrary distinctions between exogenous and endogenous variables, but such distinctions are essential in any explanatory model: we always explain phenomena in terms of phenomena which are themselves unexplained.

Part 2, subtitled "The Incompatibility of Neoclassicism and Institutional Economics," includes three other essays. Chapter 4, like Chapter 5, addresses mathematical approaches to institutions. Chapter 6, on conservation principles in twentieth-century economics, might have been included in Part 1. Chapter 7, "Philosophical Foundations of Institutional Economics," more explicitly develops Mirowski's position that there can be no complementarity between neoclassical and institutional economics. These traditions stem from incompatible philosophical roots, and the problems of "Neoclassical Economics" are, in his view, irremediable.

Part 3, "Coopting the Unorthodox," contains review essays of Donald McCloskey on rhetoric (the most penetrating in my view), Richard Nelson and Sidney Winter on evolutionary economics, and Michio Morishima on Marx. Throughout the book there is a tendency for Mirowski to get swept away in his critical exegesis—so many outrages, so little time—that his critical energies lose focus. Both Albert Einstein's theory of relativity (p. 3) and Robert Shiller's tests of market efficiency, for example, are "infamous" (p. 215).

When all of the philosophical to-and-froing has died down, the last cannon (canon?) shot fired across the bow of conventional economics, one wants to know constructively what kind of economic research Mirowski advocates. Part 4, "Historical Studies in Institutionalist Economics," is intended to address this concern. Chapter 11 uses eighteenth-century English share prices to examine how accurately Adam Smith captured trends and characteristics of firm profitability. Mirowski concludes that although Smith did well in summarizing conditions contemporaneous with the writing of the *Wealth of Nations*, he was less successful in his historical summaries; at best he was an "indifferent empiricist" (p. 206).

In Chapter 12 Mirowski again looks at time series of eighteenth-century share prices for the East India Company, the Bank of England, and the Million Bank, and, using a methodology pioneered by Shiller, he tests whether financial markets were efficient by constructing ex post rational share prices (share prices that would have been warranted, given actual dividend payouts and a discount rate estimated as the average long-term rate of interest). He finds that markets were not efficient, both in the sense that most of the Shiller variance bound tests fail, and in the sense that there were large and systematic divergences of actual from ex post rational share prices. Interestingly, he finds that although markets were not efficient, they may more closely have approximated efficiency in the eighteenth century than, according to recent research in finance, they do in the twentieth; thus the notion that there has been a historical trend toward more efficient markets is called into question. This is an important piece of research that stands on its own.

Mirowski does allude here to how idiosyncratic historical developments may explain anomalies in share prices not otherwise accounted for (p. 230). But neither of these empirical studies really serves to delineate by example the evolutionary, historical, institutional methodology advocated elsewhere in the book. And as for the book's subtitle, "Protecting Economics from Science," is not Mirowski's use in Part 4 of econometric technique and statistical data in efforts to falsify hypotheses vaguely scientific, nay, dare I say it, Popperian? The journey Mirowski has begun is thus only partially complete.

ALEXANDER J. FIELD, *Santa Clara University*

The Essential Alfred Chandler: Essays Toward a Historical Theory of Big Business. Edited by Thomas K. McCraw. Boston: Harvard Business School Press, 1988. Pp. vi, 538. $35.00.

Most economic historians know Alfred Chandler as a Pulitzer prize-winning historian who revolutionized the study of business by pioneering a new, more systematic approach to the evolution of the large, integrated corporation. I know him as a dignified, self-effacing man whose obsessive intellectual curiosity and forceful vision made him a model mentor, one as interested in learning from students as in teaching them. Thanks in part to the editorial vision of Thomas McCraw, there is now *The Essential Alfred Chandler*, a collection of his works that enables us to see more clearly where his vision came from and why it has had such an impact, not only on the study of U.S. business history but on scholars in many countries and in several disciplines as well.

McCraw accomplishes this feat by using episodes from Chandler's life and career to guide his selection, organization, and introduction of materials, which include 14 articles, chapters, or published lectures; two exchanges with other scholars; and three excerpts from *Strategy and Structure* (Cambridge, MA, 1962), *The Visible Hand* (Cambridge, MA, 1977), and the soon-to-be published *Scale and Scope* (Cambridge, MA, 1990). In a finely crafted introductory essay McCraw launches us on a picturesque and delightful "intellectual odyssey." He compares Chandler to the poet Auden, who was in Stephen Spender's words "one of those rare individuals . . . who . . . had a clear idea of what he wanted to do when he was 20 and just sat down and wrote and didn't allow himself to be diverted" (p. 3).

The collection reveals Chandler the historian as a doggedly determined hunter who has the acute sense of an accomplished tracker. His search for evidence is seldom random, guided instead by a series of specific and systematic questions about the sources of change in the strategies of businessmen and administrative structures of business organizations over time. Those questions first emerged most clearly in 1959 from the numerous company histories, corporate annual reports, and business journals that he used as the basis for "The Beginnings of 'Big Business' in American Industry."

Included among the collection is "Recent Developments in American Business Administration and their Conceptualization," (co-authored in 1961 with Fritz Redlich) and the ensuing discussion which it provoked. Chandler displayed admirable calm under fire, acknowledging the correctness of several criticisms but steadfastly holding his ground with regard to his objectives and approach. The inclusion of a series of exchanges with sociologist Charles Perrow and economist Oliver Williamson some 20 years later not only enables us to see the extent to which the issues raised by Chandler's data and approach had penetrated other disciplines, it also offers an opportunity to evaluate a fascinating debate regarding Chandler's concept of administrative coordination and the utility of transaction cost analysis.

Chandler not only faced nay-sayers in business history, he also contended with a new breed of economic historians determined to remake economic history with the modeling tools of neoclassical economics. Wedged between business historians preoccupied with individual entrepreneurship and economic historians immersed in theory, Chandler cut his own niche by concentrating on the dynamic changes in one of modern capitalism's most characteristic and defining institutions, the large, integrated corporation.

Among the handful of distinguished scholars who have trained young economic historians, Chandler has been one of the few to consider sociological theory a more important source of insights than neoclassical economics. Yet Chandler has by no means ignored economics. Indeed, he has incorporated increasingly more economics into each of his major books, making his most recent *Scale and Scope* the most methodologically integrated of them all. Not only has Chandler enlarged and refined the vocabulary of economics by making terms such as "economies of scope and speed" commonplace, he has fortified his approach by using concrete examples to demonstrate more precisely the extent to which businessmen and managers in several different economies over time have actually practiced what economists preach. While some economists will undoubtedly take issue with McCraw's assessment that Chandler's works "as economics" are "beyond significant challenge," they will have to mount the challenge against the data as well as the theory.

That none of Chandler's essays, considered individually, represents a full-blown theory suggests that his own vision of the process of theory building is far different from that of the economist. *The Essential Alfred Chandler* is appropriately subtitled "Essays Towards a Historical Theory of Big Business," and it demonstrates Chandler's view of historical theorizing as a never-ending search for evidence to support increasingly more general propositions about the process of historical change. Each of his essays widens the evidentiary base and extends the logic that links the different pieces of evidence into a unified whole. Considered together, the essays give rise to an approach that is distinctly Chandlerian, one which McCraw suggests is characterized by a focus on the anatomy of change within giant organizations, careful organization of vast quantities of information aided by charts and maps, use of sociological theory, empirical comparisons which yield theoretical generalizations, and a general lack of interest in public policy issues.

If Chandler's interest in theorizing has made his work more accessible to economists, it has also distinguished him from the majority of historians who consider theorizing a dangerous tendency, one more likely to distort than clarify the complexities of the past. Among the more trenchant criticisms of Chandler's work have come from historians who object to his narrow focus and his excessive rationalism, his lack of emphasis on the human aspect of history, and his avoidance of the issue of power. Nevertheless, even the most skeptical historian can appreciate the painstaking and laborious process involved in Chandler's attempts to generalize from the minutiae of historical detail. Without narrowing the focus, the process of understanding the evolution of corporations might well have taken even longer than it has.

As the volume shows, Chandler did not simply wake up one morning determined to theorize about large-scale organizations. We come full circle, to an understanding of the important links between the man, his life, and his career as the pre-eminent international historian of the modern corporation. First was his passionate interest in the historian's craft. Second, Chandler had the good fortune of having had supportive and well-to-do "if not very wealthy" parents, who sent him to the best private schools, where he studied with some of the best historians and sociologists and digested the theories of at least one famous economist. Third, there were Chandler's relatives, two of whom played instrumental if indirect and unexpected roles in Chandler's career. There was Great-Aunt Lucy, in whose attic Chandler discovered the papers of his great-grandfather, Henry Varnum Poor, whose career as a railroad and business analyst later provided the inspiration for some of Chandler's works. Finally, there were Chandler's life experiences, many of which he uncannily blended with his intellectual concerns to shape an especially productive career pattern. Indeed, McCraw suggests that it was Chandler's experience as an interpreter of aerial reconnaissance photos in the Navy during World War II that turned his childhood fascination with railroads into a major intellectual preoccupation with large-scale organizations.

It is to the credit of both Chandler and McCraw that this book is less a celebration of the man and his works than a carefully constructed primer on the potentialities and pitfalls of historical theorizing. Armed with *The Essential Alfred Chandler*, scholars will be better prepared than ever to enter, broaden, and deepen the debate about the historic role of managerial capitalism in the economic development of nations throughout the world.

MARY YEAGER, *University of California, Los Angeles*

GENERAL AND MISCELLANEOUS

The Development of Large Technical Systems. Edited by Renate Mayntz and Thomas P. Hughes. Boulder: Westview Press, 1988. Pp. 300. $32.50, paper.

Large technical systems are like pornography: they are hard to define, but everyone knows one when they see one. The book under review resulted from a 1987 conference at the Max Planck Institute in Cologne, which brought together historians, social scientists, and other aficionados of large technical systems to compare notes and, it was hoped, move toward a more general understanding of the subject.

At the heart of the book are six essays examining the railroad and telephone systems of the United States, France, and Germany. Another paper considers the French electrical power system, while two final contributions expand the frontiers of research by looking at the United States Air Traffic Control network and the cutting edge technology of interactive videotext. By giving accounts of the same systems in different nations and different systems in the same nation, the wide-ranging articles provide the reader with plenty of thought-provoking comparisons.

Definitions nonetheless remain something of a problem. According to Bernward Joerges, large technical systems are "systems of machineries and freestanding structures performing, more or less reliably and predictably, complex standardized operations by virtue of being integrated with other social processes, governed and legitimated by formal, knowledge-intensive, impersonal rationalities" (pp. 23–24). And that doesn't even include the meaning of large. Perhaps it is best to identify these systems by the examples which are typically studied—railroads, telephones and telegraphs, electrical power. Common characteristics include complex, science-based technology; spatial extension; functional organization; and a close relationship between the technical system and other institutions—most notably the government.

Each author uses the themes laid out by Thomas Hughes in *Networks of Power* (Baltimore, 1983) as a loose organizing principle. Major questions include: do systems go through stages of growth; is their progress inhibited by bottlenecks, or "reverse salients" in technology; do they reach a point of momentum, at which they continue to grow and expand in predictable directions; and do they vary in different political settings.

The last point Louis Galambos's paper on the United States telephone network answers with a resounding yes. From the patents that first gave the Bell Telephone Company a monopoly, to the accommodation of the Bell System to antitrust laws and regulation, to the recent breakup of AT&T, "the technological system was shaped by its political context" (p. 150). This was even more true of telecommunications systems in Western Europe. There they quickly came under state control, generally as part of a postal, telegraph, and telephone administration. State interests vied with the market and private interests to shape the structure, technology, and extent of service.

In railroading, politics contributed to system momentum, generally with negative consequences. In all three countries improved transportation helped some interests, hurt others, and led many groups to stake claims for access on their own terms. State ownership or regulation resolved these issues, usually following a period of consolidation. The railroad system was too big and important to too many interests to be left to market forces. But the resulting political compromises tended to reinforce conservatism and tradition in railroad management. The result, as Stephen Salsbury shows in the case of the Penn Central, was a refusal to use new management techniques that could have staved off financial disaster.

If public policy may sometimes drag down failing systems, it can also nurture emerging ones. All of the essays indicate that the early entrepreneurial stage of system-building is the most difficult. The need to overcome consumer skepticism and get enough of the system built to furnish economical service has frequently provided justification for strategic public intervention. In their comparative analysis of videotext, Renate Mayntz and Volker Schneider argue that in France well-considered state involvement has helped videotext take root. Overreliance on free market forces and ineffective public policy has stifled this technology in Germany, Great Britain, and the United States.

Comparisons with other systems make it clear, however, that public intervention is only one means of overcoming entrepreneurial inhibitions and reverse salients. In America, private associations have frequently accomplished what has been left to government actors elsewhere. Salsbury's study of railroads illuminates the key role of freight forwarders and the Master Car Builders' Association (a railroad organization) in standardizing track gauges and disseminating new technology, such as the air-brake, on the nation's lines.

Too often scholarship on system-building has emphasized technology at the expense of economics. Breaking with this tendency, Maurice Lévy-Leboyer argues that if technically all power systems are alike, they nonetheless may vary because of internal economic conditions. In the case of France, a late start and periodic economic downturns, coupled with demand-side constraints in provincial markets, slowed the expansion of large power grids. The author takes exception to Hughes's model, in which technology shapes the size, scale, and extent of systems, while politics modifies or interferes with that process. There is no room here for supply and demand to determine the economic size, scale, and extent of a system, which may differ from its technical capacity.

In the end the essays leave the reader with a rich, if somewhat confusing sense of system growth and change. Clearly technical factors are important—large power generators enjoy scale economies over smaller ones; extensive communications systems have clear advantages over restricted ones. Realizing this technical potential, however, is often a matter of economics. Taking account of economic forces may require looking beneath the national level, where most studies have focused, to the regional level. At the same time, politics, especially at the national level, clearly does influence the history and development of systems. As Todd La Porte cogently reminds us in his essay on air traffic control, how reliable a vital system should be, who should have access to it, and on what terms, inevitably involve matters of equity and political choice. Cold technology and hot political debate, markets and hierarchies, all contribute to the shape of systems.

KENNETH LIPARTITO, *University of Houston*

Egalitarianism and the Generation of Inequality. By Henry Phelps Brown. New York: Oxford University Press, 1988. Pp. x, 552. $72.00.

In August 1789 the French Convention proclaimed that "all men are born and continue free and equal." But the revolutionaries promptly amended the laws to make certain that slaves were not part of "all men." High-flown rhetoric and practical microbehavior have marked the tangled history of "equality" from then to the glorious celebrations of 1989.

Few revolutionary leaders in the twentieth century have been satisfied with goods and services equal to those of their fellows. Yet "egalitarianism" continues to be a catchword in most capitalist and Third World nations. (Leaders of the more hard-headed communist nations have shared Stalin's contempt for the "infantile equalitarian exercises of 'Leftist' blockheads.")

The origins of the West's fascination with equality are portrayed brilliantly, empathetically, and succinctly in Phelps Brown's magisterial study. Instead of decorating the background with words from the Sermon on the Mount, Locke, Paine, and Shelley, he integrates them into a coherent history of thought about inequality in the West. Instead of making cameo appearances in separate studies, ground rent, Speenhamland, the income tax, and the welfare state appear in relation to costs and returns of economic and social change. Quotations from Paine, Pitt, the overseers of the Poor, and Gladstone give pith and vitality to his view of the origins of upper-class English Christian socialism. Tawney's obvious successor, Phelps Brown is, however, free of Tawney's ill-concealed envy and hatred, and is much more of an economist. He is also much more concerned with illuminating how upper-class benevolence since Chadwick has affected the poor.

Part 2 reviews a host of studies on "distributions of income and wealth in the living economy." Rich in data for the United Kingdom (especially over time), it also reviews differences between nations—itself worth the price of a customary study, which is perhaps why the volume is priced so high as to preclude wide use.

As do most distribution studies, this one focuses chiefly on money income and secondarily on wealth. Its comments on trends over time and cross-national differences are therefore subject to two great, if usual, qualifications. First, it ignores capital gains and losses. That is no mean consideration since taxation eventually confiscated much of the landed wealth of the English upper classes. Nor is the omission trivial in its historical review for the United States, with its widespread home ownership, major shrinkage on farm ownership, and volatile stock market. Cross-national comparisons unwisely contrast the Pechman-Okner data on tax-income ratios in the United States, which allow for capital gains, with data for other nations, which do not. And second, it ignores what the state did with the income and inheritance taxes it collected in "the quest for equality." Asquith's great Liberal program began by using most of them to finance Fisher's dreadnoughts and the Haig-Robertson suicide campaigns in the Somme. A singularly large share of the American income tax has permitted similar transfers to the Pentagon and its predecessors.

The final section—"egalitarianism analysed and assessed"—offers a fine tour d'horizon. Its thoughtful consideration of John Rawls and so on may well induce further reading such as Kenneth Arrow and John Harsanyi on Rawls, and James Griffin's more recent *Well-Being* (New York, 1989).

Phelps Brown has compressed an immense literature on inequality, including statistical measurement of income and wealth. Those fortunate enough to begin their study of egalitarianism with this work will be prepared to tackle remaining issues. One surely involves the aftermath of the great twentieth-century successes. Having helped slash death rates among the poor of Ceylon and India in 1946–49, the United States paved the way to still greater numbers today. And while U.S. and U.K. transfer programs far exceed whatever the New Deal envisioned, they have been followed by an apparition—the new class of "problem families," the homeless, the "underclass." Who can demonstrate either a lack of relationship, or that we shall not keep on discovering "inequality"?

The religious-psychological drive for equality so well analyzed by Phelps Brown remains unsated. He quotes the U.S. Catholic bishops: "the level of inequality in income and wealth in our society and even more the inequality in the world scale today must be judged morally unacceptable." Yet neither Sweden's Social Democrats, the British Labor Party, nor Harrington's democratic socialists ever invited China's poor, or the Sudan's, to an "equal" share in their income. The United Kingdom improved its inequality index by letting Ireland go free. And the United States injures its gini-coefficients by welcoming more immigrants than nearly any other nation. The conflict over "moral acceptability" of goals continues unabated in both countries. One hopes that a suitably priced paperback edition of Phelps Brown will be available to enable a new generation concerned with egalitarianism to benefit from his wisdom, and go on from there.

STANLEY LEBERGOTT, *Wesleyan University*

Technology and the Rise of the Networked City in Europe and America. Edited by Joel A. Tarr and Gabriel Dupuy. Philadelphia: Temple University Press, 1988. Pp. xx, 338. $34.95.

The industrial revolution both spurred urbanization and ushered in the transformation of many of the services basic to the economies of cities. Waterworks replaced polluted wells; electricity competed with steam power; and the telephone threatened the livelihood of messengers. Only recently have urban historians recognized the similarities that marked the transformation of transport, sanitation, energy, and communication in urban areas after 1850: capital-intensive, networked technologies replaced the decentralized, land- or labor-intensive methods that had served as urban infrastructure for centuries. The sixteen essays of this volume—originally prepared for conference on "The City and Technology"—offer an excellent sampling of recent research on the historical origins of the networked city and its implications for future urban development.

Although relying upon disparate methods of analysis, from the archival research of Harold Platt's history of the development of electrical service in Chicago to Seymour Mandelbaum's speculations about why communications networks in American urban areas remain free of regulation, as a group these essays highlight several features common to urban networks. Traditionally composed of fixed capital installed in an area with a high density of users, the networked technologies usually offer substantial economies of scale (which at some point become diseconomies), often benefit from linkage with other networks, and frequently prompt unanticipated externalities, whether downriver pollution caused by new sewer systems or the smoke of the first generation of primitive garbage incinerators—aptly labeled "destructors." The potential for natural monopoly present in most networks has usually resulted in some governmental involvement, from granting a franchise to outright public ownership.

Historians of urban networks must meet a tall order: command of the details of the technology itself, an understanding of demand as well as costs relative to competing technologies, and an ability to sort out which institutional barriers or political considerations were instrumental in the eventual outcome. Although most essays in this volume are up to the challenge, a few are particularly successful. Letty Anderson's study of the diffusion of waterworks in New England is strong in its understanding of the basic features of the technology and the importance of the engineering profession in the delivery of the final product. Clay McShane's discussion of the development of urban parkways draws attention to the common-law barriers to limited-access highways in the United States that came down only during the 1930s. Platt's engaging account of electricity service offers a fascinating blend of entrepreneurial and economic history, as he details the steps by which Commonwealth Edison bested its competitors with path-breaking innovations in price-discriminating electrical rates and marketing.

Platt's study highlights a shortcoming of some of the other studies, which give only cursory attention at best to the determinants of demand (income and relative prices) and the costs of competing technologies. Historians of the diffusion of networked technologies can also learn from the political-economic perspective that Anthony Sutcliffe develops in his stimulating account of innovation in urban land transport after 1850. Networked technologies hold the potential for creating and redistributing urban land rents and generating other external benefits (health) and costs (smoke). In a community with any semblance of representative government, the decision to grant the tram license or locate the "garbage destructor" in a particular neighborhood will require the advice of professionals familiar with the technology's mysteries as well as a coalition of supporters standing to gain enough to override the opposition of the losers. Sutcliffe argues, for example, that the owners of horses (in demand for omnibus services in the center city), investors in suburban railways, and landholders in the city center united to stymie the construction of electrical trams in European cities for years, using arguments that the trams were an aesthetic nuisance to mask their own fears of losing rents in capital or land. U.S. cities offer a striking contrast, as the pursuit of speculative gains at the urban fringe accelerated the construction of streetcar lines to the suburbs. Dominique Larroque's essay on mass transit in Paris and Gabriel Dupuy's discussion of the influence of public utilities on the development of Andrésy (near Paris) also note the importance of urban land rents in guiding developments.

While those with an interest in urban history and the history of technology will find these contributions particularly valuable, the reader might have benefited from more care in the preparation of the volume. Some opaque translations of what may have already been difficult texts in the original French obscure the key points of some of the essays. Given the scope of the volume, this reader would have appreciated a comprehensive essay pulling together the conclusions of the research and discussion that followed, if only to assist his navigation of the pipes, tunnels, tracks, and wires that mark the networked city.

JOHN C. BROWN, *Clark University*

The Concentration Process in the Entrepreneurial Economy Since the Late Nineteenth Century. Edited by Hans Pohl and Wilhelm Treue. Stuttgart: Franz Steiner Verlag Weisbaden, 1988. Pp. 146. DM 58.

The five papers assembled here were originally presented in a section at the Ninth International Congress of Economy History in 1986; Hans Pohl has added an introduction. Each paper surveys the growth of large firms in a particular country for various periods beginning around 1880. The focus is on manufacturing, with some attention paid to particular national political environments.

Richard Tedlow reviews U.S. Census Bureau data on the concentration of economic activity among the largest manufacturing firms in the United States during the period between 1963 and 1982 and ties the recent data to previous estimates of growth in aggregate concentration between 1925 and 1972. He also summarizes Alfred Chandler's views on the growth of large American firms at the turn of the century, tying that growth to improving transportation networks and changes in production technology. But Chandler's framework refers to a period at the beginning of Tedlow's data on trends in aggregate concentration. Because they are joined in the paper, I assume that Tedlow wishes to ascribe the large firm growth in his data to Chandler's framework, but he never really makes a clear connection.

Claus Wohlert describes the growth of heavy Swedish industrial firms prior to the First World War; like Tedlow, he emphasizes Chandler's framework of transportation improvements (railway construction) that allow for the realization of scale economies embodied in contemporary technological changes. Wohlert concentrates on developments in Swedish iron, steel, and coal industries.

Hidemasa Morikawa chose a narrower focus, a discussion of the growth of the zaibatsu organizations, particularly Mitsui and Mitsubishi, in Japan between 1875 and 1930. The firms dominated some industries but not others, and Morikawa attributes their differing success to timing of entry, specific applicable corporate skills, and mergers.

Wilfried Feldenkirchen surveys the growth of large German firms between 1870 and 1938, with brief descriptions of several important industries. He discusses the role of changing technology as well as changes in cartel policy and sees a 1920s trend toward conglomerate growth as a financial phenomenon related to the inflation of the period.

Finally, Jean-Pierre Daviet provides an interesting comparison of the relative importance of large firms in economic activity in France, Germany, and the United Kingdom. He calculates that large firms grew far more slowly in France, in the early twentieth century than in Germany or the United Kingdom. Daviet relates slower French growth to factors specific to French society, including consumer resistance to standardized products, an industrial focus (comparative advantage?) in light industry when the early innovations associated with corporate growth occurred in heavy industry, and French political developments.

The papers provide useful descriptions of the growth of large firms in each country, but such descriptions are not new, and the papers rarely go beyond description. Only Daviet attempts to measure and analyze cross-national developments. With contributions covering five nations, the topic deserves more emphasis. It is also clear from the descriptions that industry-specific influences played a major role in driving the development of large firms, but the papers do not develop careful cross-industry comparisons. Finally, although each paper covers a relatively long time period, there is relatively little investigation of any temporal changes in the sources of large firm growth. Was the continuing growth in the early twentieth century simply a lagged response to transport and production innovations or did further political and commercial factors come into play? In short, while the title promises analysis of the concentration process, the papers generally deliver only descriptions. Closer interaction among the authors would likely have brought about a measurable improvement in the final publication.

JAMES M. MACDONALD, *Rensselaer Polytechnic Institute*

The Flight of International Capital: A Contemporary History. By Brendan Brown. New York: Routledge, 1988. Pp. xiv, 461. $21.50, paper.

Brendan Brown has written many books on foreign exchange and has made two major excursions into historical material. These latter have resulted in substantial studies of world currencies in the twentieth century. His first book on financial history, *Monetary Chaos in Europe* (London, 1988), covered the period 1914 to 1931. The present study takes the story from 1931 to the present day with worldwide coverage.

The treatment of the material is chronological, directed by quite a narrow view of the basic causal mechanism at work. Six chapters break the period up into the following subperiods: the 1930s; the immediate prelude to World War II; the period of controls during the war and after, when the Swiss franc was the only freely tradable currency, 1940–1957; the 1960s, or more strictly 1958–1971, when the mark-dollar axis emerged (incidentally a subject to which Brown has previously devoted a book); the immediate experience following the abandonment of the Bretton Woods system; and finally the most recent experience, the period running from 1973 to the point at which the manuscript was finished. A postscript was added to cover the two years from that point until publication.

The approach in both books has seemingly been to take a list of daily exchange rates across all the major currencies and all the major stock market data, together with a chronology of all the important events and political statements. The prices are then matched with immediately preceding events to show how investors responded to the changing political and economic environment. Indeed, a chronology is provided at the end of the book with a list of the important dates and statements—for example, "31 March 1939 British guarantee to Poland." Throughout there are cartoons reproduced from a variety of national newspapers to illustrate the times.

The primary emphasis is on "the unknown investor . . . . How did he calculate risks and returns at crucial economic and political turning points? . . . How could he have drawn on previous investment experience?" (p. 8). These are good questions, and seeking the answers are laudable ambitions. And yet an underlying hypothesis, and finally a conclusion, is that since World War II the U.S. business cycle has been the major force behind capital movements between Europe and the United States. "The secret of the U.S. cycle's continuing strong influence on the dollar . . . lies largely in a cyclicality of long run expectations" (p. 11). But why this should be so is not examined. There is no statistical analysis to support the asserted association, and in the end it is difficult to swallow this story.

The narrative is packed with detail from all around the world. There are fascinating stories, such as the bizarre episode at Paris's Le Bourget airport in 1933 with planes arriving with gold from Amsterdam as others laden with gold were leaving for Amsterdam.

But the basic objective is to account for the behavior of the investor faced with items of news. To pick one example: "How should an international investor have reacted to the looming crisis over Czechoslovakia [in 1938]?" Well, yes, how indeed? Such an investor would have been bombarded with a variety of views and left to interpret and judge and reach a decision. How much can we learn from comparing the type of comment that was available to such an investor at the time and looking at the subsequent price movements? There are subheadings such as "Portfolios adjust to Munich" and "Hungary and Suez: European Currencies Weaken." The text adds detail but what are we learning? Brown is a City economist to whom all this kind of comment is meat and drink, but at the end of the long and careful narrative about all we are able to say is that investors need to learn how to read political and economic events. That is far from easy, but the study of history is as good a way to do that as any other, and this should certainly be brought to the attention of all investment houses and business schools.

FORREST CAPIE, *City University Business School, London*

Money, History, and International Finance: Essays in Honor of Anna J. Schwartz. Edited by Michael D. Bordo. Chicago: University of Chicago Press, 1989. Pp. xi, 272. $35.00.

This collection of essays was presented to Anna Schwartz at a conference held in Oct. 1987 to honor her long and distinguished career. Schwartz has been affiliated for nearly 50 years with the National Bureau of Economic Research and has been the guiding light of the bureau's New York office. Best known to the world at large for her collaboration with Milton Friedman on *A Monetary History of the United States, 1867–1960* (Princeton, 1963), Schwartz is also renowned among economic historians for her collaboration with Arthur Gayer and W. W. Rostow on *Growth and Fluctuation of the British Economy, 1790–1850* (Oxford, 1953). Characteristic features of her work include the construction of new historical time series (not just monetary statistics, but the Gayer-Jacobson-Finkelstein price index, the Gayer-Rostow-Schwartz commodity price index, and an index of dividends and interest payments by nineteenth-century corporations), meticulous empirical work, and, since the beginning of her collaboration with Friedman, historical analysis informed by strongly held theoretical priors.

Along with an editor's introduction, personal reflections by Friedman and the late Karl Brunner, discussants' comments, and a summary of floor discussion, the volume contains five essays. The first two, by Michael Bordo and by Forrest Capie and Geoffrey Wood, review Schwartz's contributions to American and British history. Bordo offers a characteristically encyclopedic review of the literature on monetary factors in American history, concluding that Friedman and Schwartz's story survives the last quarter of a century of scholarship unscathed. The chapter features a tabulation of citations of the *Monetary History*. There can be no more impressive testimonial to the enduring influence of the book than the fact that the number of citations listed by the *Social Science Citation Index* continues to rise over time. Interestingly, the share of citations accounted for by articles in monetary economics has fallen, especially since the rational expectations revolution, while the number of citations in economic history journals and other outlets for monetary history accounts for a rising share of the total.

Bordo makes only passing reference to the methodology of the *Monetary History*, notwithstanding a penultimate sentence that reads: "In the dark age of vector autoregressions where it is no longer possible to identify truly causal relationships, turning to the record of history provides a beacon of light." Methodological aspects of the book are likely to receive new attention with the publication of a paper by Christina Romer and David Romer in which they criticize Friedman and Schwartz for (perhaps subconsciously) selecting episodes in which declines in money were followed by declines in output while neglecting episodes in which declines in output did not follow, thereby biasing the case in favor of the monetarist view.

Capie and Wood have a more difficult task. They must reconcile Gayer, Rostow, and Schwartz, for whom money played a largely subsidiary role, with Friedman and Schwartz's *Monetary Trends in the United States and the United Kingdom, 1875–1975* (Chicago, 1982), which met with a less than wholly enthusiastic reception in Britain. The most successful reconciliation comes in a comment by Walt Rostow. Rather than attempting to impute primacy to monetary factors, the authors of *Growth and Fluctuation*, according to Rostow, sought to trace the evolution of the British financial system and the shifting interactions between money, output, employment, prices, and wages.

Capie and Wood will have none of this. Citing an unpublished working paper, they impugn British critics of *Monetary Trends* who challenged Friedman and Schwartz's conclusion of a stable money demand function and of a central role for monetary factors in British macroeconomic trends. Readers of the *American Economic Review* shortly will have the opportunity to hear the other side of the debate.

The remaining essays address more specialized topics. Phillip Cagan provides a critique of the time series methods, notably vector autoregression, sometimes used in an effort to disentangle the causal interconnections between money and income. Adopting a position that will appear eminently reasonable to readers of this JOURNAL, Cagan concludes that time series econometrics is fundamentally incapable of answering questions of historical causality; rather, compelling answers can be obtained only through an accumulation of case studies of historical episodes. Michael Darby and James Lothian offer a follow-up to their previous work on the international transmission of inflation, finding, plausibly, that the move to floating exchange rates increased monetary independence. Allan Meltzer and Saranna Robinson provide a sequel to an earlier article by Meltzer on the variability and predictability of prices and output under alternative international monetary regimes. They report that the unpredictable components of output are larger for the classical gold standard period than for either Bretton Woods or the post-1973 float, while the magnitude of price forecast errors is roughly equal across regimes. Their forecasting equations, utilizing annual data, are estimated using the multistate Kalman filter. The advantage of this technique is that it allows the coefficients to drift over time. Its disadvantage is that Kalman filtering requires the estimation of a large number of parameters, which may be problematic given the availability of few observations. In an extreme case, Meltzer and Robinson have only 13 observations for the post-1973 float. They would be deserving recipients of an award bestowed upon this reviewer at a Cliometrics Conference some years ago for drawing the strongest conclusions on the basis of the least data.

A limitation of the volume is the virtual absence of substantive debate among authors and discussants. Only Robert Rasche's rebuttal to Cagan's methodological critique generates sparks. The celebratory nature of the occasion presumably accounts for the abundance of monetarists and the dirth of controversy. If none of the papers is entirely successful in combining all of the virtues of Anna Schwartz's best research—attention to the characteristics of historical data, fastidious empirical work, and rich historical narrative, all superimposed upon a coherent theoretical framework—this itself is testimony to the enduring quality of her work.

BARRY EICHENGREEN, *University of California, Berkeley*

Macroeconomic Interactions between North and South. Edited by David Currie and David Vines. New York: Cambridge University Press, 1988. Pp. xvi, 287. $49.50.

This volume contains the proceedings of a 1987 conference organized by the Centre for Economic Policy Research in Britain to discuss international economic interactions between developed countries (North) and less developed countries (LDCs or South). After a useful introductory overview by the editors, the chapters examine measures of North-South interdependence, estimated by means of a general econometric model; policy coordination in response to balance-of-payments crises; welfare aspects of commodity stabilization schemes; risk-management techniques in response to commodity price fluctuations; the effects of financial constraints on trade between North and South; the terms and availability of finance for the South; and aspects of finance in affecting LDC growth. Each paper was assigned an expert discussant.

So described—a paraphrase of the book jacket—this appears to have been an interesting conference, particularly since the general topic is timely and the participants, mostly British, were either well-known senior economists or up-and-coming junior ones. Actually the book is quite boring because, speaking generally, the paper givers used the issues the conference was intended to address to show off their econometric muscles; to a degree, many of the participants masqueraded under false colors, pretending to be interested in practical issues of North-South relations in the opening paragraph of their papers but addressing other issues thereafter. As one candidly put it after one of these excursions, "the research effort . . . should go into model building rather than policy analysis . . ." (p. 131). By the time the gigantic flaws in these models are removed, I doubt there will be any problem or urgent need for models.

As several of the discussants pointed out, the macro-model papers, of which there are five, suffer from a variety of familiar problems: overaggregation of countries into blocs; a cavalier approach to the quality of the data used for the estimations; a reluctance to use the models to make concrete policy recommendations; the omission of crucial elements—in one case, capital flows—pending "further work"; and a tendency toward excessive abstraction. A weakness of several was what Michael Beenstock, the author of the best macro paper, called the "oracular approach." This involves specifying a priori both the model and the parameters, rendering data superfluous—nice work if you can get it.

The micro papers, of which there were two, are much superior to the others. These are the ones by Andrew Powell and Christopher Gilbert on commodity contracts as a hedging device and by Winston Fritsch on Brazilian growth. They are sophisticated theoretically and technically, and the authors actually have useful points and recommendations to make. The former, however, is the more original contribution. Of the discussants, Alasdair Macbean is always worth reading, being politely dismissive of the elaborate but futile mental gymnastics displayed at the conference.

JOHN R. HANSON II, *Texas A&M University*

Fiscal Federalism: Quantitative Studies. Edited by Harvey S. Rosen. Chicago: University of Chicago Press, 1988. Pp. ix, 262. $39.95.

This volume consists of seven papers, an introduction by the editor, and comments by conference participants. Three of the papers deal with the extent of decentralization in the U.S. fiscal structure; three with the issue of the deductibility of state and local taxes; and one with the measurement of the size of the state-local government sector. This is high-quality work, but by its quantitative nature is tedious at times. Fortunately, the editor's introduction prepares the reader with a summary of the major findings.

The first paper on decentralization, by John Wallis and Wallace Oates, provides a long-term perspective on the extent and evolution of fiscal decentralization in the state and local sectors during the twentieth century. The historical data reveal that the major part of the trend toward centralization occurred in the first part of the century. The authors set up and test theories of decentralization, finding that a state's share of state and local spending is inversely related to population and urbanization. In some specifications of the model it is directly related to per capita income. Speculating on the future, Wallis and Oates conjecture that the tendency toward centralization which has already slowed may stop altogether.

The paper by Robert Inman focuses on political issues of the distribution of federal aid to state and local government. Inman tests the theoretical efficiency arguments for aid and finding little evidence that aid is so motivated, offers an explanation in terms of political behavior. Inman's discussion of the growth of aid is tied to his claim of a structural change in Congress from a strong majority-rule leadership style of budgeting to one dominated by decentralized negotiations and deal making.

The paper by Jeffrey Zax looks at the issue from the perspective of the effect of jurisdiction type and number within counties on the aggregate level of county expenditures and debt. Zax finds evidence that aggregate debt and expenditures are positively related to the number of jurisdictions per capita, and when jurisdictions have large average market shares, this power is used to enlarge the local public sector. Zax suggests that small jurisdictions are inefficient, but competitive restraint is lacking in larger jurisdictions where economies of scale should offer opportunities to lower expenditures.

The three papers on deductibility are extremely topical and contribute to the current debate on the possible effects of its elimination. Douglas Holtz-Eakin and Harvey Rosen find that deductibility does affect the choice of revenues' sources and its elimination would result in lower local collections. They did not find evidence that tax substitutions at the local level caused by its removal would work to mitigate against federal tax revenues. Finally, they found that eliminating deductibility could have major effects on local spending.

Lawrence Linday's paper on deductibility emphasizes political issues. Like Holtz-Eakin and Rosen he finds that the level of state and local spending is affected by deductibility. He also finds that voter-based measures do a better job of predicting state and local spending than aggregate measures of cost. He investigated the voting behavior of congressmen on the Tax Reform Act of 1986 with the interesting finding that regional interests were more important than class interests in explaining votes.

George Zodrow addresses the issue of deductibility in the context of a general equilibrium model. While the model is simple, it affords the opportunity to estimate the effects of the response of state and local government to the elimination of deductibility on federal revenues. He finds that the federal revenue gain resulting from the elimination of deductibility is likely to be substantially less than predicted by the partial equilibrium approach.

The final paper, by Charles Hulten and Robert Schwab, focuses on estimating income originating in the state and local sector. The paper seems somewhat misplaced in a volume on fiscal federalism. Only limited reference is made to the relationships among levels of government, but the conclusions may be important for future fiscal federalism policy. The traditional demand-side measurement of the size of the state and local sector ignores the capital income generated by this sector which Hulten and Schwab suggest is capital-intensive rather than the assumed labor-intensive. The magnitude of the understatement is significant, in recent years on the order of $100 billion. The authors argue that some unestimated amount of the understatement is offset by an overstatement in the housing sector. A subsidiary conclusion is that labor productivity in the public sector grew at an average annual rate of 0.6 percent per year in contrast to the zero growth implicit in the National Income and Product Accounts approach.

Despite the econometric problems pointed out by the discussants, these papers represent valuable additions to our knowledge in this area. At the same time, they provide us with interesting reading and a potential research agenda.

JOHN B. LEGLER, *University of Georgia*

A NOTE OF TECHNICAL CORRECTION

This note addresses technical statements in a review of Irma Adelman and Cynthia Taft Morris's *Comparative Patterns of Economic Development, 1850–1914* (Baltimore, 1988) in the September 1989 issue of this JOURNAL.

On p. 798 of the review it is stated that the subsample analyses are performed separately with a factor analytic technique. They are instead performed simultaneously, with the disjoint principal components method. The use of principal components and the simultaneity of subsample analyses alter the meaning and values of the coefficients. Ordinary principal components analysis differs from factor analysis in two ways that lead to lower coefficients. First, the squared coefficients refer to the portion of *total* variance (explained and unexplained) accounted for by a component, not as in factor analysis to the portion of total *explained* variance accounted for. (Factor analysis replaces the diagonal in the correlation matrix with the variance explained by the *retained* factors.) Second, components matrices are not rotated to maximize the large and minimize the small coefficients, as in factor analysis. High loadings are therefore lower and low loadings are higher.

Several statements on p. 799 of the review ignore the effects of the simultaneity of the subsample analyses. In a separate principal components or factor analysis, one maximizes the variance "explained" by the model. By contrast, in disjoint principal components analysis, one maximizes the variance *between observations across all the variables* by maximizing *between-sample* differences in components models. The reviewer states that the value of 0.17 used to select variables for which interpretation is "very low, . . . means that even the principal component explains less than 3 percent of the total variation of the 35 variables . . . . No conclusions at all are justified by such results." But this 3 percent has nothing to do with the variance within a single subsample. It refers to the total variance of all 69 observations, that is, to the sum of *four* sets of within-class variations *and all* between-class variations. (The number of observations is thus 69, not 12.) Therefore, the 3 percent has not the same meaning as the squared coefficients of either factor analysis or ordinary principal components analysis. The measure the reviewer seeks cannot be calculated from the coefficients in a disjoint analysis. He seeks the ratio between the variance of each variable explained by the first component within a single subsample and the total variation of that variable *within that subsample*. For example, if for the variable with the component-one loading closest to 0.17 in the class-one results of "Patterns of Industry" (table 4-2) one adjusts the loadings to reflect the explained portion of the variance *of that variable within that subsample*, the loading of 0.17 becomes 0.51. (This adjustment of course varies across variables.)

In an earlier article written with Svante Wold ("Society, Politics, and Economic Development Revisited: A Disjoint Principal Components Analysis," in L. R. Klein, M. Nerlove, and S. C. Tsiang, eds., *Quantitative Economics and Development: Essays in Memory of Ta-Chung Liu* [New York, 1980]) we calculated the combined effects of the use of ordinary principal components rather than factor analysis, and the use of simultaneous subsample analyses, using data from Morris and Adelman, *Society, Politics, and Economic Development* (Baltimore, 1967). The average coefficient for the first (disjoint) principal component across a set of three subsamples was 0.157. When three separate factor analyses were performed with the same data, the average coefficient across the three subsamples was much higher, 0.683. *But the groupings of the variables in the two sets of analyses were almost identical.* Identifying variable groupings was our major purpose in the historical work. The disjoint method also had the strong advantage of providing measures of the distances between classes and the fit of observations to individual classes, which cannot be obtained by separate analyses.

We have not compared factor analysis and disjoint principal components analysis for our historical work. But the "within-class relevance" of each variable published in tables 3-9, 4-8, 5-9, 6-8, and 7-8 of *Comparative Patterns* can be compared with the communality in factor analysis. The within-class relevance is the percentage of total within-class variations *for all four classes together* (between-class variations thus excluded) explained by the retained components. In the five tables referred to, the percentages explained for individual variables exceed 40 percent for, respectively, 19, 27, 16, 16, and 23 out of the 35 variables.

Thus, the lowness of the coefficients with the disjoint principal components method indicates neither their insignificance nor their unsuitability for the interpretive procedures we follow.

IRMA ADELMAN, *University of California, Berkeley*
CYNTHIA TAFT MORRIS, *Smith College*

1940–1990
Fifty Years of Scholarship

The JOURNAL of ECONOMIC HISTORY

VOLUME L JUNE 1990 NUMBER 2

PUBLISHED FOR
THE ECONOMIC HISTORY ASSOCIATION
IN COOPERATION WITH
RENSSELAER POLYTECHNIC INSTITUTE

PAPERS PRESENTED AT THE FORTY-NINTH ANNUAL MEETING OF THE ECONOMIC HISTORY ASSOCIATION

BARSKY AND DELONG, *Bull and Bear Markets*
CALOMIRIS, *Is Deposit Insurance Necessary?*
TEMIN, *Socialism and Wages after the Great Depression*
SUNDSTROM, *Wages in Ohio Manufacturing*
MIRON AND ROMER, *New Monthly Index of Industrial Production*
DUPRÉ, *Regulating the Quebec Dairy Industry*
SULLIVAN, *English Patenting and Invention*
SOKOLOFF AND KHAN, *Invention in the United States*
SHIELLS, *Hours in British and U. S. Iron and Steel*
WHAPLES, *Winning the Eight-Hour Day*
BERNSTEIN, *American Economic Expertise*
MAY, *Eisenhower, Economic Policy, and the 1960 Election*
NOTES AND DISCUSSION: MITCH
DISSERTATION SUMMARIES

CAMBRIDGE UNIVERSITY PRESS

THE JOURNAL OF ECONOMIC HISTORY

ISSN 0022-0507

Published for the Economic History Association in cooperation with Rensselaer Polytechnic Institute by Cambridge University Press

Aims and Scope: *The Journal of Economic History* seeks to promote the scholarly study of economic aspects of the human past from a diversity of perspectives, notably those of economists and historians. By encouraging careful formulation of issues and clear exposition of methods, the JOURNAL hopes to stimulate discourse among scholars with varied interests and modes of inquiry.

The JOURNAL is abstracted in *The Journal of Economic Literature,* which is part of the DIALOG on-line data service.

Instructions for Contributors: Articles on economic history and related aspects of history or economics will be considered for publication by the Editors on the understanding that the articles have not previously been published and are not under consideration elsewhere. Papers should indicate the wider significance of detailed original research findings as well as the logic and limitations of specialized techniques of analysis. Comments and shorter notes are also welcome. The JOURNAL does not accept unsolicited book reviews, nor can it honor requests to review particular works. Contributions should be typed double-spaced. Footnotes, also double-spaced, should be grouped at the end of the paper, along with figures and tables. Four copies of each manuscript should be submitted. Prospective contributors may obtain a copy of the Style Sheet for the JOURNAL from the Editorial Office. A submission fee of $20.00 or a year's membership (fee schedule below) is required from nonmembers of the Association.

Editorial Office Address: The Editors, *The Journal of Economic History,* Folsom Library, Rensselaer Polytechnic Institute, Troy, NY 12180-3590, U.S.A. Telephone: (518) 276-2784.

Association Office Address and Membership Information: Individuals who are members of the Economic History Association receive the JOURNAL as part of their annual dues. Membership rates (in U.S. dollars) are: $30.00 for those with income above $30,000 a year; $25.00 for those with income below $30,000; $15.00 for students and professors emeriti who have been members of the Association for 10 years; $600.00 for life membership. Payment of an *additional* $20.00 permits joint membership with the Economic History Society (UK). Applications and inquiries concerning membership should be addressed to the Economic History Association, Dept. of History, George Washington University, Washington, DC 20052, U.S.A.

Subscription, Publishing and Advertising Office Address: Cambridge University Press, 40 West 20th Street, New York, NY 10011, U.S.A.; or Cambridge University Press, The Edinburgh Building, Shaftesbury Road, Cambridge CB2 2RU, England.

Subscription Information: *The Journal of Economic History* is published quarterly in March, June, September, and December. Annual institutional subscription rate (1990) US $50.00 in the United States and Canada; UK £31.00 elsewhere. Individuals may subscribe by becoming a member of the Economic History Association (see above). Prices include surface postage and insurance.

The Journal of Economic History (USPS 279-580) is published quarterly by Cambridge University Press. Second-class postage paid at New York, NY and additional mailing offices. Postmaster: Send address changes to *The Journal of Economic History*, Cambridge University Press, 110 Midland Avenue, Port Chester, NY 10573.

Printed in the United States of America.

THE JOURNAL OF ECONOMIC HISTORY

Volume L *June 1990* *Number 2*

PAPERS PRESENTED AT THE FORTY-NINTH ANNUAL MEETING OF THE ECONOMIC HISTORY ASSOCIATION

ROBERT B. BARSKY AND J. BRADFORD DE LONG
Bull and Bear Markets in the Twentieth Century 265

CHARLES W. CALOMIRIS
Is Deposit Insurance Necessary? A Historical Perspective 283

PETER TEMIN
Socialism and Wages in the Recovery from the Great Depression in the United States and Germany 297

WILLIAM A. SUNDSTROM
Was There a Golden Age of Flexible Wages? Evidence from Ohio Manufacturing, 1892–1910 309

JEFFREY A. MIRON AND CHRISTINA D. ROMER
A New Monthly Index of Industrial Production, 1884–1940 321

RUTH DUPRÉ
Regulating the Quebec Dairy Industry, 1905–1921: Peeling Off the Joseph Label 339

RICHARD J. SULLIVAN
The Revolution of Ideas: Widespread Patenting and Invention During the English Industrial Revolution 349

KENNETH L. SOKOLOFF AND B. ZORINA KHAN
The Democratization of Invention During Early Industrialization: Evidence from the United States, 1790–1846 363

MARTHA ELLEN SHIELLS
Collective Choice of Working Conditions: Hours in British and U. S. Iron and Steel, 1890–1923 379

ROBERT WHAPLES
Winning the Eight-Hour Day, 1909–1919 393

MICHAEL A. BERNSTEIN
American Economic Expertise from the Great War to the Cold War: Some Initial Observations 407

ANN MARI MAY
President Eisenhower, Economic Policy, and the 1960 Presidential Election 417

NOTES AND DISCUSSION

DAVID MITCH
The Role of the Textbook in Undergraduate Economic History Courses: Indispensable Tool or Superficial Convenience? 428

SUMMARIES OF DOCTORAL DISSERTATIONS

LEE A. CRAIG
Farm Output, Productivity, and Fertility Decline in the Antebellum Northern United States 432

ADRIENNE D. HOOD
Organization and Extent of Textile Manufacture in Eighteenth-Century Rural Pennsylvania: A Case Study of Chester County 434

DANIEL BARBEZAT
International Cooperation and Domestic Cartel Control: The International Steel Cartel, 1926–1938 436

JEAN-LAURENT ROSENTHAL
The Fruits of Revolution: Property Rights, Litigation, and French Agriculture, 1700–1860 438

JOSHUA L. ROSENBLOOM
Labor Market Institutions and the Geographic Integration of Labor Markets in the Late Nineteenth-Century United States 440

SUSAN WOLCOTT
Keynes vs. Churchill: British Unemployment in the Twenties 442

Discussion: Philip T. Hoffman and Roger L. Ransom 444

EDITORS' NOTES 450

REVIEWS OF BOOKS

MEDIEVAL AND EARLY MODERN

ABU-LUGHOD. *Before European Hegemony: The World System A.D. 1250–1350* A. Greif 455
BAILEY. *A Marginal Economy? East Anglian Breckland in the Later Middle Ages* J. S. Hamilton 456
RAPPAPORT. *Worlds Within Worlds: Structures of Life in Sixteenth-Century London* R. M. Berger 457

MODERN EUROPE

MATHIAS AND POLLARD, Eds. *The Cambridge Economic History of Europe*. Vol. 8: *The Industrial Economies: The Development of Economic and Social Policies* A. J. Field 459
ISRAEL. *Dutch Primacy in World Trade, 1585–1740* J. M. Price 462
MARGAIRAZ. *Foires et marchés dans la France préindustrielle* G. Grantham 463

TRACY. *Government and Agriculture in Western Europe, 1880–1988* — J. J. Liebowitz 464
HAIMSON AND TILLY, Eds. *Strikes, Wars, and Revolutions in an International Perspective: Strike Waves in the Late Nineteenth and Early Twentieth Centuries* — G. Friedman 466
DAVENPORT-HINES AND LIEBENAU, Eds. *Business in the Age of Reason* — E. S. Schubert 467
RODGER. *Housing in Urban Britain, 1780–1914: Class, Capitalism and Construction* — G. Radford 468
BUCHANAN. *The Engineers: A History of the Engineering Profession in Britain, 1750–1914* — E. Robinson 470
CLEARY. *Peasants, Politicians and Producers: The Organisation of Agriculture in France Since 1918* — G. Grantham 471
CAMPBELL. *Joy in Work, German Work: The National Debate, 1800–1945* — H. W. Lepovitz 472
WEBB. *Hyperinflation and Stabilization in the Weimar Republic* — M. L. Hughes 473
TEICHOVA. *Wirtschaftsgeschichte der Tschechoslowakei, 1918–1980* — D. F. Good 475
BLANCHARD. *Russia's "Age of Silver": Precious-Metal Production and Economic Growth in the Eighteenth Century* — T. C. Owen 477
HOCH. *Serfdom and Social Control in Russia: Petrovskoe, a Village in Tambov* — E. Melton 477
URIARTE AYO. *Estructura, desarrollo y crisis de la siderurgia tradicional vizcaína (1700–1840)* — P. Hiltpold 479

MIDDLE EAST, AFRICA, AND ASIA

SHAFIR. *Land, Labor and the Origins of the Israeli-Palestinian Conflict, 1882–1914* — E. H. Tuma 480
PHILLIPS. *The Enigma of Colonialism: British Policy in West Africa* — P. D. Curtin 481
HART, TURTON, AND WHITE, Eds. *Agrarian Transformations: Local Processes and the State in Southeast Asia* — J. E. L. Campos 483

LATIN AMERICA

REINHARDT. *Our Daily Bread: The Peasant Question and Family Farming in the Colombian Andes* — R. L. Garner 485

UNITED STATES AND CANADA

NUMBERS AND SAVITT, Eds. *Science and Medicine in the Old South* — M. Fischbaum 486
RIESS. *City Games: The Evolution of American Urban Society and the Rise of Sports* — S. L. Engerman 487
CAMPBELL. *An Empire for Slavery: The Peculiar Institution in Texas, 1821–1865* — J. M. Clifton 488
SPURLOCK. *Free Love: Marriage and Middle-Class Radicalism in America, 1825–1860* — W. D. Wandersee 489
BECNEL. *The Barrow Family and the Barataria and Lafourche Canal: The Transportation Revolution in Louisiana, 1829–1925* — N. Miller 490

WARD. *Poverty, Ethnicity, and the American City, 1840–1925: Changing Conceptions of the Slum and the Ghetto* — M. J. Doucet 491
BOWMAN. *Capitalist Collective Action: Competition, Cooperation, and Conflict in the Coal Industry* — T. K. McCraw 492
KAUFMAN AND ALBERT, Eds. *The Samuel Gompers Papers*. Vol. 3: *Unrest and Depression, 1891–94* — I. N. Gang 494
TOLLIDAY AND ZEITLIN, Eds. *The Automobile Industry and its Workers: Between Fordism and Flexibility* — S. Babson 495
DUBOFF. *Accumulation and Power: An Economic History of the United States* — C. Grandy 496
PAUL AND DICKMAN, Eds. *Liberty, Property, and Goverment: Constitutional Interpretation Before the New Deal* — H. L. Platt 498
CARELESS. *Frontier and Metropolis: Regions, Cities, and Identities in Canada Before 1914* — R. Szostak 499
BOTHWELL, DRUMMOND, AND ENGLISH. *Canada, 1900–1945* — A. G. Green 501

ECONOMIC THOUGHT

MASON. *Robert Giffen and the Giffen Paradox* — R. F. Hébert 502
HOWARD AND KING. *A History of Marxian Economics*. Vol. 1: *1883–1929* — S. Resnick 503
CLARKE. *Keynesianism, Monetarism and the Crisis of the State* — H. E. Jensen 504
ABRAMOVITZ. *Thinking About Growth and Other Essays on Economic Growth and Welfare* — M. C. Urquhart 506

GENERAL AND MISCELLANEOUS

POMFRET. *Unequal Trade: The Economics of Discriminatory International Trade Policies* — N. Becker 507
ROGOWSKI. *Commerce and Coalitions: How Trade Affects Domestic Political Alignments* — D. A. Irwin 509
ADAS. *Machines as the Measure of Men: Science, Technology, and Ideologies of Western Dominance* — S. McCook 510
BOLINO. *A Century of Human Capital by Education and Training* — D. Jacoby 511
LINDER. *The Employment Relationship in Anglo-American Law: A Historical Perspective* — J. R. Grodin 513
SCHWARTZ. *In the Dominions of Debt: Historical Perspectives on Dependent Development* — D. Rock 514
DASGUPTA. *Growth, Development and Welfare: An Essay on Levels of Living* — J. Anderson 515
GALLOWAY. *The Sugar Cane Industry: An Historical Geography from its Origins to 1914* — D. O. Whitten 517
HOCH AND SLAYTON. *New Homeless and Old: Community and Skid Row Hotel* — J. Leiby 518

THE JOURNAL OF ECONOMIC HISTORY

VOLUME L | JUNE 1990 | NUMBER 2

Bull and Bear Markets in the Twentieth Century

ROBERT B. BARSKY AND J. BRADFORD DE LONG

The bull and bear markets of this century have suggested that large stock market swings reflect irrational "fads and fashions." We argue instead that investors perceived shifts in the long-run rate of future growth and that stock prices are sufficiently sensitive to expectations about the future that these perceived shifts plausibly generated the swings of the twentieth century. We document that analysts often viewed as "smart money" assessed fundamentals, based on their perceptions of future economic growth, in a way that tracked decade-to-decade swings closely.

The twentieth-century course of the U.S. stock market, as plotted in Figure 1, was volatile on a month-to-month, year-to-year, and especially decade-to-decade scale.[1] Major bull and bear movements gave 10-year real percentage changes in the Standard and Poor's (S&P)

The Journal of Economic History, Vol. L, No. 2 (June 1990). ISSN 0022-0507.

Robert B. Barsky is Assistant Professor of Economics, University of Michigan, Ann Arbor, MI 48109. J. Bradford De Long is Assistant Professor of Economics, Harvard University, Cambridge, MA 02138. They are both also Faculty Research Fellows of the National Bureau of Economic Research.

The authors wish to thank John Campbell, Barry Eichengreen, Ken Froot, James Hamilton, Bruce Lehmann, Greg Mankiw, Jeff Miron, Peter Lindert, Robert Shiller, Andrei Shleifer, and Arnold Zellner for helpful discussions.

[1] Nominal stock index values are deflated by the producer price index. The index used is a smoothed monthly version of series 6 reported in the appendix to Robert Shiller, *Market Volatility* (Cambridge, MA, 1989). The underlying nominal stock index prices are monthly average values from various issues of the *Security Price Index Record*, published by the Standard & Poor's Corporation. The S&P price index was begun in 1926; the Cowles Commission, however, extended the index before 1926 back to 1870. See Alfred Cowles, et al., *Common Stock Indices* (2nd edn. New York, 1939). We focus on twentieth-century stock prices because the pre-1900 railroad-dominated market appears to us qualitatively different from the post-1900 industrials-dominated market. There is little reason to believe that price/dividend ratios and expected dividend growth rates should bear the same relation to each other as the market shifts from being two-thirds railroads in 1890 to being two-thirds industrials in 1910. For the industrial composition of stock market indices, see Jack Wilson and Charles Jones, "A Comparison of Annual Common Stock Returns: 1871–1925 with 1926–1985," *Journal of Business*, 60 (Apr. 1987), pp. 239–58. For the rise of a market in industrial securities, see Lance Davis, "Capital Immobilities and Finance Capitalism: A Study of Economic Evolution in the United States," *Explorations in Entrepreneurial History*, 1 (Fall 1963), pp. 88–105; and Vincent Carosso, *The Morgans: Private International Bankers* (Cambridge, MA, 1987).

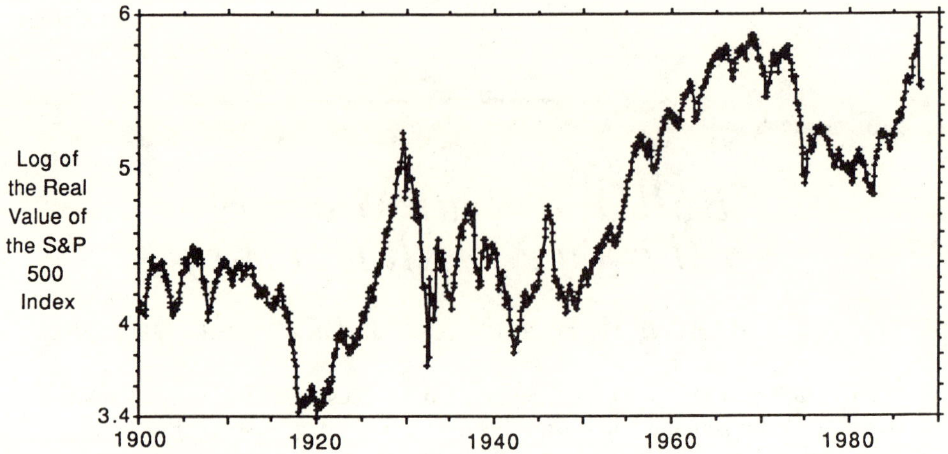

FIGURE 1

REAL UNITED STATES STOCK INDEX PRICES, 1900–1988

index a variance of 0.374—a standard deviation of more than 60 percent. By contrast, the variance of 10-year real percentage changes in national product is only 0.034. This tenfold disparity in volatility is surprising, for a broad portfolio of stocks carries ownership of a broad share of the economy. Since the productivity of the underlying assets has grown smoothly, one would expect the value of the claims to ownership of those assets traded on the stock exchange to have grown smoothly as well.[2]

Even allowing for leverage, stock prices remain volatile relative to their underlying fundamental value—the present value of the future dividends that will be paid out. Figure 2 plots the log of real January stock prices alongside the log of the ex post present value of future dividends paid, both detrended by a 30-year moving average of past dividends.[3] The present value of future dividends is nearly a constant relative to the moving average of past dividends. Major long-run stock price fluctuations, however—episodes like the major bull markets of 1949–1966 or 1921–1929 and the major bear markets of 1929–1933 or 1973–1975—are larger than and appear unconnected to fluctuations in realized fundamental values.

A view taken by observers of the stock market from John Maynard Keynes and John Kenneth Galbraith to Robert Sobel and Robert Shiller

[2] The real GNP series used is spliced together from the revised estimates of GNP in different periods made by Christina Romer and is discussed in J. Bradford De Long and Lawrence H. Summers, "How Does Macroeconomic Policy Affect Output?" *Brookings Papers on Economic Activity* (Fall 1988), pp. 433–80.

[3] Present values are calculated using a constant real discount rate of 6 percent. Figure 2 follows Shiller's "Comovements in Prices and Comovements in Dividends," in his *Market Volatility*. In Figure 2 it is assumed that the stock market's value in June 1989 accurately forecasts the present value of dividends to be paid in years after 1989.

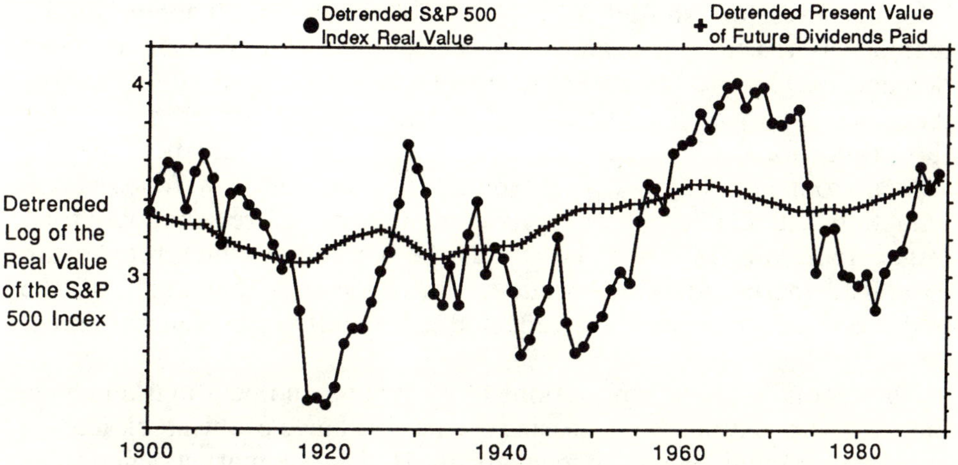

FIGURE 2

STOCK PRICES AND THE VALUE OF ACTUAL FUTURE DIVIDENDS PAID, DETRENDED BY A 30-YEAR MOVING AVERAGE OF DIVIDENDS

is that these large swings in stock prices were due to the "animal spirits" of investors. They did not reflect large shifts in the expected present value of future dividends as assessed by a cautious and far-sighted investor.[4] The stock market boomed in the 1920s not so much because of a perception of improved prospects for future earnings and dividends as because of the flow of new money into the stock market driven by the "fads and fashions" of uninformed new investors.

Sobel, for example, dismissed "fundamentalist" accounts by arguing that "had prices reflected 'realities,' the great upward move [of 1949–1966] would have begun during the war," and asserted that the post-World War II bull was not driven by good news about future growth but sprang primarily from the erosion of the memory of 1929, which had "taken on an almost mythological quality [with] Herbert Hoover . . . in the role of George III"; and secondarily from Charles Merrill's "draw[ing] . . . new capital . . . from people of moderate incomes." Merrill brought "Wall Street to Main Street—and . . . use[d] the efficient, mass-merchandising methods of the chain store to do it."[5]

An alternative view is that while irrational waves of enthusiasm or pessimism pushed stock index prices away from fundamental values in the short run (months or years), in the long run (decade-to-decade)

[4] See John Kenneth Galbraith, *The Great Crash* (Cambridge, MA, 1954); Robert Sobel, *The Big Board* (New York, 1965); John Maynard Keynes, *The General Theory of Employment, Interest and Money* (London, 1936), especially chap. 12; and Shiller, *Market Volatility*, especially the chapters previously published as "Stock Prices and Social Dynamics," *Brookings Papers on Economic Activity*, 1984 (Fall 1984), pp. 457–98 and as "Do Stock Prices Move too Much to Be Justified by Subsequent Changes in Dividends?" *American Economic Review*, 71 (June 1981), pp. 421–36.

[5] See Robert Sobel, *N.Y.S.E.* (New York, 1975), pp. 166–79.

informed investors shifted their money in response to changing fundamentals. When stocks became too expensive, careful investors reduced demand by shifting their wealth out of the market and entrepreneurs increased supply by taking more corporations public. Smart money kept the proportional differences between market prices and fundamental values from growing wider indefinitely, while shifts in fundamental valuations cumulated.[6] Shifts in fundamentals therefore accounted for a larger fraction of return variability as the horizon at which returns are examined increased. The decade-to-decade swings that made up the major bull and bear markets reflected large shifts in businesses' prospects.[7]

These conflicting interpretations of major bull and bear markets have different implications for assessing the performance of the stock market as a social capital allocation mechanism. High stock markets encourage investment. The central reason to have a stock market is that it serves as a social calculating machine that reports to firms what the market thinks of their future prospects and so governs the allocation of investment. If major swings in stock prices are driven by fads, the market is unlikely to perform well; if driven by shifts in the best guess of future cash flow prospects, the verdict may be more optimistic.[8]

The volatility of stock market indices has always been a powerful argument for the fads and fashions view. Supporters of the fundamentalist view have been hard pressed to point out the shifts in prospects that would support large bull and bear revaluations of the worth of America's corporations. As Shiller put the challenge:

> [T]he picture [our Figure 2] . . . is evidence . . . that a model that attributes all the variance of aggregate stock prices to fashions or fads is certainly at least as consistent with the data as is the efficient markets model. . . . [I]t is hard to see how a model that makes [the fundamental value of the market] roughly a trend with p [actual prices]

[6] A third view, popular among finance economists, is that stock prices always and everywhere equal the best available estimate of present fundamentals. The belief that the stock market was "the stage whereon is focused the world's most intelligent and best informed judgment of the values of . . . enterprises" and that no one has a better estimate of values than the stock market as a whole was popular in the 1920s until the crash of 1929. For example, see Joseph S. Lawrence, *Wall Street and Washington* (Princeton, 1929); Galbraith notes that after 1929 "Mr. Lawrence disappeared from Princeton. Among economists his voice was not heard again." The efficient market hypothesis did not become popular again until the 1960s.

[7] John Campbell, "Estimating the Persistence of Expected Returns" (unpublished manuscript, London School of Economics, 1989) suggests that in the United States since 1926 fads and fashions have had an expected lifetime on the order of six months, not the five to ten years required if they are to account for major bull and bear swings.

[8] Even if long swings in the stock market were primarily driven by fundamentals, sufficiently large short-run swings in stock prices could still lead to the conclusion that the economic performance of the stock market has been poor if marginal investors and firms follow short-run buy-and-sell rather than long-run buy-and-hold investment strategies. See J. Bradford De Long, et al., "Noise Trader Risk in Financial Markets," *Journal of Political Economy*, 98 (forthcoming 1990); and J. Bradford De Long, et al., "The Size and Incidence of Losses from Noise Trading," *Journal of Finance*, 44 (July 1989), pp. 681–96.

bounced around this trend by fashions or fads could ever be rejected . . . in favor of a model that says that price movements anticipated dividends. Many people . . . suppose that . . . stock price movements really do forecast dividends. . . . This might . . . have been [shown] . . . if . . . [the ex post fundamental value] moved around a lot and were substantially correlated with p [as] . . . would be expected to happen . . . if people have a lot of information about future dividend movements. If figure [2] did happen to come out that way, we could say that it presents impressive evidence for the efficient markets theory. It did not. We should not be hesitant to mention fads or fashions as the true source of the bulk of price movements that characterize the aggregate stock market.[9]

We try to answer this challenge. We argue that major bull and bear markets were driven by shifts in assessments of fundamentals; investors had little knowledge of crucial factors, in particular the long-run dividend growth rate, and their changing expectations of average dividend growth plausibly lie behind the major swings of this century.

We make our argument in two steps. First, we set out a simple model of how investors might try to forecast future dividend growth and show that if the long-run rate of future dividend growth is sufficiently uncertain, the stock market might exhibit large swings like those actually seen. Second, at least some careful investors focusing on fundamentals held expectations of future growth that validated large swings in stock prices. Some analysts whom we classify as the source of "smart money" formed forecasts that validated major market swings. We cannot disprove the hypothesis that large stock price swings have been driven by irrational fads, but we do conclude that if placed in the shoes of those past investors aiming to forecast fundamentals we would have priced the market similarly. Therefore it is very plausible to regard the large decade-to-decade swings in the past century's stock prices as a consequence of revised forecasts of fundamentals.

DETERMINING FUNDAMENTAL VALUES

An investor who expects real dividends D_t to grow in the future at a constant rate g_t and who discounts the future at a long-run real required rate of return r_t will be willing to buy stocks if[10]

$$P_t = \frac{D_t}{r_t - g_t} \tag{1}$$

Since the average price/dividend ratio over the past century is not far from 20, $r_t - g_t$ is approximately 0.05. Thus a one percentage point increase in g_t leads to a 25 percent increase in P_t/D_t. This sensitivity of equity values to expectations of the future dividend growth rate underlies our argument that we should expect to see large bull and bear swings.

[9] Robert Shiller, "Comment on Miller and on Kleidon," in Robin Hogarth and Melvin Reder, eds., *Rational Choice: The Contrast Between Economics and Psychology* (Chicago, 1987), pp. 285–315.

[10] See John Burr Williams, *The Theory of Investment Value* (Cambridge, MA, 1937).

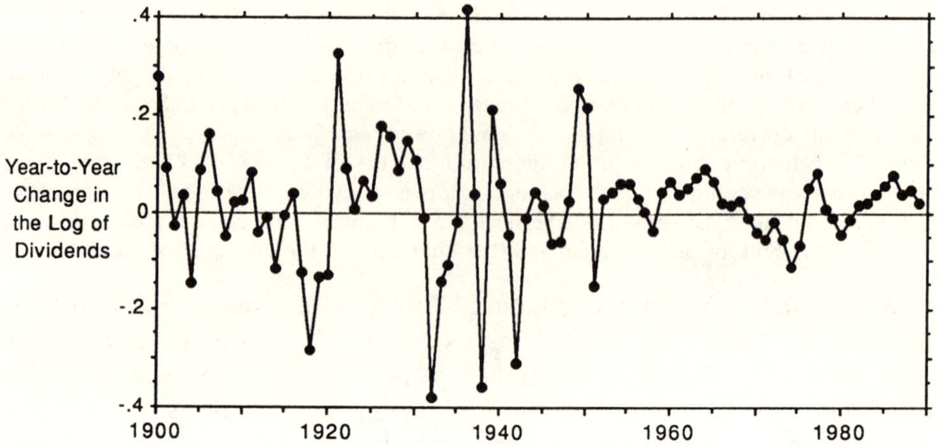

FIGURE 3

YEAR-TO-YEAR DIVIDEND GROWTH

An equivalent representation of equation 1, writing p_t and d_t for the natural logarithms of the levels of prices and dividends P_t and D_t, is

$$p_t = d_t - \ln(r_t - g_t) \tag{2}$$

We imagine that investors know the current dividend and the risk and time discount factors that they require. However, the average long-run rate of future dividend growth g_t must be estimated.

A natural way for investors to estimate expected future dividend growth g_t is to take the experience of the past and project it into the future. Such forecasts, however, should not pay a lot of attention to what the rate of dividend growth was a century before. We would be astonished if the average long-run rate of dividend growth had been the same in the Gilded Age as it is today. Forecasts reasonably take the recent past as more relevant than the distant past. A good rule of thumb is to take an average of past dividend growth rates that places more weight on the recent past, like[11]

$$g_t = (1 - \theta) \sum_{i=0}^{\infty} \theta^i \Delta d_{t-i} \qquad 0 < \theta < 1 \tag{3}$$

where Δd_{t-i} is the proportional rate of dividend growth from year $t - i - 1$ to year t.

In general, θ should be near one. Since the long-run average rate of growth shifts only slowly and most year-to-year variation in dividend

[11] John Muth, in his essay "Optimal Properties of Exponentially Weighted Forecasts," *Journal of the American Statistical Association*, 55 (Mar. 1960), pp. 299–306, showed that the forecast rule given in equation 3 would be the best that could be done forecasting from past rates of dividend growth alone as long as the rate of dividend growth is subject to independent and serially uncorrelated permanent and transitory shocks that have Gaussian normal distributions.

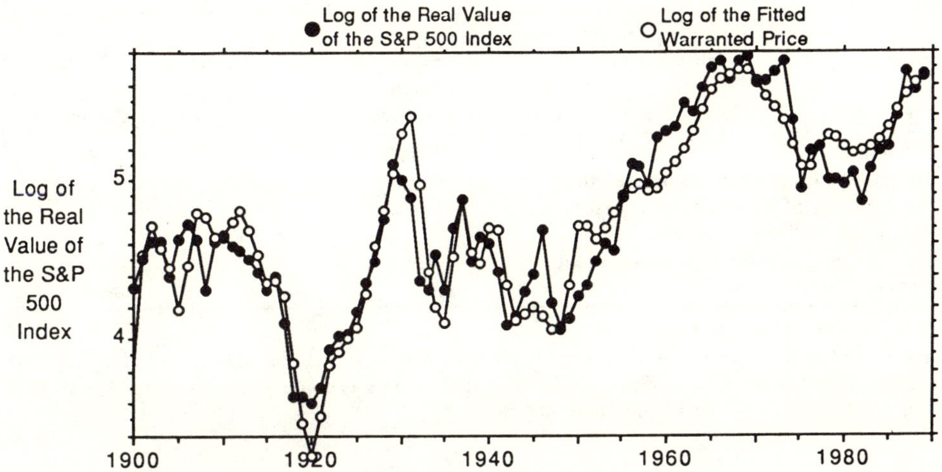

FIGURE 4

ACTUAL AND FITTED REAL STOCK INDEX VALUES

growth is transitory, the weights placed on past years should decline slowly as well. On reflection it is hard to see how an investor would forecast the long-run rate of dividend growth without using some rule of thumb like equation 3, presumably amplified by the addition of other forecasting variables. The natural way to determine what the average rate of future dividend growth will be is to look at what the average growth rate (of dividends or of the economy as a whole) has been.

As Figure 3 shows, the year-to-year rate of dividend growth has become less volatile over the course of the century as the American economy has matured. As the uncertainty associated with future dividend payments has decreased, the rate at which investors discount these future dividend payments has presumably decreased as well. It therefore seems appropriate to allow for a downward time trend in the rate of return investors use to discount future dividends r_t:

$$r_t = r_{1900} - \delta t \tag{4}$$

Our simple model of stock index prices contains three equations: equation 4 describes the possible evolution of investors' rate of discount. Equation 3 gives the rule of thumb investors use to forecast future dividend growth, and equation 2 describes how investors process their expectations of dividend growth and their rate of discount to arrive at the price at which they are willing to buy or sell stocks.[12]

Figure 4 plots actual real prices for every month alongside the prices fitted by the model for each January. The fit achieved by the model appears good (see Table 1 and Figure 4). Although formal tests of

[12] Equation 2 is used instead of equation 1 so that equal percentage deviations of prices from fitted values are counted equally in determining the fit of the model.

TABLE 1
SUMMARY STATISTICS FOR THE SIMPLE DIVIDEND-DISCOUNT MODEL

Model	Residual Variance	Estimated δ	Estimated θ
Fitted model	0.0420	0.0003	0.97
Constant estimate of dividend growth	0.0609	0.0003	1.00[a]
Constant rate of discount and constant estimate of dividend growth	0.0922	0.0[a]	1.00[a]
Variance of price around actual present value of future dividends	0.1429		

[a] Values imposed and not estimated.

Notes and sources: The model is outlined in the text. It was estimated using the extended Standard and Poor's 500 stock index and its associated dividend series as contained in appendix A of Robert Shiller's *Market Volatility* (Cambridge, MA, 1989).

hypotheses cannot be easily performed because the deviations of prices from fitted values are not independent—this year's gap between actual and fitted prices is highly correlated with next year's—the model accounts for a large share of the variance of prices about the actual present value of realized future dividends. The model accounts for 71 percent of the variance of January stock index prices about their ex post fundamental values and for more than half—55 percent—of the variance in the price/dividend ratio. About half of the variance in realized annual returns is accounted for by news about future dividend growth in our model.[13]

The estimated θ that the market appears to have used is about 0.97. This is high enough to make the market slow to change its expectations of future dividend growth. Growth during the preceding decade receives a weight of one-fourth in constructing today's estimate; years more than a decade in the past receive an aggregate weight of three-fourths. The model looks far back into the past in building its estimate of the future rate of growth of dividends, and it does not at first glance appear easy to argue that a value of 0.97 for θ is too sensitive to transitory booms and depressions to underlie a careful analysis of fundamentals.

Figure 4 shows that the long swings in stock prices can be accounted for by swings in expectations of fundamentals. If our specification of the rule of thumb used by investors in estimating dividend growth is correct, then major market movements have been closely connected to fundamentals and represent careful reassessments of the values of stocks. Our model, however, is not a complete characterization of stock prices. In our specification fundamentals change only slowly, and since monthly stock prices undergo jagged short-run fluctuations, the model

[13] On this point, see also David Cutler, et al., "What Moves Stock Prices?" *Journal of Portfolio Management*, 15 (Spring 1989), pp. 4–12.

cannot account for more than a very small fraction of the month-to-month movements.[14]

INVESTORS' EXPECTATIONS AND STOCK PRICES: BULL MARKETS

To say that over the twentieth century the stock market was very volatile in the long run is more or less equivalent to saying that the past century has seen five large revaluations of the S&P composite portfolio: five major bull and bear markets. The stock market dropped by 60 percent in real value over the 1914–1918 World War I period, rose by 500 percent in the 1920s, fell by 75 percent in the slide that opened the Great Depression, increased by 400 percent in the sustained bull market from the early 1950s to the middle 1960s, and dropped by 60 percent during the mid-1970s.

In each of these major bull and bear markets the simple rule of thumb of the previous section, with weight θ equal to 0.97, would have led careful investors to substantially revalue their fundamental-based assessments of stock market values.[15] And in fact, a number of such investors and analysts did just that. In each case they significantly revised their estimates of fundamentals and concluded that the new market levels were about right.

During and after the rapid run-up of stock prices in the 1920s the expectations held by Yale monetary economist, investor, and stock market analyst Irving Fisher were well known and have been ridiculed by many. Fisher had declared early in 1929 that stock prices had reached a "permanently high plateau." Standard histories like Sobel's see the 1920s as a decade dominated by speculation and argue that the stock market had departed far from fundamental values during the decade.[16] Such histories find Fisher, along with other economists such as Joseph Lawrence and Charles Dice, attractive targets to mock especially in view of Fisher's declaration on the eve of Black Thursday that "any fears that the price level of stocks might go down to where

[14] Campbell, "Estimating the Persistence of Expected Returns," estimates that news about future cash flows accounts for about only 30 percent of the variation in month-to-month stock returns.

[15] The 1980s have also seen a swing in stock prices larger than can be accounted for in our model. We suspect that our model's failure to fit the Reagan bull market is due to the changing role of dividends. Before 1980 cash payments to shareholders besides dividends were trivial, since 1980 they have made up a substantial part of shareholders' income. Our dividend series does not include these payments. See James Poterba, "Tax Policy and Corporate Saving," *Brookings Papers on Economic Activity* (Fall 1987), pp. 455–516.

[16] Galbraith is more cautious. He sees the rise in stock prices through the end of 1927 as largely justified by fundamentals, as does Gerald Sirkin, "The Stock Market of 1929 Revisited," *Business History Review*, 49 (Summer 1975), pp. 233–41. Joel Seligman also agrees that "overspeculation" can only be said to have begun in the spring of 1928. See Joel Seligman, *The Transformation of Wall Street* (Boston, 1982); and Eugene White, "When the Ticker Ran Late" (unpublished manuscript, Rutgers University).

it was in 1923 or earlier is not justified by present economic conditions."[17]

Shortly after the Crash, Fisher argued that the declines of October 1929 did not signal further large declines; the stock market at the end of 1929 was fairly priced given underlying fundamentals.[18] Without reference to our knowledge that the Depression had begun, his arguments for the sustainability of the January 1930 level of real stock prices appear reasonable. Fisher presented a number of reasons why investors paying the prices of stocks in January 1930 should earn acceptable returns; the 1920s had seen substantial exploitation of economies of scale resulting from mergers, the application of science and invention to industry had resulted in an acceleration of productivity growth in the 1920s, the development and application of scientific management, the shift of labor from a confrontational to a cooperative strategy of relating to management, the belief that Prohibition would decrease addiction to alcohol and increase productivity, and the increase in the rate of economic growth induced by the Federal Reserve's successful stabilization of the price level.

From any perspective except that of perfect hindsight Fisher's arguments appear reasonable. Price/dividend ratios were only a bit higher at the end of the 1920s than they had been between 1900 and 1910. Economic growth appeared strong. Although rapid growth could have been regarded as a transitional postwar phenomenon, Fisher's arguments that the systematic application of research and development to industry, the growth of scientific management, and the success of the "American system" of labor relations at taming unions and providing both high wages and high productivity had permanently raised the rate of U.S. economic growth in the 1920s seemed convincing.[19]

In retrospect, we see the "New Era" of the 1920s as brief and without foundation, but Fisher and many others thought that the economy had shifted to a new régime of rapid growth. His estimate of the long-run growth rate of the economy, and thus of dividends, was higher in 1929 than in 1924. Given this upward revision, his willingness to pay high prices for stocks does not seem surprising. And he might have been right to do so: anyone in 1956 who sold out in anticipation of the rapid end of that postwar boom made a mistake.

[17] See Sobel, *The Big Board*; Galbraith, *The Great Crash*; Charles Dice, *New Levels in the Stock Market* (New York, 1929); and Lawrence, *Wall Street and Washington*.

[18] Irving Fisher, *The Stock Market Crash—and After* (New York, 1930).

[19] An additional cause of rapid stock market growth in the 1920s may have been a general recognition that, in a turbulent time like the interwar period in which the long-run drift of the price level was uncertain, stocks were no more risky than bonds and yet promised higher expected returns. See Edgar L. Smith, *Common Stocks as Long Term Investments* (New York, 1924). The late 1920s also see the appearance of handbooks for investors that place great stress on valuing compound growth. For example, see Samuel Gould, *Stock Growth and Discount Tables* (Boston, 1931).

Fisher was not exceptional. The bull market of the 1920s had in the eyes of contemporaries ample support from the growth of the American economy.[20] Charles Dice's *New Levels in the Stock Market*, for example, argued that stock prices in the late 1920s were too low: in his view the market had not yet caught up with the ongoing triple revolutions in production, distribution, and finance that were steadily raising the fundamental value of American industry. As financial analyst George Woodruff put it, writing at the end of the 1930s:

> In 1928 and 1929 . . . the investor might read articles and books and listen to addresses, the theme of which was the new era of prosperity. . . . Now, in retrospect the prices of 1929 appear fantastic. . . . But let the investor place himself in 1928–9 and . . . blot out . . . later years. He will know . . . [i] that following World War I the United States received large shipments of gold . . . [ii] that . . . active measures were concerted . . . to forestall . . . inflation . . . [iii] that . . . the United States turned almost overnight from a debtor into a creditor [nation]. . . . And [iv] he will look back upon . . . seven years . . . of general prosperity. . . . These things together will seem to spell New Era.[21]

Even Roger Babson, the only prominent forecaster to anticipate a market break in 1929, had been bullish as late as the end of 1928 and was again bullish in 1930.[22]

Just as the 1920s were seen as a "New Era" of permanent high growth, the 1960s appeared a time in which the United States had made major steps toward solving its economic problems. Even an extremely cautious and risk-averse investor such as Benjamin Graham, who in the 1960s believed that prices in the 1920s had been unjustified, thought the economy was sound. Graham acquired his reputation by virtue of his keen eye for an undervalued company, and his firmest principle was that a prudent investor should purchase only firms with good prospects that were selling at or below liquidation value.[23] Other strategies might be

[20] A few other voices, chosen more or less at random, reaching the same conclusion are Smith, *Common Stocks as Long Term Investments*; K. S. von Strum, *Investing in Purchasing Power* (New York, 1925); William Ripley, *Main Street and Wall Street* (New York, 1927); and Kimball, Russell, and Co., *The Investment Problem—Its Solution* (Boston, 1928). After 1929 the view that the post-World War I boom would continue for a long time was easy to critique: see, for example, A. T. Miller, *What to Consider When Buying Securities Today* (New York, 1932); and Frederick Allen, *Only Yesterday* (New York, 1931). But the view found few critics before 1929.

[21] George P. Woodruff, *Investment and Speculation* (New York, 1939). The lesson Woodruff drew from the ex ante reasonableness of confidence in the "New Era" and the subsequent catastrophe of the Depression was that one could have little confidence in any fundamental-based valuation of prices, for "the rationalizing of a price level, whether it is a high one or a low one, is one of the most insidious lures . . . whenever the papers are full of a rationalizing or explaining of high prices, the investor may take it as one cue to begin selling."

[22] Galbraith, *The Great Crash*, pp. 20, 90; Roger Babson, *Business Barometers* (Wellesley, 1930); and Roger Babson, *Investment Fundamentals* (New York, 1930).

[23] See Benjamin Graham and David Dodd, *Security Analysis* (New York, 1st edn., 1934; 2nd edn., 1941); and Benjamin Graham, *The Intelligent Investor* (New York, 1954). Also see Warren Buffett's appendix to Benjamin Graham, *The Intelligent Investor* (5th edn., New York, 1987); and John Train, *The Money Masters* (2nd edn., New York, 1987).

profitable, but they were "speculation," not investment. Yet in spite of his innate caution and conservativism and his strong belief that stock markets were prone to periods of speculative overenthusiasm, he was not willing to judge the market in the early 1960s as overvalued.

Graham was of two minds in the early 1960s. Price/earnings ratios were at levels that had foretold bear markets in the past.[24] And at the end of the 1940s Graham had argued that a simple "market timing" strategy of buying when stocks were low relative to a long-run moving average of past earnings and selling when stocks rose would have outperformed a buy-and-hold strategy.[25] By 1962, however, Graham knew that any such attempt to anticipate mean reversion in stock prices would have been unprofitable in the post-World War II period; such an investor would have been out of the market while it tripled in real value. He therefore abandoned the belief that investors should be anticipating a crash, arguing instead that the situation was one of uncertainty, "old standards of valuation are no longer applicable, and new standards have yet to be tested in time." He argued that changes in the economic policy régime made it rational for investors to pay higher multiples for stocks in the 1960s than in the 1940s, 1930s, or 1920s.

> [He] believe[d] it reasonable to adopt a somewhat more generous approach to the valuation of common stocks than appeared justified in our previous edition. This conclusion is based on the assurance—not formerly present—of massive Federal intervention to prevent a serious business depression. This now appears to be a basic tenet of both political parties.[26]

In Graham's estimation, the willingness of the government to tolerate inflation in order to avoid severe depression had increased the expected long-run growth rate of the economy. Interruptions of capital accumulation and large gaps between actual and potential output like those seen in the 1930s were no longer likely. In view of this increase in the expected growth rate of the economy, a rational investor should be willing to pay a higher price/dividend or price/earnings multiple for common stocks. This point of view was common. Many analysts wrote that while "old timers say stocks selling for more than ten times earnings are overpriced . . . this view is outmoded. The proper ratio . . . [is] around fifteen or sixteen times."[27] And Babson's successors echoed

[24] See Graham, *The Intelligent Investor*; and Benjamin Graham, David Dodd, and Sidney Cottle, *Security Analysis* (4th edn., New York, 1962).

[25] Benjamin Graham and David Dodd, with the assistance of Charles Tatham, *Security Analysis* (3rd edn., New York, 1951).

[26] Graham was actually on the prudent end of commentary on the market in the early 1960s. Others urged investors to pick "stocks for the surging '60s." See Ira Cobleigh, *A Guide to Success in the Stock Market* (New York, 1961).

[27] Louis Bean, *How to Predict the Stock Market* (Washington, DC, 1962).

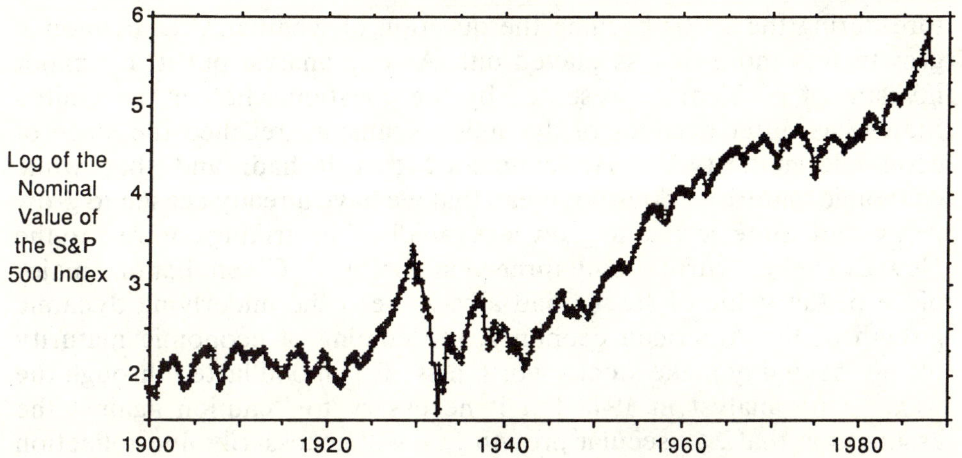

FIGURE 5
TWENTIETH-CENTURY NOMINAL STOCK PRICES

Fisher in listing seven reasons why the post-World War II "new era" would continue indefinitely.[28]

INVESTORS' EXPECTATIONS AND STOCK PRICES: BEAR MARKETS

The first of the major bear swings in the stock market was the collapse of real values during World War I. Figure 5 shows that this major swing in real values cannot be seen in the nominal stock price series. It arose entirely from the rapid inflation of World War I. Many have argued that investors during the war expected governments to substantially deflate the economy after the war.[29] Anticipated postwar deflation carries with it an expression of very high future real interest rates, and so the low real price of stocks during the war does not strike us as surprising or in need of explanation in terms of investors' expectations of future profits and dividends.

The second large bear market—the fall in the stock market during the great contraction of 1929–1933—needs no explanation. The Great Depression was an unprecedented collapse of the American economy.[30] It is difficult to say what investors' expectations should have been and how they should have valued the stock market at the bottom of the Depression. We can say little about how investors should react to economic events off the scale of previous experience.

One common response was to wonder whether the Depression heralded permanent stagnation. A common theme in investment litera-

[28] Thomas Babson and David Babson, *Investing for a Successful Future* (New York, 1959).

[29] The most recent expression of this view is Herschel Grossman, "The Political Economy of War Debts and Inflation" (NBER Working Paper 2743, 1988).

[30] See Peter Temin, *Did Monetary Forces Cause the Great Depression?* (New York, 1976); Peter Temin, *Lessons of the Great Depression* (Cambridge, MA, 1989); and Allen, *Only Yesterday*.

ture during the 1930s became the question of whether U.S. economic growth was more or less played out. As one analyst put it, a "major investment problem is presented by the question whether the United States has, after decades of dynamic expansion, reached the stage of economic maturity."[31] He concluded that it had, and that while economic maturity "does not mean that we have already ceased to grow . . . we are quite certain to grow less rapidly," in striking contrast to the New Era beliefs current only three years before.[32] Given that one major piece of the value of stocks had always been the underlying dynamic growth of the American economy, the coming of economic maturity would inevitably make stocks worth less. This mood lasted through the war.[33] One analyst in 1948 felt it necessary to "caution against the assumption that . . . secular growth . . . will necessarily find reflection in a long-term rising trend of stock prices," and forecast a gradual stock market decline over the following decade.[34] In the literature of professional economists, the same theme echoed as "secular stagnation."[35]

The final bear market—the Oil/Inflation bear market of the 1970s—is sufficiently recent to be familiar. The stock market fell steeply in response to the failure of President Richard Nixon's price control policies and to the shocks administered by the breakdown of Bretton Woods and the rise of the Organization of Petroleum Exporting Countries. During 1973 and 1974 the S&P 500 declined by 55 percent in real terms. Fundamental-based interpretations of this steep decline were common in the late 1970s. One that stressed investors' revisions of their expectations of future prospects was put forward by Andrew Tobias:

> The ability of stocks to outperform bonds—and to beat inflation—[in the pre-1973 period] . . . had much to do with America's more or less steadily improving productivity. . . . [But t]he world has changed. Resources are scarcer; foreign competition is stronger; businesses are more highly regulated . . . confidence in the future, and hence investment, is not what it was; inflation lurks. . . .[36]

As a result of this recognition that the new dimensions of political economy promised by Keynesians in the 1960s had come to an end, the market severely reduced its valuation of stock indices during 1973 and 1974.[37] As Tobias went on to argue, the fact that future growth is likely to be slow did not mean that investments in common stocks were to be

[31] Miller, *What To Consider When Buying Securities Today.*

[32] Post-1929 U.S. economic growth does not show any noticeable slackening of pace.

[33] For example, Smith, *Common Stocks as Long Term Investments.*

[34] Garfield Drew, *New Methods for Profit in the Stock Market* (Boston, 1948).

[35] See Alvin Hansen, *Economic Policy and Full Employment* (New York, 1947); and Gottfried Haberler, *Prosperity and Depression* (New York, 1958).

[36] Andrew Tobias, *The Only Investment Guide You'll Ever Need* (New York, 1978).

[37] See Walter Heller, *New Dimensions of Political Economy* (Cambridge, MA, 1965); and James Tobin and Murray Weidenbaum, eds., *Two Revolutions in Economic Policy* (Cambridge, MA, 1987).

avoided, for "the market knows all these things" and had consequently marked the prices of stocks down to levels at which they once again promised attractive long-run, albeit risky, returns.

The analysts cited—Fisher, Graham, Tobias, and the others—reassessed their own estimates of future prospects, and thus of the appropriate prices for stocks, in tandem with the major bull and bear swings of the market. They based their assessments on fundamentals, not on speculative dynamics: none of them advocated buying stocks at prices above fundamentals on the theory that someone less informed would be willing to pay even more tomorrow. To the extent that these analysts' views are representative of "smart money," the major bull and bear swings reflect shifts in the best estimate of fundamentals and not the irrational fad-driven "animal spirits" of the crowd.

Are the analysts cited representative? We cannot guarantee that they are representative smart money investors, but we can say that they are representative of those who (i) made fundamental-based as opposed to "chartist" assessments of values and (ii) wrote books on investment strategy subsequently acquired by Harvard's libraries.[38] Moreover, their judgments were shared by many of the leading economists then and now. Milton Friedman and Anna Schwartz, for example, speak of the 1920s as the "high tide of the Federal Reserve System," when economists and central bankers believed that the Federal Reserve's ability to control the money supply and the rate of interest had effectively eliminated the business cycle.[39] Popular worries that U.S. growth had been permanently derailed in the 1930s found their echo in economists' doctrines of "secular stagnation." And Graham's belief that strong growth justified high price/dividend ratios in the early 1960s is but a pale shadow of the optimism of 1960s Keynesians. If large fluctuations are driven by fashions and fads, then so are economists' forecasts. Economists, therefore, have little warrant for concluding that the stock market's performance falls short; anyone who does critique the stock market as a forecaster faces the burden of finding an alternative procedure that would have done better.

CONCLUSION

The U.S. stock market has seen five major bull and bear markets in the twentieth century. In each case, such a large revaluation of the worth of America's companies would also have been made by any investor uncertain of the possibly changing long-run dividend growth rate who estimated it by extrapolating the recent past. Such large

[38] On technical analysis, see George Goodman, "Adam Smith," *The Money Game* (New York, 1968).

[39] Milton Friedman and Anna J. Schwartz, *A Monetary History of the United States, 1867–1960* (Princeton, 1963).

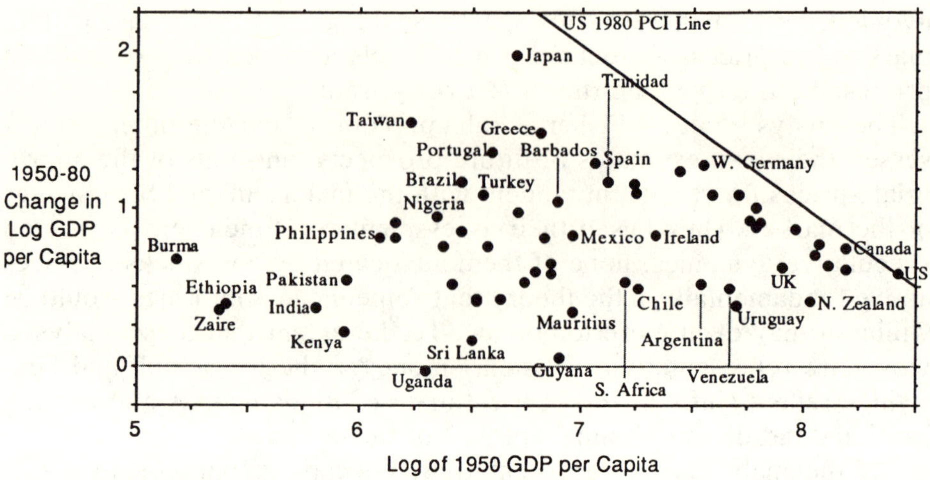

FIGURE 6

1950–1980 RATES OF PER CAPITA INCOME GROWTH FOR 62 NATIONS

revaluations were also made by investment analysts who were prominent in their day, whose acumen we respect, and who concentrated on fundamental values. Our conclusion is that major decade-to-decade stock market movements arise predominantly from careful re-evaluations of fundamentals and less so from fads or fashions.

Over the past century major market movements have been reversed more often than not. The belief that the postwar period was a "New Era" proved ex post to be correct after World War II but not after World War I. Fears of secular stagnation in the 1930s were too pessimistic in retrospect, as were fears in the late 1970s that the United States was headed for Latin American-style political gridlock and economic collapse.[40] A case can be made that the market, its analysts, and the conventional wisdom of economists overreacts, and that things are never as good as they seem in a boom or as bad as they seem in a depression.

A look at comparative economic growth over the past century, however, goes a way toward dispelling this possibility. Among the set of developed or rapidly developing nations in 1870, some—like Great Britain and Australia—have seen per capita income grow slowly; others—like Sweden, the United States, and Canada—have seen per capita income grow rapidly. The post-World War II period shows an equal spread of national growth rates. Figure 6 plots average per capita income growth rates over the 1950–1980 period for 62 countries. The differences between Uruguay and West Germany, Chile and Spain, or

[40] George Goodman, "Adam Smith," *Paper Money* (New York, 1981). Goodman, however, also accurately forecast that if the doomsday scenarios failed to come true, the 1980s "could be quite a party."

Sri Lanka and Taiwan have been much more than sufficient to drive shifts in valuation like those of the major bull and bear swings the United States has seen.[41]

Given this range of outcomes, it is understandable for investors at times to fear that whatever happened to British or Australian growth—let alone to Uruguayan—might happen here. Conversely, the tremendous surge in economic growth of the industrial revolution suggests that a further surge—an increase in per capita income growth from 2 to 2.5 percent per year, say—might be attainable with a properly managed high-pressure economy. Such fears and hopes could easily have sustained the major bull and bear swings of the past century. And the comparative growth experience of the past century suggests that such fears are not fantastic but realistic.

Our tentative conclusion—which we reach even though the New Era of the 1920s came to a rapid end and even though secular stagnation did not begin in the 1930s—is that major stock market movements arose not because investors' susceptibility to fads and fashions made the market excessively volatile, but because the future always appeared uncertain, and stock prices are extremely sensitive to expectations of what future growth will be. If this conclusion is correct, one implication is that the case against Wall Street—the belief that stock market speculation materially retards American economic growth—must focus on the short-run volatility of the market and its effect on investors' discount rates and firms' investment plans. The long-run volatility of the major bull and bear swings springs not from the poor performance of Wall Street but from unavoidable uncertainties about future economic growth.

[41] The data for Figure 6 are drawn from Robert Summers and Alan Heston, "Improved Comparisons of Real Product and Its Composition, 1950–80," *Review of Income and Wealth*, 20 (Mar. 1984), pp. 207–61.

Is Deposit Insurance Necessary? A Historical Perspective

CHARLES W. CALOMIRIS

The motivation and structure of various banking insurance experiments in U.S. history are analyzed, along with their political alternative, branch banks. In both the antebellum period and in the 1920s, insurance systems that relied on self-regulation, made credible by mutual liability, were successful, while compulsory state systems were not. Branch banking increased stability and resiliency to shocks.

Following the current savings and loan collapse, recent studies of deposit insurance funds have focused on the perverse incentives created by deposit insurance when it is not fairly priced. Insurance encourages excess risk-taking by existing banks—particularly if prior losses leave them with little capital to lose from pursuing long shots—and allows unscrupulous, or simply inexperienced, entrepreneurs to enter banking as a means to finance their risky enterprises. The discipline of the market, which normally would prevent such intermediaries from having access to funds, is removed by insurance. Depositors of insured institutions have little incentive to discriminate with respect to where and with whom they place their funds.

Careful studies of the recent federal- and state-insured thrift experiences by Edward Kane, Paul Horvitz, and others, add credence to the view that insurance itself can be destabilizing.[1] For example, bad initial realizations on investments were translated into a thrift and bank debacle in Texas because they were combined with high initial leverage and increased risk-taking by troubled institutions which responded to the initial adverse shocks by aggressively entering the speculative real estate loan market. Depositors presumably tolerated high leverage and increased risk-taking more than they would have had they not been insured. By promoting excessive leverage and increased risk-taking, deposit insurance made a bad situation much worse. The lack of political will by Congress and regulators to close insolvent institutions prolonged the "desperation" risk-taking and further magnified losses to the insurance funds.

The Journal of Economic History, Vol. L, No. 2 (June 1990). ISSN 0022-0507.

The author is Assistant Professor of Economics, Northwestern University, Evanston, IL 60208, and a member of the Research Department, Federal Reserve Bank of Chicago, 230 S. La Salle St., Chicago, IL 60604.

[1] See Edward J. Kane, "How Incentive-Incompatible Deposit-Insurance Funds Fail," mimeograph, Ohio State University, 1988; and Paul M. Horvitz, "The Causes of Texas Bank and Thrift Failures," mimeograph, University of Houston, 1989.

Renewed discussion of the purpose and proper structure of deposit insurance has focused attention on the history of financial intermediaries and their regulation. U.S. financial history contains the answers to three fundamental questions of interest to would-be reformers. Why was bank liability insurance created in the first place? What evidence supports this presumed "special" need of banks? Which experiments with insurance were most successful, and which aspects of these experiments account for the accomplishment of legitimate goals?

The answer to the first question is similar across various historical instances—bank insurance was instituted to protect the economy's payments system from financial panics.[2] Recent theoretical work on banking echoes this theme. Banks are especially vulnerable because they offer short-term (typically demandable) claims backed by longer-term assets whose value is not easily observable to depositors.[3] Thus banks are vulnerable to panics induced by depositors' uncertainty about the value of their portfolios. Disturbances that increase the probability of insolvency of some class of bank borrowers—even if they are small relative to aggregate bank assets and concentrated in only a few banks—can provoke widespread disintermediation from all banks by depositors who lack information about the incidence or degree of the shock.

The social costs of such disturbances are high because banks provide a unique source of transacting balances and commercial credit to "information-intensive" borrowers. Disruptions of banking disrupt all industries' abilities to transact and operate effectively. Not surprisingly, it was this concern for the viability of the economy's payments system (the availability of liquidity and trade credit) that prompted insurance plans, starting with that of New York in 1829, and culminating in the federal system of the 1930s.[4]

Bank insurance was not exclusively the domain of the government historically. The information externality created by depositors' confusion about the precise incidence across banks of a given shock prompted private coinsurance among banks to reduce the potential for disintermediation and to coordinate the banking system's response to such crises when they did occur. Formal coinsurance arrangements among

[2] See Carter H. Golembe, "The Deposit Insurance Legislation of 1933: An Examination of its Antecedants and its Purposes," *Political Science Quarterly* (June 1960), pp. 189–95, and Eugene N. White, "The Political Economy of Bank Regulation," this JOURNAL, 42 (Mar. 1982), pp. 33–42.

[3] The rationale behind this peculiar contracting structure is not at all obvious. For a critique of existing explanations and a new approach to this question, see Charles W. Calomiris and Charles M. Kahn, "The Role of Demandable Debt in Structuring Optimal Banking Arrangements," mimeograph, Northwestern University, 1989.

[4] The desire to insure wealth per se was not the primary motivation of bank insurance (see Golembe, "Deposit Insurance Legislation," pp. 189–95); rather, it was the desire to preserve liquidity. This explains why intermediaries other than banks (insurance companies, pension funds, and so forth) have not given rise to similar legislation.

bank clearinghouse members, and less formal arrangements among other banks—especially in the branch-banking states of the antebellum South—provided many of the features of government deposit insurance.[5] In these private insurance regimes banks agreed to make markets in each other's liabilities, to make interbank loans, and to coordinate suspensions and resumptions of convertibility to minimize disruptions during panics. In all cases, self-imposed regulations and mutual monitoring kept members of the privately established coalitions from "free riding" on the collective insurance.

It is important to note that unit banking laws (prohibitions of branch banking) increased the potential for such disturbances, and hampered banks' abilities to respond to them effectively. First, the confusion over the incidence of small shocks is accentuated in a system of many small banks, which makes runs more likely. Second, banks' abilities to coordinate behavior and coinsure depended on ease of communication and mutual monitoring (to prevent free riding), and these were hampered in systems of many, geographically isolated banks. Indeed, these barriers to private coinsurance explain why clearinghouse membership typically was limited to individual cities.

Historians long have stressed the destabilizing influence of unit banking and linked its peculiar prevalence in the United States to the unique vulnerability of U.S. banking historically.[6] Indeed, studies of the political history of deposit insurance legislation show that it was the desire to preserve unit banking, and the political influence of unit bankers, that gave rise to the perceived need for deposit insurance, both in the antebellum period and in the twentieth century.[7] It was understood early on (through observing the successful operation of branch banks in the South and in other countries) that branching—with its benefits both of greater diversification and coordination—provided an alternative stabilizer to liability insurance. But unit banks and their supporters successfully directed the movement for banking reform

[5] For discussions of clearinghouse coinsurance, see James G. Cannon, *Clearing Houses*, (Washington, DC, 1910), and Gary Gorton "Clearing Houses and the Origin of Central Banking in the United States," this JOURNAL, 46 (June 1986). For a summary of similar operations in the branching antebellum South, see Thomas Govan, "The Banking and Credit System in Georgia" (Ph.D. dissertation, Vanderbilt University, 1936), and Charles W. Calomiris and Larry Schweikart, "The Panic of 1857: Origins and Regional Responses," mimeograph, 1989.

[6] See, for example, Oliver M. W. Sprague, *History of Crises Under the National Banking System* (Washington, DC, 1910); Gaines T. Cartinhour, *Branch, Group, and Chain Banking* (New York, 1931); John M. Chapman and Ray B. Westerfield, *Branch Banking: Its Historical and Theoretical Position in America and Abroad* (New York, 1942); Milton Friedman and Anna J. Schwartz, *A Monetary History of the United States* (Princeton, 1963); Eugene N. White, *The Regulation and Reform of the American Banking System, 1900–1929* (Princeton, 1983); Charles W. Calomiris, R. Glenn Hubbard, and James T. Stock, "The Farm Debt Crisis and Public Policy," *Brookings Papers on Economic Activity*, 2 (1986); and Calomiris and Schweikart, "The Panic of 1857."

[7] Again, see Golembe, "Deposit Insurance Legislation."

toward creating government insurance funds. All six antebellum states that enacted liability insurance were unit-banking states. In the antebellum branch-banking South neither government insurance, nor urban clearinghouses, developed. Similarly, the eight state insurance systems created from 1908 to 1917 were all in unit-banking states.

In evaluating the performance of the various government-created liability-insurance schemes below, I ask two principal questions: First, which experiments failed or succeeded, and why? Here I am particularly interested in ascertaining whether the failures of insurance systems were attributable to flaws inherent in their design, or to insurmountable exogenous shocks. And second, would allowing branch banking (the perceived alternative to insurance) have provided a more effective means to protect the payments system than bank insurance?[8]

ANTEBELLUM SUCCESSES AND FAILURES

New York's Safety Fund was established in 1829, funded by limited annual contributions of members and regulated by the state government. Losses severely depleted the accumulated resources of the fund from 1837 to 1841 until, in 1842, it ceased to be able to repay losses of failed banks and thus ceased to provide protection to the payments system.

New York in 1838 created an alternative to the insured system through its free banking statute, and allowed Safety-Fund banks to switch to that system. The depletion in membership of the insured system kept its losses small during subsequent panics. After 1840 Safety-Fund banks comprised a small and continually shrinking proportion of total banks or total bank assets. Losses were also limited by the 1842 restriction on coverage of member banks' liabilities to bank notes, thus excluding the growing liability base in deposits.

Ultimately the small number of banks that chose to remain in the system and make continuing annual contributions to its fund did manage to repay in 1866 the obligations incurred some thirty years earlier, but this "success" was not anticipated in the intervening years (as shown by the high note discount rates attached to failed member-banks' notes during the 1850s), and the fund did not protect current bank liabilities or the payments system ex ante, as it was intended to do.

Not only did the system fail to provide protection to the payments system, it suffered unusually large losses due to fraud or unsound banking practices. While a supervisory authority was established to

[8] This article summarizes and extends the analysis presented in Charles W. Calomiris, "Deposit Insurance: Lessons from the Record," *Economic Perspectives*, Federal Reserve Bank of Chicago, 13 (May/June 1989), and "Do Vulnerable Economies Need Deposit Insurance? Lessons from the U.S. Agricultural Boom and Bust of the 1920s," in Philip Brock, ed., *If Texas Were Chile: Financial Risk and Regulation in Commodity-Exporting Economies* (Washington, DC, 1990).

prevent fraud and excessive risk-taking, supervision was ineffectual, and fraud or unsafe practices were common. Ten of 16 member-bank failures prior to 1842 (the period when insurance was still perceived as effective) were traceable to fraud or unsafe practices. Moreover, such problems were not detected until after they had imposed large losses on the fund.

The failure of the Safety Fund was not the fault of external shocks, severe as they were. In aggregate, banking capital was large relative to losses, and thus coinsurance among all New York banks would have been feasible. Rather it was the design of the insurance system that made it weak.[9] Upper bounds on annual premia prevented adequate ex ante insurance during panics, and ineffectual supervision allowed large risk-takers to free ride on other banks. Finally, adverse selection caused a retreat from the system through charter-switching to the alternative free-banking system once solvent banks realized the extent of losses.

Vermont and Michigan followed New York's example and suffered its problems. In Vermont, banks were even allowed to join and depart at will. It took only two bank failures—one due to fraud and the other because it joined the system after its prospects had deteriorated—to cause the dissolution of that system. Again, an incentive-compatible, broadly based system could have provided coinsurance among banks, but adverse selection and poor supervision prevented this.

Michigan's system, created in 1836, collapsed because it like the other two systems depended for its resources on accumulated contributions to the collective fund, which would be used to support banks during a crisis. The Michigan system had not time to accumulate a sufficient fund prior to the Panics of 1837 and 1839 and thus was unable to provide protection.

Not all antebellum experiments ended so disastrously. Indiana enacted a different sort of liability insurance plan in 1834, one based on the principles of self-regulation and unlimited mutual liability that would later be imitated by private clearinghouses. The Indiana system did not suffer the supervisory laxity or membership retreat of New York and Vermont, nor the illiquidity of Michigan and New York. Coverage was broad-based and there was no problem attracting and keeping members. During its 30-year history no insured bank failed. The system suspended convertibility in 1837, and again in 1839, but this was the last time banks were even forced to suspend. During the regional panic of 1854–1855 and the national Panic of 1857 all insured banks maintained operations and convertibility. During those same panics 69 of 126 nonmember, uncoordinated free banks failed in Indiana.

[9] For quantitative evidence on losses relative to bank capital for New York and other antebellum states, see Carter H. Golembe and Clark S. Warburton, *Insurance of Bank Obligations in Six States During the Period 1829–1866* (monograph, Federal Deposit Insurance Corporation, 1958).

The Indiana insurance system relied on bankers themselves to make and enforce laws and regulations through a Board of Directors and, importantly, gave the board authority to decide when to close a bank. Unlimited mutual liability provided bankers the incentive to regulate and enforce properly. The Indiana system was imitated in Ohio and Iowa, with similarly successful results. Ohio's law granted its Board of Control even greater authority than Indiana's board, allowing it virtually unlimited discretionary powers during a banking crisis, including the right to force banks to make loans to one another. Interbank loans were successfully used during the Panic of 1857 to avoid suspension of convertibility. The insured banks, it seems, even came to the assistance of nonmember banks during the Panic, as indicated by flows of interbank loans. Only one Ohio bank failed during the crisis, and it was not a member of the insured system. Iowa's system was in place for a shorter and more stable period, but its operation was similarly successful.

Like clearinghouses, these three successful insurance schemes aligned the incentive and authority to regulate and made insurance protection credible through unlimited mutual liability among banks. Like Southern branch banks in the Panics of 1837 and 1857, these systems were able to minimize systemic disruption through a coordinated, incentive-compatible response. They were brought to an end not by insolvency, but by federal taxation of bank notes designed to promote the National Banking System.

THE SECOND, POSTBELLUM WAVE OF STATE INSURANCE

The eight deposit-insurance fund systems of the early twentieth century failed to learn the lessons of the antebellum experience; they repeated and compounded the earlier errors of New York, Vermont, and Michigan. Supervisory authority was placed in government, not member-bank, hands, and often its use or disuse was politically motivated.[10] Furthermore, the numbers of banks insured were many more than in the antebellum systems (often several hundred), and this further reduced a bank's incentive to monitor and report the misbehavior of its neighbor banks, since the payoff from detection was shared with so many, and the cost of monitoring was private.

During the halcyon days for agriculture, from 1914 to 1920, deposit insurance prompted unusually high growth, particularly of small rural banks on thin capital. The insured states' banks grew faster, were smaller, and had lower capital ratios than their state-chartered counterparts in fast-growing, or neighboring states. Tables 1, 2, and 3 compare the growth, average size, and capitalization of insured state-chartered banking systems, first by comparing the highest-growth insured and

[10] For examples, see Thomas B. Robb, *The Guaranty of Bank Deposits* (New York, 1921).

TABLE 1
HIGH-GROWTH STATES: INSURED VERSUS UNINSURED

	Proportion of Assets in 1914 to Assets in 1920		Assets per Bank, 1920 ($ thousands)		Ratio of Capital to Total Assets, 1920	
	National Bank	State Bank	National Bank	State Bank	National Bank	State Bank
Uninsured						
Arkansas	0.408	0.379	$1,020	$456	0.084	0.085
Colorado	0.522	0.450	1,069	460	0.081	0.083
Idaho	0.341	0.316	1,088	487	0.059	0.088
Iowa	0.507	0.503	1,301	562	0.057	0.104
Minnesota	0.509	0.406	1,979	425	0.054	0.069
Missouri	0.490	0.540	5,507	572	0.063	0.072
Montana	0.495	0.489	761	436	0.077	0.091
New Mexico	0.501	0.352	963	347	0.073	0.119
Wyoming	0.314	0.315	1,365	300	0.048	0.090
Average	0.454	0.418	1,673	448	0.066	0.090
Insured						
Kansas	0.463	0.380	977	326	0.066	0.079
Mississippi	0.506	0.335	1,843	664	0.069	0.066
Nebraska	0.537	0.335	1,566	335	0.057	0.082
North Dakota	0.485	0.367	563	248	0.068	0.081
Oklahoma	0.309	0.259	1,096	346	0.126	0.070
South Dakota	0.400	0.351	862	376	0.053	0.062
Texas	0.414	0.391	1,588	375	0.071	0.112
Average	0.447	0.344	1,231	389	0.073	0.078

Source: Board of Governors of the Federal Reserve System, *All Bank Statistics* (Washington, DC, 1959).

uninsured systems, and then by comparing insured-banking systems with neighboring uninsured state-chartered systems and uninsured national-chartered banking in each of the states. Table 3 reports regression results that confirm the unusually high growth of state-chartered insured banks (controlling for other variables) relative to other agricultural states. A decomposition among voluntary and compulsory state insurance systems reveals that the incentives to grow were especially pronounced in the compulsory insurance systems (where the potential for cross-subsidization, or free riding through excessive risk-taking, was highest).

When agricultural prices fell, insured banking systems suffered higher rates of decline and failure than uninsured state-chartered banks in agricultural states and showed an even greater difference in the asset shortfalls (relative to deposits) of insolvent banks. All the insurance fund systems collapsed during the 1920s.[11] Insured systems also saw

[11] For summaries of the specific historical experiences, see American Bankers Association, *The Guaranty of Bank Deposits* (New York, 1933), and Federal Deposit Insurance Corporation, *Annual Report* (Washington, DC, 1956).

TABLE 2
STATE-CHARTERED REGIONAL COMPARISON: INSURED VERSUS UNINSURED

	Ratio of Assets in 1914 to Assets in 1920	Assets per Bank, 1920 ($ thousands)	Ratio of Capital to Total Assets, 1920
Uninsured			
Arkansas	0.379	$456	0.085
Colorado	0.450	460	0.083
Iowa	0.503	562	0.067
Idaho	0.316	487	0.077
Minnesota	0.406	425	0.069
Missouri	0.540	572	0.072
Montana	0.489	436	0.091
New Mexico	0.352	347	0.119
Wyoming	0.315	300	0.090
Average	0.418	448	0.084
Insured			
Kansas	0.380	326	0.079
North Dakota	0.367	248	0.081
Nebraska	0.335	335	0.082
Oklahoma	0.259	346	0.070
South Dakota	0.351	376	0.062
Texas	0.391	375	0.112
Average	0.347	334	0.081
Uninsured			
Alabama	0.553	543	0.087
Georgia	0.412	534	0.097
South Carolina	0.390	536	0.085
Average	0.452	538	0.090
Insured			
Mississippi	0.335	664	0.066

Source: Board of Governors of the Federal Reserve System, *All Bank Statistics* (Washington, DC, 1959).

greater delays in closing and liquidating insolvent banks, reminiscent of politically motivated delays during the current thrift crisis.[12]

The three states that had long-lived, free-entry, compulsory deposit insurance (which provided the worst and most prolonged incentives for risk-taking) experienced the most drastic losses by far among the state- and national-chartered systems. While several state-chartered systems experienced comparable shocks to these three (North Dakota, South Dakota, and Nebraska), in no other cases were the asset shortfalls of insolvent banks nearly large enough to threaten the capital of the banking system as a whole (see Table 4). In contrast, these three states showed shortfalls of between 1.5 and 5 times remaining bank equity of state banks.

[12] Detailed evidence on each of these points is provided in Calomiris, "U.S. Agricultural Boom and Bust."

TABLE 3
REGRESSION RESULTS: EARLY ASSET GROWTH OF STATE-CHARTERED BANKS[a]

a. Dependent variable: Growth in total assets of state-chartered banks, 1914–1920

Independent Variables	Coefficient	Standard Error	Significance Level
Intercept	0.156	0.468	0.741
National bank growth	0.682	0.147	0.000
Reserve center times national bank growth[b]	−0.115	0.063	0.080
Growth in land values, 1914–1920	0.526	0.334	0.127
Ratio of farm to non-farm population	−0.328	0.655	0.621
Presence of voluntary insurance	0.327	0.251	0.205
Presence of compulsory insurance	0.609	0.189	0.004
$R^2 = 0.683$			
$\bar{R}^2 = 0.607$			

b. Dependent variable: Growth in total assets of state-chartered banks, 1914–1920

Independent Variables	Coefficient	Standard Error	Significance Level
Intercept	0.101	0.465	0.829
National bank growth	0.681	0.147	0.000
Reserve center times national bank growth[b]	−0.132	0.060	0.038
Growth in land values, 1914–1920	0.555	0.333	0.107
Ratio of farm to non-farm population	−0.283	0.654	0.669
Presence of voluntary or compulsory insurance	0.518	0.165	0.004
$R^2 = 0.670$			
$\bar{R}^2 = 0.607$			

[a] Asset growth is defined as the log difference of total assets. All variables are defined at the state level for a sample of 32 agricultural states.
[b] National bank growth in each state is used as a control for state-chartered bank growth. In reserve-center states, national bank growth may be larger, as it reflects growth of correspondent banks outside of the state as well. To control for this difference, I interact national banking growth with an indicator variable for states with reserve centers.
Source: Charles W. Calomiris, "Do Vulnerable Economies Need Deposit Insurance?" in Philip Brock, ed., *If Texas Were Chile: Financial Risk and Regulation in Commodity-Exporting Economies* (Washington, DC, 1990).

CONTRASTING THE PERFORMANCE OF INSURED AND BRANCH BANKING

The failings of deposit insurance systems stand in sharp contrast to their perceived political alternative, branch banking. States that allowed branch banking saw much lower failure rates—reflecting the unusually high survivability of branching banks—and responded well to the agricultural crisis by consolidating banks and expanding branching systems, where this was allowed.

From 1921 to 1929 only 37 branching banks failed in the United States, almost all of which operated only one or two branches. Branching failures were only 4 percent of branch-banking facilities, almost an order of magnitude less than the failure rate of unit banks for this period. In states hard hit by the agricultural crisis, branch banks' failure rates were roughly a fourth those of unit banks. In Arizona, Mississippi, and South Carolina—three hard-hit states with existing statewide branching

TABLE 4

ESTIMATED ASSET SHORTFALLS OF FAILED BANKS RELATIVE TO REMAINING-BANK EQUITY IN "SEVERE-FAILURE" STATES

	National Banks						State-Chartered Banks						All Banks
	Deposits of Suspended Banks, 1921–30[a] ($ thousands)	Number of Liquidations Relative to Suspensions[b]	Average Size of Liquidated Banks Relative to Suspended Banks[c]	Rate of Asset Shortfall[d]	Estimated Shortfall[e] ($ thousands)	Total Bank Equity, June 1930 ($ thousands)	Deposits of Suspended Banks, 1921–30[a]	Number of Liquidations Relative to Suspensions[b]	Size Ratio[c]	Rate of Asset Shortfall[d]	Estimated Shortfall[e] ($ thousands)	Total Bank Equity, June 1930 ($ thousands)	Ratio of Shortfall to Equity[f]
Arizona	$ 1,256	0.67	0.83	0.50	$ 349	$ 3,815	$ 15,056	0.80	0.06	0.09	$ 65	$ 8,496	0.03
Colorado	11,003	0.94	0.45	0.40	1,862	13,776	12,187	0.95	0.95	0.32	3,520	10,273	0.22
Georgia	16,538	0.84	0.09	0.49	613	39,064	46,318	0.75	0.70	0.56	13,618	39,805	0.18
Idaho	10,601	0.81	0.65	0.53	2,958	4,612	9,185	0.85	0.63	0.51	2,509	4,983	0.57
Iowa	55,984	0.79	0.50	0.31	6,855	35,750	138,995	0.75	0.66	0.46	31,649	74,935	0.35
Minnesota	28,338	0.97	0.59	0.42	6,812	69,387	80,634	0.77	0.47	0.52	15,174	38,417	0.20
Montana	16,287	0.87	0.44	0.66	4,115	9,999	31,361	0.89	0.47	0.48	6,297	9,947	0.52
Nebraska	13,695	0.80	0.94	0.56	5,767	26,083	78,093	0.85	1.04	0.65	44,872	27,760	0.94
North Dakota	17,438	0.84	0.80	0.55	6,445	9,210	45,199	0.92	1.05	0.83	36,240	9,695	2.26
Oklahoma	27,364	0.72	0.70	0.57	7,861	41,251	38,986	0.79	0.28	0.44	3,794	11,493	0.22
South Carolina	12,153	0.92	0.57	0.49	3,123	11,665	50,970	0.91	0.58	0.34	9,147	17,069	0.43
South Dakota	21,109	0.93	0.60	0.49	5,772	8,477	91,619	0.77	1.00	0.76	53,615	10,848	3.07
Wyoming	9,154	0.91	0.45	0.30	1,125	4,819	7,536	0.80	0.48	0.46	1,331	3,844	0.28

[a] Deposits are defined at the time of bank suspension.
[b] The number of bank liquidations relative to suspensions measures the proportion of suspended banks that were liquidated.
[c] The average size of liquidated banks is divided by the average size of suspended banks to produce this ratio.
[d] The rate of asset shortfall equals 1 minus the ratio of the value of liquidated assets to deposit liabilities.
[e] The estimated shortfall is the product of the preceding four columns.
[f] The all-bank ratio of shortfall to equity divides estimated asset shortfall for state and national banks by the equity of surviving banks of both types.

Source: Charles W. Calomiris, "Do Vulnerable Economies Need Deposit Insurance?" in Philip Brock, ed., *If Texas Were Chile: Financial Risk and Regulation in Commodity-Exporting Economies* (Washington, DC, 1990).

networks—existing branches survived especially well, and new entry into banking (allowed only in Arizona and South Carolina) was especially strong.[13]

Table 5 reports regression results on bank growth from 1920 to 1926 and 1920 to 1930. States that permitted expansion of branching saw substantially higher (and statistically significant) asset growth relative to other states, controlling for other influences. A comparison across the two time periods shows that the influence of branching persisted and grew stronger with the passage of time. The effect of the presence of deposit insurance was negative, but this mainly reflected a temporary retreat from the state systems until after the insurance laws were repealed. By 1930 previously insured state systems had recovered to roughly the same levels of assets as other unit-banking state systems.

Contemporaries often remarked on the unusual survivability and growth of branch banks in the face of the crisis. Many states altered their branch banking laws in response to these observations. From 1924 to 1939 the number of full or limited branch-banking states rose from 18 to 36. Four of the 8 states that previously had opted for deposit insurance were among those liberalizing their branching restrictions during this period.

CONCLUSION

I conclude that unlimited branch banking, combined with the sort of privately administered insurance programs of antebellum Indiana, Ohio, and Iowa, would have been adequate to protect the payments system from exogenous disturbances that could produce banking panics.[14] The greatest threats to systemic stability historically were unit banking and ill-conceived attempts to promote stability through government-controlled insurance, which actually produced quite the opposite effect by promoting excessive risk-taking.

The problems of moral hazard and adverse selection which arise in government deposit insurance systems are likely to be even more pronounced in today's federal insurance programs. The state insurance systems of the 1920s limited interest paid on deposits, typically required ratios of capital to deposits in excess of 10 percent, and were funded by the accumulated contributions of members. Today's federal insurance plans do not restrict interest payments to depositors, require a trivial proportion of capital to deposits, and are supported by the full faith and credit of the federal government. Thus today's financial intermediaries can maintain higher leverage and attract depositors more easily by offering higher rates of return with virtually no risk of default. From this

[13] Again, for more detailed evidence, see ibid.

[14] The collapse of the 1930s demonstrates, of course, that if government policy makers want to destroy a banking system (in that case through deflation and monetary contraction) they have the power to do so.

TABLE 5

REGRESSION RESULTS: LATE ASSET GROWTH AND BANK SIZE OF STATE-CHARTERED BANK[a]

a. Dependent Variable: Growth in total assets of state-chartered banks, 1920–1926

Independent Variable	Coefficient	Standard Error	Significance Level
Intercept	0.544	0.450	0.239
National bank growth	0.602	0.235	0.018
Reserve center times national bank growth[b]	0.178	0.098	0.084
Ratio of farm to non-farm population	−0.404	0.346	0.254
Growth in land values, 1920–1925	0.037	0.541	0.946
Business failure rate, 1921–1925/ Business failure rate, 1917–1920	−0.040	0.038	0.308
Presence of deposit insurance (excluding Nebraska)[c]	−0.190	0.126	0.146
Out-of-city branch banking[d]	0.179	0.124	0.163
Within-city branch banking[d]	0.204	0.132	0.136
R^2 = 0.601			
$\bar{R}^2$ = 0.462			

b. Dependent Variable: Growth in total assets of state-chartered banks, 1920–1930

Independent Variable	Coefficient	Standard Error	Significance Level
Intercept	1.539	0.449	0.002
National bank growth	0.124	0.200	0.539
Reserve center times national bank growth[b]	0.078	0.115	0.502
Ratio of farm to non-farm population	−0.936	0.405	0.030
Growth in land values, 1920–1930	−0.386	0.551	0.490
Business failure rate, 1921–1929/ Business failure rate, 1917–1920	−0.072	0.044	0.118
Presence of deposit insurance (excluding Nebraska)[c]	−0.065	0.140	0.647
Out-of-city branch banking[d]	0.398	0.150	0.014
Within-city branch banking[d]	0.428	0.161	0.014
R^2 = 0.625			
$\bar{R}^2$ = 0.495			

[a] Asset growth is defined as the log difference of total assets. All variables are defined at the state level for a sample of 32 agricultural states.

[b] National bank growth in each state is used as a control for state-chartered bank growth. In reserve-center states, national bank growth may be larger, as it reflects growth of correspondent banks outside of the state, as well. To control for this difference, I interact national banking growth with an indicator variable for states with reserve centers.

[c] Nebraska's insured banks remained open long after they were known to be insolvent. Thus data for Nebraska on total assets of state-chartered banks overstate actual state-chartered bank assets for the 1920s. For this reason Nebraska was excluded from the group of insured states in these regressions.

[d] The indicator variable for out-of-city branching takes a value of 1 for states that allowed branching outside the home city of the bank, 0 otherwise. The within-city indicator takes a value of 1 for states that allowed branching only within a bank's home city, 0 otherwise.

Source: Charles W. Calomiris, "Do Vulnerable Economies Need Deposit Insurance?" in Philip Brock, ed., *If Texas Were Chile: Financial Risk and Regulation in Commodity-Exporting Economies* (Washington, DC, 1990).

perspective the unprecedented losses of Texas banks and thrifts in the 1980s should come as no surprise.

Reformers of current deposit insurance plans might apply the lessons of the successful antebellum insurance programs by creating a greater role for incentive-compatible self-regulation and coinsurance among banks. Today's futures clearinghouses, which regulate members' risks and provide incentive-compatible liquidity coinsurance, also successfully apply this principle.

A role remains for the government, however, in regulating bank insurance programs. At the very least the government should ensure freedom of entry into coinsuring groups of banks and competition among groups (by creating, for example, separate groups that overlap geographically). In a unit-banking scenario, the need for many groups (to keep group size small enough to encourage monitoring) dictates special attention to potential problems of local market monopolization. In contrast, today's futures clearinghouses can rely on national, and soon international, competition to limit the power of any group.

One might also argue, notwithstanding the evidence from the 1920s reported here, that government should provide some stop-gap protection against systemic collapse of the banking system—that is, shocks greater than those that could be absorbed by bank capital. To this end the government might establish an insurance plan with a "deductible." For example, coinsurance among banks would be relied on entirely for reimbursing depositors of the first banks that failed; the government would share increasingly in subsequent losses of failed banks. This would provide the incentives for interbank discipline and for market discipline of banking coalitions as a whole without risking systemic collapse.[15] Moreover, since it is likely that the government will intervene in such crises even without an explicit commitment to do so, it would be best to have that commitment spelled out. This would limit Congressional intervention to serve constituents' interests.

Absent the political feasibility of fully self-regulating, coinsuring groups of banks, some smaller steps could be taken to reduce the costs of government deposit insurance by enlisting the assistance of banks in the supervision process.[16] For example, banks could be assigned to groups, and banks within a group could be penalized (with higher insurance premia) for failing to detect and report violations or insolvency of other banks in the group. At the very least this would provide a strong counterbalance to political encouragement of excessive "forbearance" by creating an interest group that would have an incentive to monitor banks and "blow the whistle" early on insolvent institutions.

[15] I thank Henning Bohn for suggesting this to me.

[16] I thank Peter Diamond for suggesting the usefulness of state-contingent insurance premia in limited supervisory banking coalitions.

Socialism and Wages in the Recovery from the Great Depression in the United States and Germany

PETER TEMIN

The sustained unemployment in the United States during the recovery from the Great Depression has proved difficult to explain, as has the rapid elimination of unemployment in Germany. I argue that employment in the United States was restricted by high wages, which government policy raised above the level of efficiency wages. Socialist control and military expansion by the Nazis reduced unemployment, but also held down consumption.

Socialism was the common thread running through recovery policies in the 1930s. But German national socialism differed from American social democracy in many ways. Most relevant here was its emphasis on military and investment spending over consumption. The result was both lower unemployment and lower wages in Germany than in the United States. This contrast was the result of government policy rather than of efficiency wage setting by American firms. And the German economy increasingly resembled that of Russia, more conventionally socialist than either Germany or the United States. This article describes the socialist aspects of recovery policies and then focuses on wage and consumption behavior.

I

Free market capitalism and the orthodox finance of the gold standard had led to disaster in the early 1930s. Direct management of the economy could only do better. In both the United States and Germany, new and actively interventionist administrations took office in early 1933. And though there was no tight theory of a managed economy that led each country down the same path, socialist ideology led them in similar directions. I identify the following features of an economy as socialist: first, public ownership *or regulation* of "the commanding heights" of the economy, particularly of utilities and banking; second, heavy government involvement in wage determination; and third, a welfare state providing everyone with, in Oscar Lange's words, "a

The Journal of Economic History, Vol. L, No. 2 (June 1990). ISSN 0022-0507.

The author is Professor of Economics, Massachusetts Institute of Technology, Cambridge, MA 02139.

social dividend constituting the individual's share in the income derived from the capital and the natural resources owned by society."[1]

This definition differs from the one used today to distinguish Eastern from Western Europe. Instead of emphasizing the ownership of assets in a formal sense, it considers ownership in the sense of having control over an asset.[2] A nominal owner of an asset who cannot sell it and is forced to sell output through a government agency at a government-dictated price is not much of an owner. (This is a capsule description of Nazi agriculture.) The functional similarity between this concept and the more conventional one is shown by the common orientation of the Nazi and Soviet economies. Workers received Lange's "social dividend" in both Nazi Germany and Soviet Russia in the form of public monuments and military expenditures.

The Nazis seized control of an economy that already had many socialist characteristics. The Weimar government was heavily involved in mediating collective bargaining for wages throughout the 1920s. The government had virtually nationalized the banks in the wake of the currency crisis of 1931.[3] But the government's commitment to the gold standard had vitiated any gains from these policies, assuring that there was no "social dividend" to distribute.

In order to stimulate recovery, the Nazis—like the Democrats in the United States—had to establish a startling new policy regime. To do so, they destroyed many of the socialist institutions of the Weimar republic and replaced them with their own institutions that performed the functions of socialism. Personal freedom and autonomy were sacrificed in the process of controlling production and wages and distributing the "social dividend" to the populace. As Hitler is reported to have said, "Why need we trouble to socialize banks and factories? We socialize human beings."[4]

The Nazis set out to reduce unemployment by a variety of complementary actions. They centralized and appropriated the job of wage bargaining, entrusting it to a government agent, the Nazis' labor trustee. They also destroyed the unions within a few months of taking power, a form of out-socializing the socialists. The Nazis used tax incentives and propaganda to convince women to leave the labor force. And they introduced compulsory labor service in 1935.[5]

Wage payments failed to keep pace with the growth of national

[1] Peter Temin, *Lessons from the Great Depression* (Cambridge, MA, 1989), chap. 3; Oscar Lange and Fred M. Taylor, *On the Economic Theory of Socialism* (New York, 1964; 1st edn. 1938), p. 74.

[2] Sanford J. Grossman and Oliver D. Hart, "The Costs and Benefits of Ownership: A Theory of Vertical and Lateral Integration," *Journal of Political Economy*, 94 (Aug. 1986), pp. 691–719.

[3] Gustav Stolper, Karl Häuser, and Knut Borchardt, *The German Economy, 1870 to the Present* (New York, 1967), pp. 106–17.

[4] Peter Hayes, *Industry and Ideology: IG Farben in the Nazi Era* (New York, 1987), p. 73.

[5] Karl Hardach, *The Political Economy of Germany in the Twentieth Century* (Berkeley, 1980).

income, falling from 64 to 57 percent of national income between 1932 and 1938. Higher taxes on wage earners meant that consumption rose even more slowly, falling from 83 to 59 percent of national income in the same six years.[6]

The sum of investment and government expenditures thus rose from 18 to 41 percent of national income in this same period, a change in the composition of output that rivals the change under the Soviet First Five Year Plan. Productivity in the production of consumer goods, however, did not rise correspondingly. As in other socialist regimes, there was little incentive to innovate. In fact there were disincentives. High profits were taxed heavily. Good products that were competitive on world markets could not find outlets due to the extensive trade restrictions. The Nazis opted for exchange controls rather than devaluation, in part to isolate Germany from the world economy and promote their desired autarky and in part to exploit another tool for direct control over the economy.[7]

The Nazis introduced administrative controls over investment through licensing and direct allocation of raw materials. But their brand of socialism emphasized centralized control over economic activity rather than public ownership of firms. Instead of dispossessing private owners, the Nazis severely circumscribed the scope within which the nominal owners could make choices by currency controls, taxes on profits, and direct allocation measures of the state. This was nowhere more evident than in agriculture, where farms were nominally private, although they could not be sold and their output was marketed by government cartels.[8] Despite the retention of private ownership, government spending rose to one-third of GNP in 1938, while private investment rose only to one-fourth of that level.[9] As Karl Hardach noted, "In the long run, the Nazis aimed essentially at an economic system which would be an alternative to capitalism and communism, supporting neither a laissez faire attitude nor total planning."[10]

Extensive government spending did not initially mean military spending. Construction of housing and roads and the manufacture of automobiles were important sources of expansion. Hitler supported motorization for its presumed effects both on production—through imitation of Henry Ford—and on the working class, as shown by his enthusiasm for

[6] R. J. Overy, *The Nazi Economic Recovery, 1932–1938* (London, 1982), p. 34.

[7] Ibid., p. 37; Hardach, *The Political Economy of Germany*, pp. 71–72.

[8] Harold James, *The German Slump: Politics and Economics, 1924–1936* (Oxford, 1986), pp. 355–57.

[9] Overy, *The Nazi Economic Recovery*, p. 35; Charles S. Maier, *In Search of Stability* (New York, 1987), p. 98n, calculated from the same data as Overy that net private fixed investment was essentially zero through 1936. The rise in private investment was primarily inventory accumulation.

[10] Hardach, *The Political Economy of Germany*, p. 66.

the Volkswagen. Only after 1936, by which time the recovery was well under way, did the Nazis turn to preparation for war. After that time, of course, government expenditure increasingly shortchanged civilian investment in favor of the military.[11]

The American recovery under the New Deal was similar to the German expansion in its use of a socialist approach to the role of government, but it was very different in its internal dynamics. The German recovery emphasized consumption at first, only to reverse course and emphasize investment over time. The American recovery, by contrast, started with investment and went on to emphasize consumption. Germany increasingly emphasized military production; the United States did not start war production until the end of the 1930s. The German economy was subject to increasing control, while the New Deal imposed many controls all at once and withdrew partially under various pressures. The Germans kept wages low and reached full employment quickly; the Americans raised wages and had to cope with continued unemployment.

No one can doubt that Roosevelt's first hundred days comprised a whirlwind of activity. The New Deal certainly was expansionary, or "reflationist," a term that does not seem to have lasted beyond the Depression. It also took control over the economy in a way that was unprecedented.[12] The socialist elements in this extensive intervention can be seen in terms of the three attributes of socialism defined above.

Control over industry and wages in 1933 came primarily through the National Industrial Recovery Act. Control over agriculture was introduced with the Agricultural Adjustment Act, normally interpreted simply as price supports but included here as part of the growing government control over prices and marketing.

The change in the process of wage determination had a clear effect on the level of wages. Real earnings in both countries fell from their peak in 1929 to their trough in 1932 at precisely the same rate. This parallelism echoes the similar rate of deflation in the two countries, but it is remarkable in view of the well-known contrasting paths of real wages in the 1920s. Real wages in both countries started up at the same rate in 1933, but then their paths diverged. Even though prices rose under the NRA, real wages rose as well, faster than in Germany. By 1937, just before the American recession, real earnings in the United

[11] R. J. Overy, "Cars, Roads, and Economic Recovery in Germany, 1932–8," *Economic History Review*, 28 (Aug. 1975), pp. 466–83; G. F. F. Spenceley, "R. J. Overy and the Motorisierung: A Comment," *Economic History Review*, 32 (Feb. 1979), pp. 100–6; R. J. Overy, "The German Motorisierung and Rearmament: A Reply," *Economic History Review*, 32 (Feb. 1979), pp. 107–12.

[12] Peter Temin and Barrie Wigmore, "The End of One Big Deflation," *Explorations in Economic History* (forthcoming, 1990).

States were 30 percent above their 1933 level, while German real earnings were only just over 10 percent higher.[13]

The American high-wage approach therefore contrasted sharply with the low-wage program of the Nazis. The smaller gains in real wages in Germany encouraged the growth of employment, as did other Nazi policies, with dramatic effect. German unemployment fell from 30 percent to 2 percent between 1932 and 1938, while unemployment in the United States fell only from 24 to 14 percent in 1937, before rebounding to 19 percent in 1938.[14]

This capsule comparison of the New Deal and Nazi economic policy exposes a paradox. Conventional wisdom asserts that high wages raise costs and reduce international competitiveness. (This is the effect of an upward shift of the aggregate supply curve.) The American economy in the late 1930s then should have found itself with a less favorable trade balance than the Nazis. The United States should have been imposing more controls over foreign trade, while Germany was relaxing its controls. But, of course, the reverse is what we observe. The Americans passed the Reciprocal Trade Agreement Act and began to reduce tariffs, drawing back from the protectionist stance adopted under Herbert Hoover. The Nazis imposed ever more controls over their economy and over Germany's foreign trade, as each intervention seemed to create the need for another.

The contrast is sharpened by an appreciation of American business support for the high-wage component of Roosevelt's policy. Industrialists had never been as staunch deflationists as had financiers, and they supported the imposition of high wages. Firms engaged in exploiting new technology and active in international trade were not trying to cut costs by cutting wages. High wages and low tariffs were the keys to success in their eyes.[15] The United States economy was strong and progressive in the 1930s, while the normally innovative German economy began to produce lower-quality goods and found it increasingly difficult to export under the Nazis.

II

The contrast resulted from the overall policy regime in the two countries. Wages were only one aspect of national economic policies and must be seen in context. But before characterizing policy as a

[13] Gerhard Bry, *Wages in Germany* (Princeton, 1960), p. 362; U.S. Bureau of the Census, *Historical Statistics of the United States, Colonial Times to 1970* (Washington, 1975), pp. 164, 169.

[14] Brian R. Mitchell, *European Historical Statistics, 1750–1975* (New York, 1980), p. 178; U.S. Bureau of the Census, *Historical Statistics of the United States*, p. 135.

[15] Thomas Ferguson, "From Normalcy to New Deal: Industrial Structure, Party Competition and American Public Policy in the Great Depression," *International Organizations*, 38 (Winter 1984), pp. 41–94.

whole, it is necessary to show that high wages in the United States were the results of government policy.

Richard Jensen recently championed the hypothesis that the United States sustained continued unemployment because employers paid "efficiency wages," that is, wages above the market wage designed to elicit greater effort from workers. The higher pay in the United States encouraged worker productivity, giving rise to higher-quality goods.[16]

This explanation has a number of problems. Efficiency wage models are, first of all, theories of wage setting. Employers choose to pay efficiency wages in order to attract or keep hard-working employees. But, as shown above, the high wages in the United States did not result from the choice of individual firms. It was the result of legislation and the regulation that followed. True, the NRA was responsive to employer wishes, but it reflected the wish to cartelize industry more than the wish to bind the labor force to individual firms.

In addition, the efficiency wage theory predicts that efficiency wages are lower in times of high unemployment than in prosperity. The reason is clear. Employers expect loyalty and effort in response to an efficiency wage because the job and its wage are better than the worker's alternative. If the alternative is another job, then the efficiency wage must be high. But if the alternative is likely to be unemployment, then the job itself is better than the alternative. The efficiency wage need not be so high.[17] Efficiency wage theory therefore does not predict the 20 percent rise in (nominal) wages in 1934.

Finally, the evidence brought to bear on this problem to date has not examined the effort of workers, failing to demonstrate a connection between wages and effort. Many theories of the labor market imply Jensen's central finding: that employers in a slack labor market hired the best workers first. Martin Weitzman, for example, argued recently that one need only assume that wages are sticky in the short run to produce a hierarchy of jobs and conditions where employers hire the best candidates first.[18]

High wages in the United States are better seen as the result of "hysteresis." Olivier Blanchard and Lawrence Summers argue that group interests in wage setting can prevent the real wage from falling enough to restore full employment. In their model wages are set to preserve the jobs of those people already employed, not to move others out of unemployment. Workers react to negative external shocks—like

[16] Richard D. Jensen, "The Causes and Cures of Unemployment in the Great Depression," *Journal of Interdisciplinary History*, 19 (Spring 1989), pp. 553–84.

[17] Carl Shapiro and Joseph Stiglitz, "Equilibrium Unemployment as a Discipline Device," *American Economic Review*, 74 (June 1984), pp. 433–44; Lawrence F. Katz, "Efficiency Wage Theories," in *NBER Macroeconomics Annual, 1986*, Stanley Fischer, ed. (Cambridge, 1986).

[18] Martin L. Weitzman, "A Theory of Wage Dispersion and Job Market Segmentation," *Quarterly Journal of Economics*, 54 (Feb. 1989), pp. 121–37.

the deflation of the early 1930s—by accepting lower real wages, but only low enough to preserve the jobs of those still employed. The result is that the economy lacks a strong force tending to full employment.[19]

Under the NRA wages were set to serve the interests of those already employed, not those who wanted to be employed. The policies established by the AFL in the 1920s of protecting existing jobs for members and resisting wage cuts in slowdowns was generalized to industry as a whole.[20]

Just as wage patterns in the United States and Germany were the effect of government policies, the allocation of revived production followed directly from the government's aims. Germany's expansion under the Nazis was stimulated by an increasing emphasis on the military. In contrast to the United States experience, government spending was the engine of recovery.

Harold James argued recently that the Nazis expansion was not Keynesian. He asserted that the government expenditures undertaken during the later 1930s were not countercyclical in *intent*. They were directed toward the militarization of the German state and preparation for the war that the Nazis felt was both desirable and inevitable.[21] Granting James's argument, it is still true that the Nazi fiscal expansion had Keynesian *effects*.

Comparison with the United States in the 1980s makes the point. Reaganomics was hardly Keynesian in intent. The underlying theory was supply-side economics, fixated on the allocative effects of marginal tax rates. But the effect was the same as if the same dollars had been spent for the same purposes under a Keynesian banner.[22] So too in Germany in the 1930s. However baleful, political, or suicidal their intent, the Nazis expanded the economy by investing in military preparedness.

The effect on consumers was straightforward. The expansion put people back to work. But the military build-up siphoned off the goods they produced. The purchasing power of consumers was restricted and the government expanded its demand for munitions and armor. These are the products of heavy industry, which in turn depend on highly paid and highly skilled workers. Those industries thrived under Nazi control.[23]

In contrast to the experience of the 1930s, the United States has become a low-wage country in the 1980s. The two economies discussed

[19] Olivier J. Blanchard and Lawrence H. Summers, "Hysteresis and the European Unemployment Problem," *NBER Macroeconomics Annual, 1986*.

[20] Alexander Keyssar, *Out of Work* (Cambridge, 1986), p. 221.

[21] Harold James, "What is Keynesian about Deficit Financing? The Case of Interwar Germany," paper presented to the All-UC Conference in Economic History, April, 1989.

[22] Olivier J. Blanchard, "Reaganomics," *Economic Policy* (Oct. 1987), pp. 17–56.

[23] Hayes, *Industry and Ideology*.

here have begun to differentiate themselves, with the Germans specializing in products requiring highly trained and highly skilled workers and the United States expanding employment in lower skilled activities.[24] Why didn't the low-wage Nazi economy experience the same shift of resources out of heavy industry? Because there was no sign of international specialization in the 1930s to rival the shift of output mix in the 1980s. International trade ground to a halt in the Depression, breaking a critical link between the wage level and the composition of industry. Nazi Germany was among the worst offenders, sharply curtailing the opportunities for competition in foreign trade. International transactions were tightly controlled for purposes of national power and military advantage.

The Nazis' militaristic policies generated inflationary pressure on the economy. The military expansion actually created a shortage of labor, due to both the expansion of aggregate demand and the reallocation of workers. It gave rise to shortages of raw materials for the expanding industries, shortages which were compounded by the emphasis on military self-sufficiency and economic autarky.

The Nazi response was to control the German economy ever more tightly. Just as Stalin increased the centralized control of the Russian economy in the 1930s to cope with Russia's economic problems, so Hitler extended the reach of government into every corner of the German economy at the same time. Socialist as defined above, the Nazi economy increasingly resembled the paradigm of socialist economies.

The Nazis had proclaimed their economic aims long before they came to power. These plans were utopian, and they contained prominently the socialist theme of divorcing production from individual consumption, promoting instead the collective good. Once in power, the Nazis gave this a special twist; the communal aim was defined to be military expansion. This peculiar interpretation of the common good intensified the need to control ever more tightly the operation of the economy.

The Soviet government was not militaristic in the same way as the Nazis, but placed similar emphasis on heavy industry and war preparation. The USSR was second only to Germany in its munitions production in the late 1930s, far ahead of any other country.[25] Heavy industry was encouraged in Russia for its role both in war and in economic growth, but the fruits of this growth were directed toward investment and military expenditures rather than consumption. The Soviet and Nazi definitions of the public good had many similarities.

The Nazis dealt with inflationary pressure by freezing all prices in

[24] Gary W. Loveman and Chris Tilly, "Good Jobs or Bad Jobs: What Does the Evidence Say?" *New England Economic Review* (Jan.-Feb. 1988), pp. 46–65.

[25] Mark Harrison, "Resource Mobilization for World War II: The U.S.A., U.K., U.S.S.R., and Germany, 1938–1945," *Economic History Review*, 41 (May 1988), pp. 171–92.

1936. Prices quickly began to lose their economic function of allocating resources; the void was filled by direct allocation from the government bureaucracy. Purchasing permits and selling orders were needed for transactions in industry; production quotas were instituted in agriculture. Control was even tighter in foreign transactions as H. Schacht worked his magic to arrange for imports.[26]

The Nazis also refused to devalue the mark. This deflationary policy was a partial offset to the inflationary pressures of the economic expansion. The Nazis also preferred exchange controls to devaluation to insulate the German economy from the still-depressed world economy and to maximize political control over the economy. The overvalued mark, of course, made imports hard to come by, and Schacht worked on behalf of the government, not the consumer. The economic expansions in Nazi Germany and in the Reaganomic United States therefore had very different implications for consumption. The United States was flooded by imports in the 1980s, creating a consumption boom and a large foreign deficit. Nazi Germany, unable to accumulate a large foreign deficit, restricted consumption sharply. "In the end every sort of economic activity . . . was made to conform to government regulation, leaving little more than the title of private ownership."[27]

The result was a planned economy. The Nazi Four Year Plans were similar in kind and effect to the early Soviet Five Year Plans.[28] In both cases, the government sought to allocate resources by administrative means. The market and prices were abandoned as unstable and unresponsive to the national needs. Socialist planning was necessary to channel the efforts of the economy into the industries valued by the government.

Socialism was a particular approach to a planned economy, whether or not associated with explicit ownership of industrial enterprises. It was clear even in the 1930s that socialism did not necessarily mean that the workers' lot was improved. The Soviet workers suffered at least as much during the collectivization of agriculture in the early 1930s as the German workers did under the Nazis.[29] James observed that in Nazi Germany "price controls and an effective limitation of wages produced a continual worsening of qualities in consumer goods. The deterioration of textile qualities was particularly evident to the public. If, we may

[26] Larry Neal, "The Economics and Finance of Bilateral Clearing Agreements: Germany, 1934–8," *Economic History Review*, 32 (Aug. 1979), pp. 391–404.

[27] Stolper, Häuser, and Borchardt, *The German Economy*, p. 131.

[28] C. W. Guillebaud, *The Economic Recovery of Germany from 1933 to the Incorporation of Austria in March 1938* (London, 1939); Eugene Zaleski, *Stalinist Planning for Economic Growth, 1933–1952* (Chapel Hill, 1980).

[29] Michael Ellman, "Did the Agricultural Surplus Provide the Resources for the Increase in Investment in the USSR During the First Five Year Plan?" *Economic Journal*, 85 (Dec. 1975), pp. 844–63.

speculate, there had been no war, Nazi policy would have produced a society with low wages and high saving ratios manufacturing ever cheaper and shoddier goods."[30]

It is now apparent at the end of the 1980s that all socialist economies have severe problems in maintaining the quality of consumer goods produced. Centralized plans direct firms to make specified quantities of goods. These goods are then allocated to other firms or sold to consumers without competition from outside goods. Without the discipline of the market, there is no force keeping up the quality of goods. And there is every incentive to produce the needed goods at the lowest cost. The sacrifice of quality does not enter into the calculation with anything like the force it has in a competitive environment.[31]

In addition the Nazis wanted to make the German invulnerable to a wartime boycott. They promoted economic autarky to promote this end, encouraging the use of synthetic materials in place of imports. The result was higher-cost, lower-quality consumer goods made of ersatz materials. Nazi consumers therefore suffered doubly. Their wages were controlled and kept from rising in an increasingly tight labor market and they could buy only a limited range and quality of goods. The use of ersatz materials was good for defense and the foreign trade balance, but it led to inferior textiles and shoes. Inferior metals replaced gold in dental work. The normal insulation for electrical cables was replaced by "Ersatzstoffe." Cellulose replaced natural fibers; young women buying linens for their dowries discovered that they turned to pulp when washed. The Nazi economy produced progressively lower-quality products for the German consumer.[32]

III

The contrasting recovery of the United States and Germany therefore had many interconnected causes. Recovery was started in each case by a similar change in policy regime that replaced gold-standard orthodoxy by socialist measures. But the recoveries began to diverge very quickly. Recovery in the United States became based on the expansion of consumption while recovery in Germany became ever more militaristic.

The result was a contrast between the two countries in many dimensions: wage policy, exchange rates, fiscal expenditures, controls. The Nazi economy shared some characteristics of the United States under Reagan (military expansion, unwitting "Keynesianism," overvalued exchange rate) and some of the Soviet Union (direct control over the economy, low wages, military emphasis, poor consumer goods).

[30] James, *The German Slump*, p. 417.

[31] Ed A. Hewett, *Reforming the Soviet Economy: Equality versus Efficiency* (Washington, 1988).

[32] *Deutschland-Berichte der Sozialdemokratishen Partei Deutschlands* (1937); Willi A. Boelcke, *Die deutsche Wirtshaft, 1930–1945* (Düsseldorf, 1983), pp. 253–59.

High wages in the New Deal United States were the result of government policy rather than efficiency wage payments by individual American firms. And the American emphasis on consumption was reflected in a growing production of high-quality goods. The socialist control and military expansion of the Nazis, by contrast, increasingly shortchanged people as both workers and consumers.

Was There a Golden Age of Flexible Wages? Evidence from Ohio Manufacturing, 1892–1910

WILLIAM A. SUNDSTROM

Several macroeconomic studies have found evidence of diminishing cyclical wage flexibility in the United States since the turn of the century. But the importance of wage reductions during downturns must be questioned even for the era of allegedly flexible wages. This article shows that during the severe contractions of 1893 and 1908 only a small minority of Ohio manufacturing workers experienced cuts in their wage rates. The apparent downward flexibility of average earnings in these data was largely the consequence of changes in the occupational composition of the employed work force rather than pay cuts for individual workers.

The notion that the average hourly earnings of workers may be thought of as the price of something called labor has been the fiction—or more optimistically "useful abstraction"—underlying a number of exercises in historical macroeconomics. If the abstraction is to be useful, we must learn how it responds to changing demand conditions over the business cycle. If our abstraction falls only sluggishly when demand falls, then the familiar static analysis of partial equilibrium theory suggests that excess supply, or unemployment, will be the result. As John Maynard Keynes and others have argued, however, we cannot be sure that full employment will be restored by a falling wage if other prices in the economy are also slow to adjust.

Economic theory and common sense remind us that no fully integrated labor market actually exists, at least in the short run: the combined effect of industry- and occupation-specific skills, informational asymmetries, adjustment costs, and institutional structure is that there are many labor markets, not all of which will necessarily behave like the spot market of static analysis. What has not been sufficiently appreciated, however, is the extent to which empirical findings based on macroeconomic aggregates can foster misleading impressions about the microeconomic functioning of labor markets over the business cycle.

One assertion commonly made about American labor markets is that nominal wages have become less "flexible" in responding to aggregate demand conditions over the past century or so. Flexibility is usually

The Journal of Economic History, Vol. L, No. 2 (June 1990). ISSN 0022-0507.

The author is Assistant Professor of Economics, Santa Clara University, Santa Clara, CA 95053.

Helpful comments by Tony O'Brien and other participants in the session on "Wages, Output, and Macroeconomic Instability" at the 1989 Economic History Association Meetings are gratefully acknowledged.

measured as the responsiveness of average hourly earnings to changes in aggregate output or unemployment. Robert Gordon, for example, finds that the elasticity of nominal wages with respect to nominal GNP has declined substantially in the United States since the turn of the century. Related work by Jeffrey Sachs finds that the slope of the short-run Phillips curve has declined in the United States since 1890.[1] These findings conform to the diagnosis that the U.S. labor market has suffered from a progressive case of institutional arteriosclerosis, with union contracts and government regulations restricting the capacity of wages to respond rapidly to demand downturns.[2]

In this article I use disaggregated data from Ohio at the turn of the century to argue that labor markets already exhibited considerable wage rigidity by that time. For example, only a small minority of manufacturing workers in my samples experienced nominal wage reductions during the contractions of 1893 and 1908, even when output, employment, and days worked fell substantially. During the 1908 recession aggregate average hourly earnings did fall, but not because the average employed worker experienced a pay cut. Rather, average wages fell because employment fell by a much larger percentage in those industries that tended to pay higher wages. Hence the apparent downward wage flexibility was a consequence of a compositional effect, not occupation-specific wage-rate adjustments.

Because it is difficult to compare these results with more modern data, the hypothesis that wage flexibility has diminished over time is not firmly rejected here. The conclusion I wish to draw is simply that as early as the 1890s, Ohio employers were much more likely to respond to downward demand fluctuations by reducing employment, days worked, and hours than by reducing wage rates. And although Ohio is only one state, studies of other locations tend to confirm this general observation.[3] Certainly, wage hikes were likely to be put on hold during

[1] Robert J. Gordon, "Why U.S. Wage and Employment Behaviour Differs from That in Britain and Japan," *Economic Journal*, 92 (Mar. 1982), pp. 13–44; and Jeffrey Sachs, "The Changing Cyclical Behavior of Wages and Prices: 1890–1976," *American Economic Review*, 70 (Mar. 1980), pp. 78–90.

[2] In this spirit, a number of studies have pointed to the perverse effects of New Deal legislation in maintaining above-trend real wages and ignoring the root causes of high unemployment; see especially Michael M. Weinstein, "Some Macroeconomic Impacts of the National Industrial Recovery Act, 1933–1935," in Karl Brunner, ed., *The Great Depression Revisited* (Boston, 1981), pp. 262–81; and Richard J. Jensen, "The Causes of Unemployment in the Great Depression," *Journal of Interdisciplinary History*, 19 (Spring 1989), pp. 553–83. Such views have been challenged by other researchers; see Martin Neil Baily, "The Labor Market in the 1930s," in James Tobin, ed., *Macroeconomics, Prices, and Quantities: Essays in Memory of Arthur M. Okun* (Washington, DC, 1983), pp. 21–61; and Stanley Lebergott, "Wage Rigidity: Concept or Phrase?" (unpublished manuscript, Wesleyan University, Mar. 1989).

[3] Susan B. Carter and Richard Sutch, "The Labor Market in the 1890s: Evidence from Connecticut Manufacturing" (draft of paper prepared for presentation at the International Economic History Association meetings, Leuven, Belgium, 1990); and Peter R. Shergold, "Wage

bad times, and thus wage inflation decelerated; but the notion that participants in labor markets responded to excess supply by cutting the money price must be considered a very poor description of what usually occurred.

WAGE-RATE ADJUSTMENTS IN OHIO DURING TWO ECONOMIC CONTRACTIONS

From the early 1890s until 1910 the Ohio State Bureau of Labor Statistics (BLS) conducted extensive annual surveys of manufacturing establishments in the state to obtain information on wages, hours, and employment for various occupations and industries. It also collected data on wage changes by occupation. Detailed summaries of the data were published in the bureau's annual reports during the period. These data offer unusual insights into the micro-level adjustments of the labor market to macroeconomic conditions. Here I focus on evidence of wage adjustments during two very contractionary years: 1893 and 1908.

The coverage of the Ohio BLS survey seems to have changed over time, with a bias toward larger establishments during the earlier years. Beginning in 1901, however, the bureau undertook to collect responses from as many establishments as possible; moreover, amendments to the law governing the bureau's activities provided for penalties to employers who did not respond to the survey.[4] Because of this improvement in coverage, I believe examination of the time-series behavior of these data is best restricted to the period 1901 to 1910. Given the poorer coverage of the survey during earlier years, it seems safer to emphasize broad trends and cross-sectional variation rather than year-to-year changes before 1901.

Perhaps the most interesting and unusual question asked was by how much wages were increased or decreased for each occupation in an establishment during the calendar year covered by the survey. The responses were not always tabulated in a very usable form, but for 1893 and 1901–1910 one can calculate the percentage of employees who received pay cuts or raises. If the survey responses are accurate, such data provide a good approach to measuring nominal wage flexibility, since they indicate actual rate adjustments and are thus immune to problems arising from compositional effects.

The most serious issue one must confront in using such data is whether the wage changes might have been grossly underreported.[5]

Rates in Pittsburgh during the Depression of 1908," *Journal of American Studies*, 9 (Aug. 1975), pp. 163–88.

[4] More complete discussions of these sources are available from the author.

[5] In examining evidence of a similar type Mitchell expressed strong concern about underreporting: see Daniel J. B. Mitchell, "Wage Flexibility: Then and Now," *Industrial Relations*, 24 (Spring 1985), pp. 266–79.

Underreporting, which would bias the results in the direction of finding wage "rigidity," could have arisen because of ambiguities in the form of the survey question or because of careless, ignorant, or dissembling responses. The former problem seems unlikely here, because the questionnaires specifically required that the respondent write "no change" in the wage-change column next to occupations in which wages did not change. Problems of the latter type are more difficult to assess. It seems likely that the questionnaires were filled out by the factory owner or a central manager. In large plants wage setting may have been delegated to foremen, in which case higher officials would have had only limited knowledge of the details of wages and especially of changes having taken place during the year. It is conceivable that respondents attempted to conceal wage changes, but not likely because the published report did not reveal the names of employers and most industries in the reports consisted of a number of anonymous firms.

Although these remarks should serve as a caveat when interpreting my results, I think underreporting is not a serious problem. For one thing, probit analysis of the Cincinnati wage changes in 1893 shows that larger establishments were significantly more likely to report wage changes than were smaller ones. Furthermore, as I note below, the aggregate effect of the reported wage changes accounts for a large fraction of the overall change in average hourly earnings during periods of fairly stable employment (such as 1906–1907). Assuming even the worst possible underreporting, I show that wage cuts were rare, especially after 1900.

I begin with a look at the experience of Cincinnati workers during 1893. This year was severely contractionary: overall, manufacturing employment in the city fell by over 16 percent between January and December 1893; bank clearings also show a large drop. Employment statistics indicate that male workers suffered more employment loss than females, reflecting their greater concentration in durables manufacturing, with its greater cyclicality. In addition to the employment reduction, plants reduced their operating time: total days worked fell by 9.2 percent between 1892 and 1893.[6]

In spite of the large decline in activity and labor demand, relatively few Cincinnati workers experienced a cut in wages during 1893. As the first column of Table 1 shows, only 22 percent of employees experienced nominal wage reductions within their occupations. Nearly all the rest experienced no wage adjustment at all. It should be reiterated that the use of occupations as the unit of analysis implies that the data capture only changes in the wage *rates* paid for particular occupations—

[6] These figures are derived from data published in Ohio State Bureau of Labor Statistics, *Eighteenth Annual Report* (Columbus, 1895).

TABLE 1
WAGE CHANGES DURING 1893, CINCINNATI MANUFACTURING

Wage Change	All	Males	Females
Increase	1.0%	1.2%	0.04%
No Change	77.1	72.9	95.3
Decrease	22.0	25.9	4.7

Note: The wage changes occurred during the year ending Dec. 31, 1893.
Source: Ohio State Bureau of Labor Statistics, *Eighteenth Annual Report* (Columbus, 1895), pp. 143–91.

not earnings adjustments experienced by employees who were shifted between occupations.

The data suggest short-run downward wage-rate inflexibility for most workers.[7] One of the most interesting features is that women were extremely unlikely to experience a wage cut in 1893; as the third column of Table 1 shows, over 95 percent had no change in wages. Probit analysis of wage cuts by occupation and establishment indicates that the apparent gender difference reflects the fact that the establishments employing women tended to make fewer wage adjustments for both their male and female employees than did all-male establishments; there was no significant difference between the wage flexibility of men and women in plants that employed both sexes. This difference between all-male and other establishments remains even after controlling for the size of employment adjustments.[8]

The collapse of the economy in 1893 was followed by the depression of the 1890s. It would be desirable to see if there was a lagged effect on compensation, especially because economic agents might have delayed wage cuts in anticipation of price inflation during much of 1893, given uncertainties about the gold standard.[9] Unfortunately, the published reports for 1894 and 1895 do not give the number of workers experiencing wage cuts; the number of establishments reporting cuts is given, and it is very small in both years. For more complete comparability between years, however, it is better to turn to the reports from the first decade of the twentieth century, which allow us to examine wage movements during another serious contraction, that of 1908.

The first column of Table 2 summarizes changes in employment during 1901–1910 for the state of Ohio and separately for Cincinnati and

[7] During the calendar year of 1931, when the United States experienced large employment losses, only 22.8 percent of workers experienced wage changes, a figure not drastically different from that reported in Table 1. See Mitchell, "Wage Flexibility."

[8] The probit results are presented in William A. Sundstrom, "Wage Flexibility and Labor-Market Adjustments in the Contraction of 1893: The Case of Cincinnati" (unpublished manuscript, Santa Clara University, Apr. 1989).

[9] Nominal interest rates soared during early 1893, suggesting inflationary expectations. I am grateful to Charles Calomiris for calling this to my attention.

TABLE 2
PERCENTAGE OF WORKERS EXPERIENCING WAGE CHANGES, 1901–1910

Year	Percentage Change in Employment	Percentage Experiencing Wage Increase	Percentage Experiencing Wage Decrease	Ratio of Decreases to All Changes
State of Ohio				
1901		16.30%	0.44%	2.63%
1902	9.85%	30.71	0.29	0.92
1903	9.26	18.19	1.24	6.39
1904	−6.48	6.94	6.62	48.80
1905	12.13	15.42	0.71	4.43
1906	15.40	26.63	2.05	7.15
1907	3.31	22.36	1.94	7.97
1908	−16.50	6.37	7.36	53.59
1909	11.92	17.60	1.86	9.54
1910	10.12	21.20	0.83	3.77
Cincinnati				
1901		13.49	0.14	1.01
1902	9.45	20.58	0.00	0.00
1903	6.92	14.11	0.15	1.05
1904	−3.83	5.77	0.37	5.96
1905	8.80	11.66	0.45	3.70
1906	5.37	30.27	0.22	0.73
1907	0.22	17.13	1.14	6.22
1908	−14.88	6.17	4.44	41.84
1909	6.52	14.94	2.75	15.56
1910	4.40	15.40	0.88	5.41
Cleveland				
1901		23.84	0.18	0.75
1902	−1.82	29.13	0.11	0.39
1903	17.33	19.25	0.76	3.82
1904	−6.76	6.92	5.05	42.18
1905	11.17	11.84	1.21	9.31
1906	17.54	30.36	1.34	4.23
1907	1.61	18.04	1.82	9.16
1908	−18.45	4.21	7.37	63.66
1909	14.26	19.46	1.64	7.79
1910	16.83	23.86	1.24	4.92

Note: Percentage changes are calculated as differences of the natural log values for the preceding and current year.
Sources: Ohio State Bureau of Labor Statistics, 26th through 35th Annual Reports (Springfield, OH, 1903–1912).

Cleveland, as reported by the Ohio BLS reports for those years.[10] The severity of the 1907–1908 contraction is evident. Between those years the value of manufacturing output fell by 24.8 percent in the state, 13.9 percent in Cincinnati, and 21.4 percent in Cleveland. Bank clearings at the Cincinnati Clearing House fell by about 10 percent between 1907 and 1908, with the most dramatic decline coinciding with the financial crisis of October and November 1907.

[10] In 1906 Cincinnati and Cleveland together employed about 35 percent of the total workers reported for the state.

In spite of the severity of the contraction, very few wage cuts were reported. Although cuts were more common during the depressed years of 1904 and 1908 than other years, decreases were reported for less than 8 percent of workers for every year and location. Even in the most contractionary year, 1908, wage cuts make up only about half of the reported wage changes. The absencc of nominal wage reductions cannot be attributed to "stagflationary" price movements, since price indices for these years generally show deflation.

As can be seen in Table 2 the highest proportion of workers receiving reported wage increases in any year is low, on the order of 30 percent, which may reflect underreporting. An upper-bound estimate of underreporting can be made by supposing that during the years with the most reported increases *every* worker actually received an increase, but only a third of the changes were reported. If we then inflate the wage-decrease column by a factor of three to remove the largest conceivable effect of underreporting, we still find that at no time or place did the percentage of workers experiencing a cut exceed about 25 percent. The underreporting problem is certainly not that severe, but even if it were, it would seem that wage rates were sticky downward for the large majority of workers during this severe contraction.

Comparing Tables 1 and 2, there was much less wage cutting during 1908 than during 1893. In retrospect, the 1893 contraction was more long-lived and perhaps deeper, but at least in Cincinnati the initial employment loss seems to have been no worse in 1893 than in 1908. A finding of diminished wage flexibility during those 15 years would be consistent with some other findings, but further analysis of price expectations and the occupational composition of the samples is needed before any firm conclusion may be reached.[11]

AVERAGE HOURLY EARNINGS IN THE CONTRACTION OF 1907–1908

Average hourly earnings, the usual wage measure used in macroeconomic studies, can exhibit cyclical movements for a variety of reasons. Of course, individual workers may experience changes in the rate of pay on any given occupation; such changes would be captured by the wage-change question in the Ohio surveys. In addition, workers may be promoted or demoted within the firm, with less senior workers being "bumped down" the job ladder during contractions.[12] Worker mobility over the cycle may also result in workers changing employers and industries and thus pay; they may even be rehired by their old

[11] See Shergold, "Wage Rates in Pittsburgh"; and Christopher Hanes, "The Cyclical Movement of American Manufacturing Wages in the Gilded Age, 1870–1912" (unpublished manuscript, Harvard University, Mar. 1989).

[12] M. W. Reder, "The Theory of Occupational Wage Differentials," *American Economic Review*, 45 (Dec. 1955), pp. 833–52.

employers at lower wages. Finally, the composition of the employed work force may change as some subgroup of workers becomes unemployed.

These effects have very complex implications for the movement of average earnings. If one is interested in how the wage rate of a given worker of given skills changes over the cycle—which after all is really the best measure of whether the labor market is making spot-type adjustments—the changing composition of the employed work force must be carefully controlled for. The selection effect introduced by the unrepresentativeness of unemployed workers has received the most attention by researchers. Analysis using data for a recent period finds that in the economy as a whole, workers with observable characteristics associated with low pay are more likely to become unemployed during a downturn, but that workers with a large positive transitory component of pay for unobserved reasons also are selected out of the employed sample, the latter effect being stronger. In this case the combined effect of selectivity biases ordinary least squares estimates of wage changes in a procyclical direction. However, for manufacturing alone, the net bias is countercyclical; on average, that is, the lower-paid workers tend to leave manufacturing employment during downturns.[13]

As I do not have observations on individual characteristics, these sorts of controls for selectivity bias cannot be used with my data. However, the observations on wages by industry, sex, and occupation provide the raw material for a decomposition of observed changes in average hourly earnings into the effects of wage adjustments by occupation and changes in the occupational composition of the employed work force. It turns out that such a decomposition provides considerable insight into how the average hourly earnings of workers seem to have declined during the 1908 contraction when so few workers experienced wage cuts.

To see how wage changes may be decomposed, consider the change in average hourly earnings for a sample of workers between two points in time. Let w_{it} be the average hourly earnings of workers in occupation i at time t. Similarly, let p_{it} be the proportion of all employed workers at time t who hold occupation i. Then the change in average hourly earnings for all employed workers between time $t-1$ and time t is:

$$\Delta \bar{w} = \sum_i p_{it} w_{it} - \sum_i p_{i,t-1} w_{i,t-1}$$

It is easy to show that the change in average hourly earnings can be decomposed into the sum of three effects: $\Delta \bar{w} = C + E + R$, where C

[13] See Michael Keane, Robert Moffitt, and David Runkle, "Real Wages over the Business Cycle: Estimating the Impact of Heterogeneity with Micro Data," *Journal of Political Economy*, 96 (Dec. 1988), pp. 1232–66.

TABLE 3
PERCENTAGE CHANGES IN EMPLOYMENT, DAYS, HOURS, AND EARNINGS:
TEN LARGEST CINCINNATI MANUFACTURING INDUSTRIES, 1906–1910

	Percentage Change In			
Period	Employment	Days Worked	Daily Hours	Average Hourly Earnings
All Workers				
1906–1907	−1.01%	−1.02%	0.04%	2.98%
1907–1908	−17.46	−6.50	−3.21	−0.99
1908–1909	7.71	4.93	1.70	2.30
1909–1910	7.33	0.20	0.49	2.94
Males Only				
1906–1907	0.99	−1.23	−0.02	2.68
1907–1908	−22.57	−6.69	−3.28	0.58
1908–1909	9.51	4.60	2.55	0.91
1909–1910	8.64	0.93	0.54	2.26
Females Only				
1906–1907	−5.51	−0.56	0.10	0.20
1907–1908	−6.52	−6.13	−2.94	2.58
1908–1909	4.05	5.63	−0.14	4.40
1909–1910	4.54	−1.32	0.28	3.29

Notes: Percentage changes are differences of the natural log values of the variables. All figures are employment-weighted. The 10 industries included are boots and shoes; clothing; printing and binding; machinery; furniture; cigars; carriages and wagons; tools; soaps, candles, and tallow; and foundry and machine-shop products.
Sources: Ohio State Bureau of Labor Statistics, 31st through 35th Annual Reports (Springfield, OH, 1908–1912).

is a pure composition effect that holds wages at their $t-1$ values and allows the weights (proportions p) to change, E is a composition-constant pure wage-change effect that holds the weights at their $t-1$ values and allows the wage rates to change, and R is a residual effect that is a function of the time-covariance of p and w. Specifically, R would be positive if those occupations that gained representation (weight) in the sample were also occupations that tended to receive wage increases.[14]

Using the Ohio BLS reports for 1906 to 1910, I created a sample consisting of all data reported for occupations in Cincinnati's 10 largest manufacturing industries in 1906.[15] The data set is essentially a panel with a total of 2,567 separate entries disaggregated by industry, occupation, sex, and year. Table 3 shows percentage changes in employment, days worked, daily hours, and average hourly earnings for 1906 to 1910 for all occupations in the sample and separately by sex. Between 1907 and 1908 firms reduced employment dramatically; smaller but still substantial reductions were also made in the working time of those who

[14] Further details on these calculations are available from the author.

[15] The top 10 employing industries in Cincinnati in 1906, according to the Ohio Bureau of Labor Statistics, were boots and shoes; clothing; printing and binding; machinery; furniture; cigars; carriages and wagons; tools; soaps, candles, and tallow; and foundry and machine shop products. These industries employed just over half the manufacturing workers in Cincinnati in 1906.

remained employed, as indicated by total days worked and average daily hours. Employment losses were much larger for males than females, largely reflecting the fact that it was male-dominated industries, particularly producer durables, that experienced the most severe employment losses.

Overall, nominal average hourly earnings fell by about 1 percent between 1907 and 1908. Certainly, that does not seem to be a huge reduction in light of the quantity adjustments, but it does show a wage response nonetheless, and a substantial deceleration from the preceding year's 3 percent rate of increase. However, one's confidence that individual workers were experiencing reductions is eroded by the evidence on average hourly earnings by sex. The average earnings of males and females were increasing! The reason for this pattern is precisely the composition effect introduced by the differential employment adjustment by industry. Women, whose pay was on average only half that of men, comprised a growing proportion of the sample of employed workers, as they were concentrated in consumer-goods industries with much more cyclically stable employment.

Wage-change decompositions for samples of all workers and for males and females separately are presented in Table 4 for three periods: 1906–1907, 1907–1908, and 1908–1909. The sources of change are represented as percentages of the mean average hourly earnings for the two years and should add to the total percentage change in average hourly earnings. I have included the decomposition for 1906–1907 because it is indicative of a period when there was very little net total employment change.[16] The 1908–1909 change picks up the lagged effects of the contraction. The fifth column of the table shows the percentage change in average wages implied by aggregating the effects of the *reported* wage changes, holding employment composition fixed.

For the 1907–1908 decomposition it is clear that the composition effect C is responsible for the reduction in average wages. It is negative for the sample as a whole and for the separate male and female subsamples. In other words, the employment decline was greater in the higher-paying occupations. The wage effect, on the other hand, is positive: wages were rising in the average occupation. This contrasts with the net effect of the reported wage changes, which is small but negative. The difference between the wage effect of the decomposition and the net effect of reported changes could arise for a number of reasons. First, it may be that increases were underreported relative to decreases. Second, it may be that the distribution of wages within occupations was shifting, even though few individual workers experienced changes in wage rates. For example, the evidence is consistent

[16] Reported employment in these industries fell by about one percent between 1906 and 1907, reflecting the onset of the contraction by late 1907.

TABLE 4
DECOMPOSITION OF CHANGE IN AVERAGE HOURLY EARNINGS:
TEN LARGEST CINCINNATI MANUFACTURING INDUSTRIES, 1906–1909

Year	Percentage Change in Average Hourly Earnings	Source of Change			Effect of Reported Change
		C	*E*	*R*	
1906–1907					
All	2.28%	0.69%	1.87%	−0.28%	1.23%
Males	2.21	0.39	2.22	−0.40	1.37
Females	0.07	−0.51	0.44	0.14	0.67
1907–1908					
All	−0.91	−2.94	1.66	0.36	−0.11
Males	0.56	−1.08	1.17	0.47	−0.15
Producer Durables	−0.02	−0.18	−0.13	0.29	−0.95
Consumer Goods	0.59	−1.94	2.05	0.48	0.31
Females	2.26	−1.34	3.78	−0.19	0.11
1908–1909					
All	1.94	0.24	1.49	0.21	1.68
Males	0.74	−0.03	0.74	0.03	1.79
Females	5.05	−0.23	4.31	0.97	1.29

Notes: Percentage change in average hourly earnings is the total change divided by the arithmetic average for the two years. *C* is the composition effect, *E* the composition-constant wage effect, and *R* the residual, all expressed as percents of the average hourly earnings for the two years (for explanation, see text). $C + E + R$ should add to the number in the first column to within rounding error. The effect of the reported changes is the composition-constant weighted effect on average wages of the wage changes reported by employers. Producer durables industries are machinery, tools, and foundry and machine-shop products. Consumer-goods industries are boots and shoes, clothing, and cigars.
Sources: See Table 3.

with the idea that the less senior and therefore lower-paid employees in any given occupation were more likely to be laid off; their leaving could cause the occupation's average wage to rise even if those who remained on that job experienced a small reduction in pay.

By comparison with 1907–1908, the 1906–1907 and 1908–1909 changes are dominated by large positive wage effects, with the composition effects generally small for both sexes. The period 1906–1907 preceded the large employment adjustments of the recession, with employment and days worked in Cincinnati manufacturing both falling by only one percent between the two years. The reported wage changes have a larger net effect for this period and are about two-thirds the size of the wage effect. Again, this discrepancy may be attributable to underreporting of increases or composition effects within occupations. Certainly there is little reason to believe that the unreported proportion of wage changes exceeded a third.

Apparently the greater cyclicality of employment in durables manufacturing was an important factor in the decline of average hourly earnings during 1907–1908. To see if the composition effect was important within manufacturing sectors I performed the 1907–1908 decomposition on two subsamples of the male employees: first, the three producer durables industries (machinery, tools, and foundry and machine-shop products), and second, the three lighter consumer-goods manufacturing industries that employed the most women (boots and shoes, clothing, and cigars). The results are included in Table 4 with the results for 1907–1908.

The difference in the experience of male workers between the two industry groups shows the hazard of overgeneralization when describing labor-market adjustments over the cycle. In neither industry was there much change in average hourly earnings. But the similarity of this statistic masks important differences. In the producer-durables industries, despite a total employment loss of 50.8 percent, neither the composition nor wage effects were much different from zero. By contrast, there seems to have been more adjustment along both margins for men in the consumer-goods sector: the composition effect indicates that employment losses were greater for higher-paid men; but the wage effect shows that the average male worker who remained employed was experiencing a 2 percent increase in pay even as male employment in these industries fell by 9.2 percent.

Overall, the evidence from Ohio portrays manufacturing labor markets in which substantial reductions in employment, days worked, and hours were accompanied by very minimal reductions in compensation for individual workers. The most direct evidence comes from reported wage changes by occupation; to the extent that these are tainted by potential underreporting, one may have more confidence in the decomposition of changes in average hourly earnings. These indicate that nominal wages were rising during the contraction of 1908 for the average occupation. These results favor a research agenda for historical macroeconomics that focuses carefully on the micro-level responses of the labor market along various margins of adjustment without presuming spot-market fluctuations of the wage.

A New Monthly Index of Industrial Production, 1884–1940

JEFFREY A. MIRON AND CHRISTINA D. ROMER

The article derives a new monthly index of industrial production for the United States for 1884 to 1940. This index improves upon existing measures of industrial production by excluding indirect proxies for industrial activity, using only component series that are consistent over time, and not making ad hoc adjustments to the data. Analysis of the new index shows that it has more within-year volatility than conventional indexes, has relatively unimportant seasonal fluctuations, and has cyclical turning points that are grossly similar to but subtly different from existing series.

In recent years there has been renewed interest in the historical behavior of the U.S. macroeconomy. This interest reflects both a desire to use historical episodes as laboratories in which to test economic theories and a desire to understand how, and indeed if, the behavior of the U.S. economy has changed over time. To give a few examples of recent historical analyses, Bradford De Long and Lawrence Summers, Jeffrey Miron, and Christina Romer provide comparisons of output variability over time; Robert Gordon estimates the relationship between price changes and output changes in the economy since 1890; Charles Calomiris and Glenn Hubbard study the effects of credit rationing on the behavior of output in the United States before 1909; and William Schwert examines the relationship between stock market volatility and real economic events.[1] These studies

The Journal of Economic History, Vol. L, No. 2 (June 1990). ISSN 0022-0507.

The authors are Professor of Economics, Boston University, Boston, MA 02215 and Acting Associate Professor of Economics, University of California, Berkeley, CA 94720, respectively.

We thank Todd Clark and David Bowman for excellent research assistance and David Romer for helpful comments and suggestions. Financial support was provided by the National Bureau of Economic Research, the John M. Olin Fellowship at the NBER (awarded to Miron), the National Science Foundation (grants SES-8710140 and SES-8896257), and the Institute of Business and Economic Research at the University of California at Berkeley.

[1] J. Bradford De Long and Lawrence Summers, "The Changing Cyclical Variability of Economic Activity in the United States," in Robert J. Gordon, ed., *The American Business Cycle: Continuity and Change* (Chicago, 1986), pp. 679–734; Jeffrey A. Miron, "The Founding of the Fed and the Destabilization of the Post-1914 Economy," in Marcello de Cecco and Alberto Giovannini, eds., *A European Central Bank? Perspectives on Monetary Unification after Ten Years of the E.M.S.* (Cambridge, 1989); Christina D. Romer, "Is the Stabilization of the Postwar Economy a Figment of the Data?" *American Economic Review*, 76 (June 1986), pp. 314–34; Christina D. Romer, "The Cyclical Behavior of Individual Production Series, 1889–1984" (unpublished manuscript, University of California at Berkeley, 1989); Christina D. Romer, "The Prewar Business Cycle Reconsidered: New Estimates of Gross National Product, 1869–1908," *Journal of Political Economy*, 97 (Feb. 1989), pp. 1–37; Robert J. Gordon, "Price Inertia and Policy Ineffectiveness in the United States, 1890–1980," *Journal of Political Economy*, 90 (Dec. 1982), pp.

represent useful contributions in the fields of economic history and macroeconomics.

A potential weakness of much of this research, however, is the quality of the output data employed for the pre-1919 period. In 1919 the Federal Reserve Board (FRB) began to produce a comprehensive index of industrial production. For the period before 1919 there are many monthly indexes of industrial activity, but all have significant problems. For example, one of the most widely used monthly series is Roger Babson's Industrial Production Index.[2] This index, however, is based on very few physical production series before 1905. Instead, for some decades as much as 55 percent of the index is based on the behavior of the gross value of imports and exports. As a result, this series is more an index of trade than of industrial production. An additional problem with the Babson index is that, like almost all early series, it is available only in a seasonally adjusted form. This is a drawback because the seasonal movements in economic activity are themselves interesting and because early methods of seasonal adjustment involved complicated procedures that typically did more than simply remove regular seasonal fluctuations from the data.

A second measure of monthly economic activity that has been widely used in the recent literature is Frederick Macaulay's series on pig iron production.[3] The major drawback of this series is that it is based on only one commodity, whereas in most settings a more broadly based index would be desirable.

A third measure of monthly production that has been employed recently is the Index of Production and Trade constructed by Warren Persons.[4] This index is based very heavily on bank clearings. For studies of the relationship between money and output this is a particularly serious drawback, since bank clearings and money are correlated by construction. In addition, the coverage of this series changes

---

1087–117; Charles Calomiris and R. Glenn Hubbard, "Price Flexibility, Credit Availability, and Economic Fluctuations: Evidence from the United States, 1894–1909," *Quarterly Journal of Economics*, 104 (Aug. 1989), pp. 429–52; and G. William Schwert, "Why Does Stock Market Volatility Change Over Time?" *Journal of Finance* (forthcoming).

[2] Roger W. Babson, *Business Barometers and Investment* (New York, various annual issues). This series is used by Kathryn Dominguez, Ray Fair, and Matthew Shapiro, "Forecasting the Great Depression: Harvard Versus Yale," *American Economic Review*, 78 (Sept. 1988), pp. 595–612; and Schwert, "Why Does Stock Market Volatility Change Over Time?"

[3] Frederick R. Macaulay, *The Movement of Interest Rates, Bond Yields, and Stock Prices in the United States Since 1856* (New York, 1938). This series is used by Calomiris and Hubbard, "Price Flexibility"; Victor Zarnowitz, "The Regularity of Business Cycles" (NBER Working Paper No. 2381, 1987); and Gary Gorton, "Banking Panics and Business Cycles," *Oxford Economic Papers*, 40 (Dec. 1988), pp. 751–81.

[4] Warren M. Persons, *Forecasting Business Cycles* (New York, 1931). This series is used in Gordon, "Price Inertia."

significantly over the 1877 to 1918 period.[5] This change in coverage may mean that apparent changes in behavior are due to changes in the data rather than to genuine economic forces.

DERIVATION OF THE NEW INDEX

Given the limitations of the existing prewar monthly indexes of industrial production, we believe there is an urgent need for a new index. To that end this article presents a new monthly index of industrial production for the period 1884 to 1940. Our index is derived from reliable and consistent data on the monthly physical output of 13 manufacturing and mineral products. These individual physical output series are combined using value-added weights to form an aggregate index. In the derivation of this index no regression procedures are used and very few adjustments are made to the data. The new index is presented only in its seasonally unadjusted form. We carry our index through 1940, despite the existence of the FRB index of industrial production beginning in 1919, so that we can compare our index with the more comprehensive FRB series and so that there exists a consistent index that spans both the prewar and interwar eras.

Procedures

Many of the specifics of the derivation of the new index, as well as the actual data, are presented in the Appendix.[6] Nevertheless, it is useful to discuss the general procedures briefly.

The most important step in deriving the new index is deciding which component data series to collect and to include in the index. The main criterion that we use is that the series be a genuine physical output series or a direct proxy. We specifically exclude nominal value series and indirect proxies for business activity, such as bank clearings or postage stamps issued. We do, however, often use a close proxy for actual production. For example, we frequently use data on physical shipments rather than physical production because the latter data are rarely available for the prewar era. Similarly, we sometimes use a physical input series to proxy for the output of a manufactured good. For example, we use the head of cattle received by stock yards in Chicago to proxy for the output of dressed beef and the amount of raw silk imported as a proxy for the production of silk cloth. While series on shipments or inputs are obviously imperfect proxies for genuine pro-

[5] For 1877 to 1902 the Persons Index is based only on bank clearings in seven cities and pig iron production. After 1902 the index includes data on merchandise imports, railroad earnings, and employment, as well as bank clearings and pig iron production (see Persons, *Forecasting Business Cycles*, pp. 111, 131).

[6] A more detailed description of our procedures is contained in Jeffrey A. Miron and Christina D. Romer, "A New Monthly Index of Industrial Production, 1884–1940" (NBER Working Paper No. 3172, 1989).

duction, they should be much more closely related to actual production than the indirect proxies that have been used by previous authors. Indeed, one sign that the series we use are acceptable measures of production is that series like them are used even today in the derivation of the FRB index of industrial production.

A second criterion is that we collect only series for which reasonably reliable and consistent monthly data exist back to 1884. In particular, all of the series that we use are based on contemporaneous monthly surveys of major producers for the entire sample period. Most of these series were collected by trade organizations or specialized commercial news organizations. For example, the data on pig iron output were collected by *Iron Age*, the major trade publication of the iron and steel industry. Similarly, the data on sugar meltings were collected by Willett and Gray, a firm that published the *Weekly Statistical Sugar Trade Journal*. We restrict ourselves to lengthy time series because we specifically want to avoid splicing together possibly inconsistent series.

Following these criteria, we have collected monthly data on the output of 13 industrial products for the period 1884 to 1940.[7] The exact series used and the sources of the data are described in the Appendix. The series cover a wide range of goods. Among the most thoroughly represented industries are manufactured foods, textile products, iron and steel products, and petroleum and coal products. At the same time, however, there are some industries, such as forest products and stone, clay, and glass products, for which we have no series.

While we feel it is useful to leave the individual series seasonally unadjusted, it is nevertheless desirable to make the obvious correction for variations in the number of production days per month.[8] To do this we divide each of the monthly production totals by the number of calendar days in the month less the number of Sundays. While there was no doubt some variation across industries in the length of the work week, especially in the 1930s, our procedure should eliminate most of the fluctuations in production due solely to fluctuations in production days.

Aggregating the 13 individual series into an index of industrial production is accomplished by converting each series to an index and weighting each by value added.[9] This is analogous to the derivation of

[7] Several of these series are available for at least part of the period from the records of the NBER that are on a tape deposited at the Inter-university Consortium for Political and Social Research. However, we have checked all data from the NBER tape against published original sources. When there was a discrepancy between the NBER tape and the original sources, we have resolved the difference in favor of the primary sources unless there was evidence of a typographical error or other obvious flaw in the primary source.

[8] This adjustment for production days is currently done by the Federal Reserve in the derivation of its seasonally unadjusted index of industrial production.

[9] The original data on value added are from the *Census of Manufactures* or the *Census of Mines and Quarries*. We use the version of these data given by Solomon Fabricant and in *Historical*

the modern FRB index of industrial production. We choose 1909 as our base year because it is the census year nearest the middle of our sample period and because it represents a point of mid-expansion in the cycle.

While the Appendix discusses specific issues related to the assignment of weights, the basic strategy is that for each of our series we use the obvious analog in the census. For example, for our series on flour shipments, we use the value added in flour milling from the census; for our series on coffee imports, we use the value added in coffee roasting and spices. This procedure effectively weights each of our series by the value added in approximately the two- or three-digit SIC industry of which it is a component.

Benefits and Cautions

While no new index of industrial production can overcome the fundamental lack of data for the prewar era, we believe that ours represents a substantial improvement over existing ones. Most importantly, it includes only data on the output (or occasionally the inputs) of manufacturing firms and mines: it is not contaminated by other measures of economic activity such as bank clearings, prices, or the volume of foreign trade. As a result, the index can be used to test relationships that have occasionally been assumed in the derivation of other indexes. At the same time, the new index includes a fairly wide range of industrial commodities. Thus, it should yield more information about the behavior of the industrial sector of the United States than more limited series, such as the widely used pig iron series.

Second, the new index is based only on output series that are reasonably consistent over time. We do not include series that have changed significantly in coverage or definition over our sample period. This insures that the index is comparable over the entire sample period and should yield meaningful comparisons of industrial behavior in the late nineteenth and early twentieth centuries.

Finally, the new index is much less "adjusted" than other indexes. Most obviously, we do not seasonally adjust the index. More generally, the new index makes almost no adjustments to the base data. We do not use series with gaps that must be filled in by interpolation and do not impose assumptions about the smoothness of month-to-month variations in production. This lack of adjustment means that our new index should be reasonably uncontaminated by our own beliefs about the likely behavior of industrial production in the pre-World War II period.

Statistics of the United States. Solomon Fabricant, *The Output of Manufacturing Industries, 1899–1937* (New York, 1940); and U.S. Bureau of the Census, *Historical Statistics of the United States* (Washington, DC, 1975).

While the new index has many desirable features, it also has definite limitations. First, because the index is based only on series that exist over long sample periods, it misses new commodities that are introduced or new data series that become available only later in the sample period. This feature of our base data means that the index may understate the amount of growth that occurred over the entire sample period because new commodities tend to grow quickly. It may also provide less information about the precise nature of overall economic activity later in the sample period than the broader FRB index, which becomes available in 1919.

Another problem is that the focus on consistent, lengthy time series yields an index that is partially based on close proxies for actual production and is biased toward very primary commodities. The use of input series or shipments data to proxy for actual output could make the behavior of our index differ systematically from the true behavior of aggregate production if inventory fluctuations or production lags are significant. The bias toward primary commodities such as pig iron and coal could tend to make our prewar index more cyclically sensitive than the actual underlying economy because primary commodities are typically more volatile than highly processed goods.[10]

COMPARISONS WITH OTHER INDEXES

Having derived a new index of industrial production, it is useful to compare it with existing indexes. Figure 1A shows the logarithm of our index for the entire 1884 to 1940 sample period along with the Babson and Persons indexes, which are available only in seasonally adjusted form. Figure 1B shows the new index along with Macaulay's pig iron series and the FRB index of industrial production, both of which are available without seasonal adjustment.[11] The Figures suggest three key facts about how our index compares with others. First, the new index is considerably more volatile than the Babson, Persons, and FRB indexes but less volatile than the pig iron series. Second, the new index appears to have seasonal movements that are roughly as important as those of the pig iron series but noticeably less important than those of the interwar FRB series. Third, the new index appears to display cyclical

[10] See Romer, "Is the Stabilization of the Postwar Economy a Figment of the Data?" for a more thorough discussion of this bias.

[11] The exact sources of the alternative series used are the following. For the Babson index we use the version given in Geoffrey Moore, *Business Cycle Indicators* (Princeton, 1961), vol. 2, pp. 130–31. We splice ratios to the two variants of the index in Jan. 1933. For the Persons index we use the Index of Production and Trade given in Persons, *Forecasting Business Cycles*, pp. 91–167. The pig iron series is from Macaulay, *The Movement of Interest Rates*, pp. A252–A270, table 27. The FRB series is from U.S. Board of Governors of the Federal Reserve System, *Industrial Production* (Washington, DC, 1986), p. 303.

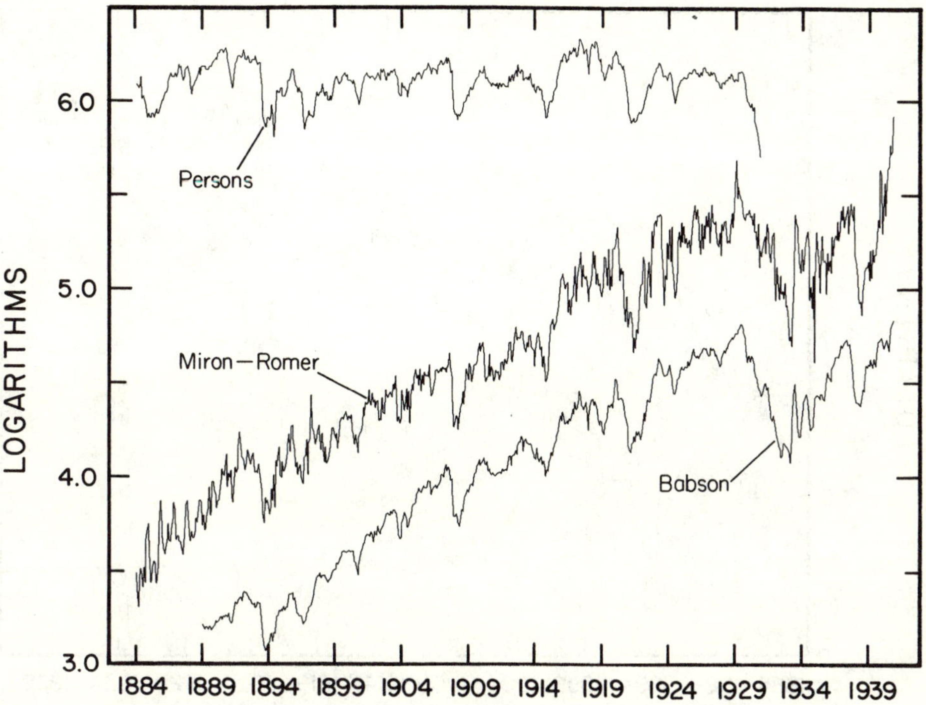

FIGURE 1A

ALTERNATIVE MEASURES OF INDUSTRIAL PRODUCTION

Note: To improve the clarity of the figure, we have added 1.5 to the logarithm of the Persons index in all years.
Sources: See the text for the sources of the Babson and Persons series and for a description of the derivation of the new Miron-Romer index.

turning points that are grossly similar to but subtly different from other series.

Volatility

Table 1 compares the volatility of different indexes by presenting the standard deviation of the growth rate of each index. In the case of the Babson and Persons indexes, we examine the volatility of the growth rate of the published seasonally adjusted indexes. For the remaining measures, we examine the volatility of both the unadjusted indexes and the residuals from a regression of the change in the logarithm of the index on seasonal dummy variables. The regressions are calculated separately for each sample period.

Table 1 shows that our monthly index is more volatile in every sample period than all of the alternative measures of monthly production with the exception of the pig iron series. This difference in volatility, however, is almost purely a within-year phenomenon. Table 1 also shows the standard deviations of the annual average of our index and

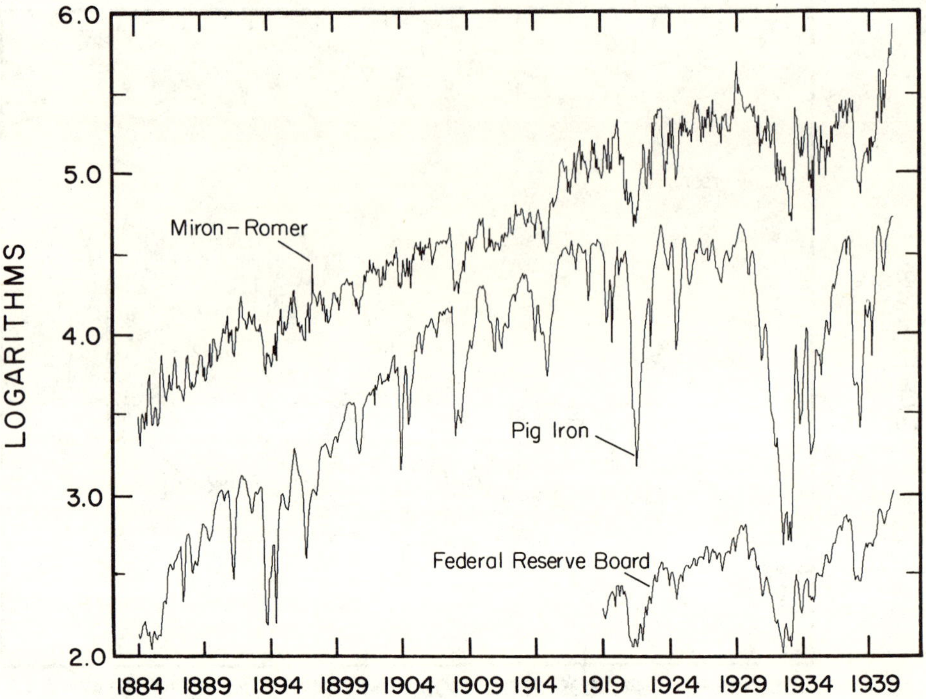

FIGURE 1B

ALTERNATIVE MEASURES OF INDUSTRIAL PRODUCTION

Note: To improve the clarity of the figure we have subtracted 0.15 from the logarithm of the Pig Iron series in all years.
Sources: See the text for the sources of the Pig Iron and Federal Reserve Board series and for a description of the derivation of the new Miron-Romer index.

the alternative indexes.[12] Using annual data, our index is typically only slightly more volatile than the others and in some cases is actually less volatile.

The greater month-to-month variation in the new index does not appear to be due to the fact that it is seasonally unadjusted: the same results hold for the residuals of the regression against seasonal dummy variables. The most likely explanation for the difference is that the seasonal-adjustment procedures used by Babson and Persons may smooth away more of the short-run variation in the data than does a simple regression against monthly dummy variables. This is a common feature of older seasonal-adjustment procedures.

While the method of seasonal adjustment is almost surely very important, some of the difference in volatility between our index and the alternatives is no doubt also due to differences in the commodities

[12] Table 1 also shows the behavior of the widely used Frickey series that is available only on an annual basis. These data are from Edwin Frickey, *Production in the United States, 1860–1914* (Cambridge, 1947), p. 54, table 6.

TABLE 1
STANDARD DEVIATIONS OF ALTERNATIVE MEASURES OF INDUSTRIAL PRODUCTION
(Growth Rates)

	Monthly Data		
Series	Feb. 1884–Dec. 1940	Feb. 1884–Dec. 1913	Jan. 1914–Dec. 1940
Miron-Romer	9.17	7.05	11.07
Miron-Romer (SA)	9.00	6.44	10.88
Babson (SA)	3.16	2.54	3.64
Persons (SA)	2.92	3.03	2.73
Pig Iron	9.33	7.86	10.73
Pig Iron (SA)	9.13	7.68	10.46
FRB			4.40
FRB (SA)			3.71
	Annual Data		
Series	1885–1940	1885–1913	1914–1940
Miron-Romer	12.91	8.96	16.30
Babson	10.86	8.23	12.84
Persons	9.61	8.67	11.25
Pig Iron	29.33	19.53	37.26
FRB			16.03
Frickey		10.04	

Notes: (SA) denotes seasonally adjusted. The seasonally adjusted results for the Miron-Romer, Pig Iron, and FRB series are based on the residuals from a regression of the growth rate on seasonal dummy variables. Because of data unavailability, the calculations for the Babson index begin in Feb. 1889, those for the Persons index end in Dec. 1930, and those for the FRB index begin in Feb. 1919. The Frickey index is available only on an annual basis. The growth rates reported in the monthly section are measured at monthly rates; those reported in the annual section are measured at annual rates.
Source: See the text for a description of the sources of the alternative series and the derivation of the Miron-Romer index.

represented. The fact that we exclude series such as bank clearings or exports may affect the volatility of our index if these series have particular volatility characteristics. Furthermore, in comparison to the FRB index for the interwar period our index is simply based on a smaller number of commodities.[13] If there is variation in each individual component that is not perfectly correlated across series, an index based on a greater number of individual series will display less volatility, holding the volatility of the individual series constant. This fact may explain why the FRB index for 1919 to 1940 is less volatile than our new index, even though both series are unadjusted.[14] It also suggests that

[13] Specifically, the FRB index in this period is based on approximately 80 series, whereas our index includes only 13.

[14] It is also important to note that for the interwar period the FRB index includes several employment series. If there is labor hoarding, then employment will tend to be less volatile than output. This feature of the FRB index could explain some of its relative stability.

our index provides a poorer indication of aggregate volatility for the interwar era than does the FRB index.

The finding that our index shows more month-to-month variation than others may alter economists' view of the pre-World War II economy. In particular, the fact that at least 13 industrial commodities appear to have fluctuated quite significantly over very short time periods may indicate that the prewar economy was buffeted by frequent shocks. That these shocks resulted mainly in intrayear fluctuations in real production suggests that the economy had a rapid, though not instantaneous, self-righting mechanism.

While the new index clearly has volatility characteristics that are different from most of the existing measures of industrial production, it is useful to note that nearly all of the indexes show a similar change in volatility between the prewar and interwar eras. Table 1 shows that every monthly index except the Persons Index of Production and Trade is more volatile after 1914 than before.[15] This finding mainly reflects the fact that the Great Depression is in the post-1914 sample period. However, even during the relatively tranquil 1922 to 1928 period the new index is slightly more volatile than during the pre-1914 period.[16] This suggests that the various structural changes that occurred around World War I, such as the rise of the Federal Reserve System, may have increased the volatility of the U.S. economy.

Seasonality

As mentioned earlier, purely seasonal movements appear to explain very little of the total month-to-month variation in our new index. This can be seen from the finding that the R^2 of the regression of the growth rate of the index on seasonal dummy variables is 0.17 in the pre-1914 period and 0.04 in the post-1914 period. At the same time, however, regular seasonal fluctuations are clearly present in the new index. In particular, the seasonal pattern of the index is large in magnitude, with an amplitude of 10 percent in the pre-1914 period and 6 percent in the post-1914 period. It is also statistically significant at the 10 percent level or better in both periods.

A comparison of the seasonal behavior of the new index with the two other available unadjusted series indicates that the new index has seasonal movements that are similar in importance to those of the pig iron series but distinctly less important than those in the interwar FRB

[15] The fact that the Persons series is more volatile in the prewar era may be due to the interaction of the use of bank clearings data and the frequency of financial panics in the period before 1914.

[16] The standard deviation of our new seasonally unadjusted index for 1922 to 1928 is 10.72. The fact that the interwar period is more volatile than the pre-World War I period has been emphasized by Miron, "The Founding of the Fed." The results presented here verify those findings with new monthly data.

index.[17] The similar importance of seasonal movements in the new index and the pig iron series could be due in part to the fact that pig iron is weighted heavily in the new index. However, this cannot be the entire explanation because the pattern of seasonal movements is quite different in the two series. In particular, the new index does not show the surge in production early in the year that is characteristic of the pig iron series, though it does show the surge in the fall that is also present in the pig iron series.

Examination of the seasonal behavior of the 13 individual series that make up the new index indicates that some of the apparent unimportance of seasonal fluctuations in the new aggregate index stems from the canceling out of individual seasonal patterns. For some of the individual series seasonal fluctuations are quite important, accounting for as much as 30 to 40 percent of the total variation in growth rates. However, the seasonal patterns differ quite substantially across the series. For example, cattle receipts and flour shipments have a large seasonal peak in the fall, wool receipts have a peak in the summer, and sugar meltings are very low in the fall but rise dramatically in the winter months.

The fact that the FRB index of industrial production shows a stronger aggregate effect of seasonal fluctuations in the interwar era may be due to differences in the composition of the FRB index and our new index. In particular, our index is more heavily weighted toward manufactured foods, which tend to have distinct seasonal cycles that vary greatly from product to product. Thus, our index may have more canceling out of seasonal patterns than the FRB index, which includes many more heavy industrial goods. One factor that does not appear to account for the greater importance of seasonal movements in the FRB index is the fact that it is only available after 1919. Between the prewar and interwar eras there is some change in the seasonality of the new index, but that change goes in the direction of making the seasonality less important over time.

To the extent that the relative unimportance of seasonal fluctuations shown by the new index is a genuine phenomenon, this finding suggests that in the period before 1940 a very small fraction of aggregate short-run fluctuations was attributable to predictable seasonal shocks and a very large fraction was due to unpredictable shocks. The most obvious place to look for such unpredictable shocks would probably be random demand shocks from both foreign and domestic sources. The importance of unpredictable shocks in the prewar era presents an interesting contrast to the postwar era, where as much as 80 percent of

17. The R^2 of the regression of log growth rates on seasonal dummy variables is 0.05 for the prewar pig iron series, 0.05 for the interwar pig iron series, and 0.29 for the interwar FRB series.

the total variation in the monthly growth rate of industrial production is due to predictable seasonal factors.[18]

Turning Points

The graphs in Figures 1A and 1B indicate that the turning points of our new index are grossly similar to those of the other indexes of production. In particular, all the indexes show significant recessions in 1893–1894, 1907–1908, 1920–1921, 1930–1933, and 1937–1938.

At the same time, however, there are some important differences between our index and various alternatives.[19] These differences are especially noticeable around the dates of major financial panics. For example, following the banking panic of May 1884, our index shows a much more immediate fall in production than does the pig iron series that has been used in other analyses. This is also the case around the panic of October 1907. The new index, like the Babson and Persons indexes, turns down perceptibly before the panic, whereas the frequently used pig iron series does not turn down until November 1907. These differences in the timing of real output movements around financial panics could have large effects in studies that seek to identify the direction of causation between panics and recessions.

A more general way to analyze the turning points of our index is to compare them to the National Bureau of Economic Research (NBER) reference dates for business cycle turning points. With respect to the most severe recessions, our index shows peaks and troughs that are quite close to those of the traditional NBER dating. In the case of the less virulent downturns, however, our index frequently has peaks and troughs that differ from the NBER dates by several months. For example, the NBER dates a peak in March 1899 whereas our index continues rising with only slight interruption until November 1899. These differences may be due to the fact that the NBER uses both real output and other indicators, such as interest rates and prices, to date cycles. Nevertheless, the finding that our new index has turning points that are sometimes quite different from NBER reference dates may alter how economists should date fluctuations in real output in the prewar era. Thus, as with the other characteristics of economic fluctuations examined in this article, the derivation of a new index of industrial production may lead to new views about the pre-World War II macroeconomy.

[18] See J. Joseph Beaulieu and Jeffrey Miron, "Seasonality in U.S. Manufacturing" (unpublished manuscript, Boston University, 1989).

[19] It is important to note that these differences in timing are not due to the fact that our index is seasonally unadjusted. The same patterns emerge when our series is adjusted using a regression against seasonal dummy variables and a linear trend.

Appendix

This appendix describes the base data and the methods used to construct our new index of industrial production. It also presents the final index.

SERIES USED AND VALUE-ADDED WEIGHTS ASSIGNED

Percentage weights are given in parentheses following the series name.

Pig Iron Capacity (31.91). For the period June 1884 to December 1940 there exist data on the capacity of pig iron furnaces in blast on the first day of the month. We average the observations for a given month and the following month to estimate the daily capacity of the average number of furnaces in blast in a given month. Since blast furnaces were typically run at full capacity, this series should provide a good measure of actual production. The data were collected by *Iron Age*, the main trade journal of the iron and steel industry. For this series we make no adjustment for production days because it is already approximately on a per production day basis. The pig iron series is assigned the value added of both blast furnace products and steel mill products because pig iron is the main input to steel production.

Anthracite Coal Shipments (9.92). This series, available for 1884 to 1940, is taken from *The Coal Trade* (later called *Saward's Annual*), a major trade publication. The only problem with the series is that no data were kept for 1924 to 1926. The anthracite coal series is assigned the value added of anthracite coal mining. This value-added figure is calculated by taking the total value added in coal mining available from *Historical Statistics* and prorating it between bituminous and anthracite coal on the basis of gross value.

Crude Petroleum Production, Appalachian Region (3.85). This series shows the output of crude petroleum in Pennsylvania, New York, Ohio, West Virginia, Kentucky, and Tennessee. These data were collected by the U.S. Geological Survey from reports of pipeline and other transportation companies. The Appalachian production series is available for 1890 to 1940. For 1884 to 1889 we splice on the output of crude petroleum in New York and Pennsylvania. This crude ratio splice is reasonable because in the 1880s New York and Pennsylvania accounted for at least 90 percent of total Appalachian production (on an annual basis). The petroleum series is assigned the value added in petroleum refining.

Sugar Meltings at Four Ports (2.53). Because the melting of cane sugar is the major step in sugar refining, this series can be used as a proxy for the output of refined sugar. The data were collected by Willett and Gray, publisher of the *Weekly Statistical Sugar Trade Journal*, and appear to be based on very detailed weekly surveys of major producers. This series is only available for 1890 to 1937. The sugar meltings series is assigned the value added in cane sugar refining and cane sugar not elsewhere mentioned.

Cattle Receipts at Chicago (5.42). The head of cattle arriving at the stockyards in Chicago should be a good proxy for the output of dressed beef because cattle were typically slaughtered soon after receipt and because Chicago was the U.S. meat-packing center in this period. This series is available for the entire sample period from the *Chicago Board of Trade Annual Report*. The cattle receipts series is assigned the value added in cattle slaughtering. This value-added figure was calculated by dividing the total value added in meat packing between beef and pork on the basis of gross value.

Hog Receipts at Chicago (7.76). The sources and issues involved in using this series are identical to those for the cattle receipts series.

Connellsville Coke Shipments (2.54). This series, only available for the period 1894 to 1935, is from the *Connellsville Courier*, a periodical covering the region. The series should provide a reasonable proxy for total coke production because the Connellsville region accounted for more than half of total production on an annual basis in the prewar period. Coke shipments are assigned the value added of coke oven products.

Minneapolis Flour Shipments (9.28). Because many of the major flour producers were located in Minneapolis in the prewar era, this series accounts for a substantial fraction of total flour production. The data are available from the *Annual Report of the Chamber of Commerce and the Board of Trade of the City of Minneapolis*. An examination of these records suggests that the series is quite complete and based on ample contemporary surveys. This series is assigned the value added in flour milling.

Wool Receipts at Boston (11.89). This series includes both the imports of wool and the shipments of domestic raw wool that passed through Boston on the way to New England textile mills. Because wool receipts at Boston account for approximately half of the domestic wool clip and between one-fourth and one-half of foreign imports, this series should be a reasonable proxy for the consumption of raw wool by textile producers. This series is available for 1888 to 1918 from the *Boston Chamber of Commerce Annual Report* and later from the *Survey of Current Business*. We assign this series the value added in woolen goods, worsted goods, wool pulling, and wool scouring.

Coffee Imports (2.18). The quantity of coffee imported is used to proxy for the production of processed coffee. The data on the physical quantity of imports for this and all the other import series are reported in the *Monthly Summary of the Foreign Commerce of the United States*. (The title of this publication and the publishing agency vary in the period before 1914.) The coffee imports series is assigned the value added in coffee roasting and spices.

Tin Imports (2.13). This series is assigned the value added of tin and other foils, tin cans, tinware not elsewhere classified, and tin and terne plate.

Crude Rubber Imports (5.97). Slight changes in coverage in both October 1890 and July 1910 are dealt with using ratio splices. Since rubber imports are used to proxy for the output of rubber goods, it is assigned the value added of all rubber products.

Raw Silk Imports (4.62). Silk imports are used as a proxy for the output of silk textiles. There is a very minor change in the coverage of this series which we correct for using a simple ratio splice in December 1924. This series is assigned the value added in the silk goods industry. This value-added figure is derived by taking Fabricant's number for silk and rayon goods combined and prorating it on the basis of the gross value of the two types of materials.

ADJUSTMENT FOR MISSING VALUES

While many of our series exist from 1884 to 1940, there is a certain amount of attrition at both ends of the index and some in the middle because of missing data on coal shipments in the 1920s. To deal with missing series we do the following. First, we recalculate the percentage weights, setting to zero the weight for the missing series. Second, to prevent discontinuous jumps in the series, we splice the series whenever there is a change in coverage. Specifically, we take the index for 1894 to 1923, for which all the series exist, as the base series and then use ratio splices on either end to append the less complete series to it.

ADJUSTMENT FOR TARIFF EFFECTS ON WOOL RECEIPTS

For most purposes, it is desirable to use our index in its least adulterated form. However, our index has a dramatic spike in mid-1897 that appears to be due to changes in the tariff on wool imports. This spike is sufficiently peculiar that it seems reasonable to present an alternative index for that year. To do this, we do not use the wool receipts series for the six months around the spike in wool receipts (February to July 1897). In making this adjustment, we use ratios to splice the series excluding wool receipts to the complete series in August 1897 but then use the complete series before February 1897 without a splice. This insures that the alternative changes only the observations for February to July 1897, not all earlier observations.

Table 2 presents the new index in both its basic form and with the minor adjustment for the effect of the tariff change on wool receipts.

TABLE 2
MIRON-ROMER INDEX OF INDUSTRIAL PRODUCTION, 1884–1940
(1909 = 100)

Year	January	February	March	April	May	June	July	August	September	October	November	December	Annual Average
1884	32.663	29.431	27.334	32.417	33.379	32.529	30.341	33.642	31.086	39.220	41.070	42.527	33.803
1885	35.326	31.070	31.372	33.941	34.757	34.386	30.918	31.329	33.523	43.127	47.974	42.973	35.891
1886	39.204	37.032	36.119	37.557	39.065	42.485	38.719	38.624	41.653	43.643	47.502	45.893	40.625
1887	39.015	39.705	39.667	38.546	38.505	37.058	36.082	39.074	41.553	47.254	48.023	43.236	40.643
1888	39.480	38.688	40.647	39.423	39.557	40.647	43.737	42.953	45.294	48.058	48.079	47.629	42.849
1889	42.128	44.540	41.061	41.480	44.462	46.024	51.524	44.493	45.283	53.171	53.015	50.542	46.477
1890	49.559	46.276	47.928	48.316	50.961	53.711	56.701	55.166	54.878	58.035	61.391	51.690	52.884
1891	55.409	54.288	56.316	48.469	47.600	51.910	57.242	55.833	56.872	64.819	69.095	64.993	56.904
1892	60.392	59.742	59.295	56.494	58.457	62.885	61.492	60.001	58.238	60.800	61.882	57.369	59.754
1893	55.857	56.202	55.670	58.165	55.306	53.950	51.272	44.536	42.720	48.753	47.575	48.109	51.510
1894	46.837	44.769	46.241	50.988	48.067	54.994	46.403	59.508	57.723	61.238	63.783	54.676	52.935
1895	54.305	59.056	56.091	56.810	58.480	61.422	65.404	68.532	62.433	71.535	71.750	66.012	62.653
1896	63.328	57.547	58.877	55.293	57.166	57.992	54.103	52.800	52.593	60.533	61.256	66.485	58.164
1897	55.224	65.597	66.613	84.313	70.553	69.415	68.310	64.985	66.984	69.954	71.567	67.950	68.455
1898	63.100	68.674	62.222	59.078	63.879	58.679	59.430	60.896	63.750	66.165	70.770	70.569	63.934
1899	68.140	66.931	68.664	63.411	67.595	73.302	74.476	74.717	74.161	75.746	77.117	74.992	71.604
1900	73.861	75.214	74.329	75.783	69.295	68.664	64.911	68.232	65.118	61.941	67.613	68.823	69.482
1901	69.643	71.739	78.872	75.537	80.885	80.181	80.838	86.653	81.543	79.826	85.057	81.344	79.343
1902	81.893	78.801		81.721	73.539	74.498	73.900	83.154	76.571	76.403	86.707	84.516	79.433
1903	83.149	84.555	85.724	84.833	83.485	89.291	87.148	93.639	87.414	73.288	75.042	72.568	83.345
1904	74.276	86.334	81.760	77.899	81.020	87.263	78.118	85.829	72.676	84.970	89.464	86.404	82.168
1905	93.714	96.550	92.465	93.843	89.031	97.103	86.292	93.886	89.297	95.278	93.436	93.880	92.898
1906	93.360	99.239	91.993	83.824	84.996	88.810	91.710	96.470	96.620	95.191	96.123	97.484	92.985
1907	95.781	97.889	96.950	97.378	95.414	97.813	99.264	105.710	97.179	93.398	81.228	71.268	94.106
1908	73.117	75.614	74.413	70.207	75.243	79.211	80.613	85.906	80.305	86.419	96.892	94.622	81.047
1909	91.660	99.782	97.895	90.816	94.327	99.274	99.357	99.562	101.209	108.008	111.270	106.841	100.000
1910	109.875	111.897	105.637	92.770	90.781	93.088	93.689	104.906	93.698	98.192	96.383	91.205	98.510
1911	92.979	96.479	95.179	95.804	91.739	94.220	100.463	100.931	96.579	102.223	100.462	99.965	97.252

1912	102.967	111.696	112.279	101.905	100.992	107.427	115.469	121.329	113.269	114.721	114.222	114.916	110.933
1913	118.687	117.834	112.744	108.121	106.299	111.631	109.059	115.755	116.286	108.856	107.716	107.199	111.682
1914	98.734	108.798	115.228	117.876	112.619	107.625	109.263	98.375	103.849	95.612	90.894	92.329	104.267
1915	95.962	112.322	122.909	123.367	126.742	119.807	122.857	124.795	129.052	134.790	145.126	156.137	126.155
1916	158.881	161.200	154.670	148.696	152.434	153.823	131.197	140.186	129.589	141.590	143.638	151.944	147.321
1917	167.560	138.983	159.420	167.068	169.931	180.591	150.507	168.540	159.861	157.079	158.831	151.446	160.818
1918	138.945	148.571	151.569	159.383	181.297	165.793	177.825	152.389	161.296	151.073	152.910	146.861	157.326
1919	142.696	149.133	175.749	174.088	165.780	151.116	183.409	147.749	158.924	151.000	184.366	183.408	163.951
1920	188.548	200.361	205.850	184.287	155.123	165.860	160.519	163.336	134.146	124.872	142.416	121.442	162.230
1921	123.392	131.139	130.893	123.679	106.174	114.304	108.381	119.869	117.457	133.106	143.169	151.867	125.286
1922	152.772	176.200	169.564	137.692	134.225	157.703	171.185	150.457	141.971	202.040	185.052	211.121	165.832
1923	213.366	207.595	219.442	218.093	220.596	218.777	183.047	164.666	136.006	159.379	156.197	189.616	190.565
1924	174.347	203.993	171.978	207.044	166.825	155.102	141.532	146.605	161.537	192.922	201.284	186.075	175.770
1925	211.625	191.158	207.232	189.900	194.892	185.285	189.792	192.751	179.293	198.567	215.119	220.923	198.045
1926	231.678	215.503	226.918	211.027	192.517	178.711	210.252	184.094	208.725	195.042	219.704	207.721	206.824
1927	223.671	190.618	202.582	232.712	212.356	209.936	213.196	201.001	189.340	187.029	200.560	177.709	203.393
1928	210.119	203.581	213.080	214.013	197.230	190.558	193.207	190.626	211.114	223.226	206.807	224.832	206.533
1929	263.791	294.849	241.635	255.798	246.418	240.253	237.105	221.448	217.829	215.283	222.017	221.397	239.819
1930	223.833	226.560	218.751	219.995	209.518	223.314	201.930	202.824	184.965	210.960	167.043	182.274	205.997
1931	176.986	185.612	192.290	197.385	179.835	210.721	202.097	179.401	172.174	180.480	198.151	201.333	189.705
1932	152.278	140.377	167.411	153.193	141.321	159.795	145.559	147.121	141.451	153.656	135.835	136.726	147.894
1933	129.017	113.479	115.877	109.910	128.269	151.576	221.452	210.920	207.182	190.378	170.434	162.880	159.281
1934	184.349	164.288	170.521	187.549	197.562	202.631	187.069	140.726	150.742	134.765	159.877	100.768	165.071
1935	164.291	201.865	184.372	171.052	146.230	170.133	198.033	172.670	173.749	171.206	145.481	180.875	173.330
1936	164.985	173.532	162.884	197.327	178.358	194.893	198.554	194.232	213.904	193.485	202.694	227.087	191.828
1937	215.962	232.051	207.278	216.205	223.829	232.285	200.692	220.668	234.997	221.343	215.345	231.944	221.050
1938	177.320	171.663	161.271	140.976	138.488	139.900	130.150	149.443	157.510	164.739	167.273	167.767	155.542
1939	172.516	156.213	182.798	158.482	184.297	172.813	179.191	179.728	192.803	215.692	207.562	281.021	190.260
1940	275.583	200.597	232.237	262.499	221.192	252.392	282.412	285.488	320.230	304.910	309.145	372.697	276.615

Index Excluding Wool Receipts for February 1897 to July 1897

1897	55.224	60.798	57.812	59.811	63.079	63.925	60.042	64.985	66.984	69.954	71.567	67.950	63.511

Source: See the text for a description of the data and procedures used to derive the new Miron-Romer index.

Regulating the Quebec Dairy Industry, 1905–1921: Peeling Off the Joseph Label

RUTH DUPRÉ

From its beginning the Quebec dairy industry was characterized by many small factories producing butter and cheese of such a low quality that the British called all bad cheese coming from Canada "Joseph." The Société d'industrie laitière, created in 1882 to promote the industry, asked the government to impose compulsory inspection, licensing, and grading. Between 1905 and 1921 the government finally but reluctantly responded.

In Quebec, as in most Western economies, agricultural policy is nowadays a matter of regulating prices and quantities in order to increase farmers' incomes. Looking back at how this policy evolved through the twentieth century, three phases can be discerned. Beginning with the century, the government first regulated quality; then in the thirties it began regulating price; and finally in the late fifties it began to control the quantity produced. This article concerns the first phase, when both the provincial and federal governments adopted a series of acts to make inspection, licensing, and grading of dairy products compulsory. How did these regulations come about, who asked for them and why, and how rapidly and enthusiastically did the government respond?

Since G. Stigler's influential contribution, the most widely accepted theory of regulation among economists is his, that "regulation is acquired by the industry regulated and is designed and operated primarily for its benefit."[1] In this model, regulation is a good for which there is a market, a political market. Some groups—industries or occupations—ask for policies to protect them from "destructive competition," uncertainty, or undesirable market fluctuations, and the politicians respond to their requests, most strongly when they feel this can be crucial for their reelection. The theory based on a "private interest" rationale has come to replace the traditional view of regulation as an instrument for correcting market failures in the "public interest."

The political-market model provides a useful general framework for

The Journal of Economic History, Vol. L, No. 2 (June 1990). ISSN 0022-0507.

The author is Assistant Professor at the Ecole des Hautes Etudes Commerciales de Montréal, 5255 Decelles, Montreal, Quebec, Canada, H3T 1V6.

She wishes to thank Lee Alston; the participants at the EHA Conference, Gary Libecap, Marvin McInnis, and Lou Cain; her colleagues, Michel Patry and Yvan Stringer; the editors for their helpful comments; and Chantal Malo for her research assistance.

[1] G. Stigler, "The Theory of Economic Regulation," *The Bell Journal of Economics and Management Science*, 2 (Spring 1971), pp. 3–21.

analyzing government intervention in agriculture because, in assuming that regulation is shaped by the forces of supply and demand, it directs attention to factors bearing on the benefits and the costs of regulation. Agriculture is an industry characterized by many relatively small producers, making private voluntary arrangements very difficult to carry out. As there are no good substitutes for regulation, the benefits of government intervention are large enough to exceed the organizational costs to obtain it, costs which increase with the number of individuals to be organized. A problem with the model is when the group to be regulated is not unanimous and does not have homogeneous interests. No farmer is against a higher price for his product and many would accept quotas in order to obtain higher prices. They do, however, have quite divergent positions about quality regulation. The Société d'industrie laitière (SIL), the group lobbying for government intervention regarding quality, was clearly a minority elite group in Quebec; it appears that the majority of the dairy producers resented being coerced. The government response then becomes a more complex problem for those who, at the time, had to decide whether to regulate and for those who now try to explain their actions.

Very little attention has been paid to the first steps in regulating Quebec agriculture.[2] Obviously, to discover the government's point of view, one would turn to the Parliamentary Debates, but the Quebec Debates were not published at the time they took place and the project to reconstitute them some years later from selected newspaper reports was completed only to 1905. I examined two Montreal daily newspapers, *La Presse* and *Le Devoir*, without much success. The absence of indexes limited the search to one month before and after each session and there were very few comments, not counting the official summaries of the laws adopted at the Assembly sessions. A systematic search of the annual reports of the Quebec Department of Agriculture yielded not much more. Although the documents are voluminous (from 325 pages in 1869 to 960 in 1930) and contain much information, most of it is of a technical or financial nature. The only useful information for the present purpose consists of some speeches by the Minister of Agriculture and of some comments scattered in the reports of the industry inspectors. It proved easier to obtain the dairy industry point of view. The SIL, created in 1882, published an annual report containing all the speeches and papers given at its annual convention as well as the whole discussion around them.[3] The association, although far from repre-

[2] The only studies which devote more than a few lines to the matter are the historical studies of regulation in general of J. A. Corry, *The Growth of Government Activities Since Confederation* (study prepared for the Royal Commission on Dominion-Provincial Relations, Ottawa, 1939) and of C. Baggaley, *The Emergence of the Regulatory State in Canada, 1867–1939* (Ottawa, 1981).

[3] The SIL documents are in French, even the few speeches originally delivered in English. I translated all the quotations.

sentative of the whole dairy community, was its only voice until the Union des cultivateurs catholiques was founded in 1923.

A PERSISTENT PROBLEM OF QUALITY

Quebec and Ontario agriculture shifted from wheat growing to dairy and livestock farming in the decades following the Confederation of 1867. Butter and cheese were produced in both provinces, but Quebec tended to specialize in butter and Ontario in cheese, especially after 1900. The two products had quite different markets. More than 80 percent of Canadian cheese was exported to Great Britain while more than 80 percent of Canadian butter went into the domestic market.[4] At the beginning both were produced on the farm, but soon production shifted to the factory, a shift more pronounced and much more rapid in cheese than in butter. In fact a significant proportion of butter continued to be "homemade" throughout the period. The first cheese factory opened in 1864 and the first butter creamery in 1871; their number increased rapidly from 25 in 1871 to 1,992 in 1901, reaching 2,142 in 1911.[5] In Quebec much more than in Ontario these factories were very small. Quite often a village contained three or four dairy factories, and they seem to have fought over the milk supply and the consumers.[6] Along with the mushrooming of small factories came a pervasive problem of poor quality. Complaints about the low quality of butter and cheese filled the official documents year after year and preoccupied the SIL. This poor quality was caused by the conditions of their fabrication: the often dirty milk sometimes came from diseased animals and was almost always diluted; the factory was badly equipped and dirty; and the manufacturer was often incompetent or lazy.[7] Moreover, before the advent in the 1900s of mechanical refrigeration in warehouses, trains, and ships, butter, even if properly made, often deteriorated badly by the time it reached the market.

It is not surprising to find a persistent quality problem in an industry with so many small producers. The literature on reputation suggests that

[4] The ratio of exports to production is calculated from the figures supplied by R. Duhaime, "Les exportations canadiennes de produits laitiers, 1867 à 1955," *L'Actualité économique*, 23 (July-Sept. 1957), pp. 248–49, for all Canada because there are no export data at the provincial level.

[5] Census data as reported in the Quebec Statistical Yearbooks.

[6] The number of dairy factories declined significantly after the turn of the century: from a peak of 2,142 in 1911 to 1,768 in 1921 and 1,318 in 1931. Their average size, however, was still much smaller in the thirties than in Ontario according to a federal government survey of cheese factories in 1932/3 reported by W. M. Drummond, "Problems of the Canadian Dairy Industry," in H. A. Innis, ed, *The Dairy Industry in Canada* (Toronto, 1937), p. 146. The average volume of production in Quebec was 23.2 tons per year, with not much difference between regions, compared to 81.5 tons in Ontario (56.3 for Eastern Ontario, 62.9 for Central Ontario, and 159.8 for Western Ontario).

[7] "Jack-of-all-trades" is perhaps more appropriate than "lazy," the latter an accusation often found in the government reports. Inspectors complained that they often found factories locked at 3:00 P.M. or looked after by a young son because the cheesemaker was working in the fields.

firms have an incentive to provide good-quality products in order to build up a good reputation, so long as the present value of the expected returns from long-term sales exceed the short-term returns from quality deception and lower cost of production.[8] For this repeat-sale enforcement mechanism to work, however, identification of the individual firm's output is necessary. If this is not possible, then quality depreciates via a standard externality argument, as G. A. Akerlof presents it.[9] When buyers use some aggregate market statistic to judge the quality of prospective purchases, producers have an incentive to provide bad-quality products since "the returns for good quality accrue mainly to the entire group whose statistic is affected rather than to the individual."[10] In this case, social and private returns differ and government intervention may increase social welfare. Did Quebec butter and cheese producers have such an externality problem? The SIL certainly thought so and used the point to argue for government intervention.

THE "SOCIETE D'INDUSTRIE LAITIERE" DEMANDS

The SIL was founded at the end of 1882 "to encourage the improvement of the butter and cheese industry." Although it refused to be considered as a political organization, it is clear that the SIL saw its role as educating not only the farmers but also the politicians. One member of the executive told the convention in 1890, "what we, members of the SIL, have to do is to persuade the two governments, provincial and federal, that the question [of bad factories] is crucial in order that they may do something," and another one said in 1904, "I do not blame the government. They cannot always realize the necessity of it [licensing]. We must inform them."[11] The group was not strictly speaking a producers' association, contrary to what the usual English translation of SIL—Quebec Dairymen's Association—suggests. Its membership never exceeded 1,600, while there were about 150,000 dairy producers in the province. Moreover, its composition was rather peculiar, consisting of course of dairy farmers and butter and cheese makers, but also of agronomists, officials from the Department of Agriculture, politicians such as the Minister of Agriculture, and members of the federal and provincial parliaments from rural ridings, Montreal butter and cheese

[8] For instance, B. Klein and K. B. Leffler, "The Role of Market Forces in Assuring Contractual Performance," *Journal of Political Economy*, 89 (Aug. 1981), pp. 615–41. This "reputation" idea seems to be gaining popularity in economic history. Three papers from the 1989 World Cliometrics Conference apply it to very different situations: Gary Libecap to U.S. government meat inspection in 1891, Akira Motomura to coinage depreciation in seventeenth-century Spain, and Avner Greif to medieval long-distance trade.

[9] See G. A. Akerlof, "The Market for Lemons: Quality Uncertainty and the Market Mechanism," *Quarterly Journal of Economics*, 84 (Aug. 1970), pp. 488–500.

[10] Ibid., p. 488.

[11] SIL Ninth Annual Report for 1890, *Quebec Sessional Papers*, 24 (1890), p. 26; and SIL Twenty-third Annual Report for 1904, *Quebec Sessional Papers*, 39 (1906), p. 139.

dealers, members of the clergy and of the liberal professions—doctors, lawyers, and notaries.

Given this composition, it is not surprising that the SIL asked the government to impose compulsory inspection, licensing, and grading in order to get rid of poor-quality producers. The "nonproducer" members did not need to care about the cost of regulation, that is, the cost of providing quality, and many of them—agronomists, inspectors, politicians—would even gain from regulation by enlarging the scope of their activities. To legitimate their demands, they argued in substance that the industry faced a free-rider problem. For instance, at the 1890 convention a cheesemaker declared that "to obtain good prices, two things are necessary: not only must we make good cheese, but our neighbor must also make good cheese." One SIL director, Father Montminy, added, "Understand me well, when we talk about those badly run factories, we want to defend the interests of the whole industry and to protect the competent producers so that we will not all be considered incompetent." At the same convention Doctor C. J. Coulombe concluded his lecture on the problem of small factories by saying that "they were the worst enemies of the dairy industry . . . because they harm our reputation in the export market considerably."[12]

Their contention rested on two types of evidence. The first was the practice, supposedly widespread, of the *achat en bloc*, that is, the buying by Montreal dealers of a whole lot of butter or of cheese from a large number—between 40 and 50—of producers, at a uniform price and without distinctions of quality. The practice was denounced by many government officials, inspectors, and members of the SIL as the source of all the industry's problems because "this average pricing is a mechanism which does not reward the competent and does not punish the incompetent."[13] Moreover, the Quebec dairy producers had a serious problem of bad reputation on the other side of the Atlantic, the British labeling as "French" or "Joseph" all bad cheese from Canada.[14]

All this might be convincing were it not for some indications in the few historical studies of the Canadian dairy industry that individual reputations could be made. In his classic study J. A. Ruddick wrote about the butter industry that "there were individuals who acquired

[12] SIL Ninth Annual Report for 1890, pp. 36, 41, 46.

[13] Inspector J. N. Allard's Annual Report to the Minister of Agriculture, in the Annual Report of the Ministry of Agriculture, *Quebec Sessional Papers*, 38 (1905), p. 131.

[14] This was stated at least twice: in the SIL Thirteenth Annual Report for 1894, *Quebec Sessional Papers*, 29 (1895), p. 56, and in the SIL Twenty-third Annual Report for 1904, p. 180; and confirmed by E. Minville, *L'agriculture, Etudes de notre milieu* (Montreal, 1943), p. 256. Joseph is the first name given at their christening to all Catholic males. As very close to 100 percent of French-Canadians were then also Catholic, Joseph was synonymous with French-Canadian.

reputations,'' and about the cheese industry that ''some individual farmers in Quebec and in Ontario earned reputation[s] for turning out high class articles . . . *the maker's identity being preserved* [emphasis added] as his product passed through the channels of trade.'' He added that ''exporters (or their representatives) located at centers such as Ingersoll, Belleville, and Brockville [all situated in Ontario] and cheese became known as 'Ingersolls' and 'Bellevilles.' ''[15] In addition, W. M. Drummond tells a fascinating story of how the Ontario local cheese auctions, trying to sell all cheese at a single price to the highest bidder, became a farce by the beginning of the twentieth century, as the best producers were selling ''on the curb'' to regular buyers. It shows that the individual producer could stand out from the crowd.[16] Although most of this latter evidence concerns Ontario, could things have been so different in Quebec? There are indications that many producers escaped the Joseph label. A good example is the Temiscouata big butter producer, given as a model of the benefits of large size by a speaker in 1894, who declared:

> I do not run after the market (I have not been to Montreal for five years) because this is the market which runs after me. It is known in the trade that I make a considerable quantity of butter. Exporters prefer to buy 20,000 pounds in one deal . . . they come to my place and my desk is inundated with orders.[17]

And beyond the anecdote, it is quite often mentioned that good Quebec cheese was sold as ''Ontario,'' a practice the Quebec Minister of Agriculture strongly deplored, but which seems to have been a way for the good producers to get a price closer to the real value of their output.

If many producers could escape the Joseph label, it was not a free-rider problem that the industry faced but a problem of competition considered by the SIL to be ''destructive.'' Complaints did indeed concern the number and small scale of firms as much as the quality of the output. For instance, Edouard A. Barnard, the most outstanding agronomist in Quebec, told the annual convention in 1896:

> I am not afraid to say that we would be in a better position if we had a third less [factories]. We would have less cheese and butter to sell, but of a better quality and perhaps for as much money as we obtain now.[18]

[15] J. A. Ruddick, ''The Development of the Dairy Industry in Canada,'' in H. A. Innis, ed, *The Dairy Industry in Canada*, pp. 33, 44, 49. He should be one of the most credible authors on the subject. As Innis wrote in his introduction (p. 10), Ruddick's curriculum vitae reads like a history of dairying in Canada: from cheesemaker in Ontario and in Quebec in the 1880s to instructor and superintendent of the Queen's University dairy school in the 1890s to federal Dairy Commissioner from the 1900s to the 1930s.

[16] Drummond, ''Problems of the Canadian Dairy Industry,'' pp. 158–59.

[17] SIL Thirteenth Annual Report for 1894, p. 49.

[18] SIL Fifteenth Annual Report for 1896, *Quebec Sessional Papers*, 31 (1897), p. 88.

A few years later, in 1902, the secretary of the SIL, J. de L. Taché, was even more explicit:

Butter and cheese factories are established anywhere they wish, hence their unreasonable multiplication in some places and a competition disastrous for everybody; anybody, with or without qualifications, can become a butter or cheese maker, hence so many inferior products. It is this situation which leads the SIL to demand that butter and cheese makers organize themselves in a closed professional association, and that the number of factories be regulated.[19]

And finally, at the 1905 Convention, the resolution was adopted unanimously that "the SIL is in principle in favor of the adoption of laws to restrict the increase of small factories."[20] The quality issue was thus most probably a facade to disguise the much less socially acceptable desire of getting rid of competition.

The SIL wanted government intervention from the beginning but prior to 1900 only discussed it and seemed very reluctant to push the idea. A resolution unanimously voted in 1884 to create a "golden book," in which the outstanding butter and cheese makers would be registered, was never implemented because it was found to be too radical. A decade later, in 1894, Doctor Coulombe still declared that "licensing would be a good thing but this falls into the sphere of arbitrariness. I still believe that persuasion is better."[21] After 1900 the SIL became much more assertive and its demands for government intervention much louder, as witness the resolution of the January 1905 convention:

It is moreover recommanded to the attention of the government that it consider the necessity, in the interest of the province of Quebec dairy industry, of imposing a license for all butter and cheese factories. The necessity of such legislation is beyond any doubt . . . the dairy interests of this province are at stake.[22]

What the resolution does not say, however, and what the discussion around it shows, is the number of members still hesitating about how strict application should be. To a member's question about what would happen if someone wanted to open a factory across the road from an existing one, the president replied that the exclusion of the incompetents would allow among other things to "space them suitably." But the secretary declared that "the regulation should not be vexatious. All those who are already there have the right to stay and no politician will want to ask the government to impose binding conditions to this examination."[23]

[19] SIL Twenty-first Annual Report for 1902, *Quebec Sessional Papers*, 37 (1904), p. 147.

[20] SIL Twenty-fourth Annual Report for 1905, *Quebec Sessional Papers*, 40 (1907), p. 193.

[21] SIL Thirteenth Annual Report for 1894, p. 46.

[22] SIL Twenty-third Annual Report for 1904, p. 145.

[23] Ibid., pp. 142–44.

THE GOVERNMENT RESPONDS

There was some government regulatory activity before the 1900s. As early as 1870 the Quebec government adopted an act to prevent the supply of watered, sour, or dirty milk to dairy factories.[24] In 1886 the federal government prohibited the fabrication, sale, import, and use of margarine, a measure highly appreciated by and very beneficial to the butter producers, and a few years later, in 1893, it adopted an act to prevent the imitation of cheese. However, the SIL-advocated measures to regulate inspection, licensing, and grading in order to improve quality came only in the period from 1905 to 1921. The measures were taken by both the Quebec and the federal governments, as both have jurisdiction over agriculture—the federal government over dairy products moving into interprovincial and export trade and the provincial government over the making of the products. The Quebec government passed three acts: the first in 1905 made inspection compulsory (5EdVII c17); the second in 1910 required permits and certificates to operate a dairy factory as of January 1912 (1 GeoV c16); and the third in 1921 integrated inspectors into the Department of Agriculture (11 GeoV c37). At the federal level, the 1914 Act (4–5 GeoV c7) made the 1893 Act more comprehensive and the 1921 Act introduced official government grading of dairy products (11–12 GeoV c28).

One cannot say that the government at either level seemed in a rush to intervene. It took 8 to 20 years from the time the SIL began its lobbying to when the governments legislated. The Quebec Minister of Agriculture's speech to the SIL for its twenty-fifth anniversary in 1906 illustrates how unenthusiastic the government was about regulating:

> I do not wish to upset or destroy anything, I have no program, I only want to improve the situation as much as possible . . . . I seriously doubt that the province has the [constitutional] power to impose certificates of competence. . . . I would recommend, instead of these certificates, to encourage the young farmers' sons to attend classes at the St-Hyacinthe Dairy School . . . . The new law on inspection will probably be sufficient: let's look at its impact for a few years before doing anything else . . . .[25]

Searching for alternatives, the government also strongly encouraged the cooperative movement.[26]

[24] As the SIL reports often point out, this legislation was seldom, if ever, enforced; the factory owners were fighting for milk and thus accepted almost anything because they feared that the farmer would otherwise go to his neighboring competitor.

[25] Excerpts from the speech by the Honorable Jules Allard, Quebec Minister of Agriculture in SIL Twenty-fifth Annual Report for 1906, *Quebec Sessional Papers*, 41 (1908), pp. 193–95.

[26] The SIL also strongly supported the cooperatives as a solution to the problems of a uniform price and of bad reputation. The Quebec Cheesemakers' Cooperative was founded in 1910 under the patronage of the Quebec Minister of Agriculture and of the SIL. J. P. Kesteman, *Histoire du syndicalisme agricole au Québec* (Montreal, 1985), p. 31, writes that it was a great success from the beginning, but a more critical reading of the Coop annual reports shows that it met with a certain success but also many difficulties.

Why was the government response not more enthusiastic? This was not, of course, a time when governments jumped into action as easily and as rapidly as they tend to do now. Beyond this one gets the impression from what the Minister of Agriculture and politicians from rural ridings said to the SIL that the government would have liked to do something for the dairy industry but was really afraid that the silent but voting majority of farmers would resent being coerced. Farmers were indeed crucial voters for two reasons. First, a large proportion of Quebec's population was still rural: 60 percent in 1901, 44 percent in 1921. Moreover, the electoral system was, in the British tradition, based on a majority of seats and not of votes, and for almost a century after Confederation rural interests had a disproportionate share of the seats. In 1867, with 12 percent of the population, Montreal was represented at the provincial elections by 3 ridings out of 65 (less than 5 percent) and in 1930, when it had 30 percent of the population, by 15 out of 90 (17 percent).[27]

The government did finally act between 1905 and 1921. More than one factor may explain why it did so then. First, SIL pressures and demands were much stronger after 1900 than before. Moreover, the 1900s were generally a turning point in the behavior of the Canadian and Quebec governments from using "willingness" to "coercion."[28] Regulation was in the air: the Quebec government also introduced regulation on work accidents in 1909 and prohibited the export of pulpwood in 1910. As for the political stakes, they may not have been as high as the above numbers suggest. In the century following the Confederation of 1867 Quebec politics was nothing if not stable. The Conservative Party ruled the province for 30 almost uninterrupted years from 1867 to 1896; the Liberal Party then followed for a 40-year reign between 1897 to 1936, and the Union Nationale of Maurice Duplessis stayed in power from 1936 to Duplessis's death in 1959, with a brief Liberal interlude from 1940 to 1944. From 1905 to 1920, the period of concern here, the same Liberal Premier Minister, Lomer Gouin, won all his elections with 80 to 90 percent of the seats (and 55 to 70 percent of the votes), two (in 1904 and 1919) by acclamation, that is, with a sufficient number of unopposed candidates to win before the polls opened. This extraordinary popularity perhaps helps explain why the government dared to do such things as regulate the dairy industry (although it may also show that the government did it cautiously enough to stay out of political trouble).[29]

[27] A. Bernard, *La politique au Canada et au Québec* (2nd edn., Montreal, 1977), p. 36.

[28] This is what Corry, "The Growth of Government," argued for Canada and J. I. Gow, *Histoire de l'administration publique québécoise* (Montreal, 1986), p. 140, for Quebec.

[29] I did an analysis of the content of Quebec electoral platforms—as compiled by J. L. Roy, *Les programmes électoraux du Québec, 1867–1966* (Montreal, 1970)—which concerned agriculture. Not surprisingly perhaps, the candidates talked very little about regulation and, later on, price fixing, and much about subsidies, agricultural credit, and electrification.

Finally, if agriculture in Quebec had been transformed, during the period when the government came to regulate quality, from the traditional diversified activity it was in the nineteenth century to a more specialized one, quality could have become an issue for a larger number of producers. But this specialization did not happen until much later, after the Second World War, and a typical Quebec farm in the twenties still produced, according to a 1925 survey of the farmers' union, "some hay, grains, potatoes, milk, livestock, eggs and wool."[30] The significant change which took place in the industry in the period of government regulation is the sharp shift from cheese to butter production beginning in the 1900s.[31] The shift was brought about by push and pull factors. On the one hand Quebec dairy producers seem to have been pushed out of cheese; they were not able to rival Ontario, much less New Zealand producers, who were to become the most important exporters to Great Britain after 1923. But at the same time a rapidly increasing population, urbanization, and a growing consumption per capita of dairy products pulled them into the production of fluid milk and butter for the domestic market.[32] The impact of this shift on the decision of the government to regulate is not easy to evaluate. All we know is that ironically, as the market was now domestic and as a significant proportion of butter was still made on the farm, quality was probably less, not more, of an issue when the government finally tried to peel off the Joseph label.[33]

[30] Reported in P. A. Linteau, R. Durocher, J. C. Robert, *Histoire du Québec contemporain* (Montreal, 1979), pp. 439–40. M. Morisset, in *L'agriculture familiale au Québec* (Paris, 1987), identifies three phases in the evolution of modern Quebec agriculture: a traditional or "self-sufficient" era from 1854 to 1939, a diversified market-oriented period from 1939 to 1966, and a specialized one from 1966 onwards. Although one can argue that 1939 is late for traditional as the dominant type, it is clear that specialization did not occur in the period under discussion.

[31] Between 1900 and 1910 the production of cheese in Quebec declined from 81 to 58 million pounds while the production of butter increased from 25 to 42 million pounds, to which should be added between 18 and 20 million pounds of homemade. The number of factories followed a similar trend, with those producing butter increasing from 445 to 787 and those producing cheese decreasing from 1,207 to 1,062 between 1901 and 1911. One cannot infer, however, from these figures any conclusion about the average scale of production because some 300 combined factories (producing both butter and cheese) should be added to the above firms but the available data do not allow us to break down the production of these "combined." See F. A. Angers, "Documentation statistique," in E. Minville, *L'agriculture*, pp. 512–13.

[32] This is what the few existing studies on the Quebec dairy industry at the time argue. See N. Perron, "Genèse des activités laitières, 1850–1960," in N. Séguin, ed, *Agriculture et colonisation au Québec* (Montreal, 1980), pp. 122–24, and Duhaime, "Les exportations canadiennes," p. 261.

[33] The proportion of butter made on the farm went from 50 percent in 1900 to 25 percent in 1920. The proportion was even larger in the rest of Canada, as homemade butter still represented 75 percent in 1900 and close to 50 percent in 1920 of Canadian production. The Quebec government regulations on inspection and licensing concerned only the factories, defined as having at least three milk and cream suppliers for butter and five for cheese.

The Revolution of Ideas: Widespread Patenting and Invention During the English Industrial Revolution

RICHARD J. SULLIVAN

Sectors of the English economy recognized as technological leaders have records of accelerated patent activity soon after 1760. But the patent record also reveals considerable inventive activity during the same period in industries not normally associated with advancing technology. It is therefore unlikely that there was a "leading technological sector." The widespread increase in patenting is consistent with macroeconomic causes of accelerated invention.

According to the most conservative of recent estimates, increased growth of productivity accounts for approximately 30 percent of increased growth of total output during the English industrial revolution.[1] Since a primary source of productivity growth is innovation, which in turn depends upon invention, eighteenth-century inventive activity remains an intriguing matter of inquiry, despite an extensive literature on the subject. Writers have been concerned with the temporal pattern of invention across the various sectors of the economy, but a lack of systematic evidence has hampered research. In this article I attack this deficiency by investigating patents and invention, from 1711 to 1850, in several prominent English industries.

In the considerable discussion of the early concentration and later extension of invention across industry, consensus favors a "leading technological sector" hypothesis: in the early years of the industrial revolution (perhaps 1760 to 1780), inventions were concentrated in a few important industries. David Landes, for example, writes that "critical innovations were concentrated at first in a small sector of the economy," with invention subsequently spreading to other industries "on an ever-widening front."[2] There is less consensus concerning the extent of the spread of invention, but the prevailing opinion seems to

The Journal of Economic History, Vol. L, No. 2 (June 1990). ISSN 0022-0507.

The author is Assistant Professor of Economics at the College of the Holy Cross, Worcester, MA 01610.

He thanks Jeremy Atack, David Wishart, Carolyn Cooper, Leslie Sullivan, Julian Simon, Tim Sullivan, Jack Powelson, Thomas Hughes, and Paul Hohenberg for their helpful comments.

[1] N. F. R. Crafts, *British Economic Growth During the Industrial Revolution* (Oxford, 1985), p. 82. The productivity measure is total factor productivity, a ratio of total output to a weighted average of inputs.

[2] David Landes, *The Unbound Prometheus* (Cambridge, MA, 1969), p. 78, 41. See also Peter Mathias, *The First Industrial Nation* (New York, 1969), p. 134; R. M. Hartwell, "The Causes of the Industrial Revolution" in R.M. Hartwell, ed., *The Causes of the Industrial Revolution in England* (London, 1967), p. 79; and Crafts, *British Economic Growth*, pp. 85–88.

hold with Donald McCloskey, that "ordinary inventiveness was widespread in the British economy 1780 to 1860."[3] N. F. R. Crafts has recently disputed this, writing that the industrial revolution does not "imply a widespread, rapid growth of productivity in manufacturing" and that "it does not seem appropriate to regard innovativeness as pervasive."[4]

The patent record shows that areas of the English economy recognized as technological leaders do, in fact, have records of early acceleration of patent activity. But it also reveals considerable inventive activity, early on, in industries not normally associated with advancing technology, casting doubt on the "leading technological sector" hypothesis, though supporting a widespread increase in invention.

SOURCES, DEFINITIONS, AND RELIABILITY OF PATENT DATA

The data are compiled from a subject index of patents for invention.[5] Because of their recognized importance, I study six industries: textiles, metals, field agriculture, ocean shipping, heavy chemicals, and railroads.[6] Following Jacob Schmookler, I have included patents in an industrial group if the industry would be expected to use the invention.[7] I also study two other important groups of inventions, steam engines and production machinery, but present their data separately from the industry data for two reasons. First, there was no production machine industry in the eighteenth century; until the development of a specialized machine tool industry, most industries built their own machines. Second, steam engines and production machinery belong in a different taxonomic scheme from the industrial groups, perhaps a scheme that defines groups by a common set of general principles of knowledge, such as mechanics.

Patents are imperfect measures of invention, so to what extent are the patent data reliable? Many inventions are not patentable; in farming, for example, many biological and organizational advances which increased productivity were not patentable. Any inferences I make from patent

[3] Donald N. McCloskey, "The Industrial Revolution 1780–1860: A Survey," in Roderick Floud and Donald N. McCloskey, eds., *The Economic History of Britain Since 1700* (Cambridge, 1981), p. 109.

[4] Crafts, *British Economic Growth*, pp. 86–87.

[5] Bennet Woodcroft, *Subject Matter Index of Patents of Invention* (London, 1857). Dates have been corrected using A. A. Gomme, "Date Corrections of English Patents, 1617–1752," *Transactions of the Newcomen Society* 33 (1932/33), pp. 159–64, and D. R. Jamieson, "Introduction," in Bennet Woodcroft, *Alphabetical Index of Patentees of Inventions* (London, 1857/1969), pp. v–xv. Definitions of the patent groups are in the Appendix. Additional detail about the source and of patent procedures is available upon request from the author.

[6] I use the industry as a basis for classification because most writing about eighteenth-century English invention focuses on industrial sectors. In his discussion of this paper, Thomas Hughes noted that classification based on productive systems (for example, motive power or machine tools) might be more appropriate.

[7] Jacob Schmookler, *Invention and Economic Growth* (Cambridge, MA, 1966), p. 20.

data are strictly limited to patentable invention. Moreover, although changes in patenting do reflect changes in inventive output, they are more closely tied to changes in the level of resources devoted to invention.[8] Throughout this article, therefore, the term "invention" refers to inventive effort represented by the resources devoted to discovery or development of new productive processes or products. Even with these caveats, however, there are concerns regarding the propensity to patent (the ratio of patents to patentable invention), both cross-sectionally and through time.

One hazardous use of patent data is a cross-sectional comparison of industrial patenting as an indication of relative rates of invention. F. M. Scherer has found that in contemporary U. S. corporations, industry-specific characteristics explain as much of the cross-sectional variation in the level of patents held by corporations as does variation in research and development expenditures.[9] Thus I make very limited comparisons of patenting experience across industry.

The ratio of patents to patentable invention was probably not constant over time. But the industry-specific characteristics noted above are apt to be stable through time relative to the changes we might expect of inventive activity. And there is little reason to expect that institutional change, or changes in the cost of obtaining a patent, changed the propensity to patent enough to mask the information in the patent data regarding the temporal pattern of patentable invention. I therefore interpret change in patents through time as a meaningful indicator of change in patentable invention.[10]

INDUSTRIAL INVENTION, 1711–1850

Textiles accounted for the largest share of patents issued, with 15 percent of the 13,023 patents issued over the period, confirming the central role that textile technology played in the industrial revolution (see Table 1). The next largest share benefited ocean shipping, followed by metals, railroads, field agriculture, and heavy chemicals.

The low shares for field agriculture and heavy chemicals deserve comment. Field agriculture's 3 percent share of total patents is small relative to its size in the economy: agriculture generated an average of

[8] See Ariel Pakes and Margaret Simpson, "Patent Renewal Data," in M. N. Baily and C. Winston, eds., *Brookings Papers on Economic Activity: Microeconomics, 1989* (Washington, 1989), p. 365.

[9] F. M. Scherer, "The Propensity to Patent," *International Journal of Industrial Organization*, 1 (Mar. 1983), pp. 107–28.

[10] Kenneth Sokoloff analyzes early U.S. invention using patent data. See Kenneth Sokoloff, "Inventive Activity in Early Industrial America: Evidence from Patent Records, 1790–1846," this JOURNAL, 48 (Sept. 1988), pp. 813–50.

TABLE 1

PATENTS ISSUED FOR INVENTIONS USEFUL IN SIX TECHNOLOGICALLY PROGRESSIVE INDUSTRIES: ENGLAND, 1711–1850

Period	Textiles N	Textiles Percent	Metals N	Metals Percent	Field Agriculture N	Field Agriculture Percent	Ocean Shipping N	Ocean Shipping Percent	Heavy Chemicals N	Heavy Chemicals Percent	Railroads N	Railroads Percent	Total Patents
1711–1720	2	4%	2	4%	3	7%	4	9%	2	4%	0	0%	45
1721–1730	11	12	9	10	9	10	11	12	2	2	0	0	93
1731–1740	3	6	5	10	5	10	6	12	1	2	0	0	48
1741–1750	14	16	5	6	6	7	2	2	5	6	0	0	85
1751–1760	8	8	7	7	4	4	5	5	2	2	0	0	98
1761–1770	23	10	22	10	8	4	14	6	5	2	2	1	221
1771–1780	51	17	33	11	7	2	18	6	13	4	0	0	299
1781–1790	65	13	43	8	20	4	24	5	15	3	2	0	512
1791–1800	88	13	36	5	30	4	34	5	23	3	2	0	673
1801–1810	118	13	46	5	43	5	58	6	24	3	3	0	932
1811–1820	126	11	90	8	39	3	79	7	17	2	18	2	1,122
1821–1830	251	16	92	6	17	1	172	11	16	1	54	4	1,533
1831–1840	497	18	164	6	57	2	206	8	108	4	156	6	2,710
1841–1850	719	15	365	8	181	4	337	7	157	3	374	8	4,652
Total 1711–1850	1,976	15	919	7	429	3	970	7	390	3	611	5	13,023

Notes: The percentages are of Total Patents for the period. Total Patents include the six industries shown in this table as well as all other industries. See Appendix for details on defining each industrial group.
Source: Compiled from Bennet Woodcroft, *Subject Matter Index of Patents of Invention* (London, 1857), with corrected dates (see fn. 5).

30 percent of total output of the economy between 1770 and 1860.[11] What invention there was in agriculture involved nonpatentable technology, as I have mentioned, but it may well be that the amount of agricultural invention was relatively low.

Heavy chemicals get a lot of scholarly attention, so their 3 percent share of patents seems small. But the industry was small, as Table 2 reveals, containing only about 8,000 workers in 1851, while the next most patent-intensive industry, railroads, had 107,000 workers. Yet the two heavy chemical patents per year per thousand workers was over six times the rate of patents issued per railroad worker. Patenting or invention per worker can overstate inventiveness in capital-intensive industries. And this statistic does not account for more complex production processes, which might mean more inventive opportunity. Nevertheless, we have to normalize the level of patenting in each industry, and the record of patents per worker in heavy chemicals makes it clearly stand out as both an extraordinarily inventive industry and one that placed heavy reliance on patents, as opposed to secrecy, to protect inventions.[12]

Table 2 also places the textile industry in better perspective; only the field agriculture industry had a lower rate of patents per worker. It does not appear that this relatively low rate was due to a maturing of textile technology. Other than railroads, the accelerated inventive experience for the industries in Table 2 had roughly similar maturities by 1841. Further, textile patents per cotton worker increased over the first half of the nineteenth century, from approximately 0.03 textile patents per year per thousand workers for 1809 to 1811, to 0.24 for 1849 to 1851.[13] The simple fact that it was a large industry helps account for the many textile patents.

Production machines, the largest group so far defined, accounted for 27 percent of total patents issued between 1711 and 1850 (see Table 3). Nonetheless, this number understates the importance of mechanical technology in patented inventions because there are other mechanical inventions. Steam engines are essentially mechanical, and account for another 7 percent of total patents. And then patents for transmission of power and for nonproduction machines ought to be included. My

[11] Phyllis Deane and W. A. Cole, *British Economic Growth, 1688–1959* (Cambridge, 1967), pp. 156, 166.

[12] Both Christine MacLeod and Harold Dutton have argued that chemical inventions were easy to keep secret, so there was less incentive to patent. On the other hand, A. E. Musson and Eric Robinson's account of invention in the alkali industry shows that there was a keen interest in the protection afforded by patents. See Christine MacLeod, *Inventing the Industrial Revolution* (Cambridge, 1988), pp. 106–7; Harold I. Dutton, *The Patent System and Inventive Activity during the Industrial Revolution, 1750–1852* (Manchester, 1984), p. 119; A. E. Musson and Eric Robinson, *Science and Technology in the Industrial Revolution* (Manchester, 1969), pp. 352–71.

[13] Employment data from G. H. Wood, *The History of Wages in the Cotton Trade* (London, 1910), pp. 127–28.

TABLE 2
AVERAGE ANNUAL PATENTS PER WORKER IN SIX TECHNOLOGICALLY PROGRESSIVE INDUSTRIES: ENGLAND, 1839–1841 AND 1849–1851

	1839–1841			1849–1851		
Industry	Employment (1841) (in thousands)	Three-Year Patent Total (1839–1841)	Average Annual Patents per Thousand Workers	Employment (1851) (in thousands)	Three-Year Patent Total (1849–1851)	Average Annual Patents per Thousand Workers
Textiles	677.4	207	0.1	1,038.3	275	0.1
Metals	142.7	87	0.2	253.1	145	0.2
Field Agriculture	1,282.2	47	0.0	1,748.9	62	0.0
Ocean Shipping				157.2	110	0.2
Heavy Chemicals				8.2	50	2.0
Railroads				107.0	98	0.3

Notes: Employment figures include men and women of all ages, for England and Wales. The available data for workers in ocean shipping, heavy chemicals, and railroads for 1841 were either unreliable or not comparable to the 1851 data, and so are not reported. Further detail on the employment data is available from the author.
Sources: Employment data: textiles, metals, and field agriculture, from C. H. Lee, *British Regional Employment Statistics, 1841–1971* (Cambridge, 1979), categories 13, 6, and 1, respectively. Ocean shipping and heavy chemicals: from the 1851 census of Great Britain (*Parliamentary Papers*, 1852–3, 88, Part I). Railroads: from Phyllis Deane and W. A. Cole, *British Economic Growth, 1688–1959* (Cambridge, 1967), p. 232. Patent data: compiled from Bennet Woodcroft, *Subject Matter Index of Patents of Invention* (London, 1857), with corrected dates (see fn. 5).

preliminary estimates suggest that mechanical technology was associated with at least 46 percent of total patents. Landes's comment that "the machine is the heart of the new civilization" is doubtlessly correct if patent numbers serve as the pulse rate.[14]

The share of machine patents remained stable over the entire period. With the exception of steam engines, which developed after 1781, machines were heavily represented in invention prior to the industrial revolution. The result deserves special notice because machines are one of two categories that come closest to being based on distinct bodies of scientific knowledge (the other is heavy chemicals). Yet there is little indication that some basic breakthrough in mechanical science led to extraordinary amounts of machine invention on the eve of the industrial revolution. To the extent that mechanical science was a key to the industrial revolution, it was based on a highly specialized form, the steam engine.

INVENTIVE ACCELERATION AND THE WIDE DISTRIBUTION OF PATENTS

It is worth looking for periods that mark sustained jumps in patenting. For example, patents per decade for ocean shipping fluctuated around

[14] Landes, *Unbound Prometheus*, p. 40.

TABLE 3
PATENTS ISSUED FOR INVENTIONS PERTAINING TO PRODUCTION MACHINES AND STEAM ENGINES: ENGLAND, 1711–1850

Period	Production Machines N	Production Machines Percent	Steam Engines N	Steam Engines Percent	Total Patents
1711–1720	11	24%	1	2%	45
1721–1730	32	34	1	1	93
1731–1740	13	27	1	2	48
1741–1750	20	23	1	1	85
1751–1760	25	26	3	3	98
1761–1770	63	29	5	2	221
1771–1780	73	24	4	1	299
1781–1790	132	26	22	4	512
1791–1800	179	27	23	3	673
1801–1810	246	26	38	4	932
1811–1820	260	23	45	4	1,122
1821–1830	414	27	117	8	1,533
1831–1840	787	29	244	9	2,710
1841–1850	1,223	26	368	8	4,652
Total 1711–1850	3,478	27	873	7	13,023

Notes: The percentages are of Total Patents for the period. Total Patents include the Production Machines and Steam Engines groups shown in this table as well as all other industries. See Appendix for details on defining the Production Machines and Steam Engines groups.
Source: Compiled from Bennet Woodcroft, *Subject Matter Index of Patents of Invention* (London, 1857), with corrected dates (see fn. 5).

an average of 5.6 between 1711 and 1760, whereas the decade from 1761 to 1770 saw 14 patents, and every decade following saw increases in patents for ocean shipping. By this standard Table 2 reveals inventive acceleration in the period 1761 to 1770 for textiles, metals, and ocean shipping; in 1771 to 1780 for heavy chemicals; and in 1781 to 1790 for field agriculture. Table 3 shows acceleration in the decade from 1761 to 1770 for production machine patenting, consistent with the fact that many of the production machine patents benefited the textiles and metals industries, and in the decade from 1781 to 1790 for steam engines. Previous writers have noted that the second half of the eighteenth century was critical to the inventive development of England, and the patent data point to the period from 1761 to 1790 as being particularly important. As might be expected, the railroad industry was a relative latecomer, experiencing its inventive acceleration in the decade from 1811 to 1820.

This chronology is consistent with early invention in strategic sectors leading to later invention in other sectors. Advances in textile production of the 1760s may have provided the incentive for the chemical industry to develop bleaching chemicals in the 1770s. New methods of making production machines in nonagricultural industries of the 1760s may have led to the development of agricultural machinery starting in the 1780s. And it is clear that the development of steam engines led to significant technological changes in the textile and ocean shipping industries in the nineteenth century.[15] But though this leader-follower theory is consistent with the patent data, it does not necessarily follow that a relatively narrow set of technologically progressive sectors provided the impetus to the industrial revolution.[16] Indeed, further investigation of the patent record suggests otherwise.

Patents were not highly concentrated in any one of our six industries—the industry that accounts for the largest share of total patents is textiles, but textiles account for only 15 percent of patents. The top three industries—textiles, metals, and ocean shipping—together account for 29 percent of patents issued between 1711 and 1850. Modern-day experience provides a contrast: electrical engineering, chemicals, and pharmaceuticals have accounted for 60 percent of patents issued since 1945 in the United Kingdom.[17]

If the narrow set of technologically progressive sectors was responsible for an acceleration of invention, then the growth rate of invention in those sectors must have been greater than the growth rate of invention in other industries, particularly for the early years of the industrial revolution, and their share of total patents would have increased. Column 2 of Table 4 shows the combined patents for the narrow set of technologically progressive sectors, and the share of total patents issued for the period from 1711 to 1850 and four subperiods.[18] Not surprisingly, the combination of patents in the narrow set of technologically progressive sectors do account for 55 percent of patents issued in England from 1711 to 1850. The share of patents issued in these categories declines slightly over the 1711-to-1820 period, suggesting that there was no extraordinary growth of invention in the narrow set of technologically progressive sectors during the critical 1761-to-1790 period, and instead that these sectors advanced at the same pace as other sectors. A significant expansion of their share of patents occurred only in the 1821-to-1850 period, reflecting the application of steam engine technology to textiles and shipping alluded to earlier, and the establishment of the railroad industry.

The time pattern of the share of total patents in a narrow set of technologically progressive sectors is not a strong test of changes in the rate of growth of invention in a technologically progressive sector of an economy, both because the choice of sectors as technologically pro-

[15] G. N. von Tunzelmann, "Technical Progress during the Industrial Revolution," in Floud and McCloskey, eds., *The Economic History of Britain Since 1700*, vol. 1, pp. 143–62.

[16] I will refer to the collective industrial, production machine, and steam engine groups of Tables 1 and 3 as the narrow set of technologically progressive sectors.

[17] Dutton, *Patent System*, p. 208.

[18] To avoid double-counting, any single patent is counted only once in the aggregated groups of Table 4. Since the groups of patents in Tables 1 and 3 are not mutually exclusive, the sum of their patents do not equal the totals in column 2 of Table 4.

TABLE 4
PATENTS ISSUED FOR INVENTIONS USEFUL IN INDUSTRIES RECOGNIZED AS TECHNOLOGICALLY PROGRESSIVE, AND FOR MACHINE INVENTIONS: ENGLAND, 1711–1850

(1)	(2) Six Industries, Production Machines, and Steam Engines		(3) Broad "Technologically Progressive" Sector		(4) Other Industries		(5)
Period	N	Percent	N	Percent	N	Percent	Total Patents
1711–1760	185	50%	315	85%	54	15%	369
1761–1790	507	49	819	79	213	21	1,032
1791–1820	1,310	48	2,113	77	614	22	2,727
1821–1850	5,187	58	7,288	82	1,604	18	8,895
Total, 1711–1850	7,189	55	10,535	81	2,483	19	13,023

Notes: The percentages are of Total Patents for the period. Column 2 includes patents for the six industries from Table 1 and the machine and steam engine patents from Table 3. To avoid double counting, any single patent is counted only once in the aggregated groups of this table. Since the groups of patents in Tables 1 and 3 are not mutually exclusive, the sum of their patents do not equal the totals in column 2. The broad "technologically progressive" sector of column 3 is defined as column 2 plus related production processes (see the Appendix for more detail). The patents for other industries in column 4 are those not assigned to column 3.
Source: Compiled from Bennet Woodcroft, *Subject Matter Index of Patents of Invention* (London, 1857), with corrected dates (see fn. 5).

gressive is somewhat arbitrary, and because there is no clear guideline for including or excluding patents from the industries. I therefore tabulated patents for a broad technologically progressive sector by expanding upon the sectors in Tables 1 and 3 in two ways.

First, since lists of progressive industries rarely define the exact production processes or products that were advanced by invention, production processes or products related to the narrow set of technologically progressive sectors are included in the broad technologically progressive sector. Examples are manufacture of clothing, transmission of power, and processing of foodstuffs. Second, technologies are interrelated, and I include production processes and products tied to the narrow set of technologically progressive sectors by a similar underlying basis (mechanical and chemical) of technology. There are numerous examples of the interrelatedness of technology. The synthesis of soda from inorganic materials in the late eighteenth century marked the beginning of the heavy-chemicals industry, and the increased supply of soda influenced a number of industries, including paper and glass.[19] Advances in transmission of power were important in making the steam engine commercially viable: Boulton and Watt's company prospered

[19] Archibald Clow and N. L. Clow, *The Chemical Revolution* (London, 1952), p. 91. Paul Hohenberg noted the same interrelated nature of chemical and other technologies in a later period; see Paul Hohenberg, *Chemicals in Western Europe: 1850–1914* (Chicago, 1967), pp. 30, 108–9, and chap. 6.

only after Watt invented and patented a way to convert reciprocating to rotary motion.[20] MacIntosh obtained naphtha as a by-product of producing alum, and found naphtha useful in making waterproofed fabrics; he obtained a patent for his process in 1823.[21] Patents for nonheavy chemicals, water, gas, and wind engines, precision machinery, and so on, are included with patents for a broad technologically progressive sector in order to account for these spillover effects.

Column 3 of Table 4 shows the combined number and the share of total patents issued for the broad technologically progressive sector, and its share also declines over the 1711-to-1820 period, even more so than the share for the narrow set of technologically progressive sectors. Invention grew more quickly in all sectors after 1760, but relatively more quickly outside even a broad definition of technologically progressive industries (column 4 of Table 4) during the 1761-to-1790 period. Invention was not only widely dispersed among the narrow set of technologically progressive sectors, but became even more widely dispersed across all industries over the eighteenth century.

This broadening of the scope of invention is further confirmed by tabulating the number of newly created classification categories in the subject index. The date of the initial patent in each category can be taken as a crude approximation to the date of the start of a new category of technology. Sixty-two percent of the 147 classification categories had been created by 1710; the large percentage is no surprise, since invention had had a long history prior to this, and so most categories of technology would have been known. Only 12 percent were created in the 50 years from 1711 to 1760, while 22 percent were created in the 30 years from 1761 to 1790. Of the 32 new categories that came on the scene between 1761 and 1790, 12 were outside the broad set of technologically progressive sectors, including categories for "drawing and photography," "type, letters, and devices," and "electricity."

THE SOURCES OF INVENTION

What do these results mean for our understanding of the sources of English invention during its industrial revolution? We do not see the increased share of patents in technologically progressive industries that must be associated with an extraordinary burst of invention. It is therefore unlikely that invention in a small number of strategic industries caused the acceleration of invention.

Inventions are adopted because they contribute to productivity, and patents useful to an industry indicate the potential profits inventors perceive they may make from creating inventions useful to that industry. The widespread increase in patenting after 1760 indicates that

[20] A. P. Usher, *A History of Mechanical Inventions* (Cambridge, 1954), p. 355.

[21] Clow and Clow, *Chemical Revolution*, pp. 251–54.

perceived profits from invention increased over the entire spectrum of industry in a relatively short period of time and suggests the work of a macroeconomic "trigger" mechanism.[22]

Previous writers have noted macroeconomic changes that might have influenced the supply of invention. Witt Bowden cited immigration of talented individuals up to the mid-eighteenth century as a source of invention.[23] D. C. Coleman, however, notes that these immigrants came mainly in the seventeenth century.[24] The influence of science on technology is a supply-side influence emphasized by A. E. Musson and Eric Robinson, who have documented the interchange between eighteenth-century scientists and inventors.[25] The patent data do not, however, reveal a pattern that suggests a large influence of scientific advance on invention. The direct link most relevant here would have been from advances in chemical and mechanical science to chemical and mechanical invention. If this were significant, we should observe increasing shares of patenting for heavy chemical and machine inventions, but the patent data show only decreasing or constant shares.

Changing attitudes towards nature may have been responsible for increased inventiveness and is a more likely supply-side influence.[26] The interchange between science and invention may have resulted not so much in an increasing ability to tackle technological problems as in an increased willingness to invest in the time and expense of invention. Christine MacLeod reviewed seventeenth- and eighteenth-century literature concerning invention and found support for this change in attitudes.[27] Writers in the early part of the period saw invention as bestowed by providence, but by the end of the eighteenth century many writers saw invention arising from human effort.

It is also possible that some trigger mechanism on the demand side was at work. For example, since invention is a type of investment, the eighteenth-century fall in the rate of interest may have stimulated the general demand for invention, as T. S. Ashton has suggested.[28] This hypothesis is doubtful, because the fall in interest rates was gradual, making it an unlikely trigger mechanism. In addition, I have done some preliminary work that ties interest rates to aggregate patenting and have

[22] "Trigger" is Mathias's term. Mathias, *First Industrial Nation*, p. 9.

[23] Witt Bowden, *Industrial Society in England Towards the End of the Eighteenth Century* (New York, 1925), pp. 54–55.

[24] D. C. Coleman, *The Economy of England, 1450–1750* (London, 1977), pp. 155–56.

[25] Musson and Robinson, *Science and Technology in the Industrial Revolution*.

[26] For example, T. S. Ashton, *The Industrial Revolution* (London, 1948), pp. 14–16; see also A. E. Musson, *Growth of British Industry* (London, 1978), p. 75.

[27] MacLeod, *Inventing the Industrial Revolution*, chap. 11.

[28] T. S. Ashton, "Some Statistics of the Industrial Revolution in Britain," *The Manchester School*, 16 (May 1948), pp. 217–18.

found a statistically significant, positive relation.[29] There is at least one possible explanation for why periods of low interest rates were also periods of small amounts of patenting. MacLeod has argued that most patented invention was aimed at saving capital.[30] If so, a fall in the rate of interest would have decreased the opportunity cost of capital and the need to save capital, and thus would have dampened the demand for capital-saving invention. Efforts to identify other demand-side influences on the aggregate level of invention (such as rising incomes, income redistribution, foreign demand, changes in consumer tastes) have not generally been successful.[31]

The acceleration of England's population growth rate in the mid-eighteenth century coincides with the acceleration in invention, and W. A. Cole has proposed that population growth stimulated invention.[32] Population growth has both supply and demand influences on invention, and both of these channels may have been at work. A larger population implies a larger demand for output, and this in turn implies a larger demand for invention. And since inventions are primarily of human origin, a larger population should lead to more invention. Within the context of English agricultural technology, the influence of population on invention has been given empirical support.[33]

CONCLUSION

England's experience with accelerated invention must be put into perspective, because invention is not innovation. The British economy was largely traditional 90 years after 1760: "the typical British worker in the mid-nineteenth century was not a machine-operator in a factory but still a traditional craftsman or labourer or domestic servant."[34] The bounty of the inventive seeds sown in the late eighteenth century was harvested slowly. Furthermore, evidence suggests that the actual experience with productivity change was more concentrated than the patent data suggest. McCloskey has found that the textile, iron, canal, railroad, and shipping industries, along with agriculture, account for 54 percent of the growth of overall total factor productivity between 1780 and 1860.[35]

[29] The model is very simple, making log of total patents a function of population, an index for time, a dummy variable for periods of war, and interest rates.

[30] MacLeod, *Inventing the Industrial Revolution*, chap. 9.

[31] Von Tunzelmann, "Technical Progress," pp. 144–46.

[32] W. A. Cole, "Eighteenth Century Growth Revisited," *Explorations in Economic History*, 10 (Summer 1973), pp. 327–48.

[33] Julian Simon and Richard Sullivan, "Population Size, Knowledge, Stock, and Other Determinants of Agricultural Publication and Patenting: England, 1541–1850," *Explorations in Economic History*, 26 (Jan. 1989), pp. 21–45.

[34] Musson, *Growth of British Industry*, p. 141.

[35] McCloskey, "Industrial Revolution," p. 114. Crafts (*British Economic Growth*, p. 86) attributes 73 percent of growth of total factor productivity to these industries, indicating an even wider gulf between invention and innovation.

Yet these industries account for only 37 percent of patents issued between 1781 and 1850. The discrepancy may have several causes, such as different rates of innovation, variation in the average contribution of patented invention to productivity, and sources of productivity growth other than patented invention.

By the early eighteenth century England had a number of characteristics in place (a market-oriented economy, a good standard of living, a significant mercantile class) that would have been required for accelerating invention. Several forces came together in the mid-eighteenth century to trigger an acceleration of invention. Important elements of these forces include an increasing willingness consciously to search for solutions to technical problems and an upturn in the growth of population. These changes manifested themselves through an increase in potential profit from invention and permeated the English economy. In a brief period of time, across a large part of the English economy, the amount of invention dramatically increased. The industrial revolution was not just advances in making cloth, or pig iron, or faster ships, or alkalies, or farm machinery, but also advances in making clothing, pins, needles, nails, coaches, roads, dyes, glass, beer, and bread, as well as advances in making building materials, building structures, making paper, printing, heating and lighting houses, making weapons, treating medical ailments, making musical instruments, and a host of other inventions. As Ashton wrote, "the industrial revolution was . . . a revolution of ideas."[36]

Appendix

DEFINITIONS OF PATENT GROUPS

Table 1: *Textiles*: carding, spinning, weaving, fulling, finishing, cutting, bleaching, dying, printing; *Metals*: production (smelting, refining, forging, casting) and fabrication (boring, turning, punching, grinding, and so forth); *Field Agriculture*: plowing, harrowing, sowing, manuring, irrigating, reaping, threshing, winnowing, cutting fodder; *Ocean Shipping*: ship building, harbor construction, navigation, working ships, loading cargo; *Heavy Chemicals*: soda, potash, sulphur, bleaches, soaps, acids; *Railroads*: locomotion, locomotives, rolling stock, rails, connections, signals.

Table 3: *Production Machines*: general production machinery (saws, lathes, drills, presses, and so forth), machinery specific to the chemical, metal and mining, textile, clothing and accessories, shipping, railroad, canal, road transport, field agriculture, and food processing industries, as well as bearings, lubrication, and machine parts (drive bands, axles, springs, hinges, steering, brakes, and so forth); *Steam engines*: boilers, furnaces, condensation, water supply, flues and vents, valves and gauges, stationary, rotary, and oscillating engines, engines applied to agriculture, railway and marine uses.

Table 4: Column 3 is column 2 plus nonproduction machinery (precision instruments,

[36] Ashton, *Industrial Revolution*, p. 16.

firearms, cooking machines, passenger carriages, and so on), road transport (building roads, bridges, viaducts, and coaches, and so on, and farriery), manufacture of clothing and accessories, mining, animal husbandry, fishing, horticulture, processing foodstuffs, nonheavy chemicals (chemical processes for glass, metal, tar, wax, and so forth, and chemically based food processes, such as brewing), chemical processes (such as condensation), chemical apparatus, water, gas and wind engines, transmission of power.

The Democratization of Invention During Early Industrialization: Evidence from the United States, 1790–1846

KENNETH L. SOKOLOFF AND B. ZORINA KHAN

The skills and knowledge necessary for patentable invention during early American industrialization were widely dispersed among the general population. This endowment permitted a rather elastic supply of patentable ideas over the relevant range as the expansion of markets induced more individuals to invent and innovate. Although a broadening of the ranks of patentees was primarily responsible for the initial acceleration of patenting, the importance of patentees with greater long-term investments in inventive activity increased during later stages of development.

Exogenous advances in knowledge, and in its diffusion, have long figured prominently in discussions of the acceleration of invention during early industrialization. Some scholars believe that at least in the American and British cases, fundamental breakthroughs in technology yielded a profusion of secondary applications.[1] They hold that these major improvements in the stock of knowledge available to "would-be" inventors, or a shifting outward of the supply curve, were the primary source of the increase in invention. Others, however, emphasize how an unparalleled expansion of markets helped frame new problems for people with ordinary skills and knowledge to resolve, and induced growing numbers of them to invest more in inventive activity.[2]

The Journal of Economic History, Vol. L, No. 2 (June 1990). ISSN 0022-0507.

Kenneth Sokoloff is Associate Professor of Economics at the University of California at Los Angeles, Los Angeles, CA 90024, and Research Associate, National Bureau of Economic Research. Zorina Khan is a graduate student of Economics at the University of California at Los Angeles.

We are grateful to James Lin for excellent assistance, and to Francesca Bray, Stanley Engerman, Naomi Lamoreaux, Pamela Nickless, Jean-Laurent Rosenthal, Michael Waldman, Gordon Wood, and Mary Yeager for helpful comments. Research support was provided by the California Institute of Technology, the Center for Advanced Study in the Behavioral Sciences, as well as the Institute of Industrial Relations and the Academic Senate at UCLA.

[1] For example, see Joel Mokyr, *The Lever of Riches: Technological Creativity and Economic Growth* (Oxford, 1990).

[2] Historians of American technology generally emphasize that much of the population was very familiar with the basic technology of the period. See David Hounshell, *From the American System to Mass Production, 1800–1932* (Baltimore, 1984). For studies of the rise in patenting, see Kenneth L. Sokoloff, "Inventive Activity in Early Industrial America: Evidence from Patent Records, 1790–1846," this JOURNAL, 48 (Dec. 1988), pp. 813–50; H. I. Dutton, *The Patent System and Inventive Activity During the Industrial Revolution, 1750–1852* (Manchester, 1984); Christine MacLeod, *Inventing the Industrial Revolution: The English Patent System, 1660–1800* (Cambridge,

Research on the role of advances in knowledge in stimulating the early rise of inventive activity has been hampered by the difficulty of distinguishing empirically between the different kinds of knowledge at issue. We try to overcome this obstacle here by using information about American patentees, including their occupation, degree of specialization in invention, and long-term commitment to patenting, to draw inferences about the knowledge they had and about other individual attributes relevant to their inventive activity. The analysis of how the characteristics of patentees varied over time and place yields much insight into their participation in invention. Particular attention is devoted to the prevalence of technical skills or knowledge which, like specific human capital, were largely restricted to members of particular occupations or industries, costly to obtain, and scarce among the general population.

We argue that the growth in patenting during the beginning of American industrialization was marked by a disproportionate increase in invention by ordinary citizens operating with relatively common skills and knowledge rather than by an elite with rare technical expertise or extensive financial resources. It was only at a later stage of development that individuals and firms with substantial investments in technical knowledge and long-term inventive activity came to receive a dominant share of patents. This interpretation is based on findings of: (1) shifts in the distributions of patentees from merchants/professionals to artisans/tradesmen and from urban to rural residents; (2) a rising share of patents to patentees with few patents over their career; (3) low specialization among patentees, with no trend over the period; and (4) a pattern of individuals with few career patents and low specialization being disproportionately represented among patentees in transitional counties which had only recently experienced substantial increase in per capita patents. These results are consistent with the hypothesis that both the state of technology and widespread familiarity with its basic elements permitted a range of relatively elastic supply of invention, through the broader participation in inventive activity induced by the early expansion of markets.

A random sample of U.S. patent records from 1790 to 1846 is the chief source of data, although additional information on many of the patentees has been added to the original data set.[3] Among the new variables are the number of career patents, compiled from a complete listing of patents through 1846, and a measure of the degree to which each

1988); and Richard J. Sullivan, "England's 'Age of Invention': The Acceleration of Patents and Patentable Invention During the Industrial Revolution," *Explorations in Economic History*, 24 (Oct. 1989), pp. 424–52.

[3] For discussions of the data set, and of the patent system during the period, see Sokoloff, "Inventive Activity."

patentee was specialized in any of five sectoral classifications. We also use a special sample of so-called "great inventors." Our key assumption is that careful analysis of patent counts can provide a valuable indicator of inventive activity over the period under study. Many scholars have found patent data useful for this and related purposes.[4]

Patent counts are not without limitations however. At least three deficiencies are relevant to the analysis presented here. First, patents do not include the many inventions for which patents are either difficult to enforce or not obtainable. Since patents are easier to enforce when they pertain to a physical product or capital equipment, they overrepresent such inventions. For this reason the use of patents may exaggerate the relative significance of inventors with large investments in skills or other capital which helped in the development of inventions (invention-generating capital).[5] Second, institutional and cultural factors can alter the proportion of inventions which are ultimately patented. Finally, patents do not contain direct information on the value of the underlying ideas, and thus patent counts provide a less reliable indicator of the value of inventions being introduced than would a series weighted by value (either ex ante or ex post). These issues are serious, but we have tried to maintain a sensitivity to them throughout our analysis. Objections to our inferences should be examined in context.

I

A salient feature of the growth of patenting in early industrial America is that it was far from continuous. As is clear from Figure 1, patenting was cyclical, with virtually all of the increase between 1790 and 1846 realized during two concentrated intervals.[6] These periods of rapid growth were not stimulated by specific breakthroughs in technology. Instead, they seem related to macroeconomic events which promoted the expansion of markets. The first upswing in patenting began slowly during the prosperous 1790s, but accelerated during the years in which

[4] For a review of the economics literature using patent data, see Ariel Pakes and Margaret Simpson, "Patent Renewal Data," *Brookings Papers on Economic Activity: Microeconomics* (1989), pp. 331–401.

[5] Invention-generating capital encompasses any human and physical capital which raises productivity in inventive activity. Such capital can be either sector-specific or general in its effects. Individuals with large investments in such capital will presumably tend to focus on ideas which involve capital equipment—both because they may have a comparative advantage in such inventions and because private returns to such inventions are easier to appropriate. For an interesting treatment of the bias under patent systems toward inventions involving large-scale or capital equipment, see Stephen A. Marglin, "What Do Bosses Do?: The Origins and Functions of Hierarchy in Capitalist Production," *Review of Radical Political Economics*, 6 (Summer 1974), pp. 60–112. For estimates of manufacturing investment in capital equipment, see Kenneth L. Sokoloff, "Investment in Fixed and Working Capital During Early Industrialization: Evidence from U.S. Manufacturing Firms," this JOURNAL, 44 (June 1984), pp. 545–56.

[6] Jacob Schmookler, among others, noted the pro-cyclicality of patenting in *Invention and Economic Growth* (Cambridge, MA, 1966).

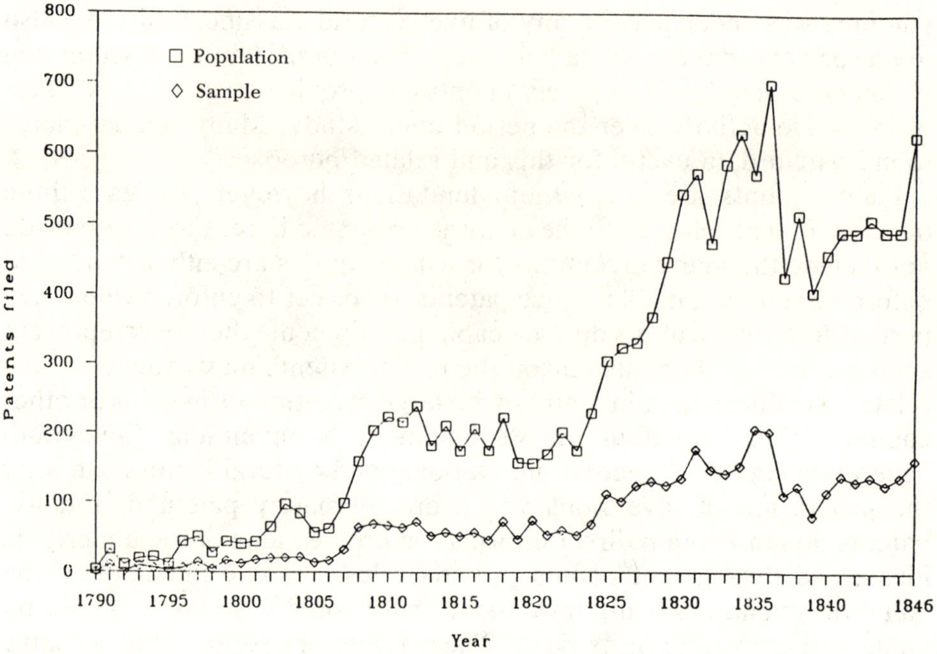

FIGURE 1

ANNUAL TOTALS OF PATENTS IN THE POPULATION AND THE SAMPLE, 1790–1846

British interference with shipping lanes and a series of non-importation acts, such as the Embargo of 1807, curtailed the supply of foreign manufactures. This interval of sustained increase in patenting was brought to an end by the War of 1812 and the long contraction which followed. The advent of the second span of rapid growth in patenting coincided with the economic recovery of the early 1820s. As the upturn in the economy continued, patenting increased steadily until a change in the patent system in July 1836 introduced more stringent requirements. The number of awards fell immediately, and then stabilized at this lower level for nearly eight years. It seems likely that the contraction, which began with the Panic of 1837 and persisted through the early 1840s, also played some role in accounting for this second spell of stagnation in patenting.

In general the tendency for patenting to increase during business expansions or episodes like the Embargo, which raised the effective demand for domestic manufacturers and encouraged the extension of domestic markets, is consistent with an emphasis on demand-induced advances in inventive activity.[7] This does not imply, however, that

[7] For more discussion of the Embargo period and cyclicality, see Sokoloff, "Inventive Activity"; Robert C. Allen, "Collective Invention," *Journal of Economic Behavior and Organization*, 4 (Mar. 1983), pp. 1–24; and Andrei Shleifer, "Implementation Cycles," *Journal of Political Economy*, 96 (Dec. 1986), pp. 1163–90. For a related theoretical treatment of trade and invention,

TABLE 1
DISTRIBUTION OF PATENTS BY PATENTEE COMMITMENT TO PATENTING, 1790–1846

Period	Number of Career Patents by Patentee: 1 Patent	2 Patents	3 Patents	4 to 5 Patents	6 to 9 Patents	More than 10 Patents
1790–1804	77	35	12	20	17	6
	46.1%	21.0%	7.2%	12.0%	10.2%	3.6%
1805–1811	186	63	50	19	19	12
	53.3%	18.1%	14.3%	5.4%	5.4%	3.4%
1812–1822	388	117	50	51	35	42
	56.8%	17.1%	7.3%	7.5%	5.1%	6.2%
1823–1829	435	132	52	58	43	28
	58.2%	17.7%	7.0%	7.8%	5.8%	3.7%
1830–1836	686	190	95	100	80	45
	57.4%	15.9%	7.9%	8.4%	6.7%	3.8%
1836–1842	416	127	61	53	28	40
	57.4%	17.5%	8.4%	7.3%	3.9%	5.5%
1843–1846	329	96	48	39	13	19
	60.5%	17.7%	8.8%	7.2%	2.4%	3.5%
All Years	2,517	760	368	340	235	192
	57.1%	17.2%	8.3%	7.7%	5.3%	4.4%

Notes and Sources: Career Patents consists of the total number of patents filed between 1790 through 1846. The figure was compiled for each patentee in the sample from Edmund Burke, *List of Patents For Inventions and Designs Issued By the United States From 1790 to 1847* (Washington, 1847). For a description of the sample, see Kenneth L. Sokoloff, "Inventive Activity in Early Industrial America: Evidence from Patent Records, 1790–1846," this JOURNAL, 48 (Dec. 1988), pp. 813–50.

supply conditions were irrelevant. On the contrary, if the level of technical knowledge previously available had not been sufficient to yield new inventions worthy of being patented (with expected private returns exceeding the cost of securing a patent), growth in market demand alone could not have produced much change in the number of patents filed. Hence the pro-cyclicality of patenting suggests that at least a significant portion of invention involved the application of known principles and techniques or modest extensions of them. In conventional economic terms the supply of patentable ideas must have been somewhat elastic, at least in the short run.

Another perspective is provided by Table 1, which presents the distribution of patents over time by classes of patentees, the latter defined by using the total number of patents ever received as a measure of long-term commitment to patenting.[8] The most important finding here

see Paul M. Romer, "Endogenous Technological Change," unpublished working paper (Chicago, 1989).

[8] Patentees active at the beginning or end of the period might have patentable ideas unrecorded in our data and accordingly have their career patents (or would-be patents) undercounted. Although careful examination indicated that patentees active after 1842 suffered from this problem

is the growing prominence of patentees with only one or two patents over their career. Whereas patentees with only one career patent took out 46.1 percent of those awarded between 1790 and 1804, their share rose to 53.3 percent during the Embargo years and remained in the high fifties and low sixties through the 1840s. This change implies that patentees with relatively small long-term investments in inventive activity responded most strongly to whatever conditions were responsible for the economy-wide increase in invention and innovation. Their sensitivity to economic conditions is shown by the contrast between the pro-cyclicality of their activity and the virtual absence of pro-cyclicality on the part of those with many awards as reflected here in the sharp rises in the share going to patentees with 10 or more patents during the two prolonged economic downturns (averaging 64 percent).

The increase in the proportion of patents granted to individuals with few career patents raises questions about how significant technical skills and knowledge were in accounting for the growth of inventive activity during the period. After all, if investment in such human capital helped generate patentable ideas (implying, on average, that patentees with more career patents had more of this human capital), and if this advantage became larger over time as technology advanced, then one would expect patentees with many career patents to have garnered an increasing share. Moreover, the same logic should apply to improvements in the diffusion of knowledge: if individuals with substantial investments in technical skills and knowledge were better equipped to understand and act on the significance of new information, then their share of patents should have risen with a geographically wider diffusion of information. Given that the proportion of patentees with multiple career patents actually declined, however, it would appear that the developments most central to the growth in patenting during the era were those which stimulated individuals with relatively modest amounts of such invention-generating capital.

It is true that patentable ideas vary enormously in both private and social returns and that the larger share of patents does not necessarily indicate an increase in the relative value of inventions contributed by "low-commitment" patentees. Indeed, some would assert that these patentees produced few important inventions and were responsible for low-value patents only. This possibility is difficult to evaluate with our current data, but indirect evidence bears against it. Since the 1836

(biasing estimates downward), no such effect was detected for those who filed before. Hence only the observations from 1843 on are suspect and deleted from the regressions below. Since any bias during the 1790s would work against us, no adjustments were made there. The 1836 change in the patent system could also explain some decline in the average number of career patents, but since most of the shift toward patentees with few patents was realized during the Embargo, it is unlikely that either this change or the cutoff at 1846 could provide an adequate explanation.

TABLE 2
DISTRIBUTION OF URBAN PATENTS BY PATENTEE OCCUPATION

	1790–1804	1805–1822	1823–1836	1836–1846
General Commerce and Professional	13	60	59	43
(merchants, doctors, gentlemen)	50.0%	38.7%	24.6%	18.6%
Artisans Working with Renewable	4	32	58	41
Materials (carpenters, shoemakers)	15.4%	20.7%	24.2%	17.8%
Precision Artisans (makers of	5	16	22	26
watches, jewelry, instruments)	19.2%	10.3%	9.2%	11.3%
Machinists/Toolmakers	1	17	34	40
	3.9%	11.0%	14.2%	17.3%
Other Producers/Dealers of Metal	2	17	40	49
Products (stove manufacturers, blacksmiths)	7.7%	11.0%	16.7%	21.2%
Other Occupations or None Listed	1	13	27	32
	3.9%	8.4%	11.3%	13.9%

Notes and Sources: Table 2 reports the number and share of patents filed by patentees of each occupational category during four subperiods. The occupations for 444 patentees were retrieved from various issues of city directories. Since the surviving directories are disproportionately from later years, it was easier to establish the occupation for patentees who were active later. Hence the increase in the number of patentees covered over time is not significant. Among the cities represented in this table are Albany, Buffalo, New York, Rochester, Troy, and Utica in New York; Newark in New Jersey; Bangor and Portland in Maine; Philadelphia and Pittsburgh in Pennsylvania; Baltimore in Maryland; Boston, Newburyport, and Salem in Massachusetts; Providence in Rhode Island; and Hartford and New Haven in Connecticut. The third subperiod runs through July 3, 1836, when the patent law was changed. Of the 1,057 patents in the sample awarded to residents of these cities over the entire period, occupations were retrieved for 458 (or 43.3 percent) of the respective patentees (with many patentees responsible for more than one patent). See the note to Table 1.

change in the patent law tightened requirements for an award, had individuals with few career patents filed patents of lower average quality, the new standards would have screened out a larger fraction of their applications. As their share did not decline, this rough test supports the inference about the increased role of inventions from those with few career patents.

Dividing patentees into occupational groups, as Table 2 does for an urban subset, reveals a major shift over time from a predominance of men of commerce to one of artisans and the like. Merchants and professionals were by far the most active up to the Embargo, with half of urban patents, but saw their proportion fall to less than one in five by the late 1830s and 1840s.[9] Since rural patentees, few of whom were merchants, also increased their share over time, the overall occupational shift was even stronger than these urban data alone indicate.

One interpretation of this change in the occupational composition is that it reflected an opening up of opportunities for deriving returns from

[9] The lack of information about the occupations of individuals who did not receive patents, as well as for most of the sample, raise questions about the interpretation of the regressions presented below.

invention. Prior to the Embargo, when domestic markets were less developed, the bulk of patenting was carried out by merchants and men of similar occupations, who were best placed to make commercial use of good ideas. Not only did they have the most direct access to wider markets, but they also were more likely to control financial resources to support inventive activity and innovation. Francis Lowell, founder of the Boston Manufacturing Company, epitomizes this class of merchant. Having decided to expand from a profitable base in foreign trade into textiles, he and a fellow merchant proceeded, without previous mechanical experience, to study the existing technology and construct their own power loom. For the most part enterprises such as Lowell's were inspired by superior business acumen, not advanced technical knowledge.

With the growth of domestic markets more and more individuals began to compete to satisfy extensive demand for their products, as well as to exploit expanded opportunities for extracting returns from invention. These developments should have boosted invention and patenting throughout the population, but such gains were likely proportionally higher for occupational groups other than commerce because they had less previous experience with the opportunities and pressures of large markets.[10] It is hardly surprising, therefore, that the major rise in patents per capita was accompanied by a shift in the occupational mix of patentees.

Prior to the Embargo the more technical groups, such as machinists and metalworkers, whose skills and knowledge were scarce and costly to acquire, received only 3.9 and 7.7 percent respectively of patents.[11] Their relative significance among urban patentees did increase substantially over time, perhaps signaling an enhanced importance of a technical background for effective invention, but even by the 1840s, when mechanization was spreading quickly, their shares had risen to only 17.3 and 21.2 percent. The totals are large, but their impact is diminished somewhat when one remembers that machinists and metalworkers/dealers were certainly overrepresented among urban patentees as compared to the general population of patentees and that the share of patents going to urban centers had declined.[12] Given these caveats, and the relatively few patents awarded to these trades before the 1830s, it is doubtful whether breakthroughs in machine and metalworking technology alone could go far in explaining the rise in patenting during the early

[10] Part of the trend in the occupational distribution may be due to the development of markets which eased capital requirements. See Dirk J. Struik, *Yankee Science in the Making* (Boston, 1948). Also see MacLeod, *Inventing the Industrial Revolution*, chap. 7, for evidence of a similar trend in England.

[11] Commercial patentees may have patented ideas conceived by others.

[12] Metropolitan patentees received 31.3 percent of all patents during 1805–1811, but only 22.1 and 28.0 percent in 1830–1836 and 1836–1842.

nineteenth century. Rather, this progress depended more on the problem-solving abilities of a kind pervasive among artisans of the era. As George Gibb suggested, "varied and dextrous mechanical abilities were all but universal . . . the Industrial Revolution in its infancy produced surprisingly few basic technical skills not already familiar to American mechanics."[13] Indeed, the major inventions of the age, such as Whitney's cotton gin or Blanchard's lathe, were typically based on commonly available information applied to a specific problem.

Another way to explore the significance of technical skills and knowledge is to examine the extent of specialization by patentees. One would expect most technical knowledge at the frontier to be sector-specific or limited in direct applicability to inventions in the same sector.[14] Hence, if such human capital did raise the productivity of inventive activity in a particular sector, and was costly to acquire, a patentee who had invested in it would tend to concentrate his efforts, as well as his patents, in that sector. For example, individuals who had acquired an expertise in power looms or sewing machines would tend to file manufacturing patents, as opposed to ones in agriculture, construction, transportation, or miscellaneous (the other four sectors in our classification). In short, the more important these sector-specific skills and knowledge, the more specialized by sector the patents of inventors were likely to be.

In Table 3 we present estimates of the proportions of patentees who were specialized—with over 75 percent of their patents in any one of the five sectors—for both the general sample and the sample of "great inventors." Opinions may vary when there is no clear standard for comparison, but the percentages seem rather low, especially during the early years when barely over half of the patentees with two patents were specialized. Even the "great inventors," who might be expected to possess highly specialized knowledge, were only slightly more specialized than the average.[15] Overall, the modest proportions of specialized patentees imply that much of the human capital tapped by inventors could be applied to problems in a wide variety of economic activities.

[13] George S. Gibb, *The Saco-Lowell Shops* (Cambridge, MA, 1950), p. 10.

[14] Although some patentable inventions could be used in more than one sector, our sectoral classification mitigates the potential mismeasurement of specialization. We were consistent about classifying closely related inventions in the same sector. Hence even though a patentee might have registered several patents for steam engines to be used in different sectors, all of his patents would be in the same category, and he would be considered specialized. Inclusion of dummy variables for sectors in the specialization regressions below did not alter the qualitative results.

[15] Dutton argued that patentees during early British industrialization were not very specialized. Although his estimates of the degree of specialization are not directly comparable, American patentees seem to have been less specialized. His data also imply that British patents were more concentrated among patentees with many career patents than U.S. patents were. Many factors may contribute to these differences, including the much higher cost of securing a patent in Britain. See Dutton, *The Patent System*, chap. 6.

TABLE 3
SPECIALIZATION OF PATENTEES IN THE SAMPLE AND AMONG GREAT INVENTORS

Patentees with		1790–1822 Sample	1790–1822 Great Inventors	1823–1846 Sample	1823–1846 Great Inventors
Two Patents	%	52.2%	62.5%	57.7%	66.7%
	N	113	8	248	21
Three Patents	%	25.6%	70.0%	43.1%	58.8%
	N	39	10	65	17
Four or More Patents	%	32.3%	30.8%	46.5%	50.0%
	N	31	26	43	44

Notes and Sources: The figures report, for the general sample and for a special group of "great inventors" responsible for especially notable patents, the number of patentees in each cell, and the proportion with over 75 percent of their patents in one of five sectors: agriculture, construction, manufacturing, transportation, and other. The number of patents refers to the total appearing in the sample. Hence the numbers of patentees with three patents refer to those individuals who had three patents appearing in the sample. The analogous percentages for all patentees with two or more patents in the sample are 40.0 percent during 1790–1822 and 52.1 percent during 1823–1846. For information on the general sample, see the note to Table 1. The list of 129 "great inventors" was drawn from inventors appearing in the *Dictionary of American Biography* (New York, 1937); and *Who Was Who in America: Historical Volume, 1607–1896* (Chicago, 1963).

Most of the skills and knowledge needed for patentable invention appear to have been either of general applicability or easily acquired.

Although these figures hint at an increase in specialization over time, the multivariate regressions presented in Table 4 reveal no trend (judging from the insignificant time period dummies). The stationary pattern may seem surprising because it conflicts with the normal conceptions of what the advance of knowledge and the development of markets lead to, but it is robust to whatever other variables are controlled for. Skeptics may question whether our measure is actually picking up specialization, but confidence in the analysis is bolstered by the finding that the degree of specialization was greater among occupations associated with technical knowledge (such as machinists), among individuals with a high career commitment to patenting (beginning to rise with six patents), and for "great inventors." All conform well with our expectations about the relationship between investments in invention-generating capital and specialization.

As patenting increased over time, two streams of development might offset each other in the time trend. On the one hand the expansion of markets, which both enhanced the commercial value of inventions and enlarged the population who could benefit from patents, attracted new patentees whose long-term investments in invention-generating capital were relatively modest and whose efforts were accordingly not as specialized as those of their more committed peers. On the other, a growing competitive advantage to technical skills and knowledge may have served over time to promote greater investment in such sector-

TABLE 4

REGRESSIONS OF SPECIALIZATION IN PATENT SECTOR, 1790–1846

Dependent Variable: Percent Specialization of Patentee	(1)	(2)	(3)	(4)
Constant	106.864	79.829	79.056	81.615
	(16.53)	(9.66)	(9.09)	(9.83)
Proportion of Labor Force in Manufacturing	−1.134	−0.176	−0.140	−0.171
	(−1.61)	(−2.12)	(−1.69)	(−2.07)
Log (Annual Patents per Million in County)		7.828	7.729	7.839
		(5.15)	(5.16)	(5.16)
(Number of Patents Over Which Index Computed)^2	0.984	0.940	1.032	1.024
	(3.84)	(3.72)	(4.12)	(4.00)
Number of Patents Over Which Index Computed	−12.00	−11.869	−12.945	−12.774
	(−4.98)	(−4.97)	(−5.46)	(−5.26)
Time Dummies				
1790–1804	−2.143	4.819	5.048	4.326
	(−0.44)	(0.97)	(1.02)	(0.87)
1805–1822	−3.542	−3.487	−2.155	−3.337
	(−1.46)	(−1.45)	(−0.90)	(−1.40)
1823–1836	3.411	1.095	2.066	1.318
	(1.63)	(0.52)	(0.99)	(0.62)
Regional Dummies				
N. New England	1.433	−2.769	−1.761	−3.119
	(0.32)	(−0.61)	(−0.40)	(−0.69)
S. New England	−2.063	−8.002	−8.969	−9.112
	(−0.72)	(−2.61)	(−2.96)	(−2.93)
New York	1.492	−2.093	−2.333	−2.453
	(0.55)	(−0.75)	(−0.85)	(−0.88)
S. Middle Atlantic	4.401	4.145	5.162	3.485
	(1.31)	(1.25)	(1.56)	(1.05)
Urbanization Dummies				
Urban	5.366	4.687	3.636	4.035
	(2.59)	(2.29)	(1.79)	(1.95)
Metropolitan	1.389	−4.662	−7.531	−4.379
	(0.66)	(−1.94)	(−3.07)	(−1.82)
Transportation Dummies				
Located on Navigable River or Canal	−7.669	−8.284	−7.006	−8.447
	(−2.36)	(−2.57)	(−2.20)	(−2.63)
Located on Ocean	−14.531	−14.087	−13.418	−13.032
	(−3.40)	(−3.33)	(−3.21)	(−3.06)
Occupational Dummies				
Commerce/White Collar			2.475	
			(0.81)	
Traditional Artisan			7.901	
			(2.83)	
Machinist/Toolmaker			13.030	
			(3.63)	
Metalworker/Dealer			20.234	
			(4.64)	
Great Inventor Dummy				6.090
				(2.00)
R^2	0.093	0.114	0.144	0.117
N	1,016	1,016	1,016	1,016

Notes and Sources: The regressions were estimated over all of the individual patent records for patentees in northeastern states who had more than one patent appearing in the sample. The constant refers to a patent filed during 1836–1846 in a rural Pennsylvania county without access to a navigable waterway by an individual for whom either no occupation was retrieved or whose occupation was different from those represented by the occupational dummy variables. The traditional artisan category refers to artisans who worked with nonmetallic raw materials or did fine crafts such as jewelry or watchmaking. For a discussion of the sample, see Kenneth L. Sokoloff, "Inventive Activity in Early Industrial America: Evidence from the Patent Records, 1790–1846," this JOURNAL, 48 (Dec. 1988), pp. 813–50, and the notes to Tables 1 and 2. Regression coefficients are reported, with *t*-statistics in parentheses below.

specific human capital and greater specialization, particularly by patentees in districts with highly developed and competitive markets. As long as the former mechanism continued to operate with sufficient strength, it might on average net out the effect of the latter in the aggregate pattern.

The regression results are consistent with this perspective. They suggest that patentees from rural counties on navigable waterways were less specialized than their counterparts in counties without such low-cost transportation. This finding is of special interest because the transitional nature of these counties captures an important stage in the process by which levels of inventive activity rose during early industrialization. As documented in previous work, rural counties realized substantial and rapid increases in patents per capita as they gained access to waterways.[16] Moreover, cities invariably emerged in these counties along the water routes, boosting patenting rates further. Whereas inventive activity appears to have risen continually once the extension of the waterways opened up an area to wider markets, the pattern of coefficients in these regressions implies that the degree of specialization by patentees did not move solely in one direction. Indeed, because the coefficient on the waterway dummy is large and negative, and those on the urban and patents per capita variables positive, the evidence indicates that the average patentee became less specialized when water transportation first became available, but that this change was reversed over time as urbanization and further investment in inventive activity progressed. Although other explanations are possible, the above hypothesis seems straightforward. With the initial phase of the increase in patenting driven by an increase in the proportion of the population awarded patents, the influx of new inventors produced a temporary shift in the composition of patentees towards individuals who had no major investments in sector-specific capital and were accordingly less specialized. During the later phases, as local populations adjusted to the greater opportunity and competition of an urban and extensive market, residents made larger investments in invention-generating capital, and focused more on their particular niches.

In Table 5 we present regressions with the log of the number of patents ever received by the patentee as the dependent variable. They reinforce the univariate analysis in indicating that the early acceleration of inventive activity was associated with a disproportionate rise in patenting by individuals without much of a previous record in invention. Perhaps most telling is the robust finding that career patents per patentee peaked during 1790–1804. In all of the specifications estimated, the coefficient on the dummy for these years was positive and statistically significant, while those for later subperiods were close to zero and

[16] See the discussion in Sokoloff, "Inventive Activity," pp. 830–47.

TABLE 5
REGRESSIONS OF NUMBER OF LIFETIME PATENTS, 1790–1842

Dependent Variable: Log of Lifetime Patents to Patentee	(1)	(2)	(3)	(4)
Constant	0.275	−0.048	−0.023	−0.026
	(3.27)	(−0.41)	(−0.20)	(−0.24)
Proportion of Labor Force in Manufacturing in County	0.001	0.001	0.002	0.000
	(0.83)	(0.52)	(1.35)	(0.41)
Log (Annual Patents per Million in County)		0.100	0.080	0.098
		(3.98)	(3.25)	(4.20)
Time Dummies				
1790–1804	0.192	0.287	0.273	0.328
	(2.16)	(3.12)	(3.04)	(4.03)
1805–1822	0.030	0.028	0.039	0.049
	(0.66)	(0.61)	(0.88)	(1.15)
1823–1836	0.027	−0.011	0.025	0.002
	(0.65)	(−0.27)	(0.60)	(0.05)
Regional Dummies				
N. New England	0.074	0.042	0.059	0.075
	(1.08)	(0.61)	(0.89)	(1.20)
S. New England	0.213	0.138	0.119	0.072
	(4.31)	(2.62)	(2.31)	(1.47)
New York	0.139	0.095	0.102	0.067
	(3.03)	(2.02)	(2.21)	(1.57)
S. Middle Atlantic	0.107	0.111	0.158	0.166
	(1.71)	(1.77)	(2.58)	(2.79)
Urbanization Dummies				
Urban	0.186	0.185	0.142	0.142
	(5.32)	(5.31)	(4.13)	(4.34)
Metropolitan	0.116	0.025	−0.088	−0.055
	(2.85)	(0.54)	(−1.88)	(−1.28)
Transportation Dummies				
Located on Navigable River or Canal	−0.001	−0.021	−0.026	−0.020
	(−0.01)	(−0.41)	(−0.52)	(−0.44)
Located on Ocean	−0.010	−0.022	−0.052	−0.060
	(−0.13)	(−0.32)	(−0.78)	(−0.97)
Occupational Dummies				
Commerce/White Collar			0.605	0.492
			(8.60)	(7.37)
Traditional Artisan			0.259	0.224
			(4.23)	(3.83)
Machinist/Toolmaker			0.830	0.607
			(9.16)	(7.72)
Metalworker/Dealer			0.420	0.330
			(3.98)	(3.19)
Great Inventor Dummy				1.009
				(18.13)
R^2	0.035	0.040	0.090	0.211
N	2,957	2,957	2,957	3,140

Notes and Sources: The first three regressions were estimated over all of the patents in the general sample; the data for the fourth regression also included the additional observations from the "great inventors" sample. The constant refers to a patent filed during 1836–1842 in a rural Pennsylvania county without access to a navigable waterway by an individual for whom either no occupation is available or whose occupation is different from those represented by the occupational dummies. See the note to Table 4.

insignificant. Evidently the decrease in the number of career patents for the average patentee during the Embargo years, when there was the first major surge in patenting, was sustained afterwards.

Although the time trend shows a decline to a lower plateau, most of the other coefficients suggest that career patents increased with conditions normally associated with development. For example, career patents were higher in urban and metropolitan areas, in counties in which patents per capita were higher, and in Southern New England and New York—the most economically developed regions. A variety of explanations could be offered for the greater commitments to patenting in such districts, including differences in occupational composition or the responses of individuals to the greater opportunities derived from larger markets and richer supplies of capital and information. Whatever the particular source, however, the small coefficient on local patents per capita implies that most of the variation in patents per capita across place and time was due to differences in the proportion of the population who patented, not to differences in the number of patents per patentee.[17]

This aspect of the spread of high levels of inventive activity during early industrialization is reflected in the performance of the dummy variable for proximity to a navigable waterway. Although such access to transportation raised county-level patents per capita between 55 and 90 percent, the regression in column 1 indicates that it did not lead to any immediate increase in career patents per patentee. Again it appears that the growth of patenting in rural counties when they were first opened up to low-cost transportation was realized virtually exclusively through individuals with limited experience in patenting. These additional patentees were like their more isolated peers in terms of their long-term commitment to invention, but there were many more of them in proportional terms.[18] Notions that the early rise in inventive activity was confined to a technical elite who were best positioned to recognize and exploit new information do not, therefore, seem to capture what happened during the first stage of the transition in rural counties.

Although individuals with a small number of career patents accounted for most of the growth in patents per capita, the regressions demonstrate that individual investments in invention-generating capital, as proxied by occupation, did yield more patentable ideas. This is a crucial point, because the inferences drawn about long-term commitments to invention from information on career patents rest on an assumption that such returns were present. The evidence consists of the large positive

[17] Accounting decompositions of the differences between metropolitan, urban, and rural counties, or between regions, yield the same conclusion.

[18] Those on waterways were less specialized, however, perhaps because they changed their livelihoods after the opening to the wider market.

coefficients on the dummy variables for machinists, metalworkers/dealers, and "great inventors," classifications we associate with investments in technical or specialized knowledge. Moreover, the greater number of career patents among inventors in commerce and the professions may reflect other sorts of investment which encouraged the development and use of patentable ideas.

II

The beginning of rapid growth in inventive activity in the United States coincided with a substantial broadening of the segments of the population who participated in patenting. Indeed, nearly all of the rise in patenting per capita during the early nineteenth century was produced by the increased proportion of the population who patented, as awards became less concentrated among commercial/professional occupations, urban residents, and individuals with multiple career patents. This shift in the distribution of patentees was especially pronounced in transitional counties which had gained access to water transportation but lacked significant urban centers. At a later stage, activity may have shifted back toward patentees with more career patents, especially in the more developed areas, because the occupational composition of the population changed and returns to investment in invention-generating capital rose.

One of the implications of these results is that the skills and knowledge necessary for patentable invention at the beginning of industrialization were widely dispersed among the population. Although training in technical occupations did yield more patents for individuals, such backgrounds were not at all required. The state of technology combined with the endowment of the population evidently permitted a rather elastic supply of patentable ideas. These special circumstances undoubtedly made it easier for the economy to realize major and broadly based increases in invention and productivity growth, once conditions raised the private return to inventive activity and encouraged a reallocation of resources in that direction.[19]

All of this enhances our understanding of the record of inventive activity, but the fundamental issue still remains. What do these patterns indicate about the source of the sharp rise in patenting during the early nineteenth century? The answer will certainly not be as simple as the question, but it is clear that the explanation will have to focus on what pulled men with relatively common skills and knowledge into invention. For this reason, the new evidence makes it more difficult to maintain that exogenous advances in technical knowledge, or in its diffusion,

[19] See Kenneth L. Sokoloff, "Productivity Growth in Manufacturing During Early Industrialization: Evidence from the American Northeast, 1820–1860," in Stanley L. Engerman and Robert E. Gallman, eds., *Long-Term Factors in American Economic Growth* (Chicago, 1986).

drove the beginning of the process. Instead, we would highlight the disproportionate response of "low-commitment" individuals during the period overall, and particularly in transitional counties. The case is not yet closed, but the greater sensitivity of this key group of patentees to economic conditions provides further evidence that the expansion of markets was a powerful inducement to the increase of inventive activity during early American industrialization.

Collective Choice of Working Conditions: Hours in British and U.S. Iron and Steel, 1890–1923

MARTHA ELLEN SHIELLS

Twelve-hour days persisted in British and U.S. iron and steel after most industrial workers worked eight-hour days. When shorter hours finally came, sooner in Britain, they came abruptly. This article presents a model of working hours as public goods; when job attributes are shared there is a collective choice problem. In Britain, a collective bargaining mechanism reconciled the preferences of workers and capital owners and facilitated the move to shorter hours. In the United States immigrants had been willing to work long hours. When immigration was cut off, the government intervened.

Traditional explanations of late and sudden hours reductions in iron and steel have dwelt on the need to move at once from twelve to eight hours and on the steelworkers' lack of control over working conditions. Although it is not clear why staggered or unequal shift lengths were felt to be impossible, there is abundant evidence that such schemes were dismissed by contemporaries as impractical and were rarely adopted.[1] At least in the United States, exploitation played a role in the persistence of long hours. John Fitch spent ten months in 1907 and 1908 surveying conditions in Allegheny County steel mills and wrote, "The steel worker sees on every side evidences of an irresistible power, baffling and intangible. It fixes the conditions of his employment; it tells

The Journal of Economic History, Vol. L, No. 2 (June 1990). ISSN 0022-0507.

The author is a member of the Research Staff, Center for Naval Analyses, 4401 Ford Avenue, Alexandria, VA 22302.

I am grateful to Joan Underhill Hannon and the editors of this JOURNAL for their valuable comments. Frank Stafford provided the initial idea that motivated the article, and most of the theoretical structure is borrowed from him and his coauthors. Gavin Wright did his best to ensure that the historical record was not sacrificed on theoretical altars. There remains little to take credit for except, of course, any remaining errors.

[1] For example, "the iron and steel manufacturer . . . did not see how he could [reduce hours] without going in one step from twelve hours to eight hours. . . . " American Engineering Council, *The Twelve Hour Shift in Industry* (New York, 1922), pp. 221–22. This and other sources discuss the work schedules of individual firms or workers, but make no mention of unorthodox shift arrangements. For the United States, see John A. Fitch, *The Steel Workers* (1st edn., 1911; reprint edn., New York, 1969); U.S. Congress, Senate, *Report on Conditions of Employment in the United States Iron and Steel Industry*, vols. 1–4, S.Doc. 110, 62nd Cong., 1st sess., 1911–1913; Interchurch World Movement, *Report on the Steel Strike of 1919* (1st edn., 1920; reprint edn., New York, 1971). For Great Britain, see [Arthur Pugh], *Men of Steel by One of Them* (London, 1951); Arthur L. Bowley, *Prices and Wages in the United Kingdom, 1914–1920* (Oxford, 1921); James Cecil Carr and W. Taplin, *History of the British Steel Industry* (Cambridge, 1962).

him what wages he may expect to receive and where and when he must work."[2]

British iron and steel was less concentrated than the United States industry. Also, British iron and steel unions were strong, while the ironworkers union in the United States never gained a strong hold in integrated steel plants.[3] These differences may explain why British workers won eight-hour days five years earlier. Nevertheless, within Great Britain short hours came later for steelworkers than for other industrial workers. Recognizing that working schedules are public goods within steel plants can enrich traditional accounts of working conditions. Great Britain had a well-developed collective-choice mechanism; eight-hour agreements were worked out in which skilled workers often subsidized the change. In the United States the recruiting of immigrant workers allowed an equilibrium in which the average worker preferred a twelve-hour day. After the cutoff of immigration, steelworkers lacked a practiced voice with which to express rapidly changing preferences. As a result, the twelve-hour day persisted until public opinion and government intervention forced a change.

A SHORT HISTORY OF WORKING HOURS

This article begins its investigation in 1890, a time when the extension of the twelve-hour day was complete. Before cheap methods of making steel were introduced, only blast furnaces generally ran two twelve-hour shifts. The twelve-hour day spread with the technological revolution in steelmaking, which brought lessened physical effort, lower skill requirements, and increased vertical integration.[4]

Figure 1 compares labor hours after 1890 in U.S. iron and steel to hours in all manufacturing industries. For manufacturing in general the greatest reductions occurred between 1910 and 1920. In iron and steel, however, average weekly hours remained constant until 1919, then fell slightly in 1920, and dramatically to 1924. Although the all-manufacturing average masks more abrupt changes in individual industries, the 12.7 percent drop in steel from 1922 to 1924 is unusual. For the twelve

[2] Fitch, *Steel Workers*, p. 232.

[3] The Amalgamated Association of Iron and Steel Workers, which was strong in the iron industry until the 1890s, lost ground after Homestead and did not survive the changes in technology and industrial organization that accompanied the transition to steel. For discussions of comparative union development, see James Holt, "Trade Unionism in the British and U.S. Steel Industries, 1880–1914: A Comparative Study," *Labor History*, 18 (Winter 1977), pp. 5–35; and Frank Wilkinson, "Collective Bargaining in the Steel Industry in the 1920s," in Asa Briggs and John Saville, eds., *Essays in Labor History, 1918–1939* (London, 1977), pp. 102–32.

[4] Discussions of hours before 1890 are found in David Brody, *Steelworkers in America: The Nonunion Era* (1st edn., 1960; paperback edn., Cambridge, 1969), pp. 35–37; and Bernard Elbaum and Frank Wilkinson, "Industrial Relations and Uneven Development: A Comparative Study of the American and British Steel Industries," *Cambridge Journal of Economics*, 3 (Sept. 1979), pp. 277–84.

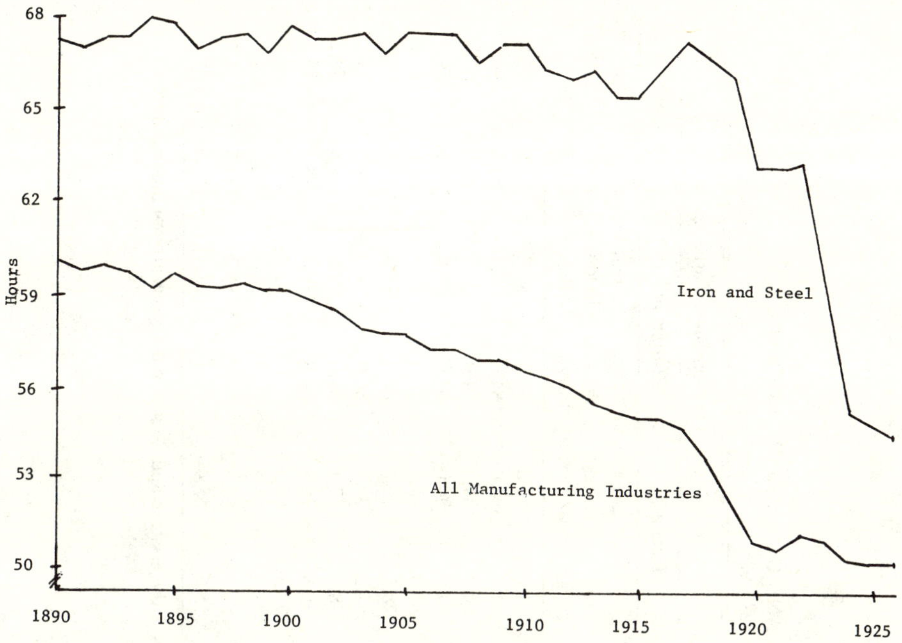

FIGURE 1

AVERAGE WEEKLY HOURS OF WORK IN IRON AND STEEL AND ALL MANUFACTURING, UNITED STATES, 1890–1926

Source: Paul A. Douglas, *Real Wages in the United States, 1890–1926* (New York, 1966), pp. 114, 116.

industries in Paul Douglas's study, the only comparable reductions occurred from 1918 to 1920 in the woolens and meatpacking industries.[5]

Average hours for the iron and steel industry also mask considerable variation among departments. Table 1 gives weekly hours for some typical occupations. Of the different operations, only blast furnaces had to be operated continuously. Even in continuous-operation departments, not all occupations were on the shift system. Many laborers, machinists, and other auxiliary workers were on one daily shift of ten hours. As Table 2 shows, 69 percent of blast furnace workers and 76 percent of open-hearth workers worked twelve-hour shifts in 1910.

Other departments, such as puddling mills, Bessemer mills, and finishing mills, had greater flexibility in setting schedules. In puddling mills, two eight- to ten-hour shifts per day were typical, with no work on Sunday. Bessemer mills worked continuously from 6 P.M. on Sunday until 6 P.M. on the following Saturday. Here most shiftworkers worked

[5] Paul A. Douglas, *Real Wages in the United States, 1890–1926* (1st edn., 1930; reprint edn., New York, 1966), pp. 92–93, 112, 114. For further discussion of data and data sources, see Martha Shiells, "Hours of Work and Shiftwork in the Early Industrial Labor Markets of Great Britain, the United States, and Japan" (Ph.D. dissertation, University of Michigan, 1985), chap. 4.

TABLE 1
AVERAGE HOURS OF WORK PER WEEK BY OCCUPATION AND GEOGRAPHIC DIVISION, U.S. IRON AND STEEL INDUSTRY, 1907–1926

	Steel Finishing Mill (Bar)						Wrought Iron		Pig-Iron Blast Furnaces					
	Catchers		Rollers		Roughers		Puddlers		Keepers		Bottom Fillers		Skip Operators	
Year	Pitts-burgh	Great Lakes/ Midwest	Pitts-burgh	Great Lakes/ Midwest	Pitts-burgh	Great Lakes/ Midwest	Pitts-burgh	Great Lakes/ Midwest	Pitts-burgh	Great Lakes/ Midwest	Pitts-burgh	Great Lakes/ Midwest	Pitts-burgh	Great Lakes/ Midwest
1907	65.9	55.4	66.9	65.6	66.4	56.7			84.0	84.0	84.0	84.0	84.0	84.0
1908	66.2	55.4	67.3	66.7	67.0	58.6			84.0	84.0	84.0	84.0	84.0	84.0
1909	66.0	55.4	66.9	66.7	66.7	58.5			84.0	84.0	84.0	84.0	84.0	84.0
1910	62.2	55.4	62.9	66.8	62.7	60.2			84.0	84.0	84.0	84.0	84.0	84.0
1911	62.0	55.4	62.2	65.8	61.9	59.8			84.0	80.3	84.0	84.0	84.0	84.0
1912	61.3	55.5	61.3	66.2	61.1	59.8			78.5	79.1	84.0	84.0	77.4	81.2
1913	61.8	56.0	61.7	60.3	62.5	55.9			84.0	79.1	84.0	84.0	84.0	81.1
1914	62.2	57.0	61.7	59.7	62.5	56.7	51.4	54.5	78.9	77.1	84.0	80.9	78.4	78.2
1915	61.5	58.3	60.9	60.4	61.8	57.9	51.7	54.5	78.8	76.3	84.0	79.4	78.7	76.8
1920	62.8	50.2	61.0	57.7	60.4	49.9	51.8		77.3	66.3		61.7	77.2	63.2
1922	57.6	54.1	56.7	58.9	56.1	53.8	46.8		75.6	71.7		70.2	76.0	71.5
1924	52.6	56.2	51.4	54.1	52.3	55.2	47.9		54.7	55.3		55.3	54.9	55.1
1926	51.9	52.7	51.0	52.9	52.8	52.5			55.5	55.4		53.0	55.8	55.4

Note: Divisions shown are the Pittsburgh district and the Great Lakes and Midwest district. Hours in the Eastern and Southern divisions are not much different than those shown from 1907–1922, but the reductions after 1922 were smaller.
Source: U.S. Bureau of Labor Statistics, Bulletin 604 (Washington, 1934), pp. 238–52.

TABLE 2
WORKERS ON TWELVE-HOUR DAYS, BY DEPARTMENT,
U.S. IRON AND STEEL INDUSTRY, 1910 AND 1920
(percentage)

	1910			1920		
	12 hours	Between 8 and 12 hours	8 hours	12 hours	Between 8 and 12 hours	8 hours
Blast Furnaces	69%	30%	1%	63%	19%	18%
Bessemer Mills	65	19	16	75	3	22
Open-Hearth Mills	76	22	2	50	20	30
Puddling Mills				20	60	20
Blooming Mills				60	15	25
Rail Mills				60	0	40
Bar Mills				over 50	under 35	15
Sheet and Plate Mills				under 10	over 25	60–70

Note: No comparison could be made between the two years for the finishing mills because the data were classified differently in the two reports.
Source: American Engineering Council, *The Twelve Hour Shift in Industry*, pp. 225–27. Compiled from U.S. Congress, Senate, *Report on Conditions of Employment in the United States Iron and Steel Industry* (vols. 1–4, S. Doc 110, 62nd Cong, 1st session, 1911–1913) and U.S. Bureau of Labor Statistics, Bulletin 205 (Washington, 1922).

twelve hours, but men who were exposed to extreme heat often had eight-hour shifts. Finishing, blooming, and rail mills, which were highly automated and often directly integrated with the steel-making departments, worked hours similar to Bessemer mills. On the other hand, in bar, sheet, and plate mills, where heavier exertion and more skill were required, hours tended to be shorter.

Statistics on hours in iron and steel are less complete for Great Britain than for the United States.[6] The existing data suggest that British and American workers had similar schedules up to 1918. Yet three shifts were adopted in some British regions as early as 1900, and work typically stopped earlier on Saturday in Great Britain.

The reductions at the end of the war show that hours remained longer in iron and steel than in virtually any other British industry. The August 1919 *Labour Gazette* gives normal weekly hours by industry and region for December 31, 1918, and July 31, 1919. During this period a standard workweek of 46 to 49 hours was established for all reporting industries, including iron and steel. Before the reductions, hours in most industries were from 48 to 58 per week, 50 to 54 hours being the most common. Only the iron and steel and tinplate manufacturing entries mention twelve-hour shifts.

[6] Board of Trade enquiries into wages and hours in iron and steel in 1886 and 1906 are in *Parliamentary Papers (Commons)*, 1890, vol. 68, p. 591, C. 375; and 1893/4, vol. 83, pt. II, p. i, C. 6889. The poor sample size in these enquiries is discussed in Donald N. McCloskey, *Economic Maturity and Entrepreneurial Decline: British Iron and Steel, 1870–1913* (Cambridge, 1973), p. 75n. Another source on hours is Ministry of Labour, "Changes in Rates of Wages and Hours of Labour in the UK," *Labour Gazette*, annually from 1893.

EXPLAINING HOURS REDUCTIONS

Standard labor supply theories assume that firms offer a constant hourly wage and that workers then choose hours to maximize utility. This theory requires that the firm not care about the working hours of an individual employee. If production depends on workers performing their tasks simultaneously, however, shift length will be a workplace public good. Working hours also concern the owners of capital, who will generally favor constant operation.

The presence of shared working conditions does not in itself imply a need for collective choice. If a continuum of job packages exists, and if workers can move between jobs, then a Tiebout local public-good equilibrium can be achieved. In this situation each worker chooses job attributes independently through a sorting of workers among firms. A static model of hours determination in which all workers in a firm have identical preferences regarding income and leisure largely captures conditions in both British and United States iron and steel in 1890. The local public-good equilibrium breaks down in a dynamic process that yields insights into the transition to eight-hour days.

Hours in 1890: A Model of Cooperating Factors

To model hours determination when two types of labor and capital must cooperate in the production process, consider a firm that uses skilled and unskilled labor in fixed proportions.[7] The proportion of skilled workers is p, hours per shift are H, and the hourly wage demanded by workers is given by $s(H)$ for skilled workers and $u(H)$ for unskilled workers. For simplicity, shift choices are restricted to twelve or eight hours. If productivity is the same on both schedules, then any difference in profits between the two- and three-shift schedules must be caused by differences in hourly wage bills. Higher labor productivity on eight-hour shifts would favor three shifts while higher fixed costs per worker would favor two shifts; these complications are omitted here for ease of exposition. The firm will work three shifts, then, if

$$ps(8) + (1 - p)u(8) < ps(12) + (1 - p)u(12).$$

The choice of shift systems depends on the skill mix and on the hourly wages that must be paid to attract eight- and twelve-hour skilled and unskilled workers.

The wage functions, $s(H)$ and $u(H)$, are derived as follows. Skilled and unskilled workers differ only in that the skilled earn higher hourly wages. By assumption, the standard labor-leisure choice model applies to both types in a large sector that provides reservation levels for hours,

[7] Alan V. Deardorff and Frank P. Stafford, "Compensation of Cooperating Factors," *Econometrica*, 44 (July 1976), pp. 671–84, develop the model of cooperating factors used here and also suggest the application to eight-hour days in steel.

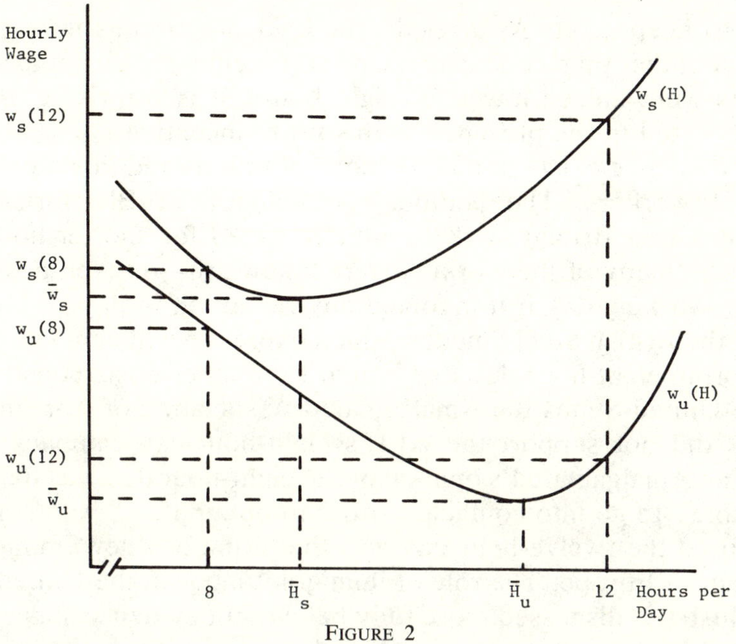

FIGURE 2

WAGE FUNCTIONS FOR SKILLED AND UNSKILLED WORKERS

wages, and utility. Also, a Tiebout equilibrium has been reached, so that all workers of a given skill type have identical wage functions. Since wage functions are derived from indifference curves attained in the standard sector, the functions reach unique minimums at the prevailing standard-sector hours. For longer or shorter hours, the wage functions indicate the compensating differentials that must be paid. If standard-sector hours are shorter for skilled than unskilled workers, then skilled workers would have to be paid a higher premium for long hours. On the other hand, unskilled workers would demand a relatively high premium for short hours.

Figure 2 pictures wage functions that may have confronted steelmakers in 1890. Premiums would most probably have been demanded for either twelve- or eight-hour days, and the average hourly wage would most likely have been lower for twelve-hour days. A ten-hour day was standard at this time for the majority of manufacturing workers in both Great Britain and the United States. If workers who were relatively less averse to long hours had been sorted into the steel industry, then higher compensating differentials would have been required for eight hours than for twelve hours.

Proving that steelworkers in 1890 demanded a lower premium for twelve than for eight hours is difficult. The existence of twelve-hour days does not prove a preference for them, since it can be argued that preferences were not realized. Even the lack of voiced opposition to long days is not conclusive, since workers and unions may have had reasons to keep quiet. As a result, the evidence on this issue may be suggestive rather than conclusive. One argument is that if compensating payments were indeed lower for eight hours, it is surprising that long hours persisted in the presence of this profit incentive.

Other evidence exists in the positions of unions and in statements of individual workers. The National Association of Blastfurnacemen, formed in Great Britain in 1888, initially called for shorter hours, but found that "many of the workers were lukewarm—or even hostile—to a shorter working day if it involved any reduction in pay."[8] Not until 1911 did the British Steel Smelters union express a willingness to accept wages for an eight-hour day that would keep labor costs constant.[9]

In the United States the Amalgamated Association of Iron and Steel Workers did not support the AFL's eight-hour-day campaign in the 1890s. The Amalgamated's opinion of the eight-hour day was that it was inadvisable "to go into conflict in order to obtain it."[10] Another factor that favored the twelve-hour day was the hiring of "new immigrants" from Eastern Europe. The role of immigrant labor in the United States steel industry is discussed more fully below, but evidence suggests that these workers were not averse to long hours.

> Russian steel laborers in Pittsburgh told an investigator they were glad to work extra days. A majority voluntarily reported on Sunday to clear yards and repair equipment. An immigrant characterized his twelve hour position: "A good job, save money, work all the time, go home, sleep, no spend."[11]

Changing Preferences

If in 1890 steel industries found themselves in equilibria in which it was cheaper to compensate workers for twelve than for eight hours, this situation could not be expected to continue. Over the next decades hours fell for almost all manufacturing workers (see Figure 1). Various explanations exist for this decline in hours, including wage increases with backward-bending labor supply curves.[12] Even if steelworkers did not have backward-bending labor supply curves, shorter hours in other industries would cause changes in reservation hours, wages, and utility. These changes would shift the wage functions in Figure 2 up and to the left, and at some point eight hours would become cheaper than twelve. Unless changes in preferences and reservation utilities happened simultaneously for all skilled and unskilled workers, however, the transition to eight-hour days would create a public-good problem.

[8] Carr and Taplin, *British Steel*, p. 137.

[9] Pugh, *Men of Steel*, p. 171.

[10] Pittsburgh *Post*, 4 July 1892, as quoted in Brody, *Steelworkers*, p. 52.

[11] Ibid., p. 100.

[12] Robert Whaples, "Winning the Eight-Hour Day, 1909–1919," this issue of the JOURNAL, pp. 393–406, presents estimates indicating that wage increases accounted for about 30 percent of the reduction in hours.

As workers' preferences and opportunities change, employers can adopt one of two strategies: maintaining a local public-good equilibrium or solving a collective-choice problem. The first option requires replacing disgruntled workers with new recruits who still prefer long hours. Either the industry as a whole can do this, or there can be a sorting of workers between firms in the industry, with more firms moving to eight-hour shifts over time. In the second option, firms retain workforces with diverse preferences regarding income and leisure. In this case there is a collective-choice problem within the firm (or within the industry if hours are set at an industry level). If worker mobility is low, or if the cost of finding and training new workers is high, the cost of compensating heterogeneous workers may be less than the cost of searching out homogeneous workers.[13]

If workers with heterogeneous preferences share working conditions, workers and firms also need some means of expressing preferences and negotiating working conditions. In this situation, the course of hours changes over time will depend on the collective-choice mechanism. If it is efficient, hours changes will reflect changes in the average worker's preferences. If workers have a poor voice or none, working conditions will reflect changing preferences poorly and a demand can arise for government intervention. Furthermore, the need to solve a collective-choice problem implies a potential demand for a union's services. Taking this into account may enrich explanations of differences in degrees of unionization.

GREAT BRITAIN: SUCCESSFUL COLLECTIVE CHOICE

In Great Britain workers with different labor-leisure preferences were not sorted among firms. With few exceptions work schedules were the same for all firms in a region. Union rules that based promotion upon seniority within a firm restricted the mobility of skilled workers.[14] As a result skilled workers could not change their hours by changing firms. Joint boards of arbitration and conciliation, established in iron and steel beginning in 1869, also encouraged similar working conditions throughout the industry. Often controlled by union and employers' associations, the boards set wages and hours for entire regions.[15]

In 1905 the employers' side of the North of England board was asked to allow one steel mill, the Port Clarence Works, to use eight-hour shifts. The request was refused: "If we were to concede it—what about

[13] Greg J. Duncan and Frank P. Stafford, "Do Union Members Receive Compensating Wage Differentials?" *American Economic Review*, 70 (June 1980), pp. 355–71, develop this model of workplace public goods, the cost of assembling homogeneous workers, and unions as mechanisms for collective choice.

[14] Wilkinson, "Collective Bargaining," p. 106.

[15] Hugh A. Clegg, Alan Fox, and A. F. Thompson, *A History of British Trade Unions Since 1889*. Vol. 1: *1889–1920* (Oxford, 1964), pp. 21–23.

other shops? You would ask it for them too . . . . We see where it will lead: a hugely increased cost and in light of foreign competition we cannot face it.''[16] The Port Clarence Works had to withdraw from the employers' association and the joint board in order to institute a three-shift system.

In Great Britain, then, hours were determined at a regional level, and within regions there must have been workers with dissimilar preferences. Regional boards reconciled the diverse preferences of employers and different groups of workers. Indeed, one reason for the strength of collective bargaining in the British iron and steel industry may have been the need to negotiate shared working conditions.

In 1917 the Iron and Steel Trades Confederation (ISTC), the principal union in the industry, adopted the eight-hour day as its primary objective.[17] The ISTC and the employers' organizations set a goal of adopting eight-hour days at the end of the war. Agreements were drafted by managers and workers at individual firms and reviewed by district and central committees. By March 1919 agreements had been adopted and the eight-hour day was in force. A common element of the agreements was that low-paid workers received constant weekly pay, implying a one-third increase in hourly pay. Most of the high-paid workers continued to earn the same hourly pay, so that their weekly pay was cut by one-third.[18] The ISTC journal noted that the lack of friction in making the arrangements was ''the highest tribute to the machinery of negotiation existing in the iron and steel trades . . . .''[19]

THE UNITED STATES: IMMIGRATION, WEAK VOICE, AND GOVERNMENT INTERVENTION

In the United States the steel industry responded to growing pressures for shorter hours by searching for workers willing to accept a low premium for twelve-hour days. From 1890 until the war the United States industry relied on a continual inflow of Eastern European immigrants to satisfy the increasingly mechanized steel plants' demands for unskilled labor.[20] The ''new immigrants'' were men who came to

[16] Pugh, *Men of Steel*, p. 137.

[17] The move to eight hours is discussed in Carr and Taplin, *British Steel*, pp. 451–56, and Pugh, *Men of Steel*, pp. 280–86.

[18] This was true for blast furnaces in South Wales, iron and steel mills in the North of England, open hearth mills in England and Scotland, and steel mills in the West of Scotland (see Bowley, *Prices and Wages*, pp. 145–47). Reductions in weekly base earnings were graduated, from no reduction for men earning under 50s ranging up to a one-third reduction for men earning 120s per week. Pugh, *Men of Steel*, pp. 611–14, reproduces the agreement that covered most workers.

[19] Pugh, *Men of Steel*, p. 286.

[20] U.S. steelmakers adopted a number of innovations that replaced skilled craftsmen and manual labor with machines and unskilled labor. These innovations and differences in occupational structures between Great Britain and the United States are discussed in Robert C. Allen, ''The Peculiar Productivity History of American Blast Furnaces, 1840–1913,'' this JOURNAL, 37 (Sept.

America "to temporarily take advantage of the greater wages paid for industrial labor in this country."[21] There were heavy concentrations of these immigrants in the steel industry, particularly in jobs and departments with twelve-hour days. In 1907/8 58 percent of all male employees in the iron and steel industry were foreign-born.[22] In the Carnegie plants of Allegheny County in March 1907, 11,694 out of 14,359 common laborers were Eastern Europeans.[23] This figure includes Italian as well as Slavic immigrants; other sources indicate that by 1910 Slavic immigrants were the predominant source of unskilled labor.[24]

The new immigration was at least partially induced by an active recruitment system. This system communicated employers' demands through a network of labor agents and steamship companies.[25] New immigrants replaced American, Irish, English, and German steelworkers, who moved into skilled jobs or into other industries. The older workers often left because of the long hours in the mills. A "Scotch-Irish furnace boss" said this about long hours:

> That's what's driven the Irish out of the industry . . . the Irish don't have to work this way. There was fifty of them here with me sixteen years ago and now where are they? I meet 'em sometimes around the city, ridin' in carriages and all of them wearin' white shirts, and here I am . . . [26]

Immigrant labor had two effects on working hours. First, it encouraged the adoption of technology that replaced skilled with unskilled labor. If premiums for long hours were lower for unskilled than for skilled laborers, then employing a higher proportion of unskilled labor would favor twelve-hour days. Furthermore, since unskilled workers

---

1977), pp. 605–33; Allen, "International Competition in Iron and Steel, 1850–1913," this JOURNAL, 39 (Dec. 1979), pp. 911–37; Allen, "Accounting for Price Changes: American Steel Rails, 1879–1920," *Journal of Political Economy*, 89 (June 1981), pp. 512–28; Bernard Elbaum, "The Making and Shaping of Job and Pay Structures in the Iron and Steel Industry," in Paul Osterman, ed., *Internal Labor Markets* (Cambridge, 1984), pp. 71–107; Elbaum and Wilkinson, "Industrial Relations;" and Holt, "Trade Unionism."

[21] U.S. Congress, Senate, *Abstract of Reports of the Immigration Commission* (vol. 1, S.Doc. 747, 61st Cong., 3rd sess., 1911), p. 24, as quoted in Michael J. Piore, *Birds of Passage: Migrant Labor and Industrial Societies* (Cambridge, 1979), p. 149. Piore, pp. 149–54, contains a general discussion of the new immigrants.

[22] Daniel Nelson, *Managers and Workers: Origins of the New Factory System in the United States, 1880–1920* (Madison, 1975), p. 80.

[23] Brody, *Steelworkers*, p. 96.

[24] Ibid., pp. 96–106. Also, John Bodnar, *Immigration and Industrialization: Ethnicity in an American Mill Town, 1870–1940* (Pittsburgh, 1977), pp. 15–17; and John Bodnar, Roger Simon, and Michael Weber, *Lives of Their Own: Blacks, Italians, and Poles in Pittsburgh, 1900–1960* (Chicago, 1982).

[25] Piore, *Birds of Passage*, p. 152. Bodnar, *Immigration and Industrialization*, describes the flow of Eastern European and black labor into Steelton. Bodnar, et al., *Lives of Their Own*, describe the recruitment of immigrant labor into Pittsburgh. Immigrants are portrayed as being aware of working conditions before their arrival.

[26] Fitch, *Steel Workers*, p. 11.

can be replaced at lower cost, it would be more feasible to discharge workers as their preferences changed. Second, immigrants provided steel companies with supplies of workers who were alike in demanding a lower premium for twelve than for eight hours.

An interesting consequence of greater homogeneity in workers' labor-leisure preferences is that the demand for a union's services is lowered. Traditional explanations of relatively late and weak union development in the United States stress the heterogeneous languages and cultures caused by successive waves of immigration that made organization difficult. A model of workplace public goods complements this explanation by pointing out the firms' incentive to recruit immigrants in order to maintain homogeneous preferences. If the workers in a department have the same preferences for working hours, they do not need a union to negotiate their working hours. Steelworkers obviously had other reasons for wanting a union, but homogeneous preferences may have worked along with cultural diversity to delay unionization.

The strategy of recruiting immigrants was shattered when immigration was cut off, first by the war, then by law in 1923. After failing to reproduce the same conditions by recruiting Southern blacks or orientals, the steel industry had to face the issue of changing preferences.[27] Initial attempts by the AFL to organize steelworkers were successful in 1918, with a popular slogan being "eight hours and the union." Although steelworkers wanted an eight-hour day and felt they needed a union to attain it, a 1919 strike failed.[28] After years of having no collective voice, steelworkers had little opportunity to learn to communicate effectively. Without a collective bargaining process, the steelworkers' hope for shorter hours lay with public opinion and government intervention.

Between the 1919 strike and the adoption of eight-hour shifts in 1923, public opinion was mobilized and government pressure exerted. An influential 1920 report by the Interchurch World Movement concluded "that the 12-hour day is a barbarism without valid excuse, penalizing the workers and the country."[29] A statement drafted by Herbert Hoover, then Secretary of Commerce, and signed by President Harding indicated the administration's position:

> It has seemed to me for a long time that the twelve-hour day and the type of worker it produces have outlived their usefulness and their part in American life in the interests of good citizenship, of good business, and of economic stability. The old order of the twelve-hour day must give way to a better and wiser form of organization of the

[27] Migrant black steelworkers are discussed in Brody, *Steelworkers*, pp. 184–87; Bodnar, *Immigration and Industrialization*, pp. 14–15; and Bodnar, et al., *Lives of Their Own*, pp. 31–36, 190–92. Brody, p. 187, discusses a proposal to recruit oriental workers.

[28] See Brody, *Steelworkers*, chap. 12; and Gerald G. Eggert, *Steelmasters and Labor Reform, 1886–1923* (Pittsburgh, 1981).

[29] Interchurch World Movement, *Steel Strike*, p. 84.

productive forces of the nation, so that proper family life and citizenship may be enjoyed suitably by all of our people.[30]

In spite of repeated hints to act voluntarily or risk direct government involvement, the steelmen hesitated. At a stockholders meeting on April 17, 1922, Judge Gary of U.S. Steel reported that although some progress had been made, the men still preferred twelve-hour shifts.[31] In May 1923 an immediate move to eight-hour days was again rejected by a committee headed by Gary. Further warnings from Harding, however, led to capitulation. In a June 27, 1923, letter, Judge Gary wrote to Harding that the twelve-hour day would be ended because of "a strong sentiment throughout the country . . . and especially because it is in accordance with your own expressed views."[32] The change to eight-hour days was completed by the end of 1923.

CONCLUSION

When working hours are a public good, hours and wages may change in ways that are not predicted by standard labor market models. A workplace public good means that either a local public-good equilibrium must be maintained or a collective-choice problem must be solved. Maintaining a local public-good equilibrium when preferences are changing requires that workers move among firms and that working schedules vary among firms. Alternatively, new supplies of workers whose preferences match existing working conditions can be recruited.

If the local public-good solution breaks down, labor market dynamics will be influenced by the collective-choice mechanism. In general, hours will decrease discontinuously after the preferences of a substantial group of employees change and a reduction is negotiated. Job attributes will tend to reflect the average worker's, rather than the marginal worker's, preferences. As a result, wages and job attributes will be less responsive to marginal changes in preferences. How well changing preferences are reflected in working conditions will depend on the efficiency of the collective-choice mechanism. If the mechanism breaks down, there is a role for government intervention.

This article illustrates the interplay between institutions, social forces, and outcomes. The presence of shared working conditions leads to different adaptions: in Great Britain, strong unions to give the workers voice; in the United States, the recruiting of immigrant workers to maintain uniform preferences. These adaptations then influence future outcomes. The British steel industry, with its internal promotion ladders and low worker mobility, used voice, rather than exit, to set shared working conditions. Here the strong choice mechanism allowed

[30] American Engineering Council, *Twelve Hour Shift*, p. ix.
[31] Eggert, *Steelmasters*, p. 155.
[32] Quoted in Brody, *Steelworkers*, p. 274.

a smoother, earlier transition to eight-hour days. With its reliance on recruitment and exit, the United States industry had little experience to draw on when changing labor market conditions increased the need to listen to workers. Ultimately, government intervention was necessary to win the eight-hour day for United States steelworkers.

Winning the Eight-Hour Day, 1909–1919

ROBERT WHAPLES

The American workers' quest for an eight-hour day finally came to an end around 1919. I argue that the most important factors behind the rapid decline in manufacturing hours in the decade before 1919 include the rapid expansion of the economy, which increased wages and drew new participants into the manufacturing sector; the reduction of immigration during the war; the growth in organized labor's strength; federal and state legislation that mandated reduced work weeks; and the electrification of the manufacturing sector.

> *The whole spirit of the time and the preponderant evidence of recent economic experience [speaks] for the eight hour day. It has been adjudged by the thought and experience of recent years a thing upon which society is justified in insisting as in the interest of health, efficiency, contentment, and a general increase of economic vigor.*
>
> —Woodrow Wilson[1]

Before World War II workers' demands for shorter hours were often advanced with greater fervor than demands for higher wages. The shorter-hours movement galvanized organized labor. It was the spark that helped found the first national labor union in the 1860s and the American Federation of Labor in the 1880s, the major issue in the steel strike of 1919, and remained important into the 1930s.[2]

The vision of the eight-hour day was especially potent. "Eight hours for work, eight hours for rest, eight hours for what we will," was the rallying cry raised immediately after the Civil War. Strain as they might, winning the eight-hour day proved very difficult for American workers. The average length of the work week inched downward, so that in 1910 the nine-hour day was still the norm. Then suddenly victory was

The Journal of Economic History, Vol. L, No. 2 (June 1990). ISSN 0022-0507.

The author is Assistant Professor of History, University of Wisconsin, Milwaukee, WI 53201.

For useful comments and advice, I wish to thank Price Fishback, Claudia Goldin, Robert Margo, Bruce Fallick, David Buffum, Laura Huntoon, Martin Eisenberg, Gerald Friedman, Richard Sutch, David Roediger, Josh Rosenbloom, and seminar participants at the University of Pennsylvania, University of Kansas, Social Science History Association Meetings, and Economic History Association Meetings. Work on this article was performed while I was an Andrew Mellon Fellow with the Program for Assessing and Revitalizing the Social Sciences at the University of Pennsylvania.

[1] President Woodrow Wilson, Aug. 29, 1916, endorsing the Adamson Act. Arthur S. Link, ed., *The Papers of Woodrow Wilson*, vol. 38 (Princeton, 1982), p. 97.

[2] Marion Cotter Cahill, *Shorter Hours: A Study of the Movement since the Civil War* (New York, 1932); and David Roediger and Philip Foner, *Our Own Time: A History of American Labor and the Working Day* (Westport, 1989), give overviews of the shorter-hours movement.

achieved. In a single decade the work week fell by six hours. In 1909 less than one-twelfth of American manufacturing workers labored 48 hours or less each week (eight hours per day, six days per week); in 1919 nearly half did.[3]

As Benjamin Hunnicutt argues, this is an important, complex, and little-studied transition. "The rapid reduction in hours of work that took place from 1900 to 1920 was accompanied by a bewildering array of social, economic, and intellectual developments each of which might have had a role in causing the phenomenon. . . . Moreover, so little work has been done on each individual strand that any hope of considering them together, judging their relative importance and their influences on one another, is remote."[4] This untangling is the task I undertake here.

Many theories have been advanced that link the events of this period to the rapid decline in the length of the work week. What were the forces behind victory in "the decisive period in the battle for the eight hour day?" I test the leading explanations and argue that the most important factors behind the rapid decline include the rapid expansion of the economy, which increased wages and drew new participants into the manufacturing sector; the reduction of immigration during the war; the growth in organized labor's strength due to a tight labor market and the federal government's wartime labor policy; federal and state legislation that mandated reduced work weeks; and the electrification of manufacturing. Each factor played a distinct role, and cumulatively they created this "Great Decline" in the length of the work week.

THE LABOR MARKET OF THE 1910s AND THEORIES OF THE "GREAT DECLINE"

The five-year period of 1914 to 1919 was an era of unprecedented growth and change in the American economy. Demand for labor grew rapidly while its supply fell with the curtailment of immigration and the expansion of the military. While over a million immigrants per year came to America from 1900 to 1914, less than a quarter of a million per year arrived from 1915 to 1919, and the armed forces employed 4.1 million by 1918. The gainful occupation rate of women climbed somewhat, but the civilian labor force, which grew at about 2.8 percent per year from 1900 to 1914, virtually stopped growing from 1914 to 1919.

[3] According to the Census of Manufactures, the average "normal" work week fell from 57.31 hours (1909) to 55.51 hours (1914) to 51.26 hours (1919). It is the census concept of normal hours which I use. The first twentieth-century industry-level data on hours are for 1909; city-level data on hours begin in 1914.

[4] Benjamin Hunnicutt, *Work Without End: Abandoning Shorter Hours for the Right to Work* (Philadelphia, 1988), p. 35.

Yet, in the face of this, manufacturing employment grew over 30 percent in these five years.[5]

The tight labor market caused unemployment to reach an all-time low of 1.4 percent in 1918 and 1919. The period of 1916 to 1919 was the first four-year period on record (Stanley Lebergott's series extends to 1890) in which the nonfarm unemployment rate did not exceed 10 percent in a single year. Real annual earnings rose as wages increased and employment filled more of the year. The long-term growth rate in earnings was greatly exceeded. The situation was especially bright in manufacturing, where the 1914 to 1919 rate of real earnings growth was 3.26 percent per year, well above the 1.4 percent annual growth rate from 1900 to 1914.[6]

Simultaneously, the federal government dramatically increased its intervention in the labor market, stipulating the basic 48-hour work week for railroad workers with the passage of the Adamson Act (1916) and actively mediating labor disputes, especially through the National War Labor Board, whose referees often awarded the basic eight-hour day. State governments tightened the restrictiveness of maximum-hours laws for women. Massachusetts, Minnesota, Oregon, and Utah, for example, reduced the legal maximum from 54 to 48 hours per week.[7] Trade unions enjoyed unprecedented political power and growth. Union leaders were courted by President Woodrow Wilson and were appointed to federal wartime agencies. Membership climbed from 2.0 million in 1909 to 4.13 million by 1919.[8]

Which of these forces were more important in the decline of the work week at the beginning of the century? Existing quantitative studies do not focus on this brief period of rapid change, looking instead at national aggregate time series data covering a half a century or more. They tend to emphasize the importance of changes in wages and generally ignore the role of organized labor and the government.[9] This is a major

[5] Immigration figures are from U.S. Department of Commerce, *Historical Statistics of the United States: Colonial Times to 1970* (Washington, DC, 1976), series C-89. Labor force figures are from Stanley Lebergott, *Manpower in Economic Growth: The American Record since 1800* (New York, 1964), tables A-3, A-5. Peak military strength is from Louis Ayres, *The War with Germany: A Statistical Analysis* (Washington, DC, 1919).

[6] Figures are from Lebergott, *Manpower*, tables A-3, A-5, A-15, A-16, A-18.

[7] The "basic eight-hour day" refers to a flat rate of pay for the first eight hours, with time-and-a-half for hours beyond eight. For state maximum-hours laws, see U.S. Women's Bureau, *Chronological Development of Labor Legislation for Women in the United States*, Bulletin No. 66-11 (Washington, DC, 1931).

[8] See Leo Wolman, *The Growth of American Trade Unions, 1880–1923* (New York, 1924), on the growth of unions; and Valerie Conner, *The National War Labor Board: Stability, Social Justice, and the Voluntary State in World War I* (Chapel Hill, 1983), on the role of union leaders in the government.

[9] For a survey, see Robert Whaples, "The Shortening of the American Work Week: An Economic and Historical Analysis of Its Context, Causes and Consequences" (Ph.D. diss., University of Pennsylvania, 1990); and John Owen, *Working Hours: An Economic Analysis* (Lexington, MA, 1979). Narrower studies which focus on the period around World War I include

omission to labor historians, many of whom agree with Marion Cahill's argument that the reduction in hours brought about by "natural" forces "has been less common than that brought about by legislative and trade-union action."[10]

A useful tool for understanding how these changes influenced the length of the work week in manufacturing is a version of the standard model of supply and demand for labor in which firms offer discrete hours-earnings packages to workers.[11] The model assumes that each worker maximizes utility subject to opportunities available within and outside the manufacturing sector. The worker's labor market behavior is summarized in his earnings curve. The earnings curve, *E*, is the indifference curve in earnings-hours space for which the worker's utility equals the reservation utility, which he is able to obtain outside the manufacturing sector. Along the earnings curve the worker is indifferent among earnings-hours packages and receives greater earnings for working additional hours. The worker will accept a manufacturing job only if its earnings-hours package is on or above this curve. The earnings curve of the marginal worker is the labor supply curve facing the firm.

Firms convert hours of labor and other inputs into output through a production function, *F*, and take the price of output, *P*, as given. It is assumed that all workers in the firm work the same hours each week.[12] Output increases as weekly hours are raised, but there are diminishing returns due to worker fatigue. The firm maximizes profit by offering the hours-earnings package at the point where the marginal cost of labor equals the value of its marginal product. In the simplest model it is assumed that the costs of other inputs are not affected by the choice of hours, so the firm maximizes profits by maximizing the difference between the total revenue per worker curve, FP/N, and the earnings curve. This equilibrium is shown in Figure 1.

Economic, technological, demographic, and other factors affect the length of the work week by determining the shape and position of the earnings curve facing the firm and its production function. As these underlying determinants change, the two curves move and the equilibrium level of hours changes. For example, as manufacturing employ-

---

Martha Shiells, "Collective Choice of Working Conditions," in this issue of the JOURNAL, pp. 379–92, and Claudia Goldin, "Maximum Hours Legislation and Female Employment in the 1920s: A Reassessment," *Journal of Political Economy*, 96 (Feb. 1988).

[10] Cahill, *Shorter Hours*, p. 27.

[11] This model is presented in Ben Bernanke, "Employment, Hours, and Earnings in the Depression," *American Economic Review*, 76 (Mar. 1986).

[12] The U.S. Bureau of the Census, *Fourteenth Census of the United States*, vol. 9, *Manufactures, 1919* (Washington, DC, 1923), reports only one level of hours for all workers in a single firm, stating, "no attention was paid to the fact that a few wage earners might have hours different from those of the majority. In most establishments, however, all the wage earners work the same number of hours, so that the figures give a substantially correct representation of the hours of labor," p. 17.

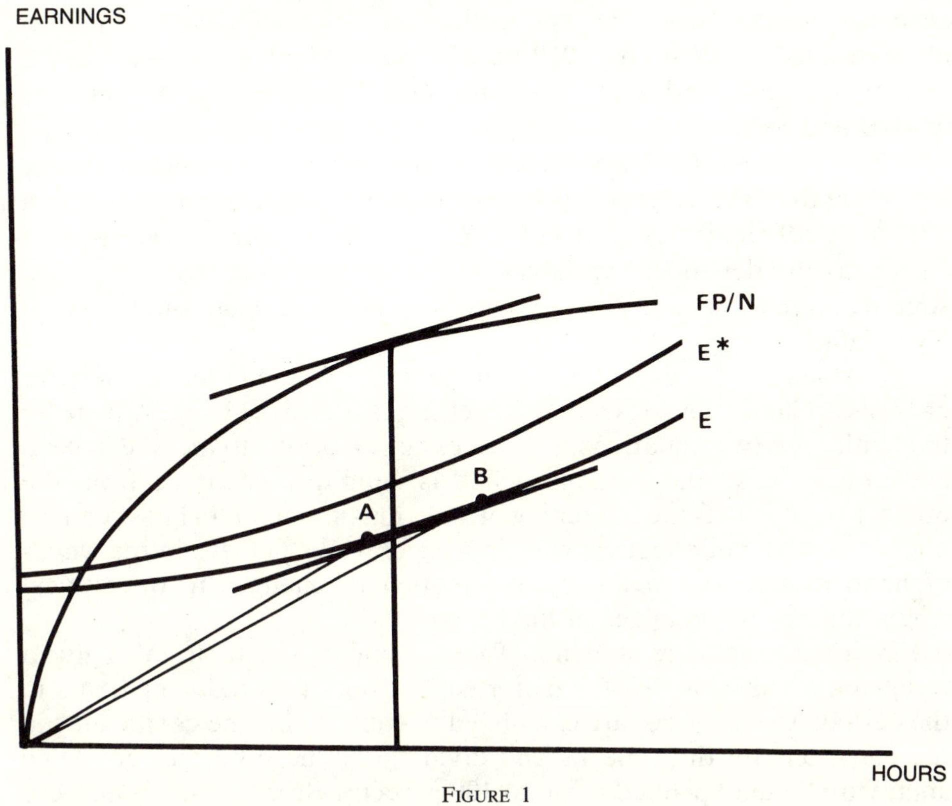

FIGURE 1

ment grew 30 percent in the late 1910s, firms were forced to hire workers whose reservation utility was previously above the earnings-hours package offered by manufacturers. These workers' earnings curves, E^*, are higher and steeper than those of the initial employees. To draw these workers into manufacturing, firms had to offer higher earnings and shorter hours. The wartime growth of the manufacturing sector should therefore be one of the reasons that hours fell.

This view of the labor market differs from the standard textbook model by recognizing that wages and hours are simultaneously determined. As hours are cut, even if the worker moves along his or her indifference curve, the hourly wage rate may change. This is illustrated by moving from point B to point A in Figure 1. The wage is the slope of the line connecting the point with the origin. Thus, the model cautions that hour and wage changes must be estimated jointly.

EMPIRICAL TESTS AND RESULTS

I examine the forces behind the decline in the work week's length using two data sets constructed from the manufacturing censuses taken in 1909, 1914, and 1919, the population censuses of 1910 and 1920, and several other sources. The first collection of data includes city-level observations for 1914 and 1919 on 274 cities which have over 25,000 residents. The second uses observations on 118 of the largest industries in 1909 and 1919.

I begin by using *HOURS CHANGE*, the negative percentage change in the length of the average work week in manufacturing in the city from 1914 to 1919, and *WAGE CHANGE*, the percentage change in real wages, as the dependent variables in a set of weighted two-stage least squares regressions and then repeat the procedure using the industry-level data.[13]

Two-stage least squares allows one to untangle the influence of wage changes on hours changes and hours changes on wage changes. In order to identify the two equations, it is necessary, a priori, to include in each equation at least one variable which is definitely excluded from the other. I assume that the tightening of state maximum hours laws reduces hours but does not effect changes in wages, while changes in the wages of nonoperative salaried workers are tied to changes in operatives' wages but not the changes in their hours.[14]

Empirical results are shown in Tables 1 and 2. The tables also give a rough approximation of each factor's contribution to reducing hours in the period. These shares are calculated by multiplying the coefficients in the equations by their means and dividing by the total change. They sum, with an unexplained term, to 100 percent. Bear in mind that these are only the direct effects of each force.

Testing the union-strength hypothesis requires the construction of industry-level unionization estimates. I begin with Leo Wolman's series on union size and make assumptions about matching census industries with unions. *UNION CHANGE* measures the growth during the decade in the percent of workers unionized in each industry outside of the South. To measure the strength of organized labor in each local labor market I estimate *STRIKE*, the number of industrial workers per capita in each city outside the South who went on strike from 1914 to 1919. (*UNION CHANGE* and *STRIKE* exclude the South because empirically neither union growth nor strikes led to shorter hours or higher wages in the South.) Both variables are statistically significant and could have a large local impact, but their total impact was rather small. Each

[13] The weights used are the number of manufacturing workers divided by the average number of manufacturing workers in the city or industry in 1919. Unweighted regressions show essentially the same patterns as the weighted equations, except that the independent variables *SHIP* and *ELECTRIFICATION* lose significance.

[14] The hours of salaried employees were set separately from those of operatives. However, salaries probably moved along with operatives' wages, since both were tied to the tightness of the local labor market and salaried workers received wage premia in industries in which operatives received wage premia. This anomaly has been noted for the postwar period in Alan Krueger and Lawrence Summers, "Efficiency Wages and Interindustry Wage Structure," *Econometrica*, 56 (Mar. 1988), and is verified using the industry-level data from 1909 and 1919.

directly accounts for less than 10 percent of the reduction in hours during the period.

Several variables suggest that the tight labor market was the most important force impelling the move toward shorter hours. *EXOGENOUS WAGE CHANGE*, the estimated exogenous increase in real wages, and *GROWTH*, the relative expansion of manufacturing employment in the city's region from 1914 to 1919, reduced the length of the work week. This reduction of hours as wages rose confirms the common finding of a backward-bending labor supply curve in this period. The city and industry equations suggest a wage-hours elasticity of about −0.10 to −0.12. Rising wages and growth of the manufacturing sector explain almost half the reduction in hours.

The jump in wages was not autonomous, however. The *WAGE CHANGE* equations indicate that the growth of unions was important in increasing wages. Unionization was responsible for about 33 percent of the increase in wages in the industry-level equation, and strikes accounted for 10 percent of the increase in the city-level equation. Adding this indirect influence on hours reductions, unionization explains up to 14 percent of the fall in hours.[15] The wage change equations show that labor markets were tightest in heavy industry. Wages rose faster in labor markets characterized by high and rising levels of capital per worker and high levels of horsepower per worker. Manufacturing wages also rose faster in oligopsonistic markets, where there was more employment in water-borne shipping and where salaried workers' wages were rising. Wages per worker declined as the share of lower-paid female workers increased. Finally, the drop in hours raised wages, though the effect is insignificantly different from zero.

The third major indication that a tight labor market drove hours down comes from an examination of immigration. Historians argue that in the early 1900s many European immigrants came to America to temporarily work and then remigrate. Their goal was to quickly amass as much earnings as possible and then return and use their wealth to establish themselves in the old country.[16] They wanted to work long hours. The war, by strangling immigration, reduced the supply of these workers in many cities and industries and trapped some immigrants in the United States. Such workers may have planned to work extremely long hours for only a short amount of time and may have been unwilling to continue

[15] This does not capture the interaction between unionization and strikes, since I cannot link strikes to industries and unionization to cities. Nor does it capture the threat effect that unionization had on nonunionized cities and industries. However, the increased unionization and strikes themselves may be a function of the labor market tightness and the actions of the federal government, so it may also overstate the role of unionization.

[16] Michael Piore, *Birds of Passage: Migrant Labor and Industrial Societies* (New York, 1979); David Brody, *Steelworkers in America: The Nonunion Era* (New York, 1960); and Shiells, "Collective Choice."

TABLE 1
CITY-LEVEL DETERMINANTS OF THE PERCENTAGE CHANGE IN HOURS AND REAL WAGES, 1914 TO 1919

	Hours Change Equation			
Variable	Coefficient	Mean	Percent Contribution Toward Reduced Hours	Wage Change Equation Coefficient
Intercept	0.8157	1	10.2%	2.5992
	(1.2193)			(4.6043)
STRIKE	0.0191*	17.7	4.2	0.0983**
	(0.0060)			(0.0442)
EXOGENOUS WAGE CHANGE	0.1206*	20.5	30.9	
	(0.0316)			
EXOGENOUS HOUR CHANGE				0.7446
				(0.6220)
GROWTH	0.0409*	31.7	16.2	
	(0.0171)			
FOREIGN BORN	0.0922*	16.8	19.4	
	(0.0207)			
FEMALE CHANGE	0.3828*	0.90	4.3	−0.8903*
	(0.1006)			(0.1894)
STATE LAW CHANGE	0.4155**	0.24	1.2	
	(0.2370)			
SHIP	0.0827*	3.09	3.2	
	(0.0215)			
WATER TRANSPORTATION	0.5264*	1.01	6.6	1.1992**
	(0.1289)			(0.6634)
OLIGOPSONY	1.7804*	0.17	3.8	0.1545*
	(0.5501)			(0.0335)
SALARY CHANGE				0.1678*
				(0.0569)
CAPITAL				−0.00056
				(0.00053)
CAPITAL CHANGE				0.1254*
				(0.0236)
HORSEPOWER				2.0267*
				(0.5268)
Number of observations	274			274
Adjusted R^2	0.414			0.396
Mean of dependent variable	7.93			18.12

* Significantly different from zero with 95 percent confidence.
** Significantly different from zero with 90 percent confidence.
Notes: Absolute values of standard errors are in parentheses. Dependent variable in hours change equation equals negative percent change in hours, 1914 to 1919. Dependent variable in wage change equation equals percent change in real wages, 1914 to 1919. The percent contribution toward reduced hours equals the mean of the independent variable times the coefficient divided by the mean percentage change in hours.
Sources: Data on hours, wages, number of workers, electricity, and oligopsony are from U.S. Bureau of the Census, *Fourteenth Census of the United States Taken in the Year 1920*, vol. 8: *Manufactures, 1919: General and Analytical Tables* (Washington, DC, 1923), and vol. 9: *Manufactures, 1919: Reports for States, With Statistics for Principal Cities* (Washington, DC, 1923); *Census of Manufactures, 1914*, vol. 1: *Report by States with Statistics for Principal Cities and Metropolitan Districts* (Washington, DC, 1918); and *Thirteenth Census of the United States Taken in the Year 1910*, vol. 8: *Manufactures, 1909: General Report and Analysis* (Washington, DC, 1913).

TABLE 1—continued

Occupational data are from U.S. Bureau of the Census, *Fourteenth Census of the United States Taken in the Year 1920*, vol. 4: *Population, 1920: Occupations* (Washington, DC, 1923); and *Thirteenth Census of the United States Taken in the Year 1910*, vol. 4: *Population, 1910: Occupation Statistics* (Washington, DC, 1914).

Population and nativity data are from U.S. Bureau of the Census, *Fourteenth Census of the United States Taken in 1920*, vol. 2: *Population, 1920: General Report and Analytical Tables* (Washington, DC, 1922); and *Thirteenth Census of the United States Taken in 1910*, vol. 1: *Population, 1910: General Report and Analysis* (Washington, DC, 1913).

Maximum hours laws are from U.S. Women's Bureau, *Chronological Development of Labor Legislation for Women in the United States*, Bulletin No. 66-11 (Washington, DC, 1931).

Number of shipbuilding workers equals the number of shipbuilding laborers and shipbuilding semiskilled operatives in cities over 100,000. Shipbuilding centers under 100,000 were identified in the Third and Fourth *Annual Report of the United States Shipping Board* (Washington, DC, 1919 and 1920). The largest firm in each of these cities was assumed to be in the shipbuilding industry.

Strike data are from U.S. Department of Labor, *Reports of the Department of Labor: Report of the Secretary of Labor* (Washington, DC, 1916–1920).

Unionization data are based on Leo Wolman, *Ebb and Flow in Trade Unionism* (New York, 1936). See Robert Whaples, "The Shortening of the American Work Week: An Economic and Historical Analysis of Its Context, Causes and Consequences" (Ph.D. diss., University of Pennsylvania, 1990), appendix 2.

working long hours indefinitely. In spite of recruiting new sources of unskilled labor including blacks, Mexicans, and farm workers, industrial employers found fewer workers who would put in long hours.

Cities with more foreign-born workers, therefore, should have seen hours fall more rapidly than others. This would occur both because the foreign born who were in the city may have wanted to reduce their hours, but especially because these were the markets to which new immigrants would have gone had the war not disrupted their plans.[17] Empirically, hours do fall more rapidly when *FOREIGN BORN*, the foreign-born share of the city's population, is higher. The disruption caused hours to fall by about 20 percent (see Table 1).

The final sign of a tight market is that *FEMALE CHANGE*, the change in the percentage of women employed in the city, is significant and positive. As more women were drawn into the city's manufacturing sector, hours fell. This may also mean that women desired shorter hours than men. In either case, *FEMALE CHANGE* had only a small effect in reducing hours.

The influence of maximum hours laws is measured by *STATE LAW CHANGE*, the estimated amount which hours would have fallen if changes in the states' laws were binding.[18] The coefficient, while

[17] See, for example, James Dunlevy and Henry Gemery, "The Role of Migrant Stock and Lagged Migration in the Settlement Patterns of Nineteenth-Century Immigrants," *Review of Economics and Statistics*, 59 (May 1977), who show that the past flow of immigration is the key predictor of its future flow.

[18] One indication that these laws were binding is seen in New England textile cities like Fall River, MA. In 1914, 90.1 percent of workers worked the legal weekly maximum for women (54 hours), in 1919, 97.2 percent worked the new maximum (48 hours).

TABLE 2
INDUSTRY-LEVEL DETERMINANTS OF THE PERCENTAGE CHANGE IN HOURS AND REAL WAGES, 1909 TO 1919

	Hours Change Equation			
Variable	Coefficient	Mean	Percent Contribution Toward Reduced Hours	Wage Change Equation Coefficient
Intercept	3.854* (0.679)	1.0	35.7%	−13.7030* (6.4342)
UNION CHANGE	0.0665* (0.0158)	13.6	8.4	0.5163* (0.1281)
EXOGENOUS WAGE CHANGE	0.1042* (0.0221)	17.4	16.7	
EXOGENOUS HOUR CHANGE				0.4882 (0.4523)
STATE LAW CHANGE	0.3902* (0.0820)	2.5	9.0	
ELECTRIFICATION	0.1252* (0.0252)	26.3	30.1	0.6016* (0.2057)
FEMALE CHANGE				−1.0767* (0.3750)
SALARY CHANGE				0.4925* (0.0694)
CAPITAL				0.0043* (0.0011)
CAPITAL CHANGE				0.1820* (0.0841)
HORSEPOWER				4.0247* (0.7741)
Number of observations	118			118
Adjusted R^2	0.667			0.821
Mean of dependent variable	10.92			17.68

* Significantly different from zero with 95 percent confidence.

Notes: Absolute values of standard errors are in parentheses. The dependent variable *HOURS CHANGE* is the negative percent change in hours, 1909 to 1919. The dependent variable *WAGE CHANGE* is the percent change in real wages, 1909 to 1919. The percent contribution toward reduced hours equals the mean of the independent variable times the coefficient divided by the percentage change in hours.

Sources: See Table 1.

significantly greater than zero, is significantly below one, suggesting that legislation was probably passed after other forces had reduced hours and had only a small additional effect. *STATE LAW CHANGE* reduced hours during the period by only 1 percent between 1914 and 1919 but by nearly 10 percent over the course of the decade.[19]

The influence of the federal government is far more difficult to measure because its programs were multifaceted and data on the number of people affected in each city and industry do not exist.

[19] This estimate is very close to that of Ethel Jones, "State Legislation and Hours of Work in Manufacturing," *Southern Economics Journal*, 41 (Apr. 1975).

Passage of the Adamson Act, which gave railroad workers the 48-hour week, was an unprecedented action by the federal government. As he endorsed it, President Wilson seemed to endorse the eight-hour day in all sectors of the economy, so it is to be expected that the effect of the act and the takeover of the railroad sector by the government during and after the war would spill beyond the transportation market to the manufacturing labor market. Although it is probable that the government's transportation policies had a widespread effect, their impact must have been nationwide, since I cannot detect any effect in local labor markets. A larger railroad sector in a city did not lead to a greater reduction in manufacturing hours in the same city. Likewise, the reduction of hours in the "railroad car building and repairing" and the "locomotive manufacturing" industries is no greater than expected due to other forces.

The federal government's maritime endeavors had a measurable role in reducing the hours of manufacturing workers. To proxy the effect of the government's provisions that its contractors employ the basic eight-hour day, I use *SHIP*, the percentage of the city's manufacturing labor force employed in the shipbuilding industry. Hours did decline more rapidly in those cities, although at the industry level the hours decline in the shipbuilding industry was not significantly faster than predicted by other forces. Hours also fell more quickly in cities where *WATER TRANSPORTATION*, the percentage of the work force employed in government-controlled water-borne transportation, was higher.[20]

Contemporaries were convinced that the National War Labor Board was extremely influential in wage and hours setting. Hours did decline much more rapidly in some of the cities where the board intervened dramatically. The unexplained drop is a hefty 10.1 percent for Bethlehem, PA. Unfortunately, much of this decline may have preceded the intervention.[21] In Springfield, MA, the federal government seized and operated the Smith and Wesson plant, after Douglas Wesson refused to

[20] George Soule, *Prosperity Decade: from War to Depression, 1917–1929* (New York, 1947), notes: "One of the main causes of the reduction in hours was a law that had been passed in 1912 making the eight-hour day . . . mandatory for those engaged in government contracts." Edmund Day, "The American Merchant Fleet: A War Achievement, A Peace Problem," *Quarterly Journal of Economics*, 34 (Aug. 1920), notes, "government control of merchant shipping . . . was absolute."

[21] See Conner, *The National War Labor Board*. The board made 384 industrial awards directly to about 600,000 manufacturing workers. Not all awards dealt with hours. The official summary and analysis of NWLB awards notes: "The umpires usually have awarded the basic eight-hour day." See "National War Labor Board," in U.S. Department of Labor, *Bulletin of the Bureau of Labor Statistics, No. 287* (Washington, DC, 1921), pp. 19, 71–85. Since the 48-hour week was more than seven hours below the average work week of 1914 and about three hours below the 1919 average, the awards probably accelerated the decline in hours. The Bethlehem, PA, case represents almost 10 percent of the workers covered by NWLB awards. Multiplying Bethlehem's effect by 10 implies that the NWLB's total impact explains about 3.4 percent of the hours decline.

deal with labor in a manner the government thought was fair and conducive to winning the war.[22] The hours decline in Springfield was 2.1 percent faster than expected, though the difference is not significant. A final case in which the government played a major role is the meat-packing industry. In March 1918 Judge Samuel Alschuler, an arbitrator selected by President Wilson, ruled that hours should be cut from 60 to 48 per week in meat-packing plants.[23] The industry-level equations show that hours in meat packing did decline about 2.7 percent more rapidly than predicted by the other forces. Together the direct impact of the state and federal governments account for about 10 to 15 percent of the hours decline.

The traditional triad of labor market tightness, union pressure, and government intervention do not exhaust the forces pushing the work week down. Two infrequently mentioned influences are of note. The first is a shift in the strategies of managers who sought to use new employment methods and to establish longer-term relations with their employees. Sanford Jacoby persuasively depicts the "personnel boom" during this period and employers' realizations that high turnover was baneful.[24] As employers sought longer, even lifetime, relationships with their employees, they came to worry more about the future productivity of these workers. This long-run concern and mounting evidence that fatigue could imperil long-term productivity may have induced some to shorten hours. This reason for offering shorter hours is hard to detect, but one group of employers, oligopsonists, had the greatest incentive to invest in future productivity through reduced hours, since they were the most likely to maintain long-term relations with their employees.[25] *OLIGOPSONY*, a dummy variable equaling one if more than half of the city's manufacturing employees work for the five largest firms, has a significant and positive effect in reducing hours, accounting for about 4 percent of the fall.[26]

[22] Conner, *National War Labor Board*, p. 133.

[23] Roediger and Foner, *Our Own Time*, p. 206.

[24] Sanford Jacoby, *Employing Bureaucracy: Managers, Unions, and the Transformation of Work in American Industry, 1900–1945* (New York, 1986). The personnel boom of the war era was largely induced by labor market tightness, but as Gavin Wright, "Labor History and Labor Economics," in Alexander Field, *The Future of Economic History* (Boston, 1987), argues, it was part of a longer-term shift toward a "high-wage-high-quality-low-turnover" employment relation.

[25] John Hicks, *The Theory of Wages* (New York, 1962), suggests just such an effect.

[26] This is not just an effect of government contracts going to larger firms; substituting a measure of the percentage of employees in large establishments yields an insignificant effect. Another indication that productivity enhancement was a goal of employers in reducing hours is that, controlling for all else, hours fell by a greater percent when they were initially above 60 per week. Josephine Goldmark, *Fatigue and Efficiency* (New York, 1912), was very influential in showing the link between hours and efficiency, as were government studies made during the war. A number of economic historians have found an inverted-U shape between hours and productivity, including Jeremy Atack and Fred Bateman, "How Long Did People Work in 1880?" (paper presented at Economic History Association meetings, 1989).

The final influence I have identified in the victory of eight hours is a technological one. *ELECTRIFICATION* measures the change in the percentage of manufacturing horsepower purchased from outside the plant. By shifting the ownership of power-generating machinery outside the firm, electrification may have helped reduce the length of the work week. This shift reduced the manufacturer's benefits from running machines (including power-generating machines) long hours in an attempt to reduce the fixed costs per unit of output. Since most firms worked only one shift, shortening machine hours meant shortening hours of labor. More importantly, electrification is also a sign that the firm had reorganized production and had adopted scientific management procedures and new technology.[27] The adoption of electricity turns out to be rather important, accounting for about 30 percent of the hours decline in the industry-level equation.

Together the effect of growth and wage increases, union growth and strikes, the intervention of state and federal governments, the interruption of immigration, and changing managerial strategies, including the adoption of electricity, account for almost all of the reduction in hours explained in the *HOURS CHANGE* equations. The division of responsibility is roughly the same at the industry and city levels, but the industry equation includes a much larger unexplained constant because it cannot measure many of the important forces, especially the effects of the immigration cut-off and oligopsony.

The most important force reducing the work week was the rise in wages, and there are a number of reasons why workers may have been especially willing to trade wages for leisure during this period. First, workers were accustomed to obtaining leisure through unemployment. They may have desired a shorter work day as a substitute for the unemployed leisure time lost during this period. Second, this period may have been especially prone to a burst in the purchase of leisure because consumption of discretionary goods was constrained. New housing and autos were rationed and often could not be purchased at any price, so leisure may have been purchased instead.[28] The psychology of the war meant that relatively less utility was derived from consumption than in nonwar periods. As Daniel Horowitz argues, spending may have been held in check during and immediately after the war by a "feeling of guilt" that consumption might deprive soldiers and that war required sacrifice from everyone. No guilt was attached to a

[27] See Warren Devine, "From Shafts to Wires: Historical Perspective on Electrification," this JOURNAL, 43 (June 1983).

[28] The auto industry reduced nonmilitary output by 50 percent in 1918 under an agreement with the War Industries Board (WIB), and home construction fell by two-thirds due to the WIB's allocation of scarce raw materials. Although the WIB was virtually dismantled by the beginning of 1919, consumer credit was rationed in 1919, so auto and new home sales remained relatively low. Bernard Baruch, *Industry in the War* (New York, 1941); and Soule, *Prosperity Decade*, p. 103.

shortened work week because public opinion asserted that it was needed for efficient work.[29] Finally, it takes time and conscious decision making to change consumption patterns and form new tastes, but as experienced consumers of leisure workers can readily expand its use.[30] Thus the greater transactions costs involved in making new and different consumption purchases made additional leisure appear relatively cheap. All these reasons argue that the same sets of influences may have reduced hours by less under other circumstances, that hours may have declined by more than normal in this period. The absence of these forces may help explain why hours stagnated during the 1920s.

Some important questions about the length of the work week have been explored here, but new ones have arisen. Why did hours stop falling during the twenties? Were technological innovations which changed the intensity of work and created a group of semiskilled operatives important in influencing hours? Did some firms reduce hours because they needed to coordinate their work day with other firms? An examination of other periods is needed to find the general and unique factors which influenced the course of the work week after this period and to understand more fully the decline of the 1910s itself.

[29] Daniel Horowitz, *The Morality of Spending: Attitudes toward the Consumer Society in America, 1875–1940* (Baltimore, 1985), p. 120. An example of this patriotic guilt is that over two million people took part in the drive to sell Liberty Bonds. Community pressure was applied so ubiquitously that nearly every household purchased bonds in lieu of spending, even though the real return on this investment was negative. This phenomenon lasted well into 1919. Twelve million subscribers, half of all American households, bought bonds in the Victory Loan drive from March to June 1919, and many of the subscribers to the loan drive of late 1918 paid in installments during the first half of 1919. Ernest Bogart, *War Costs and Their Financing* (New York, 1921), pp. 216–28.

[30] Milton Friedman, *Price Theory* (Chicago, 1962), p. 204; and Hazel Kyrk, *A Theory of Consumption* (Boston, 1923), pp. 255–58.

American Economic Expertise from the Great War to the Cold War: Some Initial Observations

MICHAEL A. BERNSTEIN

The twentieth-century American economics profession was privileged and shaped by the federal government's need to direct resources and to call on experts. Bureaucratic tendencies to classify and count had an impact on the discipline's self-concept, subdisciplines, and multiple research agendas. A consensus of professional opinion and the standardization of graduate curriculums emerged out of the involvement of economists with governmental affairs. Moreover, American economists played an important role in the reconstitution of the profession overseas after World War II.

Professional development and the maturation of intellectual disciplines are typically understood as the result of individual and collective pursuits of rationalization, precision, value-free argument, and expertise. This is especially true of studies of the history of economic analysis. The evolution of economic doctrine and practice has been predominantly understood as a sustained progression to greater and greater levels of capability, effectiveness, and sophistication. Deviations from this trend have been grasped as detours or dead ends.[1]

Historical investigations of the evolution of the economics profession itself have been no different, focusing on the results, not the processes. The emergence of a professional association, its journal, and related activities has been chronicled as part of an ideal evolutionary process in which doctrinal achievements have also been couched. Such a narrative strategy has been as much a part of histories of the American economics

The Journal of Economic History, Vol. L, No. 2 (June 1990). ISSN 0022-0507.

The author is Associate Professor of History, University of California at San Diego, La Jolla, CA 92093-0104, and currently an Andrew W. Mellon fellow at the National Humanities Center, Research Triangle Park, NC 27709.

Generous support for this research granted by the National Endowment for the Humanities, the Andrew W. Mellon Foundation, and the Office of the Dean of Arts and Humanities at the University of California at San Diego is gratefully acknowledged.

For comments on an earlier draft and on this project as a whole, I am very grateful to my friends and colleagues Amy Bridges, Paul Drake, Michael Edelstein, Steve Hahn, Carol Heim, David Luft, John Marino, Allan Mitchell, Chandra Mukerji, Terry Odendahl, Martha Olney, David Ringrose, Dan Schiller, Frank Smith, Eric Van Young, John Wallis, David Weiman, and Robert Westman, and to audiences at the annual meetings of the Economic History Association and the Social Science History Association.

[1] I have a vast amount of literature in mind as I make this claim. But a very good example of the approach to which I allude, that at the same time remains quite open-minded and intellectually generous, is Mark Blaug, *Economic Theory in Retrospect* (New York, 1978).

profession as it has been part of the histories of American economics itself.[2]

Yet focusing on the outcome of a particular professional enterprise ignores the actions, events, and forces that shape and mold that development. Exclusive attention to published mainstream works or to the public pronouncements of a professional body incorporates wholly and uncritically a virtual hagiography of professional development. It cannot and does not allow for an appreciation of historical contingency that lends a more subtle awareness of the mechanisms of so-called professionalization and scientific advancement.

A more nuanced understanding of the rise of American economic expertise in this century can be obtained by examining the interaction of American economists and the American Economic Association (AEA) with the federal government. It would be a fairly straightforward and traditional task to document and evaluate the impact that professional economists had on public policy in the first half of this century. I am, however, more anxious to contemplate the effect that involvement with the state had on the evolution of a professional ethos among economists and on the maturation of their professional society. It appears that governmental needs and objectives had as much to do with determining the character of the American economics profession as any intrinsic aspirations of economists themselves. Moreover, the intellectual growth of the discipline was powerfully affected by the actions of government agencies in times of emergency and national mobilization.

The world war episodes and their aftermaths provide initial observations of the extent to which the profession was both privileged and shaped by the needs and goals of the federal government. Persistent concerns about the practicality of the field of economics at the beginning of this century were only exacerbated by the onset of war in Europe in 1914. The chair of the Federal Reserve Bank of San Francisco, John Perrin, fired off a particularly angry note to AEA official Allyn Young in November 1915, complaining that there was nothing on the agenda of the upcoming annual association meetings in Washington, DC, on the war. Economists, he held, would be a "rather impractical lot" if they ignored such an event as this. "Here [was] a world crisis, the greatest in half a thousand years, or more." Young agreed with his colleague. "[W]e economists [have] failed in securing the influence that we might

[2] Again, it is not possible to note all of the literature which I invoke here. Notable exceptions to the general tendency I mention are R. L. Church, "Economists as Experts: The Rise of an Academic Profession in the United States, 1870–1920," in L. Stone, ed., *The University in Society*, vol. 2: *Europe, Scotland, and the United States from the Sixteenth to the Twentieth Century* (Princeton, 1974), pp. 571–609; A. W. Coats, "The American Economic Association and the Economics Profession," *Journal of Economic Literature*, 23 (Dec. 1985), pp. 1697–1727; and Mary O. Furner, *Advocacy and Objectivity: A Crisis in the Professionalization of American Social Science, 1865–1905* (Lexington, KY, 1975).

have had," he wrote to Perrin, "largely because we have neglected to attempt to secure a concert of opinion among us on important questions. . . ." The solution lay, he believed, in finding "effective ways of bringing that opinion to a focus, and expressing it in a way to secure attention."[3]

Young was content to utilize a rhetoric of expertise and scientific probity that was intrinsic to the community of economists. But war and the looming possibility of American involvement in combat overseas shifted attention from an in-house professionalizing discourse to the mobilization of experts for the prosecution of a government objective. By 1916 sessions for the annual meeting addressed problems of preparedness and the economics of warfare. And by early 1917 the AEA had set up committees of its members on "Finance and Currency, Agriculture and Food Production, Labor and Labor Legislation, Conservation of Natural Resources, [and] Corporation Finance and Regulation" to aid the war activities of the federal government. Other bodies were established to study "Cost Accounting on Government Contracts, Control of War Prices and Combinations and the Distribution of Products, [and the] Distribution of Income and Wealth as Affected by the War." Calls were issued for association representatives to be placed on the National Research Council and the Council of National Defense. Here at last were some of the mechanisms by which "a concert of opinion" among economists might be secured and deployed in such a way as to "secure attention."[4]

Yet it was the exigencies of mobilization that brought American economists into the kind of cooperation with government that would have long-run impacts on the development of their profession. Many members, both before and during the nation's involvement in the war, believed that "the Economic Association should take action to mobilize all the economists of the country for special war service." With an explicit government request to do so, the AEA canvassed its members in the early summer of 1917 with a view toward providing the Civil Service Commission with a full census of the capabilities of its constituency. By the fall an ad hoc committee composed of Frank Taussig (then of the Tariff Commission), George Barnett of Johns Hopkins, and Young was charged to sort through some 900 cards collected from the membership. The committee sought "to discard the names of persons who [did] not properly come within the classification of economic

[3] John Perrin to Young, Nov. 26, 1915; and Young to Perrin, Jan. 28, 1916, from the Records of the American Economic Association (hereafter, RAEA), Northwestern University Library, Special Collections, Box 13, Folder: "Correspondence La-Zz 1915." Where the professional affiliations in cited correspondence are not identified, the reader should assume the individuals are part of either the leadership or the membership of the American Economic Association.

[4] Henry W. Farnam to John R. Commons, Apr. 17, 1917, RAEA, Box 60, Folder: "1918"; and Henry C. Adams to Young, Apr. 4, 1916, RAEA, Box 14, Folder: "Correspondence Aa-Fz 1916."

expert, . . . classify under proper headings those who [were] trained along economic lines, and . . . make such comment in individual cases as [it] consider[ed] advisable.''[5]

The war also centralized and coordinated the various research activities of economists across the country. Yale's Irving Fisher, in May 1918, called upon his associates at the AEA to see to it that all information regarding research on war-related topics in economics be sent to his secretary. A composite file was then created, thereby establishing a national clearing house for such information.[6]

World War II brought a greater array of influences to bear on the profession and, thereby, its maturation. It was on matters of credentials and the classification of personnel that the association was first called back to wartime service by the government. Carrying on work begun almost three decades earlier, in the spring of 1940 a special executive committee of the AEA took up the matter of professional subfield classification. Fourteen major fields were identified at that time. By the fall of that year the association was approached by the National Resources Planning Board regarding the creation of a National Roster of Scientific and Specialized Personnel. Continuing with its work on field groupings, but nonetheless now aware of new and special needs attendant on the effort, the special AEA committee added six new fields to its classification list. Thus began a multiyear association with the Resources Planning Board and ultimately other war agencies whose objective was the effective utilization of economic talent for the war effort.[7]

Just before the attack on Pearl Harbor by the Imperial Japanese Navy, the National Resources Planning Board sought the aid of the association not only in classifying its membership by field but also in judging the credentials of economists of military age so that their skills and capabilities could be most effectively employed should war arise. The board was particularly anxious that the AEA nominate for such a task individuals from ''different fields of specialization within economics.'' Clyde Holmes of the National Office of Production Management approached the association two months before the outbreak of war

[5] John A. McIlhenny, president of the Civil Service Commission, to Young, Oct. 8, 1917; John B. Clark to Young, May 12, 1917; James E. LeRossignol to Young, Mar. 13, 1917; Silas L. Egley (American Telephone and Telegraph Corporation) to Davis R. Dewey, Oct. 2, 1917; Commons to Dewey, July 21, 1917; and Young to Egley, Oct. 8, 1917, in RAEA, Box 14, Folder: ''Correspondence Aa-Mz 1917,'' and Box 60, Folder: ''1917.''

[6] Fisher to members of the AEA (circular), Mar. 9, 1918; Fisher to Young, May 1, 1918; and Walton H. Hamilton to Fisher, Apr. 27, 1918, in RAEA, Box 15, Folder: ''Correspondence Fisher 1918.''

[7] Records of the Special Executive Committee Meeting on Classification, Mar. 23, 1941, and Mar. 24, 1941; and James Washington Bell to Special Executive Committee and the Editorial Board of the *American Economic Review*, Feb. 22, 1940, in RAEA, Box 57, Folder: ''1940–1944 Classification of Personnel.''

"recruiting personnel for [that] defense agency." One day after the attack in Hawaii yet another official from that office contacted Sumner Slichter (then AEA president) urging the passage of a proposal made at a recent association meeting in New Orleans that "Standards of Minimum Competence for Economists" be promulgated as soon as possible. Slichter agreed and, two weeks later, asked the association's Executive Committee to take up a rather large agenda of matters posed by "the emergency." In particular, he wished that ways be sought to provide for the effective allocation of personnel to government and military jobs and for the continued and expanded "training of as many graduate students as conditions permit."[8]

As America's participation in World War II expanded, so too did the interaction of the AEA with the federal government and the armed services. In this the association was fortunate but not unique. Most professional societies were caught up in the war effort. Early in 1942 the presidents and secretaries of all such groups were contacted directly by Steuart Henderson Britt—an official of the National Roster of Scientific and Specialized Personnel. Britt informed these men and women that it was now necessary to compile as systematically as possible information on the classification of professional personnel, where such personnel could be best recruited, and by so doing to coordinate these data with a determination of the needs of the military, industry, and civilian government agencies for professional skills. The War Labor Board also sought to recruit association members. And the War Manpower Commission, much as the National Roster had done, sought AEA help in classifying and properly tasking economists.[9]

Recruitment and utilization of personnel in wartime is one thing; the effective nurturing and the proper accrediting of talent is quite another. American economists, under the pressures of the war, quickly turned their attention to the matter of training students—most importantly, graduate students. Not surprisingly, while receiving repeated inquiries from the federal government regarding field classification and recruitment, the profession became aware of the need to maintain the supply of experts at an adequate level. And once the question of standards of

[8] Leonard Carmichael, director of National Resources Planning Board, to Bell, June 17, 1941; and Steuart Henderson Britt (National Roster of Scientific and Specialized Personnel) to Sumner Slichter, Nov. 27, 1941, in RAEA, Box 57, Folder: "1940–1944 Classification of Personnel"; Morris A. Copeland (now of the Office of Production Management) to Slichter, Dec. 8, 1941; Slichter to AEA Executive Committee, Dec. 23, 1941; and Bell to Slichter, May 1, 1941, in RAEA, Box 29, Folder: "Correspondence A-L 1941"; and Clyde E. Holmes (Office of Production Management) to Bell, Oct. 3, 1941, in RAEA, Box 29, Folder: "Correspondence M-Z 1941."

[9] Britt to Presidents and Secretaries of Professional Societies, Jan. 31, 1942, in RAEA, Box 57, Folder: "Classification of Personnel"; V. H. Yahnke (U.S. Civil Service Commission) to AEA, May 29, 1943; Bell to Yahnke, July 13, 1943, in RAEA, Box 31, Folder: "Correspondence A-L 1943"; and Carmichael (now of War Manpower Commission) to Bell, Aug. 12, 1943, in RAEA, Box 32, Folder: "Correspondence M-Z 1943."

competence for government service was raised, it was a logical next step to begin examining curriculums at both the collegiate and graduate levels.[10]

Concerned with both the training of economics students during the crisis and with bringing professional opinion to bear on major issues, the association established committees to investigate such matters. In the summer of 1943 a formal "Report on Wartime Changes in Economics Curriculum" was issued. It had been widely agreed that "the impact of the war ha[d] caused such an upheaval that [the AEA wished to] take advantage of th[e] occasion to make a thorough appraisal not only of the subject matter and the place of economics in [the] educational system and the function which it perform[ed] in society but also a reexamination of . . . teaching methods and techniques." And while it was clear that "because of the insistence of the Department of War and of the Navy there [had to] be modifications . . . for courses that [would be] immediately applicable to the two services," there was still strong feeling "for maintaining the fundamental, the eternal values even during these times of emergency."[11]

Just what those fundamental, eternal values might have been was a subject ripe for controversy and debate. While there was some consensus that the applied revisions of courses of study in economics would touch upon such matters as war aims, how the United States became involved in the conflict, economic organization for war, and postwar economic adjustment, there was genuine difference of opinion on how to teach theory. J. M. Clark rejected the idea that everything taught should be linked with "the immediate conflict," but he also felt that simply teaching "Marshallian marginalism" in a theory segment would be mistaken as well. American economists had spent "too many decades cultivating the attitude that everything . . . outside marginal system-theory [was] a problem. . . . [P]ut the Keynesian elements in front of the Marshallian," Clark told his colleagues, "as having a more direct and active relevance." War could aid the triumph of the Keynesian revolution as much on *engagé* classroom blackboards as in driving up the budget ledgers of government and military agencies.[12]

Curriculum revision and reform was a project that lasted well into the 1950s. Two months before the opening of the second front in Europe the association's Executive Committee asked that a new "Committee on Undergraduate Teaching and the Training of Economists" concern

[10] Lloyd E. Blauch (Federal Security Agency) to Bell, Aug. 9, 1943; and Bell to Blauch, Aug. 11, 1943, in RAEA, Box 31, Folder: "Correspondence M-Z 1943"; and Edwin G. Nourse to Bell, July 1, 1942; Bell to Nourse, July 3, 1942; Bell to Nourse, Apr. 21, 1942; and Nourse to Bell, Apr. 18, 1942, in RAEA, Box 30, Folder: "Edwin G. Nourse 1942."

[11] "Report on Wartime Changes in Economics Curriculum," July 7, 1943, and July 15, 1943, in RAEA, Box 32, Folder: "Correspondence M-Z 1943."

[12] Ibid.

itself with "the long run postwar period." Ultimately, of particular interest to this committee were "problems of indoctrination [of students] as to social consciousness and professional responsibility. . . ." Four months after the surrender of Japan questionnaires were sent out to 160 college economics departments to gather information on undergraduate instruction. By the autumn of 1950 plans were made for a conference on social science teaching at the precollegiate and collegiate levels. At the same time, with the support of the Rockefeller Foundation, a "Committee on Graduate Training in Economics" sought to formalize in detail the "Professional Requirements for the PhD Degree." When the committee transmitted its findings to university deans and presidents, return correspondence was grateful and enthusiastic.[13]

Hand in hand with the curriculum project went an increased concern with the "focusing of informed opinion" among economists. During World War II the AEA asked Harry Gideonse, Charles Noyes, and Frank Graham "to [consider ways of] making the informed opinion of our membership more effective in matters of public policy." As the association, by the terms of its charter, could take no partisan positions, it was felt that the "technical competence" of members could be expressed on "matters of public importance." This would require of course that "all academically respectable views on any posed controversial question be represented" on committees formed to pronounce on policy matters. Moreover, it was additionally held appropriate to "include some members not committed to any particular position on the matter at hand."[14]

Another device to increase the influence of the profession was the "Consensus Report." As the war came to a close and as attention turned to postwar economic policy needs, the association investigated the "desirability and workability" of formulating concerted opinions on major issues. There was still some concern with violating the body's charter. "A learned society could not long remain one," a committee on the matter declared, "if it passed resolutions and promoted special interest and causes. . . . Our record was . . . clean in this regard and we must keep it so." Even so, it was agreed that "[T]he professional economist has a formal background of preparation and special training which should give him [or her] competence to pass on the economic aspects of [policy] questions. Also, as a scholar, he is relatively free

[13] Horace Taylor to the AEA Executive Committee, Dec. 16, 1944; J. S. Davis to Taylor, May 22, 1944; Davis to Joseph Spengler, May 19, 1944; Davis to Paul M. O'Leary, May 19, 1944; Bell to Taylor, Sept. 20, 1944; and Davis to Taylor, Sept. 22 and 28 and Oct. 7, 1944, in RAEA, Box 58, Folder: "AEA 1944–1951 Committee on Undergraduate Teaching of Economics and Training of Economists." Also see report by the "(Ad Hoc) Committee on Graduate Training in Economics" to the AEA Executive Committee, Dec. 1, 1950, in RAEA, Box 58, Folder: "AEA 1950–53 (Ad Hoc) Committee on Graduate Training in Economics."

[14] RAEA, Box 57, Folder: "AEA 1944 Committee on Focusing of Informed Opinion."

from the influences of special interests and is qualified to view controversial questions objectively and from a broader social point of view than is the layman or the advocate."[15]

Consensus reports, it was believed, would not only educate the public but would certainly bolster the reputation of the profession. By December 1945 an effort was made to consolidate association members' opinions with regard to the government's postwar economic role, the continuation of agricultural price supports, monetary policy, and the future of the Webb-Pomerene Act. Rather than stake out a particular position on these issues, it was hoped that "something [could] be done to help the public distinguish between important and unimportant issues, recognize clap-trap arguments, and become aware of economic considerations which members of the profession [thought] significant." All in all, the "experiment" of consensus reports would "throw more evidence on the wisecrack 'Place all of the economists in the country end to end and they will arrive at no conclusion' a reference which might be true when applied to quacks but which [was] of doubtful validity when referring to professional economists."[16]

War's end also brought attention back to the matter of defining and classifying economic expertise. Officials at the War Manpower Commission, continuing their work on a National Roster of Scientific and Specialized Personnel, repeatedly contacted association leaders for information about the profession to distribute to returning veterans. The roster as well as the Federal Security Agency also had other reasons to make such inquiries. It was now hoped to maintain permanent files regarding professional personnel in the United States. As government's concerns shifted from making war to maintaining national security, continued interaction between government agencies and professional associations similarly evolved.[17]

Postwar reconstruction, moreover, brought the association into the business of aiding professionals in devastated areas overseas, and in a far more sophisticated effort than that undertaken after the Great War. For now, in addition to contributing free books and copies of the *Review* along with cash donations to scholarly libraries in Europe and East Asia, the AEA became involved in the revision of curriculums and the rehabilitation and vetting of foreign faculties. American economists going overseas, either on official or personal tours, were asked to check up on colleagues who had perhaps been imprisoned, wounded, or otherwise victimized by German national socialism and Japanese imperialism. Letters to association members from economists abroad often

[15] RAEA, Box 57, Folder: "AEA 1944–1945 Committee to Draft Consensus Report on Function of Government in the Postwar American Economy."

[16] Ibid.

[17] Bell to National Roster of Scientific and Specialized Personnel, Mar. 12, 1948, in RAEA, Box 58, Folder: "AEA 1948–50 National Roster of Scientific and Specialized Personnel."

contained information regarding colleagues who either had or had not collaborated with the enemy. Efforts were made to raise money for the relief of those who had opposed fascism and militarism. A note from a German colleague to former AEA President (and then Illinois Senator) Paul Douglas was forwarded to the association offices because in it there was "a very valuable list of economists who either opposed Hitler or kept their honor clean." American economists were now in a position not only to secure greater influence and prestige at home but also to reconstitute virtually from scratch the European and Asian branches of the guild.[18]

The reconstruction of foreign scholarly libraries prompted the American Library Association to ask professional societies to provide book lists in their fields to guide rebuilding efforts. AEA officials asked their membership for suggestions and ultimately provided such lists to the Library Association. With such books on the final list as *Stalin, A Critical Survey of Bolshevism* and *Marxism: An Autopsy*, the ideological content of the library aid effort seems clear. This is hardly surprising. The point here is not that American economists would generally be loath to suggest books that extolled Marxism or Stalin, but that Allied victory had the added impact of giving them a great deal of influence on the future course of foreign scholarship in the field. If postwar reconstruction served to recast Europe and Asia in America's image, as some scholars have suggested, the representations of that process in the academic and intellectual world should not be overlooked.[19]

Participation of the American economics profession in the emergent "Pax Americana" of the 1950s also expressed itself in a continuation and evolution of links between economists and the military-industrial establishment that had necessarily arisen in the forties. Economists participated in both the private sector and at the government level in the mobilization and allocation of resources for war. In addition, the

[18] Kenneth R. Shaffer (American Book Center for War Devastated Libraries) to Bell, Aug. 8, 1946; John O. Coppock (UN Relief and Rehabilitation Administration—Greece Mission) to the association, Aug. 13, 1946; and Joseph D. Coppock (U.S. Department of State) to E. A. Goldenweiser, Oct. 7, 1946, in RAEA, Box 33, Folder: "Correspondence A-L 1946." Robert Outsen (U.S. Army Colonel) to the association, May 3, 1951; and Bell to Outsen, May 18, 1951, in RAEA, Box 36, Folder: "American Economic Assoc. Corr. 1951, M-Z."

[19] RAEA, Box 93, Folder: "AER July 1944 AEA-ALA Book List on Economics for European Libraries." On the role of postwar reconstruction in the twentieth-century Americanization of Europe and Asia, see, for example, M. J. Hogan, "American Marshall Planners and the Search for a European Neocapitalism," *American Historical Review*, 90 (Feb. 1985), pp. 44–72; C. S. Maier, "The Politics of Productivity: Foundations of American International Economic Policy after World War II," *International Organization*, 31 (Autumn 1977), pp. 607–33; A. Rappaport, "The United States and European Integration: The First Phase," *Diplomatic History*, 5 (Spring 1981), pp. 121–49; William S. Borden, *The Pacific Alliance: United States Foreign Economic Policy and Japanese Trade Recovery, 1947–1955* (Madison, 1984); D. Horowitz, ed., *Corporations and the Cold War* (New York, 1969); Charles L. Mee, Jr., *The Marshall Plan: The Launching of the Pax Americana* (New York, 1984); and Alan S. Milward, *The Reconstruction of Western Europe, 1945–1951* (London, 1984).

profession became increasingly involved in establishing new programs of instruction at the nation's armed service academies on the economics of national security and defense. Defense-related research and support of basic economic investigations by defense agencies became more and more common. And the emergence and articulation of wholly new aspects of the discipline—such as activity analysis, linear programming, and input-output analysis—were inherent in the association of professional economics with a national security state. That is a story the full details of which have yet to be told.

An approach to the history of American economic expertise along the outlines I have sketched above affords a deeper appreciation of the profession's origins and of what it has become. It also makes for greater sensitivity to the message of critics and iconoclasts who would have moved the vocation in other directions. Characteristics of the modern profession that we take for granted—field classification schemes, conceptions of the technical rather than the partisan aspects of policy issues, involvement in government and military decision making—emerge as far more complicated and ambivalent outcomes than a teleological framework would suggest.

A more multifaceted history of expertise has the added virtue of resurrecting questions of purpose and value that have been systematically suppressed in professional communities. That the AEA would adopt a charter constraining it from taking partisan stands would appear to be a step forward for scientific precision and open-mindedness. And when the association launched campaigns to establish minimum standards for Ph.D. training in the field, the advancement of professional standards and excellence would seem to have been the result. On some levels, of course, this is all true.

On others, unfortunately, it is misleading. Scientific authority comes as much from a process of intellectual growth as from efforts of individuals to achieve prestige and sway. These efforts in turn interact with the designs and objectives of institutions—most notably appurtenances of the state—pursuing political goals as well. And ultimately the "empowerment" of some is paralleled by the "marginalization" of others. All this, to be sure, is far removed from the seemingly empyrean realm of knowledge for its own sake. Histories of authority and expertise should, among other things, remind us of these facts and make us aware of their implications.

President Eisenhower, Economic Policy, and the 1960 Presidential Election

ANN MARI MAY

This article examines economic policy in the Eisenhower years and the president's role in the 1960 election. I measure the impact of changes in fiscal policy on real GNP and show that policy in 1959 was unusually contractionary and cannot be dismissed as merely evidence of Eisenhower's fiscal conservatism.

Adlai Stevenson once described the "liberal hour" as that time before presidential elections when "even the most obsolete Republican becomes momentarily reconciled to the machine age."[1] For the most fiscally conservative president of the postwar period the liberal hour never arrived. In the 1956 and 1960 presidential elections President Dwight D. Eisenhower refused to engage in expansionary policies to enhance his or his party's chances for re-election.

Eisenhower's refusal to stimulate the economy before either presidential election raises serious questions about the validity of the political business cycle hypothesis.[2] According to this hypothesis, presidents will engage in contractionary policies in the early years of their terms to reduce inflation, then use expansionary policies before the presidential election to reduce unemployment and reap the electoral rewards of an expanding economy.

The economic policies of the Eisenhower administration provide a particularly intriguing case in the study of political business cycles because Eisenhower's policies were inconsistent with the general political business cycle pattern. Whereas real disposable income per capita increased in eight of eleven presidential and congressional election years during the administrations of Harry Truman, John Kennedy, Lyndon Johnson, Richard Nixon, and Gerald Ford, it declined in every election year during the Eisenhower administration.[3] As Stephen Weatherford points out, Eisenhower provides the deviant case

The Journal of Economic History, Vol. L, No. 2 (June 1990). ISSN 0022-0507.

The author is Assistant Professor of Economics, University of Nebraska, Lincoln, NE 68588. She would like to thank Martha Olney for helpful comments on an earlier draft.

[1] Adlai E. Stevenson, *Major Campaign Speeches of Adlai E. Stevenson* (New York, 1953), pp. 31–32.

[2] For example, see William D. Nordhaus, "The Political Business Cycle," *Review of Economic Studies*, 42 (Apr. 1975), pp. 169–90; and Edward R. Tufte, *Political Control of the Economy* (Princeton, 1978).

[3] Tufte, *Political Control*, p. 15.

because "conditions were ripe for a political business cycle in 1954, 1958, and 1960, yet he explicitly abjured the temptation."[4]

While Eisenhower had little need to stimulate the economy in 1956 with a solid lead in the polls over the Democratic front runner Adlai Stevenson, Vice President Richard Nixon could certainly have benefited from at least a momentary lapse in Eisenhower's fiscal frugality in 1960. Not only was the unemployment rate higher in 1960 than 1956, but the economy appeared to be sliding into another recession.[5] Moreover, voter surveys from August 1959 through August 1960 showed Kennedy and Nixon virtually tied in the polls.[6]

There are, of course, various interpretations of Eisenhower's economic policy actions before the 1960 presidential election. Economists have generally dismissed them as evidence of his unflinching fiscal conservatism.[7] Yet historians have consistently remarked upon the seeming ambivalence of Eisenhower toward Nixon's bid for the presidency in 1960.[8]

This article examines fiscal policy during the Eisenhower administration and explores President Eisenhower's role in the 1960 election. Impact measures are developed that provide a more complete picture of policy changes and allow us to assess their effect on economic activity and to understand the complex array of factors influencing Eisenhower's policies before the 1960 election.

OVERVIEW OF FISCAL POLICY IN THE EISENHOWER YEARS

Reflecting upon the 1960 presidential campaign Nixon later wrote: "In a losing campaign, only the candidate is responsible for the tactics that led to defeat."[9] Henry Cabot Lodge apparently agreed. Upon viewing the first Nixon-Kennedy debate Lodge erupted: "That son-of-a-bitch just lost us the election!"[10] At other times, however, Nixon expressed the belief that the outcome of the election was the result of something beyond his control—the state of the economy.[11]

The downturn which began officially in the second quarter of 1960 was

[4] Stephen Weatherford, "The Interplay of Ideology and Advice in Economic Policy-Making: The Case of Political Business Cycles," *Journal of Politics*, 49 (Nov. 1987), p. 932.

[5] The average annual unemployment rate in 1956 was 4.0 percent compared to an average annual rate of 5.4 percent in 1960. See the *Economic Report of the President*, 1988 (Washington, DC, 1988), p. 292.

[6] George H. Gallup, *The Gallup Poll Public Opinion: 1935–71* (New York, 1972), pp. 1622, 1642, 1682.

[7] For example, see Herbert Stein, *The Fiscal Revolution in America* (Chicago, 1969).

[8] See Stephen E. Ambrose, *Eisenhower: The President* (New York, 1984); and Stephen E. Ambrose, *Nixon: The Education of a Politician 1913–62* (New York, 1987).

[9] Richard M. Nixon, *Six Crises* (New York, 1962), p. 294.

[10] Fawn M. Brodie, *Richard Nixon: The Shaping of His Character* (Cambridge, MA, 1983), p. 427.

[11] Nixon, *Six Crises*, p. 310.

certainly not a complete surprise to administration officials. In February 1960 Arthur Burns, chairman of the Council of Economic Advisors during the first Eisenhower administration, advised the vice president that the economy was heading for another contraction and suggested that "steps be taken immediately" to increase federal expenditures and loosen credit.[12] Burns's advice was relayed to Eisenhower and discussed at the next Cabinet meeting.

Eisenhower did not take the advice. According to Nixon, the administration was unwilling to act to stimulate the economy until the downturn became more severe.[13] In subsequent quarters, however, unemployment increased from an already high 5.2 percent in the second quarter to 6.2 percent in the fourth quarter of 1960, and real GNP declined in the second, third, and fourth quarters.[14] The Eisenhower administration chose to deal with the economic downturn by ignoring it. Throughout 1960, until his final budget message in January 1961, Eisenhower warned of the hazards of inflation and promised not to "undermine our strength as a nation through deficits."[15]

Although Eisenhower was often accused of having a balanced budget fetish, he was, after all, a postwar Republican who, at least in principle, was willing to accept budget deficits during recessions.[16] While the actual federal budget was in surplus when economic activity was expanding, it moved to a deficit during the three recessions of 1953–1954, 1957–1958, and 1960, and there was no attempt to raise taxes to offset the reduction in revenue associated with the downturn.[17] In addition, although fiscal policy became more contractionary during the 1953–1954 recession, the full-employment budget showed a rather large deficit in early 1953. Likewise, while the full-employment budget was in surplus during the entire 1957–1958 recession, its size declined from $7.2 billion in the third quarter of 1957 to $2.4 billion by the fourth quarter of 1958.

Most interesting, however, is the full-employment budget for 1960. The full-employment budget surplus rose to $15.1 billion in the fourth quarter of 1960, its highest level of the entire Eisenhower term. Moreover, as the economy slid into recession, fiscal policy became tighter. The full-employment budget went from a surplus of $4.6 billion in 1958 to a surplus of $14.7 billion in 1960.

[12] Ibid., pp. 309–10.

[13] Ibid., p. 310.

[14] Quarterly data from Fairmodel macroeconometric model, July 1985.

[15] *Public Papers of the Presidents of the United States, Dwight D. Eisenhower*, 1960–61 (Washington, DC, 1961), p. 935.

[16] Stein, *The Fiscal Revolution*, pp. 281–84.

[17] All quarterly figures on the actual federal budget and the full-employment budget are reported in Keith Carlson, "Estimates of the High-Employment Budget: 1947–1967," Federal Reserve Bank of St. Louis, *Review*, 49 (June 1967), pp. 10–11.

IMPACT MEASURES OF FISCAL POLICY

While the full-employment budget provides a better measure of the thrust of fiscal policy than the actual federal budget, impact measures provide additional insight into the direction, magnitude, and composition of the changes in fiscal policy.[18] These measures are generated using a macroeconometric model to estimate the impact of changes in fiscal policy in a given quarter on real GNP four quarters in the future.[19]

The aggregate fiscal policy impact measure is generated by comparing simulated real GNP *with* the actual changes in fiscal policy that occurred in a particular quarter against simulated real GNP *without* them. The influence of fiscal policy in time t on real GNP Y, in period $t + j$ is thus:

$$F_y^j(t) = Y_{t+j} - Y^*_{t+j} \qquad j \geq 0$$

Ten fiscal policy variables are held constant in the Y^* simulation. They are real federal government purchases of goods, personal income tax rate, profit tax rate, indirect business tax rate, employee social security tax rate, employer social security tax rate, civilian jobs, military jobs, transfer payments to households, and grants-in-aid to state and local governments.[20]

The results presented in Table 1 indicate that fiscal policy was highly contractionary in Eisenhower's first term. Although fiscal policy in 1953 was expansionary, increasing estimated real GNP by $8.8 billion in 1954, this largely reflected the influence of the Truman administration.[21] The aggregate impact measures for 1954 reveal that fiscal policy was exceedingly contractionary, reducing estimated real GNP by $25.2 billion in 1955. This represents the largest yearly decline of the Eisenhower tenure. Moreover, fiscal policy was contractionary in every quarter of 1954—the only year in which this is true.

While contractionary policy in the early half of Eisenhower's first term is consistent with the political business cycle hypothesis, the impact measures do not indicate that fiscal policy became expansionary before the presidential election of 1956. While fiscal policy was more expansionary in 1955 and 1956 than it was in 1954, it still reduced estimated real GNP by $5.1 billion in 1956 and $490 million in 1957.

[18] The method used to estimate the impact measures is presented in Alan S. Blinder and Stephen M. Goldfeld, "New Measures of Fiscal and Monetary Policy, 1958–1973," *American Economic Review*, 66 (Dec. 1976), pp. 780–96.

[19] The four-quarter time horizon is used here because it represents a realistic impact lag and because the dynamic properties of the macroeconometric model produce highly correlated two-, four-, and six-quarter impact measures.

[20] See Ray C. Fair, *Specification, Estimation, and Analysis of Macroeconometric Models* (Cambridge, MA, 1984).

[21] When Eisenhower took office in 1953, government agencies were instructed to review their budgets and make cuts where possible. See the *Public Papers of the Presidents of the United States, Dwight D. Eisenhower*, 1953 (Washington, DC, 1960), pp. 53–54.

TABLE 1
AGGREGATE FISCAL POLICY IMPACT MEASURES ON REAL GNP
(billions of dollars)

Year	Quarters: First	Second	Third	Fourth	Yearly Total
1953	$ 3.885	$ 2.811	$−0.767	$ 2.852	$ 8.781
1954	−11.328	−8.199	−3.482	−2.177	−25.187
1955	−1.934	−3.459	2.566	−2.233	−5.059
1956	−0.400	1.360	−3.111	1.661	−0.490
1957	6.987	1.995	−1.051	2.146	10.078
1958	5.168	6.083	1.800	2.472	15.524
1959	−6.674	−1.105	−1.989	0.380	−9.388
1960	−4.927	2.162	2.375	2.524	2.134

Notes: The impact measure shows the effect of changes in fiscal policy on real GNP four quarters later. For example, fiscal policy in the first quarter of 1953 was expansionary, causing estimated real GNP in the first quarter of 1954 to be $3.88 billion higher than it would have been otherwise.
Sources: The impact measures were generated using the Fairmodel macroeconometric model, version 2.0, July 1985.

In contrast, the aggregate impact measures indicate that fiscal policy was quite expansionary in 1957 and 1958, increasing estimated real GNP by $10.1 and $15.5 billion in succeeding years. However, more interesting is the result which shows that fiscal policy in 1959 was highly contractionary, causing estimated real GNP to decline by $9.4 billion in the presidential election year of 1960. Furthermore, although fiscal policy was moderately expansionary in 1960, most of the expansionary policies occurred late in the year and would not have had an impact on the economy until after the election.

The disaggregated impact measures provide more detailed information concerning fiscal policy changes. These measures are generated in a similar fashion to the aggregate ones and allow us to isolate the impact of a single policy variable on real GNP.

The disaggregated measures in Table 2 reveal that real federal purchases of goods were indeed highly contractionary in 1954, causing estimated real GNP to decline by $28.3 billion. In addition, changes in military jobs exerted a contractionary influence early in Eisenhower's first term, reducing estimated real GNP $1.5 billion and $2.2 billion in 1954 and 1955. The reduction in federal purchases of goods and in military jobs reflects the decreased spending following the Korean conflict as well as the Eisenhower administration's attempt to reduce nondefense expenditures. In contrast, changes in transfer payments to households, personal income taxes, and indirect business taxes somewhat offset the contractionary influence of federal government purchases of goods.

In 1954 transfer payments to households increased estimated real GNP by a rather large $3.3 billion. Although this may appear to indicate

TABLE 2
DISAGGREGATED FISCAL POLICY IMPACT MEASURES ON REAL GNP
(yearly totals in billions of dollars)

Fiscal Policy	1953	1954	1955	1956	1957	1958	1959	1960
Federal Government Purchases of Goods	$ 8.390	$−28.304	$−2.819	$ 0.013	$ 3.701	$ 8.381	$−6.606	$ 0.428
Personal Income Tax Rate	0.164	0.994	−0.156	−0.385	0.065	0.306	−0.328	−0.369
Profit Tax Rate	0.097	0.118	−0.059	0.074	0.028	−0.036	0.009	0.190
Indirect Business Tax Rate	0.220	0.959	−0.232	−0.518	0.681	0.064	−0.119	−0.091
Employee Social Security Tax Rate	−0.032	−0.283	−0.070	−0.114	−0.265	0.019	−0.290	−0.489
Employer Social Security Tax Rate	0.057	−0.119	−0.042	−0.024	−0.048	0.062	−0.219	−0.213
Civilian Jobs	−0.961	−0.311	0.053	0.118	−0.353	0.153	0.297	−0.020
Military Jobs	−0.174	−1.524	−2.179	−0.811	−0.618	−0.742	−0.669	0.001
Transfer Payments to Households	1.120	3.332	0.398	1.626	4.163	3.724	1.139	2.639
Grants-in-aid to State and Local Governments	0.000	0.004	−0.002	−0.001	0.000	0.011	−0.009	0.003

Sources: See Table 1.

that discretionary fiscal policy was expansionary, it reflects instead the influence of nondiscretionary changes resulting from the recession of 1953–1954.[22]

Changes in the personal income tax rate do, however, reflect discretionary fiscal policy, and the 1954 changes exerted the largest expansionary influence of any of the Eisenhower years—increasing estimated real GNP by $994 million in 1955. This expansion does not, however, reflect countercyclical policy on the part of the Eisenhower administration. The reduction in personal income taxes was previously enacted by Congress and rather reluctantly signed into law by Eisenhower.[23]

Although the reduction in personal income taxes was offset somewhat by an increase in social security taxes in 1954, a reduction in excise taxes enacted by Congress and signed into law in March 1954 also exerted an expansionary impact on the economy. Changes in the excise tax rate during 1954 expanded estimated real GNP by $959 million in 1955—exerting the largest expansionary impact for that variable in any of the years reported. Although the reduction in excise taxes was instigated by Republicans in Congress as an antirecession action, the administration did not oppose the bill, given the state of the economy.

[22] Whereas other fiscal policy variables used here largely reflect discretionary changes in policy, transfer payments to households reflect both discretionary and nondiscretionary changes due to automatic stabilizers.

[23] See the *Economic Report of the President*, 1955 (Washington, DC, 1955), p. 19.

This result confirms Herbert Stein's observation that the "excise tax cut was the largest stimulating fiscal action of 1954 which would not have been taken if there had been no recession."[24]

The disaggregated measures provide further evidence that the contractionary policies before the 1956 presidential election were no accident. The largest expansionary influence of 1955 and 1956 came from transfer payments to households, which largely reflects nondiscretionary policy changes. All other changes in 1955, except that in civilian employment, exerted a contractionary influence on real GNP in the presidential election year of 1956.

Fiscal policy of 1957 and 1958 appears to have been quite expansionary, causing estimated real GNP to increase $10.1 and $15.5 billion. Although a significant proportion of the expansion was the result of increases in transfer payments to households and reflects the effect of automatic stabilizers, federal spending on goods was also expansionary.[25] Federal expenditures were buoyed up by an increase in the purchase of farm commodities for farm price supports, acceleration in defense contract spending, and an increase in highway expenditures.[26]

While fiscal policy was expansionary in 1957 and 1958, it became unquestionably contractionary in 1959. The disaggregated measures indicate that federal purchases of goods in 1959 were such that estimated real GNP would decline by $6.6 billion in 1960—the largest decline due to purchases for any year except the highly contractionary one of 1954. The decline in federal purchases of goods in part reflected a substantial reduction in defense-related expenditures.[27] In addition, an increase in social security taxes in both 1959 and 1960 also depressed estimated real GNP.

In 1960 changes in federal government purchases of goods were more expansionary than in 1959, increasing estimated real GNP by a modest $428 million. Most of the expansionary policies, however, came in the third quarter of 1960. Furthermore, the disaggregated figures show that increases in transfer payments to households provided most of the expansionary influence. Transfer payments to households in 1960 increased estimated real GNP by $2.6 billion, up from $1.1 billion the previous year due to the slowdown in economic activity in 1960.

The fiscal policy impact measures, along with the full-employment budget figures, provide interesting grist for our analysis of economic policy in the 1950s. Both the full-employment budget and the impact measures indicate that the policies of the Eisenhower administration do

[24] Stein, *The Fiscal Revolution*, p. 305.

[25] A proportion of the increase in transfer payments to households was due to the legislative extension of unemployment compensation payments.

[26] See Wilfred Lewis, *Federal Fiscal Policy in the Postwar Recessions* (Washington, DC, 1962), pp. 208–13.

[27] Ibid., pp. 237–39.

not correspond to the political business cycle pattern of contraction in the early years of the presidential term and expansion before the presidential election. Moreover, the fiscal policy impact measures show more clearly the highly contractionary character of policy in 1954 and 1959. While the contractionary policies of 1954 reflect the transition from a wartime to a peacetime economy, the economic policies before the 1960 election are less easily explained.

THEMES OF CONTINUITY AND DISCONTINUITY

Economists have traditionally dismissed the policies preceding the 1960 presidential election as evidence of Eisenhower's ongoing fiscal conservatism. While Eisenhower's undeniable commitment to Republican principles and his relentless budget surplus rhetoric made him appear to be "the rock of fiscal probity," the policies before the 1960 election cannot be dismissed as evidence of his conservatism.[28]

Throughout his tenure the president presented an unusually consistent theme reaffirming traditional Republican values and goals, chief among which was a belief in a minimal role for government in the economic sphere. For Eisenhower, this minimal role was inspired by the belief in the efficiency of the private sector in allocating resources and promoting economic growth.[29] Minimal taxation was desirable so as not to stifle individual initiative or put undue pressure on financial markets.[30] Moreover, the one goal which resonates throughout Eisenhower's papers is that of achieving economic growth without inflation. Maintaining a budget surplus was the primary mechanism through which low inflation was to be achieved.

Eisenhower's willingness to endure budget deficits became apparent during the 1953–1954 recession and again during the 1957–1958 recession. While it is no doubt true that a budget surplus had monumental significance to Eisenhower, as Stein points out, "the desirability of balancing the budget was not given by some eternal principle, but depended on economic conditions which would vary."[31]

In addition, the growing surpluses of the actual and full-employment budgets occurred in years when inflation became more problematic. In 1955, 1956, and 1957 the rate of inflation was above 3 percent, up from 1.6 percent in 1953 and 1954, and the full-employment budget surplus increased from \$3.9 billion in 1955 to \$6.4 billion in 1958.[32] Thus, Eisenhower's fiscal policy from 1953 through 1958 reflected consistent but flexible fiscal conservatism. The size of the budget surplus increased

[28] Jonathan Hughes, *American Economic Growth* (Glenview, 1987), p. 513.
[29] *Economic Report of the President*, 1956 (Washington, DC, 1956), pp. 72–79.
[30] *Public Papers of the Presidents*, 1960–61, p. 40.
[31] Stein, *The Fiscal Revolution*, p. 283.
[32] See the *Economic Report of the President*, 1988, p. 253.

with inflation but not during periods of recession. Fiscal policy after 1958, however, was quite different.

Both the actual and the full-employment budget figures indicate that fiscal policy became quite contractionary in 1959 and 1960. The actual federal budget went from a deficit of $10.3 billion in 1958 to a surplus of $3.4 billion in 1960 while the full-employment budget went from a surplus of $4.6 billion in 1958 to a surplus of $14.7 billion in 1960.[33] The impact measures demonstrate that fiscal policy became exceedingly contractionary in 1959, depressing estimated real GNP by $9.4 billion in 1960.

This severely contractionary fiscal policy is not consistent with the flexible fiscal conservatism of the early Eisenhower years. Whereas increases in the budget surplus were associated with increases in inflation from 1955 through 1958, as it moderated in 1958, 1959, and 1960, the surplus continued to expand significantly. Furthermore, while increases in the unemployment rate brought about more moderate fiscal policy in the first six years of the Eisenhower administration, increases in unemployment in 1959 and 1960 were met with a more contractionary policy.

It might, of course, be argued that Eisenhower was unaware of the extent to which fiscal policy was contractionary in the period before the 1960 election. After all, the full-employment budget was a new concept in the late 1950s. Nevertheless, estimates of the full-employment budget were publicly available in 1960. According to Stein, staff members of the Council of Economic Advisors presented estimates of the full-employment budget in 1960 and argued that the enlarged surplus was contributing to the sluggishness of the economy.[34]

Because fiscal policy is ultimately the result of the interaction of congressional as well as presidential action, it might be argued that fiscal policy reflected congressional rather than presidential influences. However, the contractionary fiscal policy in 1960 reflected the administration's conservative impulse more than the will of Congress. As Wilfred Lewis points out: "Congress showed far less enthusiasm for expenditure restraint in the 1960 election year than it had the year before, and appropriations were subsequently increased in virtually every category except foreign aid."[35]

Nor can it be argued that monetary policy was to provide additional stimulus to offset contractionary fiscal policy. In the period before the 1960 election, monetary policy was also exceedingly contractionary.[36] Furthermore, there appears to have been more agreement than dis-

[33] Carlson, "Estimates of the High-Employment Budget," pp. 10–11.

[34] Stein, *The Fiscal Revolution*, p. 364.

[35] Lewis, *Federal Fiscal Policy*, p. 240.

[36] See Milton Friedman and Anna J. Schwartz, *A Monetary History of the United States, 1867–1960* (Princeton, 1963), pp. 617–20.

agreement between the administration and the Federal Reserve on the thrust of monetary policy during this period. According to George Bach, "monetary authorities at the Federal Reserve by and large shared the White House view."[37]

While economists have traditionally focused on Eisenhower's ideology as an explanation for the economic policies surrounding the 1960 presidential election, historians and others have often focused on the ambivalence of Eisenhower toward Nixon's presidential campaign. Stephen Ambrose, perhaps the most thorough of Eisenhower's biographers, attributes his attitude, at least in part, to his complex and often antagonistic relationship with the vice president.[38]

Fueling the speculation about his limited endorsement of Nixon in 1960 were various public comments by Eisenhower. On the eve of the 1960 presidential election, in perhaps his most famous press conference, Eisenhower was asked repeatedly what decisions Nixon had participated in as vice president. The president finally remarked: "If you give me a week, I might think of one. I don't remember."[39] Two weeks earlier, when asked about Nixon's view on nuclear testing, Eisenhower remarked, "I can't recall what he has ever said specifically about nuclear underground testing."[40]

In reality, Eisenhower did very little to enhance the presidential prospects of Nixon and a great deal to jeopardize them. Under the guise of trying to further his vice president's career, Eisenhower suggested that Nixon take a Cabinet post to develop his administrative skills rather than remain on the ticket in 1956.[41] In 1959 Eisenhower suggested changing the structure of the administration to include two "Assistant Presidents"—one in foreign affairs and one in domestic affairs.[42] If, as Alben Barkley was fond of saying, thc vice presidency wasn't worth a "bucket of warm spit," it would certainly be worth even less with this innovation.

Although Eisenhower did not dump Nixon in 1956 and did not pursue the "Assistant President" idea in 1959, he also did not help Nixon raise campaign funds or endorse his candidacy until after the Republican Convention had nominated Nixon.[43] Eisenhower remained a distant relative throughout most of the 1960 campaign. According to Nixon, it was Eisenhower who decided when it would be time to "move into action."[44] According to Eisenhower, however, it was Nixon who

[37] George L. Bach, *Making Monetary and Fiscal Policy* (Washington, DC, 1971), p. 102.

[38] Ambrose, *Nixon*, p. 509.

[39] *Public Papers of the Presidents*, 1960–61, pp. 657–58.

[40] Ibid., p. 626.

[41] For the official and unofficial story of this event, see Dwight D. Eisenhower, *Waging Peace* (Garden City, 1965), pp. 6–9; and Ambrose, *Eisenhower*, pp. 292–93.

[42] Ambrose, *Nixon*, p. 511.

[43] Ambrose, *Eisenhower*, p. 512. Also see *Public Papers of the Presidents*, 1960–61, p. 144.

[44] Nixon, *Six Crises*, p. 349.

"suggested he stay out of the active campaign until the last few days."[45] This, of course, was not the first time they had disagreed on who was making decisions.

CONCLUDING REMARKS

The Eisenhower presidency provides a compelling counterexample to the political business cycle hypothesis that presidents will manipulate the economy to enhance their re-election prospects. While Eisenhower engaged in highly contractionary policies upon entering office, he did not engage in significantly expansionary policies before the 1956 and 1960 presidential elections.

Economists have generally been satisfied with attributing these economic policies to Eisenhower's fiscal conservatism. For many, "Eisenhower epitomized the chief executive who sets an economic policy course early in the administration and holds tightly" to its central tenets.[46] The evidence presented here, however, indicates that the highly contractionary fiscal policy before the 1960 presidential election is not consistent with the flexible fiscal conservatism exhibited throughout much of the Eisenhower presidency.

Instead, the evidence on fiscal policy is consistent with those interpretations that view fiscal policy before the 1960 election as an anomaly—possibly influenced by Eisenhower's relationship with Nixon. As Ambrose has observed: "Time and again, Eisenhower could have done things that Nixon urged on him that could have swayed votes, but he always refused."[47] It is clear that for Eisenhower as for other presidents, ideology alone provides an insufficient explanation for policy actions which must be understood in the context of other political, economic, social, and, perhaps, personal factors.

[45] Ambrose, *Nixon*, p. 558.
[46] Weatherford, "The Interplay of Ideology," p. 944.
[47] Ambrose, *Nixon*, p. 513.

The Role of the Textbook in Undergraduate Economic History Courses: Indispensable Tool or Superficial Convenience?

DAVID MITCH

Many more people read undergraduate textbooks in economic history than will ever lay eyes on a copy of this JOURNAL. And despite the many hours that we teachers of economic history devote to preparing lectures, our students may spend more hours in the library with their textbooks than they do in the classroom listening to our lectures. Students may even keep and refer back to their textbooks many years after taking the final exam. Moreover, textbooks and similar general interest books provide an opportunity for economic historians to speak to the large numbers of the educated public who will never set foot in an economic history classroom. The quality of books in economic history for students and general readers is clearly important for the intellectual impact of the discipline.

But should a textbook be used at all in teaching economic history? Can a textbook adequately capture the complexity of issues, the subtlety of argument, and the richness of evidence so as to convey to its readers the character of the discipline? This latter question is especially pertinent given history's penchant for scrutinizing sources and evidence. Some critics may regard textbooks as intellectual fast food, lacking in both flavor and nutrition. But do teachers, faced with a less selective student body, large classes, limited library resources, and limited student book budgets, have any practical alternative to a textbook?

To ascertain how undergraduate teachers of economic history were dealing with these issues and to elicit their evaluations of available textbooks, the members of the Economic History Association were surveyed. They received survey forms in May 1989 along with their registration materials for the September 1989 meeting of the Association. Eighty-one replies were received, and the results were circulated at a session of the meeting on textbooks and other readings.

Although we do not know how representative the 81 respondents are, we do know that they are heterogeneous. First, the admissions policies at the institutions they taught at ranged from egalitarian to exclusive. Twenty-two percent of the respondents taught at institutions where mean combined SAT scores were under 1000 or indicated by written comment that admissions were unselective; 50 percent taught at institutions where mean SATs were in the 1000 to 1200 range or indicated that admissions were moderately selective, and 28 percent taught at institutions where SATs were over 1200 or indicated that admissions were highly selective. Second, the institutions of the respondents ranged from small colleges to large state universities. Twenty-three percent of the respondents taught at institutions with enrollments under 5,000; 35 percent taught at institutions with enrollments of between 5,000 and 15,000; and 42 percent, at institutions with enrollments of over 15,000. Third, the respondents included both novice and veteran teachers. Forty-two percent had been teaching economic history for

The Journal of Economic History, Vol. L, No. 2 (June 1990). ISSN 0022-0507.

The author is Assistant Professor of Economics, University of Maryland Baltimore County, Catonsville, MD 21228.

My thanks to William Becker, Secretary-Treasurer of the Economic History Association, for distributing the survey forms on which this report is based and to the 81 respondents who took the time to fill them out. William Becker, Rondo Cameron, W. Drake McFeely, Charles Peake, and Richard Sutch provided helpful comments for improving the survey form. Useful editorial advice was provided by the editors and by Elisa Diehl and Virginia McConnell. The author alone is responsible for any deficiencies that remain.

under 10 years, 32 percent, between 10 and 20 years, and 26 percent, for over 20 years. Given this diversity, there is reason to think that the survey captured a meaningful range of concerns.

The respondents were diverse not only in their backgrounds but also in their practices and attitudes toward textbooks and other readings in their undergraduate economic history courses. Textbooks seem to be firmly entrenched in these courses. Of those who addressed the issue of what readings they assigned (78 out of 81 responses), 91 percent indicated that they had used a textbook recently, although 5 in this group indicated that they had not always used a textbook or might not use one in the future. But only 4 percent of these 78 indicated that a textbook was the *only* source of reading. In addition to textbooks, 49 percent also assigned books not strictly intended to be textbooks, for example, paperback monographs, as well as other materials, such as xeroxed packets and reserve readings. Another 27 percent combined a textbook with such materials as xeroxed packets and reserve readings but did not assign other types of books, and 5 percent combined a textbook with other types of books but used no other type of reading material. Overall, 54 percent of the 78 assigned reserve readings and 31 percent used xeroxed packets.

Survey respondents were also asked to identify the most important types of reading. Despite the pervasive use of textbooks in undergraduate teaching, only 32 percent of 75 respondents regarded the textbook unaccompanied by any other type of reading as the most important type of reading in their economic history courses. Nineteen percent considered journal articles the most important type of reading; 19 percent preferred textbooks and articles combined; 12 percent favored articles and monographs combined; and 11 percent stated monographs alone were the most important source of reading.

Respondents exhibited ambivalence about textbooks in attitude as well as in practice. Of the 77 responses to the question, "Do you think that the conventional textbook format is appropriate for teaching economic history courses?" 66.2 percent replied yes, 27 percent relied no, and the remaining 6.5 percent had either a mixed response or were uncertain as to what conventional meant. A higher proportion of economists (40 of the 56 responding) than of historians (5 of the 12 responding) thought the textbook format was appropriate. Those at less selective institutions (SAT scores under 1000) were more likely to consider textbooks appropriate (12 of 14 replies) than those who taught at highly selective schools (SAT scores over 1200) (9 of the 16 replying), with those at moderately selective schools (SAT scores in the 1000 to 1200 range) falling in the middle (20 of the 30 replying).

Instructors teaching at large universities clearly tended to be favorably disposed towards textbooks, but those teaching large classes were not as likely to share this attitude. The majority of instructors at relatively large institutions (enrollment over 5,000) thought textbook use *was* appropriate (35 of 49 responses) while half of the instructors at smaller institutions (enrollment of under 5,000) thought that textbooks were *not* appropriate (7 of 14 responses). The relationship between *class* size and attitudes toward textbooks differed between those teaching American and those teaching European economic history. For those teaching American economic history classes, virtually equal percentages of those with class enrollments under 20 (7 of 10 responses) and over 40 (15 of 20 responses) thought that textbooks were appropriate; only 20 of 35 respondents with 20 to 40 students considered textbooks to be appropriate. But for those teaching European economic history, 10 of 11 instructors with class enrollments over 40 thought textbook use was appropriate compared with only 4 of the 10 respondents whose enrollments were under 40. Perhaps differences in the educational environment between large and small institutions have a greater influence on attitudes toward textbooks than do the more obvious logistical considerations associated with class size.

Written comments on the survey forms reveal that different instructors in economic history courses use textbooks for different purposes. Some instructors emphasized that textbooks were far more accessible to students than other types of readings. They viewed the textbook as critical for defining issues and providing coherence in their courses. Witness such comments as: textbooks are "indispensable"; "students appreciate textbooks"; textbooks provide important "core knowledge"; and "students need the structure provided by textbooks." However, other respondents suggested that textbooks served primarily to set the stage for lectures and discussion. Some respondents in the latter group used textbooks primarily as sources of statistics and data to support class discussion. Others used textbooks as antidotes for student ignorance of geography and general history. Not all students will know what events of significance occurred in 1776 or where the Mississippi River is, especially if, as one instructor noted of her classes, many of the students are foreign.

Objectivity rather than editorializing was preferred by most, but not all, respondents. A clear majority (65.8 percent of the 76 responding) thought that textbooks and readings should strive for balance between various ideological viewpoints. Of those favoring a definite ideological perspective, 4 favored liberal values, 7 favored conservative values or a mix of balance and conservative values, and 4 favored marxist values or a mix of marxist values and balance. Another 4 respondents stated explicitly that textbooks should strive for neutrality and objectivity as opposed to a mere balance among views. One respondent did *not* want issues that were still subject to controversy to appear in textbooks on grounds that this would confuse students; in his opinion, only knowledge agreed upon by most members of the profession should appear in texts. In contrast, a few respondents welcomed books that presented issues in a stimulating and provocative manner regardless of their ideological bias. This group criticized existing undergraduate economic history texts as too dull and plastic. Available texts do seem to cater to those favoring balance: 38 of the 47 respondents who favored balance were satisfied with the ideological content of existing texts compared with only 8 of the 18 respondents who would prefer a text with a definite ideological point of view.

Economic historians vary widely in their topical and chronological interests. Moreover, the pace of research rapidly outstrips existing textbooks. One might expect under these circumstances that teachers of economic history would find textbooks both out of date and inadequate in chronological or topical coverage. On the survey, however, respondents split evenly on whether coverage was adequate (39 of 78 respondents replied yes, 37 replied no, and 2 were undecided). Furthermore, the majority (60 percent) of the 76 addressing the issue of dated texts reported no difficulty in finding up-to-date books. Some respondents explained that this was because they regarded undergraduate courses as a forum for examining issues of lasting significance rather than the most recent research. New teachers, however, were less satisfied with the coverage and currency of textbooks. Thirteen of the 19 respondents with less than 5 years of experience teaching economic history had difficulty finding a text with suitable chronological or topical coverage compared with only 27 of the 59 more experienced respondents. Similarly, 12 of 20 less experienced respondents reported difficulty finding texts that were *au courant* compared with only 19 of 56 senior respondents.

By and large, respondents seemed satisfied with the quality of existing textbooks. One group, however, was noticeably dissatisfied—those who thought available textbooks failed to integrate economic theory into the presentation of economic history or, in other words, failed to use an explicitly cliometric approach. Some in this group said that the few texts employing a cliometric approach were too difficult for their students. These teachers, who tended to come from universities with relatively open admissions, wanted a book that would explain to the *average* undergraduate economics major in their courses how economic reasoning was used in economic history. For the cliometricians, showing students how to apply economic theory was an important teaching objective of their economic history courses.

The dearth of economic content in existing texts is further suggested by the responses of 11 *historians* to the question of whether existing texts presupposed too *much* economics training: Only 2 said yes, whereas 8 replied that the level of economics training presumed was about right. In contrast, 19 of the 53 *economists* who replied indicated that existing texts presumed too *little* economics training; only 5 said too much was presumed; and 26 thought the level was about right. Among those concerned about the lack of economic reasoning in existing texts, some complained that diagrams and other apparatus of economic analysis usually appeared in appendices rather than in the main body of the text. Some respondents held the opposite opinion, arguing that undergraduate economic history courses should neither focus on applied economics nor use readings filled with diagrams and equations. Finally, of the 78 who provided information on course prerequisites, 72 percent indicated that prior course work in economics at the principles level or higher was required for enrollment in their economic history courses.

The survey suggests two contrasting results. On the one hand, the textbook seems firmly entrenched in undergraduate economic history courses. A majority of respondents both approved of and used economic history textbooks. On the other hand, respondents diverged considerably regarding the purposes for which textbooks or other readings should be used. Only a small percentage relied exclusively on textbooks. Attitudes toward textbooks ranged from those who thought them indispensable for providing coherence, to those who used them primarily for background, to those who used the term "textbook-y" pejoratively and who preferred to assign readings that they considered stimulating and provocative from other sources. Nonetheless, the majority seemed complacent about the choices of textbooks and other readings available to them. The one dissatisfied segment, the cliometricians, especially those at less selective universities, wanted economic analysis to feature more prominently and to be more fully explained in textbooks. The technicians rather than the literati in our ranks seem the most dissatisfied with the way our discipline is presented to the public in print.

Summaries of Doctoral Dissertations

Farm Output, Productivity, and Fertility Decline in the Antebellum Northern United States

Within a relatively short period of time in the nineteenth century, almost every developed country experienced a fertility transition the causes and consequences of which are still debated in the literature.[1] By estimating the economic value of children we can place fertility in an analytical framework composed of maximizing agents and capable of yielding refutable hypotheses. That children contributed to the output of the farm is not questioned, but how much did they contribute? How did their contribution change as they got older? Was there a difference between the contributions of males and females, or between regions? Did parents adjust the farm operation for differences in the size and age structure of their families? What was the net value of a child in agricultural households? These are some of the questions addressed in my thesis.

Focusing on northern farms in the antebellum United States, I estimate the value of the contribution to farm output of heterogeneous labor inputs including children by age and gender. I analyze the portfolio choices of farm households in relation to farm size, life-cycle stage, and household composition, and I present a model of the farm household with endogenous fertility and intergenerational transfers of wealth. The primary data set is the Bateman-Foust matched sample from the 1860 Census manuscripts.[2]

Answers to the questions previously posed rely on disaggregating the labor of the farm household. However, the most commonly used production relationships are nonlinear and prohibit disaggregation. I solve this problem and derive estimates of the marginal contribution of the various labor inputs by assuming constant returns to scale and estimating the resulting Euler equations. The contributions of agricultural labor by age and sex are estimated for different regions by subtracting the shares of output going to other inputs from gross revenue and regressing different classes of household labor on the remaining share.

The contribution of young children and teenage females was found to be significantly different from zero only in the region of intermediate settlement. Teenage males contributed by far the most in the most settled region. On the basis of these findings I reject the stylized fact that children contributed more to output in the least settled regions. In fact children contributed the least on the frontier. The differences in the relative contributions of young males and females are explained by the differences in the type of agriculture practiced in the various regions. Northeastern males had more improved acreage and capital to work with and were in general closer to off-farm markets than their western counterparts. This enhanced the value of any effort they put forth.

Contemporary commentators noted the relatively large quantity of structures and high quality of the homes in the Northeast relative to the Midwest. They also noted that females were more likely to perform land-clearing activities and field work in the less settled areas. The share of the total value of farms in structures was more than twice as large in the Northeast as in the Midwest, but the share of the increase in the value of the

[1] This dissertation was completed in 1989 at the Economics Department of Indiana University at Bloomington under the supervision of Elyce Rotella.

[2] Fred Bateman and James Foust, *Agricultural and Demographic Records of 21,118 Rural Households Selected for the 1860 Manuscript Censuses*, Magnetic Tape, 1974.

farm from improving acreage was nearly twice as large in the Midwest. My hypothesis is that in the Northeast young females were largely responsible for the relatively high quality of the home, and in the Midwest they were more likely to neglect home work for land clearing and crop production. I test this hypothesis by subtracting from full household income the component due to increases in the value of farmland and purging the contributions of children in land clearing from the estimates of their total contribution. As expected, I find that in the Midwest the contribution of both groups falls significantly, whereas in the Northeast there is relatively little change. More importantly, the ratios of the contributions are relatively unchanged. I conclude that young males and females were more likely to perform the same tasks in the Midwest, but in the Northeast males were more likely to specialize in market production and females in household production.

Clearly, the story of the economic role of children in the farm household is not complete without an attempt at determining what exactly the tasks of children were on the farm. Children probably did whatever they could and whenever it needed to be done; however, references to specific tasks are scarce and anecdotal at best. This problem is solved by looking at how farms with different quantities of children and children of different ages allocated the crop portfolio. In other words, the next best thing to knowing what children did is knowing what types of crops were produced on farms with different types of children. I analyze these relationships by testing the hypothesis that for different-sized farms, stages of the life cycle, and household structures the crop portfolios were the same.

Life-cycle questions are often addressed by using the age of the household head as the determining factor of life-cycle stage, but when using cross-sectional data this approach can yield misleading results. For example, a twenty-year-old head of a household and a forty-year-old head of household are at different stages in their personal life cycles, but the composition of their households could be identical if the former had a twenty-year-old son and the latter had a forty-year-old hired hand. I propose a new definition of the stage of the life cycle based on the composition of the household as well as the age of the head. The justification for this approach is that the farm was not just the home of a family of farmers but also a firm, and farmers had considerable leeway in determining the composition of the farm labor force. They could either produce labor in the form of children, or purchase labor in the spot market in the form of hired hands.[3]

The land and crop portfolio strategies chosen by antebellum farmers are shown to have depended more on region and proximity to markets than on farm size, life-cycle stage, or household composition. In almost every case the difference in the interregional distributions of the portfolio was statistically significant. Conversely, in almost every case the difference in the intraregional distributions was not statistically significant. These results contradict the argument that output mix is adjusted to the type and quantity of labor inputs.

Knowing that children contributed to farm output is not the same as their being net economic assets. In order to determine whether or not children were net economic assets, I calculate the present value at birth of a child, taking into account the value of a child's consumption, mortality, and the discounted value of future output. Only under the most favorable set of assumptions was the computed present value of a male child found to be similar to the lower-bound estimates of the value of male slaves. In no case was the present value of a female child comparable to the reported values of female slaves.

I construct a model of the farm household in which children provide utility to their

[3] The stages of the life cycle of the family are: 1) a young head but no children, 2) only young children, 3) both young children and teenagers, 4) only teenage children, and 5) an older head but no children.

parents and productive services in the operation of the farm, and parents incur costs in raising children in terms of goods, time, and a bequest payment. The model predicts that, given the same preferences and technology, fertility will be lower in the region with the greater opportunities off the farm.

The contribution of the model is that its predictions are based on an explicit calculation of the net present value of children at birth. I show that it is more likely that fertility will decrease with an increase in the level of opportunities for children off the farm if the net present value of children at birth is positive. The inclusion of a bequest motive makes this condition empirically more difficult to meet, but it does not matter whether the bequest is set up as a target or as insurance for old-age security. If parents view the bequest as a cost of raising children, the cost rises with opportunities off the farm, and opportunities vary positively with population density, then the effects of the two bequests will be observationally equivalent. However, to the extent that children rendered old-age security to parents, there would have been an offsetting increase in the value of children yielding predictions more consistent with observed behavior.

LEE A. CRAIG, *North Carolina State University*

Organization and Extent of Textile Manufacture in Eighteenth-Century Rural Pennsylvania: A Case Study of Chester County

My dissertation analyzes eighteenth-century domestic textile manufacture in rural Pennsylvania to determine how it contributed to the local economy and whether or not it could meet the colonists' requirements for cloth.[1] The notion of early household self-sufficiency continues to be a strong issue in American historiography. The existence of numerous domestic spinners and weavers, capable of producing sufficient cloth to meet the needs of rural colonists, has been an integral element of that concept. In analyzing pre-factory clothmaking, most scholars have interpreted it as an activity associated primarily with females, with little regional or temporal variation. Despite the existence of several recent studies demonstrating that many early American households did not possess the equipment to be self-sufficient in fabric manufacture, no one has attempted to estimate, in quantitative terms, the number of local textile producers and their ability to meet the needs of rural families.

Classic works on colonial American cloth production, produced in the first decades of this century, such as Arthur Cole's, *American Wool Manufacture*, and Rolla Tryon's *Household Manufactures in the United States, 1640–1860*, focused on describing the evolving mechanization that underlay industrial development. But new historical concerns and methodologies rendered it timely to reassess early American textile manufacture. In order to evaluate fully and quantify the significance of clothmaking within a regional economy, the use of imported versus locally made fabrics, and the role of gender in the labor-intensive craft, I chose to do a detailed study of a small area. Chester County, Pennsylvania provided a suitable locus since its heterogeneous rural population, reliance on mixed agriculture, and well-developed market economy made it an important basis for future comparisons with clothmaking sectors in other regions of early North America.

[1] This dissertation was completed in 1988 at the History Department of the University of California, San Diego, under the supervision of Robert C. Ritchie.

From a sampling of 825 (15 percent) of the county's 5,500 eighteenth-century household inventories and accompanying wills, I set up a computer data base to quantify cloth-related equipment and fiber owned by decedents in Chester County. By linking the probate records to tax lists and combining them with newspapers, correspondence, journals, and account books, I was able to delineate the contours of textile production in the region.

My analysis demonstrated that clothmaking in eighteenth-century Chester County does not conform to the standard view that women made the fabric required by their families. I found, instead, that this function was largely accomplished by European workers, who, after settling in the region, reestablished the system of cloth production they had known in the Old World. They divided tasks along gender lines: unskilled male and female workers processed the fiber and women spun the yarn used in weaving, while professional male craftsmen wove and finished the cloth. Weavers and fullers trained apprentices or their own sons in their crafts and, like their European ancestors, frequently hired contractual labor from outside their immediate families to assist them. In addition to textile production, the artisans owned land and engaged in mixed farming. By combining their craft with profitable seasonal agriculture, Chester County cloth workers continued to utilize a system of by-employment they had practiced prior to emigrating to Pennsylvania.

The textile sector was supported by the buoyant economy of the region. Several studies have shown that soon after establishing farms the inhabitants began to produce a surplus of wheat for sale on the Atlantic market. The money generated meant that farm families could buy many of the goods and services they would otherwise have to provide for themselves or do without. Because, for the most part, the economy continued to flourish throughout the eighteenth century, fueled largely by the ability of many farmers involved in by-occupations to accumulate capital, textile artisans had a constant local market for cloth ordered and paid for, frequently in cash, by their customers.

Despite the presence of practicing professional cloth workers, however, domestic production could not meet the community's demands for fabrics. My account-book analysis showed that weavers operated on a custom-order basis using yarn provided by their customers. But raw materials were always in limited supply as more than half the residents did not produce fiber and about 40 percent lacked tools with which to spin yarn. Moreover, the wool and flax that existed were generally low grade and farmers, concentrating on cereal agriculture, had little interest, throughout the eighteenth century, in attempting to increase the quality or quantity of the local fiber.

Finally, storekeepers' accounts, combined with inventory data, show that rural Pennsylvanians always had access to large amounts of assorted imported fabrics. These provided a source of cheap cloth for people who did not produce fiber to take to a weaver, as well as luxury textiles unavailable from local production. Rural residents participated, with their urban counterparts, in what recent scholars have called the consumer revolution of the eighteenth century and many desired to own imported luxurious clothing and fabric furnishings in order to enhance their comfort and have visible indicators of their prosperity. Therefore, even if Pennsylvania weavers could increase their output, they could never meet the demand for the fashionable and exotic fabrics available primarily through international trade.

The stable agricultural orientation of Chester County, the seasonal nature of craft work, and the availability of imported cloth, were all factors in limiting the growth of textile manufacture in the region. Never during the eighteenth century did this community begin to typify the traditional assertion that most early American households produced their own cloth. Less than 10 percent of decedents had weaving equipment and even this was used only on a part-time basis. Not until the very end of the century do we begin to see some elements of change in a system that remained relatively unaltered for over a hundred years.

My conclusions require that several long-held assumptions be reexamined. Clearly there were factors at play in determining the nature of early domestic cloth production that went beyond the boundaries of necessity or technology. We need to move away from the traditional emphasis on household self-sufficiency and continue to examine how external markets influenced local rural economies. The availability of raw materials, the accessibility of imported cloth goods, and the ability of rural households to accumulate capital with which to purchase textiles were major factors in determining the scale of local textile manufacture. By exploring more fully the contours of early regional clothmaking and the impact of changing local production and consumption practices, we will be able to trace more accurately the evolution of American consumer behavior.

ADRIENNE D. HOOD, *Royal Ontario Museum, Toronto*

International Cooperation and Domestic Cartel Control: The International Steel Cartel, 1926–1938

The First World War ended the economic and political environment that had developed over the course of the nineteenth century.[1] From 1919 through 1939 Western European nations were forced to redefine themselves and their strained relationships. They created an intricate set of international agreements and organizations, attempting to restore order to the chaotic face of Europe. One of the most important commercial agreements during this period was the International Steel Cartel (ISC), founded in 1926 by Germany, France, Belgium, and Luxembourg.

My study of the ISC is broken into three periods. The first is from 1926 to 1930, during which time the countries set up the basic structure of the cartel. The second period comes with the shock of the depression in 1930 and lasts through 1932. These were years of little international coordination, as each country was mainly concerned with its own internal collapse and less interested in maintaining its external ties. The final period is from 1933 to the eve of the Second World War and marked the period of the highest degree of international coordination. Rather than treating the ISC as a single entity with its own policies and targets, I examine each of the cartel members and how they interacted in the context of the international agreement and the economic environment. In this way the cartel is understood as a collection of separate individuals, and I am then able to compare intermember gains and losses in terms of national aims.

Over the 1920s the cartel structure was simple: each member had a fixed percentage of a tonnage program established by the executive committee of the cartel. Penalties or subsidies were paid for over- or under-quota production. I found that the Germans did pay the most penalties, as previously believed, but the amounts were not as high as reported in the contemporary press, and the payments were not made only because of large domestic demand. In addition to the production quotas, the members worked out complicated import penetration agreements. The trade limitation provided the opportunity for member countries to reorganize and operate their own domestic cartels. The international cartel provided the structure for its members to reorganize their domestic markets and to prepare for future international cooperation.

The German steel industry thrived in this environment and created a strong system of

[1] This dissertation was completed in 1988 at the Economics Department of the University of Illinois, Champaign-Urbana, under the direction of Larry Neal, Jeremy Atack, and Thomas Ulen. Financial support was provided by the Social Science Research Council.

internal product cartels, which kept the domestic price far greater than the world price for steel products. The other countries required the 1920s to rebuild and to reorganize their steel industries; it was not until after 1930 that France and Belgium could attempt global domestic steel policies. Part of their problem was that both were plagued by the small, but numerous nonintegrated steel works (called rerollers), which were basically rolling mills, requiring steel ingots as inputs for the production of finished steel products, such as thick plates; they resented policies aimed at increasing steel input prices and fought the cartels as outsiders. German steel makers had solved this problem before World War One by forcing the rerollers into concessions and by merging with them. The operation of the international cartel reflected the differences between the national groups. Using a market-share response model and calculating correlations of changes in market shares, I show that the countries with the most similar internal organizations—France, Belgium, and Luxemburg—were the most coordinated in their production and had a rival relationship with the German group, which had its own internal agenda created by its domestic cartels.

With the depression the international agreements were ignored and the countries concentrated on their own domestic markets. Although the Germans prospered in the late 1920s, they were hit most severely by the world depression. This was mainly because their rigid internal structures did not allow them the needed elasticity to adapt to the new market conditions. A graphic example of this is the agreement between the German steel producers and steel finishers, the so-called AVI agreement, which promised a finishing firm the necessary steel inputs at the world price if it had an export order. This arrangement operated well in the relatively stable 1920s but was a heavy burden when world prices dropped after 1930. I show that the actual received price for German steel was about 20 percent lower than the official prices. This helps to explain why the steel makers were so opposed to the Brüning government's *Preisabbau*; their prices had already been lowered by the AVI agreement.

Not only did the shock of the depression break the international cartel, it also marked a significant change in the relationship of the French group with the other national groups. The French took this opportunity to profit from the Germans' misfortune, and expanded output while creating their own internal cartels which operated for the rest of the decade. As the French group began to create its own domestic product cartels, it became less and less integrated with the Belgian and Luxemburg groups although it continued to have a rivalrous relationship with the German group. With the near collapse of the international market, the Belgian and Luxemburg groups clung together and their domestic cartels even met together to determine joint policy.

After the shock of the depression, the national groups were ready again to reform their international agreements under the new conditions of their own internal organizations and the changes in the international markets. In response to these changes the International Steel Export Cartel (ISEC) was created in 1933 by the original members of the 1926 cartel. (Other countries joined afterwards, for example, Britain in 1935.) The ISEC was made up of a number of individual product export cartels that set export quotas and prices for the national groups. This new arrangement continued to protect the domestic markets of each of the members, permitting them to continue the formation and operation of their domestic cartels.

For this period I first examine the domestic cartels of Belgium, France, and Germany. Each of the countries had its own internal constraints that became greater after 1936. Both Belgium and Germany seem to have succeeded in exploiting their market power, but the Belgians had to fight against their country's small domestic demand and the opposition of the rerollers, while the Germans had to adapt to increasing governmental intervention after 1936. France was struggling to maintain its internal agreements but was too weak to adapt to the internal shocks of the devaluation and the various labor conflicts after 1936. I then assess the operation of the export product cartels, using merchant bars as an example. Special emphasis is placed on the developments of the domestic steel industries and how these affected the international arrangements.

The story that emerges from these findings is that the form of the international cooperation in each period was directly linked to both the nature of the product controlled and, more importantly, the environment and goals of the various national groups. In a classic article Don Patinkin concluded that "the successful cartel must follow a policy of continuous compromise."[2] I agree and would add "and innovation in structure."

DANIEL BARBEZAT, *Amherst College*

[2] Don Patinkin, "Multiple-Plant Firms, Cartels, and Imperfect Competition," *The Quarterly Journal of Economics*, 61 (Feb. 1947), p. 203.

The Fruits of Revolution: Property Rights, Litigation, and French Agriculture, 1700–1860

The French Revolution should be assessed not simply through a debate about its economic, social, or political causes, but through its economic consequences.[1] This dissertation attempts to evaluate the Revolution by examining the political economy of drainage and irrigation. The research suggests that institutional constraints inherent to the Old Regime were responsible for the lack of investment in agriculture prior to the French Revolution. Reforms, undertaken during the Revolution of 1789, were responsible for increased investment in drainage and irrigation after 1820.

Drainage and irrigation were two types of investment in agriculture that increased the productivity of land and extended the area under cultivation. Both were identified by Old Regime reformers as important means of achieving growth in agriculture. This research shows that transaction costs involved with improving land were very high during the Old Regime, but were substantially reduced after 1789. The dissertation is organized in three parts, each of which attempts to tackle the question of institutional obstacles to investment in agriculture from a different perspective.

The first part is an empirical study of drainage in Normandy from 1700 to 1860. Using archival data, I constructed hypothetical cost-benefit series for drainage projects that run from 1700 to 1860. These hypothetical cost-benefit series suggest that drainage would have been very profitable in the absence of transaction costs during the period from 1700 to 1789, yet no drainage occurred. Based on the records of failed eighteenth-century schemes, I argue that swollen transaction costs made it impossible to drain marshes. The problems of transaction costs lay in endless litigation over property rights and the inability of property-rights owners to write binding contracts.

The ownership of marshes was highly uncertain because it involved feudal property rights that had been poorly enforced for centuries. Marshes could belong either to lords or to villages. If lords were awarded property, drainage could proceed swiftly. If villages

[1] This dissertation was completed in 1988 in the Division of Humanities and Social Sciences of the California Institute of Technology under the supervision of Philip T. Hoffman. I hold great debts to Lance E. Davis and Louis L. Wilde for advice and criticism all along the way. This research was supported by travel grants from the California Institute of Technology, a John Randolph Haynes and Dora Haynes Fellowship, and a Sloan Foundation Dissertation Fellowship.

were awarded ownership, the marshes automatically became communal property. In the case of communal marshes, drainage required that the land be divided among the villagers, a task that proved too formidable for the Old Regime. In all cases, litigation was required to sort out property rights because the judiciary systematically invalidated private contracts that resolved the question of marsh ownership. Despite frequent royal promises to reform the judiciary, the state failed to reduce the transaction costs involved with drainage. As a result, the judiciary was neither able nor willing to allocate marshes between claimants. Because customary law was unclear on the issue of marshes and because judges made money from litigation, it was always possible to appeal a verdict. In the eighteenth century, resources were thus expended to redistribute property rights rather than to make improvements. The revolutionary reforms removed all cause for litigation and gave the state the authority to enforce contracts between landowners. As a result, most of the communal marshes in Normandy were drained from 1820 to 1850.

The second part of the dissertation examines irrigation supply in Provence from 1700 to 1860. As in the first part, quantitative evidence suggests that, in the absence of transaction costs, irrigation would have been very profitable in the eighteenth century. Despite the high profits irrigation could have earned, few of the projects that were promoted in the eighteenth century succeeded. The Old Regime's failure to develop irrigation is ascribed to the division of authority over eminent domain and water rights, as well as to the inability of developers to commit to announced prices for irrigation water. Eighteenth-century Provence was in fact a collection of highly autonomous areas. Many villages had enough authority to control the right of eminent domain in their territory. Thus they were able to hold irrigation projects up for ransom. Moreover, promoters of irrigation faced problems that were similar to those of drainage promoters in Normandy. The property rights to unused water were highly uncertain because the royal government had given exclusive rights to draw water from the same river to many different parties. Again the judiciary was incapable of resolving the ambiguities of overlapping titles to water. Therefore litigation frequently dragged on for several decades, to no avail. The revolutionary reforms centralized all authority over water rights and eminent domain in the hands of the national government. From 1820 to 1860 new canals irrigated more than five times as much land as the canals built during the last century of the Old Regime. As a result, the irrigated area in Provence nearly doubled. The research on Provence also points to the dramatic consequences of the decline in transaction costs as a result of the Revolution's reforms.

The third section makes use of game theory to explain how property rights to marsh land came to rest so frequently with villages. I analyze a theoretical model of litigation and settlement that includes burden of proof as a key variable. The model describes the interaction between a landowner and a developer who has rights to the property of the landowner. In order to use the property the developer must make a settlement offer to the landowner. The landowner can either accept the developer's offer or sue in court for higher compensation. If the landowner sues, both parties may search for evidence. The court decides the level of compensation based on the evidence that the developer and the landowner bring to court. This section shows that a sequential equilibrium generically exists. Modeling expenditure decisions endogenously allows an examination of the issues of burden of proof in litigation. I show that burden of proof has substantial impact on the probability of litigation and the magnitude of the settlement offer.

More importantly, the analysis illuminates two issues relevant to the drainage of marshes. First, burden-of-proof rules seem to have played a crucial role in the high frequency of successful litigation by villages. Second, marshes that were allocated to villages could not have been drained because it was impossible to arrive at a division of village marshland that the judiciary would enforce. Moreover, the judiciary made direct bargaining between villagers and developers impossible. Thus it was rational for developers to attempt to have the rights of villages invalidated and for villages to sue. I then extend this model to examine the causes of the historical divergence of peasant property in Britain and France.

It thus seems that the French Revolution was a very important event in the economic history of France. Although the Bourbon monarchs had claimed absolute power, they never achieved the power of nineteenth-century governments. While the physiocrats and other Old Regime reformers had demanded institutional reform, they never achieved an efficient judiciary or better-defined property rights. The French Revolution did have high costs and featured significant amounts of redistribution, but it also involved institutional change. In the long run the Revolution's legacy may well be centralization of power and greatly simplified property rights.

JEAN-LAURENT ROSENTHAL, *University of California, Los Angeles*

Labor Market Institutions and the Geographic Integration of Labor Markets in the Late Nineteenth-Century United States

The late nineteenth century is widely regarded as the era in which a national economy first emerged in the United States.[1] The elaboration of national rail and telegraph networks in the decades after the Civil War lowered the cost and increased the speed of transportation and communication. While manufacturers in many industries consolidated national markets for their products, a variety of new financial intermediaries promoted increasing arbitrage in the market for capital. My dissertation examines the extent of labor market integration at this time.

There are two complementary ways of approaching the question of labor market integration. First, integration may be explored qualitatively by examining the institutions through which labor market adjustment operated. Second, the correlation of wage movements across markets and the magnitude of geographic wage differentials can be used to provide quantitative indexes of the impact of the operation of these market institutions.

In contrast to the increasing specialization and centralization of intermediation in financial and product markets, labor market adjustment continued to rely primarily on informal, word-of-mouth communication channels provided by family and friends. Although the number of employment agencies and publicly sponsored labor exchanges operating in local markets increased considerably, they played only a minor role in directing long-distance movements of labor. These formal labor market intermediaries attracted a good deal of attention around the turn of the century, and published results of a number of contemporary studies make it possible to construct a clear picture of the extent and characteristics of their activities. It appears that most job-seekers were deterred from using employment agencies by the risks of opportunistic behavior to which they were exposed. As a result, employment agencies were important only in directing the first wave of long-distance migrants. Once an established industrial work force was in place, informal communication channels replaced formal intermediaries.

[1] This dissertation was completed in 1988 at the Economics Department of Stanford University under the supervision of Paul David and Gavin Wright.

To assess the performance of labor markets after the Civil War in quantitative terms I use annual wage data collected by the U.S. Department of Labor covering 23 occupations and 12 major U.S. cities from 1870 to 1898. To adjust these data for intercity differences in the cost of living, I construct city-specific retail price indexes at several dates during this period.

Despite considerable occupational variation, year-to-year wage movements were, on average, positively correlated across cities. But this is less a reflection of labor market integration than of increasing integration in other sectors of the economy, for once I take account of the effect of aggregate fluctuations in prices and economic activity there is no perceptible correlation of wage movements.

Measurements of intercity real wage differentials for all occupations and for disaggregated occupational groups confirm the absence of labor market integration. Although real wage rates in San Francisco converged toward eastern levels following completion of the transcontinental railroad, wage differentials between other cities were large and persistent. Most striking is the finding that real wages in midwestern cities exceeded those in eastern cities by 20 to 25 percent, with no tendency toward convergence. This gap is roughly three to five times as large as the differential found between these regions in the twentieth century. It is also considerably more than the direct costs of transportation between these cities, indicating that these differentials are attributable primarily to the costs of securing information about distant employment opportunities.

Nonetheless, a considerable labor supply response is evident in the differentially rapid growth of population in the high-wage midwestern cities. The population of Chicago, for example, the midwestern city in my sample with the highest wages, grew at nearly 6 percent per year from 1870 to 1900, about twice as fast as the eastern cities in the sample. For real wage differentials to have persisted without convergence in the face of a supply response of this magnitude, there must have been persistent regional imbalances in the relative growth of labor demand.

In view of the importance of intercity differences in the rate of labor demand growth, it appears important to disentangle the contribution of imperfect labor market integration from that of exogenous supply and demand disturbances in causing the comparatively large real wage differentials of the late nineteenth century. I attempt to do this by estimating a fully identified model of local wage determination for the years 1870 to 1900, using data from the decennial censuses of manufacturing and population to measure exogenous supply and demand shocks. I then simulate the course of interregional real wage differentials from 1910 to 1940 using the actual values of the exogenous variables and the coefficients estimated for 1870 to 1900. The resulting counterfactual shows how real wage differentials would have evolved, holding the extent of labor market integration constant at its late nineteenth-century level. Since the counterfactual real wage differential closely parallels the actual course of interregional wage differentials, I conclude that the smaller magnitude of twentieth-century wage differentials was due largely to a reduction in the magnitude of exogenous labor supply and demand shocks and not to changes in the extent of labor market integration.

It is tempting to conclude that the magnitude of real wage differentials in the late nineteenth century was due entirely to the forces which produced geographic imbalances in the supply and demand of labor, but this would ignore the fact that the effects of these forces were localized because labor markets were not completely integrated. There is thus no simple answer to the question of how well late nineteenth-century labor markets worked. They worked to the extent that labor supply moved from low- to high-wage areas, and labor market institutions responded to opportunities for arbitrage. But this responsiveness was not sufficient to eliminate or even reduce interregional real wage differentials over the course of nearly thirty years.

JOSHUA L. ROSENBLOOM, *University of Kansas*

Keynes vs. Churchill: British Unemployment in the Twenties

Churchill has been associated historically with the British government's decision to return to the gold standard at the prewar parity.[1] He was Chancellor of the Exchequer in 1925 when the formal resumption occurred. Keynes was the policy's most noted contemporary critic, a self-proclaimed "Cassandra."[2] He argued that by forcing a deflation, Churchill was engineering an increase in unemployment, though he could never publicly admit the necessary causal connection. In a tongue-in-cheek parody of Churchill's advisors, Keynes suggested that they should warn the Chancellor:

> We estimate that about two years may elapse before it will be safe for you to utter in public one single word of truth. By that time you will either be out of office or the adjustment, somehow or other, will have been carried through.[3]

Churchill countered with his own accusation of duplicity:

> Let us see exactly what [Keynes' policy] means. Currency is to be the medium of adjustment—the shock absorber. How foolish to have any disputes with workmen about their wages! All you have to do is to inflate, to manipulate the currency. Immediately you depreciate the exchange, immediately you give a bounty on exports, immediately prices at home are raised, and what does that mean? . . . It means a diminution, in exact mathematical ratio, of the real wages which are received by the working classes.[4]

At the center of their debate was the question of how the government could best ameliorate the unprecedented unemployment levels, the most dramatic domestic problem the government faced in the twenties. The debate over unemployment encompassed issues other than the return to gold. In fact, the return was one of the least contested of the government's decisions. This lack of controversy was out of keeping with the fundamental importance of the decision. Not only did the revaluation affect the international competitiveness of the economy, the monetary discipline of the gold standard also determined the shape of the government's fiscal policies in the twenties, making it impossible to carry out any effective policies for alleviating unemployment, even endangering benefit payments to the unemployed.

The government returned to gold at the prewar parity because they feared the inflationary potential of the alternative. A sustained unemployment rate of 10 percent did not allay these fears. Unemployment was concentrated in just a few industries, the problems of which appeared to go much deeper than exchange-rate policy. Outside of the government there were those who came to believe that the deflation engineered to support the return to gold was related to the unemployment. But most laymen did not feel sure of themselves when debating the "mysteries of the exchange." Though skeptical, they ultimately surrendered to the advice of financial experts. Keynes exhibited no such timidity. He did not deny the "private troubles" of the afflicted industries, but he argued that there was also a "general cause" at work, which a devaluation could successfully rectify.[5] A devaluation would not be inflationary, merely stop the deflation.

Recent quantitative attempts to evaluate the merit of Keynes's argument have gone too far in simplifying his position, and they have all together ignored Churchill's fears of

[1] This dissertation was completed in 1988 at the Economics Department of Stanford University under the supervision of Gavin Wright and Gregory Clark.

[2] J. M. Keynes, *Essays in Persuasion* (New York, 1932), p. v.

[3] J. M. Keynes, "The Economic Consequences of Mr. Churchill," in *Essays*, p. 253.

[4] London, Hansard (House of Commons Debates), (1925), vol. 187, col. 1466–67.

[5] Keynes, "Consequences," p. 246.

inflation.[6] I estimate the impact of a devaluation in a manner that takes the structure of the economy into account. By modeling demand for British production as the sum of demand for its disaggregated components, and then estimating these demand curves, I am able to translate changes of demand into changes in employment and inflation. I simulate the impact of devaluations from 1 to 50 percent on the unemployment and the inflation rates. The industries that expanded most in the simulation were those with large pools of unemployed workers, suggesting that moderate devaluations would have been effective in decreasing unemployment without unduly stimulating inflation. A 20 percent devaluation would have decreased the unemployment rate from 10.2 percent to 7.5 percent, while adding only 1.3 points to the inflation rate. Devaluations of greater than 20 percent have a much larger impact on inflation while further declines in unemployment are slight. Though Churchill's fears were not ungrounded, they were excessive given the circumstances.

The still very high rate of aggregate unemployment suggests that Churchill was justified in claiming that British industry had problems beyond the reach of the government's exchange-rate policy. Five industries shared disproportionately in the general decline—textiles, mining, iron and steel, mechanical engineering, and ship building. These were referred to as the "staple trades" because they had been the staple of British industry in the prewar era. For each of these industries I estimate the change in quantity demanded due to changes in the structure of demand, which I measure by allowing for shifts in the estimated demand curves. I compare these predicted "shifts" with the predicted declines in quantity demanded due to the increase in relative price between 1913 and 1924. In every industry the declines due to price increases dominate the changes due to demand-curve shifts. British industry was declining because it had become less efficient relative to its competitors. Surmounting this relative inefficiency would have been difficult in any case. The compounding impact of a deflationary policy made recovery impossible.

To study the issue of declining efficiency in more detail, I focus on Britain's most important export market—India's demand for cotton textiles. I find only slight changes in relative costs between the British and Indian industries over the war years. The great losses British industry suffered in this market were primarily due to India's imposition of tariffs. The tariff of 1921 was 11 percent, suggesting that a moderate devaluation of the pound would have offset Britain's competitive disadvantage.

The success of an exchange-rate policy would have depended upon timing. Immediately after the war, silver prices jumped due to a contraction in supply. The silver-based rupee appreciated 100 percent relative to the gold-based pound. Though there was grumbling among the Indian merchants, the Indian government bowed to market forces and changed the official value of the rupee. Subsequently, a fall in silver prices reduced this appreciation. The Indian government's initial acceptance, however, suggests that if Britain had not forced the revaluation of sterling after the war, it would have been politically feasible for the pound to have established a new parity with the rupee more in keeping with actual conditions. It is not clear that the British government could have successfully engineered such a devaluation later in the decade.

In 1930, when asked which of the various proposed economic policies he would recommend, Keynes answered that given the situation he would have been willing to try anything, the only policy he could not countenance was a "negative one—the repelling of each of these remedies in turn."[7] This study examines the feasibility of one of the

[6] S. N. Broadberry, *The British Economy Between the Wars: A Macroeconomic Survey* (Oxford, 1986) and Donald Moggridge, *British Monetary Policy 1924–1931: The Norman Conquest of $4.86* (Cambridge, 1972).

[7] London, British Cabinet Papers, Cab. 58/11, The State of Trade, Answers by Mr. Keynes, 21 July, 1930.

policies which was rejected, a devaluation of the pound. I find that while a devaluation would not have eliminated all of Britain's economic problems, by stimulating the depressed sectors, such a policy would have given industry the breathing space it needed to deal with the problems of postwar reconstruction.

SUSAN WOLCOTT, *St. Louis University*

Comments on Craig, Hood, and Barbezat

What does one say about three excellent dissertations, three dissertations that were informative and delightful to read? If we begin with Lee Craig's, his dissertation turns out to be a model of economic history as done by economists. Tightly reasoned and ingenious in its use of theory and econometrics, it manages to tease new information and new findings from the data, findings that will be important not only for the study for fertility, but for the analysis of labor markets, of savings, and of capital formation. The admirable features in Craig's dissertation are numerous: his careful review of the literature on the fertility decline and on fertility differences in the United States is but one. Equally admirable is his painstaking calculation of gross and net farm revenue. Not content merely to read Atack, Bateman, and Faust's data into his computer, he reworks it wherever he thinks it can be improved. The care with which he proceeds may escape most readers' attention, but those who are acquainted with farm records will not fail to appreciate his efforts. As someone who has himself sweated over farm accounts, I have to applaud in particular his calculation of the profits of farm ownership.

The most stunning part of the dissertation, though, is undoubtedly Craig's calculation of wage rates for various types of household labor. His ingeniously simple method involves subtracting from gross farm revenues the amounts spent on nonhousehold inputs. The residual then represents the cost of the household inputs and it can be regressed on the quantities of household labor employed (so many adult males, so many adult females, and so forth) to calculate implicit wages (or equivalently productivities) for each category of household labor. The values Craig arrives at seem very reasonable: for example, the difference between male and female labor productivity that he calculates compares favorably, as he points out, with that derived by Claudia Goldin and Ken Sokoloff. There turn out to be important variations in Craig's wages by age, sex, and region, and he related these wage differences to farming practices and to opportunities off the farm. The wage differences between regions that he finds help explain variations in fertility, and the whole discussion underlines the importance of strategic bequests in any economic model of fertility, a conclusion that is sure to delight a number of people, including my co-discussant, Roger Ransom.

One could go on and on lauding this or that aspect of Craig's dissertation—his discussion of the life cycle, for instance—but I would rather raise one question about his method. I have one lingering (though not too serious) doubt: in all of Craig's regressions, his explanatory variables are quantities of household labor—the number of teenage boys in farm households, for example. One might wonder whether these physical quantities really were uncorrelated with the error terms in the regression, as good econometrics requires. The answer, though, is probably not. The error term might well include inputs which Craig could not observe but which were under the farmer's control. And there is every reason to believe that these unobserved inputs would be correlated with the amounts of household labor. This may seem, of course, like the usual sort of nitpicking criticism raised in any discussion of applied work, but it is a very real problem, one that affects any econometric estimation of a production function when physical quantities are involved. I am sure, however, that Lee Craig has an answer to this objection, and in the end I doubt that it will mar his findings.

If Craig's dissertation is a model of economic reasoning, Adrienne Hood's is a model of historical research. The evidence she gleans from the archives is analyzed with care and brought to bear upon a number of important questions. The heart of the research is her sample of nearly one thousand probate records from Chester County, Pennsylvania, covering the period from 1714 to 1809. Hood uses the probate documents, along with tax records and account books, to attack two ideas that have wide currency among historians: the belief in colonial household self-sufficiency and the related belief that the colonial period was a golden age for women. Despite the excellent work by Winifred Rothenberg and others, many historians still cling to the notion that colonial households were self-sufficient. Colonial households supposedly grew their own food and made their own clothing. And since it was women who made the clothing—or so many historians think—they had a special role to play in the household, one that disappeared with the extension of the market and growth of the factory. Hence the belief in the golden age of women which, despite attacks from within the field of women's history, is also widespread.

Hood attacks these two ideas by asking a series of related questions: Who made textiles in rural Chester County? What capital and skills were involved? How much was produced? The answers, which require a detailed knowledge of the textile industry and yet are told in a way that should interest any reader, cast doubt on self-sufficiency and the golden age, at least as far as Chester County is concerned. Households spun some wool and flax, often during the slack season, but they left weaving and fulling to specialists, since the skills and capital involved were large. The amount of thread or yarn the households produced was in any case minuscule relative to local demand, and most families ended up purchasing the bulk of their clothing in the market. One example of their reliance upon the market is particularly striking: the very flax they cultivated was grown less as a source of linen thread than for its seed, seed that was sold to the Irish in return for woven linens—a delightful example of the gains from trade. There was thus no self-sufficiency in Chester County and no golden age for women either, since women never provided the family with clothes.

Hood's story is told with such care and such concern to detail—yet in ever-graceful prose—that it reminded me of Jean Meuvret's *Le problème des subsistences*, recently lauded by George Grantham in the pages of this JOURNAL. Anyone interested in the textile industry will profit from this manuscript once it becomes a book. The only thing I urge Hood to do—a point which she is well aware of—is to ensure that Chester County was not completely exceptional. Other counties, more isolated from developed markets, might well conform to a different pattern.

If Hood stands out for her careful archival research and Craig for his perceptive economic reasoning, then Daniel Barbezat deserves accolades for having done both. The first thing that strikes a reader of this dissertation is the archival research. Not satisfied with merely reworking the information that one can find in the abundant multilingual literature on the European steel industry between the two World Wars, Barbezat went off to Europe and tunneled through the mountainous records—they must loom larger than the slag heaps the steel mills left behind—of cartels and companies in Belgium, France, Germany, and Luxemburg. Anyone who has toiled in archives has to admire his effort: he mastered the complexities of a number of private and public collections in four different countries. One archive alone is usually enough to daunt most researchers.

Barbezat's dissertation has other virtues as well. Unlike previous historians, Barbezat does not treat the International Steel Cartel as a single entity. Rather, he looks at the individual members of the cartel and keeps their interaction and their peculiar domestic situation always in focus. He never forgets nonmembers either, such as the steel rerollers, who bedeviled the cartel and undermined its effectiveness. Other historians have not done this. They have typically considered the cartel as a single entity or have limited themselves to an examination of steel firms in a single country. No one has managed to balance both the cartel as a whole and the peculiar domestic situations of the cartel members in the way that Barbezat does.

Barbezat should also be applauded for his clear use of economic theory. He squeezes a great deal from simple models of joint profit maximization, which—to take but one example—shed considerable light on the peculiar difficulties of cartel formation in France, where costs varied greatly from firm to firm. Equally enlightening is his discussion of the peculiar problems faced by international cartels. My only concern here is whether his analysis might profitably be rephrased in light of the recent literature on oligopoly and imperfect information—literature that Barbezat cites and is certainly aware of. One might of course object that such an exercise would merely translate his clear assertion into the murky jargon of game theory, where equilibria are multiple and conclusions vague. But it might well shed additional light on the difficulties the cartel faced in policing its collusive agreements. More important, it might raise further interesting questions. For example, might not temporary overproduction represent not the breakdown of the cartel but rather a strategy of punishing suspicious behavior? And why did the steel makers enter agreements in the first place when the agreements themselves seemed bound to fail?

I therefore hope that Barbezat will reconsider the game theoretic literature on cartels—if only briefly—when he transforms his excellent dissertation into a book. I hope too that he will tell us more about what went on outside the steel industry, outside the cartel and the steel firms. Making such a request of a dissertation writer is perhaps unfair, all the more so if we consider the prodigious amount of research that Barbezat has already done. But perhaps as he turns his dissertation into a book he can say more about how conditions outside the industry affected the cartel. How, for example, did the structure of the domestic capital markets affect the steel firms' behavior? A higher discount rate raises the incentive for cheating, and capital market regulations can obviously facilitate or hinder the task of coordinating different firms. Presumably Barbezat will want to say more about politics in his book was well. He discusses the Nazis' intervention in the German steel market, but more could be said about politics elsewhere. What, for example, were the policies of the other governments toward the cartel? Did they facilitate collusion or hinder it? If they facilitated it, what prevented consumers from organizing against the cartel and pressuring the government? Here I am not asking Barbezat to write another book, merely to add a dash of political economy to what is already an excellent dissertation.

PHILIP T. HOFFMAN, *California Institute of Technology*

Comments on Rosenthal, Rosenbloom, and Wolcott

My task is to comment on the work of Jean-Laurent Rosenthal, Joshua Rosenbloom, and Susan Wolcott. The first thing that strikes one upon reading these three dissertations is the level of intellectual craftsmanship embodied in each of them. Each author has carefully defined a specific "problem" to be examined. Each presents a carefully reasoned argument or "model" to guide their analysis using a "counterfactual" approach to underscore their findings. An impressive amount of data—including in some cases archival data—is examined using econometric techniques that only a short time ago would have been regarded as sophisticated by economic theorists, much less economic historians. Finally, it is a pleasure to report that these theses are written in a clear style that makes the arguments accessible even to one not trained in the subtleties of econometrics, game theory, and general equilibrium analysis.

Jean-Laurent Rosenthal provides us with an analysis of property rights and agricultural improvement in France between the mid-eighteenth century and the mid-nineteenth century. This is actually three distinct "economic studies": drainage in Normandy using cost-benefit analysis; irrigation in Provence, again with cost-benefit analysis; and a second look at the problem of drainage in Normandy, this time using game theory. These individual studies are then tied together with an overview of how changes in property rights brought about by the French Revolution removed the obstacles to investment.

Rosenthal's theme is that agricultural productivity in pre-Revolutionary France was stymied by a combination of ill-defined property rights, a venal judiciary that encouraged litigation, and problems of misperceptions of gains and losses on both sides. At the root of these failures, claims Rosenthal, was the decentralized authority of the *ancien régime*, which favored local, rather than global, property interest. It is easy to convince me that "market failure" might account for the failure of investment in drainage and irrigation in eighteenth-century France. Rosenthal has done an excellent job of collecting data—including 1,241 leases from Normandy—to document his argument that legal entanglements hindered agricultural improvements. While I accept his argument of market failure, I am more skeptical of his cost-benefit analysis that compares gains and losses from actions a century apart. I am reminded of the old adage that "an economist is someone who knows the *price* of everything and the *value* of nothing." This seems particularly relevant when one is dealing with perceptions of the "value" of some action that involves substantial institutional change affecting very disparate groups in very different fashions. In Rosenthal's case we are comparing the values placed on the use of common property rights by peasants on the one hand with that by the lords on the other. Peasants and lords get very different sorts of "output" from the land in question. Are they really using the same "values" (that is, market prices) to estimate the costs and benefits? While Rosenthal is convincing in his demonstration that "efficiency" in French agriculture was in fact increased through the introduction of drainage and irrigation improvements, it is less clear that the peasants ever gained the full measure of these benefits—before or after the Revolution.

Which brings us to the "Revolution." Rosenthal provides an excellent discussion of the impact of changes in property rights that emerged from the Revolution. But the Revolution itself is something of a *deus ex machina* in all this. Granted, it is unfair to expect an analysis of the Revolution in a PhD dissertation. Nevertheless, I think that the aspect of the Revolution that was crucial to Rosenthal's thesis—the centralization of state power and a willingness to enforce a narrower definition of property than existed under the *ancien régime*—is worthy of more comment than Rosenthal provides. Rosenthal notes that one of the few unequivocal gains of the Revolution was the elimination of the nobility. But was the nobility "eliminated"? Or were they able to use the centralization of property rights highlighted in Rosenthal's analysis to reassert their preeminence? I can not resist at this point a comparison with the situation of the former slaveholders in the post-bellum American South. Despite the demise of slavery, the planter class was not destroyed by the Civil War, in large part because they held on to their land. As I read Rosenthal's argument, it would appear that the same could be said of French nobility. Those who were able to retain their land (and their heads) appear to have come out of the revolutionary holocaust in a rather powerful position.

Joshua Rosenbloom also focuses on the "failure" of markets. His central question is: were labor markets "integrated" in the United States after the Civil War? His interest in this problem is motivated by an inescapable truth that emerges from the wage data: there are sizeable differentials in real wages among major cites in the United States. Moreover, after adjusting for the business cycle, wages in particular urban markets do not appear to move in any sort of synchronization that would be characteristic of a market driven by common forces of supply and demand. All of this is very puzzling because we know that large numbers of people *did* move from low-wage to higher-wage labor markets, a phenomenon suggesting that the labor market was integrated.

So why did the wage differentials persist? Rosenbloom takes up the usual impediments to explain a failure of price convergence and finds them inadequate. Imperfect information on jobs and wages was certainly a problem for those seeking employment. Yet informal networks of information systems did let people know where jobs were. A telling piece of evidence in this regard is the fact that immigrants did not just congregate in eastern cities; they moved west along with native-born workers. Transportation costs, a common source of persistent price differentials, were important in only one case—that of San Francisco.

Of course, it is always possible that the data on wages and living costs do not accurately reflect the real wage in each city. Rosenbloom recognizes this problem and offers new evidence on costs of living. However, the difficulties here go beyond shortcomings of the data (which are admittedly scanty). How does one measure the value of "amenities" offered by various locations? A large fraction of the labor force was foreign-born or first-generation. The presence of neighborhoods with common ethnic ties could be an important determinant in the decision to move to a new labor market. I suspect Rosenbloom is correct in asserting that the differentials shown by his calculations suggest that the "real" differences remain. However, his cost-of-living index still understates the impact of "nonmarket" factors on job relocation—and also the extent to which markets are not integrated.

The most likely explanation for real wage differences is that local market conditions determined wages in each city. Rosenbloom points out that, if the demand for labor was consistently outstripping supply, then persistently higher real wages in rapidly growing labor markets would be consistent with the observed flows of labor. An examination of the midwestern cities with high wages shows that this was, in fact, the case. This is an important finding—more important, I think, than Rosenbloom suggests. An in-migration of labor will not necessarily alleviate an excess demand for labor because the process of migration itself causes the demand for labor to shift. The corollary is that the regions experiencing an outflow of labor have declining population and declining demand for labor.

My final point on this question is to suggest that Rosenbloom has, in fact, found evidence of a great deal of integration in the postwar labor markets of America. The fact that the demand for labor continued to outstrip supply in western markets might best be seen as a manifestation of a general scarcity of labor in a labor market that is responding reasonably well to the incentives for change.

Susan Wolcott is also concerned with the question of labor markets—this time with a focus on unemployment and a failure of labor markets to adjust to changes in interwar Britain. Her thesis focuses on a very specific episode in economic policy: the debate between John Maynard Keynes and Winston Churchill over devaluation of the British pound after World War I.

This debate fascinates economists and economic historians for several reasons. First of all, there are the personalities involved. Keynes, who in 1920 had just written *The Economic Consequences of the Peace*, is a man who dominated intellectual agenda of economics in the mid-twentieth century just as surely as Churchill dominated the politics. A second reason for interest in the devaluation debate is that most observers—including Wolcott—agree that Britain's decision to stay with an overvalued pound was a disastrous miscalculation of economic policy that played a major role in Britain's economic problems of the 1920s. Finally, the efficacy of the gold standard, and the impact of devaluation on the stability of the world economy is a topic that will always draw a crowd of analysts interested in determining the importance of maintaining some sort of financial responsibility in the international community. I must confess at the outset that I am not part of that crowd. As a spectator, it appears to me that Wolcott's most significant contribution to this discussion is a rather convincing demonstration that although a devaluation would almost surely have benefited the British economy in 1920, it would *not* have solved the unemployment problem. In that respect, Churchill's opposition to devaluation was not entirely misguided.

Wolcott provides a sectoral analysis of the impact of a devaluation ranging from 10 to 50 percent. Though I confess that my innate skepticism of general-equilibrium models and estimates of export price elasticities have not been put entirely to rest by her analysis, I am convinced that her results—which are in line with other estimates of the impact of devaluation—seem robust enough to withstand the paucity of data. Her empirical analysis of unemployment in the staple industries supports a convincing argument that Britain's economic problems went beyond the export sector.

In fact, those problems were probably beyond the scope of policy makers—even today—to resolve. "Economic theory," she observes, "has no satisfactory explanation for the 'deplorably inelastic conditions' which Keynes believed characterized Britain's economy in the twenties" (p. 8). While I am impressed by Wolcott's econometric conclusions, I am bothered by the lack of attention she gives to the true reason for the policy disaster. Commenting on the merits of the debate, she concludes that "each of their arguments was sensible, Churchill's perhaps more so than Keynes" (p. 8). Was it, then, the force of Churchill's rhetoric and personality that carried the day? Wolcott does not seem to think so. She insists that Churchill had no deep-seated commitment to either devaluation or other policies; he called for a report on the matter from his ministers to explore possibilities. But they did not do that. After examining the interchange between Churchill and his advisors, Wolcott concludes that "the policy [of devaluation] was infeasible only because of the attitudes of policy-makers themselves. They held a conception of how the economic world operated. That conception was impervious to their economic circumstances" (p. 178).

As a historian, I can not resist asking where the advisors got their conception of how the economic world operated. The answer—which Wolcott hints at several times in her analysis but never really addresses—probably lies in the interpretation that men such as Montague Norman placed on the past performance of the international monetary system. Their faith in gold and the pound may have been misplaced—as Wolcott argues. But before I give failing grades to British policy makers in the 1920s, I am reminded of an episode where a similar stubbornness produced a very different outcome. Following the American Civil War, the United States government, led by Secretary of the Treasury Hugh McCollough, decided to drive down the "gold premium" on "greenbacks" so that the United States could return to the gold standard. Though the policy of "resumption" had its very vocal critics, it was pursued with great vigor for more than a decade. And that decade was a period of very substantial economic growth in the United States. The "lessons" of history are not always easy to understand. I would urge Wolcott to look more closely into the factors that led to the decision to remain on Gold at $4.86.

The three dissertations that I have commented on in these remarks range over a broad area of space and time. Reflecting what I have learned from reading them, I am struck by two thoughts. First, the supposed "rationality" of peasants, lords, workers, employers, and policy makers works in complex ways—if it works at all. Second, the ingenuity and skill of our most recent crop of economic historians just might be equal to the challenge posed by those complexities.

Roger L. Ransom, *University of California, Riverside*

Editors' Notes

The Editors and the Association wish to thank the following individuals who were chairs or discussants at the 1989 Economic History Association meetings. Their comments helped the authors prepare their final drafts and provided invaluable advice to the Editors.

Lee J. Alston, University of Illinois
Lance Davis, California Institute of Technology
Barry Eichengreen, University of California, Berkeley
David Felix, Washington University
Price V. Fishback, University of Georgia
Robert W. Fogel, University of Chicago
Nancy Folbre, University of Massachusetts, Amherst
Jack Goldstone, University of California, Davis
James D. Hamilton, University of Virginia
Joan U. Hannon, St. Mary's College of California
Paul M. Hohenberg, Rensselaer Polytechnic Institute
Thomas P. Hughes, University of Pennsylvania
Erika Jorgensen, World Bank
Frank Lewis, Queen's University
Harry A. Miskimin, Yale University
Pamela J. Nickless, University of North Carolina, Asheville
Anthony P. O'Brien, Lehigh University
Kerry Odell, Scripps College
Martha Olney, University of Massachusetts, Amherst
Gilles Postel-Vinay, Institut National de la Recherche Agronomique, Paris
Wayne Rasmussen, U.S. Department of Agriculture
James C. Riley, Indiana University
Anna J. Schwartz, National Bureau of Economic Research
John Joseph Wallis, University of Maryland, College Park
Steven B. Webb, World Bank
Lawrence J. White, New York University
Arthur G. Woolf, University of Vermont

ECONOMIC HISTORY ASSOCIATION MEETING

The fiftieth annual meeting of the Economic History Association will be held in Montreal, Canada, from Thursday, September 13 to Sunday, September 16, 1990. The membership should note that the meeting is both a day longer and a week earlier than in the past. The preliminary program follows:

The Structure and Organization of Agriculture

Loren Brandt, University of Toronto, "Contract Choice in Chinese Agriculture: 1930s."

Jon Cohen, University of Toronto, and Francesco Galassi, Nipissing College, "Agriculture and Institutions: Fact and Myth in Southern Italy, 1911."

Paul Thomassin, McGill University, "Impact on the Agricultural Economy of the Abolition of Seigneurial Tenure in Lower Canada: An Institutional Analysis."

Donghyu Yang, University of Seoul, "Farm Tenancy in the Antebellum North."

Trade and Tariffs

Colleen Callahan and Patrick O'Brien, Lehigh University, "The Smoot-Hawley Tariff Revisited."

John Nye, Washington University, "The Myth of Free-Trade Britain and Fortress France."

Susan Wolcott, St. Louis University, "British Culpability and the Collapse of Indian Textile Demand."

Institutions and Agricultural Innovation

Gregory Clark, University of Michigan, "The Postan Thesis Revisited: Was There an Ecological Crisis in Medieval Europe?"

William Darity, University of North Carolina, Chapel Hill, "Technical Change in Agriculture, Population Growth, and Theories of Economic History."

Donald McCloskey, University of Iowa, "Risk on the Ground: New Findings on the Institution of Open Fields."

Labor Market Dynamics

David Eltis, Queen's University, and Stanley Engerman, University of Rochester, "Gender and Age in the Transatlantic Slave Trade, 1672–1864: A Comparative Perspective."

Timothy Hatton, University of Essex, and Jeffrey Williamson, Harvard University, "Unemployment, Wage Differentials, and Labor Asymmetries: Thinking in Two Sectors."

Joshua Rosenbloom, University of Kansas, "Occupational Differences in Labor Market Integration: The United States in 1900."

Charles Roberts, Western Kentucky University, "Apparent Real Wage Rate Differentials and Convergence: Agricultural Laborers, 1870–1940."

To Market, To Market, or Not?

Anne Mayhew, University of Tennessee, and E. Friberg, General Accounting Office, "Measuring the Commercialization of Agriculture."

Hilton Root, University of Pennsylvania, "Markets and the 'Deterioration' of Peasant Norms."

Barbara Sands, University of Arizona, "Market and Extra-Market Institutions Supporting Observed Village Income Distributions in the 1930s in Rural China."

Lorena Walsh, Colonial Williamsburg, "Chesapeake Planter Response to Market Incentives, 1770–1820: Capitalist Transformation or Historical Accident?"

Agriculture and the American West

Sean Hartnett, University of Wisconsin, Eau Claire, "Land Transfers in Rock County, Wisconsin: 1840–1880."

Barbara Leibhardt, University of California, Berkeley, "Land Allotments in an Incongruous Legal System: The Yakima Indians, 1887–1934."

Donald Pisani, Texas A&M University, "The Economics of Land and Water in Nineteenth Century California."

Productivity Change and Differences

Morris Altman, University of Saskatchewan, "The Relative Prosperity of English and French Farms in Lower Canada, 1850: A Cross-Sectional Analysis of Structure, Extent, and Determinants."

James Irwin, Central Michigan University, "The Economic Consequences of Emancipation Across the South."

Nancy Virts, California State University, Northridge, "The Efficiency of Southern Tenant Plantations, 1900–1945."

Thomas Weiss, University of Kansas, "Productivity Change in Nineteenth-Century American Agriculture."

Progress Report on Recent Research on the Great Depression

Timothy Bresnahan, Stanford University, and Daniel Raff, Harvard Business School, "Understanding the Industrial Dynamics of the Great Depression: Establishment Characteristics and Compositional Effects."

Robert Margo, Vanderbilt University, "The Microeconomics of Depression Unemployment."

John J. Wallis, University of Maryland, "The Political Economy of New Deal Relief Programs."

Agricultural Institutions and the Government

Lee Alston, University of Illinois, and Joseph Ferrie, University of Chicago, "Plowing Up Paternalism in U.S. Southern Agriculture."

Elizabeth Hoffman and Gary Libecap, University of Arizona, "The History and Functioning of a Government-Sponsored Cartel: Agricultural Marketing Orders for Citrus."

Shawn Kantor, California Institute of Technology, "Razorbacks, Ticky Cows, and the Closing of the Georgia Open Range: The Dynamics of Institutional Change Uncovered."

Reputation, Money, and Financial Institutions

Michael Bordo and Eugene White, Rutgers University, "A Tale of Two Currencies: British and French Finances During the Napoleonic Wars."

Michael Haupert, University of Wisconsin, La Crosse, "The Role of Reputations in a Competitive Banking Regime."

Akira Motomura, Albion College, "Reputation and Currency Depreciation Policy in Early Seventeenth-Century Spain."

Nathan Sussman, University of California, Berkeley, "Debasements, Royal Revenues, and Inflation in France During the Second Stage of the Hundred Years War, 1415–1422."

Aspects of Agricultural Development in Land-Abundant Economies: The Case of Latin America

Samuel Armand, Stanford University, "Patterns of Rural Investment in Argentina, 1800–1850."

Stephen Haber, Stanford University, "Capital Markets and Industrial Concentration: A Comparative Study of Mexico, Brazil, and the United States, 1850–1930."

Mario Pastore, Washington University, "Foreign Trade Blockades, Public Finances, and Property Rights: The Rise of Statism in Paraguayan Agriculture, 1810–1840."

Ricardo Salvatore, University of Minnesota, "Modes of Labor Control in Open Cattle Economies: Argentina, Brazil, and Venezuela, 1780–1880."

Mechanization and Southern Agriculture

Louis Ferleger, University of Massachusetts, Boston, "Sharecropping in the Late Nineteenth-Century South."

Craig Heinicke, College of William and Mary, "Black Migration from the Rural South and Mechanization, 1940–60."

Warren Whatley, University of Michigan, "Mechanizing America's Cotton Harvest: The Impact of Institutions, Markets, and Environment."

Before and After the Famine: The Economy, The Land, and Institutions

Timothy Guinnane, Princeton University, "Land and Credit in Late Nineteenth-Century Ireland."

Kevin O'Rourke, Columbia University, " 'Burn Everything British But Their Coal!' Aspects of the British-Irish Trade War."

Peter Solar, University of Leuven, "Rent, Land Values, and the Distribution of Income in Ireland, 1780–1830."

Additional sessions in celebration of the Fiftieth Anniversary will also be held. The order of sessions in this preliminary program is subject to change.

The dissertation session will be chaired by David Weir, Yale University, and by Susan Carter, Smith College.

CONFERENCES

The International Economic History Association will hold its eleventh world congress in Milan, Italy, in August 1994 and invites proposals from scholars wishing to organize sessions. Proposals for sessions must be submitted by the following dates: A-sessions (Debates and Controversies) by March 1, 1991, B-sessions (Themes of Current Research) by March 1, 1991, and C-sessions (Workshops) by February 1, 1992. Send proposals with names of organizers and a description of the aims of the session to: Joseph Goy, General Secretary, International Economic History Association, Centre de Recherches Historiques, EHESS, 54 Boulevard Raspail, 75270 Paris CEDEX 06, France. Decisions on proposals will be taken by the Executive Committee of the International Association. Preference will be given in the selection of A and B sessions to persons who have not organized one of these sessions at the Leuven congress. Further details may be obtained from the Editors of this JOURNAL.

The Social Science History Association will hold its 15th annual conference in Minneapolis, MN, on October 18–21, 1990. Historians, economists, sociologists, anthropologists, demographers, political scientists, or others interested in participating in the program should contact Steve Rappaport, Department of History, New York University, 19 University Place, New York, NY 10003 or Laurel Cornell, Department of Sociology, Indiana University, Bloomington, IN 47405.

The Oral History Association will hold its 1990 annual meeting in Cambridge, MA, on November 8–11, 1990. For program information, contact Richard C. Smith, OHA Executive Secretary, 1093 Broxton Avenue, No. 720, Los Angeles, CA 90024.

CALL FOR PAPERS

The Oral History Association is calling for proposals for papers, panels, and speakers for its 1991 annual meeting, which will be held at Snowbird, near Salt Lake City, UT, on October 10–13, 1991. This meeting will focus particularly on women, ethnic topics, and the region of the American West. Submissions should be sent by December 1, 1990, to either of the Program Co-Chairs: Jay M. Haymond, Utah State Historical Society, 300 Rio Grande, Salt Lake City, UT 84101; or Rebecca Sharpless, c/o Institute for Oral History, Baylor University, Waco, TX 76798-7271.

GRANTS-IN-AID

The Museum of American Textile History is offering grants-in-aid for 1991 to doctoral students who are writing dissertations and to young historians who are preparing their first books. Topics of special interest include but are not limited to the following: the history of clothmaking techniques in the United States; the role of the corporation in community development; the impact of the industry on the regional economy; architecture; engineering; and labor systems. Biographies and institutional histories are also of interest. Application should be made by August 31 for projects to begin not earlier than the following January 1. To apply, write the Director, Museum of American Textile History, 800 Massachusetts Avenue, North Andover, MA 01845; telephone (508) 686–0191.

FELLOWSHIPS

The Harvard University Center for Italian Renaissance Studies at Villa I Tatti will award fellowships for independent study on any aspect of the Italian Renaissance for the academic year to run from July 1, 1991 to June 30, 1992. The fellowships are for scholars of any nationality, normally postdoctoral and in the earlier stages of their careers. Applications are due October 15, 1990; forms can be obtained from Professor Walter Kaiser, Villa I Tatti, Via de Vincigliata 26, 50135 Florence, Italy, or from Professor Dante Della Terza, Department of Romance Languages and Literatures, Harvard University, Cambridge, MA 02138, USA.

Reviews of Books

MEDIEVAL AND EARLY MODERN

Before European Hegemony: The World System A.D. 1250–1350. By Janet L. Abu-Lughod. New York: Oxford University Press, 1989. Pp. xvi, 443. $35.00.

Janet Abu-Lughod's book argues that the main reason for the "rise of the West" is the decline of the East from 1350 onwards. During the preceding century a "world system" based on international trade had reached the apogee of its development with the establishment of direct commercial ties between China and Europe. In this world system, according to Abu-Lughod, none of the parts dominated the other, and the "similarities" between them "outweighed differences" (p. 13). Thus, since variations cannot be explained by constants, to understand the eventual economic ascending of Europe one should not look for the unique Western attributes, but instead should examine the process that induced the relative economic decline of the East—mainly Egypt and China—without which the rise of the West "would have been unlikely" (p. 20). The claim is that this process was indicated by the collapse of the worldwide international trade system brought about by geopolitical factors. The demolition of the Mongolian states in Central Asia, Persia, Iraq, and China during the second half of the fourteenth century perturbed international trade and induced a contraction in the most advanced economics of the East. The latter development, intensified by the demographic contraction resulting from plague, enabled the West to "take over" and resurrect a new international trade system in which the East became a subordinate peripheral zone.

To support this thesis the author had carried out extensive historical research in secondary sources. She describes three hundred years of commercial, industrial, and institutional development in each of the three subsystems that constituted the thirteenth century world system: the European; the "Mideast Heartland," that included central Asia, Iran, Iraq, and the Mamluk Sultanate of Egypt; and "Asia," with the Indian subcontinent, the principalities along the Strait of Malacca, and China.

While this represents an impressive bibliographic effort, and provides a convenient introduction to much of the relevant literature which will be unfamiliar to nonspecialists, the information nonetheless remains inadequate to sustain the thesis, and much of Abu-Lughod's analysis seems superficial, if not misleading. To substantiate this last point, let me mention that in arguing that "similarities [between East and West] . . . outweighed differences," Abu-Lughod observes that in the East and the West alike merchants utilized money, credit, and partnerships, and that they were allowed to possess capital (pp. 15–18). These seem rather general and broad criteria for alleging similarity, especially in view of the important differences that are ignored. For example, the absence of evidence that any advance in business practices had occurred within the Muslim world for at least a century before 1350 is nowhere mentioned.

Studies by prominent historians like E. Ashtor, F. Braudel, and D. Nicholas, who on the surface at least are at odds with the author's point of view, are either ignored or cursorily dismissed. To take one instance, a central element of Abu-Lughod's thesis is that Mamluk Egypt declined due to the plague (since Egypt benefited from the decline of competing trade routes between the Mediterranean and the Far East). The other explanations for the economic contraction of Mamluk Egypt advanced by Ashtor, a leading expert on the history of Egypt, are simply dismissed. After describing Ashtor as "trying hard to blame government monopolies and taxes, corruption, and technological stagnation for the collapse of Egyptian industries," Abu-Lughod asserts that his arguments are "not fully convincing" (p. 233). Similarly, the author cites Mark Elvin to support the claim of a "radical increase" in the scale of international trade in thirteenth-century China (p. 11), ignoring the fact that Elvin was referring mainly to the trade between China, Japan, and southeast Asia, regions unaffected by the collapse of the Mongol states.

Even if one accepts all the historical details assembled in the book, they do not support the three arguments that underlie its thesis. The first argument is that Eastern economies experienced growth induced by international trade within a world system up to about 1350; the second, that destruction of the trade routes and the plague brought this growth to a halt; and the third, that these events were crucial to the relative decline of the Eastern economies. Indicating that there was trade, that there were plagues, and that certain trade routes were affected by the decline of the Mongolian states is not sufficient to document the three contentions. Furthermore, it is well known that the trade decline and the plague caused an economic contraction and social turmoil in Europe during the fourteenth century. Why was Europe's recovery so much more vigorous?

The book touches upon a fascinating period in world history. Unfortunately, the author's ideological conviction that exogenous factors promoted the rise of the West, rather than social, political, and economic factors operating within the societies of the East and the West, have skewed her historical research.

AVNER GREIF, *Stanford University*

A Marginal Economy? East Anglian Breckland in the Later Middle Ages. By Mark Bailey. New York: Cambridge University Press, 1989. Pp. xv, 350. $59.50.

East Anglian Breckland is an area poorly favored by nature. The soil is sandy, and the climate is both cold and dry, especially in the spring. It is not a region that beckons the farmer, and according to the population-resources model of economic change delineated by the late M. M. Postan, it must be considered "at the margin." If this is accurate, then economic trends in Breckland should provide an accurate barometer of demographic expansion prior to the Black Death as well as an indicator of the severity of the subsequent demographic contraction of the later Middle Ages. In a remarkably thorough study, however, Mark Bailey convincingly challenges the orthodox view of the Breckland as a marginal economy and raises important questions about the nature of economic growth and change in the later Middle Ages.

That medieval Breckland was marginal in terms of grain production is undeniable. The sandy soil over a chalk bed, coupled with low rainfall and low temperatures in spring, made this a difficult place in which to farm. Much of the region was used for arable farming, but arable and pastoral usage were well coordinated. Breckland was organized on the open-field system, but the system was very complex here, as manor and village seldom coincided. Moreover, the complexity of the system was further heightened by the relatively large proportion of free peasants. Breckland was distinctive for the use of the shift system of cropping and the foldcourse system of pasturing. Both of these devices improved the potential of otherwise unproductive land. Similarly, Breckland farmers eschewed legumes, extensive weeding, and other techniques appropriate to good soil. Increased labor or capital investments in the soil were not justified by the returns. Breckland farmers increased output through extensive rather than intensive methods.

Breckland was perhaps the most densely populated region of East Anglia during the neolithic period, and the modern distribution of Breckland villages dates to the Saxon period. There were no new medieval settlements after Domesday Book. At that time much of East Anglia averaged more than 30 tenants per thousand acres, while Breckland had less than 15. There was little assarting here during the period of demographic expansion between 1086 and 1300, yet Bailey argues convincingly that the well-documented fragmentation of holdings indicates an increase in population. This conforms to the predictions of the population-resources model. What does not conform is that prior to the Black Death the peasants of Suffolk Breckland enjoyed significantly greater per capita wealth than their neighbors in High Suffolk, while the peasants of Norfolk Breckland during this period enjoyed wealth commensurate with that of peasants elsewhere—on better soil—in Norfolk.

Since East Anglian Breckland was not a region favored with good arable farmland, it is not surprising to learn that this wealth came largely from other specializations which emerged during the later Middle Ages. Foremost among these was pastoral farming. Sheep were an essential part of the Breckland economy in two ways. Not only were their coarse, light fleeces sold, but the sheep produced sufficient quantities of manure to sustain the arable sector. And within the arable sector, Breckland farmers recognized that their barley and barley malt, low in nitrogen content, commanded prices above the going market level. Thus throughout the later Middle Ages more and more barley was grown in Breckland at the expense of other grains. Breckland also experienced remarkable success in rearing rabbits. Bailey traces the growth of this industry from the introduction of rabbits to the region in the thirteenth century to the point at which, by the sixteenth century, they verged on becoming pests. The porous, sandy Breckland soils and the relative dryness of the climate were well suited to the creation and maintenance of rabbit warrens. Despite some decline in the fifteenth century, this market remained reasonably buoyant throughout the later Middle Ages, helping to maintain the Breckland's economy at a level comparable to other nonmarginal regions. Although the economy and population both contracted, Bailey convincingly demonstrates that the desertion of Breckland villages by farmers seeking better soils was a rare phenomenon. In part, this was because Breckland was not marginal in terms of location. The region was blessed by particularly good water routes, and trade within and beyond Breckland was a boost to the economy.

This volume is an excellent addition to the growing literature on the economic history of medieval England. Not only is it well researched, thoroughly documented, and written in a highly readable prose style, but it is also that rare book which challenges assumptions and provokes thought. It is sure to inspire subsequent studies of other regions hitherto thought to have been "at the margin."

J. S. HAMILTON, *Old Dominion University*

Worlds Within Worlds: Structures of Life in Sixteenth-Century London. By Steve Rappaport. New York: Cambridge University Press, 1989. Pp. xv, 449. $54.50.

The field of early modern English urban history is becalmed. It has been crushed by the empiricism which dominates British historical research and numbed by the pointless quantification and barren sociological models which parade as scholarship in much of America. Few historians, for example, have taken up the challenge of Fernand Braudel to focus on the role of cities in the transformation of capitalism and only Charles Phythian-Adams's *Desolation of a City* (Cambridge, 1979) has excited much interest in the role of towns in these years. The most promising graduate students now study gender, mentalities, economic history, or politics. Steve Rappaport, by challenging the "desolation and decay" model advanced by Peter Clark and Paul Slack, attempts to reinvigorate our interest in premodern cities as the incubators of capitalism.

Rappaport believes that many historians, by exaggerating reports of economic decline and of poverty, have created the impression that English cities faced unprecedented difficulties. According to this thesis many towns experienced chronically depleted treasuries and chaotic administration. The fundamental structural causes of urban decay were population growth—which outstripped productivity—an insensitive and inbred political elite, and declining opportunities for social mobility. According to this consensus, discontent and social polarization reduced the stability of urban institutions and produced the potential for violent conflict.

Rappaport believes that historians have exaggerated urban social problems and nowhere is this more true than in London. He claims that there is little evidence in the capital that riots produced chronic instability or aimed at a fundamental restructuring of society. Furthermore, London's rulers were sensitive to the presence of unemployment and poverty and were willing to take remedial action to eliminate these problems. Rappaport attributes the absence of serious interclass conflict to the prevalence of two crucial stabilizing factors: disaggregated political power and opportunities for social mobility.

This study relies on a source unique to London. From an extant register of freemen for the years from 1551 to 1553 he chose 530 individuals who became citizens and members of livery companies as a representative sample of the city's adult male population. In addition, he traced the careers of the 470 men who were their masters and patrons. This group of one thousand, members of four great and four minor livery companies, constitutes the data base which Rappaport uses to explore the effects of patronage upon social mobility and to determine the causes and timing of critical changes in the status of freemen.

Rappaport's thesis is that London's fundamental stability resulted from sufficient employment opportunities, moderate price increases, and adequate prospects for social mobility. Despite population growth and the demand for employment, from 1500 to 1550 London faced no crippling instability because moderate prosperity and a liberal admissions policy—three-quarters of all applicants became freemen—reduced the potential for conflict. In short, the supply of labor and the availability of jobs remained roughly in balance. Between 1550 and 1600 high mortality and low birth rates, the migration of large numbers of apprentices, and job opportunities in the rapidly expanding service, industrial, and commercial sectors averted crippling instability. Gild masters willing to raise wages and provide poor relief to the unemployed contributed to urban harmony.

Despite complaints of poverty and unemployment after the 1570s, Rappaport believes that impoverishment caused by rising prices and falling real wages has been exaggerated. He demonstrates that prices rose gradually from 1490 to the 1540s and from the 1550s to the early 1590s. Inflation only reached crippling proportions in the mid and late 1540s and for a brief but intense period in the mid 1590s from the combined effects of wartime demand and harvest crises. For the entire century cost-of-living increases averaged only 0.5 percent per year. Because price changes were usually moderate, London's employers and laborers were able to adapt to changes in the cost of living.

Rappaport also argues that a pyramidal model of urban society is inappropriate because a majority of journeymen became householders, poor relief mitigated the most harmful effects of unemployment, and political power was decentralized. Furthermore, since one-half of London's households possessed some financial reserves there is little quantitative evidence that a majority of the population was living near the poverty line. Because of high rates of mortality and migration, ability rather than status determined the mobility of apprentices and journeymen. Later, however, patronage, status, and connections reduced the ruling element of the livery company to a relatively closed estate. Rappaport's London is a city of the middling sort, a stable urban polity ruled by responsive governors who, in establishing a consensual basis for the stratification system, eliminated the most fundamental reason for rebellion.

Although it has provided a valuable service to historians by challenging our perception of sixteenth-century urban society, this study contains four major weaknesses. First, an explanation of social and political relations in sixteenth-century London society should not rely almost entirely on an analysis of a small sample of the city's freemen. The 1551 to 1553 register, which compares unfavorably to the Florentine *catasto* of 1427 or the 1522 muster roll of Coventry, cannot be used by itself to explain the structural causes of stability or disorder in England's largest city. Second, Rappaport underestimates the ability of monarch, priest, and gildmaster together to produce that hegemony which he confuses with harmony. Third, because of its robust and diversified economy London cannot be used as a yardstick to measure the English urban experience. Enclosure riots, religious conflict, and wage disputes, while seldom resulting in open hostility, produced instability in many towns. Fourth, Rappaport's reliance on a sociological model limits the scope of his research. His adherence to quantitative methods excludes cultural variables and precludes the use of particular events around which to orchestrate dramatic narratives of contest and conflict. The choice of a freeman register upon which to construct his model of urban society encourages him to rely on a consensual theory of social relations, to neglect the working class, and to minimize evidence of class conflict.

Despite these problems, however, this is a provocative and stimulating study which cannot be adequately summarized in a brief review. It will raise challenging issues for historians and will generate much-needed debate in a field which has ignored recent advances in theory and method.

RONALD M. BERGER, *New York State University College, Oneonta*

MODERN EUROPE

The Cambridge Economic History of Europe. Vol. 8: *The Industrial Economies: The Development of Economic and Social Policies*. Edited by Peter Mathias and Sidney Pollard. New York: Cambridge University Press, 1989. Pp. xix, 1242. $125.00.

Weighing in at four-and-one-half pounds and almost four inches thick, Volume 8 of the *Cambridge Economic History of Europe* does not make for light reading. This final volume of the CEHE is a monumental undertaking constructed in sixteen parts by different architects under the coordination of two editors who, in forgoing an introduction, have left the task of interpreting or summarizing its main contribution to reviewers. That challenge is daunting, although it pales before that facing the happy soul reviewing the entire enterprise.

Volume 8 includes seven chapters with topical orientations followed by nine with a country or regional focus. Two of the chapters, at 160 and 180 pages respectively, are small books in their own right. Setting these aside, along with another that tops 100 pages, the remaining thirteen essays average just over 50 pages each in length.

We begin with two papers on trade policy: Paul Bairoch on the period from 1815 to 1914 and Charles Kindleberger on the interwar years. These are followed by two essays on national and international monetary systems: A. G. Ford on the period from 1870 to 1914 and Donald Moggridge on 1919 to 1939. Chapter 5 presents D. E. Schremmer's extensive treatise on taxation and public finance in Britain, France, and Germany. The final two topical contributions look at labor policies between 1830 and 1939 in Britain and the United States (John H. M. Laslett) and on the continent between 1800 and 1939 (Gaston V. Rimlinger). Chapters 8 to 16 comprise nine country or regional studies: S. G. Checkland on Britain, William Letwin on the United States, Tom Kemp on France, Volker Hentschel on Germany, Scott Eddie on Austria-Hungary, Alice Teichova on east central and south east Europe, R. W. Davies on the USSR, Lennart Jorberg and Olle Kranz on Sweden, and finally Seymour Broadbridge on Japan. Some overlap in treatment necessarily follows from this complementary topical/regional structure.

Bairoch's heavily descriptive survey of trade policies between 1815 and 1914 leads off the volume. Almost a monograph in itself (160 pages), this will be useful as a reference for those who wish to find in one place materials on the course of trade policies, cross-classified by country and time period. Particularly valuable will be its scope—which extends beyond intra European trade to include explicit treatment of the evolution of colonial trade policies as well as those practiced by (or imposed on) China, Japan, the United States, and other countries of European settlement.

The economic analysis, however, while sometimes insightful, is nonsystematic and frequently incomplete. In discussing Britain, for example, Bairoch argues that protectionist agricultural policies would have meant a higher purchasing power for farmers and consequently a higher demand for manufactured goods (p. 51). This ignores the beneficial impact of lower grain prices on urban incomes and purchasing power, and implies that policies protecting agriculture were desirable from the standpoint of national economies. While there may be special circumstances (such as institutional factors predisposing towards a severe underemployment of resources) that would permit such a conclusion (the opposite of that reached by Ricardo), Bairoch makes no attempt to spell them out.

Indeed, a pro-protectionist flavor runs throughout the essay. Germany's return to protection in the 1880s is at least implicitly credited with raising the rate of per capita GNP and productivity growth in that country (p. 61). Whether other factors, such as the arrival of new technologies, could have been responsible, or whether technological diffusion was itself contingent on tariff protection are matters not addressed. Again, in his overview Bairoch offers paradoxes "to diehard supporters of free trade": the resurgence of protectionist sentiment at the end of the nineteenth century coincided with a more rapid growth of trade, and the most protectionist countries experienced the fastest trade growth (pp. 88–89).

Kindleberger's article on interwar (1919 to 1939) commercial policy is much shorter and more sophisticated analytically. The material on German policies during the 1930s is particularly interesting. Neither of these first two treatments will be welcomed as assigned reading in undergraduate, or for that matter graduate, courses, however. They are best viewed, and presumably intended, as reference works.

In contrast, Ford's essay on international financial policy during the gold-standard era (1870 to 1914) could serve as supplementary reading in courses on economic history or international finance. The essay describes the effects, country by country, of "autonomous" but sometimes coinciding shocks to current and capital accounts, the strains such developments put on international adjustment under the fixed exchange rate system implied by linkage to gold, and the role that the preeminent financial center, London, as well as peripheral centers such as Paris, Berlin, and New York, played in that adjustment. Moggridge's essay on the interwar gold standard is more technically specialized, focusing on the changing nature of the settlement mechanisms themselves in the two decades between world wars.

Schremmer's monograph-length survey of public finance in Britain, France, and Germany will be a welcome addition to reading lists in economic history as well as public finance. The treatment of British finances in the nineteenth century is particularly illuminating. Schremmer chronicles the (at first premature) birth of the income tax, the principle of collection of revenues at source, the British reliance on borrowing to finance exceptional expenditures such as wars, and the decline in the proportionate share of the public sector throughout the nineteenth century, in spite of the growth of domestic responsibilities in the areas of health, education, and welfare.

The material on France and Germany develops a wealth of comparative material on the fiscal systems of these countries including France's reliance on external indicators of wealth rather than an income tax, and Germany's (Prussia's) reliance on revenues from crown lands. Focus on the nitty gritty of state revenue collection efforts serves a welcome role of demystifying "the state": observing how powerful individuals or institutions actually scramble for cash usually has this effect. Some of the treatment of German fiscal arrangements will be of principal interest to specialists, but overall this, the longest chapter in the book, is an impressive contribution. Particularly interesting is Schremmer's finding that the ratio of state spending to national income over the nineteenth century traces out a U-shaped curve closely matched by all the major European countries (p. 362).

The paper by Laslett on Anglo-American union movements is a straightforward survey of labor history that breaks relatively little new ground, although some of the comparative remarks are helpful. I found the last part of Rimlinger's survey of continental labor policy, dealing with Nazi Germany and Europe outside of France and Germany, to be of most interest.

The nine country or regional studies are somewhat shorter on average. What can one say in a short review about them? Probably the best written is Letwin's piece on the United States, which is thoughtful, contains important historiographical observations, but still cannot really be considered groundbreaking. As reference works these will all be valuable. Some go considerably beyond what has been available previously, for example in the now out-of-print *Fontana Economic History of Europe*, edited by Carlo M. Cipolla (London, 1972–76). Particularly useful will be Hentschel's treatment of Germany and Teichova's survey of east central and south east Europe, principally because they are based on foreign language materials not readily accessible elsewhere. These are also among the most up-to-date of the surveys, with coverage of the literature extending through 1986 and 1985 respectively.

Practitioners of cliometric history will find relatively little acknowledgment of their contributions here. Much of the material surveyed is necessarily documentary, rather than statistical, and so the absence of sophisticated econometrics is perhaps to be expected. And there are, to be sure, numbers, and over 152 tables. But in such a large-scale enterprise, couldn't there have been more systematic consideration of what difference all of this variation in economic and social policies has actually made? For those of us who have argued that legal systems do matter, in the sense that they influence the sectoral distribution of inputs and outputs and the rates and character of economic growth, one would have liked these pages more effectively to address the question of how much different social and economic policies mattered, and through what mechanisms.

What's missing, for example, in the contributions on commercial policy is some assessment of how much they really influenced the long-run course of national and global economic development. Tariffs and quotas can have the same economic impacts on trade as do natural barriers, but how have variations in commercial policies measured up relative to the barrier-destroying impacts of technological progress in transport and communication? A difficult question to answer, perhaps, but one can't help asking it after wading through these compendious histories of changing and varying governmental policies. The same can be said for the treatment of policy variation in other areas.

What kind of overall impression does one leave this volume with? On balance I liked the topical essays somewhat better, perhaps because they lent themselves more to comparative and analytical observations. The contributions by Schremmer on public finance and Ford on the international financial system are particularly valuable and one can recommend them without hesitation to a general audience within the profession. Letwin on U.S. public policy is also well written and relatively short. Many of the other essays, however, can be prescribed to non-historically oriented economists only with caution: these chapters, rightly or wrongly, are likely to confirm their worst suspicions about our subdiscipline.

The contributions will still be valuable as reference works, and particularly useful for their bibliographies. But a cautionary note in this regard: from the references and other notes one can infer that at least half the chapters (2, 3, 4, 6, 7, 9, 12, and 16) were completed in 1979 or earlier, a full decade before the volume went to press.

ALEXANDER J. FIELD, *Santa Clara University*

Dutch Primacy in World Trade, 1585–1740. By Jonathan I. Israel. Oxford: Clarendon Press, 1989. Pp. xxi, 462. $72.00.

By the rather restrained standards of contemporary economic historians, Jonathan Israel has been something of a publishing prodigy, with three major, highly erudite books in the past seven years. In them, in addition to his own extensive research in Dutch, Spanish, French, and English archives and in contemporary controversial literature, Israel has synthesized and reinterpreted modern scholarship in nine or ten languages. In his latest work the author invites the reader to think about the rise and fall of the Dutch world trading system in the seventeenth and early eighteenth century as a problem in political economy.

The reader must not forget, Israel reminds us, that the world trading position of the United Provinces was forged during the "Eighty Years War" with Spain. During those heroic years and afterwards the role of the federal Dutch state was crucial. Internally this role meant tax policy and quality control, whether in curing herrings or manufacturing the finest woolen cloth. Externally it meant the ability of the United Provinces' diplomacy and military and naval might to keep both seas and foreign frontiers open to their own ships and goods on advantageous terms. In Europe the Dutch wanted and very often obtained not only "most favored nation status" but also low foreign tariffs; in Asia they strove rather for a monopsonistic buying position, most successfully in Indonesia and Ceylon. Where the region involved was the sole known producer of a particular spice, this also gave the Dutch East India Company a monopolistic selling position in Europe. As their trading "system" developed, the Dutch became more than just successful merchants. They developed at home important entrepôt industries processing imported salt, sugar, and tobacco and manufacturing cloth of the first quality from imported Spanish wool. Their successful marketing of woolens, linens, and Baltic staples in Spain also earned them the large quantities of American silver needed to advance their East Indian trade.

Given the important role of the Dutch federal state, Israel sees the major phases of Dutch commercial history as delimited by events in political history from 1590 to 1784. War itself in the seventeenth century could be turned to Dutch advantage if it permitted them to close the rival harbors of Spanish Flanders and seize Spanish and Portuguese vessels with their often rich cargoes. But by the end of the War of the Spanish Succession, total Dutch effective political power was so weakened that the states of northern and central Europe could not thereafter be constrained from pursuing mercantilist protectionist measures against Dutch and other foreign manufactures. The loss of such markets led, in Israel's schema, to a decline in most Dutch industries and returned the Dutch by the end of the eighteenth century to the position they had occupied two hundred years before: except for their Asian spice trades, they were once more just builders of economical ships and efficient carriers of bulk goods.

Does such a heavily political interpretation answer all our possible questions? A considerable problem arises from the fact that for most branches of Dutch trade, Israel can offer us only physical quantities (vessels cleared, pieces of cloth manufactured, tuns of wine shipped, and so forth) rather than values. It would be extremely helpful if one could establish the relative importance of earnings from shipping and commerce against value added in manufacture. Only then could we say with some certainty whether or not the certain decline in Dutch manufactures after 1700 was or was not balanced by the continued growth of Dutch overseas trade. After all, K. Glamann's data show a continued if slowing growth of imports by the East India Company down to 1778–1780, and I have shown that British exports of tobacco to the United Provinces in 1772–1774 were almost four times as much as in 1699–1701, while Paul Butel and Robert Stein have shown comparable growth in French sugar re-exports to Holland over the same decades. How far might the income from these trading advances have gone to compensate for the income lost from declining manufactures?

Israel's emphasis on political explanations also leaves unexamined some of the underlying natural limitations on Dutch trading hegemony. How important might the republic's limited population base have been? And its limited natural resources? Weren't the provinces' peat resources, so important for many seventeenth-century manufactures, much less adequate by the eighteenth? Could not some of the fishery decline in the eighteenth century be ascribed to the migration of the herring to sites further north? A final topic left almost totally unexplored is the changing place of Amsterdam among European money markets. Did the irredeemability after 1700 of ordinary deposits at the Bank of Amsterdam have no effects on the way business was transacted?

Such questions for future work detract little from Israel's present achievement. As its stands, his is an extremely valuable book which will undoubtedly become a standard reference work for years to come.

JACOB M. PRICE, *University of Michigan*

Foires et marchés dans la France préindustrielle. By Dominique Margairaz. Paris: Editions de l'Ecole des Hautes Etudes en Sciences Sociales, 1988. Pp. 281. F150.

Before the nineteenth century, periodic fairs and local markets were the principal nodes of interregional market organization in Europe outside the great cities. Here country people conducted most of their limited exchange with the outside world; here a metropolitan cash economy intersected with informal institutions of exchange in rural communities, concentrating in time, as in space, the exchange of goods and economic information. A historical account of the replacement of such episodic economic encounters by continuous markets might shed considerable light on the differences between the economy of the past and the economy of today. The present study exploits information that resulted from the regulatory ambivalence of the French Revolutionaries with respect to the unrestricted freedom to hold fairs and markets. Faced with a proliferation of local markets resulting from the breakdown of administrative control, Revolutionary and Napoleonic governments conducted several surveys of existing fairs and markets, the records of which constitute the basis of this book.

The author has organized the data about timing and location of fairs and markets into tables and maps. Northern France had more weekly food markets per thousand inhabitants than did the more lightly settled south and west, which by contrast had more fairs to enable the pastoral farmers there to adjust their holdings of livestock. During the Revolution a number of southern towns took advantage of the distractions of the Terror and the introduction of the Republican calendar to found new fairs, but the additions did not significantly alter the overall distribution, and in the event attracted little business. The livestock fairs survived almost to the present day, whereas the fairs that organized the collection and distribution of manufactured goods have disappeared, wholesale fairs having passed through a phase of local retailing before they finally vanished. About half the book is given over to taxonomical description of the fairs and markets that characterized France's formal system of distribution in the late eighteenth century. These included the great regional fairs such as Beaucaire or Guibray, which served as wholesale markets for regional textile production, the ubiquitous livestock fairs, hiring fairs, and weekly markets for provisions. The descriptions are competent, though commonplace, and provide an introduction to the formal institutions of marketing in preindustrial France. No attempt has been made systematically to uncover changes in the volume of exchanges transacted in fairs and markets in the century before the coming of the railroad, which limits the usefulness and relevance of the descriptions.

The statistical exercises that comprise the kernel of the book are at best of moderate interest. At worst they float on what Dr. Johnson characterized as a vast sea of words. The questions that motivate the counting are contrived. Do the changes in the number of markets reflect a new "attitude" towards markets and their regulation? Was their disposition in time and space "rational"? These are not the issues most likely to provoke insightful reflection about processes of economic evolution. There nonetheless lies embedded in the details of the book elements that could enter naturally into a history of market forms. We learn that in 1764 in the remote district of St. Flour only 20 percent of transactions in wheat passed through the open market. The great wholesale fairs were already in decline by the last quarter of the eighteenth century; their diminishing volume of business is the counterfoil of the development of direct links between merchants and rural producers. By the end of the century they had become residual markets where manufacturers disposed of their "seconds." Near the great cities grain marketing was being taken over by millers; elsewhere, the emergence of rural industry called forth small weekly markets to provision workers. All this suggests a system in movement well before the great changes in transportation costs that occurred in the nineteenth century. Periodic fairs provided occasions for drawing bills, providing current cash, and settling interregional payments. There are correspondences here between the network of fairs and the extent of opportunity for multilateral settlement of debt. Changes in the volume and directionality of transactions through the nodes of the exchange system had an impact on local means of payment and the cost of credit.

To explore these connections one needs ideas and chronological precision in ordering the facts. It can be anticipated that advances in the analysis of networks and economic games characterized by increasing returns will, by drawing attention to multiple equilibria and the alternative histories they imply, reinvigorate study of the evolution of organizational forms of market exchange. In retrospect one can see that the adoption of Kuznets's national income analysis as a framework of explanation in economic history was partly responsible for the abandonment by economists of historical study of market networks because Kuznets's categories tended to reduce the economic significance of distribution to a measure of value added. Behind this, one detects the more fundamental penetration into history of static microeconomic theory, resolving institutions and their dynamical interactions down to their supposedly atomistic elements of individuals, arbitrage, and transactions cost. *Foires et marchés* bears the burdens of the school of total history that engendered it, but one doubts whether the atomistic analysis of traditional economics is itself fully equal to the task of explaining the evolution of networks where wholes are likely to exceed their totaled parts.

GEORGE GRANTHAM, *McGill University*

Government and Agriculture in Western Europe, 1880–1988. By Michael Tracy. New York: New York University Press, 1989. Third edition. Pp. xiii, 382. $50.00.

Michael Tracy has added "government" to the title of the third edition of his survey of European agricultural history. (The first editions were published as *Agriculture in Western Europe* [New York, 1964] and *Agriculture in Western Europe: Challenge and Response, 1880–1980* [London, 1982].) This is appropriate, for all three editions are concerned with the effect of government policy on farmers, as well as the impact of the latter on policy. For agriculture itself, Tracy provides little more than tables of production and land holding, yet the scope of the work and the assurance of his analysis permit Tracy's book to remain the standard in its field.

Changes from the first edition include a survey of agriculture from the Middle Ages to the mid-nineteenth century, enlarged bibliographies at the end of each chapter, a more positive view of the performance of nineteenth-century France, and an updated account of the development of the Common Market's Common Agricultural Policy (CAP). The second edition, not widely available in the United States, contains more detail on the negotiations of the 1970s, while the third emphasizes the 1980s.

These changes improve what was already a most valuable book. While the discussion of pre-1850 farming is brief, it provides a useful survey. Tracy's detailed account of the CAP benefits from the author's personal experiences as a director in the General Secretariat of the European Communities.

The book's theme is that European agriculture has faced a series of challenges since 1880 requiring "positive action by governments and by farmers themselves" (p. 360) but that the necessary structural reforms were never undertaken.

The first challenge was posed by "the immense increase in imports of cheap grain" (p. 17) starting in the 1870s. The French and Germans responded by imposing tariffs, not the optimal choice. In France protectionism diverted attention from the need to restructure fragmented holdings, while in Germany the policy "encouraged excessive production of grains [and] retarded the shift of manpower to other sectors" (p. 103). Nor was free trade alone the answer, for in Britain, where protection remained taboo, a large segment of agriculture was left to go to ruin. Danish farmers, on the other hand, saw the possibilities inherent in low grain prices. They shifted to livestock products, created cooperatives to process and market them, and found an outlet in Britain. Danish agriculture could thus contribute to that nation's economic growth.

Yet it is not certain that the solution of specialty exports, appropriate for a small country, could have worked for large producers like France and Germany. Shifting to livestock products and crops that could not be shipped long distances, a solution that had its advocates at the time, was successful for some farmers, but home markets could not have absorbed enough of such products to make it generally applicable. Nor could all the labor released by expanding the size of French farms have been absorbed by the labor market, as Tracy himself realizes (p. 79).

The interwar depression was an even more serious threat to European agriculture. Protection was strengthened and, for the first time in a century, adopted by Britain. But world prices were so low that tariffs were insufficient and had to be supplemented by non-tariff assistance. In Britain subsidies expanded production of wheat and livestock. The French combined import quotas with widespread intervention in the market for crops like wine and wheat and were able to maintain the pattern of agricultural production, though not formulate a "coherent, long-term agricultural policy" (p. 175). This the Nazis did, organizing German farmers and agribusiness in the *Reichsnährstand*, which regulated prices and markets, and establishing the *Reichsstellen*, boards that controlled imports. Though Nazi policy "was geared to the expectation of war" (p. 201) and therefore fundamentally flawed, it was efficient and served as the model for much that was done after World War II.

The persistence after 1945 of the methods developed in the 1930s ties the last part of book to the previous section. Thus the Common Market's agricultural policy was devised to support farmers through "market intervention coupled with a protective device which effectively insulated the domestic market from the world market" (p. 256). As in earlier periods, help for farmers prevented necessary structural changes, and the higher urban unemployment in the 1980s made it harder to advocate reforms that would reduce farm populations. So the CAP has helped neither the consumers, who pay higher prices, nor the small farmers, whose incomes have lagged behind those of the rest of society.

Was there another alternative? In the first edition Tracy, while condemning most politicians for their failure even to try reform, suggests that they might have succeeded had they followed the Danish example. Now he is less severe, suggesting that recent choices were limited by past policies, but also less optimistic, believing that "agricultural policy will remain, in economic terms, inefficient and wasteful of resources, and will continue to provoke political tension on both the domestic and international scenes" (p. 363).

JONATHAN J. LIEBOWITZ, *University of Lowell*

Strikes, Wars, and Revolutions in an International Perspective: Strike Waves in the Late Nineteenth and Early Twentieth Centuries. Edited by Leopold Haimson and Charles Tilly. Cambridge: Cambridge University Press, and Paris: Editions de la Maison des Sciences de l'Homme, 1989. Pp. xiv, 536. $42.50.

It is fifteen years since the appearance of Edward Shorter and Charles Tilly's landmark work, *Strikes in France*. The culmination of a large research project, *Strikes in France* changed the direction of historical research. Shorter and Tilly's use of social theory and quantitative techniques put their work on the cutting edge of social science history. And by rehabilitating the use of Marxist categories of class, working-class political action, and the state, they opened new vistas for provocative investigation.

Strikes, Wars, and Revolutions owes much to Tilly's earlier work. The first installment on a collaborative research project drawing on the work of leading scholars in seven countries, it includes studies of the great wave of labor militancy around World War I in Russia, France, Germany, Italy, Great Britain, and the United States. The result is indispensable reading for anyone interested in labor history and the evolution of twentieth-century capitalism. It establishes that the social upheavals from 1917 to 1926 were not anomalies but the culmination of a swell in labor militancy that stretched back to before 1914. Organization and collective bargaining did little to brake labor militancy. Studies of the countries with the most established reformist trade unions, including Friedhelm Boll's of Germany, James Cronin's of Britain, and David Montgomery's of the United States, show the increasing alienation of the rank and file from the union leadership and the growth of an alternative militant leadership. While the war accelerated the spread of discontent, as shown in two of the book's finest essays by James Cronin (on Britain) and Hugues Lagrange (France), radicals drew on unrest rooted in changes in the work process. Machinists and other metal workers were especially militant in resisting the rapid spread of new, American-style management techniques. Emphasizing the technological roots of labor unrest, one third of *Strikes, Wars, and Revolutions* deals directly with changes in the metal-trades sector, including fine essays by David Montgomery (United States), Keith Burgess (Britain), Elisabeth Domansky (Germany), Heather Hogan (Russia), and Leopold Haimson (Russia).

Some of the book's essays go beyond *Strikes in France*, including those by Cronin on Britain and the general remarks by Tilly and Haimson. Most, however, add little, either in methodology or theory, to the Shorter-Tilly framework. Included are the by now standard elements: strike shapes, strike waves, time-series regressions of strike activity as a function of political and economic conditions. Some of this can be exciting, especially in studies of Russia that draw on previously inaccessible material. Nonetheless, many will leave *Strikes, Wars, and Revolutions* disappointed. There are technical problems with the analysis in many essays. In most, there is little effort to relate the empirical work with theories of collective action. Even when the econometric results are presented—and in several papers they are not—it is hard to interpret findings or to understand the inclusion or omission of some variables. None of the papers controls adequately for the simultaneous relationship between strikes and independent variables, including unionization and wages. It is difficult to interpret comparisons between the countries especially when different variables are included in the different studies. And none of the papers actually tests directly the central hypotheses about the relationships among strike militancy, technological change, and political radicalism.

The study the papers present is also theoretically circumscribed. Only the work by Cronin and the remarks by Tilly and Haimson include employers and state officials as active agents. Otherwise, politics and economic militancy are presented exclusively from the worker side, a one-sided class conflict curiously dominated by labor, the weaker party. Employers and state officials appear only as one-dimensional repressive forces, never as active agents with endogenous preferences and organization.

A focus on technology also inspired the book's structure—independent national chapters tied together only by the editors' brief remarks. By preventing explicit comparisons across political systems, this approach leads to an emphasis on technological factors accounting for variations across industries within a single polity. But the real issues are cross-country. By 1920 labor strife had led to very different outcomes in, say, Russia than in Germany or the United States. The real issues in the worldwide surge in labor militancy include not only why metal workers were at the forefront, but why throughout the world workers from many industries joined in collective action. And why did labor militancy lead in some countries to communism or fascism, while in others the pillars of democratic regimes were shaken but not toppled? These questions require a more explicitly comparative approach than this work allows.

Nonetheless we can all learn much more from *Strikes, Wars, and Revolutions* about one of capitalism's truly revolutionary periods. It is an indispensable work for all historians.

GERALD FRIEDMAN, *University of Massachusetts, Amherst*

Business in the Age of Reason. Edited by R. T. P. Davenport-Hines and Jonathan Liebenau. London: Frank Cass, 1989. Pp. ix, 150. $29.50.

Within the field of economic history two forces clash. Economics emphasizes the timeless aspects of a phenomenon examined, as economic laws impose their will on societies of differing times and places; history emphasizes the uniqueness of a phenomenon examined, as the forces of politics, society, and tradition impose their will on economic interactions. In this light the economic historian has a professional duty to make historical events accessible to the nonhistorian and the economic morality tale relevant to the modern empirical economist who is trying to make sense of present-day trends within his own field.

This combination of tension and responsibility is at the essence of *Business in the Age of Reason*. The editor's introduction states that " . . . there is . . . a noticeable divide between business historians interested in the eighteenth century and those concerned with visible hands [and] managerial revolutions . . . it is to bridge this divide . . . that the present set of essays have been collected" (p. vii).

By the editor's own standard, however, only two of the book's eight essays—both by Jacob Price—are successful. In "Sheffield vs. Starke," Price examines a lawsuit caused by the liquidation of a British firm involved in the Chesapeake tobacco trade (c. 1700). He chronicles the early professional life of an apprentice in this trade and links this individual story with the change in commercial practice in the transatlantic trade during the eighteenth century. The details are put into a story that entertains the reader and will interest both the historian and the economist. Price's other essay, "Directions for the Conduct of a Merchant's Counting House, 1766," presents a brief and useful commentary on the discovery of a company's memorandum (published at the end of the essay) that details the internal organization and procedures of a British trading firm.

The other essays include an analysis of deposit banking in London, two views of the pottery trade of the eighteenth century, the creation of the fraudulent Harburgh Company during the era of the South Sea Bubble, and an examination of the growth of the nonindustrial sectors of the industrial town of Birmingham.

The strengths and weaknesses of the rest of the book are found in the best of the remaining essays, J. F. Bosher's, "Financing the French Navy in the Seven Years War: Beaujon, Goossens et Compagnie in 1759." Bosher does an excellent job in presenting the troubles of a bank—Beaujon, Goossens et Compagnie—that tried to manage its loans to a corrupt and incompetent French government. (The tale has a strong resonance today, given the resources the New York City money-center banks spent nursing their Latin American portfolios in the 1980s.) He presents the nature of the firm, the backgrounds of its leading partners, and some of the social and political pressures on the firm, all of which a historian specializing in the eighteenth century would find enlightening. The modern financial economist might find the work amusing, food for rueful reflection of the problems of modern Third World financial systems.

But, as with most of the essays in this book, the topic deserves little than a moment's thought or amusement for an economist. Bosher easily could have woven in a larger economic lesson with the smaller historical story. He missed the opportunity to compare the failure of the French government to use financial markets effectively with the success of the English government (see P. G. M. Dickson's *Financial Revolution in England* [London, 1967]). He also might have contrasted England's modern financial structure, that emphasized the rights of the holders of government debt, with France's capricious treatment of its creditors. Bosher makes no mention of Dutch lending, which both the French and the British courted during the wars of the eighteenth century in order to finance their national budget deficits. He might well have referred to James Riley's *International Government Finance and the Amsterdam Capital Market, 1740–1815* (London, 1980) and Charles Wilson's *Anglo-Dutch Commerce and Finance in the Eighteenth Century* (London, 1941).

Most of the essays are firmly in the historical camp; they provide dry exposition of the political and social impacts on eighteenth-century businesses, with relevance and interest only for specialists in eighteenth-century history. What economic issues are raised are minor.

ERIC S. SCHUBERT, *Chicago Board of Trade*

Housing in Urban Britain, 1780–1914: Class, Capitalism and Construction. By Richard Rodger. London: Macmillan Education Ltd., 1989. Pp. vii, 90. $9.95, paper.

Anyone concerned with the history of cities and especially urban housing will want to read this remarkably concise yet clearly written book, with its comprehensive annotated bibliography. It summarizes current perspectives and findings in the field of British housing history and contains a comprehensive annotated bibliography. Scholars of the U.S. urban past will find the work discussed in this volume particularly stimulating, since Rodger describes research quite different from that usually undertaken here. The British integrate social and economic factors to a greater degree, and their approach suggests promising new directions and questions for Americans.

As Rodger explains, the story of nineteenth-century housing was largely shaped by dramatic increases of urban population. During the first half of the century it was not uncommon for English towns to triple in size, and key industrial centers grew even faster. At the same time income distribution was quite skewed, with 60 percent of the population earning approximately 20 percent of the national income in 1801/3, and inequality narrowing "only marginally" over the course of the century (p. 9). Under the pressure of sheer numbers the physical unity of the preindustrial city broke down; the particular way in which this happened was conditioned by the severe income inequality. Stark contrasts in the built environment developed: both the suburbs and the slums were products of this period. At the center of the new metropolis low wages translated into a dense architecture of back-to-back terraced housing (in American terms, tiny row houses which shared back as well as side walls). Meanwhile, the middle class, motivated by desires for new kinds of personal and family life, moved from their townhouses in the urban core to residential enclaves at the outskirts of the city.

Factors on the supply side of the housing equation contributed to the development of this now familiar pattern of misery at the center and comfort at the periphery. No improvement of residential conditions for the poor was to come from the building industry. With its small firms and low levels of capitalization, this sector produced no economies of scale or technological advances comparable to those in other parts of the economy. "Consequently," Rodger explains, "building costs remained stubbornly opposed to significant long-run price falls experienced by industrial products" (p. 19).

Recent research indicates that neither the degree of crowding nor the level of rents varied in any direct way based on whether the land was held by freehold or leasehold systems. Nor did it make any difference if large holdings were developed by a single owner or small ones by many different builders. Instead, the desirability of the location determined the kind of dwellings which were erected and what was charged for them. So, for instance, "poorly drained areas were developed for industrial purposes or working-class housing irrespective of who owned the land, how concentrated the ownership was, or the nature of the tenure" (p. 15). Thus, the only factors which significantly influenced shelter conditions for the working class were wage levels and the structure of the building industry (p. 17).

Rodger describes how recent scholarship has overturned some conventional ideas about the sources of urban change, such as the idea that health dangers motivated the middle class to flee the city center. In actuality, he argues, cause and effect were the opposite. "Middle-class economic power itself contributed to precisely those living conditions from which they fled by deriving a rentier income from slums, by reinvesting business profits to the exclusion of environmental improvement, and crucially, by diverting housing investment to the suburbs" (pp. 41–42). I believe one does not have to reverse cause and effect so completely in this way to accept the importance of investment strategies as well as cultural preferences. The two can be understood as interdependent factors prompting middle class flight from the city.

The author also questions the belief that Victorian reform activities brought about those improvements in working-class living conditions which did take place. While a great quantity and variety of initiatives occurred, including model tenements, employer-provided housing, building regulations, workers' building cooperatives, municipal slum clearance programs, and garden city plans, these many efforts should be understood as indications of the severity of the housing problem and as evidence about contemporary interpretations of its causes, and not as sources of change. The actual impetus for what Rodger characterizes as "the upward drift in standards of accommodation and comfort for a majority of the population," which began in the last quarter of the nineteenth century, was higher wages combined with smaller families (p. 67). Still a matter of controversy between "optimists" and "pessimists," he notes, is the extent of improvement for unskilled workers who could not count on continuous employment (p. 12).

Small as it is, the book includes much more provocative and stimulating material than can be conveyed in a review, and should be consulted by anyone interested in the history of British cities and housing. Also, as previously noted, it will be a valuable resource to U.S. urban historians. In the early 1970s Richard O. Davies called for a new direction in historical work on American urban housing. He pointed out that while most historical research on housing (including his own) had focused on reformers and government regulations and programs, "the basic determinant in the development of

American urban housing from colonial times to the present has been private developers seeking to maximize their profits . . . " ("One-third of a Nation: The Dilemmas of America's Housing, 1607–1970," in Jerome Finster, ed., *The National Archives and Urban Research* [Athens, 1974], pp. 43–44). In general, the approach Davies criticized has remained standard practice, although some scholars have examined the ways in which market forces have been influenced by government policy and programs since the New Deal.

Overall, however, it could be argued that the impact of the market on housing in the United States has remained relatively uncharted, except for examining cultural preferences which determine the kinds of housing people desire. Yet, in fact, many other market forces significantly affect the kind, amount, and location of residential provision in cities. For instance, on the demand side, trends in wages and distribution of income determine what people can afford. In addition, changes in mortgage practices and interest rates influence what people can purchase. If producers cannot make a profit producing decent housing for a particular group, they do not build for that group. On the supply side, changes in rates of return available in *other* sectors of the economy influence investment in residential real estate, affecting the number of investors who find housing a maximally profitable use for their funds. In addition, innovations in the institutional arrangements which structure financing—such as the creation of bond funds and changes in laws governing banking activities—also have an impact on investment patterns. In turn, such patterns have powerful effects on the physical development of cites.

Until now in the United States it has been primarily political economists who have attempted to understand residential provision in relation to a wide range of market forces. Their investigations, however, have focused on the contemporary scene or recent past. Those scholars interested in expanding the field of U.S. housing history to include more understanding of economic, along with social and cultural, determinants will find the research agenda introduced in *Housing in Urban Britain* an important foundation upon which to build.

GAIL RADFORD, *Spertus College of Judaica*

The Engineers: A History of the Engineering Profession in Britain, 1750–1914. By R. A. Buchanan. London: Jessica Kingsley Publishers, 1989. Pp. 240. £25.

This book would have been more accurately subtitled "A History of Engineering Professionalism in Britain," since it is principally directed towards the study of British engineers' professional associations, the organization of engineering training and education, and the changing status of British engineers, at home and abroad, during the period. Pages 59 through 68 deal with the Society of Civil Engineers and the later Institution of Civil Engineers, which became the model for most British engineering associations; it was built primarily on the basis of the Canal Mania and strengthened by the participation of the leading canal engineers. Thomas Telford, the first President of the Institution of Civil Engineers in 1820, was its moving spirit until his death in 1834. By that time the canal age was coming to an end and the railway age had dawned.

Chapters IV and V, "The Beginning of Institutional Proliferation" and "The Fragmentation of the Profession," demonstrate by their titles that no sooner had the Institution of Civil Engineers established itself as the most important association of British engineers than the Institution of Mechanical Engineers, more closely reflecting the interests of railway engineers and manufacturing engineers, began to copy it. Apparently the story that the *doyen* of railway engineering, George Stapleton, had been spurned by the "Civils" is apocryphal, but it helped justify the creation of a new national engineering association. From that time forward, fragmentation progressed apace. Buchanan catalogues the creation of the Institution of Naval Architects, the Institution of Gas Engineers, the Iron and Steel Institute, the Institution of Mining Engineers, and the Association of Municipal and Sanitary Engineers and Surveyers. All these organizations were national, though sometimes they originated in regional societies. Differing in the extent of their membership restrictions, they were all designed to protect the professional status of their members, concerned with setting professional standards, and modeled on the Institution of Civil Engineers, with which they preserved fraternal relationships. Each new association demonstrated the maturation of another sector of Britain's engineering skills. They were born in enthusiasm and in the confidence of expansion, but the fragmentation of the profession was to have a variety of effects. Chapters VI and VII, "Divided Voices—Fragmentation Continued" and "Regional Diversification" continue the story. The strength of regionalism in Britain was at the center of its industrialization. Up until twenty years ago every manufacturing town used to reflect this just as churches and chapels reflect the religious history of Britain's varied localities.

Inevitably, however, as the author points out, this survey becomes "somewhat repetitive, because each new development of a national institution has tended to take the same form and to preserve similar patterns of evolution" (p. 121). Indeed, the repetition makes the book rather boring. Nonetheless the author has provided other scholars with a valuable guide to records.

"British Engineering Abroad," Chapter VIII of the book, offers the best short account of British engineering abroad available to date; many students will benefit from Buchanan's conclusions and from his notes. Naturally, fourteen pages, including notes, cannot be exhaustive, but it serves as a fine starting point. Buchanan is also strong on "Engineering Education and Training" and the "Ideas and Beliefs of the Engineers," although he concludes in the second of these chapters that the engineers did not have any and, outside their profession, were a rather dull lot. Perhaps the dullness lies in the biographers, not in the engineers themselves.

Except in a few isolated instances, the book tells very little about engineering practices. It will not replace the work of L. T. C. Bolt and W. H. G. Armytage. It does suggest areas of further research for those whose interests extend beyond institutions to personalities, beyond administrative procedures to the challenges of engineering concepts, and beyond educational requirements to the study of ideas. It is soundly researched and documented, but for variety, give me Samuel Smiles.

Eric Robinson, *University of Massachusetts, Boston*

Peasants, Politicians and Producers: The Organisation of Agriculture in France Since 1918. By M. C. Cleary. New York: Cambridge University Press, 1989. Pp. ix, 209.

In France the term peasant (*paysan*) is more often employed as a political than as an economic category. Prior to the Revolution, the word signified farmers, and encompassed the whole gamut of types from the small-holding day laborer to the large and wealthy capitalist tenant. During the nineteenth century the larger farm operators were increasingly called farmers (*cultivateurs*) and agriculturists (*agriculteurs*), while the word peasant (*paysan*) came to be employed as a portmanteau term denoting the agricultural and often the entire rural portion of the French electorate. In the twentieth century the term came to designate small family farmers. Because the study of the recent history of France's "peasants" has tended to be conducted more often by political scientists and sociologists whose focus of interest is the meaning of modern democracy, than by economists and economic historians interested in the mechanisms of economic growth and the distribution of income and opportunity, the term has usually referred to medium and small farmers with a view to explaining interest-group politics.

The present work is an effort of this kind. It chronicles the development of interest groups promoting the welfare of the smaller farmers in twentieth-century France.

This history is presented as an episode in the democratization of French political and economic life. Like other commentators on the change in the leadership of agricultural organizations that occurred in the 1950s, to the benefit of representatives of the more humble agricultural classes, the author emphasizes the work of the Catholic Agricultural Youth (*Jeunesse agricole catholique*) in training up a new generation of leaders to replace the traditional gentry. He argues that their success stimulated a reorientation of French farming policy from exclusive preoccupation with price supports, which benefited the largest farmers, to subsidized structural reforms intended to strengthen and ensure the survival of family farms. The reforms, however, had the ironic effect of sacrificing the smallest and least protected farmers, the remaining peasants of mid nineteenth-century France, while the amalgamation of cooperatives drew sales organizations closer to agribusiness and further from their roots in local farming communities. The interest of farm workers, as is the case everywhere, were totally neglected by the farmers' organizations.

As the history prior to the late 1950s does not differ from Gordon Wright's treatment in *Rural Revolution in France* (Stanford, 1964), the marginal contribution of this work is the account of the last quarter-century, during which time the share of the labor force in agriculture dropped precipitously. Unfortunately the author's preoccupation with the politics of farm organizations makes for an unsystematic, incomplete, and therefore unusable description of postwar agricultural policy. Economic historians seeking a detailed account of government policy toward agriculture since the end of World War I will have to look elsewhere for their facts. The book ignores issues arising out of the formation of the European Economic Community, whose impact in conjunction with modern agricultural technology dominates the postwar economic history of agriculture in western Europe. The political economy of shrinking economic sectors is a topic of considerable current importance. Cleary's book is a modest contribution to its literature, but the modern history of the shrinking agricultural sector in Europe remains to be conceived and written.

GEORGE GRANTHAM, *McGill University*

Joy in Work, German Work: The National Debate, 1800–1945. By Joan Campbell. Princeton: Princeton University Press, 1989. Pp. xi, 431. $37.50.

Campbell's book provides a masterful compendium of German responses to the concept of alienation by examining "what educated Germans thought about work" during the industrial era (p. 3). She emphasizes "the middle classes who sought to end alienation in order to *avert* social upheaval" by adopting an "anti-Marxist ideology of work based on Arbeitsfreude [Joy in Work]." Nevertheless their "shared heritage" with Marx and Engels "of romanticism, idealism, and Hegelianism," discussed briefly in the introductory chapters, gave them a similar aversion to unalleviated factory toil (p. 28). Consequently, Campbell can juxtapose the ideas of W. H. Riehl with those of Marx in a fascinating and extended overview of the former's *völkisch* contributions to shaping the Joy in Work debate as about "German work."

Later generations of middle-class theorists found little agreement with Marx's political and intellectual descendants, particularly since Engels encouraged such leaders as Karl Kautsky to emphasize "enjoyment *after* work." Most Social Democrats stressed this instead of the long hours of "enjoyable" or at least stoically Germanic assembly-line labor advocated by their more conservative opponents. Thus, they enlarged the debate to make "Joy in Life" the issue. Very sensibly, however, Campbell does not flesh out the full debate in her book, since her theme is, after all, theories of Joy in Work, particularly those that accepted the factory and sought to make it respond to its workforce. Her subjects are, therefore, frequently professionals, notably economists, psychologists, sociologists, and engineers.

Campbell focusses on the Weimar period after an overview of the prewar debate that draws reform movements and denominational reformers together with an emerging "science of work," dependent in part on questionnaires to probe "the proletarian psyche" (p. 97). After the war, "romantic longings for utopia" emerged, like Alfred Fellisch's vision of "brawny workmen, arm in arm with knights of the intellect marching into the Reich of the future" (pp. 107, 127). But common sense soon prevailed with the return to scientific thinking about the "humanization" of work, from the angle both of "restructuring the productive process," notably through "*Fordismus*," and of "reorganizing industrial relations" (pp. 134, 138). Professionals again wielded questionnaires to ascertain proletarian "attitudes toward modern work," a few even of women's. Others worried about whether work could and should be pleasurable or "preserve the vocational ethic of German labor" (p. 235). In this context the employer-oriented German Institute for Technical Industrial Training (Dinta) aimed to transform "Germany's young people into highly qualified, cooperative, and diligent members of the labor force" (p. 258).

Then came the Depression and the Nazi regime, both forces for the radicalization of attitudes toward "German work." Labor service, corporatism, "a conservative revolution to replace the despicable Weimar democracy with a corporatist new order in which the workers' estate would play a leading role," such ideas were bandied about as the Nazis moved into office. Campbell explores briefly pre-1933 Nazi contributions to the debate and their "fit" with the electorate, but this move beyond theory to impact is little grounded in the wide scholarship of the period. She soon retreats wisely to "the difficulty that educated Germans with established reputations faced" (p. 328) in adjusting to Nazi successes, then moves on to discuss the major work-related Nazi organizations, notably Robert Ley's German Labor Front. She concludes that "Ley was probably sincere in his desire to solve the problem of alienation and to make the German worker happy both as producer and consumer" (p. 332). But discussion of work-related issues continued throughout the Third Reich's stormy existence, with increasing emphasis placed on "a more rigorous ethic" of specifically Germanic work (p. 339). A "worker-warrior analogy" became ever more accurate as the war came to German society (p. 363).

Campbell's book complements her earlier work on the German Werkbund by placing in context in a very German debate that organization's desire, following Ruskin and Morris, "to restore dignity and joy to work" (pp. 68–69). Campbell challenges the reader with a dense and expository style, in keeping with her desire to "set forth" the ideas that she has uncovered. She achieves her stated objective with great skill, however, drawing on a wealth of primary documentation to provide the reader with a kaleidoscopic overview of the extended struggle with "alienated" labor of her "educated" Germans. She ends with the view that postwar German theorists about work have operated within "an international rather than . . . a German national context" (p. 383). We have yet to see whether the stunning developments of 1989 will challenge her conclusion that the traditional combination of Joy in Work with German Work "may well have been permanently broken" (p. 385).

HELENA WADDY LEPOVITZ, *State University of New York, Geneseo*

Hyperinflation and Stabilization in the Weimar Republic. By Steven B. Webb. New York: Oxford University Press, 1989. Pp. viii, 164. $29.95.

The trillion-fold inflation Germany suffered between 1914 and 1923 offers a tempting test case for current theories of inflation, and Steven Webb provides valuable insights by using it as such. But he also illuminates the historical specifics of Weimar's inflationary experience.

Webb describes clearly the fiscal and monetary mechanisms of inflation and stabilization. War and postwar budget deficits left enormous, irregularly increasing quantities of discountable debt in private hands. The central bank, the Reichsbank, was willing to monetize such debt when asked. Hence the inflation rate, Webb argues, essentially reflected private individuals' collective liquidity preferences, with Germans preferring money (for obtaining commodities) when they feared future inflation. He derives significant statistical correlations among negative financial news (an endogenous factor reflecting, he argues, expectations about future government deficits and hence future inflation), monetization of privately held debt, and the inflation rate, suggesting that rational expectations theories explain crucial aspects of Weimar's inflationary experience. He analyzes the stabilizations of 1920, early 1923, and late 1923/24 (only the last of which was successful), arguing that not the end of government deficits by itself but only a concatenation of policy changes such as happened August 1923 to April 1924, could eliminate inflation's fiscal, monetary, and psychological sources.

Webb discusses inflation's political causes with great insight. Reichsbank officials stuck with inflationary monetary policies to prevent severe recession—in order to forestall further revolution. Economically and socially conservative, they seem also to have hoped to make stabilization contingent on the reversal of the social policy gains of the 1918 revolution. Inflationary fiscal policies resulted from the inability of powerful social interests to agree on who in German society would be forced to pay the staggering costs of Germany's defeat. Webb implicitly reestablishes reparations as the major cause of inflation—not because of its direct economic effects but because it raised the government's fiscal burden beyond what Germans were willing to bear until hyperinflation forced them to come to terms with reparations. Weimar had to finance reparations, capitalism, and democracy; it could not, politically, afford all three. Because the Allies resisted reparations concessions to Weimar democracy but eventually granted a reparations moratorium to authoritarian regimes, Germany found itself after 1933 without reparations—but also without democracy (and, arguably, without capitalism).

Webb argues that inflation and hyperinflation had real effects. Inflation-induced economic uncertainty frightened and disoriented business, contributing to low investment from 1920 to 1923. He doubts the German inflation stimulated aggregate demand abroad, arguing that Germany generally ran export surpluses in the relevant years. Inflation-aggravated structural problems contributed to persistently high unemployment after 1925, and such unemployment and the disastrous contractionary policies of 1929–1932 were possible only because the experience of hyperinflation had made Germans so frightened of expansionary policies.

The correlations Webb finds among financial news, liquidity preferences, and inflation are very suggestive, but do not, of course, guarantee causal connections. Also, he talks of "people" who had rational expectations, but he never clarifies which or how many Germans were economically rational. And although he assumes Germans of the 1920s believed the quantity theory (p. 23), apparently very few did, even in the financial community. Instead, they tended to believe price rises reflected either a "dearness" of goods (resulting from war-induced shortages) or balance-of-payments disturbances (from trade deficits and reparations). Influential members of the financial community may eventually have adopted the quantity theory. But economically rational Germans of the 1920s seem more likely to have chosen to monetize debt because they expected adverse financial and political news to presage not increases in budget deficits and money supply but renewed pressure on the mark's foreign exchange rate or increased likelihood of economic difficulties or even the triumph of socialism.

Webb doubts the 1925/26 recession reflected a delayed stabilization crisis, but more research seems necessary here. Currency stabilization at one trillion to one left enterprises debt-free, and many ran up substantial new debt in 1924 and early 1925, at very high interest rates, to deal with stabilization's effects. Weak firms could have kept going for a while by deferring maintenance, running down stocks, postponing payments to suppliers, and so forth. But an inability to keep servicing their expensive new debt could have caught up with such firms by late 1925.

Webb comments, as have many, on the "proclivity of democracy for government spending and intervention in the economy." The massive debt and *dirigiste* policies of many Latin American (not to mention Eastern European) dictatorships in the 1970s and 1980s suggest that to explain these phenomena we may need another model besides the putatively unusual profligacy and ungovernability of democracies.

The German inflation's complexity ensures that it will remain controversial. But Webb's excellent study, whose richness I cannot fully explore here, significantly increases our understanding of the political causes and fiscal and monetary mechanisms behind hyperinflation and stabilization—in 1920s Germany and in the abstract.

MICHAEL L. HUGHES, *Wake Forest University*

Wirtschaftsgeschichte der Tschechoslowakei, 1918–1980. By Alice Teichova. Vienna: Böhlau Verlag, 1988. Pp. vi, 143. DM43.

Alice Teichova's economic history of Czechoslovakia is a valuable addition to the growing list of country studies available to economic historians of the twentieth century. It skillfully recounts the economic evolution of Czechoslovakia from the first days of independence in 1918 through the third decade as part of the Soviet bloc. Her main theme is one of unfulfilled expectations—the large gap between Czechoslovakia's economic potential and the reality of its actual performance.

The author correctly argues that no state in east central or southeastern Europe was better equipped to take advantage of its independence. The territories forming Czechoslovakia were among the richest agricultural and industrial regions in the Habsburg Empire, some having experienced modern economic growth from the early nineteenth century. On the eve of World War I these regions were at the level of Scandinavia and not far behind much of Western Europe. Unlike the other successor states, Czechoslovakia enjoyed considerable political stability. Popular trust in the new state and its government became obvious as financial markets easily absorbed the liberation loan of 1918. Favorable political conditions also existed immediately after World War II. The government in exile under Eduard Beneš united with emigré Communists led by Clement Gottwald behind the Košice Program as a framework for reconstruction and recovery.

By contrast, the actual performance of the economy since 1918 does seem rather disappointing. In the interwar period Czechoslovakia grew faster than Austria and most East European contemporaries, but slower than the Scandinavian and Western European economies. Most of the interwar growth came in the boom of the 1920s. The depression of the 1930s was unusually severe and the recovery so weak that by 1937 the level of output was still below that of 1929. The large income gap between the western and eastern regions inherited from the Habsburg era remained unchanged between 1919 and 1939. Czechoslovakia recovered rapidly after World War II, but grew slower than the average of both the OECD and the Soviet bloc economies in the three decades after 1950. The standard of living grew even more slowly. Wages lagged substantially behind productivity and social spending by the state did not make up for depressed private consumption. By the 1980s Czechoslovakia had dissipated much of its endowment from the Habsburg era. Not only had it failed to catch up to Western Europe, it had fallen behind the Scandinavian countries, and was losing ground to some of the rapidly growing but more backward economies of southwestern Europe.

Teichova relies on two kinds of explanations. First, the small, open economy faced unfavorable external forces. The Habsburg Empire's dismemberment created both opportunities and problems. As the successor states pursued independent economic policies, trade and investment dried up and intensified the depression. The country's increasing orientation toward Britain and France partially substituted for the lost pre-1914 economic links with Vienna, but created a new kind of dependence that led to the Munich Agreement and occupation by Germany. After World War II Czechoslovakia faced another major restructuring as part of the Council for Mutual Economic Assistance, the Soviet-led version of the ECC. Building on traditional strengths, it became the machinery and armaments supplier for much of the Soviet bloc. Yet strict orientation toward the CMEA economies isolated it from the Western technology that would have helped preserve its engineering preeminence.

Domestic policy failures compounded unfavorable international conditions. Teichova attributes much of the investment boom of the 1920s to the successful monetary reform of February 1919, which insulated Czechoslovakia from the hyperinflations suffered by Austria and Hungary. But she gives the government low marks in the 1930s for its strict adherence to financial orthodoxy as a member of the French-led gold bloc. The post-1948 planning authorities come in for the sharpest criticism. She views quite positively the two-year experiment with planning prior to the Communist takeover. After 1948, however, the loose planning mechanism gave way to a rigid, Soviet-style centralized plan, which Teichova argues was completely inappropriate for a country with a rich history of capitalist development and democratic institutions.

She regards the reform movement of the 1960s as a logical outgrowth of that history. The fourth Five Year Plan (1966–70) reflected the views of critics such as the economist Oka Sik, who favored decentralizing the planning mechanism, freeing up some prices, and using profits as a criterion for guiding resource allocation. Growing awareness that economic decentralization was inconsistent with single-party, centralized bureaucratic rule led to calls for pluralist democratic institutions. The move toward "socialism with a human face" ended, of course, with the invasion of Warsaw Pact troops in the summer of 1968.

More importantly, Teichova's reading of Czechoslovakia's history leads her to see 1968 as a foreshadowing of things to come. She closes by predicting that "in the not too distant future not only economic reform will come to Czechoslovakia but political and social democratization as well." Three years ago when these lines were written, they would have been dismissed as the wishful thinking of an incurable romantic. The events of fall 1989, of course, show Teichova to have been remarkably prescient.

We can agree with her that introducing market incentives and democratic institutions will help to close the gap between Czech economic potential and actual performance. A close reading of Czechoslovakia's interwar experience, however, suggests that she may be putting too much weight on domestic reforms. Much like Habsburg rule over east central Europe before it, the Soviet system is now disintegrating. As Czechoslovakia and other bloc economies break away from the Soviet orbit, they will have to forge institutions of international cooperation among themselves and with the developed economies of the West. The interwar years suggest how difficult that may be and how devastating may be the consequences of failure.

Written to coincide with Czechoslovakia's seventieth birthday, Teichova's book now takes on unexpected significance as the mind-numbing events in the Soviet bloc continue to unfold. A translation into English would be valuable for scholars rethinking post-1989 Europe.

DAVID F. GOOD, *University of Minnesota*

Russia's "Age of Silver": Precious-Metal Production and Economic Growth in the Eighteenth Century. By Ian Blanchard. New York: Routledge, Chapman, and Hall, 1989. Pp. xvi, 431. $79.95.

This heavy volume contains not one book, but two. The first, in Chapters One through Four, traces the extraordinarily rapid development of Russian silver and copper production to a position of leadership in the world economy. The second, in Chapter Five, offers estimates of Russian national income and per capita income in 1700, 1718, 1762, 1788, 1792, and 1800, with comparisons (in 1762 prices) forward in time to 1913. Unfortunately, the causal and logical links between the two parts remain obscure.

The early chapters tell the story of precious-metal production in the Ural region and Siberia. The narrative contains a wealth of detail, presented in many maps and tables. The reader misses, however, a sense of the entrepreneurial element in this drama. For example, Hugh D. Hudson's fine monograph on the Demidov family is absent from the list of sources.

More problematical is the author's attempt to summarize the development of Russian agriculture, industry, trade, and transport in Chapter Five. Despite some interesting descriptions of geographical variations in agriculture and handicrafts and of the creation of a unified system of river and canal transport, this chapter fails to substantiate the notion of an "agricultural revolution" and a "manufacturing-commercial revolution" (p. 233) in the eighteenth century. Particularly dubious are the author's conclusions regarding national income and per capita income. "In 1807 the average British citizen was barely richer than his Russian counterpart. The two nations—Britain and Russia—stood at the very top of the European national-income league table" (p. 282). "A century of rapid economic growth had made both Russian aristocrats and peasants the envy of visitors from the allegedly more civilized west" (p. 283).

Arithmetic comparisons obscure crucial institutional and cultural differences between the two countries, notably the lack in Russia of a free peasantry, of a banking system, of corporations, of a middle class, and of legal norms hospitable to private enterprise. How meaningful are data on per capita income in a social system based on serfdom? The tsarist aristocracy must be contrasted to the constitutional system that had evolved in Britain by 1688, masterfully examined by Douglass C. North and Barry R. Weingast recently in this JOURNAL (Dec. 89). Also, despite occasional assertions of "high correlations" among some time series, the text contains no statistical tests. Finally, the reader encounters a distressing number of errors in the transliteration of Russian names and sources, though some of these occur with such regularity that they appear to be idiosyncracies rather than lapses of scholarship.

The strength of this work lies, therefore, in its descriptions of mining and metallurgy in South America, Europe, and Russia in the seventeenth and eighteenth centuries; in its many tables and graphs of ore production, mint output, ruble stocks, and the like; and in the impressive list of sources cited.

THOMAS C. OWEN, *Louisiana State University*

Serfdom and Social Control in Russia: Petrovskoe, a Village in Tambov. By Steven L. Hoch. Chicago: University of Chicago Press, 1989. Pp. x, 220. $10.95.

Students of Imperial Russia, as well as all readers interested in agrarian societies past or present, should be pleased at the appearance in paperback of Hoch's fine study, which first came out in hardcover in 1986.

In this work, based primarily on the unpublished estate records of the Gagarin family, Hoch has opened up a crucial problem long ignored by successive generations of Russian historians—the question of seigniorial authority. Hoch confronts the issue squarely in his Introduction, when he asks, "how did landlords and bailiffs in imperial Russia get the serfs to work and behave as desired?" (p. i).

Naked force alone could not resolve the daily problems of order and work discipline on a labor-service estate. The seignior could not afford the costs of an elaborate repressive apparatus, and the instruments of the state in rural Russia were weak and primitive. The militia and gendarmes were sufficient to repress most rural disturbances, but in daily life the seignior had to depend largely on his estate manager or bailiff, who in turn needed the cooperation and assistance of the elected officials of the peasant commune.

Just how the seignior and bailiff obtained this assistance and cooperation is the subject of Hoch's book, which begins with an analysis of the cereal economy of Petrovskoe, a village in the central black soil region some three hundred miles southeast of Moscow. Based on harvest data for Petrovskoe (drawn from the Gagarin estate records), the author shows that yield ratios were much higher than the generalized estimates on which scholars have previously relied. Rye yields in the first half of the nineteenth century averaged more than six to one, while oats were nearly five to one. This data pertains to demesne lands, but since they were interstripped with peasant lands, yields on the latter were probably similar. In any case, rye and oats were the main cereals in the peasant economy, and yields of five or six to one were comparable to many areas of France and Germany in the late eighteenth and early nineteenth centuries.

Indeed, one of Hoch's strong points is his comparative approach, which yields useful insights on the relative well-being of the Russian serf. Drought and famine brought periodic subsistence crises to Petrovskoe in the first half of the nineteenth century, but, excluding crisis years (to which many European peasants were also subject), the serfs of Petrovskoe apparently ate better than their counterparts in nineteenth-century France and Belgium.

Hoch also offers detailed and convincing demographic evidence that serfdom did not have a "markedly adverse effect on mortality" (p. 69). Average life expectancy for the serfs of Petrovskoe (about 27 years) was comparable to France and England in the late eighteenth and early nineteenth centuries.

At this point, however, Hoch finds that the similarities end and the differences between Petrovskoe and Western Europe begin. The major demographic difference was at the level of family structure. As Hoch puts it, "life in Petrovskoe took place in a framework of stable and very high fertility, early and universal marriage, and large, closely related, structurally complex three generation households" (p. 89). The serfs in Petrovskoe married much earlier, and lived in much larger households than most peasants in western Europe.

For Hoch, the "complex, three generation household" provides the key to "social control" on the serf estate. The "odds of life" in Petrovskoe depended on the peasants' ability to cope successfully with specific agricultural conditions in the central black soil region. An extremely short growing season meant that the most labor-intensive period of the agricultural year was telescoped into a six-week stretch from the middle of July to the end of August. During this period, when crops were harvested and the winter fields plowed and sown, the serf household had to tend not only its own farm, but its share of seigniorial demesne as well.

This period of feverish activity imposed severe strains on the productive forces of the peasant household—its overall labor capacity, division of labor, and draft animals. For households with only one adult couple, these strains were often beyond their capacity. But the large households that dominated in Petrovskoe could usually take the strain because they enjoyed the labor capacity of at least two adult couples and often more.

In Hoch's analysis, however, the large household was more than just a labor unit; it was the crucial link in a chain of authority that enabled the seignior to exercise authority *in absentia* over the peasants. Of course, the rigors of the agricultural season also imposed their own forms of regimentation, but Hoch argues that social control rested primarily on the authority of the household patriarchs, who enjoyed nearly absolute power over their families.

Hoch shows that this power was accompanied by substantial, tangible privileges within both the household and the commune. Delegating the most onerous agricultural tasks to younger members of the household, the patriarch played a supervisory role. As a group, the patriarchs comprised a village elite, a "gerontocracy" that dominated the communal assembly and supplied the commune with its most important elected officials.

This privileged position in village and family life was upheld and sanctioned by the seignior and his bailiff, who thus provided the household patriarchs with a powerful incentive to cooperate with the estate authorities in maintaining discipline and order. Both sides worked together in upholding large households and prohibiting younger couples from leaving the patriarchal household in order to set up independent households that were smaller and thus less productive (from the seignior's standpoint). The patriarch served his own interests, as well as the seignior's, when he forced his sons to marry early and stay within his household, while enforcing the daily work discipline that was essential for an effective rendering of labor services.

Hoch admits candidly that this system of control was not airtight. The peasants of Petrovskoe were frequently subjected to corporal punishment, especially for negligent performance of labor services. But he also points out that Petrovskoe was highly profitable for its owner and required only minimal administrative costs.

Hoch documents an impressive and persuasive argument that probably applies to most labor service estates in the central black soil region, where large households dominated and where the peasant economy remained to some extent isolated from the market. It may not apply as well to monetary rent (*obrok*) estates, especially in the non-black soil region where *obrok* was synonymous with off-farm earnings in rural industry and seasonal wage labor. Such pursuits often drew peasants away from their villages for long periods of time and may thus have bred a sense of personal autonomy and independence that undermined patriarchal authority in the household.

Such regional differences would not, in any case, detract from Hoch's achievement. He has written the most thoughtful book on seigniorial authority since Otto Brunner's *Land und Herrschaft* (5th edn. 1965) explored the problem for late medieval Austria and Germany. Unlike Brunner, Hoch does not integrate his findings into larger questions of politics and state structure, but both authors, despite very different approaches, seem to reach the same conclusion—that seigniorial authority was the authority of the peasant household writ large.

EDGAR MELTON, *Harvard University*

Estructura, desarrollo y crisis de la siderurgia tradicional vizcaína (1700–1840). By Rafael Uriarte Ayo. Bilbao: Universidad del País Vasco, 1988. Pp. 328.

Although agriculture has received the lion's share of early modern historiographical attention, an increasing number of works deals with other facets of the problematical economic "decline of Spain." Rafael Uriarte Ayo's published *tesina* (short thesis) addresses the example of Vizcayan iron mining and metallurgy during the critical eighteenth century, when Spain showed signs of economic recovery under the *ilustrados*. Uriarte describes both the mining process (legally, technologically, and commercially) and the working of the metal, followed by a section on funding and marketing. It is a good book, albeit one that produces no revolutionary insights into either the Vizcayan or the Spanish economy.

Structure, Development and Crisis begins with a somewhat lengthy description of ordinances related to mining, followed by a detailed portrait of the technical aspects of mining—the hours worked, the tools used, even the number of candles necessary per day to illuminate the mines. The remainder of Part One describes the difficulties in marketing (transport, capital use, contracts, legal restrictions) and ends with a short section on the price of ore from 1710 to 1840, which might have been better left until later in the book. Part Two describes the intimate relationship between forests and foundry. Although historians of Spain need not be reminded of the problem of deforestation (beginning in the early sixteenth century in Castile), Uriarte outlines once again the failure of Vizcayan firewood and charcoal supplies.

It is in Part Three that the *tesina* finally provides the specific framework for the development of Vizcayan mining promised by the title. In what appears to be an organizational error, the last part of the work begins with a description of the technology of metallurgy (better suited for Part Two). Uriarte then discusses the *verlagssystem* of the emerging industry: capital investment, small holdings, regulation by local interests and the crown, absentee landlords, increasing consolidation of holdings as mining became more expensive. Here is an excellent example of nascent capitalism in Spain. After explaining the functions of capital and labor, Uriarte provides a Braudelian *conjoncture* for the Vizcayan iron enterprise: 1710 to 1760, a boom period as prices dropped then soared, encouraging local production in competition with the Swedes in northern Europe; 1760 to 1790, a period that sees increasing Russian production, driving the Swedes into the Mediterranean while Vizcayan ore and metallurgy were shackled by royal ordinances; and 1790 to 1840, the "crisis" in Vizcayan mining, brought on by war and the failure to accept new technologies.

As with all *tesinas*, this work suffers from a lack of breadth in secondary sources, some fumbling with evidence (especially legal evidence, although Uriarte is aware of its limitations), and organization. But it also goes beyond the typical "short thesis" in its integration of one facet of a regional economy into a global perspective. Uriarte has fulfilled his academic apprenticeship admirably. I find convincing his analysis and understanding of the place of Vizcayan iron in the global economy. Although a historian of science and technology might profit most from this study, economic historians as well will find much in the book to consider in their analyses of early modern marketing, investment, and competition in the metal industry.

PAUL HILTPOLD, *California Polytechnic State University*

MIDDLE EAST, AFRICA, AND ASIA

Land, Labor and the Origins of the Israeli-Palestinian Conflict, 1882–1914. By Gershon Shafir. New York: Cambridge University Press, 1989. Pp. xvi, 288. $44.50.

This is a provocative, well-written analytical challenge to explanations of the Palestinian-Israeli conflict that are fairly well accepted in the literature. Though the study focuses on the period from 1882 to 1914, the debate is equally relevant to later periods and events. Most of the information is secondary, but the original data and the reinterpretations are critical and enlightening. The synthesis raises questions about widely accepted explanations of the origins and development of the "Jewish" state of Israel, relations with the Palestinians, the partisan roles of various Jewish groups, and the chronic "ethnic" conflict between Ashkenazi (European) and Sephardi (Oriental) Jews. The author establishes that the main characteristics of the state of Israel were established before World War I and the Balfour Declaration of 1917, that the "return to the land" was pragmatic rather than ideological, and that the exclusivist *kibbutz* (collective) settlement whose members served as farmer-soldiers was a major guiding force in acquisition and colonization of the land and thus in planting the roots of a Jewish state in Palestine. He shows also that contrary to the myth that the migrant Jews believed Palestine to be a land without people, the leaders and immigrants knew well that there were Palestinians who would be displaced by Jewish migration and land acquisition, and that they ignored them in their vision and in planning the future for an exclusivist Jewish state.

The study progresses systematically through the last three decades of Ottoman rule in Palestine, showing how the Jewish immigrants acquired land through purchase by philanthropists and foundations, how they moved from a "plantation" form of tenure dependent on hired labor to self-employment in the collective and cooperative systems of tenure, how attempts to replace Arab labor with Yemeni Jewish immigrants failed, and how trade unions eventually merged with political parties and almost monopolized both political power and the Jewish economy. Even at this early stage the Zionist leaders aimed at the establishment of a separate Jewish economy with its own special features, but which still had something in common with white settlement in America, French colonization in North Africa, and English domination in South Africa.

The most interesting chapter is the last one, which is supposed to conclude the study but becomes a comparative analysis of the Israeli-Palestinian issue. It is a pity that this chapter was not expanded. Here we find the conflict between Palestinians and Israelis to be inherent in the dual claims to the same territory, the emerging nationalism of both peoples, the early dependence of the Jewish immigrants on the Palestinians for economic survival, and the final decision of the Jewish leaders to exclude the Palestinian Arabs from the prospective Jewish state. The fact that neither party has truly agreed to partition and coexistence on equal terms is rooted in the conflict of the early period. It is also evident that when the Jews accepted the partition of Palestine, they did so only as a strategic step toward realizing the dream of a Jewish state in the whole of Palestine.

Three forces affecting relations between the Jews and Arabs in Palestine remain unexplored even though they critically influenced the dynamics of the conflict ever since the idea of a Jewish state in Palestine came into existence. The first was the technological gap between the colonizer-settlers and the native Arabs, which made it almost unavoidable that economic and political duality would result. The second force was the role of foreign powers which had virtually dominated Ottoman politics since the last quarter of the nineteenth century and was highly favorable to Jewish settlement in the area. The third force was the interaction, including agreements and plots, between the British and French on one side and the emerging non-Palestinian Arab leaders, such as Amir Hussein and his descendants, on the other in the period under consideration. It was then that the Palestinians were being marginalized in determining their own fate and the fate of Palestine to the advantage of the Zionist movement. These comments, however, should not detract from the contributions of this book, which is a welcome addition to the small number of relatively objective studies of the Palestinian-Israeli conflict. It should be highly recommended.

ELIAS H. TUMA, *University of California, Davis*

The Enigma of Colonialism: British Policy in West Africa. By Anne Phillips. Bloomington: Indiana University Press, 1989. Pp. vii, 184. $29.95.

This book is itself enigmatic. Its subject matter would ordinarily fall under the heading of economic history; but the author is a Reader in Politics and Government, and its handling of the subject is weak—measured by the standards of either history or economics. Its intended contribution is clearly theoretical—not historical or economic—which suggests that it may be unfair to test it against the ordinary standards of economic history. It is concerned with the colonial history of British West Africa as viewed from the perspective of neo-Marxist theory. The principal sources are government despatches and memoranda; very little attention is paid to the changing economy of these four colonies.

The enigma of the title is this: "If colonialism was indeed a product of capitalist forces—as most well-thinking radicals will be likely to presume—when why were the interests of capital so ill-served?" "After eighty years of European rule, European capital had made little headway" (p. 2). The idea that capitalism failed West Africa by too little investment, rather than too much, is familiar in French Marxist literature going back to the 1960s. Anne Phillips's elaboration is new.

She holds that the fundamental necessity for capitalist development would have been to create a landless proletariat with no choice but to work for wages. The colonial administrations, however, failed to create a labor force of this kind, though "capital" urged them to do so. They failed because the colonial state lacked the coercive power to go the whole way. Faced with a danger of public disorder, the administration settled for what Phillips calls "the West Africa Policy." In place of the plantations full capitalist development would have required, it encouraged the peasantry to produce crops like cocoa and cotton and palm oil for export.

Phillips believes that communal land tenures gave virtually everyone in West Africa access to land. So long as they had access to land, they would not work for wages without coercion. Coercion required the authority of the chiefs, and the chiefs could be kept loyal only by being allowed to control the land. Without a proletariat to do the work, capital investment was limited to external commerce and mining.

The author also argues, however, that while the "West Africa Policy" prevented the capitalist exploitation of West Africa, it still served the ultimate interests of capitalist accumulation. By keeping West Africa underdeveloped, it made possible later exploitation through unequal trade with Europe. The contradictions of the West Africa Policy were, nevertheless, so serious that they, not the rise of a nationalist movement, were the real cause of African independence.

Phillips argues from the assumption that her readers already accept a neo-Marxist theory of history. Her further case is also argued without the kind of evidence economic historians normally require. She makes no attempt to show that most West Africans actually had access to enough productive land to make wage labor unattractive. Economic historians would need to know how much income was available from the land and something about the level of wages. Again and again the possible play of market forces is simply passed over. Empirically inclined economic historians will also have trouble with the idea that "capital" is an actor in history, distinct from the action of capitalists or those who spoke for them.

Phillips is also credulous in her acceptance of contemporaneous official opinion in spite of later evidence contradicting it. On the conflict between peasants and plantations as the best means of development, she accepts the official view that African farmers were backward—and "scientific" Western agronomists had the right answers. Later research has shown that the officials were often wrong, but Phillips pays no attention to such obvious recent works as Paul Richards's *Indigenous Agricultural Revolution* (Boulder, CO, 1985).

As history, the treatment of the precolonial period is riddled with inaccuracies, most of which could have been corrected by a careful reading of the works she lists in her bibliography. Nor are the bibliography and notes up to professional historical standards. She uses the "scientific" style of reference, but the reader has to look through three separate alphabetical bibliographies to find the actual citation. Page numbers are sometimes missing. "Wilks (1975)" is little help in finding information from an 800-page book. It is also curious that she limited her reading of unpublished Ph.D. theses to those presented in British universities, even though American and Canadian theses are available in Britain on microfilm.

PHILIP D. CURTIN, *The Johns Hopkins University*

Agrarian Transformations: Local Processes and the State in Southeast Asia. Edited by Gillian Hart, Andrew Turton, and Benjamin White. Berkeley: University of California Press, 1989. Pp. xv, 341. $35.00.

This collection of articles deals with the social differentiation process in rural areas of select Southeast Asian countries, namely, Indonesia, Malaysia, the Philippines, and Thailand. As is typical in classical Marxian analysis, the various authors use Hegelian dialectics. However, they deviate from classical analysis by analyzing the differentiation process within concrete situations. The classical two-class polarization model predicts that the penetration of capitalism into rural society gradually divides that society into capitalists (landowners) and the proletariat (landless workers), each class with its associated "consciousness." Many scholars who have previously studied rural differentiation have simply attempted to confirm this. The authors here unanimously reject this approach. Instead, they effectively argue that the differentiation process is profoundly influenced by economic, political, and cultural forces peculiar to a society and thus may evolve in ways that differ from those in other societies. In particular, they emphasize the role of the state in influencing the process and how the process in turn affects the character of the state. Given that states differ across countries, the differentiation process will tend to follow different paths. Hence, they concur that an analysis of rural differentiation must be flexible, not tied to a rigid paradigm. Their individual studies suggest that a general model of rural differentiation may not exist and that the most one can develop is a framework for analyzing the process that is flexible enough to encompass the contexts within which it evolves.

Rural differentiation refers to "a cumulative and permanent process of change in the ways in which different groups in rural society gain access to the products of their own or others' labor, based on their differential control over production resources and often, but not always, on increasing inequalities in access to land" (p. 20). Roughly, it refers to changes in the ways or mechanisms through which the various groups in rural society, as distinguished by their differential control over resources or access thereto, generate income. For example, in the Philippines, price controls on rice and political pressure for land reform caused many large landowners to shift their strategies for surplus extraction from sharecropping or fixed rental arrangements with tenants to rentals of farm machinery, particularly threshers, and fees for marketing services. These mechanisms yielded larger, more secure profits (Brian Fegan, Chapter 8). The same forces induced many rural villagers, particularly the landless and landowners whose landholdings were not sufficient to guarantee subsistence, to seek nonagricultural sources of income such as jobs in Saudi Arabia. A family would pool its resources by, say, selling some of its landholdings to obtain licenses for one or more members to work in Saudi Arabia. In turn, these members "repatriate" part if not most of their earnings to the family. In some cases the repatriated earnings are enough for the family to establish a business (Cynthia Banzon-Bautista, Chapter 7).

Rural differentiation, it is argued, is driven by changes in the external economic environment beyond the local level. The Green Revolution (combined with the credit institutions that were created to support it) induced changes with regard to laborsaving technology, which in turn led to significant changes in tenancy arrangements (see the Introduction). Development of the triple cropping system in Thailand led to modifications in sharecropping arrangements and increased wage labor (Anan Ganjanapan, Chapter 5). Shifts in the demand for oil may have profound consequences on surplus extraction mechanisms in the rural areas of Indonesia since Indonesia uses oil revenues to subsidize agriculture, particularly rice production. The Indonesian state's strategy of controlling the rural areas via the targeting of subsidies to the rural elite has become more costly over time; with declining oil revenues, this strategy may cease to be effective (Frans Hüsken, Chapter 14).

Furthermore, the process evolves within specific political, historical, and cultural contexts: it is subject to country-specific constraints. In the 1930s, for instance, the British introduced legislation in Malaysia that restricted the transfer of land from Malays to non-Malays. In the long run, this prevented non-Malays, particularly Chinese merchants, from accumulating land, impeded the concentration of landholdings among a small rural elite, and induced a proliferation of small farms. The net effect was to reduce the extent of tenancy (Lim Teck Ghee, Chapter 10). As another example, in order to prevent urban unrest, the Philippine government instituted price controls on rice, the major staple. This induced rural villagers to diversify into other forms of surplus extraction mechanisms (Banzon-Bautista, Chapter 7; Fegan, Chapter 8).

The basic framework of these authors is perhaps best illustrated by Gillian Hart's chapter on state patronage (Chapter 2). Hart emphasizes the dialectical nature of the state's rural sector policies and rural differentiation. He argues that the state seeks to "maintain agrarian control (via patronage of the rural elites) while simultaneously transforming the productive base of rural society" and, in typical Hegelian form, that "State patronage contains the seeds of its own destruction and is likely over the long run to generate threats to the structure of State power and hence new strategies of intervention" (p. 32). He shows, for instance, that state patronage policies in Thailand and Indonesia have induced particular mechanisms for surplus extraction—labor-tying arrangements and unproductive investments (though the particular forms these take differ because of each country's particular political, historical, and cultural forces). Labor-tying arrangements are implicit contracts between large landowners and select landless workers or land-scarce farmers that bind the latter to the landowner at a relatively low wage in return for job security and political support. While useful in maintaining political stability in the short to medium term, these arrangements alienate the rest of the rural community and thus generate the potential for rural unrest in the long run. Unproductive investments include expenditures on social festivities designed to maintain political links with state elites or political support from local citizens. While not stating this explicitly, Hart seems to suggest that such investments may have adverse long-term consequences on rural development which in turn will alter state policies.

As someone solidly trained in the neoclassical tradition, I found the book thought-provoking. It brought out the stark contrast between neoclassical analysis of tenural arrangements and Marxian analysis. I think neoclassical economists can learn something from this volume. Besides providing voluminous information, the book questions the efficiency hypothesis underlying most neoclassical analyses of tenurial arrangements. Could not tenurial arrangements be influenced by political, cultural, and historical factors as well? Could not these factors be the primary forces rather than transactions costs and information asymmetries? Could tenurial arrangements be economically irrational but politically rational? Ironically, I think the book would have had a more profound impact if it contained a chapter on neoclassical theories of tenurial arrangements and another on how these theories might be related to the analyses in the book.

JOSE EDGARDO L. CAMPOS, *University of Pennsylvania*

LATIN AMERICA

Our Daily Bread: The Peasant Question and Family Farming in the Colombian Andes. By Nola Reinhardt. Berkeley: University of California Press, 1988. Pp. xv, 308. $35.00.

Small-scale farming has survived in Latin America long after some had predicted its economic demise. Nola Reinhardt, an economist at Smith College, has set out in this book to explain why that is true in the Andean region of southern Colombia, in an area between Buenaventura on the coast and Cali in the interior. Her own field work, undertaken in the late 1970s and again in the early 1980s, concentrated on El Palmar, a community in the district of Dagua in the department of Valle del Cauca. This book is a wide-ranging inquiry because it not only presents the usual economic data on prices, incomes, costs, and yields, but also investigates family relations and household changes that influence how small-scale farmers make decisions, embrace opportunities, and even suffer failures. From a historical standpoint this book is impressive because it treats the coexistence of peasant and capitalistic agriculture as a dynamic process rather than as a linear one in which estates will eventually and inevitably destroy the small family farms. The author uses her findings to address the future of peasant agriculture, and here her approach is positive but cautious. An economic niche for small-scale farming remains in the Colombian agricultural system, but how it develops and what it achieves will depend on public policy as well as economic need.

Our Daily Bread is not as well organized as it should be for readers who are not specialists. Reinhardt does a fine job of describing the Dagua region in an introduction that precedes Chapter 1 and of assessing the large body of peasant literature, in particular its theoretical underpinnings, in the first chapter. Indeed, her analysis of the "peasant question" is one of the best that I have recently read. The concluding chapter, "Whither the Colombian Family Farm?" which weaves together the theoretical and empirical, is also well done. The chapters in between, however, must be read carefully because they shift back and forth between macro-analysis of Colombia's agricultural system and micro-analysis of El Palmar's system. The extent to which El Palmar or the Dagua district can be used to mirror broad national changes or vice versa is not always clearly explained. For example, in the late 1950s the decline in coffee and pineapple prices caused considerable economic distress in Colombian agriculture for at least a decade. The analysis of El Palmar in the 1960s against the backdrop of what happened to prices in the 1950s shows signs of economic deterioration that led to greater economic differentiation. But the analysis of El Palmar's deterioration focuses on changes in the sizes of the farms and the impact of those changes on the households. On the basis of the evidence presented for El Palmar, it is clear that for some individuals and families, especially among the young, the "economic circumstances . . . were, on the whole, dire" (p. 127). Whether these circumstances arose out of falling commodity prices received by El Palmar farmers is not specifically investigated. We learn a great deal about Colombia's agricultural sector at both levels from this book, but we cannot always be sure what the linkage is.

In tracing the history of the small family farm (actually from the fifteenth century to the 1970s) Reinhardt gives considerable attention to the way in which basically patriarchal households preserve the family holdings. The Chayanovian model, with its emphasis on the willingness of the family farm to "forego rent, profit, and even the market return to family labor" (p. 210), overlooks other behavioral patterns that concern how successful the patriarch was in organizing and exploiting the family labor supply. Clearly some were better than others at such managerial endeavors, and yet those who were most successful may have contributed to the impoverishment of those family members whose labors the patriarchs needed. And the crucial test ahead for many rural patriarchs in El Palmar (and elsewhere if the patriarchal model does apply) is how to accommodate economic and social changes (especially those relating to women) to the dual goal of keeping the family farms intact and of adapting to a more income-based rather than labor-based system of production.

Our Daily Bread must be studied rather than simply read. It contains a wealth of historical and contemporary information that will impress those who are interested in long-term developments or current policy choices. I would also direct the reader's attention to the appendices, in particular Appendix E, because it contains case studies of farmer, workers, and traders. I would add, however, that upon reading these case studies I came away with a distinctly less optimistic outlook concerning the future of the small farm in El Palmar. Perhaps at a later time Reinhardt will bring us up to date.

RICHARD L. GARNER, *Penn State*

UNITED STATES AND CANADA

Science and Medicine in the Old South. Edited by Ronald L. Numbers and Todd L. Savitt. Baton Rouge: Louisiana State University Press, 1989. Pp. xii, 370. $37.50.

This book grew out of the first two Barnard-Millington symposia held under the auspices of the University of Mississippi Center for the Study of Southern Culture in 1982 and 1983. This book on the antebellum South thus contains two distinct parts: the first six essays deal with science, while the remaining nine essays are concerned with medicine and health.

Four essays in Part 1 may be of interest to economic historians. Ronald and Janet Numbers argue that the institution of slavery did not impair scientific inquiry, but their methodology might be flawed. They correlate the number of leaders in the American Association for the Advancement of Science (AAAS) to a number of characteristics and find the strongest association to be with the degree of urbanization. In the North AAAS leaders were concentrated in the older, more settled areas—southern New England and the Middle Atlantic states. With maturation came both increased urbanization and increased scientific interest. In the South that association did not exist, towns did not develop, and Mississippi had as many AAAS leaders as Virginia. The study may confound the effects of slavery and urbanization.

Thomas Dyer studied the evolution of support for science at the University of Georgia. Comparing his results with the results of other studies in the South and Midwest, Dyer concluded that he could find no clear regional difference.

William Scarborough noted substantial accomplishments by several planters who engaged in systematic experimentation to improve crops and also a high degree of intellectual curiosity on the part of other members of the planter elite who were accomplished amateur scientists. He found the diffusion in the South of agricultural technology nonetheless deficient, with the proximate cause being the limited presence in the region of communication links—agricultural societies, farm journals, fairs—along with a dismal level of public education.

Charles Dew investigated the decline of the antebellum iron industry in Virginia. Staying with old equipment, furnaces, and forges, the region found it increasingly difficult to complete. Dew believes that detailed records from one Virginia forge provide insights into the failure to adapt new technology. Since skilled slaves were fully cognizant of their worth and in a position to sabotage output, positive incentives—cash pay for "overwork"—were more effective than the threat of the lash. Customary standards of performance could not be easily changed, which discouraged the adoption of labor-saving innovations.

The essays in Part 2 of the book are generally of high quality but treat topics that will be of interest primarily to medical and cultural historians. Topics include the evolution of regular medical practice, the arguments made for distinctively southern medical schools, the quality of southern insane asylums, domestic medicine, and black folk medicine.

Three essays deal with health status and are linked more clearly to economic conditions. David Patterson pictures the antebellum South as being most unhealthy, partially because of nutritional deficiencies but primarily because of the presence of three diseases of African origin: *falciparum* malaria, hookworm, and yellow fever. In the process of describing public health measures to contain yellow fever, Margaret Warner notes that it was an urban disease that struck new immigrants with especial severity. As knowledge of the horrendous mortality rates of deep southern cities became widespread, urban growth was restrained. Todd Savitt appraises the health of slaves, and the measures taken to deal with their sicknesses. He provides insights into old controversies regarding the adequacy of slave housing and diet.

It should be noted that a book edited by Savitt and James Harvey Young, *Southern Disease and Southern Distinctiveness* (Knoxville, 1988) covers southern health conditions more generally and treats more explicitly the relationship between health and the economy of the region. The Savitt essay appears in both books albeit under different titles. Given the time interval between the symposia and publication it is not surprising that much of the material in this book has been published elsewhere.

MARVIN FISCHBAUM, *Indiana State University*

City Games: The Evolution of American Urban Society and the Rise of Sports. By Steven A. Riess. Champaign: University of Illinois Press, 1989. Pp. xii, 332. $29.95.

City Games is the most recent publication in the very useful Sport and Society series edited by Benjamin Rader and Randy Roberts for the University of Illinois Press. Its author, Steven Riess, has written and edited other works in sports history, as well as serving as editor of the *Journal of Sports History*. Riess's central concerns here are to show that sport "is an institution that has been shaped, reshaped, and further molded by the interplay of the elements comprising the process of urbanization," and that sporting institutions "have themselves deeply influenced urban change, usually for the better, in distinctive and visible ways" (p. 259). While fully sensitive to the circumstances and ideologies affecting the links among sports, recreation, the organization of participant and spectator activities, and the changing nature of urban development, Riess is more positive about them than some other recent writers on the subject.

Although the temporal coverage of *City Games* runs from 1820 to 1980, about three-fourths of the contents deal with the period from 1870 to 1960, described by Riess as the period of the "industrialized radial city." Based primarily on the extensive secondary literature on the topics covered, the strength of the book is in covering a wide range of topics and discussing many questions of historical importance. Cases are drawn from a number of different cities and periods, and, by design, less is said about rural areas and the changes there over time, since the central argument is that the major changes and impacts occurred in the urban areas. Sports are defined broadly to include team and individual games, as well as recreational facilities and organizations. Among the basic questions examined are the different sporting activities of upper, middle, and working classes, including the class composition of baseball players; the different sporting activities of various ethnic and immigrant groups over time, pointing to the early domination of the Irish in baseball and boxing; the changing amounts of space for parks and recreational sites in urban areas and the impact of this on the patterns of recreational activities and municipal finance; and the development of organizations to channel youth sports in socially desired directions. There is a quite interesting chapter on sports, politics, and organized crime, pointing to the differing developments in baseball, boxing, and horse racing, related, in part, to the fact that the legal status of the latter two activities was often uncertain, while the development of baseball in municipal areas was influenced by politics and political decisions, even before the post-World War II changes in the financing of stadium construction. Riess is particulary interesting in his discussion of ethnic issues, as well as in the evaluation of whether to regard the failure of the attempts at urban reforms through sports and recreation as a result of their reaching too few or too many of the target populations, although the relative absence of comparisons with foreign countries and rural areas leaves some interesting questions open.

The issues discussed in *City Games* demonstrate the wide appeal that the study of sports can have for many historians. In addition to economic historians, it has something to say to social and cultural historians, as well as to those interested in ethnic history and urban history, among other areas. Whether or not one finds Riess's arguments as to the centrality of the role of the city in American sports persuasive, *City Games* presents much new analysis and information and is a book that deals in a useful scholarly manner with a quite broad range of issues.

STANLEY L. ENGERMAN, *University of Rochester*

An Empire for Slavery: The Peculiar Institution in Texas, 1821–1865. By Randolph B. Campbell. Baton Rouge: Louisiana State University Press, 1989. Pp. xii, 306. $35.00.

For over a century (beginning with Jeffrey Brackett's *The Negro in Maryland: A Study of the Institution of Slavery* in 1889), historians have been writing book-length accounts of slavery in individual states. But few can rival the competence and completeness of Randolph Campbell's effort. The publication of *An Empire for Slavery* virtually completes the picture of slavery on the state level. Only Delaware (with but 1,798 slaves in 1860) awaits a history of its slaveholding system.

Campbell early on seeks to dispel the popular misconception that Texas was not really a southern state but rather a western one, with no significant ties with the older slave states to the east nor any strong commitment to the institution of slavery. Accordingly, he argues very convincingly that while Texas was the newest of the slave states, with less than 5 percent of the South's slave population in the 1860 federal population census, its ties to the system were indeed strong. Seventy-seven percent of the heads of households in 1860 (one-fourth of whom were slaveowners) were southern born, many of these having migrated to Texas with their slaves and all the aspects of a mature slave system. Too, although the geographical extent of slaveholding included only the eastern two-fifths of the state by 1860, this was an area as large as Alabama and Mississippi combined, making it "virtually an empire for slavery" (p. 2). And the proportion of slaveholders and slaves in Texas (30 percent of the total population in 1860) was comparable to that of Virginia, oldest of the slaveholding states.

Economically, Campbell finds slavery in Texas to have been profitable: investments in slaves brought at least the earnings (6 to 8 percent) of northern investments in stocks and bonds. Moreover, the hiring out of slaves in the 1850s in Texas (which seems to have been done rather extensively) brought 15 percent of their valuation annually to their owners, twice the rate of northern investments. Too, he supports Robert Fogel and Stanley Engerman's contention in *Time on the Cross* (Boston, 1974) (and reaffirmed in Fogel's *Without Consent or Contract: The Rise and Fall of American Slavery* [New York, 1989]) that slave labor was more efficient than free labor would have been—had it been available—because the slaves were forced to work with more intensity than free laborers would have been willing to do. Texas, Campbell feels, was destined to be primarily an agricultural state with little development of industry, banking, and commerce whatever labor system was used. The development of large cotton plantations, self-sufficient in food production and operating with the slave gang labor system, served to make it only more so.

In the noneconomic aspects of slavery, Campbell devotes chapters to the material conditions and physical treatment of Texan slaves and to their family life, slave culture, and behavioral patterns and desire for freedom, all of which are quite well done. However, his understanding of each of these would surely have profited from a careful reading of Charles Joyner's *Down by the Riverside*, published in 1984 (Urbana) and called by George Rawick "the finest work ever written on American slavery." Almost as disturbing to me was the absence of any reference to the superb studies of Philip Morgan, who for the last 10 to 15 years has been one of the most productive and insightful students of American slavery.

These two omissions aside, *An Empire for Slavery* is a solid work, based on exhaustive research in dozens of manuscript collections in 17 separate depositories, numerous newspapers, county court and probate records, manuscript censuses, published primary sources, books, articles, and theses and dissertations. It is well crafted, tightly argued (with numerous supportive tables, maps, and appendices), very readable, and should immediately join ranks as one of the best histories of slavery yet written.

JAMES M. CLIFTON, *Southeastern Community College, North Carolina*

Free Love: Marriage and Middle-Class Radicalism in America, 1825–1860. By John C. Spurlock. New York: New York University Press, 1989. Pp. xiv, 277. $40.00, cloth; $15.00, paper.

John Spurlock's study of love and marriage in nineteenth-century America puts him in company with those historians who place the formation of a self-conscious and identifiable "middle class" in the antebellum period of American history. Spurlock argues, as have other scholars, that the middle class was defined more by particular values than by residence or occupation. Individual liberty and social equality were its values, and character was measured in terms of respectability and authenticity. He sees middle-class "radicalism" as both an outgrowth and a critique of these values that underlay the new middle class. For instance, marriage and family life ideally cultivated these values, but like many other institutions of the early nineteenth century, marriage came under attack by reformers and perfectionists. Radical reformers believed that marriage corrupted true love and inhibited individual freedom. Thus, those who advocated "free love" were, in fact, idealists who were striving for a perfect human community here on earth.

Spurlock notes that the utopian communities established by the followers of Owenism, Transcendentalism, and Fourierism offered an active challenge to middle-class social values, especially marriage. All three movements questioned basic assumptions of middle-class society, including its forms of family life. In addition, the nature of communal life brought marriage into question, and discussion of every aspect of life, including family life, pervaded the discourse of all of these experimental communities. Spurlock, in his effort to show the influence of these movements, notes that thousands of Americans read the socialist and transcendentalist publications, lived in communities, and questioned the middle-class consensus.

Revivalism and perfectionism provided a spiritual source of attack on marriage. Spurlock explains that while conversion *could* transform marriage into a religious vocation, for a minority, "the intense personal experience of redemption made the compromises of middle-class life seem intolerable'' (p. 73). Marriage, like intemperance and slavery, became an unnecessary evil for at least a minority of the spiritual converts.

By the 1850s marriage was so important a topic and the criticism of it came from so many sources that, according to Spurlock, an emphasis on ''individual sovereignty'' quite naturally implied a new attitude toward marriage. Free love first appeared in the community of Modern Times in New York, where pioneers gathered to test individual sovereignty in a practical setting. The Modern Times experiment gave the counterculture of free love its basic ideology. Throughout the 1850s sovereignty of the individual remained the rationale for the society envisioned by those who rejected marriage: ''The ultimate expression of middle-class radicalism was free love—the repudiation of any relations between man and woman that violated the individual sovereignty of either'' (p. 139).

Spurlock explains that free love radicalism declined after the Civil War, when the radicals lost their connections to the more moderate reformers and found themselves faced with a middle class committed to postwar nationalism and a narrowing sense of individual liberty, reflected in the Comstock Law and the various purity crusades of the late nineteenth century. Also, a new class-based economic radicalism further marginalized the free love radicals. Then, at the turn of the century new arguments for sexual liberty, based on the bohemian lifestyle of New York's Greenwich Village, made them increasingly irrelevant.

Spurlock's study is based upon the writings of free love radicals and other reformers of the nineteenth century. He makes good use of secondary sources, and, indeed, the student of antebellum reform movements will find most of the material quite familar. In his attempt to define ''middle class'' Spurlock relies heavily on the work of Stuart Blumin, Steven Mintz, Mary Ryan, and Burton Bledstein. But Spurlock never really makes clear to what extent the defining values are distinct attributes of the middle class. Finally, the connection between the middle class and the free love radicals is suggested but never clearly established. That is, the reader never gets a strong sense that middle-class families were greatly affected by the ideology of free love, or that the lifestyles of the communitarians really challenged the basis of married life in antebellum America. The problem is not unique. The most difficult part of writing about social movements of any kind is trying to measure their impact on the dominant culture. Spurlock offers an interesting attempt, and, in addition, provides an organizational schema which explains the roots of nineteenth-century free love radicalism, as well as the reasons for its decline.

WINIFRED D. WANDERSEE, *Hartwick College*

The Barrow Family and the Barataria and Lafourche Canal: The Transportation Revolution in Louisiana, 1829–1925. By Thomas A. Becnel. Baton Rouge: Louisiana State University Press, 1989. Pp. xii, 202. $27.50.

By the 1830s the flat, fertile, alluvial land-area north of the Gulf and west of the Mississippi River, interspersed with lakes and bayous in Louisiana, was sugar cane country. Where so many natural channels for water transport came free it was inevitable that planters, many of whom operated on impressive scales with work forces sometimes running into hundreds of slaves, would seek access to market—specifically to New Orleans—via canal. Such was the genesis of the Barataria and Lafourche Canal Company in 1829. At a time when enthusiasm for canal construction across the country was still intense but showing signs of modification as a result of the prospects of railroad transportation, the presence of so many lakes, bayous, and rivers slowed the shifting of interest in Louisiana from canals to railroads.

Like other states at the time, Louisiana generously subsidized transportation facilities within its borders including the Barataria and LaFourche Canal Company. Long after other states abandoned the policy of public aid to internal improvements, the state of Louisiana continued its support of the Canal Company over a period of 30 years until it reached a point where the company's obvious failure to complete the project in its entirety precluded further subsidy. Then a new company under the control of Robert R. Barrow bought the badly built, incomplete, inadequately dredged channel for a price that was far below the state's input alone. The canal remained in Barrow hands, father's then son's, until 1925, when it was taken over by the U.S. government to constitute part of the Gulf Intracoastal Waterway that crosses Louisiana.

This is essentially a study of private entrepreneurship where the corporate structure was a facade: a tale of two buccaneering, planter-businessmen, neither with more than a third-grade education. In his day Barrow senior made the most unscrupulous carpetbagger appear the soul of probity and ethical behavior. Junior, in his, could have held his own with any scoundrel of the Gilded Age. Both father and son were ruthless with competitors, calculatingly deceitful with creditors, regularly brutal with all those unfortunate enough to be engaged with them in any kind of business or financial relationship, including wives, children, and in-laws. The tale is not edifying. Yet for two generations father and son kept the canal business functioning and their plantations producing at times with sufficient success so that they lived lives of relative affluence until overtaken by conditions that they were incapable of handling.

Thomas Becnel is best in his analysis of the transportation needs of the Attakapas district which the canal was designed to serve and with the problems of topography and engineering that both canal and railroad builders confronted. His discussion of Barrow junior's involvement with the U.S. Corp of Engineers and the ultimate takeover of the canal by the federal government under desperate circumstances is also clearly rendered. He is far less successful in reaching a clear assessment of the canal as an enterprise. He is short on data and has only spotty information on costs and revenues. He makes no estimate of the impact of the enterprise on the region that the canal served. His emphasis, therefore, is excessively personal and familial, and, occasionally, he descends to the trivial.

Nevertheless, a clear message emerges from this account of business in Louisiana's cane country extending over a period of almost a hundred years: that the Barrows' view of business included the right to use to their exclusive advantage the state, local, and federal governments; the courts, debtors, and creditors; politicians; and family as they saw fit. Theirs was a particularly tawdry version of the American dream and how it might be realized, no doubt shared by vast numbers of their fellow Americans across the country.

NATHAN MILLER, *University of Wisconsin, Milwaukee*

Poverty, Ethnicity, and the American City, 1840–1925: Changing Conceptions of the Slum and the Ghetto. By David Ward. New York: Cambridge University Press, 1989. Pp. xiv, 263. $39.50, cloth; $13.95, paper.

Following almost two decades after the publication of his earlier monograph, *Cities and Immigrants* (New York, 1971), David Ward's newest book represents a return to old and familiar territory by one of the most respected urban historical geographers of the modern era.

Poverty, Ethnicity, and the American City is structured into an introduction and five substantive chapters which in turn are grouped into two parts. This organization suits the essential purpose of the book, which Ward sees as determining "how changing conceptions of the relationships between migrants and their urban environment influenced interpretations of that experience" (p. 9). Part 1, "The Relationships Formulated,'' deals with the initial recognition, between 1840 and 1875, of slums and their residents by philanthropists, charity workers, reformers, journalists, progressives, and urban planners; the struggle to define slums which took place between 1875 and 1900; and the redefinition of slums as ghettos which occurred between 1900 and 1925. In Part 2, ''The Relationships Reformulated,'' Ward examines the immigrant experience from the perspective of two social scientific groups—the Chicago School of Sociology in the 1920s and 1930s and the more recent writings of revisionist scholars from many disciplines. The result is a well-researched and well-documented synthesis of works pertaining to both the perceptions about and realities associated with the experience of migrants in urban America from the start of mass migration around 1840 until the passage of immigration restrictions in 1923–1924. *Poverty, Ethnicity, and the American City* stands as a useful contribution to our understanding of the structure, role, and character of the American inner-city neighborhood.

Ward's synthesis stems from a careful reading of an impressive body of literature. Many elements in this corpus of work—the role of the progressives, the nature of late nineteenth-century housing and land reforms, and the work of the Chicago School, to name but three—already have come under careful scholarly scrutiny. The value of Ward's contribution lies in the breadth of his approach and his success in marshaling such a diverse literature to tackle a complex and worthwhile issue.

While it would be difficult to quarrel with the nobility of Ward's effort to deal with an important topic about which we know too little, the book is not without some flaws. For one, it is written in a surprisingly pedestrian style. The vocabulary is not especially challenging and the sentence structure lacks the crispness and imagination of Ward's earlier publications. To put it bluntly, too many sentences in this book, sometimes as many as six or seven in a row, begin with ''The,'' ''This,'' or ''These,'' resulting in a difficult book to read from cover to cover. One wonders if this is not a residual effect of years spent in administration.

Ward includes 46 illustrations in this book. While he is careful to discuss the meaning of each in his text, the quality of the illustrations is not so uniform. The graphs and diagrams that are included were not redrawn for this book and some are less useful as a result. A few of the photographs suffer from a lack of sharpness. None of the illustrations is original to this volume, which stands in marked contrast to Ward's earlier publications. Surely a fresh schematic ''model'' could have been drawn to summarize the new insights that Ward verbally provides into our understanding of inner-city neighborhoods.

In spite of these shortcomings, *Poverty, Ethnicity, and the American City* is a useful addition to scholarly research dealing with life in American cities. Ward's sensitivity both to neighborhoods as living places and to their residents as individuals who were capable of responding in different ways to similar circumstances is commendable. This book should be read by all who share an interest in such concerns.

MICHAEL J. DOUCET, *Ryerson Polytechnical Institute*

Capitalist Collective Action: Competition, Cooperation, and Conflict in the Coal Industry. By John R. Bowman. New York: Cambridge University Press, 1989. Pp. xvii, 253. $37.50.

John Bowman is a Marxist scholar trained at the University of Chicago. In this book, a revision of his 1984 doctoral dissertation, he employs standard Marxist paradigms plus the tools of industrial organization economics (especially the ''New I.O.,'' which emphasizes game theory), to analyze competitive patterns in the U.S. bituminous coal industry from the 1880s to 1940. The result is an insightful study more important for its innovative methodology than its substantive findings.

Bowman argues that while capitalism does indeed array workers against capitalists, it also compels capitalists to fight each other in competitive markets. He believes that by closely analyzing specific competitive situations, scholars "can achieve a richer understanding of a political reality that includes cleavages among capitalists, and alliances between workers and capitalists, as well as conflict between workers and capitalists" (p. xii). Bowman's overall concern here "is with organizational solutions to capitalist collective action problems" (p. 33). Such solutions, when they can be worked out successfully, permit effective competition among companies but still enable them to act cooperatively in their common interest.

Given its structure, the bituminous coal industry affords an appropriate setting for such a study. It has low entry barriers yet high fixed costs. Its product is a commodity, yet one with several hundred different grades. The industry is plagued with extreme cyclicality owing to derived demand and variations in weather. It exhibits strikingly different cost patterns across numerous firms, depending on location, strip versus shaft mining, and quality of coal. It is staffed by a large and militant work force whose degree of unionization was almost as cyclical as the demand for its product.

Bowman begins his book with two methodological chapters which, considering that he is a political scientist and not an economist, exhibit an impressive grasp of industrial organization. Here he lays out a predictive game-theoretic model addressed to the "principal collective action problem faced by capitalist firms" (p. 30). This problem is not how to organize against the workers but rather how firms themselves can keep their own markets sufficiently stable so that the behavior of participants is predictable and profits are high enough for all to prosper. The structure of the bituminous coal industry, a notoriously "sick" patient during most of the period covered, created a situation in which the incentive for collective action persisted at a high level, yet the inducement to defect from price, wage, and output agreements remained even higher. Hence, there ensued a chronic Prisoner's Dilemma and a decades-long quest for stability.

Bowman posits a hierarchy of preferred solutions, ranging from agreements internal to the industry (which failed because of divergent interests among northern, midwestern, and southern operators); price and wage agreements enforced by the United Mine Workers (one chapter is charmingly titled "Workers Organize Capitalists"); and, as a last resort, government action. Both operators and workers typically appealed to the government in crisis situations, most notably the Great Depression. Bowman perceptively argues that, while government intervention was much the most effective disciplinary device, it also represented the one most hazardous to the interests of capitalists. It introduced the possibility that "hostile actors" (workers and consumers) would gain influence over policy, and it "deprive[d] individual firms of their dominant defection strategy" (p. 237), the power to cut prices and wages.

Given the inherent drama of the story and Bowman's manifest talent as a writer, his tale might easily have been made vivid and exciting. Yet throughout its length, the book proceeds on an unnecessarily abstract level. The "firm" is never a flesh-and-blood entity with a particular kind of management and a certain number of employees. Instead, it is a disembodied player in an abstracted game. The word "capitalist" occurs hundreds of times, but not a single actual capitalist is ever delineated. In chronicling the history of the industry, the author relies too heavily on a small number of sources, principally the trade journal *Coal Age*. In Chapter 6, 74 of the 84 citations are to this single source, a circumstance that in one stretch of footnotes produces 35 consecutive ibid.'s.

At times Bowman's argument seems overconceptualized, his Marxist and game-theoretic apparatus constituting superfluous embellishments of a straightforward story. Yet the model here is extremely useful and may well be widely generalizable. Thus it is a pity that additional commentary on comparable research sites is almost entirely absent. Reading this book, one is repeatedly struck by potential parallels with agriculture, oil and gas, cotton textiles, and the garment trade. In each of these, internal efforts to organize markets persistently failed, and external forces—grain and cotton exchanges, labor unions, government agencies—were brought into the game. Bowman hardly refers at all to any of these parallels except for a single cursory passage about the garment trade. Nor does he explore the history of the coal industry in other countries, despite the rich and convenient secondary literature on coal in Britain and Germany. Overall, therefore, this is a very good book that might easily have been an even better one.

THOMAS K. MCCRAW, *Harvard University*

The Samuel Gompers Papers. Vol. 3: *Unrest and Depression, 1891–94*. Edited by Stuart B. Kaufman and Peter J. Albert. Champaign: University of Illinois Press, 1989. Pp. xxxii, 764. $49.95.

The Samuel Gompers Papers project, housed at the University of Maryland under the editorship of Stuart Kaufman and Peter Albert, is a massive attempt to collect and disseminate the Gompers documents. This is the third volume of a subset of these documents selected and annotated by the editors for print. (The first two volumes were edited by Kaufman alone.) The first volume, *The Making of a Union Leader, 1850–1886* (Champaign, 1986), covered Gompers's early life up to his election as president of the newly formed American Federation of Labor (AFL) [see this JOURNAL, 47 (June 1987), pp. 570–71]. Volume 2, *The Early Years of the American Federation of Labor, 1887–1890* (Champaign, 1987), covered AFL relations with the Knights of Labor and socialist parties plus the eight-hour day movement [see this JOURNAL, 48 (Dec. 1988), pp. 975–76].

This third volume picks up on these themes in displaying documents relating Gompers to the Populist movement. While the documents, primarily letters from Gompers, are arranged chronologically, each section emphasizes its particular theme. In addition to Gompers's views on populist movements, other themes covered are the labor upheavals of 1892, Gompers's role in the arbitration of labor disputes, the depression of the 1890s, the AFL's political program, and the Pullman strike.

Over and over again in his letters, articles, and speeches Gompers emphasized the need for a labor movement free from political parties, the peculiar role of the AFL as a governing body, the righteous struggle for the eight-hour day, and the common interests of the working person, whether male or female, black or white (but not Chinese). He appeared optimistic on the chances of the eight-hour movement and respectful of his loss of the AFL presidency. The letters remind us of the number of sincere and interesting actors involved in the formation of the modern American labor movement. Examples include John McBride, head of the United Mine Workers, who defeated Gompers for the AFL presidency, and George Norton, who worked to organize black workers along the Ohio and Mississippi rivers. We find also a record of both the gains labor achieved and the constant pummeling those gains faced by business, trade associations, and the government, as well as jurisdictional disputes by other labor organizations.

As in the previous volumes, each section is introduced by an informative but brief essay and the volume itself is introduced by a piece outlining the major themes. Annotated footnotes following each document are one of the best features, working to define the actors and placing the documents in some context. The glossary profiles the major and minor actors and organizations. A warning, however, is in order. While the volume stands on its own, there is only a hint of its place in the Samuel Gompers Papers project. For information on the project and what the published volumes contain and lack, the reader is forced to refer back to the first volume. Volume 3 of *The Samuel*

Gompers Papers provides a convenient, if somewhat incomplete, reference tool for researchers and good reading for students looking for topics to research.

IRA N. GANG, *Rutgers University*

The Automobile Industry and its Workers: Between Fordism and Flexibility. Edited by Steven Tolliday and Jonathan Zeitlin. New York: St. Martin's Press, 1987. Pp. viii, 335. $45.00.

To the degree that auto manufacturing has become a truly international industry, only a comparative analysis can capture its global dynamics. Accordingly, Steven Tolliday and Jonathan Zeitlin have collected detailed studies of work organization and labor relations in the United States, western Europe, and Japan.

To provide continuity, the editors have divided their collection into three chronological sections. Part 1, "The Rise of Fordism" (1896–1939), indicates the degree to which European automakers adapted Fordist practice to suit their national markets; Part 2, "Industrial Relations in the Age of Fordism" (1945–1975), examines the contrasting labor relations systems in Europe, the United States, and Japan; and Part 3, "Beyond Fordism?" focuses on current strategies for restructuring work and redefining labor relations in each of these varied settings.

Tolliday establishes the critical themes in Part 1 with his opening essay on "Management and Labour in Britain." Here, Morris and Austin adapted Fordist methods to their own unique variant of volume production. Both companies introduced specialized machine tools but primarily to increase the quality of machined parts rather than their quantity; both also subdivided tasks, but cycle times were longer, and body work in particular required skill and labor-intensive methods.

Above all, both companies sought greater productivity, not through close supervision and high day wages, but through piece-work incentive systems that allowed greater self-supervision. Unions did not veto the Fordist alternative; they could not, as Tolliday indicates, since union density in the auto industry was generally quite low. The market was the determining factor: as elsewhere in Europe, restricted demand for varied and well-equipped cars required production flexibility at relatively low volumes. Ford's capital-intensive methods were too expensive and too rigid.

The essays in Part 2 link the contrasting production systems in Europe and America with their equally divergent labor-relations systems. In Italy and Britain unionized workers established a decentralized and steward-based bargaining presence by the late 1960s and early 1970s, in contrast to a more centralized and bureaucratic system in the United States. While Nelson Lichtenstein identifies the latter with the United Auto Workers' declining ability—and will—to defend the shop-floor power of its stewards, Tolliday and Zeitlin argue that American labor historians underestimate the "job control" inherent in the UAW's seniority and job classification systems and overestimate the durability of steward-based job control in Italy and Britain. Ultimately, the steward's leverage was so dependent on piece-rate bargaining that when management moved toward measured day rates in the 1970s, union power declined accordingly.

In Japan yet another system prevailed, as described in Reiko Okayama's study of enterprise unionism at Toyota. Okayama chronicles the strike-breaking efforts in the early 1950s that favored company-dominated unions, but he also examines human-relations techniques and company efforts to redefine foremen as managers rather than skilled workers. With this redefinition, the foreman's role in the all-grades enterprise union shifted toward a pro-management posture.

Koichi Shimokawa's following essay, "Product and Labor Strategies in Japan," obscures this history: unions, he says, simply "realized" the virtues of company growth and cooperative relations. Noting the absence of union work rules and strikes since

1953, he insists "this is not due to weakness on the part of the labour unions" (p. 242), an assertion the reader will have to ponder in light of Shimokawa's earlier acknowledgment that foremen predominate in union leadership.

Shimokawa is more persuasive when he argues that cooperative labor-management relations are a precondition of just-in-time (JIT) manufacturing. JIT, he argues, is not a mere inventory-control measure, for it "also plays an important role in uncovering waste of time and materials" (p. 233). By generating "unavoidable pressures to maximize uptime," workers are "compelled to try to thoroughly eliminate waste" (p. 235). Since the system's intended vulnerabilities demand continual diligence from workers, JIT also "necessitates . . . loyalty to the company and a very low rate of absenteeism" (p. 235).

It remains to be determined what the *negotiated* basis of cooperation will be in European and American plants. Several of the essays in Part 3 attempt a prognosis, with varying results. Harry Katz's mid-1980s assessment that the Big Three's recovery "will depend heavily" (p. 300) on work-rule changes and new forms of work organization does not describe the subsequent performance of Ford—which devoted less attention to these matters than General Motors but gained market share by developing successful products and operating at full capacity.

Even so, Katz and other contributors to Part 3 amply demonstrate the complexities of the auto industry's current restructuring. Alternative proposals for new work organization confront the conflicting agendas of corporate officers, plant managers, union leaders, skilled tradesmen, and production workers, all bound by national cultures and political-economic structures that confound easy generalization. Among its many merits, this collection of essays makes a substantial contribution toward understanding the global dimensions of that evolutionary process.

STEVE BABSON, *Wayne State University*

Accumulation and Power: An Economic History of the United States. By Richard B. DuBoff. Armonk, NY: M. E. Sharpe, Inc., 1989. Pp. xii, 223. $38.50.

As the title may suggest, this work relates a highly interpretive economic history of the United States. The author takes an explicitly nonneoclassical perspective shaded with Marxian allusion and Keynesian thought. In a peculiar synthesis of macroeconomic and interpretive history, Richard DuBoff presents the American economic record as the story of relentless profit seeking by corporations. Although more convincing for the twentieth than the nineteenth century, the book does not quite succeed at supplying both a general economic history and an interpretive analysis.

DuBoff uses the first chapter to state forthrightly his view of the "flow of economic history," which he claims differs "radically" from that of new economic and business historians. For DuBoff, "the *purpose* of the new economic history has been to show how the American economy achieved its size and efficiency through a process of 'free,' unregulated decisionmaking" (p. 3, emphasis mine). This may surprise readers who thought the new economic history's innovation had more to do with explicit modeling of historical hypotheses and the empirical testing of their implications. New business historians (read Alfred Chandler) receive similar treatment, DuBoff seeing the "strategy and structure" theme as the complement of the "market rationality" presumption of new economic history. Instead, DuBoff argues that the capitalist goals of accumulation and monopolization, as pursued by corporations, dictated the dynamics of American economic history. Succeeding chapters only partially fulfill promises to explore the social implications of these dynamics.

For a radical interpretive history, the next three chapters tell a surprisingly familiar, if incomplete, tale of the nineteenth century. Beginning with a market-oriented mercantile economy in the years before 1840, the railroad and telegraph expanded markets and began the transition from small-scale manufacturing to larger firms. Indeed, we learn that the telegraph sparked "spectacular reduction[s] in intermarket price differentials, information costs, and transactions costs" (p. 21). Apparently, new economic historians have ignored such phenomena. The author takes exception to the traditional view of the Grand Traverse that explains the large savings and investment ratios of the late nineteenth century by the rise in personal savings due to innovation in financial intermediation (p. 30). DuBoff prefers a story in which investment demand generates heightened income and savings, but he cites for support economic historians Moses Abramovitz, Paul David, and Jeffrey Williamson (pp. 31–32). Unfortunately the story leaves much out: the labor movement receives a four-line paragraph (p. 34); farmers and small business played a role in the Interstate Commerce Act, but, apparently, in little else. This is one of the major disappointments: the book neglects important political and economic phenomena to the point of suggesting that big business arose unopposed, occasionally assisted by a compliant government.

The three chapters discussing the inherent cyclical crises of American capitalism in the twentieth century form the strongest portion of the book. Indeed, these three chronological chapters treat the crisis theme so consistently that DuBoff gives each the same title, "Investment, Growth, Instability." A growth-producing process (usually led by investment) characterizes the up side of the cycle. DuBoff illustrates with electrification and automobiles in the 1920s, government investment in the form of the military and the national highway system in the 1950s and 1960s, and debt-financed, consumption-oriented growth in both the private and public sectors in the 1970s and 1980s. Excess capacity and crisis characterize the second stage of the cycle. The 1930s provide easy examples; while government spending tended to forestall such episodes thereafter, the relatively severe recessions of the mid-1970s and early 1980s attest to capitalism's inherent tendency toward crisis. DuBoff documents the argument with a full panoply of statistics. Unfortunately, the description sometimes overshadows the theme. In spite of occasional assertions about the decisive role of corporations in determining investment and consumption flows, the link between the dynamic of the economy and corporate organization is weak. Here the macroeconomic view could benefit from a micro-level perspective.

The arguments of inherent overproduction in a capitalist economy and the government's assistance in resolving business problems come together most closely in the single chapter on foreign trade and investment. From the search for markets at the turn of the century; to political and economic dominance through the Marshall Plan, the North Atlantic Treaty Organization, and Bretton Woods; to the loss of influence in the face of revitalized Japan and Europe (particularly the Europe of 1992); DuBoff tells this part of the story well. The decision to confine the international discussion to a single chapter gives the author a chance to review previous themes while telling the story in a tight, organized fashion.

DuBoff concludes that the social problems of the corporate political economy persist because government plays a relatively small role in the U.S. economy. Where Joseph Schumpeter and Chandler see positive net benefits to the process of corporate "creative destruction," DuBoff questions their social arithmetic. Because of low levels of government involvement, the U.S. economy faces the contradiction of high per capita incomes and low job security, relatively unequal income distribution, high poverty incidence, low life expectancy, high infant mortality, and so on. "If the analysis in the preceding chapters holds," DuBoff can explain all this by "the nature and exercise of corporate power" (p. 185). Unfortunately, the analysis is incomplete and unconvincing. DuBoff paints a macroeconomic history of the United States with a Marxist brush. But he has *not* explained the process by which corporate activity leads to the social contradiction described in this chapter. Ultimately, his indictment rests on circumstantial evidence.

True to the dialectical method, this book contains a number of contradictions. It aspires to be "an economic history of the United States," but it essentially neglects the role of small business, agriculture, labor, and politics. At least in the first half, the book attacks the perspective of the new economic historians, but it relies on their quantitative (and, occasionally, interpretive) results. The author wants to place the profit-seeking behavior of corporations at the center of the story, but he ends by making weak inferences about their relationship to a fairly familiar macroeconomic history. Those who prefer to teach American economic history from a Marxist, or "alternative," perspective should consider this book, but they will only want to use it in conjunction with more detailed works.

CHRISTOPHER GRANDY, *Barnard College*

Liberty, Property, and Government: Constitutional Interpretation Before the New Deal. Edited by Ellen Frankel Paul and Howard Dickman. Albany: State University of New York Press, 1989. Pp. viii, 303. $57.50, cloth; $18.95, paper.

Like the return of the living dead in one of George Romero's "campy" horror flicks, the ghosts of laissez-faire constitutionalism are again stalking the land. Efforts to resurrect doctrines of economic liberty buried 50 years ago by the New Deal Supreme Court cannot be dismissed lightly, because the shifting composition of the federal judiciary portends a sympathetic reception of ideological positions on the right. Moreover, the proponents of a new-style, old legality are turning ambiguities in the intellectual legacy of the free-wheeling Earl Warren Supreme Court era to advantage. The revival of long-rejected notions of the Constitution's contract, commerce, due process, and "takings" clauses is drawing strength from recent rulings which gave those clauses new meaning on behalf of minorities and other disadvantaged groups. Now, the warnings of the Warren court's critics about needs for greater judicial craftsmanship are coming back to haunt its liberal defenders as reactionaries attempt to dismantle the welfare state.

Liberty, Property, and Government is a book about the use of history in this policy debate over the proper balance of power between the protection of private rights and the promotion of the public welfare. Stretching back to the framers, this controversy gives expression to fundamental issues of who rules the state and for what purposes. The eight essays contained in the volume revolve around the new-fashioned, laissez-faire position of Richard Epstein. His contribution here on the commerce clause complements his earlier work on the power of eminent domain, the so-called takings provisions. He goes much further than simply calling for a rollback of constitutional interpretation to pre-1936 days; he would like to relegate government completely to the sidelines of the economic arena. According to Epstein, the founders and succeeding generations of Americans leading up to the New Deal intended to limit government to an umpire's role, allowing it to act only to protect the individual from "force or fraud" in the marketplace (p. 162).

Either directly or indirectly, the other seven authors show that Epstein has callously abused history. While the bench and bar have made a common practice of skewing interpretations of our legal heritage, Epstein's brand of history descends to a new and dangerous level of anti-intellectualism. As Harry Scheiber contends in his essay on evolving concepts of eminent domain, Epstein and fellow advocates of laissez faire "make a wise move when they largely block history out" (p. 217). Scheiber and the other authors agree that economic liberty in the American experience has meaning only within a context of a constant tension between individual property rights and community values. In a concise and useful summary of his previous studies of the takings clauses, Scheiber demonstrates that scholars must look beyond the often mythical rhetoric of the black letter law to investigate the law in action. Glen Robinson also makes a direct attack on the conservative's myopic, one-sided view of the framers' intent. His essay on the due process clause provides a reasoned explanation of why the search for the "original" meaning of the Constitution represents a "misguided strategy. . . . It really comes down to a choice of fictions" (pp. 66–68). While Robinson is sympathetic to conservative efforts to root social stability in constitutional notions of fundamental values, he believes that this search must be based on a concept of historical continuity as an evolving process of democratic choice.

Three contributions to the book indirectly dispute Epstein's use of history by offering case studies that follow Robinson's alternative approach. Alan Jones examines the constitutional politics of the railroad in the Midwest during the middle of the nineteenth century, and Tony Freyer evaluates the antitrust movement during its closing years. Both focus on republicanism as a powerful counterweight to doctrines of laissez faire. In an excellent piece of original research, Jones shows how midwesterners gave contemporary meaning to the revolutionary ideology of the founders. Echoing President Andrew Jackson's battle against the bank, farmers and local merchants used the power of government to curb perceived abuses of the common welfare by private business interests. Freyer's analysis of antitrust law from 1880 to 1925 reinforces the idea that there has been an ebb and flow in the constitutional balance of power. Building on William Letwin's work on the Antitrust Act of 1890, he details how contemporaries adapted traditional, republican values to the needs of a modern economy dominated by large scale, corporate enterprise. Paul Murphy's essay neatly assesses the contributions of Oliver Wendell Holmes, Louis Brandeis, and Roscoe Pound to this evolutionary process.

Two additional pieces underscore the importance of history in the current policy debate on the proper balance of power. Harold Hyman sheds new light on the 1873 bench mark *Slaughterhouse* decision by illuminating the interdependence between economic liberty and civil rights. His ingenious reinterpretation of this multifaceted case shows how the postwar ascendancy of laissez-faire economics contributed to an atrophy of constitutional safeguards of individual rights for African-Americans, women, and other minority groups. A century later, according to Mary Porter, a similar rising tide of conservatism threatens to reverse the Warren court's extension of civil rights to disadvantaged groups. Its open-ended use of substantive due process to embrace the "new property" of government entitlements sets precedents that may now be employed to produce just the opposite results. It is ironic that perhaps the most important legacy of the *Slaughterhouse* ruling was Justice Samuel Miller's warning to avoid turning the court into a "perpetual censor" of a democratic society's evolving policy preferences.

HAROLD L. PLATT, *Loyola University of Chicago*

Frontier and Metropolis: Regions, Cities, and Identities in Canada Before 1914. By J. M. S. Careless. Toronto: University of Toronto Press, 1989. Pp. xiii, 132. $22.50.

In a career spanning more than four decades J. M. S. Careless has been one of the best-known and most influential scholars of Canadian history. In 1987 he presented the Donald Creighton Lectures at the University of Toronto. This slim volume comprises those three lectures, as well as an edited version of a fourth lecture presented at the University of Victoria. Together, they provide Careless with a forum for outlining the broad themes which have guided his research career.

The key word in this volume, as it has been throughout his work, is metropolitanism. Careless emphasizes the pivotal role played by dominant metropolitan centers in shaping the historical development of particular regions and of Canada itself. Cities, of course, do not exist without a hinterland. Careless feels that frontierism and metropolitanism should not be viewed separately, but that we should recognize the reciprocal links between the two. In this relationship metropolitanism is neither naturally benign nor naturally exploitive, but some of each. He disagrees with those who have ascribed to the frontier the key role in shaping history. In Canada, especially, he maintains, frontier expansion was quite capital-intensive and therefore strongly directed by metropolitan forces. Those on the frontier were not economically self-reliant but depended vitally on trade. Careless devotes much of the second lecture to discussing how his conception of Canadian history differs from the perspectives of other leading Canadian historians. Harold Innis (and staple theory) is mentioned only in passing, but S. D. Clark, A. R. M. Lower, D. Creighton, and W. L. Morton are discussed at greater length. While there are no footnotes or bibliography, some brief mention of their major works is made in the text.

Much of the book is devoted to describing the development of regional and national identities. In a country which might aspire to the world record for the longest-running identity crisis (p. 70), this is laudable. Cities become the foci of regional identity. While their own hinterlands may rebel against them, these cities become the self-proclaimed centers of regional protest. Several cities may serve this role for a particular region; due to shared grievances Atlantic Canada develops a regional identity despite having no one dominant metropolis.

Development of a national identity must also occur across a number of cities and is limited by the existence of a small number of large cities, each with different regional loyalties.

Careless notes in the foreword that he is aiming for the big picture and may be in error in some particulars. One example must suffice. In attributing the defensive-assertive nature of French Canadian identity to the predominance of English-speaking people in Quebec's largest city in the nineteenth century, Careless is likely at least partly correct. In severely downplaying the role of the rural habitant in that period, however, he seems to ignore the fact that Quebec was over 80 percent rural at Confederation and saw substantial rural-urban migration thereafter.

The final chapter shifts the focus from the nineteenth to the seventeenth and eighteenth centuries. Students of Canadian history are well aware that (most of) the key decisions affecting Canadian development in that period were made in Europe. To learn that these decisions were made in European cities, and indeed in a large number of different cities, may add little to our understanding. Recognition that agents in North America often acted against the interest of European cities (p. 108) only reinforces the impression that the concept of metropolitanism provides little additional insight.

With books such as this, it is always unclear what the ideal audience is. Those who are familiar with the work of Careless may find little that is new in this volume. Others are likely to find themselves left unconvinced. Most of the space is devoted simply to defining what frontierism, metropolitanism, and other terms mean in historical context. There is no space in this volume for the detailed examination of particular historical cases which could show how this historical approach yields a better understanding than alternative approaches. Economic historians especially may object to the descriptive rather than analytical nature of the work. It is, indeed, difficult to imagine what counterfactuals might even be posed. Hopefully, the appetite may be whetted for further reading of Careless's work, though the lack of a bibliography will not be helpful there. While the book focuses on Canada, the themes discussed do have a wider applicability, especially to other lands of new settlement. All those who read the book will be rewarded by a fine writing style. Donald Creighton had argued that historical work should be both readable and evocative, and that historians should display both imagination and scholarship. In presenting the Creighton lectures Careless achieves all of these goals.

RICK SZOSTAK, *University of Alberta*

Canada, 1900–1945. By Robert Bothwell, Ian Drummond, and John English. Toronto: University of Toronto Press, 1987. Pp. x, 427. $30.00.

With the publication of this book together with an earlier work, *Canada Since 1945: Power, Politics and Provincialism* (Toronto, 1981), the authors have completed their surveys of twentieth-century Canadian history. These are comprehensive investigations embracing economic, social, political, and cultural developments in Canada since the turn of the century.

In the volume reviewed here the authors not only comment on the main economic events of the first half of the century—the opening of the Canadian West, the Great Depression of the 1930s—but also cover in depth the impact on the country of World Wars I and II. Little is left uninvestigated. We are treated not only to the standard interpretations of the boom that accompanied western settlement and the bust of the thirties, but to the role of religion, especially the rise of the social gospel movement, literacy, and corruption among politicians. This is a truly eclectic treatment of Canadian history during the first half of the century.

What do we learn from this narrative? Certainly we are exposed to a lot of facts; at times the detail is overwhelming. Why the authors chose to include the background to the Spanish Civil War to explain Canadian foreign policy during the thirties or run on endlessly with a string of indigestible facts about economic conditions during the thirties is confusing. Unlike the earlier work there is really no systematic treatment of Canadian development. Where, for example, is the chapter on economic growth and change that "set the scene" for postwar developments?

The hope, one gathers, is that this collection of information will throw light on the evolution of Canada during these critical decades. Certainly someone reading Canadian social and economic history for the first time will be informed. Unfortunately, at least for non-Canadian economic historians, they will be left with the impression that not much research has gone on in this field in the last 20 years.

In their annotated bibliography, the authors state that since the literature on economic history of the period 1900 to 1945 is dominated by questions of economic policy, then extant texts are unable to provide "a complete coverage of actual economic events." This is a strange statement given the breadth of work that the new economic historians have done since the mid-sixties. The authors must obviously believe what they say since no reference is made to any of this work. What happened to research on the delay of Prairies settlement, or revisions to our understanding of the role of railroads, or the wheat boom itself, or the revisions to our understanding of the opening decades that has emerged since publication of the revised national accounts estimates for this period? The absence of this whole body of literature seriously weakens the value of this text for classroom use.

Finally, the authors by their own admission are not free of biases in their interpretation of observed events. This is fine. It is enjoyable to read how they interpret the origins of the rise of social gospel or the impact of foreign investment. However, for those not familiar with Canadian developments during these decades, the interpretation can be misleading. In a number of cases new research has moved well beyond the generalizations presented here.

Both volumes are impressive. They represent the collective reasoning of three lively scholars and so are worth reading. However, a healthy dose of skepticism is a necessary companion as the reader moves through this volume.

A. G. GREEN, *Queen's University*

ECONOMIC THOUGHT

Robert Giffen and the Giffen Paradox. By Roger S. Mason. Totowa, NJ: Barnes & Noble Books, 1989. Pp. xi, 153. $27.50.

The subject of Giffen goods and of Giffenesque behavior can be approached at two very different levels: first, as a fact of experience, capable of being identified in historical context with modern statistical and econometric tools; or second, as a theoretical curiosum, by which economists (chiefly Alfred Marshall) confronted challenges to the "universal" law of demand. In this slim volume, Roger Mason examines the Giffen paradox, as well as the man behind it, from both perspectives. His effort has not been unproductive. Within the brief compass of approximately 150 pages Mason weaves the disparate strands of a somewhat abstruse topic into a compact, concise, and readable history that commands the attention of economic historians and economic theorists alike. His conclusion is that Robert Giffen (1837–1910) has been systematically underestimated as an economist and as a statistician, despite the fact that the paradox in economic theory which bears his name is commonplace in economics textbooks.

Following a cogent (albeit brief and nontechnical) review of demand theory that clearly delineates between Giffen-type phenomena and other proposed "exceptions" to the law of demand, Mason traces the somewhat muddled history of the origin of the Giffen paradox. He shuns George Stigler's denunciation of Giffen as the author of the paradox but admits that the actual roots of the paradox are deeply hidden in economic literature and cannot be traced in overt *written* fashion to Giffen himself. Instead, Mason makes the case for authorship by association, adding marginal, documentary support to Marshall's incontrovertible, though ambiguous, attribution of the paradox to Giffen in the third edition of *Principles of Economics*. Insofar as the development of economic theory is concerned, Giffen's paradox entered economic analysis when Marshall responded to a criticism by J. S. Nicholson regarding the nature of changes in the marginal utility of money as purchases occur.

A major part of the book is devoted to the empirical validity of the Giffen paradox. This core discussion will appeal to economic historians, because it contains a wealth of detail on the living standards of nineteenth-century British wage earners. Historians of thought, too, should note the outright misrepresentations of Giffenesque behavior (in terms of Ireland and potatoes) by contemporary economists who should know better. Mason denies that potato consumption in Ireland, Scotland, or any other country ever conformed to the requisites of the Giffen paradox. At this juncture the exposition becomes a bit repetitive, but Mason provides abundant detail on bread versus potatoes in the diet of the British urban laborer during the first half of the nineteenth century. Minutiae of this kind notwithstanding, what emerges from the sea of detail is the fact that Giffen maintained a running commentary and debate for almost 40 years on the condition of the urban poor in England. He asserted that a dramatic rise in the living standard of the British wage earner occurred in the second half of the century, and although he was roundly attacked on many sides, Giffen never wavered in this basic supposition.

The empirical validity of Giffenesque behavior runs intermittently throughout the book and is never far below the surface, even in the chapters that concentrate on the more narrow intellectual history of the subject. Theorists and intellectual historians will be particularly attracted to Chapters 5 and 8, which deal, respectively, with Marshall's introduction of the paradox in 1895 and with postwar attempts to rehabilitate the idea in the wake of theoretic innovations in modern demand theory (for example, Hicks, Lancaster, and others).

In the final analysis, what emerges from Mason's pen is a book that stands on its own merits as a scholarly and probing history of its subject. At the same time, it may force economists to confront and perhaps reassess several broader aspects of economic analysis. Can economists and historians afford to ignore the symbiotic relationship between the development of economic theory and the growth of empirical data? Does economic theory give sufficient emphasis to the symbiosis between multifarious items that compete daily for consumers' expenditures (although the importance of complements and substitutes is commonly acknowledged in economic analysis, how frequently or carefully is the subject researched in any concrete way)? Finally, from the standpoint of economic history, is Giffen-type behavior passé, or is it relevant to contemporary experience in less-developed nations? This brief review does not afford the opportunity for definitive answers to these questions. Suffice it to say that Mason's book has raised them to the surface of economic inquiry, where they may now be ignored at the economist's peril.

ROBERT F. HÉBERT, *Auburn University*

A History of Marxian Economics. Vol. 1: *1883–1929*. By M. C. Howard and J. E. King. Princeton: Princeton University Press, 1989. Pp. xiv, 359. $45.00, cloth; $14.95, paper.

Reading a good book in the history of economic thought permits one to have a better understanding of the tensions, conflicts, and temporary resolutions that give a theoretical tradition its excitement and development. M. C. Howard and J. E. King have produced such a book. They succeed in creating a history of the Marxian tradition from Karl Marx's death to 1929 that is very much alive with its practitioners' different and often contending insights into the structure and development of capitalism and the transitions from capitalism to socialism. Consider some of the authors discussed: Friedrich Engels, Eduard Bernstein, Karl Kautsky, Rosa Luxemburg, Georgi Plekhanov, Vladimir Lenin, Leon Trotsky, and Nikolai Bukharin. These are not what one would call minor characters in the history of the Marxian tradition. Indeed, their contributions and differences not only have helped to constitute Marxism as a theoretical discourse but, as recognized in this book, have played a significant role in shaping differing political movements, parties, and strategies on the left.

For those who would like an erudite, well-researched, and readable book on the intellectual history of Marxism, they will not be disappointed in Howard and King's contribution. It includes a fascinating analytical description of early theorists' struggles to produce a logically consistent value theory; a critical presentation and evaluation of Marxian economists' longstanding search to discover the essential cause of capitalist crises; a proper emphasis on the continual attempts of almost all writers after Marx's death to make sense of and integrate into a coherent theory capitalism's monopolistic features and its imperialist drive; and, perhaps most important of all from a Marxian perspective, a superb and again critical historical analysis of differing Marxists striving to understand the issue of societal transition, in this case both to and from capitalism.

These and still other topics are discussed within a framework of a dialectical struggle between Marxism's so-called orthodox and revisionist positions. The latter are presented first in terms of their German and then their Russian origins, and finally in terms of developments after 1917, in particular the Russian revolution. In this context the book discusses, albeit briefly, key historical events that allow one to understand better the complex relationship between these produced Marxisms and the societies in which they developed and, in turn, helped to change.

Despite the virtues of this book, there are two problems that deserve mention, precisely because of their historic importance within Marxism. Although the issue of determinism is recognized by Howard and King, they fail to consider its longstanding, pernicious influence on Marxism and its politics. They also miss an opportunity to present as a recurrent theme the tension produced within the Marxian tradition by some theorists' struggles to produce a dialectical theory freed from the reductionist legacy bequeathed by Engels and others. Here Lenin especially comes to mind as one who attempted to free Marxism from its ontological and epistemological essentialism.

A second problem concerns their failure to recognize Marxism's use of different and contending definitions of class, certainly no minor matter in a tradition presumably devoted to analyzing and changing class. A related but different point concerns their uncritical acceptance and use of terms such as "peasants," "landlords," "bourgeoisie," and "proletariat." Such "class" categories abstract from the different capitalist and noncapitalist class positions occupied by the individuals they aggregate according to criteria other than class. For example, an individual may appropriate feudal surplus labor and also rent land to industrial capitalists. Placing such an individual in a landlord category obscures the different noncapitalist and capitalist class positions occupied. It also may produce analyses of transitions that have little to do with movements among these class positions.

STEPHEN RESNICK, *University of Massachusetts, Amherst*

Keynesianism, Monetarism and the Crisis of the State. By Simon Clarke. Aldershot, England: Edward Elgar, 1988. Pp. viii, 368. $49.95.

Simon Clarke notes that "over the past decade Keynesian full employment policies have been abandoned in one country after another, to be replaced by monetarist policies that place a premium on price stability. . ." then poses the question: "How are we to understand this development, and what is its significance?" (p. 1). Forming his image of capitalism on the basis of a decidedly post-Marxian economic sociology, Clarke argues that a key to an answer to these questions is found in the circumstance that the "social power of capital is . . . embodied . . . in the social power of money. The fundamental theoretical problem is therefore that of the relationship between the social power of money and the political power of the state." This relationship, he argues, has been a "persistent theoretical, political and ideological issue since the first emergence of commerce" and it was "raised [most recently] by the crisis of Keynesianism and the rise of monetarism" (p. 17).

Because of its "ideal-typical" history, Clarke focuses his inquiry on the experience of Great Britain, which, he argues, has been characterized by a "cyclical pattern of growth" since 1823 (pp. 19, 83). Clarke identifies the causes of this pattern as an "insatiable thirst of capital for surplus value" which engendered an "incessant accumulation of capital" that inexorably turned into "overaccumulation" because of a "constant tendency for capital to revolutionise the methods of production" in an effort to " 'capitalise' a competitive advantage" (pp. 101, 102, 105).

The Keynesians' "commitment to full employment" (p. 289) remained just a commitment because they mistook the manifestations of overaccumulation for the causes thereof. Clarke defines Keynesianism as an "ideological expression of institutionalised forms of regulation of capitalist production, which embodied working class expectations of rising wages, increasing standards of public provision, and employment opportunities." These institutionalized forms he dubbed the "Keynesian Welfare State" (p. 285). But just like capitalism, the Keynesian Welfare State suffered from contradictions. On the one hand, "accumulation remained subject to the law of value imposed by the rule of money" for the sake of profit generation, a rule that forced the government to implement even closer "wage regulations." On the other hand, the "regulation of the reproduction of the working class," that is, its standard of living, "was achieved [by the government] through . . . [an] increasingly pervasive system of social administration." Furthermore, swings in employment, the balance of payments, and the price level forced the government to engage in stop-and-go macropolicies (p. 298). Because of its schizophrenia, the Keynesian Welfare State collapsed into "stagflation" that intensified the "class struggle" (pp. 302, 304).

This event "opened the way for the rise of the New Right, whose monetarist ideology" replaced the Keynesian ideology when Margaret Thatcher assumed the premiership (p. 307). At first Thatcherism was cast in the mold of Milton "Friedman's simplistic monetarism." Because of its ineffectiveness, Friedmanism was scuttled in 1982. Instead, the Thatcher government turned toward Friedrich Hayek's "neo-Austrian" doctrine, which focused on the "supposed monopoly power of trades unions" (p. 329). Hence laws were passed in 1982 and 1984 that placed such severe restrictions on the activities of unions that they "were in full retreat" by the latter year. As a result, "union power had been so reduced that it could no longer be plausibly blamed for anything" (pp. 336, 337). Consequently, the "focus of the government's offensive shifted . . . to the state itself" and took the form of attacks on all "forms of public provision." The efforts to dismantle the welfare state were accompanied by extensive "privatisation of public monopolies" (pp. 337, 338). Variants of Thatcherism were put in place in other countries. But like Keynesianism, Thatcherism has "not removed the tendency to the overaccumulation of capital or confined accumulation within the limits of the market" (pp. 356, 357). Thus the basic problem of capitalism is still with us.

On this note, Clarke ends his book rather abruptly by concluding that the "necessity of socialism has never been more urgent. The objective . . . [and] subjective conditions for socialism are also more fully developed [today] than in any previous period in history" (p. 359). As he sees it, socialism is a necessity because it is the only solution to the contradictions of capitalism. As far as the subjective conditions are concerned, despite "political defeats, workers . . . seek to realise their hopes and aspirations through trades unions and . . . the 'new social movements' " because "monetarism has politicised . . . [their] struggles to an unprecedented degree." With regard to the objective conditions, Clarke is of the opinion that the path to socialism has been eased by the fact that "concentration and centralisation of capital has socialised production to an [equally] unprecedented degree." Moreover, the computer "provides the instrument that makes it possible to bring the complex apparatus of social production under democratic rule," in the process in which "formal democracy" will be transformed into "social democracy" (pp. 359, 365).

Within the limits imposed by his concept of reality, Clarke provides some very interesting insights into the relationships among economic theory, ideology, policy, and politics in the history of capitalism, relationships that could be touched upon only superficially in this brief review. Hence even *some* of those who reject Clarke's image of capitalism might be stimulated by his book to take a fresh look at *some* aspects of their own image of capitalism, its processes, and its history.

HANS E. JENSEN, *University of Tennessee, Knoxville*

Thinking About Growth and Other Essays on Economic Growth and Welfare. By Moses Abramovitz. New York: Cambridge University Press, 1989. Pp. xviii, 377. $39.50.

In the editors' words, "*Thinking About Growth* brings together Moses Abramovitz's principal essays on long-term economic change, and introduces them with a new and previously unpublished piece," the publication dates spanning the period of 1952 to 1989. The essays are divided into four categories under labels attached by the author: growth and the economists—two essays, summarizing the author's views of the status of growth theory in 1952 and 1988; studies in long-term growth—five core essays; long swings in economic growth—two essays; and growth and welfare—four essays.

At the outset, one must note Abramovitz's style. On the one hand, he makes great use of available quantitative historical data, believing they are essential for understanding growth. On the other hand, he is not a high theorist in his use of data: he draws inferences for growth from the data against a background of economic theory but without use of high-powered statistical or econometric method. His awareness of the limitations of the data themselves, both in their quality and in what has not yielded to quantification, on occasion leads him to becoming encyclopedic in discussing them. For instance, in the two essays on the status of growth theory he ranges over the relevance of such items as industrial, commercial, and financial organization, of class structures and goals of behavior, and of the political framework.

I make only two points about the essays of Part 1. First, the newly written essay (1989) is best left until the other essays have been read: the latter provide much of the background to it and, while it is a most erudite work, I do not feel it adds much itself. Second, the other essay, written in 1952, stresses the undeveloped state of growth theory at the time and, in itself, emphasizes the role of capital formation; thus, it is perhaps a good starting point.

In my view, the most interesting and most significant of Abramovitz's contributions are in the group of essays on long-term growth. The first in this group (1956), on resource and output trends in the United States since 1870, is the seminal paper of his work. It sets out to answer three sharply defined questions. How large has been the net increase in output per capita? Is there evidence of trends in growth rates of per capita output? Have there been long-term fluctuations in growth? The first question was the important one. From observed data, Abramovitz decided that increased output per capita could not be explained by increased inputs of labor and capital but was largely a result of technological change. Two points on Abramovitz's pioneer discovery of the important productivity factor merit attention. First, he emphasizes the crucial importance of having Simon Kuznets's and Kendrick's long-term quantitative data available to him in arriving at his conclusions. Second, Abramovitz did not perhaps reap the kudos he deserved since he used an arithmetic weighting of labor and capital inputs to measure joint inputs rather than make formal use of a production function. The next two essays on growth deal with explanations of the productivity factor, such as the role of education, improved quality of labor with shorter working hours, market size, research and development, and so forth. One paper is a review of Edward Denison's measures of such items. The quantitative data here being less good and their relevance less clear, the conclusions are less certain. The final two essays of the group, in somewhat similar manner, try to explain the high growth rates of productivity following World War II in the United States and in other developed countries. The importance of "social capability" as well as technological potentials is stressed. There is some tendency to revert to attempts at the previously noted comprehensiveness, which I find distracting.

The two essays of Part 3 on Kuznets cycles (18- to 20-year cycles) and growth are, in my view, the least satisfying of the book. They provide respectively an argument that such cycles existed before 1914 (1961 essay) and that they were absent probably after

1914 and certainly after 1945 (1968 essay). Much of the explanation of change is based on the country having changed from a period of the railway, large immigration, and predominantly goods production to the mixed economy with substantial government involvement and a dominant service sector. While the cases are well argued, given the data available, one needs to keep an open mind about the significance of the conclusions. The pre-1914 data on which the argument is based are not of high quality; and the years 1914 to 1945 were characterized by two wars and a great depression, leaving only the years 1945 to the mid-sixties (roughly one cycle period) on which to make a good data-based judgment about the disappearance of fluctuations.

Abramovitz's interest in growth and welfare, addressed in the final group of essays, began quite early. He was a leader, in 1958, in noting that the quintupling of output per head over the previous 100 years had meant great changes in life patterns and in policy problems. In particular, he saw a larger role for governments accepted by the public and justified by the rising per capita income, a theme to which he returned in his presidential address to the American Economic Association in 1980. Two years later he noted the development of considerable reservation about the role of government in the mixed economy, a reservation exacerbated by the slowdown of growth at the time. In these essays Abramovitz casts his net widely indeed in his consideration of the core items of welfare: efficiency and equity. He points out the deficiencies for welfare judgments of the measured data and then a host of welfare considerations that are either unmeasured or immeasurable.

These essays present an interesting example of the development of one man's thought over a lifetime devoted to understanding economic growth. They raise the major issues related to economic growth and provide us with considerable knowledge about its nature. They are far from being definitive on all matters, as the author strongly urges: *vide* our lack of understanding of growth and the environment. They have the merit of attempts to use evidence for testing analysis where possible; they may be thought a bit old-fashioned in their absence of use of high theory. However, they stand as a challenge to others to proceed to a greater understanding than we have now in this relatively new line of endeavor. We have so much unused data with which to proceed.

M. C. URQUHART, *Queen's University*

GENERAL AND MISCELLANEOUS

Unequal Trade: The Economics of Discriminatory International Trade Policies. By Richard Pomfret. New York: Basil Blackwell Ltd., 1988. Pp. x, 227. $39.95.

In this book Richard Pomfret warns the reader about the dangers of the increased use of geographically discriminating trade agreements (GDAs). The increase in the popularity of GDAs is well documented in the book, but the dangers of these trade policies are not made clear. He identifies three possible costs of GDAs: welfare costs from resource misallocation; higher transaction costs from attempts to avoid discrimination; and political costs of singling out countries for differential treatment. The value of this book is in stimulating further research by first convincing the reader that GDAs are important and then by showing that little is known about their effects.

The book is divided into three sections. The first and longest section presents the history of geographically discriminating agreements since 1860. Rather than forming the basis of his analysis, this section serves to convince the reader of the prevalence of GDAs. Pomfret traces the increasing level of protection up to 1930, which made discrimination more valuable to the favored country. The trade wars of the 1930s resulted in an attempt to back away from discriminatory policies through the General

Agreement on Trade and Tariffs (GATT). The General Agreement does, however, allow some discrimination under some articles, and GATT has not been very discriminating in the application of these articles. Pomfret correctly concludes that the signators to GATT subvert its intentions.

In considering postwar trade relations, the book focuses on U.S. and European community trade policy. While the European community did make some effort to comply with GATT regulations covering customs unions, its external relations, especially with associated overseas territories, are discriminatory and criticized. For its part, the United States has instituted discriminatory agreements under the Caribbean Basin Initiative, the United States-Israel free trade area, and the United States-Canada free trade area. The net effect of these agreements and others, Pomfret argues, is that over 50 percent of current trade takes place under discriminatory agreements.

Having established the practical importance of GDAs, the second section of the book examines the resource costs of discrimination by reviewing the theory of discriminatory agreements and empirical examination of the welfare costs of existing GDAs. Although the author states that this section is the core of the book, it is relatively short and offers only a basic review of the literature. Pomfret presents the theory of GDAs, concentrating on Viner's notion of trade creation and diversion. He also summarizes recent work on higher dimensional and increasing returns to scale industries models. The theory sheds little light on the likely welfare effects of GDAs, however, as almost anything can happen in the second-best world that GDAs inhabit.

Turning to empirical estimates of the welfare effects of GDAs, Pomfret finds that they are not persuasive. Ex ante studies suffer from an inability to specify an accurate elasticity of substitution between imported goods, while ex post studies cannot present a relevant counterfactual trade flow. Most of the estimates assume away any terms of trade effects and are not well grounded in the theory. Pomfret concludes that welfare losses from GDAs are probably larger than the small estimates given in these studies but laments the lack of precision of any estimate of welfare changes.

The final section of the book considers possible explanations for GDAs. Pomfret finds four possible categories of explanation: optimal tariff motivations, export gains motivations, bargaining motivations, and political motivations. He dismisses the first three, concentrating on political models of tariff creation, arguing that most discriminatory agreements are the result of special-interest politics. He also argues that discriminating trade policy has become viewed as a low-cost foreign policy, especially by the United States.

The book concludes with some projections of future trade policy, examining the forces resisting and promoting the spread of GDAs in the trading community. He predicts that the threat of regionalization of trade that results from GDAs is not great, as it is swamped by the reduction of transportation costs, information costs, and the rise and fall of new markets. He also predicts that GATT will not die under the threat of GDAs but worries that it will suffer a gradual apathy. There is an appendix which considers United States-Canadian trade relations.

There are several problems with Pomfret's case against GDAs. He puts a great deal of emphasis on political bad feeling which may result from the tariffs. There is little evidence to support these costs in the book. The possible gains from discrimination that do not involve increases in economic efficiency are ignored. It may well be the case that discrimination in response to a specific country's tariff change could reduce political friction by only punishing the deviating country. Attempts to avoid nondiscrimination requirements may also result in a less efficient tariff policy being used. At the end of the Chicken wars, the United States imposed a series of nondiscriminatory tariff increases which were designed to limit the impact on countries other than France, rather than any efficiency-motivated reason. Finally, tariff agreements made under GATT may be limited by the free-riding behavior of countries that benefit from nondiscriminatory reductions without making concessions themselves. Restricting agreements to be nondiscriminatory among rational actors can only hurt their efficiency.

This book is important because of the questions that it raises. Although all discriminatory agreements are treated alike in the analysis, there are fairly clear motivational differences between different agreements. The process of economic integration in Europe, for example, is a different type of discriminatory agreement from the voluntary export restraint on Japanese automobile imports in the United States, which differs from retaliatory discriminating tariff increases under article 19 of GATT. These different types of discrimination have their own costs and benefits associated with them and are not well understood. This book gives a warning about GDAs, but the warning is based on vague suspicions rather than concrete information about their consequences.

NEAL BECKER, *University of Kansas*

Commerce and Coalitions: How Trade Affects Domestic Political Alignments. By Ronald Rogowski. Princeton: Princeton University Press, 1989. Pp. xvi, 208. $24.50.

Ronald Rogowski's slim book is the most recent in an expanding literature by political scientists on politics and international trade. The book begins by posing the question of why labor, industry, and agriculture conflict with each other in different coalitional combinations at various points in history. Rogowski employs the logic of the Stolper-Samuelson theorem along with some notion of a country's relative factor endowments to explain these domestic political "cleavages." For example, an economy abundant in both capital and labor but scarce in land (relative to the rest of the world) can expect an "urban-rural" conflict, pitting industrialists and urban workers against landlords and farmers. An economy abundant in labor but poorly endowed with capital and land can expect "class" conflict, where workers oppose capitalists and landlords. As an economy's factor endowment changes over time, through accumulation of capital or loss of productive agricultural land, the configuration of domestic political alignments changes.

Rogowski applies this framework in chapters devoted to the nineteenth-century expansion in world trade, the decline in trade during the interwar period, the post-World War II revival in trade, and to earlier periods of changing trade (ancient Greece, the Roman Empire, and sixteenth-century Europe). In each case Rogowski categorizes countries according to their relative endowment of factors. He then uses Stolper-Samuelson reasoning to predict what type of cleavage will arise and assesses this prediction against evidence gleaned from a wide reading of secondary sources. In the nineteenth century, for example, expanding world trade meant that in capital- and labor-rich countries industrialists and workers would unite to support free trade and landed interests would support protection. Rogowski shows that events in Britain, Belgium, Switzerland, and part of France support this thesis. Economies abundant only in labor could expect class conflict, where labor's support for free trade would be opposed by capital and land. Rogowski again marshalls evidence from Germany (the "iron and rye" protectionist coalition), Europe, and Asia to suggest that this was indeed the case. Economies abundant only in land, such as North America and Oceania, could expect domestic politics to be shaped by conflict between free-trading farmers and a protectionist alliance of labor and capital. The author demonstrates that these conflicts also spill over into issues other than trade policy.

The book's chief merit is its repeated use of a simple framework, set out in detail in the first chapter, to different periods in recent and ancient history. Economists will not be entirely surprised that the Stolper-Samuelson theorem proves useful in understanding history, but will be impressed by exactly how easily and generally it lends insight into past events. I found particularly refreshing Rogowski's application of the analysis to Latin America, Asia, and Africa, thereby going beyond the well-known examples of Western Europe and North America. Rogowski prudently states that noneconomic factors may at times determine coalitions and candidly admits when events cannot be fully reconciled with his framework. But I found Rogowski's own twist—when world trade expands, abundant factors become politically more assertive than scarce factors; and when trade declines, scarce factors assert themselves more than abundant factors—less compelling. Is it not also plausible to posit that because scarce factors have the most to lose from expanding trade that they have a greater interest in becoming politically assertive to promote measures that will preserve their economic position?

For such an enthusiastic proponent of an economic theorem to explain political alignments, Rogowski reveals scant awareness of the work by economic historians on the topics under consideration (such as general equilibrium modeling of policy changes). So great is his regard for the original Stolper-Samuelson theorem that Rogowski too quickly rejects alternative models, such as the specific-factors model, that are simply variations on the two-good two-factor Stolper-Samuelson framework. Rogowski himself implicitly uses a three-factor (land, labor, capital) model, known to international trade economists as Anne Krueger's model of trade and development.

Rogowski states that his only concern is about why political alignments arise and change, and not about the "outcomes" of the conflicts that these alignments create (although he often comes close to crossing this line). One of the things Rogowski would have discovered from a closer examination of the literature in economics on the political economy of trade policy is that economists have gone beyond just identifying the various coalitions that arise depending on factor endowments and have tried to endogenize policy itself, so that outcomes are determined within the model.

However, the book is aimed at political scientists and historians, not economists. Rogowski performs a valuable service in doing what economists generally neglect to do—bringing together a good dose of historical evidence to show how useful a theory can be in interpreting the broad sweep of events. Rogowski has done this with brevity and clarity, allowing the relevance and insight of the economic approach to shine through.

DOUGLAS A. IRWIN, *Federal Reserve System*

Machines as the Measure of Men: Science, Technology, and Ideologies of Western Dominance. By Michael Adas. Ithaca: Cornell University Press, 1989. Pp. xii, 430. $29.95.

From the fifteenth through to the twentieth centuries Europeans have dominated the globe. They attributed their success to racial superiority, as manifested in both the moral and the scientific and technological realms. *Machines as the Measure of Men* explores how this perception shaped the way that Europeans saw non-European cultures and interacted with them.

The geographical range and temporal scope of this work are immense, covering the five hundred years from the first western voyages of exploration to the present day and sub-Saharan Africa, India, and China. The book is divided into three distinct but not discontinuous periods: before the industrial revolution, the age of industrialization, and the twentieth century.

Using explorers' accounts, Adas vividly characterizes the constantly changing ways in which Europeans related to other cultures. In their earliest contacts with the Chinese and Indians, some European technology was decidedly inferior to that of the host countries. In cases such as this, the Europeans stressed the moral superiority of Christianity and played down the technological side.

As time went on, the Europeans began to build faster ships, bigger guns, and more complex machines. These new developments provided the Europeans with a material basis for their moral claim to superiority. In the eyes of the Europeans, lack of technological or scientific development became equated with moral degeneracy.

Skillfully interweaving material from a number of fields, including thinkers such as Mill and Voltaire, explorers such as Livingstone and Park, and popular writers such as Kipling and Conrad, Adas paints a colorful and diverse picture of the attitudes of the colonizers towards the colonized.

European imperialism during the age of the industrial revolution was justified by the "civilizing mission." Europeans saw themselves as having a duty to bring the moral and material benefits of Western civilization to "backward" cultures. Mastery of science and technology symbolized the defeat of irrationality and superstition by the forces of Christian, rational thought.

The notion that the Western races were somehow uniquely superior began to crumble in the late years of the nineteenth century. By a little after 1900 Japan, supposedly one of the inferior races, was competing economically with the European nations and had defeated one of them, Russia, in a war.

The biggest blow to the moral authority of science and technology, and consequently to the civilizing mission, came from World War I. Disillusioned Europeans realized that their scientific and technological developments simply facilitated mass slaughter rather than bringing the war to a quicker end. For all their material achievements many Europeans came to doubt their moral superiority over any other people.

The use of science and technology as measures of development continued in the United States, which had built much of its national success on these foundations, and which had escaped largely unscathed from the First World War. The civilizing mission survived here in a modified form: the philosophy of modernization, which continues to this day.

The only serious problem with the book is the lack of a bibliography. The footnotes are thoroughly done, but they are overwhelming. A critical bibliography would have greatly helped the reader pursue in greater detail any of the myriad topics Adas discusses.

Adas has dealt carefully and thoughtfully with possible objections to his statements throughout the book. For example, he deals with the apparent sexism in the title of the book by explaining that scientific standards have, for the periods which he discusses, largely been applied "by males to activities presumed to be dominated by males" (p. 13).

By showing how science and technology are used in power relations, Adas does a beautiful job of illustrating their inherently political nature. This important sub-theme runs through the whole work and yet the author never discusses it explicitly. The central value of the work is that it provides a broad understanding of the roles of science and technology in shaping how Europeans understood themselves in relation to the rest of the world.

STUART MCCOOK, *Rensselaer Polytechnic Institute*

A Century of Human Capital by Education and Training. By August C. Bolino. Washington, DC: Kensington Historical Press, 1989. Pp. xii, 332. $30.00.

What institutions have fostered the development of skills and why have they changed over time? Although the literature on human capital has burgeoned over the past 30 years, economic historians have made few attempts to synthesize developments in this vast field. Although August Bolino's work yields reasonably comprehensive histories for several of the past century's American human capital institutions, these accounts are only partially satisfying. A weak statistical base makes it difficult to completely specify and delineate the accomplishments of particular forms of training and then to integrate these findings into a coherent whole.

The book is divided into four sections. The first provides an overview and a brief history of the American high school. The second discusses the various providers of human capital including corporations, the military, and school-based training in both the public and private sectors—although curiously absent is any discussion of professional training in colleges and graduate schools. The third section ostensibly addresses the recipients of training. Chapters are dedicated to immigrants, women, and the minorities. The last of these chapters more properly belongs in the section on suppliers because it is an overview of government manpower programs rather than a synopsis of the differential effects such programs have had on distinct minority groups. The final section includes a single chapter dedicated to the economics of training.

This survey usefully puts together a wide variety of sources and statistical evidence. Many of the chapters neatly tie together the disparate programs, policies, and legislation that constitute the checkered quilt of American human capital institutions. For example, Bolino's discussion of corporation schooling and apprenticeship is thorough and enlightening. Likewise, the chapter on the economics of training provides an excellent guide to related research. For the most part, the text ably reviews the relevant literature, but unfortunately the synthesis which would crystallize our understanding of the vocational mosaic fails to emerge. The parts remain larger than the whole. If, as Bolino suggests, his concern is "the role of the education and training [sic] in raising the quality of the American labor force," the underlying issues must be cast in sharper relief (p. 4). Without this, Bolino's conclusions—that "training in the United States has taken a great variety of forms and that the private sector has been a major contributor of our economic well-being by providing opportunities for less skilled workers to become more skilled"—are too vague to support any specific policy prescriptions (p. 258).

Seventy years ago Paul Douglas wrote *American Apprenticeship and Industrial Education* (1921). Like Bolino, Douglas focused on the acquisition of blue-collar skills on and off the job. However, where Bolino's accounts are primarily descriptive, Douglas offered pungent analyses of the various means by which youth were prepared for work. For example, Douglas clearly outlined the pros and cons of corporate training in order to conclude that although "thoroughly practical," such training "does not provide broad vocational or civic training" which workers need "to protect themselves against unemployment" and "as citizens." Bolino, by contrast, proffers the mealy finding that "American corporations were primary suppliers of human capital in this century" (p. 38).

Bolino's rejoinder to the critics of corporate and vocational training is too brief. By siphoning minorities and lower-income youth into less challenging educational paths that dampen aspirations for greater social mobility, these critics insist that early vocational preparation perpetuates societal inequalities and undermines America's democratic ideals. To such charges, Bolino responds that "only 20 percent of high school graduates receive a college degree, and 40 percent go directly into the labor force." Do, as Bolino suggests, such statistics really, "tell us that it is unrealistic and economically unwise to require all youth to take a classical program in high school" (p. 117)? This fundamental controversy could fruitfully withstand greater elaboration. It would be instructive to see how Bolino would use the information he has garnered to counter the points raised by critics such as Brint and Karabel (1989), Grubb (1984), and Bowles and Gintis (1976).

The publishers at Kensington have done a disservice to this book first, by failing to edit and arrange the text more carefully, but second and more fundamentally, by failing to insist that issues be sharpened. Despite such flaws, the text provides a useful introduction to an unwieldy field.

DAN JACOBY, *University of New England*

The Employment Relationship in Anglo-American Law: A Historical Perspective. By Marc Linder. Westport: Greenwood Press Inc., 1989. Pp. xv, 294. $45.00.

The title is a bit misleading. Except incidentally, this is not a book about the legal aspects of the employer-employee relationship. Readers expecting to find, for example, a historical treatment of contract principles applicable to the employment context will be disappointed. Rather, the book tells how the law has historically defined (or attempted to define) the boundary between employees, on one side, and independent contractors or entrepreneurs on the other.

But that is an enormously important and interesting topic. Much of labor and employment law (not to speak of antitrust law) is predicated on employee status. One must be an employee, for example, in order to have bargaining rights under the National Labor Relations Act, or to claim protection under the Fair Labor Standards Act, the Occupational Safety and Health Act, or the Civil Rights Act, or to obtain benefits under the various workers compensation or unemployment compensation statutes, or to be eligible for the labor exemption from the federal antitrust laws, and so on.

Lovers of formal symmetry may find comfort in the knowledge that in nearly all relevant contexts the distinguishing factor of employee status is said to depend upon the same test: whether the putative employer has the "right to control" significant aspects of performance. Anyone who has had occasion to study or apply the control test, however, knows that it is singularly elusive, highly manipulable, variable from one statutory context to another, and capable of producing results which, in terms of the policies which presumably inspired the particular statute, seem quite arbitrary. As legal regulation of the workplace expands, employers become increasingly motivated to avoid employee status in order to escape the legal consequences that attach, and the resulting problem is of more than academic interest.

Marc Linder, an attorney in the Farmworker Division of Texas Rural Legal Aid, found his interest sparked in a very immediate way, by legal disputes in which farmers and other employers denied the existence of an employment relationship with migrant farmworkers. His investigation led him deep into the misty past of the fourteenth-century Statute of Laborers, the Statute of Artificers of 1563, through the various English and American regulatory statutes of the nineteenth century, and into the origins of the control test—which, as he demonstrates, is of fairly modern growth. It has its roots in the doctrine of vicarious liability, where it was employed as a means of limiting the liability of entrepreneurs to third parties. Reliance upon the right to control as the litmus test of coverage under twentieth-century labor protective statutes, Linder argues, is perverse and dysfunctional.

The United States Supreme Court, in the wake of New Deal legislation, suggested that if the humanitarian objectives of that legislation were to be realized the common law test should be relaxed in favor of a broader, more functional standard that looked to the economic reality of dependence: whether the workers claiming coverage, even though not subject to managerial control, were "subject, *as a matter of economic fact*, to the evils the statute was designed to eradicate." But a Republican-controlled Congress was incensed with the Supreme Court's approach. It reacted through the Taft-Hartley amendments to the National Labor Relations Act, and later through a "Status Quo Resolution" pertaining to the Social Security Act, both of which made clear the dominance of the common law criterion.

Linder is not an advocate of the "economic reality of dependence" standard, though he would obviously prefer it over its common law rival. The standard is, he observes, lacking in limits or precision: "it has no operationally useful stopping point" (p. 235). At the same time, and more fundamentally in Linder's view, it is flawed because it is overly narrow in its focus upon whether a worker is economically dependent on a particular business or employer, "rather than on the employing class as a whole" (p. 237). The real answer, Linder argues in the book's conclusion, is to abandon employee status altogether as the touchstone for benefits, and to move toward the European model of an income security program which makes benefits available on the basis of need.

Linder's final leap from a critique of criteria to the advocacy of their wholesale abandonment is a bit breathtaking. He does not explain, for example, what we should do with the National Labor Relations Act if we eliminate the employment relationship as the predicate for social legislation, and even as to entitlements (which are, to be fair, the author's main concern) the argument is a bit elliptical even if the conclusion is correct. The author's reliance upon the indeterminacy of the dependence standard, for example, is not persuasive; we do not get rid of the First Amendment simply because we have difficulty in defining freedom of speech.

These are minor shortcomings, however. This is a scholarly work which, before arriving at its policy conclusions, traverses relatively unexplored historical territory. While the style is a bit heavy at times, the author succeeds in illuminating the economic assumptions, political biases, and inconsistencies that lurk beneath the surface symmetry in this highly significant area of the law.

JOSEPH R. GRODIN, *University of California, Hastings College of Law*

In the Dominions of Debt: Historical Perspectives on Dependent Development. By Herman M. Schwartz. Ithaca: Cornell University Press, 1989. Pp. x, 295. $39.95.

Dominions of Debt responds to the pleas of dependency theorists to test their ideas in concrete historical situations. Schwartz's study covers Australia, New Zealand, Argentina from about 1880 to 1914, and South Korea in the 1960s and 1970s. The four are examples of what he calls "middling countries" that combine successful growth and development, at least for long periods, with other features typical of dependent peripheral nations. The dependency theorists often found such countries difficult to place in their models, since they reveal few of the classic traits of underdevelopment, but remain nevertheless in an unequal relationship with the imperialist "core." Dependency, Schwartz suggests, takes root in such countries primarily through foreign indebtedness, and "debt dependency," he continues, represents another category of dependency that earlier theorists have failed to address.

Debt dependency develops as states pursue foreign investment to speed development while relinquishing control of the returns on investment to private interests, usually financiers or land speculators. To repay the debt, states then inflict heavy exactions on the population at large led by labor and domestic manufacturers, but in doing so weaken domestic accumulation and destroy the "national bourgeoisie." Escaping debt dependency, Schwartz argues, rests on the capacity of those confronted by these exactions to resist them and then to force the state to minimize future debt and to support higher levels of domestic accumulation.

The crucial issues in debt dependency are who pays the debt, who controls the state, and who will control the state in the future. If those who benefit from indebtedness lose power to those willing to support domestic accumulation, debt dependency can be surmounted. But if the beneficiaries of debt keep control and succeed in forcing others to pay it, dependency will continue.

Schwartz views Australia as a nation that escaped debt dependency, but Argentina, South Korea, and to a lesser extent New Zealand as debt dependency's victims. In

Australia rapidly rising foreign debt promoted by landed and railroad interests provoked upheaval in the 1890s when, having lost control of land and railroad revenues, local colonial governments found themselves unable to make debt repayments. The crisis persisted throughout the decade amidst steeply falling land values, bank failures, and growing labor agitation provoked by falling wages and rising taxes. In 1900 the groups wanting to place the burden of debt repayments on the country at large led the campaign to establish the federation. But this new government fell partly under the influence of manufacturing interests and labor tied to national capital. From 1900 to 1913 there were prolonged, indecisive conflicts over Protection and Imperial Preference in Australia, but the "nationalists" finally achieved the Conciliation and Arbitration law offering labor higher wages in return for an end to strikes. The legislation encouraged rising productivity and launched a period of rapid industrial growth. After 1900 Australia thus underwent a successful shift from debt dependency to capitalist development.

In Argentina, by contrast, a similar crisis in the 1890s left the distribution of power unchanged and the beneficiaries of foreign debt in control of the state. Argentina therefore failed to achieve the same transition as Australia. Schwartz sees some parallels between Argentina and modern South Korea in that both relied on a continuing influx of foreign investment to maintain export-led growth. In New Zealand the conflicts over debt in the late nineteenth century failed to induce a strong labor movement, and labor unrest was instead diverted into the expansion of rural smallholdings. In the 1880s manufacturing production expanded in New Zealand, but then stagnated when foreign borrowing—used here to settle landless workers on smallholdings—began to increase. From this account of New Zealand labor represented the critical difference between Australia and the other three cases: the only successful challenge to pro-debt interests sprang from a strong labor movement. Schwartz argues elsewhere, however, that "Argentina's crucial difference with the Antipodes revolved around the absence in Argentina of a strong imperial or central state that could control landownership and maintain a stable currency" (p. 195).

Which then is crucial, labor or the state? The book contains some ambiguities and contradictions, but its chief failure is methodological. Schwartz does not provide a homogeneous framework to identify, classify, and compare the power groups in the four countries. A clearer comparative framework would probably show that already by the beginning of Schwartz's period the labor and manufacturing classes in Australia were much stronger than those elsewhere. As a result the same groups in Australia were much better placed to challenge pressures to force them to pay the foreign debt. Rather than focusing almost entirely on the period from 1890 to 1913 Schwartz might have spent more time on the period from 1850 to 1880 since at this point, not later, the basic class configurations appeared that were ultimately decisive to development. The four countries are treated unevenly: the book looks as if it began as a study of Australia alone with the other countries and the attempt at theory tacked on later. Nevertheless, Schwartz offers many valuable and provocative ideas, and he correctly focuses on the issues of class alliances and the state.

DAVID ROCK, *University of California, Santa Barbara*

Growth, Development and Welfare: An Essay on Levels of Living. By Ajit K. Dasgupta. New York: Basil Blackwell, 1988. Pp. xi, 211. $49.95.

Few would argue that GNP per capita is a completely satisfactory measure for comparing levels of social welfare across countries and over time, and many have suggested alternative or supplementary social indicators for use in such comparisons. Ajit Dasgupta's concern is that "statistical" issues in choice of indicators have been addressed to the neglect of "conceptual" ones (p. 1). He seeks to remedy this by examining the principles of "social welfare" (interchangeably called "wellbeing" and "level of living" in the text) upon which the use of various indicators may be justified. The main arguments are found in Chapter 3's examination of general principles, while Chapter 4 discusses grounds for and against employing two specific indicators: the adult literacy rate and life expectancy. Chapter 5 considers the extent to which GNP per capita and several social indicators vary together across countries and over time, both in currently developing countries and in Europe between 1850 and 1929. These three core chapters are preceded by two tangential ones defending the "economic approach" against wide-ranging "attacks."

According to Dasgupta, social states may be evaluated with regard to four principles: satisfaction of individuals' desires, fulfillment of basic needs, protection of rights, or achievement of excellence. Satisfaction of desires is the guiding principle for practitioners of the "economic approach," who have been characterized as choosing GNP per capita as their index of social welfare. The use of other social indicators must be justified either by establishing that GNP per capita fails as a desire-based indicator or by arguing that the principles of needs, rights, and excellence are compelling and are not well captured by GNP.

The author's primary aim is to discuss definitions of the alternative principles and dismiss miscellaneous objections to their validity. Basic needs are minimum targets for consumption of goods and services that intuition links with some notion of "urgency" not captured in preferences (p. 56) and are more easily defined by example: food, clothing, shelter, water, sanitation, primary education, and health care (p. 52). Rights are moral entitlements that supercede other claims. "Positive rights" and basic needs are much the same, while "negative rights" refer to freedoms as from coercion or from harassment on account of race or sex. Excellence has to do with attaining high standards in the arts, competitive games, or academic research. The author considers all of these principles to be valid means of justifying the use of social indicators other than GNP per capita when evaluating social welfare but does not discuss explicitly the links between principles and measurement.

The author's decision to presuppose interest in an unspecified set of social indicators and work backwards to some principles upon which their use may be justified has unfortunate consequences for the scope, logic, and exposition of the exercise. A more systematic progression from well-defined notions of social welfare to the selection of sets of indicators sufficient for ranking social states would have prevented the obvious omission of income distribution and poverty from the discussion; might have reined in the unequal and sometimes rambling treatments of needs, rights, and excellence; and might have led to precise links between guiding principles and practical measurement choices. The premise of the exercise, that social indicators can be justified one at a time by choosing appropriately from the set of guiding principles, is unsettling. It also leads to some ambiguity about the sense in which an indicator is justified, as becomes apparent in the author's "application" to life expectancies. Arguments justifying life expectancy as a substitute for GNP per capita are intermixed with those justifying it as an important complementary index.

The empirical work is a run-of-the-mill study of correlations between per capita GNP and other social indicators, in this case poverty headcount ratios, adult literacy rates, and life expectancies at birth. As far as possible the author avoids attributing cardinal significance to the indicators, presenting rank correlations and lists of country pairs for which the signs of differences on two indicators diverge. Inference from cross-section correlations about how well changes in one indicator will predict changes in another is troubling, as is the occasional "dash of causality" (p. 135) in interpretation. It is unclear how either the principles or the data inform the conclusion, "according to my results while a strictly deterministic interpretation of the relationship between GNP per head and other level-of-living indicators is unconvincing, the view that they are unrelated is absurd" (p. 137).

Dasgupta has read broadly, and most readers will be intrigued by some reference to research in anthropology, biology, economics, history, philosophy, psychology, or sociology. At times adequate citations for follow-up reading are absent. This is one symptom of the broader failure to choose an audience. If he were writing to economists he might have related his principles in a more precise way to the framework of economic analysis. If he is writing to noneconomists, as suggested by the two-chapter defense of economics, then he should have stated the assumptions behind economic theorems, rather than merely referring to their importance and should have defined technical terms or avoided jargon altogether.

JULIE ANDERSON, *Stanford University*

The Sugar Cane Industry: An Historical Geography from its Origins to 1914. By J. H. Galloway. New York: Cambridge University Press, 1989. Pp. xiii, 266. $44.50.

Sugar, like petroleum, fuels the modern world. Sugar cane and sugar beets are the sources of that fuel. J. H. Galloway has written a historical geography of sugar cane but includes sugar beets to complete his study. The work is not limited by continent or hemisphere but encompasses the world supply of and demand for cane sugar in the years before World War I. Although not economic history, the book has value for economic historians.

The Sugar Cane Industry is divided into two numbered parts preceded by an opening section comprising an introduction and two chapters. The main parts are divided into the industrial development of sugar cane in the West and the East. The introduction is explained by its subtitle, "the taste for sweetness." Galloway outlines the role of sweeteners in the increasingly westernized world since the Industrial Revolution. He also outlines his thesis and prepares the reader for the work that follows. In the first chapter he sets out the rudiments of sugar cane cultivation—what it needs to grow and where those needs are met—and manufacture. The second chapter sets out the origins of sugar cane and its processing—cane can be traced to circa 1500 B.C. and manufacturing to circa 500 B.C.

Five of Galloway's nine chapters are devoted to the sugar industry in the West. He begins with the rise and demise of Mediterranean sugar (c. A.D. 700 to 1600) and links that development with the beginnings of a sugar industry in the Atlantic on the islands off Europe and Africa (c. 1450 to 1680). He then connects these beginnings to the eighteenth-century American sugar industry. Chapter 6 is especially valuable to economic historians and historians of technology—"The Innovations of a Long Nineteenth Century: 1790–1914." The transition discussion that ties Chapter 5 on American sugar to Chapter 6 is an excellent summary of the history of the sugar cane industry until 1914. Two chapters present the history of sugar in the East: one covers Asia from circa 1750 to 1914; the other, the Indian Ocean and Pacific colonies from 1800 to 1914. The book closes with a brief conclusions chapter and an appendix on the price of sugar. Galloway supports his narrative with 18 pages of references, 16 tables, 12 plates, 9 tables, and 2 graphs.

Galloway reports on the composition of the labor supply, its treatment, and its response to that treatment. Although Galloway estimates population flows, he does not include labor costs for free men or slaves. He discusses the development and adoption of technology and attempts to trace financing but provides no figures on costs or returns. He notes the role of land and land ownership in the development of relationships between workers, planters, mill owners, and investors but offers few figures on land costs and returns. He reports that large central mills were expensive but does not provide costs of engines and machinery. There is little economic data or economic analysis in what is an excellent historical geography. A similar economic historical study of sugar cane is yet to be done. Galloway has prepared the ground.

DAVID O. WHITTEN, *Auburn University*

New Homeless and Old: Community and Skid Row Hotel. By Charles Hoch and Robert A. Slayton. Philadelphia: Temple University Press, 1989. Pp. ix, 299. $32.95.

The authors of this book, a sociologist and a historian, are evidently, in addition to their academic jobs, involved in organizing the homeless. They write in the spirit of neighborhood organizers of the 1960s, full of dark thoughts about "liberal" professionals and bureaucrats as well as "conservative" downtown business interests, but they give plausible accounts of those points of view and also criticize their radical friends. Their argument about policy toward the homeless is well founded and forceful and leads to proposals that seem reasonable and feasible.

They believe that the core of the problem of the homeless is the far-reaching destruction of a variety of single-room occupancy (SRO) accommodations that clustered in particular areas (skid row). The authors argue that these took form as businesses in a market economy; the SROs and their neighborhoods had important economic and social functions and institutionalized positive economic and social values. Their residents were soon subjects for both philanthropic and punitive reforms, however, because reformers misunderstood the neighborhood. "Skid row" was supposed to contain a residue of failure and deviance that was pitiful and dangerous.

Failures and deviants were indeed conspicuous among the residents, but they were not the representative or essential part, the authors say. They go on to explain the positive values and functions of the SROs and their neighborhoods, why reformers overlooked them, how the mistaken view informed policies that destroyed them, how their destruction was an important factor of the current problem of the homeless, and how different policies might support and improve the representative and positive functions to the advantage of everyone, especially the many poor people who now suffer from shelter deprivation.

History enters the argument in two ways. Chapters 2 through 6 (two-fifths of the book) describe the development of skid row and the reformers' views of it; Chapters 7 through 12 are a more detailed analysis of the 1980s and include a lot of contemporary history. Ironically, the second part is better history than the first: it is a primary source by reflective advocates and organizers. In the first part the authors go looking for evidence to support their thesis; instead of reconstructing events as they appeared to people of the time, they project their analysis upon the past. They do pull together a lot of literature on the subject, and their account of sociological research and its relation to policy is sound and relevant to their purpose.

Essentially they challenge a line of research, culminating in the 1950s, which described SRO residents and those who lived on the street as disaffiliated and anomic. They follow (and contribute to) another line of research, which revealed that the residents found satisfactions in their privacy and autonomy, miserable as their circumstances might be, even in comparison with the more regimented life of the missions and philanthropic shelters; moreover, the residents experienced a rudimentary community of interdependence and mutual aid that avoided the indignity of dependence on charitable agencies. The pursuit of autonomy and privacy are core values of our culture, not deviations, the authors say (the real problem is lack of security and opportunity in their pursuit, which results from inequitable and unwise social and economic policies). Not quite: historically autonomy and privacy were honored in a context where family responsibilities and the economic self-sufficiency of families were prior; housing reformers who condemned SROs wanted private dwellings for families as a support for family life and its values (they criticized hotel life among the rich on the same grounds).

More generally the authors do not account for how English experience and ideas of the nineteenth century influenced American reformers; they do not mention the English argument over Poor Law reform and the offer of the workhouse, or the distinction made by Thomas Chalmers and his later followers in charity organization societies between "natural" and "artificial" forms of helping, or the popularity of the little tramp portrayed by Charlie Chaplin. These facts might support their thesis; my point is that their history is deficient because they did not properly reconstruct people's ideas and actions.

On the other hand, some reviewers might argue that this book is simply not economic history, in the narrow sense of using historical data to test economic theory. I think it merits the attention of economists as do works of institutional economists. In any case, many economists will support their proposals to improve the SRO sector of the housing market.

JAMES LEIBY, *University of California, Berkeley*

QUESTIONNAIRE FOR POTENTIAL REVIEWERS

Insofar as possible the Editors will select reviewers from among readers of the JOURNAL. They therefore request all who would be willing to write reviews to fill out and return this form to Paul Hohenberg, JOURNAL OF ECONOMIC HISTORY, Folsom Library, Rensselaer Polytechnic Institute, Troy, NY 12180-3590.

Name (last name first): ____________________

Address: ____________________

Institutional affiliation (if not in address) and academic status: ________

Areas of reviewing competence in economic history (specify country and place): ____________________

Languages other than English in which you have a reading proficiency: ____________________

Representative recent publications (maximum of five):

OFFICERS AND TRUSTEES OF THE ECONOMIC HISTORY ASSOCIATION 1989–1990

Wolf-Rüdiger Baumann

The Merchants Adventurers and the Continental Cloth-trade (1560s-1620s)

European University Institute,
Series B (History) 2

1990. 23 x 15.5 cm. XIV, 425 pages. Cloth. DM 176.00. Approx. £ 60.00
ISBN 3 11 012582 X

Everyone has heard of the English naval victory over the Spanish Armada, which marked the start of the decline of Spanish and the rise of English world power. But not so many people know that most of the English ships that won the battles in the channel in 1588 were used in pacetime for exporting woollen cloth of the Merchants Adventurers Company to the Netherlands and Germany.

Everyone has heard of the Mayflower, the famous English ship that carried the first Pilgrim Fathers from Plymouth, England, to New England in 1620. But how many people know that the Mayflower regularly sailed to the German North Sea ports of Emden and Stade on contract to the Merchants Adventurers?

This important British trading company, erected by a 1564 charter from Queen Elizabeth into a "body politic", a sort of statutory corporation, with a monopoly on exporting English cloth, is the subject of this book.

The importance of woollen cloth for the English economy of the time cannot be rated highly enough. In 1565 81.60% of total exports were accounted for by it. It is hardly surprising that there was bitter fighting over this market among the great merchant "nations" of the time, and that foreigners – particularly the German Hanseatic merchants – were a thorn in the flesh of the Adventurers. They endeavoured by every economic and political recourse to get ride of the competition. The outcome was that foreigners' share in this lucrative business fell to 5.14% in the years 1598–1600, whereas fifty years earlier the Hanseatic share alone had been around 21%.

The Merchants Adventures managed not only to squeeze the Hanse out of their old, established rights in England, but to establish their company in Germany itself, in Emden and even the Hanseatic cities of Stade and Hamburg. As if that were not enough, the Adventurers became increasingly involved in internal trade, made direct contact with producers of goods and brought some manufactories, and later even guilds, for instance in Saxony, Silesia, Lausatia and Bohemia, under their control.

The work – based largely on hitherto untapped primary sources – centres round trade and commerce between England and Germany and English internal trade in Germany, especially in the second half of the 16th and the early 17th centuries. Much light is thrown on the influence of this trade on individual branches of industry and on the economic development of Germany as a whole.

ECONOMICS AND PHILOSOPHY

Cambridge Journals

EDITORS:
Daniel Hausman, *University of Wisconsin*
Michael McPherson, *Williams College*

Economics and Philosophy is designed to foster collaboration between economists and philosophers and to bridge the increasingly artificial disciplinary boundaries that divide them. Frequently, economists acknowledge that their work in both positive and normative economics depends on methodological and ethical commitments that demand philosophical study and justification. Philosophers increasingly insist that philosophy of science must be informed by and tested against studies of current science and of its history, while ethics and political philosophy must depend on what we know about human aims and interests and about the principles, benefits, and drawbacks of different forms of social organization.

Selected papers:

Should Social Preferences be Consistent?, *John Broome*

Imperfect Choice and Self-Stabilizing Rules, *Ronald A. Heiner*

How to Combine Rhetoric and Realism in the Methodology of Economics, *Uskali Mäki*

Economic Methodology: Rhetoric of Epistemology?, *Steven Rappaport*

Economics Is Too Important to Be Left to the Rhetoricians, *Alexander Rosenberg*

Economics and Philosophy (ISSN 0266-2671) is published twice a year. Subscription to Volume 6, 1990 (US and Canada only): $55 for institutions; $29 for individuals; single parts $30.

Back Volumes: 1-5 (1985-1989) $49 each.

Send order to:
Journals Department
Cambridge University Press
40 West 20th Street, New York, NY 10011, USA; or
The Edinburgh Building, Cambridge CB2 2RU, UK

1940–1990
Fifty Years of Scholarship

The JOURNAL of ECONOMIC HISTORY

VOLUME L SEPTEMBER 1990 NUMBER 3

PUBLISHED FOR
THE ECONOMIC HISTORY ASSOCIATION
IN COOPERATION WITH
RENSSELAER POLYTECHNIC INSTITUTE

ELTIS
Welfare Trends among the Yoruba
COWAN
Nuclear Power Reactors
HARRISON
The Volume of Soviet Munitions Output, 1937–1945
BROWN
The Condition of England and the Standard of Living
ROSENTHAL
The Development of Irrigation in Provence, 1700–1860
NOVAK
The Real Takeover of the BIA
NOTES AND DISCUSSION: THORNTON AND THORNTON, COSGEL, HETHERINGTON, CAMPA, HUBERMAN, TEMIN, CARRUTHERS
REVIEW ARTICLE: BOGUE

CAMBRIDGE UNIVERSITY PRESS

THE JOURNAL
OF ECONOMIC HISTORY
ISSN 0022-0507

Published for the Economic History Association in cooperation with Rensselaer Polytechnic Institute by Cambridge University Press

Aims and Scope: *The Journal of Economic History* seeks to promote the scholarly study of economic aspects of the human past from a diversity of perspectives, notably those of economists and historians. By encouraging careful formulation of issues and clear exposition of methods, the JOURNAL hopes to stimulate discourse among scholars with varied interests and modes of inquiry.

The JOURNAL is abstracted in *The Journal of Economic Literature,* which is part of the DIALOG on-line data service.

Instructions for Contributors: Articles on economic history and related aspects of history or economics will be considered for publication by the Editors on the understanding that the articles have not previously been published and are not under consideration elsewhere. Papers should indicate the wider significance of detailed original research findings as well as the logic and limitations of specialized techniques of analysis. Comments and shorter notes are also welcome. The JOURNAL does not accept unsolicited book reviews, nor can it honor requests to review particular works. Contributions should be typed double-spaced. Footnotes, also double-spaced, should be grouped at the end of the paper, along with figures and tables. Four copies of each manuscript should be submitted. Prospective contributors may obtain a copy of the Style Sheet for the JOURNAL from the Editorial Office. A submission fee of $20.00 or a year's membership (fee schedule below) is required from nonmembers of the Association.

Editorial Office Address: The Editors, *The Journal of Economic History,* 211 Watkins Home, Hall Center for the Humanities, University of Kansas, Lawrence, KS 66045, U.S.A. Telephone: (913) 864-4798.

Association Office Address and Membership Information: Individuals who are members of the Economic History Association receive the JOURNAL as part of their annual dues. Membership rates (in U.S. dollars) are: $30.00 for those with income above $30,000 a year; $25.00 for those with income below $30,000; $15.00 for students and professors emeriti who have been members of the Association for 10 years; $600.00 for life membership. Payment of an *additional* $20.00 permits joint membership with the Economic History Society (UK). Applications and inquiries concerning membership should be addressed to the Economic History Association, Dept. of History, George Washington University, Washington, DC 20052, U.S.A.

Subscription, Publishing and Advertising Office Address: Cambridge University Press, 40 West 20th Street, New York, NY 10011, U.S.A.; or Cambridge University Press, The Edinburgh Building, Shaftesbury Road, Cambridge CB2 2RU, England.

Subscription Information: *The Journal of Economic History* is published quarterly in March, June, September, and December. Annual institutional subscription rate (1990) US $50.00 in the United States and Canada; UK £31.00 elsewhere. Individuals may subscribe by becoming a member of the Economic History Association (see above). Prices include surface postage and insurance.

The Journal of Economic History (USPS 279-580) is published quarterly by Cambridge University Press. Second-class postage paid at New York, NY and additional mailing offices. Postmaster: Send address changes to *The Journal of Economic History*, Cambridge University Press, 110 Midland Avenue, Port Chester, NY 10573.

Printed in the United States of America.

THE JOURNAL
OF ECONOMIC HISTORY

Volume L *September 1990* *Number 3*

ARTICLES

DAVID ELTIS
Welfare Trends among the Yoruba in the Early Nineteenth Century: The Anthropometric Evidence 521

ROBIN COWAN
Nuclear Power Reactors: A Study in Technological Lock-in 541

MARK HARRISON
The Volume of Soviet Munitions Output, 1937–1945: A Reevaluation 569

JOHN C. BROWN
The Condition of England and the Standard of Living: Cotton Textiles in the Northwest, 1806–1850 591

JEAN-LAURENT ROSENTHAL
The Development of Irrigation in Provence, 1700–1860: The French Revolution and Economic Growth 615

STEVEN J. NOVAK
The Real Takeover of the BIA: The Preferential Hiring of Indians 639

NOTES AND DISCUSSION

M. K. THORNTON AND R. L. THORNTON
The Financial Crisis of A.D. *33: A Keynesian Depression?* 655

METIN M. COSGEL
Scattering and Contracts in Medieval Agriculture: Challenges Ahead 663

BRUCE W. HETHERINGTON
Bank Entry and the Low Issue of National Bank Notes: A Re-examination 669

JOSÉ MANUEL CAMPA
Exchange Rates and Economic Recovery in the 1930s: An Extension to Latin America 677

MICHAEL HUBERMAN
Vertical Disintegration in Lancashire: A Comment on Temin 683

Peter Temin
Product Quality and Vertical Integration in the Early Cotton Textile Industry: A Reply 691

Bruce G. Carruthers
Politics, Popery, and Property: A Comment on North and Weingast 693

REVIEW ARTICLE

Allan G. Bogue
Fogel's Journey through the Slave States 699

EDITORS' NOTES 711

REVIEWS OF BOOKS

ANCIENT, MEDIEVAL, AND EARLY MODERN

Bergier, Ed. *Montagnes, fleuves, fôrets dans l'histoire: Barrières ou lignes de convergence?* P. Kooij 713
Hallam, Ed. *The Agrarian History of England and Wales.* Vol. 2: *1046–1350* J. L. Langdon 714
Shatzmiller. *Shylock Reconsidered: Jews, Moneylending, and Medieval Society* G. I. Langmuir 715
Hybel. *Crisis or Change: The Concept of Crisis in the Light of Agrarian Structural Reorganization in Late Medieval England* E. B. DeWindt 717
Matossian. *Poisons of the Past: Molds, Epidemics, and History* G. Grantham 718
Camporesi. *Bread of Dreams: Food and Fantasy in Early Modern Europe* G. Grantham 718
van der Wee, Ed. *The Rise and Decline of Urban Industries in Italy and in the Low Countries (Late Middle Ages-Early Modern Times)* M. Howell 720
Kindleberger. *Spenders and Hoarders: The World Distribution of Spanish American Silver, 1550–1750* D. O. Flynn 721

MODERN EUROPE

Curtin. *Death by Migration: Europe's Encounter with the Tropical World in the Nineteenth Century* D. Eltis 724
Chalklin and Wordie, Eds. *Town and Countryside: The English Landowner in the National Economy, 1660–1860* A. Kussmaul 726
Weatherill. *Consumer Behaviour and Material Culture in Britain, 1660–1760* D. H. Sacks 727
Hudson, Ed. *Regions and Industries: A Perspective on the Industrial Revolution in Britain* J. Humphries 729
Cairncross and Watts. *The Economic Section, 1939–1961: A Study in Economic Advising* C. E. Heim 730
Hayward. *The British Aircraft Industry* E. H. Lorenz 732
Ollerenshaw. *Banking in Nineteenth Century Ireland: The Belfast Banks, 1825–1914* D. J. Moss 734
Press. *The Footwear Industry in Ireland, 1922–1973* K. O'Rourke 736

WEISSBACH. *Child Labor Reform in Nineteenth-Century France: Assuring the Future Harvest* C. Tuttle 737
LEBOUTTE. *Reconversions de la main-d'oeuvre et transition démographique: Les bassins industriels en aval de Liège XVIIe–XXe siècles* E. Accampo 739
MORI, Ed. *Prato: Storia di una città*. Vol. 3, Parts 1 and 2: *Il tempo dell'industria (1815–1943)* F. L. Galassi 740
DON AND KARADY, Eds. *A Social and Economic History of Central European Jewry* C. E. McClelland 741
EDELMAN. *Proletarian Peasants: The Revolution of 1905 in Russia's Southwest* W. J. Kelly 743
SNOWDEN. *Violence and Great Estates in the South of Italy: Apulia, 1900–1922* W. J. Kelly 743
DAVIES. *The Soviet Economy in Turmoil, 1929–1930* P. R. Gregory 744

AUSTRALIA

NICHOLAS, Ed. *Convict Workers: Reinterpreting Australia's Past* S. L. Engerman 745

LATIN AMERICA

DUPUY. *Haiti in the World Economy: Class, Race, and Underdevelopment Since 1700* F. W. Knight 747
GOOTENBERG. *Between Silver and Guano: Commercial Policy and the State in Postindependence Peru* M. J. Gonzales 748

UNITED STATES AND CANADA

RUSSO. *Free Workers in a Plantation Economy: Talbot County, Maryland, 1690–1759* P. C. Mancall 749
CARR, MORGAN, AND RUSSO, Eds. *Colonial Chesapeake Society* C. Wetherell 751
GOODSTEIN. *Nashville, 1780–1860: From Frontier to City* R. D. Green 752
WILKINS. *The History of Foreign Investment in the United States to 1914* M. A. Yeager 754
SCHULTZ. *Constructing Urban Culture: American Cities and City Planning, 1800–1920* L. Cain 757
FOX-GENOVESE. *Within the Plantation Household: Black and White Women of the Old South* D. F. Weiman 759
MOODY AND KESSLER-HARRIS, Eds. *Perspectives on American Labor History: The Problems of Synthesis* G. Friedman 761
DE LEÓN AND STEWART. *Tejanos and the Numbers Game: A Socio-Historical Interpretation from the Federal Censuses, 1850–1900* J. E. Crisp 762
WARREN. *The American Steel Industry, 1850–1970* D. R. Meyer 764
KLEINBERG. *The Shadow of the Mills: Working-Class Families in Pittsburgh, 1870–1907* J. T. Cumbler 765
ANDERSON AND HILL. *The Birth of a Transfer Society* E. D. Berkowitz 766
YOUNG. *Pure Food: Securing the Federal Food and Drugs Act of 1906* G. D. Libecap 767
GROSSMAN. *Land of Hope: Chicago, Black Southerners, and the Great Migration* W. C. Whatley 768
CLARK. *Unions and Communities Under Siege: American Communities and the Crisis of Organized Labor* D. Nelson 770

LAXER. *Open For Business: The Roots of Foreign Ownership in Canada* — P. Wylie 771
BASKERVILLE, Ed. *Canadian Papers in Business History.* Vol. I — R. Dupré 772

ECONOMIC THOUGHT

NIEHANS. *A History of Economic Theory: Classic Contributions, 1720–1980* — G. Mongiovi 773
ROY. *Philosophy of Economics: On the Scope of Reason in Economic Inquiry* — A. Cudd 775
SHAW. *Keynesian Economics: The Permanent Revolution* — T. Mott 777
STEEDMAN. *From Exploitation to Altruism* — B. Roberts 777
FLANDERS. *International Monetary Economics, 1870–1960: Between the Classical and the New Classical* — L. H. Officer 779

GENERAL AND MISCELLANEOUS

TEICHOVA, LEVY-LEBOYER, AND NUSSBAUM, Eds. *Historical Studies in International Corporate Business* — V. N. Bandera 781
EICHENGREEN AND LINDERT, Eds. *The International Debt Crisis in Historical Perspective* — C. P. Kindleberger 782
FISHER, Ed. *Innovation in Shipping and Trade* — C. K. Harley 784
LOCKE. *Management and Higher Education Since 1940: The Influence of America and Japan on West Germany, Great Britain and France* — A. W. Niemi 785
POHL, Ed. *Die Bedeutung der Kommunikation für Wirtschafts und Gesellschaft* — G. Rosseger 785
KUZNETS. *Economic Development, the Family, and Income Distribution: Selected Essays* — M. R. Haines 787

THE JOURNAL OF ECONOMIC HISTORY

VOLUME L SEPTEMBER 1990 NUMBER 3

Welfare Trends among the Yoruba in the Early Nineteenth Century: The Anthropometric Evidence

DAVID ELTIS

Analysis indicates that the Yoruba were taller than other West African peoples in the early nineteenth century. Disease, workloads, and environmental or genetic factors explain little of this differential. Rather, it appears due to a superior nutritional status made possible by Yoruba social structures, in particular, Yoruba towns. Yoruba stature declined both absolutely and relatively over the forty years corresponding to the collapse of the Oyo Empire. Regression analysis suggests a systematic relationship between these two events.

There is now a substantial literature on measuring secular trends in welfare in premodern societies by means of anthropometric data—usually data on human stature. In recent years scholars have used height, weight, and the pace and timing of changes in both for historical assessments of nutritional status and disease environment.[1] Indeed, some have made a strong case for using such data to measure standard-of-living trends as a supplement, at least, to the more orthodox indexes of real wages, per capita food consumption, or per capita national income.[2] Sweden, the Austrian Empire, the United Kingdom, the English-speaking Caribbean, and the United States have yielded most of the data on which anthropometric studies of this type have been based.

The Journal of Economic History, Vol. L, No. 3 (Sept. 1990). ISSN 0022-0507.

The author is Associate Professor of History, Queen's University, Kingston, Ontario K7L 3N6.

Earlier versions of this article were given at meetings of the Queen's University Economic History Seminar, the Canadian African Studies Association in Ottawa in May 1989, and the Social Science History Association in Washington in November 1989. Comments from participants, especially Martin Klein, improved the article. I am also indebted to Stanley L. Engerman, Henry A. Gemery, and Richard H. Steckel for valuable suggestions. Queen's University Statlab prepared Figure 1. The funding for the research was provided by the Social Science and Humanities Research Council of Canada.

[1] See, for example, Robert William Fogel, "Nutrition and the Decline in Mortality since 1700: Some Preliminary Findings," in Stanley L. Engerman and Robert E. Gallman, eds., *Long-Term Factors in American Economic Growth* (Chicago, 1986), pp. 439–527. The basic reference work on the physiology of this issue is P. B. Eveleth and J. M. Tanner, *Worldwide Variation in Human Growth* (Cambridge, 1976).

[2] Richard H. Steckel, "Height and Per Capita Income," *Historical Methods*, 16 (Winter 1983), pp. 1–7.

For some periods and some regions, however, neither the orthodox indexes nor the materials necessary for their construction are ever likely to exist. In several such cases anthropometric data are the only nonqualitative evidence of welfare trends that we have, and among these are several West African societies of the early nineteenth century.

A quick review of the broad trends of recent research is appropriate. Native-born U.S. white males at the time of the American Revolution approached the physical stature of their modern counterparts. Native-born U.S. blacks at the end of the eighteenth century were slightly shorter than whites (as well as having markedly different childhood growth patterns), but taller than their contemporaries in the Caribbean. Whites in the Americas, however, had a considerable height advantage over whites of the same genetic base in Europe until the early twentieth century. And mirroring this pattern, blacks in both the United States and the Caribbean were substantially taller than slaves born in Africa, after controlling for the considerable human diversity between regions in that continent. This last holds true whether the comparison is with slaves who had never left Africa or with slaves born in Africa and transported to the Americas. Indeed, this differential continues today between peoples of African descent in the Americas and some descendants of populations in Africa on which the slave trade drew, although well-fed subpopulations in Africa (usually urban based) do have similar stature to Europeans and North Americans. Scholars have also uncovered variations between classes and regions within particular countries, and between rural and town populations on the one hand and large-city populations on the other.[3]

The trend in human stature from the eighteenth to the twentieth century exhibits some striking intercontinental differences. The European secular trend has shown pronounced but irregular gains. Stature in the United States, on the other hand, has changed little for males of both European and African ancestry in the long run but has varied considerably in the short and medium term. In Africa modern stature in rural areas is also little different from what it was 150 years ago, but though the evidence is much less substantial, we might reasonably assume that over shorter time periods stature has varied as much there as in other parts of the Atlantic basin. Phillip Tobias has argued for substantial

[3] Robert W. Fogel et al., "Secular Changes in American and British Stature and Nutrition," in Robert I. Rotberg and Theodore K. Rabb, eds., *Hunger and History: The Impact of Changing Food Production and Consumption Patterns on Society* (Cambridge, 1983), pp. 247–83; and the articles in the special issue of *Social Science History*, 6 (Fall 1982), edited by Robert W. Fogel and Stanley L. Engerman; B. W. Higman, "Growth in Afro-Caribbean Slave Populations," *American Journal of Physical Anthropology*, 50 (Mar. 1979), pp. 373–85; David Eltis, "Nutritional Trends in Africa and the Americas: Heights of Africans, 1819–1839," *Journal of Interdisciplinary History*, 12 (Winter 1982), pp. 453–75; T. O. Johnson, "Height and Weight Patterns of an Urban African Population Sample in Nigeria," *Tropical and Geographical Medicine*, 22 (Mar. 1970), pp. 65–76; Eveleth and Tanner, *Worldwide Variation in Human Growth*, p. 340.

short-term fluctuations as well as the possibility of a negative secular trend in twentieth-century Africa.[4] In Europe and North America urbanization, industrialization, the disease environment, and to a lesser extent social stresses resulting from war have all contributed to shifts in the time trend. These factors would not necessarily be of the same relative importance in Africa, however.

In the African context, not only are historical data less abundant than elsewhere, but there are major explanations for differences in stature in Africa that have little to do with nutrition. "Human diversity"—to use Jean Hiernaux's phrase—rooted in genetic adaptation is probably greater in the African context than it is anywhere else. To put this differently, stature differences among most African ethnic groups probably have a stronger genetic basis than stature differences among equivalent European and perhaps Asian peoples.[5] While much attention has been given to the gains in stature experienced by the descendants of Africans taken to the New World, little attempt has been made to sort out the nutritional and genetic contributions to the much larger differences among African populations in Africa.

A fuller examination of regional and ethnic differences as well as time trends in Africa is, however, possible. One source from the first half of the nineteenth century in particular draws on a wide band of West African societies located mainly between Guinea-Conakry and the eastern limits of Nigeria. As part of a long campaign to suppress the slave trade, the British negotiated treaties with several countries to provide for courts of mixed commission which would adjudicate cases involving suspected slave ships. The data for the present study come from copies of the records of the courts at Sierra Leone, deposited at the Public Record Office in London. Between 1819 and 1845 British cruisers landed almost 60,000 Africans at Sierra Leone, most of whom had been recaptured while en route to the Americas or to islands off the African coast. The age, height, name, sex, distinguishing body marks, and in a few cases the country of origin of 56,935 of these Africans were officially registered by the courts. The motives for this were probably to provide evidence of the freedom of an individual in an environment where re-enslavement was always a risk, as well as to provide statistics for both the British diplomatic campaign to suppress the traffic and the payment of bounties to the naval personnel responsible for capturing the slave ships. Because the slaves were registered by the ship on which they were found, it is possible, by checking the official trial report for

[4] Phillip V. Tobias, "The Negative Secular Trend," *Journal of Human Evolution*, 14 (May 1985), pp. 347–56. It might be noted that very few West African and no Yoruba peoples are included in the Tobias survey.

[5] Jean Hiernaux, *La diversité humaine en Afrique subsaharienne: Recherchés biologiques* (Brussels, 1968). See further development of this point below.

each ship, to determine the date, as well as the port of embarkation for every slave registered.

Earlier studies based on parts of these data contain fuller discussions of reliability and possible bias.[6] Here I use an expanded data set of measurements of 47,000 individuals—most of those registered at Sierra Leone—and focus in particular on a subset of 4,053 records of male adult Africans put on board slave ships between 1821 and 1845 at two embarkation points in the Bight of Benin: Badagry and Lagos. The focus on two ports in the Bight of Benin is due to the clear inference that may be drawn (see below) that almost all persons entering the slave trade there were Yoruba. Children are excluded from the study because estimates of childrens' ages in the registers are not reliable; at the very least there is clear evidence of reporting bias.[7]

The reason for concentrating on the Yoruba requires fuller elucidation. As already noted, the range of anthropometric patterns in Africa is probably greater than in any other continent. Terminal heights vary considerably for genetic reasons, with climate being a major selective agent. According to Hiernaux, shorter stature is associated with the more humid forest zones and an absence of seasonal extremes. Taller stature is linked with the drier and more seasonal savanna regions.[8] However, variations that are probably genetically based may be observed within these zones and even within the same ethnic or language group. Of the three major Ibibio divisions, for example, the one best represented among the Sierra Leone recaptives, the Anang, are today among the shortest of southern Nigerians. Statistically significant differences of between four and five centimeters existed between the Abadja and the Edda Unwano divisions of the Igbo in the mid-twentieth

[6] See David Eltis, *Economic Growth and the Ending of the Transatlantic Slave Trade* (New York, 1987), p. 400; and Eltis, "Nutritional Trends in Africa and the Americas," pp. 453–57. The copies of the registers are scattered in the Foreign Slave Trade series (FO 84) of the British Public Record Office, volumes 4, 9, 15, 21, 38, 63, 64, 76, 86, 87, 98, 100, 101, 102, 110, 116, 127, 134, 135, 147, 166, 189, 212, 231, 269, 273, 308, 310, 345, 346, 393, 450, 507, 559.

[7] Children's growth curves calculated from the Sierra Leone data are improbably steep as well as bimodal in distribution. The reporting bias that almost certainly lies at the root of these features likely has two sources. First, the British paid their naval crews a bounty for each slave landed alive. This bounty was greater for adults than for children (see Christopher Lloyd, *The Navy and the Slave Trade* [London, 1949], pp. 79–84), and it is possible that to reduce costs, court officials underestimated the ages of young adults. Second, European unfamiliarity with the growth patterns of Africans, and the fact that officials had in any event to estimate African ages, could also have contributed to reporting bias.

[8] Heat dissipation occurs through the skin. A low mass-to-surface ratio, which facilitates cooling, is a characteristic of both shorter body types and tall, slender physiques. According to Hiernaux, which of these adaptive routes is taken depends on humidity, because in hot dry climates sweating is a more efficient method of cooling than in humid environments. For a full review, see the work of Jean Hiernaux, in particular *La diversité humaine* and the summary in *The People of Africa* (New York, 1974), pp. 65–90.

century.[9] All of these groups lived in the humid forest zone, broadly defined. Any attempt to measure time trends among such groups presupposes that it is possible to identify the subethnic division, or at least location of the group, with some precision. If this is not done, then observed variation over time may simply reflect the changing ethnic or regional composition of the sample rather than real changes in nutritional status. The nineteenth-century data generally do not permit such precision.

For one large ethnic group, however, the Yoruba, the regional variations within the group are remarkably small, despite the fact that the Yoruba have long occupied parts of both savanna and forest zones. In the 1950s, for example, differences in the mean heights of six separate regional subgroups of Yoruba were less than two centimeters.[10] This lack of regional variation means that changes over time in Yoruba stature cannot be explained by shifts in the regional composition of the sample, and for the broad picture it is enough simply to isolate the Yoruba component of the Sierra Leone recaptives.[11]

I begin by comparing the stature of the Yoruba with other peoples from Africa or of African descent at this time. Table 1 summarizes the extant data on early nineteenth-century heights, with Section I including only slaves born in Africa and Section II including only those born in the Americas. Panel Ia breaks down the data by ethnicity according to information in the Sierra Leone registers on country of origin together with reasonable inferences from port of embarkation.[12] Panel Ib provides a regional breakdown. This additional breakdown is offered

[9] For twentieth-century data on stature, see Eveleth and Tanner, *Worldwide Variation in Human Growth*, pp. 338–39; P. A. Talbot and H. Mulhall, *The Physical Anthropology of Southern Nigeria* (Cambridge, 1962), p. 82; Hiernaux, *La diversité humaine*, pp. 167–76.

[10] See citations in fn. 9. These data are conveniently drawn together in Eltis, "Nutritional Trends in Africa and the Americas," p. 462.

[11] Over half of the Sierra Leone recaptives spoke Yoruba dialects. Data on countries of origin in the Sierra Leone registers indicate that all Yoruba left from the six major embarkation points for slaves in the Bight of Benin. The registers also show that the most easterly of the six, Benin, shipped some Igbo peoples as well as Nupe and Hausa, though most of these left from points farther east. We can infer that the two westernmost, Little and Grand Popoe, must have been the source of the significant Ewe, Gun, and Adja populations at Sierra Leone. Some Adja may have left Whydah and this embarkation area also is ignored. The Yoruba must have made up the overwhelming majority of those leaving Badagry and Lagos because few ports in this region other than the ones discussed embarked slaves, and the large numbers of Yoruba could not have set sail from anywhere else. There were relatively few Nupe, Hausa, and other peoples living to the north of the Yoruba at Sierra Leone, and some of these embarked in the Bight of Biafra rather than points to the east. See Sigmund W. Koelle in *Polyglotta Africana*, Philip E. H. Hair and David Dalby, eds. (Sierra Leone, 1963); P. E. H. Hair, "The Enslavement of Koelle's Informants," *Journal of African History*, 6 (No. 2, 1965), pp. 193–203; Philip D. Curtin and Jan Vansina, "Sources of the Nineteenth Century Atlantic Slave Trade," *Journal of African History*, 5 (No. 2, 1964), pp. 185–208; Eltis, *Economic Growth*, pp. 165–80. For the purposes of this study, then, "adult Yoruba" are defined as Africans embarking at Badagry and Lagos (even though only Lagos was actually a Yoruba town) in the period from 1821 to 1845, with a recorded age of between 23 and 40.

[12] See Eltis, "Nutritional Trends in Africa and the Americas," for a fuller discussion of this.

TABLE 1
HEIGHTS OF ADULT MALES OF AFRICAN DESCENT, EARLY NINETEENTH CENTURY
(in centimeters)

	Number	Mean	Standard Deviation
	I. Born in Africa		
a. Ethnicity			
Malinke, 1813	423	166.4 cm	7.8
Nupe and Hausa, 1819–23	22	162.3*	6.1
Popoes,[a] 1822–29	80	163.2*	6.4
Igbo, 1821–32	973	162.8*	7.3
Ibibio, 1821–22	37	163.1*	7.0
N.W. Bantu, 1819–23	12	159.2*	5.7
Yoruba, 1821–45	4,053	166.6	6.7
b. Region of Embarkation			
Senegambia, 1813	568	166.1	8.4
Sierra Leone, 1819–45	1,751	164.9	7.1
Windward Coast, 1813	302	162.6	7.9
Gold Coast, 1813	364	163.6	8.1
Bight of Benin, 1819–45	6,302	166.1	6.9
Bight of Biafra, 1821–44	7,059	163.7	6.9
West-central Africa, 1813	985	161.8	7.9
Mozambique, 1836	141	165.3	5.8
c. Inferred Region of Disembarkation[b]			
French Caribbean, 1780–99	n.a.	163.5	n.a.
United States, 1804–7	n.a.	164.2	n.a.
British Caribbean, 1800–7	n.a.	162.9	n.a.
Cuba, 1821–40	n.a.	164.7	n.a.
Bahia, 1821–40	n.a.	165.9	n.a.
Brazil, south of Bahia, 1821–40	n.a.	162.7	n.a.
	II. Born in the Americas		
United States, 1828–60[c]	780	170.8	8.0
Trinidad, 1813	128	165.6	7.6
St. Lucia, 1815	1,284	164.8	9.1
Berbice, 1819	230	163.2	8.3

* Significantly different from the Yoruba mean at the 1 percent level on the basis of two-tailed *t*-test.

[a] "Popoes" refers to Africans embarking at both Little and Grand Popoe. Ethnicity is not defined, but is probably Fon, Gun, or Adja.

[b] This panel is made up of weighted means, with the weights determined by the share of slaves arriving in the regions listed from each of the African embarkation zones in Panel b. The French, British, and U.S. categories refer to slave trades rather than regions in the Americas controlled by these nations.

[c] An undetermined number (but certainly a small minority) of African-born are included in this sample.

Notes: Year is for year of measurement. Definitions of adult vary, but all are older than 22 and younger than 50.

Sources: Row 1: Gerald C. Friedman, "The Heights of Slaves in Trinidad," *Social Science History*, 6 (Fall 1982), p. 487; Rows 2–6: David Eltis, "Nutritional Trends in Africa and the Americas: Heights of Africans, 1819–1839," *Journal of Interdisciplinary History*, 12 (Winter 1982), p. 460; Rows 7, 9, 12, 13, 15: Calculated from data set of slaves landed at Sierra Leone (see text); Rows 8, 10, 11, 14: B. W. Higman, "Growth in Afro-Caribbean Slave Populations," *American Journal of Physical Anthropology*, 50 (Mar. 1979), p. 374; Rows 16–21: see text; Row 22: Richard H. Steckel, "Slave Height Profiles from Coastwise Manifests," *Explorations in Economic History*, 16 (Oct. 1979), p. 368; Rows 23–25: B. W. Higman, *Slave Populations of the British Caribbean, 1807–1834* (Baltimore, 1984), p. 281.

because people with the same ethnicity left from more than one region on the coast, and conversely most major ports of embarkation saw people of several different ethnicities pass through in any given year. For regions where there was no or little slave trading after 1820, the panel relies on Barry Higman's means calculated from the British West Indian slave registries. It should be noted that although the slaves in the West Indian data were measured in 1813, most of these slaves probably left Africa between 1797 and 1807, earlier than the post-1818 departures recorded in the Sierra Leone data.[13] Despite this time difference and therefore the possibility of time trends developing, there are no statistically significant differences for the African-born leaving from the same African region where the Sierra Leone and West Indian data overlap. Panel Ib also shows that the standard deviations in the regional groupings are larger than the same statistic in the ethnic groupings in Panel Ia. This is to be expected, given the fact that different ethnic groups, often of different genotypes, normally left from the same region.

Unlike the rest of Table 1, Panel Ic is based on inference rather than observation. It is an attempt to estimate the mean heights of Africans arriving in the major slave-importing regions of the Americas in the late eighteenth and early nineteenth centuries. The point of this operation is to establish a base for measuring changes in the stature of Afro-Americans that might be associated with their experience in the New World. The means in Panel Ic are weighted averages, with the weights determined by the share of arrivals in each American region accounted for by the African areas shown in Panel Ib.[14] It should be noted that there were often quite dramatic shifts in African provenance zones in the nineteenth century as suppression made its gradual impact. Heights of the average African adult male would therefore also vary substantially. Thus the Cuban mean in Panel Ic is for a period when few slaves from west-central Africa arrived in Cuba and it suggests accordingly

[13] These data are from Trinidad, which received most of its slaves between the British takeover of the island in 1797 and 1805, when an order-in-council prohibited direct shipments of slaves from Africa. For a few years thereafter slaves arrived from other British territories, though many of these slaves had been born in Africa.

[14] The latest information on this is in David Richardson, "Slave Exports from West and West-Central Africa, 1700–1810: New Estimates of Volume and Distribution," *Journal of African History*, 30 (No. 1, 1989), pp. 1–22. For the U.S. distribution, Richardson uses Elizabeth Donnan, *Documents Illustrative of the History of the Slave Trade to America*, 4 vols. (Washington, 1935), vol. 4, pp. 474, 475, 477, 490, 504, 508, 513–15, 521–22, 633. The African distribution of the British slave trade is explained more fully in David Richardson, "The Eighteenth Century British Slave Trade: Estimates of its Volume and Coastal Distribution in Africa," *Research in Economic History*, 12 (1989), pp. 151–95. As pointed out in the notes to Table 1, the U.S. and British weights are based on the share of each country's slave trade rather than arrivals in U.S. and British territory. The British Caribbean was overwhelmingly supplied by British slavers at this time, however. In the U.S. case the British and Americans were together responsible for most of the slaves arriving in the early nineteenth century, but the distribution of the two trades is rather similar. For the African origins of the Cuban and Brazilian traffic in slaves after 1820, see David Eltis, "The Export of Slaves from Africa, 1821–1843," this JOURNAL, 37 (June 1977), p. 423.

that Africans arriving in Cuba were relatively tall. If, however, the large-scale west-central African arrivals from before 1821 and after 1840 are allowed for, then the mean would be substantially lower. Similarly, the greater stature of African arrivals at Bahia was probably a nineteenth-century phenomenon. Before 1800 the bulk of slaves leaving the Bight of Benin were probably drawn from the Adja-Ewe and other groups to the west of the Yoruba. These were of shorter stature than the Yoruba.[15]

Table 1 shows that the Yoruba were generally taller than other Africans. Indeed, they were so much taller that the absence or presence of Yoruba people explains much of the difference in the mean stature of African arrivals in the regional Americas—at least after the traffic to Senegambia shut down in the late eighteenth century. Yoruba males were taller even than creoles in newly developing British Caribbean sugar colonies, though it is likely that the height gains experienced by Africans coming to the Americas were smallest of all in such environments.[16] Africans arriving in the British Caribbean were probably shorter than those arriving anywhere else in the Americas except for south-central Brazil.[17] The intriguing question, taken up below, is how much of this taller stature of the Yoruba was due to differences in relative nutrition and how much to genetic adaptation to the environment.

I turn next to an examination of trends over time. Given the importance of the childhood experience in the determination of final heights, time trends of stature are normally plotted against the year of birth. Figure 1 shows a time trend for 4,053 recaptive Yoruba males fitted with a second-degree polynomial (significant at the 5 percent level) on year of birth. Two other time trends are included in the figure for comparative purposes. The first is computed from the manifests of ships

[15] In the eighteenth century St. Domingue drew heavily from the Bight of Benin, and slaves from this area were not noted for their tall stature. See the discussion in Jean Fouchard, *The Haitian Maroons: Liberty or Death*, trans. by A. Faulkner Watts (New York, 1981), pp. 177–81.

[16] Barry Higman, *Slave Populations of the British Caribbean, 1807–1833* (Baltimore, 1984), pp. 282–83, shows that slaves born in non-sugar colonies were taller than those born in newly developing sugar-producing regions. The evidence is not conclusive, however, as slaves on Trinidad sugar estates were taller than those on non-sugar-producing units. See Gerald C. Friedman, "The Heights of Slaves in Trinidad," *Social Science History*, 6 (Fall 1982), pp. 482–515; and A. Meredith John, *Plantation Slaves in Trinidad, 1783–1816: A Mathematical Inquiry* (Cambridge, 1988), pp. 117–18.

[17] While it is not my main concern here, it is worth noting that about a quarter of the difference in height between slaves in the United States and slaves in the British Caribbean is explained by the shorter initial stature of new arrivals in the British Caribbean compared to those arriving in the United States. Indeed, after allowing for the unrepresentativeness of the Cuban data (see text), it is clear that slaves arriving in the United States were generally taller than slaves arriving in any other major region in the Americas apart from Bahia. The tall stature of U.S. and Bahian arrivals is explained by the fact that the United States drew heavily from the Senegambia and Sierra Leone areas, where the taller Susu and Mandingo peoples embarked, and Bahia drew almost exclusively from the Bight of Benin—which in the nineteenth century meant Yoruba—regions.

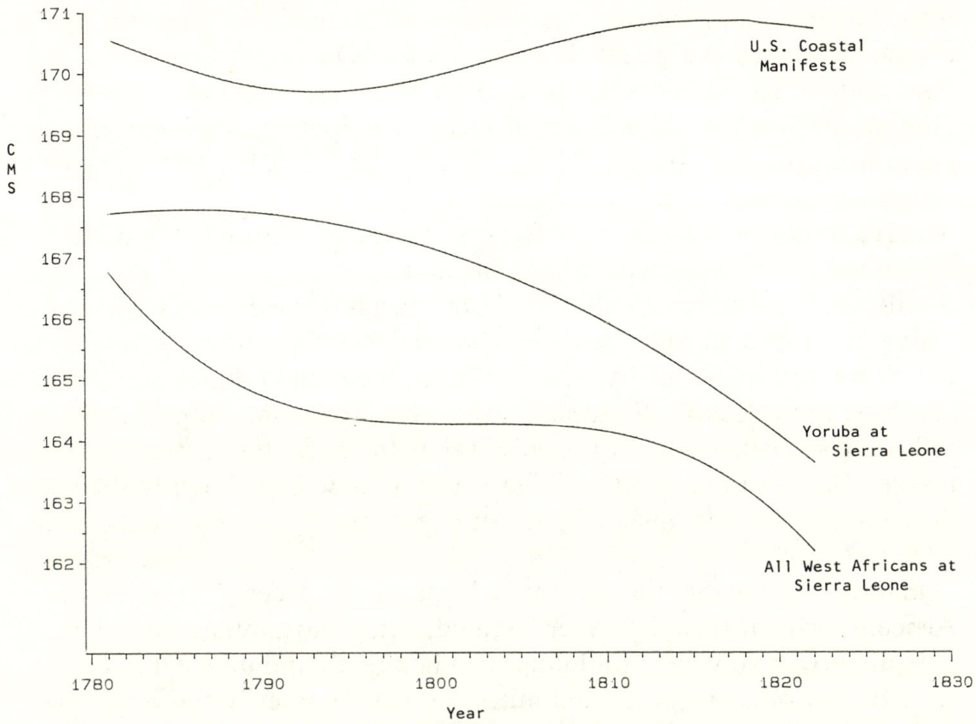

FIGURE 1

TIME PROFILES OF ADULT MALE HEIGHTS: SELECTED POPULATIONS OF AFRICANS AND AFRICAN DESCENT
(in centimeters)

Sources: U.S. slaves: Robert A. Margo and Richard H. Steckel, "The Heights of American Slaves: New Evidence on Slave Nutrition and Health," *Social Science History*, 6 (Fall 1982), pp. 522–23; Yoruba and West African recaptives: computed from copies of Sierra Leone registers of liberated Africans located in British Public Records Office, Foreign Slave Trade series FO 84, vols. 4, 9, 15, 21, 38, 63, 64, 76, 86, 87, 98, 100, 101, 102, 110, 116, 127, 134, 135, 147, 166, 189, 212, 231, 269, 273, 308, 310, 345, 346, 393, 450, 507, 599.

involved in the coastal U.S. trade and almost all of these slaves would have been born in the United States.[18] The second time trend, a third-degree polynomial on year of birth significant at the 1 percent level, is for 11,734 adult males embarked at ports other than Badagry and Lagos and subsequently registered at Sierra Leone.[19] This is a crude representation of the trend in mean stature of non-Yoruba. The sample is drawn mainly from those entering the slave trade from regions north of Cape Lopez—in other words West Africa as the term is usually used.

The American sample includes some individuals born in Africa who

[18] Robert A. Margo and Richard H. Steckel, "The Heights of American Slaves: New Evidence on Slave Nutrition and Health," *Social Science History*, 6 (Fall 1982), pp. 522–23.

[19] Time profiles for both non-Yoruba and Yoruba data were fitted with higher-order polynomials, but no improvement in significance levels resulted.

were shorter than those born in the United States. This gives the U.S. profile in Figure 1 a slight downward bias. On the African side, the non-Yoruba data contain only a few hundred measurements from the 45 percent or so of all slaves carried to the Americas in this period who came from regions south of Cape Lopez, and, as Table 1 shows, who were shorter than their West African counterparts. These few hundred observations of west-central Africans, moreover, are clustered at the end of the period covered and help account for the post-1813 dip in the profile. It is therefore likely that both African-based time profiles lie above the trend in final heights of slaves leaving Africa as a whole. Bearing in mind that few Africans going to the United States came from south of Cape Lopez, the non-Yoruba time trend may come close to reflecting the true trend for arrivals in the United States alone. Thus the top and bottom time trends in Figure 1 may understate slightly the true differential between final heights in the United States and those in Africa.[20]

Figure 1 shows that the difference in stature between U.S. slaves and African-born groups, however defined, was substantial, and that it extended over 40 years straddling the eighteenth and nineteenth centuries. Both work intensities and nutrition were greater in the Americas, but a net gain in nutrition must have occurred as a consequence of the forced migration. More important in the present context, the decline in the final heights of male Yoruba over the period was quite marked, amounting to about four centimeters over the period, with most of the decline occurring in the last 15 years. A time trend for females, not shown here, also shows a decline, but it is less pronounced, partly because the female sample is smaller and does not include all the years covered by the male sample.[21] It is unlikely that regional shifts in the composition of the Yoruba groups caused these differences. As already

[20] One indeterminate, but probably small, influence would result in some further understatement of the difference. Mortality rates in Trinidad were greater for slaves of shorter stature; see Friedman, "The Heights of Slaves in Trinidad," p. 488. There is the possibility that the substantial mortality associated with the slave trade yielded a survival group in the Americas slightly taller than the African population from which these survivors were drawn. Most of the Sierra Leone sample had already undergone this selection process because the ocean voyage to Sierra Leone from most parts of Africa was as severe in terms of duration and loss of life as the transatlantic voyage; see David Eltis, "Mortality and Voyage Length in the Middle Passage: New Evidence from the Nineteenth Century," this JOURNAL, 44 (June 1984), pp. 301–8. None of the samples of the African-born in Table 1 were collected in the homelands before the slave trade took its effect. Thus the height difference between the Sierra Leone sample and samples from the Americas could understate the true difference between Africa and the Americas. It should also be noted that very few Africans arrived in the United States after 1807 and even fewer after the Piracy Act of 1821—the period covered by the Sierra Leone data. Thus the non-Yoruba series as used in this context is a projection for comparative purposes based on pre-1807 trends of U.S. imports.

[21] A second-degree polynomial significant at the 1 percent level suggests a 2.3-centimeter decline between 1801 and 1821.

noted, subgroups of Yoruba exhibit much smaller height differences than the decline implied by Figure 1.

Preliminary analysis of the data thus indicates first that the Yoruba were taller than most other West African groups, and second that this stature advantage diminished in the early nineteenth century. The data also suggest a major differential in stature between Africa and the Americas, but this matter has been explored elsewhere. Four broadly competing (though not entirely exclusive) explanations might account for these results: genetic variations, differences in either the work or the epidemiological environment, and, finally, fluctuations in nutritional intakes. Scholars have given most emphasis to genetic adaptation to climatic biotopes in their attempt to explain differences in stature within Africa. Yet the data presented here do not entirely support this approach. From the genetic standpoint shorter stature is associated with forest conditions (and the climate producing these) and taller stature with a savanna or at least a thinner forest environment. As noted above, the Yoruba occupied both types of biotopes. A strict application of the Hiernaux hypothesis would lead us to expect the following: first, a large variation in final heights among the Yoruba (in other words, a higher standard deviation than for other groups); second, a Yoruba advantage over the more northerly Nupe and Hausa, as well as over the unidentified eastern group—the latter presumably being drawn from the area where the savanna penetrates to the ocean; third, that the Yoruba as a group would be taller than the Igbo, all but the most northerly of whom are forest dwellers.

A quick look at Table 1 shows that only the third of the above expectations is met. Panel Ia shows heights of a small sample of Hausa and Nupe, living to the north of Yorubaland, and Igbo, living to the east. In addition we have heights for an unidentified group which embarked from Little Popoe and Grand Popoe, drawn, certainly, from an area west of Yorubaland.[22] In the 1820s all these groups were significantly shorter than the Yoruba, and the relatively low standard deviations for Yoruba heights have continued into the twentieth century. It is possible to conclude that, as for other human populations, genotypes may have set limits on stature, but it is necessary to look elsewhere for explanations of at least some of the differences between Yoruba and non-Yoruba.

A genetically based hypothesis that would account for the time profile is even harder to visualize. A decline over such a short period could only result from a rather sudden influx into the gene pool of shorter-statured populations, or, alternatively, a shift in the slave catchment zone from regions occupied by taller individuals to those occupied by shorter ones. There is no evidence of the former having occurred, and

[22] See fn. 10.

to argue for the latter one must assume that height differences between Yoruba subgroups were significant—a position that the cross-sectional analysis does not appear to support. Even if we accept for the moment that stature differences within the Yoruba were significant, Peter Morton-Williams has argued on the basis of field work and oral traditions that the eastern Yoruba areas fell victim to slave trade first. These were the forest and forest fringe areas that the Hiernaux hypothesis associates with shorter stature. Yoruba lands to the north and west, associated with taller stature, were pulled into the slave trade in the late eighteenth century, a period when the stature of deportees was in fact declining.[23]

The second and third of the possible explanations for Yoruba stature look no more promising than the first. Human capacity for recovery from severe illness in childhood is truly remarkable. For disease to affect final heights the insult to the body must be prolonged.[24] Certainly, solid evidence exists of both severity and regional differences in African epidemiological environments, but there is a poor fit between Yoruba and non-Yoruba height differentials and the distribution of pathogens and disease vectors.[25] The epidemiological environment of the Niger Delta is, and was, severe, but it is nevertheless highly unlikely that the pathogens faced by the Yoruba and their western neighbors in the Niger Delta, the Igbo, differed sufficiently in type and intensity to explain height differences of four centimeters between the two groups. It is even less likely that the similar advantage that the Yoruba had over the Nupe and Hausa to the north, and other groups to the east, can be explained in epidemiological terms. Indeed, as one moves east from the Yoruba region (and among the shorter-statured groups) the disease environment becomes more, rather than less, benign. As for the work environment, there is nothing to suggest a differential in Africa of the order of magnitude that produced height differences between Caribbean slaves working under sugar and nonsugar regimes.

As for the time profile, it is certainly conceivable that epidemics—perhaps in conjunction with nutritional stress—induced a decline in stature, and this issue is joined below. Changes in work regimes or crops, on the other hand, are less likely to have contributed to the observed decline. Commodity exports such as palm oil products were simply not important during the period covered here—at least in the

[23] Peter Morton-Williams, "The Oyo Yoruba and the Atlantic Trade, 1670–1830," *Journal of the Historical Society of Nigeria*, 3 (Dec. 1964), pp. 25–45, reprinted in J. E. Inkori, ed., *Forced Migrations: The Impact of the Export Slave Trade on African Societies* (New York, 1982), pp. 167–86.

[24] Richard H. Steckel, "A Peculiar Population: The Nutrition, Health, and Mortality of American Slaves from Childhood to Maturity," this JOURNAL, 46 (Sept. 1986), pp. 721–41.

[25] Philip D. Curtin, "Epidemiology and the Slave Trade," *Political Science Quarterly*, 83 (June 1968), pp. 190–216.

Bight of Benin hinterland—and there is no evidence of a dramatic change in crops or production technologies within that part of the economy producing for the domestic or trans-Saharan markets.

At first sight the nutritional explanation of both cross-sectional and time series patterns looks as unpromising as the genetic, disease, and work-regime approaches. Throughout rural eastern and western Nigeria in the mid-twentieth century starchy roots and fruits accounted for 60 percent or more of the calorie intake. Cereals did form a more important portion of the remainder of the Yoruba diet than in non-Yoruba regions farther east, and there are well-known qualitative differences in nutrition between yams, plantains, and manioc on the one hand and maize, millet, and sorghums on the other. But there are three problems with using this approach to explain height differentials. First, nutritionally inferior root crops were usually dominant even where cereals were grown (though root crop yields are higher on the forest fringe than further south). Second, in other regions, notably the Ivory and Gold Coast hinterlands and areas north of the Igbo, a similar mix of cereals and root crops was not associated with taller stature.[26] Third, Yorubaland incorporates a wide range of crop regimes, some of which are very close to those governing adjacent cultures such as the Igbo and Hausa. Height measurements from the mid-twentieth century indicate that, as in the early nineteenth century, variations among different groups of Yoruba were much less significant than differences between the Yoruba as a whole and other groups. Nor are standard deviations for twentieth-century Yoruba samples large, compared to a very wide range of heights of ethnic groups from all over twentieth-century Africa.[27] This would suggest that despite the size of Yorubaland and the wide range of biotopes and disease environments it incorporated, the height advantage of the Yoruba people was broadly based.

The contrast between the Yoruba and the adjacent Igbo is particularly striking. As already noted, while most Igbo are forest dwellers, the northern Igbo live on the forest fringe. Africanus Horton—a rare environmentalist in an age of European scientific racism—noted significant differentials in Igbo heights following a north-south pattern; consistent with this, the large Igbo sample in Table 1 has a greater standard deviation than the Yoruba data.[28] In the mid-twentieth century

[26] W. B. Morgan and J. C. Pugh, *West Africa* (London, 1969), pp. 112–13. For height data on Gold Coast slaves, see Higman, "Growth in Afro-Caribbean Slave Populations," p. 364.

[27] See fn. 10.

[28] "In stature the Egboes differ very considerably according to the region whence they are taken. In Isuama and the north-central districts the inhabitants are tall and majestic looking, some well formed and shaped. . . . In other parts they are of middling size, averaging five feet two. In the delta of the river the inhabitants are short and stout . . . scarcely above four and a half feet." *West African Countries and Peoples* (Edinburgh, 1969, reprint of 1868 edition), p. 157. It might be added that both the Sierra Leone and modern data suggest that Horton somewhat exaggerated the intra-Igbo differentials.

the Yoruba did tend to have a higher, though still small, proportion of their caloric intake in the form of meat and fish. Bruce Johnston attributed this to the relative prosperity of cocoa farmers in the 1950s, but the fact that height differences between the Yoruba and the Igbo at this time were close to those computed for the 1820s indicates that nutritional differences, whatever their source, were not of recent origin.[29] This suggests that instead of focusing on genetic adaptation to biotopes or what the Yoruba shared with their neighbors, such as crop regimes and pathogens, we should consider Yoruba sociocultural factors as these impinged on the economy.[30]

The common strand binding the Yoruba together and distinguishing them from other West African groups over time was probably social and economic organization, particularly as this pertained to cities. Clearly it was not the presence of urban centers per se that made Yoruba society unusual in the broader region—much less regional population densities. Towns were not uncommon outside Yorubaland in a belt from Kumasi far to the west through Kano to the north and Onitsha to the east, and the heaviest population densities in sub-Saharan Africa were among the Igbo and Ibibio.[31]

The economic history of the Yoruba has received much less attention than political, military, and constitutional events in the historiography.[32] Nevertheless, some characteristics of Yoruba urbanization appear distinctive and hint at a specialization of labor that was more common outside Africa than within it in the early nineteenth century. In the first place, Yoruba cities were large by West African standards (though not, as noted below, by North Atlantic standards). The three largest centers in the 1850s, according to the missionary William Clarke, were Ilorin with 80,000, Abeokuta with 60,000, and Ibadan with 50,000 inhabitants.[33] These and other smaller towns had probably grown in the preceding half-century because the nineteenth-century wars generated refugees that fled to the towns. But the impressions of H. Clapperton

[29] Bruce F. Johnston, *The Staple Food Economies of Western Tropical Africa* (Stanford, 1958), pp. 55–90.

[30] There is also the point that the Oyo absorbed several non-Yoruba groups into the Yoruba socioeconomic "system" during its period of hegemony. On the basis of the above evidence, these non-Yoruba were very probably of shorter stature than the dominant group. Once more the relatively low standard deviations in the Yoruba Sierra Leone data indicate that such non-Yoruba groups quickly came to share in the Yoruba advantage over neighboring peoples.

[31] For 1911 and 1921 data, see P. Amaury Talbot, *The Peoples of Southern Nigeria*, 4 vols. (London, 1926), vol. 4, pp. 1–15.

[32] The fullest assessment of the historical Yoruba economy is in Robin Law, *The Oyo Empire, c. 1600–c. 1836* (Oxford, 1977), pp. 202–36, but the orientation of both this and the same author's "Slaves, Trade and Taxes: The Material Basis of Political Power in Precolonial West Africa," *Research in Economic Anthropology*, 1 (1978), pp. 37–52, is toward explaining the sources of state economic power.

[33] W. H. Clarke, in *Travels and Exploration in Yorubaland (1854–1858)*, J. A. Atanda, ed. (Ibadan, 1972), p. xxxviii.

suggest that the size advantage of Yoruba over non-Yoruba cities in the mid-twentieth century goes back some time.[34]

More important, a greater proportion of Yoruba than other West African societies lived in such communities. In the 1850s over half of the population of Yoruba province lived in Ibadan, Abeokuta, and Oyo, and while only the latter existed in the early nineteenth century, a high urban ratio had long been a feature of Yoruba life.[35] Furthermore, occupational census classifications are notoriously unreliable in an African context, where individuals typically perform several different tasks. But there seems little doubt that Yoruba urban dwellers had a much larger ratio of nonagriculturalists than might be found in other West African towns. Consistent with this, population densities of Yoruba cities are higher than elsewhere in West Africa. These last comments are based mainly on mid-twentieth-century data, but while European colonialism likely increased administrative occupations in cities such as Ibadan, overall, colonial domination could easily have meant a fall in the proportion of nonagricultural pursuits, particularly in urban-based manufacturing.[36]

The precise connection between urbanization and a welfare differential in favor of the Yoruba must remain speculative. The disease environment is not likely to have been more benign in urban as opposed to rural areas, and the most likely link is the high degree of specialization of tasks in the production and distribution of food required by cities the size of Oyo, Ilorin, Owo, Ife, and many others. This also ensured nutritional gains for the population at large, notwithstanding the fact that until well into the twentieth century much of the specialized food production was carried out by slave labor.[37] Perhaps it was not only in

[34] Law, *The Oyo Empire*, pp. 8–10; H. Clapperton, *Journal of a Second Expedition into the Interior of Africa* (London, 1829), p. 13; William Bascom, "Urbanism as a Traditional African Pattern," *The Sociological Review*, 7 (July 1959), pp. 29–43.

[35] See the missionary map of Yorubaland containing population estimates for urban centers from the early 1850s reproduced in Clarke, *Travels and Explorations*, p. xxxviii; also T. J. Bowen, *Central Africa: Adventures and Missionary Labours* (Charleston, 1857), p. 218.

[36] E. P. Skinner, "West African Economic Systems," in M. J. Herskovitz and M. Harwitz, eds., *Economic Transition in Africa* (London, 1964), p. 97; Akin Mabogunje and J. D. Omer-Cooper, *Owu in Yoruba History* (Ibadan, 1971), pp. 42–43.

[37] Urbanization might increase the incidence of diseases spread by congestion, such as intestinal complaints, though presumably nothing like the conditions in the slave trade that produced enormous mortality rates from dysentery existed in cities or indeed anywhere else in Africa under normal conditions. The major diseases in West Africa tend, in any event, to be endemic rather than epidemic, and it is hard to see how urbanization would reduce their impact. Johnston, *Staple Food Economies*, pp. 55–90, 200–1; B. M. Nicol, "Nutrition of Nigerian Peasant Farmers, with Special Reference to the Effects of Vitamin A and Riboflavin Deficiency," *British Journal of Nutrition*, 3 (1949), pp. 25–43; idem, "The Nutrition of Nigerian Peasants, with Special Reference to the Effects of the Vitamin B complex, Vitamin A, and Annual Protein," *British Journal of Nutrition*, 6 (1952), pp. 34–55; U.S. Department of Health, Education, and Welfare, *Republic of Nigeria: Nutrition Survey: February-April 1965* (Washington, 1967). Regarding specialized food production, see Talbot, *The Peoples of Southern Nigeria*, vol. 3, p. 699.

the Americas that coerced labor could be compatible with improvements in nutritional status. For John Iliffe the "high degree of occupational specialization" provided a "wealth of opportunities for independent survival" and ensured that the poor were "less numerous and visible" than elsewhere in Africa.[38]

This argument raises a fascinating point of comparison around the Atlantic basin. Urbanization in nineteenth-century European and North American cities usually meant a net welfare loss for most inhabitants, often associated with the income inequalities and unhealthiness of large urban areas. Was the African experience different? There are two possible answers. Mid-nineteenth-century Yoruba cities were not large in comparison with what they were to become, nor compared to their overseas counterparts. In North America and Europe, small-scale urbanization was actually associated with improvements in welfare—the deleterious impact being largely confined to centers in excess of 10,000.[39] If Yoruba towns were below this threshold, then perhaps the American, European, and Yoruba experiences were subject to similar constraints. But if Yoruba towns were in excess of 10,000 at this time, then an alternative interpretation emerges. In contrast with North America and Europe, the Yoruba urban environment may not have generated the income inequalities and unsanitary conditions of the larger centers of the North Atlantic. As an average population greater than 10,000 is likely, urbanization in Yorubaland may well have had different social implications from the same phenomenon in the North Atlantic.

There is the additional possibility that the relative absence of the Yoruba from the transatlantic traffic before the nineteenth century ensured an undisrupted economy and some nutritional security compared to less fortunate groups. This is an attractive hypothesis. However, while the Yoruba share of the slave trade increased after 1800, it was not insignificant before 1800, and the hypothesis cannot explain the continuation of greater Yoruba stature, albeit on a diminishing basis, after 1800.[40] In any event there is clearly a case for evaluating human diversity in historical Africa in terms of nutrition and disease, as well as genetic variation.[41]

[38] John Iliffe, *The African Poor: A History* (Cambridge, 1987), pp. 85–86.

[39] Steckel, "Height and Per Capita Income"; Robert A. Margo and Richard H. Steckel, "Heights of Native-Born Whites During the Antebellum Period," this JOURNAL, 43 (Mar. 1983), pp. 167–74.

[40] Nearly 12 percent of a sample of 13,334 slaves on eighteenth-century St. Domingue plantations have been identified as Yoruba; see David Geggus, "Sex Ratio, Age and Ethnicity in the Atlantic Slave Trade: Data from French Shipping and Plantation Records," *Journal of African History*, 30 (No. 1, 1989), p. 32.

[41] A similar case could be made for a nutritional component in the height advantage of West Africans as a whole compared to those from west-central Africa. Specialization in the production of both food and nonfood items seems to have been greater in most West African societies compared to most west-central African groups. Genetic variation was probably greater in the latter

As for the decline of Yoruba stature over time, a plausible explanation does exist in the historical record that incorporates elements of both nutritional status and perhaps the disease variable. The Oyo Empire that dominated Yorubaland from the north in the mid-eighteenth century and imposed a pax Oyo on the region went into irrevocable decline at the end of the century.[42] Internal dissension initiated the process, but the latter was accelerated by losses to the Nupe and Borgu in the north, a Fulani jihad, attacks from Dahomey in the west, and full-scale conflicts among Yoruba communities in the south and east. The city of Oyo itself was taken by the Fulani only in 1835, but a general deterioration of public order and the appearance of marauding bands of "war-boys" were a feature of life in many areas long before this point. The independence asserted by Afonja at Ilorin and the subsequent emergence of that city as a center of Fulani opposition began in the first decade of the nineteenth century. More generalized warfare, spreading through the southern and eastern regions which owed allegiance to old Oyo, is usually thought to have begun in 1810 with the two phases of the Owu wars. These lasted most of the following decade and included long sieges. Intensification of the disturbances in the north dates from the Muslim rebellion of 1817. In the 1820s the campaigns and lawlessness spread to the Egba region, with the destruction of Ikija and Orun among other centers. This is the era which saw the founding of, or huge expansion of, what were virtually refugee settlements at Ibadan and Abeokeuta.

Large areas of Yorubaland were unaffected at first. There are few hints of disruption in the western Yoruba societies through which Clapperton and the Landers passed in the 1820s. And even when the troubles were at their height there would always have been regions in which agriculture and trade could be conducted normally. These regions, however, were not the ones from which the slaves measured at Sierra Leone were likely to have been drawn. War captives may not have formed the majority of those entering the transatlantic slave trade, but in nineteenth-century Yorubaland the link between war and the slave trade seems to have been strong.

The acceleration in the decline of the Yoruba trend line in Figure 1 coincides with the intensification of the Oyo conflict and its shift southward. The horizontal axis in the figure shows year of birth, and the

---

region than the former, but it would be difficult to argue that the humidity and heat combinations discussed by Hiernaux explain stature differences between these two broad nineteenth-century slave provenance zones.

[42] The following is based on Robert S. Smith, *Kingdoms of the Yoruba* (3rd edn., Madison, 1988), pp. 109–24; Mabogunje and Omer-Cooper, *Owu in Yoruba History*, pp. 19–82; and especially Law, *The Oyo Empire*, pp. 245–77.

insult to physical maturation would have occurred in the first 10 or 15 years of life. The years from about 1810 to about 1830 emerge as the critical era in literature on the collapse of Oyo. In this period war became more generalized and would have had a more disruptive impact than the disputes between royalty and aristocracy and the localized military initiatives that preceded 1810. Figure 1 implies that the Yoruba lost most of their height advantage over non-Yoruba males entering the slave trade at this period. Since much of the decline after 1813 in the non-Yoruba profile in Figure 1 is explained by the inclusion of the whole limited subsample from west-central Africa in these years, the decline in the differential between Yoruba stature and stature of other *West* African peoples is not fully captured in Figure 1. In absolute terms the Yoruba decline after about 1805 was rather more severe than short-term declines experienced by both blacks and whites in the nineteenth-century United States.[43] It might be inferred that the dislocation to the Yoruba system and more specifically to food supplies was of major proportions.

One quantitative attempt to link trends in stature with the collapse of old Oyo is possible. Captives from the wars fed the transatlantic slave trade, or perhaps the slave trade triggered the wars that generated captives. Before the decline of the Oyo Empire relatively few Yoruba entered the slave trade, and Lagos and Badagry were minor embarkation points in the traffic. To the extent that the volume of slaves leaving these ports reflected disorder, and disorder had an impact on Yoruba stature, then we might expect to find a negative relationship between stature of cohorts grouped by year of birth and the volume of exports. In addition, the beginning of more generalized warfare in Yorubaland after 1810 should also have had a depressing impact on mean stature.

Export data for individual ports to test for this relationship are not available, but annual estimates of slave departures from the Bight of Benin exist for the years from 1811 to 1822. For the period before 1810 we know that the Portuguese were the major, indeed after the demise of the French and Dutch traffics in 1793 virtually the only, purchasers of slaves in the Bight of Benin. Their shipments from this region went almost entirely to Bahia.[44] Estimates of annual arrivals of slaves at Bahia, 1793 to 1810, do exist, and, with the addition of an allowance for mortality, these may be accepted as a proxy for departures from the

[43] Robert William Fogel, "Nutrition and the Decline in Mortality since 1800: Some Preliminary Findings," pp. 497–502; idem et al., "Secular Changes in American and British Stature and Nutrition."

[44] The only other active slave traders at this time were the British and the Americans. In the 1790s and early 1800s neither group traded heavily in the Bight of Benin. See Richardson, "Slave Exports from West and West-Central Africa." For slave departures from the Bight of Benin after 1810, see Eltis, *Economic Growth*, p. 250.

Bight of Benin.[45] Because of the activities of the French and the Dutch, no attempt is made to extend the series back before 1794. We thus have 30 observations between the period 1793 and 1822. A crude allowance for the effect of the more generalized phase of warfare can be made with the inclusion of a dummy variable, with the period after 1810 set equal to one. The effects of time are captured with the inclusion of a time trend variable entered as 1 for the year 1793 to 30 for 1822. An ordinary least squares regression equation was estimated with mean final heights in centimeters grouped in year of birth as the dependent variable, and three independent variables: first, the dummy variable for intensification of the war; second, annual slave departures from the Bight of Benin in thousands; and third, a time-trend variable. The equation was also estimated with slave departures lagged, that is, stature dependent on departures in the previous year, or departures two or three years before. The best result was obtained with slave departures lagged by one year, though significant results were obtained with greater lags. With this format the coefficients for slave exports, the time trend, and the intercept were significant at the 5 percent level, and the dummy variable for the effects of war was weakly significant at the 20 percent level. The result was (standard error in the first set of parentheses, *t*-statistic in the second):

$$\text{Mean height} = \underset{\substack{(0.738)\\(229.9)}}{169.6} - \underset{\substack{(0.099)\\(-2.1)}}{0.209}\ \text{slv exp (lag)} - \underset{\substack{(0.044)\\(-2.1)}}{0.093}\ \text{time} - \underset{\substack{(0.696)\\(-1.3)}}{0.92}\ \text{war}$$

$N = 30 \quad R^2 = 0.73$

Evaluated at the mean this result suggests that for every increase in slave departures of 1,000, mean heights of the birth cohort declined by more than one-fifth of a centimeter, and the onset of a more intensive phase of the Yoruba wars resulted in a nearly one-centimeter decline in mean heights. However, the time-trend variable suggests a decline of less than one-tenth of a centimeter each year attributable to other factors. These could have included the onset of drought or unrest arising from a long-term expansion of domestic slavery. The historical record does not support speculation on the issue. No less than 73 percent of the variation in mean heights of the Yoruba in this period is explained by the equation.[46] Since correlation does not imply causation, the result does

[45] Eltis, *Economic Growth*, p. 243.

[46] The omission of the dummy variable from the equation does nothing to impair the systematic relationship between final heights and slave departures. A simple regression of mean annual stature on slave exports yielded a reduced R^2 of 0.34, but a slave export coefficient significant at the 0.001 level.

nothing to settle the question of whether the slave trade was responsible for the decline in stature, or whether the war, or more precisely the collapse of Oyo, created conditions that both reduced the nutritional status of the Yoruba and made possible an increase in the number of Yoruba slaves shipped to the Americas. Certainly the demise of old Oyo has long been attributed to the slave trade, but more recent assessments have raised awkward questions of timing and linkages for those supporting this position.[47] The above regression provides ammunition for both sides in the debate on the impact of the slave trade on Africa.[48]

In summary, the anthropometric evidence supports two hypotheses. First, the Yoruba as a group had a higher level of material welfare than their West African neighbors; second, the dislocations following the collapse of the Oyo Empire were severe enough to reduce that material welfare. The first of these two positions will probably be subject to closer scrutiny than the second. While this second point is not particularly startling, new quantitative evidence has not always confirmed what has long been discussed in the qualitative literature. To conclude on a speculative note, it is possible that these results provide a rare empirical hint, in this part of Africa at least, of the inappropriateness of the Malthusian model. As the Yoruba height advantage may be discerned in the mid-twentieth century (though less pronounced) as well as the early nineteenth, in the long run there is a suggestion that the advantage survived both war and population pressures. The collapse of Oyo apparently did not have a permanent impact on the Yoruba welfare differential. Though a transatlantic gap remained, rapid population growth in the later nineteenth and early twentieth centuries did not permanently erode the Yoruba advantage under Oyo.

[47] Law, *The Oyo Empire*, pp. 305–6; Eltis, *Economic Growth*, p. 74. The traditional view is represented by I. A. Akinjogbin, "The Prelude to the Yoruba Civil Wars of the Nineteenth Century," *Odu*, 2nd series, 1 (1964), pp. 24–46.

[48] A third possible interpretation is that as the volume of slave exports increased, slave traders were forced to take shorter slaves. Given the fact that the final heights here are grouped into year of birth cohorts, this is very unlikely. If this tendency was in fact a feature of the trade, we would expect final heights grouped by year of export (rather than year of birth) to vary inversely with annual slave departures. To test for this, an ordinary least squares regression equation was estimated with mean heights in year of departure as the dependent variable, and annual slave departures from the Bight of Benin as the independent variable. The sign of the coefficient was negative, but the result was nonsignificant and the R^2 less than 0.02. Rerunning the regression with lagged values did not improve the result. It should also be noted that the distribution of slaves from all regions was normal, whereas a predisposition for taller slaves would have made the distribution of recaptives skewed. See Eltis, "Nutritional Trends in Africa and the Americas," for a discussion of this last point.

Nuclear Power Reactors: A Study in Technological Lock-in

ROBIN COWAN

Recent theory has predicted that if competing technologies operate under dynamic increasing returns, one, possibly inferior, technology will dominate the market. The history of nuclear power technology is used to illustrate these results. Light water is considered inferior to other technologies, yet it dominates the market for power reactors. This is largely due to the early adoption and heavy development by the U.S. Navy of light water for submarine propulsion. When a market for civilian power emerged, light water had a large head start, and by the time other technologies were ready to enter the market, light water was entrenched.

The history of nuclear power generation can be seen as a competition among several technologies to capture the market. This competition, which began immediately following World War II, was eventually won by the light water technology. At a 1982 conference on nuclear power experience a U.S. delegate claimed: "In retrospect, choosing the LWR [light water reactor] was a wise decision. Not only is the LWR used almost exclusively in the USA today, but this type, based largely on technology developed in the USA, is being used for about 80 percent of all the reactors built or under construction in the world today."[1] While an appropriate decision at the time, it now seems that light water may have been an unfortunate choice. One of the interesting features of this history is the belief held by many that light water is not the best technology, either economically or technically. The evidence in support of this belief, while not incontrovertible, is strong enough to support the contention that light water is not the superior technology. This suggests that other technologies should still be present in the market. Light water, however, has taken virtually the entire market.

COMPETING TECHNOLOGIES

The Stanley Steamer, direct current electricity, and gas graphite reactors were, at one time, considered the best available technology by

The Journal of Economic History, Vol. L, No. 3 (Sept. 1990). ISSN 0022-0507.

The author is Assistant Professor of Economics, New York University, 269 Mercer Street, New York, NY 10003.

The author wishes to acknowledge the many useful comments of Brian Arthur, Tim Bresnahan, John Connelly, Mario Rizzo, two anonymous referees, and the editor of this JOURNAL. I also acknowledge the able research assistance of Sabyasachi Ray. This research was funded in part by the Social Sciences and Humanities Research Council of Canada and the C. V. Starr Center for Applied Economics.

[1] International Atomic Energy Agency, *Nuclear Power Experience, Proceedings of a Conference on Nuclear Power Experience* (Vienna, 1983), vol. 1, p. 51.

knowledgeable people.[2] They also share the feature of being technologies that are not used today.

Important in the competition between direct and alternating electric current were changes in the environment in which technologies operated, altering which aspects of the technology were desirable and which ought to be considered "best."[3] Initially, when electricity transmission took place over short distances, direct current seemed to have an advantage, as it was technically better equipped to meet peak loading problems. As transmission distances grew, however, alternating current gained the upper hand, to a great extent due to its ability to transmit at high voltages and then use step-down transformers to lower the voltage for consumers, thus circumventing the problems of voltage loss. Now, however, direct current is making somewhat of a comeback, with very long-distance, very high-voltage transmission. Similar changes have occurred in the case of nuclear reactors, but here they are more clear cut. Everywhere except in Canada, military issues were the first to be considered—in France and the United Kingdom weapons-grade fissionable material was in demand; in the United States naval propulsion was the main application. When these demands had been relieved or were no longer so pressing, civilian power emerged as the main consideration, and the important characteristics of reactors became cost and safety. After a market for civilian nuclear power was established, these concerns remained in the forefront. Very important in the development of nuclear power, though, was the early interest in military applications. The effects which followed from the military's definition of "best" have been felt ever since.

One part of the explanation for the demise of the Stanley Steamer early this century was the reluctance on the part of the Stanley brothers to adopt high volume manufacturing.[4] Another lies in what Brian Arthur refers to as "historical small events." The steam car fared poorly in important races against petrol cars, and at a crucial time there was an outbreak of hoof and mouth disease in the northeastern United States. This closed the horse troughs which were used to refill the boilers of steam cars. The outbreak lasted six months in 1914, long enough to do

[2] For other case studies of competing technologies, see Paul David, "CLIO and the Economics of QWERTY," *American Economic Review*, 75 (May 1985); Morris Teubal and Edward Steinmueller, "Government Policy, Innovation and Economic Growth: Lessons From a Study of Satellite Communications," *Research Policy*, 11 (Oct. 1981); and S. H. Karlson, "Adoption of Competing Inventions by United States Steel Producers," *Review of Economics and Statistics*, 68 (Aug. 1986).

[3] See Paul David with Julie Bunn, "The Economics of Gateway Technologies and Network Evolution: Lessons from Electricity Supply History," *Information Economics and Policy*, 3 (No. 2, 1988).

[4] See Brian Arthur, "Competing Technologies and Economic Prediction," *Options*, International Institute for Applied Systems Analysis (Laxenburg, Austria, 1984); and Charles McLaughlin, "The Stanley Steamer: A Study in Unsuccessful Innovation," *Explorations in Entrepreneurial History*, 7 (Oct. 1954).

irreparable damage to the reputation of the steam automobile. Similar events shaped the outcome of the nuclear reactor competition. First, Hyman Rickover was put in charge of the U.S. naval propulsion program in 1946. His preference for light water was central to most of the history that followed. Second, the explosion of the Soviet nuclear bomb in 1949 caused a civilian power project to be rushed forward, before the physicists involved were ready to make a choice among the available technologies, effectively forcing the choice of light water.

Finally, direct current and the Stanley Steamer technologies and gas graphite and heavy water reactors share one further characteristic. They were all new technologies, competing with other new ones, all operating under dynamic increasing returns.

COMPETING TECHNOLOGIES AND INCREASING RETURNS

Recent theoretical work on competing technologies has focused on situations in which superior technologies can disappear from the market.[5] If technologies operate under dynamic increasing returns (often thought of in terms of learning-by-doing or learning-by-using), then early use of one technology can create a snowballing effect by which that technology quickly becomes preferred to others and comes to dominate the market.

Following Arthur, consider a market in which two types of consumers adopt technology sequentially. As a result of dynamic increasing returns arising from learning-by-using, the payoff to adopting a technology is an increasing function of the number of times it has been adopted in the past.[6] Important with regard to which technology is chosen next is how many times each of the technologies has been used in the past. Arthur shows that if the order of adopters is random (that is, the type of the next adopter is not predictable) then with certainty one technology will claim the entire market. He also shows that both technologies have a positive probability of dominating. Thus the market can get locked into an inferior technology.[7]

[5] For a survey of the recent competing technologies literature, see Brian Arthur, "Competing Technologies: An Overview," in G. Dosi, et al., eds., *Technical Change and Economic Theory* (London, 1988). "Superior" here means "inherently superior." Theoretical results indicate that under a variety of conditions, only one technology will survive in the market. Given this result, the superior technology is that which, if it were to be the surviving one, would maximize net benefits from the technology choice process. This is an ex post definition of "superior."

[6] "Technology" here is a generic term. Following Kenneth Arrow: "At any moment of time, the new capital goods incorporate all the knowledge then available, but once built their productive efficiency cannot be altered by subsequent learning." Kenneth Arrow, "The Economic Implications of Learning by Doing," *Review of Economic Studies*, 29 (June 1962), p. 157. Technologies improve but particular instances of them do not.

[7] This model is presented in Brian Arthur, "On Competing Technologies and Historical Small Events: The Dynamics of Choice Under Increasing Returns" (International Institute for Applied Systems Analysis Working Paper WP-83-90, 1983); and in Brian Arthur, "Competing Technolo-

In this model it is assumed that the future payoffs to a technology are well known.[8] Typically, however, when a technology is introduced its future payoffs are not well known. Though it is safe to assume that payoffs will increase with use, the degree of improvement is often difficult to predict. Thus a second type of learning common to new technologies is learning-about-payoffs. As a technology is used more and more, the uncertainty about its benefits is reduced. This feature has been modeled as a multiarmed bandit which allows explicit recognition of two effects of every adoption: the adopter receives an immediate payoff, and more information is generated about the inherent "goodness" of that technology.[9] This model shows that even if there is a powerful central authority managing these two features optimally, the results of the earlier model remain: one technology takes the entire market, and each technology has a positive probability of being dominant. An inferior technology can dominate the market if when first used the inherently superior technology's payoff causes the decision maker to lower his estimate of how good it "really" is. As a consequence he switches to the other technology which may produce results good enough that the estimate of its value is not lowered. Because the superior technology is not being used, it cannot prove its superiority or advance along its learning curve. If the results of the inferior technology are good for long enough, the decision maker will eventually have very strong beliefs that it is better than the first technology. Thus he will never switch back to the initial, superior technology, and the inferior technology will dominate the market. This mechanism operates a fortiori in the absence of a central decision maker.

Both types of learning—learning-by-doing and learning-about-payoffs—were present throughout the history of nuclear power, and so theory predicts that one technology, not necessarily the best, would come to dominate the market. Theory also suggests that events early in the process can be crucial in determining the long-run outcome. This

---

gies, Increasing Returns, and Lock-In by Historical Events," *Economic Journal*, 99 (Mar. 1989). It is possible to find sets of parameters and functions such that only one technology is ever used, and so these results will be violated. The results are very general, however.

[8] Many other models make the same assumption. See, for example, Joe Farrell and Garth Saloner, "Standardization, Compatibility and Innovation," *Rand Journal of Economics*, 16 (Spring 1985); Joe Farrell and Garth Saloner, "Installed Base and Compatibility," *American Economic Review*, 76 (Dec. 1986); Michael Katz and Carl Shapiro, "Network Externalities, Competition and Compatibility," *American Economic Review*, 75 (May 1985); and Michael Katz and Carl Shapiro, "Technology Adoption in the Presence of Network Externalities," *Journal of Political Economy*, 94 (Aug. 1986).

[9] See Robin Cowan, "Backing the Wrong Horse: Sequential Technology Choice Under Increasing Returns" (Ph.D. diss., Stanford University, 1987). The multiarmed bandit is a problem studied in probability theory, characterized as a slot machine with several arms. The arms are assumed to have different probabilities of paying out, and the object is to play the arms one at a time in any order so as to maximize the expected present value of the winnings.

seems to have been the case with nuclear power. The early choice of light water for the U.S. naval program resulted in considerable learning about this technology very early in the competition. When the push for civilian nuclear power emerged in the early 1960s light water was well advanced along its learning curve while the other technologies were late entrants which failed to catch up.

LIGHT WATER, HEAVY WATER, AND GAS GRAPHITE

Nuclear reactors are classified by two of the materials used in their construction: the coolant used to transfer heat from the reactor core; and the moderator used to control the energy level of the neutrons in the reactor core.[10] In a light water reactor both coolant and moderator are light water—H_2O. In a heavy water reactor both are heavy water—D_2O.[11] In a gas graphite reactor the coolant is a gas, usually helium or carbon dioxide, and the moderator is graphite. These three types of reactor—light water, heavy water, and gas graphite—while not the only technologies used or feasible were the most extensively developed as competitors in the nuclear power reactor market.

There has always been doubt as to the superiority, both technical and economic, of the light water reactor.[12] It is difficult to document the claim that light water is inferior in an ex post sense—light water may be relatively good now but had a different technology dominated, we would have an even better reactor. Nonetheless, there are indications that this hypothesis is true. In the fifties, following a debate on the relative merits of enriched uranium (light water) and natural uranium (heavy water and gas graphite), the journal *Nucleonics* stated that "to the observer of this debate it seems that enriched reactors must rely heavily upon their development potential to do much better than match the power costs of natural uranium systems."[13] Further, the cost estimates made throughout the fifties, detailed later, by no means pointed to light water as the most efficient technology.

[10] When an atom is split, neutrons are released which bombard other atoms, causing them to split and so creating a chain reaction. The chain reaction generates considerable heat which is used to turn turbines which generate electricity. To sustain a chain reaction there is an optimal speed, or energy level, for the neutrons. By causing the neutrons to travel through particular substances in the reactor core (moderators), this optimal energy level can be obtained. For an easily accessible account of the technology of nuclear power reactors, see Irwin Bupp and Jean-Claude Derian, *Light Water: How the Nuclear Dream Dissolved* (New York, 1968), chap. 1, fn. 3.

[11] Deuterium is a naturally found isotope of hydrogen. D_2O is found in nature, in the ratio of approximately 1 part in 5,000 parts H_2O.

[12] The sources for the following paragraphs are *Nucleonics*, 15 (June 1957); W. Marshall, ed., "Reactor Technology," *Nuclear Power Technology*, vol. 1 (Oxford, 1983); Alan Cottrell, "The Pressure on Nuclear Safety," *New Scientist* (Mar. 25, 1982); David Green, "AGR v PWR: The Debate Continues," *Energy Policy*, 14 (Feb. 1986); M. Piran and W. Murgatroyd, "Fuelling Costs of Nuclear Reactors," *Energy Policy*, 12 (Mar. 1984); and International Atomic Energy Agency, *Nuclear Power Reactors in the World* (Vienna, 1987).

[13] *Nucleonics*, 15 (June 1957), p. 71.

Both the gas graphite and heavy water reactors have much lower volumetric power densities (the ratio of power output to core volume) than do light water reactors. While this tends to raise capital costs and reduce design flexibility, it also provides a safety advantage. In the event of a coolant loss, the core will provide a much larger heat sink (particularly in the case of the graphite core) and so the temperature transients will be much smaller, giving operators more time to effect an adequate response. The use of a gas coolant also has the advantage of being safe from phase changes with changes in pressure or temperature. Thus under many fault conditions cooling can be maintained in the gas graphite reactor, when it would be lost with liquid coolant technologies. A second, related advantage of gas coolants is that they can be heated to higher temperatures, which gives the advanced gas graphite reactors a higher thermal efficiency than others.

An element of considerable concern during the British debate over the merits of light water and gas graphite technologies was the steel pressure vessel of the pressurized water reactor (PWR—Westinghouse's light water reactor). The safety principle in the PWR was, and still is, that the vessel never comes close to failure. If a crack does happen to reach the critical size (much smaller than the thickness of the vessel), however, it can grow at speeds up to the speed of sound. There would be no time for reaction. To manufacture a vessel sufficiently free of flaws to be safe from this problem requires very high-technology manufacturing abilities, which are beyond the capabilities of many countries and were beyond most countries in the fifties. Both the Canadian heavy water reactor, the Candu, and the second-generation British gas graphite reactor, the AGR, avoid this problem through systematic redundancy. The Candu uses many pressure tubes rather than a single vessel. The failure of a single tube is not critical and gives warning of other potential failures. This makes Candu less prone to meltdown due to coolant loss. The AGR uses a prestressed concrete pressure vessel. There is considerable mechanical redundancy in the system of steel load-bearing cables. Cables can be replaced individually, and again, the failure of a single cable is not fatal and gives warning of other potential failures.

In terms of operating experience, light water has not been significantly better than the other technologies in spite of having logged many more reactor years—an order of magnitude more than heavy water and three times more than gas graphite. While occupational radiation exposure with light water has been approximately equal to that of heavy water, it has been more than 10 times that of the British gas graphite reactors. The annual load factor of a reactor is the ratio of the total amount of power produced in a year to the amount it would have produced had it operated at full capacity, never shutting down, throughout the year. This is the standard measure of reactor availability. The average annual load factors of light water and gas graphite reactors have been approximately equal at 63 percent. Heavy water reactors, however, have had an average annual load factor of 73 percent.[14] This difference is due in part to the on-load refueling capabilities of the Candu, which have been adopted for the AGR.

Hugh McIntyre estimated that the heavy water Candu reactors at Pickering near Toronto generate power at about 75 percent of the cost of the light water reactors of equivalent size at the Zion 2 generating station in Illinois.[15] This is consistent with analyses done by Ontario Hydro, which suggest that if Ontario Hydro had a mature light water reactor program, the costs of nuclear electricity would be 20 to 25 percent higher than with the current heavy water systems.[16]

There is considerable evidence, then, that other technologies have inherent advantages over light water and that with equivalent amounts of development and use might well have proven to be better.[17] While it is not possible to document definitively that light water is an inferior technology, it seems clear that the dominant position held by light water cannot be due to a unanimous belief in its technical and economic superiority.

THE DOMINANCE OF LIGHT WATER

At the 1955 Peaceful Uses of the Atom Conference in Geneva about 100 different reactor types were judged not obviously impractical. In 1958, at the second Geneva conference, only about 12 types were seriously considered.[18] In the late 1950s the U.S. Atomic Energy Commission (AEC) was doing research on several different types of reactors, while the United Kingdom and France were working independently on gas graphite reactors and Canada was working on heavy water reactors. By 1960 serious research had been done or was being done on

[14] The source for these figures is International Atomic Energy Agency, *Nuclear Power Reactors in the World*, table 17. A reactor is included in the average for the entire time it is connected to the electricity grid up to 1987. These figures do not control for things such as different regulatory regimes. If the average performance within a country is used as an observation point, light water looks much better, largely due to extremely good performance in Belgium and Sweden, though still not as good as heavy water.

[15] Hugh McIntyre, "Natural-Uranium Heavy-Water Reactors," *Scientific American*, 233 (Oct. 1975).

[16] G. R. Fanjoy, "Generating Costs From Candu," *European Symposium on the Candu Reactor*, London (Mar. 1982); and Ontario Hydro, "Ontario Hydro CANDU Operating Experience," NGD-9 (1987). The higher estimate uses the world average load factor; the lower estimate assumes that the annual load factor would be higher under Ontario Hydro management policies.

[17] For more discussion on the merits of other technologies, see Harold Agnew, "Gas-Cooled Nuclear Power Reactors," *Scientific American*, 244 (June 1981); Alvin Weinberg and Irving Spiewak, "Inherently Safe Reactors and a Second Nuclear Era," *Science*, 29 (June 1984); and Eliot Marshall, "The Gas Reactor Makes a Comeback," *Science*, 29 (May 1984).

[18] See Phillip Mullenbach, *Civilian Nuclear Power: Economic Issues and Policy Formation* (New York, 1964), p. 39.

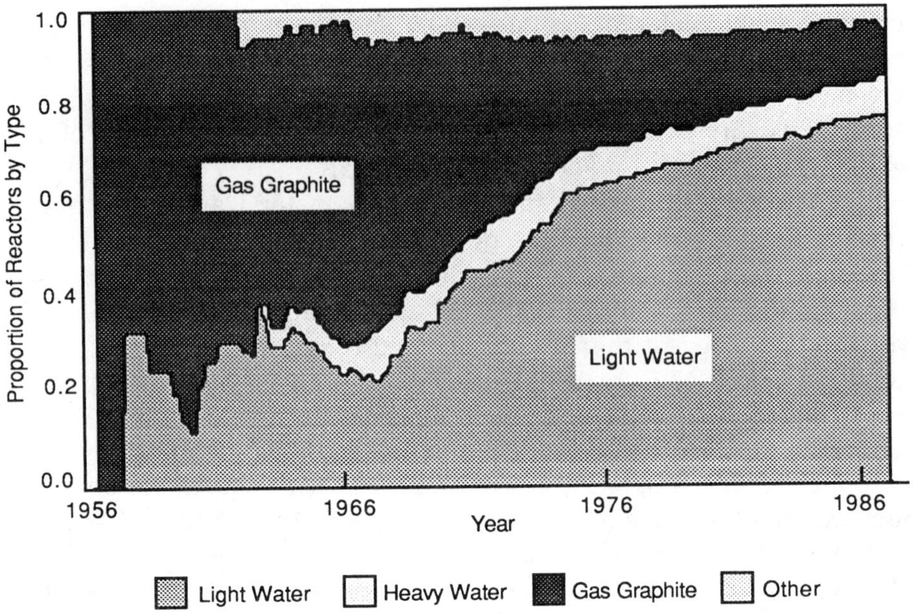

FIGURE 1A

PROPORTION OF THE INSTALLED BASE BY REACTOR TYPE

Source: International Atomic Energy Agency, *Nuclear Power Reactors in the World* (Vienna, 1987).

about a dozen reactor types. Of these technologies, six have been used in generating stations (one, the light water graphite reactor, is used only in the Soviet Union), but Irwin Bupp and Jean-Claude Derian stated that by 1975 there were only two distinct reactor types in the marketplace—the light water, basically of U.S. design, and the Canadian Candu, a heavy water reactor.[19] Indeed, in 1986 of the 101 power reactors under construction in the world (excluding the Soviet Union), 81 were light water. Of the 56 planned but not yet under construction, 48 were light water. Light water has taken the lion's share of the world reactor market.

The first reactor to be connected to a power grid was the gas graphite reactor at Calder Hall in the United Kingdom in August 1956. The second was a light water reactor at Shippingport, Pennsylvania, in the United States in December 1957. In the very early days of nuclear power, gas graphite had a small advantage over light water in terms of number of generating stations, but light water was rapidly accumulating experience through its use by the U.S. Navy.

In the early 1960s light water began to be commercialized. Under the 1958 Euratom accord and the 1954 Atoms for Peace program light water

[19] See Bupp and Derian, *Light Water*, p. 6.

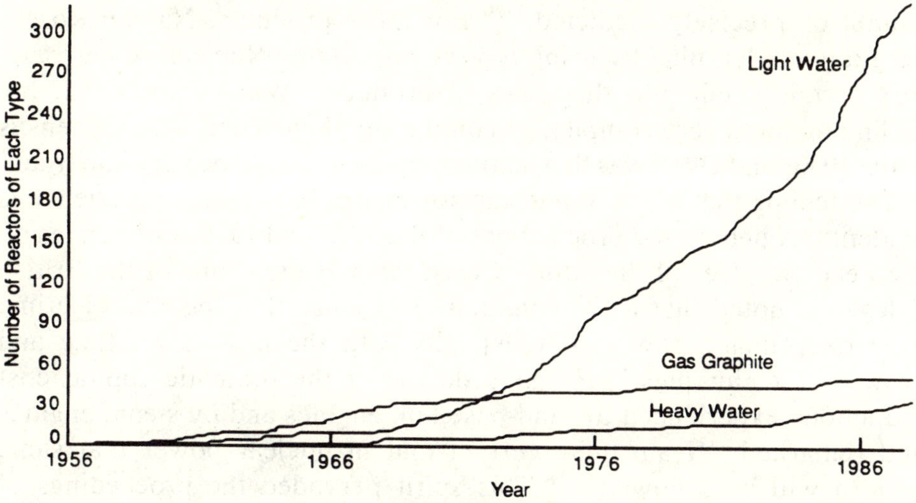

FIGURE 1B

NUMBER OF REACTORS BY TYPE

Source: International Atomic Energy Agency, *Nuclear Power Reactors in the World* (Vienna, 1987).

was introduced to Europe and was quickly accepted by those countries not having indigenous reactor programs. U.S. utility companies began a serious move toward nuclear power in the early 1960s and had ordered 18 reactors by the end of 1965. All of them were light water. About this time France was beginning to have doubts about the economic viability of gas graphite and in 1969 abandoned it for light water. By 1970 only two of the major consumers of nuclear power, Canada and the United Kingdom, had not chosen light water as the technology on which to base their nuclear generating capacity. Canada brought the first full-scale Candu reactor on line in 1967, but by then it was a late entrant into the market. It continues to be the only reactor used in Canada, but it has not had a big impact on the world market. The United Kingdom, by contrast, entered early with a gas graphite technology. The second-generation reactor was plagued with problems, however, and in 1978 the United Kingdom switched to light water. Canada remains the only country marketing a technology other than light water. Figures 1A and 1B illustrate the progressive dominance of light water in the power reactor market between 1957 and 1987.

INCREASING RETURNS IN NUCLEAR POWER

"For a range of products involving complex, interdependent components or materials that will be subject to varied or prolonged stress in extreme environments, the outcome of the interaction of these parts cannot be precisely predicted.''[20] For these products, Nathan Rosenberg argues, learning-by-using is very important. Nuclear power reactors certainly fall into this class of products. When introduced, the technology was very complex and unlike any then in use. The consensus in the 1950s and 1960s was that learning-by-using would be very important.

The feeling that costs of nuclear power would fall with experience is evident throughout the proceedings of the 1955 and 1958 conferences on the Peaceful Uses of the Atom. Christopher Hinton, one of the British delegates, noted that it ''is common experience that the cost of prime movers [primary power sources] falls with the passage of time and growth of techniques.'' He gave details of the dramatic capital cost reductions experienced by land-based oil engines and by steam engines and remarked: ''I am quite certain that in nuclear power that same pattern will be followed.''[21] This spirit pervaded the proceedings of those two conferences.

In a 1962 study the AEC claimed that the cost of electricity generated by light water reactors had fallen from 50 mills per kilowatt-hour (kWh) to less than 10 mills per kWh between 1958 and 1962.[22] Even critics of the cost estimates for nuclear power accepted the belief ''that 'learning effects' would help reduce costs in the early years of nuclear plant construction.''[23] The four reactor units installed at the Pickering generating station provide evidence. For the first unit the time elapsed between going critical and generating full power was 91 days. For the second unit this time was cut to 53 days; the third and fourth units were 18 and 12 days, respectively.[24] As the designs of these units were virtually identical it seems appropriate to ascribe this improvement to learning.

A simple examination of generating-cost data would not provide evidence of learning. While one would expect learning to drive costs down over time, there are several factors which have applied upward pressure. The early generating stations were sold on a turnkey basis, which amounted to a very large discount on the capital cost for the

[20] Nathan Rosenberg, *Inside the Black Box: Technology and Economics* (Cambridge, 1982), p. 122.

[21] Hinton also added: ''Let us remember that the first movement onward from the Bolton and Watt engine was really made by Trevithick when he built his high-pressure steam engine on the Thames, with its cast iron boiler which blew up, killed eight men, nearly ruined him and set back the development of the steam engine by a great many years. We must make certain that we do not do that sort of thing. . . .'' United Nations, *Proceedings of the Second International Conference on Peaceful Uses of the Atom* (Geneva, 1955), p. 368. See also the proceedings of the First Conference.

[22] See Bupp and Derian, *Light Water*, p. 45.

[23] Ibid., p. 46.

[24] Peter DeLeon, *Development and Diffusion of the Nuclear Power Reactor: A Comparative Analysis* (Cambridge, MA, 1978), p. 200.

utilities.[25] Thus the cost to the utilities of generating power for 13 of the first stations were artificially low and did not represent true costs. In addition, increased concern with safety over time has resulted in more stringent regulation which has raised costs. For these and other reasons, the cost of nuclear energy, in spite of any learning that might have taken place, has not declined over time. Econometric studies, however, indicate that learning has been important in nuclear reactor technology in several ways. Paul Joskow and G. A. Rozanski estimated learning both by operators and by suppliers of power stations.[26] Their concern was with load, or capacity, factors. In their model any particular plant has a maximum achievable capacity factor, which they call its asymptotic capacity factor. When a utility begins to operate a plant, the operators spend several years "working the bugs out," and the annual capacity factor rises, approaching the asymptotic capacity factor. This is the first type of learning. The second type of learning has to do with the suppliers of nuclear generating stations. As it gains experience, a supplier is able to build plants with higher asymptotic capacity factors—plants of higher quality. Using data on 72 reactors that began operation before December 1975, Joskow and Rozanski found that there "is evidence of an industry learning curve, with technological improvements increasing ultimate [asymptotic] capacity factors of new plants at a rate of about 5 percent per year."[27]

W. E. Mooz found that doubling the number of plants built by an architect-engineer (that is, a firm such as General Electric [GE] or Westinghouse) reduced construction time by about 10 percent and total capital costs by about $55 per kilowatt, or about 10 percent.[28]

Martin Zimmerman's study of the early stages of commercialization of nuclear power in the United States found that "learning-by-doing associated with the first one or two plants was . . . substantial."[29] Moreover, there was a second type of learning. Learning-about-costs reflects the fact that the benefits accruing to users of a new technology are not well known until the technology has had considerable use. This idea is central to the multiarmed bandit model of technology choice described earlier. Zimmerman found that learning-about-costs was also important in the early reactor market.

[25] A turnkey contract is one in which a price is fixed before construction begins, and any unforeseen costs are borne by the designers, in this case Westinghouse and General Electric.

[26] Paul Joskow and G. A. Rozanski, "The Effects of Learning by Doing on Nuclear Plant Operating Reliability," *Review of Economics and Statistics*, 61 (May 1979).

[27] Ibid., p. 167.

[28] W. E. Mooz, *Cost Analysis of Light Water Reactor Power Plants* (Prepared for the Department of Energy, Rand Corporation, R-2304-DOE, Santa Monica, 1978).

[29] Martin Zimmerman, "Learning Effects and the Commercialization of New Energy Technologies: The Case of Nuclear Power," *Bell Journal of Economics*, 13 (Autumn 1982). He estimates that the completion of the first plant reduces the cost of future plants by 12 percent. Completing the second plant reduces costs further by 4 percent.

There is a form of increasing returns from learning common to any technology competing in the research and development stage of a product's life. In the presence of discounting, a technology that is marketable earlier is of more value than one that takes longer to bring to the market. Thus simply working on a technology increases its value by bringing its completion date closer and increases the incentive to do further work on that technology. This was a factor in the dominance of light water.

It is occasionally suggested that network externalities are also important in nuclear power. The network in this case has to do with information. Information about operating performance, appropriate accident response, and safety regulations can be passed among users of the same technology. This was seen (at least in retrospect) as a key factor in the explanation of the Belgian and Swedish decisions to adopt light water: "The best counter measure against technical problems is to have a production system which is common all over the world. . . ."[30]

Nuclear reactor technology presents a case of a technology subject to strong increasing returns and early uncertainty about the level of its payoffs. There were, and still are, dynamic increasing returns, largely learning economies, particularly in the research and development and early commercialization stages of the technology.[31] Economic theory suggests that the history of this technology will exhibit several characteristics: a tendency for the market to lock in to one of the technologies, not necessarily the best one; early tilting of the process toward one of the technologies (this tilting may be caused by events, which at the time did not appear to be crucial to the coming history); and finally, early inability to see (without the benefit of hindsight) which of the technologies will eventually dominate.

HOW DOMINANCE OF LIGHT WATER CAME ABOUT

In 1958, after three years of negotiations, six European countries signed the Euratom accord. Euratom was to be an intercountry agency whose mandate was to develop European nuclear power.[32] In 1957, prior to the signing of the accord, *A Target for Euratom* was written, recommending that Euratom cooperate with the U.S. nuclear reactor programs. That the three prominent European authors advocated close cooperation with the United States provided a strong challenge to the view then current in Europe that British and French gas graphite

[30] International Atomic Energy Agency, *Nuclear Power Experience*, vol. 1, pp. 137, 170.

[31] Strong static increasing returns are present as well but are of less interest from the point of view of this article.

[32] At the time, there was a single European reactor technology, namely the French gas graphite. The French saw Euratom, in part, as a way to get their technology adopted throughout Europe.

technologies were the most advanced.[33] Cooperation with the United States, of course, meant embracing light water. This embrace was tightened in late 1958 when the Euratom High Commission signed an accord with the U.S. government which proposed that one million kilowatts of nuclear generating capacity be built. These plants were to be built under U.S. patents and, as it turned out, largely by the European subsidiaries of Westinghouse and GE. Under this agreement the United States was to provide (tied) technical and financial aid, and indeed this was the source of half of the Euratom budget for research and construction.

The first reactor built under the auspices of Euratom was at Garigliano, Italy, and initially both British gas graphite and light water designs were considered. The choice of light water was another serious challenge to the view that gas graphite was the more advanced technology. "For the first time in Europe, light water reactors achieved technical respectability. . . ."[34] The three plants built under the auspices of the U.S.-Euratom agreement contributed crucial momentum to changing European views about the viability of light water. The final nail in the coffin of European gas graphite technology, however, was the apparent breakthrough signaled by the bandwagon market in the United States.[35] By the mid-1960s light water had become the technology of choice within Europe.

There are two noteworthy features of this period in Europe. The first is the attempts of a central authority, Euratom acting in concert with the U.S. government, to steer the adoption process. Financial aid and technical assistance lowered the cost of developing and using light water, improving its status relative to gas graphite.[36] This was enough to provide light water with a significant entry into both the European consciousness and market.[37] The second feature has to do with uncertainty. In 1960 it was still not clear which of the viable technologies—gas

[33] This report was jointly authored by Franz Estel, German vice president of the European Coal and Steel Community; Francesco Giordiani, former president of the Italian Atomic Energy Commission; and Louis Armand, president of the French National Railroad Company.

[34] Bupp and Derian, *Light Water*, p. 37.

[35] Particularly important was the Oyster Creek station, announced in 1963. This was an early turnkey plant built by GE which promised power at 4 mills per kWh. This was a decrease of 60 percent from the costs quoted by the Atomic Energy Commission in 1962. The "bandwagon market" refers to the time 1962 to 1965 during which U.S. utilities ordered 13 generating stations.

[36] There is a distinct similarity between the actions of the U.S. government in this role and those of General Electric and Westinghouse in offering turnkey contracts. U.S. government subsidies applied only to reactor varieties tested in the United States. (R. G. Hewlett and F. Duncan, *Nuclear Navy, 1946–1962* [Chicago, 1974], p. 135.) This policy gave considerable assistance to Westinghouse and General Electric and their European subsidiaries.

[37] The faith in the light water technology displayed by European willingness to abandon their own gas graphite technology could only encourage utilities in the United States to believe that light water was good. The apparent breakthrough in light water, evidenced by the rash of orders in the United States, in turn encouraged the Europeans to continue to use the U.S. technology.

graphite or light water—was preferable. Three events—*A Target for Euratom*, the Garigliano decision, and the bandwagon market—were all interpreted in Europe as evidence of the inherent superiority of light water.

Before the Euratom accord the European reactor story was English and French. Technology choice for both countries was, to a large extent, influenced by military considerations. The refusal of the United States to share uranium enrichment technology forced both France and the United Kingdom to pursue natural uranium technologies. Both countries felt the need to develop an atomic bomb, and both, through the Manhattan Project, had had experience with gas graphite. This was the obvious initial choice for their civilian power programs.

The only first-generation reactor pursued by the *Commisariat à l'Energie Atomique* was gas graphite. As nuclear power began to be commercialized in the 1960s, French industry and the *Electricité de France* (EdF) raised concerns over export possibilities. As remarked earlier, network externalities were thought to be important in the reactor market. One of the concerns of a reactor importer is to be part of a large information network and so it prefers to import a commonly used technology. For good reason, the EdF feared that if France became technologically isolated, the potential export market would rapidly disappear. In addition, the Garigliano decision and the U.S. bandwagon market were both seen as evidence supporting the view that light water was economically superior to gas graphite. A third economic issue was that the relative costs of fuel had been changed by the U.S.-Euratom accord. Enriched uranium was now available and at subsidized prices. Thus the fueling costs of light water reactors (which needed enriched uranium) relative to gas graphite reactors (which used natural uranium) was significantly improved. The light water arm of the multiarmed bandit appeared, judging by the actions of others, to be having very good results.

These considerations were countered by the desire to retain an indigenous technology, something favored by French President Charles de Gaulle. When he died, however, the tide turned, and in 1969 the government announced that France would no longer pursue the gas graphite technology. When France joined Euratom in 1957 it had hoped to have the French technology adopted as the European standard. This did not happen, and the French nuclear program, one of the most successful in the world, is based almost entirely on light water technology.

The history of nuclear power in the United Kingdom looks very much like a multiarmed bandit, as first one technology and then another was tried and discarded, occasionally being picked up again later.[38] Devel-

[38] This section draws heavily on R. Williams, *The Nuclear Power Decisions: British Policies, 1953–78* (London, 1980).

opment resources were shifted among technologies, depending upon beliefs about the viabilities of the different technologies.

For reasons similar to those relevant in France, there was an early commitment to Magnox, a gas graphite reactor, for the first generation. For the next generation three technologies were actively considered in the late 1950s—heavy water, gas graphite, and breeder reactors. Significantly, as part of the early decision to concentrate on Magnox, plans to build a prototype heavy water reactor in 1953 were shelved. Early results with Magnox were good, however, and so the high-temperature gas reactor (HTR) was given high priority. In 1959, though, the HTR was shunted aside to make room for the advanced gas-cooled reactor (AGR), which was seen as technologically intermediate between Magnox and the HTR. To develop the HTR an international project, Dragon, funded by the United Kingdom, Euratom, and other European countries, was organized in 1959.

For the first reactors of the second generation gas graphite was again chosen in 1965. Heavy water was not yet sufficiently developed, no doubt due in part to the 1953 decision, and light water was thought inferior in terms of safety and long-run development potential. The second-generation gas graphite reactors, the AGR, suffered serious failures. This version of the gas graphite technology was much more expensive than had been anticipated, and the problems of scaling up a 32 megawatt (MW) prototype plant to a full-scale 600 MW generating station proved more difficult than was expected. This resulted in a shift away from gas graphite to heavy water, at least until more advanced technologies appeared. But the decision in 1974 to make this shift for the short run, by creating a large demand for resources to develop the heavy water reactor (SGHWR), effectively ended the long-run prospects of the HTR. "Thus the HTR, the one reactor favored by virtually everybody in the early seventies, was the one decisive casualty of the 1974 decision."[39] The problems of the British heavy water reactor seem to have been generated by lack of experience.[40] Research on this technology had for two decades been shunted aside in favor of work on the gas graphite technology. This hurt its prospects but to make matters worse, light water had been the subject of massive amounts of research and development over those two decades. When the time came for the United Kingdom to move away from the trouble-plagued AGR, there were two options: heavy water, which would need considerable devel-

[39] Ibid., p. 234.

[40] Interestingly, in 1962 this reactor was considered by the Atomic Energy Agency to have better development potential than light water. (Ibid., p. 197.) In 1971 it was referred to as "the best of American BWR [a light water technology], Canadian and British technologies." See p. 213.

opment before it was ready for commercial use, and light water, which could be used immediately.[41] Finally, in 1977 light water was chosen.[42]

Canada has pursued a single technology, namely heavy water, throughout its nuclear program. There was no desire for nuclear weapons, there was an abundant supply of hydro-electric power, and the security concerns of the United States were not present in Canada. These three factors allowed Canada to proceed at a slower pace, while other countries were forced to adopt strategies which would produce nuclear technology quickly. At the beginning of the bandwagon market in 1962, five years after Shippingport, the first commercial heavy water reactor was brought on line. As a small, 22 MW reactor, it was a prototype rather than a serious competitor in the power reactor market. The first full-scale heavy water reactor, a 206 MW Candu brought on line in January 1967, was only the fourth commercial heavy water reactor in the world. (All of the others were designed to produce less than 55 MW.) By this time there were 10 commercial light water reactors in service, four of which were greater than 100 MW. The second nonprototype heavy water reactor was brought on line in April 1972.[43] By this time there were 27 full-size light water reactors in commercial use outside Canada. Though heavy water is the only technology used in Canada and has been exported, mostly to middle-income countries, it has not been a large presence on the world market. In this it exhibits the problems associated with a late entrant in an increasing returns process.

During the late forties the primary concerns of the U.S. AEC were military. All branches of the armed services were interested in nuclear energy, and their projects were being undertaken at several different national laboratories. The high priority given to military tasks meant that there were few resources available for the study of civilian power reactors. In April 1951 Lawrence Hafstad, the AEC director of Reactor Development, wrote that "the cost of a nuclear power plant is essentially unknown. We have never designed, much less built and operated, a reactor intended to deliver significant amounts of power economically."[44] In this aspect, early developments in nuclear power resemble the early stages of a multiarmed bandit—many arms seem feasible, very

[41] Ironically, recent experience with the AGR has been very good. In terms of reliability and availability, it has looked better than other technologies since the mid-1980s.

[42] This decision was reconsidered in the 1980s but was not in the end changed.

[43] In 1964 Sweden completed a 10 MW reactor which was shut down 10 years later. In France in August 1967 a 70 MW heavy water moderated, gas-cooled reactor was brought on line. Later in 1967 the United Kingdom brought on line a 92 MW heavy water prototype similar in design to the Candu.

[44] Lawrence Hafstad, "Reactors," *Scientific American*, 184 (Apr. 1951), p. 43. Quoted in Bupp and Derian, *Light Water*, p. 32.

little is known about the payoffs of any of them, and resources are devoted to reducing this uncertainty.

During the forties and early fifties the AEC was engaged in several reactor projects. While GE's intermediate breeder reactor was the only project aimed specifically at civilian power, four of the technologies under study were important to its future development.[45] In the early fifties, though, the demands of the military were gradually being met, and the AEC began to evaluate the economic prospects of various reactor technologies. This went on throughout the decade. One of the first analyses was made by a group of firms, between 1951 and 1953, on the basis of which the AEC chose four technologies for further development.[46] These industry teams concluded that economically competitive nuclear electricity was a long way off, but that given the state of development of the various reactor types, the light water reactor promised the cheapest electricity.[47]

Cost estimates presented at the first Geneva conference in 1955, however, told a different story. Using data presented at this conference J. A. Lane made cost estimates for various reactor types, under uniform assumptions about prices and operating conditions.[48] He concluded, using the lower bound of his range of estimates, that by far the cheapest electricity, 4.7 mills per kWh, would be produced by gas graphite reactors. The next cheapest, 6.3 mills per kWh, would come from the aqueous homogeneous reactor, although that reactor posed many technical problems, particularly when compared to gas graphite. Water reactors, both heavy and light, were expected to be relatively expensive. The lowest cost estimate for a light water reactor was 14.7 mills per kWh.[49]

Because the AEC was prohibited from building and operating full-scale power plants by itself it was committed to involving industry in the development of nuclear energy and in September 1955 issued an invitation to industry to build demonstration power plants. In response

[45] The technologies were being studied under the GE project; in naval work on gas and light water coolants; and in AEC work on graphite reactors and its work on light water.

[46] These were light water; liquid-metal-cooled, graphite-moderated; aqueous homogeneous; and fast breeder reactors. See Mullenbach, *Civilian Nuclear Power*, p. 131.

[47] Theodore Stern, "Appraisal of Reactor Systems for Central-Station Power Plants," *Chemical Engineering Progress Symposium Series*, part 1, 54 (Nov. 1954), summarized these studies. The cheapest electricity, 6.4 mills per kWh, would be generated by boiling water, a light water technology. The next cheapest would be a fast breeder, 6.5 mills per kWh, followed by pressurized water, another light water technology, 6.8 mills per kWh. The most expensive was the sodium-graphite technology at 10.3 mills per kWh. Stern noted, though, that in analyses of this sort the difference between 6.4 and 10.3 "may not be out of the margin of uncertainty."

[48] J. A. Lane, "An Evaluation of Geneva and Post-Geneva Nuclear-Power Economic Data," *The Economics of Nuclear Power*, series 8 (New York, 1957).

[49] In defense of water reactors, their cost estimates assumed plants with relatively small generating capacity, which, given the faith in increasing returns to scale, would appear to put them at a disadvantage.

seven proposals were submitted, each suggesting a different reactor type.[50] Clearly there was no consensus about which type of reactor was best.

In 1957 Project Size-Up was commissioned. One of the goals of Project Size-Up was to compare the light water reactor at Shippingport, the first nuclear generating station in the United States, with Calder Hall, the gas graphite reactor which had gone on line in the United Kingdom a year earlier. The study found that if both had been built in the United Kingdom, the gas graphite reactor would have produced electricity at a significantly lower cost than would a light water plant (8.0 mills per kWh as opposed to 13.1 mills). In the United States, however, gas graphite would still have been less expensive but the difference was considerably less pronounced (17.9 versus 19.6 mills per kWh).

At the same time, a formal debate was sponsored by the journal *Nucleonics* about the relative merits of enriched and natural uranium reactors.[51] The conclusion of the debate was that it was by no means clear that enriched uranium reactors, which the AEC was heavily backing, were inherently superior to natural uranium reactors. It appeared "that of the design concepts conceived so far, none makes an economic advantage for the enriched uranium reactor a foregone conclusion."[52]

Throughout the fifties comparisons of the various reactor types were continually being made, based both on engineering studies and on the performance of the few existing plants. By no means, however, had they found the light water technology superior to other technologies. Indeed, in 1954 Alvin Weinberg declared that "the choice of water cooling and moderation for PWR [the Shippingport reactor] was dictated by the requirement that the reactor demonstrate reliable nuclear power rather than cheap nuclear power."[53] Interestingly, he suggested that possible improvements on the Shippingport design (made possible by learning-by-using) include using heavy water instead of light water as coolant and moderator. Many arms of the multiarmed bandit were examined during the fifties, but there was no consensus as to their relative merits. Nonetheless, one arm—light water—was adopted by a major player, the U.S. Navy.

[50] The types were liquid-metal-cooled, heavy water moderated; gas graphite; graphite moderated, liquid-metal fuel; homogeneous; two variants of light water; and an organic hydrocarbon cooled and moderated reactor. Lane, "An Evaluation of Geneva."

[51] The participants in the debate were J. R. Menke, president of the Nuclear Development Corp., and W. B. Lewis, vice president of Atomic Energy Canada Limited, both of whom spoke in defense of natural uranium reactors; and Chauncey Starr of North American Aviation and W. E. Shoupp of Westinghouse, both of whom spoke in defense of enriched uranium reactors. See *Nucleonics*, 15 (June 1957), p. 68.

[52] Ibid., p. 70.

[53] Alvin Weinberg, "Power Reactors," *Scientific American*, 191 (Dec. 1954), p. 36.

THE ROLE OF THE U.S. NAVY

The duration of underwater operation of conventional submarines is severely limited because they are forced to run on batteries when submerged. By the end of World War II the U.S. Navy was concerned with this problem and saw nuclear propulsion as a possible solution.[54] Captain Hyman Rickover, in charge of the navy's new nuclear propulsion program, wanted to produce a nuclear submarine as quickly as possible.

In Rickover we see one of Jonathan Hughes's vital few, someone who was crucial to the development of an innovation.[55] To a very great extent his was the voice that mattered when it came to technical decisions within the navy's propulsion program. His commitment to pursue nuclear submarines meant that nuclear power technology (in addition to nuclear weapons) would be developed quickly after the war. His preference for light water caused it to be the only technology available when a civilian power reactor was demanded immediately in 1949 by "national security." By pulling General Electric into light water technology he effectively prevented the company from developing any other technology and set the stage for its battle with Westinghouse. In effect, the history of nuclear power in the United States follows on the work of Rickover in the 1940s and 1950s. His contribution came at a crucial time. Before anyone else was prepared to make a commitment to any particular technology, he did. He forced his project to be successful and in so doing gave a sufficient lead to light water. The backers of light water power reactors were able to use this advance along the learning curve and the dynamic increasing returns inherent in the technology to capture the market.

After spending several months at the Oak Ridge National Laboratory in 1946, Rickover was convinced that enough was known to build a prototype reactor. He felt that light water was the technology he wanted, but in 1946 there was certainly no consensus among the physicists that it was the best. They felt that much more study was needed before a sensible choice could be made. Harold Etherington, head of the Naval Reactor Division at the Argonne National Laboratory, was still conducting studies of six reactor types in 1949. His preliminary study of light water (the first that he completed) indicated that there were no insurmountable problems in using this technology for

[54] There are two other technologies that overcome this problem. One is the closed cycle submarine, in which diesel exhaust gas is recycled and mixed with oxygen which has been stored in cylinders, and then re-used. The second is a snorkel submarine, in which air for combustion while the submarine is submerged is obtained from a snorkel arrangement which trails the submarine on the surface. After the war, the U.S. Navy was working on all three of these technologies, only one of which has survived.

[55] Jonathan Hughes, *The Vital Few: The Entrepreneur and American Economic Progress* (New York, 1986).

submarine propulsion.[56] Rickover, too, was aware that many technologies were feasible and had arranged to have several laboratories working on various aspects of gas-cooled, liquid-metal-cooled, and sodium-cooled systems, in addition to the Westinghouse work on light water. Diversity notwithstanding, Rickover was determined to build a reactor as quickly as possible. To this end he got a letter from a reluctant Walter Zinn, the director of the Argonne laboratory, stating that on the basis of existing knowledge, light water seemed to be the most promising. This was enough for Rickover. He was able to get approval for Westinghouse to build a prototype submarine reactor on land.

This prototype, known as the Mark I, was tested in early 1953, and its successor, the Mark II, was installed in the submarine *Nautilus*. The *Nautilus* was launched in early 1954 and had no major problems in its sea trials. Performance of the first two nuclear reactors made the light water arm of the multiarmed bandit look very good.

During the time that Westinghouse was working on the Mark I and Mark II, technical problems had forced General Electric to abandon its civilian reactor project and turn its energies to its own naval reactor, the Mark A, a liquid-metal-cooled, beryllium-moderated reactor. The Mark A was successfully tested in June 1955, but as it continued to be used, problems developed. The second nuclear submarine, the *Seawolf*, was launched in July 1956 with the GE Mark B as its propulsion unit. Problems with this reactor were so severe, however, that late in 1956 Rickover had it removed from the ship and replaced with a Westinghouse light water reactor.

The competition with regard to submarine reactors was over. The initial competition took place on paper as Etherington and others studied the feasibility of various coolants. Rickover decided in favor of light water. In the second competition between actual working reactors, the problems with the Mark B caused Rickover to decide against liquid metal for submarines. This decision effectively spelled the end for liquid-metal-cooled reactors.

This was not the end for General Electric in the reactor business, however. While working on the Mark A and Mark B, the company had also been developing the submarine advanced reactor—a light water reactor. Despite problems with this reactor and the feeling that the work could have been done much more quickly by Westinghouse, Rickover kept the project alive. One of his chief motives was to bring GE into competition with Westinghouse in light water technology. Although this reactor was never extensively used as a propulsion unit, it did provide

[56] His other studies were not completed before Rickover had made his decision.

GE with the experience necessary to enter the civilian market with the light water technology.[57]

While the work on submarine reactors was going on, the navy was also considering the feasibility of nuclear-powered surface ships. The need was less severe than for submarines, but it was felt that a nuclear-powered surface ship would be faster and could stay at sea longer than a conventional ship. The work focused on developing a nuclear-powered aircraft carrier. Westinghouse had been doing initial work on six different coolants for this reactor, but once again Rickover favored the light water technology.

Since the early 1950s interest had been expressed in a dual purpose reactor—one which would be a prototype for both a large shipboard plant and for a power reactor. Rickover had, until 1954 at least, been successful in vetoing that idea. But throughout this time two things were happening. The utilities were beginning to show interest in acquiring nuclear power, and the Soviet nuclear program was seen as more and more of a threat to U.S. national interests. In 1952 the AEC had moved civilian power from last to first priority and by 1953 was making plans to build a power reactor jointly with industry.[58] The carrier reactor project had been put on the shelf, for the time being at least, in order to provide funds for the civilian project. Two approaches were available to the AEC for the power reactor. The first was to adopt Rickover's suggestion to transform the carrier reactor into the civilian reactor, with few if any major changes.[59] This would have produced a reliable reactor quickly but would not have provided cheap electricity.[60] The other approach was to take more time and to explore further the work that had been done at the Argonne National Laboratory on light and heavy water moderators and coolants. It was thought that this approach would be far more likely to generate electricity that would be competitive with conventional sources. Hafstad favored the latter approach and was supported by his staff, but Rickover prevailed. The civilian reactor, "now called the pressurized-water reactor, would follow the carrier reactor design and . . . it would be assigned to the naval reactors branch. . . ."[61] This battle was won so handily by Rickover that while still an active naval officer, he was put in charge of the construction of the first nuclear generating station in the United States. Needless to say, the technology used was light water.

[57] Combustion Engineering had also been drawn into light water by the navy and developed a reactor for the hunter-killer submarine, *Tullibee*, which was launched in 1960.

[58] R. G. Hewlett and F. Duncan, *A History of the United States Atomic Energy Commission*, vol. 2: *Atomic Shield, 1947/1952* (University Park, PA, 1969), p. 226 ff.

[59] Rickover did not want to abandon the carrier project in favor of Shippingport. His proposal was a fall-back position in which he could work on a reactor which would provide valuable information for any future carrier project if the current one was put on the shelf.

[60] See Weinberg, "Power Reactors."

[61] Hewlett and Duncan, *A History of the United States Atomic Energy Commission*, p. 231.

SHIPPINGPORT AND THE SOVIET BOMB

On theoretical grounds, one might expect that the stronger the increasing returns early in the life of a technology, the faster it will become dominant.[62] Nuclear reactor technology in the 1950s was still very new and very complex. Building a complete power station would involve a considerable advance along what was sure to be a steep learning curve. The first technology in the United States to make this advance was light water.

In the 1940s and early 1950s the AEC had advocated a cautious approach to civilian nuclear power, arguing that much laboratory work was needed before a sensible decision could be made about which technology was best suited for civilian use. It was forced to make an early decision, however, by the National Security Council.

After World War II the United States believed that if it kept its nuclear knowledge secret, it would enjoy a 20-year monopoly in nuclear technology. This it did, refusing to share either uranium enrichment or reactor technology with its wartime allies. U.S. secrecy explains in part why nuclear programs in the rest of the world focused on natural as opposed to enriched uranium reactors. Under the Atoms For Peace program this changed—the United States was willing to guarantee supplies of enriched uranium and provide other reactor technology.

This change, it seems, was brought about by the Soviet nuclear weapon test. In 1949 the Soviet Union exploded its first nuclear bomb and exploded as well the U.S. dream of a monopoly in nuclear technology. In 1953 the United Kingdom exploded an atomic weapon. There was also evidence that both of these countries were developing civilian power capabilities. It is necessary to remember that in the late forties and early fifties there was a tremendous faith that nuclear energy could do much good, for example providing inexpensive power to the Third World that would facilitate economic growth. This possibility, combined with the apparent prowess of the United Kingdom and the Soviet Union in the nuclear power field, caused great alarm in the United States. There was a fear that if the world perceived the Soviets to be winning the race for nuclear energy (which the United States had not yet seriously entered), it would draw nonaligned nations, particularly Third World countries, into the Soviet camp. This would do no end of damage to U.S. interests. AEC Commissioner T. Murray stated: "Once we become fully conscious of the possibility that power-hungry [that is, energy scarce] nations will gravitate towards the USSR if it wins the nuclear power race, it will be quite clear that this race is no Everest-climbing, kudos-providing contest."[63] Indeed, Murray thought

[62] See Cowan, "Backing the Wrong Horse," chap. 4; and Rosenberg, *Inside the Black Box*.

[63] M. Hertsgaard, *Nuclear Inc: The Men and Money Behind Nuclear Energy* (New York, 1983), p. 25.

that permitting the Soviet Union to be first in the race to civilian power would do more damage to U.S. interests than had the Soviet atomic bomb.

Suddenly a new priority had been forced on the AEC. The National Security Council had decided that a strong civilian reactor program was vital to national interests and that it was imperative to get the program going. To this end the Shippingport generating station was built with the idea "to prove American nuclear superiority, not to lower energy costs."[64] Any reactor would do, as long as it was known to be reliable. Clearly the obvious choice was the light water reactor, with which there had been the most experience.

While fear of Soviet superiority led to the choice of the light water reactor for the Shippingport plant, it also led to the desire to have U.S. technology spread throughout the world. As pointed out in reference to Euratom, this resulted in enormous subsidies to Europe to encourage the adoption of American technology. Learning-by-doing was very important in the early stages of the industry, and Europe provided a location in which this learning could take place. If enough plants could be built quickly, U.S. technology would improve rapidly and become the standard for the first generation, until more advanced reactors—breeders or high-temperature gas-cooled reactors—could be developed. Unfortunately, this choice "gave the light water model a head start and momentum that others were never able to match and led the industry to base its commercial future on a reactor design that some experts have subsequently suggested was economically and technically inferior."[65]

In the early 1950s the AEC was given new priorities under which civilian power reactor development became very important. Atoms For Peace, the U.S.-Euratom bilateral accord, and Shippingport were all a result of a new desire that the United States win the race for nuclear power and that its technology should spread throughout the world. Within the country, however, only light water was sufficiently developed to be the standard bearer.

Within the United States, the early years of reactor development were under control of the AEC. Throughout the fifties, based on a continual series of cost estimates and projections, the AEC had a fluid opinion about which technology was best and shifted its research program accordingly. Military demands, however, resulted in considerable work on light water. In 1954, when priorities changed, security decisions demanded an immediate payoff. The potential for using the first generating station as a way of learning about different technologies

[64] Ibid., p. 27.
[65] Ibid., p. 28.

was sacrificed to the need for a reliable reactor.[66] Because of the experience on submarines, there was confidence in light water's reliability, though not in its ability to produce inexpensive power, even in the long run. At the same time, foreign policy called for the spread of U.S. technology, and again there was a bias toward immediate payoff. This was less conscious than the Shippingport decision, but part of spreading U.S. technology involved building demonstration plants, and only light water was sufficiently advanced.

By 1962 light water had a large head start over all other technologies, with the exception of gas graphite. The latter was being pursued seriously only in the United Kingdom, and its demise was detailed earlier. Good results early on with light water, combined with the problems of other technologies that had been tried, enhanced the relative position of light water in the beliefs of the decision makers. Westinghouse and General Electric, fearing the advent of a new and better technology, adopted a successful loss-leader, pre-emptive strategy. They are effectively the only reactor designers in the United States, and the descendants of their technologies are the only ones currently being built in Europe.

THE UNITED STATES AFTER 1960

The nuclear power reactor market in the United States after the early 1960s can be seen as the tail end of an increasing returns process. If one technology, in advance of its competitors, makes a large movement along its learning curve, the others will be hard pressed to compete, finding it difficult if not impossible to enter the market. The first technology to get significantly ahead of its rivals is likely to dominate the market.

By the early 1960s General Electric and Westinghouse had amassed considerable technical expertise in nuclear technology, almost all of it using light water technology. Their work for the navy and to a lesser extent their work in Europe had given them enough experience to feel that they had a product for which the market was ready.[67] They thought that there were huge profits to be made in nuclear energy but that a great deal of learning was necessary before the costs would be brought down enough to make it competitive with conventional energy. They had other concerns as well:

> We had a problem like a lump of butter sitting in the sun. If we couldn't get orders out of the utility industry, with every tick of the clock it became progressively more likely

[66] Recall that the Atomic Energy Commission wanted to do more research before building Shippingport but was overridden.

[67] By the end of 1960, 13 nuclear ships had been launched, and a further 33 were under construction. The two firms had completed or begun construction on eight power reactors in Europe and the United States.

that some competing technology would be developed that would supersede the economic viability of our own. Our people understood this was a game of massive stakes, and that if we didn't force the utility industry to put those stations on line, we'd end up with nothing.[68]

Thus GE and Westinghouse were willing to offer turnkey contracts. They sold 13 plants on this basis and suffered tremendous losses but by doing so were able to precipitate the Great Bandwagon Market in 1963. In the late 1960s General Atomic attempted to enter the market with a high-temperature gas graphite reactor. By 1975 it had orders for seven power stations, and in 1976 the Fort St. Vrain station came on line. By then, however, all of the other orders had been cancelled, and Fort St. Vrain remains the only high-temperature gas graphite reactor operating in the United States.[69]

Within the United States after 1960 we see two firms competing for market share. Using variants of the same technology, they were competing both with each other and with other technologies. They had a tremendous technological head start over their competitors and worked hard to capitalize on this advantage. In an attempt to make further advances along what they were sure were steep learning curves, they sold early power stations at very low prices. The utilities were very receptive. Light water advanced rapidly along its learning curve, and by the time other technologies tried to compete, it was too late.

SUMMARY AND CONCLUSION

The history of nuclear power reactor technology has several branches, primarily representing different countries, which slowly intertwine. In essence, the story is one of competition among several technologies, each of which operates under strong dynamic increasing returns, with one coming to dominate the market.

The light water reactor satisfied the U.S. Navy's needs for a small reactor which would be ready for use very quickly. The navy expended considerable resources on the development of this technology, and as a result, it was the only one available at a critical moment—when national security demanded a nuclear power station. The same national security concerns prompted the U.S. government to force light water into Europe. In the late 1950s and early 1960s three forces came together: questions about the economics of the first generation of gas graphite reactors; large U.S. subsidies of light water in Europe; and claims by the

[68] John McKitterick, General Electric vice president for corporate planning, quoted in Hertsgaard, *Nuclear Inc*, p. 42.

[69] Significantly, three of the six utilities involved had, at the same time, plans to build other generating stations using light water. None of these plans were cancelled, and by 1974 construction had begun on all of them.

producers of very large decreases in the cost of their reactors.[70] There followed a rash of orders in Europe and the United States, a significant advance along the learning curve, and, equally important, an apparent reduction in the uncertainty about the benefits of light water. This was enough to push virtually the whole market into light water, and by 1969 Canada and the United Kingdom were the only holdouts.

For many years the United Kingdom was determined to use its own technology. Throughout the 1970s, however, there was ongoing debate about which technology to use for its second-generation reactors. Both gas graphite and heavy water were chosen and pursued. Both presented technical problems, however, and it became clear that the development of either would be very expensive. Since light water had been thoroughly developed elsewhere, the United Kingdom finally adopted it.

The heavy water reactor prevailed in Canada, but by the time it was ready for commercial use, light water had been in use for 10 years, and dozens of light water reactors were under construction. Heavy water's late entry into the competition and its lying outside the mainstream of reactor technology explain its lack of export success.

Recent theoretical developments in the area of competing technologies suggest that if increasing returns are strong, one technology will dominate the market, and it is not possible to predict which of the technologies will do so. It is likely, however, that the technology which first makes large advances along its learning curve will emerge dominant. In the three decades since the first nuclear power station, the light water technology has come to dominate the power reactor market. This has occurred in spite of the fact that from its very first use there were serious doubts as to its technical or economic superiority.

Its rise to pre-eminence can be attributed to three things: the choice by the U.S. Navy in the late 1940s of light water for its propulsion program and its subsequent research on that technology; the desire, following the Soviet bomb, for quick construction of a nuclear generating station; and the subsidies given by the U.S. government in an attempt to have light water pre-empt other technologies domestically and in Europe. The first two, at the time, were not generally thought to be as significant as they have turned out to be. At the time of Shippingport, light water was considered an interim technology, and it

[70] Bupp and Derian, *Light Water*, are also convinced that the current dominance by light water is due to its early acceptance in the United States, and subsequent rapid spread into Europe. They emphasize, however, the way in which reactors were built largely on expectations of future performance. Many reactors were ordered based on the claims of manufacturers that the next, bigger generation had achieved enormous cost reductions. These claims turned out to be far from true. The degree to which orders (both in the United States and Europe) preceded experience is astounding. In 1968, for example, the largest light water reactor that had been operating for a year or more was 200 MW. In contrast the mean size of reactor ordered that year was 926 MW (see figure 4-1, p. 73). This sort of advertising (and to be fair, the willingness to accept it) generated enough light water orders, that, again, other technologies were left behind.

was expected that very soon other technologies would take its place. These three things combined to give light water a tremendous advantage in terms of development resources and time. When these other, potentially superior, technologies were developed to the point of being marketable, it was too late. Light water was entrenched.

The Volume of Soviet Munitions Output, 1937–1945: A Reevaluation

MARK HARRISON

The only official measure of overall Soviet munitions output in World War II, first published in 1965, was based on changes in values, not volumes, and grossly understates change in the level of real Soviet war production. Subsequently published official data on production of ground and air munitions in physical units, supplemented by information about real spending on naval munitions, provide foundations for a new index. During the war the USSR produced more munitions than Great Britain or Germany, but much less than the United States.

The only available summary measure of the total Soviet output of munitions in World War II is an index first published in 1965, in the sixth, final volume of the *Istoriia Velikoi Otechestvennoi voiny Sovetskogo Soiuza, 1941–1945* [History of the Great Patriotic War of the Soviet Union, 1941–1945], hereafter called the *Istoriia* index. It covered the years from 1940 to 1944 and was said to be based on the output of the four main commissariats supplying the ground and air forces—the aircraft, tank-building, armament, and ammunition industries. Published with it were subindices showing the output of each of the four commissariats separately for the years from 1940 to 1945. The *Istoriia* index and its four subindices are reproduced in Table 1.

The *Istoriia* index was probably first compiled during or immediately after the war. It showed that the output of Soviet ground and air munitions at the 1944 peak stood at 251 (1940 equals 100). This formed the basis for N. A. Voznesenskii's statement in 1947 that "war production in the eastern and central areas of the USSR alone increased during the Patriotic War two and a half times over in comparison with the 1940 production level for the whole of the USSR."[1] After Voznesenskii's book about the war economy there was a blackout on the publication of

The Journal of Economic History, Vol. L, No. 3 (Sept. 1990). ISSN 0022-0507.

The author is senior lecturer in Economics at the University of Warwick, Coventry, England CV4 7AL.

I wish to thank the following for help and advice: Correlli Barnet (Cambridge), Alec Cairncross (Oxford), Robin Clifton (Warwick), Julian Cooper (Birmingham), Peter Fearon (Leicester), Michael Kaser (Oxford), Peter Law (Warwick), Alan Milward (LSE), Austin Robinson (Cambridge), the late Kenneth Usherwood (formerly Director of Statistics in the wartime Ministry of Supply), and Hugh Weeks (another former Director of Statistics, Ministry of Supply). I owe a special debt of gratitude to Peter Wiles (LSE) for his guidance, criticism, and support. I am also grateful to the University of Warwick for leave of absence during which work for this article was undertaken.

[1] N. A. Voznesenskii, *War Economy of the USSR in the Period of the Patriotic War* (Moscow, 1948), p. 63.

TABLE 1
THE *ISTORIIA* INDEX OF SOVIET MUNITIONS OUTPUT, 1941–1945
(1940 = 100)

Year	*Istoriia* Index	Industrial Commissariat: Aircraft	Tank-Building	Armament	Ammunition
1941	140	126	112	145	152
1942	186	178	184	191	218
1943	224	223	234	200	264
1944	251	239	296	206	310
1945		177	276	156	171

Source: *Istoriia Velikoi Otechestvennoi voiny Sovetskogo Soiuza, 1941–5* (Moscow, 1965), vol. 6, pp. 45, 52.

further statistical information from the war period, which explains the long delay in full publication of the *Istoriia* index.

The *Istoriia* index has continued to be republished in official statistical handbooks and to be cited as authoritative to the present day. (In subsequent publications the *Istoriia* index has often been represented as an index of total munitions output rather than of the main types of ground and air munitions.) Soviet writers have never questioned its reliability as a guide to Soviet munitions output in wartime.

It is, however, far from clear what these index numbers were meant to measure. Whatever else, it is certain that they *do not* satisfactorily measure quantities of weapons produced. Detailed time series for different lines of war products, denominated in physical units, have been published subsequently in the official twelve-volume *Istoriia Vtoroi Mirovoi voiny, 1939–1945* [History of the Second World War, 1939–1945].[2] These make it absolutely clear that the *Istoriia* index numbers greatly understate the growth of munitions production from the beginning of the war to the wartime peak in 1944.

For example, four times as many military aircraft were produced in 1944 as in 1940, compared with the peak output of 2.4 times the 1940 level recorded by the *Istoriia* index for the aircraft industry. A larger discrepancy is found in the case of armored fighting vehicles; more than ten times as many units were produced in 1944 as in 1940, while the industry's *Istoriia* index grew to only three times. The armament industry's *Istoriia* index for 1944 stands at only twice the 1940 level, yet six times as many heavy guns were produced in 1944 as in 1939. Light guns were nearly eight times the 1939 level even though more guns were manufactured then than in 1940. The 1944 output of machine pistols was 24 times the 1940 level, that of machine guns three times, and only the

[2] See relevant sections of *Istoriia Vtoroi Mirovoi voiny, 1939–1945* (hereafter *IVMV*) (Moscow, 1973–82), vols. 1–12. Detailed series of physical output are brought together from this and other sources in Mark Harrison, *Soviet Planning in Peace and War, 1938–1945* (Cambridge, 1985), pp. 250–52.

increase in supply of rifles and carbines falls below the index. As for ammunition, the official *Istoriia* index shows 1944 output to be three times the 1940 level, but this is somewhat less than the increase in the supply of shells and mines recorded for 1944 over 1941; the output of shells taken separately had expanded to more than nine times 1940 output already by 1943.

Discrepancies on this scale and pattern cannot possibly be explained by changes in either the composition or the quality of Soviet munitions produced in wartime. Only in the aircraft industry was there any shift away from bigger, more complex and expensive types of output to cheaper types, and the scale of the shift was too slight to account for more than a small part of the gap between change in numbers produced and change in the industry's subindex. Overall, the quality of Soviet munitions rose during the war, and should have further boosted the valuation of real munitions output above any measure based on crude numbers of products.

The physical product series provide the basis for a revised index of the volume of total Soviet finished output of munitions. First, however, I wish to explain the character of the *Istoriia* index of total output and the four industry subindices.

THE *ISTORIIA* INDEX

There are two problems with the *Istoriia* index: prices and coverage. First, what price set was used to compile it? The context of its first publication made it look like a volume index calculated at fixed prices, although nothing was said in writing. It was entered in a table as a subindex of gross industrial production (normally measured for this period at the so-called fixed prices of 1926/27), alongside various other indicators of wartime economic activity, for the most part denominated in fixed prices (such as national income, measured at "1926/27" prices) or in physical terms (millions of people in employment). Yet we have seen that the expansion of the *Istoriia* index lags too far behind the reported growth in physical output of war products for it to be understood as a measure of volumes.[3]

Second, what was the *Istoriia* index intended to cover? It was originally published in the form of a weighted sum of the four subindices for the industries supplying aircraft, tanks, guns, and ammunition. This too may have been misleading.

If the *Istoriia* index is really the weighted average of the four subindices, then there must be a mistake in the reported totals. Simple algebra shows that the behavior of the *Istoriia* index as reported cannot

[3] Previously I considered various possible explanations—that the *Istoriia* index was based on changes in values, not volumes, or that its behavior was seriously affected by changing boundaries in the administration of war production. See Harrison, *Soviet Planning*, pp. 119–21.

TABLE 2
NKO EXPENDITURE ON MUNITIONS AND THE *ISTORIIA* INDEX COMPARED, 1938–1945

	Istoriia Index		*Finansovaia sluzhba* Index of NKO Expenditure on Munitions at Current Prices	
	Original	Recalculated to show 1944 = 100	Original	Recalculated to show 1944 = 100
1938			100.0	15.1
1939			177.6	26.9
1940	100	40	217.9	33.0
1941	140	56	361.2	54.6
1942	186	74	507.5	76.8
1943	224	89	591.0	89.4
1944	251	100	661.2	100.0
1945			471.6	71.3

Notes and sources: For the *Istoriia* index, see Table 1. For the *Finansovaia sluzhba* index, see *Finansovaia sluzhba Vooruzhennykh Sil SSSR v period voiny* (Moscow, 1967), p. 66. When the *Istoriia* index is regressed against the NKO expenditure index over the years from 1940 to 1944, with the latter as the independent variable, the regression is highly significant, and the constant term is not significantly different from zero at the 10 percent level. When the constant term is dropped, the regression is significant, and the regression coefficient is insignificantly different from one, at almost any meaningful level.

in fact be explained by the variation in the four subindices. One possible way out of the inconsistency would be to assume an error somewhere, whether deliberate or typographic. The likeliest candidate for a mistake is the 1941 entry of the *Istoriia* index, which is too high.[4] This hypothesis is attractively simple, but I reject it in favor of the following alternative.

The four subindices are measures of defense industry production, but the *Istoriia* index measures munitions expenditure. The coverage of production was less comprehensive than that of expenditure. Expenditure was measured at current prices, production at the so-called unchanged prices of 1926/27.

What is the evidence for this? Table 2 compares the *Istoriia* index, recalculated with 1944 as the base year, with an official index of defense commissariat (NKO) expenditure on munitions at current prices; this

[4] The entries of the total index for 1940 to 1943 can be taken as the right-hand sides of four simultaneous equations, with the four 1940 weights of the subindices as unknowns. In this case there is no set of nonnegative solutions which can satisfy the constraints. Moreover, the entry for total munitions output in 1944 of 251 cannot be matched by combining the subindices using weights imputed in this way. When the entries of the total index for 1940 and 1942–1944 are taken as the right-hand sides of the four simultaneous equations, again with the four 1940 weights of the subindices as unknowns, feasible and realistic weights result, but now the entry for total munitions output in 1941 is estimated at 130, not the 140 given. This might be consistent with a typographic or arithmetic error in the official index for 1941. The "feasible and realistic" 1940 weights are: aircraft—45 percent, tanks—23 percent, guns—23 percent, ammunition—9 percent.

excludes only naval munitions, procured by the commissariat for the war fleet (NKVMF). Except in 1940/41, the two indices move almost exactly in step.[5] The fit is too good to be a coincidence, even though I cannot explain the 1940 gap.

I think it likely, however, that the four subindices were based on production. While the behavior of the *Istoriia* index can be clearly associated with a published expenditure series, the same is not true for the four subindices.[6] They were explicitly classified by commissariat, that is, by production branch. Even if the underlying price set were the same, the difference between a production classification and an expenditure classification would be sufficient to explain some discrepancy between the four subindices and the *Istoriia* index.[7]

At what prices were the four subindices calculated? It is certain that they were not compiled using genuinely fixed prices, but this still leaves two alternatives—current prices, and the prices of "1926/27."

It is possible that the four subindices measure reported output at current prices. The *Istoriia* index and the subindices diverge, but their divergence from each other is arithmetically small and is far less than their common divergence from series for reported physical output of munitions. Therefore the subindices could have employed a price set similar to the *Istoriia* index, that is, transfer prices at current rubles. The discrepancy between them could be due entirely to the various sources of a production-expenditure gap.

More likely, however, are "1926/27" prices. In theory these were product prices actually prevailing in 1926/27 or, for new products introduced after that year, notional prices based on 1926/27 factor costs. However, new products were actually incorporated into the "1926/27" price set at current prices, not the prices which would notionally have prevailed in 1926/27.[8] Moreover, in munitions at least, the replacement of old products by new ones was quite rapid; as a result, by 1940 there

[5] This was drawn to my attention by Peter Wiles. I owe him special thanks for giving me access to the rare and invaluable *Finansovaia sluzhba Vooruzhennykh Sil SSSR v period voiny* [Financial service of the USSR Armed Forces in the period of the war] (Moscow, 1967), from which this and other evidence is derived.

[6] The four subindices shown in Table 1 are not significantly associated with indices of current NKO expenditure on munitions under comparable headings, 1941–1945, based on budget outlays derived by Frank Doe, "Understanding the Soviet View of Military Expenditures" (Washington, DC, 1982), table 4.

[7] Reported munitions output (Q) and expenditure (E) could be expected to diverge because of defective products included in reported output but remaining unsold (DP), because of civilian products of defense factories counted in output of munitions branches of industry (CIV), and military products of civilian industries not counted in munitions output but purchased as munitions out of the defense budget (MIL), because of exports (EX) and imports (IM), and because of the lag between production and procurement:

$$E_n = Q_{n-1} - DP_{n-1} + (MIL_{n-1} - CIV_{n-1}) + (IM_n - EX_n)$$

[8] Naum Jasny, *The Soviet Price System* (Stanford, 1951), pp. 96–97.

were probably no products included in the "1926/27" price set which were actually priced in 1926/27. Thus the prices of "1926/27" amounted in reality to no more than a kind of moving average of new product prices over a past interval of variable length. The more rapid the diffusion of new products, the more closely would "1926/27" prices approximate to current prices. Prewar evidence suggests that product innovation and diffusion were sufficiently rapid in the Soviet engineering industry to make current and "1926/27" prices virtually indistinguishable.[9]

In summary, the *Istoriia* index is based on the current ruble value of defense commissariat total expenditure on ground and air munitions. The four subindices which accompanied it are production indices covering a substantial subset (but not all) of the munitions subject to NKO procurement. The subindices may have been calculated at current prices or, more likely, at "1926/27" prices which, in the case of munitions and other products of engineering, may have come to nearly the same thing.

MUNITIONS PRICES IN WARTIME

If values lagged behind volumes, then ruble prices of Soviet munitions must have fallen substantially in wartime. Here is something that we know about. Munitions prices were already being pushed down when war broke out. Downward pressure intensified during the war when trade commissar and Deputy Prime Minister A. I. Mikoian was appointed in March 1942 to check the dizzying rise in ruble costs of NKO procurements. He found multiple prices for identical products and huge price-cost margins in which NKO officials acquiesced. Meanwhile unit costs in the munitions industries were falling smartly, mainly because of the transition to serial production.[10]

The most comprehensive information on trends in munitions prices appears in Soviet estimates of cost savings accruing to the munitions budget in each year of the war as a result of buying current output at current prices rather than prices of the previous year. These can be compared with each year's total cost of munitions procurement to yield a chained Paasche index of prices for ground and air munitions, shown in Table 3. An index of naval munitions prices, chained back to 1941 equals 100, is also shown in Table 3. These indices confirm significant, sometimes dramatic price reductions for Soviet munitions in every year of the war and suggest that the general decline in munitions prices was of the order of 40 percent.[11]

[9] Donald R. Hodgman, *Soviet Industrial Production, 1928–1951* (Cambridge, MA, 1954), pp. 9–11.

[10] *Finansovaia sluzhba*, pp. 78–79.

[11] Abram Bergson, *The Real National Income of Soviet Russia Since 1928* (Cambridge, MA, 1961), p. 74 and appendix E, reckoned 1944 munitions prices at above the 1942/43 level and only

TABLE 3
SOVIET PRICE DEFLATORS AND REAL MUNITIONS EXPENDITURE, 1940–1945

	Price Deflators		
	Ground and Air Munitions	Naval Munitions	Real Expenditure on Ground and Air Munitions
1940	100.0		100.0
1941	84.5	100.0	196.2
1942	65.8	86.0	354.2
1943	60.4	79.1	448.9
1944	59.0	75.2	514.3
1945	56.8		380.8

Notes and sources: For Price Deflators, see the Appendix. For Real Expenditure, see index of NKO expenditure on munitions at current prices (Table 2), recalculated to show 1940 equals 100, divided by the appropriate price index.

According to an official calculation, the total accumulated saving from price reductions through the war years amounted to 50.3 billion rubles.[12] This is comparable to a saving of 51.0 billion rubles which can be estimated from Table 3 when we take 1941 (rather than 1940) as the base year and calculate the cumulative sum saved on NKO procurements through to the end of May 1945.[13]

These indices are also in the same general range as more fragmentary data compiled on an unknown basis, and released by Voznesenskii after the war. For example, according to the latter, the prices of defense industry products had fallen in 1942 to 72 percent of the 1940 level (as against a figure of 65.8 shown in Table 3).[14] For 1940 to 1943, Voznesenskii reported figures suggesting a cumulative 42.6 percent fall in unit costs in machine building and metal working (that is, military and civilian engineering), compared with the estimated 39.6 percent fall in munitions prices shown in Table 3.[15]

The behavior of Soviet munitions prices, estimated in this way, was sharply at variance with other price trends. Some relevant comparisons are as follows. By 1944 wholesale prices of civilian machinery, of basic industrial goods, and of fuel and power were slightly above the 1940 level; railway charges per ton-kilometer had risen by a quarter.[16]

---

20 percent below the 1940 level. This figure seems arbitrarily conservative. Also arbitrary, but in the other direction, is the estimate of P. Krylov, "Bor'ba za ekonomiiu v voennye gody" [The struggle for economy in the war years], *Planovoe khoziaistvo*, 3 (1985), p. 34; he suggests that during the war the wholesale prices of "the most important types of weapons and ammunition" fell by more than half.

[12] *Finansovaia sluzhba*, p. 87.

[13] This means the sum of $[(E_n/P_{1941}) - E_n]$ in each year from 1942 to 1944, plus five-twelfths of $[(E_n/P_{1941}) - E_n]$ for 1945 (for notation, see the Appendix).

[14] Voznesenskii, *War Economy*, p. 102.

[15] Ibid., p. 108.

[16] Independent estimates reported by Bergson, *Real National Income*, pp. 350, 367–68.

Monthly ruble earnings of industrial workers were more than 50 percent above the prewar benchmark.[17] As for the cost of living faced by public sector employees, it stood in 1944 at almost six times the prewar price level.[18]

Possibly there was some cheating involved in the munitions price cuts claimed. Certainly this was Naum Jasny's belief.[19] Some reductions may have been achieved at the expense of unpaid overtime and subsidies to defense producers and suppliers to the defense industries. At the same time, even taking into account rising wages and nonlabor input costs, the suggested decline in unit procurement prices was not at all implausible. It is supported both by claimed reductions in unit labor requirements of individual weapons, and by claimed improvements in finished output per worker in the munitions sector.[20] Nor are these Soviet claims out of line with international experience in World War II.[21]

The official index of reported NKO expenditure on munitions (Table 2) can be divided by the ground and air munitions price index (Table 3). The result is a chained Laspeyres index of real expenditure on ground and air munitions. In 1944 it stands at roughly 5.1 times 1940 expenditure.

We can almost certainly do better than this, however, by producing a new index of the volume of total munitions produced. We can base it on available physical product series and published information about ruble weapons prices and expenditure shares in different years. We can take into account the fluctuating supply of naval munitions—the only line of

[17] Voznesenskii, *War Economy*, p. 94.

[18] Eugène Zaleski, *Stalinist Planning for Economic Growth, 1933–1952* (London, 1980), p. 452 (table 118, row 22).

[19] Jasny, *The Soviet Price System*, p. 107.

[20] For reductions in labor requirements of Soviet weapons from 1941 to 1943, see Voznesenskii, *War Economy*, p. 92; according to *Istoriia Velikoi Otechestvennoi voiny Sovetskogo Soiuza, 1941–1945* [History of the Great Patriotic War of the Soviet Union, 1941–1945] (Moscow, 1965), vol. 5, p. 375, finished output per worker in Soviet defense industries rose by 121 percent between May 1942 and May 1945.

[21] In the United States, contract prices for the War Department, Army Air Force, and Ordinance fell by 25 to 40 percent in three and a half years (January 1942–August 1945), despite a 50 percent increase in weekly earnings in manufacturing industry (data reported by Bergson, *Real National Income*, pp. 373–74). Behind this lay a doubling of output per worker in munitions in just two years, 1942–1944, with only a small increase in the length of the working week. (According to charts published in *American Industry in War and Transition, 1940–50*, Part II: *The Effect of the War on the Industrial Economy* [Washington, DC, 1945], p. 10, "productivity" [whether per worker or per hour worked is not specified] in munitions industries in 1944 stood at approximately two and one-half times the 1942 level, while average hours worked in durable goods manufacturing rose over the same two years from roughly 45 to 47 hours.)

In Germany, too, output per munitions worker doubled between 1941 and 1944, without any increase in hours worked. German munitions output trebled between the end of 1941 and mid-1944; see *Die deutsche Industrie im Kriege, 1939–1945* (Berlin, 1954), p. 191. Meanwhile, between mid-1941 and mid-1944 the German munitions work force grew by only 44 percent (from 2.7 to 3.9 millions), according to Burton H. Klein, *Germany's Economic Preparations for War* (Cambridge, MA, 1959), p. 217.

Soviet defense output to decline during the war years. We can also examine the sensitivity of these estimates to whether "early" or "late" prices and values are used to weight the index.

RELIABILITY OF PHYSICAL PRODUCT SERIES

Before arriving at a new munitions index, we have to satisfy ourselves as to the reliability of its statistical foundations. How trustworthy are the available time series for physical output of tanks, planes, guns, and shells?

A Soviet historian, B. V. Sokolov, has recently expressed distrust on the following grounds. Assuming their reliability, Soviet production figures for combat aircraft and armored fighting vehicles may be used in combination with data on Soviet combat stocks and imports to estimate Soviet losses of these munitions in each period of the war.[22] Sokolov then compares Soviet equipment losses estimated in this way with German losses on the eastern front. He finds that estimated Soviet losses far exceeded German losses over equivalent periods, regardless of whether Soviet forces were losing or winning the war, often by a factor of two or three to one, occasionally by more.

Sokolov ascribes a part of the excess of estimated Soviet over German losses to the same Stalinist deformations in the military sphere which were associated with heavy expenditure of soldiers' lives—excessive centralization and despotic use of authority, unthinking obedience, the low valuation of life itself in the wake of the mass repressions of the 1930s. He judges, however, that it is impossible to ascribe all the estimated disproportion to such factors. He believes the Soviet losses estimated in this way are implausibly high and concludes that the fault lies with the underlying production data, which must be exaggerated. The contribution to Soviet victory of the Soviet munitions industries should be downgraded (and that of the Soviet military should presumably be upgraded correspondingly).

I find this chain of reasoning doubtful. There are significant problems of methodology involved in the estimation of losses by Sokolov's route, but they are not conclusive.[23] For the sake of argument, therefore, let us

[22] B. V. Sokolov, "O sootnoshenii poter' v liudiakh i boevoi tekhnike na Sovetsko-Germanskom fronte v khode Velikoi Otechestvennoi voiny" [On the correlation of losses of people and combat equipment on the Soviet-German front in the course of the Great Patriotic war], *Voprosy istorii*, 9 (1988), p. 123. Define CS_n as the level of combat stocks at the end of period n, and assume that there are no other stocks held in the rear or in reserve; the number of units produced during each period is given by Q_n, imported units by IM_n, and the number of losses by L_n. Then the following would obtain:

$$L_n = Q_n + IM_n - (CS_n - CS_{n-1})$$

[23] Hidden assumptions are made about initial reserves and rear formations, and the change in their level in each period of account, and about noncombat losses. At the same time it is true that

take for granted that when Soviet munitions losses are estimated on the basis of production series they look disproportionately high. Is this unbelievable?

Modern Soviet military commentators do not find disproportionate rates of combat expenditure of Soviet munitions in World War II implausible. In one view, the Red Army wasted its armored resources as a result of strategic and logistic errors. Excessive losses arose in the early period of the war because of the incorrect use of tanks, deficiencies of leadership, and the lack of spare parts. The wasteful deployment of tank units continued through 1942; even after 1943, when fully motorized and independently operating tank formations were created, they continued to be used inappropriately, for example, for assaults on large cities, right through 1945. As a result, "the Soviet tank forces suffered impossibly heavy losses throughout the war."[24]

German evidence supports the proposition that Red Army aircraft were easier to shoot down than those of the RAF and USAAF, and not only in June and July 1941. In 1942 Hitler decorated Adolf Galland, the Luftwaffe fighter ace, considering that his 94 air victories "were achieved exclusively against the western enemy and were therefore to be valued more highly." Galland himself described the Soviet losses as "astronomical," and sustainable only because of the remoteness of the Soviet centers of aircraft production: "It was as if one tried to exterminate a nest of ants by killing them one by one without being able to get to their heap."[25] In 1943/44, when the war in the air was at its most intense, the Luftwaffe "used Russia as a school for inexperienced

---

the possibility of bias introduced as a result of hidden assumptions may diminish with the length of the accounting period. In the long run both imports and changes in combat and reserve stocks were small relative to output, and it is output which therefore dominates (in an accounting sense) the determination of losses. Over the period of the war taken as a whole, these are unlikely to be significant sources of bias. The relative importance of combat and noncombat losses, however, will remain undetermined. For further discussion of this methodology, see Harrison, *Soviet Planning*, pp. 110–15, 256–66, where Soviet wartime losses of combat aircraft, armored fighting vehicles, and guns are similarly estimated.

[24] Vitalii Shlykov, "On the History of Tank Asymmetry in Europe," *International Affairs* (Moscow), 10 (1988), pp. 112–13. My thanks to Julian Cooper for this reference. Shlykov's assessment that the Soviet Army possessed a numerical advantage in tanks over the Wehrmacht on the eve of war has been subjected to detailed criticism by V. P. Krikunov, " 'Prostaia arifmetika' V. V. Shlykova" [The 'simple arithmetic' of V. V. Shlykov], *Voenno-istoricheskii zhurnal*, 4 (1989), pp. 41–44. The part of Shlykov's argument which is significant for this article rests in part on direct military estimates of average monthly permanent losses of aircraft, tanks, and guns on the front line, detailed in *Voennaia strategiia* [Military strategy] (Moscow, 1963), p. 427, as follows: aircraft—21 percent, tanks—19 percent, guns—9 percent. It is true that these are substantially lower than the equivalent rates implied by Sokolov and estimated by Harrison, *Soviet Planning*, p. 265, using the same methodology as Sokolov. It is possible, however, that the military estimates refer only to combat losses.

[25] Adolf Galland, *The First and the Last* (London, 1970), pp. 71, 91. My thanks to Robin Clifton for this and the following reference.

pilots. There they could build flying and fighting skills before being thrown into the cauldron of western air battles.''[26]

Sokolov, however, does not believe his own estimates of Soviet munitions losses; he considers them too high. He believes that numerical advantage must have reduced Soviet losses below the German level after 1942. If estimated losses are too high, the reason must be that reports of munitions output were exaggerated. He considers production exaggerated first of all at the enterprise level:

> Inflated reports [*pripiski*]—a defect inherent in our national economy as in the prewar, so in the postwar period, were apparent also in wartime when obligations were often handed down to enterprises subject to shortage of resources for their fulfilment and without taking account of real possibilities. The arbitrary administrative principle was triumphant, and on the fulfilment of these often unbalanced plans hung the fate, in the literal sense of the word, of enterprise leaders. Under such circumstances inflated reports were an inevitable evil.[27]

I do not agree. I tend to evaluate positively the reliability of Soviet data for munitions output in physical units for two reasons. First, a military inspectorate was already installed in Soviet defense factories in 1939, charged with control over both quantity and quality of munitions output.[28] This system of "consumer sovereignty," unique to the munitions industries in the Soviet economy, made it much more difficult for the defense factory to record fictitious output than for its counterpart in the civilian sector. Military inspection could be so strict, on occasion, as to prove an independent factor delaying the handing over of finished output and accentuating munitions shortages in wartime.[29]

Second, there was no obvious reticence of enterprises and ministries when plans failed, even in the most critical months of 1941/42. Plan failure was reported, not concealed. Underfulfillment of quarterly and monthly plans for shell production by wide margins was reported period by period in the second half of 1941. By December 1941 the reported output of aircraft was down to two-fifths of ministerial targets, and that of aircraft engines was down to one-quarter.[30] Such reports are inconsistent with the view that industrial leaders inflated output returns to show 100 percent plan fulfillment because their lives depended on it.

"We all know that the assignments are impossible," wrote one participant; "if they can be met only by 75 percent, there will be

[26] Williamson Murray, *Luftwaffe: Strategy for Defeat, 1933–1945* (London, 1988), p. 371.

[27] Sokolov, "O sootnoshenii poter'," p. 125.

[28] *IVMV*, vol. 2, p. 189; Julian Cooper, "Defence Production and the Soviet Economy, 1929–1941," Soviet Industrialisation Project Series no. 3 (University of Birmingham, 1976), pp. 26–27.

[29] A. P. Kovalev, "V Gosplane v to pamiatnoe vremia" [In Gosplan in that memorable time], *EKO*, 5 (1988), pp. 22–23, reports the case of a nonferrous metal works where, in the early months of the war, delays in military inspection of ammunition cases aggravated the already severe shell famine.

[30] *IVMV*, vol. 4, pp. 150–51.

rejoicing and bonuses and Orders of Merit."[31] In fact, some of the most important peacetime obstacles to the reporting of true output were absent. Norms and targets were set, but workers and managers alike were praised and rewarded for producing as much as possible, not for mechanically fulfilling the plan. Underfulfillment of the plan generated less disgrace than slacking and working below capacity. Mechanically fulfilling the plan did not guarantee immunity from inspection.[32] Traditional incentives to falsify reports may have been to some extent neutralized.[33]

Clearly, many Soviet wartime economic series need revision, but I would be surprised if data for physical output of munitions required radical surgery. I am inclined to see them as a relatively reliable foundation for what follows.

FIVE NEW SUBINDICES

The first result of the revision process is five new indices covering the wartime supply of aircraft, armored fighting vehicles (AFV), armament and ammunition from 1940 to mid-1945, and naval munitions from 1940 to 1945. They can also be extended back to 1937, accepting somewhat lower standards of coverage, detail, and reliability. (Sources and methods are further summarized in the Appendix and detailed in a statistical supplement available from the author.)

The period beginning in 1940 is the best-documented one as far as munitions output in physical units is concerned, and it gives correspondingly reliable results in terms of index numbers.

For 1940 and the war years, I use three different methods. Available time series for physical output of aircraft, AFV, and armament are valued on the basis of 1941 munitions prices and added up to give series for total finished output of the industrial branch in 1941 rubles. The process is repeated using 1944 munitions prices. When divided by base-year output, the result is two indices, one set to 1941 equals 100 and the other set to 1944 equals 100.

In the case of ammunition, no prices are available for either 1941 or 1944; the only near-continuous time series denominated in physical units for the war years shows the supply of "shells and mines." I assume this series to be representative of ammunition supply as a whole. Therefore, the problem of weighting and adding up different series does not arise at this stage. Indices are generated with both 1941 and 1944 as base years, but the difference is purely formal.

[31] G. S. Kravchenko, *Ekonomika SSSR v gody Velikoi Otechestvennoi voiny (1941–1945 gg.)* [The economy of the USSR in the years of the Great Patriotic War (1941–1945)] (Moscow, 1970), pp. 410–11.

[32] See V. V. Kolotov, *Nikolai Alekseevich Voznesenskii* (2nd edn., Moscow, 1976), p. 267.

[33] David Dyker, review of Harrison, *Soviet Planning*, in *Slavonic and East European Review*, 75 (1987), p. 309.

For naval munitions we face a choice between an index based on numbers of warships of the "basic classes" (that is, excluding mosquito craft) completed in each year, or an index of current expenditure deflated by a chained index of procurement costs which can be reckoned in terms of a base year either in 1941 or in 1944. For various reasons I prefer the method of expenditure deflation.

The choice of naval index is awkward and makes quite a lot of difference. The published series for warships of the basic classes shows a continuous, year-by-year, dramatic fall in vessel completion from 41 in 1941 to only 4 in 1944. In contrast the index of deflated naval munitions expenditure shows a substantially lower level of procurement in 1941/42 compared to 1940, then near-recovery by 1944.

In principle I would prefer unambiguous physical product series to expenditure series, however accurately deflated, for the foundations of a revised munitions index. In this case, however, I prefer deflated expenditure. The disastrous fall in warship completions would certainly be misleading as a measure of both naval munitions consumption and supply. Although the Soviet war fleet played no strategic role in World War II, it played a major tactical role, especially in support of the ground forces. At some moments this tactical role could be decisive. In the winter of 1941, for example, the Baltic fleet's artillery was central to the defense of Leningrad. The acquisition of new ships became less important than their supply with naval guns, ammunition, and other means of war. The latter are captured by the method of expenditure deflation, but would be lost otherwise (for example, the artillery series used for my new "Guns" subindex in Table 3 explicitly excludes naval guns).

It may be that imports sustained 1944 expenditure on naval munitions above the level of domestic production. This is undoubtedly true, but I do not believe the effect to be very significant. The share of vessels (including merchant vessels, not chargeable to war-fleet expenditures) in the dollar value of United States Lend Lease shipments in 1944 was less than 6 percent.[34] This was similar to the navy's share in overall munitions outlays, and it suggests that any overstatement of naval munitions production in 1944 arising from the use of deflated expenditure will be minor.

The new subindices for 1940 to 1945 are shown in Table 4. Also shown in the table are results of their extension back to 1937. Index numbers given for the period before 1940 are certainly less reliable than for the war years themselves. Before 1940 three of the five subindices (aircraft, AFV, and ammunition) rely on a single series showing units produced under some heading which is assumed to be representative, and the aircraft series is inflated in the early years by inclusion of civilian types.

[34] Harrison, *Soviet Planning*, p. 259.

TABLE 4
NEW SUBINDICES FOR FINISHED OUTPUT OF GROUND, AIR, AND NAVAL MUNITIONS, 1937–1945

	Aircraft	Armored Fighting Vehicles	Guns	Ammunition	Naval Munitions
At Constant Prices of 1941					
1937	29	15	13	13	58
1938	36	21	30	32	64
1939	68	28	44	29	92
1940	69	26	43	36	131
1941	100	100	100	100	100
1942	141	381	282	190	89
1943	186	375	288	310	113
1944	218	465	280	326	124
1945	219[a]	501[a]	260[a]	287[a]	161
At Constant Prices of 1944					
1937	13	3	5	4	46
1938	16	5	12	10	52
1939	30	6	17	9	74
1940	31	6	16	11	106
1941	46	22	38	31	81
1942	64	82	102	58	72
1943	84	81	104	95	91
1944	100	100	100	100	100
1945	101[a]	108[a]	93[a]	88[a]	130

[a] First six months, at annual rate.
Source: See the Appendix.

Only the armament index maintains relatively full coverage before as after 1940.

The prewar subindex for naval munitions is based on an official index of gross value of output of the shipbuilding industry. The prices at which gross value of output is calculated are unspecified, but are probably those of "1926/27." Output is also inflated in the early years by inclusion of civilian types. It excludes naval munitions other than warships, but I do not consider this to be a source of major distortion under peacetime conditions. A case could be made for dropping the prewar years from the naval munitions subindex altogether and simply assuming that the prewar supply of naval munitions grew in line with a weighted average of ground and air munitions. In fact, its inclusion will not make much difference over the period from 1937 to 1940, when shipbuilding output shown in the industry subindex grew 2.3 times, compared to 2.5 times for other munitions types taken together. It is true that the year-to-year movement of the shipbuilding subindex is quite different from that of other subindices, but this is information which seems relevant and interesting.

Of course even in 1940 and after the new subindices are still not perfect. They are based on 16 underlying time series (of which 15 show physical output of munitions, and one shows deflated munitions expenditure). Out of 96 observations required (16 series times the five years from 1940 to 1944, and one half-year, 1945), no less than 33 have been estimated or interpolated. All the estimated observations, however, are anchored in at least one other officially reported observation on either side (intertemporally or simultaneously).

For the war years the best of the new subindices are those covering aircraft, AFV, and guns. Least satisfactory is the ammunition subindex, which is based on a single physical product series. I am unable to judge precisely the reliability of the naval munitions subindex, but I am sure that the evaluation of total munitions output is improved by its inclusion. For the prewar years the only reliably based subindex is the one for guns. Two of the five, the prewar subindices for aircraft and naval munitions, certainly understate output growth before 1940 because of the inclusion of civilian types, the relative importance of which was greater in earlier years.

The most important and ineradicable common defect of the new subindices is their neglect of changing product quality. This is taken into account only when qualitative improvement in weaponry resulted in the expansion of one measured line of output at the expense of another—for example, the growth of medium and heavy tank output relative to that of light tanks. Otherwise it is entirely ignored. Undoubtedly the Soviet fighter-bomber, tank, and gun of 1944 were very different products from those which took the field in 1941. I cannot myself find any way of taking this systematically into account. Nor do I find any solution to this problem in statistical work on the munitions production of other countries in World War II. Thus the new subindices still do not pretend to measure anything more than the volume of output in a relatively crude sense, and represent a lower bound on the true (quality-adjusted) growth of munitions produced.

Still, I believe that for the period from 1937 to 1945 the problem of qualitative change in weaponry is not so great as to destroy the value of a new index of munitions output based on change in the numbers of units produced. It is true that, if we were to try to extend the index further back into the prewar decade, the rapid qualitative improvement then taking place in military technology would begin to represent an uncontainable problem. This is why I take no year earlier than 1937 for the new subindices' starting point.

The extent of the new subindices' deviation from the old ones is quantified in Table 5. This confirms the utter unreliability of the old ones as guides to the volume of output.

TABLE 5
THE NEW AND OLD SUBINDICES COMPARED
(1944 as percentage of 1940)

	Aircraft	Armored Fighting Vehicles	Guns	Ammunition	Naval Munitions
		Istoriia Subindices			
	239	296	206	310	
		New Subindices			
At 1941 prices	315	1,771	652	902	95
At 1944 prices	323	1,698	611	902	95

Notes and sources: For the *Istoriia* subindices, see Table 1; for the new subindices, see Table 4.

TABLE 6
EXPENDITURE WEIGHTS FOR THE NEW MUNITIONS INDEX, 1941 AND 1944

	1941	1944
Percent of Outlays on Ground and Air Munitions		
Aircraft	35.2%	27.1%
Armored Fighting Vehicles	11.7	12.9
Guns, Ammunition	41.9	43.7
Guns	16.8	17.5
Ammunition	25.1	26.2
Vehicles, Other	11.2	16.3
Total	100.0	100.0
Percent of Total Outlays on Munitions		
Ground and Air Munitions	88.5	93.4
Naval Munitions	11.5	6.6
Total	100.0	100.0

Source: See the Appendix.

TOTAL MUNITIONS OUTPUT—A NEW INDEX

The new subindices can now be combined using appropriate expenditure weights. These weights, shown in Table 6, are derived from officially reported percent shares of the annual munitions budget. The main area of uncertainty is the relative weighting of guns and ammunition. In Table 6, expenditure on guns is divided from expenditure on ammunition in the ratio of 2 to 3 in both 1941 and 1944. This seems consistent both with Soviet evidence and with the available World War II experience of other nations.

Computation proceeds notionally in two stages. First, I combine the subindices of ground and air munitions, incorporating the assumption that the supply of vehicles, tractors, and "other" armament grew at the same rate as the output of other items. Then I combine the resulting index of real output of munitions for the ground and air forces with the naval munitions subindex for the index of total (ground, air, and naval) munitions output, shown in Table 7.

TABLE 7
THE NEW INDEX OF TOTAL SOVIET FINISHED OUTPUT OF MUNITIONS, 1937–1945

At Prices of	1941	1944
Index Numbers		
1937	24	10
1938	36	14
1939	52	21
1940	59	24
1941	100	39
1942	199	73
1943	247	91
1944	274	100
1945[a]	269	98
1944, Percent of		
1940	466	424
1937	1,147	1,042

[a] First six months, at annual rate. Here I assume that the production of naval munitions was evenly spread through the year. This was not the case for ground and air munitions, the year's production of which was heavily concentrated (70 percent) in the first six months; see *Istoriia Vtoroi Mirovoi voiny, 1939–1945* (Moscow, 1980), vol. 11, p. 348. However, the procurement of naval munitions was clearly on a different, and probably rising, trend in 1945.
Source: The five new subindices (Table 4), summed using appropriate expenditure weights (Table 6).

There are two versions of this index, based on the relative munitions prices of 1941 and 1944 respectively. When the base year is 1941, the index shows that Soviet munitions output expanded rapidly in the last prewar years before slowing in 1939/40. The expansion of two and a half times from 1937 to 1940 shown in Table 7 is a little less than that estimated by Abram Bergson.[35]

At the outbreak of war, Soviet munitions output began to grow with still greater rapidity, even taking into account the early decline in output of naval munitions. The period of fastest growth was 1941/42 when real output doubled. Taking the war as a whole, the year of peak output was 1944. In that year munitions output stood at 4.7 times the 1940 level, and 11.5 times the level already achieved in 1937.

When munitions output is revalued in the prices of 1944, the picture changes only a little. The period of most rapid growth is still 1941/42, and the year of peak output is still 1944. Expansion in 1941/42 is estimated at just under 90 percent; in 1944 peak output still stood at 4.2 times the 1940 level and 10.4 times the level of 1937. Thus the use of

[35] Bergson, *Real National Income*, p. 371, gave real Soviet munitions output in 1940 as 2.8 times the level of 1937. Bergson's estimate was based partly on official reports of production (measured in "1926/27 rubles"), partly on reported budgetary appropriations. Some understatement of prewar munitions output growth is likely in Table 7 because of the inclusion of civilian aircraft production, relatively more important than combat types in the earlier years, and the very large weight of aircraft production in prewar rearmament.

"late" prices makes the growth record look a little more modest, but the overall effect is small.

These results are not overly sensitive to substantial variation of assumptions about the relative weights of guns and ammunition. In Table 6 expenditure on guns was divided from expenditure on ammunition in a ratio of 2 to 3 in both 1941 and 1944. Alternatively, spending on guns may be divided from spending on ammunition in the ratios of 3 to 2 or 1 to 4. When the base year is 1941, the only wartime index number to be seriously affected is that for 1942, when the extent of possible bias is plus or minus 3.9 percent. In other years the range of error is less than 1.5 percent. When the base year is 1944, varying assumptions about the relative weights of guns and ammunition have greatest effect again in 1942 (plus or minus 5.9 percent); in other war years the range of error is 2.2 percent or less.

The behavior of Soviet munitions output can be compared with the expansion recorded in some other countries. This is shown in Table 8. According to index numbers shown in the top half of this table, in the United States the production of armaments in 1944 was roughly 6.7 times the 1941 level. British munitions output is known to have peaked in the first quarter of 1944 at 6.5 times the 1939 (fourth-quarter) level; taking 1943 as the calendar year of peak output, the equivalent figure was an expansion factor of 6.0 times. In each case the expansion of munitions output from the outbreak of hostilities to the wartime peak was more rapid and compressed than that of Germany, where the index of munitions output shows peak output in 1944 at 6.3 times the level of 1938. (Table 8 does not, however, take into account any effects arising from Germany's access to weapons produced in Italy or occupied Europe.)

A similar (sevenfold) increase in Soviet munitions output up to the 1944 peak was probably achieved in the period from 1938. This was an interval similar to that required by Germany. The time taken partly reflects the fact that, like Germany, the Soviet Union was an early starter in the interwar arms race and had already built up a relatively high level of output in the late 1930s. By 1941 each country had achieved a similar expansion over 1938. After 1941, however, the munitions indices of the two countries behaved quite differently. Soviet output surged ahead; Germany's delayed burst of effort in munitions production in 1943/44 came too late to reverse the outcome.

The level of munitions output achieved by the warring powers in various years can also be compared. The index numbers shown in the top half of Table 8 can be combined with a rough estimate of relative levels of munitions output of the great powers in 1944. This yields the figures in the bottom half of Table 8, which show each country's munitions output in each year in proportion to that of the United States in 1944. (The table leaves out of account a number of secondary factors:

TABLE 8
THE TOTAL OUTPUT OF MUNITIONS: UNITED STATES, UNITED KINGDOM, USSR, AND GERMANY, 1937–1944

	United States	United Kingdom	USSR	Germany
Index Numbers, Based on	Mid-1945[a]	Jan.-Mar. 1941[a]	1944	Jan.-Feb. 1942[a]
1937			10	
1938			14	16
1939		17[b]	21	20
1940	7[c]	42[c]	24	35
1941	15	54	39	35
1942	53	86	73	51
1943	91	102	91	80
1944	100	100	100	100
Percent of United States Munitions Output in 1944				
1937			3	
1938			4	3
1939		3[b]	6	4
1940	7[c]	8[c]	7	8
1941	15	10	12	8
1942	53	17	22	11
1943	91	20	28	17
1944	100	19	31	21

[a] For ease of comparison, non-Soviet indices have been recalculated to show 1944 equals 100.
[b] Fourth quarter of 1939, at annual rate.
[c] Second half of 1940, at annual rate.
Sources: United States: calculated from constant price dollar values in R. Elberton Smith, *The Army and Economic Mobilization* (Washington, DC, 1959), p. 7. United Kingdom: calculated from a quarterly index in Mark Harrison, "A Volume Index of the Total Munitions Output of the United Kingdom, 1939–1944," forthcoming in the *Economic History Review*. USSR: Table 7. Germany: taken from *Die deutsche Industrie im Kriege, 1939–1945* (Berlin, 1954), p. 191. Each country's total (ground, air, and naval) 1944 munitions output is expressed in standard aircraft units, then calculated as a percentage of United States total munitions output in that year. See further the Appendix.

the Canadian contribution to Allied mutual aid; German weapons procurement in Czechoslovakia, France, and Italy; and the Italian and Japanese contributions to Axis strength.)

The table shows that, despite big differences in the scale and pace of prewar rearmament, by 1940 each of the four countries was producing munitions at roughly the same absolute level. This meant that Germany was already being outproduced by three to one (and neither Italy nor even Japan contributed much to offset this disproportion), but of course Germany was not yet actively engaged on land with any of the three future Allies. After 1940, as first Russia then America entered the war, the German disadvantage was compounded and multiplied. In 1942 even the weakened Soviet economy managed to double the effort of German war industries. Thus the table confirms that Germany's failure to win the war in Russia by the end of 1941 was already decisive in its loss of control over the war's outcome.

In 1943/44, as Anglo-American resources were thrown into the balance, the German disadvantage became overwhelming in spite of increasingly frantic efforts. Of the weapons supplied by the three Allies after 1941, two-thirds came from the war industries of the United States alone. One-fifth was supplied by the Soviet Union, and the remainder (one-seventh) came from Great Britain. However, Soviet munitions were also significant out of all proportion to their numerical weight because of their role in the destruction of Germany's fighting strength on land.

Appendix

Tables 3 through 8 rest upon a statistical supplement not reproduced here for reasons of space but available on application to the author. Its contents are briefly summarized below.

A. PRICE DEFLATORS FOR SOVIET MUNITIONS, 1940–1945

For ground and air munitions, a chained Paasche price index of unit procurement costs, 1941–1945 (1940 equals 100) is calculated from the estimated change in prices in each year over the previous year (P_n). The latter is derived from comparing total munitions expenditure of the defense commissariat in period n, in current rubles (E_n), with the ruble saving on NKO munitions expenditures attributed in each year to price reductions over the previous year (S_n). The relationship between these terms is therefore as follows:

$$E_n = \Sigma p_n q_n$$

$$S_n = \Sigma p_{n-1} q_n - \Sigma p_n q_n$$

$$P_n = \Sigma p_n q_n / \Sigma p_{n-1} q_n$$

$$= E_n/(E_n + S_n)$$

For naval munitions an index of procurement costs, 1942–1944 (1941 equals 100), is obtained by chaining together reported figures representing annual percentage price reductions.

B. SOVIET MUNITIONS PRICES, IN RUBLES, 1941–1945

Officially reported ruble prices are listed for nine selected types of aircraft, AFV, and guns in most years, 1941–1945.

C. NEW SUBINDICES OF SOVIET MUNITIONS OUTPUT, 1940–1945

The physical output of different types of aircraft, AFV, and guns is listed as reported, or estimated where official reports are missing, then aggregated and evaluated in index number form on the basis of officially reported ruble prices from B, above. For ammunition, a single physical output series is listed and expressed as an index number.

For naval munitions an index of realized expenditure is derived from official reports and deflated on the basis of estimated trends in procurement costs from A, above.

D. EXTENDING THE NEW SUBINDICES OF SOVIET MUNITIONS OUTPUT BACK FROM 1940 TO 1937

The subindices already derived in C, above, are extended back to 1937. For aircraft, AFV, guns, and ammunition the methodology in each case is consistent with that already applied to the war years. For naval munitions an official index of gross value of output of the shipbuilding industry (1937 equals 100) is employed.

E. ESTIMATING EXPENDITURE WEIGHTS FOR THE NEW MUNITIONS INDEX

The relative weights of the new subindices are established on the basis of officially reported budget data for 1941 and 1944. The relative shares of aircraft, AFV, guns, and ammunition in ground and air forces' expenditure are officially reported or, where missing, estimated on the basis of plausible assumptions and comparative information. The sensitivity of final results to assumptions made at this stage is established.

The share of naval munitions in ruble spending on munitions in 1941 and 1944 is also obtained after considerable further processing of available budget indicators.

F. THE LEVEL OF MUNITIONS OUTPUT IN CROSS-COUNTRY COMPARISON, 1944

Available information on the munitions output of different countries in 1944, expressed in comparable physical units, is presented. Difficulties in using these to establish reliable measures of the relative levels of munitions output in different countries in 1944 are considered, together with alternative solutions and a past precedent.

The method chosen begins with conversion of each country's 1944 aircraft output into internationally standard units of single-engined aircraft equivalents. The latter figure, divided by the share of aircraft in total munitions procurement or supply of each country in 1944, then yields each country's total (ground, air, and naval) 1944 munitions output, expressed in common units of single-engined aircraft equivalents, when each country's ground and naval munitions output is converted to single-engined aircraft equivalents at national prices or costs.

The Condition of England and the Standard of Living: Cotton Textiles in the Northwest, 1806–1850

JOHN C. BROWN

This article examines the workers' standard of living in the cotton textile industry of Northwest England from 1806 to 1850. Hedonic earnings regressions using 1835 data suggest that power-loom weavers required substantial compensation for the high rents and poor sanitation of urban locations. Adjusting earnings in the factory sector for the impact of urbanization cuts growth in living standards by 10 percent, or up to one-quarter of gains realized by 1850. Inclusion of those employed in the handloom sector implies that any improvements in the living standards of all workers in the industry appeared only during the 1840s.

Much historical debate has sought to clarify the impact of industrialization on the living standards of English workers. The debate originated in a wide-ranging public discussion during the 1830s and 1840s over the "Condition of England": what, people asked, was the impact of the demographic revolution and the advance of the factory system in the late eighteenth century on the well-being of the poorer members of English society?[1] J. L. and Barbara Hammonds' answer in 1925 arose out of their belief that laissez-faire urbanization, the rigors of factory work, and the decline of domestic industry canceled the material benefits generated by the industrial revolution: "The new factories and the new furnaces were like Pyramids, telling of man's enslavement, rather than his power."[2] J. H. Clapham and subsequent scholars countered this critique of unregulated economic development with real-wage series indicating that the average English worker experienced a modest increase in his material living standard during the seventy years prior to 1850. As long as estimates of gains in real earnings remained relatively low, however, historians such as E. P. Thompson could plausibly argue that the reduction in the quality of life because of

The Journal of Economic History, Vol. L, No. 3 (Sept. 1990). ISSN 0022-0507.

The author is Assistant Professor of Economics at Clark University, Worcester, MA 01610.

He thanks Steve Webb, Jeffrey Williamson, John Lyons, participants at the 1984 Cliometrics Conference, three anonymous referees, and the editor for helpful comments. Errors remaining are his alone.

[1] See Gertrude Himmelfarb, *The Idea of Poverty: England in the Early Industrial Age* (New York, 1983), for a discussion of the contemporary debate over the "Condition of England"; and David Cannadine, "The Present and the Past in the English Industrial Revolution," *Past and Present*, 103 (May 1984), pp. 131–72, for a review of the subsequent historical literature.

[2] See J. L. and Barbara Hammond, *The Rise of Modern Industry* (9th edn., London, 1966), p. 232.

industrialization more than canceled any gains to welfare from increased consumption.[3]

In the early 1980s Peter Lindert and Jeffrey Williamson announced that the debate was over. Primarily because of the strong deflation evident in their cost-of-living indices after the Napoleonic Wars, they concluded that living standards for "blue collar workers" rose from 60 to 90 percent after 1810. They argued further that the differential in nominal wages between the city and country offered a reliable measure of the welfare cost the migrant would experience in the move to the city with its "long rigid hours," "disruption of traditional family roles," and "noise, filth, crime, and crowding of urban slums." They applied estimates of this compensation—either 7 to 10 percent from Williamson's previous work or an upper bound of 65 percent (the differential between the pay of a laborer in Manchester and a farm worker in the South)—to the earnings of those making the move, whether into industry or into the cities. The calculation implied that changes in "the quality of life" eroded living standards by a modest 6 to 10 percent, leaving impressive gains in welfare intact. Their cost-of-living index suggested further that even the handloom weavers—the foremost case of domestic industry in distress—"may not have suffered any further net losses after 1820."[4]

Those familiar with the contemporary debate among intellectuals over the "Condition of England" have had difficulty reconciling this account of dramatic improvements in well-being with the pessimism and social unrest of the years before 1851, when the Crystal Palace exhibition marked "an extraordinary chronological frontier" at the beginning of the widely shared prosperity of the mid-Victorian era. Some have accepted the conclusions of the new optimism and ascribed the ferment to "cultural lag."[5] Others have challenged the new optimism, taking a cue from T. S. Ashton's perspective that assessments of living standards must recognize the uneven impact of the industrial revolution across regions and occupational groups.[6] They argue that

[3] See E. P. Thompson, *The Making of the English Working Class* (New York, 1966).

[4] See Peter Lindert and Jeffrey Williamson, "English Workers' Living Standards During the Industrial Revolution: A New Look," *Economic History Review*, 36 (Feb. 1983), pp. 1–25; and Peter Lindert and Jeffrey Williamson, "English Workers' Real Wages: Reply to Crafts," this JOURNAL, 45 (Mar. 1985), pp. 145–53, for the evidence on real wages. Jeffrey G. Williamson, "Urban Disamenities, Dark Satanic Mills, and the British Standard of Living Debate," this JOURNAL, 41 (Mar. 1981), pp. 75–83; and Jeffrey G. Williamson, "Was the Industrial Revolution Worth It? Disamenities and Death in 19th Century British Towns," *Explorations in Economic History*, 19 (June 1982), pp. 221–45, provide evidence on the compensation estimated from hedonic regressions of earnings paid laborers in 1909 and 1834. The estimates range from 13 percent in the far North to 7 to 10 percent in the Midlands, Lancashire, Cheshire, and Yorkshire, and a –2 percent in the South and East for moves to London.

[5] See Himmelfarb, *Idea of Poverty*, p. 137.

[6] See T. S. Ashton, "The Standard of Life of the Workers in England, 1790–1830," this JOURNAL, 9 (Supplement 1949), pp. 19–38; and T. R. Gourvish, "Flinn and Real Wages in Britain,

neither labor nor goods markets were sufficiently well integrated to ensure that the experience of one region or industry could fairly represent living standards in all of England. Indeed, despite evidence of convergence during the late 1700s, significant interregional differences in real agricultural earnings remained across England until after 1850.[7]

The few regional studies that do exist have failed to uncover the pattern of substantial growth in living standards after 1810 suggested by the new optimism. R. S. Neale maintains that contrary to the Lindert and Williamson series for common labor, the real earnings of laborers in Bath and Glasgow register little improvement until after the mid-1830s. Evidence on the real earnings of wool weavers in Gloucestershire and female domestic servants in Bath tells a similar story. Neale concludes that evaluations of living standards relying primarily on earnings series for adult male wage earners may seriously distort the picture for the labor force as a whole, which included a substantial contingent of women, children, and the self-employed. John Walton's social history of Lancashire likewise finds little evidence for a surge of real wages during the "difficult transitional years" before 1850. On the basis of price data and scattered evidence on rents, he suggests that the deflation evident in the Lindert and Williamson price indices, which are based primarily on London prices and on rents from cottages in rural Staffordshire, began only after 1830 in Lancashire. The detailed studies of living standards in 1850 that do exist for Oldham and Preston document a high level of poverty that is inconsistent with a virtual doubling of real wages during the preceding forty years.[8] Joel Mokyr's recent reappraisal of statistics of tea, sugar, and tobacco imports provides some support for this skepticism on a national basis. Only during the 1840s do these proxies for consumption—and living standards—reveal a noticeable upward trend.[9]

The region of dramatic urbanization and economic transformation that so stimulated contemporary debate, the cotton Northwest of

---

1750–1850: A Comment," *Economic History Review*, 2nd Series, 29 (Feb. 1976), pp. 135–45. G. N. von Tunzelmann, "Trends in Real Wages, 1750–1850, Revisited," *Economic History Review*, 2nd Series, 32 (Feb. 1979), pp. 37–49, concludes from principal-components analysis of wage series of town laborers from six towns that regional variation in real nonagricultural wages was more likely influenced by differences in prices than in wage rates.

[7] See N. F. R. Crafts, *British Economic Growth during the Industrial Revolution* (Oxford, 1985), pp. 105–7 and Jeffrey G. Williamson, "Did English Factor Markets Fail during the Industrial Revolution?," *Oxford Economic Papers* 39 (Dec. 1987), pp. 641–78.

[8] See R. S. Neale, *Writing Marxist History* (Oxford, 1985); John Walton, *A Social History of Lancashire, 1558–1939* (Manchester, 1985), chap. 9; and Richard K. Fleischman, *Conditions of Life Among the Cotton Workers of Southeastern Lancashire, 1780–1850* (New York, 1985).

[9] Joel Mokyr, "Is There Still Life in the Pessimist Case? Consumption during the Industrial Revolution, 1790–1850," this JOURNAL, 48 (Mar. 1988), pp. 69–92; and Joel Mokyr, "Has the Industrial Revolution been Crowded Out? Some Reflections on Crafts and Williamson," *Explorations in Economic History*, 24 (July 1987), pp. 293–319.

England—Lancashire and the adjoining areas of Yorkshire, Cheshire, and Derbyshire—provides an ideal testing ground for these objections to the new optimism. Detailed information on earnings in the factory sector and piece rates from the handloom sector provide the raw material, but developing these data into plausible conjectures about living standards requires consideration of the impact on the market for textile labor of both the relocation of the textile industry into urban areas after 1815 and the protracted decline of handloom weaving. Looked at this way, living standards in the cotton Northwest improved only marginally, and then only during the 1840s.

URBANIZATION, HANDLOOM WEAVERS, AND THE LABOR MARKET

The Condition of England captured by accounts of the crowded cities and impoverished handloom weavers of the Northwest marked the outcome of the double transformation of the cotton textile industry that set in toward the end of the Napoleonic Wars: the reversal of both the industry's geographic dispersal and its reliance on hand labor. During the initial period of rapid growth from the late eighteenth century until about 1815, spinners sought out water-power sites that were increasingly available only along streams in the rural uplands of Lancashire and the adjoining counties.[10] In addition, the industry's expansion during these years prompted a quadrupling of the weaving population, to about 200,000. Although considerable diversity still characterized handloom weaving in 1815, it appears that high earnings had led most weavers to abandon part-time farming and relocate to Bolton and to handloom villages located in northeastern Lancashire. The transformation of the industry meant that by 1850, both spinning and weaving had moved to primarily steam-powered mills that were concentrated in a heavily urbanized belt extending 20 to 30 miles around Manchester; the army of weavers had shrunk to a corps of about 35,000.[11]

The adoption of steam power and Manchester's rise as a center of the cotton industry prompted the geographic concentration. The expanded demand for mule-spun yarn and the diffusion of the power loom after 1820 hastened the growth of the steam-powered sector of the industry, which located primarily in those areas of southeastern Lancashire where coal was readily accessible.[12] Use of steam power also conferred

[10] See D. A. Farnie, *The English Cotton Industry and the World Market: 1815–1896* (Oxford, 1979), pp. 52–57; and G. N. von Tunzelmann, *Steam Power and British Industrialization to 1860* (Oxford, 1978), pp. 137–38, who notes that the strong demand for water-power sites after 1790 led to the construction of mills in northern Wales and the far north of Lancashire.

[11] See A. J. Taylor, "Concentration and Specialization in the Lancashire Cotton Industry, 1825–1850," *Economic History Review*, 2nd Series, 1 (1949), pp. 114–22.

[12] See Taylor, "Cotton Industry," pp. 114–16; and von Tunzelmann, *Steam Power*, pp. 64–67. The estimates of fuel usage in Andrew Ure, *The Cotton Manufacture of Great Britain* (London, 1836), vol. 1, p. 306; and the price of calico found in Edward Baines, *History of the Cotton*

competitive advantages. While adjustment of rents on water-power sites tended to equalize the average total cost of water relative to steam power, the two sources remained imperfect substitutes. Even when not afflicted with a summer dry spell or winter flooding, water-power sites were rarely able to deliver the horsepower combined spinning and weaving firms required to attain scale economies.[13] The strict limitations on the hours of work of children and young people included in the Factory Acts of 1833 also undermined the competitiveness of rural mills, since they were no longer able to use longer working days or night work to make up for time lost due to adverse weather conditions.[14]

Manchester's eclipse of London as the industry's center of marketing after 1800 promoted geographic concentration as well, since firms in nearby towns could enjoy ready and inexpensive access to cloth and yarn markets. Despite a well-developed network of roads and waterways, as late as the mid-1830s the cost of transporting cloth to Manchester could account for 3 percent of its value for a firm located in Preston, only 31 miles away.[15] As the center of the specialized machine-making industry that emerged during the 1820s, the Manchester area also offered firms the services of skilled labor for repair and new innovations.[16] These influences—the rise of steam and the premier position of Manchester—prompted a degree of locational concentration

Manufacture in Great Britain (2nd edn., New York, 1971), p. 407, imply that in 1833, for each 10 shillings' reduction in the price of a ton of coal, the firm would realize a savings of 1 percent on the sales price of calico.

[13] See R. Lloyd-Jones and A. A. Le Roux, "The Size of Firms in the Cotton Industry, Manchester: 1815–1841," *Economic History Review*, 2nd series, 33 (Feb. 1980), pp. 72–82; von Tunzelmann, *Steam Power*, pp. 124–47; V. A. C. Gatrell, "Labor, Power, and the Size of Firms in the Lancashire Cotton Industry in the Nineteenth Century," *Economic History Review*, 30 (Feb. 1978), pp. 95–139; and Stanley D. Chapman, "The Cost of Power in the Industrial Revolution in Britain: the Case of the Textile Industry," *Midland History*, 1 (Autumn 1971), pp. 1–23. By 1850 specialized weaving firms accounted for only one-fifth of power looms, an estimate that appears to be consistent with Horner's 1841 survey as well. See Taylor, "Cotton Industry," p. 122.

[14] See Howard Marvel, "Factory Regulation: A Reinterpretation of Early English Experience," *Journal of Law and Economics* (Oct. 1977), pp. 379–402; and von Tunzelmann, *Steam Power*, pp. 172–73.

[15] See Farnie, *English Cotton Industry*, pp. 60–66; Michael M. Edwards, *The Growth of the British Cotton Trade: 1780–1815* (Manchester, 1967), pp. 111–21, 171–77; and Edward Baines, *Baines' Lancashire* (1st edn., 1824, 2nd edn., Newton Abbot, England, 1969), vol. 2, p. 135. John Lyons, "The Lancashire Cotton Industry and the Introduction of the Power Loom" (Ph.D. dissertation, University of California at Berkeley, 1977), pp. 195, 246, provides data from Horrocks' of Preston on the weight, cost of transport, and market price of printers' calico.

[16] See Edwards, *Cotton Trade*, pp. 201–2. John S. Hekman, "The Product Cycle and New England Textiles," *Quarterly Journal of Economics* (June 1980), pp. 697–717, stresses the importance of access to machine-makers located in the Boston area for explaining the geographic concentration of the New England textile industry during this period. Over one-half of the machine-making firms and iron founders serving the Northwest textile area who were listed in *Baines' Lancashire* lived within 10 miles of Manchester, and three-quarters lived within 20 miles.

in the English cotton textile industry that was never equaled on the continent or in the United States.[17]

The industry's shift to urban areas after 1815 spurred the unprecedented urbanization of Northwest England, as most cities tripled in size between 1800 and 1850 and Lancashire became England's most urbanized county.[18] The growth in population often overwhelmed the wells and privies that the population traditionally relied upon for water and disposal of waste.[19] As late as the mid-1840s, one-half of Preston's houses lacked piped water and 80 percent were without sewers and drains. In Ashton-under-Lyne, although the construction of housing by local millowners ensured that most houses received piped water, two-thirds still wanted sewers.[20] These sanitary conditions contributed to the steep adult and child mortality gradient between urban and rural areas. Adult male mortality in the registration districts including Preston and Ashton-under-Lyne, for example, was one-third to one-half higher than in the rural Lancashire district of Fylde and Garstang, with the gap between Manchester and the area surrounding it even higher.[21]

The urbanization of the cotton textile industry casts the trade-off between industrialization's material benefits and its impact on the quality of life in a spatial context: how much did the welfare cost to workers from the higher rents, poorer sanitation, and higher mortality of urban areas offset the gains in consumption arising from the productivity advantages of the cities? Urban economics has developed a model of the supply and demand for labor in regional labor markets that suggests

[17] See Gerhart von Schulze-Gävernitz, *The Cotton Trade in England and on the Continent* (London, 1895), for a comparison of the English with the other leading industries in Europe.

[18] See Fleischman, *Conditions of Life*, pp. 297, 313.

[19] See Alan Anderson, *The Origins and Resolution of an Urban Crisis* (Baltimore, 1977), for a general discussion of these issues.

[20] See the report on Ashton-under-Lyne by J. R. Coulthart in the "Appendix to the First Report of the Commissioners of Inquiry into the State of the Large Towns," *Parliamentary Papers*, 1844, vol. 17; the report on Preston of the Rev. J. Clay, "Appendix to the Second Report of the Commissioners of Inquiry into the State of the Large Towns," *Parliamentary Papers*, 1845, vol. 18; and the comments on Ashton by Angus Bethune Reach, *Manchester and the Textile Districts in 1849* (Helmshore, Lancs., 1972), pp. 71, 76.

[21] The *Seventh Annual Report of the Registrar-General* (London, 1847), p. 330, provides the data on adult male mortality for ages 15 to 65 for Manchester and the surrounding townships, and the *Ninth Annual Report of the Registrar-General* (London, 1849), pp. 230–33, provides the same data for the registration districts of Lancashire. The gap between urban Preston and rural Garstang is noteworthy given the continued prevalence of low-quality "mud and thatch" housing in Garstang. See Walton, *Social History of Lancashire*, p. 173. Whether the urban-rural difference prevailing in the early 1840s is the outcome of a deterioration in cities of the same size class is unclear. Fleischman, *Conditions of Life*, pp. 278–79, uses evidence on the age structure of mortality to argue that life expectancy in several Lancashire towns fell slightly between 1800 and 1840. Williamson and Lindert argue that the lengthening of life expectancy in all of England up to 1820, and only a modest dip thereafter, suggests an *improvement* in urban living conditions well before environmental reform got underway after 1860. Robert Woods, "The Effects of Population Redistribution on the Level of Mortality in Nineteenth-Century England and Wales," this JOURNAL, 45 (Sept. 1985), pp. 645–51, concludes that the arithmetic of population growth and redistribution does not rule out rising life expectancies in cities of particular size classes after 1820.

an approach to measuring this trade-off.[22] For a worker with a skill level—and attainable well-being—of u_o considering a number of jobs that differ only by the quality of working conditions (indexed by f_{ij}), the quality of life in the factory town (indexed by q_i), and the cost of living (c_i), the lowest wage she would accept for working at factory j in town i would equal the following:

$$w_{ij} = g(c_i, q_i, f_{ij}, u_o) \qquad (1)$$

The more unpleasant her surroundings at work and at home, the higher the minimum wage she would be willing to accept. During industrialization, the wage offer of the cotton mill owner deciding on how much to pay a worker with her skill level would also vary with the location. Supposing that the prevailing level of profits in the industry is π_o, the wage offer would be lower for a higher distance from Manchester (d_i), reliance on waterpower (p_{ij}), and a smaller firm size (s_{ij}):

$$w_{ij} = f(d_i, p_{ij}, s_{ij}, \pi_o) \qquad (2)$$

If the maximum wage offer at a particular location at least matched the minimum acceptable wage, the worker would be hired. The market-clearing range of wages—highest in the most unpleasant surroundings and in the most advantageous locations—would result when no worker had an incentive to move elsewhere, no firm was making above- or below-normal profits, and the wage offers of firms matched the reservation wages of workers. The model suggests that the cost-saving advantages of an urban location would accrue to workers as higher earnings to the extent required to compensate them for the disutility of life in the city. This compensation should be available to all workers at that location, not just the mover.[23] Implementing the model empirically, by regressing the wage for a particular skill level on the locational characteristics appearing in equations 1 or 2, offers a way to evaluate the argument that the higher living costs and poorer quality of life in the cities offset the benefits of the productivity gains offered by urban locations.

Several historians have questioned whether static equilibrium models of this kind are appropriate for the labor market during industrialization, since they rely upon strong assumptions of rational migration behavior, a willingness of workers to accept more compensation in exchange for

[22] See J. Vernon Henderson, "Evaluating Consumer Amenities and Interregional Welfare Differences," *Journal of Urban Economics*, 11 (Jan. 1982), pp. 32–59; Jennifer Roback, "Wages, Rents, and the Quality of Life," *Journal of Political Economy*, 90 (Dec. 1982), pp. 1257–78; and Glenn C. Blomquist, Mark C. Berger, and John P. Hoehn, "New Estimates of Quality of Life in Urban Areas," *American Economic Review*, 78 (Mar. 1988), pp. 89–107.

[23] The compensation will actually equal the workers' valuation of conditions if differences across communities are capitalized entirely in wage rates and all workers have similar tastes. Those preferring other aspects of "country living" would require an even larger payment than those who chose to live in the city. See Henderson, "Interregional Welfare Differences," pp. 36–44.

poorer working conditions, and market equilibrium.[24] The last assumption is perhaps most troubling in the context of cotton textiles during a period of dynamic change and will be taken up in the regression analysis. The model does offer one reason why mill owners such as the Ashworths and the Gregs were willing to continue investing in rural mills that relied primarily upon water power. Their mill villages at Egerton and Styal offered the employee a healthful environment with "epidemics rare" and "no ruinous and squalid hovels." In return, they were able to pay wages "a trifle below those paid in the towns."[25]

The relocation of the factory sector to the cities after 1815 coincided with the crisis and then decline of the handloom weaving sector. Historians concur that at its peak in the 1820s, the army of 200,000 handloom weavers far outnumbered the factory labor force in the cotton Northwest. They disagree over the significance of the collapse of the nominal piece rates earned by the weavers—on the order of 80 percent between 1810 and 1833—for living standards in the industry as a whole. Duncan Bythell's revisionist history of handloom weaving argues persuasively that the traditional view of the weavers as highly skilled craftsmen immiserated by steam applies only to a small group weaving high-quality fancy goods. He maintains instead that for most of the century the cotton textile industry drew upon a dualistic labor market. The factory sector employed a skilled, full-time labor force. Handloom weaving, as an easily acquired skill, relied primarily upon a part-time, "casual" labor force engaged in the trade as a "by-occupation" when freed from other responsibilities. Countering the view that the Irish were particularly important during the last decades of decline, Bythell argues that throughout the years after 1815 most weavers were women and children; adult males were important as weavers of fancy goods. The casual nature of their employment—and implicitly, the low opportunity cost of their time—ensured that most weavers were particularly

[24] See Sidney Pollard, "Sheffield and Sweet Auburn—Amenities and Living Standards in the Industrial Revolution: A Comment," this JOURNAL, 41 (Dec. 1981), pp. 902–4, who questions the use of the spatial labor market model in Williamson, "Urban Disamenities" and "Disamenities and Death." Mary MacKinnon and Paul Johnson, in "The Case Against Productive Whipping," *Explorations in Economic History*, 21 (Apr. 1984), pp. 218–23, doubt whether the bargaining relationship between children and factory managers would allow for the compensation for corporal punishment reported by Clark Nardinelli, "Corporal Punishment and Children's Wages in Nineteenth Century Britain," *Explorations in Economic History*, 19 (July 1982), pp. 283–95.

[25] See *Report of the Registrar-General*, 1854, for the data on migration and George Henry Wood, *The History of Wages in the Cotton Trade During the Past One Hundred Years* (London, 1910), table 35, for the data on interregional earnings. Reach, *Textile Districts*, pp. 66–68, provides a description of conditions at the Ashworths' mill at Egerton near Bolton and Frances Collier, *The Family Economy of the Working Classes in the Cotton Industry, 1784–1833* (Manchester, 1964), describes conditions at the Greg mill at Styal. Price V. Fishback and Dieter Lauszus, "The Quality of Services in Company Towns: Sanitation in Coal Towns During the 1920s," this JOURNAL, 49 (Mar. 1989), pp. 125–44, provide evidence of firm efforts to influence local living conditions in the United States.

"willing" to accept the collapse in piece rates. Those adult male weavers who were caught by the decline in piece rates were able to find alternative employment in factories or elsewhere.[26]

John Lyons's recent research undermines both the traditional and revisionist perspectives. Abandoning Bythell's model of a dualistic labor market, Lyons suggests instead that the occupational choice of both children and adults in the cotton textile region is best understood as the outcome of a family strategy to maximize earnings. Before 1820 handloom weaving was the appropriate choice for all household members and the industry remained concentrated in weaving hamlets and villages in northeastern Lancashire. During the 1820s the earnings of children and youths in the factory rose most, relative to what they could earn at the loom. Since children also had easier access to entry-level positions, the family now chose to send its children to the factory—even if it meant relocating the household to nearby factory towns—while adult family members remained at the looms. Quantitative evidence from 1817 to 1851 offers support for the family-economy view. While the typical weaver was always an adult male, the share of children in the labor force appears to have declined.[27] These competing interpretations of the handloom weaving labor force hold differing implications for the spatial market for factory labor. The dualistic labor market hypothesis implies that concentrations of weavers would have little impact on earnings in the factory sector, while the family-economy approach suggests that the wages of younger workers in handloom weaving areas would be depressed as weaving families sought employment for their children.

ESTIMATING COMPENSATION AND PRODUCTIVITY DIFFERENTIALS

Regression analysis of the supply and demand sides of the spatial market for cotton textile labor sketched out by equations 1 and 2 addresses the two issues key to the debate over the impact of urbanization and the decline of handloom weaving on living standards. How much compensation did factory workers require for the poorer quality of life in the cities? Were the markets for hand and factory labor integrated? An 1835 survey of earnings in power-loom weaving offers data on the number of looms, type of cloth woven, and weekly earnings for several age groups for over 200 firms in 60 towns in Lancashire and West Yorkshire that are particularly well-suited for examining both of these issues. With earnings about one-half those of the elite mule

[26] See Thompson, *English Working Class*, chap. 9, for a restatement of the traditional view; and Duncan Bythell, *The Handloom Weavers: A Study of the English Cotton Industry during the Industrial Revolution* (Cambridge, 1969), pp. 60–64.

[27] See John Lyons, "Family Response to Economic Decline: Handloom Weavers in Early Nineteenth-Century Lancashire" in *Research in Economic History*, 12 (1989), pp. 45–91.

spinners, power-loom weavers in the mid-1830s were representative of the semiskilled workers who predominated in the cotton textile labor force.[28]

The specification of the supply equation 1 includes variables capturing spatial differences in living costs, the quality of life, working conditions on the job, and local concentrations of weavers. By the early 1840s differentials in rents were chiefly responsible for differences in living costs in the Northwest. A regression model relating weekly rents from two surveys of the mid-1830s to density variables serves to predict rents for the remainder of the towns in the sample.[29] Rather than using these estimates to deflate the earnings data with an index of living costs that may prove to be arbitrary, the predicted *RENT* appears directly in the earnings regressions. Following the practice of public health reformers, who recognized the incidence of waterborne diseases as a barometer of inadequate sanitation, the regressions use *WATERDISEASE*, the average mortality rates from cholera and dysentery from 1838 to 1842.[30]

[28] Baines, *Cotton Manufacture*, pp. 229–37, and Lyons, "Introduction of the Powerloom," p. 167, describe the power-loom sector. The survey covers two-thirds of the parishes in Lancashire and West Yorkshire and is included in the "Returns Relative to Power Looms Used in Factories," *Parliamentary Papers*, 1836, vol. 45. Pigot and Company, *National and Commercial Directory for the North of England* (London, 1834), provides the names of towns for mills in West Yorkshire.

[29] See the "economiser" indices for provisions for the North, the Northwest, and the industrial North in N. F. R. Crafts, "Regional Price Variations in England in 1843: An Aspect of the Standard of Living Debate," *Explorations in Economic History*, 19 (Jan. 1982), pp. 51–70. The data on rents are from the Manchester Statistical Society, *Report on the Condition of the Working Classes in an Extensive Manufacturing District* (London, 1838); and Joshua Milne, "Survey of the Condition of the Poor in Thirty-Three Townships of the Manufacturing Districts," *Parliamentary Papers*, 1833, vol. 6, pp. 664–67. The regression model of rents used to predict rents for the entire sample, with *t*-statistics in parentheses, is as follows:

$$\underset{(12.9)}{RENT = 15.2} + \underset{(4.17)}{2.51\log(\text{town density})} + \underset{(2.18)}{4.63\log(\text{parish density})}$$

$$\text{Adjusted } R^2 = 0.64 \quad N = 32$$

Data on population and area are from the *Abstracts of the 1831 Census*, *Parliamentary Papers*, 1833, vols. 36–38.

[30] See Edwin Chadwick, *Report of the Sanitary Conditions of the Laboring Population of Great Britain*, in M. W. Flinn, ed. (1st edn., 1842; London, 1965), pp. 8, 148–49. Although infant mortality is also cited as an indicator of the quality of life, it depends upon other influences, such as breast-feeding practices, income, and female labor-force participation, that are only partially related to urban environmental conditions. A puzzle for historians of nineteenth-century demography, for example, is the failure of urban infant mortality to fall until after 1900, over 30 years after most English cities had installed modern water supply and sewer systems. See Robert Woods and John Woodward, "Mortality, Poverty and the Environment," and Barbara Thompson, "Infant Mortality in Bradford," in Robert Woods and John Woodward, eds., *Urban Disease and Mortality in Nineteenth-Century England* (London, 1984), pp. 1–36 and 120–47, respectively; and Anthony Wohl, *Endangered Lives: Public Health in Victorian Britain* (Cambridge, MA, 1983), pp. 10–42. Mortality from typhoid fever is another indicator of local sanitary conditions, but was not reported separately from typhus during this period. The mortality data by registration district are from "Abstracts of the Causes of Death," *Reports of the Registrar-General* for 1838–42.

FINES, the sum of penalties levied on each firm as a result of violations of the reporting and child labor provisions of the Factory Acts, captures work site conditions that also may have influenced earnings.[31]

Reliable information on where handloom weavers lived is available only from the 1851 census, when the weaving population had declined to about one-fifth of its size in 1835 and relocated from weaving hamlets and villages into mill towns. The Poor Law Commissioner for Lancashire suggested an alternative measure of concentrations of handloom weavers in 1834, when he noted that "poor-rates have been greatly augmented by the transition from hand to power-loom weaving." Because local poor law authorities typically supplemented the earnings of weaving families in Lancashire with outdoor relief, per capita poor law payments were usually higher in handloom weaving centers. The level of per capita poor law relief (*RELIEF*) in a town is thus used in the labor supply equations as a proxy for concentrations of handloom weavers.[32]

The specification of the demand side of the market (equation 2) includes variables measuring the relative attractiveness of a location: *DISTANCE*, which is measured in miles from Manchester; *SHAREWATER*, the share of water power in total horsepower in the parish in which the mill was located; and the number of *LOOMS*, a measure of potential scale economies. Mill owners—usually those reliant on water power—attempted to circumvent the restrictions of the Factory Acts on hours worked by child labor by employing children and youths in "relays," or shifts. *RELAYS*, a dummy variable, should be negatively correlated with the earnings of older workers, as millowners used the system to substitute the labor of younger workers.[33]

The continued high rates of in-migration into the cotton towns during the 1830s and the high levels of investment in the power-loom sector

[31] See A. E. Peacock, "The Successful Prosecution of the Factory Acts, 1833–1855," *Economic History Review*, 37 (May 1984), pp. 197–210; and Marvel, "Factory Regulation," p. 387. The data for *FINES* for the period 1834 to 1837 are from the *Reports of the Inspectors of Factories*, *Parliamentary Papers*, 1836, vol. 45; 1837, vol. 50; and 1837–38, vol. 45.

[32] *RELIEF* was, for example, 1.7 to 2 times higher in the handloom weaving centers of Padiham and Burnley than in Bury, which by the mid-1830s had few handloom weavers. See Bythell, *Handloom Weavers*, p. 57; the "Reports of Assistant Commissioners: Report of G. Henderson," *Report from His Majesty's Commissioners for Inquiring into the Administration and Practical Operation of the Poor Laws*, appendix A (London, 1834), pp. 909–10A, 922–24; Walton, *Social History of Lancashire*, pp. 194–95; and Fleischman, *Conditions of Life*, pp. 329–35. *RELIEF* is the per capita amount "Expended for the Relief of the Poor" for 1835–36 found in the Appendix, *Second Annual Report of the Poor Law Commission*, *Parliamentary Papers*, 1836, vol. 29.

[33] The data for *SHAREWATER* for weaving and integrated mills are available by parish for most of the sample area from "Appendix to Mr. Horner's Report," *Reports of the Inspectors of Factories*, *Parliamentary Papers*, 1842, vol. 22. The power-loom survey provided data on the number of looms. See B. L. Hutchins and A. Harrison, *History of Factory Legislation* (London, 1911), pp. 70, 79–80, and Bayson, *Ashworth Cotton*, p. 164, for discussions of relays. The data on relays are for those factories identified as using them for children on July 1, 1836, by the *Report of the Inspector of Factories*, *Parliamentary Papers*, 1837, vol. 50, pp. 193–95.

until the slump of 1839–1842 both raise the possibility that the labor market was actually in disequilibrium in 1835. If, for example, in-migration was responding to excess demand in the cities, the correlation of above-equilibrium wages with a poor quality of life could lead to an overstatement of the compensation required to make workers as well off as in the countryside. Excess supply of labor in the country—perhaps unemployed handloom weavers—could also trigger migration, depressing urban wages and leading to an understatement of compensation. Unequal returns to capital across locations could likewise bias estimates of the relative cost advantage enjoyed by urban areas. The reports of the Factory Inspectorate from the 1830s provide two measures of disequilibrium at the parish level that can be used in the earnings regressions: the percentage increase in the textile labor force between 1835 and 1838 (*EMPLOYGROWTH*) and in horsepower (*POWERGROWTH*), which is used in studies of the period as a proxy for fixed capital. If earnings were above market-clearing levels because of excess demand for labor, we would expect earnings to be higher in towns with substantial growth in the labor force and in the capital stock.[34] Following the practice of other earnings equations, the regression analysis uses the natural log of earnings as the dependent variable. In addition, dummy variables control for weavers of high-value small wares and for differences in age (and skill) within the four subgroups chosen for analysis: adults, those aged 17 and 18, teens with average earnings, and those aged 13 and under.[35]

The results of the earnings regressions in Table 1 for the supply side and in Table 2 for the demand side of the spatial market for power-loom labor offer strong evidence that the mill's location mattered the most for explaining the earnings of those 17 years and older. The coefficients on *RENT* imply that a 10 pence increase in weekly rents prompted a 12-

[34] See Gatrell, "Size of Firms." The *Report of the Inspector of Factories* for 1835 and 1838, *Parliamentary Papers*, 1836, vol. 45; 1839, vol. 42, provides parish-level data on the numbers employed and on horsepower. I am grateful to an anonymous referee and the editor for bringing this issue to my attention.

[35] The survey includes earnings for three age groups: adults 18 years or older, teens 13 to 17 years, and children under 13 years. Of the 195 factories in the sample, 65 report a range of earnings for each age group that bracket what are apparently the average earnings reported for the remaining 130 factories. The age-earnings profile resulting from the wage regressions supports this interpretation. The predicted ratios of earnings of 9-, 12-, and 13-year-olds to 18-year-olds from the regressions for Manchester are all within 10 percent of the ratios found in Stanway's 1833 survey of children employed in factories in Stockport and Manchester in the "Report of the Factory Commission," *Parliamentary Papers*, 1833, vol. 20, pp. D1 87–88. Chow tests determined the appropriate breakdown of the data into subsamples. In each of the four resulting subsamples, coefficients were stable across potentially smaller subgroupings at better than a 5 percent level of significance. Since the observations on earnings were averaged over differing numbers of looms, one might expect heteroskedastic error terms that would lead to biases of an unknown direction in the *t*-statistics. The Goldfeld-Quandt test failed to reject the hypothesis of homoskedasticity at a 5 percent level of significance. See Jan Kmenta, *Elements of Econometrics* (2nd edn., New York, 1986), pp. 292–94.

TABLE 1
THE IMPACT OF LOCATION ON EARNINGS OF POWER-LOOM WEAVERS: SUPPLY SIDE

	Age Group			
Variable [Mean]	Adult	17/18	Teen	Children
RENT	0.010	0.010	0.002	−0.002
[22.4 pence]	(5.26)	(3.20)	(0.69)	(−0.37)
WATERDISEASE	0.797	−0.130	0.155	−1.329
[0.139 per 1,000]	(3.43)	(−0.60)	(0.65)	(−3.58)
FINES[a]	0.012	0.003	−0.002	0.000
[£2.16]	(2.02)	(1.20)	(−1.04)	(−0.10)
RELIEF	0.239	−0.008	−0.275	−0.950
[£0.13 per capita]	(1.18)	(−0.04)	(−1.83)	(−2.28)
EMPLOYGROWTH	−0.021	0.031	−0.006	−0.037
[24 percent]	(−0.81)	(0.76)	(−0.28)	(−1.02)
SMALL WARES	0.277	0.092	0.116	−0.020
[0.05]	(5.25)	(1.12)	(1.28)	(−0.12)
Constant	4.726	4.563	4.608	4.687
	(67.7)	(51.8)	(63.8)	(37.1)
Mean Earnings	147	123	104	69
Adjusted R^2	0.45	0.12	0.01	0.38
N	195	132	116	99

[a] The coefficient on *FINES* was −0.007 (2.89) for the lower-paid group of adult workers.
Notes: *t*-statistics are in parentheses. The dependent variable is the log of weekly earnings in pence. The constants for the other groups were 4.50 for lower-paid adults, 4.58 for lower-paid 18-year-olds, 4.52 for the highest-paid children, 4.15 for the middle group of children, and 4.29 for the lowest-paid children.
Source: Results of ordinary least squares estimation.

pence increase in earnings of adults and a 10-pence increase in the earnings of those 17 to 18 years old. This high degree of responsiveness suggests that the correlation of rent with other density variables may be capturing some of the influence of congestion. Adult weavers living in mill towns with double the sample average of *WATERDISEASE* received earnings about 12 percent higher. The earnings of the most highly skilled weavers were about 2 percent higher at mills paying the sample average of *FINES*.[36] The coefficients on *DISTANCE* in Table 2 imply that the earnings of those 17 and older fell about 9 pence for every 10 miles from Manchester (or 6 to 7 percent) and earnings of teens fell about one penny (1 percent). For a mill located 31 miles away from Manchester, the implied reduction in earnings would offset up to one-half of the cost of transporting the weekly output of an adult weaver and her teen assistant. Given the high correlation of *RELAYS* with the use of water power, it appears that the combined impact of exclusive reliance on water power and use of relays would lower earnings of adults 13 percent and earnings of 17- to 18-year-olds 6 percent. The elasticity of adult earnings with respect to *LOOMS*—the proxy for firm

[36] Note, however, that the average-skilled weavers received no compensation for high levels of Factory Act violations.

TABLE 2
THE IMPACT OF LOCATION ON EARNINGS OF POWER-LOOM WEAVERS: DEMAND SIDE

Variable [Mean]	Age Group: Adult	17/18	Teen	Children
DISTANCE	−0.007	−0.005	−0.001	0.004
[11.4 mi.]	(−5.18)	(−2.63)	(−0.41)	(0.91)
SHAREWATER	−0.039	0.022	−0.226	0.125
[10 percent]	(−0.31)	(0.23)	(−2.20)	(0.60)
RELAYS	−0.119	−0.080	0.006	−0.025
[0.16]	(−2.93)	(−2.41)	(0.18)	(−0.35)
LOOMS[a]	0.025	0.027	−0.007	0.001
[240]	(3.20)	(3.02)	(−0.77)	(0.54)
POWERGROWTH	−0.057	0.002	0.005	−0.033
[44 percent]	(2.84)	(−0.06)	(.25)	(−1.51)
SMALL WARES	0.332	0.162	0.095	−0.057
[0.05]	(5.89)	(2.16)	(1.06)	(−0.28)
Constant	5.196	4.827	4.675	4.256
	(140)	(94)	(111)	(51.3)
Mean Earnings	148	126	104	68
Adjusted R^2	0.46	0.13	0.01	0.30
N	180	122	107	94

[a] Looms are measured in 100s.
Notes: *t*-statistics in parentheses. The dependent variable is the log of weekly earnings in pence. The constant was 4.93 for lower-paid adults, 4.82 for lower-paid 18-year-olds, 4.05 for the highest-paid children, 3.81 for the middle group of children, and 3.83 for the lowest-paid children.
Source: Results of ordinary least squares estimation.

size—is about 5 percent, which is consistent with the modest economies of scale for combined spinning and weaving firms found by R. Lloyd-Jones and A. Le Roux in their recent study.[37]

The supply-side results in Table 1 also offer evidence on the degree to which the markets for hand and factory labor were integrated. The coefficients on *RELIEF* for teens and children support Lyons's view that the markets for handloom and factory labor were integrated. Earnings of adult power-loom weavers were slightly higher in towns with high levels of poor law relief (and concentrations of handloom weavers), but a little lower for teens, and 5 to 9 percent lower for those 13 and under.[38]

The impact of the variables measuring disequilibrium in the labor market is modest. Increasing *POWERGROWTH* by its sample mean, for example, would lower earnings about 2 percent. Although the negative correlation between subsequent expansion of the industry and high earnings may seem surprising, it is consistent with the shift in the center of the industry's growth to towns 20 to 30 miles from high-wage

[37] See Lloyd-Jones and Le Roux, "Size of Firms," p. 78.

[38] The differentials in earnings are based upon a comparison of the handloom weaving towns of Padiham and Burnley with the factory town of Bury.

Manchester after the mid-1830s, particularly as the power-loom sector expanded into former handloom weaving areas.[39]

THE IMPACT OF THE MOVE TO THE CITIES ON LIVING STANDARDS

The regression results for the spatial market for power-loom labor suggest that the trade-off between the quality of life and productivity in urban locations was significant in the cotton Northwest during the 1830s. If urban locations prompted substantially higher earnings to compensate for living conditions, the urbanization of the industry after 1815 might have exacted a significant cost in welfare; indices of real wages may thus overstate the gains in living standards in the cotton industry.

One commonly used approach to summarizing the estimated impact of living conditions on earnings is to calculate the wage gradient that rises with higher living costs and a poorer (urban) quality of life. For the average-skilled adult power-loom weaver in 1835, for example, the gradient would begin at the village of Barrowford, where predicted weekly earnings were about 110 pence, and rise to almost 160 pence at Hulme, located just outside of Manchester. If compensation reflected the cost differentials between locations, as the spatial labor market model predicts, the earnings gradient estimated for the demand side of the market should about equal that estimated for the supply side. We can approximate the earnings gradients for the four age-skill groups by assigning the 64 mill towns for which the necessary rent and mortality data are available to three parish types representative of the range of locations available to workers. The lowest-rent communities with the best sanitary conditions provide characteristics of a "rural" parish, which includes villages in the Whalley and Lancaster parishes, the West Riding of Yorkshire, and Derbyshire. Those cities with the highest rents and mortality, including Manchester, Bolton, and Stockport, are assigned to a "dense urban" parish. The remaining cotton towns, including Preston and Wigan, provide the characteristics for an intermediate "urban" parish.[40]

A comparison of the supply- and demand-side characteristics of the three parishes suggests a correlation between poorer urban living conditions and lower-cost locations. Rural mill workers paid rents one-half those in the dense urban parish and faced a much lower risk of mortality from waterborne diseases. Rural mill owners paid higher

[39] Taylor, "Cotton Industry," pp. 117–18.

[40] Towns with a value of *WATERDISEASE* or *RENT* greater than one standard deviation above the mean were assigned to the dense urban parish; those with either value more than one standard deviation below the mean were assigned to the rural parish. The remaining towns were assigned to the urban parish. Dividing the towns into seven representative locations did improve the approximation of the wage gradients, but led to only slightly higher estimates of compensation.

TABLE 3
EARNINGS DIFFERENTIALS IN THE SPATIAL MARKET FOR POWER-LOOM WEAVERS

Characteristics of Representative Parishes

Parish	Supply of Labor: *RENT* (pence per week)	Supply of Labor: *WATER-DISEASE* (deaths per 1,000)	Demand for Labor: *DISTANCE* (miles from Manchester)	Demand for Labor: *SHARE-WATER* (share of horsepower)	Demand for Labor: *RELAYS* (share of firms)	Demand for Labor: *LOOMS* (per firm)
Dense Urban	29	0.20	6	0.04	0.03	340
Urban	18	0.16	15	0.06	0.14	221
Rural	13	0.06	29	0.34	0.22	182

Predicted Compensation by Age Group and Location

Parish	Adult S[a]	Adult D[b]	17/18 S[a]	17/18 D[b]	Teen S[a]	Teen D[b]	Children S[a]	Children D[b]
Dense Urban	30%	26%	15%	18%	5%	7%	−18%	−10%
	(5.5)	(4.8)	(7.1)	(5.4)	(5.2)	(5.0)	(7.2)	(7.4)
Urban	15	13	5	9	3	6	−13	−8
	(3.0)	(3.7)	(3.3)	(3.5)	(2.9)	(3.9)	(4.0)	(5.8)
Rural Earnings in Pence	112	112	109	108	99	96	85	81

[a] Using results of the supply-side earnings regressions.
[b] Using results of the demand-side earnings regressions.
Notes: Standard errors of compensation are shown in parentheses. For a description of the procedure used to calculate compensation, see text.
Source: Results of regressions reported in Tables 1 and 2. Standard errors are approximated by a Taylor expansion. See Jan Kmenta, *Elements of Econometrics* (New York, 1971), p. 444.

transport costs, relied more heavily on water power and relays, and were less likely to achieve significant scale economies than those in more urbanized parishes. Using the results from the earnings equations, the lower section of Table 3 translates these characteristics into estimates of the percentage compensation paid workers living in unhealthy and expensive cities relative to rural areas.

The estimates of compensation and their accompanying standard errors provide evidence that the rural-urban earnings gradient for adult weavers was relatively steep and statistically significant. High living costs and poor sanitation in the cities prompted compensation that approached one-third of adult weavers' earnings. The parallel set of estimates calculated using the demand-side characteristics tell virtually the same story for those 17 and older. The close match between the demand- and supply-side estimates suggests that payments to workers partially offset the cost advantages of urban location. Only the small (or even negative) estimates for teens and children provide support for the hypothesis that workers were not compensated for urban living conditions.

How much of the compensation payments presented in Table 3 may have simply covered the higher rents and how much they may have reflected the disutility of sanitary conditions in the city is difficult to surmise, given the interactive semi-log specification and the correlation of rents with crowding and congestion. At the minimum, the coefficient on *WATERDISEASE* implies adult earnings 11 percent higher in dense urban parishes and 8 percent higher in urban parishes because of differences in sanitation. If instead the payment for the disutility of living in the city is treated as the residual remaining after subtracting higher urban rents, the compensation for sanitary conditions rises to 16 percent for the weaver of average skill paying all of the rural-urban rent differential and 23 percent for the weaver paying one-half of the differential and relying on other household members to pay the rest. All three estimates exceed the 7 to 8 percent initially estimated for Lancashire and Cheshire using earnings of day laborers, but are much closer to Williamson's recently revised estimates for northern England.[41]

Even a weekly compensation of about 34 pence per adult weaver posed a significant cost to the millowner in a dense urban parish. Lyons has estimated that a state-of-the-art power-loom mill in the mid-1830s would yield a weekly value-added per weaver of about 370 pence. For an average weaver, the compensation for living in a dense urban parish would thus account for almost one-tenth of value-added. Despite a regulatory environment hostile to the irregular work hours of isolated rural mills dependent upon water power, savings in labor costs of this magnitude may help explain their continued viability through the Cotton Famine of the 1860s.[42]

The crux of the argument of the Hammonds and other critics of industrialization was that the conditions of rapid urbanization characteristic of the cotton textile industry after 1815 forced large numbers of workers to accept the poorer quality of life and higher cost of living in the cities in return for factory wages. The steep rural-urban wage gradient for the semiskilled power-loom weavers suggests that as the industry relocated to the cities, a rising share of the wage bill may have gone to compensation. For this reason, the net improvement in welfare (W^*) would be less than the increase in real wages (W). In terms of the compensation (C) and the real wage W, the welfare in any year would equal the following:

$$W^* = W[(1 + C_d)\sigma_d + (1 + C_u)\sigma_u + \sigma_r]^{-1} \quad (3)$$

[41] Williamson, "Factor Markets," pp. 648–54. The revised estimate of compensation is 30 percent for "the North," which arises from a different specification of the hedonic regression and a modified definition of the compensation.

[42] See Lyons, "Introduction of the Powerloom," table A.II.3, and p. 185, for estimates of the output per weaver.

TABLE 4
URBANIZATION AND THE LIVING STANDARDS OF FACTORY WORKERS, 1806–1850

Year	Nominal Earnings[b]	Cost of Living	Real Earnings[c]	Share of Employment: Dense Urban	Share of Employment: Urban	Adjusted Earnings[a]: Nominal[b]	Adjusted Earnings[a]: Real[c]
1806	125	162	77	0.35[d]	0.04[d]	113	69
1810/16	131	183	73	0.35[d]	0.04[d]	118	65
1817	129	149	86	0.34[d]	0.05[d]	116	78
1818/20	128	156	83	0.34	0.05	115	74
1821/22	127	129	99	0.36	0.06	114	89
1823/26	121	139	87	0.41	0.08	107	77
1832/33	117	118	99	0.48	0.10	101	86
1836	120	119	101	0.50	0.12	103	86
1839/41	115	140	82	0.54	0.17	97	69
1849/50	115	101	114	0.52	0.23	96	96

[a] Earnings net of compensation for rents and sanitary conditions in urban areas.
[b] Weekly earnings in pence.
[c] Real weekly earnings in 1850 pence.
[d] Estimated.
Notes: For explanation of calculation of adjusted factory wage, see text.
Sources: For share employed in dense urban and urban parishes: G. W. Daniels, "The Cotton Trade and the Close of the Napoleonic Wars," *Manchester Statistical Society Transactions* (1917–18), pp. 1–30, for the number of mills in Manchester in 1802, which was multiplied by the employment per mill for 1816 found in "Special Committee on the State of Children Employed in Manufactories," *House of Lords Sessional Papers,* vol. 110, appendices 32, 33; Stephen Kinney, "The Evolution of the Lancashire Cotton Industry ca. 1750–1900: A Study in Locational and Organizational Change" (M.A. thesis, University of Manchester, 1975), table 4, for employment in 1818–20; "Returns Relating to Factories," *Reports of the Inspectors of Factories, Parliamentary Papers*, 1836, vol. 45 for 1835; "Returns of the Numbers Employed," *Reports of the Inspectors of Factories, Parliamentary Papers*, 1839, vol. 42, for employment in 1839–41; and Census of 1851, *Parliamentary Papers*, 1852–53, vol. 100, for 1850. Intervening years are estimated by linear interpolation. Total employment and nominal factory earnings are from George Henry Wood, *The History of Wages in the Cotton Trade During the Past One Hundred Years* (London, 1910), tables 37, 38, 41. I adopt Wood's assumption that 83 percent of total industry employment is in the Northwest. For the cost-of-living index, see fn. 43 and text.

where σ_i is the share of employees receiving compensation and locations are indexed by *d* for dense urban, *u* for urban, and *r* for rural.

George Henry Wood developed a comprehensive series of nominal earnings for cotton textiles in the Northwest available for several years from 1806 through 1850 that appears in the second column of Table 4. Data on prices for provisions available for Manchester and Bolton permit calculation of the regional index of living costs in column 3.[43]

[43] The nominal wage series is from Wood, *History of Wages*, tables 37, 38. The series relies upon wage data from Manchester prior to 1833 and assumes that the gap in wages between southeastern and northeastern Lancashire in 1833 prevailed for the period from 1806 to 1833. See Fleischman, *Conditions of Life*, chap. 4, for the data on prices for Manchester and Bolton for 1806 through 1834; and William Neild, "Comparative Statement of the Income and Expenditures of Certain Families of the Working Classes in Manchester and Dukinfield, in the Years 1836 and 1841," *Journal of the Statistical Society of London*, 4 (Jan. 1842), pp. 320–34, for the data for 1836 and 1841. Data on

The resulting real-earnings series (*W*) registers continued growth throughout the first half of the nineteenth century, with most improvement occurring after 1815, in a pattern similar to Lindert and Williamson's blue-collar workers.

Of course, real earnings rose the most during the three decades when the factory sector relocated to the cities. Reliable data on the distribution of factory employment by parish (σ_i) are available for 1818, the 1830s, and 1850, while the lack of construction of mills during the turbulent years of the Napoleonic Wars (1803 to 1815) suggests that the distribution in 1818 had changed little from 1806.[44] On the basis of the average values of *WATERDISEASE* and *RENT* for the late 1830s and early 1840s, every parish in the Northwest is identified as a dense urban, urban, or rural parish. If rapid population growth prompted a deterioration of conditions and higher rents prior to the 1830s, this approach would understate the adverse impact of urbanization on living standards.

As the data on the distribution of employment suggest, the urbanization of the industry focused initially on the large cotton centers such as Manchester, but shifted after the mid-1830s with the growth of powerloom weaving toward smaller cities such as Preston, Ashton-under-Lyne, and Blackburn. By 1850, although Manchester's share of employment had fallen, the expansion of the other cotton towns had boosted the share of employment in urbanized parishes to about three-quarters.

A conjecture about how much the move of the industry to the cities may have undercut living standards appears in column 8. Urbanization of the industry dampened the growth in living standards most strongly during the two decades following the end of the Napoleonic Wars. Taking account of the influence of urbanization lowers growth in living standards about 3 percent from 1836 to 1850, but about 6 percent between 1818/20 and the mid-1830s. Overall, the calculations suggest that accounting for urbanization cuts back improvements in living standards by one-quarter between 1818/20 and 1850 and by one-fifth over the entire period 1806 to 1850. Viewed from the perspective of the industry, the estimates in Table 4 suggest as well that a large and rising share of the wage bill (10 percent in 1806 and 17 percent in 1850) went for compensation. A substantial part of this cost was rents, which may have contributed to the relative decline of Manchester as a center of

---

rents and the "northern urban" budget weights are from Williamson, *British Capitalism*, appendix tables A.3 and A.1 respectively. Data on coal prices in Manchester are from von Tunzelmann, *Steam Power*, pp. 96–97. Arthur D. Gayer, W. W. Rostow, and Anna Jacobson Schwartz, *The Growth and Fluctuation of the British Economy, 1790–1850*, microfilmed supplement (Oxford, 1953), table 123, provides the data on the price of tea inclusive of duties; the index of clothing prices is from Williamson and Lindert, "Reply to Crafts," pp. 148–49. The regional cost-of-living index is linked to Williamson and Lindert's "southern urban" price index to extend it from 1842 to 1850.

[44] See Edwards, *Cotton Trade*, p. 212.

manufacturing. Some part of it, however, stemmed from the poor sanitary conditions of the cities that were not rectified until the last third of the nineteenth century.

HANDLOOM WEAVING AND LIVING STANDARDS

Despite the attention the conditions in the factory towns have received in historical accounts of industrialization, it was the plight of

TABLE 5
LIVING STANDARDS OF HANDLOOM WEAVERS AND ALL WORKERS, 1806–1850

	Handloom Weavers					All Workers	
		Piece Rates		Earnings[a] of Weavers of			
Period	Share of Employment	Coarse/ Medium	Cambric (1832/33 = 100)	Coarse/ Medium	Cambric	Coarse/ Medium[b]	Cambric[c]
1806	0.67	407	345	144	119	96	83
1810/16	0.67	327	288	103	88	76	66
1817	0.66	207	161	82	62	78	57
1818/20	0.66	226	170	88	64	74	55
1821/22	0.65	215	165	105	78	76	64
1823/26	0.59	147	149	70	68	59	59
1832/33	0.51	100	100	62	61	67	67
1836	0.46	106	84	66	51	70	64
1839/41	0.32	82	111	41	59	57	62
1849/50	0.13	68[d]	111[d]	58	82	89	92
Percent Change							
1806–1836						−28	−23
1806–1850						+11	−7

[a] Real weekly earnings of an adult male weaver in 1850 pence.
[b] Average real weekly earnings in 1850 pence, assuming handloom weavers are weaving only coarse and medium cloths.
[c] Average real weekly earnings in 1850 pence, assuming handloom weavers are weaving only cambrics.
[d] Estimated.
Notes: Coarse and medium cloths include calico, shirtings, and fustians.
Sources: G. Henry Wood, *The History of Wages in the Cotton Trade During the Past One Hundred Years* (London, 1910), table 40, provides data on employment in the hand and factory sectors. The piece-rate series are based on simple averages of the series available for these cloths from Edward Baines, *History of the Cotton Manufacture in Great Britain* (2nd edn., New York, 1971), pp. 438, 489, 490, for three calico series and three series for cambrics (60 and 80 reed); Richard Guest, *A Compendious History of the Cotton Manufacture* (Manchester, 1823), p. 35, for 60 reed cambric; and John Lyons, "The Lancashire Cotton Industry and the Introduction of the Power Loom" (Ph.D. dissertation, University of California at Berkeley, 1977), appendix tables B.II.1 for calico, shirting, and fustian; B.II.2 for 48, 56, and 70 reed, and an unidentified cambric. Earnings for handloom weavers are taken from the piece-rate indices adjusted for a 30 percent increase in hours worked per week between 1820 and 1829 and assuming adult male earnings of 72 pence in 1833. The earnings for all workers are the weighted sum of the earnings of weavers, which have been adjusted for the relative productivity and age distribution of the handloom labor force, and factory earnings adjusted for urbanization from Table 4. The productivity and age distribution data are from John Lyons, "Family Response to Economic Decline: Handloom Weavers in Early Nineteenth-Century Lancashire," *Research in Economic History*, 12 (1989), pp. 45–91, tables 3, 7, and 8. Earnings are deflated by the cost-of-living index in Table 4.

the handloom weavers that most strongly colored the public's perception of the "Condition of England." G. Himmelfarb's intellectual history of the contemporary debate argues that the plight of the weavers "cast a pall over the entire period and over all the working classes."[45] As Table 5 suggests, the handloom weavers remained a large share of the labor force in cotton textiles through the end of the 1830s, even as nominal piece rates for the most commonly woven coarse cloths—calicos and shirtings—and cambrics plummeted to less than one-half the level of the early 1800s.

Although there is general agreement over the magnitude of this collapse, the question of how steeply the earnings of the weavers declined during this period remains unresolved.[46] Bythell's discussion suggests several obstacles that stand in the way of computing reliable estimates of earnings from piece rates. While piece-rate series and estimates of weekly productivity allow calculation of gross earnings, the net earnings remaining after deducting other inputs purchased by the weaver—coal, candles, and soap—depended upon prices that may have varied considerably over time. In addition, if the labor supply curve of the typical weaver was backward bending, as some accounts of weavers' desultory work habits during the years of high earnings imply, the collapse in piece rates may have prompted increases in the hours worked that cushioned the fall in earnings. Finally, the diversity of the weaving labor force makes it nearly impossible to estimate a typical weaver's earnings, since output (and earnings) depended heavily upon the age and sex of the weaver.[47]

While these difficulties may prevent calculation of a definitive earnings series for all handloom weavers, the abundant evidence on piece rates for the plain cloths woven by most weavers makes it possible to develop estimates of trends in the earnings of adult males that will, however, tend to understate the fall in earnings after 1800. Since the prices for other inputs fell less rapidly than piece rates during the deflation after 1815, expenses may have actually increased their bite of gross earnings by the mid-1830s.[48] It is also unlikely that work effort rose by more than 30 percent in response to the sharp drop in rates most evident during the 1820s.[49] Adjusting the indices of piece rates in Table

[45] Himmelfarb, *Idea of Poverty*, p. 137.

[46] See Lyons, "Family Economy," p. 51.

[47] See Bythell, *Handloom Weavers*, pp. 115–22. The output of a child weaver was typically less than one-half the output of an adult male.

[48] Fleischman, in *Conditions of Life*, pp. 129–33, provides the price data. Weavers testifying to Parliament argued that the cost of inputs as a share of gross earnings was 8 to 25 percent higher in 1833 than in 1814. See the "Report of the Select Committee on the Present State of Manufactures, Commerce, and Shipping in the United Kingdom," *Parliamentary Papers*, 1833, vol. 6, pp. 605, 665.

[49] Bythell, *Handloom Weavers*, p. 117, accepts this estimate as a "plausible guess." The assumption does contradict the 1833 testimony of handloom weaver Richard Needham that there

5 downward before 1820 to account for lower work effort, applying the evidence from the early 1830s that adult male weavers netted on average 72 pence per week, and accounting for changes in the cost of living yields the real earnings series for weavers of coarse and medium cloths and cambrics appearing in columns 5 and 6.[50] Except for a brief respite during the early 1820s, real earnings for an adult weaver of finer-quality cambric fell or stagnated until the late 1830s, while the pay of those weaving coarse cloths fell continuously until the 1840s.

Even a rough guess at how much the obvious decline in the handloom sector eroded living standards in the cotton industry as a whole requires adjusting the earnings series for adult male weavers for the age-mix of the labor force; only then will it be compatible with Wood's factory series, which includes earnings for all age groups. A survey from 1818 and comprehensive census information from 1851 offer information on the distribution of handloom weavers across five productivity categories: male household heads, their wives, adult children, teenaged children, and children under 14 years. Weighting the relative productivity of each age group by its estimated share in the labor force suggests that the earnings of the average weaver were about three-quarters of the earnings of an adult male household head in 1818, rising slightly to four-fifths by 1851.[51] When the adjusted average earnings in the handloom sector are combined with the factory series from the last column of Table 4, the series in the final two columns of Table 5 result. They offer alternative views of living standards for all workers in cotton textiles.

The "cambric" series in column 8 of Table 5 presents the most optimistic appraisal of living standards in the industry, while the "coarse and medium" series is most likely representative of conditions in the industry after the mid-1820s as the output of handloom weavers shifted toward low-quality calicos and shirtings in response to export opportunities in India and the Far East.[52] Both series record substantial declines in living standards from 1806 to 1818/20 and at best modest recovery through the mid-1830s. Only when the rapid shrinkage of the handloom sector set in after the crisis of 1838 did living standards in the industry begin to improve. On the reasonable assumption that two-thirds of those at the loom in the late 1830s were weaving coarse and medium plain cloths, there was virtually no improvement in living

---

had been no productivity growth in the weaving of cambric since 1800. See "Report of Select Committee," *Parliamentary Papers*, 1833, vol. 6, p. 700.

[50] See Wood, *History of Wages*, table 41.

[51] See Lyons, "Family Response," tables 3, 7, 8, for the data on the relative productivity and age-mix of weaving household members from a survey of 142 weavers in Tottington in 1818 and the census of 1851.

[52] See Farnie, *English Cotton Industry*, pp. 101–2.

standards in cotton textiles until at least the 1840s and for perhaps the entire first half of the nineteenth century.[53]

CONCLUSIONS

In cotton textiles, the industry occupying center stage in the debate over the Condition of England, both urbanization of the industry and the decline of the domestic sector significantly undermined living standards. If real factory earnings rose about 50 percent over the period, adjusting real earnings for the welfare cost of urbanization trims the improvement to 40 percent, and taking account of the decline of handloom weaving as well means that living standards rose at best 10 percent—or even fell. Fragmentary data for agricultural laborers in the Northwest and laborers in Manchester also suggest that earnings of much of the labor force registered at best modest gains between the Napoleonic Wars and the 1830s.[54] This pattern is consistent with Mokyr's recent finding that the per capita consumption of luxuries acting as proxies for living standards showed little increase before the 1840s. These results underscore the need to account for regional variations in assessments of living standards during the first half of the nineteenth century, a perspective suggested as well by the revision in the historiography of the industrial revolution that has emphasized its uneven impact on the English economy.

A final question posed by the early historians of the industrial revolution is whether different governmental policies could have improved upon this record. While the plight of the handloom weavers exerted the most profound influence on living standards in cotton textiles, most historians agree that efforts to halt the fall in piece rates—as the weavers demanded throughout the period—would only have stretched out what was already a painful decline.[55] The response

[53] Assuming a weekly output of four pieces per adult weaver of calico and one piece per weaver of cambric, and that power-loom production was exclusively calico, production of cambric and fancy goods would occupy at most one-third of the weaving population. See Lyons, "Power Loom," p. 247; Bythell, *Handloom Weavers*, p. 115; and Baines, *Cotton Manufacture*, p. 407.

[54] Annual growth in real agricultural wages in West Yorkshire, Lancashire, Cheshire, Cumberland, and Westmoreland from 1795 to 1833 was from 0 to 0.6 percent; growth rates more than doubled after 1833. A time series from Cumberland suggests a pattern of improvement from 1795 to 1806–1810, little growth up to the mid-1830s, and then rapid growth of about 2 percent until 1850. See Arthur L. Bowley, "The Statistics of Wages in the United Kingdom during the last Hundred Years: Part I, Agricultural Wages," *Journal of the Royal Statistical Society*, 61 (Dec. 1898), pp. 702–22. From 1818–1820 to the mid-1830s earnings of Manchester porters rose 6 percent, while earnings of bricklayers' laborers apparently stagnated. Most of the growth in earnings of town laborers between 1805 and 1850 occurred after 1831. See Fleischman, *Conditions of Life*, pp. 188–89, Baines, *Cotton Manufacture*, p. 438; and von Tunzelmann, "Trends in Real Wages," p. 46.

[55] Paul Richards, "The State and Early Industrial Capitalism: The Case of the Handloom Weavers," *Past and Present*, 83 (May 1979), pp. 91–115; and Thompson, *English Working Class*,

of local governments to the "most urgent of problems generated by the Industrial Revolution"—the sanitary state of the cities—has been subject to more debate. Some have argued that "ignorance rather than avarice" stymied effective action until the 1860s and 1870s, decades after conditions in the large towns had been well documented.[56] Others are more critical, pointing to Parliament's failure to consolidate widely scattered local authority for public health interventions and overcome the difficulty municipalities encountered borrowing capital. At the local level, they argue that a short-sighted "economy" party blocked action in town councils.[57]

A simple benefit-cost calculation suggests that, whatever the reason, the failure to act was costly. The regression results imply that workers in towns such as Preston and Ashton-under-Lyne were receiving compensation of at least 8 to 11 percent for poor sanitary conditions, or 6 to 9 pence per week for an average weaver. Observers estimated in the 1840s that the cost of sanitary improvement in these towns—cleaning out cesspools, building sewers, and laying on water mains—would have raised weekly rents about 2 to 2.5 pence.[58] Even if such a thorough program of sanitary reform cut these payments by only one-half, it would have paid for itself in reduced costs of labor, not to mention savings in human capital from a reduction in untimely adult mortality and work time lost to illness. The poor quality of urban life most likely did not cancel improvements in living standards even for the workers in the mill towns of Northwest England, but this evidence does argue for a closer examination of the response of authorities to urban growth during the industrial revolution.

---

pp. 295–305, do contend that state intervention, whether through continuation of supplements to income under the Old Poor Law or mandating minimum earnings, would have been appropriate.

[56] See R. M. Hartwell, "The Rising Standard of Living in England, 1800–1850," *Economic History Review*, 2nd Series, 13 (May 1960), pp. 397–416.

[57] See the Hammonds, *Modern Industry*, p. 223; François Vigier, *Change and Apathy: Liverpool and Manchester during the Industrial Revolution* (Cambridge, MA, 1970); Wohl, *Endangered Lives*, chap. 7; and Jeffrey G. Williamson, "Underinvestment in Britain's Cities during the Industrial Revolution?" mimeo, Cambridge, MA, 1987.

[58] Fn. 20 provides the sources for the estimates for Ashton-under-Lyne and Preston. "The Return of the Average Rate of Expense of Combined Works of Drainage and Water Supply for Towns under the Public Health Act . . .," *House of Lords Papers*, vol. 31, 1852, p. 305, suggests that these estimates are consistent with the actual costs reported for several unnamed towns.

The Development of Irrigation in Provence, 1700–1860: The French Revolution and Economic Growth

JEAN-LAURENT ROSENTHAL

Quantitative and qualitative evidence suggest that the returns to irrigation in France were similar during the eighteenth and nineteenth centuries. The Old Regime failed to develop irrigation because of fragmented political authority over rights of eminent domain. Since many groups could hold projects up, transaction costs increased dramatically. Reforms enacted during the French Revolution reduced the costs of securing rights of eminent domain.

Historians and economic historians hotly debate the issue of the French Revolution's contribution to economic growth. Most view the French Revolution either as testimony to the Old Regime's inability to survive in the world created by the Industrial Revolution, or as the unfortunate result of poor political calculations on the part of the nobility or the king's ministers.[1] Hence scholars have focused on the causes of the Revolution. As Alfred Cobban argues, however, the true measure of such an event probably lies in its consequences.[2] Although economic historians have tended to point to technological change as the crucial source of economic growth, more and more attention is being paid to the development of markets and to the relationship between institutional change and economic growth.[3] One important area where it has been argued that institutions held back development in Old Regime France is agriculture. This article attempts to assess the impact of the Revolution of 1789 on a specific agricultural investment—irrigation in southeastern France. I show that both quantitative and qualitative evidence suggest that irrigation was profitable under the Old Regime. To

The Journal of Economic History, Vol. L, No. 3 (Sept. 1990). ISSN 0022-0507.

The author is Assistant Professor of Economics, UCLA, Los Angeles, CA 90024.

This article is a revised version of the fourth chapter of my Ph.D. dissertation, "The Fruits of Revolution: Property Rights, Litigation and French Agriculture (1700–1860)" (Caltech, 1988). I would like to thank Philip Hoffman and Lance Davis for their guidance, as well as Ken Sokoloff and two referees and the editors for very helpful suggestions. The archival research was made possible by two travel grants from the California Institute of Technology and by the John Randolph and Dora Haines Fellowship.

[1] See, for example, Donald Sutherland, *France 1789–1815: Revolution and Counterrevolution* (Oxford, 1985); and Michel Vovelle, *La Chute de la monarchie, 1787–1872* (Paris, 1972).

[2] Alfred Cobban, *The Social Interpretation of the French Revolution* (Cambridge, 1968), p. 67.

[3] See Douglass North, *Structure and Change in Economic History* (New York, 1985); see also Philip Hoffman, "Institutions and Agriculture in Old-Regime France," *Politics and Society*, 16 (June-Sept. 1988), pp. 241–64.

explain the lack of growth in irrigation before 1789, I explore legal constraints and argue that divided authority over rights of way was the most important factor responsible for hindering agricultural growth.

The narrowness of the topic—irrigation in Provence—is dictated by the need for precise knowledge of institutions and their historical context. Since law and the distribution of political power varied greatly across regions in Old Regime France, a national approach to institutional problems would miss details that might explain the diversity of regional performance and failure. My conclusions, however, should hold for most of eighteenth-century France, because any investment project that featured externalities would have been plagued by the same problems that plagued irrigation.

IRRIGATION AND PROVENÇAL AGRICULTURE

Considered from a geographic point of view, Provence, one of France's more arid regions, was an area where development of an irrigation network should have had the greatest impact before 1789.[4] Years when rainfall is negligible from June to October are frequent, restricting agricultural production to grains, grapes, and olives on dry fields. The obvious remedy to the arid climate was, and remains, irrigation. Until the twentieth century the main source of irrigation water was the Durance River, a tributary to the Rhône.

Because the water of the Durance is very silty, it acts as a natural fertilizer, which permitted eighteenth-century farmers to avoid the biennial fallow on irrigated plots. The abandonment of the fallow alone indicates how dramatic an impact irrigation could have on total output. Yet the value of output would have probably more than doubled because irrigation also allowed farmers to abandon traditional crops in favor of fodder grasses, peas, beans, and other high-value crops. These more valuable crops require both the warmth of the summer and significant amounts of water. Thus irrigation could lead to substantial per-acre increases in output.

A more accurate measure of the increase in efficiency associated with irrigation involves estimating the rise in total factor productivity, a measure of productivity change that takes into account the fact that more labor and capital were applied to irrigated than to dry land. Using sharecropping contracts to trace changes in the quantity of labor and capital applied to the land, I estimate that total factor productivity per acre

[4] Throughout the article Provence will denote the present-day *départements* of the Vaucluse and the Bouches du Rhône. While these departments represent only lower Provence, the rest of southeastern France, namely, the Côte d'Azur and upper Provence, has a much lower potential for irrigation development.

would have risen at least 30 to 40 percent as a result of irrigation.[5] Thus irrigation would have represented a significant increase in efficiency.

Unlike farmers or landowners, Old Regime royal governments may have been less concerned with increasing production on specific plots of land than with raising regional agricultural output. Using data from the 1870s I compute a conservative estimate of the change in total factor productivity as a result of the development of irrigation after 1789 (see the Appendix for details). Had the canals planned or proposed under the Old Regime, but only realized after 1789, been built in the eighteenth century, the increase in total output in the region would have been more than 7 percent.[6] While an output increase of 7 percent at the regional level may seem small, it would have significantly eased any short-term Malthusian constraints on the population, the very problem that concerned so many government officials.[7] A qualitative survey of the geography and economy of eighteenth-century Provence thus suggests that irrigation should have seen greater development under the Old Regime. The benefits of irrigation were well known long before 1820, when the development of irrigation began in earnest. Indeed, some of the canals of southeastern France dated back to the Middle Ages.[8] Many irrigation projects were proposed between 1700 and 1789, so we must look to something other than ignorance to explain why irrigation grew so slowly before 1789.

PROFITABILITY

Improvements in technology, credit markets, or relative price changes are all potential causes for the sudden development of irrigation canals after 1820. Using data from projects built between 1760 and 1860, we shall see that neither profits nor techniques, nor even credit was the determining factor in the timing of irrigation development.

Let us first assume that there was little technical change and that credit was easily available and present the data collected to examine the issue of profits.[9] Too few canals were built between 1700 and 1860 to measure directly the profitability of irrigation projects. Moreover no

[5] Abandoning the fallow leads, over two years, to twice the output on the same piece of land but at the cost of more labor and capital. Farmers probably invested some labor and capital on the fallow, so irrigation would not double labor and capital inputs. Because I want to compute a lower bound for total factor productivity growth, I assume that labor and capital inputs double. The assumption that nonland inputs double is consistent with estimated labor and capital inputs from rental contracts.

[6] Provence was a net importer of grain throughout the eighteenth century. Thus the increased output could have been either consumed locally or used to purchase more food.

[7] Not surprisingly, Old Regime government officials promoted irrigation, but royal government protection proved insufficient to overcome institutional obstacles.

[8] The canals of Saint-Julien in Cavaillon and l'Hôpital in Avignon were built between 1200 and 1350.

[9] I defend these assumptions in the section titled "Technology and Credit."

irrigation projects were realized until 1765 in Provence. It is possible, however, to estimate the level of profits that projects would have earned had they been started earlier than 1765. Estimating rates of return requires three kinds of data: price series for the inputs and outputs of canal construction; factor shares for each canal; and an interest rate series (because the costs and benefits are spread over time).

Unfortunately, canal accounts are not very detailed. Except in the case of skilled and unskilled labor, it is difficult to get factor shares for such things as quarried stone, lime, wood, and other material inputs. However, since nonlabor inputs were mostly used on bridges and in a few buildings, land and labor comprised nearly all the costs of canal construction. The measure of costs for a canal includes building costs and maintenance costs. For the jth construction year expenditures are divided between man-days spent digging using unskilled labor (d_u^j), man-days of construction, which requires skilled labor (d_s^j), and the amount of land consumed by the canal (n). Man-days of labor and acres of land are bought at market prices w_u^t, w_s^t, and p_i^t (all land bought for the canal is assumed irrigated, which biases the rates of return downward). The present value of future maintenance costs is the yearly maintenance cost (m) divided by the interest rate r^t.

The social return to building a canal is taken to be the increase in the price of land when it becomes irrigated ($p_i^t - p_d^t$). Since land is the only input in fixed supply, in the long run the net increase in output from irrigation should accrue to the owner of the land. Thus if N acres of land become irrigated, the social return will be N times ($p_i^t - p_d^t$). Given these assumptions one can compute the hypothetical benefit-cost ratio, R^t, had the project started in year t and taken T years to complete:[10]

$$R^t = \frac{N(p_i^t - p_d^t)/(1 + r^t)^T}{\sum_{j=0}^{T} (d_u^j w_u^t + d_s^j w_s^t + np_i^t)/(1 + r^t)^j + \dfrac{m}{r^t(1 + r^t)^T}}$$

To estimate hypothetical profits, I was able to construct two different wage series, using data from Avignon, a large town in the middle of the area.[11] The data consist of wage bills for unfed labor from the account

[10] The hypothetical internal rate of return is simply the r^{t*} that sets R^t equal to 1.

[11] For any year wages are nearly identical across sources in the area. Avignon, the major city, has the most abundant sources, and the ones which were used to construct the series. The noticeable intraregional pattern was that unskilled labor was somewhat cheaper in nearby villages but skilled labor was more expensive there than in Avignon. There was considerable seasonal fluctuation in wages, partially due to variation in the working day. For further detail, see the Appendix.

books of religious and municipal organizations.[12] Religious institutions owned medieval canals and they hired labor by the day for maintenance work. Thus the wage data come from the very professions involved in canal construction and maintenance. These data have been sorted into two series: skilled and unskilled workers (see Table 4). The first, unskilled labor, was constructed from the wages of laborers, road gangs, and levee maintenance workers. The second was constructed from skilled workers' wages (masons, miners, carpenters, gang bosses, and so on).[13]

The data for the land price series are taken from a sample of land-sale and land-lease contracts negotiated between 1700 and 1855 that were found among the archives of *notaires* in Cavaillon, the town with the largest amount of irrigated land in southeastern France both in the eighteenth and in the nineteenth century.[14] The choice of Cavaillon allows us to ignore any local market effects on the price of improved land. If anything, the fact that Cavaillon had more irrigated land than other areas should bias the price of irrigated land downward and thus underestimate potential canal revenues.[15]

Calculating hypothetical profits also requires data on the costs and revenues of canals built between 1700 and 1860. Data are available for two eighteenth-century projects, Cabedan-Neuf and Crillon, and for two projects proposed in the eighteenth century but not realized until the nineteenth, Plan-Oriental and Carpentras. While there are insufficient data to estimate the profits of other projects, my sample of canals is representative of most canals built between 1700 and 1860, in terms of size, location, and timing. The canal of Carpentras is as large as any in Provence and the smaller ones of Cabedan-Neuf, Crillon, and Plan-

[12] Most of the workers who received food were paid not on a per-diem basis, but on a monthly or yearly basis. Not knowing how many days of work corresponded to a year's wages, I did not use wage bills of workers who received food as part of their compensation.

[13] The data also reflect some of the extraordinary levels of inflation associated with the French Revolution, unlike most series previously published. One excellent source for wage data is René Baehrel, *Une Croissance: La Basse Provence rurale (1650–1789)* (Paris, 1962). Unfortunately Baehrel's data stop in 1789. The sources used for wages came from the *Archives Départementales* in Avignon. The sources include the accounts books of the city of Avignon (AC Avignon, CC 550 to CC 805, *pièces à l'appui des Comptes*), religious institutions (AD Vaucluse, H Bompas 182–185; H Cordeliers Avignon, 62–64), and the hospital of Avignon (AD Vaucluse, H sup. Hôpital Ste Marthe E 103, M 6–18).

[14] Cavaillon is a local market town located 17 miles to the east of Avignon, 30 miles northwest of Aix, on the banks of the Durance River.

[15] In Old Regime France transportation costs were high. If only a small portion of a given area was irrigated, such land would fetch a very high price. When the irrigation network was completed the price would fall dramatically; thus we want to use a price for irrigated land that is close to the price irrigated land would have fetched after the network was completed and a price for dry land that is the price of irrigable dry land. By 1700, 15 percent of the area of Cavaillon was irrigated. The large area irrigated suggests that most irrigation-specific goods would have commanded only a competitive price. Moreover, most of Cavaillon's nonirrigated land under cultivation was irrigable, so we are in fact measuring the price difference between irrigable and irrigated land with reasonable confidence.

Oriental are similar in size to most other projects.[16] Table 1 displays in condensed form all the project-specific data used in the construction of hypothetical profit streams.

The only other data necessary are interest rates. These are taken for the eighteenth century from *rentes* data collected in Provence that have been sorted into decadal averages, and in the nineteenth century from French government bond data.[17]

I estimated both benefit-cost ratios and internal rates of return.[18] All projects were profitable during nearly the entire period under study. But the projects were more profitable before 1750, when they were not carried out, than after 1820, when they were. Although some projects are always more profitable than others, changes in profit rates are similar for all projects. In addition, the profitability of an irrigation canal does not seem to depend on the scale of the project. Profits for any project vary significantly from one estimate to the next, but the benefit-cost ratios are less than 1.2 in fewer than 20 percent of the years. The estimates suggest that any uncertainty about the profits of a canal concerned their magnitude rather than their existence. The dispersion of rates of return and benefit-cost ratios is largely due to variations in the increase in the value of land as a result of irrigation (75 percent of the variance of the benefit-cost ratios is explained by a regression of the ratio on land prices). Because the hypothetical profits of Old Regime projects are similar to the hypothetical profits realized by projects built after 1820, it is unlikely that changes in technology played a major role in irrigation development. Had there been a lot of technological change, later projects should have been much more profitable.

As Table 2 suggests, the highest profits came in the early eighteenth century between 1700 and 1730. During the years 1735 to 1755 projects were less profitable—though not unprofitable—than at any other time except for the Revolutionary period. A number of projects built after

[16] Cabedan-Neuf irrigated 600 hectares in and around Cavaillon and was built from 1764 to 1766; Crillon irrigated 1,000 hectares around Avignon and was completed in 1777. Plan-Oriental, another canal in Cavaillon, watered 800 hectares to the north of Cavaillon; it was built in 1823. Carpentras was very large; built in the 1850s, it irrigated more than 4,500 hectares.

[17] The interest rate data for the eighteenth century comes from J.-L. Rosenthal, "Credit Markets in Southeastern France, 1650–1788" (UCLA Dept. of Economics Working Paper No. 589). For the nineteenth century I have relied on Stanley Homer, *A History of Interest Rates* (New Brunswick, 1977), pp. 156–57, 172, 195–96, 222–23. I preferred to ignore the interest data in David Weir and François Velde, "The Financial Market and Government Debt in France, 1750–1793" (Paper presented at the Second International Cliometrics meeting, Santander, 1989). The data they present come from government interest rates that are significantly affected by the government probability of default. As a consistency check I did estimate benefit-cost ratios using these data with results similar to those from using the *rentes* data. In fact, none of the results depend strongly on the choice of an interest rate, provided it is less than 8 percent. An interest rate of 8 percent is higher than any paid in the eighteenth century by the French government (except in 1770) or by private borrowers.

[18] The data and results are presented in detail in the Appendix.

TABLE 1
CANAL COSTS

Canal	Date of Completion	Land Irrigated (in hectares[a])	Total Building Costs (in francs)	Capitalized Maintenance Costs (in francs)
Cabedan-Neuf I	1767	500	822,300[c]	97,200
Cabedan-Neuf II[b]	1767	270	172,490	97,200
Crillon	1779	1,000	400,000	400,000
Plan-Oriental	1821	590	138,595	100,000
Carpentras	1857	5,000	5,297,011	100,000

Canal	Years Under Construction	Skilled Labor (in man-days per year)	Unskilled Labor (in man-days per year)	Land Requirements (in hectares)
Cabedan-Neuf I	2	88,815	73,053	27.0
Cabedan-Neuf II	2	21,410	19,824	27.0
Crillon	3	35,088	41,190	49.5
Plan-Oriental	2	63,561	46,631	9.7
Carpentras[d]	6			
First 3 Years		61,341	224,242	96.7
Last 3 Years		221,852	112,403	73.3

[a] One hectare equals 2.4 acres.
[b] Cabedan-Neuf I and Cabedan-Neuf II are the same canal, but the various sources on construction accounts could not be reconciled. Not knowing which one was more accurate I present results based on both sets of sources.
[c] All costs are given for the year in which they were incurred. There was no need to deflate them because they are converted into quantities of labor.
[d] Carpentras was a very large canal. For the first three years work focused on the main canal. Only in the next three years were branches built. See René Caillet, *Le Canal de Carpentras* (Carpentras, 1925), vol. 1, pp. 69–70.
Sources: For the first estimate of the costs of Cabedan-Neuf: Jean-Auguste Barral, *Les Irrigations dans le Vaucluse* (Paris, 1876), pp. 539–44. For the second estimate of the costs of Cabedan-Neuf: *Syndicat du Canal de Cabedan-Neuf, Archives et Documents 1230–1883* (Cavaillon, 1883), pp. 45–52. For the canal of Crillon: A. Reboulet, "Le Canal de Crillon," in *Mémoires de l'Académie de Vaucluse* (33, 1914), pp. 37–40; and Barral, *Les Irrigations dans le Vaucluse*, pp. 326–27. For Plan-Oriental: André Martel, "Les Origines du Canal de Plan-Oriental," in *Actes du Congres des Societés Savantes* (Avignon, 1955), pp. 394–95; and Barral, *Les Irrigations dans le Vaucluse*, pp. 545–47. For Carpentras: René Caillet, *Le Canal de Carpentras* (Carpentras, 1925), vol. 2, pp. 199–201; and Barral, *Les Irrigations dans le Vaucluse*, pp. 325–26.

1760 were proposed during this intermediate period, suggesting that investors, at least, found it profitable to attempt irrigation development. The last decades of the Old Regime between 1760 and 1785 show high internal rates of return and high benefit-cost ratios. The rates of the late eighteenth century, were in fact higher on average than those of the nineteenth century when most of the development actually took place. After 1785 the rates of return were highly erratic until 1820, no doubt because of the uncertainties provoked by the Revolution.

The high levels of estimated profits through most of the Old Regime, and in particular during the years from 1700 to 1730, suggest that changes in relative prices were not responsible for the late development of irrigation in southeastern France. During most of the eighteenth

TABLE 2
AVERAGE HYPOTHETICAL INTERNAL RATES OF RETURN
(in percent per year)

Canal	Periods 1700–1730	1735–1755	1760–1785	1790–1820	1820–1855
Cabedan-Neuf I (1767)	113.0	32.5	77.8	11.0	63.3
Cabedan-Neuf II (1767)	60.0	2.1	35.3	−16.0	24.2
Crillon (1779)	91.8	33.8	68.6	10.7	57.8
Plan-Oriental (1821)	126.9	49.9	104.0	25.3	78.9
Carpentras (1857)	32.0	13.4	30.0	−1.4	25.0
Interest Rate	5.0	5.1	5.0	7.5	4.3

Sources: Table 6.

century rates of return were in fact higher than they were in the nineteenth century. Yet irrigation development was much more limited from 1700 to 1789 than it was from 1820 to 1860. Indeed, despite the fact that hypothetical rates of return before 1760 were well above the interest rate, no canal was built before that date. Thus some sort of a market failure in the supply of irrigation must have been at work in the eighteenth century.

TECHNOLOGY AND CREDIT

Given the high levels of hypothetical profits, it is important to examine the validity of assumptions made about technology and credit availability. The design of French transportation canals was very sophisticated; these canals involved locks, dams, bridges, and complex water management.[19] The technology of transportation canals was also greatly improved between 1700 and 1855. By contrast, the technology of irrigation seems to have remained the same from the Middle Ages to the late nineteenth century. The methods used between 1700 and 1860 resembled those used in the thirteenth century in building the canals of Saint-Julien and l'Hôpital, or in the sixteenth century in building the canal of Craponne.[20] From 1200 to 1870 all new irrigation canals were unlined dirt ditches, where water flowed by gravity alone. Stone masonry was used only for bridges. The only dams in use, flimsy dirt levees that captured the water from the Durance River, had to be rebuilt after every large flood. They diverted part of the river's flow but made no attempt to retain water in a reservoir.

Agricultural development simply could not support the innovative,

[19] A valuable source on eighteenth-century canal technology is Delalande, *Des Canaux de navigation* (Paris, 1777). See also André Maistre, *Le Canal des deux mers: Canal royal du Languedoc, 1666–1810* (Toulouse, 1968), chap. 3.

[20] Jean Rigaud, *Le Canal de Craponne, Etude historique et juridique relative aux concessions complexes des arrosages communaux d'Istre et Grans* (Aix-en-Provence, 1934); Roger Caillet, *Le Canal de Carpentras* (Carpentras, 1925), chaps. 2, 3.

but very expensive, technologies used for urban water supply and transportation. In contrast to the low levels of technological sophistication utilized in agricultural projects stands a set of urban projects that overlaps both geographically and temporally with those under study. One project, the canal of Marseille (1840 to 1848), a joint urban and rural water-supply project, offers a good example of the technologies available in the nineteenth century yet not used in agriculture. The canal of Marseille featured a large dam and a permanent reservoir, many bridges, and it ran underground for 25 percent of its length. The project was financed by the city of Marseille, which attempted to sell excess water to farmers. The city also wanted farmers to pay a share of the building costs equivalent to their share of the water. This led to a price for water 15 times the cost of water on other agricultural projects. As a result, the scheme to retail excess water to farmers failed.[21]

Despite the available technology the methods used to build irrigation canals did not change. Yet it is possible that experience gained from past canal construction led to smaller engineering errors. The resulting reduction in risk would have increased the viability of projects by lowering the risk premiums demanded by investors. Yet technological risks—the risks associated with the construction phase of the project—seem to have been very limited. Even in the eighteenth century the relationship between technology and cost was well established. Engineering costs could be predicted with a good deal of confidence because of the experience gained from transportation canals, which were much more complex and thus riskier. Irrigation projects were by contrast very simple, even when there were unanticipated delays or higher-than-expected costs.[22] It thus appears that between 1700 and 1860 change in the methods of irrigation canal construction was limited, and technological risk did not threaten irrigation projects or constrain the supply of irrigation.

Because the construction of irrigation canals involved considerable cash outlays, the assumption that credit was easily available is crucial for my argument. While Old Regime France lacked a well-developed, centralized credit market, the limited development of credit markets did not block the expansion of the irrigated area of Provence.[23] In defense

[21] Paul Masson, *Encyclopédie des Bouches du Rhône* (Paris, 1929–1930), vol. 7, pp. 162–67. This canal ran nearly 100 kilometers through a very rugged part of Provence to deliver water to Marseille.

[22] The canal of Boisgelin, the most ambitious canal realized prior to the Revolution, shows that risk was small. The engineer, Brun, had warned of the very large costs associated with the tunnel. Yet he did not doubt that the tunnel could be built. BM Méjanes, Ms. 840(853). My section titled "Institutional Failure: Eminent Domain and Rent-seeking" will discuss how institutional factors raised costs on this canal.

[23] Pierre Goubert, *L'Ancien Régime* (Paris, 1973), vol. 2, chap. 7, offers an introduction to Old Regime finance. See also Guy Chaussinant-Nogaret, *Les Financiers du Languedoc au XVIII*^{eme} *siècle* (Paris, 1976).

of this position one can marshal four different kinds of evidence. First, the credit demands of most irrigation canals were tiny relative to the credit demands of Provençal villages that borrowed extensively during the Old Regime. Second, credit markets based on mortgages, which were very active in rural France, could have provided significant sources of capital for irrigation promoters, who were often wealthy landowners.[24] Third, Jewish agents were directly involved in making loans to at least one promoter in the 1780s. These loans did not have the collateral of land and the promoter paid an interest rate double that of the mortgage rate—8 to 10 percent as compared to 5 percent. Fourth, the high nobility was also able to finance projects directly in the case of many of the smaller projects, perhaps putting its vast wealth at the disposal of canal promoters because irrigation canals did not carry the stigma attached to many other forms of investment.[25] Therefore, it seems there were sufficient sources of capital (though not necessarily through organized markets) to carry out irrigation projects.

Finally, the apparent market failure in irrigation cannot be ascribed to a lack of acumen on the part of Old Regime investors. In fact the magnitude of entrepreneurial activity is striking when it is contrasted with the failures endured by canal promoters before 1789. Every canal built after the Revolution can be traced back to a serious promoter under the Old Regime who had expended considerable resources attempting to secure all the authorizations needed to build the canal. These promoters failed overwhelmingly, if we measure success by the ability to build a canal and earn a profit. The failure rate remains very high even if we demand only that a canal be built. Indeed, the pre-Revolutionary expansion of the irrigated area represents only 16 percent of what was actually planned before 1789 and built before 1860. Simple economic arguments do not seem to explain the failure of irrigation development under the Old Regime or its success after the Revolution. Instead, it seems that the peculiar fragmentation of power that characterized the Old Regime constrained Provençal canal promoters.

[24] The canal of the Midi was primarily financed by the estates of Languedoc through loans. See Robert Forster, *The Nobility of Toulouse in the Eighteenth Century: A Social and Economic Study* (Baltimore, 1960), pp. 66–74; William Beik, *Absolutism and Society in Seventeenth-Century France: State Power and Provincial Aristocracy in Languedoc* (New York, 1985), pp. 292–97; and Maistre, *Le Canal des Deux Mers*, chap. 4.

[25] See Paul Masson, "Le Canal de Provence," in *Revue historique de Provence* (Aix-en-Provence, 1901), pp. 423–25; Hubert Elie, "La Spéculation sous la Régence: l'Affaire du Canal d'Avignon à la Mer," *Provence Historique*, 3 (1953), pp. 112–13; and A. Reboulet, "Construction du Canal de Crillon," *Mémoires de l'Académie de Vaucluse*, 33 (1914), pp. 46–47. In the case of the canal of Crillon, 25 percent of the construction costs was advanced by Jews and another 25 percent by nobles and bourgeois. Landowners were the largest source of credit in France because they could borrow money through mortgages. Had promoters been able to interest more than a small number of landowners, the credit problem would never have existed.

INSTITUTIONAL FAILURE: EMINENT DOMAIN AND RENT-SEEKING

While the failure of the supply of irrigation had multiple causes, the most important, I would argue, lay in the division of authority over rights of eminent domain.[26] This problem was well understood before 1789, yet resolution was elusive because eminent domain authority was embedded in the Old Regime structure of privileges.

The woes of a sixteenth-century canal builder illustrate the costs of divided authority. In 1554 Adam de Craponne, a Provençal nobleman and engineer, received a royal grant to draw water from the Durance. In order to secure eminent domain rights for his canal, Craponne had his grant acknowledged by the local assembly—the Estates. Yet some Provençal communities (called *Terres Adjacentes*) did not come under the jurisdiction of the Estates as far as eminent domain was concerned. These villages delayed the project until Craponne gave farmers there unlimited, free access to the canal's water.[27]

Despite these outlandish concessions Craponne completed his canal in 1559 and sold a number of irrigation rights. In dry years, however, *Terres-Adjacentes* villages used up most of the canal's capacity, and with no water to deliver, Craponne had to renege on his other contracts. The resulting suits led Craponne to an early bankruptcy and discouraged other investors from pursuing irrigation projects. From the standpoint of *Terres-Adjacentes* villages, the whole affair was a free ride. Although Craponne's bankruptcy saddled them with part of the maintenance costs, they now received irrigation water without the burden of any construction costs. Divided authority over eminent domain could indeed create severe problems for canal developers.

The structure of authority Craponne encountered in the sixteenth century was a legacy of medieval state building, and it remained in place until the Revolution of 1789. After the division of Provence between the Pope and the counts of Provence in the twelfth century, the Pope's share became known as the *Comtat* Venaissin (hereafter the *Comtat*). The *Comtat* corresponds to the present-day *département* of the Vaucluse. The counts of Provence retained control of the *Comté* of Provence and the *Terres Adjacentes*. The western half of the *Comté* of Provence (hereafter the *Comté*) and the *Terres Adjacentes* make up

[26] Other causes of failure were the costs associated with securing water rights and the severe revenue problems related to the fact that most of the costs of the network were sunk when the builder bargained with landowners to sell them water rights. Although these other causes were important, they were due to the same division of authority that encouraged rent-seeking over rights of eminent domain. Focusing solely on rights of way simplifies the argument.

[27] On the canal of Craponne see J.-B. Bertin and P. Autier, *Adam de Craponne* (Paris, 1904); Rigaud, *Le Canal de Craponne*; Jean de Villeneuve, *Encyclopédie des Bouches du Rhône* (Marseille, 1825–1829), vol. 3, pp. 698–714; and Masson, *Encyclopédie*, vol. 7, p. 148.

what is now the *département* of the Bouches du Rhône.[28] In 1481 the king of France inherited the *Comté* and the *Terres Adjacentes*.

The geographic divisions outlined above corresponded to organizational divisions that seem to have determined the transaction costs of irrigation. Prior to the Revolution, two organizations alone should have decided the fate of irrigation projects in the *Comtat*, although, as this article will make clear, their authority was far more limited. These organizations were the Estates of the *Comtat*, a representative assembly in charge of taxation, and the Apostolic Chamber, the *Comtat*'s final court of appeals. The approval of the Estates was necessary to secure financial or legal support for irrigation projects, but the Pope and his local representative (the vice legate) had veto power over decisions by the Estates, a veto power they regularly exercised. Similarly, the Apostolic Chamber was a court of last resort and should have enforced all contracts relating to irrigation. In fact, appeals were possible either to the Chamber itself or in some rare cases to papal courts in Rome.[29]

The *Comté* of Provence had organizations similar to those of the *Comtat*. As a French *Pays d'Etat* it had, like the *Comtat*, a fiscal and legislative body—the *Assemblée du Pays*. Like the Estates of the *Comtat*, the *Assemblée du Pays* could provide a locus of bargaining for institutional change. As far as the judicial system in the *Comté* was concerned, the final court of appeals was the *Parlement* of Aix.[30]

The final area under study, the *Terres Adjacentes*, was classified as a *Pays d'Election*. These communities were directly under the authority of the king and had no Estate. In these villages the division of judicial authority among the king, the villages, and the *Parlement* of Aix was very ambiguous. Most importantly for this study, individual villages rather than a central authority seem to have controlled eminent domain rights. In the Middle Ages the *Terres Adjacentes* had been autonomous and had in fact decided issues of eminent domain alone. Under the Old Regime the extent of local autonomy was uncertain and subject to erosion by the Crown. Yet the *Terres-Adjacentes* villages were well organized and could credibly threaten to sue anyone who did not secure rights of eminent domain from them.

One might assume that the political border that ran between *Comtat* and *Comté* was the root cause of the institutional problems, but in fact

[28] The *Terres Adjacentes* were a set of administratively independent communities that included Marseille, Arles, and a number of villages on the border between the *Comté* and the *Comtat*. These communities had never been directly incorporated into Provence. In fact, until they became part of France, the *Terres Adjacentes* recognized only the direct authority of the Count of Provence. The best reference detailing the political divisions of Provence is Edouard Baratier, *Histoire de la Provence* (Toulouse, 1969). For more detail, see Masson, *Encyclopédie*, vol. 4; and Villeneuve, *Encyclopédie*, vol. 3.

[29] Elie, "La Spéculation sous la Régence," pp. 112–13; and Reboulet, "Construction du Canal de Crillon," pp. 37–50.

[30] Masson, *Encyclopédie*, vol. 7.

the two territories were divided by the Durance River. Thus most canals were either in the *Comtat* or in the French part of Provence, even though nearly all drew water from the Durance. So most *Comtat* affairs were strictly *Comtat* affairs and the same was true in the French part of Provence. Moreover, the problems of eminent domain were sufficiently important within each political division that we can ignore the effect of the *Comtat*'s independence from France. Let us, for example, consider rights of eminent domain in the *Comté*. Since any canal on the southern side of the river would irrigate land mostly in the *Comté*, the king, the Estates, and the *Parlement* would all be involved in granting rights of way; however, the need to cross the *Terres Adjacentes* added a further cost. In the *Comté*, the best sites from which to draw water from the Durance were in, or led into, the *Terres Adjacentes*. Thus villages that ruled over eminent domain in the *Terres Adjacentes* could block or delay projects.[31]

The hypothesis that divided authority over rights of way made it very difficult to build irrigation canals is difficult to test. Nonetheless it is possible to examine the history of five Old Regime canals to see whether institutions significantly raised the costs of irrigation. One relationship emerges from these histories: the more institutional boundaries canals crossed, the more difficult they were to build.

Of the four small canals completed under the Old Regime, three were in the *Comtat* and the fourth in the *Comté*. Each of the four projects distributed water to, at most, a few communities. They did not cross any important political boundaries, yet even among the four projects delays and transaction costs rose with size.

The two smallest canals, Janson and Cambis, were each only a few kilometers long and faced only minor transaction costs. Each was entirely financed by the principal landowner—the Marquis of Janson and the Duke of Cambis—who wanted to irrigate his very large estate. The marquis and the duke both maintained strong political ties to the French royal court, and they successfully lobbied for water grants. Their large estates eliminated the free-rider problem and allowed each nobleman to internalize most of the benefits of his irrigation canal. In his grant application the Marquis of Janson argued that the benefits to his estates would more than suffice to cover the construction costs.[32] He did allow the neighboring community to use the canal for irrigation purposes, no doubt to facilitate his use of rights of eminent domain. But there is no evidence to show that he or Cambis failed to make a profit from the canals, even though the villages did not contribute to construction costs. In any case, unlike the other examples, these two small

[31] Bertin and Autier, *Adam de Craponne*, p. 113.

[32] AN H[1] 1515 (March 1780).

canals were completed swiftly and experienced little in the way of transaction costs.

The third project actually completed was the canal of Cabedan-Neuf, built in the *Comtat* around 1765. Although it affected only three communities—Cavaillon, Les Taillades, and Merindol—it was large enough to create problems with eminent domain. The canal was built by an association of landowners under the tutelage of the city of Cavaillon. Because most of the land irrigated by the canal was either in the territory of Cavaillon or in that of Les Taillades, costs of the canal were apportioned between the two villages according to the area irrigated. The third village involved, Merindol, enjoyed a generous free ride. Much of the canal passed through Merindol, which, unlike Cavaillon, lay in the *Comté* not the *Comtat* and thus was not subject to the powers of eminent domain of *Comtat* authorities. Not surprisingly Merindol sued Cavaillon over rights of eminent domain. The issue was settled out of court: Merindol received water from the canal, but it did not contribute anything to the project.

Except for the redistributive implications, the free-riding by Merindol was relatively unimportant: it did not stop the project. Litigation was avoided because Cavaillon alone could have paid for the entire canal and still benefited from the project.[33] Yet the history of Cabedan-Neuf demonstrates that the involvement of a mere three communities was enough to drive institutional costs higher than when only one community was involved. These institutional costs were associated with scale because of the extreme division of authority in the region.[34]

The fourth canal, the canal of Crillon, delivered irrigation water to Avignon and surrounding communities. It was built by the Duke of Crillon, descendant of an old line of *Comtat* noblemen who had led the French king's armies. Using his favor at court, Crillon secured a grant to draw water from the Durance. He then had the grant registered in the *Parlement* of Aix. Next he secured rights of way from the city of Avignon that were recognized by the Estates of the *Comtat* and the vice legate. The canal, however, ran through several communities and challenged the water monopolies of a number of seigniors and monasteries, all of whom held the project up for ransom by attacking it in court. The most important suit was brought by the Duke of Gadagne, Lord of Vedene, one of the communities traversed by the canal. Gadagne contested Crillon's right both to cross into Vedene and to cross

[33] *Syndicat du Canal de Cabedan-Neuf, Archives et Documents 1230–1883* (Cavaillon, 1883), pp. 48–69. Cavaillon chose to bargain with Merindol directly rather than with the *Assemblée* for a right of eminent domain. Presumably both Merindol and the *Assemblée* were seeking rents and Merindol proved cheaper to pay off.

[34] Across the Durance, in the *Comté*, the town of Châteaurenard also attempted to build a canal in the 1780s. Châteaurenard was also forced to negotiate over rights of way and water rights with the nearby town of Noves and its seigniors. See Jean-Auguste Barral, *Les Irrigations dans les Bouches du Rhône* (Paris, 1875), vol. 1, pp. 370–71.

Gadagne's irrigation canal. The suit was temporarily settled out of court in 1777, and in the settlement Gadagne granted rights of way in return for water rights. The settlement was not fully executed by either party and the case was still being litigated after the French Revolution.[35]

The canal of Crillon demonstrates the need for precise geographical and historical detail. Gadagne could litigate against Crillon only because the canal's rights of eminent domain had been granted first by the city of Avignon and only then approved by the Estates. Avignon and the Estates had a complex relationship because the city was in fact a *Terre Adjacente* of the *Comtat*, having been bought by the Pope from the counts of Provence in 1348. As a result the authority of the Estates over Avignon was unclear. Although the Estates and other *Comtat* organizations had approved the canal, they had not specifically granted rights of way in the *Comtat*. Thus the validity of the Duke of Crillon's rights of eminent domain was subject to dispute and formed an open avenue for anyone to attack the project.

The history of the canal of Boisgelin, my fifth example, shows the costs of fragmented authority in a large-scale project, built in the *Comté* under the financial authority of the *Assemblée du Pays* after a number of other attempts had failed. The proposed canal had two possible routes: one ran through the *Comté* alone; the other crossed the *Terres Adjacentes*. While the latter would have been cheaper, it involved bargaining with the *Terres Adjacentes* for rights of eminent domain. Rather than bargain with each village in the *Terres Adjacentes*, the *Assemblée du Pays* avoided the issue but paid a very high price.[36] The *Assemblée* opted for the all-*Comté* route—much more expensive from an engineering standpoint because it involved tunneling through about one kilometer of solid rock near the village of Orgon. The cost of tunneling totaled nearly 400,000 livres and absorbed half the yearly budget of the canal for eight years.

Yet piercing the rock of Orgon allowed the promoters to avoid the *Terres-Adjacentes* villages of Sénas and Salon, where the cheaper route lay. Once the tunnel was built, the *Assemblée* had the ability to exclude the *Terres Adjacentes* from the benefits of the new canal if they did not contribute to its cost. Not surprisingly, the *Terres-Adjacentes* communities did purchase a significant amount of water from the canal just before the French Revolution, and a branch canal through Sénas and Salon was built.

Unlike all other irrigation projects, which involved little more than the digging of ditches, the canal of Boisgelin had to resort to an extraordinarily costly technology, a technology imposed by institutional

[35] BM Cecano, Ms. 2549. Appeals were heard in the Apostolic Chamber and then in Rome throughout the 1780s. Again the settlement gave free water to Gadagne.

[36] See Villeneuve, *Encyclopédie*, vol. 3, pp. 714–21.

constraints. Once again the division of authority led to much higher transaction or institutional costs than if only a small canal had been built. In this case these institutional costs took the indirect form of digging a tunnel at Orgon rather than bargaining or litigation.

Thus the histories of a few projects make it clear that the institutional environment blocked irrigation by raising the cost of canal building. The obstacles had their origins in the long-term development of institutions in southeastern France. One either had to pay off obstructionist villages, as Craponne did, or bear much higher construction costs, as did the promoters of the canal through Orgon.[37] The presence of organizations like the Estates and the *Parlement* did allow for some institutional change. It was, after all, possible to build the canal of Boisgelin. But the sort of institutional change that would have substantially reduced costs lay outside the authority of these organizations. In fact, not even the king, the *Parlement*, or the *Assemblée* could reform the *Terres Adjacentes*. Their peculiar status indeed constituted a *privilège*, something only the Revolution would change.[38]

Irrigation was an easy prey for rent-seeking villages because it involved both economies of scale and significant geographical specificity. Canals were networks; hence the costs involved in building the main canals did not rise as quickly as the irrigated area increased. Moreover, because canals relied on gravity to move water, each area usually had a single most economical drawing site from the river. As a result villages close to the Durance could credibly threaten irrigation projects with much higher costs or insurmountable engineering problems if they refused to grant rights of eminent domain. Most often villages were in a position of such strength that promoters could only give in or give up.

The phenomenon of villages holding irrigation projects up for ransom was not due to the specific form of village organization in eighteenth-century Provence. In fact, as the well-known examples of the sale of judicial offices and the monopolies of craft guilds suggest, rent-seeking was commonplace under the Old Regime.[39] Ironically, in the case of irrigation the greatest rent-seeker of them all, the Crown, was generally allied with canal promoters against local powers that were holding up the projects. Yet the Crown proved powerless to resolve the problem in the case of irrigation.

[37] BM Cecano, Ms. 1605 2459, 4°6198; and Reboulet, "Construction du Canal de Crillon," pp. 41–44.

[38] The *Terres Adjacentes* took advantage of Provence for much more than irrigation. See Villeneuve, *Encyclopédie*, vol. 3, pp. 755–61.

[39] See, for example, Roland Mousnier, *La Venalité des offices sous Henri IV et Louis XIII* (Paris, 1971); and Gail Bossenga, "La Révolution française et les corporations: Trois examples lillois," *Annales ESC*, 43 (Mar. 1988), pp. 405–26.

THE REVOLUTION AND IRRIGATION

For 25 years after 1789 there was no increase in irrigated area in Provence and those networks already in use were very poorly maintained.[40] Revolutionary turmoil during the years from 1789 to 1795 was violent in Provence. Moreover, starting in 1792, warfare drained away manpower and drove up the price of labor relative to land, a problem that grew even worse during the Napoleonic period (1798 to 1815). Yet even though the Revolution caused delays in the extension of the irrigation network, it was bringing about institutional reforms that would set the stage for future development, notably the construction of a number of new irrigation canals after 1820.

Institutional reforms, initiated by Revolutionary regimes and continued by Napoleon, would drastically cut the institutional costs of irrigation in the nineteenth century, consolidating all powers of eminent domain in the hands of the central government and destroying the old organizations and institutions that had prevented reforms. In Provence the annexation of the *Comtat* and the abolition of the peculiar status of the *Terres Adjacentes* removed two major obstacles to development of irrigation. For the first time since the early Middle Ages a single authority could decide all issues of property rights in Provence. Beyond the simplification of regional boundaries, the most important single Revolutionary reform was the centralization of legal and political power. Although centralization had been one of the goals of the absolutist monarchy, and although the king had held veto power over virtually all economic activity, he had never been able to eliminate local organizations like the *Parlement*, the *Assemblée du Pays*, the Estates, or even village councils. Centralization during the Revolution eliminated these local organizations and replaced them with a single pyramidic administrative structure headed by the Ministry of Interior. In the case of rights of way, the agent of the government at the local level—the prefect—was now charged with making all decisions.[41] The destruction of all other veto players freed irrigation development from the shackles of strategic behavior. Towns and villages near rivers could no longer refuse rights of way for new irrigation projects simply to protect the market value of their older irrigated land or, even worse, to siphon off part of the profits.

Revolutionary reforms gave prefects complete authority over projects until they were built and removed the judiciary from the planning stages of irrigation, making it difficult for local groups to delay projects through litigation. Local groups could appeal a project only before the prefect,

[40] AD Vaucluse S (Usines et Cours d'Eaux, Cavaillon and L'Isle sur Sorgues). The series S was being classified and sorted at the time I looked through it, thus no precise references can be given.

[41] Jean Petot, *L'Administration des ponts et chaussées* (Paris, 1958), pp. 383–87; Louis Bergeron, *L'Episode napoléonien: Aspects intérieurs* (Paris, 1972), p. 33; Sutherland, *France 1789–1815*, p. 345; and AD Vaucluse S, Usines et Cours d'Eaux.

whose approval was thus sufficient to guarantee the success of an irrigation project. Litigation—when it occurred—did not start until after the canal was built and the social gains were realized. Moreover, conflicts over technical and engineering issues could no longer be litigated but were decided by French administrators. After the Revolution the central administration not only had the power to provide promoters of irrigation with the property rights they needed, it also had the power to enforce the contracts.[42]

After the end of the Napoleonic regime in 1815, and under many different governments, irrigation in southeastern France flourished. State help was considerable, including engineering advice, administrative oversight, and the full power of its newly centralized authority. One form of support, however, was conspicuously absent: the government offered very few subsidies for the development of irrigation. By and large the irrigation canals of the nineteenth century seem to have been paid for by the landowners whose fields were irrigated, further evidence that institutions rather than technology or profits had caused the earlier market failure.

Whether in the case of a small project such as the canal of Plan-Oriental, or in the case of a large project such as the canal of Carpentras, state approval was decisive. The Plan-Oriental canal involved only a small amount of land (800 hectares) and delivered water to fields only in a few villages. The project was quickly approved by the prefect and completed in 1823, less than four years after initiation. In contrast, the canal of Carpentras involved more than 4,000 hectares in many different communities. Although the size of the canal slowed development, the state showed the flexibility of its new power by designing organizations with authority over many communities and many canals. For example, an organization was created that legally grouped all the canals drawing water from the Durance at the site originally used by Cabedan-Neuf alone, thereby allowing an efficient sharing of this desirable site.[43] Because the promoters were able to rely on the support and authority of the national government the Carpentras canal was completed in 1865, less than 20 years from its launching.

The overall success of irrigation in the nineteenth century is striking: more than 16,000 hectares, at least half of all the land irrigated from the Durance by 1875, received water from canals completed between 1820 and 1860. In all, more than 80 percent of the increase in irrigated area between 1700 and 1860 came after 1820.

[42] Fernand Ponteil, *Les Institutions de la France de 1814 à 1870* (Paris, 1965), pp. 30–34.
[43] René Caillet, *Le Canal de Carpentras*, pp. 75–76.

CONCLUSION

Under the Old Regime the division of authority over rights of eminent domain limited the scale of irrigation development. In Provence the political division of authority—a legacy of the Middle Ages—gave ample opportunities to a variety of groups to hold up projects. Villages successfully used this position to extract rents from canal promoters.[44]

Only local irrigation projects could avoid the costs associated with divided authority over rights of eminent domain. As a result, the transaction costs associated with irrigation development increased dramatically when projects crossed authority boundaries. Irrigation promoters were forced to face these transaction costs because the state proved incapable of reform.

The problems of eminent domain were simply not resolved before the French Revolution, which makes it surprising that any irrigation projects were developed before 1789. By contrast, the nineteenth century witnessed substantial growth in irrigation in southeastern France without significant litigation and with much shorter delays than had been customary in the previous century. Between 1820 and 1865 the area irrigated in Provence more than doubled and all the water in the Durance was used. Hence, insofar as irrigation is concerned the Revolution seems to have been a turning point. While the contribution of the Revolution to economic growth still eludes us, it appears that 1789 had a dramatic effect on transaction costs in irrigation.

Appendix

INCREASES IN IRRIGATED AREA

The studies of irrigation by J.-A. Barral offer good data to estimate the increase in total output as a result of irrigation because he investigated irrigated acreage thoroughly for each canal. In 1875 the total irrigated area for the region was about 52,700 hectares, or 18 percent of the total cultivated area.[45] To evaluate total output changes we must know the increase in area irrigated, not only from the Durance (a figure that is available and presented in Table 3), but also from other rivers. The increase in irrigation from other sources is not known precisely, so I present two estimates. The first concerns the impact of the increase in Durance irrigation, while the second estimates the increase in output that would have occurred if irrigation from all sources had grown at the same rate

[44] Veto power was widely used to extract rents from developers in Old Regime Provence; see Baehrel, *La Basse Provence rurale*, pp. 450–56; René Pillorget, *Les Mouvements insurrectionnels de Provence entre 1596 et 1715* (Paris, 1975), pp. 196–207; Maurice Agulhon, *La Vie sociale en Provence intérieure au lendemain de la Révolution* (Paris, 1970), pp. 43–59.

[45] One hundred forty thousand acres. The total cultivated area in the Bouches du Rhône and the Vaucluse was 201,000 hectares (excluding olive groves and vines). Since I was concerned with output that could be increased by irrigation, I excluded both olives and vines from my measure of total cultivated area. J.-A. Barral, *Les Irrigations dans le Vaucluse* (Paris, 1876), pp. 323–34; idem, *Les Irrigations dans les Bouches du Rhône*, pp. 83–87, 511–12.

TABLE 3
INCREASES IN AREA IRRIGATED FROM THE DURANCE
(in hectares)

Region	Periods 1100–1700	1700–1789	1790–1820	1820–1860
Vaucluse	3,835	2,253	0	9,105
Bouches du Rhône	10,624	1,765	0	8,211
Total	14,459	4,108	0	16,316

Sources: See Appendix text; Jean-Auguste Barral, *Les Irrigations dans le Vaucluse* (Paris, 1876), pp. 323–34; and Jean-Auguste Barral, *Les Irrigations dans les Bouches du Rhône* (Paris, 1875), vol. 1, pp. 86–91, 511–12.

as Durance irrigation. Since irrigation at least doubled output we know that the increase in output will be close to the ratio of newly irrigated area to total cultivated area. The early nineteenth-century canals added 16,314 hectares of irrigated land from the Durance compared with 3,211 for the eighteenth century as a whole. The Durance's increase alone would have led to a 7.7 percent increase in total output for Provence. If non-Durance irrigation witnessed the same growth, total output would have increased by about 12 percent.

LAND PRICES

Sampling and Sorting

At least four notarial *études* (practices) were active in Cavaillon between 1700 and 1855. However, gathering data from all land contracts for Cavaillon from 1700 to 1855 would have taken at least two years' research. Sampling was therefore necessary. The data represent a complete, quinquennial sample of both land-sale and land-rental contracts from one *étude* from 1700 to 1855. Up to 1720 I sampled two *études* because the first had too few land contracts. The total sample contains 1,781 observations. To obtain both an irrigated- and a dry-land price series, it was necessary to distinguish sales and rental of irrigated land. Before 1800 such sorting was relatively easy since the contracts all contained detailed information about the quality of the land. After 1800, however, notaries ceased recording such information regularly. I therefore relied on location data to distinguish between irrigated and dry land after 1800. Such sorting by location is imperfect, making the irrigated series a downward-biased estimate of irrigated land prices and the dry series an upward-biased estimate of the price of dry land after 1800.

Constructing the Series

The land prices were estimated with a simple procedure that allowed me to use data both from rental contracts that predominated before 1789 and from sales contracts that predominated after the Revolution. For rental contracts the value of a transaction was computed by capitalizing the rent using the interest rate. Such a procedure ignores capital gains; thus the price series for dry and irrigated land will be downward-biased. If anything this will reduce the absolute value of the difference in these prices, which will bring down the estimated rates of return. For sales, the value of land was simply the price. For each year for each type of land (dry or irrigated), average prices were

TABLE 4
PRICE SERIES FOR PROVENCE, 1700–1855

	Daily Wages (unfed, in francs)		Land Prices (in francs per hectare)	
Date	Unskilled	Skilled	Dry	Irrigated
1700	0.61	1.00	511	2,153
1705	0.77	0.90	814	2,730
1710	0.76	1.07	1,080	2,201
1715	0.74	1.00	851	2,819
1720	0.75	1.00	1,510	2,590
1725	0.74	1.12	939	2,297
1730	0.79	1.11	1,031	2,202
1735	0.76	1.22	1,598	2,407
1740	0.73	1.10	1,320	2,355
1745	0.92	1.25	1,538	2,477
1750	0.88	1.14	1,827	2,694
1755	0.94	1.25	1,827	2,694
1760	0.76	1.30	1,934	2,857
1765	0.93	1.25	1,410	2,867
1770	1.09	1.25	2,361	3,854
1775	1.12	1.60	2,081	3,055
1780	1.12	1.50	2,203	5,003
1785	1.18	1.50	1,604	4,328
1790	1.14	1.50	2,756	3,271
1795			4,365	6,309
1800	1.66	2.41	1,910	2,963
1805	1.15	2.24	2,044	5,438
1810	1.59	2.16	2,698	4,097
1815	1.61	2.43	2,640	3,831
1820	1.78	2.27	2,420	3,677
1825	1.74	2.22	2,985	5,100
1830	1.73	3.18	2,590	4,411
1835	1.89	3.00	2,450	4,469
1840	1.78	2.60	2,399	5,149
1845	1.77	3.00	2,621	5,192
1850	1.88	3.00	2,679	5,400
1855	1.86	3.00	2,900	5,470

Sources: See text, fn. 13, and the Appendix text.

calculated for each type of contract as the sum of the value of all transactions divided by the total area sold.

WAGES

The sample contains 851 bills of wages for 13 professions, covering roughly 150 years for a total of over 60,000 man-days. The bills were sorted into skilled and unskilled and the reported wages are the ratio of the total wage bill for a given year divided by the total number of days worked. To the extent that canals were built solely in the winter—when wages were lower than average—the rates of return would be even higher than estimated. Yet since winter and summer wages seem to move in tandem, the trends in the wage bills should not depend on the aggregation procedure. Since we care most about the trend in benefit-cost ratios, the procedure used here seems adequate. Table 4 presents both wage and land prices.

TABLE 5
HYPOTHETICAL BENEFIT-COST RATIOS FOR IRRIGATION PROJECTS

Date	Cabedan-Neuf I	Cabedan-Neuf II	Crillon	Plan-Oriental	Carpentras
1700	3.85	3.20	3.66	3.82	3.13
1705	4.01	3.45	3.91	4.34	3.33
1710	2.06	1.83	2.06	2.27	1.75
1715	3.96	3.42	3.88	4.24	3.30
1720	1.91	1.80	1.99	2.29	1.71
1725	2.57	2.24	2.53	2.74	2.17
1730	2.14	1.88	2.12	2.32	1.82
1735	1.29	1.20	1.34	1.49	1.14
1740	1.82	1.67	1.87	2.07	1.59
1745	1.08	0.92	1.04	1.23	0.88
1750	1.30	1.23	1.36	1.58	1.16
1755	1.22	1.14	1.27	1.45	1.07
1760	1.33	1.28	1.42	1.60	1.20
1765	2.24	2.02	2.26	2.53	1.93
1770	1.96	1.92	2.11	2.48	1.78
1775	1.15	1.06	1.18	1.33	1.01
1780	3.31	3.10	3.44	3.93	2.92
1785	3.43	3.04	3.42	3.82	2.92
1790	0.56	0.55	0.60	0.70	0.51
1795					
1800	0.87	0.75	0.85	0.92	0.70
1805	3.02	2.65	3.00	3.27	2.49
1810	1.19	1.09	1.22	1.37	1.02
1815	0.95	0.85	0.96	1.06	0.80
1820	1.03	0.91	1.03	1.14	0.86
1825	1.71	1.57	1.75	1.99	1.49
1830	1.29	1.14	1.28	1.37	1.10
1835	1.46	1.27	1.44	1.55	1.24
1840	2.18	1.92	2.16	2.36	1.86
1845	1.88	1.67	1.87	2.02	1.62
1850	1.92	1.69	1.91	2.07	1.63
1855	1.81	1.62	1.82	1.98	1.57

Sources: Tables 1 and 2.

CANAL CONSTRUCTION ACCOUNTS

Number of Man-Days

Canal construction accounts rarely itemized costs beyond excavation (*terrassement*) and skilled construction (*ouvrages d'arts*). As the former was done by unskilled labor, I divided those costs by the wage for unskilled labor for the period in which the project was carried out to get an an estimate of the quantity of labor employed. To simplify the calculation of the rates of return, I assigned all skilled construction and administrative costs to skilled labor. Skilled construction involved the building of bridges for roads over canals and aqueducts for canals over small rivers and valleys. Such jobs were clearly the domain of skilled masons. Nonlabor inputs were also assigned to skilled labor, because the primary input of canals other than labor was quarried stone. Quarrying was an extractive industry that required only skilled labor and some transportation. Thus the cost of quarried stone should closely follow the price of skilled labor. The sum of nonlabor inputs, skilled labor, and administrative expenses was divided by the skilled wage to get an estimate for the number of skilled man-days.

TABLE 6
HYPOTHETICAL INTERNAL RATES OF RETURN FOR IRRIGATION PROJECTS

Date	Cabedan-Neuf I	Cabedan-Neuf II	Crillon	Plan-Oriental	Carpentras	Interest Rate
1700	157.5%	84.6%	120.4%	156.1%	50.1%	5.36%
1705	166.0	102.4	127.2	185.0	54.1	5.15
1710	77.9	35.4	68.8	94.3	30.1	5.30
1715	157.3	93.2	121.0	173.0	51.5	5.30
1720	61.3	27.9	58.2	86.5	25.8	4.62
1725	95.5	45.0	80.5	105.0	34.8	4.62
1730	77.3	32.4	67.6	89.4	29.2	4.94
1735	25.3	−3.7	27.6	41.3	10.2	4.94
1740	55.6	19.0	52.3	71.3	22.7	4.90
1745	35.5	3.1	35.8	50.9	14.4	4.90
1750	26.7	−0.8	29.6	47.5	11.3	5.51
1755	21.4	−6.7	24.1	38.8	8.3	5.51
1760	32.6	6.0	35.7	57.5	14.7	5.04
1765	88.5	47.1	77.6	111.0	34.4	5.04
1770	64.0	35.9	62.1	98.4	28.7	5.03
1775	17.1	−11.1	19.6	32.6	5.8	5.03
1780	127.1	85.3	106.7	164.2	48.0	5.01
1785	138.5	84.7	111.2	161.0	48.5	5.01
1790	−36.3	−53.4	−44.2	−24.0	31.2	6.87
1795						
1800	−6.9	−36.5	−12.1	−0.9	10.8	9.30
1805	93.5	39.8	77.8	98.6	32.8	8.70
1810	12.7	−17.4	13.4	23.1	2.4	6.15
1815	−7.8	−10.6	−10.2	15.3	−8.3	7.40
1820	17.6	−12.5	18.9	29.9	5.3	6.70
1825	58.4	24.8	55.7	81.5	24.6	5.09
1830	49.7	15.2	47.9	67.8	20.4	5.16
1835	58.9	21.1	54.6	75.4	23.5	4.33
1840	89.3	44.7	77.3	107.4	33.9	4.58
1845	59.2	17.7	53.6	67.4	22.9	3.62
1850	66.6	24.2	59.6	77.1	25.7	3.57
1855	61.4	21.9	56.1	76.2	24.1	4.41

Sources: Tables 1 and 2.

Land Consumed by Canals

The main canal of Carpentras, the largest canal in my sample, was only 7.5 meters wide. Including the embankments, it occupied an area less than 17 meters across for the first quarter of its length. The rest of the main canal occupied an area less than 10 meters wide, and its branches were even smaller. Other canals were less than 4 meters at their widest and their branches were much smaller than that. I assumed that all canals required a band of land 15 meters wide and the length of the canal and its main branches. This simplifying assumption, by reducing the estimated profits, can only strengthen any finding that irrigation was profitable before 1760.[46]

[46] Caillet, *Canal de Carpentras*, pp. 194–212.

Uncounted Revenues

I disregarded certain revenues accruing to canals that are difficult to estimate. These revenues came from the sale of water-power rights on the canal to mill owners. To be sure, mills were an important source of revenues for some canals. They brought in revenues equal to one-sixth of maintenance costs on the canal of Crillon. A mill was worth above 20,000 livres in the eighteenth century or more than 5 percent of the cost of a small canal.[47] The size and value of mills varied greatly. Moreover, the value of a mill is not a good indicator for the rent of the fall, which is what accrues to the canal owner. Therefore one would need not only the rental contracts of the mill but also their agreement with the canal to know what they paid for the fall. The archival research effort to secure rental contracts would thus be very large for little gain. Obviously the omission will push my hypothetical rates of return downward.

Maintenance Costs

Some maintenance costs already appear in the price of irrigated land. Indeed the price of a particular piece of irrigated land is equal to the discounted stream of profits from using that land minus the capitalized value of whatever maintenance costs are assessed on that land. If all irrigated land were assessed uniformly there would be no need to count maintenance costs, but such uniformity was far from prevalent in Cavaillon, where each canal had a different organization dealing with maintenance. Each organization assessed landowners on a yearly basis for contributions, but it did not assess land uniformly, either over time or across parcels. Thus the land price series reflect only maintenance costs as assessed by the institutions governing canals in Cavaillon. It is clearly wrong to assume that the maintenance costs already affecting the irrigated price series are the correct ones for all projects. As a result it seemed best to assume that the price series reflect the discounted future revenues from land and to account for maintenance costs explicitly. To do this, and to simplify the calculation of internal rates of return, I assumed that the promoters created a sinking fund to pay for the future maintenance costs.

[47] AD Vaucluse, I doc. 221. See also AD Vaucluse, S, Usines et Cours d'Eaux (Avignon, canal de Crillon, 1820).

The Real Takeover of the BIA: The Preferential Hiring of Indians

STEVEN J. NOVAK

An early long-running federal social policy experiment was the preferential hiring of American Indians at agencies, reservations, and schools. This government employment was designed to accelerate the assimilation of the natives and to reduce their resistance to education and economic change. Instead, the program inadvertently created a form of dependency. This ironic outcome was due to the power of the natives to shape the policy according to their needs and values.

In November 1972 hundreds of American Indian Movement militants occupied and trashed the Washington, DC, offices of the Bureau of Indian Affairs (BIA). Ironically, at that time the majority of BIA employees, many in positions of power, were of Indian extraction. Just over a decade later, James Watt, President Ronald Reagan's vocal secretary of the Interior, accused Indian bureaucrats of retarding tribal progress in order to retain their positions. He alleged that they were guilty of "keeping this group of people assembled on a desert environment where there are no jobs, no agricultural potential, no water, because if Indians were allowed to be liberated, they'd go and get a job and that guy wouldn't have his handout as a paid government official."[1]

When the government designed the policy of preferential hiring for Indians, it had no intention of keeping thousands of natives on the civil service list. But unexpectedly, today the BIA, the Indian Public Health Service, and Indian schools are the largest source of Indian employment. The 1980 census revealed that a higher proportion of American Indians worked for federal, state, and local government than any other ethnic group.[2] The rise of this Indian bureaucracy, especially the slow infiltration of the BIA, resulted from one of the nation's oldest experiments in social policy: the preferential hiring of Indians. Despite the program's apparent success, it is little known, misunderstood, and rather unappreciated. A look at the historical origins and evolution of Indian preferential hiring suggests that the social policy took ironic twists and began to reflect the goals of its recipients more than those of

The Journal of Economic History, Vol. L, No. 3 (Sept. 1990). ISSN 0022-0507.

Steven J. Novak is an Editor of the Oral History Program, University of California, Los Angeles, CA 90024.

[1] *New York Times*, Jan. 25, 1983, p. 16; see also Jan. 19, 1983, p. 19, and Jan. 26, 1983, p. 13.

[2] In 1980, 29 percent of all employed Indians worked in the public sector, as opposed to 27 percent of blacks, 18 percent of Asian-Americans, and 16 percent of whites; U.S. Bureau of the Census, *General Social and Economic Characteristics of the 1980 Census of Population*, vol. 1, part 1 (Washington, DC, 1983), pp. 99–100.

its creators. In that sense the BIA might be seen as a case of so-called "captive bureaucracy."[3]

The preferential hiring of Indians began as a minor clause in the 1834 act organizing the Department of Indian Affairs (variously called the Indian Office, the Indian Service, and later the BIA). The BIA was created in order to "civilize" the Indians. The migration of Euro-Americans across the continent, spreading disease, usurping the best lands, and depleting game, drove American Indians into death and dependency. Rather than restrain this demographic movement, which was largely outside its control, the government tried to lessen the financial and social costs by negotiating the peaceful transfer of lands and helping the natives adapt to living on leftovers. In exchange for their territory, Indian treaties provided tribes with cash annuities, mills, plows, looms, and the aid of blacksmiths, farmers, teachers, and physicians, usually on a temporary basis. Although almost every tribe had practiced some agriculture, the government's objective was to transform migratory communal huntsmen into settled individualistic farmers requiring no government aid. The focus was on changing the Indian work ethic. Once natives had taken up their yeoman farms, they would be absorbed into white society, regain their independence, and allow the transitional government programs to end. The BIA was meant to be short-lived.[4]

This dream of a rapid transformation proved illusory. The government failed to understand how, with a few exceptions such as the

[3] Recent efforts to explain the poverty of domestic minorities have employed a colonialism model in which the colonizers first rob the subject peoples of their resources and then keep them dependent by strangling them with bureaucracy and appeasement benefits such as welfare, jobs, and schools. For example, Gary Anders likened American Indians who participated in BIA programs to the compradors of the Spanish Empire whose alliance with the conquerors promoted "the interests of the white economy at the expense of the tribe," see Gary C. Anders, "Theories of Underdevelopment and the American Indian," *Journal of Economic Issues*, 14 (Sept. 1980), p. 694; see also Michael K. Brown and Steven P. Erie, "Blacks and the Legacy of the Great Society: The Economic and Political Impact of Federal Social Policy," *Public Policy*, 29 (Summer 1981), pp. 299–329. There are two main problems with using the colonialism model to explain Indian employment in the BIA. First, North American whites had little interest in exploiting Indian labor. Cardell Jacobsen, Matthew Snipp, and Stephen Cornell have pointed out that the U.S. government sought to expropriate the Indian lands but not their labor. The government hoped to handle the Indian peoples as quickly and cheaply as possible; see Cardell K. Jacobsen, "Internal Colonialism and Native Americans: Indian Labor in the United States From 1871 to World War II," *Social Science Quarterly*, 65 (Mar. 1984), pp. 167–68; Matthew Snipp, "The Changing Political and Economic Status of the American Indians: From Captive Nations to Internal Colonies," *American Journal of Economics and Sociology*, 45 (Apr. 1986), p. 151; and Stephen Cornell, *The Return of the Native: American Indian Political Resurgence* (New York, 1988), pp. 28, 30, 54. Second, the colonialism model stresses the power of the colonizer and minimizes the strength of the colonized, when in some instances colonizers are not omnipotent or colonized totally impotent.

[4] On Indian policy, see Francis Paul Prucha, *The Great Father: The United States Government and the American Indian*, 2 vols. (Lincoln, NE, 1984); Brian W. Dipple, *The Vanishing Americans: White Attitudes and U.S. Indian Policy* (Middletown, CT, 1982); and Robert F. Berkhofer, Jr., *The White Man's Indian: From Columbus to the Present* (New York, 1977).

Cherokee and Creek, the powerful Indian culture would cause natives to resist the civilization program. Though they readily accepted annuities, advisers, and goods, most of them refused to break up their tribes or to rely on the plow exclusively. Sioux Chief Big Eagle complained that "the whites were always trying to make the Indians give up their life and live like white men—go to farming, work hard and do as they did—and the Indians did not know how to do that, and did not want to anyway." Indian identity was closely tied to the means of subsistence. With a thousand-year-old culture, Indians saw no need to change. Natives were perceived as lazy because they did not work like whites. Indians had communal premodern values; they tended to labor in groups and to share the fruits of their labor. Arapaho artist Carl Sweezy explained that "it took years to learn to settle down on a farm and work alone and see one's neighbors only once in a while. Neither we nor our dogs nor our ponies understood this new way of the white people. To us it seemed unsociable and lonely, and not the way people were meant to live."[5]

Indians worked in spurts, alternating bursts of intense effort with long periods of leisure. Lacking means of storing or transporting a surplus, Indians only produced what they could immediately use. Work was a means to an end rather than an end in itself. Sweezy said, "white people . . . . thought we were all lazy . . . . because we took a different attitude toward time than theirs. We enjoyed time; they measured it." Indians tended to be risk averse and to prefer a diversified economy. Rather than put all their eggs in one basket, they planted, hunted, trapped, fished, gathered, and harvested, each in due course. They garnered immediate results from their work, distrusting postponed gratification. Sex roles were also strictly defined. Though there were areas of overlap—men might break the ground, women dress the skins and butcher the kill—in general the men hunted and the women farmed. That was what had worked best over the centuries, and to ignore these norms was to invite disaster. In 1853 the Potawatomie agent reported how Indian traditionalists vandalized the agency's model farm: "early in the spring a few commenced ploughing; the chiefs sent their braves into the field, cut up their harness, broke ploughs, and whipped them out, saying that they had disgraced themselves, the women alone should work." Unfortunately, the government's civilization program flew in the face of almost all these Indian values.[6]

[5] Quoted in Return I. Holcomb, ed., "A Sioux Story of the War," *Minnesota Historical Collections*, 6 (1894), p. 384; and Carl Sweezy, *The Arapaho Way: A Memoir of an Indian Boyhood*, edited by Althea Bass (New York, 1966), p. 38.

[6] Sweezy, *The Arapaho Way*, pp. 17–19, 27–29; Luther Standing Bear wrote that "because the Indian was unable, and in some cases refused, to accept completely the white man's ways which were so contrary to his heritage and tradition, he earned for himself the reputation of being lazy," *Land of the Spotted Eagle* (Lincoln, NE, 1978; 1st edn., 1933), pp. 166, 168; and *Annual Report for the Commissioner of Indian Affairs for 1853* [hereafter cited as *Annual Report*] (Washington, DC,

As they lost faith in Indian adults, government officials and reformers turned their hopes to the rising generation of youths. But again they were quickly disappointed as Indian students became known for high absenteeism and slow progress. When the graduates of boarding schools came home, they often succumbed to peer pressure and "returned to the blanket"—reverted to Indian ways.[7] Teachers felt that young Indians had ability but lacked motivation, and that graduates needed a way to use their education in order to apply themselves. Stephen Riggs, who taught the Sioux, observed that "education is not valued as it ought to be, even by those who have learned to read, and one reason undoubtedly is, that it has not been brought into use. The 'Cui bono' is not yet understood by them." Riggs and other officials urged the government to reward returned students by helping them find jobs.[8]

About this time, the government, for obscure reasons, took its first short step toward employing native Americans. Section 9 of the 1834 Reorganization Act declared that in the appointment of interpreters, blacksmiths, teachers, and other agency personnel "a preference shall be given to persons of Indian descent, if such can be found, who are properly qualified for the execution of the duties." The rationale behind Section 9 was not explained, but it seems to be that the government hoped to speed assimilation. Agency employment would spur effort and prevent a return to the blanket. In 1835 President Andrew Jackson glibly minimized the hardships entailed by Indian removal, arguing that Section 9 would serve as a "stimulus for exertion."[9]

It is extremely hard to ascertain the effects of Section 9 in the early years. Its administration was left to the local Indian agents who were ordered to list annually their native employees, though the published documents of the Indian Office took little note of the data. A thorough search of the personnel lists and letters in the *Annual Reports* of the

---

1853), p. 324. Further examples of Indian resistance to the civilization program are in *Annual Report 1841*, pp. 401, 336; and T. W. Davenport, "Recollections of an Indian Agent," *Oregon Historical Quarterly*, 8 (Mar. 1907), p. 5.

[7] Ronald N. Satz, *American Indian Policy in the Jacksonian Era* (Lincoln, NE, 1975), pp. 258–78. Federal records are full of complaints such as that of the Quapaw agent in 1852 that "all who have been educated at this school, except the present United States interpreter, have resumed all their original habits," *Annual Report 1852*, p. 395.

[8] Riggs quoted in *Annual Report 1858*, p. 537. For added remarks on the need for employment assistance, see the following *Annual Reports: 1842*, p. 509; *1845*, p. 521; *1846*, pp. 264, 334; *1851*, p. 381; *1852*, p. 395; *1855*, p. 497; and *1858*, p. 491.

[9] Francis Paul Prucha, ed., *Documents of United States Indian Policy* (Lincoln, NE, 1975), pp. 70, 72. On the hopes raised by Section 9, see *Annual Report 1833*, pp. 169–70; *1834*, pp. 241, 262–63; and *1835*, p. 283.

commissioner of Indian Affairs has revealed that at least 253 natives worked for the BIA before the Civil War.[10]

Most of the Indians employed at agencies and reservations held one of three positions: 40 percent were blacksmiths, 28 percent interpreters, and 24 percent teachers. They were paid the same as whites, which indicates that their hiring was not an economy move. The 1850 salary scale was $480 for blacksmiths, $300 for interpreters, and $500 for teachers—fairly low for whites but high for Indians. Although there was rapid turnover of both races, at least 50 natives held their positions for over a year.

The program was small at first; a couple of hundred participants was merely a drop in the bucket compared to the thousands of needy Indians. The BIA itself was miniscule, numbering only 358 employees altogether in 1859. Despite its small size, the program worked; being placed on the payroll altered the outlook of an Indian. Federal agents marveled that the natives preferred to work for wages than to farm for themselves. John Foreman, the government farmer for the Sac and Fox, frustrated by having shown them how to farm to no avail, advised that the only way to get the Indians to work was to hire them as farm hands "even if at an extravagant price." Philander Prescott, the farmer for the Santee Sioux, repeatedly hit the same stumbling block: "ask the man why he does not assist the work, the answer generally is, 'Will you pay me for it?'" Section 9 had the effect of increasing acceptance of the civilization program.[11]

What federal work might mean to an individual Indian may be seen in the career of Andrew Jackson Blackbird, an Ottawa. In 1840 he was appointed as apprentice blacksmith at the Chippewa agency by John Johnstone, a native himself. Blackbird arrived in Grand Traverse at the center of a controversy.

> [The Chippewa] were getting up remonstrances and petitioning the Government against my appointment, setting forth as reason for their complaint that I did not belong to that tribe of Indians, and was therefore not entitled to the position, and they would rather have one of their own boys belonging to the tribe put to the trade. But my friend

[10] Besides the *Annual Reports* of the commissioner of Indian Affairs, after 1834 the secretary of War published a somewhat less useful list of "Persons Employed in the Indian Department." To my knowledge the BIA never published a memorandum on the effects of Section 9 preferential hiring. My compilation required judgments about the ethnicity of the employees. Sometimes their Indian name is obvious (Wah-pe-ka-no-sho-may, a Menominee blacksmith of 1847), or the name might be translated (Jerry Crow, a Seneca blacksmith that same year). For natives with Anglicized names, race or tribe might be given in parentheses. Thus the 1839 personnel list contained Choctaw teacher "T. McKenny (native)" and interpreter "James Vallier (a Quapaw)." Place of birth is another clue, as with the 1855 interpreters Joseph W. Bourassa, born in "Pottawatomie nation," and Baptiste Peoria, nativity "Indian country."

[11] Foreman quoted in *Annual Report 1845*, p. 487; and Prescott in *1850*, p. 119. For further observations on the impact of governmental wages, see the following *Annual Reports*: *1834*, pp. 238, 255; *1839*, p. 84; *1842*, pp. 412, 436; *1845*, p. 579; *1851*, p. 347; *1855*, p. 86; *1857*, p. 404; and *1859*, p. 95.

Johnstone told me 'not to mind anything, but to go about my business. The blacksmith shop had been established here for more than two years, and they should have thought of putting their boy in the shop long before this.'

Blackbird served as an apprentice from 1840 to 1845 at $240 a year. After working his way through school as a journeyman blacksmith, he ended up as a federal interpreter and postmaster. Far from being mollified, he was mobilized by public service. He became a lifelong activist who successfully lobbied to win citizenship for Michigan Indians in the state constitution of 1850.[12] Apparently Blackbird's Chippewa critics also learned a lesson about the possibilities of Section 9. In their next treaty the tribe was allowed "to employ their own farmers, mechanics, and teachers."[13]

After the Civil War the remaining western tribes were subdued one by one and government responsibility increased. As before, officials tried to turn the natives into farmers. The failure of Washington's plan left it begrudgingly feeding 100,000 Indians. Although it anticipated giving temporary support, quite often its rations "had to continue indefinitely, for the conversion to agriculture came slowly if at all." Without a constructive role to play, "large numbers of the formerly energetic and aggressive warriors became enervated dispirited recipients of the dole."[14]

Rather than revise its plans, the BIA redoubled efforts. In the late nineteenth century the government and social reformers intensified the civilization program. In 1875 Indians were included in the Homestead Act and allowed to stake 160-acre claims if they left the reservation and renounced their tribe.[15] When few took advantage of this bounty, Congress passed the ill-fated Dawes Act of 1887 which authorized President Grover Cleveland to divide tribal lands into 160-acre allotments which Indian families would farm as private property.[16] Millions of acres of remaining tribal lands were then sold to outsiders as surplus. In theory private property was supposed to unleash Indian enterprise, but in practice few earned enough to live on their allotments. Many tried to lease or sell their land. Far from being enriched, the tribes whose lands were allotted were further impoverished.

[12] Andrew Jackson Blackbird, *History of the Ottawa and Chippewa Indians of Michigan* (Ypsilanti, MI, 1887), pp. 56, 59–70.

[13] Charles J. Kappler, ed., *Indian Treaties, 1778–1883* (Washington, DC, 1904), p. 689. By the 1840s several tribes tried to place members in agency positions. See *Annual Reports*: *1840*, p. 480; *1845*, p. 502; *1847*, pp. 912–13; *1848*, p. 474; and *1849*, p. 1054.

[14] Prucha, *The Great Father*, vol. 2, p. 656. The BIA's long struggle to transform Indians into farmers is analyzed in R. Douglas Hurt, *Indian Agriculture in America, Prehistory to the Present* (Lawrence, KS, 1987). Although natives farmed both before and after government programs, Hurt concludes that federal efforts failed because they were tried on infertile lands and because they "required too great a cultural change," p. 233.

[15] Alice C. Fletcher, *Indian Education and Civilization* (Washington, DC, 1888), p. 137.

[16] D. S. Otis, *The Dawes Act and the Allotment of Indian Lands*, edited by Francis Paul Prucha (Norman, OK, 1973); and Leonard A. Carlson, *Indians, Bureaucrats, and Land: The Dawes Act and the Decline of Indian Farming* (Westport, CT, 1981).

Congress also expanded the Indian school system and added the first compulsory attendance laws for Indians. Between 1880 and 1900 the number of Indian schools almost doubled to 307, while daily attendance quadrupled to 21,568. Congress also created special off-reservation training institutes where Indian youths could acquire the vocational skills demanded by an urban-industrial economy. Hampton Institute took its first Indian pupils in 1878; the next year Richard Pratt opened Carlisle Institute. By 1890 there were over 2,000 Indians enrolled in seven institutes at an annual cost of $300,000. With their heavy emphasis on jobs, the schools inaugurated the so-called outing system in which Indian pupils spent their summers working for the local whites. Congress felt sure that with all this aid the natives would soon be on their feet again.[17]

But the vocational schools continued to confront the nagging problem of what would become of their graduates. Critics complained that many students, like those before them, simply went back to the reservation and donned the proverbial blanket. On March 11, 1886, four congressmen attacked the appropriation for the BIA on these grounds. Representative Joseph Cannon claimed that "the Indian children educated at Carlisle, Hampton, and elsewhere off the reservation, *who were not given employment by the Government*, at a very early period lapse into barbarism."[18]

Supporters of the institutes rallied to their defense with statistics showing that many of the graduates had found useful careers. However, their data actually substantiated the high correlation between the acculturation of educated Indians and their employment by the government. In 1886 almost one-third of the graduates from Hampton and two-thirds of those from Carlisle who were employed at all worked for the federal government. Helen Ludlow, who taught Indians at Hampton, pointed out that there were two ways to view this correlation. Why apologize for the failure of the schools rather than applaud the success of preferential hiring? Federal Indian employees retained the lifestyle and skills they acquired in the schools. On the other hand, congressmen

[17] See *Annual Reports*: *1891*, pp. 57–59; *1892*, pp. 156–58; *1907*, p. 45; and David Wallace Adams, "From Bullets to Boarding Schools: The Educational Assault on the American Indian Identity," in Philip Weeks, ed., *The American Indian Experience* (Arlington Heights, IL, 1988), pp. 218–39. For general background on this phase of policy, see Henry F. Fritz, *The Movement for Indian Assimilation, 1860–1890* (Philadelphia, 1963); Loring Benson Priest, *Uncle Sam's Stepchildren: The Reformation of United States Indian Policy, 1865–1887* (New Brunswick, NJ, 1942); Francis Paul Prucha, *American Indian Policy in Crisis: Christian Reformers and the Indian, 1865–1900* (Norman, OK, 1976); and Frederick E. Hoxie, *A Final Promise: The Campaign to Assimilate the Indians, 1880–1920* (Lincoln, NE, 1984).

[18] *Congressional Record*, 49th Cong., 1st sess. (1886), vol. 17, part 4, pp. 2268, 2272, 2305–13, emphasis added. Cannon's colleague William Holman echoed his sentiment, "unless the Government gives to the Indian girl or boy employment, in other words, unless they are supported by the Government, they relapse into barbarism when they return to the tribe."

TABLE 1
BUREAU OF INDIAN AFFAIRS PERSONNEL

Year	Indians	Total	Indian Share
1892	1,932	4,453	43%
1909	1,920	4,746	40
1927	1,700	5,000	34
1934	2,100	6,500	32
1940	3,000	5,000	60
1970	8,282	15,523	53
1980	13,602	17,438	78
1990	11,841	14,232	83

Sources: *Annual Report 1892*, pp. 95–97, 818–75; *Annual Report 1909*, p. 91; *Annual Report 1927*, pp. 16, 56; Wilcomb E. Washburn, ed., *The American Indian and the United States: A Documentary History*, 4 vols. (New York, 1973), vol. 3, p. 1966; *Annual Report 1941*, p. 439; Sar A. Levitan and Barbara Hetrick, *Big Brother's Indian Programs—With Reservations* (New York, 1971), p. 157; Francis Paul Prucha, *The Great Father: The United States Government and the American Indian*, 2 vols. (Lincoln, NE, 1984), vol. 2, p. 1126; and telephone interview, U.S. Department of Equal Employment Opportunity, Bureau of Indian Affairs, Jan. 24, 1990.

and no doubt most Americans of that day did not want the Indians rewarded with public service jobs.[19]

Despite such opposition, the number of Indians employed by the BIA rose dramatically. The commissioners' annual reports began to include occasional personnel summaries which listed the workers by race and showed impressive gains by the Indians. Although most of the natives were at the bottom of the ladder, by 1892 almost 2,000 Indians worked for the BIA, over 40 percent of the whole. This is not surprising considering that the law continued to require the preferential hiring of natives. For instance, Section 232 of the 1880 code said that "no work must be given white men which can be done by Indians." The 1909 *Annual Report* explained that "Indians are given the preference to all positions in the Indian Service which they are competent to fill." Despite the law, it seems that the proportion of Indians in the BIA actually declined around the turn of the century. Table 1 indicates that the proportion fell from 43 percent in 1892 to 32 percent in 1934. Though the law mandated Indian preference, this was checked by three countervailing trends.[20]

First, the BIA personnel were increasingly stratified by skill. Whereas much of the late nineteenth-century growth was in relatively semiskilled

[19] Herbert Welsh, *Are the Eastern Industrial Training Schools for Indian Children a Failure?* (Philadelphia, 1886), pp. 9–12, 14, 36; also R. H. Pratt, *Seventh Annual Report of the Carlisle Indian School* (Carlisle, 1886); and Helen Ludlow, *Twenty-Two Years Work of the Hampton Normal and Agricultural Institute* (Hampton, 1893), p. 488.

[20] Prucha, *The Great Father*, vol. 2, p. 719; and *Annual Report 1909*, p. 6. For similar provisions, see Karl A. Funke, "Educational Assistance and Employment Preference: Who is an Indian?" *American Indian Law Review*, 4 (Jan. 1976), pp. 1–45; and Kevin N. Anderson, "Indian Employment Preference: Legal Foundations and Limitations," *Tulsa Law Journal*, 15 (Summer 1980), pp. 733–71.

TABLE 2
BUREAU OF INDIAN AFFAIRS PERSONNEL BY RACE AND SKILL

Year	Skill	Indians	Total	Indian Share
1888	Blue Collar	1,376	1,931	71%
1888	White Collar	218	857	25
1909	Blue Collar	1,479	2,532	58
1909	White Collar	441	2,214	20

Note: In the original documents, the 1909 list contained reservation judges and police, but the 1888 list did not. For the sake of consistency, I added to the 1888 figures the judges and police in 1892, the nearest date available. There is no reason to think that this was significantly different.
Sources: *Annual Report 1888*, pp. xx–xxi; *Annual Report 1892*, p. 95; and *Annual Report 1909*, p. 91.

positions such as police, cooks, seamstresses, laundry workers, and laborers, in the early twentieth century the demand shifted to professionals—clerks, teachers, principals, superintendents, physicians, and nurses (see Table 2). It was difficult for natives to qualify for such positions. From 1888 to 1909, 69 percent of the new positions in the BIA were in white-collar fields, but Indians accounted for only 18 percent of the gain.[21]

Second, qualifying was even harder after 1891 when the BIA was included in the new civil service system, forcing natives to compete for positions by taking tests. The goal of civil service reform was to eliminate corruption and raise standards, but it also threatened to undermine Indian hiring and cost hundreds of natives their jobs. Luther Standing Bear, a Sioux teacher thrown out of work, recalled the change bitterly:

> [In] 1894 word came that the Government were [sic] going to hold civil service examinations for all teachers. It really was not necessary for the primary education of the smaller Indian children. I had proved this by holding competitions between my own scholars and those taught by the white teachers . . . . Soon afterward, many white people were sent out from the East to teach our schools . . . . While they knew quite a bit about book-learning, and could pass the civil service examinations, that was about the extent of their knowledge.

Some natives passed the tests, of course, while some whites failed. But the mere existence of the tests deterred some Indian applicants. The Pawnee agent reported that "a number of our Indians are holding positions in the Indian Service. There are others who would like similar

[21] In the late nineteenth century the entire American society went through a broad shift toward white-collar work. See Burton J. Bledstein, *The Culture of Professionalism: The Middle Class and the Development of Higher Education in America* (New York, 1976). Indians had some new career opportunities as in the 1870s part-time Indian judges and police were hired on reservations; see William T. Hagan, *Indian Police and Judges: Experiments in Acculturation and Control* (New Haven, 1966). After the Civil War the U.S. Army hired hundreds of Indian scouts; see Thomas W. Dunlay, *Wolves for the Blue Soldiers: Indian Scouts and Auxiliaries with the United States Army, 1860–90* (Lincoln, NE, 1982).

employment, but hesitate to take the necessary civil service examinations. Some have tried the examinations and failed."[22]

The third constraint was the rising concern of top BIA officials that preferential hiring of Indians was not turning out as planned. The government had expected public service positions to serve as an avenue to self-employment or private sector work, but the Indians seemed to regard the federal jobs as sufficient in themselves. Two turn-of-the-century Indian Affairs commissioners worried about this development. They realized that the BIA had few openings, that it existed at the whim of Congress, that the policy of preferential hiring might be reversed, and that public employment continued the Indian dependence on the government. Thomas Morgan, commissioner from 1889 to 1893, and Francis Leupp, from 1904 to 1909, accepted the Social Darwinist assumption that Indians had to learn to compete. Morgan warned returning students that if they were "unable or unwilling to sustain themselves, they must go to the wall" (face starvation). Likewise, Leupp avowed that Indians had to "stand on their own feet like other men."[23] They urged the Indians to leave the reservations, go where the work was, and not expect it to come to them. Morgan promoted the outing system; Leupp created an employment bureau in 1905. Neither of these programs, however, was very successful. Most of the private sector jobs they found were for unskilled low-paid migrant farm hands and maids. Indian participants not only suffered loneliness and culture shock but often barely earned enough to cover their expenses.[24]

Despite these three constraints—stratification, civil service, and misgivings—the preferential hiring of Indians received a boost from other government officials who realized that it was a vital prop to Indian schools and indeed to the entire civilization program. The Social Darwinism of Morgan and Leupp was politically unpalatable: if returning Indian school graduates lacked the chance to work for the government, they would not be magically transformed into entrepreneurs but rather sink into unemployment. This would fuel the outcry that the money for their schooling had been wasted. Thus the civil service rules were relaxed. Loopholes were placed in the laws so that an Indian could qualify for BIA employment by passing a noncompetitive test, earning

[22] Luther Standing Bear, *My People the Sioux* (New York, 1928), pp. 239, 241; and "Unpublished Annual Report 1910," National Archives, Record Group 75, M1011, reel 100, p. 4.

[23] *Annual Report 1891*, p. 7; and *1905*, pp. 4–5; see also, *1892*, pp. 94–97. On the commissioners, see Robert M. Kvasnicka, et al., *The Commissioners of Indian Affairs, 1824–1977* (Lincoln, NE, 1979), pp. 193–203, 221–32.

[24] Robert A. Trennert, "Educating Indian Girls at Nonreservation Boarding Schools, 1878–1920," *The Western Historical Quarterly*, 13 (July 1982), pp. 271–90, 288; Robert A. Trennert, "From Carlisle to Phoenix: The Rise and Fall of the Indian Outing System, 1878–1930," *Pacific Historical Review*, 52 (Aug. 1983), pp. 267–91, 277; and Hoxie, *A Final Promise*, pp. 201–7.

an institute diploma, or being bilingual.[25] Commissioner Robert Valentine, Leupp's successor, re-emphasized preferential hiring. By "the employing of Indians in the service," he said, "the department is only supplementing the work of the schools and furthering its policy of educating the Indians in a broad and practical way." It was a mistake to divorce education from employment.[26]

There is no doubt that finding work for the graduates was a major boon to Indian schools. Hervey Peairs, the superintendent of Haskell Institute, frowned on his students taking federal jobs but had to admit that when they got them it increased the applications from their tribesmen:

> [W]herever the graduates are employed the Indians become more friendly to schools and more ready to put their children in school. [In 1900] 110 ex-Haskell students were employed in the agency and school service, and as a result Haskell was flooded with applicants for enrollment, especially from vicinities where those graduates were located.[27]

In other words, preferential hiring let Indians see the benefit of school. Likewise, the superintendent of Pierre School in South Dakota reported that his Sioux graduates "are scattered throughout the Northwestern Agencies and they are good boosters for Pierre." Education and eventual employment were inextricably linked.[28]

Yet critics such as Morgan, Leupp, and later Watt had a point: there was something paradoxical about this social program. The BIA was meant to dissolve once the natives regained their independence, and government officials always dreamed that it was near its end. In 1913 the secretary of the Interior prayed that "the Indian Bureau should be a vanishing bureau."[29] In 1946 Congressman George Schwabe promised "to get rid of the Indian Bureau as fast as possible." Schwabe was one of the architects of the post-World War II termination program which settled thousands of natives in cities and then tried to cut off federal

[25] U.S. Department of Interior, *Federal Indian Law* (Washington, DC, 1958), pp. 532–39; U.S. Civil Service Commission, *Tables Showing the Number of Persons Not Under Civil Service* (Washington, DC, 1933); and *Annual Report 1941*, p. 440, which declared that "the Civil Service will exact no standard or requirement of Indians of one-fourth or more of Indian blood."

[26] *Annual Report 1912*, pp. 41–42. On Valentine, see Kvasnicka, *Commissioners of Indian Affairs*, pp. 233–42.

[27] *Annual Report 1901*, p. 537; Loretto Mary Granzer examined Haskell students seeking federal exploymemt in "Indian Education at Haskell Institute, 1884–1937" (M.A. thesis, University of Nebraska, 1937), pp. 241–52. A sociologist tracking Haskell graduates in the 1920s found that two-thirds of those employed held government positions. See Frank Wilson Blackmar, "The Socialization of the American Indian," *American Journal of Sociology*, 34 (Jan. 1929), pp. 657, 659.

[28] "Unpublished Annual Report 1914," National Archives, Record Group 75, M1011, reel 104, pp. 2–3.

[29] Hoxie, *A Final Promise*, pp. 173, 179.

funds to their tribes.[30] But termination was not a panacea, and the BIA persisted. By an odd twist, the BIA had become a self-perpetuating bureaucracy, at least partly because preferential hiring had made it essential to the Indians.

The need for continuation of the bureau arose in part because government hiring undermined Indian farming. A good illustration of this is what happened in the early twentieth century when the government undertook irrigation projects in the west, in order to bring water to arid reservations to help the natives farm. A 1908 provision specified that on Bureau of Reclamation projects "as far as possible Indian labor shall be employed."[31] But to build the dams, Indians neglected their ranches and farms. In 1914 the Crow agent noted that "there is much less land in cultivation now than there was eight to fifteen years ago . . . . I am told that employing Indians on the irrigation project at good wages . . . was the beginning of the decline of agricultural work."[32] In 1929 the agent for the Kaibab Indians reported that their progress in public works was offset by their abandonment of ranching: "they are clamoring to dispose of their herds and devote their time to manual labor."[33] In terms of the government's overall strategy, preferential hiring seemed counterproductive. The government was getting the Indians to work, but not the work it wanted.

The fact is that, given their meager alternatives, many Indians preferred to work for the BIA or other federal agencies. There were both economic and cultural reasons for this choice. Most Indian reservations were at remote undeveloped sites which offered few employment options. An official wrote from Minnesota in 1900 that "the Indians have been without work except what little could be given them at this agency."[34] According to a South Dakota agent in 1892, "the few positions authorized at the agencies which the Indians are competent to fill are eagerly sought after by them."[35] One reason Indians preferred agency jobs was that it allowed them to work together and preserve their communities. The Oregon superintendent of schools reported:

> [T]he one cry of these Indians is for shops and trades for their children, but they want them right here . . . . All of these people are industrious, anxious to work for wages, and clamorous for the few jobs the Government has to offer.[36]

[30] Donald L. Fixico, *Termination and Relocation: Federal Indian Policy, 1945–1960* (Albuquerque, 1987), pp. 16, 32.

[31] Department of the Interior, *Manual of the United States Reclamation Service* (Washington, DC, 1911), pp. 500, 499–512.

[32] "Unpublished Annual Report 1914," pp. 25–26.

[33] "Unpublished Annual Report 1929," National Archives, Record Group 75, M1011, reel 97, p. 15.

[34] *Annual Report 1900*, p. 258.

[35] *Annual Report 1892*, p. 433.

[36] *Annual Report 1901*, p. 356.

It also seems that government employment was less risky, better paying, and more prestigious than farming or outside manual labor. The Apache school superintendent wrote from Arizona in 1904 that "we are making effort to have our boys and girls see and feel that there is as much dignity in the labor of the farmer and stock grower as there is in the work of the literary teacher, the clerk, or the physician."[37]

Somehow, to the horror of the government, Indians had begun to regard federal jobs as an entitlement. A North Dakota agent wrote in 1891 that the students "labor under the impression . . . that the Government should provide a paying position at the agency for each, upon his return home."[38] Public service employment partly satisfied the native sense of justice, restoring a bit of the wealth that was lost when the white man took their lands. Thus, when the Crow agent upbraided shirking Indian line riders for not earning their pay, they indignantly replied, "it is our money anyway." Strictly speaking, their salaries did not come from tribal funds, but from the Indian perspective, wages were something they were owed.[39]

Furthermore, Indians felt increasingly empowered by holding BIA positions. Of his appointment as assistant clerk, Standing Bear wrote that "all the Indians were proud to have one of their own race in positions where he could compete with the white people."[40] Potawatomie Chief Joe Mack Ignatius thought that the more Indians there were in the BIA, the better reservations would be managed.

> I think Indian ought to do for himself. His welfare will be better. Of course we will be under the government forever. We ought to have our own Indian employees, Indian teachers, Indian blacksmiths, Indian wagonmakers, Indian superintendents, and Indian inspectors.[41]

As Ignatius implied, Indians sought not only more but higher BIA positions. Attorney John Oskison (Cherokee) urged that the Indian Office should "make special efforts to use the capable men and women of the race—not merely as policemen and tailors and cooks and laundry helpers, but in positions of leadership."[42] Ironically, Indians came to embrace preferential hiring not as a means of destroying Indian culture, or as a path of assimilation, but as a chance for greater self-determination and the preservation of their culture. Standing Bear implored that:

> Indians should teach Indians . . . Indians should serve Indians . . . [E]very reservation could well be supplied with Indian doctors, nurses, and engineers, road- and bridge-

[37] *Annual Report 1904*, p. 132.

[38] *Annual Report 1891*, p. 511.

[39] "Unpublished Annual Report 1914," pp. 32–33.

[40] Standing Bear, *My People the Sioux*, p. 243; also see pp. 192–95, 239–43. See also Standing Bear, *Land of the Spotted Eagle*, pp. 252–54.

[41] *American Indian Magazine*, 1 (Jan.-Apr. 1913), p. 48.

[42] John M. Oskison, "In Governing the Indian, Use the Indian!" *Case and Comment*, 23 (Feb. 1917), p. 726.

builders, draughtsmen, architects, dentists, lawyers, teachers, and instructors in tribal lore, legends, orations, song, dance, and ceremonial ritual.[43]

When Standing Bear's plea was published in 1933, the federal government was receptive. President Franklin Roosevelt's New Deal program was also meant to be a new regime for Indians. Roosevelt's commissioner of Indian Affairs, John Collier, wanted to preserve the Indian culture. Reversing previous policies, he tried to strengthen tribal governments, increase communal lands, and safeguard Indian religion. But he continued preferential hiring. In 1934, exactly 100 years after the passage of Section 9, the preferential hiring of Indians was reaffirmed in the revolutionary Wheeler-Howard Act. Section 13 of the act circumvented civil service laws for Indian applicants and stated that "such qualified Indians shall hereafter have the preference to appointment to vacancies in any such positions."[44] Collier retained preferential hiring not as a means of assimilation but as a step toward Indian self-determination. Though many tribes rejected certain Collier proposals, Indians were responsive to preferential hiring. Philip Deloria (Standing Rock Sioux) recalled that "a generation or more of Indian leaders had made a commitment to working for the BIA. They wanted to help their people by fulfilling the intent of John Collier . . . to have Indians administer their own affairs."[45] By 1940 the Indian share of the approximately 5,000 BIA employees had risen to 60 percent (see Table 1).

CONCLUSIONS AND IMPLICATIONS

The history of Indian preferential hiring in the century after 1834 provides a unique opportunity to examine the effect of a social policy experiment and reveals lessons for other social programs. Social policy experiments may require a long time to take hold and may have unintended side effects. In the case of Indian preferential hiring, it took generations for natives to overcome their distrust of the government and to gain the necessary qualifications. The BIA programs being administered by fellow Indians did much to dispel suspicion and suggests that social programs are more effective when administered by members of the affected group.

As the BIA became "Indianized," there was a very real danger that its policies would be ineffective. For instance, there were many complaints that Indian teachers were too lenient with the pupils and did not

[43] Standing Bear, *Land of the Spotted Eagle*, pp. 252–54.

[44] *Congressional Record*, 73rd Cong., 2nd sess. (1934), vol. 78, part 11, pp. 11, 725. On the Collier reforms, see Kenneth R. Philp, *John Collier's Crusade for Indian Reform, 1920–1954* (Tucson, 1977).

[45] Deloria quoted in Kenneth R. Philp, ed., *Indian Self-Rule: First Hand Accounts of Indian-White Relations from Roosevelt to Reagan* (Salt Lake City, 1986), p. 197.

always abide by the "English-only" rules. Such lapses, however, were more than offset by the advantages of having a teacher who could establish rapport with the students, respect their culture, speak their language, and serve as a role model. In 1901 a Hampton educator concluded that "it goes without saying that we must have teachers who are educated Indians . . . . The first Indian school should have a good deal of Indian and not much white man in it."[46] Although it took time for such attitudes to gain acceptance, by the 1930s the government was trying to base Indian education on respect for Indian culture.[47] Allowing Indians to run the BIA programs risked its becoming a "captive bureaucracy," but this may have been a small price to pay in order to mobilize a weak minority.[48]

Some have seen BIA Indian employees as victims of co-optation by the system, labeling them collaborationists and "Uncle Tomahawks." The opposite is closer to the truth. Indians employed in the BIA have been activists for native rights. For example, nearly all the founders of the American Indian Association (1911), the birth of the Pan-Indian movement, launched their careers in government work. Although the association was divided on the role of the BIA, most of the leaders insisted that those Indians working at the BIA were just as loyal to their people and just as critical of the government as anyone.[49]

Indian infiltration of the BIA continues. In 1980 natives accounted for 78 percent of its employees, in 1990 over 83 percent. This dominance makes it difficult for Indians to consider the bureaucracy as just a tool of outside oppression. As Helen Peterson (Oglala Sioux) remarked, "many people do not realize that the Bureau is staffed by Indians. Almost all the area directors, superintendents, and division chiefs are Indians."[50]

Perhaps the most important effect of Indian preferential hiring was to pour federal funds into impoverished reservations. In 1960 Navajo BIA employees earned $7,590,000, almost twice what the tribe earned from livestock and farming combined. In 1970 federal employment accounted for 65 percent of all the income at the Pine Ridge Reservation and 72 percent at Fort Belknap.[51] Rather than being the cause of Indian poverty, government employment has been one of the cures. It seems

[46] *Annual Report 1901*, pp. 439, 471–74.

[47] Margaret Connell Szasz, *Education and the American Indian* (Albuquerque, 1977).

[48] On the concept of captive bureaucracy, see Fred Thompson, *Regulatory Policy and Practices* (New York, 1982), pp. 93–129.

[49] Hazel W. Hertzberg, *The Search for an American Indian Identity* (Syracuse, 1971), pp. 19, 79–99, 136–54.

[50] Peterson quoted in Philp, *Indian Self-Rule*, p. 170.

[51] Garrick Bailey and Roberta Glenn Bailey, *A History of the Navajos: The Reservation Years* (Santa Fe, 1986), p. 257; and Alan L. Sorkin, "The Economic Basis of Indian Life," *Annals of the American Academy of Political and Social Science*, 436 (Mar. 1978), p. 7. See also Ernest L. Schusky, *The Forgotten Sioux: An Ethnohistory of the Lower Brule Reservation* (Chicago, 1975), pp. 198, 222, 228–29.

obvious that Indian poverty would have been far worse without preferential hiring.

Yet preferential hiring inadvertently perpetuated Indian dependency. Overcoming this dependence is currently a major policy goal, but one which echoes the futile nineteenth-century struggle to turn the natives into farmers.[52] Perhaps the time will come to abolish the BIA and to set the natives "free."[53] If so, this will not so much prove the failure of BIA Indian preferential hiring as its success. American Indians had a proud history of resistance but eventually embraced preferential hiring. Their involvement caused this social experiment to grow larger and last longer than the government ever intended. Public employment seems to have fit the cultural values of the Indians better than private enterprise.

[52] D'arcy McNickle Center for the History of the American Indian, Occasional Papers in Curriculum Series, 9, *Overcoming Economic Dependency* (Chicago, 1988); Richard J. Margolis, "Native Profit," *Foundation News* (Jan./Feb. 1988), pp. 19–23; James Cook, "Help Wanted—Work, Not Handouts," *Forbes* (May 4, 1987), pp. 68–71; and Daniel Cohen, "Business: Tribal Enterprise," *The Atlantic* (Oct. 1989), pp. 32–43.

[53] This is the recommendation of a recent Senate report, see U.S. Senate, Select Committee on Indian Affairs, Special Committee on Investigations, *A New Federalism for American Indians* (Washington, DC, 1989).

The Financial Crisis of A.D. *33: A Keynesian Depression?*

M. K. THORNTON AND R. L. THORNTON

In A.D. 33 a major economic and financial crisis struck the City of Rome, capital of the Roman Empire.[1] The crisis must have made a tremendous impression on the world at the time; otherwise, the three great historians of the period (Tacitus, Suetonius, and Dio) would not have highlighted it. Ancient writers were not commonly interested in economics.

Modern historians, writing of the premodern period, have spent little effort on financial crises. While the historians have written of the seventeenth-century tulip crisis in Holland, the Mississippi Bubble in France, and the South Sea Bubble in England, these are important but rare exceptions. The financial crisis of A.D. 33 is another and very much earlier exception. Here, extensive and surprisingly sophisticated reporting from the time of the crisis has made possible substantial modern analysis.

The actual crisis consisted of a sudden shortage of money and a contraction of credit which threatened to bankrupt some of Rome's most respected citizens. In evaluating this crisis, modern analysts have focused much of their work on calculations of the money supply at the time, a logical approach since the crisis had as its proximate cause a money shortage. Lacking direct monetary data, they generally rely on numismatic evidence as provided by records of issuance of coins.

Various scholars, among them Tenney Frank, Michael Crawford, Cosmo Rodewald, and Barbara Levick, have suggested different causes for the crisis.[2] Although Frank mentions in passing that Augustus spent far less on buildings than the *Res Gestae* would suggest and that Tiberius was constantly accused of stinginess, he seems to attribute the reduced money supply to an outflow of gold and silver in payments for imports.[3] Crawford denies that the money supply in Rome was varied intentionally by the state at any time other than to cure (rather than to cause) the crisis of A.D. 33. Governmental expenditures are to him devoid of any impact on the money supply. He states: "There are no grounds for the old view of the story as evidence for a general currency shortage and its remedy.[4] Rodewald has a lengthy discussion on the crisis in which, basing his

The Journal of Economic History, Vol. L, No. 3 (Sept. 1990). ISSN 0022-0507.

M. K. Thornton is Professor of Classics, Miami University, Oxford, OH 45056. R. L. Thornton is Professor of International Business, Miami University, Oxford, OH 45056.

The authors gratefully acknowledge the helpful comments and editorial assistance of Paul Hohenberg, Richard Ehlers, and this JOURNAL's referees.

[1] Throughout this note we have referred to the economic unit under discussion as Rome or the Roman Empire. Speaking practically, we are reasonably certain that the actual economic unit was the city and the "close-in" area of Italy surrounding the city. We believe with some confidence that this is correct economically. Shipments from the edges of the empire were between economic units, thus imports, not intra-country movements.

[2] For the most widely accepted modern discussion of the crisis, see Tenney Frank, "The Financial Crisis of 33 A.D.," *American Journal of Philology*, 56 (Oct. 1935), pp. 336–41. Frank also incorporated this article in his volume *Rome and Italy of the Empire* in *Economic Survey of Ancient Rome* (Baltimore, 1940), pp. 32–35; Michael Crawford, "Money and Exchange in the Roman World," *Journal of Roman Studies*, 60 (1970), p. 76; Cosmo Rodewald, *Money in the Age of Tiberius* (Manchester, 1976), pp. 1–17; Barbara Levick, *Tiberius the Politician* (London, 1976), p. 133.

[3] The *Res Gestae* is an account of his stewardship left by the Emperor Augustus and preserved in a copy chiseled upon the walls of the Temple of Rome and Augustus in the modern Angora in Asia Minor. Frank, "Financial Crisis," p. 337.

[4] Crawford, "Money and Exchange," p. 76.

opinion on numismatic evidence, he attacks Frank's view.[5] Levick presumes that a shortage of money in the hands of Tiberius caused his frugality. She then suggests, however, that "it might have been more advantageous to the Roman economy if Tiberius had hoarded less." She believes that Tiberius solved his alleged money shortages by confiscations.[6]

We are fortunate to have so well documented a crisis. Just as important, the crisis was the reverse of the other pre-industrial examples in that it was a crisis of economic depression—possibly a Keynesian one—rather than one of unjustified speculation.

Our attempts to obtain deeper insight into the economic implications of the crisis produced a hypothesis that we use in evaluating the case.

HYPOTHESIS

A severe reduction in governmental building programs following a period of very high investment created an economic condition of sharply reduced liquidity. In an economy where most construction labor is slave, loss of government contracts put severe pressure on slaveowners who had been contractors for government projects. The investment hiatus was then followed by a separate government decision to reduce interest rates in Rome below their natural rate and to require immediate renegotiation of existing loans down to this legal maximum. Lenders then moved their money to outside uses. The resulting panic was relieved by sharp, heavy infusions of government cash into the economy.

THE CHARACTERISTICS OF THE ROMAN ECONOMIC SYSTEM

Some general information about the Roman economic system will help to evaluate the above hypothesis. After the Roman Revolution there had to be a readjustment from Republic to Empire. The final accession of Augustus ended the period of conflict, both foreign and domestic, which characterized the Roman Revolution. Government needs for funds and for legions to fight wars subsided. The emperor had to redeploy resources to peaceful uses.

Within the Empire, in exchange for peace and governmental services, Rome received payments from its provinces in several ways. The provinces contributed grain, in kind, to the city, and the grain was distributed directly to the free citizens in the city. No money was involved. The provinces also paid monetary taxes and tribute to the city. These payments were made to the government, although the official collecting them was expected to profit personally in the process. The state used provincial taxes to pay residents of Rome for such things as construction, arms, and government wages. The tax money citizens in Rome received returned to the provinces as private payments for imported goods and services. To the extent that cash flow "out" did not equal cash flow "in," standard balance-of-payments effects on prices and employment should have occurred. During the period of the crisis, price-level changes are not known.[7] Our expectation of unemployment is part of the core of our argument.

At this time perhaps one-third of the population was slave.[8] Slaves did not receive free food; their master met their consumption needs by purchasing food and other necessities in the open market. In times of unemployment a master was required to

[5] Rodewald, *Money in the Age of Tiberius*, pp. 1–17.

[6] Levick, *Tiberius the Politician*, p. 133.

[7] M. I. Finley, *The Ancient Economy* (London, 1973), p. 142.

[8] M. I. Finley, "Slavery," *Oxford Classical Dictionary* (Oxford, 1970), p. 995.

support his slaves, through dissaving if necessary.[9] Should he free his slaves, they were eligible for the food dole, but slaves were expensive and a master would be reluctant to free able-bodied ones except in times of extreme crisis. Slaves could be sold if a suitable market existed.

Tribute and booty money accruing to the state did not enhance the well-being of Rome until it was spent. Thus for Rome to profit from its tribute the state had to spend its income. When the money came directly to the emperor or to the state, assurance that the money would be spent was not guaranteed.[10] Early in the Empire Augustus made it quite clear that he understood this elementary principle: a state cannot afford to run a long-term surplus; if it has no direct needs as a government, it should take steps to transfer the surplus to its people for spending, either employing them, for example, on building programs, or by means of tax reductions or other means. Suetonius confirms that Augustus understood this:

> For example, by bringing the royal treasures to Rome in his Alexandrian triumph he made ready money so abundant, that the rate of interest fell, and the value of real estate rose greatly; and after that, whenever there was an excess of funds from the property of those who had been condemned, he loaned it without interest for fixed periods to any who could give security for double the amount. . . . He often gave largess to the people, but usually of different sums: now four hundred, now three hundred, now two hundred and fifty sesterces a man; and he did not even exclude young boys, though it has been usual for them to receive a share only after the age of eleven. In times of scarcity too he often distributed grain to each man at a very low figure, sometimes for nothing, and he doubled the money tickets.[11]

Upon his accession in A.D. 14, Tiberius repudiated Augustus's policies. The pattern of government building expenditures in Rome throughout the Julio-Claudian period is known from research reported in this JOURNAL. We summarize this pattern in Figure 1.[12] Note the enormous strength of the building programs during Augustus's reign followed by their precipitous decline during Tiberius's hegemony. They were near zero during the eight-year period immediately preceding the crisis of A.D. 33. It is important to note that the Augustan building program actually ended with the death of his powerful subordinate Agrippa in 12 B.C. After the work in progress—two aqueducts—had been completed in 4 B.C., Tiberius was actually in charge of building program planning. Thus for evaluative purposes the sharp decline in construction from 4 B.C. until the death of Tiberius in A.D. 37 reflects Tiberius's preferences.

In Rome the "new rich" traditionally translated their recent wealth into land. As P. Garnsey and R. Saller say: "In such societies, as was the case in pre-industrial Europe, land is valued as a source of prestige and political power. The conversion of profits won in commerce into landed wealth often heralds the arrival of a new family into the aristocracy. In such cases the acquisition of property may be followed by the purchase of office and the forging of marriage connections into the upper class. The process of assimilation into the aristocracy might take a generation or more."[13] The profits from the building programs of Augustus, which frequently went to freedmen or their sons,

[9] P. A. Brunt, "Free Labour and Public Works at Rome," *Journal of Roman Studies*, 70 (1980), p. 85.

[10] E. R. Boak and W. G. Sinnigen, in *A History of Rome to A.D. 565* (New York, 1965), p. 161, said that as early as 133 B.C. Rome was experiencing a critical situation because it had no way to give money to the lower classes.

[11] *Augustus* (henceforth Suet. *Aug.*) 41. Translated by J. C. Rolfe, *Suetonius*, Loeb Classical Library (1964), vol. 1, p. 189. Other biographies by Suetonius are from the edition and will be cited as Suet. and the subject's name.

[12] M. K. Thornton and R. L. Thornton, "Manpower Needs for the Public Works Programs of the Julio-Claudian Emperors," this JOURNAL, 43 (June 1983), p. 376.

[13] P. Garnsey and R. Saller, *The Roman Empire* (Berkeley, 1987), p. 44.

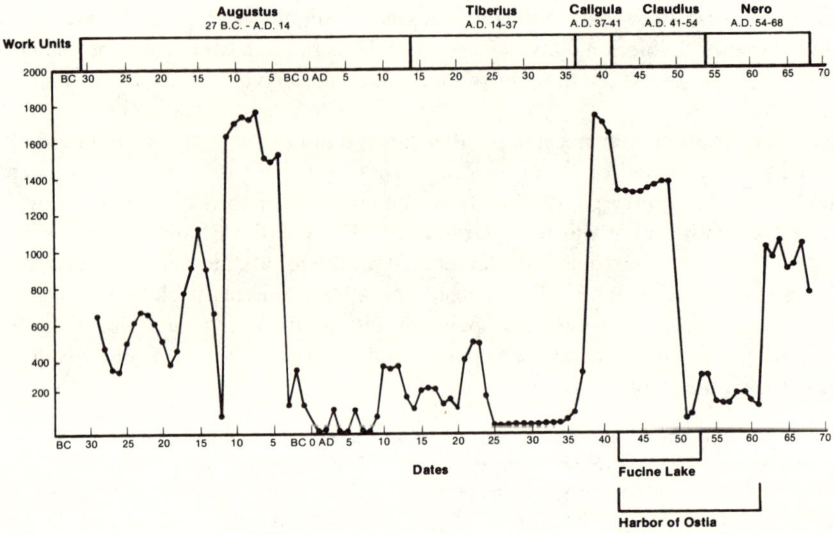

FIGURE 1

TOTAL ANNUAL WORK UNITS, JULIO-CLAUDIAN EMPERORS

Notes: Work units represent index numbers; 60 work units represent the manpower required to construct the Maison Carrée project. The Fucine Lake and the Harbor of Ostia projects are not quantified on the figure.
Source: M. K. Thornton and R. L. Thornton, "Manpower Needs for the Public Works Programs of the Julio-Claudian Emperors," this JOURNAL, 43 (June 1983), p. 376.

would have been converted into land insofar as possible. Petronius invented such a case, using his freedman Trimalchio as the spokesman:

> I made a clear ten million on one voyage. I at once bought up all the estates which had belonged to my patron. I built a house, and bought slaves and cattle; whatever I touched grew like a honey-comb. When I came to have more than the whole revenues of my own country, I threw up the game: I retired from active work and proceeded to finance freedmen.[14]

THE CRISIS

Recognizing the characteristics of the Roman economy, we can now evaluate the crisis itself. We must first consider whether a shortage of money prevented Tiberius from spending more. The evidence is clear that the policy change enacted by Tiberius did not result from a shortage of money. First, we know that in A.D. 14 Tiberius inherited from Augustus 100,000,000 sesterces (a modest sum for an emperor) in the emperor's privy purse.[15] Second, we know that in A.D. 37 Tiberius left to Caligula at least 2,700,000,000 sesterces.[16] If we subtract the 100,000,000 sesterces Tiberius had at

[14] *Satyricon* 76. Translated by W. H. D. Rouse, *Petronius*, Loeb Classical Library (1969), pp. 177, 179.

[15] Suet. *Aug*. 101.2.

[16] Suet. *Caligula*, 37.3. Rodewald, in *Money in the Age of Tiberius*, p. 11, questions whether the two figures represent the same depository. He suggests that they may not. In view of the mixing of money during the Early Empire between the *fiscus* (the imperial treasury) and the *aerarium* (public treasury) we cannot be absolutely certain. However, Caligula's sudden outpouring of money during the first year of his reign on particular buildings suggests a large usable inheritance from Tiberius.

the beginning of his reign from the 2,700,000,000 sesterces which he left to Caligula, we get a 2,600,000,000-sesterce gain. Thus on average, Tiberius ran a surplus of over 110,000,000 sesterces per year throughout his reign.

In comparison, we learned from Pliny that the large aqueduct Aqua Claudia cost 350,000,000 sesterces.[17] Thus Tiberius could have financed a major aqueduct in a little over three years simply by balancing his budget. It is interesting to note that his successor Caligula started two aqueducts immediately upon his accession.[18]

The second possibility is that Tiberius saw no reason for change, even though there is good evidence that Tiberius had to be aware that the food supply of Rome was inadequate. Serious wheat shortages occurred in A.D. 5, in A.D. 6, and again in A.D. 19.[19] Tiberius needed to spend some of his stored-up money to solve Rome's food crisis. Claudius, succeeding to the imperium four years after Tiberius's death, immediately started two major food supply projects, the Harbor of Ostia and the draining of the Fucine Lake, both of which had been considered at the time of Julius Caesar (who died in 44 B.C.).

We can conclude from this that the sharp policy change between Augustus and Tiberius should have resulted in a classic cash squeeze. Much of the money supply would have vanished into Tiberius's coffers as a budgetary surplus and would thus have been sterilized. The actual catalyst that changed the squeeze to a crisis was a sudden government decision to reduce interest rates sharply on real estate loans by directing immediate renegotiation of existing mortgages. The resulting shift in available funds away from real estate was near disastrous. Tacitus gave us an account of the situation:

> Hence followed a scarcity of money, a great shock being given to all credit, the current coin too, in consequence of the conviction of so many persons and the sale of their property, being locked up in the imperial treasury or the public exchequer. Creditors however were suing for payment in full, and it was not respectable for persons when sued to break faith. So, at first, there were clamorous meetings and importunate entreaties; then noisy applications to the praetor's court. And the very device intended as a remedy, the sale and purchase of estates, proved the contrary, as the money lenders had hoarded up all their money for buying land. The facilities for selling were followed by a fall of prices, and the deeper a man was in debt, the more reluctantly did he part with his property, and many were utterly ruined.[20]

Tiberius eventually cured the crisis with a well-recognized maneuver: the instant provision of large amounts of cash. As Dio stated: "After this Tiberius adopted a more moderate policy with regards to loans and gave the public treasury 100,000,000 sesterces to enable senators [counting houses] to make loans to applicants for three years free of interest."[21] Obviously Tiberius knew what the problem was and how to solve it.

Who were the people affected by this crisis? The Roman government transferred income from its coffers to its citizens in several ways: Augustus literally threw it to the people. Later Roman emperors (for example, Caligula and Claudius) built it away. Reducing taxes, the modern way to transfer excess money to the people, was not a solution.[22] The population in and around the City of Rome paid no taxes. Among others the newly wealthy put their money into land, so builders, who had put their money acquired from earlier prosperous times into land, would have been much affected.

As soon as Tiberius could be removed, his successor, Caligula, returned to a vigorous

[17] Pliny, *Historia Naturalis* (henceforth *NH*) 36.122.

[18] M. K. Thornton, "Julio-Claudian Building Programs: Eat, Drink, and Be Merry," *Historia*, 35 (1986), pp. 37, 43.

[19] Dio, *Roman History* 55.26.1–3, 55.26.1 ff; Pliny, *NH* 7.129; Tacitus, *Annals* 2.87, translated by A. J. Church and W. J. Brodribb, *Complete Works of Tacitus* (New York, 1942), pp. 204–5; and Suet. *Tiberius*, 48.

[20] Tac., *Ann.* 6.17.

[21] Dio, *Rom. Hist.*, 58.21.4–5. Translated by Rodewald, *Money in the Age of Tiberius*, p. 2.

[22] Rome had sumptuary taxes. For a discussion of them, see Tacitus, *Ann.* 3.52–4.

policy of expenditure on public construction and the remaining Julio-Claudian emperors continued to follow a policy of forceful, well-planned public construction (see Figure 1). The construction of the harbor of Ostia (not quantified in Figure 1) covers the apparent building hiatus during Nero's reign.[23]

We infer from the above events that a long-standing economic policy confrontation had existed in Rome between the reactionaries who favored strict state fiscal restraint and those others who backed a policy of fiscal responsiveness to needs. The old guard were senators and traditionalists, while those favoring fiscal responsiveness were the upstarts who had made their money during the Augustan building boom. Augustus had given the nouveau riche their chance by opening the purse under his control and by taking control of most building programs away from the Senate.[24] When the imperium passed to Tiberius, a conservative patrician in every sense, he changed the economic direction abruptly and transferred power to those favoring restraint.[25] The crisis of A.D. 33 destroyed the conservatives' position, but power did not actually revert until Tiberius was assassinated in A.D. 37.

THE CAUSE OF THE CRISIS

We suggest two alternative reasons for the crisis of A.D. 33. In the pure money case the crisis was a simple cash squeeze caused by the event suggested in the ancient sources—the sudden decision to enforce an old law requiring cash backing for real estate loans.[26] In this scenario the ultimate cause of the crisis is the same as the proximate one: an uncomplicated money squeeze which gave citizens insufficient time to liquify investments and to meet unexpected demands.

The other explanation is a more Keynesian one: a failure of investment (or of alternative ways to transfer money from the Imperial Treasury to the public) over a long period so reduced the money supply that when an event triggered a sudden demand for cash the underlying malaise of the economy surfaced. In this explanation the ready assets of businessmen—builders, suppliers of materials, and tradespeople—had been so eroded by a long-continued lack of profitable work that they could not deal with the sudden shock.

If we had evidence of a continuing malaise starting with the sharp drop in construction at the end of Augustus's reign and continuing to the end of Tiberius's reign, we could accept the Keynesian explanation for the events in A.D. 33. We have no such evidence. We can be sure that the sharp drop in public building would have required readjustments by the construction industry. Unfortunately we have no evidence of a reorientation. Frank addresses the problem and discusses the Schumpeterian explanation of private investment in private housing which must have been set off by the earlier boom in public works and the consequent movement of labor to the city.[27] We believe redundant public

[23] See M. K. Thornton, "Nero's Quinquennium: The Ostian Connection," *Historia*, 38 (1989), pp. 117–19.

[24] D. E. Strong, in "The Administration of Public Building in Rome During the Late Republic and Early Empire," *Institute of Classical Studies*, 15 (1968), pp. 97–109, describes the process by which Augustus transferred construction decisions from the Senate to the emperor.

[25] As noted before, the actual policy change started in 12 B.C. with the death of Agrippa. Construction after that date was principally clean-up work on projects started under him, which strongly suggests Agrippa was the real policy maker for Augustus on building programs. The unproductive years at the end of his reign were overseen by Tiberius.

[26] For a detailed discussion of the specific law involved, see Rodewald, *Money in the Age of Tiberius*, pp. 1–4.

[27] Frank, *Economic Survey of Ancient Rome*, V, p. 19.

works labor might have been absorbed in other ways, but we have no original source evidence to confirm them.[28]

In either event Tiberius's action in A.D. 33 should have solved the immediate problem. However, in the "pure money" case the problem would have been but an incident. The immediate cure would have been sufficient, without long-term effects. We have no evidence of any follow-on problems with the economy from the date of the crisis to the death of Tiberius, so it would be easy to accept the "pure money" case. It obeys the law of parsimony and seems to cover the facts adequately. For a society in which economic data are almost never available, however, it would be inappropriate to accept a general lack of information as providing much confirmation.

We prefer an alternative source of evidence to the direct one of economic malaise. It assumes that the Roman managers were fully aware of their problem and were prevented from solving it by the obduracy of Tiberius. There is no doubt as to Tiberius's conservatism. The evidence of his unwillingness to spend money is as close to incontrovertible as we are likely to get anywhere. Given this fact, the precipitous way in which Caligula and Claudius rushed into building programs offers clear evidence that something was badly wrong in the latter half of Tiberius's reign. We believe that Rome did not simply need facilities but that it needed continuity in programs, and this belief is strengthened by the smooth nature of the building load from the end of Tiberius's reign through the end of the Julio-Claudian dynasty and into the following one. In the words of the Emperor Vespasian (A.D. 69–79) when he refused to require the use of a device which would have saved a large amount of labor, "You must let me feed my poor people."[29] The Romans were well aware of the need for workload management.

Before we can legitimately ascribe as the underlying cause of the crisis the collapse of public building under Tiberius we must establish the matter of timing. Thirty-seven years elapsed between the initial reduction of building and the Tiberian crisis, and eight years between the complete cessation of building in A.D. 25 and the crisis of A.D. 33. In most economies the crisis would have been felt more quickly. Further, such a crisis should have been characterized by severe unemployment, which in a modern economy is very quickly evident after the collapse of building. We think the slave system accounts for the long delay between the cessation of building and its effect on employment. Unemployment would not have become immediately apparent in the suffering of the labor force. Slaveowners would protect this labor from hunger and want until their own resources descended to crisis levels.[30] They had a remedy for the drain of their resources—freeing the slaves—but until things got really bad they would instead have spent their own cash reserves. This theory offers a possible added explanation for the cash shortages of A.D. 33. By that time the additional cash spent in caring for underemployed slaves would aggravate the crisis and Caligula would be welcomed.

We hold that the crisis of A.D. 33 was ultimately caused by a failure of investment and by an abandonment of Augustan innovation and hence is best classified as a Keynesian trough, not unlike the worldwide Depression from 1929 to 1939.[31] Because we now have available a quantified measure of the government building programs of the period, we need no longer rely on suspect and inadequate estimates of the money supply. The usual tool for estimating the money supply, numismatics, is a poor data source.

Clearly, the failure of Tiberius to keep the working stock of money resupplied through building expenditures could have caused a classic money-supply problem. From a

[28] M. K. and R. L. Thornton, *Julio-Claudian Building Programs: A Quantitative Study in Political Management* (Wauconda, IL, 1989), pp. 36–37.

[29] Suet. *Vespasian*, 18.

[30] Seneca, *Dialogus* 9.8.8.

[31] K. K. Hulley, in "Tacitus on the Depression," *Classical Journal*, 27 (Oct. 1932), pp. 525–26, refers to Herbert Hoover.

Keynesian perspective the problem would have been accompanied by joblessness among the work force. In the "money-supply" hypothesis, the key factor could have been the short-term distress of debtors unable to borrow immediately needed capital.

It would be helpful if price data were available. For this period we have only a report of rising prices, which is not the expected direction to support the money-supply hypothesis, and only for grain. Since the grain supply of Rome was at the time in critical condition, with many minicrises, such data can reasonably be presumed to indicate only specific price changes in a short commodity, not a change in the general price level.

Replacing the numismatic data used by earlier scholars with a reasonable portrayal of government expenditures puts the analysis of the circumstances surrounding the crisis of A.D. 33 on a more economically respectable footing. It does not, however, tie the crisis solely to decreased economic activity due to the disappearance of the building programs. The alternative or supplementary explanation would be that the severe reduction of the money supply because of its disappearance into the state's coffers stifled the normal array of commercial and private transactions of the city independently of building activity. If this were true, the crisis might be considered a straightforward money-supply crisis.

Scattering and Contracts in Medieval Agriculture: Challenges Ahead

METIN M. COSGEL

Among the issues involved in understanding the organization of medieval agriculture, two have particularly interested economic historians: the manorial contractual arrangements between the lord of the manor and the peasants, and the scattering of peasant land holdings on open fields. While our understanding of each issue has improved, the symmetry between them needs further attention. Examining the issues separately is only a necessary first step; it is also important to consider their interdependence.

I argue below that the explanations offered by Stefano Fenoaltea, Donald McCloskey, and Douglass North and Robert Thomas all need modification to address more adequately the facts of the *overall* organization of medieval agriculture.[1] Note, however, that my goal here is simply to alert future researchers to the symmetry between open fields and the manorial organization. Pointing out the incompleteness of earlier explanations offers a way to reopen the debate.

MANORIAL RELATIONSHIPS AND FARMING

The regularities observed by economic historians in the contractual relationships between the lord and the peasants in a "classic" manor were quite peculiar to medieval agriculture. The land in a typical manor was usually divided into two parts. The lord kept one part as his demesne and let the remaining arable land to tenants. The peasants' labor was likewise divided into two parts: the tenants cultivated both the lord's demesne and their own holdings. The characteristic feature of this type of contracting was that it mixed wage and rent contracts. It also differed from sharecropping, since the total output was not distributed between the lord and the peasants in fixed proportion. Instead, each party was entitled to output accruing to his own land, plus wages or rent from the other party.

Historians have traditionally been reluctant to offer general explanations of the organizational structure of medieval agriculture. The reluctance often leads them to explain the variations in the relative importance of the lords' demesne by local circumstances such as topographical, soil, and climate conditions, and the contractions and expansions of the demesne over time by population pressures or the changes in relative prices. Economists, on the other hand, contributed a new dimension by

The Journal of Economic History, Vol. L, No. 3 (Sept. 1990). ISSN 0022-0507.

The author is Assistant Professor of Economics, University of Connecticut, Storrs, CT 06269-1063.

Helpful comments from Donald N. McCloskey, Stefano Fenoaltea, and Douglass C. North are gratefully acknowledged. In addition, the author would like to thank S. R. H. Jones, S. Y. Wu, and the editors of this JOURNAL for helpful suggestions.

[1] I choose these authors since their works have been the most influential, and at the same time the most representative of the partial explanations offered in the literature. See, in particular, Stefano Fenoaltea, "Authority, Efficiency, and Agricultural Organization in Medieval England and Beyond: A Hypothesis," this JOURNAL, 35 (Dec. 1975), pp. 693–718; Stefano Fenoaltea, "Transaction Costs, Whig History, and the Common Fields," *Politics and Society* (Summer 1988), pp. 171–240; Donald N. McCloskey, "English Open Fields as Behavior toward Risk," in P. Uselding, ed., *Research in Economic History* (Greenwich, CT, 1976), vol. 1, pp. 124–70; and Douglass C. North and Robert P. Thomas, "The Rise and Fall of the Manorial System: A Theoretical Model," this JOURNAL, 31 (Dec. 1971), pp. 777–803. The symmetry has actually been recognized by some of these authors. See, for instance, Fenoaltea, "Transaction Costs." Also see Carl J. Dahlman, *The Open Field System and Beyond* (Cambridge, 1980), especially chap. 2.

searching for a theoretical model to explain the organization of the "classic" manor as well as to account for the observed variations in the system. They asked a different question: why this particular system?

North and Thomas, for example, expressed their discontent with the particularistic aspect of the literature and the lack of a consistent theoretical foundation. They proposed a model of the rise and fall of the manorial system that emphasized transaction costs to explain the sharing of inputs between the lord and the peasants. They viewed input-sharing as the dominant contractual structure in medieval agriculture on the basis that it was the cheapest to negotiate.

North and Thomas's model has been criticized on various grounds. Fenoaltea notes, for instance, that the costs of negotiation were not so high as to have a determining effect.[2] A further complication arises from North and Thomas's model: it fails to consider the totality of the exchange relationships within a manor. In particular, the model neglects the peasants' side of the economy. The known facts about open-field farming seem to contradict their hypothesis. It is well known, for instance, that the peasants exchanged land and employed each other's labor, which points to the role of relative prices of land and labor. One might point out that North and Thomas's explanation rests on the absence of goods markets, and not land or labor markets. The absence of the goods market, however, is important to the extent that it increases the cost of exchanging land and labor (which makes direct exchange cheaper). The exchange among peasants was not in the form of input-sharing. The effect on North and Thomas's model of the presence of an interpeasant market is clear: when negotiating with the lord, the peasants did not have to incur any additional costs to determine the relevant prices.

Fenoaltea agrees that transaction costs were important but emphasizes enforcement rather than negotiation costs as the critical component. He is more sensitive to the interrelatedness of open fields and the manorial system, having contributed to our understanding of both.[3] But parts of his argument are still open to criticism from my perspective.

Fenoaltea's focus on enforcement costs alone explains the superiority of fixed rents over other types of contracts. The sharing of inputs then must have had other offsetting benefits. For this Fenoaltea offers another hypothesis: the advantage of exercising authority over the labor force. The lord's advantages for his hierarchical position were, in fact, twofold: his authority over peasants (required for long-run social stability) and his differential expertise in production. After specifying costs and benefits, Fenoaltea asserts that their balance determined the institutional structure and the size of the lord's demesne.

Fenoaltea's argument justifies demesne agriculture so long as the benefits to the lord of direct farming exceed its costs. That, however, is precisely the reason why his explanation of input-sharing needs additional hypotheses. It is not obvious how the balancing of costs and benefits takes place to determine the size of the lord's demesne. If the expertise of the lord is superior for each type of land and for all crops, then the only way the lord would not cultivate all the available land is if at some point costs outweighed benefits. Fenoaltea's hypothesis, however, is based rather on the difference in the required expertise between different crops. The peasants generally did not

[2] See Andrew Jones, "The Rise and Fall of the Manorial System: A Critical Comment," this Journal, 32 (Dec. 1972), pp. 938–44; and Stefano Fenoaltea, "The Rise and Fall of a Theoretical Model: The Manorial System," this Journal, 35 (June 1975), pp. 386–409, for criticisms of the North-Thomas model. North answers the criticisms and modifies his argument somewhat in his later work, *Structure and Change in Economic History* (New York, 1981), particularly pp. 129–31.

[3] Furthermore, he uses the symmetry to criticize McCloskey's and Dahlman's explanations of open fields. See his "Transaction Costs."

possess the necessary skills and information in growing certain crops such as wheat, causing a differential expertise in production. Thus the lord's benefits exceeded his costs for such crops, but not for others. The peasants needed supervision in growing wheat, but their skills were sufficient to undertake production of other crops independently. The question needing to be answered is this: why did the differences in expertise persist?

Fenoaltea's argument is essentially dynamic. Differential information could exist in a changing environment if the lord introduced a technological innovation first. The important question, however, is the longevity of the differences in technique. Peasants were not innovators perhaps, but that should not exclude them from the possibility of imitating the new techniques. Two reasons could explain the longevity of the lord's differential expertise. Either the peasants did not know the new techniques or they refused to adopt them. The first cannot be true, since peasants worked on the lord's land as well as on their own. A typical peasant, according to Fenoaltea, was a "casual" worker on the lord's demesne. Casual or not, peasants had to be taught the new methods in order to labor effectively. The relevant issue might be the timing of agricultural operations. This argument seems contradictory, however, in juxtaposition with the facts of peasant farming. The peasants were in the same business of agricultural production as the lord, and acted as independent producers on their own land. They made decisions as to the choice of crops and the timing of agricultural operations. The argument may hold true for some peasants but does not explain the existence of others who held large quantities of land and employed (and supervised) others' labor.

The second reason, the appeal to peasant conservatism, is not convincing either. According to Fenoaltea, "[t]he master may deem his method successful, but the workers might refuse to replicate it, even if they could, until they had enough evidence to convince them that it was indeed superior to the method that had proved itself since time out of mind."[4] The peasants were conservative perhaps, but that in itself does not explain why they would refuse to accept a change for so long. To see that the new technique was indeed superior, they needed only to observe for "some" years the increase in agricultural output or the saving in labor required for a specific job.

It is also not clear why input-sharing should be desirable to peasants as well. Even if we accept Fenoaltea's explanation of why the lord would lease part of the land, the fact remains that he needs a leaseholder. Therefore the peasants' side of the adjustment and the conditions under which the peasants might cultivate the land left vacant by the lord need to be explained. His hypothesis amounts to justifying demesne agriculture but not the sharing of inputs.

The foregoing argument suggests, therefore, that a proper treatment of peasant farming is essential for the history of medieval agriculture—in particular, for a complete account of the plausibility of input-sharing arrangements. Both North-Thomas's and Fenoaltea's models neglect farming by the peasants.

What we can learn from a partial analysis of the manor is limited, since the changes could not be made unilaterally. The lord certainly had the authority, especially over dependent tenants, to design and change things to his taste, but there were limits to his decision-making power. It is important to understand the constraining factors. The gains and losses resulting from a decision by the lord depended on how the peasants were affected by the decision and how they reacted.

FARMING BY THE PEASANTS

Peasant farming becomes an important consideration in an explanation of the peculiar locational distribution of land holdings. The peasants often preferred to hold their land

[4] Fenoaltea, "Authority, Efficiency," p. 700.

in scattered rather than consolidated plots. A typical villager held twenty or so plots of land, less than an acre each, separate from one another and widely scattered on the village arable.

McCloskey was first among economists to address the problem by pointing to the importance of risk in agricultural production and the absence of insurance against it. While earlier historians searched for the system's origin, McCloskey questions its persistence and decline. The persistence of scattering for many centuries implies that it was a purposeful action. Any account of peasant land holdings, therefore, must explain not only how the peasants scattered, but also why. He observes that the land within a village had varying characteristics, as did the weather. A typical peasant would be averse to the risks of poor yield, high prices, and so on, which he would assume if he were to specialize in one crop and one crop area. Therefore the scattered holdings by the peasants had a purpose, namely, to insure against disaster.

McCloskey formulates a "risk-aversion hypothesis" to represent the peasants' desire for safety. His formulation, however, neglects an important consideration, namely, the presence of the lords. The peasants already had a "safe asset" in their portfolio: labor income. If the peasants were concerned with "safety first," they could easily achieve it by working for the lord. It is true, of course, that if the land had varying characteristics the variance of the output from the peasants' land could be reduced by scattered holdings. But his formulation is nevertheless incomplete if the problem of allocating resources is taken to include the distribution of land and labor among individuals as well as different locations. The incompleteness associated with the neglect of peasant farming discussed earlier is reversed here, as McCloskey neglects farming by the lord.

Fenoaltea offers a different explanation of scattering on open fields, based on the peasants' pursuit of productivity. He views scattering as a means of stabilizing the peasants' individual labor needs. He notes that "[s]ince the village arable is heterogenous—in chemistry, drainage, exposure to wind and sun—different parts of it are best worked at different times, and productivity depends critically on the careful allocation of labor over space as well as over time.[5] He notes that peasants could keep consolidated land holdings and hire each other as workers to meet individual labor requirements when needed. Such an arrangement, he argues, could not be optimal because of the costs of supervising outside labor. Thus private scattering, according to Fenoaltea, is designed to maximize productivity by optimizing self-employment.

Fenoaltea's argument is plausible. Fenoaltea's and McCloskey's arguments can actually be seen as complementing each other to a degree. Fenoaltea shows the advantages of scattering with self-employment. McCloskey explains scattering (and diversification by crops) regardless of how employment and land ownership were related. Fenoaltea's argument, like McCloskey's, is an explanation of why peasants scattered land, given that they had some. On this basis, however, it is open to criticism. Recall the criticism of the previous section, only this time see the problem as caused by the neglect of the lord's side. If supervision was costly, but the lord had offsetting advantages in employing peasants as workers, then why did the lord not employ all the villagers? Depending on weather conditions, he could direct labor around the village for the desired optimal allocation. With his superior technology he could reap all benefits from scattering despite the costs of supervision.

A similar issue remains open even if we accept Fenoaltea's justification of demesne as constituting only part of the land. We would expect the lords to scatter their land holdings to benefit from the advantages of scattering. Fenoaltea's discussion of demesne agriculture, however, argues the contrary. He states: "where the qualities of the soil (including exposure and drainage) vary over small distances, even a scattered demesne

[5] Fenoaltea, "Transaction Costs," pp. 190–91.

could well represent a selection of relatively homogenous land.[6] The two hypotheses Fenoaltea employs to explain demesne agriculture and open fields seem to argue against each other here: the lords' desire to exploit the systematic differences in expertise (by selecting homogenous land) and the advantages of scattering (by selecting heterogenous land). Why, then, would the lords ignore the possible advantages of scattering by choosing only a certain type of land?

The lord's employment of peasant labor has further implications for Fenoaltea's argument. Most peasants, if not all, worked for the lord (and for each other) part of the time. Fenoaltea notes that "the lord exercised his prior claim to labor at the busy times of the agricultural cycle."[7] In other words, if conditions were ripe for work on a particular type of land, then the peasants needed to finish the work on the lord's land first. Fenoaltea does not discuss whether and how the lord's priority would interfere with the optimality of the peasants' allocation of labor on open fields. The peasants, after all, may not even have had enough time to exploit the advantages of the conditions on their own land.

Both McCloskey's and Fenoaltea's explanations of scattering on open fields, therefore, need modification.

THE SYMMETRY IN THE ORGANIZATION OF MEDIEVAL AGRICULTURE

My critical review suggests that the questions asked by economic historians have biased their answers. The problem is to determine the relevant decision makers for a particular issue. Should the peasants be viewed as involved in the decision-making process in a manor, or was the lord the only relevant decision maker? The question is implicitly answered by the problem chosen. Explanations of scattering neglect the lord's side, yet the manorial contractual arrangements are viewed from the lord's side only. As a result the economic explanations of the allocation of resources in medieval agriculture become partial accounts of its organizational structure.

The problem associated with the improper neglect of one of the potential decision makers generates a problem of inconsistency in the explanations of the two issues. Input-sharing, after all, concerned the division of resources between the lord and the peasants, and scattering concerned the locational allocation of those resources. If an explanation of one issue fails to consider the known regularities concerning the other, then the picture of the organization of medieval agriculture is likely to be incomplete.

My examples show that leaving the lord or the peasants out of the picture has far-reaching consequences. North and Thomas's hypothesis becomes incomplete because it neglects the transactions among peasants and between the lord and the peasants. Similarly, Fenoaltea's explanation of the sharing of inputs explains demesne farming only. Thus the neglect of the peasants makes the explanations offered by North and Thomas and by Fenoaltea an unsatisfactory account of the sharing of inputs.

Explanations of scattering are incomplete as well. McCloskey's explanation, based on *his* formulation of the risk-aversion hypothesis, remains incomplete, since the peasants' desire for safety could be achieved through other contractual arrangements with the lord. Similarly the presence of the lord weakens Fenoaltea's claim that the open fields were designed to maximize productivity, because of the constraints the lord's presence places on the maximization. The pioneering efforts of North and Thomas, Fenoaltea, and McCloskey in explaining the organization of medieval agriculture need completion by considering all relevant decision makers and the wider set of exchange relationships.

[6] Fenoaltea, "Authority, Efficiency," p. 703.

[7] Stefano Fenoaltea, "Risk, Transaction Costs, and the Organization of Medieval Agriculture," *Explorations in Economic History*, 13 (Apr. 1976), p. 132.

One might argue that mere criticism without showing a way out is an incomplete procedure in itself. While criticism is valuable, proposing alternative hypotheses is more satisfying. I now turn to that task. It is at least possible to offer some general remarks about the direction in which future research might lead. I have argued that explanations of scattering must be compatible with the lord's interests, and that the proposed benefits of the sharing of inputs must be plausible to the peasants. It is important to determine who the decision makers are on a particular issue and to decide whether a proposed explanation remains consistent within the constraints of the system as a whole.

One promising line of research would be to examine the risk-sharing properties of the overall organization of medieval agriculture. A brief preface to such an inquiry can be given as follows.[8] In the absence of any means to prevent, transfer, or avoid agricultural risks, the organizational structure of medieval communities would be affected by and would respond to these factors. A lord and his peasants could deal only internally with the risks; they could share the risks only among themselves.

As McCloskey argues, given the variability of land the peasants could reduce the variation in their personal incomes by scattering their land holdings. Yet this could not eliminate the risks altogether. A reinterpretation of McCloskey's risk-aversion hypothesis is necessary to include the contractual arrangements between the lord and the peasants. Risk aversion does not necessarily imply that a person would try to minimize risks. Given that the lord and the peasants had risky as well as safe income sources, risk aversion means that each party preferred a combination of the two rather than wholly risky or wholly sure income. Portfolio theory supports the argument: a good analogy, for instance, is a risk-averse investor's decision to invest in a combination of stocks and bonds rather than only stocks or only bonds.

The contractual arrangements between lords and peasants gave each party a further chance to adjust the allocation of resources to their risk attitudes. In order for both parties to achieve the desired allocation of risks, the contractual structure had to take the form of input-sharing rather than wage, rent, or sharecropping contracts. Input-sharing contracts—in addition to scattering—observed in medieval agriculture provided lords and peasants with the opportunity to allocate risks optimally within the manor. This argument, therefore, may explain the overall organization of medieval agriculture by extending McCloskey's hypothesis to include the peasants' relationships with the lord.

Clearly, the explanation above demands a more thorough and rigorous treatment, which is beyond the scope of the present study. But the brief discussion here does suggest the possibility of a comprehensive treatment of the issues examined. Further progress in understanding the organization of medieval agriculture will require that the symmetry between open fields and the manorial organization be considered.

[8] What follows is a brief description of work currently in progress. For a more extensive treatment, see Metin M. Cosgel, "Risk-sharing Properties of the Organization of Medieval Agriculture" (Unpublished Manuscript, University of Connecticut, June 1990).

Bank Entry and the Low Issue of National Bank Notes: A Re-examination

BRUCE W. HETHERINGTON

Economic historians have long been puzzled by the low issue of national bank notes between 1882 and 1891. Circulation fell over 50 percent from $360 million in 1882 to $171 million in 1891 (see Table 1). Yet over that same period the number of national banks more than doubled. In 1890, when circulation had almost reached its lowest point, a confused Comptroller of the Currency wrote that new banks "are now being organized with greater rapidity than in any time for the past twenty-five years."[1] Since bank note issue was the major privilege associated with a national bank charter, the anomaly of record numbers entering the system and ignoring note issue has puzzled historians.

There are two long-standing theories explaining low note issue. The comptroller's theory links bank note profitability to the price of U.S. government bonds used as collateral to back note issue.[2] Bond prices began rising in the mid-1880s, making note issue less profitable. Banks sold their bonds at a premium and circulation contracted. Note issue rebounded when the bond premiums disappeared after the treasury ran deficits for four consecutive years following the Panic of 1893. This theory was unchallenged until John James focused on the local lending rate as the key variable in determining profitability.[3] James argued that a national bank faced two options after accepting a deposit: loan the deposit directly or purchase U.S. bonds as collateral and issue notes. The wider the spread between the loan rate and the bond rate, the more likely a bank would loan the deposit directly rather than tie up funds in low earning bonds. This opportunity-cost approach predicts that note issue should have been lower in regions with higher local lending rates (the South, Midwest, and Pacific). As regional interest rate differentials narrowed, around the turn of the century, note issue became more profitable in the South and West and circulation increased.

Local lending rates and bond prices were important variables in determining profitability, but they ignored bank entry and have not adequately explained changes in circulation. I argue that changes in the regulatory environment help greatly to explain the movements in circulation and increased bank entry. The reduction in circulation can be traced to an 1882 change in the law that allowed banks to divest their bond holdings. The law also reduced barriers to entry and made national banking attractive to potential entrants. Circulation rebounded in 1900 when another change in the law made note issue more profitable and induced new banks to enter the system.[4]

The Journal of Economic History, Vol. L, No. 3 (Sept. 1990). ISSN 0022-0507.

The author is Associate Professor of Economics, Oglethorpe University, Atlanta, GA 30319.

The majority of the work done on this note was completed while the author was a visiting scholar at Clemson University, Fall 1988. I am indebted to David N. Laband, Clark Nardinelli, John James, and the editors and referees of this JOURNAL for their helpful comments on earlier drafts. The usual disclaimer applies.

[1] *Report of the Comptroller of the Currency* (Washington, DC, 1890), p. 9.

[2] *Report of the Comptroller of the Currency* (Washington, DC, 1883), pp. ix–xii. The comptroller's theory has been supported by several contemporary authors. See Paul Studenski and Herman Krooss, *Financial History of the United States* (New York, 1952), pp. 176–81; and Sidney Homer, *A History of Interest Rates* (New Brunswick, 1963), p. 315. Phillip Cagan revised the comptroller's theory to allow repeated issue, or leveraging of capital devoted to bond purchases. See Phillip Cagan, "The First Fifty Years of the National Banking System—An Historical Appraisal," reprinted in Deane Carson, *Banking and Monetary Studies* (Homewood, IL, 1963), pp. 22–23.

[3] John James, "The Conundrum of the Low Issue of National Bank Notes," *Journal of Political Economy*, 84 (Apr. 1976), pp. 360–67.

[4] James, "The Conundrum of the Low Issue"; and Richard Sylla, "Federal Policy, Banking Market Structure, and Capital Mobilization in the United States, 1863–1913," this JOURNAL, 29 (Dec. 1969), pp. 657–86, emphasized the importance of the Monetary Reform Act of 1900 on national bank profitability and bank entry.

TABLE 1
NUMBER OF NATIONAL BANKS BY STATUS AND NATIONAL BANK NOTE CIRCULATION, 1876–1907

	Number of National Banks				
Year	New Banks	Voluntary Liquidation	Insolvent	In Active Operation	Bank Note Circulation
1876	36	32	9	2,089	$319.2
1877	29	26	10	2,080	315.8
1878	28	41	14	2,053	319.6
1879	38	33	8	2,048	335.1
1880	57	9	3	2,090	342.0
1881	86	26	0	2,132	358.9
1882	227	78	3	2,269	360.9
1883	262	40	2	2,501	350.8
1884	191	30	11	2,664	332.5
1885	145	85	4	2,714	314.9
1886	174	25	8	2,852	301.0
1887	225	25	8	3,049	271.7
1888	132	34	8	3,140	239.0
1889	211	41	2	3,290	201.7
1890	307	50	9	3,540	179.5
1891	193	41	25	3,677	171.9
1892	163	53	17	3,773	172.0
1893	119	46	67	3,781	208.7
1894	50	79	21	3,755	207.1
1895	43	49	36	3,712	213.5
1896	28	37	27	3,676	234.4
1897	44	70	38	3,610	230.0
1898	56	69	7	3,535	239.5
1899	78	64	12	3,595	242.9
1900	383	43	6	3,871	331.6
1901	394	39	11	4,221	359.8
1902	470	71	2	4,601	380.4
1903	553	72	12	5,042	419.5
1904	431	65	20	5,412	457.2
1905	506	121	22	5,757	524.4
1906	455	81	8	6,137	583.1
1907	516	84	7	6,544	609.9

Note: Bank note circulation is in millions of dollars and is the stock on or around October 1 of each year.
Sources: New Banks, Voluntary Liquidation, and Insolvent figures are from *Report of the Comptroller of the Currency* (Washington, DC, 1907), p. 111. Number of National Banks in Active Operation are from *Report of the Comptroller of the Currency* (Washington, DC, 1908), pp. 500–21. Circulation is from *Report of the Comptroller of the Currency* (Washington, DC, 1914), p. 110.

A MODEL LINKING REGULATION AND NATIONAL BANK NOTE ISSUE

Charles Calomiris has recently developed a model for determining the aggregate supply of bank notes under suspension of convertibility and exogenous greenback supply.[5] Borrowing from Calomiris and others, I have modeled the aggregate bank note supply under the gold standard as a negative function of the interest rate on demand deposits (see Figure 1). The logic for a negative sloping supply curve is that as the

[5] Charles W. Calomiris, "Price and Exchange Rate Determination During the Greenback Suspension," *Oxford Economic Papers*, 40 (Dec. 1988), pp. 189–220.

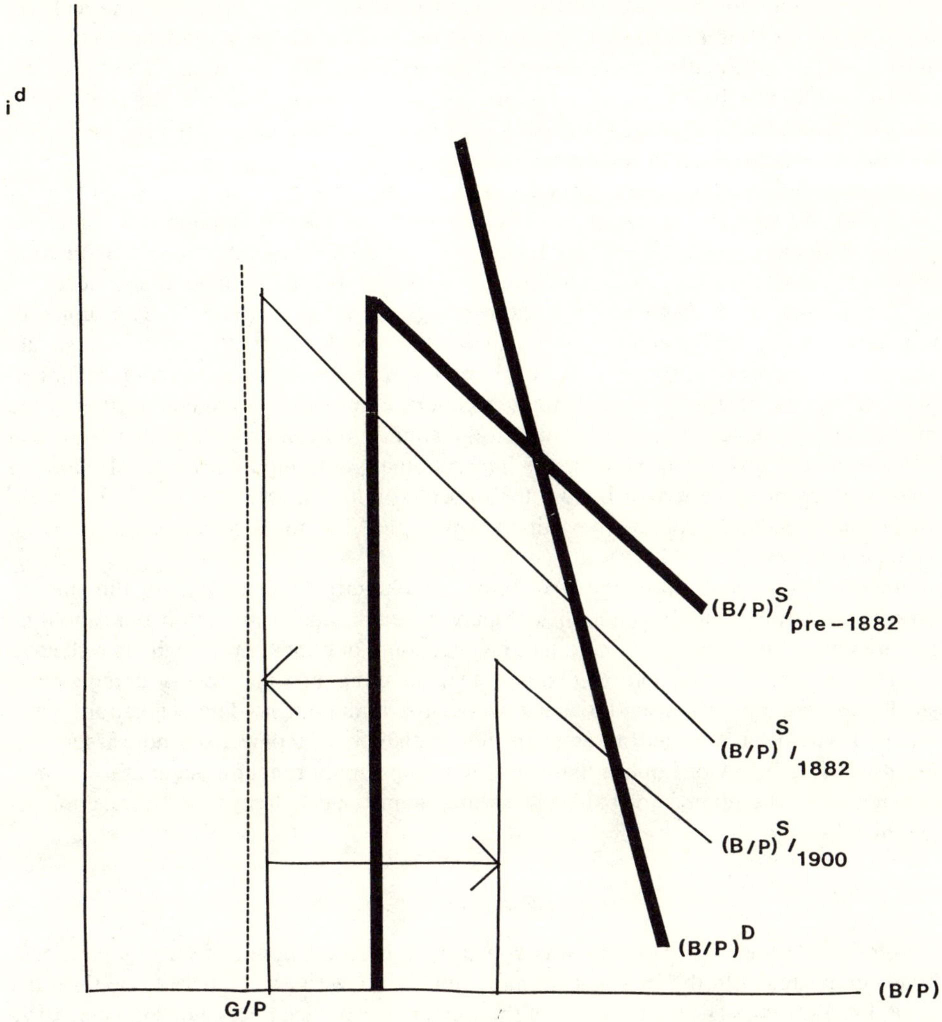

FIGURE 1

THE MARKET FOR REAL PAPER MONEY

Notes: The interest rate paid on deposits is i^d. (B/P) represents real paper money. $(B/P)^D$ is the demand for real paper money. $(B/P)^S$/pre-1882 represents the supply of real paper money before the Act of 1882, $(B/P)^S/1882$ represents the supply of real paper money after the Act of 1882. $(B/P)^S/1900$ is the supply of real paper money after the Monetary Reform Act of 1900. (G/P) is the real greenback supply.

opportunity cost of diverting bank capital to note supply rises, the marginal banks drop out of the note supply business.

For any bank, the real rate of profit per unit of bank capital diverted to bond purchases can be expressed as in equation 1:

$$\text{Real Profit Rate} = L[b - (0.9t)r - 0.009] - p \tag{1}$$

where L is a leverage coefficient, t is the greenback reserve ratio, 0.009 is the annual note tax (in units of bonds purchased), p is the expected inflation rate, b is the nominal yield on government bonds, and r is the local lending rate. James argued that r varied regionally while Calomiris argued that *b* was exogenous to note supply and the real rate of profit for the marginal bank was given exogenously. Calomiris and Glenn Hubbard argued that under the classical gold standard *b* and *p* can be determined internationally (within bounds).[6] Given these assumptions and the average spread between the interest rates on bank loans and demand deposits, the supply curve of bank notes can be plotted as a decreasing function of the demand deposit rate.

The demand for real paper money $(B/P)^D$ consisted of the demand for national bank notes (*N*) and greenbacks (*G*) and can be written as a negative function of the interest rate on demand deposits, a positive function of the price level, and a positive function of real income. With a gold standard, it is reasonable to assume that prices are exogenous and that income would be exogenous to paper money supply. The supply of real paper money will be kinked (assuming that the greenback supply is not interest-rate sensitive). In order to ensure stability of the equilibrium, let the demand function for real paper money be steeper than the supply function. Figure 1 plots the equilibrium in the market for real paper money, from which the equilibrium supply of nominal notes can be determined, given real income, the internationally determined price level, nominal interest rates on government bonds, the expected inflation rate, the supply of greenbacks, the exogenous real rate of profit on bank capital, and the endogenous interest rate on demand deposits.

Some national bank note supply occurred involuntarily, not as part of the smooth downward sloping supply function in Figure 1. Banks faced minimum bond holding requirements. Once they were holding a given amount of bonds, they might as well have used them as backing for national bank notes, since the marginal cost of doing so was small. Some national banks (those for whom the minimum holding regulations were binding) would have issued notes even though their net income from note issue was negative. This behavior implies that the kink in the supply function occurs farther out, depending on the number of banks, their minimum bond holdings, and the supply of greenbacks.

DETERMINANTS OF NOTE ISSUE

Before 1882 the issue of notes was constrained by the amount of U.S. government bonds deposited with the treasury. Bond requirements were the higher of one-third the capital or $30,000.[7] The Comptroller of the Currency provided notes equal in value to 90 percent of the market or par value of the deposited bonds, whichever was lower.[8] Two amendments to the national banking system are critical in explaining the decline in notes issued along with the simultaneous increase in bank charters and the subsequent rebound in circulation after 1900. The Act of July 12, 1882, explains the decline, and the Monetary Reform Act of 1900 explains the rise. Both explain new bank entry.

The 1882 Act reduced the minimum bond requirement that national banks had to deposit with the treasury to 25 percent of capital with a $50,000 cap. With bond premiums ranging between 20 and 30 percent, banks made significant capital gains by

[6] Charles W. Calomiris and Glenn R. Hubbard, "Evaluating Theories of International Adjustment Under the Classical Gold Standard" (NBER Working Paper No. 2206, Apr. 1987).

[7] In order to receive a national bank charter, minimum capital requirements had to be met: $50,000 in areas where population was less than 6,000 (nonreserve city banks) and $150,000 where population exceeded 6,000 (reserve city banks).

[8] After setting aside a 5 percent redemption fund against notes outstanding (the bank would usually exchange 5 percent of its own notes for gold) the bank would loan the remaining national bank notes.

selling bonds and retiring circulation.[9] The act also reduced barriers to entry for marginal banks that had not entered previously because of the prohibitive costs of diverting capital to bond holdings. Since banks no longer had to tie up as much capital against which nothing could be issued, existing national banks divested their bond holdings, which reduced the supply of real paper money, while new entrants worked to shift the supply to the right. On balance, the former effect was greater than the latter and the supply shifted to the left as illustrated in Figure 1.

The Monetary Reform Act of 1900 brought three changes: banks were allowed to receive notes equal in value to the bonds deposited with the treasury; the tax on notes outstanding was reduced from 1 to 0.5 percent; and minimum capital requirements were reduced to $25,000 in areas where population was less than 3,000 inhabitants. Existing banks began at once to circulate their additional allotment of notes and the rate of entry into the system increased.[10] As a consequence the supply function shifted down due to the reduced tax on notes and the increased leverage coefficient and shifted left with the new entries. The effects are illustrated in Figure 1.

There are four empirical implications of the preceding discussion. Two deal with entry: (1) bank entry should have been greater in regions where local lending rates were higher since banks could have loaned their capital stock directly rather than tie it up in bonds; and (2) because of high bond prices new banks should have deposited the legal minimum in bonds in order to avoid tying up their capital stock. Two deal with note issue: (1) banks in operation before 1882 should have divested their bond holdings and reduced circulation, and (2) there should have been a greater reduction in circulation for reserve city banks.

EMPIRICAL TESTS

Some evidence on bank entry and circulation was shown in Table 1. Bank entry was sluggish before 1882, grew rapidly between 1882 and 1891 (the period of low note issue), declined during the depression years from 1893 to 1899, and then experienced its greatest period of growth between 1900 and 1907, finally slowing down during the Panic of 1907. It should be no surprise that the first period of rapid bank entry began in 1882, the second in 1900. Circulation on the other hand increased before 1882, contracted by over 50 percent between 1882 and 1891, increased somewhat sporadically during the 1890s, and exploded after 1900.[11] By the time the Federal Reserve System replaced the National Banking System in 1914, circulation was well over $1 billion. Again it is no coincidence that circulation began its decline in 1882 and rebounded in 1900.

Before the Act of July 12, 1882, there were 2,298 national banks operating nationwide,

[9] The Act of July 12, 1882, was especially favorable to reserve city banks, those with capital in excess of $200,000, for no matter how large such a bank was, after the act it only had to hold $50,000 in government bonds to secure circulation. Reserve city banks stood to make considerable windfalls by divesting their bond holdings.

[10] New entry was especially rapid in areas where population was less than 3,000 inhabitants.

[11] The $70 million increase in circulation between 1892 and 1899 was not the result of increased note profitability. Instead, banks increased circulation as a means to pay off depositors following the panics of 1893 and 1897. In the 1899 Annual Report the comptroller stated that national banks, in 1893, paid off $31.2 million in depositors by increasing circulation. An additional $11 million would have been issued to pay depositors, but the comptroller's office experienced a printing delay. *Report of the Comptroller of the Currency* (Washington, DC, 1899), p. xii. A similar incident occurred in 1897 and 1898 when state banks gave national banks U.S. bonds in exchange for national bank notes. State banks then paid off their depositors with national bank notes. For further detail of these two incidents, see *Bradstreet's*, Aug. 15, 1893; *Financial Review* (New York, 1901), pp. 61–63; and Charles Hoffmann, *The Depression of the Nineties—An Economic History* (Westport, CT, 1970), p. 207.

TABLE 2
NATIONAL BANK ENTRY BY REGION, 1882–1891 AND 1900–1907

Region	1882	1891	1900	1907	Changes 1882 to 1891	Changes 1900 to 1907
East	558	585	568	489	27 (5%)	−79 (−14%)
Mid Atlantic	690	884	973	1,478	194 (28%)	505 (52%)
South	213	562	544	1,334	349 (150%)	790 (145%)
Midwest	778	1,384	1,296	2,512	606 (78%)	1,216 (94%)
Pacific	59	278	220	837	219 (371%)	617 (280%)
United States	2,298	3,693	3,601	6,650	1,395 (61%)	3,049 (85%)

Notes: The East region is Maine, New Hampshire, Vermont, Massachusetts, Rhode Island, and Connecticut. The Mid Atlantic states are New York, New Jersey, Pennsylvania, Maryland, Delaware, and the District of Columbia. The South region is Virginia, West Virginia, North Carolina, South Carolina, Georgia, Florida, Alabama, Mississippi, Louisiana, Arkansas, Texas, Tennessee, and Kentucky. The Midwest states are Ohio, Indiana, Illinois, Michigan, Wisconsin, Minnesota, Missouri, Iowa, Kansas, Nebraska, North Dakota, and South Dakota. The Pacific states are Colorado, Nevada, Oregon, Utah, Idaho, Montana, Wyoming, New Mexico, Washington, Arizona, and California.
Source: Computed from annual balance sheet data for each individual national bank. The evidence was reported on or around September 1 of each year and includes entries that occurred over the preceding 12 months.

with 1,050 of them operating in the South, Midwest, and Pacific regions (see Table 2). There were 1,395 national banks chartered between 1882 and 1891, and, as expected, over 80 percent (1,174) were chartered in the South (349), Midwest (606), and Pacific (219) regions. By comparison, only 27 banks were chartered in New England and 194 were chartered in the Mid Atlantic section of the country. The Act of 1900 reduced capital requirements from a minimum of $50,000 to $25,000, and national banks were made increasingly competitive in more rural areas. Two-thirds (2,063) of the 3,049 banks chartered between 1900 and 1907 had a capital stock less than $50,000 and accounted for almost one-third of all national banks in 1907. Bank entry was again greatest in the South (790), Midwest (1,216), and Pacific (617) regions. It is important to note that bank entry after 1900 was prompted by reduced barriers to entry and not from excess profit from note issue (although a greater rate of return could be made from note issue after the Monetary Reform Act than before). This was especially true for new entrants with the highest opportunity costs, that is, banks in the South, Midwest, and Pacific regions of the country. Banks in these regions stood to gain little by diverting capital to the purchase of bonds to support note issues. Having to hold bonds was still a bitter pill to swallow but less so after the Act of 1990.

The second conjecture, concerning the amount of bonds deposited to secure circulation after the 1882 Act, also holds up well. After a brief adjustment period in 1883 and 1884, national banks did not deposit more than 10 percent of the legal minimum until after 1891. In fact, after 1887 national banks were never in excess of 1 percent of the legal minimum.[12]

[12] *Report of the Comptroller of the Currency* (Washington, DC, 1891), p. 44.

TABLE 3
NATIONAL BANK NOTE CIRCULATION BY REGION, 1882–1891
(in millions of dollars)

Region	1882	1891	Decline	Percent Decline
East:	$128.69	$47.10	−$81.59	−63%
Reserve City	30.44	4.05	−26.38	−88
Nonreserve City	98.24	43.05	−55.20	−56
Mid Atlantic:	128.20	52.42	−72.78	−59
Reserve City	43.83	10.12	−33.71	−77
Nonreserve City	81.37	42.30	−39.06	−48
South:	31.56	9.95	−21.60	−69
Reserve City	5.40	0.88	−4.52	−83
Nonreserve City	26.16	9.07	−17.08	−66
Midwest:	70.87	29.48	−41.39	−58
Reserve City	8.52	1.54	−6.98	−82
Nonreserve City	62.35	27.94	−34.40	−55
Pacific:	4.65	2.37	−2.28	−55
Reserve City	0.25	0.04	−0.21	−83
Nonreserve City	4.29	2.33	−2.07	−45
National Banking System:	361.00	141.34	−219.39	−61
Reserve City	88.46	16.65	−71.81	−81
Nonreserve City	272.41	124.69	−147.58	−53

Notes: Banks chartered after 1882 are not included. The numbers in the columns may not add due to rounding errors. See Table 2 for regional definitions.
Source: Computed from balance sheet data for each individual national bank for the 1882–1891 period.

National banks operating before 1882 reacted to the legislation by reducing their circulation by $219.4 million, and, as predicted, reserve city banks reduced circulation more than did nonreserve city banks. The figures in Table 3 show this. Reserve city banks reduced circulation 80 percent ($71.8 million) while nonreserve city banks reduced circulation only 53 percent ($147.6 million).

CONCLUSION

I have argued that regulatory changes help to explain swings in national bank circulation and entry. High premiums on U.S. government bonds caused banks to divest some bond holdings but cannot alone account for the entire national bank note decline. Without regulatory changes the decline would have been greatly reduced in magnitude. My findings are consistent with James's that entry was greatest in regions with high interest rates, but reduced entry barriers also had an effect. With the reduction in the required amount of capital tied up in bonds many banks that would not have entered before the legislative changes sought national bank charters.

This still leaves unanswered exactly why national bank charters were so attractive. The re-emergence of state chartered banking between 1875 and 1900 provided a viable alternative, and most state banks faced less regulation, had lower capital requirements, and were allowed branch banking and mortgage lending. Yet national banks grew in number. Further research about national bank profitability and the emergence of checkbook money might clarify this phenomenon.

Exchange Rates and Economic Recovery in the 1930s: An Extension to Latin America

JOSÉ MANUEL CAMPA

In a study of ten European countries during the 1930s Barry Eichengreen and Jeffrey Sachs show that devaluation benefited the initiating countries and that there can be no presumption that depreciation was beggar-thy-neighbor.[1] I apply their methodology to ten Latin American countries.

Examining the behavior of the Latin American economies is important in several respects: these countries were hit first by and reacted earlier to the effects of the Depression; they were part of the "periphery" and their policies did not directly affect the behavior of the "center"; and their experience during the 1930s led them to select a subsequent inward-oriented path of development, based on import substitution.[2]

This model of development built upon a particular set of social and economic structures that were seen as shaping the world economic order, notably a center and a periphery with different structures of production. Unlike those of the periphery, the industrialized economies of the center are self-sustained; specifically, the periphery is constrained by an export sector confined to a very small range of goods and offering only limited backward and forward linkages with the rest of the economy.[3]

This note shows that Latin America reacted in the same way to depreciation as did Europe, and so offers evidence against the argument that Latin American economies were structurally constrained during this period.

I. LATIN AMERICAN DEPRECIATIONS IN THE 1930s

Latin American countries varied greatly in their ability to manage their economic policies independently. Countries which either were relatively large, such as Brazil, or

The Journal of Economic History, Vol. L, No. 3 (Sept. 1990). ISSN 0022-0507.

The author is a graduate student in the Department of Economics, Harvard University, Cambridge, MA 02138.

I am grateful to Paul Hohenberg, Eric Rice, Wendy Wisbaum, and the referee for their comments. I am specially indebted to Jeffrey Williamson for his encouragement and advice.

[1] Barry Eichengreen and Jeffrey Sachs, "Exchange Rates and Economic Recovery in the 1930s," this JOURNAL, 45 (Dec. 1985), pp. 925–46.

[2] The causes were a deterioration in the terms of trade due to the fall in primary commodity prices in 1929, a decline in foreign lending from the United States in 1928, and later the emergence of protective tariffs in industrial countries. The terms "center" and "periphery" were used in this context by Raúl Prebisch, *The Economic Development of Latin America and its Principal Problems* (New York, 1950), to refer to the industrialized countries and to the developing world, respectively.

[3] The "structuralists," as this school of thought came to be known, describe the structure of production in the periphery as poorly integrated and very specialized, characterized by exports of primary products and imports of manufactures. Because demand for imports in developing countries tends to grow faster than the demand for exports, the periphery terms of trade deteriorate, resulting in a structural external disequilibrium. The only long-term alternative is for the developing country to satisfy its highly income-elastic demand for manufactures through a process of industrialization and import substitution. For an explicit description of the structuralist framework, see Raúl Prebisch, "International Trade and Payments in an Era of Coexistence," *American Economic Review*, 49 (May 1959), pp. 251–73; and Raúl Prebisch, "The Economic Development of Latin America and its Principal Problems," *Economic Bulletin for Latin America*, 7 (Feb. 1962), pp. 1–22. Good economic critics of Prebisch's work are Robert E. Baldwin, "Secular Movements in the Terms of Trade," *American Economic Review, Papers and Proceedings*, 45 (May 1955), pp. 259–69; and G. Haberler, "Terms of Trade and Economic Development," in H. S. Ellis, ed., *Economic Development of Latin America* (New York, 1961), pp. 275–97.

TABLE 1
PRINCIPAL MEASURES AFFECTING EXCHANGE RATES AND MONETARY GOLD RESERVES

Country	Suspension of Gold Standard	Exchange Controls	Depreciation Relative to Gold	Central Monetary Gold Reserves[a]
Argentina[b]	Dec. 1929	Oct. 1931	Nov. 1929	0.50
Bolivia	Sep. 1931	Oct. 1931	Mar. 1930	0.25
Brazil[b]		May 1931	Dec. 1929	0.09
Chile[b]	Apr. 1932	Jul. 1931	Apr. 1932	2.43
Colombia[b]	Sep. 1931	Sep. 1931	Jan. 1932	0.38
Costa Rica[b]		Jan. 1932	Jan. 1932	
Cuba	Nov. 1933	Jun. 1934	Apr. 1933	
Ecuador	Feb. 1932	May 1932–Jul. 1936	Jun. 1932	2.00
Guatemala[b]			Apr. 1933	
Honduras[b]		Mar. 1934	Apr. 1933	
Mexico[b]	Jul. 1931		Aug. 1931	2.14
Nicaragua[b]	Nov. 1931	Nov. 1931	Jan. 1932	
Panama			Apr. 1933	
Paraguay		Aug. 1932	Nov. 1929	
Peru	May 1932		May 1932	0.57
Salvador, El[b]	Oct. 1931	Aug. 1933	Oct. 1931	0.80
Uruguay	Dec. 1929	Sep. 1931	Apr. 1929	0.56
Venezuela		Dec. 1936	Sep. 1930	1.67

[a] Ratio of 1935 to 1929 gold reserves
[b] The country has been used below for my analysis.
Source: League of Nations Economic Intelligence Service, *Monetary Review* (Geneva, 1937), appendix tables I, VI.

had autonomous public sectors, such as Costa Rica and Uruguay, followed more active exchange rate policies. Carlos Díaz-Alejandro calls these "reactive" countries. Small countries, like Honduras, or those with highly dependent governments, such as Cuba, followed much more passive policies.[4]

Table 1 shows the timing of depreciations in Latin America. A decrease in foreign capital inflows, a small decrease in the quantity of exports, and a sharp decline in export prices were the precipitating forces. By December 1929 Argentina and Uruguay had suspended gold payments and both had suffered a depreciation. Paraguay and Brazil devalued their currencies shortly thereafter. In 1930 Bolivia and Venezuela had to devalue officially. All of these devaluations preceded Britain's departure from the gold standard in 1931. These precocious Latin American countries faced great pressure from the balance of payments.

The second round of depreciations started with the devaluation of the British pound in September 1931. Countries that had their currency tied to sterling and had already devalued, like Argentina and Bolivia, were forced to do it once more. Mexico, Costa Rica, Colombia, and Peru followed within six months. Most of these countries suspended their currency's parity with gold as well.

The fall of the U.S. dollar in 1933 provoked a new round of depreciations among the Latin American economies. All Central American currencies were pegged to the U.S. dollar, and some had not even developed their own monetary policies. Therefore their

[4] Carlos Díaz-Alejandro, "Latin America in the 1930s," in Rosemary Thorp, ed., *Latin America in the 1930s, The Role of the Periphery in World Crisis* (Oxford, 1984), chap. 2.

currency immediately depreciated with respect to gold.[5] Argentina, Colombia, Mexico, and Uruguay suffered new depreciations during that year.

Beginning in 1933 most countries implemented complex systems of exchange controls, with multiple and preferential exchange-rate regimes. These regimes were intended to promote import substitution and economic activity or to avoid currency speculation and capital outflows. The official rate was applied to certain "official" imports, and the lower free trade rate was used for all other commodities, as in Colombia and Argentina. In Uruguay the free rate was de facto a multiple exchange rate, with a different rate depending on the type of transaction. Most countries distinguished between import and export rates, and among the commodities being traded. Moreover, the exchange rates also differed depending on the partner country. Chile, for instance, in addition to the official exchange rate had three other exchange rates: the "export rate" for transactions with the United States and the United Kingdom, the "compensation rates" for transactions with other European countries, and the "free rates" for other transactions.[6]

II. COUNTRY-SPECIFIC EFFECTS OF DEPRECIATION

Eichengreen and Sachs use a simple two-country model based on the work of Robert Mundell and J. Marcus Fleming.[7] In each country wages adjust slowly, but prices move to clear the commodity markets. Eichengreen and Sachs show that devaluation in a country has either a positive effect or no effect on domestic output, and can have a positive or negative effect on foreign output, depending on the monetary measures that accompany the devaluation. In particular, whether the devaluation is unilateral or simultaneous and whether it is "sterilized" or not determines the kind of effect the devaluation will have.[8] Then they proceed to analyze the response of industrial production, real wages, export volume, discount rates, Tobin's q, and gold reserves for ten European countries.

I explore the same issues for ten Latin countries: Argentina, Brazil, Chile, Colombia, Costa Rica, Guatemala, Honduras, Mexico, Nicaragua, and El Salvador. Data constraints make it possible to examine only the effects of depreciation on industrial production and export volume. I assume that unilateral devaluations by Latin American countries had no effect on the rest of the world.[9] Therefore I focus only on the devaluating country's domestic economy.

A currency depreciation causes an increase in the price of imports relative to domestic goods, an aggregate-demand switch toward domestic goods, and a total increase in employment and output. Excess demand raises domestic commodity prices, stimulating aggregate supply and moderating the inflationary impact. Resources move

[5] One may conjecture that these were not important, real depreciations. It is fair to say that Central America followed a passive exchange-rate policy because even in the countries where the exchange rate was allowed to float, Costa Rica and El Salvador, it did not change very dramatically. See Victor Bulmer-Thomas, "Central America in the Inter-War Period," in Thorp, *Latin America in the 1930s*, p. 289.

[6] For a more detailed explanation of the different exchange-rate regimes applicable in each country, see League of Nations Economic Intelligence Service, *Monetary Review* (Geneva, 1937).

[7] See Robert Mundell, "Capital Mobility and Stabilization Policy under Fixed and Flexible Exchange Rates," *Canadian Journal of Economics and Political Science*, 29 (Nov. 1963), pp. 475–85; and J. Marcus Fleming, "Domestic Financial Policies under Fixed and under Floating Exchange Rates," *International Monetary Fund Staff Papers*, 9 (Nov. 1962), pp. 369–79.

[8] A devaluation is sterilized when the depreciating country adjusts its money supply in order to leave unchanged the ratio of gold backing to money in circulation.

[9] This small-country assumption seems realistic since all of these countries were part of the periphery.

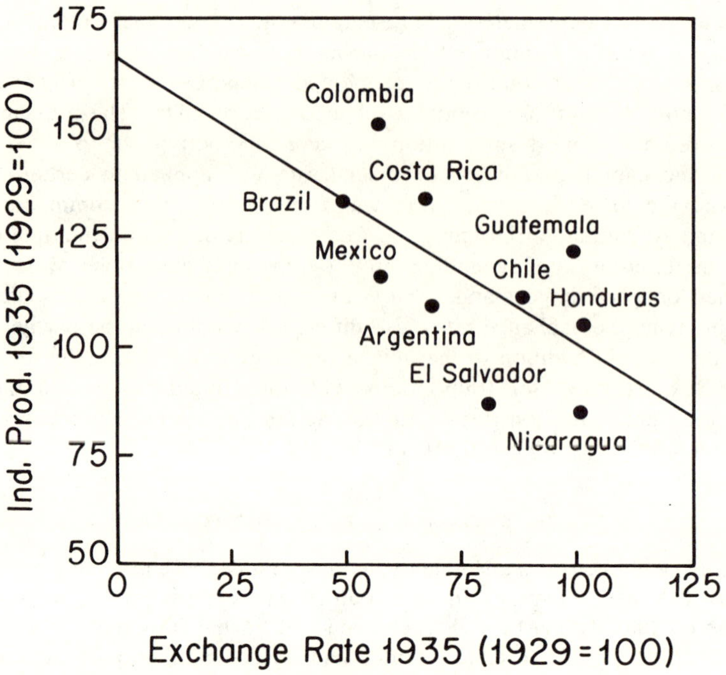

FIGURE 1

CHANGES IN INDUSTRIAL PRODUCTION, 1929–1935

from the nontraded sector toward the traded sector. Since manufactures constituted the main imports of most Latin American countries, this import-substitution effect served to reallocate resources from the primary sector to the industrial sector.[10]

Figure 1 shows the relationship between depreciation and the index of industrial production. The variables are defined the same way as in Eichengreen and Sachs.[11] A clear negative relationship exists. Reactive countries which devalued more performed better than passive countries. All countries except for El Salvador and Nicaragua experienced a relative increase in their industrial sector during this period, reflecting the shift in resources described above.[12]

[10] There is a general agreement that the import-substitution policies followed by the governments of the Latin American countries as an answer to the Depression were basically correct. These policies did not come from an existing theoretical framework but were the reaction to enormous macroeconomic imbalances. For a better description of the general policies, see Díaz-Alejandro, "Latin America in the 1930s." For a detailed description of individual countries' policies, see Angus Maddison, *Two Crises: Latin America and Asia, 1929–38 and 1973–83* (Washington, DC, 1985), pp. 23–32.

[11] A depreciation is expressed as the gold price of domestic currency in 1935 as a percentage of the 1929 parity. A value of 69 for Argentina indicates a 31 percent depreciation. Industrial production is the ratio of the production index in 1935 to that of 1929 multiplied by 100.

[12] El Salvador is a special case in the sense that it suffered a 17 percent reduction in industrial production in spite of an almost 20 percent depreciation. This was probably caused by the government's decision to keep promoting coffee production despite the drop in coffee prices. A more detailed exposition of the policies followed by the Salvadorian government in this period can be found in E. A. Wilson, "The Crisis of National Integration in El Salvador, 1919–35" (Ph.D. dissertation, Stanford University, 1970).

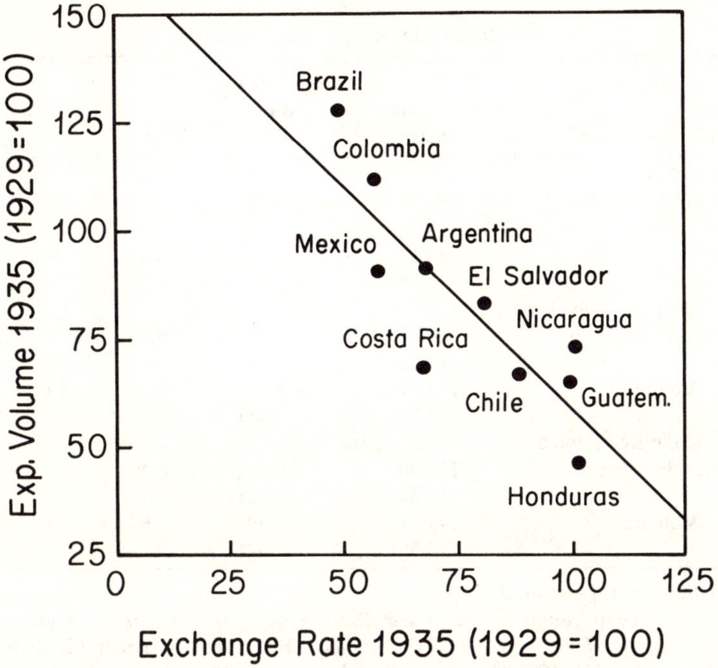

FIGURE 2

CHANGES IN EXPORT VOLUME, 1929–1935

Figure 2 shows the relationship between export performance and exchange rates. The vertical axis reflects the ratio of export volume of 1935 to the export volume of 1929, and the horizontal axis represents the same variable found in Figure 1. There is a clear negative relationship between the two variables, demonstrating that a higher currency depreciation served to improve that country's exports.

In order to analyze whether the Latin American countries reacted in a different manner to the depreciations than the European countries, I pooled my Latin American sample with the Eichengreen and Sachs European sample. Table 2 shows the results of simple OLS regressions. Regressions 1 and 2 reflect the results of the European sample used by Eichengreen and Sachs.[13] Regressions 3 and 4 correspond to the results using only the Latin American countries. Finally, regressions 5 and 6 correspond to the results of the pooled sample of European and Latin American countries, where the coefficients are restricted to be equal for both subsamples.

Taking as the null hypothesis that the structural coefficients are not different, the *F*-ratio test gives a value equal to 2.96 for the case of industrial production and 0.48 for export volume. In both cases the null hypothesis cannot be rejected at the 1 percent level of confidence. This implies that there is no statistical evidence of different behavior by the Latin American countries when compared to the European countries. One should realize, however, that even though there is no statistical difference in the behavior of both sets of countries, the underlying mechanism was somewhat dissimilar since the Latin nations traded less among themselves than the European countries.

Two straightforward conclusions emerge from these results. First, they show the robustness of the framework developed by Eichengreen and Sachs. This framework not

[13] These regressions reproduce equations 1 and 5 in table 3 of their paper.

TABLE 2
REGRESSION RESULTS, 1929–1935

Dependent Variable	Constant Term	Exchange-Rate Term	R^2	N	Sum Square Residuals
Ten European Countries					
(1) Industrial Production	153.55	−0.71	0.63	10	1349.285
	(14.59)	(−3.66)			
(2) Export Volume	140.87	−0.80	0.63	10	1714.387
	(8.56)	(−3.67)			
Ten Latin American Countries					
(3) Industrial Production	166.79	−0.66	0.40	10	2334.101
	(7.22)	(−2.29)			
(4) Export Volume	162.91	−1.04	0.71	10	1515.124
	(8.75)	(−4.45)			
The Twenty Countries Pooled					
(5) Industrial Production	156.40	−0.63	0.40	20	5048.950
	(10.84)	(−3.42)			
(6) Export Volume	149.44	−0.89	0.65	20	3424.112
	(12.56)	(−5.82)			

Note: *t*-statistics are in parentheses.
Sources: For European countries: Exchange Rate: League of Nations Economic Intelligence Service, *Monetary Review* (Geneva, 1937); Industrial Production: Brian Mitchell, *European Historical Statistics, 1750–1975* (2nd rev. edn., London, 1981); and H. W. Methorst, *Recueil international de statistiques économiques, 1931–1936* (The Hague, 1938); Export Volume: League of Nations, *Review of World Trade 1936* (Geneva, 1937). For Latin American countries: Exchange Rate: J. Wilkie, "Statistics and National Policy," in *Statistical Abstract of Latin America*, supplement 3 (Los Angeles, 1974); Industrial Production: Index value in Rosemary Thorp, ed., *Latin America in the 1930s, The Role of the Periphery in World Crisis*, appendix (Oxford, 1984); Export Volume: for Argentina, Brazil, Chile, and Mexico, index of export volume quantum in ECLA, *Economic Survey of Latin America 1949* (New York, 1950), for Colombia, export quantum index in M. Urrutia and M. Arrubla, eds., *Compendio de estadísticas históricas de Colombia* (Bogota, 1970), for the rest an export volume index was computed taking the ratio of real export values in 1935 over real export values in 1929 from Wilkie, "Statistics and National Policy."

only applies to a few European countries, but it can be generalized without altering the results. Second, although Latin American countries were hit first by and reacted earlier to the Depression, their response to exchange rate policies cannot be distinguished from that of European economies. Thus there is no evidence here to support the popular view that the Latin American economies were structurally constrained in the interwar period.

Vertical Disintegration in Lancashire: A Comment on Temin

MICHAEL HUBERMAN

In a recent article in this JOURNAL Peter Temin examined the determinants of vertical integration in the British and American cotton textile industries.[1] Temin found that spinners of coarse yarn and large firms were more likely to integrate (combine spinning and weaving) than were spinners of fine yarn and smaller firms. For the British case Temin relied on an 1833 survey of firms. In this note I reformulate and estimate Temin's model using evidence from a much larger survey of firms available for 1841. The reformulated model does not hold for the later survey. While the results for 1841 are not sufficient to overturn Temin's findings for 1833, they do raise questions about Temin's model of integration and whether it holds over time.

Temin's approach assumes that the proportion of integrated concerns remained roughly stable during the nineteenth century. This is an accurate description of industrial organization until mid-century, but the proportion of integrated firms and the percentage of total employment at these mills declined from 1850 on even though the number of integrated concerns increased steadily into the 1870s, as shown in Table 1.[2] The 1841 survey shows early signs that new firms in Lancashire had a greater tendency to be specialized than before.

I suggest that after mid-century new firms tended to specialize in spinning or weaving because large integrated firms faced a managerial constraint. Temin ignored these managerial limits in large part because he was concerned with a period when even integrated firms were small. After 1850, however, size became a problem, and firms tended to specialize in either spinning or weaving. First, I demonstrate that Temin's model does not hold for the 1841 survey, then I argue that integration was discouraged because, as the optimal size of combined spinning and weaving operations expanded after 1850, large integrated firms found themselves unable to monitor and supervise their work forces effectively.[3] Not surprisingly, the response was specialization.

The Journal of Economic History, Vol. L, No. 3 (Sept. 1990). ISSN 0022-0507.

The author is Associate Professor of Economics, Trent University, Peterborough, Ontario, Canada K9J 7B8.

Funding for this research was provided by the Social Sciences and Humanities Research Council of Canada. I would like to thank Jon S. Cohen, John S. Lyons, and Denise Young for their comments on earlier versions of this note. Robyn Dubrule assisted with the compilation and analysis of the data. All errors are my own.

[1] Peter Temin, "Product Quality and Vertical Integration in the Early Cotton Textile Industry," this JOURNAL, 48 (Dec. 1988), pp. 891–907.

[2] William H. Lazonick, "Industrial Organization and Technical Change: The Decline of the British Cotton Industry," *Business History Review*, 57 (Summer 1983), pp. 199–200.

[3] The standard analysis of the managerial constraint and firm expansion is Edith T. Penrose, *The Growth of the Firm* (Oxford, 1980). Sydney Chapman gave an early version of the Penrose effect in cotton: "We may lay it down as a rough approximation to the truth that in each industry and branch of an industry a typical magnitude tends to be attained. Where this magnitude is surpassed the waste involved in defective supervision begins to counterbalance the economies of further specialization." Sydney J. Chapman, *The Lancashire Cotton Industry* (Manchester, 1904), p. 168. For a more recent statement on the Penrose effect, see Roger Lloyd-Jones and M. J. Lewis, *Manchester and the Age of the Factory: The Business Structure of Cottonopolis in the Industrial Revolution* (London, 1988), pp. 206–7.

TABLE 1
INTEGRATED FIRMS IN THE BRITISH COTTON INDUSTRY

	Integrated Firms			Percentage of Total Employment in Integrated Mills
	Number	Mean Employment per Mill	As a Percentage of all Mills	
1824/25	321[a]		40.00[b]%	
1841	321	349	32.92	59.40%
1850	573	332	37.95	60.80
1878	597	354	23.68	43.73
1890	438	437	18.47	36.75

[a] Includes spinning firms (*N* equals 240) integrated with hand-loom weaving.
[b] Factory sector totals (excludes specialized hand-loom weavers).
Sources: The data for 1824/25 are from John S. Lyons, "Vertical Integration in the British Cotton Industry, 1825–1850: A Revision," this JOURNAL, 45 (June 1985), p. 420; for 1841 data, see V. A. C. Gatrell, "Labour, Power, and the Size of Firms in Lancashire Cotton in the Second Quarter of the Nineteenth Century," *Economic History Review*, 30 (Feb. 1977), p. 127; 1850 and 1878 data are from Thomas Ellison, *The Cotton Trade of Great Britain* (London, 1886), p. 72; and 1890 data are from "Reports of the Inspectors of Factories," *Parliamentary Papers*, vol. 17 (1897), p. 546.

I

Temin hypothesized that integration was a function of the type of yarn spun and firm size. Firms spinning coarse yarn found it more advantageous than did fine spinners to combine with weaving because power looms of the period were efficient only for weaving coarse yarn. Moreover, the costs of capital improvement were substantial, and larger firms that had access to credit could more easily finance an expansion into weaving. Temin wrote the argument in the following logit formulation.

$$\text{Prob}\ (INTEGRATE = 1) = f(a - b\ COUNT + c\ SPINNERS + u)$$

in which the probability of integration (where *INTEGRATE* takes the value of one if a firm integrates and zero otherwise) is hypothesized to be a negative function of the fineness of yarn or *COUNT* spun and a positive function of firm size, which is measured by the number of *SPINNERS* employed.

Temin used John Cowell's survey of 1833 to estimate the model but recognized that the survey had limitations.[4] Cowell's survey was restricted to the south and contained a relatively high proportion of large firms. Its snapshot view of firms would portray accurately the changes over time only if the period or industry was stable. Despite these limitations, Temin asserted that the 1833 survey provided a reasonable view of the industry and imparted no biases in the estimation.

The second quarter of the nineteenth century was not a stable period in the history of the cotton textile industry. Power-loom weaving, self-actor spinning, and longer mules which were to alter permanently the face of the industry were being introduced around the time of the 1833 survey. The period also marked the beginnings of regional specialization in the industry with northern Lancashire taking the lead in weaving and the south in spinning. An extensive survey is available which captures these changes. In late 1841, under the supervision of Leonard Horner, the factory inspectors conducted a survey of nearly 1,000 firms of all sizes in all the textile regions of Lancashire.[5] The

[4] Temin, "Product Quality," p. 893.

[5] "Reports of the Inspectors of Factories," *Parliamentary Papers*, vol. 22 (1842), pp. 370–99. For a detailed study of the 1841 survey, see V. A. C. Gatrell, "Labour, Power, and the Size of

survey is generally acknowledged to be comprehensive and so provides us with a sound body of data with which to test the explanatory power of Temin's model and to assess whether it holds over time.

The surveys are not directly comparable. While the 1833 survey records the actual counts spun for all types of firms, the 1841 survey notes only whether spinning firms spun fine or coarse yarn, and for integrated concerns gives no indication of the type of yarn spun. As reported in Table 2, however, the location of the industry can be used as a reasonable proxy for count. Bolton firms spun almost exclusively fine yarn, while those in Oldham concentrated on coarse yarn.[6] Manchester, a much larger city, contained firms that produced all types of yarn. Using 1841 data, therefore, Temin's model can be reformulated with Oldham and Bolton firms representing coarse and fine yarn production. The additional virtue of this specification is that it highlights any relation that may exist between local or urban specialization and vertical integration in the industry.

Columns 1 to 6 in Table 3 show the comparability of the two surveys and check the accuracy of using location as a proxy for counts spun. Column 1 reports Temin's results, and column 2 shows the logit results for a slightly modified sample of firms designed to be comparable to the 1841 survey.[7] Column 3 reports Temin's model estimated for 1833 for Manchester, Bolton, and Oldham only. The estimated coefficients are similar to those for the entire 1833 sample reported in column 1. Column 4 reports the estimation of the 1833 data for the three towns, but using dummy variables for Bolton and Oldham firms to represent fine and coarse spinning. Manchester is taken as the bench mark in the estimations. It had a large number of coarse spinning firms and a small group of large firms which spun the finest yarn in Lancashire. Indeed, as found in Table 2, the yarn spun by the latter group was so fine that the average count spun in Manchester was slightly above that found in Bolton. Because of the strong presence of fine spinners in Manchester, Temin's model would predict there would be no difference between the probability of integration in Bolton and Manchester, but that there would be a significant and positive difference between Manchester and Oldham where coarse spinning dominated. The results are in accord with Temin's hypothesis. The coefficient of the worker and the Oldham variables are positive and significant (at the 0.10 level), while that of the Bolton variable is insignificant. Finally, the predictive power of Temin's model and the model with proxies (columns 3 and 4) is identical. Note that column 5 reveals that the inclusion of the dummy variables for Bolton and Oldham adds to the predictive power of the model.[8] As expected, the dummies do contain more information than *COUNT*; nevertheless, neither of the town variables is significant in column 5.

Firms in Lancashire Cotton in the Second Quarter of the Nineteenth Century," *Economic History Review*, 30 (Feb. 1977), pp. 95–139.

[6] Douglas A. Farnie, *The English Cotton Industry and the World Market, 1815–1896* (Oxford, 1979), p. 303. Fine yarn is defined as counts above No. 60.

[7] John Cowell's survey of 1833 is reproduced in Andrew Ure, *The Cotton Manufacture of Great Britain* (London, 1836), vol. 1, pp. 334–42. My calculations are based on the 144 firms listed in Ure. Temin added 21 firms from the original survey, but the estimation results of the larger and smaller samples do not differ greatly. The estimation results of columns 2–6 in Table 3 are for the smaller sample. In his estimation Temin used the number of spinners to capture the size of firm effect. Because the 1841 sample gives only the total number of workers (spinners and weavers) in integrated firms, I have re-estimated the model for 1833 using total workers. For 1833 the number of spinners and workers are highly correlated (R^2 = 0.86).

[8] Following Temin's original model, column 6 reports the estimation of the 1833 survey using spinners as a measure of the size of firms. The coefficients have the predicted sign, although the spinner coefficient is significant at the 0.15 level. In general, the estimation of the reformulated model for 1833 using spinners does not perform as well as the model with total workers. This may be the result of using data for the three towns only to estimate the reformulated model.

TABLE 2
SIZE OF FIRMS AND TYPE OF YARN SPUN IN THREE TOWNS IN SURVEYS OF 1833 AND 1841

	1833					1841		
	Number of Firms	Number of Integrated Firms	Average Count Spun	Percentage of Fine Spinners	Mean Employment Size	Number of Firms	Number of Integrated Firms	Mean Employment Size
Manchester	38	14	78.90	44.74%	406.45	84	35	341.97
			(68.84)		(377.57)			(280.15)
Bolton	12	3	71.92	100.00	455.75	41	12	200.76
			(29.56)		(430.21)			(176.00)
Oldham	21	11	33.86	9.52	170.05	107	32	118.12
			(10.08)		(179.01)			(141.19)
All Firms	71	28	64.40	43.67	344.85	232	79	213.78
			(55.45)		(356.27)			(230.12)

Notes: Standard deviations are in parentheses. The category of fine spinners includes those firms that spun both fine (above No. 60) and coarse yarn. Mean size is calculated using total employment figures (spinners and weavers).

Sources: The 1833 data are from John Cowell's survey reprinted in Andrew Ure, *The Cotton Manufacture of Great Britain* (London, 1836), vol. 1, pp. 334–42. The 1841 data are from "Reports of the Inspectors of Factories," *Parliamentary Papers*, vol. 22 (1842), pp. 370–99.

TABLE 3
LOGIT ESTIMATES OF THE DETERMINANTS OF INTEGRATION IN LANCASHIRE, 1833 AND 1841

	1833						1841
	(1)	(2)	(3)	(4)	(5)	(6)	(7)
Constant	1.22	1.01	0.623	−1.1951	0.2766	0.6019	−1.652
	(3.24)	(2.98)	(1.27)	(−2.48)	(0.463)	(1.125)	(−4.42)
Count	−0.0431	−0.0347	−0.0421		−0.0416	−0.0271	
	(−4.07)	(−4.05)	(−3.41)		(−3.32)	(−3.26)	
Oldham				1.030	0.6158	0.4889	0.3127
				(1.72)	(0.937)	(0.794)	(0.847)
Bolton				−0.6976	−0.8674	−0.7011	−0.0942
				(−0.884)	(−0.841)	(−0.8279)	(−0.213)
Spinners	0.00306					0.0012	
	(2.78)					(1.45)	
Workers		0.0021	0.0032	0.0016	0.0038		0.0039
		(2.07)	(2.67)	(1.97)	(2.91)		(4.36)
Number of Observations	165	144	71	71	71	71	232
Percent Predicted Correctly	71%	70%	82%	82%	100%	100%	41%

Notes: For all regressions the dependent variable is *INTEGRATE*, which takes the values one and zero depending on whether or not the firm was integrated. The *t*-statistics are in parentheses. Column 1 is Temin's results for 1833 with spinners as a measure of size. Columns 2–5 are the estimation results of Temin's model for 1833 with total workers as a measure of size. Column 3 uses the 1833 survey data for Manchester, Bolton, and Oldham only. Column 4 uses the 1833 survey data with dummy variables for Oldham (=1; 0 otherwise) and Bolton (=1; 0 otherwise) firms. Column 5 uses the 1833 survey data for all variables. Column 6 uses the 1833 survey data with dummy variables and with spinners as a measure of size. Column 7 uses the 1841 survey data with dummy variables for Oldham (=1; 0 otherwise) and Bolton (=1; 0 otherwise) firms.
Sources: See Table 2.

The results in column 7 suggest that Temin's model may not explain the behavior revealed in the 1841 survey. There was a positive relation between workers and integration, in fact a much stronger one than revealed in the results in column 3. The Oldham coefficient, however, has the right sign but indicates that there was not a significantly different relation in Oldham and Manchester between count spun and integration. Similarly, fine spinning Bolton did not differ significantly from Manchester. The three towns specialized in different types of yarn production, but there appears to be no relation between counts spun and integration in 1841.

The Temin model might still be appropriate if the average size of firms in Oldham was small enough to offset the positive effect on integration of the low count production in the town. It is well known that the average Oldham firm was much smaller than those in Manchester and Bolton, and this may have discouraged integration. Separate regressions run for both surveys indicate that for all towns there was a significant positive relation between the size of establishments, measured by workers, and integration. In any event, historians of the Oldham industry report that during the late 1830s and through the 1840s the average size of mills was increasing.[9]

A related explanation why Temin's results for 1833 do not hold for 1841 is that the distribution of firms was different in the two samples. The 1841 sample may include a significantly higher proportion of smaller firms than that of 1833 and this may impart a bias in estimation. A goodness-of-fit test between the two surveys could not, however, reject the hypothesis that the distribution of firms in the two surveys was similar.[10]

It remains possible that the results of Table 3 indicate simply that the reformulated model for 1833 does not perform well for 1841, but there is additional support for the logit results. Using evidence on investments in new machinery and plant contained in the reports of the factory inspectors, H. B. Rogers found that coarse spinning towns like Oldham were not adding weaving facilities in the 1840s but were becoming more specialized in spinning production.[11] Rogers concluded that the inverse relation between integration and count spun found in 1833 was short-lived.

II

A widely held explanation of the changing pattern of industrial organization which can be traced to Alfred Marshall is that the benefits to integration were always small, but after 1850 there existed external economies for firms that specialized in spinning or weaving. These benefits included financial services, market exchanges, transportation networks, and readily available supplies of cotton, machinery, and industrial workers.[12]

[9] Edwin Butterworth, *Historical Sketches of Oldham* (Oldham, 1856); and sources cited in John Foster, *Class Struggle and the Industrial Revolution* (London, 1974), p. 230.

[10] For the 1833 and 1841 samples firms were grouped into four categories: firms with less than 100 workers; 100 to 199; 200 to 299; and greater than or equal to 300 workers. The actual values of 1833 were compared to their expected values, which were calculated using the distribution of firms found in the 1841 sample. The calculated chi-squared statistic is 9.18 with three degrees of freedom. The null hypothesis that there was no difference between the two samples could not be rejected at the 0.025 level of confidence.

[11] H. B. Rogers, "The Lancashire Cotton Industry in 1840," *Transactions and Papers of the Institute of British Geographers*, 28 (1960), pp. 135–55.

[12] Easy access to capital encouraged the entry of specialized firms after 1850. Alfred Marshall's views on specialization are summarized in Lazonick, "Industrial Organization," p. 200; and D. A. Farnie, "The Structure of the British Cotton Industry, 1846–1914," in Akio Okochi and Shin-Ichi Yonekawa, eds., *The Textile Industry and its Business Climate* (Tokyo, 1982), p. 59. For an assessment of the external economies of specialization, see C. H. Lee, "The Cotton Textile Industry," in Roy Church, ed., *The Dynamics of Victorian Business* (London, 1980), pp. 172–80. Lee rejected transportation and organizational factors and argued instead that after 1850 demand

An alternative explanation of the rise of specialized firms which has received less attention centers on the monitoring problems of large firms. Recent research on the cotton textile industry has established the importance of the managerial factor in insuring the smooth flow of output.[13] In the heyday of industrialization, however, there was little innovation in managerial methods of supervision or monitoring. In production processes such as spinning, which demanded a core group of skilled adult male workers, firms had to rely on an internal subcontract system to insure the flow of output. Adult males who were paid by the piece recruited, supervised, and paid their younger assistants or piecers. Relative to spinning, weaving demanded a larger proportion of unskilled operatives, usually women. Weaving firms had no "superior caste of employees" comparable to the spinners, and managers had to supervise operations themselves.[14]

The supervision problem, in conjunction with technical change in spinning, had implications for the organization of the industry. As long as the optimal size of the firm was small, it was possible for the managers of integrated or specialized firms to directly oversee their weavers. However, by 1850, if not earlier, the diffusion of the self-actor had led to an increase in the optimal size of specialized spinning and integrated firms.[15] Spinning operations were easily expanded because the adult male spinners were responsible for supervision, but weaving departments in integrated concerns could only expand if they could add managerial inputs. The available evidence suggests, however, that overseers were scarce.[16]

The managerial constraint on weaving operations created an imbalance in combined firms. Evidence on the number of spindles and power looms in the industry after 1850 suggests that integrated firms produced an excess supply of yarn.[17] In most large integrated concerns, according to S. J. Chapman and T. S. Ashton, weaving and spinning were two completely separate operations, in which "the whole or the bulk of the yarn [was] sold, while for the weaving the whole or the bulk of the yarn [was] bought."[18] As large integrated concerns could not realize the full benefits of integration, it was likely that firms entering the industry would specialize either in spinning or weaving.[19]

---

for yarn stabilized and it was no longer necessary for spinning firms to expand into weaving. Recent research has raised doubts about Lee's view that integration was a defensive strategy. John S. Lyons, "Vertical Integration in the British Cotton Industry, 1825–1850: A Revision," this JOURNAL, 45 (June 1985), pp. 419–26.

[13] William H. Lazonick, "Industrial Relations and Technical Change: The Case of the Self-Acting Mule," *Cambridge Journal of Economics*, 3 (Sept. 1979), pp. 231–62. Michael Huberman, "How Did Labor Markets Work in Lancashire? More Evidence on Prices and Quantities," *Explorations in Economic History*, 27 (forthcoming, Jan. 1991).

[14] Farnie, *English Cotton*, p. 297.

[15] Stanley D. Chapman, *The Cotton Industry in the Industrial Revolution* (2nd edn., London, 1987), p. 25.

[16] Chapman, *Lancashire Cotton*, p. 163, wrote that integration "implies a minute knowledge of machinery and hands, of what they can do, and of the stage to which the work in hand has progressed; a knowledge which is seldom consistent with the management of very large works." Real wage patterns are consistent with the managerial constraint hypothesis. Between 1833 and 1849 real wages of overseers in Manchester remained stable, but wages of spinners fell. For wages, see G. H. Wood, *The History of Wages in the Cotton Trade During the Past Hundred Years* (Manchester, 1910), pp. 14–15. For price index, see the Rousseaux index in B. R. Mitchell, *Abstract of British Historical Statistics* (Cambridge, 1962), p. 471.

[17] Lee, "Cotton Textile Industry," p. 177.

[18] S. J. Chapman and T. S. Ashton, "The Size of Businesses, Mainly in the Textile Industries," *Journal of the Royal Statistical Society*, 77 (Apr. 1914), p. 501.

[19] The methods of supervision in spinning and weaving had implications for the regional organization of the industry. An alternative way of monitoring workers was to use the threat of

III

In sum, Temin's model of integration works well with the 1833 survey, but when the model is adapted for use with the data for 1841, its performance is less satisfactory. This does not imply that if comparable data were available Temin's model would be rejected for 1841, but it does take issue with Temin's explanation of the course of integration over time. I have suggested that managerial inputs need to be considered explicitly in accounting for the declining share of integrated concerns. There are other explanations for the rise of specialized firms after 1850. It remains for future research to document more fully how the managerial constraint evolved and to assess its relative contribution to the changing pattern of integration.

---

dismissal. The threat was more likely in weaving because it demanded a larger proportion of unskilled operatives. But to enforce the threat, firms required an excess supply of labor. After 1850 weaving became increasingly concentrated in northern Lancashire where there was a surplus of young adults and women workers. Farnie (*English Cotton*, pp. 295–301) gives evidence to support the view that weaving firms migrated north to tap the excess supply of workers. Integrated and weaving firms in the south could not attract workers because labor was immobile, as evidenced by the persistence of wage differentials (ibid., p. 296).

Product Quality and Vertical Integration in the Early Cotton Textile Industry: A Reply

PETER TEMIN

Two cheers for Michael Huberman. His comment on my article makes two valid points but fails to preserve its internal consistency in its extrapolations from them.[1]

First, Huberman has replicated the principal empirical findings of my article. Such replication should become more common in economics and economic history. I welcome it here, of course, because my conclusion that integration in 1833 was related to product quality in the textile industry can be replicated easily. Huberman even shows that this finding is robust under alternate specifications.

Second, Huberman compares my principal regression for 1833 with a new regression for 1841. I did not use the 1841 survey in my work because it did not contain the data that my hypothesis required. Huberman has dealt with this problem in the spirit of Christina Romer, degrading the 1833 data to make them comparable with the 1841 data.[2] Regressions on these limited data (in columns 4 and 7 of his table 3) are not very good for either year. And they are less good for 1841 than for 1833.

What should we conclude from this difference? Neither regression on these incomplete data is well specified. Location is used as a proxy for product quality even though there was a range of quality in each location. The standard deviations of the count spun in a town was 69, 30, and 10 in Manchester, Bolton, and Oldham, respectively, in 1833. The ratio of the standard deviation to the mean in the three towns was 0.9, 0.4, and 0.3.[3] This independent variable, in other words, was very roughly measured, biasing its coefficient and *t*-statistic toward zero. In addition, Huberman uses all workers as a measure of size. I used spinners in order to avoid simultaneity coming from the presence of weavers in integrated establishments. The 1841 data do not allow this. Using workers as an independent variable introduces positive feedback into the regression, enhancing the measured significance of this variable.

Huberman finds that this imperfect regression works less well for 1841 than for 1833. But there is no test statistic for comparing poorly specified regressions. There is no way of knowing whether this difference represents chance, problems with the imperfect data, or changes in the structure of the cotton industry. Huberman's regression result, while interesting, does not provide a solid foundation for a new interpretation of the industry.

Nevertheless, Huberman is correct to emphasize the historical nature of my conclusion. The cotton textile industry was evolving rapidly, and the correlation between product quality and vertical integration that I found was a product of the then current technology. It is only natural to expect this relationship to evolve over time as power looms became more able to weave finer counts. I believe I emphasized the historical nature of my conclusions—that I was describing and analyzing economic conditions of the 1830s—but it is well to have that point emphasized.

This brings us to the problem with Huberman's argument. Starting from this highly imperfect evidence, he suggests that "the monitoring problems of large firms" can

The Journal of Economic History, Vol. L, No. 3 (Sept. 1990). ISSN 0022-0507.

Peter Temin is Professor of Economics, Massachusetts Institute of Technology, Cambridge, MA 02139.

[1] Michael Huberman, "Vertical Disintegration in Lancashire: A Comment on Temin," this JOURNAL, 50 (Sept. 1990); and Peter Temin, "Product Quality and Vertical Integration in the Early Cotton Textile Industry," this JOURNAL, 48 (Dec. 1988), pp. 891–907.

[2] Christina D. Romer, "Is the Stabilization of the Postwar Economy a Figment of the Data?" *American Economic Review*, 76 (June 1986), pp. 314–34.

[3] Huberman, "Vertical Disintegration," table 2.

account for "the rise of specialized firms." It is not clear what phenomenon is being described. On the one hand, Huberman's data refer to 1841. But, as I noted in my article, vertical integration was still *increasing* in Lancashire during the 1840s. There was no increase in vertical specialization to explain at the time of Huberman's regression.

On the other hand, if Huberman is discussing trends after 1850, he has fallen into the pit that he dug for me. He has made the implicit assumption that conditions remained the same over time so that his regression result for 1841 illuminates trends some decades later.

The monitoring cost argument also has other problems. Huberman cites evidence that supervisors were hard to get. But cotton textile firms were small among industrial firms. Expansion of the industry came from increases in the number of firms rather than the size of firms. The argument from monitoring costs would be stronger if cotton mills employed thousands rather than hundreds of workers.

The average employment of spinning factories in 1890 was about 150, small enough for personal supervision by a very few managers. Worrall's directory reports cotton mills of widely different sizes, from 50 to 750 employees, suggesting a more or less flat average cost curve in this range. Many integrated firms also survived, employing fully 30 percent of the spindles and 38 percent of the workers in the industry in 1890.[4] There does not seem to be a *prima facie* case in favor of a uniform firm size and configuration.

There surely were monitoring costs in cotton textiles, as there are in all industrial plants, but the decreasing integration of the Lancashire cotton industry in the late nineteenth century still awaits an explanation.

[4] Douglas A. Farnie, *The English Cotton Industry and the World Market* (Oxford, 1979), pp. 215, 317; and *Worrall's Cotton Spinners and Manufacturing Directory* (Oldham, 1890).

Politics, Popery, and Property: A Comment on North and Weingast

BRUCE G. CARRUTHERS

In a recent article Douglass North and Barry Weingast offered an intriguing interpretation of political and economic institutional change in seventeenth-century England.[1] Their central point is that the institutional arrangements that constrain government action have important implications for individual property rights and for the development of markets. They illustrate this argument using the example of constitutional change during the Glorious Revolution of 1688 and the subsequent development of public and private capital markets in England. I wish to discuss certain of the limitations to the North-Weingast argument.

North and Weingast assert that the development of markets is heavily influenced by the extent to which rulers abide by the rules that govern economic exchange.[2] Economic growth is reduced if rulers can unilaterally alter property rights whenever it suits them. Growth is enhanced if property rights are secure. Political institutions determine the extent to which rulers can revise property rights and hence also determine the trajectory of economic growth. They do this by structuring the incentives that face a ruler. Does a sovereign have an incentive to renege on his or her obligations, or is it in the sovereign's interest to live up to them? In the former situation, property rights will likely be violated. In the latter, they are secure.

North and Weingast apply this argument to the case of seventeenth-century England. They argue that political institutions changed during the Glorious Revolution in such a way as to alter fundamentally the incentives faced by English monarchs. They pay particular attention to capital markets and to public indebtedness since "capital markets are especially sensitive to the security of property rights."[3] Capital markets serve as a kind of litmus test. Before 1688 Stuart monarchs were frequently tempted to alter the terms of loans unilaterally, to grant monopolies, and to impose new taxes in order to solve their financial problems.[4] This demonstrated their willingness to alter property rights in their favor.

After 1688 constitutional changes shifted the position of the Crown relative to Parliament in such a way as to reduce the incentive to alter property rights. Parliamentary supremacy was established, Parliament gained a central role in public finances, various prerogative powers were eliminated or curtailed, and the judiciary gained its independence from the Crown.[5] The wealth holders represented by Parliament gained greater control over the government, enhancing the security of their property rights. Public creditors were now assured that the terms of their loans would be honored. The result was a tremendous development in the system of public finance, with more money being borrowed at lower rates of interest. North and Weingast summarize the develop-

The Journal of Economic History, Vol. L, No. 3 (Sept. 1990). ISSN 0022-0507.

The author is Assistant Professor of Sociology, Northwestern University, 1810 Chicago Avenue, Evanston, IL 60208.

The financial and institutional support of the American Bar Foundation is gratefully acknowledged. My thanks to Jack Knight and Jack Goldstone for helpful comments.

[1] Douglass C. North and Barry R. Weingast, "Constitutions and Commitment: The Evolution of Institutions Governing Public Choice in Seventeenth-Century England," this JOURNAL, 49 (Dec. 1989), pp. 803–32.

[2] Ibid., p. 803.

[3] Ibid., p. 819.

[4] Ibid., pp. 809–12.

[5] Ibid., pp. 816, 829.

ments of the "Financial Revolution" to show just how much public finance changed. In addition, the emergence of a market for public debt facilitated the emergence of the private capital market. North and Weingast present evidence from the English stock market to show how the expansion of private capital markets paralleled that of public capital markets.

North and Weingast set out a general argument and exemplify it with a single case. This case involves a comparison of an ex ante with an ex post situation. England before 1688 is contrasted with England after 1688. The difference between the two is then attributed to a particular set of constitutional changes that occurred between the two situations. Of course many events occurred after the fiscal depredations of James I and Charles I but before the financial developments of the reigns of William and Mary and Anne. Two in particular are relevant to North and Weingast's argument but receive scant attention.

I will focus upon these two events. One involved a default on Crown debts (the Stop of the Exchequer) and a protracted legal battle as Crown creditors sought to recover their loans. It raised virtually all the issues that North and Weingast address and so its neglect is unfortunate. The second involved an additional set of political changes. North and Weingast stress the constitutional changes that resulted in a shift in political power from the Crown to Parliament, but they ignore the issue of how Parliament's newly acquired power was organized. A major change in this period, the development of political parties, organized Parliament along Whig and Tory party lines. Party strife was an important factor in the development of public finance and capital markets, and so North and Weingast's political argument does not go far enough.

I will also focus upon North and Weingast's decision to set aside the question of religion and religious conflict, which lay at the heart of their historical case. Fears about James II's Catholicism, and not just his attitude toward property rights, motivated opposition to him before and during the Glorious Revolution. A direct comparison of the importance of religion and property rights is possible since Parliament considered both shortly after the Stop of the Exchequer.

The first omitted event would appear to strengthen the North-Weingast argument. It started in 1672 with the "Stop of the Exchequer": a unilateral suspension of repayment of debts owed by Charles II to a group of goldsmith-bankers. When the debt was finally calculated in 1677 it totaled over £1.3 million, then a vast sum.[6] Charles's revenues were heavily encumbered, and the Stop freed up the money necessary for the war he was about to launch against the Dutch.[7] Initially, payments were suspended for a single year, but repayment was postponed further. Starting in June 1674, pending final determination of the exact amount owed, £140,000 was paid out annually to the creditors as interest on their loans.[8] In April 1677 letters patent setting aside revenues from the hereditary excise were issued to pay 6 percent interest on the total debt due to the goldsmith-bankers, payable in quarterly installments. There was no provision to repay the principal of the loans, but nevertheless the action was a very welcome one to the bankers and their creditors.[9]

These payments were met fairly regularly through the rest of Charles II's reign, but

[6] See W. A. Shaw, ed., *Calender of Treasury Books* (London, 1908), vol. 3, p. xlviii.

[7] The connection of the Stop with the Third Dutch War is consistent with North and Weingast's point that wars raise the discount rate of rulers and make repudiations of sovereign debt more likely.

[8] J. Keith Horsefield, "The 'Stop of the Exchequer' Revisited," *Economic History Review*, 35 (Nov. 1982), p. 514.

[9] The terms of the letters patent allowed the goldsmith-bankers the option of assigning a portion of the interest payments they received directly to their own creditors, most of whom were former depositors.

only a few were made during the reign of James II. By the time of the accession of William and Mary in 1689, the payments were in considerable arrears.[10] When Parliament used the hereditary excise as backing for a loan without making any provision for these debts, it was clear that legal action would be necessary.

The legal options available to a Crown creditor were not very satisfactory. If the Crown defaulted on its debts, traditionally there was one avenue open: the petition of right. Sovereign immunity meant that a Crown creditor could not sue as when dealing with an ordinary debtor.[11] A king could not be sued in his own courts.

In a petition of right the petitioner would make his or her case to the Crown, establishing and documenting the claim as if in a court of law. Procedurally all advantages lay with the Crown. Proceedings were complex, lengthy, and could be suspended at any time. The burden of proof lay with the petitioners. Even if the case were proven, it was still up to the discretion of the Crown whether or not to grant the request.[12] If the Crown defaulted on a loan, creditors were in a very difficult position.

The bankers and their assignees brought a suit of *monstrans de droit* in the Court of Exchequer in 1691 for payment of the arrears.[13] They did *not* present a petition of right to William and Mary. It was easy to establish their claim to the interest payments, but the outcome of the case rested primarily on the question of whether they had followed the legally correct procedure.[14]

The Court of Exchequer decided that they had followed the correct procedure and so ruled in favor of the bankers. The decision was appealed to the Court of Exchequer Chamber by the Attorney General. This court consisted of the Lord Treasurer and the Lord Chancellor (or Lord Keeper), advised by the judges of the King's Bench and Common Pleas. Both the Treasurer and the Chancellor were political offices. The Treasurer was in commission, and so when Sir John Somers was appointed Lord Keeper in 1693 the appeal came before him. Somers rejected the advice of the other judges and ruled in 1696 that a petition of right was the correct procedure, and therefore that the *monstrans de droit* filed by the bankers was not.[15] Somers's ruling was widely regarded as politically motivated, since the government's finances were severely strained by the war effort against France.[16]

In 1699 the bankers and their assignees used their final option and brought an appeal to the House of Lords. In early 1700 the Lords reversed the decision of the Court of Exchequer Chamber and ruled in favor of the bankers.[17] This final decision recognized a *monstrans de droit* brought in the Court of Exchequer as a legal alternative to the petition of right.

This case, called the Bankers' Case, established a more satisfactory procedure for sovereign creditors. It gave them more easily enforceable property rights. The features of the Stop of the Exchequer–Bankers' Case episode are consistent with the North-Weingast argument: claims against the Crown were not very enforceable and the property rights of sovereign creditors were abused. When the creditors sought redress,

[10] Horsefield, "The 'Stop of the Exchequer,' " p. 517.

[11] C. G. A. Clay, *Economic Expansion and Social Change: England 1500–1700* (Cambridge, 1984), vol. 2, p. 277.

[12] Sir William Holdsworth, *A History of English Law* (3rd edn., London, 1944), vol. 9, pp. 8–15, 22–23.

[13] The Court of Exchequer had jurisdiction over cases involving Crown revenue. A *monstrans de droit* was a fourteenth-century offshoot of the petition of right. For some situations it provided an alternative remedy against the Crown. See Holdsworth, *A History*, p. 25.

[14] Ibid., p. 33.

[15] William L. Sachse, *Lord Somers: A Political Portrait* (Manchester, 1975), p. 75.

[16] Horsefield, "The 'Stop of the Exchequer,' " pp. 519–20.

[17] See the Historical Manuscripts Commission, *Manuscripts of the House of Lords*, new series (London, 1905), vol. 3, pp. 407–9.

they were defeated by a politically controlled court system until they reached the highest court: the House of Lords. It is not clear that the eventual success of the bankers was due to the constitutional changes associated with the Glorious Revolution, and, as will be discussed below, some aspects of the Stop are inconsistent with their argument. But nevertheless, given North and Weingast's agenda, the Stop and its consequences warrant much more than the simple mention they provide.[18] At issue in the Stop was the security of property rights.

If the episode of the Stop can buttress the North-Weingast argument, an even more important development of the period could well erode it. Much emphasis is put on the shift in political power from Crown to Parliament. But there is no examination of how parliamentary political power was organized. In this connection the most striking feature of late Stuart England was the emergence of two political parties: the Whigs and the Tories.[19] Parliamentary power was organized by the conflict between these two parties.

The genesis for party politics lay in the Exclusion Crisis in the late 1670s and early 1680s, before the Glorious Revolution. Led by Lord Shaftesbury, a Whig party was organized to exclude Charles II's younger brother James from the succession.[20] Opposition to the Whigs was organized into the Tory party. The Whigs were unable to win Charles II over to their position, and so James succeeded to the throne in 1685.

For a variety of reasons James II managed to alienate many of his Tory supporters.[21] The combination of Whigs and disaffected Tories was sufficient to generate very considerable opposition to James by 1688. During the reigns of William and Mary, and later William III, party distinctions were somewhat confused. Parliament was divided along Whig and Tory lines, but also along Court and Country lines.[22] During the reign of Anne, however, party differences were clear, and party conflict intense.[23]

From the perspective of the North-Weingast argument, the development of parties would be a largely irrelevant occurrence (one that happened to overlap with the important constitutional changes) were it not for the fact that party conflict had many repercussions in the area of public finance. To begin with, a number of the institutions involved in public finance had strongly partisan connections. The Bank of England played a central role in the management of the public debt and made substantial loans to the government. It was a Whiggish institution established by a Whig ministry.[24] The Tories made several moves to undermine the Bank, including an attempt to establish a rival Land Bank.[25] A group of Bank directors publicly attempted to influence Anne's

[18] North and Weingast, "Constitutions and Commitment," p. 820.

[19] I. F. Burton, P. W. J. Riley, and E. Rowlands, *Political Parties in the Reigns of William III and Anne* (Bulletin of the Institute of Historical Research, Special Supplement No. 7, London, 1968), pp. 1–3; Richard R. Johnson, "Politics Redefined: An Assessment of Recent Writings on the Late Stuart Period of English History, 1660 to 1714," *William and Mary Quarterly*, 35 (Oct. 1978), pp. 705–7.

[20] J. R. Jones, *The First Whigs: The Politics of the Exclusion Crisis, 1678–1683* (London, 1961), pp. 2, 4, 214.

[21] W. A. Speck, *Reluctant Revolutionaries: Englishmen and the Revolution of 1688* (Oxford, 1988), pp. 66, 128.

[22] Henry Horwitz, *Parliament, Policy and Politics in the Reign of William III* (Newark, 1977), pp. 217, 316–17.

[23] Geoffrey Holmes, *British Politics in the Age of Anne* (London, 1967), p. 63; W. A. Speck, *Tory and Whig: The Struggle in the Constituencies, 1701–1715* (London, 1970), pp. 1, 22.

[24] Horwitz, *Parliament, Policy and Politics*, pp. 130–31; Dennis Rubini, "Politics and the battle for the Banks, 1688–1697," *English Historical Review*, 337 (Oct. 1970), p. 694.

[25] Geoffrey Holmes, *British Politics*, p. 27; B. W. Hill, *The Growth of Parliamentary Parties, 1689–1742* (Hamden, 1976), p. 69.

selection of ministers in favor of the Whigs on the grounds that a Tory ministry would not be able to maintain public credit.[26]

The South Sea Company was also centrally involved in public finance. Its establishment in 1711 was part of a refinancing operation that converted short-term unfunded public debt into long-term debt.[27] It was also a deliberate political strategy on the part of the Tory minister Robert Harley to cultivate a Tory-controlled constituency in the money market.[28]

The East India Companies were also embroiled in party conflict and played a role in public loans. The old East India Company had strong Tory connections and was closely identified with James II at the time of the Revolution.[29] The new East India Company, established in 1698, was tied to the Whigs and to the Bank of England.[30] The rivalry between these two companies greatly enlarged the size of the loans the government received and also had beneficial consequences for the English balance of trade during the War of the Spanish Succession.[31]

In the period of English history North and Weingast analyze, each of these three joint-stock companies played a large role in public borrowing. But those roles are only explicable in terms of the political rivalry that existed between Whigs and Tories, a rivalry that North and Weingast scarcely mention. The significance of the Whig-Tory split applies equally to private capital markets, since the three most important companies whose shares were traded on the stock market were the Bank of England, the East India Company, and the South Sea Company. The development of public finance and capital markets was accelerated by a party conflict whose origins predated the events of 1688.

My final point concerns the cause of the constitutional and institutional changes North and Weingast focus upon. Who pushed for the new constraints on the Crown introduced in 1688 and why? North and Weingast's point is to show "how, given the means, motives, and behavior of the king during this century, the institutional changes altered the incentives of government actors in the manner desired by the winners of the Revolution."[32] The winners were the wealth holders represented by Parliament, and their goal was to make Crown commitments more credible and to increase the security of property rights.

The winners also wanted to remove the religious threat that James II's Catholicism represented. Indeed, a very strong case can be made that the issue of religion was primary. Whig opposition alone was insufficient to dislodge James II. It was James II's consistent support for Catholicism that alienated his own Tory supporters.[33] In his pursuit of a more Catholic England, James was willing to violate the rights of his subjects. But it was his Catholicism more than his absolutism that turned his subjects against him.[34] The wealth holders of England who engineered the Glorious Revolution were more concerned with popery than with property.

[26] Sir John Clapham, *The Bank of England* (Cambridge, 1945), vol. 1, pp. 74–75; B. W. Hill, "The Change of Government and the 'Loss of the City,' 1710–1711," *Economic History Review*, 24 (Aug. 1971), p. 395.

[27] P. G. M. Dickson, *The Financial Revolution in England* (London, 1967), p. 65.

[28] John Brewer, *The Sinews of Power: War, Money and the English State, 1688–1783* (New York, 1989), p. 120; John G. Sperling, *The South Sea Company* (Boston, 1962), pp. 7, 14.

[29] Henry Horwitz, "The East India Trade, The Politicians, and the Constitution: 1689–1702," *Journal of British Studies*, 17 (Spring 1978), p. 1.

[30] Ibid., pp. 10–11.

[31] Henry Horwitz, *Parliament, Policy and Politics*, pp. 232–33; D. W. Jones, *War and Economy in the Age of William III and Marlborough* (Oxford, 1988), pp. 221, 301.

[32] North and Weingast, "Constitutions and Commitment," p. 804.

[33] John Miller, *Popery and Politics in England, 1660–1688* (Cambridge, 1973), pp. 197, 202, 250; Speck, *Reluctant Revolutionaries*, p. 128.

[34] Speck, *Reluctant Revolutionaries*, pp. 233, 235.

Attitudes toward other religious groups were also important. Tory suspicions of the stock market were fueled by the prominence of Huguenot and Jewish financiers and brokers.[35] The Stop of the Exchequer was as clear-cut a violation of creditor property rights as one can imagine, but when Parliament reconvened in 1673 there was remarkably little mention of it.[36] The Commons directed its attention to the Declaration of Indulgence issued by Charles II shortly after the Stop. This declaration was an attempt to grant a measure of toleration to dissenting Protestants and so raised questions of religion. Even a major violation of property rights took a back seat to religious policy.

North and Weingast consider religion only in passing. They note the importance of religious issues but save these for a "more thorough study."[37] The consideration of religious issues should not have been postponed. They are central to the Glorious Revolution and the constitutional changes it wrought.

Each of the three limitations I have discussed involve aspects of the historical case which North and Weingast neglected. One limitation involves a missed opportunity: most aspects of the Stop of the Exchequer fit in with the logic of their analysis. Another involves an unfortunate omission. One cannot gloss over the question of religion and correctly understand the Glorious Revolution. The final limitation provides an invitation for further theoretical development. North and Weingast demonstrate the importance of political institutions for the development of markets. The role of political parties in the development of public debt suggests that it was not simply parliamentary power which mattered, but how that power was organized. The specific structure of political institutions influenced markets in ways we do not yet entirely understand. North and Weingast have taken a first step, but there is much more to be done.

[35] J. A. Giuseppi, "Sephardi Jews and the early years of The Bank of England," *Transactions of the Jewish Historical Society of England*, 19 (1955–59), pp. 53–54; A. C. Carter, "The Huguenot Contribution to the Early Years of the Funded Debt, 1694–1714," *Proceedings of the Huguenot Society of London*, 19 (1955), p. 22.

[36] Maurice Lee, Jr., *The Cabal* (Urbana, 1965), p. 159.

[37] North and Weingast, "Constitutions and Commitments," p. 805.

Fogel's Journey through the Slave States

Without Consent or Contract: The Rise and Fall of American Slavery. By Robert W. Fogel. New York: W.W. Norton, 1989. Pp. 539. $23.00.

For some 20 years Robert W. Fogel was more successful in bringing his research agenda to the attention of other economic historians than was any other member of that guild. His audacious re-evaluation of the role of the Union Pacific Railroad entrepreneurs and his ingenious research design and startling findings about the general contribution of railroads to American economic growth during the late nineteenth century were controversial.[1] In some readers his work inspired admiration or emulation; others, who regarded the counterfactual as a breach of sacred trust, responded with outraged anguish. Those who braved the DC3s of Lake Central Airlines and the uncertain late winter climate of West Lafayette, Indiana, to attend Cliometrics meetings during the mid-1960s remember Fogel in youthful prime, standing at the blackboard, plump, flushed, tousle-haired, in rumpled clothes, but unfailingly buoyant, as he parried the queries of as keen and cutthroat an assembly of young scholars as perhaps ever assembled in American academia.

Fogel also revealed a pronounced talent for academic entrepreneurship. He became chairman of the History Advisory Committee of the Mathematical Social Science Board (MSSB), and he and his colleagues supervised the planning, preparation, and publication of a series of volumes designed to combine innovative methods and substantive content in those areas of history where quantitative analysis promised useful results. Although hardly equivalent in stature or impact to those famous landmarks, volumes 24 and 30 in the *Studies in Income and Wealth* series of the National Bureau of Economic Research, the MSSB books were influential, bearing on almost every area in which quantitative analysis became important in history during the 1960s and 1970s.

Despite such achievements, it was *Time on the Cross*, prepared in collaboration with Stanley Engerman, that made Fogel's name a byword in the history profession. This book, noted eminent reviewers in this JOURNAL, brought "to a close an historiographic cycle that began with the publication of Ulrich Bonnell Phillips' *American Negro Slavery* (1918)."[2] Like the premature report of Mark Twain's passing, that statement was something of an exaggeration. *Time on the Cross* could, and probably should, have ended argument over some long-debated aspects of slavery, but in reality it precipitated one of the most notable scholarly controversies in American historiography. Seldom if ever did so diverse an array of critics bring a scholarly work of history under such intense scrutiny. The debate was not mere happenstance. Endowed with a keen promotional sense, Fogel and Engerman (and who can blame them) were delighted to have their work subjected to analysis by conference panels and symposia speakers. And if some of the evaluations were emotionally negative, so happy a warrior as Fogel was eager to do battle for his positions.

The Journal of Economic History, Vol. L, No. 3 (Sept. 1990). ISSN 0022-0507.

[1] Robert W. Fogel, *The Union Pacific Railroad: A Case in Premature Enterprise* (Baltimore, 1960); and Robert W. Fogel, *Railroads and American Economic Growth: Essays in Econometric History* (Baltimore, 1964).

[2] Robert W. Fogel and Stanley L. Engerman, *Time on the Cross*. Vol. 1: *The Economics of American Negro Slavery*; Vol. 2: *Evidence and Methods* (Boston, 1974). Paul A. David and Peter Temin, "Slavery: The Progressive Institution?" this JOURNAL, 34 (Sept. 1974), pp. 739–83. See p. 739 for quoted passage.

Firmly believing that social science is cumulative, Fogel and Engerman announced that *Time on the Cross* was not the last word on the subject and noted that some of the issues treated in their work would reward further study. They displayed a willingness to explain technical aspects of their research and to make their data available to other scholars, which was unusual among social scientists and almost unknown among more traditionally oriented historians. Most of the critics took their shots and moved on. Fogel, however, had not lost his flair for agenda-setting. He succeeded in attracting investigators from among his graduate students and interested scholars to the issues that remained unsettled during the early controversy over *Time on the Cross*. Although shifting his own interests to some extent, he exercised a coordinating influence over these scholars and continued to broaden his own understanding of the history of American Negro slavery. *Without Consent or Contract: The Rise and Fall of American Slavery* is, Fogel tells us, the culmination of this work—his final authoritative statement on the subject.[3]

As a final statement the book will take some time for digestion. Also offered to this reviewer was the copy-edited manuscript of a companion volume on *Evidence and Methods*, still in press, and the table of contents of two additional volumes of technical papers. Thirty-five scholars collaborated with Fogel and Engerman in the production of the 74 items in the volume dealing with evidence and methods and the 34 technical papers in the last two projected volumes.

Since the contribution of *Without Consent or Contract* is best understood in the light of the professional and popular evaluation of *Time on the Cross*, it is well to refresh our memories about the reception and contents of that work, which was published in 1974 and soon awarded the Bancroft Prize. Its initial reception, it can be argued, represented a kind of high watermark in the acceptance of quantitative analysis in the history profession generally. But perceptions changed as peer reviews began to appear, critical attention was focused on the book at various professional meetings or symposia, nonquantitative students of American slavery realized its threat to established positions, and minority scholars and spokespeople concluded that some of the Fogel and Engerman positions compromised both cherished beliefs and action agendas.

Fogel and Engerman published *Time on the Cross* in two volumes—a procedure destined to draw considerable fire since it separated the nontechnical text of the first volume from the notes and discussions of research methods and procedures in the second. The authors laid out their basic theses in the Prologue—hardly as many as Martin Luther once nailed to a cathedral door but sufficient to fuel the fires of controversy to this day. According to Fogel and Engerman, the slavery years had been America's "time on the cross." The devastating war that ended the institution took a tremendous toll of life and property and indeed threatened the very existence of the Union. Understandably, hundreds of historians had probed the background of the conflict, including slavery, and a "traditional interpretation" of that institution had emerged, though scholars of course often disagreed on specifics. The publication of *Time on the Cross* came, its authors explained, after some 15 years of "critical review" of slavery sources and scholarship by "historians and economists . . . trained in the application of quantitative methods to historical problems." The "new techniques and hitherto neglected sources" had allowed Fogel and Engerman to contradict "many of the most important propositions in the traditional portrayal of the slave system." Indeed, they wrote: "The reconstruction which has emerged is so much at variance with common beliefs, and its implications are so central to the understanding of contemporary issues, that we believe the new findings should no longer be restricted to the pages of esoteric scholarly journals" (pp. 3–4).

Fogel and Engerman specifically listed 10 "principal corrections of the traditional

[3] Fogel, *Without Consent or Contract*, p. 13.

characterization of the slave economy." In summary these were: slavery was a rational, profitable institution, never more profitable than immediately prior to the Civil War, and was maintained by southerners who were optimistic about both their own future and that of the slave system. There was no indication during the 1850s that internal weaknesses would bring slavery down in the foreseeable future. "Slave agriculture [was] 35 percent more efficient than the northern system of family farming." Nor was slavery incompatible with urbanization and industrialization. "The belief that slave-breeding, sexual exploitation, and promiscuity destroyed the black family [was] a myth. The family was the basic unit of social organization under slavery." "The material (not psychological) conditions of the lives of slaves compared favorably with those of free industrial workers." Expropriation of income was "much lower than has generally been presumed," about 10 percent over the course of the "typical" field hand's lifetime (pp. 4–6). The southern antebellum economy was not stagnant; per capita income in the region increased more rapidly during the years from 1840 to 1860 than elsewhere in the nation.

How could earlier historians have misunderstood crucial elements of the story? Fogel and Engerman explained that bias to some degree was involved, but more important was the fact that historians had lacked the research tools available to econometric historians. Nor was misunderstanding confined solely to the study of slavery. Its "reexamination . . . [was] part of a more ambitious effort to reconstruct the entire history of American economic development on a sound quantitative basis" by scholars variously called "new economic historians," "econometric historians," and "cliometricians" (p. 6). These scholars brought new insights and research tools to their work but also "amassed a more complete body of information on the operation of the slave system than [had ever] been available to anyone interested in the subject." "This enormous body of evidence" was "the source of many of the new discoveries." Some of these, they confided, "were at one time as unbelievable to the cliometricians as they [would] be to the readers" (p. 8). The euphoric, even messianic, overtones in such passages were perhaps no more than a reflection of naiveté, but some read them as condescension or even imperialism.

If Fogel and Engerman were unfortunate in the tone of their introduction, their interpretive conclusion provoked further ire. They had sought "to strike down the view that black Americans were without culture, without achievement, and without development for their first two hundred and fifty years on American soil." "Pecuniary income, diet, health, skill acquisition, and other aspects of the material conditions of life [had] been worse for blacks . . . after emancipation than it had been under slavery." Black slaves had made southern agriculture more efficient than that of northern free farmers. That was impressive. It was "time to reveal not only to blacks but to whites as well . . . the record of black achievement under adversity" (pp. 258, 262, 264).

Institutional and social historians of American slavery were quick to argue that Fogel and Engerman's depiction of a "traditional interpretation" suggested a degree of agreement among historians past and present that was contrary to fact. L. C. Gray and others, for example, had argued that slavery was indeed profitable during the late antebellum years. Here there was a pronounced difference in research style at issue—traditional historians willing to emphasize the exceptional case; the cliometrician seeking a mean judgment.

Cliometric reviewers did not question the profitability of slavery and the general prevalence of prosperity within the South during the late antebellum period. Various econometric historians had made these points prior to the publication of *Time on the Cross*. But some, notably Paul David, Peter Temin, and Richard Sutch, challenged the measurement techniques and findings of Fogel and Engerman concerning the relative efficiency of northern and southern agriculture, as well as their estimates of the nutritional adequacy of the slave diet, the relative severity of the plantation work regime, and the proportion of slaves in supervisory or "elite" occupations. Other critics argued that by charging the cost of rearing to working age against the slave's account, the authors had grossly underestimated the amount of expropriation of income involved in the slavery system. Fogel and Engerman's treatment of various aspects of slave family life drew fire as well. They had failed to determine the full extent of slave breeding, the number of families broken by the workings of the domestic slave trade, and the amount of sexual molestation and exploitation at the hands of the master class. Their "systematic" evidence on the amount of whipping suffered by slaves rested on the records of but one plantation. As the debate moved beyond the initial reviews and cliometricians reworked elements of the research, criticism became more pointed. Sutch attempted to "replicate the results of Fogel and Engerman's cliometric experiments" in a minute "dissection of about half-a-dozen major issues raised in *Time on the Cross*." He reported that he had "found so many errors of computation or citation, data so selectively weak, and the presentation of results so distorted that [he had] been forced to conclude that *Time on the Cross* [was] a failure."[4]

Fogel and Engerman used an impressive array of data sets in their research—some developed by other historians, as in the case of the Parker-Gallman census sample of 5,229 southern farms in 1860, and various others either prepared under their immediate supervision or at their instigation. Particularly interesting in this last category were samples drawn from the probate records of southern states, from invoices of slave sales at the New Orleans slave market, and from the shipping manifests of the coastwise slave trade. Reviewers in general praised the diversity and range of data utilized but were less satisfied with various subsamples, particularly one based on the records of 30 southern plantations. There were objections also that conclusions sometimes exceeded the capacity of the data, and particularly that volume two inadequately explained complex or sophisticated quantitative manipulations. Non-cliometricians generally agreed on this last point and one team of reviewers suggested in exasperation and apparent ignorance of modern Concord that Fogel and Engerman's "computers badly need a quiet period of reflection by Walden Pond."[5]

The debate over *Time on the Cross* raged at various levels of professional and popular attention. Among the social and institutional historians of slavery, within the broader academic community, and throughout the public sectors dedicated to social and political reform on behalf of minorities, there were many individuals who found the book to be either threatening or requiring difficult conceptual or ideological adjustments. When Fogel summarized the findings of *Time on the Cross* at a meeting of the Board of Directors of the Social Science Research Council, a distinguished black anthropologist angrily declared: "I can never forgive Fogel for what he has done to my people."[6] Nor was the cliometric community less free of those minor, yet sometimes determinative, considerations of old school tie, ambition, and personality that are found in academia generally. In addition the cliometrics community was a passionate one—imbued with the fervor and dedication typically present in the founding generation of a successful cult. The "truth" was terribly important and individual cliometricians were prepared to fight for their version with no holds barred. Thus the technical disputes over *Time on the Cross* were bloody and not well understood by the other interested public groups whose

[4] Richard Sutch, "The Treatment Received by American Slaves: A Critical Review of the Evidence Presented in *Time on the Cross*," *Explorations in Economic History*, 12 (Oct. 1975), pp. 335–438. See p. 339 for quote. More extended development of the critique is to be found in Paul A. David, et al., *Reckoning with Slavery: A Critical Study in the Quantitative History of American Negro Slavery* (New York, 1976); and Herbert G. Gutman, *Slavery and the Numbers Game: A Critique of Time on the Cross* (Urbana, 1975).

[5] John H. Pruett and Robert M. McColley, "Review," *Journal of Southern History*, 40 (Nov. 1974), p. 639.

[6] Personal conversation with Allan G. Bogue.

members found it easy to seize upon seemingly damning, if incompletely understood, criticisms and circulate them as matters of established fact. Sutch's judgment became widely accepted throughout the scholarly community.

To the charges that they had made computational errors, mispecified models, or used the wrong ones Fogel and Engerman responded that even the suggested corrections would do little to change the general picture. Had most of the criticism been valid (and much of it was not), *Time on the Cross* should not have been dismissed as a scholarly failure. None henceforth dared to argue that the peculiar institution was unprofitable or that its economic underpinnings were about to collapse. If a major purpose of the scholarly enterprise is to advance understanding of a subject, *Time on the Cross* in retrospect was a considerable success. Its publication greatly intensified the re-evaluation of the history of American slavery then underway. *Without Consent or Contract* and its supporting volumes can be evaluated on their own terms, but their reception at the hands of qualified critics will also allow us to evaluate the contribution of *Time on the Cross* more realistically than ever before.

In contrast to the "Gee Whiz" tone of the Prologue to *Time on the Cross* the Foreword of *Without Consent or Contract* is sober and tentative. Here Fogel tells us the book presents "one picture of the emerging synthesis" developing among scholars concerning the history of American slavery. For Fogel it is the close of "an intellectual journey that . . . lasted more than two decades" (pp. 12–13). He tells us that it is a book with three subplots: slavery as economic and social system; slavery as the focus of ideological and political struggle; and slavery as the subject of scholarly reinterpretation—the search for the "true story"—during the last three decades. *Time on the Cross* was focused primarily on the first of these subplots with some attention given to the third. The high voltage of the debate that it inspired, Fogel suggests, reflected the fact that the institution of slavery involved significant moral implications and, indeed, that "the ultimate issues" considered in *Without Consent or Contract* are moral ones (p. 10). Thus only the first half of this volume is devoted to the explication of slavery as an economic institution and related historiographic developments. Since slavery's successful economic performance in America provided no rational explanation for its demise, Fogel devotes the second half of the book to description and explanation of the ideological and political struggle that finally brought abolition.

Chapter 1 of *Without Consent or Contract* describes the importation of slaves and the development of slave systems in the Caribbean and Hispanic America as well as within the mainland British colonies. Fogel suggests minor upward revisions of Phillip Curtin's estimates of the numbers involved in the international slave trade and notes the large movement of slaves into the mainland settlements after 1780. The advantages of slavery as a mode of industrial production are noted, but the gang system must be appropriate for the crops under cultivation; demand must be strong for these products; the legal-political context must be supportive; the application of industrial discipline and physical coercion condoned; supplies of slaves must be adequate; and planters must be able to reallocate labor supplies as market forces dictate. Harking back to the controversies over *Time on the Cross*, how harsh were working conditions on the plantations of the American South? On cotton plantations in the United States "the average work week during the spring, summer, and fall was about 58 hours, well below the 72 hours thought to have prevailed in English textile mills during the first quarter of the nineteenth century and also below the 60-hour week of northern commercial farmers in the United States during the first quarter of the twentieth century" (pp. 28–29).

In the remainder of Part 1 of *Without Consent or Contract* Fogel devotes chapters to occupational patterns, "economic riddles," the development of the southern economy, population questions, and "changing interpretations of slave culture." In these chapters we discover Fogel's current positions on the more contentious historiographic issues of the recent past, as well as in those areas in which knowledge has advanced substantially since 1974. In contrast to the five pages devoted to occupational structure in volume 1 of *Time on the Cross*, Chapter 2 of *Without Consent or Contract* provides 18 pages of discussion of the subject, and a simple breakdown of "about 1850" for males is replaced by comparative data on both males and females for four plantation economies—the U.S. sample drawn from 60 intermediate and large plantations over the span of 1797 to 1865. The exhibit in *Without Consent or Contract* suggests a somewhat more diverse occupational hierarchy in America than originally suggested and the most varied as well in the cross-country comparison.

In the chapter devoted to "Unravelling Some Economic Riddles" Fogel considers the general patterns of development and profitability in the West Indies and the United States and defines the American institution as a "flexible, highly developed form of capitalism" in which supplies of labor moved rapidly to the point of most profitable use and slave prices closely reflected the productive capacities of the individual slave (p. 64). Fogel notes continuing disagreement among cliometricians about the details of interregional slave migration—the proportion managed by slave traders as compared to that transported west in the course of planter family migration. He rejects the view that soil exhaustion or land shortage played much part in the movement of resources westward, arguing that the "struggle over the expansion of slavery into the territories . . . was almost a purely political issue" (p. 71). The discussion of labor efficiency is enriched in this volume, but once more Fogel argues that in a comparison of the technical efficiencies of agriculture in the North and in all farms in the South the latter region had an advantage of about 35 percent. Nor were the critics correct in maintaining that slaves endured a more taxing work regime than northern farmers and that a longer growing season in the South necessarily indicated a greater total of work hours for the bondsman than for the free agriculturist of the North. He acknowledges, however, that total hour comparisons are complicated by the difficulty of evaluating intensity of work and that the "gang system," on which southern efficiency rested, was designed to produce intense work.

Fogel pictures an antebellum southern economy in which rich individuals were more numerous than in the northern United States. Military defeat reversed this picture rather than postwar changes in market structures. Fogel rejects the contention that the mid-century South suffered from "colonial dependency." The basic issue in evaluating southern viability, he suggests, was the question of whether slaves should be considered persons or intermediate goods, a quintessentially moral judgment. The southern economy of the antebellum years was flexible, highly capitalistic, and capable of reallocating productive resources rapidly between regions and major crops. Although not rejecting the suggestion that at times "insufficient demand" for cotton affected southern development, Fogel is in general unsympathetic to that contention. He believes that the postbellum problems of the economy occurred because the New South failed to extract effort from its labor force comparable to that obtained during the antebellum period. Southern urbanization and industrialization did not lag because of the inappropriateness of slave labor in such settings but because of intense demand for labor in the production of the major southern staples. Industrialization in the northeastern states involved integration of women into the factory system; in the South women contributed more effectively in agriculture. Fogel tentatively accepts the suggestion of various radical historians, however, that a precapitalist crisis of modernization may have occurred within the southern yeoman farm sector.

Fogel begins his chapter on demographic issues with some discussion of contemporary views on the issues of natural increase and mortality, beginning with Benjamin Franklin's ideas and moving through Theodore Dwight Weld's indictment of American slavery to the position of antebellum southern sociologists. The factual picture which follows represents one of the great contributions of the Fogel group during the last 20 years. Although the southern slave population showed earlier and greater rates of natural increase than did those of the Caribbean plantation areas, mortality was higher indeed than Weld had imagined. But that fact primarily reflected high levels of infant and early childhood mortality. Southern planters worked women in the field gangs to very advanced stages of pregnancy, the surviving babies tended to be small and weak, and early childhood diets were inadequate. Slave children reached ages of eight or nine significantly retarded in growth, but then access to adult slave diets redressed the situation; their mature stature was little less than that of adult white southerners. The life expectancy of the adult slave was hardly inferior to that of the comparable white southerner and considerably better than that of industrial workers in most areas of Europe at the time.

Birth rates in the southern slave populations were higher than those in the British West Indies, although the latter have been underestimated, Fogel notes. The southern planter's use of family cabins in contrast to the barracks of the Caribbean plantation raised fertility levels. If slave breeding was present in North America it was not sufficient to shape demographic trends. The master's greatest interference in family development involved the domestic slave trade—the working of that institution accounted for one-third of the single parent households represented in the Works Progress Administration's slave narratives. Fogel now argues for a rate of natural increase within the slave population in North America that remained relatively constant from the 1730s to the 1830s, declining somewhat thereafter, apparently because of the movement of the slave labor force increasingly into cotton production and the growth in population on large plantations. Slave demographics were far more complicated than either contemporaries or the early historians of North American slavery realized. That being the case, argues Fogel, it is not surprising that the contemporary solution was ultimately a political one.

The final chapter in the first half of the book surveys the changing scholarly interpretations of the institution, beginning with the works of James Ford Rhodes, Ulrich Phillips, W. E. B. DuBois, Franklin Frazier, and Carter Woodson and continuing through the modern panoply of opinion setters, Herbert Aptheker, Melville Herskovitz, Kenneth Stammp, Eugene Genovese, Stanley Elkins, Herbert Gutman, John Blasingame, and Thomas Webber, among others. Here the emphasis is upon the nature, preservation, and development of a slave culture, resistance as opposed to co-option, and the degree to which slaves created a fostering context of community. That remnants of African culture, the fusion of religious practices, word patterns, and the barriers of race could provide foundations for cultural independence and community and that slaves developed patterns of resistance, Fogel does not dispute. On the other hand, the masters had their arsenal of countermeasures—work-free half-days and weekends, garden plots, and permission to work for wages. But, argues Fogel, whatever the gambits of resistance and however cleverly the barriers were raised between the slave quarters and the big house, the system in general worked as the planters wished. It made them rich. If the objective of resistance was to thwart the master, it failed. Nor, given the actual ownership patterns of slavery, could the community within a community pictured by some recent writers have been a reality for any but a very small percentage of American slaves.

"Within the span of a little more than a century, a system that had stood above criticism for 3,000 years was outlawed everywhere in the Western world" (p. 205). That development did not occur, Fogel argues in the first half of *Without Consent or Contract*, because slavery was an unprofitable institution. Rather, the emancipation process was essentially political, and in the first four chapters of the book's second section Fogel attempts to describe and explain the politics of antislavery. After a short summary of the progress of emancipation in the western world, Fogel devotes most of a chapter to the British campaign to outlaw slavery within the British possessions. He sketches its roots in the Quaker sect and its spread to other dissenting religious elements, particularly the Methodists. He traces it through the British Parliament's decision to outlaw the international slave trade in 1807, a period of quiescence, efforts in the early 1820s to ameliorate conditions on the West Indies plantations, and the final parliamentary act of abolition in 1833. Although the British dissenters provided the shock troops of the abolition movement in Great Britain, so few of them served in Parliament that the actual implementation of emancipation there was the work of gentry trying "to control an expanding, increasingly complicated, and highly volatile civility" (p. 221).

As the British members of Parliament wrestled with the problems generated by economic distress among the lower classes, restoration of the right of political participation to Roman Catholics, extension of the general suffrage in the Reform Act of 1832, and the challenge of peacefully absorbing the new electoral sector, the antislavery movement among the dissenters became more radical, particularly within Methodist congregations. Now the abolitionists endorsed immediatism and when nonconformist missionaries suffered persecution following the slave revolt in Jamaica, antislavery sentiment reached fever pitch. Since dissenters constituted 21 percent of the British electorate, the parliamentary leadership was willing to make concessions to keep them from making common cause with the spokesmen of radical labor. Thus began the parliamentary maneuverings that produced the act abolishing slavery in the British colonies in 1838.

Eric Williams maintained that British capitalists deserted the West Indian planter interest because of their belief that high sugar prices would impede their efforts to lower wages. In response, Fogel reports that emancipation actually raised sugar prices very materially due to the use of sugar duties to finance emancipation and particularly as a result of the diminished productivity that developed in the British Caribbean sugar industry following emancipation. Results do not necessarily conform to intent, but Fogel notes that radical labor leaders were at the time hostile to the emancipation movement. The British "Emancipation Act brought no real economic advantages to domestic interests" (p. 231), and the "upper-class evangelicals" who provided much of the leadership of the antislavery movement in Britain displayed an altruism that to Fogel was narrowly focused. Although prepared to sacrifice much of their own wealth, as well as that of the planters to effect abolition, they favored the sternest of repressive measures to check the spread of lower-class radicalism in England. Once success was won the British abolitionists tried to carry their message abroad with mixed success. They made some progress in India and in suppressing the Islamic trade, but their activities in the United States were in Fogel's eyes counterproductive, stimulating xenophobic and nationalistic sentiment.

When he turns to the American campaign against slavery, Fogel notes the very different conditions prevailing in America as contrasted with Great Britain. Here political power was more diffused, the electorate "diverse in economic interest, religion, ethnicity, and political culture" (p. 239). Although natural rights philosophy encouraged the abolition of slavery in various northern states during the revolutionary and early national period, the net effect of the American Revolution was retardative. Deistic in inclination and endorsing a rationalist philosophy of natural rights, the revolutionary leaders despiritualized the antislavery cause. Provisions in the federal constitution and other institutional developments of the late eighteenth century seemed to set slavery securely within the framework of American government and legal-judicial practice.

In the new nation institutional antislavery effort became concentrated in the activities of the American Colonization Society, committed to a gradualist and indirect program that never provided a serious threat to slavery. Recognition of the society's inadequacies did not become general until the late 1820s, when new currents of religious activism had revitalized antislavery sentiment—the Second Great Awakening, the rise of

Methodism and the Baptists, and the institutional and doctrinal readjustments of the Congregationalists and Presbyterians and their exemplification in the revivalism of Charles Finney. Fogel describes the reawakened abolitionism of the 1830s in terms of the competitive interplay of the Tappan, Garrison, and Gerrit Smith groups, northern successes and southern failures, and growing denominational schisms. But the abolitionists failed to win the support of the churches en masse during the 1830s. Abolitionist strategies during that decade ranged from continued adherence to the radical doctrines of natural rights and root-and-branch denunciation of the sin of slavery as found among the Garrisonians, through Weld's collection of slavery horror stories, *Slavery as it Is: Testimony of a Thousand Witnesses*, to the political activism endorsed by amateurs who with great prescience and comparable naiveté decided to found an abolitionist political party. Moral suasion, they believed, had failed.

Fogel describes the development of the American political campaign against slavery, presenting a broadly based synthesis of the relevant historiography. General understanding of the constitutional provisions concerning slavery, and the national party system that developed during the first 50 years of the Republic inhibited the acceptance of abolition as a major political issue. But the Louisiana Purchase, the Missouri controversy, the emergence of southern sectionalists, as illustrated by the Old Republicans and South Carolina's national spokesmen, all suggested that slavery might indeed achieve salience. Then came the territorial expansion of the 1840s and a national political crisis far greater than those thus far sustained. Its severity, maintains Fogel, "was more extended and far more destabilizing politically than the Missouri crisis, partly because of changes that had occurred in the political cultures of the North and the South during the intervening decades, and partly because of changes in the political balance between the sections" (p. 301).

The rapid growth of the American economy, Fogel notes, was destabilizing national politics, changing the sectional balance of population, and rendering the old national party issues of banking and tariffs less important. Particularly he emphasizes the growing urbanization and industrialization of the North and the impact of the flood of immigrants from abroad both in the labor market and as a focus of nativist political activity. Ethnicity and religion "became the principal basis for urban politics in the late antebellum era" (p. 308). "It was the huge influx of foreigners into the North after 1820, rather than the northern rate of natural increase, that gave the North its increasing predominance in the struggle for power and made it possible for a party based exclusively in the North to gain control of the federal government" (p. 319).

In Chapter 10 Fogel forges "a victorious antislavery coalition" (p. 320). By the early 1850s the old national economic issues that had divided Whig from Democrat had lost their binding power. Although the wide-sweeping economic changes of the past decades had spawned economic issues, their political interplay took place during the early 1850s at the local and state level. In the national political arena in the North realignment proceeded as voters chose between the options advanced by those who sought to "establish a new national coalition on an anti-Catholic, anti-foreign-born program" and those seeking to weld "a purely northern coalition on an antislavery program." Ingenuity, luck, "unintended help" from proslavery adversaries, and favorable contingent circumstances all were to play important roles in the final outcome (p. 322).

In moving to this final result Fogel examines the ways in which the antislavery appeal was broadened, the indictment of southern morality and culture, the constitutional rationalizations for federal action against slavery, and the development of a slaveholder conspiracy thesis and counterstrategies. Unusual in his account is the attention devoted to "the 'hidden' depression and the political revolt of the northern workers," which was a "triple crisis for native, non-farm workers in the North, 1848–1855" (pp. 354–55), reflecting immigrant competition, soaring food prices, and deteriorating health conditions. These circumstances led, in part at least, to unrest mirrored in strikes, the land reform movement, and the rise of benevolent associations. Such was the background of political activity that culminated in the formation of the Know-Nothing political movement. It was, however, to be the architects of antislavery politics whose maneuvering was ultimately crowned with success in the precarious victory of 1860. That election, argues Fogel, "turned on less than 1/2 of 1 percent of the northern ballots cast in the popular contest" (p. 382). Regression inference analysis using the base vote of 1852 suggests to Fogel that the Free Soil and Whig constituencies accounted for some 89 percent of Lincoln's vote and that some 11 percent was derived from former Democrats (see Table 7, p. 383). About two-fifths of the Republicans were former Know-Nothings. Essential to the whole process of realignment was the radicalization of a significant segment of the northern electorate on the subject of slavery.

Fogel's Afterword is titled "The Moral Problem of Slavery" and blends personal reminiscence, speculation about history that might have been, and the author's suggestions as to what a modern indictment of slavery should involve. The dilemmas and paradoxes that recent scholarship has revealed in the history of slavery have been discomforting, he maintains: antislavery leaders who were less than perfect, the decline in economic productivity subsequent to abolition in the American South and other slave plantation regions, antislavery's links with imperialism abroad, and the distressing tendency of free labor leaders to truckle with slaveholding interests. Although post-1950s scholarship has shown that the material basis of the nineteenth-century indictment was erroneous, slavery was a moral abomination. Since the abolitionists strictures were in part false, Fogel tells us why he believes that we should consider it so today. "Slavery permitted one group of people to exercise unrestrained personal domination over another group of people" (p. 394). Second, it denied economic opportunity to the members of the latter group. Slaves also suffered "denial of citizenship" as well as denial of "cultural self-identification" (pp. 396, 398). These charges, Fogel believes, are more consonant with the facts of slavery and mutually less inconsistent than the charges of the abolitionists. Fogel's indictment places much less emphasis on physical maltreatment than did the abolitionists: "exaggerations of the severity of slavery divert attention from the novel forms of exploitation that replaced it, from the long period during which the occupational opportunities, the real income, and the life expectations of freed blacks deteriorated, and from injustices of our own time which are often more a product of recent policies than a legacy of slavery" (p. 406).

Fogel considers some of the ironies apparent in the final stages of the emancipation movement—advocates of moral righteousness arguing that emancipation in the West Indies had been economically beneficial when they knew that the contention was false, and the Republican party gaining power, ostensibly for a righteous cause but pandering to Negrophobia and nativism in the process. Finally, he adds his answer to those of historians who have in some way asked whether the human and material costs of the Civil War were justified. Alternative but less apocalyptic scenarios, thinks Fogel, would not have worked, and the outcome might have been even more unfortunate had the South been allowed to secede peacefully, establishing itself as an expansionist bastion of forced labor and antidemocracy and utilizing its control over the cotton market to disrupt northern growth and industrialization and to support reactionary elements in Europe.

This reviewer was provided with a copy of the companion volume, *Evidence and Methods*, in copy-edited typescript. Exceeding 1,000 pages in this form it is a fascinating manuscript, containing 70-plus sections, varying in length from a few typed pages to more than 150. Fogel provides a substantial introduction "On The Art of Empirical Research during an Age of Plunging Costs in Data Processing" and the other material deals with the more technical aspects of the methods used by him and his associates in their 20 years of research on the history of slavery. Some of this material is written by Fogel, and some by Fogel and Engerman, or by Fogel and other collaborators; many pieces are the independent work of members of the Fogel group. The findings are not always congruent, as Fogel points out, reflecting the fact that informed opinion still varies on appropriate methods and answers in this area of research. When published this volume will be the richest introduction to the methods and materials of quantitative history ever produced, its discussions ranging far beyond the boundaries of slavery research. It will be in reviews of *Evidence and Methods* that debate on technical issues will be most appropriate.

One of the most commendable features of *Without Consent or Contract* is Fogel's effort to place American slavery within comparative perspective, particularly in contrast with slavery in the western hemisphere but to some degree with other contemporary labor systems. Readers will be struck as well by the great difference in tone between *Time on the Cross* and *Without Consent or Contract*. If Fogel and Engerman appeared to be arrogant in the first volume, now Fogel lays out his positions in measured sometimes cautious terms—carrying circumspection almost to a fault on occasion, in my opinion, by showing deference to the work of some recent authors that may in the end prove to be undeserved.

But what of *Time on the Cross*? In what respects were the critics right and in what were they mistaken? Only the reader with minute recall and the gift of close reading will be able to answer these questions from *Without Consent or Contract*. True, there is some low-keyed rebuttal within the narrative—our attention is drawn for example to the deficiencies of Herbert Gutman's sampling procedures and quiet dissent expressed concerning the full range of Gavin Wright's demand-side argument. Generally Fogel gives us a statement of what he considers to be the best current answers to the various controversial issues raised in *Time on the Cross* without detailed reference to past controversies or specific confrontation with onetime critics. He explains that his position has indeed been sometimes modified or supplemented by the reconsideration and research that has been ongoing since 1974. For more detailed assessment of the criticisms raised by Temin, David, Sutch, and others one must look to *Evidence and Methods* where one does find contributions addressed specifically to major points at issue in the initial controversy over *Time on the Cross*. This being the case, it is disappointing that the two volumes could not have been published simultaneously. But if Fogel's current positions are somewhat more qualified in some respects and in others changed or expanded, he believes (correctly I think) that the initial positions on efficiency, labor productivity, and the material condition of southern slaves were much more nearly correct than a reading of the critics of *Time on the Cross* would suggest.

The second half of *Without Consent or Contract* combines a skillful synthesis of the contributions of political and intellectual historians on the subject of slavery during the last 50 years with Fogel's understanding of the economic context as developed by the members of the cliometric community. It is this last dimension that gives these chapters unique value, as well as Fogel's comfortable handling of the electoral realignment of the 1850s. No doubt there will be quibbling among reviewers from the political and intellectual history camps concerning the emphasis or lack of it that Fogel places on particular aspects of the story. In general, however, it is a very balanced account and marked by his rejection of simple economic determinism as governing the behavior of major actors. He quite rightly emphasizes, however, the destabilizing influence of economic growth and particularly the impact of large-scale immigration upon the position of native labor and the problems and challenges that political managers faced in socializing the new electorate.

Fogel explains that he has in effect "melded" the positions of the ethnocultural school with that of historians who still see class issues as dominant, noting less basic difference between the camps than the campers have believed to be the case. Fogel has brought greater statistical skills to the application of regression inference in analyzing the party antecedents of the voters of the Republican coalition of 1860 than any of the political historians who have preceded him. What is not so clear is the degree to which ethnocultural-religious groups actually served as building blocks of the parties of the 1850s and the extent to which those particular aggregations held firm or changed allegiance. Data problems multiply in this game and the Tad Blalocks of the world continue to view regression inference with some skepticism. But the paper in *Evidence and Methods* on these matters, co-authored with Ralph Galantine, moves beyond previous research in various respects, particularly concerning the relations between laboring men and the Know-Nothings during the 1850s.

Not all will accept the position that Fogel takes implicitly by assuming that Republican victory in the presidential campaign of 1860 foreordained the end of slavery. The Democratic party was defeated by a narrow margin, as Fogel notes, and the Civil War would prove its resilience. Secession was not the only option available to the southerners in 1860. If one crucial act among alternatives must be chosen, it was perhaps the decision to secede rather than the election of Abraham Lincoln that brought a speedy end to slavery in the United States. The election did not necessarily predestine emancipation.

In his introduction Fogel tells us that with the publication of *Without Consent or Contract* and its companion volumes an "intellectual journey" of "more than two decades" will end. That journey has been a most remarkable one, symbolizing in its way modern problems of race in the American polity, a revolution in historical methods, and both the changeability and pettiness of the historical profession, as well as its potential grandeur. This first volume of the *Without Consent or Contract* series may well be the finest union of quantitative and conventional historical analysis thus far produced in the "new" histories. In retrospect, despite its very real contributions, *Time on the Cross* perhaps should not have won a major prize; conversely *Without Consent or Contract* should be an award winner. Given the book's controversial origins, however, that may not be in its future—such an outcome would be a shame.

ALLAN G. BOGUE, *University of Wisconsin, Madison*

Editors' Notes

ESSAY PRIZE

The National Federation of Independent Businesses and the Association of Private Enterprise Education is offering a $1,000 prize for the two papers which the editorial board of the *Journal of Private Enterprise* judges best address the issue of entrepreneurship and public policy. The papers will be presented at APEE's annual meeting, April 7–9, 1991, in Nashville, TN, and will be published in the *Journal of Private Enterprise*. Submissions should not exceed 6,000 words and the deadline is November 15, 1990. Awards will be announced in January 1991. Please send submissions to Professor Gerald Gunderson, Editor, *Journal of Private Enterprise*, Trinity College, Hartford, CT 06106.

CALL FOR PAPERS

Siena College is sponsoring its sixth annual multidisciplinary conference on the 50th anniversary of World War II. The focus for 1991 will be the year 1941, though papers dealing with broad issues of the earlier years will be welcomed. Possible topics include Fascism and Nazism; the war in Asia; literature; art; film; diplomatic, political, and military history; popular culture and women's and Jewish issues during the era. Asian, African, Latin American, and Near Eastern topics of relevance are solicited. The collaboration and collaborationist regimes, the events in Greece, Yugoslavia, and the Balkans in general as well as North Africa, and the invasion of Russia and Pearl Harbor will be of particular relevance. The deadline for submissions is December 15, 1990. For further information, write Professor Thomas O. Kelly, II, Department of History, Siena College, Loudonville, NY 12211.

FELLOWSHIPS

The Woodrow Wilson International Center for Scholars is offering fellowships in the humanities and social sciences for 1991–1992. Applicants must hold a doctorate or have equivalent professional accomplishments. Stipends follow the principle of no gain/no loss, with the average yearly stipend approximately $36,000. Travel expenses for Fellows and their families are also provided. Deadline for applications is October 1, 1990; decisions will be made by March 1, 1991. For further information, contact The Fellowships Office, The Woodrow Wilson Center, Washington, DC 20560; telephone (202) 357–2841.

CONFERENCES

The University of Pennsylvania is holding a conference on "The Workplace before the Factory: Proletarianization in an Age of Manufactures, 1500–1800" on October 11–12, 1990. For further information, write Professor Thomas Max Safley, Department of History, 207 College Hall, University of Pennsylvania, Philadelphia, PA 19104-6379.

The International Union for the Scientific Study of Population (IUSSP) will, in commemoration of the 500th anniversary of Columbus's landing in the Americas and in cooperation with several other organizations, be holding a conference on the "Peopling of the Americas" in Veracruz, Mexico, in March-April 1992. The conference will take a multidisciplinary approach to examine population settlement and growth in the Americas from pre-Columbian times to the present. Planned sessions will cover demographic transition, fertility and mortality decline, family structure, rural-urban migration, and urbanization, as well as slavery, the consequences of conquest and contract, pre-Columbian population estimation, the political economy of international migration, the survival of the Amerindians, and population and environmental issues in the Amazon. For further information, write Bruno Remiche, Executive Secretary, IUSSP, 34 rue des Augustins, B-4000 Liège, Belgium.

EIGHTEENTH-CENTURY BRITISH BIOGRAPHY

The Eighteenth Century British Biography project (EBB), initiated at the University of Newcastle upon Tyne in February 1990, aims to bring together the personal records of the English-speaking peoples of that period. It will include individuals who lived in areas that were then colonies as well as those who lived in the United Kingdom. The project will begin by creating a file of all local and national directories and all book subscription lists of the period. The project invites contributions of biographical records. For a more detailed description of the project, write the Project Office, Park House, Ashow Nr. Kenilworth, Warwickshire, CV8 2LE, United Kingdom.

Reviews of Books

ANCIENT, MEDIEVAL, AND EARLY MODERN

Montagnes, fleuves, fôrets dans l'histoire: Barrières ou lignes de convergence? Edited by Jean-François Bergier. St. Katharinen: Scripta Mercaturae Verlag, 1989. Pp. 214. DM39.

At a section of the XVI International Congress of Historical Sciences in 1985 at Stuttgart, ancient and medieval historians discussed the role of mountains, rivers, and forests in history. Eighteen papers presented there are gathered in this book. They are written in English, French, or German, with clear summaries in the other languages.

The central question posed was whether mountains, rivers, and forests acted as obstacles or unifiers. A convincing answer is not given, but what becomes clear is that none have been insurmountable boundaries. What were they then? The articles differ too much in point of view, in scope, in time period, in region, and also in length to offer more than global generalizations. Every situation seems to have been unique.

The eight articles which primarily deal with mountains may elucidate that. Paola Sereno shows that mountains provided refuge for the indigenous population during the colonization of Sardinia in the Roman period; Chryssa Maltézou holds the same was true of Crete during its colonization by the Venetians. This was also the case in the process of state building in medieval Spain (Miguel-Ángel Ladero Quesara). Two other articles, however, stress the function of mountains in stimulating nation building. Michael Toch maintains that the Tyrol was colonized between the sixth and thirteenth centuries by Bavarian farmers who developed a semi-independent societal organization. Şt. Ştefănescu notes how the Carpathians formed the axis of the Danubian marsh area. In central Asia as well, mountains did not obstruct cultural and economic contacts (Sh. Bira).

Jacqueline Christien's contribution, based on epigraphical and archeological evidence, shows that even in ancient times technological development permitted people to overcome mountainous obstacles. Around Sparta a network of grooved tracks for wagon wheels was constructed which covered the whole of Laconia, including a "railway" across the Taygetus mountains. Michael Jameson shows how the Greek city-states integrated the adjacent mountains into the local economy and culture.

All of the contributions implicitly present mountains in the same way: a mountain is a mountain. Only the author discussing the Carpathians mentions their relatively small height as a reason for their not being a real obstacle. But he does emphasize the relative isolation of this area in which old cultural values persisted and which was to be the cradle of the 1918 Roumanian state.

All the articles on Eastern Europe have a broader scope and for that reason can be considered to form a cluster within the book. A fine article on medieval Bohemia investigates the function of mountains and other physical-geographical properties in unifying the area. But the argument does not result in geographical determinism thanks to the attention paid to the growing influences from outside (Leoš Jeleček and Zdeněk Boháč).

J. J. Khak's contribution on the Baltic area tells mostly of the tragic fate of the Slavs living there, but implicitly shows that forests, rivers, and marshes were no obstacle to economic and political colonization. Joachim Hermann gives some interesting hypotheses on rivers, mountains, and seas as factors in state building in Central Europe. North-south rivers were important channels of communication. But the east-west connections consisted of seven to eight land roads. From the ninth century onward, economic and cultural exchange has taken place along these routes. But political unification, which endeavored to follow the same paths, failed because of specific traditions developed during ages of relative isolation. Unfortunately the role of rivers in this process is not worked out.

Rivers were indeed the way by which the Slavs in the sixth to the ninth centuries moved southward. According to archeological evidence, in doing so they changed their agricultural methods (D. A. Avdusin). Thérèse Dunin's article on the Vistula in Poland fits less well into this cluster. It is mainly an evaluation of archeological investigations as well as a program for further research in that field.

The other articles on rivers—forests are underrepresented—all concern Western Europe. In Roman Gaul the development of smaller urban centers was promoted by the north-south traffic from one river to another. Rivers flowed east-west in that area (Tønnes Bekker-Nielsen). William Harris explains that the relative unimportance of the river Po as a transport route within the Roman empire resulted from the structure of the economy and the Po's distance from Rome.

Peter Laven gives a full account of the functions of the Venetian rivers in the sixteenth century, including the river Po. The regulations made by the authorities with regard to these rivers also provide clear insight into the Venetian way of government.

Dietrich Lohrmann holds that the watershed between the rivers Scheldt and Somme is one of the few cases in which rivers acted as a frontier. But this boundary between France and Flanders was only partly natural. In greater part it resulted from fortifications and the creation of wetlands.

The volume ends with T. C. Lounghis's effort to provide the first systematic quantification in the field of medieval geography. This contribution again stresses the heterogeneity of the book. But, as Bergier tells us in his short introduction, the volume must be considered a first stocktaking. Material for further research is now available.

PIM KOOIJ, *Groningen University*

The Agrarian History of England and Wales.Vol. 2: *1046–1350*. Edited by H. E. Hallam. New York: Cambridge University Press, 1988. Pp. xxxix, 1,086. $135.

Normally the appearance of a new volume in the *Agrarian History of England and Wales* series would be warmly welcomed. A definitive work of reference, combining the fruits of recent research plus the endeavors of the individual contributors, would have provided an excellent springboard for future research. Indeed, at first glance, the book is promising. It includes a much-needed chapter on pre-Conquest agriculture; a chapter on Domesday England; long chapters on the settlement of new land, farming techniques, and social structure; a chapter on population trends and one on prices and wages; a chapter on rural buildings; and even one on the life of rural people. The crucial topic of marketing is omitted, but, as the editor indicates, this will be covered in Volume 3, which is soon to appear.

Unfortunately, as the reader will soon discover, the volume is faulty on a number of crucial points. First, despite claims that the book represents the state of research in the late 1980s, long delays since the volume's inception in the mid-sixties have meant that it is sadly out of touch with recent work in the field. In truth, it is far more representative of the limits of research in the 1970s, since most of the contributions were written in the early part of that decade. An opportunity was given for chapters to be updated in 1983, but relatively little was changed, as the editor himself admits in his own case when referring to works of Bruce Campbell from the early 1980s (p. xxvii). The impact of all this can readily be seen in the bibliography, which is woefully deficient in works since 1980.

Second, the volume is very poorly edited. Contradictory views among the contributors abound. Some of these are acknowledged, as in the treatment of settlement names

(p. 23) or in the use of surveys in determining population trends (pp. 235–37), but others, more seriously, are simply ignored, as in the lack of coordination between population figures given by Hallam and David Farmer (Chapter 5 and pp. 718–19). The volume desperately needed a strong concluding chapter to bring these differing views and perspectives together and to suggest where research has headed most recently. Hallam's attempt to provide this fell far short of what was required, being principally a tedious recitation of statistics, most of which were already given in the book.

Third, the book lacks balance. Owing to contributors dropping out, the editor ended up writing nearly half of the chapters himself. This lopsidedness is unfortunate, because Hallam's adventurous, not to say eccentric, treatment of his materials sits very oddly with the more cautious, traditionally oriented approach of the other contributors. This is not necessarily a bad thing, but, in the absence of a strong editorial hand, the difference in approaches produced a very uneven result.

Finally, one almost feels that this book should carry some sort of academic health warning. It is not a volume that one can easily recommend to readers not thoroughly versed in the field, most crucially students. The problems not only lie on the level of factual errors and distortions, of which there are a number, but also stem from the overall lack of focus and direction. Uninitiated readers are likely to emerge hopelessly confused from the mass of ideas and statistics presented.

All these negative observations, however, do an injustice to the good work of individuals and, to a certain extent, to the volume as a whole. All the contributors thoroughly plumbed the archives, and as a result the book is a mine of information. There is some fool's gold in this mine, but researchers reading it will be rewarded with useful new references on a whole host of matters. Many of the individual contributions are very fine indeed. In particular, Farmer's immensely industrious and sensitively considered chapter on prices and wages is easily the highlight of the volume and will be required reading for anyone remotely concerned with or interested in the subject. Similarly fine contributions on other aspects include John Hatcher's sections on the Southwest and Christopher Dyer's on the West Midlands. Providing new material on a lightly researched area, the sections on the Welsh experience by Ian Jack are likewise very welcome.

In conclusion, this volume will become an essential work of reference for experts in the field, if not for the general public. But it is still a large disappointment, particularly when compared to the glories of Volume 4, published over two decades ago. Perhaps the lesson is that the time for such huge, overarching surveys may be past. As the general editor of the series, Joan Thirsk, writes in her preface (p. xxvi), this volume was much delayed as a result of the mounting responsibilities, teaching and otherwise, that are part of the life of today's researcher. This sad truth is not going to change in the near future, given trends in student enrollments and university funding, and perhaps some fundamental changes in strategy will be required to provide such surveys in the future. It will be interesting to see whether the imminent publication of Volume 3 (covering the period 1350 to 1500) will confirm this suspicion.

JOHN L. LANGDON, *University of Alberta*

Shylock Reconsidered: Jews, Moneylending, and Medieval Society. By Joseph Shatzmiller. Berkeley: University of California Press, 1990. Pp. viii, 255. $30.00.

In 1317 Laurentius Girardi charged that Bondavid of Draguignan, a Jew and prominent moneylender in Marseilles, was demanding repayment of a debt of 60 shillings that Laurentius claimed he had already repaid. Notarized reports of the testimony of witnesses in Bondavid's behalf, but not the final decision, are extant in Marseilles's municipal court records. Joseph Schatzmiller, who has done so much work on the Jews of Provence, uses those records and other records from Marseilles and nearby regions, as well as the extensive work by other scholars on Jewish moneylending in Mediterranean Europe, to provide a richly detailed description of the practice of moneylending in Provence, the law relevant to it, and attitudes toward it.

Bondavid's 24 witnesses were there to testify to his good reputation and the bad reputation of Petrus Guizo, Laurentius's only witness that he had repaid. These Christian witnesses, who included some of the most prominent citizens of Marseilles, depicted Petrus as a heavy drinker who frequented loose women and was an obsessive gambler. By contrast, they described Bondavid as a very honest and generous man. Although one witness believed that Bondavid lent money at usury "like all other Jews" (p. 119), another, a cleric, deposed that "he never met or saw a Christian more righteous than he" (p. 118). If some of that testimony may be "too good to be true" (p. 3), it was generally so favorable as to provide an obvious contrast to the Shylock stereotype.

There were hundreds of loans a day in Marseilles (p. 22), and indebtedness in some form was so common in southern France as to be the normal condition (p. 70). Courts, even episcopal courts, enforced repayment, and disputes about whether a debtor had or had not repaid were frequent. A creditor who falsely demanded repayment of a repaid loan would be punished as a false creditor, which would damage his reputation and his standing in any later case, as would testimony that he was a manifest usurer. To avoid that latter stigma, loan contracts camouflaged how much of the amount to be repaid was principal and how much interest. Attitudes toward lending at interest in Marseilles were obviously highly ambivalent. Officially condemned, it was taken for granted and enforced.

The three chapters devoted to Bondavid and conditions in Provence, together with the 38 pages of appendices in Latin (the court record and the will of Bondavid's father) constitute a scholarly monograph based on careful research in the primary sources and addressed primarily to scholars in the field. But two of Schatzmiller's five chapters are devoted to a rapid description of reactions to moneylending throughout Europe. Relying heavily on secondary sources, he sketches the demand for credit, ecclesiastical attitudes to usury, governmental regulation and exploitation of moneylending, the involvement of northern Italians, the social status of those who borrowed from Jews, and the attacks on, defense of, and expulsions of Jews. Though most of the matters discussed will be familiar to scholars working in medieval Jewish history, Shatzmiller's synthesis should be very helpful to those outside the field. He also provides an excellent bibliography that will be valuable for both those who are familiar with the field and those who are not.

To offset the Shylock stereotype, Schatzmiller argues that because of the need for credit, ambivalence to Jewish moneylending similar to that documented at Marseilles characterized opinions about Jewish moneylending throughout Europe from the twelfth to the fourteenth century. He thus implies that Jewish lenders in northern Europe were regarded as favorably as was Bondavid in Marseilles, which seems debatable. Mediterranean Europe was long familiar with commerce and credit—as the moneylending of northern Italians and the Cahorsins of southern France makes obvious. Provence fell outside the kingdom of France, and despite considerable friction at times, Jews were typically treated very well there and only moderately exploited up to the end of the thirteenth century.

In much of northern Europe, however, where Jews were even more disproportionately engaged in moneylending and kings and major nobles exercised direct jurisdiction over them, kings and barons exploited Jews heavily by taxes, fines, and confiscations in the thirteenth century. To come up with those large sums, Jews had to pass much of the burden on to their debtors. Moreover, where royal-baronial control was strong, muncipal governments were denied jurisdiction over Jews, which made many townsmen want to see them expelled. This apparently made Jews much more unpopular in northern than southern Europe in the thirteenth century. One indication is the local expulsions in the north. Another is the fantasies of ritual murder and profanation of the host which originated and spread widely in northern Europe, leading to the death of many Jews by 1300. In Mediterranean Europe, by contrast, the mendicant friars had only limited success in propagating such fantasies, and Jews were being invited to come and lend in Italy just when they were being expelled from northern Europe.

GAVIN I. LANGMUIR, *Stanford University*

Crisis or Change: The Concept of Crisis in the Light of Agrarian Structural Reorganization in Late Medieval England. By Nils Hybel. Aarhus, Denmark: Aarhus University Press, 1989. Pp. xxiv, 260. DKK 220.

The England of the late thirteenth, fourteenth, and fifteenth centuries has long been a scholarly battlefield. With its population shifts, plagues, foreign and domestic wars, nincompoop kings, and even climatic changes, late medieval England has been seen as encompassing a period of dramatic and near-revolutionary upheavals—politically, economically, and socially. It is a period often described as one of crisis. Onto this battlefield, and into this landscape dotted with a wide variety of alleged crises, strides Nils Hybel. He sets out to determine whether it is possible to speak of a general social crisis in England in the late Middle Ages. Defining "crisis" as both society's inability to reproduce its members ("the reproductive crisis of feudal society") and as the inability of the agrarian relations of production to reproduce themselves (the "reproductive crisis of the feudal system") (p. xiv), and basing his approach on the conviction that solving complex problems can best be done by a thorough analysis of existing historical theories, including their "theoretical and empirical presuppositions," and not merely by "fact-oriented studies of primary sources" (p. xv), Hybel proceeds to describe and critique the wide range of historical reconstruction and interpretation of late medieval English socioeconomic historiography from the 1860s to the 1980s.

The book is divided into eight chapters, each focusing on a specific, often overlapping time period and on the dominant theories—and their challenges—produced at the time. Chapter 1 covers the years 1865 to 1885 and devotes extended attention to the work of Frederic Seebohm and to the subsequent critical response to it, primarily exemplified by the research of J. E. Thorold Rogers. This period witnessed the emergence of the "neo-classical theory" of late medieval crisis, which posited a specific crisis of the landlords and the manorial system. In Chapter 2, covering the years from 1888 to 1890, Hybel turns his attention to the emergence of what he calls a "political theory" of crisis. As primarily embodied in the work of W. Denton and W. Cunningham, it viewed late medieval English social and economic malaise as an agricultural crisis, but one especially triggered by and continuously affected by the political-constitutional and military turmoil of the time, although it also finds room for advancing a notion of soil exhaustion as part of the overall picture. Chapter 3, from 1884 to 1915, introduces the "epidemiological theory" of Charles Creighton, which again thrust the question of plague to the forefront, an approach downplayed subsequently in the works of scholars such as A. E. Levett (Chapter 4, 1915 to 1930). From Chapter 5 (covering the years from 1930 to 1950) onward, Hybel steers the reader through the rough seas churned up by the still-thriving theories on the one hand of M. M. Postan, beginning with the positing of an agricultural crisis in England antedating the Black Death by at least a generation and reaching final form in what is labeled the "neo-Malthusian" theory, and on the other of the so-called "neo-Marxist" school, associated with Maurice Dobb and his views on the "inefficiency of feudalism as a mode of production" (p. 152) and continuing to the present-day work of R. H. Hilton and others. I will not attempt to summarize Hybel's own summaries of these historians' labors. Suffice it to say he does a creditable job.

At the end of his extended survey, Hybel—noting that much historical research today incorporates elements of virtually all the previously advanced theories and avoids monocausal explanations—concludes that there was, in fact, no socioeconomic crisis in late medieval England. Instead, he suggests the necessity of viewing the whole range of economic and social development as a series of regular ups and downs ("S curves," p. 295) rather than as a pattern of gradual rise from 1000 to the fourteenth century followed by a steady decline. This is a useful recommendation, but it is not going to come as a shock or revelation to the current generation of medieval agrarian, economic, and social historians represented by such men and women as Bruce Campbell, Kathleen Biddick, Christopher Dyer, Paul Glennie, and Richard Britnell.

Hybel has produced a both useful and provocative book. It is useful because it provides a truly comprehensive survey of a century's research on the late medieval English economy. It is less successful regarding social history, to be sure, but one cannot blame Hybel for restricting himself to what one mere mortal could reasonably expect to accomplish in a limited time. As a quick guide to the work of major scholars—an exalted version of "Cliff Notes"—the book is truly valuable. It is also provocative, insofar as it rejects the notion of crisis for late medieval England. Here, however, one must proceed with caution. It is a very *specific definition* of crisis, one not all readers will accept, that is found inapplicable.

Finally, although this is a useful book, it left me with a sense of uneasiness. I do not feel comfortable with historical writing that exists in fundamental isolation from primary sources. The author confesses that he has not had ready access to English sources (p. xv) and has thus depended on the reliability of the historians he is discussing. This is a questionable practice. It adds yet another type of scholar to Braudel's classifications of the historian as parachutist and the historian as truffle digger: the historian as voyeur.

EDWIN B. DEWINDT, *University of Detroit*

Poisons of the Past: Molds, Epidemics, and History. By Mary Kilbourne Matossian. New Haven: Yale University Press, 1989. Pp. xiv, 190. $22.50.

Bread of Dreams: Food and Fantasy in Early Modern Europe. By Piero Camporesi. Translated by David Gentilcore. Chicago: The University of Chicago Press, 1989. Pp. 209. $27.50.

Humankind may be a social animal, but it is also a plain vanilla animal, affecting and affected by the biological environment. The crumbled remains of long-vanished civilizations and mounting evidence of feedback effects operating through the impact of modern economic activity on the atmosphere and the food chain remind us that human history has been influenced by hidden natural forces. Of these, few are as potentially powerful as the influence of the kinds of food we eat. Two recent books explore the possibility that, within the recently recorded past, fungal poisoning of foods influenced the social behavior of Europeans. The conjectures are daring, the evidence slender, and the case not proved.

Poisons of the Past proceeds from the supposition that infection of the rye crop by molds of the genus *claviceps* may have been extensive enough before the late nineteenth century to cause outbreaks of ergotism among the populations that consumed bread prepared from contaminated flour. The book also raises the possibility that the colonization of cereal stands by certain species of *fusarium* molds gave rise to a form of immune deficiency known as alimentary toxic aleikiia (ATA). Neither of these diseases would be of more than anecdotal significance unless it were extensive enough to depress natural rates of increase or induce episodes of socially bizarre behavior among masses of people that lasted long enough to affect the course of history. Matossian claims that this was indeed the case.

Her chain of reasoning is based on the epidemiology of mycotoxicity and immune deficiency, which provides a loose but not implausible connection between observed weather conditions and observed symptoms of food poisoning. In wet years grain yields usually declined and parasite molds flourished. The resulting contraction of food supply forced populations to substitute inferior grades of rye, some of which may have contained toxins from diseased plants, in their diet. It follows that cold and wet winters should be associated with outbreaks of ergotism and ATA among the affected population. As there can be no question of obtaining observations, accurate or otherwise, of the extent of myco-intoxication of the populations of the past, historical investigation of the conjectures described necessarily depends on the above linkage. Matossian presumes that since wet and cold winters appear to have been conducive to the propagation of *claviceps*, any conjunction of wet weather and events that may be interpreted as the results or symptoms of ergotism or ATA is evidence of possible mass poisoning. The episodes include the demographic depression of the later Middle Ages (which she suggests may have been due more to immune deficiency caused by wet-weather molds than to the virulence of the plague), the demographic stagnation of the later seventeenth century, witch hunts in early modern Europe and colonial Massachusetts, the Great Fear in France in July 1789, and the convulsive religious revival of the Great Awakening in New England in 1741.

The problem with all this is that the power of the author's tests, to use statistical language, is exceedingly low. We are presented with possibilities, not probabilities. To take but one example: the proposition that witchcraft trials in the early seventeenth century might be explained by the importance of rye in local diet is based on quarter-session records from one English county that grew some rye, which is meaningless in the absence of statistics constructed out of court records from other counties. Similar problems attend the other hypotheses. The tendency of plague to decimate children at 12- to 15-year intervals in the years following its first appearance in 1348 is more likely to have resulted from lack of immunity among generations born after the previous outbreak than to acquired immune deficiency caused by eating too much poisoned bread. Ergotism may have been present in New England during the Great Awakening of 1741, but the underlying phenomena of mass conversion and revivalism there had its roots in the ironies of predestination and the Puritan Covenant, and in Jonathan Edwards's novel appeal to the sensory evidences of God's action in converting souls, both of which predate the rural howling of 1741; and there is no evidence that subsequent shriekings and shakings were ergot-induced. None of this is to say that food poisoning was absent in the episodes under consideration, but more proof is required for one to accept that it was important. The correlation coefficients developed from the evidence of late nineteenth-century Russia are impossible to interpret. Nevertheless, despite flaws in statistical procedure and inadequate consideration of alternative hypotheses, *Poisons of the Past* is worth reading because it just might be true. The history of science contains too many examples of eccentric ideas—plate tectonics comes immediately to mind—for which proof was lacking but that later turned out to be true for one to be complacent about current verities.

This much cannot be said for Piero Camporesi's *Bread of Dreams*, which is not so much a hypothesis as a series of unsystematic meditations on the hallucinogenic effects of food poisoning. One has the impression that this book, which appears to have been sent to the JOURNAL under the illusion that it has something to do with food and economic history, was composed in a psychedelic trance. There is no discernible argument or pattern to the order and contents of the chapters. The author's vision is that the life of the poor in early modern Europe was one long hunger-ridden nightmare, punctuated by episodes of mass violence and possibly alleviated by drug-induced sexual perversions. From this ramble one obtains an early modern pharmacopeia of mind-enhancing natural substances and an uncoordinated assortment of what the French call *petits faits*. Perhaps the author was attempting an intellectual history of hunger-affected minds; if so, he succeeded only in reproducing the breakdown of man's rational faculty without early modern man's excuses.

GEORGE GRANTHAM, *McGill University*

The Rise and Decline of Urban Industries in Italy and in the Low Countries (Late Middle Ages-Early Modern Times). Edited by Herman van der Wee. Leuven: Leuven University Press, 1988. Pp. 400. BEF 1.350. (paper).

The papers in this volume commence an important project: a systematic comparison of economic, demographic, and social developments in the urbanized Low Countries and Italy during the early modern period. They emerged from a conference at Antwerp in 1984 (held in preparation for the Ninth International Congress of Economic History in 1986), the theme of which was "The Dynamics of Urban Decline in the Late Middle Ages and Early Modern Times: Economic Response and Social Effects." This theme, along with the question of whether and why protoindustrialization took place in early modern Europe, provide the volume's unity.

Six essays on Italian developments (in the regions of Genoa, Venice, Tuscany, Lombardy, Naples, and Milan) begin the volume, and a seventh offers a synthesis. Following this group are seven essays treating the Low Countries (Tienen, Bruges, Antwerp, Brussels, Brabant and Flanders together, Brabant alone, and the Netherlands) and a last, rather more conceptual essay which provides a general overview and a test of several theories that have been proposed to explain the patterns of urbanization and industrial development between about 1500 and 1800 in the Low Countries. Each article provides a solid guide to the research which has been done on these cities and their environs.

Yet, as each author almost invariably reminds us, in no case is the evidence sufficient for confident generalizations even about the facts, much less about the correct interpretation of these facts. Part of the difficulty can be attributed to the project; the set of problems the authors were asked to address was in many cases not their own, and neither their own evidence nor that on which they could draw easily accommodated the questions of urban decline and the role of rural protoindustrialization in the process. The hesitancy and occasional incoherence which characterizes this volume does not, however, render it useless. On the contrary: taken together, the articles sketch a meaningful scenario.

They offer tentative confirmation that protoindustrialization occurred in many places as some historians have proposed, with the transfer of urban industry, especially textiles, to the countryside where an impoverished peasantry took on piecework under a *Verlagssystem*, thereby destroying urban craft guilds and corporative structures built on them and allowing the expansion of an export industry producing cheap, low-quality goods. The evidence from Italy seems by and large to lend itself rather comfortably to the theory. In Genoa the epidemics of the sixteenth and seventeenth centuries drove workers to the countryside, and the resistance of guilds to the proletarianization of labor encouraged merchants to organize their production outside of cities. Venice lost its traditional wool industry as a *Verlagssystem* in the countryside developed to meet competition from the North; Florence faced similar pressures from the Tuscan countryside. In Lombardy and in the area around Naples the story appears to have been similar: plague, urban guilds, and northern competition combined to drive industry from the city to the countryside, where wages were lower and production methods could be easily altered. In the Low Countries we also have some examples of a similar process, whereby international competition and changes in the availability of raw materials led industry away from urban craftspeople and into the hands of merchants and wage-dependent peasants; in both Brabant and Flanders, for example, the eighteenth century saw the displacement of urban textile industries by rural centers.

But the evidence from the Low Countries also provides potent evidence that the story of urban decline and rural industrialization is not so simply told, and it is this kind of nuancing that constitutes the book's real strength. In particular, the cities of the Low Countries seem often to have successfully adapted to changing markets and difficulties with raw material supplies. In some cities (Bruges, for example), new textile industries grew up outside of the traditional corporative structure, in a form of urban *Verlagssystem*; in others, such as Antwerp, a whole new range of urban luxury trades emerged to meet new regional and international demands, alongside an urban *Verlagssystem* producing first linen and then cotton textiles. In Brussels, the guilds both participated in the construction of urban *Verlagssysteme* and allowed new branches of the textile industry to grow up outside of their corporate structures. In short, the evidence from the eight chapters on the Low Countries tells of urban diversification, resistance, innovation, and differentiation in a difficult and changing environment, but it does not add up to a tale of woe.

The final chapter, by the book's editor, Herman van der Wee, emphasizes the general point that economic change—both decline and expansion—during this period cannot be explained simply by an appeal to the "market." Instead we must look at institutional conditions, in particular at the varied responses possible at different moments and at the way choices made in any particular instance. This is not to say that the increased international demand for cheap textiles, the emergence of the English cloth industry with the attendant decline in the export of English wools, and the demographic shifts of the period were not instrumental in changing the balance between city and countryside and in undermining traditional forms of production in the cities. But these changes alone account neither for the histories of the various cities of the period nor for the pace of industrialization in the regions thereafter.

Economic historians will be grateful for this volume because it provides convenient access to much of the existing scholarship about economic change in Italy and the Low Countries during the early modern centuries and directs this information toward the larger questions which ought to inform that scholarship. As the authors are aware, the collection leaves much unanswered, but it points toward what we need to know and why we need to know it.

MARTHA HOWELL, *Columbia University*

Spenders and Hoarders: The World Distribution of Spanish American Silver, 1550–1750. By Charles P. Kindleberger. Singapore: Institute of Southeast Asian Studies, 1989. Pp. 91. $7.00.

Charles Kindleberger opens with a characteristic, modest claim that he is not an economic historian at all; rather, he is an economic theorist interloping in unfamiliar territory—this time the global flows of precious metals in the early modern period. The flow of precious metals (mostly silver) from the New World—through Europe and also over the Pacific Ocean and ultimately to Asia—was massive and endured for more than two centuries. Kindleberger uses evidence from the secondary historical literature in order to identify and analyze the core issues. In less than one hundred pages, he unabashedly attacks competing views and weaves his own eclectic version of events. Some aspects of his interpretation are vulnerable to criticism, but his overall argument is perceptive and provocative, even for those who remain unconvinced on particular points.

Kindleberger rejects the tradition which sees money as the sole causative factor in treasure's flow from the West to the East, particularly the Humean price-specie-flow variant. At the country-to-country level, the specie-flow argument says that an influx of specie raises the monetary stock in the recipient nation and in turn the price level. Higher domestic prices encourage imports and discourage exports, thereby causing a trade deficit that drains specie back out of the country. It is thus futile for a country to try to accumulate specie because the price mechanism will simply drive it elsewhere, perhaps back whence it came. Kindleberger argues against the specie-flow doctrine by altering the unit of analysis. He points out that precious metals flowed from the Western hemisphere to the Eastern hemisphere in gargantuan quantities for centuries. Since we know that the metals were not returned to the West in conformity with the price-specie-flow prediction, Kindleberger reaches the reasonable conclusion that a more comprehensive model is needed: "The central issue is whether there is one balancing model of the balance of payments—the price-specie-flow model in the period concerned—or three, with persistent surpluses and persistent deficits also with balance. The analysis runs in terms of Alexander's absorption or spending propensities rather than the elasticities implicit in Hume's model based on prices" (p. 3). Kindleberger argues persuasively that we must look at both monetary and nonmonetary phenomena, especially regarding the intense demand for precious metals in the Far East.

It is when he reaches this point—the social forces behind Asian demand for precious metals—that his argument becomes most contentious. Is movement of the precious metals into and within the Far East explainable via the same cause-effect mechanisms applicable to Europe—as K. N. Chaudhuri, Frank Perlin, Om Prakash, and others have insisted—or is the Far East qualitatively different from the West? Kindleberger concludes that the Far East in general, and India and China in particular, are psychologically different in one important respect—Asians were and are notorious *hoarders* (thus the book's title). And it is this hoarding of precious metals that must be taken into account when explaining the massive flow of precious metals from the West to the East over the centuries. Modern-day India furnishes perhaps the most obvious evidence in our times: "The rankest of amateurs is persuaded of the Indian propensity to hoard from the experience of the twentieth century . . ." (p. 62).

On the surface it does not sound like much to observe that utility functions differ by culture. But for Kindleberger, hoarding of precious metals correlates with backwardness:

> This brings us to the central issue, whether the traditional view that hoarding in India and China was a reflection of financial lack of sophistication or that their use of precious metals was much the same as that in Europe (p. 35).
>
> The amount of specie hoarded in a country relative to that which circulated as money is most uncertain, although the ratio probably varied negatively with the state of development (p. 38).
>
> Precious metals of all kinds were a sign of prestige, still used in the rather medieval way, which, in the West, was slowly giving way to a more economical lifestyle (p. 48).
>
> [In Europe a] transition was under way from a traditional society based on self-sufficient peasants at the bottom to a market society using money to buy mass consumption goods, not only in food but also in the new instead of the old draperies. As part of this transition, monetization increased, hoarding decreased (p. 7).
>
> Hoarding in modern times has been studied analytically for Southeast Asia by P. J. Drake who explains it as a traditional stage in very poor countries between saving in real forms such as stores of goods and land, and saving through financial institutions . . . (p. 64).
>
> What needs to be explained is why the silver stops when it comes to China. . . . Not until the opium period of early nineteenth century was silver exported in large amounts. . . . It would appear that silver was as addictive as opium (p. 69).
>
> In China, silver was spent primarily for opium, one addictive substance exchanged for the other. The answer to the puzzle may lie less in economic theory than in psychological and psychoanalytical regions (p. 79).

These quotes paint a pretty clear picture. Advancing Europe was successfully shedding the anti-development habit of hoarding in early modern times, while Asia's addiction to hoarding gold and silver continued, presumably dooming the Eastern hemisphere to backwardness for centuries. So threatening is the label "hoarder" that Eli Heckscher once denied that Norway was guilty of it, "insisting that the Baltic was not India" (p. 45).

It is not terribly surprising that scholars who have long studied or lived in India—Chaudhuri, Perlin, and J. F. Richards are singled out by Kindleberger—take exception to the hoarding thesis (p. 63). For one thing, hoarding can be construed as a pejorative pinned on nonwhite (later colonized) societies by chauvinistic Europeans. One might wonder why rational Europeans "hold" precious metals in inventories, while Asians "hoard" like addicts, when both are doing the same thing. Chaudhuri, Perlin, Richards, and all feel that Asians resemble Europeans when it comes to the laws of supply and demand. To play devil's advocate for a minute, if Asians are really guilty of the sin of hoarding, then what exactly is hoarding? It is not a term one finds in economic theory, as far as I know, and I find no definition or description in *Spenders and Hoarders*. At times hoarding seems to be a nonmonetary phenomenon: "As part of this transition [European development], monetization increased, hoarding decreased" (p. 7). Yet at other times it is clear that money itself can be hoarded: "after 1600 silver was minted into coins in Surat, and used as money as well as hoarded. . . . There was undoubtedly some hoarding of the rupees passed northward along the caravan trail to Agra . . ." (p. 61). There are hints that hoarding somehow involves burying the coins (p. 33). From a theoretical point of view, one might ask the difference between burying one's money in the ground or warehousing it in an interest-free bank account. Since hoarding plays such a central role in this book, Kindleberger should really have defined the term.

In addition, the alleged backwardness of Asia is particularly confusing in light of the author's quotes (pp. 52–53) on the sophistication of China compared with Europe during this period.

Moreover, a key player in the world silver market—Japan—is only mentioned in passing (especially on p. 57 in a chapter on India). Japanese silver production, for a time perhaps half that of all Spanish America, was also destined for China (and perhaps to a lesser extent India). Japan and Spain were silver-based competitors in the same global market. If Asians had some sort of propensity to hoard silver, why were the Japanese not infected? Europeans were middlemen in the flow of Japanese silver to China, just as they were in the flow of American silver to China. The intra-Asian silver trade can be viewed as one facet of the world silver market and the flows through Europe to the East a second. Kindleberger rightly emphasizes a third facet—the route of the Manila galleons via Acapulco and over the Pacific Ocean—probably as large a flow at times as the flow through Europe (pp. 23–25). In all three facets of the silver trade Europeans served merely as middlemen. Why does the author consider European middlemen so rational compared with Asian buyers and sellers? We are not told whether residents of silver-producing areas—the New World and Japan—are rational or irrational. Like people in Europe, residents of America and Japan traded their silver for goods from China and India. Were these Asian goods held or hoarded in America and Japan?

Kindleberger acknowledges (pp. 51–52) that at times substantial quantities of gold flowed *out* of Asia and *into* Europe. This was in fact the pattern from the mid-sixteenth to the mid-seventeenth century. Not mentioned, but equally true, is the fact that Japanese copper (much of it coined in Spain) became a major competitor with Swedish copper in seventeenth-century Europe. Were Europeans hoarders of copper? What we find, therefore, is one coinable metal traveling from the West and Japan (silver), while two other coinable metals traveled to the West (gold and copper). This circumstance lends additional credence to Kindleberger's rejection of the price-specie-flow argument—why should not all coinable metals move in the same direction? Moreover, the simultaneous, contrary movements of precious metals makes a shambles of all macroeconomic arguments because macro approaches aggregate the metals and treat them as one concept—"money." Perhaps instead we need a microeconomic theory that is global in scope: treat each metal as an individual product irrespective of whether some of it is coined. Even this may not satisfy Kindleberger, however, because he is reluctant to acknowledge a world market for precious metals. He again rejects Chaudhuri's global-market approach by citing John Munro to the effect that "arbitrage in the modern sense was impossible" (p. 51). But if arbitrage—which is just another name for profitable trading—was impossible, then what nonprofit motive made merchants move the metals to and through markets all over the world? As Kindleberger's Chapter XII shows in summary, bimetallic ratios converged at about 13 to 1 throughout the world by about 1640. If market forces did not generate this convergence of values, what did?

Part of Kindleberger's anti-arbitrage argument is based on criticism of the sort of microeconomic model I proposed earlier. He claims that there was no Asian inflation as a counterpart to Europe's price revolution: "While the prices of gold and silver shifted against one another in Asia, prices of other goods rose only slightly against the two metals. This is what needs to be explained" (p. 78). In other words, precious metals generated price inflation when they hit Europe, but did not have the same result in Asia. But Kindleberger's allegation is not true for China or Japan and it is probably not true for India either. Chinese rice prices converted into silver-content terms reveal about a 250 percent price inflation (M. Cartier, "Les importations de metaux monétaires en Chine: Essai sur la conjoncture Chinoise," *Annales E.S.C.* [mai-juin 1981], pp. 454–66), much like that found in Europe, the Middle East, and elsewhere. As for India, Om Prakash and others at the April 1989 New Delhi Conference on Monetary History said that there is no consensus at all on the issue of silver-content price inflation in early modern times; data are too sketchy to substantiate or refute claims of secular price inflation in India. The solid evidence that we do have elsewhere points to converging bimetallic ratios all over the world by the middle of the seventeenth century and a (silver-content) price revolution on all continents. It is therefore hard to accept Kindleberger's contention that world markets were not integrated during this period.

In sum, *Spenders and Hoarders* contributes to our understanding of global precious metals flows by refocusing attention on the often neglected nonmonetary aspects of the trade. I would prefer that he had stuck with Alexander's unemotional "absorption" terminology, rather than the pejorative word "hoarding," but the emphasis on nonmonetary factors is healthy nonetheless. If the reader can be persuaded either to accept or ignore the emotional issue of Asian hoarding and underdevelopment, there is a great deal of substance in this small, provocative book.

DENNIS O. FLYNN, *University of the Pacific*

MODERN EUROPE

Death by Migration: Europe's Encounter with the Tropical World in the Nineteenth Century. By Philip D. Curtin. New York: Cambridge University Press, 1990. Pp. xix, 251. $39.50, cloth; $11.95, paper.

Interest in secular trends in vital rates and comparisons of these across regions has scarcely lagged since Malthus, but has shown particular strength in the last decade. Because the present study is the first of a projected trilogy, we need not fear a weakening in such interest. This volume focuses on white (or more precisely British, French, and, to a much lesser extent, Dutch) military mortality in the nineteenth century, when the most dramatic fall occurred in the death rates of Europeans relocating in the tropics. Subsequent studies will extend the analysis by comparing the mortality and morbidity experiences of Europeans and indigenous peoples in the tropics and by examining the experiences of migrating Africans.

Having become a major figure in British imperial history, and then in that of Africa and Afro-American slavery, Philip Curtin is now heading for similar status in this new field. "New," of course, is not strictly correct. Apart from recent articles, his 1968 essay on historical epidemiology in the *Political Science Quarterly* is still widely quoted; indeed, the present work begins where that article left off. The raw data are the records of morbidity and mortality among military personnel stationed in Europe on the one hand, and a wide range of European tropical dependencies on the other. The book is divided temporally into the nineteenth century before and after 1870, with each of these sections containing chapters comparing trends in Europe and the tropical world, changing attitudes toward tropical disease, and policy shifts. A lengthy and useful tabular appendix comprises more than one-quarter of the book.

The dramatic drop in mortality among Europeans relocating in the tropics has become well known. This study shows the drop to have been rather larger than many have realized. In less than a century after 1820 mortality rates fell by about 90 percent, with almost all of those affected being in the 20- to 30-age group. It also shows that despite this decline, the differential between deaths at home and deaths in the tropics expressed in ratio terms remained remarkably constant—improvements in life expectancy for military personnel staying in Europe at this time were nearly as dramatic as for those relocating. A further conclusion here is that most of this drop in mortality came in the mid-nineteenth century rather than later, and can be explained not by pharmacological prophylactics or antidotes, but rather by empirical measures put into practice without contemporaries knowing why such measures were effective. Authorities implemented public health measures—troops housed at higher altitudes, clean water, clean air, and sewage disposal—which reduced fevers, in particular, long before they knew the epidemiological justification for doing so. Pharmacological victories over typhoid, malaria, and yellow fever came much later and were of smaller significance by comparison.

The author plausibly points out that improvements in nutrition cannot explain much of the mortality decline among European service personnel. Indeed, the thrust of the argument is very much against Thomas McKeown's position in *The Modern Rise of Population* (New York, 1976) and in favor of the improvements-in-public-health-measures explanation of the revolution in human mortality. Nevertheless, the findings in Curtin's study are not necessarily inconsistent with the latest formulation of the nutritional hypothesis. Robert Fogel's recent work attributes 40 percent of the decline in mortality within Europe over a longer period than that covered here to improved nutrition, with much of this effect concentrated in reduced mortality among infants—a group that does not feature in the present study. It might be noted that the drop in mortality among civilians in Europe over the same period was much less than that experienced by the military groups in Europe examined here. Thus improved life expectancies of civilian and military groups in Europe may have occurred for different reasons, as indeed with the same phenomenon for service personnel at home and in the tropics. But these fascinating possibilities are left for others to develop more fully.

There are important implications in Curtin's book, not just for historical demographers but for students of migration, particularly economic historians. It also has considerable significance for historians of colonization, especially African colonial history. It provides, for example, grounds for widening the explanations for European partition of that continent. Scholars will be impatient to see the remaining volumes of Curtin's trilogy.

David Eltis, *Queen's University, Kingston*

Town and Countryside: The English Landowner in the National Economy, 1660–1860. Edited by C. W. Chalklin and J. R. Wordie. Winchester: Unwin Hyman, 1989. Pp. xiii, 224. $55.00.

Landowners' economic functions ranged widely: most obviously, they managed the use of their land (directly or through proxy agents or entrepreneurs), whether for urban residential development, for agriculture, for mining, or for transportation improvements. Some disseminated new techniques, enforcing their use through covenants in leases. Some raised mortgages and invested in new sectors. Parliament in most of the 200 years covered by the book was more controlled by landowners than by any other interest. The nine essays of this volume tend to celebrate landowners more than consider land as a factor of production or examine the links between town and countryside, as the main title somewhat misleadingly suggests. The subject can be approached in several ways—considering landowning in town and country (and in agriculture or mining in the countryside), landowners private and corporate, landowners large and small—and the volume offers a good balance among these.

Four of the essays treat urban landowners; three explicitly look at the corporate owner, and if the fourth does not, it is because Chalklin provides an overview of three provincial towns (Birmingham, Bristol, and Liverpool) that bucked the trend of slow urban growth in the eighteenth century. Jane Longmore's essay on the Liverpool Corporation will most engage economic historians: she traces the Corporation's success in building dock after dock, wet and dry, allowing the city to expand from a modest port in the shadow of Chester in the early eighteenth century to overtake Bristol by the fourth quarter of that century. (She exhibits a slight delicacy in her reference to the city's merchants' "trading to Africa" (p. 125) and defensiveness in the unsurprising finding that merchants in the slave trade also profited from other trades.) S. T. Blake's essay on Crown and Corporation estates in Reading is, I trust, as absorbing to the seven of nine other contributors with past or present connections to the University of Reading as a detailed history of my own urban surroundings would be to me and my neighbors.

B. E. S. Trueman's subject, Guy's Hospital in London, was comfortably saddled with an endowment from the bookseller who had added to his fortune in the South Sea Bubble; it suffered only one small thorn, the constraint placed on the Corporation to transform its endowment into land at a time of rising land prices. The hospital corporation purchased, in its first 30 years, 23,000 acres in Essex, Lincolnshire, and Herefordshire. So here is the rural-urban connection, but turned on its head, urban corporation as rural landholder. The corporation is seen enforcing fallow courses, with interesting details on estate management, including mortgage loans.

Four other essays are more completely concerned with the countryside. The rural landowners of these essays range from the very large (the third Earl of Spencer and the Leveson-Gowers) to the large. P. J. Keeley moves quickly through nine generations of the latter—the Northcotes of Devon as judges, baronets, MP's, gamblers, debtors. The family recovered in the late eighteenth century to link up with entrepreneurs in developing manganese mines on the family property and to move into banking. Janie Cottis offers less drama but more economic detail in an account of an individual landlord, a contemporary of Coke of Norfolk, but a squire, as she points out, on intractable clay in Berkshire, not a free-spending noble on improvable sands. Here, there is much of interest in the use of covenants to leases to govern the use of land and to enforce a switch to permanent grass. E. A. Wasson sketches in the third Earl of Spencer, aristocratic activist, proponent of agricultural change (through the Smithfield Club and the Royal Agricultural Society), architect of the Reform Act and the new Poor Law, opponent of the Corn Law and eventual supporter of universal manhood suffrage, who had amassed a debt of £60,000 by 1833.

In addition to a comprehensive introductory essay (treating economic policymaking among other things), Wordie contributes a most fascinating essay on the relationship between three generations of fast-rising and well-documented aristocratic landlords and their less well-documented entrepreneurs and estate agents (themselves gentlemen landlords) in east Shropshire during its brief run as Cradle of the Industrial Revolution; we see them developing coal mines and involved in canal schemes.

As is almost inevitable, the volume's introduction promises more than the book delivers. The introduction develops an important point on the importance of land as a producer of timber—for building, for machine-making, for fuel—in what A. E. Wrigley has called the "advanced organic economy" of the eighteenth century, but this is taken up only in passing within the essays.

ANN KUSSMAUL, *Glendon College, York University*

Consumer Behaviour and Material Culture in Britain, 1660–1760. By Lorna Weatherill. New York: Routledge, 1988. Pp. xii, 252. $47.50.

We human beings have always been consumers, dependent on our capacity to use and use up what we have killed, grown, or made. But we have lived in modern consumer societies—societies organized around mass markets for the acquisition of material possessions—only in relatively recent times. Much current scholarship traces the birth of mass markets to seventeenth- and eighteenth-century Europe, focusing particularly on the Netherlands and Great Britain. Lorna Weatherill's book contributes significantly to this work. Using evidence derived from handbooks of household advice, probate inventories, private account books, diaries, memoirs, and genre painting among other sources, she explores patterns of consumption and consumer behavior in a variety of rural and urban communities in early modern England and Scotland. She pays particular attention to the middling sort, whom she defines as ranging from husbandmen and small craftsmen at the bottom to the lesser gentry at the top. Her main aim is to situate the consumption habits of this broad group within the context of their social and economic lives and to elucidate the cultural "meaning of ownership" (p. 5) for them in social terms.

Within this framework Weatherill gives us a useful and balanced account of some important features of the so-called consumer revolution of this period. She provides significant evidence of increases in the number and value of household items owned by members of the middling sort, of new products entering into everyday use, and of new attention being given to their presentation for public view in what she calls the "front stage" rooms of their houses. But in contrast to Margaret Spufford and D. E. C. Eversley, she sees laborers, wage-earners, and even small farmers very largely excluded from the market for consumer items. As a result, she argues, fluctuations in agricultural incomes and even in food prices probably made a smaller difference to consumption patterns in this period than many scholars have assumed. However, she leaves this important claim to her concluding remarks, and so does not work it out fully. Weatherill also finds that ownership of consumer goods did not map neatly onto the conventional social hierarchy of status and wealth. Families in the commercial and dealing trades often possessed household wares and personal effects in greater number and more variety than did the members of the higher-status gentry and professions, while yeomen followed those in the lesser trades. This suggests that cultural and economic differences between rural and urban settings were crucial to the developments that Weatherill describes. Unfortunately her chapter on this subject merely touches on the mechanisms involved, apparently because her research design was not initially intended to test for a rural-urban dichotomy in consumption patterns.

The limitations in social coverage of this study, many of them dictated by Weatherill's reliance on probate inventories drawn from individual dioceses and London's Court of

Orphans, necessarily leaves the consumer behavior of Britain's nobility and county gentry (whose wills normally were proven in the Prerogative Courts of Canterbury or York, not in diocesan courts) almost completely dark to us. But this fact inevitably blinds us to the role of social emulation in shaping the consumer markets. On her evidence, we cannot know whether Britain's great families operated in an entirely separate consumer market of refined taste, exquisite workmanship, and exotic luxuries while the rest of society plodded along with more mundane and more affordable wares, or whether the more fashionable members of the middling sort simply bypassed the backwoods gentry and looked to the national elite for their paragons. We simply need to know more about the tastemakers of this period and how their preferences were communicated to others.

Weatherill's method for tracing consumption habits also has its flaws, especially for understanding the social and cultural meanings attached to the ownership of material goods. To provide a firm basis of comparison over space and time, she chose to study the ownership of a group of seventeen items, all household wares, selected because they were "reliably and consistently listed in the documents" and were "representative of other goods or of people's domestic behaviour" (p. 3). But we cannot tell what weight particular items were given by different individuals and groups, since the overall pattern of consumption remains unknown. Nor can we know the importance of a household's material possessions without seeing them in relation to other forms of consumption, say of food and drink or of those kinds of cultural production, like songs or sermons, which can be enjoyed without being possessed materially. Weatherill tries to make up for these methodological shortcomings by studying a small number of household account books, an admittedly rare source. Here at least we can see in money terms how particular households handled their expenditures. But her use of this evidence still leaves open the question of what constituted "consumption" in her period, since not every item a household consumed was paid for in cash, whether one construes "consumption" narrowly or broadly. From sources like these, moreover, we can hardly determine to what degree members of the middling sort still lived in a culture of gift and barter and not a market exchange economy; obviously we can say nothing at all about the socioeconomic lives of those who lacked the skills or reasons to keep such records. Nor does Weatherill's use of other kinds of sources overcome this limitation. Handbooks of household advice and even diaries and memoirs conform to literary conventions and didactic purposes that keep them from being straightforward representations of actual social and cultural practices; equally problematic are genre paintings, which for all their apparent visual realism have iconographical meanings and moralizing aims that make them exceptionally tricky guides.

A further problem in interpretation arises because "consumption," for all its uses as a term of analysis, is never an entirely independent category. Its proper study cannot be divorced from examination of the processes of production, accumulation, and distribution of wealth that make consumption possible and condition its meanings and functions. But use of probate inventories has the effect of isolating consumption from other economic activities in just this way. For a book concerned with cultural meanings, moreover, the absence of information about real estate and indebtedness creates special problems. The possession of land and other kinds of real property surely was one of the greatest forms of social display in this period. Its ownership may well account for the fact that the lesser gentry did not indulge themselves in the purchase of new consumer items to the same degree as did those engaged in the leading commercial and dealing trades. At the same time, shopkeepers, artisans, and traders regularly owed money to their suppliers just as they were owed money in turn by their customers. In consequence, it was essential for those engaged in commercial dealing at every level to uphold their reputations as good credit risks. Can it be that the relatively heavy investment these figures made in purchases of goods for the "front stage" rooms of their houses, where friends and neighbors would have been entertained, was part of complex strategy used to demonstrate economic worth? Members of the gentry and the professions, who were much better established in status and reputation and somewhat less dependent on credit for their livelihoods, would not have needed to follow this practice to the same degree. Nothing in Weatherill's approach allows us to evaluate the practices of possession in light of these other important socioeconomic considerations.

Finally, a word must be said about Weatherill's understanding of cultural "meaning." As she uses the term, it often seems to stand for, or be reduced to, social function. But functions are not meanings. The ownership of a clock, for example, may mark one's status in the social hierarchy, as Weatherill argues, but the meaning of the clock surely has something to do with a particular conception of time and perhaps also with a particular fascination with measurement and interest in the workings of machines, all situated in a particular view of the world. The ownership of a clock, then, meshes with a variety of other cultural proclivities and must be interpreted discursively, semiotically, or symbolically. To count the number of clocks owned by the members of different occupational groups shows us something important about early modern Britain's consumer economy, but cannot reveal the way this instrument resonated with other aspects of their mentalities and ideologies or tell us why there was a market for clocks in the first place. This is to say that the serious study of consumer society demands attention to the market for culture broadly defined as well as to the culture of the market.

But it would be wrong to end this review on too negative a note. Weatherill has made a useful contribution to our understanding of the emergence of a consumer society in early modern Britain. Despite its imperfections, her book should be read by anyone interested in this important field.

DAVID HARRIS SACKS, *Reed College*

Regions and Industries: A Perspective on the Industrial Revolution in Britain. Edited by Pat Hudson. New York: Cambridge University Press, 1989. Pp. xiii, 277. $49.50.

Industrialization in Britain, contend Pat Hudson and her contributors, began in regions rather than in the national economy. The currently fashionable view of the Industrial Revolution as a phenomenon seen through aggregate data necessarily conflates the diverse experiences of industries as well as regions as it aggregates up to the national economy. Variation, the red meat of this volume's approach, is wiped out in the averaging needed to produce macroeconomic estimates of changes in growth, productivity, investment, and real wages. The regional studies, in turn, nag and niggle at contemporary orthodoxy: they excoriate the glacial contours of the gradualism which has become the hallmark conclusion of the macroeconomic school.

In the first chapter Hudson makes a convincing case for the regional perspective on the Industrial Revolution, and in the process criticizes the approach and the findings of the macroeconomic school. John Walton then asks whether the idea of proto-industrialization fits the case of Lancashire. Here transition from a preindustrial through a proto-industrial to an industrial economy was most likely to occur in its pure form, uninhibited by prior developments elsewhere. In the third chapter, Hudson summarizes her comparative work on the woolen and worsted areas of the West Riding. Chapter 4 moves to the West Midlands, where, as Marie Rowlands shows, regional experience confirms the findings of recent aggregate analyses of industrialization: a stress on the importance of economic growth and structural change before 1760 and the suggestion that between 1760 and 1850 growth was slower and innovation more piecemeal than was formerly believed. John Marshall, in Chapter 5, uses a model of industrial evolution to question whether the concept of proto-industrialization applies to Cumbria. Brian

Short's study of the Weald, 1600–1850, provides an example of a failed transition from proto-industrialization to full industrialization, and one where commercial agriculture did not replace industry. Short uses his example to explore possible causes of deindustrialization. Adrian Randall's discussion of resistance to technological change in the West Country illustrates that the attitudes of workers to machinery are contingent not only on the organization of the industry but also on the control of work and the character of the community within which work takes place. A comparison between Wales and the northeast of England allows Neil Evans in Chapter 8 to identify the distinctiveness of Wales and deepen understanding of its economic experience. In Chapters 9 and 10, Ian Whyte and Leslie Clarkson analyze the early industrial development of Scotland and Northern Ireland respectively.

Although Hudson promises, and implicitly the studies do deliver, a challenge to established views on industrialization, only Rowlands, whose conclusions are by and large supportive, explicitly confronts the macroeconomic school. The other authors choose instead to organize their analyses around the central hypotheses of the proto-industrialization model. It is left to the reader to draw the revisionist inferences for contemporary orthodoxy with its emphasis on evolution, not revolution, and its dichotomization of the economy into modern and traditional sectors. Perhaps Hudson's contributors are less concerned than she is with economists' economic history. As for the concept of proto-industrialization, it grows through these studies. Invariably associated hypotheses are revealed as too simplistic and too crude, but these authors' findings refine and elaborate the original concept rather than undermine it.

In other ways *Regions and Industries* is demanding of its readership. A macroeconomic exercise which involves the comparison of a handful of estimates with a few older figures is relatively easy to digest even if inquiring minds are drawn to investigate the changed assumptions or new data that underpin the revisions. Well written as the book is, readers will have to wrestle with the text to extract the main lines of the arguments. In the process nuggets of interesting information, useful to a variety of research agendas, can be turned up, a bonus for the diligent reader.

In the end, of course, the questions and criticisms of the macroeconomic school which emerge emanate less from the focus on regions as the unit of analysis than from other related differences in approach. The macroeconomic school focuses on the aggregate economy because it conceptualizes industrialization principally in terms of significant breaks in economic time-series. Hudson and her contributors focus on regions because their understanding of industrialization is more complex, and therefore less easily presented, covering changes in industrial organization, technology, and class relations.

JANE HUMPHRIES, *Cambridge University*

The Economic Section, 1939–1961: A Study in Economic Advising. By Alec Cairncross and Nita Watts. New York: Routledge, Chapman and Hall, 1989. Pp. xii, 372. $56.00.

Prior to 1940 the British government lacked a full-time staff for economic advising at the center of government, and virtually no professional economists were employed by government departments. By 1989 the Government Economic Service employed nearly 400 economists. A central place in the intervening evolution was occupied by the Economic Section, whose history is chronicled by Alec Cairncross and Nita Watts in this book. Located in the Cabinet Office until 1953, when it was transferred to the Treasury, the Economic Section was a small (12- to 15-person) team of economists who developed a unified view of economic issues and were the primary source of professional advice from 1940 until 1964, when employment of other economists began to increase.

The authors draw upon their own experiences as former members of the Economic Section, although the story is mainly traced, with abundant references, from archival sources in the Public Record Office and the Bank of England. The work of the Section is discussed under four main areas: monetary policy, fiscal policy, external economic policy, and incomes policy. Both its role in major policy decisions and its day-to-day influence are described. As the authors explain, the book is not a complete history of policy formulation, and nonspecialist readers may well need to "seek amplification elsewhere" (for example, in Cairncross's own *Years of Recovery: British Economic Policy, 1945–51* [New York, 1985]). What the book does provide is a careful account of the contributions of the Economic Section, and some valuable insights into the conditions under which successful policy advising may occur.

The most important of the Section's activities (especially under Robert Hall's directorship, from 1947 to 1961) was advising on the annual budget. National income forecasts and annual economic assessments developed by the Section became vital background to the budget-making process. Hunches and economic intuition nonetheless played an important role. The authors discuss in detail the budgets from 1947 to 1958. In 1951 the Section had a major impact, arguing against large tax increases despite rearmament and other increases in government spending. In general, the Section recommended relatively small changes in the budget (no more than £150 million up or down, when national income was £10,000 to 20,000 million). It took a Keynesian approach, and one very interesting theme in the book is the Section's role in the transition from wartime physical controls and manpower budgeting (a conceptual framework retained by many ministers after the war) to financial controls and demand management of the economy. The authors might have linked these points with the recent literature on the nature and timing of the "Keynesian revolution."

In external economic policy the Section's influence is harder to identify, partly because other departments advised in this area as well. But it had major impacts in urging the 1949 devaluation and accompanying expenditure cuts, encouraging British membership in the European Payments Union, and helping to block the Robot scheme during the 1951/52 balance-of-payments crisis. In monetary policy the Section appears to have held fewer strong positions, though it was concerned about inflation and saw credit controls (more than high interest rates) as a useful weapon. It faced opposition, however, from the Bank of England, which was unwilling to exert strong control over the commercial banks and which argued that the government's financing requirements made such control difficult.

Advice was least successful in the area of incomes policy, despite considerable efforts. The Section advocated creation of a wages advisory council and mobilization of public support for moderate wage settlements. The failure is intriguing, especially since the conflict between full employment and price stability remained a central long-term policy problem. The authors note the contrast between peacetime and wartime policymaking, with multiple objectives replacing the single aim of military victory. They might have gone on to explore whether in peacetime, political constraints (or opportunities) from outside government play a more important role in some policy areas, such as incomes policy, than others. Such analysis of the political and institutional context would have broadened the reader's understanding of the Section's effectiveness.

More generally, policymaking within the book seems almost insulated from politics; it is not entirely clear whether this reflects historical realities, or primarily the authors' delimitation of their subject matter. Readers seeking a richer understanding of the politics (and personalities) of the period may wish to consult recently published diaries and papers of key figures: *The Robert Hall Diaries, 1947–53*, edited by Alec Cairncross (Winchester, 1989); *The Collected Papers of James Meade*. Vol. 4, *The Cabinet Office Diary, 1944–46*, edited by Susan Howson and Donald Moggridge (Winchester, 1990);

and Edwin Plowden, *An Industrialist in the Treasury: The Post-War Years* (London, 1989).

Apart from its impact on major policy decisions, the Section also contributed to the provision of an adequate statistical basis for policymaking and to the general level of economic education through its participation in interdepartmental committees. Before 1940 economic data were scarce, and almost entirely annual rather than quarterly or monthly. World War II had a major impact, as had World War I, with urgent wartime demands for economic data—some prepared by the Section and its antecedents—carrying over into peacetime practice.

The Section's effectiveness was bolstered by its command of these data, and by its "collective memory" of policy history. A foundation in economic theory undoubtedly helped, although an interesting point made by the authors is the extent to which policy continued to be formulated on the basis of inadequate concepts (for example, ministers' preoccupation with the budget surplus or deficit "above the line" as opposed to a measure of the budget's overall impact on final demand and macroeconomic activity). Trust, based on character and temperament as well as technical expertise, and access to ministers were crucial. Good relations between Lionel Robbins, the Director from 1940 to 1945, and Sir John Anderson, Lord President in charge of economic affairs from 1940 to 1943, and between Hall and numerous ministers during his 14-year directorship, greatly increased the Section's influence.

Interdepartmental relations also played a role. Between 1945 and 1947, for example, the Treasury was reasserting itself as the central economic department and rejected Economic Section advice. The Inland Revenue Service, which disliked using taxes for economic ends, opposed Economic Section proposals in the mid-1950s for investment tax credits. A key turning point for the Section's influence came in 1947 when economic crises led to a shake-up in the governmental machine. Economic and financial policy were united under a new Chancellor (Sir Stafford Cripps) who worked closely with the Section's director (Hall), and the Treasury acquired a planning staff which collaborated with the Section and came to rely on it for professional advice.

One finishes the book with a thorough understanding of the activities of the Economic Section, and with many questions about the overall nature and purposes of economic advising, including how these changed over time. What factors outside government influence economic advising and policymaking? Has economic advising improved with the great increase in the quantity of advisors since the 1960s? While it could not be based upon Public Record Office sources, a chapter on the Economic Section since the 1960s would have been fascinating, both completing the Section's own history and indicating how advising and its effectiveness changed when the Economic Section lost its "virtual monopoly" of the process. Did advisors continue to be interested in ends, as the authors argue was true for Economic Section members before 1961, and not only means? Was there any shift in the importance of the two approaches—technocratic, and representative of outside interests—described on p. 10? Perhaps most important, why has economic advising (both in the time period covered by the book and later) on long-term issues and problems, such as growth and competitiveness, regional decline, or incomes policy, not been more successful?

Carol E. Heim, *University of Massachusetts, Amherst*

The British Aircraft Industry. By Keith Hayward. Manchester: Manchester University Press, 1989. Pp. xiv, 221. $59.95.

Keith Hayward has performed a valuable service. Not only has he provided the first history of the British aircraft industry from its origins before World War I to the present, but he has also attempted to identify the economic forces accounting for its evolution.

Hayward's basic thesis is straightforward. Large initial investments in research, development, and tooling in aircraft production, and the importance of the learning curve, make scale of paramount importance. British aircraft producers were at a disadvantage relative to American producers after World War II because of Britain's fragmented industrial structure and the small size of the domestic market. This led inevitably toward increasing concentration in Britain and toward international collaborative projects. Government support for the industry proved a mixed blessing. While government played a crucial role in providing launch aid (by the 1980s airframe producers faced a one-time R&D cost of about $1.5 billion), the vagaries of its policy increased the burden of uncertainty in an industry where the initial cost is not recovered for ten years.

Hayward develops this thesis in four well-organized chapters. The first covers the industry's formative years through World War II. It points to the importance of rearmament and the war in expanding the scale and technical capabilities of the industry. Chapter 2 traces the events leading up to the restructuring of the industry at the end of the 1950s. Britain's increasing involvement in European collaborative projects during the 1960s, including the Concorde, Airbus, and the Anglo-French military package, are described in Chapter 3. The fourth chapter discusses the events leading to the bankruptcy and nationalization of Rolls Royce in 1971, the nationalization of the airframe industry with the formation of British Aerospace under Labour in 1976, and the subsequent privatization of Rolls and BAe under the Thatcher government. A final chapter assesses the industry's economic performance and the impact of government.

Hayward presents a great deal of interesting information about the beliefs and aims of the key individuals in business and government responsible for the development of the British aircraft industry. At times, however, his account appears schizophrenic. While he discusses the beliefs of these individuals as if they did matter, he nonetheless maintains that competition from the United States ineluctably pushed the British aircraft industry toward greater concentration and international collaboration. If the march of history is determined by impersonal market forces, then the views of individual entrepreneurs and politicians is just so much froth. Does a desire to downplay the apparent inconsistency explain Hayward's lack of attention to some glaring anomalies for the market structure argument?

First, there is the unexplained success of Rolls Royce. A table showing the world market shares of the "big three" in aircraft engine production since World War II would be helpful here. The figures would reveal that Rolls, ranked ahead of General Electric in 1960, subsequently increased its world market share at the expense of Pratt and Whitney.

Second, there is the remarkable success of Airbus Industrie's A300 series of airframe, introduced in 1975. The A300, a collaborative project of France and Germany which Britain eventually bought into with a 20 percent share, was the first European airframe to seriously challenge U.S. market dominance, and Airbus Industrie emerged as Boeing's main competitor during the 1980s, leaving Lockheed and McDonnell Douglas a distant third and fourth.

The success of the collaborative A300 project seems to support Hayward's contention that Britain's former inability to compete with the United States can be explained in terms of industrial fragmentation and the small size of the domestic market, but a more careful look at the evidence suggests that this is overly simplistic. The key breakthrough for Airbus was an order by an American airline, Eastern, which established the A300's market acceptability. It was only subsequent to this in 1978 that the French government redirected resources into the program, with an order from Air France for 24 A300s, and that Britain decided to buy into the program.

Arguably a key factor in the success of the A300 series was the entrepreneurial vision of the project's director, Henri Ziegler. The A300, the only advanced twin-engine, wide-bodied airplane on the market in the mid-1970s, addressed a market segment that was poorly covered by U.S. manufacturers. When Boeing introduced its competitive wide-bodied 767 in 1982, Airbus Industrie was well along its learning curve and was easily able to compete with Boeing on price, quality, and delivery.

Hayward could have drawn on recent theoretical work on path-dependency and increasing returns, particularly by W. Brian Arthur and Paul David, which shows in a tractable manner that for increasing returns industries small-chance events (for instance, entrepreneurship or a crucial order) early in the history of a technology can tilt the competitive advantage.

Hayward also fails to come to grips with the evidence he presents on comparatively low British productivity. Hayward expresses incredulity: "If the productivity of BAe and Rolls was so poor, they could hardly have competed on price in international markets . . ." (p. 197). Part of the answer is on the previous page: "French industry could be up to one and a half times more productive than the British, although the French advantage was balanced by higher wage costs."

The British aircraft industry is certainly a post-World War II success story, but one should be wary of drawing implications from this for the debate on British decline. The industry has benefited from exceptionally high levels of subsidization and the British government is by far its largest customer. It is striking that, in common with such "nonstrategic" sectors as cars, shipbuilding, and steel, productivity is low in the British aircraft industry relative to its principal competitors. By exploring the reasons for this, Hayward might have transformed a creditable account of a somewhat idiosyncratic case into an analysis with much wider implications for British economic performance. As British manufacturing continues its downward slide, this wider analysis is of the utmost importance.

EDWARD H. LORENZ, *University of Notre Dame*

Banking in Nineteenth Century Ireland: The Belfast Banks, 1825–1914. By Phillip Ollerenshaw. Manchester: University of Manchester Press, 1987. Pp. xi, 263. $19.95.

It has been fashionable to decry the publication of doctoral theses in recent years on the grounds that they are too detailed and overly pedantic even when recut to suit the market. This book should, however, be given a more favorable reception. Although there are a number of studies of individual banks in Ireland, including the Bank of Ireland, Ollerenshaw rightly notes in his introduction that very little has been published which links the banks with the growing Irish economy. To correct this oversight, he examines a group of banks based in Belfast. Generalizing from this data base, he ambitiously confronts traditional historiography by arguing that banks did contribute to the development of the Irish economy and that the view of Joseph Lee, among others, is "both simplistic and wide of the mark" (p. 186). The banks adopted a "flexible and extensive lending policy" (p. 196), did their best to meet the needs of industry, and were not "sterile" establishments as alleged in most business histories. His conclusions rely heavily on an analysis of the ratio of lending to deposits, the quality of management, and the similarity in practice to the Scottish banks, whose contributions to economic growth are, he claims, generally praised. The greatest weakness in the acceptance of his thesis is, perhaps inevitably, the narrow base, Belfast; it is a problem compounded by the city's geographical location, which gave a Lancashire–west of Scotland orientation to business connections. Nevertheless, the approach is challenging and should encourage a reconsideration of a number of thorny questions relating to the role of banking in Ireland in the nineteenth century.

The book follows a fairly standard chronological format. The peculiarities of the Irish system as it developed in the eighteenth century are well known and Ollerenshaw moves quickly to the creation of the Belfast banks: one note-issuing bank was formed in 1808 and two more appeared in the city in 1809. The repeal of the more restrictive clauses in earlier legislation by the Irish Banking Act of 1824 led to the city's first joint-stock company, the Northern, founded in the same year and based on one of the private banks, Montgomery's. The other two amalgamated in 1827 as the Belfast Banking Company. Ollerenshaw succintly analyzes the background to these decisions and suggests that the reason for this swift conversion was the perception that the private approach was unable to supply sufficient capital for the growing market. To bolster his position, he emphasizes the links between the Presbyterian merchants of the city and the banks. The argument is persuasive but there does not seem to be much concrete evidence of a shortage of capital; other factors, including the desire to spread the risk of operation, may have played a part.

The most interesting aspect of the early chapters is the discussion of the mechanics of joint-stock banking in Belfast. The author presents a wealth of statistics from each bank's records in 39 tables and 2 figures which are models of clarity. The gradual expansion of business, including the decision to open branches outside the city, the competition with rival establishments created during the joint-stock boom of the 1830s, and the responses to the various financial crises in the period to 1857, are treated thoughtfully. The author recognizes a seasonal cycle of business, even in Belfast, due to the connection with agriculture, either directly or through particular industries, flax spinning among others. He also notes development of an unusual management structure. In each bank an elected committee of leading shareholders, separate from a permanent board of directors, kept in touch with the needs of the community. Thus, the directors were free to devote themselves solely to the business of banking. Ollerenshaw suggests that this two-tiered approach helped the banks avoid the failures that became commonplace elsewhere. Other questions within the overall argument deserve more extensive examination—for example, the problems of tax collection, which have liquidity and credit/time implications, and the vexatious questions of specie payments. But the analysis is generally thorough.

The second half of the book examines more closely the relationship between the bank and the economy. It is difficult to quarrel with the author's general position that the banks did participate in economic development. In the technical discussion of the reasons behind this participation, the evidence is fairly straightforward. Lending policy and support in periods of crisis depended on the size of the firm and the degree to which it was known and valued as a customer by the bank's officers. The banks adopted a "pragmatic" approach and were loath to do anything that might upset the market. Furthermore, for most of the period lending balances exceeded those of deposits. This, of course, stands at variance with the usual interpretation of banks in Ireland, which describes them as generally indifferent to business, with their assets kept locked in their vaults. The crucial distinction for the general thesis relies on the definition of "support." Ollerenshaw presents a picture of partnership in which the legitimate needs of business were satisfied, on the odd occasion even without collateral security; in that sense, the term "conservative" is not necessarily pejorative. Moreover, on the vexed question of long-term lending by overdraft rather than fixed term in Ireland, he joins those who claim that it was a fairly common practice throughout the period. Further to this conclusion, he takes issue with W. P. Kennedy on the consequences of the 1878 failure of the City of Glasgow bank for lending policy. There was a decline in the amount advanced but this can easily be explained by reference to the economic conditions (reductions can be noted prior to the crisis) and there did not appear to be any reevaluation of the general approach. In sum, he concludes, the banks did all that could be expected of them, with safety, for businessmen.

The argument is attractive, but occasionally Ollerenshaw is on weaker ground. In

1825 the three banks, soon to become two, agreed to limit the payment of interest on deposit accounts to 2 percent. Thirteen years later, in 1839, this collusion was extended to eliminate price competition altogether. The agreement survived the period under discussion and the author credits it with preventing both "excessive competition" and an early encroachment by stranger banks. In neither instance does he provide much evidence as to the value of this successful adoption of monopoly banking except in terms of each bank's dividends and the structure of accounts. The Scottish system chose a similar approach at about the same time and became heavily cartelized as a result. The topic reappears in his discussion of practice after 1850, the impact of competitors and their co-option into the system, for example. It is given more satisfying treatment here but some worrying inconsistencies could still force a modification of his general conclusions. The statement that Belfast banks sought to "preserve collusive agreement at all costs" (p. 123) sits oddly with the conclusion that they tried to operate with "flexibility in order to maintain customer loyalty" (p. 194). It is noted elsewhere that the banks were forced to adopt some unusual and awkward arrangements in order to circumvent their own restrictions. The apparent contradiction is quite important, as responsiveness to economic conditions is rarely shown by establishments hedged around with self-imposed restrictive practices. To argue otherwise is to suppose that stability is the primary contribution that banks can make to the economy. Although this aspect of service is undoubtedly important, it does not necessarily invalidate the criticisms of conservatism which Ollerenshaw is trying, for the most part successfully, to refute.

Overall, the book does provide a good analysis of banking in Belfast and, by extension, Ireland. The reader may take issue with the unsatisfactory explanation of the continuance of small notes in Ireland after 1826 and the weak comparison with English practice in the second half of the century, but these are minor flaws. The strengths, which are considerable, lie in the provision of much useful data on the financial system and its interplay with the business sector. As Ollerenshaw himself is aware, much work is still to be done. This carefully researched and well-written study has provided a valuable base upon which future explanations of the role of banks in the economic development of Ireland can be built.

DAVID J. MOSS, *University of Alberta*

The Footwear Industry in Ireland, 1922–1973. By Jon Press. Dublin: Irish Academic Press, 1989. Pp. 229. $39.50.

Ireland's failure to industrialize relative to Britain and the rest of Europe remains a historical puzzle. The value of case studies of individual Irish industries should therefore be obvious. Unfortunately, the Irish historical literature contains relatively few company histories, and even fewer industry histories. Jon Press's work on the Irish footwear industry thus assumes a greater importance than might be obvious at first glance. Historians in search of explanations for Ireland's mostly dismal twentieth-century economic performance will profit from this well-written and thorough book, which is also quite suggestive about the strategies which successful Irish firms of the future will need to follow.

The book's organization is particularly useful. Successive chapters examine how the industry's fortunes varied in response to changes in Ireland's economic relationship with the outside world. Thus Chapter 1 deals with the early development of the industry, in the years prior to Irish independence and in the first, relatively free-trading, decade of the new state. Chapter 2 describes the rapid growth of the industry from 1932 to 1936, the first years of the protectionist experiment in Ireland. Chapter 3 chronicles the recession that followed, as the industry ran into the constraints imposed by the size of the home market, while Chapter 4 recounts the experience of the industry during World War II. Chapters 5 and 6 describe the shakeout which occurred in the changed postwar economic environment, and the gradual development of export markets corresponding to the opening of the national economy in the latter half of the 1950s. Chapter 7 considers the rapid export-based expansion of the 1960s. Since 1973, when Ireland joined the European Community, the industry has experienced decline. This is dealt with in a distressingly summary fashion in the concluding chapter.

The book is particularly useful in its treatment of the links between Irish and British firms. Economists tend to analyze the movement of entrepreneurs, skills, and technology across national frontiers less than they do similar movements of labor and capital, although it is surely of great importance; a major contribution of history can be to redress the balance. British firms such as Clarks licensed their technology to the more successful Irish firms, providing training (and occasionally brand names and quality-control services) to their Irish counterparts. Just as important was the knowledge of international market conditions foreigners could bring to Ireland.

The story of the industry's most successful product of the 1960s, the "Wallabee" shoe, is instructive. Padmore & Barnes, a Clarks affiliate, started exporting this product to North America shortly after a former export manager of Clarks Overseas Shoes took over as managing director: no coincidence. The new boss knew the leading European shoe manufacturers and obtained the Wallabee's design from a German company; the decision to focus on the American market was surely due to his experience in international marketing. By 1970 this one product accounted for nearly half of total Irish shoe exports to North America (pp. 159–60). The most fundamental constraint facing the Irish economy may well be expertise (as in the modern knowledge-based theories of economic growth). The extent to which such expertise can be imported thus becomes of crucial importance in the process of industrial development.

The most important British player on the Irish scene, Clarks, has been out of Ireland since 1973 (p. 173). The post-1973 decline of the industry thus stands in contrast to the optimistic picture of the 1960s which the book stresses. One wishes the author had discussed the latter period more, even though it was not included in his original brief. A cynic may, perhaps unfairly, suspect that Clarks, who funded the project, did not wish to see this experience unduly emphasized.

The author, a business historian rather than an economist, does not provide the analysis economists look for, but this is hardly fair criticism, given the book's aims. More irritating is the study's occasional uncritical acceptance of what one assumes is conventional wisdom. Is it really true that "the events of the 1920s had clearly demonstrated the dangers of allowing foreign firms to commence operations behind the tariff wall" (p. 34)? Or that "it is generally accepted that a move towards economic nationalism was inevitable and indeed desirable in the 1930s" (p. 55), or that at the time protectionism "had the blessing of contemporary economists" (p. 30)? Readers may be surprised to learn that governmental "techniques of economic planning have progressed considerably in recent decades" (p. 59). These are minor complaints, however. The author and Clarks are to be congratulated on the book, which one hopes will inspire similar studies for other industries in the future.

KEVIN O'ROURKE, *Columbia University*

Child Labor Reform in Nineteenth-Century France: Assuring the Future Harvest. By Lee Shai Weissbach. Baton Rouge: Louisiana State University Press, 1989. Pp. xv, 268. $35.00.

In this well-written general historical analysis of child labor reform in post-Revolutionary France, Lee Shai Weissbach thoroughly summarizes the arguments and events of each stage of social reform from the recognition of child abuses in factories in 1840 to the enforcement of the Child Labor Law of 1874. He provides a chronological study of the various proposed and legislated child labor laws with an extensive discussion of the men who supported or opposed such "social" legislation. Unfortunately, his methodology is simple and lacks sophistication and his arguments are all too familiar to scholars of child labor in Great Britain. The discussions noticeably lack models and theories which would have provided testable hypotheses. An attempt at using cliometrics (applying statistical analyses to historical events) was made once (p. 162) and demonstrated the author's misconceptions about this methodology. Nevertheless, Weissbach has made a noteworthy contribution because he provides the first comprehensive study of child labor in France, which historians, economic historians, sociologists, and cliometricians will use for further research on the issue of child labor, the family economy, social reform, and political voting preferences in nineteenth-century France.

The first part of the book is the weakest because Weissbach does not convince the reader that child labor was or should have been a burning issue requiring legislation. In the first chapter he presents employment statistics which illustrate that only 11.7 percent of the total work force in 1845 was under 16 years of age (pp. 17–19). Obviously, reformers needed to prove the children were ill-treated to generate national concern for this silent and naturally submissive minority. Here, Weissbach needs to draw a stronger association between the poor health of industrial child laborers (as reflected in military rejection rates) and work in the factory. More statistical and anecdotal evidence on the atmosphere in the factories (heat, ventilation, and machine safety) and on the conditions of employment (hours, recesses, and holidays) is necessary to document the nature and extent of the abuses. Thus, contrary to Weissbach's claim in Chapter 3, it is not surprising that the Inquiry of July 31, 1837 revealed "widespread apathy about child labor reform" (p. 41) and that early socialists, Utopians, and the Catholic Church remained silent on the issue of child labor (pp. 56–57).

The author's strengths and expertise become evident in Chapter 4, where he eloquently develops the issues surrounding the Child Labor Law of 1841. The discussions of the full Chamber of Peers over the scope of child labor legislation (local or national), the inclusion of compulsory education in the law, and the infringement on entrepreneurial rights (but not parental rights) are presented in an interesting sociopolitical framework. The author makes several insightful comparisons with Great Britain, where compulsory education was distinctly separate from the child labor laws and where the infringement of parental rights, not entrepreneurial rights, impeded child labor reform. In Chapter 5 Weissbach discusses the limitations of the 1841 law and society's increasing awareness of the plight of the young. Especially illuminating are the selected literary pieces that portray the emotional and physical deterioration of the child laborer (pp. 100–3).

Unfortunately this vigor does not continue. The remaining chapters provide little insight regarding the enforcement and socioeconomic impact of the reforms. In Chapter 7, "The Dilemma of Enforcement," the arguments are weak, overly general, and lacking in statistical evidence. Weissbach needs better support for his observation that "noncompliance seemed to pervade the entire country" (p. 124). Too often he refers to possible evidence contained in government inquiries without attempting to present or summarize the findings. The reader's curiosity is heightened but hardly satisfied when Weissbach states that "an 1853 inquiry into the implementation of the apprenticeship law revealed that dealings between masters and their apprentices were virtually unaffected by the new legislation" (p. 126) or "there is fragmentary evidence of a government study in 1860 of labor conditions that also confirmed the need for a system of centralized inspection" (p. 138). Finally, in discussing the impact of the Child Labor

Law of 1841 and 1874, Weissbach further muddles the issue by generalizing. Instead of supporting a specific hypothesis with his information on enforcement and employment (Tables 3 and 4), Weissbach concludes that conditions for children improved and employment fell for *all* the reasons given in the literature on Great Britain: child labor laws, advances in technology, and changes in popular attitudes (p. 229). At the least the author should have referred to the contemporary debate over Clark Nardinelli's argument in the 1980 issue of this JOURNAL regarding "Child Labor and the Factory Acts." Nardinelli claims it was not the laws which decreased the employment of children in British textile mills but changes in technology. By skirting the issue of causality, Weissbach's conclusions in Chapter 11 that the total number of children under 12 working decreased and that the educational level of young workers seemed to improve significantly (p. 221) seem misplaced.

CAROLYN TUTTLE, *Lake Forest College*

Reconversions de la main-d'oeuvre et transition démographique: Les bassins industriels en aval de Liège XVIIe–XXe siècles. By René Leboutte. Paris: Société d'Edition "Les Belles Lettres" 1988. Pp. 519.

René Leboutte examines how inhabitants of the Liégois region experienced industrialization and the demographic transition from the perspective of their everyday lives. Geographically he focuses on two sets of villages located on the Meuse River between Liège and the Dutch border: those in the basin downstream from Liège—the Bassin aval—and those located on the lower part of the river, the Basse Meuse. Leboutte uses a combination of aggregate data and family reconstitution to examine nuptiality; fertility; mortality; household size and structure; population structure according to age, sex, and matrimonial status; and migration. But his inquiry goes far beyond the statistical analysis of demographic patterns. Dissatisfied with economic and demographic theories explaining the demographic transition, Leboutte focuses on changes in culture and mentalities that, he argues, are inherent to the transition. In this regard he makes use of a very rich and interesting source: the daily chronicle of Gaspard Marnette, a modest gunsmith, who between 1865 and 1903 recorded hundreds of facts he witnessed or heard rumor of in the village of Vottem.

One of Leboutte's main arguments is that between 1850 and 1870 industrialization in this region created a marked rise in the standard of living and the inhabitants of this region experienced a passage "from a society of mass poverty to a society of relative mass abundance" (p. 141), which in turn created a fundamental change in mentality. The population no longer felt a need to resign itself to poverty, but instead believed that incomes would continue to rise. Workers acquired new habits of consumption and developed a taste for luxury. They also developed a new attitude toward children, seeing them as objects of investment rather than as sources of wealth. The new socioeconomic environment of prosperity made small families a rational choice, and fertility began to decline. Education and increased literacy reinforced these attitudes. The great depression from 1873 to 1890 further intensified them because expectations had permanently risen. The population coped with the depression by exercising tighter control over family size, resulting in still fewer children. Workers and artisans adopted new attitudes not just through simple imitation of the petite bourgeoisie with whom they intermingled, but through a logical response and adaptation to a changed socioeconomic environment.

Leboutte's exhaustive statistical analysis certainly demonstrates that a conjuncture of various economic and demographic changes occurred between 1850 and 1870 and that the demographic transition began with this conjuncture. He links the onset of new demographic behavior to the process of industrialization. The industrialization he chronicles, however, produced little upheaval. Industries in the Bassin aval and Basse Meuse included coal, iron, and textiles, the latter two of which were organized on the basis of the putting-out system. Mechanization caused a rapid disappearance of the wool industry in the beginning of the nineteenth century, but other home-based industries—especially straw plaiting, hat making, and arms manufacturing—survived until the twentieth century. The author argues that the distinction between proto-industry and industrialization is a false one, for the "light industries" studied here not only survived through conversion and adaptation, but thrived because of industrialization.

Thus the workers whose daily lives Leboutte seeks to understand are not the proletariat one usually associates with mechanized factory labor, but artisans who continued to work in their homes, often assisted by their wives and children. One of this book's many merits is to document how proto-industrialization did not simply precede full-scale industrialization, but continued as an inherent part of that process. One cannot, however, assume from this study that workers elsewhere experienced industrialization—and its cultural consequences—as did the people in the Liège region.

Leboutte boldly integrates cultural and demographic explanations and assumes a direction other scholars will surely follow. But the rise in real wages he documents and Gaspard Marnette's testimony do not convince me that living conditions improved and cultural attitudes changed as dramatically as he suggests they did. Some of his own evidence is contradictory. He points out, for example, that putting-out industries were able to survive precisely because workers remained economically subordinate to merchants and became more pauperized and proletarianized with the sweating system (p. 133). Moreover, infant mortality, "the best indicator of the sanitary condition of a population" (p. 418), did not decline until the twentieth century. His assessment of industrialization seems too optimistic, and he overstates the case that change in cultural attitudes toward the family could come only with a marked rise in the standard of living.

These reservations do not detract from the book's significant contribution. Leboutte presents a masterful synthesis of work in demographic history, and the systematic comparison of his own findings with other local, regional, and national studies is extremely useful. His major conclusions are also convincing: though the demographic transition is a universal phenomenon that transcends the extraordinary diversity of demographic and socioeconomic conditions, the desire to establish a unique explanatory model is illusory. "The demographic transition is not an isolated phenomenon, it is part of a broader transitional process that is cultural . . . the whole mental apparatus that permits a group to exist while adapting to its environment" (p. 484).

ELINOR ACCAMPO, *University of Southern California*

Prato: Storia di una città. Volume 3, Parts 1 and 2: *Il tempo dell'industria (1815–1943)*. Edited by Giorgio Mori. Florence: Le Monnier, 1988. Pp. xiv, 1563. L.380,000.

The town of Prato already occupies a position of some significance in economic and social history, thanks mainly to its most celebrated citizen, Francesco Datini, and to his largesse. That heritage alone would be enough to give any city a good place in the sun, but the town has always felt overshadowed by its more powerful neighbor, Florence. Prato's tradition of intense municipal attachment and civic pride, in some ways unusually intense even for a deeply "urban" society like Italy's, finds its roots in the need to define a distinct, non-Florentine identity. Motivated at least in part by this tradition, the Commune of Prato has in the last few years financed the publication of what is evidently intended to be the definitive history of the town. So far only the second and third volumes have appeared, dealing with the years from 1494 to 1943. Completion is expected in 1991.

Volume 3 is a collection of essays on the life of Prato from the Restoration of the Hapsburg-Lorraine dynasty in 1815 to the fall of Fascism in Italy. The work describes in systematic and painstaking detail the economic, political, social, cultural, demographic, and religious trends that shaped the town during those 130 years. In fact, after 1,500 pages the reader cannot fail to conclude that very little of what happened in Prato during this time must have escaped the attention of the contributing authors. Individual sections deal with the evolution and cyclical crises of the woolens and straw-weaving industries; with the role of foreign capital and entrepreneurship in industrial development in the first half of the nineteenth century; with the tensions between the urban economy tied to the fluctuations of the export markets and the more stable world of sharecroppers in the surrounding countryside; with the painfully slow evolution of banking and credit institutions (in Datini's own town!); with the development of the network of municipal utilities; with the building of the transportation infrastructure, both within and outside the town; with the politics of the municipal council; with demographic change, public hygiene, welfare and medical assistance, social mores, church attendance.

The strength of the work is in its thoroughness and careful research. Beautifully illustrated and complemented by scores of maps, it offers a living picture of Prato in the minutest detail, following events year by year, and almost day by day. Individuals, families, public officials, political leaders, shopkeepers, parish priests, unionists, entrepreneurs, are all studied with the same attention. The picture that emerges is one of a society where the "old order" of landowners, clergy, and bureaucrats never gave way to the rising industrial elites (such as there were), who for their part liked things well enough as they found them, and never really challenged the status quo. Only with the spread of socialist ideas and organizations around the turn of the century did this paternalistic social harmony suffer somewhat, though the advent of Fascism forcibly reimposed a social peace of sorts. Thus the general approach of the book loosely follows Gramsci's view of Italian unification as a revolution manqué, but because the authors consistently refuse to come to grips with the counterfactual issue, the work ends up lacking incisiveness.

This is precisely the basic weakness of the book: its detail is fascinating, but it is difficult to sustain the reader's interest with detail alone, and this work is as lavish in microscopic scrutiny as it is stingy with analysis. This is a book likely to attract the interest of only an extremely restricted circle of scholars, not because its focus is too narrow (it isn't), but because it fails to draw from its subject matter any conclusion of more than strictly parochial import.

In spite of its multiple authorship the book is uniformly poorly written: simple ideas are discussed in an unnecessarily convoluted language, and jargon, eruditon, and verbosity take precedence over clarity of presentation. It is, fundamentally, a book that owes more to civic boosterism than to scholarly necessity.

FRANCESCO L. GALASSI, *Nipissing University College*

A Social and Economic History of Central European Jewry. Edited by Yehuda Don and Victor Karady. New Brunswick: Transaction Publishers, 1990. Pp. viii, 262. $34.95.

The historical study of the social and economic structure of Central Europe has been a casualty of neglect, Cold War politics, and the relatively feeble interest of scholars in Communist societies in non-Marxist interpretative models. Recently, however, the new social history has begun to awaken interest in ever broader scholarly circles both inside and outside the Soviet bloc countries. Presumably the next few years will witness a swelling torrent of studies on various aspects of modern social history, for which sources are often abundant, because of the liberation of historical scholarship from the constraints imposed by Communist parties—a process that had already begun some years ago in such places as Hungary and Poland. Access to rich sources ought in future be much easier, particularly in the countries that used to comprise the Austro-Hungarian Empire.

It is these countries, particularly the "core lands" of Austria, Hungary, and Czechoslovakia, that constitute the geographical focus of this collection of papers originally presented at an international conference in Paris during 1986. The papers focus on the last half of the nineteenth century and the decades leading to the virtual liquidation of Central European Jewry during World War II.

Other limitations suggest that the rather sweeping title of this volume is misleading. The articles concentrate on urban, modernizing Jews who were physically and mentally moving away from the rural, eastern parts of Central Europe, such as Galicia, and into the great cities of Austria-Hungary: Vienna, Budapest, and, to a somewhat lesser degree, Prague. Here Jews tended to work in commerce, light industry, and the free professions. The role of Jews in finance and heavy industry was (to judge by the essays of Yehuda Don and György Lengyel) less notable than in Germany at the same time. (A useful recent work for comparison is George E. Mosse's *Jews in the German Economy* [Oxford, 1987].) Almost no attention is given to the many Jews still living in economically backward parts of the Empire, hence my quibble with the title.

Most of the contributors stress the "intermediate" position of "Central European" (really Austro-Hungarian) Jews between the numerically smaller and somewhat better-integrated communities to the west (England, France, probably also Germany) and those further east, including the hinterlands that provided considerable in-migration to Austrian, Bohemian, and Hungarian cities. (Victor Karady provides a very thorough essay on work still needing to be done on historical demography and social mobility.) Oddly, only one contribution (Maria Kovacs on lawyers in Hungary) specifically addresses Jews (and anti-Semitism) in the free professions, although this area of economic activity was of great importance to the social mobility of Jews. Don's attention to the Kuznets "model" of Jewish economic activity may explain why he tends to slight professional work.

About half the essays deal with social (and even sociocultural) matters, such as whether or not the fin-de-siècle Viennese educated middle class (*Bildungsbürgertum*) was primarily Jewish in composition and origins; Stephen Beller argues for, Gary Cohen against the thesis. Tensions within the various religious factions of observing Jews around 1900 in Vienna are nicely explored by Harriet Pass Freidenreich, as are similar fissures in the identity of Hungarian Jewry by Jacob Katz. William McCagg links structural changes between the Jewish and other communities in the successor states to the decline in Jewish power and influence after 1918.

It is regrettable that this book took nearly four years to be published, since some of the contributors' work then in progress (that of McCagg and Kovacs) has since appeared in fuller form. Yet it provides a good, if slightly dated, index of the state of research in this area beyond the usual confines of one nation-state and over a considerable range of time. Readers up to date with the most recent literature in English will still find here many fresh arguments, new interpretations, and statistical information not readily available elsewhere. Although a familiarity with *Mitteleuropa* English is helpful in some of the passages, and typographical errors abound, the volume is for the most part readable and straightforward in style. It is a welcome addition to the literature and one which all social and economic historians of Europe will want to consult.

CHARLES E. MCCLELLAND, *University of New Mexico*

Proletarian Peasants: The Revolution of 1905 in Russia's Southwest. By Robert Edelman. Ithaca: Cornell University Press, 1987. Pp. xv, 195. $28.95, cloth; $9.95, paper.

Violence and Great Estates in the South of Italy: Apulia, 1900–1922. By Frank M. Snowden. New York: Cambridge University Press, 1986. Pp. x, 245. $42.50.

Although these two books analyze events in two different countries and do not reference each other, they are remarkably similar in many respects. Both deal with agricultural labor unrest in the early twentieth century, and both focus on the role of wage-earning farm workers in strikes and other forms of protest.

Edelman's study deals with Russia's 1905 Revolution, especially the agricultural disturbances in the right-bank Ukraine (that is, the provinces of Kiev, Podol'e, and Volynia). After the 1861 emancipation of the serfs, this part of the Russian Empire became increasingly oriented toward capitalist agriculture, with the nobility holding on to their land and successfully raising cash crops, such as wheat, tobacco, hops, potatoes, and—most important for this story—sugar beets. At the same time, the growing population of peasants, who were unable to feed themselves on a constant amount of land, became increasingly involved as wage-earning laborers on the large landed estates. The revolutionary years from 1905 to 1907 in this part of the Russian Empire were marked by modern strikes, and Edelman is especially interested in the degree of involvement in these strikes of truly landless agricultural workers as opposed to members of peasant communes who had some land but not enough to live on. Throughout the study Edelman contrasts the views of Marxists and "culturalists" on the motivations of rural workers.

Snowden's study focuses on the agricultural labor disturbances in southern Italy's Apulia, comprising the provinces of Bari, Foggia, and Lecce, during the years from 1900 to 1922. Although much of this part of Italy was not opened to cultivation until 1865, by the end of the century most of the land was in the hands of a limited number of wealthy families who used it to raise sheep, wheat, grapes, and other cash crops. The landownership situation was even worse than in the Ukraine, with 70 to 85 percent of agricultural workers having no land at all and surviving only by working as day laborers for the wealthy *latifondisti* or their capitalist tenants, who rented and cultivated large blocks of land.

In both regions wages and standards of living were low, while the move to capitalistic farming led to enclosures of common pasture lands and a loss of access to common woodlands and ponds. As a result in both cases low current standards of living were accompanied by a sense of deprivation of a past golden era that the agricultural workers had lost through treachery and theft by the wealthy landlords (and the social institutions that supported them).

The traditional peasant reaction to such circumstances has been spontaneous elemental rage reflected in poaching, illegal fishing, theft of wood, forced occupation and cultivation of idle land, arson, and even murder. Some of this did occur in the Ukraine and in Apulia, but what is more noteworthy is the heavy emphasis on a more modern weapon—the strike.

In both regions workers were able during this period to formulate realizable demands and to organize strikes to make employers listen to them. The success of these strikes depended on timing them to coincide with periods of strong seasonal demand for labor and on measures (sometimes violent) to keep away strikebreakers. In both cases the agricultural workers mastered the mechanics of strikes and, for a while, were highly successful, particularly in raising wages. In time, however, opposing elements of society organized to counter the workers. In the case of the Russian Empire, after several years of conflict with the local police, cossacks, and the army, the peasant movement became exhausted and the peasant rebellion died down until 1917, when it recurred in a much more violent form and without the strike. In the case of Italy, social reaction came in a variety of forms, including lockouts, encouragement of sharecroppers, and a fascist movement that set about destroying the economic and political gains of the agricultural workers (and many other reforming groups) through threats, intimidation, and violence.

The situations in the two regions were not identical. In Apulia the degree of landlessness and proletarianization was much more extreme, and agricultural workers lived in towns (which facilitated communication) rather than in the countryside. In the Ukraine, the peasant commune (*gromada*) continued to function, and the assembly of heads of households (*skhod*) often served as a strike committee.

One of the general conclusions, especially of Edelman, is that peasants act differently depending on the circumstances that they confront. The peasants in the right-bank Ukraine initially were in a traditional setting and behaved in the manner that the culturalists would predict. But as circumstances changed (growing demographically based land hunger combined with increasing opportunities for wage labor), they adapted to these new circumstances and behaved in ways that were closer to what the Marxists predicted.

Both authors found that the poorest rural elements were seldom leaders in the strikes, and the truly landless often were called in as strikebreakers. Peasants who had a little land to fall back on or, in the case of Italy, workers who had returned from work in America with a nest egg, were more willing to strike and more daring in their behavior in general. The peasants who had substantial amounts of land generally did not participate in these activities.

Both books appear to be well researched, with heavy use of local and regional archival materials and other primary sources. The authors back up their assertions with tables of statistics, but neither work gets into statistical tests of hypotheses.

The books do have some shortcomings. Edelman's work is repetitious in places, and his tables are not always clearly labeled, while Snowden's study would benefit from a longer wrap-up section at the end. But these deficiencies are not serious and are far outweighed by the good points of the two studies.

These books will be of interest to students of the economic and political histories of the respective countries and to those studying the history of the labor movement, peasant economics, or, in the case of Snowden, anarcho-syndicalism and the rise of Fascism. Both books are well written and are not excessively long and hence could reasonably be assigned to graduate or undergraduate students as supplemental readings.

WILLIAM J. KELLY, *Battelle, Columbus, OH*

The Soviet Economy in Turmoil, 1929–1930. By R. W. Davies. Cambridge, MA: Harvard University Press, 1989. Pp. xx, 610. $69.50.

Robert Davies's account of the Soviet economy in turmoil is the third in his Industrialization of Soviet Russia series. The first two monographs dealt with agriculture during the socialist offensive. This volume deals with developments in the nonagricultural sectors, the creation of the Stalinist "administrative-command system," and the ideology and politics of rapid industrialization. Building on the writings of Naum Jasny, Eugene Zaleski, and Alexander Erlich, the author provides the most detailed account to date of the adoption of the Stalinist command model of forced industrialization.

Davies presents the Soviet decision to abandon the NEP system in favor of forced industrialization through the eyes and ears of the Soviet leadership in the late 1920s and early 1930s. He appears to accept the Soviet proposition that rapid industrialization would not have been compatible with a market-driven economy and that the Soviet leadership had legitimate reasons for opting for superindustrialization. He cites the low level of industrial labor productivity on the eve of the Five Year Plan era (the Soviets estimated their own workers at one-seventh the level of American workers). Davies argues that the socialist offensive did not proceed solely from Stalin; rather it was an outgrowth of the Russian totalitarian system, the embedded preference for state ownership, and the desire to eliminate monetary exchange in favor of natural exchange.

The author describes the emergence of the basic features of the Stalinist command system—unrealistic, taut plans; lack of attention to profitability; the disappearance of private ownership and enterprise—emphasizing the unrealistic nature of planning during the initial years of the first Five Year Plan. Heroic assumptions were made about when capital investment programs would be completed and associated increases in labor productivity occur. Davies also points to the major assumptions behind Soviet planners' miscalculation: substantial productivity advances would be forthcoming; rapid inflation would serve the useful function of destroying money as a medium of exchange; and the move away from economic accounting would not reduce cost efficiency. By 1930 it had become dangerous to criticize planning goals as unrealistic, critics being referred to as wreckers.

It is useful that such a detailed account of the creation of the Soviet administrative-command model appears at the very time efforts are under way to dismantle it; reconsideration of its adoption gives us clues to the sources of resistance to its abandonment. Yet Davies fails to offer a modern perspective on the Soviet experiment. He explains why the Soviet leadership of the time, with its ideological bent and with the information at its disposal, opted for the administrative command model and failed completely to anticipate its negative consequences. It would have been useful had Davies applied the lessons of hindsight to the Soviet experiment so that we could better interpret it in a modern context.

PAUL R. GREGORY, *University of Houston*

AUSTRALIA

Convict Workers: Reinterpreting Australia's Past. Edited by Stephen Nicholas. New York: Cambridge University Press, 1989. Pp. x, 246. $44.50.

In *Convict Workers* Australians are promised "a radical reinterpretation of our convict past," a point agreed upon in the foreword by the prime minister of Australia. The volume contains thirteen chapters (plus a statistical appendix) by seven different authors, although the principal work of research, writing, and organization was undertaken by Stephen Nicholas, who is responsible for nine of the chapters, five in co-authorship with Peter R. Shergold. Given the central role of convict labor in Australian history and historiography, such an ambitious attempt to describe the characteristics of the individuals transported, their labor performance and material treatment after arrival, and the efficiency of the market for coerced workers is bound to attract attention and debate.

The authors range widely in primary and secondary sources, but the statistical core of their contributions comes from a sample of 19,711 convicts transported to New South Wales from England, Scotland, Wales, and Ireland in the period between 1817 and 1840. This is over 30 percent of the numbers shipped to New South Wales and one-fifth of all those sent to Australia in that period, and about one-eighth of the overall total sent to Australia. The indents include data on, among other items of interest, age, sex, literacy, occupation, height, town and county of birth, county of trial, and criminal background.

These data are examined in various chapters, with detailed breakdowns presented in the statistical appendix.

Among the most important revisionist claims made in regard to convicts are that "convicts transported to Australia were ordinary British and Irish working class men and women" (p. 7); that convicts were skilled, educated, and physically fit workers; that "most transported females were not prostitutes" (p. 10); and that "an English labour aristocracy" came "with a unique system of values" (p. 10). In regard to what happened after arrival it is claimed that "the labour market was efficient" (p. 10); that a system of incentives, rewards, and punishments developed, with a judicious use of the lash; and that, in terms of food allotment, barrack space, medical care, and hours of work, the convicts fared rather well in comparison with workers in Britain. It is argued by Nicholas that acceptance of these propositions will correct a distortion of the past, of "convicts as unskilled professional criminals" (p. 199), and of "convict society as brutal, unproductive and sterile" (p. 199).

A number of issues are raised by Nicholas's revisionism. There is first the question of how well supported by data and convincing is the test of each hypothesis. Then, if a hypothesis is regarded as acceptable, is it to be considered a dramatic revision of historical views or rather a general restatement of them? In some cases the arguments in the book are based upon materials drawn from the indents and compared to relevant British data, frequently from the Census of 1841, and the standards of comparison are clearly defined. In the critical matter of whether the convicts were a "criminal class," less of the statistical data from the indents is presented and the appropriate standard of reference is more obscure. The test for the efficiency of labor markets is based upon a comparison of the Australian and British occupations of the convicts, with no comparative standard provided for purposes of judgment. And in some cases, while the conclusions seem quite plausible based on what has been learned about various other forms of coerced labor or in comparison with what seem to other scholars to have been previous overstatements or overgeneralizations, they sometimes appear to be accepted without any fully convincing new evidence being presented. In addition to the more controversial presentations, the examination of the characteristics described in the convict indents and the information drawn from primary sources in chapters dealing with early views of the transportation process, "public employment and assignment to private masters," and the hiring of convict labor by the Australian Agricultural Company add to the usefulness of this book.

Nicholas and Shergold also present some quite interesting material on "Transportation as Global Migration," describing various other streams of penal labor in the course of the nineteenth century. While the movement of convicts from Britain to Australia was the largest of these transoceanic movements, it does pale compared with the numbers sent to Siberia. It is unfortunate that A. Roger Ekirch's fine study, *Bound for America: The Transportation of British Convicts to the Colonies, 1718–1775* (New York, 1987) was not available for comparisons of these two British streams of convict labor movement. Clearly the stream to Australia had a more significant impact upon the colonial economy, with convicts and ex-convicts forming, according to Noel Butlin's estimates, the major part of the labor force throughout the period studied. Given this economic and social importance, *Convict Workers* will attract considerable attention and it will generate considerable discussion among Australian historians and economists, providing a useful supplement to the works of other historians and economic historians, including Butlin and A. G. L. Shaw, on this subject. And, since it deals with an important set of issues related to labor migrations and labor markets, it will also be of interest to scholars in other countries.

STANLEY L. ENGERMAN, *University of Rochester*

LATIN AMERICA

Haiti in the World Economy: Class, Race, and Underdevelopment Since 1700. By Alex Dupuy. Boulder: Westview Press, 1989. Pp. ix, 245. $42.50.

Few countries have experienced as complex and disappointing a history as that of Haiti. Forged heroically during the chaotic days of the French Revolution as the second independent state in the western hemisphere—and the first established by Afro-Americans anywhere in the Americas—Haiti has had, as Alex Dupuy skillfully describes here, a most difficult time overcoming the unfortunate circumstances of its creation. It began its integration into the wider Atlantic community as the virtually abandoned western part of the Spanish island colony of Santo Domingo. By the middle of the seventeenth century French corsairs and freebooters had begun to encroach over much of the area. After several unsuccessful attempts to destroy the fledgling foreign colonies, the Spanish finally ceded the territory to France at the Treaty of Ryswick in 1697. Throughout the eighteenth century the French colony, called Saint-Domingue, flourished. In 1789 it was the most prosperous colony of the grandest empire at that time. The colony generated enormous wealth from its 793 sugar plantations, 3,150 indigo plantations, 3,117 coffee plantations, 789 cotton plantations, and work force of some 450,000 slaves. It was the tropical plantation colony par excellence. The envy of the region, its fields seemed more verdant, its soils more fertile, and its economy more robust than any other Caribbean colony. Then the revolution came, destroying everything: the system of slavery and the slave society; the productive plantation economy; and the structural organization of the French Caribbean colony. Recovery and reconstruction proved eternally elusive. Two hundred years later, dominated by an unenlightened military regime, Haiti has the dubious distinction of being the poorest country in the hemisphere.

Dupuy sets out to explain this puzzling history in an informative, challenging, and provocative study that covers the period from the Treaty of Ryswick to the military overthrow of the five-month government of Leslie Manigat in June 1988. He candidly concedes the theoretical assumptions that underlie his work. "In the renewed effort to understand the associated processes of development and underdevelopment, four models became highly appreciated: dependency theory, world system theory, modes of production theory, and plantation economy theory. It was the fourth perspective that became widely used by indigenous and foreign scholars to account for the peculiarities of the Caribbean economies" (p. 1). The argument revolves around four neatly summarized postulates: Haiti's persistent underdevelopment was caused by its peripheral relations to the "capitalist world economy" that relentlessly inhibited the creation of a complex, consumer-driven industrial economy; "Haiti's underdevelopment was also caused by the emergence there of specific class, racial/color, and political relations and structures that reproduced the economy's extroverted and unintegrated characteristics and its dependence on foreign capital"; class, color, and race generated conflicts that inhibited capital formation; and the political culture of using control of the state both as a form of compensation for rival factions prevented the establishment of a local economic group able to withstand the penetration of foreign interests (pp. 210–11).

Haiti and the World Economy has much to recommend it. It takes the reader through the confusing course of the revolution and the nineteenth century with admirable verbal economy. Based on extensive reading of a wide variety of secondary works, it insightfully discusses the complex problems of establishing the new state and a viable economy against the conflicting wishes of a new black and mulatto managerial cadre with a rational economic view and the rising, predominantly rural peasant group with an understandable reluctance to be re-enslaved in fact if not in law. "Louverture considered work necessary and virtuous and agriculture the basis of economic growth and prosperity'' (p. 53), but ''left to their own device the former slaves would not choose to work on the plantation, and the government could not count on moral or economic compulsion to insure an adequate supply of workers for the plantations'' (p. 57). Eventually the peasants won the conflict, especially since the successive governments proved fleeting, powerless, and ineffective. Haiti became extremely vulnerable both to inside and outside influences.

Although forcefully rephrased and recontextualized here, many of the observations will appear familiar to the specialist reader. Moreover, many of the assumptions and assertions raise unanswered questions. Is it correct to speak of French merchant capital as ''foreign capital'' before 1804 when Haiti was an integral part of the larger French economic community? Are the overworked concepts of ''bourgeois,'' ''development,'' ''underdevelopment,'' and ''class'' aptly applied in the situations described? Was Saint-Domingue really ''peripheral'' to the French economy in 1789? And is economic dependency unavoidably a determinant of underdevelopment? What emerges from this study is less that Haiti's experience was unique but rather that it was an extreme case of the difficulty of establishing consistent economic growth without political stability. Dupuy's descriptions are good, but his diagnosis of the cause of Haitian poverty and political weakness is not fully persuasive, and he is too apt to confuse theories of change with laws of change.

FRANKLIN W. KNIGHT, *The Johns Hopkins University*

Between Silver and Guano: Commercial Policy and the State in Postindependence Peru. By Paul Gootenberg. Princeton: Princeton University Press, 1989. Pp. x, 234. $39.50.

Paul Gootenberg ventures onto terra incognita in his study of international trade, commercial policy, and national politics in Peru from 1820 to 1850. Historians have assumed that the economic decline of the period was caused in part by Lima's acceptance of economic liberalism and the subsequent infusion of cheap foreign goods and destruction of domestic industry. Gootenberg shows, however, that Peru initially pursued nationalist and protectionist trade policies and only turned to the free market in the 1840s. He believes that this early failure of protectionism in Peru (and elsewhere) made economic liberalism more attractive and helped condemn Latin America to long-term dependency.

The initial triumph of protectionism can be attributed to the success of Lima merchants and large landowners (*hacendados*) at lobbying and bankrolling the central government, and to the failure of foreign interests and exporters to sell free trade. Gootenberg argues that the wealth of foreign merchants only made them vulnerable to exactions by military strongmen (*caudillos*); and that foreign envoys and governments, despite their aggressiveness, could not force generals into lowering tariffs or prevent them from defaulting on loans. Exporters (mostly Southerners) were equally unsuccessful at seizing control of the government and implementing free-trade policies. Moreover, other advocates for liberalism, such as Bolivarians and internationalists, failed because they lacked an adequate social and political base.

Peruvian merchants and landowners, on the other hand, succeeded in getting protective tariffs as safeguards to national interests. Their most effective lobby was the Lima merchants' guild, which Gootenberg calls ''the single most organized and influential interest group for the Lima state'' (p. 42). An important guild project was the commercial treaty with Chile which offered an exchange of Peruvian sugar for Chilean wheat, thereby cutting out North Atlantic traders. The guild also established a special fund for making loans to the state, which gained it substantial political influence.

Gootenberg views the numerous civil wars of the period as struggles over trade policy between nationalist *caudillos*, backed by *limeño* merchants and northern *hacendados*, and liberal *caudillos*, supported by Southerners and foreign interests. Nationalists won primarily because they controlled Lima with its "elaborate administrative, financial, and military apparatus" (p. 75).

Merchants were key supporters because they supplied the state with "short-term loans, customs, and tax bonds" (p. 104). These were the only dependable sources of income for Peru's military presidents, who could no longer borrow abroad. For merchants, however, this was a double-edged sword: *caudillos* supported protectionism, but demanded increasing sums of money in the 1840s.

The state eventually exhausted its merchant-creditors and forced them to turn to liberalism and foreign interests to make money and "to help restructure Peru's unruly relations of State to society" (p. 113). Peruvian merchants supported the sale of guano on consignment because it restored Peru's credit abroad and freed them from predatory *caudillos*. Merchants remained on good terms with the state and managed to reap instant fortunes through the consolidation of the internal debt in the 1850s.

Gootenberg has written one of the few truly innovative works on early republican Peruvian history. He replaces assumptions based on little research with bold and innovative conclusions based on an impressive array of primary sources. He brings coherence to a understudied and chaotic period and revises important aspects of early nineteenth-century economic history. We now know substantially more about Peruvian merchants, commercial policy, and *caudillo* politics.

The boldness of the book is both its strength and its weakness. The purported theoretical contribution is unclear because of the difficulty of judging to what extent the failure of protectionism facilitated the acceptance of liberalism. Peru is not the best test case, because guano could only be marketed effectively by large foreign merchant houses with established contacts in European markets. I am also unconvinced that trade issues alone caused civil strife, and that all non-Southern elites were protectionists. Planters and miners sought markets for their products wherever they could find them, and Southerners were not just free traders but devout Catholics opposed to secular intrusions on ecclesiastical prerogatives. I also wonder to what extent the debate over the abolition of Indian tribute, a crucial source of government revenue, influenced conflict between Lima and the provinces.

Despite these reservations, this is one of the best books in recent years on Peruvian history, and a valuable contribution to nineteenth-century commercial and financial studies.

MICHAEL J. GONZALES, *Northern Illinois University*

UNITED STATES AND CANADA

Free Workers in a Plantation Economy: Talbot County, Maryland, 1690–1759. By Jean B. Russo. New York: Garland Publishing, Inc., 1989. Pp. xi, 486. $76.00.

Jean Russo's study of Talbot County, Maryland, describes the role of free labor in a slave-based economy. As Russo ably demonstrates, the extant records of the county provide excellent evidence for this subject, and she complements the primary sources with a wide range of secondary sources touching on matters of economic history and the history of artisans and their work. References to artisans in Europe and in other parts of early America allow Russo to place her study into a larger historical context. While the heart of the study is Russo's careful explication of primary source materials, her references outward from this evidence allow her to reconstruct successfully the world of artisans.

The prime achievement of the work is Russo's demonstration that artisans constituted an important and often vital element of the colonial work force in Talbot County. Through selected case studies, often traced through court records, Russo shows the range of clients who hired artisans. Some artisans failed, mostly because they offered services not needed by county residents at the time; thus a goldsmith who came there in the 1720s soon left, and watchmakers and coachmakers did not find much work until later. Further, some artisans could not succeed because their wares could not compete with imported goods; here Russo notes the failure of those who produced hats and gloves.

Yet while some artisans failed, Russo's story details many who succeeded. This group was composed of local residents who often remained in the county for many years, as she shows in a comparison of persistence rates (see, for example, her tables on pp. 380 and 389). Those who succeeded did so because local residents needed their services and, just as important, they could take advantage of local resources. Not all succeeded equally: shoemakers encountered competition from planters seeking to make their plantations more self-sufficient; weavers rarely became prosperous. But blacksmiths and wheelwrights fared very well in general; they faced little competition from either imported goods or planters who pursued other investments instead of trying to become self-sufficient in these skills. Most significant among the groups Russo studied were those who worked with wood, especially ship builders and carpenters. With a rise in tobacco prices from the 1720s on these groups sat perfectly positioned to build the ships that would transport tobacco to markets and the houses and public buildings that the community desired in greater quantity and elegance to befit their rise in wealth.

Russo's work succeeds, in part, because she demonstrates the connection between artisans and their community and because she is conscious of the overall structure of the tobacco economy. She thus traces the demographic history of the county, carefully showing connections between internal developments and outside factors, such as the price of tobacco and the availability of work in other colonies. While the story she tells is thus solidly grounded in the economic history of the Chesapeake, one of the book's strengths is its attention to the necessities and opportunities of the artisans. Here Russo's attention to detail in documentary evidence is at its best. She uses, for example, inventories of estates to trace the dispersion of tools across the county (see especially table 3.2, p. 159), demonstrating that many owned woodworking tools but far smaller numbers had the equipment necessary to be blacksmiths or tanners. She excels too at showing the range of jobs performed by artisans; carpenters built rudimentary structures, such as tobacco sheds, as well as the finer buildings on the plantation such as the planter's household; even small planters paid carpenters for work when one might have expected that, given the limits of their resources, they would have gotten by with buildings of their own construction. Such activity, Russo reminds us, is striking in an economic system where planters could have employed their servants or slaves to perform much of this labor. Russo's description of the extensive ties between artisans and their clients solidifies her assertions about the importance of free laborers in this plantation economy.

Planters in Talbot County employed artisans of various types because they wanted the labor of those who professed "the art and mystery" of diverse crafts. On this point Russo makes perhaps her finest contribution. Artisans, she tells us, were held in high esteem because their skills set them apart from common laborers. Planters, rich and poor alike, might have been able to get by without employing artisans as much as they did, but such practices would have made little sense. The planters of Talbot County bound themselves into a transatlantic world of commerce; they wanted the rewards that went along with production for that market. Thus it should surprise no one that these planters desired the finer accouterments of life. Some, such as hats and gloves, they could import. But others, such as finely built houses, required the presence of skilled artisans who could create in this county on the edge of the Atlantic world the outward appearance of a successful community. When public and church officials hired skilled woodworkers to construct their buildings, they were making a statement: they too could live like proper Englishmen, even if they happened to inhabit an English world located on the shores of the Chesapeake. Russo declares this in her discussion of church buildings. These edifices, she writes, "served as statements to the community, both about the role of the church within that community and about the civilized state of the community as a whole. They stood as an affirmation of the colonial society's ability to recreate in visible form the institutional structure of the metropolitan society in a manner that approximated the expression of skill and control embodied in the structures of the metropolis" (p. 343). Looked at from this perspective, the role of free workers in this plantation economy becomes self-evident. Without these workers, planters would have failed to live like the landed gentry they aspired to be.

This book, Russo's 1983 dissertation (with an index and new preface), is published as part of a series edited by John Murrin titled "Outstanding Studies in Early American History." The price of individual volumes in this series places them, in all likelihood, beyond the range of many younger scholars and graduate students, but Russo's work should find a place in any research library. It is a model of careful research and contributes to the explosion of works describing the Chesapeake region in the colonial period.

PETER C. MANCALL, *University of Kansas*

Colonial Chesapeake Society. Edited by Lois Green Carr, Philip D. Morgan, and Jean B. Russo. Chapel Hill: University of North Carolina Press, 1988. Pp. xii, 512. $29.50.

Colonial Chesapeake Society, a collection of essays drawn from two 1984 conferences, contributes both large and small pieces to an emerging narrative of the history of the colonial Chesapeake. The essays treat subjects as diverse as early Anglo-Indian relations, diet, living standards, inheritance patterns, immigration, community networks, and slavery. All provide insight and most enhance our understanding of the social, economic, and material worlds of the seventeenth- and eighteenth-century Chesapeake. Specialists will probably want to read the entire volume. Newcomers to the field should start with the especially good introduction that provides an overview of work done between 1975 and 1987.

The broad interpretation the editors and contributors present follows a rough line from a highly unstable society in the seventeenth century, through the development of stabilizing institutions and profound demographic and economic change in the decades immediately surrounding the turn of the eighteenth century, to an era of economic prosperity and rapid cultural integration in the British Atlantic world, but one that started to deteriorate by mid-century in the wake of increasing regional diversity. Following the Revolutionary War the region's economic importance and political influence declined. By the early nineteenth century the "kinetic energy that had characterized the early Chesapeake had been transferred—along with many of its residents and much of its heritage—to the southwest" (p. 16). Although the editors admit to "overschematization," they think it "preferable to fragmentation" (p. 15). Here is where they run into trouble.

The editors and many of the contributors are major players in the field, and the ones who have been engraving the main interpretative points into the literature for some time. Indeed, they sketched the essence of their interpretation in the late 1970s and early 1980s. Now, however, they have trouble weaving diversity of opinion and sometimes fundamentally opposing views into their story. Seeming to subscribe to the notion that the best way to counter an interpretation is to subsume it, the editors call for a "more subtle and complex narrative" that will be able to "encompass temporal and spatial change, linear and lateral developments," leading ultimately to "a fully integrated human history" (pp. 33, 45). An admirable goal, to be sure, but practically this position often translates into an unwillingness to engage directly conflicting views. Getting the facts and causal relationship right ought to come first.

If the demographic regime of the region improved so dramatically in the eighteenth century, why did life expectancy not rise? Certainly Henry Miller's convincing argument that Chesapeake residents enjoyed a better diet than their English counterparts suggests that the demographic foundations of the larger interpretation need more consideration. Similarly, Lois Green Carr's argument that economic diversification, as evidenced by more and different kinds of crafts, crops, and goods, led to increased local exchange is difficult to reconcile with that of others who maintain that diversification led to greater self-sufficiency. One strategy might involve employing more sophisticated quantitative methods to test causal relationships. Summary counts and aggregate tabulations are the standard. Russell Menard employs regression in arguing immigration responded to changes in real wages, but he never demonstrates that the time series he uses are not autocorrelated and so renders his analysis suspect. By and large, the contributors to *Colonial Chesapeake Society* have not learned how to count much better than they did a decade ago. Instead, they opt for variety and elaboration. Yet the field might be better served by more rigorous analyses than by focusing, as Douglas Deal does, on the very, very few free blacks on Virginia's Eastern shore.

In setting out the future agenda, the editors suggest that historians should direct attention to the mental worlds of Chesapeake colonists. Such a call proceeds from the assumption that the big picture is clear. It is not. How can we expect existing anomalies to be reconciled by following this approach? If the objective realities of Middlesex, Lunenberg, Surry, and Somerset colonists differed so much, can their subjective realities be delved effectively? Embracing variety rather than rethinking positions threatens to rob colonial Chesapeake history of the energy it once had.

CHARLES WETHERELL, *University of California, Riverside*

Nashville, 1780–1860: From Frontier to City. By Anita Shafer Goodstein. Gainesville: University of Florida Press, 1989. Pp. xv, 278. $29.95.

Nashville's thorough scholarship makes it the new standard antebellum history of Tennessee's proudest city. The first four chapters trace the evolution of Nashville from frontier settlement to urban village, with leadership passing swiftly from pioneers and Indian-fighters to land speculators and profiteers; the fourth chapter focuses on the black history of this period (1779–1830) in an innovative effort which provides a sorely needed model for other historians. Succeeding chapters summarize economic, institutional, and political developments through the 1840s for the established white population, describe the emerging class and ethnic conflicts that surfaced during the last antebellum decades as Irish and German immigration swelled the town's population, and return to Nashville's black history with an emphasis on the grim 1850s. The last part of the book (Chapters 8 and 9) traces the remarkable persistence of Whig power in this southern city up to secession.

Anita Goodstein's work reflects the historian's love for recounting major historical phenomena in a multifaceted way. She deftly weaves anecdotes (those from free black barber James Thomas are particularly striking), aggregate statistics, political speeches, church records, personal papers, and other primary sources to create a well-rounded, valuable urban biography.

But does this splendid portrait of one city offer broader implications about the period for historians (economic and otherwise) of the antebellum South? Unfortunately, one completes this volume with the feeling of having learned little more than the history of the city of Nashville. Goodstein rarely engages in interpretative debates. For instance, she says little about the vital issue of the degree of compatibility of slavery, urbanization, and industrialization. She does provide tantalizing anecdotes about slave insurrection panics in 1835 and 1856, laws banning slave self-hiring, restrictions of black assemblies on Sunday on the town square, and generalized repression of blacks; the alert reader can spot intriguing evidence of free and slave black cooperation in resisting slavery's conditions, and even black-white mixing in one important ward. Unfortunately, it is hard to tell whether any of this presented the Whig leadership with serious problems of social control. Perhaps Nashville, relatively small, not strongly industrial, and quite distant from the centers of both Virginia cavaliers and Mississippi planter-capitalists, never developed sufficiently for potential incompatibilities to become actual. Or perhaps there was no potential incompatibility. In any case, Goodstein does not advance this important debate despite having gathered evidence that bears on the issue. Hopefully she will have more to say about it in another forum.

She does address the question of black family integrity and offers evidence that Nashville blacks worked hard (and successfully) at maintaining solid families. But stressing this seems a bit patronizing given the state of the debate today, especially since urban blacks had better opportunities in this regard than their rural counterparts.

Goodstein nicely traces the evolution of Nashville's municipal politics. The clubby oligarchy of post-frontier times was challenged briefly after the Panic of 1819 by the mechanic class, and a ward system enabled new political faces to emerge. But despite national and local Jacksonian impulses, Nashville politics remained under the firm hand of the lawyer/merchant monopoly which maintained its power by (among other things) eliminating hundreds of voters from the rolls by suffrage restrictions. The prowess of this Whig establishment in maintaining power is impressively documented, from their deft control of political party ward organizations to their cooptation of churches, fire companies, and other urban institutions. But several questions remained unanswered. Was it primarily the Whiggish self-help, upward mobility cant that won the apparent loyalty of artisans and upwardly aspiring native white workmen? Why was the appeal of Jacksonian democracy so weak among the mechanics and workmen? Are there explanations of Whig power other than raw political power plays? Did the Whigs succeed in this town by cementing an all-class, white-over-black herrenvolk ideology among the relatively established white nonelites? Goodstein provides no clear answers to such questions, giving instead an extensive empiricist chronicle of Whig control of Nashville institutions. More analysis might have better explained the apparent social stability of antebellum Nashville.

The book is generally organized around political not economic themes, thus reducing its appeal to economic historians. We learn a great deal about the political structures among the frontier speculators which developed into the Whig clique that dominated the city, but not as much as we might like about the intricacies of an emerging urban economy in a plantation slavery environment. Goodstein describes the economic development of Nashville extensively but not in sufficient detail to enable the reader to understand the class conflicts of the period. By her account, merchants, land speculators, planters, industrialists, and bankers all seem to have gotten along quite well, and even mechanics and workmen (except for a few who participated in minor but fascinating labor actions) seemed to share the general Whiggish interest of internal improvements and personal progress (blacks and recent immigrants were of course outside this apparent consensus). Yet conflicts of interest always exist in some form among economic classes, be it bankers versus planters, merchants versus industrialists, or capitalists versus workers. The elaboration of such conflicts in antebellum Nashville awaits the hand of one who focuses on economic processes as the driving force of historical development.

RODNEY D. GREEN, *Howard University*

The History of Foreign Investment in the United States to 1914. By Mira Wilkins. Cambridge, MA: Harvard University Press, 1989. Pp. xxiii, 1055. $65.00.

Mira Wilkins has long trespassed the national boundaries that have straitjacketed so much of American business and economic history. During the 1960s, when Alfred Chandler was reconceptualizing business history and Edith Penrose was refining the theory of the firm, Wilkins teamed up with Frank Ernest Hill to produce the first study to focus exclusively on the firm's international activities. Shortly thereafter she explored the origins and spread of all American multinationals, gathering, compiling, and cataloguing the data that came to gird every subsequent study of American multinational investment. Now, some 10 years after completing that two-volume study, Wilkins has produced the first of a projected two-volume history of foreign investment in the United States.

Just as her earlier volumes on multinationals soft-pedaled the controversial issues of political economy that engaged so many scholars of the sixties, *The History of Foreign Investment* does not directly engage current policy debates regarding the role of direct foreign investment in the United States. Nevertheless, her evaluation of the record of foreign investment offers timely relief for sufferers of antiforeign paranoia. Foreigners have provided impressively continuous and high-volume flows of capital to the United States with significant and, Wilkins argues, largely beneficial results for both the American economy and the investing nations, at least until 1914, when this history ends. Only after World War I, Wilkins reminds us, did the United States emerge as a creditor nation.

Fundamental to the transition from debtor to creditor nation was an arduous and risky learning process that channeled foreign capital into productive investments. There was "nothing inevitable" about the expansion of foreign investment. "It was all a reinforcing process," Wilkins explains, "with new foreign investment creating an infrastructure that encouraged more foreign investments." Far from retarding growth, foreign debt in nineteenth-century America acted like a magnet, attracting foreign capital without distorting the domestic growth process. Although then as now there were some policy makers who worried about the growing foreign debt, the simultaneous growth of American exports seemed to promise relief. The more important role of income growth in debt repayment, on the other hand, seems not to have received much attention from policy makers.

Why foreign debt proved to be a boon for American development in the nineteenth century and a drag on the development of so many of today's developing economies is not the central question of Wilkins's book. In tracing the history of foreign investment in America, however, Wilkins provides at least a few answers which should be of interest not only to historians and economists but to policy makers in both the developed and developing economies.

No scholar knows better than Wilkins the challenges of documenting the historical record of foreign investment in America. There have been endless debates about the nature and meaning of the term foreign investment and about the analytical strategies that best capture the significance of foreign investment. Although histories and theories of direct foreign investment abound, most have been built with only bits and pieces of the larger historical puzzle. They have focused primarily on portfolios rather than direct foreign investments and upon quantifying changing capital flows rather than identifying the changing patterns and levels of investment over time.

Wilkins casts her research net as broadly as possible, sweeping into her history nearly everything that any scholar might consider as nonresidentiary long-term foreign investment. By long term she means an investment that survives anywhere from five to 300 years. She treats long-term private and public investments, excluding only short-term commercial credits, foreign holdings of U.S. Treasury notes, and foreign bank deposits, which at least for this period are probably insignificant. She covers portfolio investments, where foreigners make loans or invest in securities or equity controlled by the recipient, as well as direct investments, which involve both the ownership and control or at least the potential for control over securities or real assets.

Having set her parameters as widely as possible, Wilkins then painstakingly reconstructs the entire jigsaw of foreign investment, piece by piece, from the histories of individual investors, firms, and industries found in the public and private archives of eight nations, from trade journals, annual reports, newspapers, directories, encyclopedias, bulletins, and hundreds of primary and secondary articles, books, dissertations, and public documents. The result is a massively dense 1,000-page study (one-third of which consists of notes and bibliography), which describes changes in the patterns, level, national origins, geographical, and sectoral composition of foreign investment and in American attitudes and responses to those changes from the time of the first direct investment by the Virginia Company in 1618 to the outbreak of World War I in 1914.

The picture of foreign investment which emerges is pointillistic, with the broad contours of foreign investment emerging from a myriad of details, only a handful of which retain individual significance either in terms of the level of investments or the role of these investments in the larger economy. Considered together as they are presented over time, however, these constantly changing details open a window on the world through which to view American history.

The 1870s emerge as the pivotal decade, when the United States went from being a "developing country" to "the greatest debtor nation in the world." Wilkins accords the United States "greatest debtor" status on the basis of the (net) level or stock of foreign investment. She uses only 138 pages to cover the 267-year period before 1870, subdividing this period at the Revolution, the Louisiana Purchase, and the Civil War. Each of these events provoked changes in foreign investment behavior that altered the level, sectoral composition, national origins, and geographical distributions of investments.

The much shorter 35-year period after 1875 requires 484 pages and is organized to reflect the sectoral spread of foreign investments. A summary chapter describing "The Setting" paves the way for 10 chapters that follow individual investors into railroads and land; precious metals and coal, iron, steel; other minerals from copper to oil; food, drink, tobacco, and grocery products; textiles, apparel, leather goods, and related products; and chemicals, banking services, financial, commercial, and communication services. So as not to miss anything, she includes two chapters that sweep into residual "other" categories, foreign investments in such areas as advertising, insurance, power and light, and electric transportation services.

For Wilkins, each major period of foreign investment generates ambiguous public responses that have only a limited impact upon public policy. Favorable attitudes co-existed and comingled with unfavorable reactions. The populist-agrarian sentiments against monopoly and wealth concentration that appeared after 1870 had their origins in the pre-1870 period. Although hostility toward foreign investors, especially with regard to investments in lands and banks, seems to have intensified and increased in significance after 1870 (the Contract Labor Law of 1885, the Land Alien Act of 1887), Wilkins argues that the "net" impact upon the pattern of growth of foreign investment remained minimal. So concerned were Americans with the distribution of domestic income, domestic monopoly, and national competition, she explains, that foreign investors and investments tended to remain "on the fringe rather than at the core of major controversies" (p. 585).

Wilkins offers several reasons why the 1870s mark a turning point in the history of foreign investment and demand a different organizing strategy. Until the 1870s the level of investments had grown rapidly from a small base: from $1.1 million or 1 percent of total colonial wealth in 1776, they climbed to $65–70 million in 1803, $222.2 million in 1853, to reach $1.4 billion or (depending on figures) 1 to 4 percent of national wealth by 1869. Investments were easily dominated by the British, concentrated in trade, banking, land, and transportation. The public sector, particularly state banking and transportation securities, attracted by far the lion's share of foreign investment. Foreign capital flows tended to be relatively volatile, ebbing and flowing with financial booms and busts and with the Civil War.

After 1870 foreign investment as a percentage of national wealth inched up only an additional 1 percent to reach 5 percent in 1914, but the level of investment hit $7 billion. The investments in the United States were "large enough" by this period, she argues, "to have had economic impacts on capital exporting countries" (p. 616). Great Britain invested between one-fourth and one-fifth of its national wealth abroad, much of it in the United States; the Dutch invested 17.5 percent, with one-third flowing to the United States; the Germans, 8–12 percent; the French, about 15 percent, with most in Russia. Moreover, not until the 1870s did foreigners undertake significant direct investments in manufacturing. After the 1870s foreign investments spread geographically to the U.S. West and South, across many more sectors of the economy. Although the impacts of these investments varied from sector to sector, she singles out the following: British investments in railroads (beginning in the 1850s with the Illinois Central and later in Hill's railroads), the southern iron and steel industry, in crucible steel, in borax ("the only United States mineral virtually entirely in foreign [British] hands," p. 281), in soap (Pear's), and in thread (J. P. Coats); and German investments in metals (as traders, through the American Metal Co.), in chemicals ("no other American industry was as influenced by European business enterprise," p. 411), and in pharmaceuticals (Bayer aspirin); and the Swiss in condensed milk and baby foods (Nestle).

Although direct investments remained quantitatively less significant than private portfolio investments throughout the entire period, Wilkins argues that after 1870 direct foreign investments in manufacturing industries had a much more significant impact on the country's long-run institutional development. Unlike the earlier direct investments in manufacturing, such as those made by the British in the Principio Iron Company in the 1700s, many more investments after the 1870s were made as part of a long-term multinational strategy, which meant greater vertical integration and greater interest on the part of foreign investors to exercise control along with ownership.

For Wilkins, the United States became the world's largest debtor during this period because it proved to be the safest and most lucrative haven for investment in the world. Although occasionally she cites the importance of factors which "push" foreign capital to America (for example, the German capital that flowed into America after 1848), she clearly believes that most foreign capital was "pulled" to America by a set of unique conditions and opportunities. Among the most important of these are: (1) the country's growth-oriented system of political federalism, which constrained the role of the federal government and enabled the states to compete as conduits for foreign capital; (2) the role that the political system played in keeping markets and competition relatively free and open; (3) the size of the market and the abundance of human and natural resources; (4) the primary role played by private enterprise in developing and organizing economic activities; (5) the nature of American banking and banking laws, which kept control in American hands and prevented branch banking; (6) the nature and geographical spread of industrialization from east to west to south, which renewed and generated new opportunities for investment; (7) the muted and ambiguous nationalism that evolved with the growth of the economy; and (8) the existence of a relatively free and open international market.

Except in a very general way, Wilkins does not concern herself with conditions in the capital exporting countries. She follows foreign capital and particular investors to America in order to better observe the domestic patterns of foreign investment over time. She also comes close to suggesting that culture itself played a role in shaping investment patterns by identifying and contrasting a "British and German way" of investing.

Wilkins does not, however, provide an analytical framework that enables her to compare systematically the patterns of foreign investment, either by nationality, sector, or in terms of the interrelated forces of markets and technology that shaped investor strategy over time. Nor does she develop a consistent set of criteria by which to judge the significance of the details she documents. Readers have to follow her in following history wherever it leads. That it leads her into and out of many nooks and crannies which others might find insignificant does not bother her in the least. As she insists repeatedly, she "did not set out to re-write American history" (p. 297).

Perhaps that is her problem. Given her pioneering efforts to document the record, she could hardly do more. She has shown that foreign investment played a "material and consequential role" in American economic development; that foreign investment was more critical to the development of some sectors than others; that some foreigners played a more important role than others; that the patterns and level of foreign investments varied over time and across industries and also by nationality; and that some investments proved more profitable than others for different reasons. She has shown that benefits and costs change over time and differ according to country, region, and sector.

She has challenged others to think more systematically about the relationship between domestic and foreign capital and about the actual mechanisms by which levels and flows of capital exert their effects, not only upon recipient countries but upon capital exporting nations as well. By paving the way for others, Wilkins has gone a long way toward building a truly international economic history. That history has not divided the world into discrete camps of developed and developing economies frozen in time and place, nor has it forced analytical distinctions that are difficult to track in the evidence. Rather, it has viewed the histories of national economies as interrelated parts of a changing world economy. Just how interrelated the world has become will undoubtedly become clearer as Wilkins tracks foreign investments in the United States over the course of 70 more years.

MARY A. YEAGER, *University of California, Los Angeles*

Constructing Urban Culture: American Cities and City Planning, 1800–1920. By Stanley K. Schultz. Philadelphia: Temple University Press, 1989. Pp. xviii, 275. $34.95.

Stanley Schultz's extended essay is a multidisciplinary, impressionistic collage. His approximately 200 pages of text are well written and easily read. His craftsmanship and years of attention to detail are revealed in the 45 pages of notes. There are few discursive notes, and given the difference in the size of type, the ratio of text to notes is a formidable three to one. His clever use of layers and textures conveys a larger meaning than the four distinct images that meet the eye.

What meets the eye is Schultz's integration of "intellectual, legal, medical, and technological history to illuminate general patterns." The patterns are those through which our conception of the city evolved from the Jeffersonian agrarianism of 1800 to the "normalcy" of industrial America in 1920. Urban centers grew intensively and extensively throughout this period. Technological change contributed to this growth and ultimately helped solve many of the problems growth created. Along the way Americans were "forced to think in new ways about the quality of their lives and of their environments." If, as seemed likely, the city was to emerge as the hub of American civilization, then it was important to attempt to plan and to control the unknown and uncertain changes that lay ahead.

The four images Schultz presents, "Imagining, Regulating, Sanitizing, and Engineering" the city, each consists of two chapters. Through these Schultz portrays "the discourse, the people, the planners, and their cities." The first image, "Imagining the City," examines the changes in the intellectual conception of cities through a review of the utopian, or "urbtopian," literature of the late nineteenth century. The juxtaposition of these novels' ideal worlds and the real world in which their authors lived proves an effective way of presenting perceptions about what facets of urban life could be changed and how they might be changed. One of Schultz's underlying assumptions is that what populations wish were true is often of greater consequence than what is true. He uses this assumption most effectively within this first image, where wishes were unconstrained by technological reality and where technological progress was customarily equated with progress of the human spirit.

The second image stems from legal history. "Regulating the City" depicts the ideological innovations in the law derived from urban growth. Schultz makes a strong case that this emergent body of urban law was central to the creation of urban culture. He details the difficulties the law had coming to grips with eminent domain and public nuisances, how the law adjusted to changes in the land-use pattern, and how urban areas "crafted" the police power to give them some control over their futures.

"Sanitizing the City" reveals the problems of urban disease and health in the years before the germ theory was accepted (near the end of the nineteenth century). Five specific "perils" are considered: epidemics, the condition of the streets, waste disposal, air pollution, and the sudden appearance of slums. The competing hypotheses as to the causes of perils led to different conclusions with respect to cure and prevention. Schultz presents the agendas of sanitarians such as Edwin Chadwick, Lemuel Shattuck, John Griscom, and George Waring Jr. Many of their conclusions advocated proper measures, if for the wrong reason. Most argued the need for planned, concerted action.

The final image, "Engineering the City," represents the emergence of the municipal engineer, who became responsible for recommending and implementing technological responses to physical problems in the urban environment. Three problems were paramount by the turn of the century: water supply, sewage disposal, and street paving. The technology of water supply and wastewater removal required the functions we now associate with modern municipal administration. To Schultz, the wave of public works projects that characterized the turn of the century is the manifestation of the acceptance of planning as an effective solution to society's problems. We would later extrapolate from the success of this approach to physical problems to attack social problems. While that story lies beyond Schultz's period, it does suggest the validity of another assumption underlying his study, that the ideas articulated for improving the urban environment were derived from "a desire to improve the moral nature of human beings."

Many of the raw materials Schultz uses in this collage will be familiar to economic historians: Edward Bellamy's *Looking Backward* and Charles Fourier's associationism, the legal debates concerning the definition and limitation of property rights and the state's police power, the urban death rates of the late nineteenth century, and the urban expenditures on public works of the early twentieth century. Much less familiar are Chauncey Thomas's *The Crystal Button* or King Gillette's *The Human Drift*, Dillon's rule of municipal corporate law, the political strength of the sanitarians, and the ascendancy of municipal engineers in the city planning process.

Schultz assumes that attitudes had to be altered before actions could be adopted to change the urban environment. If economic historians arguably are familiar with most of the results, the same cannot be said about the general environment from which these results emerged. Historians adopted the "White City" of Chicago's 1893 Columbian Exposition as the image of the origins of American city planning and point to the First National Conference on City Planning and the Problems of Congestion in 1909 as the event where it became a meaningful entity. After years of work, Schultz convincingly depicts the origins as having occurred many decades earlier, perhaps as early as the 1820s. In a few hours of enjoyable and profitable reading, Schultz will convince you that comprehensive thought about the urban environment occupied the entire nineteenth century.

LOUIS CAIN, *Loyola University, Chicago and Northwestern University*

Within the Plantation Household: Black and White Women of the Old South. By Elizabeth Fox-Genovese. Chapel Hill: University of North Carolina Press, 1988. Pp. xi, 544. $34.95, cloth; $12.95, paper.

Economic and social historians of the slave South have for generations carefully and insightfully dissected the formative institutions of that "peculiar" society. Based on their research we now better comprehend the economic and demographic dynamics that fueled the reproduction and expansion of households—both free and slave—across the southern states. Yet, by the very nature of its methods and sources, social science history has been notably silent on another critical question: how southerners formed their sense of self and assumed their roles within the distinct but intersecting spheres of family, class, and polity. If we take them at their word, it is the very question of individual identity and place in society, and not just the economic value of their slaves, that drove southern whites to fight a second war of independence.

In *Within the Plantation Household* Elizabeth Fox-Genovese masterfully bridges the gap between the study of individual identity and the economic and social milieu. A history of antebellum southern women, free and slave, this prodigious effort takes as its object the mapping of gender relations and roles in that society. These "most fundamental relations among individual[s]" (p. 29), she convincingly demonstrates, can be depicted with the same care and clarity as say the cultivation of cotton and corn and the distribution of slave and real wealth.

Fox-Genovese opens *Within the Plantation Household* with an exegesis of the diary of Sarah Gayle, a lady of the plantation, and concludes with a reading of the published works of Harriet Jacobs, an ex-slave. Neither of these women, nor the lives which they record, are representative of free and slave women of the Old South. Yet, as Fox-Genovese painstakingly shows, their experiences, perceptions, and aspirations, as well as those of the countless other women whose diaries, letters, narratives, and published works she has digested, give personal expression to the forces of gender differentiation that defined what it meant to be a woman (and implicitly a man) in the South. Additionally, the view from within the household provides a fresh but complementary perspective on such issues as the organization of gang labor and plantation production, the geographic mobility of planters, the material well-being of slaves, and the integrity of the slave family, to name a few.

These assorted and often diverse narratives are tied to the central theme of gender relations in the Old South through the analysis of the slave system developed in the first chapter. The discussion is predicated on the notion of gender, the socially and culturally constructed distinctions between men and women. Gender relations, Fox-Genovese remarks, are both characteristic and constitutive of society. How women of the Old South formed their identities, she elaborates, depended on the specific institutions and structures that constrained their relationships to each other and to men. Their most intimate thoughts and feelings, in turn, were manifest in myriad social relationships and so reflected the milieu in which they lived.

This milieu, Fox-Genovese argues, differed fundamentally from the ascendant bourgeois society to which it was tied economically and politically. The slave South, as she puts it, was a distinct social formation, located "in but not of" the capitalist economy (p. 55). In contrast to northern society, which professed at least the principle of universal equality, the South developed a "hybrid" political culture of paternalism, which extended these individual rights to *white men* only and preserved "corporatist values that legitimated men's personal power over dependents"—their wives, children, and slaves (p. 63). This political dualism had its economic correlate. The southern household exhibited an enduring "vigor" as a unit of production under the authority of the male head. "[A]s the institutional consolidation of a distinct set of social relations of production and reproduction" (p. 58), the southern household was a bulwark against the corrosive influence of market relations and created the space, a network of private "enclaves," for the development of a distinct way of life.

Fox-Genovese explains the peculiar structure of southern households by the region's low rate of urbanization and the almost complete absence of local city systems. Isolated economically and geographically, rural households remained the principal loci of production for the market, as well as for domestic consumption. Additionally, the dispersion of population across the countryside restricted the opportunities for women to meet and organize collectively and thereby establish an independent identity. Confined by their social geography, southern women, both black and white, on plantations and family farms, defined themselves within the private world of the household and highly localized and informal networks of neighbors and kin. These constraints, in turn, reinforced a "natural" order of paternalism in which white male heads reigned supreme. Slave women suffered a "double oppression" (p. 49). Without denying their heroic struggles for self-determination, Fox-Genovese regards slaves as members of an extended plantation household under the legal authority of the master. Unable to form independent households and communities, slaves forged gender roles and identities in relationship to their masters, as well as to one another.

By penetrating the veil of the household, Fox-Genovese presents a refreshing and promising alternative to the static view of the slave South as either a precapitalist mode of production or a specialized region of an expanding capitalist economy. She is especially critical of the latter position, associated with much of the New Economic History. She hints, not too subtly, that the inability of cliometricians to grasp the distinctive features and pathologies of the slave system stems from their failure to look in the right place—the household. Her focus on urban development in the Old South sounds a similar chord.

Any book of such scope will inevitably leave many questions unanswered or only partially settled. In closing, I would like to raise three. First, despite the title, Fox-Genovese seeks to generalize her claims beyond the plantation household to encompass black and white women on farms of all sizes and in all regions of the South. At the same time, she repeatedly qualifies these claims by at least recognizing "discontinuities in the experience of women of different classes" (p. 39). Her very formulation, however, presumes that gender relations within the plantation defined the norm, a kind of central tendency around which the experiences of women who lived and worked under very different material conditions coalesced. Fox-Genovese cannot substantiate this conjecture, for her sources not surprisingly were penned almost exclusively by southern "ladies" of the plantation.

Second, Fox-Genovese treats gender relations of blacks and whites within the plantation household asymmetrically. White women, she holds, developed their gender identities and roles in relationship to other whites. By contrast, "slave women's primary gender struggles . . . were [also] deeply affected by their common confrontation with white men and women'' (p. 97). This distinction undermines the compelling notion of a unified plantation household. What is more, it is contradicted by numerous examples throughout the text which clearly illustrate how slaves directly mediated the relationships between white men and women. Indeed, as she herself notes, whites' images of blacks often reflected their own ambivalent attitudes toward their gender identities.

Finally, in her analysis of the slave system, Fox-Genovese implies that because of its peculiar structure, the southern household resisted full integration into the expanding world market and thus impeded urban development in the Lower South. At the same time, we are told, the sparse network of cities and towns accounts for the ''strength'' of the household to resist market pressures. Having specified both sides of the reciprocal and cumulative process of regional development, Fox-Genovese offers no way out of this vicious circle. This omission weakens her argument. Moreover, it is surprising, because the answer, it seems to me, lies ''within the plantation household.'' Pooling the considerable resources and incomes of their slaves into a single household, masters transformed their landed estates into ''a township of itself'' (p. 104). This plantation household, as Fox-Genovese abundantly illustrates, usurped town functions and thereby displaced towns from the countryside.

By failing to incorporate slaves fully into the plantation household, Fox-Genovese further restricts the scope of the book to life in the ''Big House.'' Yet, even while falling short of its aims, *Within the Plantation Household* offers a penetrating and highly original theoretical framework, elaborated by a wealth of historical insights. An impressive contribution, this book will certainly help to transform our understanding of the economic, social, and political dynamics of the slave system.

DAVID F. WEIMAN, *Yale University*

Perspectives on American Labor History: The Problems of Synthesis. Edited by J. Carroll Moody and Alice Kessler-Harris. DeKalb: Northern Illinois University Press, 1989. Pp. xix, 237. $28.50.

Since 1963 Edward Thompson's *Making of the English Working Class* (London) has sparked a transformation in the field of labor history. Following his counsel to study class formation ''from the ground up'' as a subjective process reflecting popular actions and ideas rather than immutable laws of economic development, labor historians have revised the history of American workers. Rejecting the materialist models of John Commons and Selig Perlman and their focus on formal organizations and labor unions, practitioners of the New Labor History (NLH) have uncovered an American record of social conflict and popular resistance to capitalist industrialization. By demonstrating the strength of popular resistance to capitalist hegemony, the NLH has forced a re-examination of established views of American society and has brought labor history to the cutting edge of American historiography.

Perhaps it is only inevitable that disappointment should follow such an exciting beginning. After innumerable case studies of popular (white, male) culture and community resistance to rapacious capitalist individualism, many have been led to ask: so what? The NLH's insights have been slow in entering the canon of historical record not only because it has been detached by choice from the touchstones of traditional history, political events, and institutional development, but because its focus on tradition, discrete cultures, insular communities, and spontaneous local resistance has inhibited the creation of an alternative synthesis or a new model of social change. Instead of studying history as change and developing a model of social change to illuminate the nature of social conflict and change, the NLH has cultivated a strong antiquarian bias, more interested in the roots of popular protest in traditional cultures and communities than in the process of social change. As a result, while there are many fascinating and sometimes stirring case studies, little effort has been made to integrate this material into a story of how America became a modern capitalist industrial power. While discrediting the Commons/Perlman model, the NLH has remained without an alternative model of historical change. But without such a model it cannot establish an alternative synthesis of labor history or produce a new American history.

Perspectives on American Labor History marks an attempt to build a new synthesis by presenting alternative visions of labor history. Based on papers presented at a conference held in 1984 at Northern Illinois University, the book includes five major papers by some of the brightest stars of the younger generation of labor historians bracketed by three shorter essays introducing and discussing the papers. While all the papers are interesting, they reveal the discipline's disarray. In separate papers Leon Fink and Sean Wilentz recapitulate the field's greatest success by using the concept of "republicanism" to integrate nineteenth-century labor struggles; while worthwhile introductions to the NLH, they carry the field no further. Mary Jo Buhle's paper and Alice Kessler-Harris's discussion are more promising by suggesting ways to use the concept of gender to expand the scope of labor history. Unfortunately, these too lack the element most wanting in the NLH: an explanation for social change. Such an explanation is found in the papers by Michael Reich and Alan Dawley, but it is one distant from the discipline's roots and with little room for its focus on community protest and subjective consciousness. Writing at a high level of generalization, dealing with class conflict and political events at the level of the state and the national economy, Reich and Dawley explain macro-social change as the result of the creation and breakup of national capital-labor compromises. While their papers are important, not least for bringing material structures as well as employers and state officials back into labor history, their work can only disappoint active labor historians. They develop a model of social change to replace Commons's and Perlman's, but it is one that largely abandons the NLH's original inspiration about the importance of popular action, culture, and communities.

There have been reports that participants at the conference were disappointed; the conference revealed the extent of the field's disarray without signs of an emerging synthesis. This volume will provide little comfort. There are a host of exciting ideas but little sign of a model to integrate material structures with subjective consciousness and popular action. The book that does this will shake the field as surely as did Thompson's, and it is yet to be written.

GERALD FRIEDMAN, *University of Massachusetts, Amherst*

Tejanos and the Numbers Game: A Socio-Historical Interpretation from the Federal Censuses, 1850–1900. By Arnoldo De León and Kenneth L. Stewart. Albuquerque: University of New Mexico Press, 1989. Pp. xi, 119. $24.95.

Arnoldo De León and Kenneth Stewart risked guilt by association when they chose "Tejanos and the Numbers Game" as the title for their collaborative effort. Though their obvious titular archetype is *Slavery and the Numbers Game: A Critique of Time on the Cross* (Urbana, 1975), Herbert Gutman's blistering critique of *Time on the Cross: The Economics of American Negro Slavery* (Boston, 1974), it is unfortunately with Gutman's target—the ill-starred joint venture of Robert Fogel and Stanley Engerman—that the comparison is more likely to be made.

Perhaps anticipating the worst, Stewart and De León offer their title as a sort of disclaimer, noting that its "lamentable" appropriateness is due to the fact that "Mexican-American history is such a young field with such limited understanding that any new quantitative findings are subject to quick re-evaluation." Regrettably, this vulnerability is not the only characteristic of *Time on the Cross* that is shared by *Tejanos and the Numbers Game*. Emulating Fogel and Engerman, De León and Stewart set up and knock down more than a few straw men, hang arguments on evidence that will not bear the weight, and occasionally jump to conclusions in apparent defiance of the laws of logic.

It would be unfair to press the analogy too far. Stewart and De León have written a short and unpretentious book, which seeks no cliometric counterrevolution. Instead, they attempt to steer a quantitative middle course between the rhetorical extremes that have characterized academic discourse on the "Mexican problem" in the United States (p. 7). Unfortunately, this is where the straw men make their appearance. The authors note the dominance earlier in this century of a school of "cultural determinists" (p. 91) who blamed the "problem" on the victims by branding Mexicans' values "backward and regressive" (p. 4), their culture "tradition-bound and maladaptive" (p. 92), and their homelife and heritage "pathological" (pp. 50, 57, 65).

The difficulty here is that at no point in *Tejanos and the Numbers Game* do these presumably ethnocentric social scientists speak with their own voices or are directly cited in the notes! The descriptions and citations are instead drawn from the other side of this polarized debate: the revisionist "El Grito school" (p. 5) of young Chicano historians who began in the late 1960s to attack the assumptions of the determinists by pointing to the bitter legacies of racism, discrimination, and oppression. The issue here is not which side is more "right," but that De León and Stewart have done both the determinists and their own readers a disservice by allowing Charybdis to sculpt Scylla!

The authors are certainly justified in claiming that their examination of over 100,000 census returns (drawn at random from three centers of Tejano population in central, west, and south Texas) puts to rest any lingering monolithic explanations based exclusively on either Hispanic cultural deficiency or Anglo-Saxon racial hegemony. Tracing patterns of immigration, occupational status, education and wealth, marriage and fertility, residential segregation, and socio-cultural assimilation, they have confirmed that "the Chicano experience [has been] . . . complex and fundamentally diverse" (p. 97). They argue that the detrimental effects of racial prejudice were overshadowed for most Chicanos by the impersonal forces of urbanization and economic change; they also provide impressive cumulative evidence that the Tejanos' behavior was shaped more by rational strategies for coping with historical circumstances and the necessities of life than by any regressive features of their Hispanic culture.

Yet *Tejanos and the Numbers Game* remains a frustrating and often disappointing book, not only because the authors have oversimplified the historiographical debate but also because they rely far too exclusively on census data. They give only cursory reference to the rapidly growing historical literature (such as David Montejano's *Anglos and Mexicans in the Making of Texas, 1836–1986* [Austin, 1987]) which could provide a far richer contextual grounding for their evidence. This inadequate integration into their text of the most important recent scholarship in Mexican-American history too frequently causes their quantitative contributions to appear simplistic or incomplete. (Stewart and De León refer in their "Epilog" to a larger manuscript in progress and hint that it will take more direct issue with Montejano's thesis that the shift from commercial agriculture toward urban industrialism in Texas was associated with a decline in segregation and inequality.)

Even within the self-imposed limitations of the present volume, however, there are some curious omissions. Although their running comparison of Tejano and Anglo statistics provides important correctives to popular stereotypes and constitutes one of the book's greatest strengths, the authors inexplicably fail to provide any comparative Anglo data in their discussion of women in the work force (pp. 44–46) or of female-headed households (pp. 82–84), despite their argument that in both cases the Tejano census figures suggest destitution and domestic stress among Hispanic Texans.

JAMES E. CRISP, *North Carolina State University*

The American Steel Industry, 1850–1970: A Geographical Interpretation. By Kenneth Warren. Reprint. Pittsburgh: University of Pittsburgh Press, 1989. Pp. xiii, 337. $34.95.

First published in 1973, this reprint remains a valuable contribution to the study of the iron and steel industry. Within an overall chronological organization, the discussion follows the changing fortunes of the industry in each district, occasionally focusing on particularly important components of the industry such as the rail trade and structural steel.

Although transportation costs for raw materials and products rightly receive extensive attention, Kenneth Warren expands the discussion of locational principles relevant to the development of the iron and steel industry beyond these costs to include factors such as technological change, entrepreneurial initiative, and government policy. Regrettably, labor costs receive scant attention, other than a brief reference to east-west and north-south differentials. Following a short summary of locational principles in the first chapter, the next chapter sets the stage for subsequent coverage of the steel districts by surveying the development of the iron industry in the East and Midwest up to the mid-nineteenth century.

The changing geography of the steel industry over the next century and more has long been explained as a complex result of several key factors, including a shift in fuel from charcoal to coke; the growing dominance of the Connellsville coal region; the rise to prominence of the upper Michigan and later the Mesabi iron ore districts; the growth of midwestern steel markets, especially along the Great Lakes; and gains in fuel economy which resulted in a declining relative importance of coal supplies as an attraction for steel mills. Warren brings these factors to life, along with other factors such as technological change and government policy, by a richly documented discussion of the different districts. Moving from the eastern anthracite and Philadelphia area districts to the Pittsburgh district to the Valley district (between Pittsburgh and Cleveland) to the Lake Erie Shore district to the Chicago district, he demonstrates that they have been in constant flux. Firms in these districts faced seemingly never ending alterations in raw material sources and pricing, markets, transportation costs, and technological change. Periods of stability seldom lasted more than several decades. The competitive position of eastern steel mills declined relative to mills in the Midwest in the late nineteenth century only to revive by the 1920s. While the Pittsburgh district ascended to its prominence during the late nineteenth century, Chicago mills steadily grew in size and numbers, becoming market threats to Pittsburgh mills.

Warren makes a convincing case that the U.S. steel industry was not a simple outgrowth of natural resource abundance. Rather, successful firms in the different districts had to carefully calculate their raw material, production, and marketing costs. Mindless location in an environment of seemingly abundant natural resources was a recipe for failure. Given the availability of resources, the thread running through the discussion is that the profitable steel mills had markets in close proximity. The limited development of steel districts outside the manufacturing belt until well into the twentieth century thus can be explained by the small widely dispersed markets. The effects of government policy on the steel districts during World War II provided a warning about the dangers of subsequent intervention. New mills founded under federal sponsorship in Utah and Texas had a precarious postwar existence. For the most part, fortunately, the government followed the cheaper path of encouraging the expansion of existing plants concentrated in the manufacturing belt, thus leaving these well-placed mills to battle for markets after the war.

Warren weaves a finely textured picture of the rise, decline, and persistence of steel districts. Abundantly documented with data in the text and in 133 tables (most quite small) and richly illustrated with 40 maps and diagrams (reprinted with sharp clarity), the character of the districts over time becomes vivid. They are not simply measured by tonnage of steel output but are composed also of firms strung along river valleys, railroad lines, furnaces, and ore storage yards. This book is an example of description in the best tradition, assembling numerous facts from industry trade publications, weaving them together in an interesting story, and providing interpretations based on concepts (locational in this case). Readers wanting a tightly argued explication of the dynamics of the steel districts will be disappointed. The theory used is specified too loosely to meet that demand. Indicative of this is Warren's failure to generalize adequately from his own evidence about the continual changes in the steel districts. He predicted in 1973 that the Pittsburgh district would continue as a leading steel district into the twenty-first century, and he failed to predict the subsequent dramatic effect of foreign competition on the steel districts, even though he recognized that this competition was increasing. The book nonetheless provides a wealth of well-organized information and interpretation for scholars to use for identifying hypotheses and building theories of urban, regional, and industrial development.

DAVID R. MEYER, *Brown University*

The Shadow of the Mills: Working-Class Families in Pittsburgh, 1870–1907. By S. J. Kleinberg. Pittsburgh: University of Pittsburgh Press, 1989. Pp. xxv, 414. $49.95.

S. J. Kleinberg has made a significant contribution to social and urban history. Looking at the families of industrial Pittsburgh between 1870 and 1907, Kleinberg provides a detailed study of how the industrial economy of the pre-eminent heavy-industry town shaped the lives of all its inhabitants.

Pittsburgh was a city of iron and steel; as such its paid labor force was predominantly male. The work in the mills became increasingly dangerous, hard, long, and unskilled as the city switched from iron to steel. The workers in the mills were increasingly immigrants, particularly from southern and eastern Europe. They were valued not for their skills but for their brawn and endurance.

The story of the 12-hour days and seven-day weeks has been told before. Kleinberg tells us about the impact of those days on the families of Pittsburgh. Kleinberg reminds us again and again how the work in the mill had its complement in work in the home. The men who labored seven days a week for 12 hours a day were supported by women who worked just as hard and as long at home. If conditions in the mills were unnecessarily horrendous (there was no technological reason not to run three eight-hour shifts, thus increasing the safety of the work), so were the conditions at home. Low wages and the assumptions of city leaders that resources and city services should be provided on a "buy as you go" system meant that working-class women struggled with lack of water (even what they got from corner pumps was often polluted), sanitation, clean air, adequate refrigeration, heating, and cooling. Within this system of resource deprivation working-class women were expected to maintain a home, raise children, and often supplement the male's wage by taking in boarders or laundry.

If the rise of industrial capitalism separated the spheres of men and women, industrial Pittsburgh carried that separation to an extreme. For the men of Pittsburgh life was lived in a public sphere of work, taverns, and fraternal lodges. For the women of the city, life was lived in a very private sphere of family and home.

Faced with the immense burden of work (paid and unpaid) and inadequate resources, both the men and women of Pittsburgh did what they could to control their environment and make a world for themselves. They formed and joined benefit societies, helped their neighbors, raised local money for the sick and widowed, sent children into the labor market, and took in boarders and laundry. Kleinberg is no romantic. Backing up her argument with a large amount of quantitative data, she shows that ultimately it was the larger industrial economy which shaped the lives of working-class steel city denizens. Although much of this work is about people trying to take control of their lives, the message is clear that it was the making of steel and the structure of industrial capitalism which ultimately determined the destinies of the Pittsburgh working class. It subordinated women to men and men to the dictates of industry.

Kleinberg has dug deep in her study of Pittsburgh. She shows us the impact of death and sickness on Pittsburgh's families, the consequences of inadequate services, and a public sector committed to the values of the marketplace. She looks at how a variety of variables from charity to schools to job options for men and women affected the family. Although Kleinberg is sensitive to the issue of culture, she puts culture within the context of the larger industrial setting. When looking at women's employment, she notes that culture had an impact, yet "where the economy provided employment opportunities women were more likely to work regardless of cultural background" (pp. 145–46). Kleinberg's work brings balance to much recent labor and family history which tends to see the working class or the working-class family as if the larger capitalist structure did not exist.

Although this is not an easily read book (the wealth of detail and methodological discussion often bogs down the reader), it has much to offer. As eastern Europeans abandon the failures of a centralized command economy, they should read this work before they rush in the opposite direction into a private-market-driven society. Kleinberg clearly shows that when the dictates of the market and industrial capitalism dominate without the countervailing force of a strong public-oriented state and a powerful institutional voice for the collective interests, the costs are immense. True, there were always food and goods in Pittsburgh's stores, but Kleinberg's families could not afford most of them. And the dirty, polluted cities of eastern Europe would have a tough time competing with turn-of-the-century prosperous Pittsburgh for the title of filthiest city.

JOHN T. CUMBLER, *University of Louisville*

The Birth of a Transfer Society. By Terry L. Anderson and Peter J. Hill. Lanham, MD: University Press of America, 1989. Pp. xv, 114. $9.75, paper.

America gave birth to a transfer society, Terry Anderson and Peter Hill argue in this reissue of a 1980 monograph, in the late nineteenth and early twentieth centuries. The Progressive Era, rather than the New Deal, produced the legal innovations that effectively diminished the protection against transfers provided by the Constitution. In making this argument Hill and Anderson distance themselves both from Jonathan Hughes's "nothing new under the sun when it comes to non-market social control" theme and from historians who date the rise of the transfer society from the second New Deal of 1935.

In the beginning things worked. There may have been maximum hour laws and the like on the books, but no one took them seriously. Meanwhile, the John Marshall court honored such notions as freedom of contract. Then things fell apart. In common with Harry Scheiber and others, Hill and Anderson see the 1877 *Munn v. Illinois* case as a great turning point: the moment when the court turned away from tight Lockean doctrine and began to invent reasons, using suitably opaque Latin, to condone the actions of state legislatures. The Granger cases begot the Brandeis brief and soon there was intellectual chaos and economic grief.

All in all, this monograph is an accessible application of public choice principles to the problems of legal history. The reader will believe the argument to the extent that he or she believes, in the author's terms, that transfers are almost always "negative sum" and that sooner or later excessive transfers catch up with a society and reduce its wealth and productivity to a dangerous degree. When the book first appeared, I suspect that its tone was considered outrageous by the liberal academic establishment; now it seems of a piece with other forms of political commentary. My only objection is that the authors do not take the Supreme Court cases of 1937 very seriously; they assert that only two cases of this era (*Nebbia* and the case upholding the Wagner Act) were important to the economy. What about *Helvering v. Davis* and its companion cases that upheld the social insurance programs of the 1935 Social Security Act?

Historians, unused to short global treatments of large subjects, such as most of Douglass North's later books, will of course react adversely to the book's quick pace and rather cavalier treatment of complex events. Even more than in 1980, this book cuts against the current historiographic grain. More and more, historians write social histories, with mincing little descriptions of small places over short periods. I find Hill and Anderson's book to be a refreshing antidote to the social history approach. They write about what might be called "the rules of the game" that influence entire societies over great sweeps of time. As they note: "If economists have anything to offer society, it is way of thinking" (p. xiii). I agree, and I applaud the authors' efforts to argue, so cogently and clearly, for their side. Those who think differently are, of course, free to choose.

EDWARD D. BERKOWITZ, *George Washington University*

Pure Food: Securing the Federal Food and Drugs Act of 1906. By James Harvey Young. Princeton: Princeton University Press, 1989. Pp. xiii, 312. $29.95.

This is an important book by a person who has long studied the history of food and drug regulation in the United States, James Harvey Young. Young relies on congressional documents and hearings, as well as on the large secondary literature, to address the events leading to the enactment of the Pure Food and Drugs Act of 1906. There are 12 chapters, beginning with "A 'Murderous Traffic in Imported Drugs,' " which discusses some of the factors behind the 1906 law. These include new scientific knowledge and an associated research revolution, greater production complexity, and increased competition for established "natural" products from new, "adulterated" products. Examples are the competitive rivalries between butter and oleomargarine, between sugar and glucose, and among pharmaceutical companies and peddlers of patent medicines. Young briefly describes how crusaders, such as Harvey Washington Wiley, head of the Bureau of Chemistry in the U.S. Department of Agriculture, became involved in these rivalries and in the political lobbying for federal intervention. Young argues that the process began in 1848 with a federal law to regulate drug imports. Chapter 2 discusses what Young believes was a growing anxiety among Americans about food quality in the late nineteenth century, and he points to specific cases regarding controversial additives to chocolate and flour and a feared contamination of milk. Chapters 3 and 4 examine various political and (to a much less degree) scientific battles between established and new, adulterated products. Chapter 5 describes how new technologies, which were often poorly understood, were rapidly changing the marketplace and inviting opposition from established firms. Crusaders, such as Wiley, became central in this debate. Chapters 6 through 11 examine the political process by which maneuvering by various interest groups moved slowly but inexorably at the state and federal levels, culminating in the final enactment of the Pure Food and Drug and Meat Inspection acts of 1906. Pure Food Congresses were organized, especially by makers of existing, "natural" products; congressional hearings were held on food quality and the impact of preservatives on health, on alleged quackery, and on proposed taxes on adulterated products; and muckrakers, such as Upton Sinclair, vilified the Chicago packers and helped to organize public opinion for direct federal government intervention. Young describes the provisions of the Pure Food and Meat Inspection laws and claims that they were aimed primarily at safeguarding the nation's food supply. Chapter 12, in many ways the capstone of the book, describes the extensive and often conflicting historiography of the Pure Food and Meat Inspection acts.

Although I applaud Young's work, many of the problems he raises in the last chapter about the existing literature remain unsettled in this book. Most critical is the nature of the health hazard posed by the new, adulterated products. The Pure Food and Drugs and Meat Inspection acts were enacted along with other Progressive Era legislation at a time when interest groups were gaining in political influence and when political parties were declining in authority. New technologies brought winners and losers, and the latter had incentives to organize to block or at least to mold the paths these technologies would take. There was clearly a growing consumer information problem regarding the evaluation of the wholesomeness of new additives and new products, but just how serious was the problem, how extensive consumer concerns were, and in what ways consumer interests were involved in the enactment of this so-called consumer legislation remain unclear. The actions of various self-interested groups and individuals, such as pharmacists, makers of straight whiskey, and the Bureau of Chemistry in the Agriculture Department, are clear in the record, even if their motives are subject to more dispute. Accordingly, while not dismissing the possibility that a broad and growing health threat provided the basis for the new legislation, the competing hypothesis that commercial rivalries and bureaucratic goals had more to do with the enactment of pure laws than did consumer concerns cannot be rejected. On this critical issue much more remains to be done.

GARY D. LIBECAP, *University of Arizona*

Land of Hope: Chicago, Black Southerners, and the Great Migration. By James R. Grossman. Chicago: University of Chicago Press, 1989. Pp. xiii, 384. $29.95.

Land of Hope is about the transformation of poor southern black farmers into poor northern factory workers in the city of Chicago. To economic historians this would be the story of migration, North-South labor market integration, unions, schooling, jobs, and wages. For historian James Grossman there is more. He wants to "explore the meaning of the Great Migration from the perspective of its participants with a particular focus on their adjustments and on their perceptions of their place in that City" (p. 4). What the reader gets is less attention to racial differences in socioeconomic outcomes and more attention to the migrants' perception of opportunities and the evolutionary dynamics of their world view.

It is not always easy for economists who are trained to extract the kernel from the mystical shell to read a book like this. In this case, however, the reward is often worth the anxiety. The main journey is refreshingly straightforward. To summarize, blacks moved to Chicago with a sense of cautious optimism. In the South they had learned to distrust whites, but they also believed race relations in the North were different. This expectation evolved into the view that Chicago offered blacks the freedom to limit their social interaction with whites to settings essential to economic and political citizenship. "At home," recalled Mahilia Jackson, a black worker "could lay down his burden of being a colored person in a white man's world, and live out his life." In the South this was not possible. I only wish Grossman had flushed out the fuller implications of this hypothesis.

Grossman begins with the southern origins by asking: if you were a black southerner in 1910, what would your life be like in 1920? First of all, you would probably still be a southern farmer of some kind, but you would certainly know someone up North. People thought about leaving the South long before the war, but few had the means. Most of the wartime studies of the Great Migration de-emphasized the decades of "fundamental unrest" in the South and refused to ascribe the migration to Jim Crow segregation and racial inequalities. Why? Because most of the studies were conducted by federal agents like Emmett Scott and George Haynes, who reflected the Woodrow Wilson administration's hope that the migration would abate after the war boom.

Most public figures (both white and black) advised you to stay in the South, so your northern trek appeared leaderless. In reality a new class of leaders was emerging—the migrants themselves. By 1917 you were part of an information network through which migrants learned about northern job availability, quality of life, schooling, and so forth. Did you meet a labor recruiter along the way? Probably not. The widespread use of labor recruiters is a myth, says Grossman; a myth created by the way northern and southern labor markets integrated. There was also a racial component. Read this part of the book; it is intriguing.

Grossman also argues that the migration was not dominated by "floating young men" but often consisted of entire communities. This is controversial, but letters show that once community members began to move, others tended to follow because the social structure to which they had become accustomed began to disappear. Most likely, your last image of home was not an emotional farewell from friends and relatives at the railroad station, but a traumatic encounter with a white South reluctant to lose its labor force. You left a known world of limited opportunities for an unknown world believed to offer somewhat better opportunities. This discussion is interesting, but I could not help wanting some comparisons with the farewell experiences of other emigrant groups so we could put the southern black experience into perspective.

Upon arriving in Chicago you initially experienced a strange new world where the outward signs of apartheid were not immediately visible. A new sense of freedom—to sit anywhere on a streetcar, for example—invoked wonder. Your first impulse was to test your new freedoms in other areas of social life. Those impulses, however, were systematically "guided" by the small, yet established, black middle class in Chicago. They saw the migrants as potential votes and customers. They had much to gain but also much to lose because of their concern for respectability, reflecting the tenuous nature of their acceptance in the city. They feared that you, as a poor southerner, would go too far in testing your new freedom, so they lectured you on how to be respectable in public and how to be an inconspicuous as possible. "The migrants represented a 'trial' for the race . . ." you were told (p. 146). You listened to them because the black middle class was your means to economic and political citizenship. For example, if you arrived in the city and randomly searched for a job, you ran the risk of immediate rejection because of the color of your skin. Black-owned employment agencies sprang up as efficient mechanisms for matching worker and employer preferences. By 1917 at least six agencies, nearly all located in a ten-block area of State Street, catered to black Chicagoans. Finding a job was made easier, but the expression of employer preferences for workers of different races was also made easier—as easy as listing different jobs at different employment agencies. Stereotypes about the kind of a worker you were influenced the kinds of jobs you were offered, and your successful performance on the job only further convinced employers that their race-based priors were correct. Economic citizenship was achieved through racially segregated labor markets, but segregation had long-term consequences for the structure of job opportunities afforded black workers.

The book ends with a discussion of the educational opportunities and union struggles of black Chicagoans during this period. But the best part of the book is the middle section, which uses letters, newspaper articles, and other historical documents to paint an intriguing picture of how race shaped the opportunities of blacks in a large industrial northern city. Grossman gives us a fine glimpse into the origins and evolution of the racial planes of life during and immediately after World War I. As such, it is a welcomed addition to a long tradition in this area.

WARREN C. WHATLEY, *University of Michigan*

Unions and Communities Under Siege: American Communities and the Crisis of Organized Labor. By Gordon L. Clark. New York: Cambridge University Press, 1989. Pp. xvii, 309. $44.50.

Why has organized labor done so poorly in recent years? With this monograph, Gordon Clark joins the army of analysts who have tried to explain the remarkable decline of the labor movement in the 1970s and 1980s. Clark's distinctive contribution is an emphasis on the local context of industrial relations, leading him to argue persuasively against any theory of union decline that does not recognize this reality and to advance a more complex interpretation of recent events. He stresses the negative impact of three different but interrelated trends: the changing legal and political climate of industrial relations, which requires a decentralized, localized approach to organizing and bargaining despite the increasingly national and international scope of business; the restructuring of American industry, which has reduced union membership and made new members harder to recruit; and the lethargic, legalistic, and increasingly pro-management operations of the National Labor Relations Board (NLRB). Though he believes the convergence of these trends in the 1980s was largely coincidental, he is not optimistic about the future. He describes the congressional stalemate that has thwarted reform and the limited potential of novel union services such as associate memberships and concludes that the "crisis" is likely to continue, perhaps worsen.

As this summary suggests, Clark's principal contribution is the documentation of local and regional trends in organizing. Utilizing information on representation elections, for example, he shows that the record of industrial unions in the 1980s is even worse than summaries of their overall experiences suggest. He also assembles useful data on labor law and the NLRB, though his analysis here is less persuasive. Like many union partisans, he recalls a golden age when the board operated as it was supposed to operate and unions fared better. But as James Gross, Christopher Tomlins, and other historians of the law have emphasized, the NLRB was conceived in controversy and never created more than a fleeting consensus on its role and purpose. Lawyers and legalistic procedures have always beset it and the pro-management decisions of the Ronald Reagan appointees are only the latest phase in the cycles of partisanship that have characterized the board since its origin.

Clark's prognosis also seems unnecessarily bleak. It is unrealistic to assume that the political climate will not change and unwise to disregard, as he does, the successes of government and other service sector organizations in recent years. Even if Clark is right about the downward spiral of industrial unionism, the labor movement will not necessarily be enfeebled. It will more closely resemble the labor movement of the first third of the century, which was neither powerless nor incapable of adjustment as circumstances changed.

Despite its virtues, *Unions and Communities Under Siege* lacks a sharp focus, not because Clark does not know what he wants to say but because he is preoccupied with theory and methodology and writes for the 20 other people working on the same problems. A union leader or human resources manager, attracted by the title, would soon find the author's frequent digressions and opaque language impossible obstacles. There is valuable ore in this mine but only for the prospector with the persistence of a Klondike veteran.

DANIEL NELSON, *University of Akron*

Open for Business: The Roots of Foreign Ownership in Canada. By Gordon Laxer. Toronto: Oxford University Press, 1989. Pp. viii, 247. $16.95, paper.

According to Gordon Laxer, Canadians failed to resist foreign ownership in their first half-century of development to 1914, at great cost to Canadian economic independence, because they were such weak nationalists. Canadians lacked nationalism because Confederation in 1867 was not an agrarian-democratic movement but rather the project of business interests. Laxer highlights the especially weak influence of farmers in Canadian politics and argues that in countries of strong farm populism (for example Sweden, Japan, and the United States) state policies of easy credit, foreign ownership restrictions, economy in government, and military preparedness were followed. These helped foster industrial, technological, and economic independence. In Canada farm populism was weak, hindered by its association with disloyalty to Britain and by internal cultural and linguistic conflicts.

The argument that weak nationalism was the cause of Canada's high levels of foreign ownership is convincing, and although not new, it is explored in detail by Laxer. He emphasizes the cultural, political, and social determinants of Canadian economic development so often ignored in Canadian economic history. He finds the lack of Canadian nationalism disquieting and a mark of economic failure, but it can be seen in a more positive light. It meant less self-defense militarism, the seeking of allies rather than enemies, and less discrimination against foreigners. A more nationalistic and militaristic Canada that blocked foreign investment and gave preference to national industry through easy banking and credit would probably have been more like Mexico or Argentina rather than Sweden or Japan.

In Chapter 1 Canada's increasingly unfavorable balance of trade in finished manufactures is ascribed to the impact of branch-plant foreign investment and taken as an index of economic failure. It should alternatively be seen as an index of the success of the Canadian economy, since increasing exports of wheat and resource products were being exchanged for imports of finished manufactures. Canada's share of world manufacturing production rose impressively to 1914 in spite of wheat and resource export booms, hardly a sign of industrial regression. To argue that Canada should run a positive trade balance in finished goods is in any case a coals-to-Newcastle economic absurdity, since it implies net imports of raw materials.

In Chapters 2 and 3 it is shown how other countries became net exporters of finished manufactures through farm populism, nationalism, and militarism. For example, compared to Canada's social and cultural heterogeneity and weak nationalism, Sweden was homogeneous and nationalistic. But the Swedish comparison is problematic. A more relevant comparison might be Sweden to Ontario, since Sweden was the dominant industrial region of Scandinavia in the same way as Ontario was of Canada. Moreover, Canada compares unfavorably with Sweden in exports of finished manufactures because Canada had a larger number of additional export sectors. To view Canada as an economic failure to 1914 and Sweden as a success ignores the fact that many Swedes chose to emigrate to Canada in these same years. Laxer's comparative analysis fails to consider per capita levels of economic well-being, the most relevant index of comparison.

In Chapter 6 Canadian banking is shown as a sector where foreign ownership was effectively blocked but in Chapter 5 as a sector that contributed critically to Canada's industrial failure by remaining dominated by a domestic elite and failing to extend adequate credit. There is praise for the more flexible U.S. banking system; hence it is somewhat ironic that foreign investment might have been beneficial in Canadian banking. The reader is left with the suspicion that if Canada had blocked foreign investment in manufacturing and resources as they did in banking, these sectors would have been similarly conservative, elitist, and inefficient.

In Chapter 5 the timing of Canadian prairie settlement is linked to foreign investment and industrialization in Canada. It is argued that had the CPR (Canadian Pacific Railway, completed in 1885) been financed by bond guarantees rather than by land grants, run through the northern prairie rather than close to the U.S. border, and not have included the expensive north of Lake Superior section, more homesteads would have been available on better land and freight rates would have been lower, ensuring earlier prairie settlement. This would have fostered earlier and stronger growth of an indigenous Canadian manufacturing sector better able to withstand foreign investment. But recent scholarship has shown that the delay in prairie settlement had little to do with government policies, that bond-guaranteed railways were particularly prone to failure, and that Canada industrialized more in spite of rather than because of the prairie wheat boom. Whereas elsewhere in the book Laxer is acutely aware of the political and strategic realities of state economic policy, he chooses to ignore their critical influence in the decision for an all-Canadian, southerly route for the CPR.

This book represents a welcome and rare attempt to see Canadian economic development in its cultural, political, social, and internationally comparative context. In a true Canadian self-effacing manner the author consistently criticizes Canadian economic policies and development and praises the economic policies and development of other nations. Non-Canadians might find this fascinating and corrective reading, for they are more likely to see virtue in Canada's nonnationalistic tendencies and to regard Canadian economic development as a story of success rather than of failure.

PETER WYLIE, *Trent University*

Canadian Papers in Business History. Vol. 1. Edited by Peter Baskerville. Victoria, British Columbia: The Public History Group of the University of Victoria, 1989. Pp. vi, 269. $19.95 (Canadian).

Coming out of the Second Canadian Business History Conference held in Victoria in 1988, this is the first volume of what is intended to be a regular collection of essays in Canadian business history.

Four essays explore decision making in a context of uncertainty. Mark Cox examines the short-lived experience (1919–1920) of a governmental agency, the Board of Commerce of Canada, whose objective was to put some order in the economic system by determining "fair" prices and profits. The scheme failed and Cox believes that it was because of its innovative character, but one gets the impression that it simply was an impossible mission. Eric Sager argues that declining profits are not a complete explanation for the decline of the Atlantic shipping industry and that the pessimistic perceptions of the merchant shipowners about the fate of the industry must be considered. This is a good idea, but his attack on neoclassical economics seems out of proportion: is it really necessary to call comparative advantage a "hoary chestnut?" (pp. 62–63). Ian Radforth's captivating essay on the management problems associated with long distance narrates the relationship between Robert Hay, owner of the Toronto furniture firm Jacques and Hay, and his brother-in-law, manager of its New Lowell logging and sawmill plant, 45 miles north of Toronto. Hay's letters from 1853 to 1873 are a litany of complaints about his in-law's managerial mistakes. Yet he did not fire him because of the Scottish strong sense of family, Radforth explains. Under the striking title "A Merchant of Death in the Peaceable Kingdom," Graham Taylor examines Canadian Vickers, a British-owned arms manufacturer in the period 1911 to 1927. This is an excellent case of decision making under uncertainty because, from the 1910s "Canadian navy" project which never materialized to the 1920s conversion to peacetime, the environment Canadian Vickers faced was anything but stable. Taylor's story of continuous problems with an elusive Canadian government and of much autonomy vis-à-vis the British parent firm does not fit well with its introductory statements about the "military-industrial complex" and the problem of foreign control.

In addition to Taylor's, three other essays have a Marxist flavor. Ronald Rudin's Caisses Populaires of Quebec are a good illustration of the tradeoff faced by most cooperative movements between local autonomy and centralization. But Rudin's interpretation of a shift in the control of the Caisses in the period 1900 to 1945 from the "petite bourgeoisie"—conservative and nationalist—to the more audacious middle class who would eventually usher the province in the Quiet Revolution is not really convincing for two reasons. First, as he recognizes, the tradeoff seems to be inherent in this form of organization: it was present from the beginnings and, one may add, is still very much alive today. Moreover, the struggle took place, and still does, between Montreal and Quebec city. Montreal's rejection of centralization seems more than anything else a rejection of any attempt of control by Quebec, a "big village" in Montrealers' eyes. Richard Rajala's essay asks whether the logging engineer appeared between 1900 and 1930 because the industry needed someone who knew about logging and railways or because it needed control over the workers. The two rationales are present in the essay, but Rajala clearly favors the latter and many of his arguments will seem far-fetched to non-Marxist readers. The same can be said about Phillip Wood's essay on the Maritime provinces' "failure" to industrialize. The few comments on the problems of the cotton textile firms are buried in a grandiose comparison of the rates of exploitation in the Maritimes and the American South. The reader needs to have faith since there is not a single explanation of the assumptions underlying the calculations.

Two essays are about women's history. Brian Young's examination of the case of married women traders in mid-nineteenth-century Lower Canada shows the dichotomy between the rise of "bourgeois law" and the legal incapacity of married women. Janine Grant and Kris Inwood's essay wishes to challenge conventional wisdom that cloth home production was insignificant by 1870 and that hand-loom weaving was dominated by males. The essay should have been tightened: many statistical tables are unrelated to the questions asked and 10 successive footnotes giving all the references on women's work history are clearly superfluous. Finally, there are two descriptive essays by Ian MacPherson and John Herd Thompson, who draw a picture of the business of farming in the prairie over the period 1880 to 1950, and by Douglas McCalla, who describes the establishment of the insurance industry in Upper Canada from 1832 to 1868.

To sum up, there is in business history a little something for many people: economists will consider the issues in Cox's and Rudin's essays very real; management theorists will find useful Radforth's and Taylor's case studies; Canadian economic historians will recognize their topics in the essays by MacPherson and Thompson and by Sager; and social historians will appreciate the essays by Young and Rajala.

RUTH DUPRÉ, *Ecole des Hautes Etudes Commerciales de Montréal*

ECONOMIC THOUGHT

A History of Economic Theory: Classic Contributions, 1720–1980. By Jürg Niehans. Baltimore: Johns Hopkins University Press, 1990. Pp. x, 578. $59.95.

In his preface to this book Jürg Niehans appears to endorse the view that economists can benefit from an understanding of the history of their discipline. He does not carry this claim beyond the preface, however, and the book's tone reflects nearly the opposite point of view. Starting from a "toolbox" conception of science, Niehans traces the process by which various analytical devices were invented, refined, and finally incorporated into the mainstream of economics. Modern mainstream theory is uncritically adopted as the standard of scientific achievement, and theories are judged to be sound or useful on the basis of a naive survivor test: tools that proved serviceable became permanent elements of the science; ideas that were discarded must have been worthless.

The development of economics is divided into three stages, each defined by a central theme or leitmotif. Classical theory, according to Niehans, focused on the circular flow of income in an economy conceptualized as an interdependent system. This characterization makes sense in connection with Richard Cantillon, François Quesnay, and perhaps Karl Marx but is less appropriate for Adam Smith, David Ricardo, or Thomas Malthus; a more striking feature of classical analysis—its concern with the creation, distribution, and accumulation of a social surplus—is not even mentioned. The leitmotif of marginalism lies in its attempt to understand the behavior of individuals and firms in terms of a calculus of constrained optimization. Finally, the era of formal model-building, from about 1930 onward, is marked by an increasing application of axiomatic methods to theory construction.

Niehans rejects the notion that the transition from any one stage to the next constitutes a paradigm shift. He sees instead an unbroken chain of scientific progress, running from the scholastics through to Kenneth Arrow and Gerard Debreu, in which the most useful achievements of earlier periods are assimilated into newer and better theoretical frameworks. (General equilibrium theory, for example, is interpreted as a synthesis of marginalist microfoundations and classical insights about the circular flow of income.) Facts which do not fit this reading are ignored, a case in point being the role of surplus in classical theory.

Niehans admits to being interested in earlier theories only insofar as they anticipate modern developments. Not surprisingly, this attitude often results in an inaccurate presentation of older theories; there is a noticeable tendency to project modern views onto writers of the past. The principal casualties belong to the classical period. A downward-sloping firm demand curve is imputed to Smith (p. 66). Ricardo's theory of value is interpreted as a special case, in which demand is irrelevant, of the more general supply-and-demand theory (pp. 89, 104), his growth theory is presumed to coincide with Paul Samuelson's "canonical classical model," and Niehans comes close to suggesting that distribution could be regulated in a classical model by the marginal productivity of inputs (pp. 93–99). There is a vast secondary literature which addresses these issues and challenges the positions taken by Niehans, but he never confronts knotty interpretational problems. Much recent debate has centered on the possibility that the classicals were not groping toward modern supply-and-demand theory—that they might have had a fundamentally different understanding of how a market economy operates. Niehans seems unwilling to acknowledge even the existence of interpretations which leave room for the idea that nonneoclassical perspectives can be scientifically valid.

This modernist bias often takes the form of an irritating smugness about the technical handicaps under which earlier writers labored. When the work of, for example, Ricardo is judged against a standard that was established 150 years after his death, it is easy to underrate the genuine brilliance of what he did accomplish *with the tools then at his disposal*. For example, Niehans misses the fact that both Ricardo and Marx were able, by expressing their accounts in units of embodied labor time, not only to refute Smith's incorrect "adding-up" theory of price but also to derive the main propositions of Samuelson's nonsubstitution theorem.

The chapters on Marx and John Maynard Keynes are illustrative of the book's shortcomings. Niehans makes no effort to understand the theoretical aims of these writers or to appreciate the difficulties they faced at the times they wrote; he dismisses their scientific work in patronizing terms and confines their importance to the areas of ideology (Marx) and polemics (Keynes). The chapter on Marx opens with an unsympathetic sketch of his life, drawn from Raddatz's notoriously hostile biography; there is also an irrelevant (and in my view off-target) attack on Marx's literary style. His value theory is treated in a cursory manner, and no stand is taken on its analytical function. Marx's cycle theory is mentioned only to be unfavorably compared with that of Clément Juglar. The one theoretical innovation credited to Marx, his two-sector balanced growth model, is said to be developed in a "clumsy, fragmentary and almost unintelligible fashion" (p. 155); his overall contribution is described as "mediocre." Innuendoes and sweeping generalizations abound; readers looking for an impartial and balanced assessment of Marx will be disappointed. Keynes does not fare much better. The significance of the effective demand mechanism is played down (almost to the point of invisibility), and Keynes's argument is reduced to the uninteresting assertion that wage rigidity impedes equilibration in the labor market.

On the positive side, the book is well organized. Its chapters on monetary topics and marginalist writers are balanced and informative. Many economists neglected in other histories are here given their due: Johann von Thünen, Hermann Gossen, Rudolf Auspitz and Richard Lieben, and Ragnar Frisch. (Friedrich Von Hayek, though, is unaccountably shortchanged.) As a convenient desk reference, this book has much to offer, provided the above-mentioned limitations are kept in mind.

In the epilogue Niehans restates and attempts to make a case for his belief that modern economics is the culmination of a steady process of scientific advance. But of course the survivor test upon which this conclusion rests is a tautology. Modern economics has more than its share of problems. Intellectual history is hardly useful if it does nothing more than reassure us about our own preconceptions; it ought to foster a critical attitude and give a fresh perspective on familiar ideas. The last thing economists should be doing these days is patting themselves on the back.

GARY MONGIOVI, *St. John's University*

Philosophy of Economics: On the Scope of Reason in Economic Inquiry. By Subroto Roy. New York: Routledge, 1989. Pp. ix, 236. $37.50.

There is near consensus among economists today that economics is a positive theory which cannot and should not make normative claims. This book seeks to understand the philosophical roots of this consensus and to show that it is mistaken. Subroto Roy argues that modern (twentieth century) economists agree on two claims which come from David Hume: first, all normative economic judgments rest ultimately on subjective evaluations of the good; and second, these subjective evaluations are immune to rational criticism. He denies both claims, using contemporary philosophy, as best represented by Cambridge philosopher Ludwig Wittgenstein and Harvard philosopher W. V. O. Quine, to show that objective knowledge is possible in all areas and that no claim is immune to criticism.

Roy traces the Humean consensus among economists to the rejection of Platonism. Plato held that there are objective values which only specially talented and educated persons could come to know. He argued that these persons should rule the state to achieve the highest good of the state. Roy argues that in the Middle Ages Platonism inspired the authoritarian rule of the Church and its claim to know objective value. He presents a whirlwind history of economic thought from mercantilism through the marginalist revolution, arguing that the rejection of dogmatism resulted in modern moral skepticism, which he takes to be equivalent to the Humean idea that values are completely subjective. This argument strains the history of ideas and fails adequately to treat the serious ontological problems with objective values. Furthermore, it is not clear that holding that value is subjective entails moral skepticism. There are contemporary moral theories which are not skeptical and hold that value is subjective.

Roy presents two arguments against moral skepticism. First, moral skeptics cannot make moral prescriptions, since they deny the possibility of moral knowledge. But moral skeptics claim that economists *ought not* make policy decisions—a moral prescription. Thus moral skepticism is inconsistent. Second, if one takes a skeptical attitude toward moral knowledge, then one ought also, to be consistent, see if epistemological skepticism is warranted. The problem of induction shows that empirical knowledge is uncertain. Thus if one is a moral skeptic one ought also be an epistemological skeptic, so that the possibility of all economic knowledge is equally dubious. Both arguments are problematic as arguments designed to defeat moral skepticism, and even more so as arguments against the subjectivity of value, if subjectivity does not entail skepticism. Moral skeptics grant that they cannot make normative prescriptions about what economists ought to do, but they claim that the policy prescriptions of economists rely on subjective values. There is no inconsistency in that. As for the second argument, there is no connection between the arguments for subjective value and for epistemological skepticism, so a person may consistently reject one and hold the other.

The central argument of the book shows that the skepticism/dogmatism choice is a false dichotomy, that one need not embrace dogmatism in order to have objectivity or give up objectivity for freedom. Roy argues that moral skeptics fail to distinguish between the claim that there is objective knowledge from claims about who has access to it. He takes the Wittgensteinian view that objective knowledge is guaranteed by the language games we use in serious discussion. These games require a great deal of agreement on many things (mostly unspoken), and this agreement is proof of objective knowledge. Since language is essentially a public, collective activity, objective knowledge is only determinable by social consensus. Roy sees this as the nonskeptical antidote to dogmatism: "Ultimately all theory is (or ought to be) 'Critique of Language' " (p. 165).

In the final section of the book Roy applies his critique of Humeanism and positive epistemological views to several debates in economics. Chapter 8 presents the development of macroeconomics from John Maynard Keynes to the present through a dialogue between economists of opposing schools, designed to show that there is a broad base of objective fact about macro-policies on which both agree. Chapter 9 is a rich, wide-ranging discussion of mathematical models in economics. It begins with the debate over the use of mathematics in economics, then moves to the debate over interpretations of probability, and ends by discussing models in economics—whether they are meant as normative ideals or empirical descriptions. This last topic is especially important, though neglected and misunderstood by economists. Chapter 10 discusses the foundations of welfare economics, including the debate between Marshallian cardinal utilities and Hicksian ordinal utilities, and the Pigou-Robbins debate on the uses by the state of welfare economics based on their differing views of interpersonal comparisons of utility.

This book is an interesting discussion of philosophical assumptions which underlie modern economics. Roy shows how philosophical mistakes can lead economic thought astray, even though some of his arguments are also unsound. As a philosopher I find it encouraging to see an economist apply recent developments in epistemology to economic debates.

ANN CUDD, *University of Kansas*

Keynesian Economics: The Permanent Revolution. By G. K. Shaw. Brookfield, VT: Gower Publishing Co., 1988. Pp. xi, 155. $33.95, cloth; $11.95, paper.

This book covers the major interpretations of John Maynard Keynes, the empirical problems which confronted the dominant interpretation, the theoretical challenges raised by monetarists and new classicals, the New Keynesian reinterpretation, and the failures of the Margaret Thatcher and Ronald Reagan programs in implementing anti-Keynesian policies. G. K. Shaw argues that Keynesianism has successfully survived and is improved from the monetarist and new classical challenges. The book is marketed as a survey of current macroeconomic controversies for second- or third-year undergraduates.

I am sympathetic with the author's aim, and I find much to like and recommend in the book. The collection of doctrinal history and the related presentations of many of the specific issues certainly could be of great help in, for example, an intermediate macroeconomics course, though to reach North American undergraduates at least, the book generally needs more clarity and thoroughness. It could be read in the later stages of such a course after the students have achieved some familiarity with IS-LM and AD-AS analyses, but still I fear they would have trouble with some of the exposition.

I particularly like Shaw's discussion of the treatment of expectations in Keynes and its contrast with the development of adaptive and then rational expectations models and his presentation of the new classical macroeconomics. I also applaud his forays into presenting and analyzing the empirical results of the application of Keynesian and then anti-Keynesian ideas, though each story needs a little more work, I think. I would also like to see more of the empirical studies that have been done on the new classical hypotheses reported.

The advent of the "New Keynesian" macroeconomics is an important link in Shaw's argument that Keynesian ideas are resilient. Shaw's presentation of New Keynesianism mentions only new arguments for wage and price stickiness. While not denying that these points are important, I think there is both more to New Keynesianism and less to the necessity of imperfect price flexibility to support Keynesian arguments than Shaw seems to allow.

Shaw himself recognizes the tension over price flexibility in Keynesian economics in his discussion of Keynes versus his interpreters. He fails to note, however, that there has been quite a bit of research arguing that price flexibility in Keynesian models may actually be destabilizing.

Furthermore, there is some New Keynesian work, mainly by Bruce Greenwald and Joseph Stiglitz, which does not rely on price inflexibility to achieve Keynesian results. This work, based on credit rationing and equity rationing under asymmetric information, is a very significant contribution of the New Keynesian school but is ignored by Shaw.

When surveying the various interpretations put forth by followers of Keynes, Shaw discusses very briefly "Neo- and Post-Keynesian interpretations." Steven Fazzari and I have argued that there are some remarkable similarities between certain aspects of the Post and New Keynesian schools. My emphasis is on the correspondence of Greenwald and Stiglitz's ideas with those of Michal Kalecki. Here is a "Keynesian" revolution not based on price inflexibility (though improperly flexible mark-ups are necessary) but on limits on the access to capital. This I think is an aspect of Keynesian economics that Shaw would well profit from looking into.

TRACY MOTT, *University of Colorado, Boulder*

From Exploitation to Altruism. By Ian Steedman. Boulder: Westview Press, 1989. Pp. ix, 249. $47.50.

Few volumes of collected essays have both the coherence and the intellectual punch of this one. Eleven of Ian Steedman's previously published articles appear here, some well known, others not previously readily accessible. The order of presentation follows roughly the chronological order of the ideas discussed. One essay, "P.H. Wicksteed's Jevonian Critique of Marx," appears for the first time and functions as a bridge between the broadly classical and neoclassical sections of the volume.

Steedman's familiarity with the history of economics is impressive; while particular attention is given to David Ricardo, Karl Marx, Stanley Jevons, and Philip Wicksteed, other authors of almost every period and persuasion make appearances. As the title suggests, the topics considered span an enormous range, from exploitation and issues of concern to "surplus theory" to altruism and questions arising in the neoclassical analyses of rational individual action.

The essays are decidedly not conventional history of economic thought. Steedman is principally concerned with theoretical propositions of contemporary relevance to work in both classical and neoclassical traditions, and at times he does discuss points of theory largely without reference to the texts associated with the ideas under scrutiny. Thus his famous demonstration of "positive profits with negative surplus value" proceeds on the assumption that the Marxian context of the problem is both known to the reader and adequately represented by the formulas employed. Similarly his lucid summary of the case for the intrinsically nonautonomous nature of preference concludes with the strong claim that "the conventional structure of microeconomic theory" is "incoherent" and not "rationally acceptable" (pp. 214–15), but the relatively brief consideration given to the reasons why that structure evolved and the possible rationales of its proponents probably will undermine the essay's intended purpose of stimulating change.

Still, every essay contains at least something of interest to the historian of thought. Even when theory itself is his focus, Steedman as a rule displays uncommon interest in and reliance on both the insights and the blind spots of past thinkers. Thus, rather than simply launching into a theoretical critique of the Ramsey formula and other conclusions based on "the assumption . . . that consumption is the sole end of economic activity" (p. 222), Steedman first surveys 15 major theorists, from David Hume and Adam Smith through Irving Fisher, Frank Knight, and John Maynard Keynes, to demonstrate the historical pedigree for his inclusion of wealth as an explicit argument in the intertemporal utility function. Similarly, in an essay principally devoted to enumerating the difficulties faced by contemporary work on the stability of classical models of "center of gravity" prices, he firmly roots the issue in the problematic assumption, common to Smith, Ricardo, and Marx, that the deviations of prices and profits from their natural competitive levels must always have the same sign.

Since his task is frequently critical and his tone often polemical, clarity concerning the nature of the criticisms offered is essential. Steedman is on solid ground in suggesting that if the arguments of a theory or the concepts on which those arguments rest can be subjected to logical criticism of their coherence, consistency, generality, and so on, then—absent a reformulation—there is reason to jettison them or at least to contemplate doing so. But it is a different sort of criticism to suggest that one should jettison concepts or forms of argument which (the word "merely" can be read between the lines) constitute "description" as distinct from "explanation." Are the two so clearly distinct, and are they always distinguishable on the same grounds? Neither events nor algebra provide their own descriptions, so *how* we describe is not a trivial matter. Similarly, agreement on an "explanation" (for example, that "the classical, given real wage . . . and the conditions of production suffice to determine the rate of profit and all relative prices" [p. 81]) is not enough to settle all issues of how to *interpret* the relations agreed upon. Steedman is always careful to criticize only those descriptive concepts which in his view masquerade as explanation, but one still wishes that at some point he would address, with the same precision and rigor evident in his discussions of particular theories, the more general and largely implicit methodological premises underlying his own view of what constitutes good theory or good explanation.

On the whole, though, the volume is a striking success. It is hard to see how anyone with a serious interest in economic theory can read these essays without on numerous occasions being stimulated to new insights, some of which will surely arise in the process of "talking back" to the author. Steedman is, as always, provocative in the best sense of the word.

BRUCE ROBERTS, *College of William and Mary*

International Monetary Economics, 1870–1960: Between the Classical and the New Classical. By M. June Flanders. New York: Cambridge University Press, 1989. Pp. xii, 368. $49.50.

This book is an admirable undertaking. June Flanders exposits and interprets a body of literature tremendous both in sheer quantity and in the power of its accomplishment. While Flanders is decidedly presenting a history of ideas rather than events, her continuing or recurrent themes—how the balance-of-payments adjustment process actually (or ought to have) worked and how the Bank of England actually (or ought to have) behaved—are certainly of interest to historians. Flanders does nothing less than build a railroad pulling the classical balance-of-payments adjustment model of the nineteenth century up to the modern adjustment process that culminated in the 1950s and 1960s. A bibliography of several hundred items itself indicates the vastness of the task.

Flanders does more than simply exposit and interpret; she uses an explicit framework (what I called the railroad) to process the literature. The author moves from a protomodel that began with Isaac Gervaise in the early eighteenth century. This model involves endogeneity of a given country's money supply under a fixed exchange rate. There is a separation of monetary and real sectors, and equilibrium does not occur until international payments are in balance (the sense in which Flanders uses the term "proto"). The protomodel gave rise to two, concurrent, lines of economic thought. Discussed first in the introductory chapter but later in the body of the text is stream F ("formal"), involving analytical model building, equilibrium, and the long run. The other line, stream P ("policy-oriented"), is normative and concerned with disequilibrium or short-run equilibrium. The streams converge in the 1950s and 1960s. It would be an oversimplification, however, to view the schema as the usual one of thesis (F stream) generating antithesis (P stream) and conjoining as synthesis. Rather, the two streams were chronologically and analytically coexistent. Both stemmed from classical roots, which Flanders puts at the beginning of the F stream.

Specifically, the F stream has four component theories: classical, late classical, Ohlin, and small-k keynesian (emphatically not Keynes himself). In her discussion of the "classical mainstream," Flanders confines herself to existing surveys: Frank Fetter, D. P. O'Brien, and Jacob Viner. Even so, it is distressing how little space is devoted to the bullionist controversy. (It is also unfortunate—though in keeping with the book's Anglo-American orientation—that the earlier bullionist controversies in Sweden and France are not even mentioned.) More attention is given to the banking-versus-currency schools; but the author relies heavily on O'Brien. The classical approach involved payments imbalances corrected quickly by price changes so that long-run equilibrium was reached rapidly in real time. International capital movements, central banking, and the interest rate were generally ignored.

The bulk of the book is devoted to stream P, which follows the chapter on the classical approach. Thus the rest of stream F (following the classicals) is interrupted by stream P. (This organization might seem illogical, but it did not disturb me.) Stream P also has four components: the neoclassicals, anti-classicals, Keynes himself, and the crisis writers.

The neoclassical tradition begins with Walter Bagehot and includes Alfred Marshall, the Cunliffe Committee, and the Macmillan Committee. The neoclassicists incorporated interest-rate effects (on domestic investment spending and international capital flows) into the classical model through the discount-rate (Bank Rate) policy of the central bank (Bank of England). To Flanders's credit, she pays careful attention to R. S. Sayers's masterful study of the Bank of England in the heyday of the gold standard, 1890 to 1914. For the economic historian, her synopsis of Sayers is perhaps the most interesting part of the book. Sayers shows that the Cunliffe Committee description of the Bank routinely raising Bank Rate to defend its gold stock whenever threatened is incorrect. Because Bank Rate was a penalty rate, the Bank had to tighten the money market considerably to achieve a response of the market rate to Bank Rate. Bank Rate changes were not the only policy; there were gold-point manipulations and open-market operations. Further, the Bank was as concerned with internal as with external balance: "The theme of avoiding action because of the internal effects is a constantly recurring one in Sayers" (p. 80). Flanders sees a need for more historical study on the extent to which the "rules of the game" of the prewar gold standard were observed: "The debate is far from over regarding the role played by the Bank of England in particular (and other central banks in general) in the Game and the extent to which they abided by its Rules" (p. 84). She documents the striking difference between the Cunliffe and Macmillan Reports in describing the international gold standard in the last few postwar decades.

Friedrich Hayek and Ralph Hawtrey began the neoclassical approach. They believed in the prewar classical mechanism historically and normatively, and blamed institutional factors (exchange rates not rigidly fixed, fractional-reserve banking) for its problems. The revisionists (Arthur Bloomfield, William Adams Brown, Jr., Robert Triffin, Barrett Whale) argued that historically the neoclassical position was incorrect. Keynes was neoclassical in his early writings. Later, in the *Treatise*, he provided a combined Wicksellian and Marshall-Lerner analysis that Flanders examines in detail. Keynes's model involved the current account dependent on relative prices and the capital account varying with relative interest rates. The final stage in stream P, the crisis writers, includes Marco Fanno, Bloomfield, Ragnar Nurkse, and Charles Kindleberger (as well as part of Keynes). For these authors, short-term capital flows are destabilizing and the classical view of rapid, real adjustment is the opposite of reality.

Flanders then returns to stream F, beginning with Frank Taussig and his students (James Angell, Viner, Harry Dexter White, John Williams)—the late classicals. They add to the classical approach fractional-reserve banking, international (but largely exogenous) capital flows, and a conviction that historical study is required to test the validity of the classical (or any) adjustment process. Flanders is most impressed with White:

> In reading his book, one is continually struck by the recurring tension between what he says he believes the adjustment mechanism to be, a product, apparently, of his training seasoned by his original thoughts on the subject, and what he feels he can document historically and factually (p. 237).

The anticlassicals were succeeded by Bertil Ohlin and the keynesians. Flanders exposits and interprets the much-neglected monetary part of Ohlin's theory and concludes:

> If we must summarize, Ohlin parted company with the classicals in that he did not *assume* full employment; in this, and in his interest in the determinants of expenditure, he was keynesian. In his emphasis on the monetary mechanism he was classical. And (while the reader may on occasion wish he had a greater penchant for simplification and abstraction) in his awareness of the

complexity of the general-equilibrium system and the importance of intersectoral adjustments he was unique (p. 256).

The keynesians were many—Roy Harrod, Michal Kalecki, Frank Paish, Colin Clark, Dennis Robertson, Nurkse, Gottfried Haberler, Joan Robinson, A. J. Brown, early Lloyd Metzler, Fritz Machlup, William Salant, Kindleberger, Jacques Polak, Hans Neisser, and Franco Modigliani. They applied Keynes's *General Theory* to an open economy. Fittingly, their models involved rigid prices and ignored or neutralized monetary effects of payments imbalances (the opposite of the classical approach).

Finally, the two streams are merged in the post-Keynesian work of Metzler, James Meade, and Robert Mundell, who made capital flows and the money supply endogenous. Thus the keynesian approach is linked to the protomodel, with payments imbalances changing the money supply.

Flanders includes an excellent introductory chapter, a useful summary or equivalent section in each chapter, and an "ex post" chapter posing unanswered questions and suggesting future research. It is hard to criticize a work so well done. Where the book does have shortcomings, Flanders readily admits them: neglect of important writers, old and modern, such as Bresciani-Turroni, Cassel, and Johnson; little attention to economists (or events) outside the Anglo-American category; omission of such topics as purchasing power parity and devaluation; and the subjective nature of her F-P schema. These limitations should not dissuade economic historians from reading Flanders's book. In particular, historians investigating the international gold standard or the Bank of England will find the study an especially useful history-of-thought companion.

LAWRENCE H. OFFICER, *University of Illinois, Chicago*

GENERAL AND MISCELLANEOUS

Historical Studies in International Corporate Business. Edited by Alice Teichova, Maurice Levy-Leboyer, and Helga Nussbaum. New York: Cambridge University Press, 1989. Pp. vii, 252. $37.50.

The present volume constitutes a sequel to *Multinational Enterprise in Historical Perspective*, published in 1986 and reviewed in this JOURNAL (June 1988). Being a collection of 19 research reports and survey essays, the book covers diverse aspects of corporate business as it developed in the context of international political economy.

As observed by Barry Supple in the introductory chapter, multinationals not only have history, but they also exist in history. Thus the contributing authors examine the origins and the development of multinational enterprises and investments in various countries. They grapple with such questions as these: Why do multinationals evolve? What explains their various forms? What determines their success and failure? Although econometricians and model builders in their devious ways are also concerned with those questions, the crucial additional question that is being uniquely illuminated by the historical studies in the reviewed collection is What have been the political ramifications of multinational business in the twentieth century?

The multinational enterprise appears as a truly global phenomenon. Thus, K. Wohlert traces how the Swedish corporations were entangled in multi-country financing, trade, and diplomacy. G. D. Feldman shows how foreign expansion of German enterprises in the interwar period spread the fear of their domination. C. A. Wurm discusses British involvement in international industrial cartels, a process with significant political overtones. R. P. T. Davenport-Hines, using the cases of Vickers and Schneider, offers a comparison of British and French multinational strategies from 1916 to 1926. Emma Harris recounts how J. & P. Coats Ltd of Scotland, specializing in thread production, had to relocate operations from the lost Russian imperial market in 1918 to Poland and Latvia; it would have been helpful to present this case against the background of East European economic history, which is poorly appreciated in the West.

Of special interest are two chapters pertaining to multinational business in Latin America. S. J. Randall's short article interprets the role of private corporations in U.S. policies toward the developing oil industry in Latin America. Focusing on the cigarette industry, P. Shepherd's study analyzes the interaction between transnational enterprises and government-promoted domestic monopolies. These two chapters allow the reader a glimpse into the complex political economy in Latin America, characterized by frustrated economic development, governmental interference with free markets, and the intrusion of powerful multinationals.

Finally, very welcome is the inclusion of three case studies of Japanese international enterprises before the Second World War. N. Kawabe explains how Mitsui and Mitsubishi operated in the United States and Canada as an extension of a family of companies, the *zaibatsu*. As such, these trading companies proved to be effective conduits of technology, and they served as suppliers of primary products for Japan's ambitious industrial establishment.

The collection of current historical studies underscores two conclusions. First, it is obvious that the MNC as a modern form of global business has its origins well before World War II. And second, the multinational approach to business is not merely an Euro-American phenomenon, but a mode of enterprise that extends into, and is being adapted by, countries on all continents. The wide-ranging scope of multinational business requires the historical and institutional methods of study, especially if we are to grasp the significance of such things as the intricacy of Japanese business organizations or the intrusion of politics into the game of global business.

VLADIMIR N. BANDERA, *Temple University*

The International Debt Crisis in Historical Perspective. Edited by Barry Eichengreen and Peter H. Lindert. Cambridge, MA: MIT Press, 1989. Pp. ix, 282. $25.00.

This is not a particularly original book. *Finance and Development* for March 1990 reports that the IMF–World Bank Joint Library has 548 books in its collection under the catalogue entry of "external debt" and 2,975 articles and working papers on the subject, 2,940 of the latter published since 1982. This JOURNAL itself has published 32 articles and reviewed 17 books in the field since its March 1982 issue (p. 12). Many of these books and articles, moreover, have been written by the same distinguished cast of economists brought together by the editors in a conference in California in the spring of 1987, largely along similar lines as those presented here.

The historical perspective offered is not especially wide, being confined for the most part to Latin American borrowing, British lending in the nineteenth century, and U.S. lending in the twentieth. French lending to Russia at the end of the nineteenth and beginning of this century and U.S. bonds issued for Germany, followed by short-term debt, are barely mentioned. Nor are such devices as payments agreements, used by Germany to collect debt service from Latin America, and by such countries as Switzerland to squeeze some payment out of Germany, given attention. For Latin America it seems curious that the Argentine choice to buy back British railroads rather than pay off debt with the cash piled up in World War II is ignored, along with the point that much Argentine borrowing also involved Argentine lending, not only in the nineteenth century as D. C. M. Platt has discussed, but also since World War II, as noted by Carlos Díaz-Alejandro, with U.S. banks lending to Latin America in the 1970s while Latinos exported capital to U.S. banks.

The general conclusions of the conferees are more or less widely held but well summarized by Peter Lindert in regressions, tables, and figures. First, nineteenth-century lending in bonds differed markedly from twentieth-century lending through banks in that the former was largely ignored by governments while the latter, because of the threat to the banking system, could not be. Second, a number of the debtor countries currently transfer net resources to the creditors, but most avoid such transfers by borrowing interest and any principal payment, rolling over debt as it matures, and in crisis rescheduling through the Paris club for government debt or negotiations with banks for private. Third, creditor pressure to force adjustment has slowed down debtor-country growth, up to 1990 at least, but continued growth in the creditor countries has avoided the double hit of 1929–1932. And finally, the papers demonstrate great sympathy for the debtor countries and criticism of the creditors for "muddling through" or just "muddling," despite the Baker and Brady plans—but apart from Eliana Cardoso and Rudiger Dornbusch, none of the essayists offers alternative plans to join the hundreds of those catalogued in *The International Economy*.

One point new to me, though Albert Fishlow has published it earlier, is his distinction between "revenue defaults" and "developmental defaults." Presumably the former arise when a country spends on consumption, the latter when there is an external shock that slows down development. The distinction may be overdrawn. Investment in uneconomic projects ("industrial pyramids" or "big-dam foolishness") are in effect consumption that produce no income from which debt service can be subtracted. In simple economies close to the subsistence level one should forgive consumption borrowing which otherwise piles up debt through compounding, but contract to collect part of the earnings of productive investments made with loans. The comparison of new loans with debt service in any given year is valid only if past borrowings have been consumed or wasted.

Along with most of the rest of the world, the authors believe that the present crisis first became recognizable in 1982 and had its origins in the OPEC oil price rise of 1973. Lindert, for example, writes of the growth of debt from 1974 to 1982. But this overlooks the contribution of Stephen Goodman, then of the Export-Import Bank, who organized a conference on LDC debt in 1977 that produced a book edited by him, *Financing and Risk in Developing Countries* (New York, 1978), and the fact that the bubble began in 1970–1973 with easy money in the United States (to help in Nixon's re-election) coinciding with tight-money policies at the Bundesbank. Dollars poured from the United States, flooded the Euro-currency market, and drove bankers worldwide in search of loans. The beginnings of the debt crisis at this time are visible in the Cardoso and Dornbusch essay on Brazil, in table 5.1 and figures 5.4 and 5.5.

The conference on which the volume is based was held about the time of the May 1987 massive Citicorp write-off on its portfolio of LDC loans that initiated a widening process among money-center banks, leading from the Baker to the Brady plan. Lindert's table 8.2 notes that the major creditors (excluding the IMF or the World Bank, the numbers for which are not included) wrote off 44.7 percent of loans to Ghana between 1966 and 1974, 56 percent of loans to Indonesia between 1966 and 1970, and 45 percent of those to Turkey between 1959 and 1965. Why are these not called 100 percent, since the resources borrowed were entirely wasted?

The book jacket is adorned with encomia from distinguished social scientists, largely economists, which include such phrases as "scholars who think clearly and write lucidly," "authoritative and well-written essays," "uniformly excellent," and "a valuable resource for policymakers." On the first three descriptions I demur on the ground that there is some unevenness in the essays. If by "a valuable resource for policymakers" is meant Vinod Aggarwal's essay on the use of game theory in interpreting the course of debt negotiation with Mexico, some reservation is possible. For one thing, even a limited knowledge of government makes it evident that no high-up policymaker will find the essay in the sea of articles and books on debt. Second, the author himself recognizes that the model furnishes only broad conclusions.

I have not found space to comment on Erika Jorgensen and Jeffrey Sachs's paper on Latin American bonds in the interwar period; on Barry Eichengreen and Richard Porter's essay on default, negotiation, and adjustment in the same period; on Cordoso and Dornbusch's paper on Brazilian debt crises, or on Charles Lipson's contrast, from the point of view of political science, of Britain as a lender in the Victorian period and the United States as lender after World War II. They are, along with most of the others, uniformly excellent and lucidly written.

CHARLES P. KINDLEBERGER, *Massachusetts Institute of Technology*

Innovation in Shipping and Trade. Edited by Stephen Fisher. Exeter: University of Exeter Press, 1989. Pp. vi, 177. £7.50.

This volume consists of a collection of essays on maritime economic history presented at several of the annual Dartington maritime history conferences organized by the Department of Economic and Social History of Exeter University. There are seven essays on a variety of topics ranging from ancient Greece through sixteenth-century Britain and nineteenth-century South Africa to twentieth-century Britain. Inevitably such a collection fails to present a very coherent whole and it will prove to be a reference volume for specialists.

Most readers will find the two essays and two briefer commentaries, on the role of the Admiralty in the adoption of screw propulsion for steam vessels, the most interesting. In separate articles Basil Greenhill and Andrew Lambert, the two leading experts on the Royal Navy's adoption of steamships, draw on Admiralty archives to dispel the popular notion that the navy was at least backward, and perhaps hostile, in adopting steam propulsion. The navy was actively involved in the technological developments but constrained by worldwide commitments and the technological limitations of the early engines. These articles, along with the brief introduction by Greenhill and a summing-up by Ewan Corlett, will be of considerable interest to students of both nineteenth-century marine technology and the Royal Navy.

The lead article, "Some Possible Technical Features of a Salamis *Trieres*," by naval architects K. H. Hamilton-Smith and E. C. B. Corlett, is a fascinating, and to this uninformed reader technical, discussion, complete with extensive line illustrations, of the likely performance characteristics of these Greek vessels. Examination of likely design and discussion of probable configuration of rowers indicate high propulsive efficiency. Calculations of likely power output and hull resistance suggest that the vessels were capable of considerable performance. Attack speeds of 10.6 knots could be achieved briefly; fast cruising at 8.1 knots would be sustainable for up to 6 hours; and the vessel could cruise at 7.2 knots almost indefinitely. These calculations lend plausibility to classical accounts that some modern accounts have questioned.

Four additional essays complete the volume. Alison Grant provides a useful account of John Delbridge of Barnstaple's part in the emergence of the transatlantic trade in the late sixteenth and early seventeenth centuries. He was a major figure in the early English colonies in America and his career helps place the role of the outports in sharper focus. David Williams convincingly argues that Edwardian postcards should be taken seriously as a visual source for historical work. Somewhat lesser essays, by E. A. G. Clark on port establishment in South Africa in the early nineteenth century, and by Stephanie Jones, on the unsatisfactory performance of the P & O during the last years of Lord Inchcape's chairmanship after the First World War, round out the volume.

C. KNICK HARLEY, *University of Western Ontario*

Management and Higher Education Since 1940: The Influence of America and Japan on West Germany, Great Britain and France. By Robert R. Locke. New York: Cambridge University Press, 1989. Pp. xiii, 328. $59.50.

Robert Locke has written an interesting and very detailed history of the development of management education in West Germany, Great Britain, and France. The book should attract scholars and educators with an interest in the historical evolution of higher education, the development of management education, and the development of the three leading industrial nations of Europe.

The subtitle is misleading: very little deals with the influence of America and Japan on the development of management education in West Germany, Great Britain, and France. To be sure, several references support the notion that the German approach to business education resembled the Japanese approach and that the French and British more closely followed the lead of the Americans. These cross-cultural relationships, however, do not appear to be very strong, and most of the book is devoted to explaining the differences in management education in West Germany, Britain, and France.

Locke shows how the approach to and development of management education were rooted in the culture and institutions of each of the three leading industrial nations. While using the same basic paradigm of managerial science formulated in America, each nation developed a unique approach to management education, differences largely reflecting cultural and institutional factors. Higher education in Germany emphasized scientific research; in Britain universities sought to educate gentlemen; and in France the main function of universities was to train public servants. The sharp differences in culture and institutional purpose led to very different approaches to management education.

Locke traces the development of engineering education in the three nations to dramatize the impact of cultural forces. Germany developed a strong engineering program by combining formal scientific education and lengthy on-the-job training. The British never really saw much need for engineering and therefore accomplished very little. The French were moderately successful and developed *grandes écoles* for the elite and lower-level schools for the masses. These same basic patterns were followed in developing formal programs of study in business and management.

The Germans implemented the new management science paradigm quickly by combining strong educational programs with practical technical competence. According to Locke, the emphasis on practical experience in Germany was similar to the Japanese model. In contrast, British universities were prejudiced against management education because the culture emphasized the school one attended rather than the subject one studied. The French were also very status conscious about schools. Locke contends that the French and British approaches to management education were modeled roughly after the system found in American business schools.

The similarities in approach to management education in the leading European nations, Japan, and America are easily overemphasized. Locke's careful research makes it clear that differences in cultural and institutional factors created a unique approach to management and management education in each nation.

ALBERT W. NIEMI, JR., *University of Georgia*

Die Bedeutung der Kommunikation für Wirtschafts und Gesellschaft. Edited by Hans Pohl. Stuttgart: Franz Steiner Verlag, 1989. Pp. 485. DM 128.

This excellent collection of papers presented at the 1987 meeting of the German *Gesellschaft für Sozial- und Wirtschaftsgeschichte* deals with various aspects of "the significance of communication for economy and society." Even while recognizing the volume's contributions to this subject, I must issue a caveat: the definition of *Kommunikation* chosen by the editor as a unifying framework (". . . *alle Formen von Verkehr, Verbindung, Vermittlung und Verständigung*" [p. 7]) is so broad as to encompass virtually every kind of social interaction. Although in their paper titles and introductions most of the authors bow to the general theme, a good deal of their research lies well outside the conventional boundaries of the history of communication. Therefore, specialists may find less than expected on account of the book's title, but nonspecialists should not be put off by it.

The diversity of contributions forces me to start with a listing of topics (freely translated), so that readers of this review can decide whether there is anything of interest to them: "Travel, messengers, mails and correspondence in the Middle Ages and in early modern times"; "The significance of *Kontoren, Faktoreien*, company outposts, markets, fairs, and exchanges in the Middle Ages"; "The significance of pilgrimages, crusades, and other forms of migration (for example, of journeymen) for communication in the Middle Ages and in early modern times"; "The Hanseatic League and the *Reich* from the perspective of communication"; "Communication at the Church councils of the late Middle Ages"; "European traditions and 'German university space': forms and phases of academic communication"; "Economic literature and communication to 1800"; "Travel and housekeeping literature in early modern times"; "The social significance of communication in civic societies and clubs, from the 18th to the early 20th century"; "The development of message transmission and its significance: letter mail and telecommunications in the German Empire, 1871–1918"; "New means of transportation in the 19th and 20th centuries: steamship, railroad, bicycle, automobile, aviation"; "Communication through tourism: the history of organized travel in the 19th and 20th centuries"; "Markets, exchanges, fairs, exhibits, and conferences in the 19th and 20th centuries"; "The role of 19th- and 20th-century educational institutions in communication"; "The significance of the old and new media for economy and society."

The list also suggests that it is quite impossible in a brief review to summarize and evaluate these wide-ranging forays into social and economic history. Nevertheless, a few general observations are appropriate.

First and foremost, I find it easy to skip the usual cautionary reference to "the obvious unevenness in the quality of papers." Without exception, the authors deserve high marks for having written scholarly, interesting, and informative treatments of their subjects. One approaches with some skepticism a paper that purports to cover the impact of all modern means of transportation in the space of 37 pages, but even this *tour de force* by W. Treue (Göttingen) comes off as a fine summary of some important German developments.

Second, I was impressed again and again by the authors' thoroughness in the exploration of sources and by their diligence in weaving together often disparate bits and pieces of evidence into coherent stories. Anyone interested in the evolution of social institutions, in the history of technology, or indeed in delightful historical trivia, will find this volume a veritable gold mine. Although my own work could not be further removed, chronologically and topically, from the Middle Ages, the papers dealing with that era provided me with a host of clues, insights, and relevant bits of evidence. I am thinking here, for example, of a recurrent theme—the tension between the communicative potentials of new institutions and new technologies on the one hand, and the jealous guarding of intellectual property by parties of interest, on the other.

And third, virtually all of the papers place their sometimes quite specialized subjects into a wider context of salient historical trends, thus providing even the nonspecialist with a useful frame of reference. Even when it does so only implicitly, every one of the contributions serves as an illustration for the complementarity of theory and history.

How much modern economists could learn from these accounts, if only they had the time and inclination to interest themselves in the past!

Having heaped such unequivocal praise on the volume, I cannot conclude without expressing puzzlement over some major omissions in a collection intended to cover communication in the broadest possible sense of the term. In only one paper is there scant mention of radio and television. Even more surprising is the complete absence of a treatment of film, a medium to whose technical and artistic development Germany has made such significant contributions.

These remarks are not meant as an unfair criticism of what the book is not about. Rather, they suggest that what is in any event a superb display of German historical scholarship might have gained in appeal from the inclusion of subjects very much in the forefront of attention elsewhere.

GERHARD ROSEGGER, *Case Western Reserve University*

Economic Development, the Family, and Income Distribution: Selected Essays. By Simon Kuznets. New York: Cambridge University Press, 1989. Pp. viii, 463. $54.50.

This selection of essays by Nobel laureate Simon Kuznets (1901–1985) was published posthumously through the cooperation of his widow, Edith Kuznets, with Moses Abramowitz, Richard Easterlin, and Robert Fogel (the latter two being students of Kuznets). While the essays represent more recent work by Kuznets, they do cover a number of the topics that motivated his enormously productive lifetime of research (exemplified by his output of over twenty books and several hundred articles). Familiar issues reappear—concern with measurement, structural change during economic development, economic-demographic interactions, and the sources of modern economic growth. A major theme of this volume (and of 7 of the 11 essays) is the interaction of population growth and structure with income distribution and inequality.

The book opens with a brief preface by Louis Galambos and Robert Gallman, providing some background on the book and a few comments on the life of Simon Kuznets. This is followed by a short, informative preface by Richard Easterlin, which gives an overview of the topics of the essays as well as some observations on the Kuznets tradition in economics today.

> Kuznets's approach to research, with its strong empirical emphasis, may be contrasted with that dominant in economics today. Currently the focus is wholly on hypothesis testing—statement of a formal model rooted in economic theory followed by empirical testing using the latest econometric methods. Could a doctoral student today present for a dissertation topic a purely measurement thesis? Consider a topic at the heart of chapter 11 and the focus of a lively debate currently in the United States—the economic welfare of children. Would a dissertation devoted purely to establishing the facts on this question be acceptable in a graduate economics program? One suspects not. . . . But where would economic science be today if Kuznets and all those he influenced had been discouraged from the pursuit of quantitative facts? (pp. 5–6).

In a similar vein, a concluding essay titled "Afterword: Some Notes on the Scientific Methods of Simon Kuznets," by Robert Fogel, provides another assessment:

> Kuznets was impatient with economists who became infatuated with elegance and forgot that the aim of theory was to promote the search for tested knowledge about economic behavior. There was a limit to how far theory in economics could become separated from the product which the patrons of economics—the policymakers—demand of the discipline . . . . One may quarrel about the proper way to measure the payoff to pure theory, but as a practical matter the resources available for such work are heavily dependent upon the volume and quality of that part of the output of scientific disciplines whose social usefulness is readily apparent to policymakers. It is not the pure theorists but the experimentalists and empiricists whose output is directly keyed to societal demands that have been most effective in convincing policymakers to support those seemingly

dainty and irrelevant exercises (the pure theory) that they neither understand nor are inclined to support (pp. 433–34).

The body of the book consists of 11 essays. The first 4 deal with topics familiar in Kuznets's work: the lessons of history for the study of economic growth (essay 1), the contributions of structural shifts in the composition of labor force and product for economic growth and inequality in both developed and less-developed countries since World War II (essays 2 and 3), and the obstacles to, and prospects for, modern economic growth in today's developing nations.

The remaining 7 essays constitute, in essence, a second part to the book. They deal with the relationship of population growth and age and family structure to inequality, a subject which occupied Kuznets later in his career. The issue of measurement is prominent. Essays 7 through 11 address the establishing of the basic facts on income inequality. Indeed, Kuznets has repeatedly reminded us of the shortcomings of our measures of inequality and the often wretched quantity and quality of the data used to describe this topic of policy concern. One essay (7) reprints a long (94-page) 1976 paper from *Economic Development and Cultural Change*, which is concerned with the general issues of the impact of family and household size and composition on measures of the size distribution of income across families, households, and individuals. To carry the comparison to individuals, some consumer equivalence scaling is suggested, as well as taking into account age of household head (or life-cycle stage). As usual, the work is heavily bolstered with statistical data, although, as essays 7 to 9 suggest, good-quality data were still not overly abundant in the 1970s. I might add that more current work in income inequality has moved in the directions that Kuznets suggested, although the inextricable relationship of demographic structure to inequality of income and resource distribution is still too often overlooked.

Although all of these papers appear to have been published elsewhere, this volume is a most convenient collection. It complements several previous anthologies of his essays and is a must for libraries and for serious students of economic development, inequality, and the demographic aspects of modern economic growth. The 20-page bibliography of Kuznets's works is alone worth the price. We all mourn the passing of one of the great figures of economics, demography, economic history, and economic development. This volume is a fitting memorial.

MICHAEL R. HAINES, *Colgate University*

Announcing

AMERICAN NATIONAL BIOGRAPHY

To be published under the auspices of the AMERICAN COUNCIL OF LEARNED SOCIETIES

ANB

This new biographical dictionary, which will contain sketches of approximately 20,000 persons, will be published in twenty volumes by Oxford University Press.

It will cover the entire sweep of American history from the first explorations to the present, and include persons prominent in every field of human activity.

Already under consideration for inclusion are all persons in the *Dictionary of American Biography, Notable American Women*, and other important collections. But the editors are eager to locate significant people whose careers have not been described in these reference works. Readers of this journal who have come across such persons in the course of their research are urged to nominate them by writing to:

John A. Garraty, General Editor
American National Biography
Center for the Social Sciences
Columbia University
New York, NY 10027

Please include a brief explanation of why each nominee merits inclusion.

*

The editors are also eager to locate scholars who would be interested in writing biographies for *American National Biography*. Such persons should write to Mark C. Carnes, Managing Editor, at the above address, indicating their fields of special competence. In particular the editors are hoping to locate scholars who would be willing to prepare sketches of persons in fields where there are relatively few academic experts.

1940–1990
Fifty Years of Scholarship

The JOURNAL of ECONOMIC HISTORY

VOLUME L DECEMBER 1990 NUMBER 4

PUBLISHED FOR
THE ECONOMIC HISTORY ASSOCIATION
IN COOPERATION WITH
THE UNIVERSITY OF KANSAS

REDISH
The Evolution of the Gold Standard in England

BRANDT AND SANDS
Inequality in Early Twentieth-Century Rural China

LA CROIX AND ROUMASSET
The Evolution of Private Property in Nineteenth-Century Hawaii

CARLOS AND NICHOLAS
Agency Problems in Early Chartered Companies

GREASLEY
British Coal-mining Productivity before 1939

HEIM
British New Town Building in the 1950s

NOTES AND DISCUSSION: GARRETT, OVERTON, O'BRIEN, MAYER AND CHATTERJI

CAMBRIDGE UNIVERSITY PRESS

THE JOURNAL OF ECONOMIC HISTORY

ISSN 0022-0507

Published for the Economic History Association in cooperation with The University of Kansas by Cambridge University Press

Aims and Scope: *The Journal of Economic History* seeks to promote the scholarly study of economic aspects of t human past from a diversity of perspectives, notably those of economists and historians. By encouraging caref formulation of issues and clear exposition of methods, the JOURNAL hopes to stimulate discourse among scholars wi varied interests and modes of inquiry.

The JOURNAL is abstracted in *The Journal of Economic Literature*, which is part of the DIALOG on-line data servic

Instructions for Contributors: Articles on economic history and related aspects of history or economics will considered for publication by the Editors on the understanding that the articles have not previously been published a are not under consideration elsewhere. Papers should indicate the wider significance of detailed original resear findings as well as the logic and limitations of specialized techniques of analysis. Comments and shorter notes are al welcome. The JOURNAL does not accept unsolicited book reviews, nor can it honor requests to review particular work Contributions should be typed double-spaced. Footnotes, also double-spaced, should be grouped at the end of t paper, along with figures and tables. Four copies of each manuscript should be submitted. Prospective contributors m obtain a copy of the Style Sheet for the JOURNAL from the Editorial Office. A submission fee of $20.00 or a yea membership (fee schedule below) is required from nonmembers of the Association.

Editorial Office Address: The Editors, *The Journal of Economic History*, 211 Watkins Home, Hall Center for t Humanities, University of Kansas, Lawrence, KS 66045, U.S.A. Telephone: (913) 864-4798.

Association Office Address and Membership Information: Individuals who are members of the Economic Histc Association receive the JOURNAL as part of their annual dues. Membership rates (in U.S. dollars) are: $30.00 for the with income above $30,000 a year; $25.00 for those with income below $30,000; $15.00 for students and professo emeriti who have been members of the Association for 10 years; $600.00 for life membership. Payment of an *additio* $20.00 permits joint membership with the Economic History Society (UK). Applications and inquiries concerni membership should be addressed to the Economic History Association, Dept. of History, George Washingt University, Washington, DC 20052, U.S.A.

Subscription, Publishing and Advertising Office Address: Cambridge University Press, 40 West 20th Street, New Yo NY 10011, U.S.A.; or Cambridge University Press, The Edinburgh Building, Shaftesbury Road, Cambridge CB2 2R England.

Subscription Information: *The Journal of Economic History* is published quarterly in March, June, September, a December. Annual institutional subscription rate (1990) US $50.00 in the United States and Canada; UK £31 elsewhere. Individuals may subscribe by becoming a member of the Economic History Association (see above). Pri include surface postage and insurance.

The Journal of Economic History (USPS 279-580) is published quarterly by Cambridge University Press. Second-class postage pai New York, NY and additional mailing offices. Postmaster: Send address changes to *The Journal of Economic History*, Cambr University Press, 110 Midland Avenue, Port Chester, NY 10573.

Printed in the United States of America.

THE JOURNAL
OF ECONOMIC HISTORY

Volume L December 1990 Number 4

ARTICLES

ANGELA REDISH
The Evolution of the Gold Standard in England 789

LOREN BRANDT AND BARBARA SANDS
Beyond Malthus and Ricardo: Economic Growth, Land Concentration, and Income Distribution in Early Twentieth-Century Rural China 807

SUMNER J. LA CROIX AND JAMES ROUMASSET
The Evolution of Private Property in Nineteenth-Century Hawaii 829

ANN M. CARLOS AND STEPHEN NICHOLAS
Agency Problems in Early Chartered Companies: The Case of the Hudson's Bay Company 853

DAVID GREASLEY
Fifty Years of Coal-mining Productivity: The Record of the British Coal Industry before 1939 877

CAROL E. HEIM
The Treasury As Developer-Capitalist? British New Town Building in the 1950s 903

NOTES AND DISCUSSION

MARTIN A. GARRETT, JR.
The Mule in Southern Agriculture: A Requiem 925

MARK OVERTON
Re-estimating Crop Yields from Probate Inventories: A Comment 931

ANTHONY PATRICK O'BRIEN
Were Businessmen Afraid of FDR? A Comment on Mayer and Chatterji 936

THOMAS MAYER AND MONOJIT CHATTERJI
Reply to O'Brien 942

EDITORS' NOTES 945

REVIEWS OF BOOKS

MEDIEVAL AND EARLY MODERN

HERLIHY. *Opera Muliebria: Women and Work in Medieval Europe* — K. Biddick 948
CIPOLLA. *Money in Sixteenth-Century Florence* — L. Martines 950
CIPOLLA. *Le tre rivoluzioni e altri saggi di storia economica e sociale* — L. Martines 950
VANNINI MARX, Ed. *Trasporti e sviluppo economico: Secoli XIII–XVIII* — T. W. Blomquist 951

MODERN EUROPE

ZANINELLI, Ed. *Da un sistema agricolo a un sistema industriale: Il comasco dal settecento al novecento*. Vol. II: *La lunga trasformazione tra due crisi (1814–1880)* — A. I. Grab 953
LEPETIT. *Les villes dans la France moderne: 1740–1840* — L. H. Lees 954
BAMFORD. *Privilege and Profit: A Business Family in Eighteenth-Century France* — T. J. A. Le Goff 956
ZILCH. *Die Reichsbank und die finanzielle Kriegsvorbereitung 1907 bis 1914* — G. D. Feldman 957
OFFER. *The First World War: An Agrarian Interpretation* — R. M. McInnis 959
CAIRNCROSS, Ed. *The Robert Hall Diaries, 1947–53* — S. Howson 960
HARVEY AND TURNER, Eds. *Labour and Business in Modern Britain* — J. Schneer 961
CHIROT, Ed. *The Origins of Backwardness in Eastern Europe* — D. F. Good 962

ASIA, AFRICA, AND AUSTRALIA

BROEZE, Ed. *Brides of the Sea: Port Cities of Asia from the 16th–20th Centuries* — L. C. Johnson 963
LINDBLAD. *Between Dayak and the Dutch: The Economic History of Southeast Kalimantan* — M. M. Khan 964
RAWSKI. *Economic Growth in Prewar China* — B. Sands 966
GREGORY AND BUTLIN, Eds. *Recovery from the Depression: Australia and the World Economy in the 1930s* — M. A. Bernstein 969

LATIN AMERICA

SLICHER VAN BATH. *Real hacienda y economía en Hispanoamérica, 1541–1820* — P. Gootenberg 971
JOHNSON AND TANDETER, Eds. *Essays on the Price History of Eighteenth-Century Latin America* — R. J. Salvucci 972
WOOD AND CARVALHO. *The Demography of Inequality in Brazil* — E.-S. Pang 973

UNITED STATES AND CANADA

WILLIAMS. *Americans and Their Forests: A Historical Geography* — A. F. McEvoy 975
GALLAY. *The Formation of a Planter Elite: Jonathan Bryan and the Southern Colonial Frontier* — L. S. Walsh 976

MATSON AND ONUF. *A Union of Interests: Political and Economic Thought in Revolutionary America*	J. N. Rakove	978
THORNTON. *Cultivating Gentlemen: The Meaning of Country Life among the Boston Elite, 1785–1860*	G. J. Kornblith	979
PALLADINO. *Another Civil War: Labor, Capital, and the State in the Anthracite Regions of Pennsylvania, 1840–68*	P. S. Paludan	980
RANSOM. *Conflict and Compromise: The Political Economy of Slavery, Emancipation, and the American Civil War*	J. M. McPherson	982
MILLER. *Soldiers and Settlers: Military Supply in the Southwest, 1861–1885*	P. N. Limerick	984
GARVEY AND GARVEY. *Economic Law and Economic Growth: Antitrust, Regulation, and the American Growth System*	M. R. Burns	985
BEAN, MINEAU, AND ANDERTON. *Fertility Change on the American Frontier: Adaptation and Innovation*	L. A. Craig	987
EMMONS. *The Butte Irish: Class and Ethnicity in an American Mining Town, 1875–1925*	G. R. Mormino	988
MORGAN. *Eisenhower Versus 'The Spenders': The Eisenhower Administration, the Democrats and the Budget, 1953–60*	A. M. May	989
MEYER. *Evolution of United States Budgeting: Changing Fiscal and Financial Concepts*	W. E. Brownlee	990
STONE. *Wrong Number: The Breakup of AT&T*	G. D. Smith	991
AKENSON, Ed. *Canadian Papers in Rural History.* Volume VII	C. A. Wilson	992

ECONOMIC THOUGHT

KADISH. *Historians, Economists and Economic History*	A. W. Coats	994
COLANDER AND COATS, Eds. *The Spread of Economic Ideas*	K. J. Stirling	995

GENERAL AND MISCELLANEOUS

BORIS AND DANIELS, Eds. *Homework: Historical and Contemporary Perspectives on Paid Labor at Home*	D. S. Cobble	996
SMITH ET AL., Eds. *Racism, Sexism, and the World-System*	S. B. Carter	997

INDEX TO VOLUME L 999

CONTRIBUTORS TO VOLUME L 1009

CONTENTS OF VOLUME L

Number 1, March

ARTICLES

SUSAN B. CARTER AND ELIZABETH SAVOCA	Labor Mobility and Lengthy Jobs in Nineteenth-Century America	1
JANE HUMPHRIES	Enclosures, Common Rights, and Women: The Proletarianization of Families in the Late Eighteenth and Early Nineteenth Centuries	17
WARREN C. WHATLEY	Getting a Foot in the Door: "Learning," State Dependence, and the Racial Integration of Firms	43
NACHUM T. GROSS	Israeli Economic Policies, 1948–1951: Problems of Evaluation	67
JOSHUA L. ROSENBLOOM	One Market or Many? Labor Market Integration in the Late Nineteenth-Century United States	85
ROBERT A. BLACK AND CLAIRE G. GILMORE	Crowding Out during Britain's Industrial Revolution	109
GEORGE K. DAVIS AND GARY M. PECQUET	Interest Rates in the Civil War South	133
EDWIN S. HUNT	A New Look at the Dealings of the Bardi and Peruzzi with Edward III	149

NOTES AND DISCUSSION

MARGARET PATTERSON AND DAVID REIFFEN	The Effect of the Bubble Act on the Market for Joint Stock Shares	163

REVIEW ARTICLE

JOEL MOKYR AND JOHN V. C. NYE	La Grande Quantification	172

EDITORS' NOTES 177

REVIEWS OF BOOKS 182

Number 2, June

Papers Presented at the Forty-Ninth Annual Meeting of the Economic History Association

ROBERT B. BARSKY AND J. BRADFORD DE LONG	Bull and Bear Markets in the Twentieth Century	265
CHARLES W. CALOMIRIS	Is Deposit Insurance Necessary? A Historical Perspective	283
PETER TEMIN	Socialism and Wages in the Recovery from the Great Depression in the United States and Germany	297
WILLIAM A. SUNDSTROM	Was There a Golden Age of Flexible Wages? Evidence from Ohio Manufacturing, 1892–1910	309
JEFFREY A. MIRON AND CHRISTINA D. ROMER	A New Monthly Index of Industrial Production, 1884–1940	321
RUTH DUPRÉ	Regulating the Quebec Dairy Industry, 1905–1921: Peeling Off the Joseph Label	339
RICHARD J. SULLIVAN	The Revolution of Ideas: Widespread Patenting and Invention During the English Industrial Revolution	349
KENNETH L. SOKOLOFF AND B. ZORINA KHAN	The Democratization of Invention During Early Industrialization: Evidence from the United States, 1790–1846	363
MARTHA ELLEN SHIELLS	Collective Choice of Working Conditions: Hours in British and U.S. Iron and Steel, 1890–1923	379
ROBERT WHAPLES	Winning the Eight-Hour Day, 1909–1919	393
MICHAEL A. BERNSTEIN	American Economic Expertise from the Great War to the Cold War: Some Initial Observations	407
ANN MARI MAY	President Eisenhower, Economic Policy, and the 1960 Presidential Election	417

NOTES AND DISCUSSION

DAVID MITCH — The Role of the Textbook in Undergraduate Economic History Courses: Indispensable Tool or Superficial Convenience? 428

DOCTORAL CANDIDATES — Summaries of Doctoral Dissertations of Lee A. Craig, Adrienne D. Hood, Daniel Barbezat, Jean-Laurent Rosenthal, Joshua L. Rosenbloom, and Susan Wolcott 432

Discussion by Philip T. Hoffman and Roger L. Ransom 444

EDITORS' NOTES 450

REVIEWS OF BOOKS 455

Number 3, September

ARTICLES

DAVID ELTIS — Welfare Trends among the Yoruba in the Early Nineteenth Century: The Anthropometric Evidence 521

ROBIN COWAN — Nuclear Power Reactors: A Study in Technological Lock-in 541

MARK HARRISON — The Volume of Soviet Munitions Output, 1937–1945: A Reevaluation 569

JOHN C. BROWN — The Condition of England and the Standard of Living: Cotton Textiles in the Northwest, 1806–1850 591

JEAN-LAURENT ROSENTHAL — The Development of Irrigation in Provence, 1700–1860: The French Revolution and Economic Growth 615

STEVEN J. NOVAK — The Real Takeover of the BIA: The Preferential Hiring of Indians 639

NOTES AND DISCUSSION

M. K. THORNTON AND R. L. THORNTON — The Financial Crisis of A.D. 33: A Keynesian Depression? .. 655

METIN M. COSGEL — Scattering and Contracts in Medieval Agriculture: Challenges Ahead 663

BRUCE W. HETHERINGTON — Bank Entry and the Low Issue of National Bank Notes: A Re-examination 669

JOSÉ MANUEL CAMPA — Exchange Rates and Economic Recovery in the 1930s: An Extension to Latin America 677

MICHAEL HUBERMAN — Vertical Disintegration in Lancashire: A Comment on Temin 683

PETER TEMIN — Product Quality and Vertical Integration in the Early Cotton Textile Industry: A Reply 691

BRUCE G. CARRUTHERS — Politics, Popery, and Property: A Comment on North and Weingast 693

REVIEW ARTICLE

ALLAN G. BOGUE — Fogel's Journey through the Slave States 699

EDITORS' NOTES 711

REVIEWS OF BOOKS 713

Number 4, December

ARTICLES

ANGELA REDISH — The Evolution of the Gold Standard in England 789

LOREN BRANDT AND BARBARA SANDS — Beyond Malthus and Ricardo: Economic Growth, Land Concentration, and Income Distribution in Early Twentieth-Century Rural China 807

SUMNER J. LA CROIX AND JAMES ROUMASSET — The Evolution of Private Property in Nineteenth-Century Hawaii 829

ANN M. CARLOS AND STEPHEN NICHOLAS — Agency Problems in Early Chartered Companies: The Case of the Hudson's Bay Company 853

DAVID GREASLEY — Fifty Years of Coal-mining Productivity: The Record of the British Coal Industry before 1939 877

CAROL E. HEIM — The Treasury As Developer-Capitalist? British New Town Building in the 1950s 903

NOTES AND DISCUSSION

MARTIN A. GARRETT, JR. — The Mule in Southern Agriculture: A Requiem 925

MARK OVERTON — Re-estimating Crop Yields from Probate Inventories: A Comment 931

ANTHONY PATRICK O'BRIEN — Were Businessmen Afraid of FDR? A Comment on Mayer and Chatterji 936

THOMAS MAYER AND MONOJIT CHATTERJI — Reply to O'Brien 942

EDITORS' NOTES 945

REVIEWS OF BOOKS 948

THE JOURNAL OF ECONOMIC HISTORY

VOLUME L DECEMBER 1990 NUMBER 4

The Evolution of the Gold Standard in England

ANGELA REDISH

In 1816 England officially abandoned bimetallism and made silver coins into tokens that were only limited legal tender. Earlier monetary authorities had lacked the ability to manage a subsidiary coinage, a necessary complement to the monometallic gold standard. A successful token coinage must be both costly to counterfeit and credibly backed to ensure that the tokens do not depreciate to their intrinsic value. These problems were solved in the nineteenth century through the introduction of steam-driven stamping presses and with the assistance of the Bank of England.

In 1816 England ended its official policy of bimetallism and adopted a single gold standard with a gold coinage complemented by a token silver coinage. This monetary system was so successful that it has become the benchmark against which monetary regimes are measured. Yet despite extensive analysis of the gold standard, few economists or economic historians have questioned why this apparently ideal system took so long to emerge. In this article I argue that the critical characteristics of the nineteenth-century gold standard were that it enabled coins of a variety of denominations, in convenient sizes, to circulate at par and that the relative values of coins were expected to remain fixed. I argue that these characteristics could not both be achieved by a single-commodity money; therefore, the gold standard's success depended on the concurrent circulation of the token silver coinage. Finally, I argue that it was not feasible to establish a stable token coinage prior to the nineteenth century.

The historical literature has typically explained the emergence of the gold standard as a matter of happenstance: the legislation of 1816 merely ratified the de facto gold standard that had existed in England since

The Journal of Economic History, Vol. L, No. 4 (Dec. 1990). ISSN 0022-0507.

The author is Associate Professor of Economics at the University of British Columbia, Vancouver, BC, Canada, V6T 1W5.

I would like to thank the Archives of the Bank of England for permission to use their materials, and Bob Allen, Michael Bordo, Ardo Hansson, Knick Harley, Jeremy Rudin, Ron Shearer, the editor and anonymous referees of this JOURNAL, and participants at the NBER Mini-Conference on Macroeconomic History (June 1989) for useful comments. Financial support from the Social Sciences and Humanities Research Council of Canada is gratefully acknowledged.

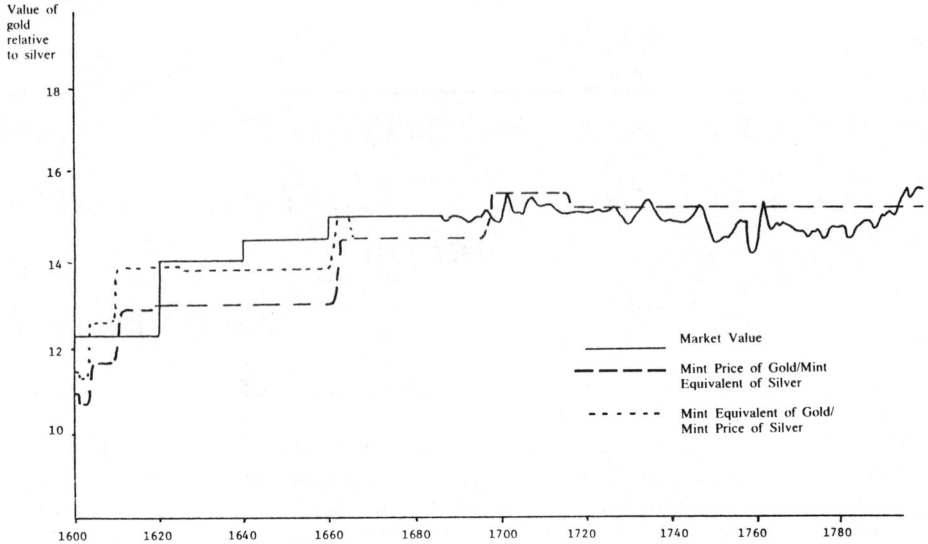

FIGURE 1

ENGLAND'S VALUATION OF GOLD, 1600–1800

Sources: Mint prices, mint equivalents: A. Feavearyear, *The Pound Sterling* (Oxford, 1963); Market value: J. Laurence Laughlin, *The History of Bimetallism in the United States* (New York, 1885).

Newton's "inadvertent" overvaluation of gold at the beginning of the eighteenth century.[1] This analysis is incomplete for several reasons. First, it ignores earlier monetary history. In the early seventeenth century England had overvalued gold, and silver coin had been driven from circulation (see Figure 1), yet England did not adopt a gold standard. Second, there is no explanation of why the decision to ratify did not occur until 100 years after the overvaluation of gold. Finally, the legislation did not merely ratify the existing monetary system. Under the de facto eighteenth-century gold standard, high-denomination gold coins circulated, but virtually no small-denomination coins were in circulation.[2] The significance of the 1816 legislation is that it introduced token coins that provided a small-denomination medium of exchange. It is the gold standard of the nineteenth century, under which coins of high

[1] Richard N. Cooper, *The International Monetary System* (Cambridge, MA, 1987), pp. 44–45. Similarly, Feavearyear argued that "England did not establish the gold standard by any conscious and deliberate act, and it is doubtful whether anyone foresaw that it would establish itself"; Sir A. Feavearyear, *The Pound Sterling* (Oxford, 1963), p. 142. See also Charles P. Kindleberger, *A Financial History of Western Europe* (London, 1982), p. 59.

[2] It is not clear what people used in the absence of small-denomination coins. Various authorities discuss the manufacture of lightweight counterfeits of farthings and halfpennies (for example, see Peter Seaby, *The Story of British Coinage* [London, 1985]), and presumably there was some demonetization of this part of the economy. For a discussion of these issues, see Angela Redish, "The Monetary Economy of the Labouring Poor in England, 1500–1800" (Ms., University of British Columbia, 1990).

and low denomination circulated concurrently, that is held up as a benchmark, not the monetary chaos of the eighteenth century.

Frank Fetter and Derek Gregory have previously noted that the decision to adopt the gold standard was made "largely on the basis of details of small coin convenience, and not on larger issues of economic policy."[3] But they preface this conclusion with the comment that "It is amazing that a decision of such importance for England, and by England's example for the entire world, should have been made without benefit of full analysis."[4] I maintain that the basis for the decision is not at all amazing: it was the problem of small-coin convenience that had prevented England from adopting a monometallic standard centuries earlier.

A gold standard with token silver coinage would provide a more convenient and therefore less costly medium of exchange than a bimetallic standard. Technological difficulties (the threat of counterfeiting) and institutional immaturity (no guarantor of convertibility), however, made management of such a coinage impossible prior to the nineteenth century. At the turn of the century improvements in minting technology and the Mint's acceptance of its role in maintaining the value of the tokens led to the success of the token coinage.

I. THE MECHANICS OF BIMETALLISM

Under a bimetallic standard, coins of two metals are given legal tender values in the unit of account. For example, in England in 1615 the silver sixpence and the gold unite were legal tender. The sixpence was $^{11}/_{12}$ pure (or fine) silver, weighed 46.8 (Troy) grains, and was valued at six pence. (The unit of account was the pound sterling, comprising twenty shillings [20/-], each of twelve pence [12d].) The unite was made of 22-carat gold, weighed 140.8 grains, and was valued at 20 shillings. Coinage was free in the sense that anyone could bring metal to the Mint for coining—at a price.[5] The Mint bought fine gold at 72/- per Troy ounce (of 480 grains) and fine silver at 64.91d per Troy ounce. The ounce of fine silver was coined into 11.19 sixpenny pieces worth 67.13d (called the mint equivalent [ME] of silver), and therefore there was a residual of 2.22d per ounce to cover Mint expenses and the king's seignorage. Similarly, the ounce of gold that the Mint bought for 72/- was coined into 3.72 unites worth 74.4/- (the ME of gold).[6]

[3] Frank W. Fetter and Derek Gregory, *Monetary and Financial Policy* (Dublin, 1973), p. 16.

[4] This is a view more recently espoused by M. Friedman, "Bimetallism Revisited," *Journal of Economic Perspectives* (forthcoming).

[5] Free coinage refers to the Mint being required to buy metal from all sellers, not to gratuitous minting. See further.

[6] The quantity of gold and silver coin in circulation was determined by market forces. The Mint should be thought of as an agency that for a fee stamped out coins from metal brought to it. The exchange rate was determined by the numeraire values attached to silver and gold coins by

The objective of adopting a bimetallic standard was to permit concurrent circulation of gold and silver coins at par, thus providing an efficient medium of exchange. Consider the alternatives. If only gold coins were minted, the coins for small retail transactions would be tiny: in 1615 the smallest gold coin—the half crown—weighed 1.14 grams, had a diameter of 16 millimeters, and was valued at 2/6. (Today's Canadian dimes weigh approximately 2.3 grams.) A smaller gold coin would have been very inconvenient, yet 2/6 represented four days' wages for a laborer.[7] On the other hand, if only silver coins were minted, they would be very cumbersome for mercantile trade. Silver coins would have weighed thirteen times the same value in gold coin.

A third possibility would be a silver standard in which silver coins were complemented by gold coins with gold coins not given a legal tender value. (If it wished to, the Mint could continue to charge its minting fees.) This would effectively demonetize the gold coin. While demand might exist for such coins, to obviate the costs of using large amounts of silver coins for high-value transactions, it would be less than if gold and silver coins were both given legal tender values because agents would bear information costs in determining (or bargaining over) the value of their coins as well as their merchandise. In addition there would be risks of capital gains and losses to which those who received payments in one metal and made payments in the other would be particularly vulnerable.[8]

The objective of concurrent circulation imposed constraints on the choice of Mint prices (MP) and Mint equivalents of the two metals, and only one of the four variables was a free parameter that the monetary authority could set arbitrarily. To be more precise, define as correct a setting of mint prices and mint equivalents such that agents with foreign debts are indifferent between exporting gold and silver. Those who are owed debts, it follows, are also indifferent between importing gold and

individual nations. Such terms as "guaranteeing convertibility" or "maintaining the exchange rate" have no meaning in this context.

[7] Henry Phelps Brown and Sheila V. Hopkins, *A Perspective of Wages and Prices* (London, 1981), p. 11. The attempt to introduce a quarter-guinea coin weighing 2.09 gms failed in 1718: "A piece so tiny, and so readily lost, was entirely unacceptable to the British public." J. Craig, *The Mint* (Cambridge, 1953), p. 21. Notwithstanding this small size, essayists in the mid-eighteenth century recommended minting such a coin to reduce the scarcity of small change (*Gentlemans' Magazine*, 1761, p. 615); see also J. Waugh, "Reflections on Coins in General" (London, 1762), reprinted in *A Select Collection of Scarce and Valuable Tracts on Money* (New York, 1966). The quarter guinea (worth 5/3) weighed less in 1718 than the 1616 crown (worth 5/-), because the price of gold rose by 16 percent between 1661 and 1717.

[8] Although such a system was occasionally considered, notably in France in 1803, it was never officially implemented because of these costs. The costs of varying rates of exchange between two coins are very similar to those imposed today by the multiplicity of national monetary units. Under flexible exchange rates, agents who wish to use a foreign currency must bear both the costs of finding out the exchange rate and the risks of depreciation or appreciation. Of course today, forward markets reduce the latter costs.

silver. Thus, if there is initially concurrent circulation of gold and silver coins, both will remain in circulation.

Now consider a small open economy in which the monetary authorities establish a fixed mint equivalent of gold ($\overline{MEg}$). Assume that there is a large world bullion market in which the relative price of gold to silver is R.[9] Further, ignore for the moment all transactions costs other than domestic minting fees (seignorage and brassage), denoted by s_i, where i equals silver or gold. In the event of a balance-of-payments deficit a domestic (goods) importer will have to make payments by shipping either gold or silver. By definition of R, if the foreign debt requires payment of X ounces of gold, it could be paid with R times X ounces of silver. Payment in gold would require melting down coins worth X times $\overline{MEg}$, while payment in silver would require melting down coins worth R times X times MEs. The domestic importer will do whichever is less costly and will be indifferent between the two options if

$$MEs = (1/R)\ \overline{MEg} \tag{1}$$

A balance-of-payments surplus implies that a foreigner must ship gold or silver to England. If the foreigner's debt is £X, the foreigner can ship (X/MPg) ounces of gold or (X/MPs) ounces of silver. For the foreigner, one ounce of gold is worth R ounces of silver, and the foreigner will be indifferent between shipping gold and silver if ($R \cdot X/MPg$) equals (X/MPs), or

$$MPs = (1/R)\ MPg \tag{2}$$

The final constraint on the actions of the monetary authorities is the threat of counterfeiting. Assume that counterfeiting is costly but feasible, and let c_i, where i equals silver or gold, represent the costs of producing counterfeit coins from one ounce of metal i. Counterfeiting is profitable whenever

$$MPi + c_i < MEi \tag{3}$$

so that the amount of minting fees (s_i) must be less than or equal to c_i.[10] As MEi equals MPi plus s_i, if equation 3 is binding, equation 1 to equation 3 establishes MPg, MEs, and MPs in terms of the exogenous variables $\overline{MEg}$, R, S_s, S_g, C_s, and C_g.

[9] This simplifying assumption obviates the need for dealing explicitly with mint prices and mint equivalents in other countries and implicitly assumes that the foreign buying and selling prices of gold and silver are the same.

[10] The condition for profitable counterfeiting is more accurately stated as $Pi + c_i < MEi$ (where Pi is the market price of the metal), but when ratings are correct, Pi equals MPi. When ratings are incorrect, for the relatively overvalued metal MP equals P, so that this condition constrains seignorage on the overvalued metal. Other factors affected the level of minting fees, particularly competition between national mints. From 1666 to 1816 such fees were zero for both gold and silver coins in England.

If transactions costs are incorporated, the conditions are slightly more complex. Let d_i, where i equals silver or gold, represent transactions costs (in domestic unit of account per ounce) of exporting or importing gold and silver, respectively. These costs include transportation, insurance, interest on metal at the Mint waiting to be coined, commissions, and so forth. Traders in this environment will be indifferent between shipping gold and silver if

$$R = (\overline{MEg} + d_g)/(MEs + d_s) = (MPg - d_g)/(MPs - d_s) \tag{4}$$

Given values of R greater than 1, if d_s equals d_g, the rate of seignorage on silver (per £) must be lower than the seignorage on gold to offset the high transportation cost (per £).

If the monetary authorities chose the mint equivalents and mint prices correctly, and if there were initially concurrent circulation of gold and silver, then continued concurrent circulation was ensured. The impact of incorrect ratings depended on the margin of error. If the ratings were slightly (as defined below) wrong, there would be a tendency for the currency to degenerate toward monometallism. For example, if gold were undervalued (that is, $R > [\overline{MEg}/MEs]$) it would be exported in years of balance-of-payments surplus, while silver would be imported in years of balance-of-payments deficits. The progression toward monometallism would typically take a number of years, as the size of balance-of-payments deficits and surpluses was small relative to the money stock.

If, on the other hand, coin ratings were more than slightly incorrect, bilateral arbitrage—the export of one metal to import the other—would be profitable and the currency would very quickly degenerate into monometallism. Again, temporarily ignore transactions costs other than domestic minting fees. It would be profitable to export one ounce of gold to import R ounces of silver (for sale to the Mint) if R times the mint price of silver exceeded the mint equivalent of gold ($\overline{MEg} < R \cdot MPs$). Similarly, the export of silver for gold would be profitable if the mint price of gold divided by R exceeded the mint equivalent of silver ($MEs < (1/R) \cdot MPg$). Using the relationship MEi equals MPi plus s_i, bilateral arbitrage would be profitable if

$$MEs < (\overline{MEg}/R) - (s_g/R)$$

or

$$MEs > (\overline{MEg}/R) + s_s \tag{5}$$

Again, allowing for transactions costs makes the condition more complex. Arbitrageurs would export gold if $\overline{MEg}$ plus d_g plus R times d_s were less than R times MPs, and would export silver if MEs times R plus

d_s times R plus d_g were less than MPg. Thus, bimetallic arbitrage would be profitable if

$$MEs < (\overline{MEg} - s_g - d_g)/R - d_s$$

or

$$MEs > (\overline{MEg} + d_g)/R + s_s + d_s \qquad (6)$$

That is, if the mint equivalent of silver were low enough to cover the seignorage and transaction costs, it would pay to export silver coins and import gold for sale to the Mint. Alternatively, if the mint equivalent of silver were sufficiently high, it would be profitable to export gold and import silver. Transactions costs expand the range within which an incorrect rating would not lead to bimetallic arbitrage.

Figure 1 shows the available annual data on the relative price of gold and silver from 1687 to 1800. Even if the ratings were correctly set at one point in time, the fluctuations in R would require changing the mint equivalents and mint prices if the ratings were to remain correct: that is, if R rose (fell), either the mint equivalent of gold must rise (fall) or the mint equivalent of silver must fall (rise). The monetary authority could raise the mint equivalent of gold by raising the legal tender value of each gold coin ("calling up" the coin) or by reminting the gold coins and making coins of the old value with a lower gold content. Coin values were frequently chosen to be aliquot (dividing evenly without a remainder) parts of the unit of account, and calling up coins might yield coins of nonaliquot or awkward values. (For example, calling up a penny by 5 percent would yield a coin worth 1.05d.) This was particularly problematic for the lower-denomination coins. On the other hand, reminting coins involved real resource costs, and to encourage coin holders to sell their old coins to the Mint the mint price would need to be raised at least to the old mint equivalent.

The mint equivalent of silver could be lowered by calling down the silver coins (and possibly losing their aliquot property) or by reminting them with a lower silver content. The political unpopularity of calling down the money and the costs of reminting meant that the adjustment was most frequently made by calling up the undervalued coin. If this were done on an annual basis to correct the coin ratings, however, the currency would have a persistent tendency to depreciate—that is, for the amount of specie per unit of account to decrease. To illustrate this process, I calculate the effect of adhering to such a rule over the period from 1687 to 1800 (a period for which there are annual data on the gold-to-silver ratio). If the monetary authorities adjusted the coinage according to the rule above once a year, the gold content of the pound would have fallen by 40 percent, even though the relative market value of gold rose only 5 percent (from 14.94 to 15.68 times the value of silver).[11] In practice the depreciation would probably have been greater, as the monetary authorities would have had to adjust the coinage more frequently than once a year.

In practice the costs of keeping the coin ratings correct meant that over much of the early modern period the monetary authority did not adjust the coin ratings when they became incorrect, and the undervalued coins were driven from circulation. When silver coin was undervalued it was exported or melted and there was a scarcity of small coins. Undervalued gold coins, however, were not all melted or exported; some circulated at a premium, entailing the same information and risk costs (described above) as a silver standard with gold coins that were not legal tender.

The history of bimetallic standards shows that they rarely accomplished the objective of concurrent circulation of high- and low-denomination coins circulating at par.[12] A monometallic gold standard accompanied by a managed subsidiary coinage could, however, provide a medium of exchange with coins of a convenient size for both large and small transactions, no need for recoinage or revaluation of coins if the relative price of gold and silver changed, and coins that circulated at par rather than at some varying premium. Because neither a bimetallic standard nor a monometallic (gold or silver) standard alone could offer all these advantages, the gold standard with token silver provided a better medium of exchange.[13]

It is important to note here that the medium-of-exchange function is only one of the functions of money. Money also acts as a unit of account, and for that function other properties, such as stability of value, are important. Which properties matter most depends on the relative importance of the two functions. Before the nineteenth century the importance of coins as a medium of exchange caused economists and policy makers to emphasize the properties that characterized a useful medium of exchange. Fetter, in his study of monetary theory in the nineteenth century, notes

[11] The silver content of the pound would have fallen by 36 percent. This calculation uses Soetbeer's annual data on the relative values of gold and silver and omits the initial depreciation necessary to bring the coin ratio up to the market ratio in 1687. Soetbeer's data are reprinted in J. Laurence Laughlin, *The History of Bimetallism in the United States* (New York, 1885).

[12] Friedman argues that bimetallic standards were far more stable than is conventionally believed. His only evidence for this argument is the experience of France between 1800 and 1875. I believe he overstates that evidence and that the experience of most European countries before and during the nineteenth century (and that of the United States) suggests that bimetallism typically resulted in a de facto monometallic standard with a "scarcity" of either gold or silver coins. Friedman, "Bimetallism Revisited."

[13] A monometallic silver standard with token gold coins would have many of the same advantages. If gold coins were tokens, however, they would by definition be worth less on the international market than domestically, so agents would either bear the costs of silver for international exchange or accept the losses from using gold. A monometallic gold standard with token silver would avoid these costs.

I find practically no mention in any literature before 1797 of the idea that figured in discussions for a few years before and after the resumption of 1821, and was so prominent in the bimetallic controversy in the last quarter of the nineteenth century: that one metal would give more stable prices than would the other, or that the use of two metals as a standard would give greater price stability than would a single gold or silver standard.[14]

To understand the evolution of the gold standard, it is therefore appropriate to emphasize the superiority of the gold standard with token silver as a medium of exchange.[15]

II. THE MECHANICS OF A TOKEN CURRENCY

If a monometallic currency complemented by a token currency offers a more efficient medium of exchange than a bimetallic currency, why were bimetallic standards so common before the nineteenth century? The answer lies in the difficulty of managing a token currency that was not subject to widespread counterfeiting, was not melted down or withdrawn from circulation, and maintained its value. I will examine these problems in turn.

Under a monometallic gold standard the unit of account is defined as a fixed weight of gold. Gold is the numeraire. The market price of silver (Ps) must equal the mint equivalent of gold divided by the ratio of the market price of gold and silver: Ps equals $\overline{MEg}/R$. A token coin can be defined as one whose legal tender value exceeds the market value of its components. A silver coin is a token if MEs is greater than Ps. As noted earlier, the difference (MEs less Ps) is limited by the threat of counterfeiting. If, over the planning horizon, the price of silver is expected to lie within the range (Ps^L, Ps^H), the monetary authority must set MEs less than Ps^L plus c_s to avoid counterfeiting. If, on the other hand, the coin is to remain a token, the authorities must set MEs greater than Ps^H. (If MEs is less than Ps, the tokens will be melted down or exported.) These two conditions imply that a token coinage is possible only if the costs of counterfeiting are large relative to the expected fluctuations in the price of silver. I will argue later that technological changes in the early nineteenth century significantly increased the costs of counterfeiting, making a token coinage feasible in that century.

The remaining task facing issuers of a token currency is to ensure that the token does not depreciate. Consider the problem of an "automatic" token currency: that is, assume that the monetary authority wishes the quantity of tokens in circulation to be established by market forces rather than by government fiat. To prevent the token coins driving the gold coin out of circulation, the authority must set the mint price of

[14] Frank W. Fetter, *The Development of British Monetary Orthodoxy* (Cambridge, MA, 1965), p. 3.

[15] The corollary of course is that during the nineteenth century, as coins became dominated by notes and cheques in the stock of media of exchange, these properties became less important.

silver less than or equal to the market price. Silver will not be sold to the Mint, however, if the mint price is less than the market price. Therefore a supply of tokens requires that the Mint buy silver at exactly the market price. Because the monetary authority must change the mint price regularly to ensure the supply of tokens, this system would not be automatic but would require constant monitoring by the monetary authorities.

Typically, monetary authorities attempted to alleviate the need for the mint price to reflect the market price by introducing limited legal tender laws. A law that limited the legal tender of tokens (for example, to amounts less than 40/-) would reduce the de facto mint price of silver, because individuals bringing one ounce of silver to the Mint would get coins valued at *MPs*, but those coins could only be used for small transactions. Thus, it was hoped, a mint price above the market price of silver would not cause a flood of silver to the Mint. Rather, the amount of silver brought in would be limited to "the needs of the circulation."

Although framers of limited legal tender laws typically justified them in this way, theory suggests (and experience bears out) that such laws were likely to be less than completely effective. For example, employers could pay their wages in silver and would, if *Ps* were less than *MPs*, buy silver to have it minted for such payments. Workers would spend the coins at retail stores, however, and retailers would have difficulty spending the silver, as their purchases would tend to be amounts larger than forty shillings. They could spend the silver by selling it at a discount, which would be limited by the intrinsic value of the coin. Thus limited legal tender laws alone would not achieve the objective of par circulation of coins. Rather, they would imply that instead of undervalued coins circulating at a premium, the overvalued coins (the tokens) would circulate at a discount.

While limited legal tender laws could accompany free coinage of silver, an alternative supply strategy would be for the monetary authority to eliminate the free coinage of silver. The monetary authority would purchase silver at the market price and have it coined into tokens according to the needs of the circulation. This would prevent the overissue (and consequent depreciation) possible under free coinage with limited legal tender laws. It would require, however, that the monetary authority correctly anticipate the "needs of the circulation," a task demanding at least as much monitoring and action as maintaining the mint price of silver equal to its market price.

An alternative strategy would be for the monetary authority to guarantee the value of the coins; for example, by making them convertible into gold. This would require that the guarantee be credible and that the guarantor control the supply of coins. Such a guarantee is therefore incompatible with the free coinage of silver, with or without limited legal tender laws.

III. THE NINETEENTH-CENTURY TOKEN COINAGE

Throughout the eighteenth century the overvaluation of gold had caused a scarcity of silver coins, but the costs involved in correcting the coin ratings had forestalled a change that might have permitted the concurrent circulation of gold and silver coins.[16] In 1816 the government introduced legislation aimed at eliminating the scarcity of small change. By raising the mint equivalent of silver and leaving the mint price unchanged, the legislation made silver coins into tokens. Simultaneously their legal tender status was limited. The government had introduced tokens before (for example, the copper tokens coined by the Royal Mint after 1672), but these had been counterfeited or depreciated. The silver tokens were not widely counterfeited and circulated at par. The success of the tokens was due both to changes in minting technology that made counterfeiting more costly and to the Mint's willingness to guarantee the convertibility of the tokens.

The Technology

Before 1800 the major change in the technology of minting dated back to the 1660s.[17] At that time the old process of making coins by hammering (a blank was placed between two dies and the imprint made by a hammer blow struck on the upper die) was replaced by a more mechanized process. The blanks were struck by a fly-press, and the edges of coins were engraved (or "milled"). While there was some gain in uniformity, the major advantage of the mechanization was that the blanks were exactly centered under the die, so the coins had sharp edges and clipping of coins became more obvious and therefore less common. Culling (sorting out the heavier coins for export or melting down), however, remained a profitable operation and, because the fly-press was also used in many branches of manufacturing, many people had the tools necessary for counterfeiting.

In the 1780s the scarcity of small-denomination coin led to the creation by the Privy Council of a Select Committee of Council on Coin (SCC). This committee did little until it was reconstituted in 1798, when it decided that improvements in the stock of coin required the introduction of new minting methods. After examining European practice, the committee asked the advice of Matthew Boulton (of Boulton and Watt fame). In 1786 Boulton had established a private mint at Soho, near Birmingham, which he used primarily for coining copper tokens for private and foreign orders. The Soho mint had the unique feature of

[16] The monetary problems of the eighteenth century were induced in part by the monetary authority's decision not to charge minting fees for coining either gold or silver. As equation 6 shows, this implies that from an initially correct rating even a small change in the relative price of gold and silver could trigger bimetallic arbitrage.

[17] See Craig, *The Mint*, chap. 9.

employing steam power for the rolling mills, the cutting presses (that made the blanks), and the coining presses. Boulton extolled the advantages of his mint to the committee:

The work performed by the Steam Engine will also be perfectly uniform, But that of the Men will vary as their strength respectively does; and even the work of the same Men will not be constantly uniform as there must unavoidably be a difference between the blow of a Man coming fresh to his Work and when fatigued in several hours severe labour: the effect of which will appear in the difference of Diameter and Thickness of the pieces of Coin when examined by a correct steel gauge; whereas if a Steam Engine be used a proper proportion of Power may be measured out for the different sorts of Coin, and when duly adjusted, every blow will be uniformly the same and consequently will produce uniform effects upon the Coins.[18]

Later an independent report commissioned by the Committee supported this claim, stating that, if the coining presses were steam powered, "not only a great saving would be made in manual labour, but the Coin would be much more perfect—advantages which need not be pointed out to Your Lordships."[19] The *Encyclopedia Britannica* of 1875 listed among Boulton's achievements that he erected coining machinery "so extensive and complete that the operation was performed with equal economy and precision, and the coins could not be imitated by any single artist for their nominal value."

In addition to using a screw press with the steam engine, Boulton recommended the use of steel collars:

To make counterfeiting more difficult and at the same time facilitate the detection of false money, I advise that the pieces be made perfectly round and of the same exact diameter and thickness and to this end that they be struck in Polished Steel Collars. The highest possible Polish and Beauty ought also to be given to the Coin, such Coin being more difficult to counterfeit and more easily detected than Coin of inferior Workmanship. It has been objected that the use of steel collars exposes the Dies to break and become rough at the Edges; but this I can effectually prevent by a contrivance I have very lately invented so that I can now affirm that I can strike millions of pieces of money without breaking the edge of the Die or any way injuring it by the steel collars. And this new method being secret, the difficulty of counterfeiting will be thereby much increased.[20]

These improvements, he argued, would enable the Mint to do away with milling the edges of coins.

I recommend that instead of milling the edges should be made perfectly smooth. Milling is of no use whatever but it is in itself a defect in coining as it tends by its roughness to cause friction and waste from which a perfect piece of coin ought to be as far as possible

[18] Board of Trade, "Minutes of the Privy Council Committee on Coin," vol. 6 (henceforth BT6), 118, p. 108, 9/5/1798.

[19] Ibid., p. 166, 10/7/1798.

[20] Ibid., p. 107, 9/5/1798.

intirely free. Indented inscriptions on the Edges would be much more durable as well as Neater than milling and are subject to no inconvenience.[21]

Boulton later wrote, concerning the minting of gold coins,

I have also made more experiments relative to the Coining of Gold upon the Construction which I advised in my reply to Question Number 2 to which I beg leave to refer and am more and more convinced of the Importance and the Superiority of it over all others that have hitherto been practiced, insomuch that I am fully persuaded that all great Nations will sooner or later make their money upon that Plan and work their Presses by my new Method.[22]

In a further letter he argued that of the three popular methods for reducing the weight of coins (that is, by shaking them in a bag, filing and milling the edges, and dissolving a part from the surface in aqua regis), "it is impossible to perform either of those Operations upon Guineas of my Construction without rendering such operation visible to the Eye of the Peasant and easily detectable by the steel gauge."[23]

Boulton's advice was accepted by the committee and between 1805 and 1811 the new Royal Mint, virtually a carbon copy of the Soho mint, was erected.

Between 1798 and 1816 the SCC seemed content to address the problems of the copper coinage and the renovation of the Mint, but with the return of peace in 1816 they once again considered renewal of the silver coinage. Following the Bank of England's successful management of the silver-token coinage during the Napoleonic Wars, the committee suggested in May 1816 that "the Bank take upon itself the Coinage." But the Bank's Committee of Treasury resolved "that the Bank ought to decline taking upon itself the responsibility of the silver coinage but that they shall be much disposed, without making any change to offer their best assistance to carry so desirable a measure into effect."[24]

The SCC then reported to the House of Commons, recommending a general recoinage and reorganization of the silver currency. The committee recommended "gold coin alone to be the standard coin of the

[21] Ibid., p. 110, 9/5/1798.

[22] Ibid., p. 157, 5/7/1798.

[23] Ibid., p. 159, 10/7/1798.

[24] Bank of England, "Minutes of the Committee of the Treasury" (henceforth MCT), G8/18, p. 121, 17/5/1816. During the Napoleonic Wars, the Bank of England had attempted to alleviate the inconvenience caused by the lack of a small-denomination medium of exchange by issuing stamped dollars. The dollars were valued at 5/- until 1811 and 5/6d after 1811. After 1811 the Bank also provided tokens valued at 1/6d and 3/-. (They were not permitted to coin tokens that were aliquot parts of the official coinage.) These coins, struck by both the Royal Mint and a private mint owned by Matthew Boulton, were all overvalued (that is, the value of their silver content was less than the value at which the bank accepted them), and they were withdrawn after 1817. It is possible that the experience with token coins during the war was influential in the introduction of the token coinage in 1816. It is clear, however, that Lord Liverpool's recommendations preceded that experience and that he expected his proposals to be accepted. In Feb. 1798 Bank of England officials returned from a meeting with the SCC saying that a coining of silver at a new standard was imminent. Bank of England, "Minutes of the Court Directors" (henceforth MCD), vol. Z, G4/27, p. 351, 22/2/1798.

realm, and that the silver coins are hereafter to be considered merely as representative coins and to be a legal tender only in payment of sums not exceeding two guineas.''[25]

The Coinage Act closely followed the committee's recommendations, though it reduced the legal tender limit on silver to £2.[26] The weight of the silver coins was reduced so that 5/6d was coined from one ounce of sterling silver. The mint price remained at 5/2d per ounce of sterling silver. The old silver coin was to be brought in and exchanged for new at par. In February 1817 the government announced its readiness for the exchange to begin and allowed two weeks for individuals to bring in their old silver coin to exchange it for the new.[27]

Convertibility

The Act of 1816 creating the token silver coinage was based on Lord Liverpool's proposal to the SCC in 1798.[28] He recommended that one ounce of sterling silver be made into 66d (rather than 62d), that seignorage be charged on the coinage, and that silver coin be legal tender only for payments of up to two guineas.

If the Coinage Act had been implemented as envisioned by Lord Liverpool and the SCC, the gold standard would have been very short-lived. In 1817 the market price of silver was 5/-, and therefore the mint price of 5/2d would have induced many people to sell silver to the Mint. The limited legal tender of token silver might have limited sales somewhat, but it is likely that silver coin would have been used

[25] The Committee's recommendations are in the Mint Records, ''Privy Council on Coin Papers—Miscellaneous,'' vols. 1–54 (henceforth M1–54), 3rd head, pp. 156–59, 10/5/1816.

[26] 56 Geo. III c. 68.

[27] The exchange was fraught with difficulties. The banks, which had promised to assist, avoided the ''odium and responsibility'' (MCT, G8/18, p. 178, 6/2/1817) of allowing the exchange to take place on their premises, as it would mean throwing open their buildings to ''all Ranks of the Community'' and ''their Property would be endangered'' (M1–54; 6th head, p. 418, 21/2/1817). This attitude stands in contrast to their cooperation with the gold exchange in 1774, doubtless because gold coin was not held by ''all ranks of the community.'' A second difficulty in implementing the recoinage concerned whether or not to accept the counterfeit coin and indeed how to distinguish it from the Royal Mint coin. The Master of the Mint suggested that if a teller were uncertain a coin was good, he should call in an intelligent shopkeeper: ''such a person probably would be a better judge upon such a subject than a more scientific man'' (M1–54; 6th head, p. 351). The Master of the Mint (W. W. Pole) also recommended that tellers be given instructions to give those bringing in coin the benefit of the doubt, with the proviso that ''you will be very careful not to divulge the nature of your instructions. Were the full extent of the indulgence to be granted known it is to be feared that many attempts would be made to pass large Counterfeits in the exchange.'' Nicholas Vansittart, the Chancellor of the Exchequer, commented on these instructions that ''it is vain to expect that a secret entrusted to so many will be kept'' and suggested that giving express authority to be indulgent was ''quite unnecessary and liable to abuse'' (M1–54, 6th head, p. 373, 23/9/1816). Lord Liverpool agreed with Vansittart: ''it would be by no means expedient to give as great a latitude as Pole proposes''; the final instructions reflected these views.

[28] BT6–127, pp. 1–12, 7/2/1798. Lord Liverpool subsequently expanded these ideas and, after a four-year illness, published them. Charles Jenkinson, *A Treatise on the Coins of the Realm* (1805, reprinted in New York, 1968).

whenever possible and would have accumulated in the pockets of retailers, who would be able to dispose of it only at a discount.

At the proclamation of the Coinage Act, however, the clause allowing the public to sell silver to the Mint was reserved, as the Mint was busy preparing for the exchange; it was never subsequently promulgated. The Mint bought silver at the prevailing market price in the quantity it thought necessary and believed that by limiting the quantity of silver coin supplied it could maintain the value of the coins above the value of their silver content; that is, the supply limitation would give value to the fiat component of the currency. In 1819 the Master of the Mint explained the process in a memo to the Secret Committee of the Lords on Resumption:

> The Mint, having constant communication with the Bank and the London Bankers is enabled to afford information on the state of the silver currency to the Lords of the Treasury; and their Lordships being also in possession of other means of knowing the wants of the country, regulate the issues in such manner as they conceive will best afford the necessary accommodation throughout the Kingdom for the facility of exchange and Commerce without throwing into circulation any superabundance of silver. The silver coinage can never therefore while it is preserved upon its present footing exceed the amount which the Government, from the best information they can procure, conceive to be necessary for the accommodation of the Public.[29]

By the 1830s the Treasury had realized that supply limitation was not sufficient to maintain the value of the silver coin and that in fact it was the willingness of the Bank of England to guarantee implicitly the convertibility of the coins, at par, into gold that gave the silver coin its value. The bank did this through its willingness to accept silver in unlimited quantities at par. In 1831 Lord Althorp (then Chancellor of the Exchequer) noted that "if the Bank of England refused to receive the silver coin of the Realm in larger sums than that for which it is a legal tender the greatest confusion would be produced in the retail trade of the Metropolis."[30] Indeed, the Governor of the Bank of England reported explaining to Lord Althorp "the necessity of the Bank receiving such coin in order to prevent its being depreciated in the general currency of the Country, to which Lord Althorp assented and admitted the necessity."[31]

The conflict between the bank's behavior and profit maximization came to a head in the 1830s. By 1831 the bank's acceptance of silver coin had yielded an inventory of about £1 million in silver coin.[32] These coins could not be paid out by the bank in exchange for its notes, and the market value of the silver coins was about 10 percent less than their official value. The difference was owing to a decrease in the weight of

[29] M1–54, 6th head, pp. 594–95, 3/5/1819.

[30] Treasury Papers (henceforth T1), 3141/6277; 3/3/1831.

[31] MCT, G8/26, p. 55, 6/3/1833.

[32] MCD, Eb G4/56, p. 258, 2/1/1834.

the coin as a result of wear and tear and the difference between the mint equivalent of the coins and the market price of silver (still about 5/-). The bank wished to sell £600,000 of this silver to the Mint and, perhaps foolishly, suggested that "it should be left for the future decision of their Lordships whether any and what allowance should be made to the Bank to repay them for the loss."[33] Noting that the question of compensation required "deep consideration," the Lords of the Treasury agreed to reserve the question.

The bank sold the silver coin at its market price to the Mint; that is, silver coin they had accepted for 5/6d was sold to the Mint for less than 5/-. Two years later, when the bank wished to increase its supply of silver coin, they argued that they should not have to pay the official value (5/6d per ounce) for the coins. The bank accompanied its request with a not-so-subtle threat:

> Should Lord Althorp not deem it expedient to adopt that course or to take any other measure for discharging the debt now due to the Bank, and at the same time to relieve them from future responsibility, The Court request the Governor and Deputy Governor respectfully to represent that they must decline the general receipt of Silver further than may suit their own convenience; and the Court will from time to time apply to the Master of His Majesty's Mint for any supplies of silver coin which they may require for the use of the public.[34]

The argument over the "debt" raged on for several years until in 1833 a general operating principle was agreed on: "The Bank shall be at liberty at their discretion to return all silver coin [to the Mint at its par value] which they may receive from the Public above a balance to be retained by the Bank of £250,000."[35] The monetary authorities had

[33] T1 3141/6277; 3/3/1831.

[34] MCD, Eb G4/56, p. 218, 5/12/1833.

[35] MCT, G8/26, p. 55, 6/3/1833. Their Lordships had replied to the bank's threat by stating that they could not give the bank special privileges with respect to the price at which they bought and sold silver; that they thought that the renewal of the Bank Charter had "cancelled all former claims"; and that if a proposal of the kind the bank suggested were put to Parliament, "the proposition would be rejected" because

> the melting of the silver coin [in 1831] was adopted at the suggestion and for the convenience of the Bank;—as it was effected at the expense of the public, and as it now appears that this measure was decided upon an erroneous view of what were to be the permanent wants of the public; at least in the extent to which the operation was carried it would not be just to saddle the country with the expense consequent upon this transaction. (MCD, Eb G4/56, p. 255, 2/1/1834)

The bank agreed that "so long as the Mint continues to issue silver coin at a seignorage, and the publick are allowed to pay an unlimited amount of that Coin into the Bank at its current value in exchange for Notes or gold; So long will common justice require that the Bank should be allowed to throw back upon the Mint at the same value any excess beyond the fair wants of the publick" (MCD, Eb G4/56, p. 257, 2/1/1834). In 1834 a tentative agreement was reached. The Mint would coin £600,000 without charging the bank seignorage, but the bank would pay the expenses of coining. The bank agreed so long as it had the right to send in any excess over £250,000 (MCD, Eb G4/56, p. 281, 18/1/1834). Finally the bank accepted the terms and in Jan. 1836 sent the Mint finally learned that for silver tokens to circulate at a value in excess of the market value of their silver would require not only limited legal tender and controlled supply but also an agency that would convert them on demand into a money form that was unlimited legal tender.

IV. CONCLUSION

I have argued that England abandoned bimetallism in 1816 because a gold standard with a complementary token silver coinage offered the possibility of a medium of exchange with high- and low-denomination coins circulating concurrently. The gold standard succeeded because the new technology employed by the Mint was able to make coins that counterfeiters could not copy cheaply and because the Mint accepted the responsibility of guaranteeing the convertibility of the tokens.

This thesis raises two interesting questions that are beyond the scope of this article. The first pertains to the experiments with copper tokens in early modern England. From Elizabethan times until the nineteenth century, the government had attempted to establish a coinage of copper tokens to provide a medium of exchange for transactions for which silver was too valuable. I would interpret the failure to establish such a currency as support for the hypothesis that it was not technically or institutionally feasible to manage a token currency prior to the nineteenth century, but this requires further examination. Second, we should inquire about international experience. Boulton and Watt exported steam-powered mint machinery to some European mints in the 1830s, so presumably the technology to make expensive-to-counterfeit coins was widely accessible. Why, then, did other European and North American countries not follow Britain and adopt the gold standard in the first half of the nineteenth century? Only a detailed examination of the technical, political, and institutional constraints on the choice of monetary standards in those countries can answer this question.

£600,000 to be coined. The bank would bear the costs of coining, of loss from wear and tear, and the interest on the deficiency of silver (MCD, Gb G4/58, p. 328, 7/1/1836).

Beyond Malthus and Ricardo: Economic Growth, Land Concentration, and Income Distribution in Early Twentieth-Century Rural China

LOREN BRANDT AND BARBARA SANDS

The article reexamines the connection between rural landownership and income distribution in light of recent evidence suggesting economic growth in China in the early twentieth century. The study utilizes a government-organized national survey of landholding and income-earning in 1930s' China and three household-level village surveys conducted by Japanese researchers in the 1930s. Our investigations produce evidence contrary to the currently held view of substantial (and increasing) income inequality. We suggest an alternative scenario of economic opportunities.

> *There is reason to think that in the [last] twenty years . . . occupying ownership has lost ground. . . . The fact of concentration can hardly be questioned. . . . Over a large part of China, tenancy of one kind or another undoubtedly predominates and it appears everywhere to be increasing.* (Richard Tawney, *Agrarian China*, 1938)

Histories of China in the late nineteenth and early twentieth centuries are filled with concerns for the increasing concentration of rural landholdings said to be taking place. Upon closer inspection we see these concerns are not just for landownership per se, but for the worsening distribution of economic welfare that increasingly concentrated landholding implies. This is because both Chinese and Western accounts of this historical economy characterize it as a predominantly agricultural one experiencing diminishing returns under increasing population pressure. Such a Malthusian perspective directly ties households' economic welfare to their landholdings, in that land is seen not only as the most important form in which households hold their wealth but also as the best indicator of households' income-earnings. Thus, an increasing concentration of landholdings naturally implies an increasing concentration of economic welfare.

The current Chinese version predictably has a distinct Marxist flavor. In late nineteenth-century China increased population pressure on a

The Journal of Economic History, Vol. L, No. 4 (Dec. 1990). ISSN 0022-0507.

The authors are Associate Professor of Economics, University of Toronto, Toronto, Canada M5S 1A1, and Assistant Professor of Economics, University of Arizona, Tucson, AZ 85721, respectively.

We thank Canada's Social Sciences and Humanities Research Council for financial support, and Albert Barry, James Irwin, Ramon Myers, and Thomas Rawski for helpful comments.

fixed amount of land provoked progressively unequal contests over land's ownership. Certain groups—namely, landlords, compradores, usurers, and merchants—wrested land away from the peasantry, forcing more and more of them into poverty and debt. With only meager savings to improve their farms, farmers' agricultural productivity declined and their living standards worsened.[1]

The Western version generally suggests the same story. Mark Elvin's term "high-level equilibrium trap," for example, describes the trouble China's primarily agricultural economy experienced in accommodating population growth over the course of the late nineteenth and early twentieth centuries. Dwight Perkins's estimates of 0.6 percent each for population and agricultural output annual growth rates for this period support the view of a no-growth economy. Concerns for individual households' economic welfare naturally follow. After all, when incomes in general are stagnating, an increasingly unequal distribution portends much more dire welfare consequences than when incomes are increasing.[2]

Works focusing on China's current situation reflect these views of the past. In his political-economic history of modern China, for example, economist Carl Riskin argues of the early twentieth century: "Chinese rural society was hardly egalitarian with respect to the distribution of income and wealth: and although characterized by substantial social mobility, the predominant direction for the latter was downward, at least in relative terms." Harry Harding, a political scientist, similarly notes in his book on China's contemporary political situation: "Though still prone to drought, flood, and plague, China's rural economy could, in most years, also produce the surplus to support one of the world's

[1] See Li Lichung, "Guanyu Zhongguo Nongcun Shehui Xingzhi" (Concerning the characteristics of Chinese rural society), *Zhongguo Jingji*, 11 (Dec. 1936), pp. 113–15, for a pre-1949 Chinese view along these lines. For the post-1949 view, see Chen Shaowen and Guo Xianglin, eds., *Zhongguo Jindai Jingji Jianshi* (Chinese modern economic history) (Shanghai, 1983); History Research Center of the Chinese Social Science Academy, *Ming-Qing Shidai de Nongve Zibenzhuyi Mengya Wenti* (The question of Ming and Qing dynasties' capitalist sprouts in agriculture) (Beijing, 1983); and Wei Yongli, *Zhongguo Jindai Jingji Shigang* (Modern Chinese economic history outline) (Lanzhou, 1983).

[2] See Mark Elvin, *The Pattern of the Chinese Past* (Stanford, 1973), for his definition of "high-level equilibrium trap." Note that he dates economic decline in China from the early nineteenth century. For a discussion of the term applied to the early twentieth century, see Robert Dernberger, "The Role of the Foreigner in China's Economic Development, 1840–1949," in Dwight Perkins, ed., *China's Modern Economy in Historical Perspective* (Stanford, 1975), pp. 19–47. See also Dwight Perkins, *Agricultural Development in China* (Chicago, 1969). Note that most of the growth in output Perkins finds for the late nineteenth century and after occurs in newly settled areas of Manchuria and therefore the rate of growth of output for China proper was less than that of population. Philip Huang, in *The Peasant Economy in Prewar China* (Stanford, 1985), is the most recent to make the connection between landholdings and economic welfare. See Ramon Myers, *The Chinese Peasant Economy: Agricultural Development in Hopei and Shantung, 1890–1949* (Cambridge, 1970) for an early view somewhat similar to the one we advocate here.

most advanced urban civilizations and most highly bureaucratic states. But the distribution of that output was increasingly unequal."[3]

Recent work by both Thomas Rawski and Loren Brandt suggests, however, that the economic history of China's late nineteenth and early twentieth centuries may warrant a rewrite.[4] Both argue the economy fared much better than previously implied. In fact, they suggest per capita incomes increased by a third or more over this period and that despite impressive rates of growth in the emerging modern manufacturing sector, much of this growth occurred in agriculture and traditional industry. Underlying the economic expansion was the rapid commercialization and increasing specialization of economic activity fostered by new market opportunities at both the national and international level and by a secular rise in the terms of trade in agriculture's favor. The result was increasing productivity of labor and rising real wages.

Several kinds of evidence provide support for this view, including rising real wages. Between 1929 and 1933 John L. Buck, an American agricultural economist, carried out an extensive survey of almost 17,000 farms in 167 localities in 153 countries in 22 provinces. Roughly two-thirds of the hundred localities for which Buck was able to compile long-term wage data show not only rising real wages, but real wages that were rising at an accelerating rate. For the entire sample, real wage growth averaged slightly less than 1 percent for the years between 1901 and 1931.[5] In addition to time-series data, cross-sectional data for the early- to mid-1930s reveal real wages at least two-thirds higher than in the late 1880s, and higher still compared to wages a century before that.[6]

Also signaling an increase in the return to labor were increases in labor productivity in the rural handicraft textile sector, perhaps the most important rural industry. This increase can be attributed to two important factors—first, the substitution of manufactured for handicraft yarn in handicraft cloth production and a reallocation of labor time into

[3] See Carl Riskin, *China's Political Economy* (New York, 1986), p. 32; and Harry Harding, *China's Second Revolution: Reform After Mao* (Washington, DC, 1987), p. 13.

[4] Thomas G. Rawski, *Economic Growth in Prewar China* (Berkeley, 1989); and Loren Brandt, *Commercialization and Agricultural Development, Central and Eastern China, 1870–1937* (Cambridge, 1989).

[5] See John L. Buck, *Land Utilization in China: Statistical Volume* (Chicago, 1937); and T. Rawski, *Economic Growth in Prewar China*, chap. 6.

[6] Extensive wage data for the 1930s can be found in Chen Zhengmo, *Ge Sheng Nonggong Guyong Xiguan Ji Xugong Zhuankuang* (Customary practices and demand and supply for farm labor in different provinces) (Beijing, 1935); and "Ge Sheng Nonggong Gongzi Tongqi" (Statistics on agricultural wages in different provinces), *Tongqi Yuebao*, 13 (Sept./Oct. 1933), pp. 99–106. These data have been deflated by provincial grain prices compiled by Thomas Wiens, "The Microeconomics of Peasant Economy: China, 1920–1940" (Ph.D. dissertation, Harvard University, 1973). Cross-sectional data for the 1880s can be found in George Jamieson, "Tenure of Land in China and the Condition of the Rural Population," *Journal of the China Branch of the Royal Asiatic Society*, 23 (1889), pp. 58–143. For earlier periods, see Kang Chao, *Man and Land in Chinese History: An Economic Analysis* (Stanford, 1986), pp. 218–19. The difference in wage levels between the 1880s and 1930s implies real wage growth just in excess of 1 percent per year.

weaving, in which labor productivity was higher; and second, the rapid dissemination of new looms, originally imported from Japan and later manufactured domestically, which increased labor productivity several-fold.

Finally, the commercialization of the period generated a host of new income-earning opportunities, of which transportation was one of the most important. Rawski estimates that trade grew roughly 2.5 percent per year during the early twentieth century, with the rate of growth in the traditional sector only modestly below that in the modern manufacturing sector (2.2 percent versus 3.0 percent).[7] By the 1930s as many as 8 or 9 million people were involved in traditional transport.[8]

Neither Rawski nor Brandt suggests uniform economic growth throughout China—large parts of the Chinese countryside remained largely isolated from the forces described above. In addition, other factors, such as increased market uncertainty, partially mitigated the benefits of the higher return to labor. Nevertheless, they make the case that the return to labor increased over the course of the late nineteenth and early twentieth centuries, implying economic growth.

If we are to change our minds about China's aggregate economic performance in the late nineteenth and early twentieth centuries, perhaps we should also rethink our understanding of the distribution of economic welfare. The traditional histories place China in Malthusian conditions, thereby conferring economic power on a single factor of production, land; ownership of land serves as a proxy for economic welfare. In fact, however, the connection between landownership concentration and the economic welfare of rural households rests on a weak empirical foundation. First, it is not clear whether landownership actually became more concentrated during the late nineteenth and early twentieth centuries, and second, the accuracy of landholdings as a proxy for household economic welfare has never been established.

Such need not be the case. Data from the 1930s allow estimates of the degree of dispersion of both land and incomes in the rural sector. These include the survey of the National Land Commission that provides provincial-level data, and village-level surveys carried out by the South Manchurian Railroad in North China. Although these two data sources differ in a number of respects and the latter is confined to North China, they complement each other in allowing both macro- and micro-level assessments of the degree of concentration of incomes and land ownership in the rural sector in the 1930s. We use both sources to

[7] Rawski, *Economic Growth in Prewar China*, chap. 6.

[8] Liu and Yeh estimate that in the 1930s there were 87.5 million male "man-labor" units solely in agriculture and an additional 43.0 million jointly in agriculture and subsidiary occupations. Of this latter group, 2.8 million "man-labor" units were in trade and transportation. In other words roughly 8.5 million males devoted a third of their time to this sideline. See T. C. Liu and K. C. Yeh, *The Economy of the Chinese Mainland* (Princeton, 1965), pp. 184–85.

review critically the hypothesis of increasing landownership concentration during the late nineteenth and early twentieth centuries as well as the implied link between landownership and material welfare in the rural sector.

INCREASING CONCENTRATION OF LANDHOLDINGS

Concerns over an increasing concentration of landholdings and rise in tenancy were voiced in China centuries prior to the current one. During the late Ming (1368–1643) and Qing (1644–1911) dynasties, for example, government officials regularly expressed alarm over what appeared to be an increasing accumulation of land by the wealthy and decline in holdings of smaller farm households.[9] For the late nineteenth and early twentieth centuries, the suggested increasing concentration of landholdings was linked to forced land sales. Farm households borrowed for a number of reasons: to obtain working capital, to meet consumption needs in times of emergency, and in some cases to help cover major ceremonial expenses such as a wedding or funeral. Land was frequently pledged as collateral. In other cases, the rights of land use were ceded to the lender, with the income generated from the land serving as the interest. Once the loan was repaid, rights of land use reverted back to the original owner. In many cases, borrowers were unable to service these loans. Chen Hansheng's description is typical: "When a poor peasant in China mortgages his bit of land, he has practically no hope of ever getting it back. Everything conspires against him in his frantic effort to meet the interest charges, and eventually he loses not only the land but also this additional fruit of his labor."[10] These difficulties are quite often related to declining economic fortunes associated with the opening up of the rural sector to international market forces and still further commercialization. With the loss of their land, small cultivators were forced either to rent back the same land from the new owners or possibly hire out as wage laborers if the landlords decided to cultivate the land instead of renting it out. This explains the link implicit in the opening quote from Tawney between rising tenancy (or perhaps wage labor) and a growing concentration of landholdings. Are the data consistent with this view of a secular rise in land concentration?

Reasonably good information on private land ownership exists for the early twentieth century. On the basis of data compiled by the National Land Commission in 1934 on almost 1.75 million rural households residing in 16 provinces, Table 1 presents an estimate of the size

[9] See, for example, Yang Yi, "Qingchao Qianqi de Tudi Zhidu" (Land system of early Qing China), *Shehui Yuekan*, 7 (1958), pp. 21–26; and Fu Yiling, "Guanyu Mingmo Qingchu Zhongguo Nongcun Shehui Guanxi de Xin Guji" (A new assessment of rural social relationships in late Ming and early Qing China), *Xiamen Daxue Xuebao*, 6 (1959), pp. 57–70.

[10] Chen Hansheng, *Landlord and Peasant in China* (New York, 1936), p. 95.

Table 1
DISTRIBUTION OF OWN LANDHOLDINGS FOR RURAL HOUSEHOLDS, 1930s

Size of Holdings (in *mou*)	Average Size (in *mou*)	Percentage of Households	Percentage of Land
Landless		25.8%	0.0%
0–5	2.7	16.4	6.2
5–10	7.2	17.8	11.4
10–15	12.3	9.8	10.6
15–20	17.4	5.9	9.2
20–30	24.3	6.1	13.2
30–50	38.0	4.6	15.5
50–70	58.6	1.6	8.4
70–100	82.6	1.0	7.2
100–150	120.2	0.5	5.7
150–200	172.0	0.2	2.8
200–300	241.0	0.2	3.2
300–500	378.4	0.1	2.6
500–1,000	671.9	0.0	2.3
Over 1,000	1,752.7	0.0	1.8

Note: A *mou* equals one-sixth of an acre.
Source: Tudi Weiyuanhui, *Quanguo Tudi Diaocha Baogao Gangyao* (Summary report of the nationwide investigation of land) (Nanjing, 1937), tables 21, 23.

distribution of private landholdings for rural China. These aggregate data are complemented by similar data compiled by the National Agricultural Research Bureau (NARB) in the 1930s and by several hundred village-level surveys undertaken during the 1920s and 1930s.[11] Both kinds of data confirm what others have long argued: in absolute terms, the distribution of land ownership in rural China was highly unequal; and on the surface they are consistent with the view that distribution may have been worsening. For the distribution in Table 1, the gini coefficient is equal to 0.72. The top 1 percent of rural households owned 18.5 percent of the land, the top 5 percent owned 38.7 percent, and the top 10 percent owned 53.4 percent. By contrast, slightly more than a quarter of all rural households were landless and an additional quarter owned less than 5 *mou*.[12]

[11] The results of 47 surveys carried out between 1931 and 1941 are reported in Kang Chao and Chen Chungyi, *Zhongguo Tudi Zhidu Shi* (History of China's land system) (Taipei, 1982), pp. 234–38. A majority of these are the product of the research efforts of the South Manchurian Railway and can be found in *Mantetsu Chosa Geppo* (Monthly survey reports).

[12] By international comparison, however, the concentration of landholdings in China does not seem so extreme. It is markedly less than that in Mexico in the 1920s, where the top 10 percent owned an estimated 64 to 99 percent of landholdings and 79 percent were landless, or Victorian England (excluding London), where 85 percent owned no land and the top 10 percent owned 82 percent of the land; and is actually slightly better than that estimated separately for both farming households and the entire rural population in the United States (whites only) in both 1798 and 1860. In many respects land distribution in China in the 1930s is very similar to that estimated for post-independence India. Data on Mexico, Victorian England, and the United States are taken from Peter Lindert, "Who Owned Victorian England? The Debate Over Landed Wealth and

These data suffer from a number of omissions. On the one hand, they do not include the holdings of some absentee landlords, or any publicly owned land (*gongdian*). Other data in the survey, however, suggest that these holdings were nearly equal to each other and together amounted to slightly less than one-fifth (18.8 percent) of total cultivated area, or just in excess of three-fifths (61.5 percent) of total rented area. Depending on the size distribution of the landholdings of the omitted absentee landlords, overall concentration was probably higher than that suggested by the data for the rural households alone.

On the other hand, no allowances are made for the multiple layers of land ownership. In some regions of China, property rights were divided between topsoil and subsoil rights. Topsoil rights entitled an individual to rent the land from the owner (who owned the subsoil rights) at a fixed rent for long periods of time, sometimes even in perpetuity. These rights could be sold or mortgaged by the tenant and were also inheritable. If many smallholders enjoyed these rights, Table 1 would provide a slightly biased assessment of the degree of land concentration.[13]

Unfortunately, comparable information on the distribution of landholdings in the past does not exist. We have only a handful of observations at the county or village level, and these do not easily lend themselves to intertemporal comparison.[14] Nevertheless, additional information on such things as the percentage of land that was rented out and the amount of long-term labor hired in, either or both of which typically accompany an increasing concentration of landholdings, suggests no long-term rise between the 1880s and 1930s. Estimates of land rental, for example, reveal that in both periods approximately a third of cultivated acreage was rented in, two-thirds of which was from absentee landlords.[15] We have not uncovered estimates of the number of long-term agricultural laborers for the 1880s, but of the 1.75 million rural households surveyed by the National Land Commission (*Tudi Weiyuanhui*) in the 1930s, only 1.6 percent were classified as landless laboring households, that is, households earning a living as long-term agricultural laborers. Finally, over the 25-year period between 1912 and 1937, the

---

Inequality," *Agricultural History*, 61 (Fall, 1987), pp. 25–51; data on India are taken from P. K. Bardhan and T. N. Srinivisan, eds., *Poverty and Income Distribution in India* (Calcutta, 1974).

[13] In the three densely populated provinces of the Lower Yangzi (Jiangsu, Zhejiang, and Anhui), for example, land rental contracts covered slightly less than half of cultivated area, of which 40 percent conferred on tenants topsoil rights in some form. See Tudi Weiyuanhui, *Quanguo Tudi Diaocha Baogao Gangyao* (Summary report of the nationwide investigation of land) (Nanjing, 1937) p. 45.

[14] In fact, some provide evidence contradicting the suggestion of increasing concentration of landholdings. See, for example, the data for Huailu county, Hebei province, for the early 1700s and 1930s provided in Brandt's review of Philip Huang's *Peasant Economy and Social Change in North China* in *Economic Development and Cultural Change*, 35 (Apr. 1987), pp. 670–82.

[15] For the 1930s, estimates have been made on the basis of additional data contained in the Summary Report of the National Land Commission. For the 1880s, see Zhang Zhongli (Chang Chungli), *The Income of the Chinese Gentry* (Seattle, 1962), p. 145.

percentage of households classified as owner-operators failed to decrease.[16]

On the basis of these very limited data, mostly highly aggregate in nature, we do not want to push any view very far, especially one suggesting that the degree of concentration of landholdings remained constant for fifty years, let alone several hundred years, throughout all of China. Over the long run a number of processes simultaneously influenced landholding concentration and it would be odd if these were exactly offsetting.[17] Nonetheless, the point needs to be made that data presently at our disposal do not support the popularly held view that the high degree of concentration of landholdings observed in the 1930s was the product of several decades (or centuries) of increasing inequality. By most indications, land distribution in the 1930s looked very much as it had a half century earlier.

LAND AND INCOME DISTRIBUTION IN RURAL CHINA

The fact still remains that land was unequally held in late nineteenth- and early twentieth-century China. Were incomes so distributed as well? We use information from our two surveys to address the suggested link between landholdings and income distribution in early twentieth-century China.

We first looked at the concentration of landholdings reported in the National Land Commission survey. Unfortunately, the Summary Report of the National Land Commission provides a distribution of private landholdings only for the country as a whole (see Table 1). Provincial-level information, however, is provided on the distribution of operational holdings, the sum of self-owned and rented land that a household cultivates. The survey reports the number of households in each of thirteen size categories. We modified these data slightly to include households that did not farm, that is, that had zero operational holdings, and then calculated gini coefficients for the new distributions.[18] These estimates are provided in Table 2, along with information on land rental.

It is widely agreed that land rental provided more equal access to land; thus, the distribution of operational holdings should be more equal than self-owned land. This is borne out by the data: the gini coefficient for land ownership is 0.72, while that for operational holdings is 0.61.

[16] *Nongqing Baogao* (Dec. 1937), p. 330.

[17] We have discussed these in some detail in an earlier paper prepared for the ACLS/SSRC conference on Economic Methods for Chinese Historical Research, 1988.

[18] Most computational formulas for the gini coefficient based on grouped data such as these underestimate the degree of inequality because they ignore intra-group inequality. We have followed Kakwani in correcting for this, using the midpoint of each interval as an estimate of its mean. See Nanak Kakwani, "On the Estimation of Income Inequality from Grouped Observations," *Review of Economic Studies*, 43 (Oct. 1976), pp. 483–92.

TABLE 2
DISTRIBUTION OF CULTIVATED HOLDINGS AND INCOMES PER HOUSEHOLD, 1930s

Province	Gini Coefficient		
	Cultivated Holdings	Incomes	Percentage of Land Rented
1. Jiangsu	0.57	0.43	42.2
2. Zhejiang	0.57	0.42	51.3
3. Anhui	0.54	0.47	52.6
4. Jiangxi	0.53	0.34	45.1
5. Hunan	0.60	0.43	47.8
6. Hubei	0.53	0.39	27.8
7. Hebei	0.60	0.46	12.9
8. Shandong	0.54	0.45	12.6
9. Henan	0.60	0.44	27.3
10. Shanxi	0.53	0.52	na
11. Shaanxi	0.56	0.42	16.6
12. Chahar	0.44	0.65	10.2
13. Suiyan	0.64	0.50	8.8
14. Fujian	0.56	0.35	39.3
15. Guangdong	0.42	0.34	77.0
16. Guangxi	0.54	0.45	21.2
Arithmetic Average	0.55	0.44	32.9
Pooled Sample	0.62	0.46	30.7

Source: Tudi Weiyuanhui, *Quanguo Tudi Diaocha Baogao* (Summary report of the nationwide investigation of land) (Nanjing, 1937), tables 15, 33.

For a majority of provinces the gini coefficient for operational holdings is between 0.55 and 0.60.

In general, we expect the difference between the gini coefficient for self-owned and operational holdings to be positively correlated with the percentage of land rented; in other words, the more land that is rented out, the lower the concentration of operational landholdings associated with any given level of inequality of private landholdings. Since the gini coefficients for operational holdings for the provinces of North China and the Yangzi (see Table 2) are almost the same, the fact that a much higher percentage of land was rented in in the Yangzi than in North China (45 percent versus 15 percent) would suggest that land ownership was more concentrated in the former. The gini coefficient for land ownership in the Yangzi was probably in excess of 0.75, while that for North China was nearer to 0.65.

But what about incomes? Were they just as concentrated as private landholdings in China's rural areas? Again drawing on data compiled by the National Land Commission, we calculated gini coefficients for household incomes for each of the 16 provinces. These estimates are also reported in Table 2. With one exception they reveal a degree of income inequality much lower than that suggested by the land data alone. For a majority of the provinces the gini coefficient for household income was between 0.40 and 0.45, while the gini coefficient for the pooled data is 0.46.[19] These estimates are 35 to 40 percent lower than the provincial gini coefficients for private landholdings. Geographically, the degree of income dispersion appears to be slightly lower in the more densely populated areas of the Yangzi and southern China, and modestly higher in the North and Northwest.

In a number of respects these estimates are not entirely satisfactory. On the one hand, it is not clear from the Summary Report what measure of income was used: net or gross, cash or total (which includes income in kind). Charles Roll has argued that households probably reported their total net income, yet the difficulty of accurately estimating all in-kind income and production expenditure should not be underestimated.[20] On the other hand, if household incomes and family size are systematically related, the distribution of household income may provide a misleading indicator of income distribution on a per capita basis. From a welfare perspective, it is the latter distribution with which we are concerned. We therefore turn to other data, namely, three village surveys undertaken by the Japanese-owned South Manchurian Railroad in the mid-1930s in Hebei province, for information on these questions.[21]

The three villages selected by the SMR for detailed examination include Michang village in Fengrun County, Dabeiguan village in Pinggu County, and Qianlianggezhuang village (Lianggezhuang, for short) in Changli County. All are located in northeastern Hebei within a radius of 100 to 150 kilometers of each other and are less than several hundred kilometers from Tianjin. Despite some obvious similarities, there are marked differences between the villages, some of which are captured by Table 3.

Dabeiguan in the 1930s was a relatively poor farming village with a low-level commercial structure. For the most part, every household in

[19] In calculating the gini coefficient for the pooled data, we have taken a weighted average of the percentage of households in each province in each size category, using as weights the percentage of the total rural population in each province. Rural population estimates are based on provincial population estimates contained in Dwight Perkins, *Agricultural Development in China*, p. 212, and estimates of the percentage of population classified as rural provided in Wu Baosan, *Zhongguo Guomin Soude, 1933* (China's national income, 1933) (Shanghai, 1947), vol. 1, p. 151.

[20] Charles Roll, "The Distribution of Incomes in Rural China" (Ph.D. dissertation, Harvard University, 1974).

[21] See Minami Manshū tetsudō kabushiki kaisha, Kitō nōson jittai chōsahan, *Dainiji kitō nōson jittai chōsa hōkokusho: tōkeihen. Dai ichiban. Heikoku ken. Dai sanban: Hōjun ken. Dai yonban: Shōrei ken.* (Report on the second investigation of actual conditions of northeastern Hebei villages: Statistical volume. First group: Pinggu County. Third group: Fengrun County. Fourth group: Changli County.) (Dalian, 1937). These surveys are part of an enormous collection of materials on social and economic life in China compiled by the SMR during the late 1930s and early 1940s. Of particular use is Minami Manshū tetsudō kabushiki kaisha, Kitō chiku nōson jittai chōsahan, *Kitō chiku nai nijūgo ka son nōson jittai chōsa hōkokusho* (Report on the investigation of actual conditions in 25 villages of the northeastern Hebei area) (Tianjin, 1936), 2 vols., which provides slightly less detailed information on an additional 25 villages in North China. For introductions to these materials, see Philip Huang, *The Peasant Economy and Social Change in North China* and Ramon Myers, *The Chinese Peasant Economy: Agricultural Development in Hopei and Shantung, 1890–1949*.

TABLE 3
DESCRIPTIVE STATISTICS OF THREE VILLAGE ECONOMIES

	Michang	Lianggezhuang	Dabeiguan
1. Percentage of Land Rented	32.1%	49.1%	5.1%
2. Hiring-in/out of Labor:			
Annual (number of laborers)	34/17	8/0	18/11
Monthly (in months)	10/10	1/0	12/19
Daily (in days)	807/2959	561/4096	342/2610
Net: Importer(−)/Exporter(+) (expressed in terms of annual labor)	−8.04	+9.65	+3.03
3. Labor Hired as a Percentage of Total Village Labor	14.8%	5.7%	10.1%
4. Number of Village Members who had Migrated	37	19	4
5. Number of Households Borrowing/Lending	49/27	65/47	44/43
6. Net Borrowing(+)/Lending(−) (in *yuan*)	+4,185.0	+1,267.0	−3,510.0
7. Draft Animal Rental (in days)	132	0	10
8. Percentage of Agricultural Output Marketed	47%	11%	13%
9. Self-sufficiency in Grain Production (percentage of total consumption self-produced)	69%	28%	90%
10. Percentage of Gross Income earned in cash	76%	69%	35%

Note: A *yuan* equals 0.20 1936 U.S. dollars.
Source: Minami Manshū tetsudō kabushiki kaisha, Kitō nōson jittai chōsahan, *Dainiji kitō nōson jittai chōsa hōkokusho: tōkeihen. Dai ichiban: Heikoku ken. Dai sanban: Hōjun ken. Dai yonban: Shōrei ken*. (Report on the second investigation of actual conditions of northeastern Hebei villages: Statistical volume. First group: Pinggu County. Third group: Fengrun County. Fourth group: Changli County) (Dalian, 1937).

the village engaged in farming and most families worked their own land, used their own family labor, and directly consumed the products of their efforts. Michang, on the other hand, was a richer, more commercialized village. Not all of Michang's households were engaged in farming. Moreover, a majority of those that specialized in growing cotton for export imported foodgrains from outside areas. Lianggezhuang, the third village, was also commercialized, but very differently than Michang. In the past Lianggezhuang had provided both goods (pears) and labor to northern markets. When the Japanese established the state of Manchuguo in 1932, however, access to these markets was severely restricted. By the time of the 1936 survey Lianggezhuang's economy was experiencing a downturn—its pear orchards lay neglected and villagers sought work in surrounding villages and nearby cities.

What is unique about these surveys is that they enumerate every household in each village and provide information on individual landholdings and in-kind and cash incomes and expenditures, thus allowing complete description of each household's economic position.[22] Com-

[22] An earlier estimate of the degree of income inequality in a North China village made by Marc Blecher suffers in both regards because it is based on a stratified sample for a village in which larger

TABLE 4
ASSET AND INCOME DISTRIBUTION GINI COEFFICIENTS[a]

	Michang	Lianggezhuang	Dabeiguan
1. Household Size	0.30 (6.4)	0.27 (5.3)	0.26 (6.1)
2. Labor Power[b]	0.33 (2.9)	0.32 (2.1)	0.24 (4.1)
Male Laborers	0.29 (2.2)	0.33 (1.7)	0.25 (2.1)
Female Laborers	0.64 (1.1)	0.64 (0.6)	0.32 (3.2)
3. Draft Animals	0.72 (0.5)	0.81 (0.3)	0.49 (0.8)
4. Own Land	0.75 (15.3)	0.75 (19.5)	0.58 (23.6)
5. Operational Holdings	0.55 (21.4)	0.53 (15.5)	0.51 (24.9)
6. Capital Borrowed	0.82 (93.9)	0.76 (151.8)	0.76 (49.5)
7. Capital Lent	0.90 (57.2)	0.85 (164.4)	0.77 (85.3)
8. Net Cash Income	0.60 (153.8)	0.52 (101.1)	0.60 (37.4)
9. Net In-kind Income	0.46 (98.8)	0.56 (61.4)	0.45 (123.2)
10. Net Income	0.49 (252.7)	0.41 (162.5)	0.44 (160.6)
11. Net Income per Capita	0.39 (37.3)[c]	0.35 (32.8)	0.35 (26.4)
12. Consumption Expenditure	0.44 (178.4)	0.35 (139.8)	0.39 (129.9)
13. Consumption Expenditure per Capita	0.30 (27.0)	0.29 (29.6)	0.33 (24.6)

[a] Village averages are in parenthesis. Land is measured in *mou* and incomes and expenditures in *yuan*. Unless otherwise noted, the gini coefficients are for distributions at the household level.
[b] Labor power is defined to be the number of laboring males plus 0.65 times the number of laboring females in the household.
[c] The figure reported in the table is the average of net income per capita for all households. Net income per capita for each village (in the order they appear in the table) is 39.23, 30.71, and 26.50 *yuan*.
Notes: One *yuan* equals 0.20 1936 U.S. dollars. One *mou* equals one-sixth of an acre.
Source: Minami Manshū tetsudō kabushiki kaisha, Kitō nōson jittai chōsahan, *Dainiji kitō nōson jittai chōsa hōkokusho: tōkeihen. Dai ichiban: Heikoku ken. Dai sanban: Hōjun ken. Dai yonban: Shōrei ken*. (Report on the second investigation of actual conditions of northeastern Hebei villages: Statistical volume. First group: Pinggu County. Third group: Fengrun County. Fourth group: Changli County) (Dalian, 1937).

bined with the information in Table 2, the surveys allow us to discuss the degree of income inequality in rural China at the household level on a per capita basis. The surveys also help explain why the concentration of incomes observed in Table 2 was so much lower than that suggested by the data on land ownership alone. And finally, they illustrate the impact of economic growth on the relationship between landholdings and income distribution in the rural economy.

What can we say about the distributions of land and incomes in these three villages and how do they compare to the aggregate estimates for Hebei provided by the National Land Commission survey? In Table 4 we report estimated gini coefficients for asset holdings (land, draft animals, and labor power) and incomes, both at the household level and on a per capita basis for each of the three villages. Mean values of each variable are reported in parentheses. The table shows that in Michang and Lianggezhuang average landholdings were smaller and land owner-

farms were overrepresented, and because household income is measured simply by the gross agricultural output of each household. See Marc Blecher, "Income Distribution in Small Rural Chinese Communities," *China Quarterly*, 68 (Dec. 1976), pp. 795–816.

ship much more concentrated than in Dabeiguan. In all three villages, however, land rental helped to equalize access to land among households; this effect is most pronounced in Michang and Lianggezhuang, where one-third and one-half of land was rented in, respectively. In Michang, for example, the gini coefficient for landholdings was 0.745, while that for operational holdings was 0.547; in Lianggezhuang, 0.752 and 0.528, respectively. The mean operational holding in Michang was also much larger than the mean land ownership because of the substantial holdings of absentee landlords. In Lianggezhuang the relationship was the exact opposite, since a quarter of the land was rented out to nonvillagers who were not included in the survey.

Rows 8 through 11 of Table 4 report gini coefficients for household income and household income on a per capita basis.[23] The gini coefficients for household income are consistent with the estimate suggested by the National Land Commission data for Hebei. As reported in Table 2, the gini coefficient for the distribution of rural incomes in Hebei is 0.458, while that for each of the three villages is 0.488, 0.409, and 0.436. Yet it is the distribution of household incomes on a per capita basis that concerns us and here we observe in every case a much lower degree of inequality on a per capita basis than on a household basis: Michang, 0.391 versus 0.488; Lianggezhuang, 0.346 versus 0.409; and Dabeiguan, 0.349 versus 0.436. These contrasts pose several immediate questions. Why is the degree of inequality of incomes on a per capita basis much lower than that at the household level? Why are household incomes distributed so much more equitably than landholdings? And what forces acting on the village economies of Michang and Lianggezhuang produced a degree of dispersion in incomes similar to that observed for Dabeiguan, despite more concentrated landholdings in the former?

Until the work of Simon Kuznets, the influence of the size distribution of households on income disparities was relatively neglected.[24] Most estimates of income inequality were calculated using income per household. Since households differ in size, this can provide a very misleading indicator of the degree of dispersion of incomes on a per capita basis. In general, family size and incomes are highly and positively correlated. In the three villages examined, the highest-income households are usually those with ten or more members. The most obvious reason for this is that larger families typically have more members of working age who can add to the household's income. In China these households were typically extended, multi-generational households that had not recently

[23] The details of the income calculations are included in a lengthy appendix provided on request.

[24] Simon Kuznets, "Demographic Aspects of the Size Distribution of Income: An Exploratory Essay," *Economic Development and Cultural Change*, 25 (Oct. 1976), pp. 1–94. See also Gautam Datta and Jacob Meerman, "Household Income or Household Income per Capita in Welfare Comparisons," *Review of Income and Wealth*, 26 (Dec. 1980), pp. 401–18.

divided.[25] If incomes increase more than proportionally with household size, the dispersion of incomes on a per capita basis will actually exceed that on a per household basis. But this is typically not the case; rather, incomes increase less than proportionately, and family size and per capita incomes are negatively associated. Indeed, some of the poorest households on a per capita basis in these villages are among those identified as having the highest total household incomes. Although it need not always be the case, under such conditions the dispersion of household incomes on a per capita basis can be less than that for total household incomes. This is in fact what we observe for all three villages.

The remaining questions concerning the link between landownership and income earnings inequality benefit from a brief discussion of what we mean by income. Conceptually, income can be thought of as a stream of earnings generated by all owned factors of production. In a primarily agrarian economy, the key factors of production are land, labor, and capital (the last including such things as farm implements and draft animals). A household's income, therefore, is positively related to how much of each factor it owns as well as to the returns to each factor.

Income distribution, on the other hand, depends on the distribution of these factors of production, their returns, and the correlation of factor ownership across households. Clearly, the distribution of incomes is more concentrated the more concentrated land ownership is, and the higher the percentage of income for which land accounts. A high correlation of landholdings with ownership of other factors of productions would only reinforce the influence of a high concentration of landholdings on incomes. This, of course, would be mitigated by a more even distribution of ownership of other factors of production, a higher percentage of output captured by them, and a weaker correlation of factor ownership across households.[26] We turn to the data to determine the actual factor ownership situations prevailing in the three villages.

In Table 4 we observe that labor power (and therefore income from labor) was much more evenly distributed across households than was land. The gini coefficients for labor power per household were 0.328, 0.322, and 0.237, for Michang, Lianggezhang, and Dabeiguan, respectively, or less than half those observed for land. Draft animal ownership,

[25] The custom in China was for households to split up after the death of the household head.

[26] This discussion can be addressed more formally through a decomposition of the gini coefficient for household income. Let G_k ($k = L, H$, and K in all cases) be the concentration index (or gini coefficient) for earnings, y_k, from labor, land, and capital, respectively; u_k be the mean earnings of each factor; s_k be the earnings of each factor as a percentage of total earnings; and C_k be the correlation between y_k and the ranking of Y, total income. G^y, the concentration index for total incomes is then equal to: $G^y = (1/u)\,\Sigma(s_k \times C_k \times G_k \times u_k)$. Income inequality is higher the more concentrated income from land ownership is and the higher the percentage of total income captured by land; in addition, income inequality will be higher the more highly correlated income from land is with the ranking of overall income, which depends pivotally on the correlation of income from land with that from other factors of production.

on the other hand, was about as unequally distributed as landholdings in the three villages. The strength of these additional influences on income distribution, however, clearly depends on the portion of output that the inputs capture. If labor power were more evenly distributed across households, but the portion of output it captured were relatively small, any equalizing effect on incomes would be relatively modest.

In rural North China in general, land captured about half of agricultural output, labor a third, and the remainder represented the return to draft animals and other forms of farm capital.[27] These estimates are slightly misleading for our purposes, however, because agriculture was not the only source of income. In all three villages a variety of sidelines offered subsidiary sources of incomes, most of it representing returns to labor (capital inputs were modest). As a percentage of total net village income, land rents (paid and imputed) were only about a third, while wage incomes represented more than half. The exaggerated importance attached to land ownership in the determination of rural income distribution can be attributed primarily to the failure to recognize the more even distribution of labor power in the village economy and to an overestimation of the portion of rural incomes captured by land.

Inter-village differences along these same lines help to explain why the much higher concentration of landholdings in Michang and Lianggezhuang did not generate higher degrees of income concentration. In Michang, annual land rents averaged between 4 and 5 *yuan* per *mou*, while an adult male long-term laborer could expect to earn 45 to 50 *yuan* in cash, plus an in-kind component of perhaps equal value. In Dabeiguan, by contrast, land rents were slightly less, 3 to 3.5 *yuan* per *mou*, but wages paid long-term agricultural laborers were only about half that in Michang. In Lianggezhuang, on the other hand, land rents averaged between 2 and 2.5 *yuan* per *mou*, while wages (cash component only) paid long-term agricultural laborers were 30 to 35 *yuan*. These differences in the wage-rental ratio are ultimately reflected in output shares: the share of agricultural output going to land in Michang and Lianggezhuang was roughly 40 percent, while in Dabeiguan it exceeded 50 percent.[28]

Nonagricultural activities and remittances played a similar role. In both Michang and Lianggezhuang, 40 households were engaged in nonagricultural activities either as a sideline or on a full-time basis.[29]

[27] These estimates are taken from Loren Brandt, "Farm Household Behavior, Factor Markets, and the Distributive Consequences of Commercialization in Early Twentieth-Century China," this JOURNAL, 47 (Sept. 1987), p. 731.

[28] Average land rents were computed from detailed land contract information provided by the surveys. Land's share was then calculated by dividing average land rent into average output per unit of land.

[29] The percentage of households in Michang and Lianggezhuang engaged in nonagricultural activity on a full-time basis (3.5 and 7.4 percent, respectively) was actually relatively low compared to that in other North China villages. The average for 30 villages examined by the South

TABLE 5
CORRELATIONS OF HOUSEHOLD-HOLDINGS OF FACTORS OF PRODUCTION[a]

	Pearson Correlation Coefficients		
	Draft Animals	Landownership	Female Agricultural Labor
Own Landholdings	M. 0.55[b] L. 0.10 D. 0.80[b]		
Labor Power (measured in adult male equivalents)	M. 0.38[b] L. 0.32[b] D. 0.57[b]	M. 0.49[b] L. −0.03 D. 0.61[b]	
Male Agricultural Labor			M. .54[b] L. .32[b] D. .49[b]

[a] M. is Michang; L. is Lianggezhuang; and D. is Dabeiguan.
[b] Statistically significant at 1 percent level.
Source: Minami Manshū tetsudō kabushiki kaisha, Kitō nōson jittai chōsahan, *Dainiji kitō nōson jittai chōsa hōkokusho: tōkeihen. Dai ichiban: Heikoku ken. Dai sanban: Hōjun ken. Dai yonban: Shōrei ken.* (Report on the second investigation of actual conditions of northeastern Hebei villages: Statistical volume. First group: Pinggu County. Third group: Fengrun County. Fourth group: Changli County) (Dalian, 1937).

Both villages also experienced substantial out-migration: 19 household members from Michang and 37 from Lianggezhuang had migrated, and typically remitted a healthy portion of their labor earnings back to the village. A disproportionate number of these villagers were from households with less-than-average landholdings. In contrast, only four village members from Dabeiguan had migrated. The higher the percentage of income generated from nonagricultural sources and received in the form of remittances, the weaker the influence of land concentration on the overall dispersion of incomes. In Lianggezhuang, nonagricultural activity and remittances represented 42 percent of gross household income, while in Michang they amounted to 17.4 percent; in Dabeiguan, in contrast, they totaled only 6.1 percent.

Finally, Table 5 reveals that the correlation between landownership and the other factors of production was also much weaker in Michang and Lianggezhuang than in Dabeiguan. The same is also true for the relationship between labor power and draft animal ownership. While factor ownership was positively correlated, the probability that a household with substantial landholdings simultaneously had more than

Manchurian Railway is 13.7 percent. In a number of localities, 20 percent or more of households were classified solely as nonagricultural. These include Macun in Huailu County, 21.8 percent; Zhongliangshan in Changli County, 26.8 percent; Huzhang in Ninghe County, 31.2 percent; and Dongjiao, located just outside Shijiazhuang, 46.8 percent. In a 1936 survey of 22 villages in Northeast China, 16 percent of all labor (not households) was classified as nonagricultural.

average labor power and draft animals was significantly lower in either Michang or Lianggezhuang than in Dabeiguan. When combined with the higher return to labor relative to land and the higher percentage of income earned from nonagricultural sources, this pattern of factor ownership helped reduce the influence of a more concentrated landownership in both Michang and Lianggezhuang and produce a degree of income inequality not much different from that in Dabeiguan. In summary, the above calculations show that the distribution of land can be a misleading indicator of the degree of income inequality in China's early twentieth-century rural economy. Commercialization not only increased the returns to land, but also raised the productivity of labor, generating new off-farm opportunities—both in the village and outside—in the process. By increasing the demand for labor and increasing the percentage of output that it captured, commercialization had basically the same impact on income distribution in these rural economies as a "labor-using" technological change.

LANDHOLDINGS, SAVING, AND GROWTH

We have shown that the distribution of land ownership exerted less influence on the distribution of incomes in at least three rural twentieth-century villages than was previously thought. Does this mean land's concentrated ownership produced no deleterious effects on China's early twentieth-century economy? In fact, much of the discussion regarding the failure of this historical economy to grow more rapidly has centered on questions of saving and the negative influence of concentrated land ownership on this activity. In some histories of the period the low saving rates are attributed to a highly skewed distribution of income in favor of a "parasitic" landlord class with a low propensity to save. One example of this argument is as follows: "In sum, then, the distributionist position sees the peasant as a 'helpless prey to the evil gentry, the tax collector, and any man with a gun—soldier or bandit,' as the victim of a 'rural triple alliance between the gentry, village usurers . . . and local government underlings' that milked the surplus of the rural economy and used it for personal aggrandizement and familial fortune."[30] Although our information is limited to three villages, we detected interesting differences in saving behavior that bear on the suggested long-run relationship between landholdings, income concentration, and economic growth.

The saving rates in the three villages shown in Table 6 include both stock and flow measures. Category one in the table reports the stock of households' savings at the beginning of 1936; category two reports net saving flows during 1936; and category three lists the savings stocks at

[30] See Carl Riskin, "Surplus and Stagnation in Modern China," in Dwight Perkins, ed., *China's Modern Economy in Historical Perspective* (Stanford, 1973), pp. 50–84.

TABLE 6
VILLAGE SAVINGS AND ACCUMULATIONS, 1936[a]
(in *yuan*)

	Michang	Lianggezhuang	Dabeiguan
1. Accumulated Holdings at the Beginning of 1936			
Cash	2,558.2 (22.2)	751.6 (7.4)	n.a.
Grain	2,109.2 (18.5)	694.5 (6.9)	4,030.7 (41.1)
Total	4,667.2 (40.9)	1,446.1 (14.3)	n.a.
2. Savings during 1936			
Cash	7,433.3 (65.2)	1,683.5 (16.7)	898.4 (9.2)
Grain	756.7 (6.6)	658.0 (6.5)	2,073.1 (21.2)
Total	8,190.1 (71.8)	2,341.5 (23.2)	2,971.5 (30.3)
3. Year-end Totals			
Cash	6,506.7[b] (57.1)	3,026.5 (30.0)	3,327.5 (34.0)
Grain	2,866.0 (25.1)	1,352.5 (13.4)	6,103.9 (62.3)
Total	9,372.7 (82.2)	4,379.90 (43.4)	9,431.0 (96.2)
4. Village Savings Rates			
As a percent of total village income	29.4%	14.0%	19.1%
Household arithmetic average	16.7%	−1.0%	3.7%
5. Number of Households Dissaving in 1936	29	31	37

[a] Household averages are in parenthesis.

[b] In Michang, the sum of cash holdings at the beginning of 1936 plus cash saving in 1936 were less than year-end cash holdings. This difference represents savings that went to retire debt, were lent out, used to buy land and livestock, or used for other investment purposes. In Lianggezhuang, the exact opposite was true, reflecting an increase in cash holdings from asset sales, loan repayment, and so forth.

Note: One *yuan* equals 0.20 1936 U.S. dollars.

Source: Minami Manshū tetsudō kabushiki kaisha, Kitō nōson jittai chōsahan, *Dainiji kitō nōson jittai chōsa hōkokusho: tōkeihen. Dai ichiban: Heikoku ken. Dai sanban: Hōjun ken. Dai yonban: Shōrei ken.* (Report on the second investigation of actual conditions of northeastern Hebei villages: Statistical volume. First group: Pinggu County. Third group: Fengrun County. Fourth group: Changli County) (Dalian, 1937).

the end of 1936. The village saving rates (category four) report the flow of savings in 1936 as a percentage of total village income. All measures include both household cash and grain savings. Note that in all three villages the overall rate of saving was positive: it was highest in Michang, where 29.4 percent of village income was saved, followed by Dabeiguan's 19.1 percent and Lianggezhuang's 14.0 percent.

Yet saving in the three villages differed remarkably in composition and reflected distinct differences in their commercial orientation. In Dabeiguan, the least commercialized of the three villages, much of the saving took the form of grain. That is, out of total village savings in 1936 valued at 2,971.5 *yuan*, 2,073.1 *yuan*, or slightly more than two-thirds, represents the value of the increase in grain holdings. Added to the carryover from the previous year, villagers kept on hand roughly 60 percent of a year's grain consumption.[31] In Michang, on the other hand, cash savings in 1936 were 7,433.3 *yuan*, nearly ten times the value of the saving in grain (756.7 *yuan*). The total value of grain holdings at year's end was 2,866.0 *yuan*, or slightly more than a quarter of a year's consumption. Households in Michang not only depended much more heavily on the market to meet their grain consumption needs (31.0 percent in 1936 versus 10 percent in Dabeiguan), but they also tied up a much smaller portion of their savings in the form of grain. Finally, in Lianggezhuang, out of total savings in 1936 of 2,341.5 *yuan*, 28 percent was in grain and the remainder in cash. Lianggezhuang also had the lowest level of accumulated holdings at the beginning of the year, reflecting a succession of poor years during which households appear to have drawn down their stocks to maintain consumption levels. As in Michang, nevertheless, less than a third of total year-end holdings were in grain.

Not only did grain holdings constitute a much higher percentage of total savings in Dabeiguan, but, as Table 3 shows, there was a net outflow of capital (total lending less total borrowing) from the village. In the case of Michang, an inflow of capital supplemented villagers' own high saving rates. This behavior reflects inter-village differences in investment and income-earning opportunities, and more generally, differences in commercial orientation. Michang households held a much higher percentage of their annual saving in the form of cash for, among other things, use as working capital to buy fertilizer and hire labor, the demand for which increased significantly with the expansion in cotton acreage. Households in Dabeiguan, on the other hand, while marketing modest amounts of cotton and sesame, were clearly much more subsistence-oriented, as reflected by the larger percentage of their annual saving and year-end holdings in grain.

But who was doing the saving and to what extent was it tied to landownership? In Table 7 we provide information on average saving rates by income classes and landholdings. As expected, saving rates do rise with incomes, with the highest income group saving roughly a third of their incomes. At least for these few villages, concerns that high-income households were dissipating incomes on luxuries seem slightly unjustified. There are, however, fundamental differences between the villages in the relationship between landholdings and saving rates. In Dabeiguan, average saving rates rise with landholdings and are actually negative for the first two landholding categories. In Michang, however, saving rates and landholdings are much less systematically correlated; excluding a few outliers, they are fairly constant across landholding groups. This reflects differences in the importance of land in the generation of income in the two villages, with land clearly much less

[31] A small portion of the stock represents next year's seed requirements, by Buck's estimate 3 to 4 percent of annual output in the winter wheat-millet area of North China.

TABLE 7
AVERAGE SAVING RATES BY INCOMES AND LANDHOLDINGS[a]
(percentage of net household income)

	Income Category (in *yuan*)					
	0–50	50–100	100–150	150–250	250–350	over 350
Michang	−0.13	0.08	0.11	0.15	0.30	0.36
	(7)	(20)	(18)	(34)	(16)	(17)
Lianggezhuang	−0.72	−0.10	0.08	0.10	0.27	0.29
	(10)	(27)	(28)	(20)	(7)	(9)
Dabeiguan	−0.37	−0.02	0.11	0.15	0.21	0.32
	(12)	(34)	(18)	(20)	(7)	(7)
	Landholding Category (in *mou*)					
	Landless	1–10	10–30	30–50	50–70	over 70
Michang	0.10	0.18	0.23	0.17	0.26	0.21
	(41)	(32)	(23)	(4)	(7)	(5)
Lianggezhuang	0.03	−0.14	0.01	−0.07	0.28	0.23
	(28)	(30)	(21)	(3)	(4)	(9)
Dabeiguan	−0.41	−0.04	0.07	0.11	0.43	0.42
	(5)	(37)	(36)	(12)	(3)	(5)

[a] Number of households in parenthesis.
Notes: One *yuan* equals 0.20 1936 U.S. dollars. One *mou* equals one-sixth of an acre.
Source: Minami Manshū tetsudō kabushiki kaisha, Kitō nōson jittai chōsahan, *Dainiji kitō nōson jittai chōsa hōkokusho: tōkeihen. Dai ichiban: Heikoku ken. Dai sanban: Hōjun ken. Dai yonban: Shōrei ken.* (Report on the second investigation of actual conditions of northeastern Hebei villages: Statistical volume. First group: Pinggu County. Third group: Fengrun County. Fourth group: Changli County) (Dalian, 1937).

important in Michang than in Dabeiguan. Regardless of the size of their landholdings, households were saving substantially in Michang in order to take advantage of the new market opportunities that commercialization was opening up. In Dabeiguan, in contrast, saving and incomes alike were much more tightly linked to landholding, and households much more preoccupied with meeting subsistence needs than with exploiting new commercial opportunities.

SUMMARY

Couple the view of a predominantly agricultural economy with an observed increase in population and a story of economic stagnation (if not absolute decline) emerges. Add to this a "fact" of increasing inequality of landownership and the pessimism of the story is compounded. While this has been the accepted scenario for China's late nineteenth- and early twentieth-century economic history, our empirical investigations suggest it may not be the correct story.

We would like to suggest an alternative view, emphasizing commercially induced, regionally differentiated economic growth, with some areas benefiting from lower-cost exchange opportunities and others remaining largely unaffected by the changes surrounding them. Yet overall, the productivity gains induced by these changes were sufficient to deliver aggregate economic growth.

What is the link between landownership and income in our new story? Land in early twentieth-century China was becoming only one among several investment opportunities, in some places no longer even the most important one. Some rural households responded to increased nonfarm economic opportunities and directed not only their efforts but their savings toward these opportunities. As a consequence, like any other specialized factor of production in an increasingly complex production system, land became less uniformly owned. Rather than heralding economic decline, however, such inequality in land ownership signified a change in economic structure, new production opportunities, and (with measured hindsight) economic growth.

In a number of respects our scenario for much of China over this period parallels a process that Peter Lindert has described for Great Britain.[32] As early as the eighteenth century the "drift toward human skills and away from land" in the economy had a slight income-leveling effect in a society otherwise dominated by landed wealth. The rise in real wages beginning in the 1820s, some 60 years after the start of the Industrial Revolution, only accelerated the process and contributed further to the increasing unimportance of land.

While late nineteenth-, early twentieth-century China had yet to undergo an industrial revolution, similar changes were taking place, albeit in more subtle form. Rural real wages began to rise before the manufacturing sector had grown significantly as a portion of the economy. Much of the growth (in absolute terms) in the economy was, in fact, in agriculture and the rural sector and tied to economywide increasing specialization and exchange.

As always in any empirical investigation, a story is only as good as theory and data allow. Here we have used a mix of macro- and micro-level data reporting households' landholdings and incomes for the early twentieth century. While our micro-level data cover only three North China villages and our macro-level data are subject to problems of interpretation, their evidence is mutually consistent and sufficiently contrary to the currently held view of China's late nineteenth-, early twentieth-century economic history to provoke a reconsideration of that view. While we believe the alternative outline of cause-and-effect consistent with our reported data to be quite plausible, we recognize it remains a task for future research to confirm or discard this new view of China's recent past.

[32] Peter H. Lindert, "Unequal English Wealth since 1670," *Journal of Political Economy*, 94 (Dec. 1986), pp. 1127–62.

The Evolution of Private Property in Nineteenth-Century Hawaii

SUMNER J. LA CROIX AND JAMES ROUMASSET

Population pressure has been identified as a major force behind the transition from traditional property rights in land to exclusive, transferable property rights. This article examines the case of Hawaii where the transition to private property in land occurred while its population was rapidly declining. That transition was driven by new market opportunities and considerations of public finance. The shift in comparative advantage to sugar production increased the rents associated with private land rights, while declining tax revenues prompted the king and his government to pursue property rights reform to gain additional revenues.

When Captain James Cook made the first western contact with the Hawaiian Islands in 1778, he found several small political entities with a common cultural and institutional heritage. Hawaii's agricultural economy was organized around a hierarchical kinship system. A ruling chief controlled the land and distributed revocable land grants to lesser chiefs. The grants specified certain rights of use for the chiefs and allowed them to collect taxes from extended families of commoners who also retained restricted rights of occupancy and use. Yet by 1855 the land institutions observed at contact had disappeared, replaced by a system of exclusive, transferable private property rights. Historians have pointed to a variety of forces which placed pressure on traditional institutions governing land use. The influence of western ideas, pressure by western governments, fears of annexation, and the desire to secure capital investments specific to land have been identified by various observers and authors as the critical factors.[1] Historians have, however, ignored the possible influence of other demographic and economic factors that had major impacts on Hawaii's economy and governmental institutions. Our review of historical sources provides some support for the traditional explanations but also provides evidence that powerful

The Journal of Economic History, Vol. L, No. 4 (Dec. 1990). ISSN 0022-0507.

The authors are Professors of Economics, University of Hawaii, Honolulu, HI 96822.

Comments which significantly improved the article were received from several anonymous referees, Harry Ball, Richard Dowell, David Feeny, D. Bruce Johnsen, Pauline King, James Mak, John Palmer, Mark Plummer, Subroto Roy, John Wallis, Thomas Weiss, Calla Wiemer, and participants in seminars at the University of Hawaii, the University of Canterbury, the University of New South Wales, the University of Newcastle, Flinders University, the East-West Center, the 1983 meetings of the Western Economics Association, and the 1986 meetings of the Public Choice Society.

[1] See R. S. Kuykendall, *The Hawaiian Kingdom* (Honolulu, 1938), vol. 1, pp. 269–98; Gavan Daws, *Shoal of Time* (Honolulu, 1968), pp. 124–28; Edward D. Beechert, *Working in Hawaii* (Honolulu, 1985), pp. 29–36; and Theodore Morgan, *Hawaii: A Century of Economic Change: 1778–1876* (Cambridge, MA, 1948), pp. 123–39.

demographic and economic forces influenced the course of institutional development.

Economists have often portrayed the transition in property rights to land as an efficient response to changing economic and demographic factors.[2] Population pressure, which usually brings an appreciation of land rents and a decline of real wages and thus an incentive to define property rights more precisely, has frequently been regarded as a major force behind the transformation. In the case of the English enclosures, Douglass North and Robert Paul Thomas concluded that the transition from a system of open field property rights to one of exclusive, transferable property rights was driven at least in part by rising population; Ricardian forces drove up land rents and the negative externalities of open field systems became large enough to warrant the costs of changing to more efficient institutional arrangements.[3] For Thailand, Burma, India, and the Philippines, David Feeney concluded that "the growth of population [and the increase in the terms of trade] were indeed associated with a rise in real land prices" and that land scarcity induced changes in the institutions governing its use.[4]

In those cases population was increasing and land was becoming more scarce relative to the population. In Hawaii, however, private property emerged during the 1840s and 1850s after a 75-year period of severe population *decline*. As a result, the Hawaiian case presents an opportunity to explore two other economic factors that enhance the advantages of private property over collective arrangements. First, an economy's comparative advantage may turn away from goods that can be efficiently produced under traditional property rights. Hawaii's rapid transition from a closed to an open economy removed the close association between land rents and population density. In an open economy land rents are linked to movements in the terms of trade as well as to changes in population.[5] Second, the timing of the property rights transition may be influenced by considerations of public finance. Changes in population and the terms of trade affected the income earned by members of various social groups as well as the king and his government. These effects prompted the king and his government to promote a change to private property rights to allow net government revenue collections to increase.

The specific episode investigated here is the evolution and redistri-

[2] We define efficient actions as those which maximize the society's wealth, without regard to the actual distribution of the gains and losses.

[3] Douglass C. North and Robert Paul Thomas, *The Rise of the Western World: A New Economic History* (Cambridge, 1973); Douglass C. North, *Structure and Change in Economic History* (New York, 1981); and J. D. Chambers, "Enclosure and Labour Supply in the Industrial Revolution," *Economic History Review*, 2nd series, 5 (1953), pp. 319–43.

[4] David Feeny, "The Development of Property Rights in Land: A Comparative Study," in Robert H. Bates, ed., *Toward a Political Economy of Development* (Berkeley, 1988).

[5] Ibid., pp. 273–82.

bution of property rights in Hawaiian land over the period 1778 to 1855. These changes in land tenure began with the dismantling of the traditional structure of rights of use and ended with the establishment of exclusive, transferable property rights in land. To understand why the institutional structure changed so rapidly, we sketch a picture of the changes in Hawaii's economy and property institutions from 1778, the year of "contact" with the outside world, to 1855, when the "Great Mahele" (Division) was completed. We also examine traditional explanations for the transformation of property rights and analyze how changes in factor scarcity and product prices affected that process and how considerations of public finance provided incentives for the king to capitalize rights in the land. Finally, we discuss how this case study may contribute to a more general understanding of institutional change and the evolution of property rights.

I. THE PRE-CONTACT ECONOMY AND POPULATION DECLINE

In 1778 Captain Cook's ships encountered a group of eight small tropical islands populated by a people with social and political institutions remarkably similar to those in other more distant Polynesian societies. Although several distinct political entities actively competed with each other, the people of Hawaii participated in a common culture. In each polity the populace was divided into three classes: chiefs (*ali'i*), commoners (*maka'ainana*), and priests (*kahuna*).[6] Each polity was led by a ruling chief (*ali'i'ai moku*), who held title to all lands and goods. In the manner of a feudal society, the ruling chief gave temporary land grants to lesser chiefs (*ali'i'ai ahupua'a*), who then gave temporary land grants to their land managers (*konohiki*). The *konohiki* then subleased the land to commoners to grow sweet potatoes and taro.[7] Usually the managers retained an active role in the management of their diverse lands (*ahupua'a*) which extended from the mountains to the coral reef fishing grounds. The common people worked in a variety of occupations (canoe building, home building, bird catching, fishing) with the bulk of the work being the cultivation of the land.

Work, like most other activities, was organized around an extended family unit, the *'ohana*. The term *'ohana* was used to cover relatives by blood, marriage, and adoption.[8] Many communal activities were conducted by the *'ohana* such as planting and harvesting crops, clearing land, constructing irrigation works, and fishing beyond the shoreline's coral reefs. Land managers collected the chief's share of output from the family's headman (*haku*) rather than from individual farmers. The

[6] There was also a third very small class of slaves (*kauwa*).

[7] See William Davenport, "The 'Hawaiian Cultural Revolution': Some Political and Economic Considerations," *American Anthropologist*, 71 (Feb. 1969), p. 5.

[8] Some controversy exists as to whether the *'ohana* represents a single extended family or a group of extended families. See Beechert, *Working in Hawaii*, p. 7.

'ohana facilitated specialization in work activities and ensured the ability to consume a somewhat varied market basket of goods and, in the absence of organized market institutions, acted to reduce the cost of exchange among family members. In a similar fashion, the inclusion of diverse lands in the *ahupua'a* helped to make this production unit generally self-sufficient; without extensive market institutions linking the *ahupua'a*, organization of production under the auspices of one large diversified firm further facilitated the expansion of opportunities for individual workers and consumers. While occasional market fairs (where participants exchanged cloth, mats, baskets, pigs, dogs, dried fish, vegetables, poi, canoes, paddles, and spears) allowed for some regional specialization in production, the institutions of the *'ohana* and the *ahupua'a* were vital given the rough geography and shifting political boundaries in Hawaii.

Two missionary observers believed that the chiefs managed, via taxes, arbitrary confiscations, and voluntary offerings, to appropriate about two-thirds of the *'ohana's* output.[9] There is some evidence that the net appropriation may have been lower, as the chiefs stored and ultimately redistributed a large fraction of their share of the produced goods. Marshall Sahlins has speculated that the storage and redistribution of goods was intended to redistribute income, to provide revenue for public works projects, and to ensure adequate stores during times of war and famine.[10] In any case, even with these substantial taxes and land rents, the common people lived well above subsistence levels. Even if the chiefs did appropriate two-thirds of the physical goods produced, a significant portion of income in the Polynesian economic system is leisure, which is excluded from the tax base. Tales of starvation are absent from the renderings of pre-1778 Hawaiian history. Theodore Morgan has observed that "[i]n good times the food supply was adequate in quantity and variety."[11] Ralph Kuykendall has emphasized that the common people "were probably less downtrodden than

[9] See William Richards, letter to Charles Wilkes, U.S.N., Commander of the U.S.A. Exploring Expedition (Mar. 15, 1841), in Marshall Sahlins and Dorothy Barrere, "William Richards on Hawaiian Culture and Political Conditions of the Islands in 1841," *Hawaiian Journal of History*, 7 (1973), p. 23; and Sheldon Dibble, *A History of the Sandwich Islands* (Honolulu, 1909), p. 74. Since Richards's letter was written in 1841, the two-thirds figure may not be applicable to earlier periods. Unfortunately, his figure is not based on empirical investigations, and there are no other contemporary sources with which to compare his estimate. It should be noted that the two-thirds share is considerably higher than the one-half share commonly observed in modern share-tenancy contracts.

[10] A more complete discussion of the role of the *ali'i* in the Hawaiian economy can be found in Marshall Sahlins, *Stone Age Economics* (Chicago, 1972).

[11] See Morgan, *Hawaii*, p. 51. An evaluation of the nutritional merits of the ancient Hawaiian diet reveals that it meets modern (1927) standards. See C. D. Miller, *Food Values of Poi, Taro, and Limu*, Bernice P. Bishop Museum Bulletin (Honolulu, 1927).

the lower classes of Europe in the eighteenth century,'' noting that they ''regularly had time for cultural activities, sports, and games.''[12]

Common people were not bound to the soil, unlike the serfs in Europe during the Middle Ages, and their relative mobility understandably contributed to their real incomes. While migration was infrequent, the common people were free to seek better opportunities or escape oppressive conditions. Some families worked plots of land under different chiefs (or on different islands) as insurance against both arbitrary behavior by their landlord and local famine or drought.[13] The commoners' ability to vote with their feet placed constraints on the ability of chiefs to extract all income above subsistence levels; at the same time, the high transportation costs associated with moving to another district allowed chiefs to extract a portion of the common people's income above the subsistence level.

If the chiefs attempted to extract additional income, commoners had an additional option besides moving. The historical record contains numerous stories of rebellions against chiefs who oppressed the common people. David Malo, an early chronicler of ancient Hawaii, wrote that ''[f]or this reason . . . some of the ancient kings had a wholesome fear of the people.'' [14] As in other societies, competition between the ruling chiefs was not confined to the labor and product markets. Constantly waging war on each other, the ruling chiefs attained power by assembling loyal armies composed of large numbers of chiefs. In pre-contact Hawaii, chiefdoms expanded and contracted, formed and broke alliances, and apparently maintained this state of affairs for many centuries.

Thus, on eight small isolated islands in the middle of the Pacific Ocean, without mineral resources but with a complex agricultural technology, there existed for many centuries four to six competing polities in a common cultural and economic environment. The Hawaiians cultivated numerous tropical root, tuber, and tree crops in ''irrigated valley lands ranked among the most productive agricultural ecosystems anywhere in Polynesia.''[15] While the commoners were poor, competition between the chiefs for their services prevented their incomes from being pushed to subsistence levels. Numerous institutions, such as the *'ohana* and the *ahupua'a*, were developed to exploit

[12] Kuykendall, *The Hawaiian Kingdom*, vol. 1, p. 9.

[13] See Sahlins and Barrere, ''William Richards,'' p. 23. They qualified Richards's statement with the observation that testimony ''before the land commission (1848–1854) will not support the contention that people commonly held land in different *ahupua'a*. What sometimes occurs is that siblings and first cousins from locally important families are dispersed among several *ahupua'a* of a district (such as *'Ewa*). On the other hand, ordinary *maka'ainana* did often have claims in different [parts] of the same *ahupua'a*, a distribution which . . . might place them under two or more chiefs at once'' (p. 38).

[14] David Malo, *Hawaiian Antiquities* (Mooelo Hawaii) (Honolulu, reprinted 1971), p. 195.

[15] Patrick Vinton Kirch, *Feathered Gods and Fishhooks* (Honolulu, 1985), p. 2.

economies of scale in food production. To some observers, Hawaii's complex civilization with its highly developed technology, hierarchical, social, and political organizations, art and culture, religious beliefs, and temple rituals was an amazing achievement for a group of people isolated in the middle of the Pacific Ocean.[16]

Contact with the western world set in motion forces that rapidly changed the society of pre-contact Hawaii. Among other things, it led to the formation of the nation-state in 1795, while access to western markets increased the benefits of a cartel among the chiefs.[17] Access to western military technology lowered the costs to the chiefs of maintaining a political coalition, with one of the chiefs, Kamehameha I, dominating the others.[18] The king maintained the cartel by allocating several *ahupua'a* on different islands to each of his chiefs, thereby making it more difficult for a particular chief to acquire a strong base of support on a single island. Kamehameha, by requiring powerful chiefs to join his court on Oahu and to travel with him to other Hawaiian Islands, prevented his rivals from accumulating power.[19] After unification, the chiefs' cartel made it feasible to enforce higher labor taxes, thereby pushing the commoners closer to subsistence.[20]

The decline in population of indigenous Americans and Pacific Islanders after contact with westerners was a universal and tragic occurrence. Exposure to western diseases and reduction of living standards after contact also led to a massive decline in the native population of Hawaii. While the population estimates at the time of contact vary, the extent of the population decline is enormous regardless of which figure is adopted (see Table 1). Two officers on Cook's

[16] See, for example, ibid., p. 7.

[17] Sumner J. La Croix and James Roumasset, "An Economic Theory of Political Change in Premissionary Hawaii," *Explorations in Economic History*, 21 (Apr. 1984), pp. 151–68. The island of Kauai remained independent until 1810.

[18] See D. Bruce Johnsen, "The Formation and Protection of Property Rights Among the Southern Kwakiutl Indians," *Journal of Legal Studies*, 15 (Jan. 1986), pp. 41–67, for an analysis of a similar response to western contact. He argued that the opportunities presented by trade and the threat presented by the new settlers in Canada would increase expenditures to enforce property rights in fishing and hunting territories. Johnsen observed that the use of violence to settle disputes about property rights fell as a result of the decline in the Kwakiutl population. His explanation for the change was that violence is "a relatively labor-intensive input in protecting exclusive property rights" (p. 65). The Canadian government's sanctions on violence between tribes also contributed to a shift away from its use.

[19] The system of separated strips also facilitated the king's monitoring of each chief's managerial efforts.

[20] See accounts of the commoners' burden in Kuykendall, *The Hawaiian Kingdom*, vol. 1, pp. 89–90. The decline in population probably had mixed effects on living standards. In a simple Malthusian general equilibrium model, population decline should lead to increased wages and higher standards of living. The decline in population may, however, also generate a host of effects that would reduce living standards. Incentives to accumulate human capital and to work intensively on the job may be impaired and individual specialization may decrease as market size declines. Long-term sequelae of the diseases (or their treatments) can adversely affect health status and labor productivity and therefore living standards.

TABLE 1
POPULATION BY ISLANDS, 1778–1849

Island	1778 (Schmitt)	1778 (Nordyke)	1778 (Stannard)	1805 (Youngson)	1823 (Census)	1832 (Census)	1836 (Census)	1849 (Census)
All Islands	225,000	310,000	795,343	264,160	142,050	130,313	108,579	80,641
Hawaii	90,000	120,000	403,800	100,000	85,000	45,792	39,364	27,204
Maui	52,500	70,000	125,021	48,000	20,000	35,062	24,199	21,047
Lanai	3,500	4,000	13,950	7,000	2,500	1,600	1,200	604
Molokai	9,000	15,000	44,387	25,000	3,500	6,000	6,000	3,540
Oahu	42,500	60,000	121,540	40,000	20,000	29,755	27,809	25,440
Kauai	25,000	40,000	82,995	40,000	10,000	10,977	8,934	6,956
Other	750	1,000	3,650	4,160	1,050	1,127	1,073	714

Sources: Robert C. Schmitt, *Demographic Statistics of Hawaii: 1778–1965* (Honolulu, 1968), p. 42; and David E. Stannard, *Before the Horror: The Population of Hawai'i on the Eve of Western Contact* (Honolulu, 1989), table 1.

ships offered very different estimates. Captain James King estimated the population at 400,000, while Lieutenant William Bligh suggested the correct figure was closer to 200,000. Three recent reviews of historical sources have arrived at vastly different population estimates: Robert Schmitt proposed between 200,000 and 250,000; Eleanor Nordyke, 310,000; and David Stannard, 795,000.[21] Since Schmitt's figures form the lower bound among the three modern estimates and are the least favorable to our analysis, we adopted his mean figure (225,000) as our benchmark.

The first missionary census in 1831–1832 revealed a population of only 130,313 people, a sharp decline from the 1778 level.[22] Battlefield deaths during Kamehameha I's wars of unification, starvation during famines, and human sacrifices contributed to the decline but were probably minor factors. Since the Hawaiian language was first transcribed in 1823, records of these events do not exist and their importance cannot be quantified. A substantial portion of the decline can be attributed to a series of epidemics beginning after contact. The epidemic of 1804 (the *oku'u*) decimated an army assembled by Kamehameha on Oahu to invade the last independent island, Kauai. This dysenteric disease, thought by modern analysts to have been cholera, took between 5,000 and 15,000 lives.[23] Schmitt related that in 1825 and 1826

[21] Robert C. Schmitt, "New Estimates of the Pre-Censal Population of Hawaii," *Journal of the Polynesian Society*, 80 (June 1971), pp. 237–43; and David E. Stannard, *Before the Horror: The Population of Hawai'i on the Eve of Western Contact* (Honolulu, 1989).

[22] The 150,000 figure is the "official" missionary estimate. Other estimates are as low as 130,000. James Jackson Jarves's estimate of 142,050 has been widely cited. See Robert C. Schmitt, *Demographic Statistics of Hawaii: 1778–1965* (Honolulu, 1968), pp. 22–25.

[23] Robert C. Schmitt, "The *Oku'u*: Hawaii's Greatest Epidemic," *Hawaii Medical Journal*, 29 (May–June 1970), pp. 359–64. Schmitt disputed accounts that the 1804 epidemic killed 175,000 people. He presented evidence indicating that historians' accounts of the episode have become increasingly exaggerated. Two visitors to Hawaii in 1822 (17 years after the epidemic) indicated that a yellow fever "swept away more than two thirds" of the 8,000 assembled troops. See Daniel

thousands "died of an epidemic of 'cough, congested lungs and sore throats.' A net population loss of 22,000 between 1832 and 1836 has been attributed to whooping cough, measles, or social disintegration, depending on the source."[24] In 1839 an epidemic of mumps spread through the populace, and in 1848 outbreaks of measles and whooping cough were followed by epidemics of diarrhea and influenza. Contemporary observers believed that "[t]en thousand would be a low estimate for 1848 and 1849 which those epidemics took away."[25]

Another factor which contributed significantly to the population decline was the decrease in the crude birth rate. Schmitt argued that "crude birth rates must have remained below 30 per 1000 most of the time and may have fallen to as low as 15 per 1000. Specific factors probably included sterility (caused by gonorrhea), a high proportion of fetal deaths (from syphilis), and induced abortion."[26] Introduced by Cook's crew, venereal disease was previously unknown in the Islands. In addition to the fall in the crude birth rate, infanticide may also have contributed to the population decline, although contemporary observers disagreed as to its significance.

The demand by visiting foreign ships for seamen also reduced the resident population. Romanzo Adams estimated that the number of Hawaiian men absent from the Islands "increased from 200 in 1823 . . . to 600 in 1836, 3,500 in 1848, and 4,000 in 1850. The latter figure amounts to almost 5 percent of the total Hawaiian and part Hawaiian population at that time, and 12 percent of all Hawaiian males 18 years of age."[27] Immigration was insufficient to offset this outflow; by 1850 only 1.9 percent of the population was foreign-born. The first accurate census conducted in the Islands revealed a population of 80,641 in 1849. The native population reached its nadir in 1900 when the U.S. census revealed only 37,656 full or part Hawaiians.

II. CHANGING LAND TENURE: 1795–1855

Prior to the establishment of a unified Hawaiian kingdom by Kamehameha I in 1795, several competing political entities existed, all with similar land institutions. The ruling chief made revocable land grants to lesser chiefs, who hired land managers to oversee production by commoner families residing on the land. Land rights were not hereditary, and the ruling chief could redistribute land at a chief's death or at any other time. Commoner tenants were required to labor on the ruling chief's (and his retainers') lands and fish ponds. In addition, commoners

Tyerman and George Bennet, *Voyages and Travels*, compiled by James Montgomery (Boston, 1832), vol. 2, pp. 48–49.

[24] Schmitt, "The *Oku'u*," p. 363.

[25] *The Friend*, vol. 7, no. 10 (Nov. 15, 1849), p. 79, as quoted in Schmitt, "The *Oku'u*," p. 363.

[26] Schmitt, "New Estimates," pp. 238–39.

[27] As quoted in Schmitt, *Demographic Statistics*, p. 39.

owed a portion of their production to the *ahupua'a* chief. Rights to collect taxes from commoners on the land and to use the land could not, however, be transferred between chiefs. While commoners were free to move to other districts or islands, Malo observed that the commoners "were the fixed residents of the land; the chiefs were the ones who moved about from place to place."[28]

Abraham Fornander related that "[i]t has been the custom since the days of Keawenui-a-Umi on the death of a Moi (King) and the accession of a new one, to redivide and distribute the land of the island between the chiefs and favorites of the new monarch."[29] Following this ancient practice, Kamehameha I (who united all but one of Hawaii's small polities in 1795) redistributed rights in land to chiefs in his army after conquering islands governed by rival chiefs. Samuel Kamakau and John Ii, two contemporary Hawaiian observers, told us who got what in many cases.[30] Yet during Kamehameha's subsequent long reign (1795–1819), "the leading families of chiefs enjoyed a greater degree of permanence and security in the possession of their lands than had been previously known."[31] This conclusion is based on the observation that Kamehameha I implicitly recognized hereditary rights to property (by allowing the deceased's family to retain the property) and did not arbitrarily redistribute land. The rationale for Kamehameha's change in practice is unknown.

The second major change in the land tenure system came in 1819 with the death of Kamehameha I and the transition to the rule of Kamehameha II. Instead of redistributing land to form a viable coalition of chiefs to support his rule, the new king chose to solidify his support among the existing coalition of chiefs by relaxing his control over the chiefs' sandalwood trades with foreign merchants.[32] By ignoring one of the major options open to a new king, Kamehameha II weakened the prerogative of redistributing land for future rulers. This de facto security of tenure in the land was reinforced in 1825, when Kamehameha II and his queen succumbed to measles while visiting London. Neither the regent, Kaahumanu (who governed until the successor reached age 18), nor the young king, Kamehameha III, redistributed property during their reigns.

[28] As quoted in Beechert, *Working in Hawaii*, pp. 9–10.

[29] Abraham Fornander, *An Account of the Polynesian Race: Its Origins and Migrations*, 2 vols. (Tokyo, 1969), vol. 2, p. 300. Fornander, a newspaper editor and judge, was a dedicated student of Hawaiian history in the middle to late nineteenth century. In his 1878 work he compiled genealogies and recorded oral traditions for many pre- and post-contact events. His accounts are only as reliable as the oral traditions.

[30] See Samuel M. Kamakau, *Ruling Chiefs of Hawaii* (Honolulu, 1961), p. 175; and John Papa Ii, *Fragments of Hawaiian History*, edited by Dorothy B. Barrere (Honolulu, 1959), pp. 13–14, 20, 26, 69–70.

[31] See W. D. Alexander, "A Brief History of Land Titles in the Hawaiian Kingdom," in Thomas G. Thrum, ed., *Hawaiian Annual for 1891* (Honolulu, 1890), p. 108.

[32] La Croix and Roumasset, "An Economic Theory of Political Change," p. 164.

In 1845 a proposal to convert customary rights in land into private property rights came from Hawaii's Minister of the Interior, Dr. Gerrit Judd; a constitutional monarchy having been established in 1840. Judd called for a law permitting the sale of land "as freehold property forever" to Hawaiian subjects.[33] Later that year the legislature passed a law establishing a board of commissioners which would award title to various tracts of land. A valid claimant would receive a "Land Commission Award," which could be exchanged for a title upon payment to the government of one-third of the value of the unimproved land. But how was the Land Commission to divide land among the three parties (king, landlord, tenant) holding an interest in the land? After several meetings of the King's Privy Council in December 1847, the council adopted a set of rules to facilitate the land division. They are aptly summarized by John Chinen:

> (1) The King was to retain all of his private lands as his own individual property, subject only to the rights of the tenants. (2) One third of the remaining lands was to be for the Hawaiian Government; one third for the chiefs and the konohikis; and one third to be set aside for the tenants, the actual possessors and cultivators of the soil. (3) The division between the chiefs and konohikis and their tenants under Rule 2 was to take place whenever any chief, konohiki, or tenant desired such a division, subject only to confirmation by the king in privy council. (4) The tenants of the King's private lands were entitled to a fee simple title to one third of the lands possessed and cultivated by them, which was to be set off for the tenants in fee, whenever the king or any of the tenants desired such a division. (5) The divisions prescribed in the foregoing rules were not to interfere with any lands that may have been granted in fee simple by the king or his predecessors. (6) The Chiefs and konohikis were authorized to satisfy the commutation by either the setting aside of one third of their lands to the government or by the payments of one third of the unimproved value of their lands. (7) The lands of King Kamehameha III were to be recorded in the same book as all other allodial titles, and the only separate book was to be that listing the government lands. It was Kamehameha III who insisted upon the seventh rule, as a means of protecting his private lands in the event of an invasion by a foreign power.[34]

[33] Kuykendall, *The Hawaiian Kingdom*, vol. 1, p. 278. After the Declaration of Rights of 1839 and the constitution of 1840 transformed Hawaii's government, several missionaries entered the king's government service including Judd, Lorrin Andrews, Richard Armstrong, and Edwin Hall. Daws observed that each man, "as a condition of his employment, had signed an oath of allegiance to the king. Among the noisy expatriates of the foreign community this was enough to ruin any man's reputation." See Daws, *Shoal of Time*, p. 108, and pp. 106–12 for a full discussion of the role of the missionaries in Kamehameha III's government. R. C. Wyllie, the minister of foreign affairs, also argued in a report dated Dec. 1, 1847 (in *Reports of the Minister of Foreign Affairs, 1852–62*, p. 67) that land reform would have salutary effects on Hawaiians. "Thus even the poorest of Your Majesty's subjects would stand on a footing of independent right—he would know that the land which he cultivated was his own, and could not be taken from him; and he would have the powerful stimulus of self interest to improve it, and to put a good dwelling on it; every child would be of value to him as he grew up, to help him in cultivating the ground; laborers would be induced to marry, in order to have children to help them; those children would be better taken care of, and would become more moral by being removed from the haunts of vice in the seaports."

[34] Jon J. Chinen, *The Great Mahele* (Honolulu, 1958), pp. 15–16. Other important renditions of the Great Mahele are Kuykendall, *The Hawaiian Kingdom*, vol. 1, chap. 15; Morgan, *Hawaii*, chap. 8; and Daws, *Shoal of Time*, pp. 124–27.

On January 27, 1848, "245 landlords came forward to arrange their lands and divide with the King."[35] By March 7, 1848, the "Great Division" or "Great Mahele" was completed. The next day the king divided his lands into Government lands and "Crown lands," the latter and smaller portion to be his private lands. The process of division between the king and his landlords ended in the summer of 1850. "Many of the chiefs surrendered to the government portions of their land, which were accepted by the privy council as full commutation of the government's interest, and fee simple titles were accordingly given to those chiefs for the lands which remained to them."[36]

The Privy Council resolutions of December 21, 1849, specified procedures for tenants to claim land shares. These resolutions provided for

> fee simple titles free of commutation, (to) be granted to all native tenants for the lands occupied and improved by them, but not including houselots in Honolulu, Lahaina and Hilo. . . . The resolutions further provided that some government land on each island should be set aside to be sold in fee simple in lots of from one to fifty acres to such natives as were not otherwise furnished with sufficient lands at a minimum price of 50 cents per acre.[37]

The housing lots carried a commutation fee of one-fourth their unimproved value. In 1855 the completed division of lands was as follows: Crown Lands, 984,000 acres; Chiefs' Lands, 1,619,000 acres; Government Lands, 1,495,000 acres; Kuleanas, which were the land grants to commoners, 28,600 acres. The Mahele principles provided for commoners to receive one-third of the lands they occupied and cultivated, yet their final allocation was only a very small proportion of the total arable land. There are three reasons behind this disproportionate allotment. First, some commoners were unaware of the Mahele process and/or did not understand how to file claims. Second, many surveyors allocated only one-third of the tenants' *cultivated* lands to the tenants. Lands lying fallow were not counted as being under cultivation by some surveyors, and, consequently, large errors were made in the actual allocation of land. Third, the lands received by commoners were valuable agricultural lands. Although commoners received only a small proportion of the Islands' acreage, they received a higher proportion of total land value.[38]

[35] Kuykendall, *The Hawaiian Kingdom*, vol. 1, p. 288.

[36] Ibid., p. 289.

[37] Ibid., p. 291.

[38] Ibid., p. 294. This allocation is consistent with John Umbeck's prediction about property rights allocation. See John Umbeck, "Might Makes Rights: A Theory of the Foundation and Initial Distribution of Property Rights," *Economic Inquiry*, 19 (Jan. 1981), pp. 38–59. On p. 46 he showed that when property is being allocated among a group of individuals, those people receiving "more productive land will get less land than others whose holdings are not so productive." See also James Roumasset and William James, "Explaining Variations in Share Contracts: Land Quality,

In 1847 the legislature passed an act allowing foreigners to keep lands which they possessed, but they could sell such land only to native subjects. New lands could not be acquired. Kuykendall argued that the boom in the demand for Hawaii's agricultural products between 1848 and 1850 prompted a reconsideration of earlier positions regarding foreign ownership. The editors of the *Polynesian*, the major weekly newspaper, supported plans to allow foreign acquisition and conveyance of land to attract foreign capital and enterprise to agriculture. Legislation allowing foreigners to hold and convey land was rejected in 1848 but approved in 1850.[39]

III. INSTITUTIONAL CHANGE: TRADITIONAL AND ECONOMIC EXPLANATIONS

The traditional explanations offered by Hawaii's historians identified the major forces behind the evolution of land rights, but we argue that two economic forces were also important determinants of the transition in land rights: the effect of an open economy on factor and product prices; and the effect of population decline on factor prices, public finance, and social organization.

According to some historians, the intellectual influence of western visitors and missionaries after 1822 was important in the transition to constitutional government and in the transformation of land rights.[40] The proposal for the Great Mahele came from Interior Minister Judd, formerly an American medical missionary. William Richards, an American missionary living in Lahaina since 1823, became the king's teacher and advisor in 1838 and was an important influence on the transition to constitutional government. He regularly delivered lectures to the king and chiefs on government and political economy, emphasizing the advantages of free trade. Moreover, numerous young Hawaiians who became advisors to the king were educated by American missionaries at the Lahainaluna school. Visiting ship captains regularly advised the king to adopt liberal economic policies, including the establishment of secure rights to property.[41]

Pressure by the British, French, and American consuls to institute fee simple titles for foreigners' building lots and farms caused numerous unpleasant episodes for the king.[42] Conflicts with British Consul Rich-

Population Pressure and Technological Change," *Australian Journal of Agricultural Economics*, 23 (Aug. 1979), pp. 116–27.

[39] *Penal Code of the Hawaiian Islands, Passed by the House of Nobles and Representatives on the 21st of June, A.D. 1850; to which are appended the Other Acts Passed by the House of Nobles and Representatives during their general Session for 1850* (Honolulu, 1850), pp. 146–47. See the discussion in Kuykendall, *The Hawaiian Kingdom*, vol. 1, pp. 294–98.

[40] Kuykendall, *The Hawaiian Kingdom*, vol. 1, pp. 153–69.

[41] See the discussion in ibid., pp. 153–59.

[42] Earlier disputes between the Hawaiian government and foreign governments had resulted in foreign warships visiting the Islands to "influence" the course of negotiations. Two American

ard Charlton led to a provisional cession of the Islands to Great Britain on February 25, 1841. While the king's sovereignty was restored on July 31, 1841, the episode surely left an indelible impression on the king and chiefs.

The nontrivial probability of an unfriendly annexation in the 1840s undoubtedly increased the king's desire to secure his land holdings. If Hawaii had been annexed by a foreign power, "public" lands would have been appropriated by the new authorities, and the king would have lost his main source of income—land rent. This explanation is credible because the probability of annexation by a foreign power was significant when private property was established in the 1840s.

Foreigners also pushed for alienable property rights on economic development grounds. Some missionaries who responded to R. C. Wyllie's questions on the subject concluded that an influx of foreign capital could not be expected until transferable ownership rights were secured. Other missionaries responding to Wyllie's survey believed that establishment of private property rights in land was one way of motivating Hawaiians to work.[43]

While these explanations all have relevance, most of them concentrate on outside cultural and political influences and fail to examine the broad array of economic and demographic forces transforming Hawaii's economy that also played a significant role in the evolution of a system of private land rights. Between 1778 and 1857 structural change in Hawaii's economy was driven by two forces: changes in the terms of trade and persistent population decline. Both forces affected factor and product prices which, in turn, induced institutional change. Unfortunately, in Hawaii, as in other Asian/Pacific economies, there is a paucity of factor price time-series data so our analysis is indirect, arguing that changes in factor endowments and the terms of trade affected Hawaii's economy.[44]

The change from autarky to trade after 1778 induced major changes in Hawaii's economy. The observations of contemporary observers made clear that living standards of commoners fell from the early 1790s until the sandalwood trade effectively ended in the late 1820s.[45] The decline in living standards was unusual as the change from autarky to trade, the expansion of a labor-intensive sector of the economy (sandalwood

---

warships arrived in 1826 to press for the repayment of debts incurred by the chiefs in the course of sandalwood trading. Ships returned later in the year and in 1829 to remind the chiefs of their unpaid obligations. Questions about the treatment of native Catholics, French priests, and foreign consuls produced a succession of visits by American, French, and British ships during the 1830s.

[43] R. C. Wyllie, *Answers to Questions Proposed by R. C. Wyllie* (Honolulu, 1848), pp. 7–13.

[44] See David Feeny, *The Political Economy of Productivity: Thai Agricultural Development, 1880–1975* (Vancouver, 1982), chap. 3, appendix 2, for a more complete discussion concerning the inference of factor prices from sparse data.

[45] La Croix and Roumasset, "An Economic Theory of Political Change," pp. 161–64.

harvesting), and the decline in population were all forces that normally should have produced higher living standards.

The lot of the chiefs was improved by the sandalwood trade. While sales to foreigners were maintained as a monopoly by Kamehameha I, 60 percent of the revenue was given to the chiefs who harvested the wood. Kamehameha II gave up control of the trade to enhance his support among the major chiefs. He allowed individual chiefs (instead of the king) to negotiate sales, but the king retained 40 percent of the gross revenue. Given their revocable land grants the chiefs vigorously competed to remove sandalwood from the mountainous regions of their *ahupua'a*. The additional income from sandalwood sales was welcome to the chiefs, as the decline in population had led to many agricultural lands being abandoned. Since most chiefs were granted an *ahupua'a*, a thin slice of land stretching from the mountains to the ocean reef, the decline in the value of portions of their agricultural land was offset by the increased value of sandalwood in the mountains of the *ahupua'a*.

When the sandalwood industry began to decline, Hawaii became the base for the northcentral Pacific whaling trade. The impetus for the new trade was the 1818 discovery of the "Offshore Ground" west of Peru and the 1820 discovery of rich sperm whale grounds off the coast of Japan. The first whaling ship visited the Islands in 1820, and by the late 1820s over 150 whaling ships were stopping in Hawaii annually. Table 2 documents this new sector's importance to Hawaii's economy.[46] Although the number of whaling ships visiting Lahaina and Honolulu fell from over 200 in 1832 to less than 90 in 1840, by 1843 over 350 whaling ships annually visited both ports.

One consequence of this growth was an increased demand for labor to service the ships.[47] Foreign traders and entrepreneurs, mostly from the United States, competed with the chiefs for labor, thereby reducing and finally eliminating the chiefs' monopsony power. The continuing decline in population, the collapse of the chiefs' labor cartel, and the replacement of one labor-intensive traded good (harvested sandalwood) by another (services to ships) points to increasing wages for commoners. In

[46] Morgan, *Hawaii*, p. 76. In addition, he noted: "By 1838, with diminishing returns from the Japan and Yellow Seas, the rich Kodiak or Northwest Coast ground off the Russian possessions had been discovered, 30 days sail from Hawaii." With the exhaustion of the Northwest Coast grounds in the late 1840s, ship visits declined until news of the 1848 opening of the Arctic Ocean north of the Bering Strait brought forth a renewed round of visits in 1852. Whaling ship visits began to permanently decline in 1859 and, with the exception of a brief revival in the late 1860s, continuously declined thereafter.

[47] Growth in whaling ship visits varied (see Table 2). From 1824 to 1833 ship visits increased from 104 to 189, but then declined steadily over the next seven years, bottoming out at 86 in 1840. From 1843 to 1854 an average of 419 ships visited Honolulu and Lahaina annually. While the decline during the 1830s is substantial, it is important to remember that whaling ships did not visit the Islands prior to 1820. The period 1820–1842 might be characterized as the "establishment" period of the industry in the Islands, while the decade after 1843 might be identified as the industry's "mature" period.

TABLE 2
WHALERS AND TRADING SHIP ARRIVALS IN HAWAII, 1824–1847

Year	Whalers	Traders	Total
1824	104	17	121
1825	78	18	96
1826	138	37	175
1827	98	23	121
1828	157	37	194
1829	173	32	205
1830	157	39	196
1831	159	37	196
1832	198	37	235
1833	189	35	224
1834	111	31	142
1835	76	33	109
1836	73	39	112
1837	129	32	161
1838	148	23	171
1839	116	33	149
1840	86	31	117
1841	133	31	164
1842	172	46	218
1843	383	37	420
1844	490	42	532
1845	542	41	583
1846	596	53	649
1847	406	67	473

Notes and Sources: Theodore Morgan, *Hawaii: A Century of Economic Change: 1778–1876* (Cambridge, MA, 1948), appendix 2, pp. 225–26. The traders data included only ships arriving at Honolulu while the whalers data included ships arriving at both Honolulu and Lahaina. Whalers data for 1834 to 1836 included only ships arriving at Honolulu.

the agricultural sector the decline in population reduced product demand, which, coupled with increased competition for labor, should have led to a decrease in land rents.[48] There is no systematic evidence concerning land rents and wages during this period, but lower land rents can be inferred from the large amount of agricultural land abandoned during the first 45 years of the nineteenth century.[49] The change in population and comparative advantage points to the conclusion that throughout the 1830s and early 1840s the income of the king and the chiefs fell, while the lot of the commoner improved. Without sufficient skills and capital to begin new enterprises and with epidemics periodically affecting all native Hawaiians, the chiefs began to consider new commercial ventures that would increase their incomes.

The first major attempt to grow sugar commercially in Hawaii was by the American mercantile firm of Ladd & Company in 1835. While this

[48] Demand by visiting ships for food supplies offset some of the decline in demand from other sources.

[49] See Andrew Lind, *An Island Community: Ecological Succession in Hawaii* (Chicago, 1936), pp. 61–62.

venture cannot be judged a success as it lasted only until 1844, it stimulated interest in sugar production. Numerous small sugar mills were established by missionaries and chiefs between 1835 and 1840. Sugar grown by commoners on chiefs' lands was milled on shares by these establishments. Population increases in Oregon and California created potentially large markets for commercial agricultural products, thereby enhancing the comparative advantage of exporting sugar.

While the Hawaiian government and the missionaries were adamantly against foreign ownership throughout the 1830s and 1840s, vigorous discussion took place over the necessity of stimulating the interest of the common people toward commercial agriculture. Considerable capital investment was required to mill and manufacture sugar. Changes in the methods of milling and manufacture came rapidly in the early nineteenth century, and J. H. Galloway stated that the new technology "created larger mills and factories than the industry had known before and they demanded a more extensive hinterland of cane-pieces."[50] Without alienable land, however, it was difficult for a chief or commoner to assemble enough land to enable the new mills to operate near capacity. Commoners, who had traditional use rights in the lands which they occupied, could not be compensated for the loss of these rights, as they were inalienable. Moreover, chiefs who did not have a comparative advantage in producing sugar or organizing sugar milling and manufacture could not capitalize their rights in the land. Given the declining income of chiefs during this period, the opportunity to move their lands into more valuable uses gave additional impetus to the movement to define alienable land rights. Even without such rights 11 mills for the manufacture of sugar had been established by 1846: two on Kauai, six on Maui, and three on Hawaii.[51]

The declining demand for agricultural products came to a halt in the late 1840s due to the sudden appearance of a market for agricultural products in California during the 1849–1851 gold rush.[52] After 1851, as California's demand for Hawaii's agricultural exports fell, there is evidence that land rents resumed their downward path. Letters written by prominent residents of Hawaii to Joel Turrill, U.S. consul in Hawaii

[50] J. H. Galloway, *The Sugar Cane Industry: An Historical Geography from its Origins to 1914* (New York, 1989), p. 135.

[51] See Kuykendall, *The Hawaiian Kingdom*, vol. 1, pp. 315–16.

[52] Morgan, *Hawaii*, pp. 154–58, presented data on exports of important agricultural products which indicate that the increased "[d]emand was bunched into a three-year interval, from the fall of 1848 through part of 1851, though it continued at a higher level after 1851 than it had before 1849." An additional effect of the gold rush was to stimulate migration of Hawaiians to California and southern Oregon. See G. V. Blue, "Early Relations Between Hawaii and the Northwest Coast," *Hawaiian Historical Society Report No. 33* (Honolulu, 1924), p. 20.

from 1846 to 1850, repeatedly indicated that land prices continued falling until 1858.[53]

Economic changes in the early 1800s then tended to undermine the traditional Hawaiian social structure. First, agriculture was in decline due to a smaller population and increased competition for labor from the whaling services sector. These forces point to a decline in rental income for the king and chiefs and an increase in the real incomes of commoners. Second, prospects for commercial sugar production became evident as the population of the North American West Coast increased. Hawaiian land-use rights were, however, not structured to facilitate large-scale sugar production.

Other changes were occurring in social institutions that contributed to the transition in land rights. Hawaii did not have any substantial urban population in 1778, and given the subsequent decline in population, there seemed little prospect of urbanization. Yet three large, growing villages (Honolulu on Oahu, Lahaina on Maui, and Hilo on Hawaii) arose in the 1820s in the midst of the continuing population decline.[54] Declining population and its increasing concentration in growing villages meant, of course, a decline in rural population. The shift in population from rural to urban areas had two important repercussions. The movement to urban areas disrupted the relationship between chiefs and commoners, inducing the development of new governmental institutions, and the rural population decline stimulated competition between chiefs for tenants. Chiefs competed to increase tenant compensation by adjusting the traditional package of tenant obligations and taxes.[55]

Changes in Hawaii's government were prompted by the necessity to devise new institutions capable of governing and providing services to an urban population. Traditional systems of governance based on the hierarchy of common people and chiefs broke down with the rural exodus. As more common people pursued activities outside the traditional economy and divisions over the development of a code of law among chiefs grew, the enforcement of the law by local chiefs began to break down in the late 1820s. When the regent, Kaahumanu, died in 1832, the new king and his Council of Chiefs responded to the confusion over law enforcement by promulgating new laws designed to protect public order and settle private disputes. Informal district courts had

[53] See the letters sent to Joel Turrill by his friends in Hawaii in "The Turrill Collection, 1845–1860," *Hawaiian Historical Society Report No. 66* (Honolulu, 1957).

[54] Reliable population estimates do not exist for any of the three villages.

[55] The term "wage rate" refers to the shadow price of a commoner's time, not to the actual method of compensation for agricultural work. Since a worker on the land owed labor dues (which are not fixed in value) to the chief and to the king, workers could be characterized as sharecroppers. "Rents" refer to a combination of taxes and rents prior to the constitution of 1840, as the finances of the chiefs, king, and the government were not separated until 1842. After 1842 rents refer to the shadow price of the land's services.

already been established in 1829 and were formally instituted in 1840. The existence of a rudimentary court system was important to land reform, as it provided a mechanism of rights enforcement and dispute resolution, thereby lowering the transaction costs associated with the innovation in property rights.

Kamehameha III, with the approval of Hawaii's important chiefs and the assistance of Richards, promulgated the "Declaration of Rights and the Laws of 1839," which defined and secured certain rights for the people, including protection of property. Government by the king and his ministers was formalized by the establishment of the 1840 constitution; while most existing institutional arrangements were retained, a House of Representatives chosen by the people was established as one branch of a two-branch legislature that included the existing Council of Chiefs.

Establishment of the rule of law in urban areas and the rise of constitutional government reduced the power of the chiefs over the common people. Tenants who were dissatisfied with their role in the traditional economy migrated to urban areas. Moreover, rising tenant compensation, prompted by increased competition for labor from urban areas, reduced land rents earned by chiefs. Thus the decline in the chiefs' power was accompanied by a decline in their income.

The decline in land rents also reduced government revenues. Taxes collected by the king were directly tied to the number of commoners working in agriculture, as agricultural workers were obligated to work in the king's fields. With increased competition from the whaling services sector for labor and a declining total population, it was in the chiefs' interest to adjust the traditional obligations and taxes paid by tenants. In addition, since government is a labor-intensive enterprise, higher wages increased expenditures just as revenues were falling.

In response to the rising budget deficit, the new legislature enacted a series of sweeping tax laws. Two distinct stages of change in the taxation system were important components of these institutional developments. First, the "Laws of 1839" codified the tax owed by various individuals, while (partially) converting most taxes from in-kind obligations to monetary payments. Taxes and land rents were collected in several ways; commoners usually worked 52 days on the king's land (taxes), 52 days on the land manager's land (rents), and made harvest "offerings." North and Thomas have argued that the shift from in-kind to monetary taxation can usually be explained by the growth of factor and commodity markets.[56] Rulers could then use the proceeds from

[56] North and Thomas, *The Rise of the Western World*, pp. 39–40, argued that part of the shift from in-kind to other forms of taxation is explained by the growth of commodity and factor markets. Rulers could more efficiently collect money taxes and then use the proceeds to purchase the goods and services they needed as markets became better developed relative to the earlier period in which taxes in kind may have been used to minimize the transaction costs of revenue

money taxes to purchase required goods and services. In pre-contact Hawaii in-kind taxes were used to reduce the higher transaction costs associated with contracting in the absence of well-functioning markets. Given the absence of such markets in Hawaii prior to the sandalwood trade and their subsequent development, North and Thomas's analysis is consistent with the timing of this shift in taxation methods.

Second, the "Laws of 1842" reduced the overall level of taxes owed by rural agricultural families and increased that owed by urban families. From 52 days owed to the landlord (for help on large projects and work on the landlord's fishponds and fields) and an equal number to the king, the Laws of 1842 reduced the required number of days to 36 for each.[57] The effect of the law was to reduce a tenant's rental and tax payments by equal amounts, thereby increasing real wages in agriculture. These changes provide corroborating evidence for our earlier inference of rising real wages during this period.

The establishment of a poll tax in the 1839 declaration and its continuing presence in the Laws of 1842 is a product of this migration of workers from their traditional residences in the fertile mountain valleys to urban areas.[58] The new tax was supported by the Council of Chiefs as a measure to maintain land rents and taxes (as migrants to urban areas did not owe the in-kind taxes) by stemming the flow of migration from the rural areas. Other provisions in the Laws of 1842 reinforced this goal by prohibiting tenants from leaving the land without cause.[59] These attempts by the chiefs and the king to ameliorate problems stemming from rising wages and declining land rents were not unusual; similar laws were common in Europe in the late fourteenth century when wages were increasing and land rents were falling.[60] Such laws are consistent with our earlier inference that wages rose and land rents fell as Hawaii's population declined.

Another provision of the Laws of 1842 provided a total exemption from taxes for families with more than three children.[61] A reduction in the cost of raising additional children stimulates population growth and tends to stem the upward pressure on wages and relieve the downward pressure on rents, thereby improving the future lot of the chiefs. These changes in Hawaii's institutions and laws suggest that rents had

---

collection. While North has recently acknowledged (*Structure and Change*, pp. 129–31) timing problems with the application of his analysis to Europe, the criticisms do not apply to the Hawaiian case.

[57] Lorrin A. Thurston, ed., *Constitution and Laws of 1842*, in *The Fundamental Law of Hawaii* (Honolulu, 1904), chap. 3, sec. 3.

[58] Ibid., chap. 3, sec. 1.

[59] Ibid., chap. 3, secs. 5 and 6.

[60] See, for example, the Statutes of Labourers considered by virtually every English Parliament between 1350 and 1380.

[61] *Constitution and Laws of 1842*, chap. 3, sec. 4.

declined and that the chiefs, whose income was primarily derived from land rents, influenced the legislature to prevent further declines.

The adjustments in traditional tenant obligations reduced rents available to the chiefs and taxes paid by the chiefs to the government. In 1842 revenue collected to finance the king's and the government's expenditures amounted to only $41,000. To increase government revenues the legislature approved an ad valorem duty of 3 percent on all imports, effective at the beginning of 1843. Tax revenue increased to $50,000 in 1843, while government expenditures increased to $80,000. Although a bond issue was floated to cover the shortfall, a debt of this magnitude could not be regularly financed by the government unless it wished to compromise its independence from foreign powers. Other taxes were subsequently imposed. A tax on whaling activities was collected by arresting sailors from whaling ships for no apparent reason and then releasing them upon payment of a fine. The tariff was raised from 3 to 5 percent in 1845, and in 1855 some imported articles had duties of 10 and 15 percent imposed on them, with heavier charges imposed on wines and spirits. Chattel taxes on horses, mares, cattle, dogs, and cats were imposed in 1846.

The possibility of creating alienable property rights provided two new potentially additional sources of revenue to the Hawaiian government. First, the capitalization of the right to receive land rents enabled the government to sell a large proportion of its land during and after the Great Mahele. Indeed, W. D. Alexander stated that "between the years 1850 and 1860, nearly all the desirable Government land was sold, generally to natives."[62] Kuykendall supported this view, noting that evidence of active sales of public land was documented in "official records and in the newspapers, letters, and other contemporary writings."[63] These anecdotal reports are corroborated by more direct, quantitative evidence found in an 1881 private compilation of government land sales (also known as "royal patent grants") and the 1858 Report of the Minister of the Interior.[64] The 1881 survey indicates that 654,622 acres, or 44 percent of the original 1,495,000 acres awarded to the government, were sold between 1841 and 1886.[65] The bulk of the sales occurred between 1846 and 1861 when the government sold 420,781.76 acres, approximately 31 percent of its total holdings. The 1858 interior minister's report contains annual data on acreage sold and revenue received from sales on each island (see Table 3). A significant

[62] Alexander, "A Brief History," p. 119.

[63] Kuykendall, *The Hawaiian Kingdom*, vol. 1, p. 298.

[64] See Surveyer General, comp., *Index of All Grants Issued By the Hawaiian Government Previous to March 31, 1886* (Honolulu, 1887). The two sets of data correspond almost exactly. The only discrepancies are in the 1849 Maui acreage and the 1857 Molokai acreage. Review of these entries indicates that the private report probably double counts acreage for those two observations.

[65] A small amount of acreage was sold prior to the institutional reforms in 1847, but we have been unable to discover how such sales were executed.

TABLE 3
GOVERNMENT LAND SALES, 1846–1857

	Oahu	Hawaii	Maui	Kauai	Others	Total
1846						
Acres	850.54	10.00	0.00	0.00	0.00	860.54
Revenue	526.00	50.00	0.00	0.00	0.00	576.00
1847						
Acres	171.53	763.75	1,365.00	0.00	0.00	2,300.28
Revenue	2,207.88	752.15	1,839.41	0.00	0.00	4,799.44
1848						
Acres	488.40	14.00	213.36	201.51	0.00	917.27
Revenue	1,782.25	50.00	207.97	366.50	0.00	2,406.72
1849						
Acres	2,022.22	232.75	4,867.76	8.50	0.00	7,131.23
Revenue	12,935.78	303.07	4,596.61	17.50	0.00	17,852.96
1850						
Acres	15,330.66	1,859.15	6,988.87	1,028.50	1,371.00	26,578.18
Revenue	17,626.13	4,215.55	11,165.75	3,243.29	489.00	36,739.72
1851						
Acres	5,567.81	5,285.10	6,569.55	2,634.38	92.46	20,149.30
Revenue	6,933.60	5,568.00	11,100.99	3,004.86	164.88	26,772.33
1852						
Acres	7,938.87	20,790.93	2,599.32	301.72	358.45	31,989.29
Revenue	7,765.22	19,075.55	4,402.29	274.00	1,128.12	32,645.18
1853						
Acres	1,447.01	3,260.82	6,142.59	834.31	316.14	12,000.87
Revenue	3,739.25	2,624.04	6,468.08	551.88	579.00	13,962.25
1854						
Acres	1,610.13	3,976.11	16,930.87	710.00	0.00	23,227.11
Revenue	8,181.08	2,595.00	18,885.30	428.22	0.00	30,089.60
1855						
Acres	3,842.42	15,753.37	3,616.12	3,960.60	646.44	27,818.95
Revenue	4,839.77	8,570.86	6,242.63	1,058.09	1,062.05	21,773.40
1856						
Acres	1,889.90	14,427.23	3,329.87	119.90	331.70	20,098.60
Revenue	5,367.80	6,111.89	3,745.90	389.95	365.31	15,980.85
1857						
Acres	478.10	8,115.87	320.39	44.42	1.64	8,960.42
Revenue	6,724.68	4,420.72	514.87	153.90	1.75	11,815.92
Grand Totals						
Acres	41,637.59	74,489.08	52,943.70	9,843.84	3,117.83	182,032.04
Revenue	78,629.44	54,336.83	69,169.80	9,488.19	3,790.11	215,414.37

Notes and Sources: Data, which are from Sept. 1846 to Dec. 1857, are taken from *The Report of the Minister of the Interior* (Honolulu, 1858). Revenue is in U.S. dollars, the unit of account in Hawaii.

proportion of government revenues during this period was derived from land sales (see Table 4).[66]

Second, the change to alienable private property rights also created *additional* land rents. Governments seldom encounter such favorable

[66] The figures from 1853–1857 should be interpreted cautiously. In 1856 the government halted the sale of large tracts of land. It adopted a policy of leasing the remaining lands in response to the lower land prices prevailing during this period. The land sales reported for 1855 and 1857 were actually made in 1854 and 1855 but were reported in later years due to a delay in the issuance of royal patent grants.

TABLE 4
GOVERNMENT REVENUE AND LAND SALE REVENUE, 1846–1857

Year	Government Revenue	Land Sale Revenue	Land Commission Net Revenue	Revenue from Land Sales as a Percentage of Government Revenue
1846	$75,000	$576		0.77%
1847	127,000	4,799		3.78
1848	155,000	2,407		1.55
1849	166,000	17,853		10.75
1850	194,000	36,690		18.91
1851	284,000	27,772		9.78
1852	278,934	32,645	−$3,232	10.54
1853	326,620	13,962	523	4.43
1854	323,393	30,090	−214	9.24
1855	419,228	21,773	3,454	6.02
1856	319,521	15,981		5.00
1857	319,521	11,816		3.70

Notes and Sources: Government revenue data are taken from *The Report of the Minister of Finance*, various years, 1847–1860. The remainder of the data is taken from *The Report of the Minister of the Interior*, various years, 1847–1860. Government revenue for 1852 was calculated by adding one-fourth of the revenue from the Mar. 1851 to Mar. 1852 revenue to the reported data for the period Mar. to Dec. 1852.

opportunities. In his neoclassical model of the state, North analyzed the trade-off usually encountered by governments seeking to raise additional revenue.[67] He found that "the property rights structures that will maximize rents to the ruler (or the ruling class) are in conflict with those that would produce economic growth."[68] To survive the state must encourage economic growth and generate sufficient flows of tax revenue to maintain its position against competitors.

As North observed, declining land rents and increasing wages tend to generate a budget deficit in agrarian societies where property taxes are an important component of state revenue and state expenditures are labor-intensive. North cited several instances of these induced deficits, such as the fiscal crisis faced by European kings in the fourteenth century in the wake of Europe's declining population. He concluded that tax revenues were in "[d]ecline . . . as a result of the fall in land rents due to a declining population . . . at precisely the time when more revenues were required for survival."[69]

In Hawaii the fiscal crisis also was due, at least in part, to a fall in land rents stemming from a declining population. That crisis, however, coincided with economic changes that rendered alienable property rights in land more attractive. The Hawaiian rulers were able to sell land to commoners partly because commoners could resell the land to

[67] North's theory was presented in detail in *Structure and Change*, chap. 3.
[68] Ibid., p. 28.
[69] Ibid., p. 139.

foreigners in the face of new prospects for commercial agriculture. The revenue from land sales and tax revenue from an expanding agricultural economy enabled the government to finance its increased expenditures without resorting to the instruments of mercantilism. This contrasts with the European case where monarchs did not face the same favorable opportunities encountered by the Hawaiian king. In Europe they sold licenses, monopoly rights, and other restrictions on commerce to raise revenue, thereby sacrificing economic growth for the maintenance of the state.[70] Their maximization of tax revenues was generally in conflict with efficient incentives for private economic activity. The Hawaiian case provides an interesting counterexample wherein the revenue-seeking interests of the monarch had a positive effect on private investment and economic growth.

IV. LESSONS FOR THE NEW POLITICAL ECONOMY

Early contributions to the new political economy have been criticized as "spontaneous order" theories for relying on efficiency as the primary engine of change.[71] Our framework relies instead on generalized rent-seeking as the engine of change. Rent-seeking may be broadly construed as creating rents as well as capturing them. By changing property rights in land and selling public land, the Hawaiian monarchy was able to raise additional revenue without imposing dead weight losses on producers and consumers. Pursuit of self-interest by government officials accelerated the transition from a complex system of traditional use rights to a system of exclusive, transferable property rights. Thus while the rent-seeking objectives of the ruling class are ordinarily in conflict with efficient economic growth, occasions may arise in which the conflict is absent.

The evolution of private property rights in nineteenth-century Hawaii also illustrates that the comparative efficiency of private property depends on external market conditions as well as population pressure. In Hawaii the transition to alienable, private property rights was driven by new market opportunities rather than population growth. The shift in comparative advantage toward sugar meant that agricultural production would be more capital-intensive and would require land improvements. Since capital-intensive production is usually more efficient with commercial cultivation, the increase in sugar cultivation opportunities led to a greater demand for the institutions of private property.

[70] Ibid., pp. 138–42.

[71] The "new political economy" is an umbrella term for public choice, economics of property rights, law and economics, political economy of regulation, the new institutional economics, and the new economic history. See James M. Buchanan, *Explorations into Constitutional Economics* (College Station, 1989), p. 61; and Robert P. Inman, "Markets, Governments, and the 'New' Political Economy," in Alan J. Auerbach and Martin Feldstein, eds., *Handbook of Public Economics* (New York, 1987), vol. 2.

In conventional welfare economics, central government control and free markets are viewed as alternative forms of economic organization. This may be misleading since, as we have suggested above, the evolution of private property and market exchange may be highly interdependent with the evolution of government. New external trading opportunities may induce, in combination with other factors, increased centralization of government *and* simplified, private property rights. As the gains from specialization grow, so does the role of central government in providing the institutional prerequisites for market exchange.[72] Thus growth of governmental institutions may be a coevolutionary phenomenon which accompanies the rise of private property rights.

[72] This perspective suggests due caution in generalizing about the minimal efficient degree of central control independent of an economy's state of development. See James Roumasset and Sumner J. La Croix, "The Coevolution of Property Rights and Political Order: An Illustration from Nineteenth-Century Hawaii," in Vincent Ostrom, David Feeny, and Hartmut Picht, eds., *Rethinking Institutional Analysis and Development* (San Francisco, 1988), pp. 315–36.

Agency Problems in Early Chartered Companies: The Case of the Hudson's Bay Company

ANN M. CARLOS AND STEPHEN NICHOLAS

The problem of controlling overseas managers confronts all multilocational firms. Historians have argued that because of the extreme time lags in communication, chartered companies were unable to control managerial behavior. We argue that not only did the Hudson's Bay Company understand the agency problem but also put into operation strategies designed to attenuate opportunistic behavior. The company used employment contracts and control systems and established a social structure compatible with the company's aims.

INTRODUCTION

England emerged as an important trading nation during the reign of Charles II, 1660 to 1688. Although England already had a sizeable textile trade with Europe, the Restoration saw a movement into what have been called the "distant trades." By 1700 one-third of England's imports came from North America, the West Indies, and the East; these imports and their growth over the ensuing century made England a world entrepôt.[1] The work of economic historians has ably documented the rise, course, and structure of these trade patterns. As far back as 1954 Ralph Davis asked "why was it possible to expand these distant trades?" and over the years economic historians have advanced many explanations of this important but yet unanswered question, including supply- and demand-side changes in the market, innovations in transport and technology, and the general organization of commerce.[2]

This last factor has attracted considerable attention, since the growth of foreign trade coincided with the rise of the chartered trading

The Journal of Economic History, Vol. L, No. 4 (Dec. 1990). ISSN 0022-0507.

Ann M. Carlos is Associate Professor of Economics, University of Colorado, Boulder, CO 80903; and Stephen Nicholas is Associate Professor of Economic History, University of New South Wales, Kensington, New South Wales 2033 and currently Visiting Fellow, Australia-Japan Research Institute and Economics/Economic History Research School of the Social Sciences, Australian National University, Canberra, Australia.

The authors would like to thank Lou Cain, Knick Harley, David Laidler, Douglas McCalla, James Markusen, the participants of the many seminars at which this article was given, five unknown referees, and an exceedingly patient editor for their many insightful comments. All errors unfortunately remain our own. Ann Carlos would like to thank the Social Science and Humanities Research Council of Canada for its funding for this project (410-89-0371).

[1] Ralph Davis, *England's Overseas Trade, 1500–1700* (London, 1973), pp. 5–32.

[2] Ralph Davis, "English Foreign Trade 1660–1700," in Walter E. Minchinton, *The Growth of English Overseas Trade in the 17th and 18th Centuries* (London, 1969), p. 80. See also Minchinton's "Introduction" in the same volume. Charles Wilson, *England's Apprenticeship, 1603–1763* (Oxford, 1965); and Peter Mathias, *First Industrial Nation: An Economic History of Britain, 1700–1914* (Mathuen, 1969).

companies and was accompanied by a decline in the old "regulated" companies, such as the Levant and Eastland companies, which had formerly conducted the European trades.[3] Davis thought that the English East India Company and the charter companies in aggregate made a "large" contribution to Britain's overseas trade, while Charles Wilson was even more emphatic about the charter companies: "Without the resources which only the joint stock Company could mobilise, the expansion of trade in far-distant and turbulent lands would, at this stage, have been impossible."[4]

An equally strong view is that these companies were nothing more than monopoly franchises seeking rents. This theme is exemplified in economic writings as early as the work of Adam Smith. Continuing a tradition which had started at the beginning of the eighteenth century, Smith argued that the companies existed only because of their monopoly position, without which they could not have survived in the face of competition from individual traders. He wrote:

> The directors of such companies, however, being the managers rather of other people's money than of their own, it cannot well be expected, that they should watch over it with the same anxious vigilance with which the partners in a private copartnery frequently watch over their own. Like the stewards of a rich man, they are apt to consider attention to small matters as not for their master's honour, and very easily give themselves a dispensation from having it. Negligence and profusion, therefore, must always prevail, more or less, in the management of the affairs of such a Company.[5]

Switching his attention from the directors to the overseas managers of the trading companies, Smith argued that exclusive privilege brought mismanagement and allowed "negligence, profusion and marversion of their own servants," which the companies were unable to control.[6]

Although Smith was arguing against monopoly and for competition, he identified the two major problems facing all multilocational and multinational companies. The first is the problem of control being separated from ownership; the second is how the directors or owners at home can ensure that their agents abroad work for the benefit of the company and not in their own self-interest.

Many economic historians concur with Smith's judgment about the early trading companies, arguing that they were unsuccessful because they were inefficient, evidenced by their inability to control their agents overseas. E. L. J. Coornaert wrote that "seldom or never did the companies set up a rigorous hierarchy. . . . For the most part the bonds between these agents and their companies were exceedingly tenuous;

[3] Wilson, *England's Apprenticeship*, p. 172. Regulated companies can be thought of most easily as licensing institutions. Merchants, on payment of an entry fee, were admitted to the company but thereafter traded on their own account. There was no joint ownership of stock.

[4] Davis, *England's Overseas Trade*, p. 43; and Wilson, *England's Apprenticeship*, p. 173.

[5] Adam Smith, *Wealth of Nations* (Homewood, IL, 1963), book 5, chap. 1, part 3, p. 255.

[6] Ibid., p. 265.

distances were often immense, and everywhere the companies' representatives of all ranks were empowered to carry on trade for their private accounts and were often, in effect, the most dangerous rivals of their own companies."[7] The historian of the Royal African Company, Keith Davies, argued specifically that the company failed because "too much had to be left to the discretion of employees abroad who for the most part followed their own concerns to the detriment of the Company's."[8] Wilson reached the same conclusion about the Royal African Company but also pointed out that even the successful companies had to face the same problems in that their "servants were remote, [the] accounting system and methods of control inadequate."[9] Indeed, the most serious problem identified by historians seems to have been private trade by managers; for example, K. N. Chaudhuri identified private trade by the English East India Company's Asian managers as a major area of conflict, and Thomas Stuart Willan thought that the real evil for the Russia Company was private trade by its managers.[10] The major problem confronting the trading companies, therefore, was that of managing their managers at a distance.

Of course, it is important to remember that controlling managers of overseas branches is a problem for all multinational firms, whether early trading companies, nineteenth-century industrial multinationals, or today's transnational firms. For contemporary international firms, Richard Caves has written that the "cost of information and supervision, the difficulty of working out employment contracts that align the efforts of employees with the goals of the firm . . . limit the firm's pursuit of its ultimate goals."[11] Before the age of modern communications and transport, the problems of managing at a distance were in many ways more acute for the seventeenth- and eighteenth-century firms than for their modern counterparts. It is also important to realize that the seventeenth century witnessed the formation not only of English firms but of similar long-distance trading companies in the Netherlands, Sweden, Prussia, Portugal, Spain, and France.[12] These companies similarly grappled with the problem of controlling their overseas managers.

Yet, in spite of the assertions that the early trading companies failed or suffered from their inability to control their managers, there has been very little archival work done to ascertain whether the directors

[7] E. L. J. Coornaert, "European Economic Institutions and the New World: The Chartered Companies," in *Cambridge Economic History of Europe* (Cambridge, 1967), vol. 4, p. 262.

[8] Keith Davies, *The Royal African Company* (Oxford, 1957), p. 165.

[9] Wilson, *England's Apprenticeship*, p. 176.

[10] K. N. Chaudhuri, *The Trading World of Asia and the English East India Company, 1660–1760* (New York, 1978); and Thomas Stuart Willan, *The Early History of the Russia Company* (Manchester, 1956).

[11] Richard Caves, *Multinational Enterprise and Economic Analysis* (New York, 1982), p. 70.

[12] Coornaert, "European Economic Institutions," vol. 4.

understood the nature of the agency problem and what steps, if any, they took to control the problem.[13] This article examines the agency problem that the Hudson's Bay Company faced because its directors were located in London, while the acquisition operations occurred around Hudson Bay in Canada. In at least this particular case, the company recognized the agency problem and looked for ways to control managerial behavior. We describe the ways in which this company sought to put into operation incentives and mechanisms designed to attenuate the problem.

BEARING THE CHARGE WITHOUT HAVING THE ADVANTAGE

Long-distance trade requires that managers have some discretionary power, at the same time directors must ensure that such power is used to the best advantage of the company. This is the economics of the agency problem.[14] The stress put on this issue in the literature on the early chartered companies is easy to understand. For these companies there existed a tremendous time lag between the issuance of orders in England or in Europe and the appearance of commodities from afar. The turnaround time could take anywhere from eighteen months to two and a half years.[15] Even when the commodities arrived, the directors still had to ascertain whether the output before them was the maximum amount they should have received or whether their managers had cheated them. Cheating could involve mere shirking of effort or could involve a more active policy of trading for commodities on one's own account at the expense of the company. This latter problem (private trade) is believed by most historians of the chartered companies to have been serious. According to Thomas Stuart Willan, although the Russia

[13] As a corollary, there has been no questioning of the types of situations in which agency problems are likely to arise. It is unclear whether economic historians thought that all multilocational trading companies faced an agency problem of the same magnitude or whether the magnitude (and the ability to control the agency problem) was related to the particular reasons for each company's existence. In this article we are taking, as given, the hierarchical structure of the Hudson's Bay Company, which implies a principal/agent relationship between the factories and the head office. The extent to which this was the most beneficial organizational structure is discussed in Ann M. Carlos and Stephen Nicholas, "Giants of An Earlier Capitalism: The Early Chartered Companies as an Analogue of the Modern Multinational," *Business History Review*, 26 (Autumn 1988).

[14] This section relies on Kenneth Arrow, "The Economics of Agency," in John Pratt and Richard Zeckhauser, eds., *Principals and Agents: The Structure of Business* (Boston, 1984), pp. 27–51; Neil Strong and Michael Waterson, "Principals, Agents and Information," in Roger Clarke and Tony McGuinness, eds., *The Economics of the Firm* (Oxford, 1987), pp. 18–61; Michael Jensen and William Meckling, "Theory of the Firm: Managerial Behavior, Agency Costs and Ownership Structure," *Journal of Financial Economics*, 3 (Nov. 1978), pp. 305–11; Stephen Ross, "The Economic Theory of Agency: The Principal's Problem," *American Economic Review*, 63 (May 1973), pp. 134–49; Oliver Williamson, *The Economic Institutions of Capitalism* (New York, 1985), chaps. 2, 3, 7, 8; and Eugene Fama and Michael Jensen, "Separation of Ownership and Control," *Journal of Law and Economics*, 25 (June 1983), pp. 301–26.

[15] Carlos and Nicholas, "Giants of An Earlier Capitalism," gave a description of the physical organization of the long-distance trades.

Company was concerned about "horedom [sic], incontinency, drunkenness, and idleness, the greatest evil was private trade."[16] In 1710 the Dutch East India Company accused its Bengali factories of putting aside the most profitable assortment of textiles for their own benefit.[17] The English East India Company complained that the inter-Asian trade was poorly developed because of private trade.[18] In 1691 the Royal African Company wrote: "We have reason to complain that our factors and some of the chiefs manage private trade which is the way to encourage interlopers and ruin our stock by bearing the charge without having the advantage."[19]

The Hudson's Bay Company was no exception. Douglas MacKay called private trade the "gravest of all Company offenses."[20] Edwin Ernest Rich, the company's main historian, wrote that "the business of private trade was a perpetual worry to the Company, as it always was to the East India Company. . . ."[21] In describing the letter of recall written to Charles Bayly in May 1674 Rich wrote: "He is to hand over all trade goods, stores and papers, and to 'bee assistante' to Lydall [new governor] in discovereing & preventeing private trade. *Always private trade*."[22]

The ability of agents to behave in their own self-interests occurs in situations of asymmetrical information and uncertainty. In asymmetrical situations the information between any two contracting parties is unequal. For the chartered companies, managers had more and better information about the foreign location, while the directors had more information about the firm. The presence of uncertainty meant that outputs could not be linked invariably with inputs or efforts of managers. For example, in the fur trade the harvest of furs was somewhat random. The severity of the winter, disease, or the activity of Indians or competitors had an impact on the level of trading activity. Only the managers in Canada observed the true harvest, not the company. If the supply of furs shipped was low, the directors could not have known whether this was because the harvest was low or because its managers were engaged in private trade. Informational asymmetries allowed the private trade problem to exist.[23] The resulting opportunism by managers

[16] Willan, *The Early History of the Russia Company*, p. 37.

[17] Kristof Glamann, *Dutch Asiatic Trade 1620–1740* (The Hague, 1981), p. 147.

[18] Chaudhuri, *The Trading World of Asia*, p. 208.

[19] Davies, *The Royal African Company*, p. 255.

[20] Douglas MacKay, *The Honourable Company* (Toronto, 1949), p. 67.

[21] Edwin Ernest Rich, ed., *Minutes of the Hudson's Bay Company, 1671–74* (London, 1942), vol. 5, p. 101.

[22] Ibid., pp. 101, 112, emphasis is added.

[23] An alternative way to phrase the problems arising from asymmetrical information and uncertainty is in terms of moral hazard and adverse selection. Moral hazard relates to the work effort of the agent, while adverse selection relates to informational asymmetries between counteracting parties. Thus the adverse selection problem allows the moral hazard problem to

reduced company profits and increased returns to managers. Firms, therefore, needed to find ways to control their managers or to reduce the level of private trade.

An obvious place for any firm to exercise control is with the employment contract. The remuneration package and work provisions in employment contracts are critical in reducing opportunism and encouraging managers to work in the best interests of the firm by making it expensive for the worker to cheat. Firms can use both fixed and incentive fee payments to encourage managers to work hard. However, when information is asymmetric, changes in managers' efforts will remain less than perfectly detectable. Thus pay for performance systems may still invite shirking or in fact induce counterproductive efforts.[24] For their part, managers promise, as a condition of employment, to work hard and in the best interest of the company. Such promises are, of course, open to evasion.

Since employment contracts do not necessarily solve the problem of private trade, firms need to generate supplemental sources of information: systems of internal controls to monitor managers. Written records of decisions and notification of compliance to formal rules and procedures (accounting procedures, inventory systems, and fee-incentive structures) provide a flow of information to the head office. Thus output levels and information derived from the records form two separate but interdependent methods of checking on the work activity of managers. This can be further supplemented by seeking reports on managers from other employees and from third parties.

Not all monitoring and control devices which reduce shirking operate on the system of economic rewards and punishments. Firms are also social systems and have a social hierarchy and unique "culture," in which there are mores and values which sanction and prohibit certain types of behavior. Frequently directors try to create an ethical system, especially when the firm is a family concern.[25] Insofar as managers conform to the mores of the firm, they are constrained in their behavior and monitoring costs are reduced. An internal social system which instills values directly into managers is a powerful instrument used in a company's attempts to reduce private trade, to attenuate opportunism, and to encourage high levels of effort on the part of managers.

While there are ways in which firms can control the opportunistic tendencies of its managers, to do so is not costless. Incentives, such as high salaries or bonuses, and monitoring procedures all are costs to the firm. The profitability of the firm will depend on both the effectiveness

---

exist, which, in turn, can result in self-seeking behavior by agents and a resulting loss in profits for the firm.

[24] George P. Baker, Michael C. Jensen, and Kevin J. Murphy, "Compensation and Incentives: Practice vs. Theory," *Journal of Finance*, 42 (July 1988), p. 599.

[25] Peter Buckley and Michael Casson, "A Theory of Co-operation in International Business" (University of Reading Discussion Paper in International Business, No. 102, Jan. 1987), pp. 1–39.

of such measures and their costs. The key question therefore is the circumstances under which incentives and monitoring will be effective relative to costs.

Two features of the external environment are important in determining profitability: the cost effectiveness of monitoring, and the ease with which managers may engage in private trade. Both of these factors differed widely among the chartered companies and may help explain differing company successes.[26] The more highly cost effective monitoring is, the higher the firm's profitability for a given level of monitoring. In addition, the firm can change the level of monitoring (an endogenous choice variable) as its effectiveness changes and further increase its profitability. If private trade is costly and inefficient, we would expect less of it at any given incentive and monitoring levels by the firm, and hence higher profitability. Reductions in the efficiency of private trade in turn imply optimal changes in the incentives and monitoring strategy that further increase the firm's profits. Thus firm profitability and success may be fairly sensitive to exogenous environmental factors dictating the effectiveness of monitoring and the efficiency of private trade.

Taken together these two parameters go a long way toward explaining when a hierarchical-firm structure will succeed and when a firm will break apart. In short, when monitoring costs are low and the efficiency of private trade is low, a hierarchical firm is more likely to succeed.

Whether monitoring costs are high or low depends, in part, on the physical environment in which the managers operate. To the extent that operations take place in an environment with few contact points with the outside economy or when all managerial activity can only be conducted through a very small number of channels, then monitoring costs will be lower than in an environment in which this is not the case. Thus one would expect monitoring costs to be low, all else being equal, for the Hudson's Bay Company, whose managers were relatively isolated around Hudson Bay and were dependent on the company ship for communication.

It must be recognized, however, that Hudson Bay's isolated environment does not mean that the private trading problem can be ignored. The nature of the market in which a firm operates determines the impact of any level of private trade on profitability. In a very profitable environment a firm can afford to ignore some given level of private trading by its managers, but in a more depressed environment no level of private trade can be tolerated. Indeed, it is the nature of the market

[26] The Royal African Company, which was chartered in 1672, two years after the Hudson's Bay Company, faced a serious agency problem. Monitoring was difficult and agents could easily engage in private trade. For a discussion of that company's efforts to control its agency problem, see Ann M. Carlos, "The Royal African Company and Its Managers" (University of Western Ontario mimeo, Mar. 1990).

in which the Hudson's Bay Company operated which helps to explain why this company was quickly unwilling to permit any private trade by its managers.

With its charter of 1672 the Hudson's Bay Company was given a monopoly position within England to carry on a fur trade in Hudson Bay. The charter did not free the company from competition in either its input or output market. The Hudson's Bay Company faced from its inception almost continuous French competition. This rivalry was very intense. This took the form of traders approaching the Bay overland from the St. Lawrence River and coming into Hudson Bay by ship. It also involved war. "In the twelve years, 1686–97, the French attacked Moose, Rupert and Albany Rivers, New Severn, and York Fort three times; only once, at York in 1690, did they fail. The English sent two expeditions to the Bottom of the Bay and one against York Fort; only that of 1688 failed. . . ."[27] The wars with France brought financial problems. The price of furs fell while the price of the trade goods rose. Shipping and insurance costs rose, while in some years the company was unable to send even one ship to Hudson Bay. Indeed, Rich argued that the company's "survival was due to its mastery of the essentials of its trade as much as to the privileges which it enjoyed. . . ."[28] One of the essentials was "its firm adherence to close control" and "in particular, the increasing resistance to private trade by ships' captains and other servants of the Company. . . ."[29] Thus it is within the context of a war-troubled market that the company instituted a set of policies designed to reduce at least the level of internal competition in the company.

A SYSTEM OF CONTROL

Contracts and Incentives

The managers or "officers" at Hudson Bay were employed to perform two functions. The most important was trading for furs with the Indians, while the secondary function, also viewed as important by the London Committee, was managing the work force at the Bay. Inadequate performance and opportunism could occur in either of these areas, and it was the committee's job to decipher from the information flows what actually was occurring.

An examination of labor-management activity gives some insight into the way the London Committee operated. The committee had very strict expectations about the behavior of its workers. They were

[27] Edwin Ernest Rich, ed., *Hudson's Bay Copy Booke of Letters, Commissions, Instructions Outward, 1688–1696* (London, 1957), vol. 20, p. xx.

[28] Edwin Ernest Rich, *The History of the Hudson's Bay Company, 1670–1870* (London, 1958), vol. 1, p. 57.

[29] Ibid., p. 55.

supposed to be sober, industrious, and, by and large, celibate; for example, a letter written by the committee in 1714 and read to the men required that "(a) all persons to attend prayers, (b) 'To live lovingly with one another not to swear or quarrel but to live peaceable without drunkenness or Profaneness', (c) No man to meddle, trade or affront any of Indians, nor to concern themselves with women."[30] Initially, the expectations of the committee were infrequently, if ever, met. The managers, in letters to the committee, claimed that they were unable to control the labor force because the workers were unsuitable for their jobs. The committee then had to use the information flows to determine to what extent its managers were to blame or its work force was unsuitable. Since most servants had been hired in London and were used to a life that countervened the requirements of prayer, sobriety, and peacefulness, the London Committee chose to give its managers the benefit of the doubt.

Instead of chiding the managers for allowing the men to get drunk, the committee pursued a strategy designed to alleviate the problem and to make easier both the supervisory task of the manager and the deciphering task of the committee. The committee changed its labor force, trying to find workers who were more ideally suited to life on Hudson Bay. Within a few years of operation, the committee started to hire from Scotland, the view being that Scots would be more used to the cold. This did not solve all problems. By 1700 the company started to hire from the Orkney Islands, which quickly became the sole source of labor.[31] Conditioned by life on the Islands, Orcadians were particularly suited to the conditions at Hudson Bay. Now, the committee was better able to judge the performance of its manager. To the extent that brawling, drunkenness, or other forms of "loose living" occurred, the manager was deemed responsible and might be brought home or sent to another post as a second-in-command.

The primary function of the managers on Hudson Bay was to acquire furs for the company, and it is in this area that the problem of opportunistic behavior loomed large. To counteract this behavior, the London Committee used a variety of contracts and incentives to ensure adequate performance by its managers.

[30] Harold A. Innis, *The Fur Trade in Canada* (Toronto, 1930), p. 135. For a more detailed discussion of the Orcadians in the Hudson's Bay Company, see John Nicks, "The Role of Orcadians in the Fur Trade," in Arthur Ray and Carol M. Judd, eds., *Old Trails and New Directions: Papers of the Third North American Fur Trade Conference* (Toronto, 1980); and Rich, *The History of the Hudson's Bay Company*, vol. 1, pp. 377–92. These regulations reduced the problems that can occur when small groups of individuals live together in crowded circumstances for long periods of time. The use of Orcadians may have further reduced the tensions that could have arisen.

[31] The desire to change the work force was reinforced by the wars with France. Due to the wars men were no longer easily available in London because of press gauges, and the route north was safer than going south along the British channel.

Each individual hired by the Hudson's Bay Company was given a formal contract that specified the number of years to be spent on the Bay, the salary, and any other stipulations that might have been negotiated, such as care of a wife or children in the event the man died. The money wages paid underestimated the real wages since the company provided housing, food, and transportation to and from the Bay and a multiyear contract. Even so, in comparison to a list of wages for British workers, the managers were very well paid for the period.[32] Charles Bayly, the first governor at Hudson Bay, was initially given a salary of £50 per annum, but that was quickly raised to £200. A successor, John Nixon, had an initial salary of £100, which was raised to £200 in his second year of office.[33] High salaries, by increasing the opportunity cost of opportunistic behavior, helped potentially to reduce such activity. The fact that men regularly throughout the eighteenth century renewed their contracts at the Bay is further evidence that salaries were generous and perhaps that opportunism was not a problem.

The policy of high salaries was reinforced both by salary increases and commendations and by gratuities. During the early years of the company's history, the committee seemed to have had a deliberate policy of encouraging increased effort through end-of-year monetary rewards, which were not necessarily tied to increased output levels. The company's belief that such a policy increased work effort is evident in a letter of 1690 to George Geyer, governor of York Factory:

> Having Resolved on our parts not to faile of giveing encouragement to all whome wee find dilligent and active to promote our Interest, Wee have amongst others taken into Consideration Mr. Lawson the warehousekeeper and being well satisfied of his Carraidg and Care in the station, have ordered him a gratuity of Twenty pounds, and moreover Complyed with his humble request in Increasing his sallary to Forty pounds p. Ann.[34]

Making the same point, the company wrote to one Mr. Walsh in the same year, "you may see our Resolves to Leave noe merritt unrewarded for your further encouragement in the Preservation of our Rights and Encrease of the trade wee have voted you fifty pounds Gratuity, over and above your Fixed salary."[35] Not only were gratuities commonplace but they were large. In the examples presented here gratuities ranged from 50 to 100 percent of salary.

In addition to high real wages and gratuities which should have

[32] Jeffrey Williamson, "Structure of Pay in Britain, 1710–1911," in Paul Uselding, ed., *Research in Economic History* (Greenwich, CT, 1982), vol. 7, p. 48, appendix table 4. Salaries for the men at the Bay are found in Innis, *Fur Trade in Canada*, pp. 124, 125; and in Rich, ed., *Hudson's Bay Copy Booke*, vol. 20.

[33] Rich, *The History of the Hudson's Bay Company*, vol. 1, pp. 81, 92.

[34] Rich, ed., *Hudson's Bay Copy Booke*, vol. 20, p. 103.

[35] Ibid., p. 105. Mr. Walsh was in charge of the factory at New Severn in 1690, earning a salary of £50 per annum.

discouraged opportunism, contracts originally gave the men the right to trade for furs on their own account. In its instructions to the first ships sent out to the Bay, the company wrote:

> Some small private adventures may be also carryed by you and your men which wee doe not refuse to allow but doe absolutely restraine all persons from tradeing themselves with the Indians because thereby our Trade may be distroyed and the said Mr. Gooseberry [Grosseilliers] and Mr. Radisson loose theire credit with the Indians. Private ventures were therefore to be "disposed of in a like manner as our owne goods are."[36]

Why the committee allowed such a policy is still unresolved. It may have been that Grosseilliers and Radisson negotiated private trade as part of their contract or that the company was copying a policy to be found in other overseas chartered companies, such as the East India Company. In any event, private trade encouraged opportunism. Opportunistic managers, by purchasing the best furs for themselves and devoting a disproportionate amount of time to their private trade, reduced company profits. The London Committee quickly recognized that allowing private trade was not a useful policy, and within two years it was declared illegal.[37]

Even though the company banned private trade by its managers in 1672, it was not easy to eradicate the problem. The London Committee first looked for a solution within the formal contract structure by requiring that all managers and ships' captains take an oath declaring that they would not engage in private trade. The use of such an oath started very early in the company's history. In 1683 Captain Samuel Edwards, commander of the *Friendship*, appeared before the "Committee and made oath neither Directly or indirectly to derive any private trade outward or homewards dureing the present Expedition and to use all possible meanes he can to prevent private trade in others."[38] The success of oaths in reducing opportunism depends on the mores of the period and the character of the individual. Certainly some managers treated the oath seriously. For example, in 1685 Radisson and his group of Frenchmen initially refused to take the oath of fidelity which required them to restrain from private trade.[39] The company eventually came to an agreement with Radisson which excluded the right to private trade.

As well as having to take an oath, early managers were asked to post bonds. Indeed, in 1685, the same year in which Radisson and his men

[36] Rich, *The History of the Hudson's Bay Company*, vol. 1, p. 55. Médard Chouart Grosseilliers and Pierre Esprit Radisson sailed to London in the 1660s and were instrumental in launching a British attempt to get furs in northern Canada. Their efforts resulted in the formation of the Hudson's Bay Company.

[37] Rich, ed., *Minutes, 1671–74*, vol. 5, p. 38.

[38] Edwin Ernest Rich, ed., *Minutes of the Hudson's Bay Company, 1679–1684*. First Part: *1679–1682* (London, 1945), vol. 8, p. 228.

[39] Rich, *The History of the Hudson's Bay Company*, vol. 1, p. 179.

had originally refused to take the oath of fidelity, the group was asked to put up bonds. Radisson gave a bond of £300 that he would make the voyage and a further bond of £2,000 that he would fulfill his covenant. The other Frenchmen were required to put up bonds of £500. Such bonds were asked not just of groups such as the French, who had shown a reluctance to abandon private trade, but of many of the company's early managers. As early as 1674 William Lydall, who had been chosen as governor to replace Bayly and was to be the second governor at the Bay, was asked to put up a bond of £1,000.[40] We have found little evidence that those bonds were forfeited, implying that they were successful in reducing opportunism. With the emergence of a professional managerial class within the company by the end of the eighteenth century, the use of bonds seemed to disappear.

Further experimentation by the London Committee led to the introduction of a new incentive within the formal contract structure. As well as multiyear contracts in which managers were well paid and abundantly supplied with commodities for their own tables, they were allowed to trap their own furs.[41] Rich argued that the company introduced private trapping as an incentive designed to keep men working in Hudson Bay during a time of possible French attack. Private trapping would raise men's income in a manner thought to be costless to the company. It also would increase the number of small furs which were selling well in England and possibly teach the men survival skills which would allow them to winter away from the posts.[42]

Although trapping increased managers' income and thus raised the opportunity cost of losing one's job, it brought the London Committee face to face, once again, with the issue of opportunistic behavior. Private trapping gave managers a mechanism for masking private trade and also opened the opportunity for unscrupulous managers to substitute company furs for their own poorer quality furs. To attenuate this problem, the conditions for private trapping and the penalties for cheating were carefully specified. In the letter of instructions sent out in 1701, the committee encouraged trapping "all sorts of small ffurs as ffox woolfe quickahash [Wolverene] Martin ffeathers, &ca." "All skins except those of foexes were to be delivered into the warehouse by the end of February and each man's catch would be sent to London under his own mark. One half of the proceeds from the sale by candle of these small furs and feathers would be paid to each man's order in London. If skins were concealed instead of being delivered into the warehouse the

[40] Ibid., pp. 79, 179.

[41] The letters sent to the Bay listed the commodities sent out for the managers' table, for example, "Clarett, Hock, Sack Soe and Sherry." See Rich, ed., *Hudson's Bay Copy Booke*, vol. 20, p. 234.

[42] Rich, *The History of the Hudson's Bay Company*, vol. 1, p. 374.

offender would not only forfeit them but also all his wages."[43] By requiring all furs to be in the warehouse before the Indians came to trade and by specifying penalties for abuses, the committee hoped to control private trapping. Nevertheless, private trapping was open to abuse and was, without monitoring, of questionable success in increasing managerial effort on behalf of the company. The company realized this and instituted a system of internal control to enhance the supervision of its managers and to curtail private trade and abuses of private trapping.

Monitoring and Internal Controls

At the heart of the company's ability to control the conduct of managers and to ensure that they performed satisfactorily lay a system of monitoring and internal controls. Private trapping had reintroduced the problem of private trade because privately trapped furs could not be distinguished in London from privately traded ones. As we said earlier, wiping out private trade was not easy. This was due both to the distances involved and the particular difficulties in monitoring ships' captains. The captains of the ships that arrived annually at the Bay acted as the main conduit for privately traded furs either by providing unofficial trade goods or by purchasing the furs from the managers for resale on the continent. Beginning in 1683 the men at the Bay were warned that all their baggage would be searched for contraband trade goods or illegal furs. This, however, only diverted the trade to the ships' captains. To combat this the committee searched the ships before they left London for contraband brandy and trade goods and for furs when they returned. The procedure for searching returned vessels was highly organized. The company minutes for December 1679 reported:

> Charles Wilmott and Jeremy Griffith being appointed to goe on board the *John and Alexander* and to stay there to prevent all Frauds and Embezelments, tooke their Oathes so to doe and carried with them a Letter to Capt. Walker to receive them on board.[44]

The oath the "waiters" took specified clearly what was expected. "I doe Sweare to be true to the Governor & Company of Adventurers of England trading into Hudsons Bay I will go on board the ship *John & Alexander* as Soone as conveniently I can, and I will endeavour to my power to discover and prevent all frauds & Embezlements wch. are or may be comitted by any person or pesons there and I shall not come from on board the Sayd Ship untill she be delivered or I receave farther orders."[45] In addition, the committee sealed all legal consignments of

[43] Keith G. Davies, ed., *Letters from Hudson Bay, 1703–1740* (London, 1965), vol. 25, p. 11. "Sale 'by the candle' was a system in which an 'upset price' was called as the candle was lit and bids were made as the candle burned. Whoever had made the highest bid when the candle guttered out was the purchaser." Rich, *The History of The Hudson's Bay Company*, vol. 1, p. 68.

[44] Rich, ed., *Minutes, 1679–84*, vol. 8, pp. 11–12.

[45] Ibid., footnote on p. 11.

liquor and trade goods before consigning them aboard ships in an effort to discover illegal trade goods when the ships were searched before departing for Hudson Bay. In spite of the precautions, some furs were still smuggled into England. In a report to the committee in 1682 Governor John Nixon wrote, "indeed most or all of them [men] have got private trade more, or less, which I cannot possibly come to the knowledge of, they being great with the masters and the ships company. . . ."[46]

The committee also had to prevent high-quality Indian furs being substituted for low-quality private furs and had to prevent trade goods being used for purposes of private trade, with the furs then being shipped as the returns on private trapping. These areas were difficult to monitor. In cases where the committee was suspicious of the size of private trapping, it demanded assurances from its managers that they had actually trapped all the furs and had not received them in exchange for presents or in gratitude from the Indians. According to Rich, the committee refused to believe, probably correctly, that a man could trap £100 worth of furs a year in addition to his ordinary work. In 1679 a martin skin, which was one of the most valuable of the small skins, sold for four shillings a skin in England. To earn £100, a man would have had to trap 500 good-quality skins during the winter months. In comparison Fort Albany received 915 martin skins in trade in 1701 and 369 in 1702. In those same years, Eastmain received 411 and 207 skins.[47] The problem of managers substituting low-quality furs for the company's furs does not seem to have been too serious. The London correspondence before 1763 recorded only one case of significant theft. In 1721 Mr. Hall, the warehouse keeper at York Factory, was accused of "taking ye best of ye comps out of ye Bundles and puting his worst Martins Instead thereof. . . ."[48]

The penalties for engaging in private trade were, from the company's perspective, severe ranging from reprimands to loss of posted bonds to demotion or dismissal. The severity of such penalties for the individual, however, depended on the availability of alternative opportunities. Clearly, opportunities were greater for ships' captains than for managers, since many more openings existed in the maritime trades for skilled captains, proven by the journey to Hudson Bay, than existed for the skills acquired by managers in fur trading.[49] Even if a man was not

[46] Ibid., appendix A, p. 244.

[47] Rich, ed., *Minutes, 1679–84*, vol. 8, appendix B, pp. 320–27, detailed the prices paid for furs at the sale held Feb. 3, 1679. See Arthur J. Ray and Donald Freeman, *"Give us Good Measure": An Economic Analysis of Relations Between the Indians and The Hudson's Bay Company Before 1763* (Toronto, 1978), p. 168, table 18.

[48] Ray and Freeman, *Good Measure*, p. 115.

[49] Hugh G. T. Aitken, "Defensive Expansionism: The State and Economic Growth," in Hugh G. T. Aitken, ed., *The State and Economic Growth* (New York, 1959), commented on the fact that

dismissed for private trade, he could be held under suspicion by the company, which could mean denial of promotion. Of course, the company was well aware that it could use positive as well as negative incentives. For example, ships' captains were promised 20 percent of the value of any illegal furs confiscated. In spite of this incentive, no captains brought forward confiscated furs.

Private trapping was finally declared illegal in 1770. Its existence for 50 years suggests that the negative aspects of the scheme could not have outweighed the positive gains for the company. In fact, to compensate for the end of private trapping, the committee revised the salary scales. Managers now received £130 per year while ships' captains got £12 per month and £100 gratuity with extra allowances in lieu of their customary "presents." A bonus system was also introduced. Each manager received a bonus of three shillings per score of beaver traded and a ship's captain one shilling sixpence. In 1770–1771 this amounted to £172 for each chief factor, which was forfeited if the person took part in any illegal trade. However, this was an unusually large sum. This bonus scheme existed in some form until 1810, when for a number of years the company went back to a straight wage contract, but one in which the salaries were adjusted to take account of what could be earned under the bonus scheme. In 1810 the two superintendents (governors) each received £400 per annum, with chief factors receiving £150. These salary figures suggest that only a manager sure of remaining undetected would cheat; the opportunity cost of losing one's job was very high.[50] The change in schemes was part of a more complete change in the orientation of the company. The year 1763 marked the British conquest of French Canada and by 1770 an organized British trade from the St. Lawrence basin based along the lines of the previous French trade was well organized and already threatening to encircle Hudson's Bay Company posts around the Bay. In response the company finally started to establish permanent inland trading posts.

While the London Committee could and did search ships, baggage, and letters, it further enhanced its ability to control the conduct of its managers by determining the price at which the managers traded commodities for furs. From the first the committee wanted its methods of trade to be both conservative and consistent.[51] This resulted in two standards of trade: the *Official Standard* which valued all trade goods in the company's unit of account, a "Made Beaver" (the price of a single prime male beaver skin), and the *Comparative Standard* which assigned made beaver values to all furs received from the Indians. The establish-

---

some Hudson's Bay Company factors went to London to act as buying agents for the company, using the expertise gained in trade. These numbers, however, were never very large.

[50] Rich, *The History of the Hudson's Bay Company*, vol. 1, p. 602, and vol. 2, pp. 103, 291–92.

[51] Rich, *The History of the Hudson's Bay Company*, vol. 1, p. 64.

ment of such standards helped to control the discretionary behavior of managers by making it more difficult to cheat and by eliminating competition which maximized the profits of branch plants at the expense of the company. These fixed price standards also satisfied the Indians' demand for certainty of the prices that they would receive for the skins.[52]

By exactly specifying the values of all furs and trade goods, the company controlled the discretionary behavior of its managers. The volume of furs received combined with the volume of trade goods sent gave the committee a high level of information about its managers. At the same time, as these fixed standards reduced the possibility of cheating by managers, they removed, however, all discretion over the terms of trade both from the company and the managers. Thus managers were denied the ability to give presents or, as Rich said, the scope to leave items around for the Indians to pick up in passing. The Indians, while enjoying fixed prices for furs, wanted a ceremonial aspect to the trade which required gift giving and presents.[53] The committee's motive for wanting to change the standard was the price inflation during the wars with France, which increased the price of trade goods and the costs of shipping while depressing fur prices. The lack of discretionary power by either managers or the London Committee operated to the company's disadvantage.

A study of the *Official Standard* shows that it neither varied much over time nor between posts.[54] But this invariance disguises the true nature of the trading relationship and, in particular, the ability of the London Committee to control its agents. Due to the war, the committee allowed the factors to depart from the official prices, writing that "the method of which is however left to your discretion so to manage as not to give any disgust to the natives."[55] As a result, the factor essentially tried to obtain what the market would bear from the Indians, being at all times circumscribed by the fact that the Indians knew the official prices for furs and what was received at other posts. Thus, what has become known as the *Factor's* or *Double Standard* occurred in those commodities most amenable to slight variations such as brandy, cloth, and tobacco, giving the factors goods on hand for ceremonial gift giving and discretionary presents.

The existence of the *Factor's Standard* reduced the company's control over its managers in that it created a bundle of trade goods

[52] Thus, just as the very existence of the branch plants around the Bay signified a long-term commitment on the part of the company, so too did these standards. See Arthur J. Ray, *The Indians and the Fur Trade* (Toronto, 1974), chap. 3, for a more complete discussion of these standards.

[53] Ibid., chap. 5.

[54] A. Rotstein and D. Foot, "The Two Economies of the Hudson's Bay Company" (University of Toronto Working Paper Series, No. 8710, July 1987).

[55] Rich, ed., *Hudson's Bay Copy Booke*, vol. 20, p. 78.

which the managers could use to their own advantage, such as in private trade. To ensure that this was not the case, the committee had requested that the clerks and managers keep an itemized record of exactly what trade goods were sold for which furs in the *Account Book*. This proved to be impossible since a large volume of trade took place within a very short period of time, and the Indians were anxious to complete transactions quickly and start on their journey home. The committee then allowed the chief factor to make an inventory of the trade goods and furs at the end of each trading period. The account books, then, record the furs obtained, commodities traded, the goods remaining for both trade and post use, and the bundle of trade goods freed up by the use of the *Double Standard*. Arthur Ray and Donald Freeman described how this was done.

> The total quantity of each type of fur or country produce brought in by the Indians is . . . listed along with the aggregate M[ade] B[eaver] value of the commodities as determined according to the comparative standard. The value of the goods traded (priced according to the standard of trade) is then subtracted and the remainder is termed the "overplus". If all of the goods and furs had been exchanged according to the official standards listed in the account books, then the value of the furs received should have equalled that of the goods traded and there would be no overplus.[56]

Thus for each post each year a balancing item in the account books is the level of the overplus. The company sought to ensure that it received this information by laying down precise regulations and rigorous standards governing the way that the account books, post journals, and *London Correspondence Inward-Official* were kept.

For the *London Correspondence Inward-Official*, the company required that the letters be written in paragraphs, each coinciding with that in the *Correspondence Outward*. John Knight, chief factor at York in 1716, wrote in one of his letters: "I shall endeavour to follow your instructions as near as I can so I hope you'll excuse me from answering to every particular paragraph of your letter." In the 1730s James Isham, governor at Churchill, was repeatedly reproved by the committee for not writing his general letter home "in paragraphs in the approved manner."[57] The annual letter sent to each post at the Bay contained both the committee's instructions to that post and any questions, queries, or comments that the committee might have had concerning the account books received. These letters contained information relating to the regulation of the trade, the wages of men to be rehired, and the state of the market in England. For example, certain posts might be asked to

[56] Actual quantities of overplus made can be found in the factory accounts, with some amounts being given in Rich, ed., *Hudson's Bay Copy Booke*, vol. 20, p. xliv. A very detailed discussion of the composition of the accounts and derivation can be found in Ray and Freeman, *Good Measure*, chap. 9.

[57] Davies, ed., *Letters form Hudson Bay*, vol. 25, p. 58; and Rich, *The History of the Hudson's Bay Company*, vol. 1, p. 543.

develop a timber trade or to increase trade in certain items such as feathers, whale oil, or castoreum. The *Correspondence Inward* were the factors' responses to the committee's yearly letter. The factors' letters usually began by acknowledging the receipt of the packet sent out and by detailing what documentation they were sending to England. Joseph Myatt's letter from Albany Factor in 1727 in its first paragraph stated that the committee "will find here enclosed together with the journal, weekly allowance, bill of lading, invoice and indent."[58] These letters then gave the number of Made Beaver shipped, explaining why the post had such a poor return or congratulating themselves on their hard work which had produced good results. They talked about how orders had been followed; for example, Myatt wrote in paragraph five: "According to your orders I have sent home six samples of the England brandy which came over this year with the number of each cask fixed to every sample and have likewise sent you a sample of the brandy which came over last year, but it is everyone's opinion it is nothing near so good as that which came over the year before. . . ." From these letters one can obtain a detailed picture of the way in which the managers at the Bay complied with the instructions sent out to them.

It was through comparison of the account books, the *Correspondence Inward*, the actual quantities of furs shipped from the Bay, and the committee's records of the trade goods sent from England that the London Committee was in a position to judge how their managers were handling the trade at the Bay and whether any manager was defrauding the company. This information flow gave the potential to audit each manager's performance, and the records indicate that the company used it to monitor its managers and make it more difficult for them to cheat, in particular through private trade. One way to monitor their performance was through examination of a number of indices that allowed comparisons through time and to reprove, dismiss, or identify inexperienced managers. One such index has been described by Ray and Freeman. They argued that the committee compared the level of overplus for each post with its level of expenses and used the resulting net return as a decision-making tool. Table 1 shows these figures for Fort Churchill during the decade 1721 to 1731. The overplus column measures the bundle of trade goods freed up by paying the Indians below the *Official Standard*. Some of these freed-up goods, however, were used in the gift-giving ceremonies associated with trade and were an expense of the trade. The table shows a dramatic reversal in the level of the net return in 1722, which continued for four years. Richard Norton was the chief trader during these years; in 1727, when he was relieved of his command, the committee wrote:

[58] Davies, ed., *Letters from Hudson Bay*, vol. 25, pp. 121–23.

TABLE 1
FORT CHURCHILL: EXPENSES AND OVERPLUS

Date	Overplus	Expenses	Net Return
1721	$2,826	$1,140	$1,686
1722	696	1,747	−1,051
1723	630	1,365	−735
1724	567	1,341	−774
1725	634	1,853	−1,219
1726	601	1,722	−1,121
1727	2,017	908	1,109
1728	4,135	898	3,237
1729	3,131	896	2,235
1730	2,650	894	1,756
1731	4,769	1,956	2,813

Notes: The Hudson's Bay Company's official rates of exchange for trade goods and furs remained fixed for long periods of time. The actual rates of exchange on trade goods could vary. The amount by which the actual exchange rate differed from the official rate was termed overplus. Not all of this reflected a gain for the company, as some had to be used in gift-giving ceremonies and thus constituted an expense.
Source: Arthur J. Ray and Donald B. Freeman, *"Give us Good Measure": An Economic Analysis of Relations Between the Indians and The Hudson's Bay Company Before 1763* (Toronto 1978).

We observe in the Accounts you have sent us, that your over Trade hath been every year very small compared, with that of our other factories, and former Accts. from the fort you are at, . . . we have therefore ordered that you shall be removed to York Fort, and their, to be under the direction of Governor. Macklish, which we are certain, will be very much to your advantage, and improvement, in the knowledge of our Trade and Accounts.[59]

Anthony Beale, Norton's replacement, was able to reverse the net returns. When he died in 1731, he was replaced by Thomas Bird and three months later by Richard Norton once again, who was to maintain the level of net returns.

Although the level of net returns for a post provided information about a manager's performance, the size of the overplus and expenses for any post was affected directly by the amount of competition the company faced. An alternative measure was to look at the total return for the post in comparison to the merchandise exported to that post. Thus a post could have had a low net return due to intense competition, which would have lowered the overplus and raised expenses, but still have a reasonable terms-of-trade index between the fur return and the trade goods supplied. The policy was that a certain quantity of trade goods should receive a given quantity of furs in return. In Table 2 we have calculated such an index for the Eastmain and Albany factories for the decade 1804 to 1814. The existence of the official and comparative standards allow all fur returns and all trade goods to be denominated in Made Beaver equivalents. The standard used is that for 1801. The

[59] Ibid., p. 121.

TABLE 2
COMPARISON OF TRADING PERFORMANCE

	Ratio of Beaver Returns to Merchandise Exported	
	Albany Factory	Eastmain Factory
1804	2.3	2.3
1805	2.1	2.1
1806	2.0	2.6
1807	1.8	2.0
1808	1.9	1.8
1809	1.5	1.1
1810	3.9	2.1
1813	3.1	1.3
1814	4.9	

Notes: The ratios are denominated in "Made Beaver" equivalents. A Made Beaver was the standard unit of account employed by the Hudson's Bay Company. A Made Beaver was the value of a prime beaver skin. All furs and trade goods were given a Made Beaver equivalent.
Source: Public Archives of Canada HBC MG20A53, MG20A25. Fur returns are missing for 1811 and are incomplete for 1812.

indices for each factor show a similar pattern of decline to 1810, then Eastmain and Albany diverge. In 1810 John Hodson was informed that he was no longer employed as chief trader at Albany, the committee writing that "for some time past there has been a want of that activity and vigour which can alone retrieve the hitherto declining trade from your parts."[60] The committee also expressed concern over the management of the Eastmain Factory. The response to the continuing decline of the index at Eastmain was to change its status from that of an independent factory to that of the trading district under Moose Factory.

These examples show how the accounting systems were used to monitor behavior and the flexibility of the committee in handling cases. The committee did not assume automatically that its managers were trying to defraud the company. The effectiveness of these monitoring and control systems improved over the eighteenth century, not just because the London Committee gained experience and improved their record keeping but because the committee tried to create an environment in which managers were less likely to cheat.

A Social System

We argued earlier that if firms can create an ethical system to which the managers conform, the necessity for close monitoring will be lessened. In a family concern such a social system can be created by making family members partners and managers of the various plants.[61] Although the Hudson's Bay Company was not a family concern, the

[60] *London Correspondence Outward-Official*, Public Archives of Canada, Hudson's Bay Company MG20A6 (Albany, 1810).

[61] A very good history and analysis of such a family concern can be found in Douglas McCalla, *The Upper Canada Trade, 1834–1872: A Study of the Buchanans' Business* (Toronto, 1979).

directors definitely tried to create a social system in which the managers and workers were made to feel part of a family. The attempt to create a "family environment" was particularly evident during the French wars when the committee wrote:

> [A]nd for the better encouragement of your men in their Duty Wee doe hereby promise and assure you and them, that Wee will take Care by way of Pension for such of them as haveing behaved themselves with Courage and fidelity shalbe wounded and the Wives and Children of those whoe shall happen to bee killed in our Services . . . be Confident that noe brave action pformed in defence or recovery of any places or Factoryes shall passe ungratifyed.[62]

Indeed, all the correspondence is replete with positive encouragement to the men and managers, commenting on their work, commending them, and rewarding them with the large gratuities mentioned earlier.

A homogeneous social group was created when the London Committee's search for a labor force led to the hiring of Orcadians. As well as hiring suitable servants, the committee also tried to ensure that it would have suitable managers. The committee needed people who could manage the labor force and trade for furs and were sufficiently educated that they could keep the account books and post journals. The men who were promoted from the ranks were very often able traders but fell short on the other two counts. In fact, the committee took the trading ability of the men from the ranks as a base, believing that more suitable managers should be able to do better. To this end the committee started to indenture apprentices. In 1689 the company sent four apprentices from Christ's Hospital in London to Hudson Bay. These "Blue Coat Boys" were educated in writing and arithmetic and usually started in the company at the age of 14, although John Hindson, a "Parish boy" from Essex, is said to have started as young as eight. In the general letter of 1689 the committee described its view of these apprentices:

> [T]hey all write faire haudes and Cast accompts, and being young will easily attaine the Lingua and bee trained up in our service and if you think such Ladds may bee useful in a few years to send up with the Indians wee have thoughts yearely or every other year to take the like or a greater number from the said Hospital.[63]

By the end of the eighteenth century it was from this group that many of the company's major officers, including Henry Kelsey and Richard Norton, regularly came. Indeed, recent work by Jennifer Brown confirmed that the company actively pursued a policy directed toward creating a set of shared values and apparently was successful in this.[64]

[62] Rich, ed., *Hudson's Bay Copy Booke*, vol. 20, p. 51.

[63] Ibid., p. 79; and Davies, ed., *Letters from Hudson Bay*, vol. 25, p. 76.

[64] Jennifer Brown, *Strangers in Blood: Fur Trade Company Families in Indian Country* (Vancouver, 1980).

Not only did the Hudson's Bay Company actively try to create a managerial class with a set of shared values, it encouraged any complaints that its managers might have concerning the behavior of peers or supervisors. The company tried to create a moral code governing both private and work behavior and encouraged managers to report on each other. A recurring theme in the eighteenth-century correspondence was the number of men who were recalled to London to answer questions concerning their moral conduct or alleged private trade on the basis of complaints by other employees. Examples of this abound. In 1685, when Governor Sargeant accused James Knight, chief factor at Albany and deputy governor at the Bay, of private trade, Knight was called to London to answer the charges. Three years later Radisson accused Governor Geyer of the same and Geyer too was brought home to answer the charges. In the 1730s chief factor Macklish had to go to England to explain how he had trapped so many furs, and in 1745 chief factor Isham was called to London in regard to private trade and his general behavior.[65] In some cases the answers were found satisfactory and in others not. But the committee made it very clear that it was willing to listen before it acted.

A social system has positive and negative attributes. Insofar as managers perceived themselves to be part of a "family," opportunistic behavior was mitigated. Of course, such a system was open to abuse by managers when reporting meant that diligent managers would be called home and supervision would be more lax. However, the company often replaced recalled managers with personnel from other posts, providing the London Committee with an independent auditing of work practices at that post.

CONCLUSION

The motivation behind this article came from the generalized statements found in the literature that one of the major problems facing chartered companies was that of private trade by their own managers. We have examined the issue of private trade for one of these chartered companies, the Hudson's Bay Company, which saw private trade as a serious problem and tried to eradicate it by employing a range of strategies to deal with the problem.

One device was the formal contract structure. High real wages and large gratuities paid by the company increased the opportunity cost of losing one's position because of private trade and so should have reduced the level of opportunism. The company also required that its managers take an oath swearing that they would not engage in private trade and reinforced these oaths by requiring that the managers post large bonds that would be lost if the person was found to have engaged in private trade. Again these strategies should have helped to reduce the level of opportunistic behavior.

[65] Rich, *The History of the Hudson's Bay Company*, vol. 1, pp. 182, 259, 543, 546.

Nevertheless, high salaries, gratuities, bonds, and oaths need not have reduced the level of private trade if managers believed there existed little possibility of being caught and losing their salary.

A second approach was to monitor the activities of its managers. This was done through such straightforward monitoring devices as searching incoming and outgoing ships and the men's baggage for illicit trade goods or furs and reading men's letters for any information concerning possible private trade. Again such activity on the company's part should have reduced the level of private trade by managers. The company also monitored its managers' activities by putting into place a set of internal control mechanisms designed to account for the use of all trade goods sent to Hudson Bay. To this end the managers were required to follow rigorous standards in the maintenance of post records and in particular of all account books. Through these records the company could monitor the trading activity of individual managers, and, as we argued, devise indices based on the accounts to be used as monitoring devices. Such close scrutiny of managerial activity should have helped further to reduce the level of private trade.

Finally the company attempted to reduce the level of private trade by creating a social structure within the company, the mores of which dictated against such behavior. The Hudson's Bay Company tried to engender the view of the company as family and to create the existence of a set of shared values. Both the policy of hiring lower-level workers solely from the Orkney Islands and of apprenticing boys from Christ's College in London to form a future managerial class helped to create a "family" structure. The more successful was this policy, the less likely was private trade to occur.

The physical environment in which the company operated with its limited access and few contact points with the outside enhanced the likelihood that a strategy for controlling private trade would succeed. It is unlikely, however, that any strategy would have succeeded alone. More likely, success depended on the application of a judicious mixture of all the policies described earlier. The Hudson's Bay Company treated its managers well, especially by the standards of the time, and kept a watchful eye on what was happening in each of its posts, but did all of this in the context of a "caring" environment. The social structure which the company created was, we would argue, an integral part of its ability to attenuate opportunistic behavior by its managers. All of this suggests that the Hudson's Bay Company had succeeded in controlling private trade by the end of the eighteenth century. The company is still in operation today, suggesting that it was able to exert enough control over opportunistic behavior to remain viable. Survivorship gives a lower bound on success and in subsequent work we anticipate being able to provide a better quantitative assessment of those efforts.

Fifty Years of Coal-mining Productivity: The Record of the British Coal Industry before 1939

DAVID GREASLEY

A downward trend in British coal-mining productivity was reversed between the world wars. Declining productivity before 1914 was accompanied by wide regional differences, especially at the coalface. Scotland attained the best overall productivity, while coalface productivity was highest in Durham and Northumberland. Regional differences narrowed by the 1920s but re-emerged in the 1930s, as mines in the North Midlands outpaced the productivity gains made elsewhere. Only a multifaceted interpretation can explain these distinctive patterns—over time, between regions, and at different stages of the coal-mining operation.

British coal mining's productivity record in the half-century before 1939 has attracted considerable attention. The interest stems in part from the dominant position coal had attained in the British economy by the early twentieth century. Judged by its contributions to energy supply, male employment, and overseas earnings, coal reigned supreme in 1913. Yet doubts about the industry's longer-term prospects were beginning to surface before World War I. American output surpassed that of Britain in 1900, and German production was fast catching up by 1913, the year in which British coal output peaked. Before 1914 there was little sign of decreased demand for British coal, but the industry's supply-side performance caused concern. A report from the Royal Commission on Coal Supplies, 1903/05, eased worries about resource depletion, but the secular decline in output per labor year from the 1880s (see Figure 1) cast a shadow over future prospects. Prosperity was not immediately undermined, but the translation of productivity weakness into higher coal prices and revenue in the era of buoyant demand prior to 1914 abruptly ended with the collapse of the postwar boom. Thereafter declining exports and stagnant domestic demand stimulated a search for lower wages and higher productivity. The resulting social tensions ensured coal-mining productivity a place in the limelight during the years of declining output, low profitability, and unemployment between the wars. Indeed, productivity improved in the troubled years after 1914.

The Journal of Economic History, Vol. L, No. 4 (Dec. 1990). ISSN 0022-0507.

The author is Lecturer in Economic History at the University of Edinburgh, Edinburgh, Scotland.

He would like to thank Professor C. H. Feinstein, members of the Warwick University Economic History Workshop, and this JOURNAL's editorial team for advice.

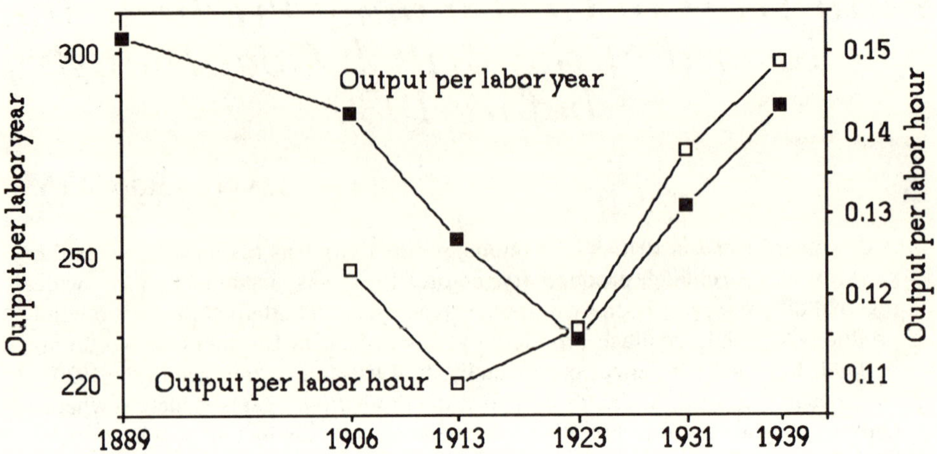

FIGURE 1

LABOR PRODUCTIVITY IN BRITISH COAL MINING (TONS)

Historians' explanations for the fluctuations in British coal-mining productivity are divided by the watershed in the industry's fortunes that World War I represented. For the prosperous years between the 1880s and 1914, analysts primarily attributed falling productivity to resource depletion and diminished labor effort. Miners working less strenuously, argued both Arthur Taylor and Rhodri Walters, exacerbated the effects of longer underground haulage requirements and thinner seams in Great Britain and South Wales.[1] Donald McCloskey and Brian Mitchell emphasized the deleterious influence of the resource endowment, whereas Barry Hirsch and William Hausman stressed the role of reduced work intensity.[2] Roy Church took a different view, arguing that productivity decline was largely confined to the 1880s and that a judicious concentration of investment and production offset the effects of resource depletion.[3]

On the far side of the watershed, deterioration of the industry's financial performance between the wars was accompanied by rising productivity. Neil Buxton credited mechanization for the upturn; contemporaries emphasized the benefits from amalgamating colliery enter-

[1] Arthur J. Taylor, "Labour Productivity and Technological Innovation in the British Coal Industry, 1850–1914," *Economic History Review*, 14 (Aug. 1961), pp. 48–70; Rhodri Walters, "Labour Productivity in the South Wales Steam Coal Industry, 1870–1914," *Economic History Review*, 28 (May 1975), pp. 280–303.

[2] Donald N. McCloskey, "International Differences in Productivity? Coal and Steel in America and Britain before World War I," in Donald N. McCloskey, *Essays on a Mature Economy: Britain after 1840* (London, 1970), pp. 285–304; Brian R. Mitchell, *Economic Development of the British Coal Industry* (Cambridge, 1984); Barry T. Hirsch and William J. Hausman, "Labour Productivity in the British and South Wales Coal Industry, 1874–1914," *Economica*, 50 (May 1983), pp. 145–59.

[3] Roy Church, *The History of the British Coal Industry 1830–1913* (Oxford, 1986).

prises.[4] Maurice Kirby and Walford Johnson questioned the importance of mechanization to the upswing, citing as evidence the findings of the Samuel Commission and the Reid Inquiry.[5] More recently Ben Fine and Trevor Boyns have stressed the advantages of scale, though Michael Dintenfass demurred from their point, postulating instead the efficacy of machines.[6]

To some extent the tendency to divide British coal-mining history into pre-1914 and interwar segments hinders the analysis of productivity. While the financial fortunes of the industry declined sharply between the wars, this resulted, as Barry Supple plausibly argued, from the vagaries of market demand.[7] Changes on the supply side, notwithstanding the productivity upturn in the 1920s, were less dramatic. Individual influences on productivity—coalface mechanization, resource depletion, and regional disparities in hours and work practices—originated before the war. The longer-term effects of these forces are obscured by the artificial division in the literature. An examination of the causes of productivity during the 50 years prior to 1939 demonstrates the limitations of focusing on singular short-term explanations and suggests that interaction between a wider range of variables shaped British coal-mining productivity. In isolation mechanization had little impact; it failed, for example, to halt productivity decline in the years before 1914. Eventually, integrated machine-mining systems offset resource depletion, and productivity rose between the wars. Yet the gains from mechanization, even when accompanied by wider reorganization, failed to eliminate disparities in productivity. These disparities, already apparent in the era of hand hewing, persisted to the 1930s, indicating that organization and conditions of work influenced productivity. The underground "landscape," shaped by geology and previous mining, along with the organization of the mining operation and mechanization, interacted to pattern the contours of productivity in the 50 years before 1939. Before the forces governing productivity can be explained, the record itself needs to be established.

[4] Neil K. Buxton, "Entrepreneurial Efficiency in the British Coal Industry between the Wars," *Economic History Review*, 23 (Feb. 1970), pp. 476–97.

[5] *Report of the Technical Advisory Committee* (P.P. 1944–45, IV, London). *Report of the Royal Commission on the Coal Industry* (P.P. 1926, XIV, London); Maurice W. Kirby, "Entrepreneurship in the British Coal Industry between the Wars," *Economic History Review*, 25 (Nov. 1972), pp. 655–57; Walford Johnson, "Entrepreneurial Efficiency in the British Coal Industry between the Wars: A Second Comment," *Economic History Review*, 25 (Nov. 1972), pp. 665–68.

[6] Trevor Boyns, "Rationalisation in the Inter-War Period: The Case of the South Wales Steam Coal Industry," *Business History*, 29 (July 1987), pp. 282–303; Michael Dintenfass, "Entrepreneurial Failure Reconsidered: The Case of the Interwar British Coal Industry," *Business History Review*, 62 (Spring 1988), pp. 1–34; Ben Fine, *The Coal Question* (London, 1990).

[7] Barry Supple, *The History of the British Coal Industry 1914–1946* (Oxford, 1987).

TABLE 1
OUTPUT PER LABOR HOUR
(tons)

	1906	1914	1923	1931	1938
Durham	0.127	0.113	0.115	0.137	0.135
Lancashire & Cheshire	0.114	0.097	0.097	0.108	0.126
Northumberland	0.126	0.117	0.112	0.141	0.143
North Midlands	0.131	0.112	0.124	0.153	0.173
Scotland	0.146	0.127	0.133	0.154	0.156
South Wales	0.097	0.092	0.102	0.111	0.120
Great Britain	0.123	0.109	0.116	0.138	0.149

Source: See Appendix A. Note that the data for Great Britain are weighted averages of the six regions.

MEASURING COAL-MINING PRODUCTIVITY

Labor Productivity

Historians adopt a variety of approaches to measure labor productivity in British coal mining. Output per labor year (O/Y) traditionally serves, in the absence of labor shift data, for the years prior to 1914. For the interwar period, output per labor shift (O/S) provides the standard measure but lacks some utility, as shift lengths varied between regions and over time. More useful are output per labor hour (O/H) data, and constructing these for several British regions yields new insights into coal-mining productivity (see Table 1 and Appendix A). For the British industry overall, the results show falling labor productivity up to 1914 and then a recovery that becomes marked after 1923. Overall, O/H rose around 21 percent between 1906 and 1938, compared to static O/Y between those dates. For the interwar years, especially, the O/H figures cast British coal mining's productivity in a better light relative to both other nations' coal industries and the overall British economy.

Regional productivity patterns evolved as well. The regions in Table 1 produced 85 to 90 percent of British coal, and the relative contribution of each district changed little (see Figure 2). Only the share of the North Midlands (comprising the counties of Yorkshire, Derbyshire, and Nottinghamshire) noticeably increased, from 26 to 32 percent. Strikingly wide productivity differences between regions appeared before World War I. Scotland did best, achieving 50 percent higher O/H in 1906 than the lagging South Wales field. Durham and Northumberland were above-average areas before the war, overtaking the North Midlands' productivity levels by 1914. O/H in Lancashire and Cheshire fell comparatively sharply by 1914 to a level not much above that of South Wales.

Labor productivity stagnated in most regions from the onset of war to 1923, and actually fell in Northumberland. Overall, the British industry's O/H rose just 6 percent between 1914 and 1923, mostly because of

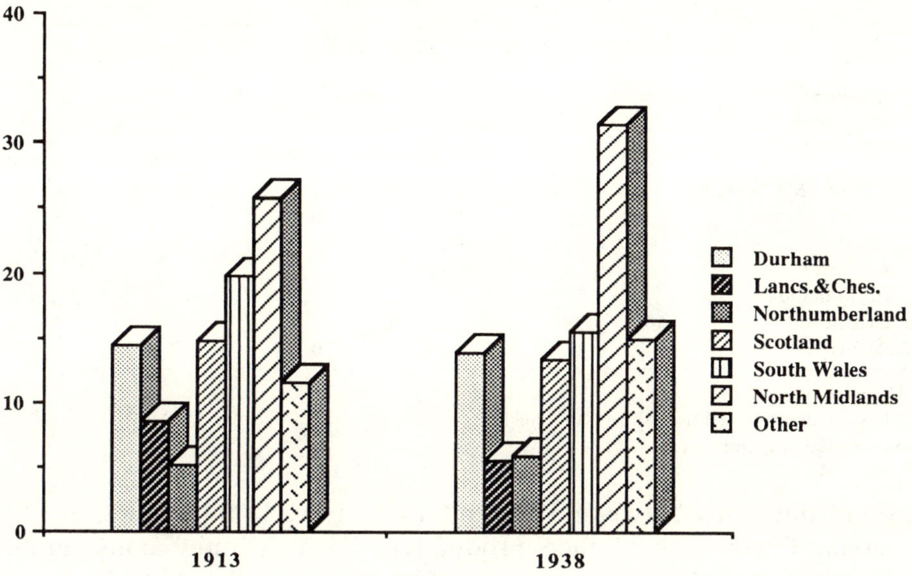

FIGURE 2

BRITISH COAL OUTPUT BY REGION (PERCENT)

the increases recorded in the North Midlands and South Wales. Recovery was stronger thereafter, and all fields experienced productivity gains in the 1920s; however, these varied, and regional differences, which had lessened by 1923, resurfaced. Relatively fast productivity growth in the North Midlands led to levels there similar to those in high-productivity Scotland by 1931. Northumberland also made useful gains, whereas productivity levels in South Wales and Lancashire and Cheshire languished 40 percent below the highest levels in 1931. Productivity gains were more patchy in the 1930s, and overall growth lower than in the 1920s. Growth was maintained in the North Midlands, and productivity there was well above that in other areas by 1938. Productivity in Durham, Northumberland, and Scotland was stagnant in the 1930s, but the low-productivity South Wales and Lancashire-and-Cheshire fields made some gains. Widening productivity dispersion within British coal mining by the end of the 1930s thus arose from the singular achievements of the North Midlands' pits.

A further labor productivity index can usefully be added to the indicators presented so far. Output per labor hour at the coalface—$(O/H)_f$ —shows different spatial and temporal patterns from overall productivity (see Table 2). These differences shed light on the determinants of productivity, as two of the influences that commentators stress—the use of coal-cutting machines and the efforts expended by coal hewers—directly impinge on coalface productivity. Face productivity for the industry generally shows a smaller decline than overall productivity up to 1914, and subsequently a faster recovery, rising by

TABLE 2
OUTPUT PER LABOR HOUR AT THE COALFACE
(tons)

	1906	1914	1923	1931	1938
Durham	0.43	0.40	0.37	0.40	0.40
Lancashire & Cheshire	0.26	0.27	—[a]	—	—
Northumberland	0.36	0.39	0.32	0.39	0.39
Scotland	0.28	0.26	0.29	0.37	0.36
South Wales	0.20	0.20	0.23	0.26	0.27
North Midlands	0.27	0.24	0.31	0.37	0.46
Great Britain	0.289	0.271	—	—	—
Great Britain[b]	0.293	0.271	0.298	0.353	0.391

[a] Data are not available.
[b] These data exclude Lancashire and Cheshire.
Source: See Appendix A.

around one-third between 1906 and 1938. Equally interesting are the regional differences in face productivity, which show considerably greater range and different rankings from the overall O/H figures.

Durham and Northumberland attained high face productivity in the period before World War I. Clearly a smaller proportion of the work force was employed at the coalface in these two northeastern counties, because overall productivity there was close to the national average. The estimates suggest that Durham face workers in 1906 produced twice as much coal per hour as their counterparts in South Wales. By 1914 Northumberland's $(O/H)_f$ was also approaching twice the South Wales level. Moreover, as the average age of pits was greater in the northeastern counties, coalfaces there were farther from mine shafts, which meant longer underground travel for face workers and suggests that their productivity was understated by the figures, which do not allow for travel time. Regional disparities do lessen by the 1920s. During the period from 1914 through 1923 face productivity fell in the northeast, whereas most other areas experienced modest gains and the North Midlands recorded a 29 percent increase. Indeed by 1931, with the exception of South Wales, face productivity levels were remarkably similar throughout the British coalfield, with Scotland achieving substantial gains in the 1920s. Face productivity then stagnated in all but one region through the 1930s. Only the North Midlands continued to record gains to become, by a clear margin, the highest face (and overall) productivity area within the British industry before the end of the decade.

Multifactor Productivity

Shifts in labor productivity partly reflect changes in the use of complementary inputs. The influence of land resources is considered under "Explaining Coal-mining Productivity." Machine inputs can explicitly be incorporated into the productivity indexes. Ideally this would be done for both overall and face productivity indicators, but limited data restrict us to measuring multifactor productivity at the coalface. The mechanization of coalface operations in the early decades of the twentieth century initially involved coal cutters and later face conveyors. Machine cutting made only limited progress in Great Britain before 1914, but there were regional differences. In 1914, 8 percent of British coal was machine cut; in Scotland the figure was 20 percent. The use of mechanical conveying trailed behind machine cutting, except in South Wales. By 1938, 60 percent of British coal was machine cut and 54 percent machine conveyed. Again there were regional variations, with 26 percent and 90 percent, respectively, of South Wales's and Northumberland's coal being cut by machine in 1938.

Annual multifactor face productivity indexes incorporating coal cutter and face conveyor as well as labor inputs are reported in Figure 3 and Table 1 of the Appendix. The multifactor indexes confirm the productivity diversity within British coal mining. Between 1902 and 1939 face multifactor productivity growth ranged from −20 percent in Durham to 55 percent in the North Midlands. Multifactor growth rates were below those for $(O/H)_f$, because coalface operations became more capital intensive. Both northeastern counties, for example, had static $(O/H)_f$ between 1914 and 1938 but experienced 20 percent falls in multifactor productivity. In the North Midlands $(O/H)_f$ almost doubled between 1914 and 1938, but the multifactor index rose only 58 percent. Over the years from 1902 to 1914, multifactor face productivity was stable in the majority of regions but grew 17 percent in Northumberland and 6 percent in South Wales and held up well for most of the war years before falling heavily in 1918 and 1919. All fields, Durham apart, experienced face productivity growth after 1923, though the gains in South Wales and Scotland were fewer than in the North Midlands. Multifactor face productivity trends were less impressive in the coalfields of northeastern England. The gains made in Northumberland before 1917 were lost, and productivity there returned to 1902 levels by 1938. Durham fared worst of all, with a 25 percent face productivity loss between 1917 and 1938.

These disparate trends are reflected in the evolving regional pattern of face productivity levels. The cross-sectional multifactor face productivity indicators in Table 3 show relative regional levels. Face productivity appears to be strikingly higher in northeastern England before World War I. Durham achieved 56 percent more face productivity than the average for the five regions in 1906. While Durham produced 19.7 percent of the five regions' coal, it used only 12.5 percent and 10.8 percent of the face labor and coal cutter hours, respectively. Northumberland's prewar face productivity gains strengthened the northeast's relative position by 1914. Regional differences in face productivity do narrow by the 1920s, as gains were made outside Northumberland and

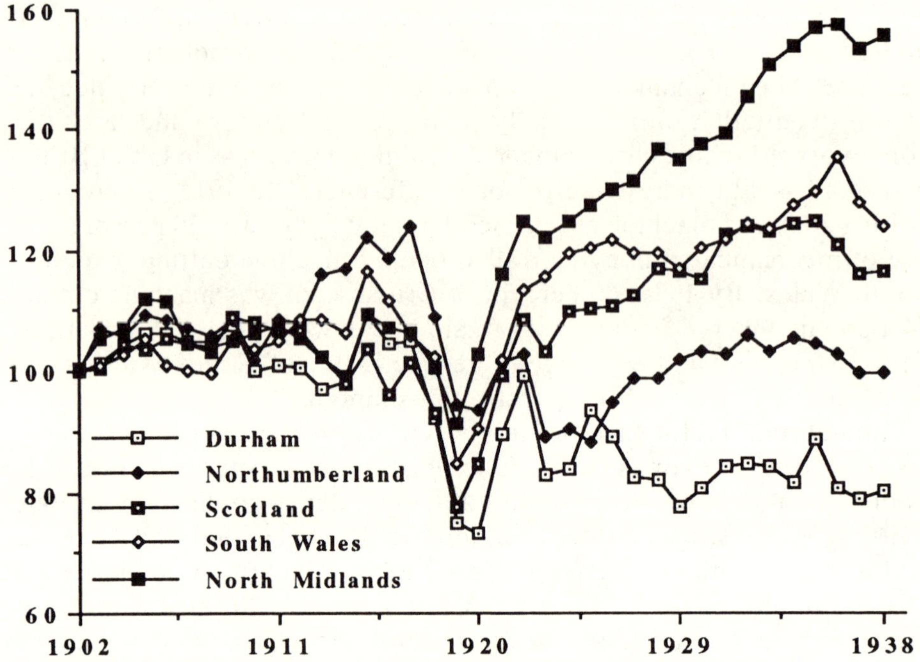

FIGURE 3

INDEX OF COALFACE MULTIFACTOR PRODUCTIVITY
(1902 = 100)

Durham. By 1931 only South Wales's face productivity was markedly below levels achieved elsewhere. In the 1930s regional disparities started to widen again. All fields lost ground relative to the North Midlands, which became the British coal industry's high-productivity area.

TABLE 3
MULTIFACTOR PRODUCTIVITY AT THE COALFACE AS A PERCENTAGE OF AVERAGE LEVELS

	Durham	Northumberland	Scotland	S. Wales	N. Midlands
1906	157.9[a]	131.3	101.2	73.5	98.6
	158.1[b]	131.2	100.4	75.4	98.3
1914	157.7[a]	151.8	101.9	79.7	93.4
	160.7[b]	150.3	99.8	82.4	93.2
1923	126.9[a]	110.7	99.5	80.0	106.4
	127.4[b]	109.0	96.2	83.8	106.7
1931	118.2[a]	111.9	106.7	74.1	109.6
	118.2[b]	104.9	100.0	80.6	112.3
1938	107.3[a]	102.0	95.4	72.8	121.8
	107.6[b]	96.6	91.3	78.3	122.9

[a] Data are based on the least capital intensive weights.
[b] Data are based on the most capital intensive weights.
Source: See Appendices A and B.

TABLE 4
AVERAGE SEAM THICKNESS
(inches)

	Durham	Northumberland	Scotland	S. Wales	N. Midlands
1913	47.4	42.0	43.2	58.9	52.8
1924	45.2	41.8	39.6	54.1	48.5
1944	43.2	39.6	43.8	52.8	47.9

Source: *Royal Commission on the Coal Industry* (London, 1925), vol. 3; Kenneth Lomax, "Coal Production Functions for Great Britain," p. 348; *Journal of the Royal Statistical Society*, ser. A (Part 3, 1950), p. 348.

EXPLAINING COAL-MINING PRODUCTIVITY

A plausible explanation of British coal-mining productivity should account for the disparities in regional levels and trends, be consistent with the evidence for coalface productivity, and hold true for the years before as well as after World War I. The interpretations of coal mining's productivity variations offered by the literature can be grouped under three headings: the influences of land, of labor, and of machines. As none offers an entirely satisfactory explanation, a multivariable hypothesis would seem logical.

Productivity and Land

Geological conditions are commonly assumed to determine coal-mining productivity, though a rigorous measurement of their contribution is seldom possible. However, McCloskey treated the geological input explicitly, contending that differences in labor productivity between the British and U.S. industries may be explained by the size and especially the quality of that input.[8] Quantifying the coal industry's natural resource endowment would ideally incorporate a wide range of geological characteristics. Most of these—for example, the texture, inclination, and faulting of coal seams—are not amenable to precise measurement. Fortunately, some progress can be made by measuring seam thickness, generally reckoned a factor of prime importance and clearly pertinent when measuring coalface productivity (see Table 4). McCloskey, for example, argued that more than half of the American productivity advantage over the British industry lay in the New World's thicker seams. To quantify the effect of seam thickness, note that output was proportional to thickness (other things being equal), as coal cutting was an undermining operation before the advent of shearing technology, except in South Wales.[9] Hence for a given lineal distance undercut, whether by hand or machine, the volume of coal was in proportion to seam thickness.

[8] McCloskey, "International Differences," p. 294.

[9] David Greasley, "The Diffusion of Machine Cutting in the British Coal Industry, 1902–1938," *Explorations in Economic History*, 19 (July 1982), pp. 246–68.

Seam thickness does not appear to be a major factor explaining regional productivity differences. Scotland apart, average seam thickness decreased between 6 and 10 percent in each district between 1913 and 1944. Face productivity, given a unit elasticity of output with respect to seam thickness, would also fall 6 to 10 percent, all else being equal, as seams narrowed. Clearly the face productivity declines of around 15 percent and 20 percent, respectively, in Durham and Northumberland between 1913 and 1938 and the advances elsewhere (except perhaps in Scotland) cannot substantially be explained by changes in average seam thickness. The North Midlands 50 percent face productivity increase, for example, occurred despite a 9 percent fall in average seam thickness. Average seam thickness in Scotland shows a pattern different from that of the other fields, falling before 1924 but then recovering as a greater proportion of Scottish coal was mined in the Lothians and Fife. It seems unlikely that the 10 percent improvement in the average thickness of Scottish seams after 1924 explains the concurrent productivity growth, because declining seam thickness in earlier years was also accompanied by productivity growth.

Regional differences in face productivity are no better explained by differences in seam thickness. South Wales and the North Midlands were the areas most favored by thick seams. The case of South Wales is unusual, as the friable coal there generally precluded undercutting the face. Hence thicker seams did not reduce the amount of work required to extract a particular volume of coal. Yet even in districts where undermining was the norm, face productivity levels depended on more than just seam thickness. Before 1914 face productivity in the North Midlands was below that of most other districts despite its thicker seams. Scotland, for example, attained greater face productivity while its seams were only 80 percent the thickness of those in the North Midlands. And by the 1930s, when Scotland was less disadvantaged by thin seams, the productivity rankings favored the North Midlands. Although seam thickness measures only one dimension of resource quality, it appears unlikely that trends and regional disparities in productivity were dominated by geological conditions at the coalface.

Productivity and Labor

Explanations of British coal-mining productivity for the period up to 1914 that look beyond the resource endowment stress the influence of labor. A reduction in work effort and hours worked is often offered as the cause of productivity decline. The less strenuous effort by miners and their greater absenteeism rate are blamed on the industry's prewar prosperity. Better wage rates enabled earnings to be maintained with less effort, and analysts claim that the miners preferred greater leisure. Taylor suggested that productivity fluctuated inversely with wage rates over the business cycle, and that secular wage growth from the 1880s had a longer-term detrimental effect on productivity.[10] Walters as well as Hirsch and Hausman supported Taylor's interpretation with evidence for the South Wales coalfield.[11] The data for face and overall O/H cast doubt on these views, however.

The notion that absenteeism rose and fell with wage rates over the business cycle is particularly vulnerable to a more precise measurement of labor utilization. Taylor noted parallel movements of absenteeism and wage rates in the Durham coalfield in the decade spanning the 1900 cyclical peak, but the varying proportion of shifts missed by miners was entirely offset by pits working more days when trade was better. The attendance of Durham miners was stable over the business cycle. But the possibility remains that miners worked less on the job when wages were better. Coalface workers were generally paid by piece rates and could vary their effort because they had little supervision.[12] In the short term, miners' efforts did fluctuate. Walters showed that productivity rose in South Wales in the weeks before Christmas and after trade disputes. The productivity upsurge in the early stages of World War I also suggests a greater effort by labor. It seems less likely that secular productivity trends, however, were influenced by the variation in miners' efforts. Measuring labor utilization more precisely weakens the theory that declining productivity before the war was a result of diminished labor effort. In particular, the hourly productivity of face workers, who could vary their efforts, needs to be considered.

Data for overall output per labor year (O/Y) do show a secular decline prior to 1914. A peak of 333 tons per miner was reached in the 1880s; the average miner produced only 260 tons in 1913. During this long-term 22 percent decline, O/Y fluctuated inversely with the state of trade. Moreover, miners' wage rates exhibit a secular growth from the trough of the 1880s and in the shorter term follow the swings in the business cycle. However, little can be adduced about miners' work effort from the inverse association between wages and overall O/Y. The recent work of Church suggested that O/Y considerably overstates the extent of productivity decline.[13] O/H, Church argued, fell only 8 percent between the 1880s and 1914. My own estimates, which show an 11 percent fall in O/H between 1906 and 1914, indicate that Church perhaps went too far. (The differences between Church's estimates and mine are considered in the Appendix.) The decline in coal-mining productivity up to 1914 was genuine and needs to be explained.

The main reason that less strenuous effort by miners cannot explain

[10] Taylor, "Labour Productivity," p. 53.

[11] Hirsch and Hausman, "South Wales Coal," pp. 145–59; Walters, "Labour Productivity," pp. 288–91.

[12] David Greasley, "Wage Rates and Work Intensity in the South Wales Coalfield, 1874–1914," *Economica*, 52 (Aug. 1985), pp. 383–89.

[13] Church, *British Coal Industry*, p. 477.

this decline is that productivity at the coalface does not show the same decline as overall productivity. The difference, as Walters demonstrated for South Wales, results from smaller proportions of the work force being employed at the coalface by 1914. Increased proportions of on-cost workers resulted from the aging of collieries, which led to greater underground haulage requirements. More workers had to be used to transport the coal from the face to the mine shaft. Walters did provide limited productivity data for the principal class of face workers, coal hewers, but these are annual figures and are presumed to show diminished effort. Hewers' annual product fell 2.5 percent and 1 percent, respectively, between 1889 and 1905 and between 1905 and 1914 in South Wales according to Walters. These declines seem modest in light of the likely reduction in hours worked. The year 1905 was the nadir of the first twentieth-century business cycle, and hours declined a further 12 percent in South Wales between 1905 and 1914 due to the enforcement of the Eight Hours Act. It seems unlikely that South Wales hewers' effort and productivity declined prior to 1914. The multifactor face productivity data presented in Table 1 of the Appendix show a modest increase during the final prewar decade, suggesting—for South Wales at least—that declining overall O/H was not attributable to miners working less strenuously.

The hewers' productivity appears to have declined more sharply in Durham. Using the records of the Coalowners Association, Taylor reported a 13.3 percent decline in output per shift between 1889 and 1906 and further drops up to 1914. These figures indicate a smaller discrepancy between face and overall productivity trends in Durham, reflecting the smaller rise there in numbers of on-cost haulage workers. However, Durham's hewers were spending fewer hours per shift cutting coal by 1906. Official reports suggest that hewers' net working time at the coalface was reduced by 13.6 percent between 1889 and 1906, a decrease that closely matches the decline in shift productivity.[14] The reduction in hours was the result of shorter shifts and the increased travel time to the face as pits aged. Because haulage workers benefited comparatively less in Durham from reduced hours before the Eight Hours Act, face and overall annual productivity trends show less difference there. The absence of a decline in the hourly productivity of hewers further weakens the theory that miners worked less hard in the period before 1914.

Legislation was one cause of the reduction in miner work time. Much of the discussion of the effects of the Eight Hours Act has focused on its detrimental consequences for annual productivity. Taylor, for example, suggested that a large part of the 9.2 percent fall in British coal-mining

[14] *Royal Commission on Labour* (P.P. 1890, LXVIII, London); *Report of the Eight Hours Day Committee* (P.P. 1907, XIV, London).

productivity between 1904/08 and 1909/13 could be attributed to the Eight Hours Act.[15] Brian McCormick and John Williams argued that the Act increased the number of workers at the face, causing the output per worker to fall sharply below trend in 1909/10.[16] South Wales, according to Walters, was severely affected, though output per labor year did fall less there than in Britain overall between 1908 and 1913. The Act's impact on hourly productivity is less certain. Miners outside of Durham and Northumberland strongly favored the legislation, anticipating that their productivity would be greater in a shorter day.[17] Hewers in northeastern England did not benefit, because they were already working fewer hours than the maximum laid down by the Act.[18] Otherwise miners (including those in South Wales, where hours were most reduced) expected their earnings to be maintained through higher productivity. The owners disagreed, contending that bottlenecks in haulage and winding capacity would preclude hourly productivity gains.

Regional data for hourly multifactor productivity suggest that the owners' worst fears about the Eight Hours Act were not realized and that the judgments of historians are unduly pessimistic. Face productivity following the enforcement of the Eight Hours Act rose in most districts.[19] Rather surprisingly, the Act appears to have been most advantageous in South Wales, where hours were reduced most, and most detrimental in Durham, where hewers' hours were unaffected.[20] Scotland's and South Wales's face productivity rose 5 percent and 4 percent, respectively, between 1908 and 1910, while that of the North Midlands increased by 2.5 percent. Hence productivity improvements were significant enough to maintain earnings in most fields in which hewers' hours were reduced. In South Wales, however, the productivity gains were insufficient to offset the effect of reduced hours on earnings. Face productivity falls 7 percent and 6 percent, respectively, in Durham and Northumberland between 1909 and 1910. The disruption was most serious in Durham, as productivity rapidly recovered in Northumberland, and resulted from the legal necessity to reduce the hours of haulage workers. Generally the solution was to employ two shifts of support workers for every three specialist hewer shifts, as

[15] Arthur J. Taylor, "The Coal Industry," in Derek H. Aldcroft, *The Development of British Industry and Foreign Competition* (London, 1968), p. 54.

[16] Brian McCormick and John Williams, "The Miners and the Eight Hour Day," *Economic History Review*, 12 (1959–1960), pp. 223–37.

[17] Eric Evans, *The Miners of South Wales* (Cardiff, 1961), p. 191.

[18] McCormick and Williams, "Eight Hour Day," p. 235.

[19] The Act became effective in most areas, including South Wales, on July 1, 1909. In Durham and Northumberland the legislation was applied from Jan. 1, 1910.

[20] Martin J. Daunton, in "Down the Pit: Work in the Great Northern and South Wales Coalfields, 1870–1914," *Economic History Review*, 34 (Nov. 1981), p. 593, took the alternative view.

opposed to the earlier one-for-two arrangement.[21] For Durham, the detrimental effect on face productivity makes the hewers' opposition to the Act there understandable, though levels of face productivity in the northeast remained well above the national average. Otherwise, the effects of the Eight Hours Act were modestly beneficial for O/H. In sum, the influence of labor, whether through hours worked, absenteeism, or work intensity, cannot by itself account for the downward trend and regional disparities in British coal-mining productivity before 1914.

Productivity and Machines

Mechanical coal cutting and conveying became commercially viable technologies around the start of the twentieth century, though their adoption was modest before 1914 and patchy between the wars. Overall, less coal was machine cut in Britain than elsewhere in Europe. Buxton argues that regional variations in British coal-mining productivity between the wars and Britain's internationally slow productivity growth were both related to mechanization.[22] He suggests that Scotland, Yorkshire, and Northumberland were the most mechanized British districts and achieved the highest O/S. The idea of a simple link between mechanization and productivity is dubious, however. Mistrust stems partly from the indicators Buxton used to measure mechanization, as others show a different picture. Electric horsepower per worker, for example, was 40 percent higher in Durham and South Wales in 1921 than in Yorkshire or Northumberland, and the Northumberland figure did not exceed that of Durham until 1933. The proportion of output mechanically conveyed was also greater in South Wales than in Yorkshire until 1923. Viewing Scotland, Yorkshire, and Northumberland as the most mechanized districts rests, then, on attaching primary importance to machine cutting.

Even if coal cutters are viewed as central to mechanization, the alleged link to productivity still appears questionable. By the 1930s Buxton's highly mechanized regions—Scotland, Northumberland, and Yorkshire did achieve high levels of O/S, but it seems unlikely that these resulted from a greater use of coal cutters. If machine cutting were the key to higher productivity, it would also be reflected in coalface productivity, that part of the production cycle most directly affected by machine cutting. Estimates for proportions of output machine cut (see Table 5) in conjunction with those for face productivity (see Table 2) demonstrate the weakness of the proposed link between machine cutting and productivity levels. For example, face productivity in Durham always exceeded the levels attained in Scotland, the region that

[21] Increased refinement in the division of labor in the northeast created greater interdependence between hewers and other underground workers. Reduced hours for support workers generally disrupted face operations.

[22] Buxton, "Entrepreneurial Efficiency," p. 482.

TABLE 5
PERCENTAGE OF COAL OUTPUT MACHINE CUT

	1906	1914	1923	1931	1938
Durham	2.5	4.9	13.9	29.1	41.9
Lancashire & Cheshire	3.5	8.1	15.1	27.7	67.6
Northumberland	4.2	13.8	24.5	70.5	91.2
Scotland	8.0	23.7	44.9	66.4	80.2
South Wales	0.2	1.2	4.1	11.8	26.0
North Midlands	6.9	10.6	14.7	29.7	65.1

Source: *General Reports and Statistics of Mines and Quarries in the United Kingdom* (P.P. 1907, XCVII; 1908, CXII; 1914–16, LXX, London); *Annual Reports of the Secretary for Mines* (Board of Trade, London).

led the way with machine cutting. Overall O/S was greater in Scotland, even in the 1930s when Durham miners no longer worked shorter shifts, but face productivity was lower. Clearly a greater proportion of Scottish miners was employed at the coalface. Durham, where large pits and scattered workings meant long underground haulage, had the smallest proportion of face workers in the British coalfield. An absence of machine cutting did not preclude high levels of face productivity in Durham, but overall productivity was adversely affected by haulage requirements.

In response to criticism Buxton switched his attention from regional levels to coalfield trends, suggesting that productivity increased as mechanization developed.[23] However, the Reid Committee failed to find a simple link between the growth of O/S and the diffusion of coal cutters. Nor does the evidence on face productivity support Buxton's view. For example, face productivity trends in Northumberland and Durham were similar between 1914 and 1938 despite dramatically different mechanization experiences. For Scotland face productivity was roughly stable before 1923, while machine cutting advanced rapidly. South Wales, the field that made least use of coal cutters, experienced a face productivity growth exceeded only by that of the North Midlands. Buxton also explained divergent productivity trends within the European coal industry by mechanization.[24] A modest 16 percent O/S increase in Britain between 1913 and 1936, contrasted with the 80 percent and 50 percent achieved by the Ruhr and Belgium, respectively, allegedly demonstrates the advantages of more widespread machine cutting. Yet in the Ruhr productivity growth accelerated after 1929, when face mechanization was virtually complete. Belgium's coal industry achieved modest productivity growth before 1932, while output machine cut was rising to 95 percent. Similarly, 85

[23] Neil K. Buxton, "Avoiding the Pitfalls: Entrepreneurial Efficiency in the British Coal Industry Again," *Economic History Review*, 25 (Nov. 1972), pp. 669–73.

[24] Neil K. Buxton, *The Economic Development of the British Coal Industry* (London, 1978), p. 180.

percent of France's coal was cut by machine by 1932, but productivity grew modestly. The hypothesized link between the adoption of coal cutters and productivity growth appears to be weak in both British and European contexts. British coal-mining productivity did recover between the wars, but machine cutting by itself does not provide a satisfactory explanation.

TOWARD AN OVERALL ASSESSMENT

The chief characteristics of British coal-mining productivity in the 50 years before 1939 were rich regional diversity and a reversal between the wars of the downward productivity trend. Together these features suggest a partial modernization of the British coal industry. On the average British coal mining's productivity between the wars appears less bleak than most commentators suggest, though a wide distribution around average performance persisted. The use of O/H to measure productivity confirms the clear decline up to 1914 but suggests a stronger upturn in productivity between the wars. O/H rose 37 percent in the British industry overall between 1914 and 1938: around twice the increase shown by O/S. By most conventional yardsticks the O/H figures portray a reasonably respectable performance for British coal mining by the 1930s.

International productivity comparisons are difficult exercises, but the O/H data cast the relative British performance in better light. Annual growth of British O/H between 1923/31 and 1931/38 averaged 2.2 and 1.1 percent, respectively—close to the labor productivity growth John Kendrick reported for the U.S. bituminous coal industry of 2.4 percent and 0.9 percent per annum, respectively, for the periods of 1919/29 and 1929/37.[25] In Europe, France and Belgium achieved 24 percent and 48 percent O/S increases between 1913 and 1938, respectively, comparable to the 37 percent British productivity increase indicated by the O/H figures. Nevertheless, the British O/H increase was clearly below the 80 percent O/S gain recorded in the Ruhr. Uncertainty surrounds the precise relation between the O/H and O/S indicators. Britain's prewar O/S data, based on the operations of a limited sample of collieries in June 1914, are unreliable.[26] They suggest that British O/S was 10 percent greater than that of the prewar Ruhr and provide a high base from which to measure subsequent British growth.[27] Shift lengths also varied across Europe.[28] Hours worked came down less quickly in

[25] John W. Kendrick, *Productivity Trends in the United States* (Princeton, 1961), p. 152.

[26] Only two-thirds of collieries were covered by the sample, and those data specifically pertained to June 1914.

[27] Prewar output per labor year in Britain and Germany was almost identical.

[28] For details see *Royal Commission* (1926), p. 170, and *International Labor Office Yearbook 1937–38* (Geneva, 1938).

Germany after 1913, which favored the growth of shift productivity there, though it might have deterred hourly productivity. Even so it can hardly be claimed that British coal mining achieved productivity growth similar to that of Germany in the quarter-century following 1914, though the North Midlands, with a 54 percent O/H increase between 1914 and 1938, may not have fallen far short of the German performance. Obviously these international comparisons are imprecise, but their tone seems clear enough. British coal mining's productivity growth was not very different from the average American and European performance but, for the industry as a whole, was below the best achievements elsewhere, especially those of the Ruhr and Holland.

British coal-mining productivity also looks reasonable in comparison with productivity elsewhere in the British economy.[29] Coal mining's O/H averaged a 1.7 percent per annum growth between 1923 and 1938. In the total economy O/H increased 0.7 percent per year between 1924 and 1937. Even compared to manufacturing, in which O/H averaged a 1.8 percent annual growth between 1924 and 1937, coal mining, as an extractive industry, looks respectable. The O/H figures offer little support for the idea that labor was overcommitted to the interwar coal industry, though it must be admitted that, relative to manufacturing, mining became more capital intensive between the wars. Recent estimates suggest that mining and quarrying's total factor productivity growth averaged 1.2 percent per annum (compared to manufacturing's 1.9 percent) for the period between 1924 and 1937. Coal mining's specific position is uncertain, because the multifactor data presented here are only for the coalface, where mechanization advanced relatively rapidly. Even so the North Midland's face multifactor productivity grew 1.6 percent per annum between 1924 and 1937, though other fields, Durham especially, did less well. As with the international comparisons, a comparison with productivity within the British economy suggests that performance for the coal industry as a whole was satisfactory despite the variability of the industry's achievement.

The upshot would seem to be that substantial modernization took place in British coal mining in the quarter-century after 1914, but that diversity was as much a feature in the 1930s as it had been at the turn of the century. Productivity gains were made in all fields between the wars, but the dispersion around the average increase and the limited regional restructuring of the industry constrained overall productivity growth. Mechanization, working practices and organization, the efforts made by labor, and the resource endowment cannot singly account for the productivity record, but each has a role to play in a multifaceted interpretation.

[29] The noncoal productivity data is from Robin C. Matthews, Charles H. Feinstein, and John C. Odling-Smee, *British Economic Growth, 1856–1973* (Oxford, 1982).

The shift from declining productivity in the years prior to 1914 to an upward trend indicates some modernization within British coal mining between the wars. Better technology, to an extent, countered the deleterious effect of resource depletion. Yet modernization failed to dent regional productivity dispersion. Substantial regional differences in work organization and mining conditions existed in the early years of the twentieth century, and subsequently modified the benefits gained from machine technology. In the years of hand hewing, variation in organization and circumstance led to productivity dispersion, both overall and at the coalface, against a backdrop of falling levels as resource depletion took its toll. The application of modern machine-mining systems between the wars generally raised productivity and led to greater uniformity in work practices. Nevertheless, regional productivity differences remained and widened during the 1930s, indicating that a complex interaction between mechanization, the resource environment, and working practices shaped coal-mining productivity in the half-century up to 1939.

Disparities within traditional mining systems, and the concomitant productivity dispersion, presaged subsequent productivity patterns. Many elements in the coal-mining cycle were craft oriented at the turn of the twentieth century. Manual skills predominated, and the variety of tasks offered ample scope for labor specialization, especially at the coalface. Apart from cutting and loading, face operations involved removing and setting props and other hewing preparation—the so-called deadwork. Regional diversity in the division of deadwork and hewing was marked.[30] Specialization was most extreme in Durham and Northumberland, where hewers did not do deadwork. Hewers there were able to concentrate on cutting coal and, helped by shorter shifts, achieved relatively high hourly productivity. At the other extreme the low-productivity hewers in South Wales also performed most of the deadwork and had longer shifts. The resource environment was partly responsible for differences in work organization. Friable coal in South Wales made roof falls there more likely, making it sensible for hewers to attend to deadwork immediately rather than wait for support workers. Consequently face productivity languished at half of Durham's level in the years prior to 1914, though the overall productivity gap was smaller. Clearly the interplay between mining conditions and work organization led to productivity dispersion in the era of hand cutting.

Replacing manual with machine systems of mining eventually reduced the scope for diversity in the organization of work. However, in the years prior to 1914 the limited use of machines was not accompanied by widespread reorganization. Initially machines were a simple replacement for hand cutting in difficult conditions. Pits with thin, hard seams,

[30] See Daunton, "Down the Pit."

such as Govan Collieries in Scotland, Ashingtons in Northumberland, and William Briggs in West Yorkshire, were the first to adopt machines.[31] The productivity effects, in the absence of reorganization, were not substantial. Coalface productivity in Scotland, for example, remained below average despite the prevalence of machines. So long as machines simply replaced one element in traditional mining systems, the scope for productivity gains was limited because the machines could not work to capacity.

Realizing the potential of machines required the reorganization of mining as an integrated system. Contemporaries well understood that an efficient cycle of coal cutting, loading, conveying, and winding was needed to make maximum use of machines.[32] Machine systems were introduced between the wars, and the heterogeneity of working practices in British coal mining, along with regional differences in hours worked, diminished. Twenty-four-hour cyclic systems, in which separate shifts machine-cut the coal, loaded it onto conveyors, and prepared the face for further cutting, became the norm.[33] The result was productivity advance and some decline in regional productivity differences by the early 1920s. Yet disparities remained—South Wales only attained 77 percent of Scotland's O/H in 1923—and widened in the 1930s as productivity gains in the North Midlands outpaced those elsewhere. By 1938 South Wales had only achieved 69 percent the O/H of the North Midlands. These disparities were not simply the result of new technology patchily applied; Northumberland and Scotland, where machine use was widespread, also failed to keep up. The absence of a linear relation between advances in machine cutting and productivity indicates that the gains from modern mining systems were heterogeneous.

Eventually, in the 1930s, pits in the North Midlands took fuller advantage of better conditions. In 1929 the average product of rotary coal cutters was only 10,000 tons in the North Midlands, whereas in Scotland and Northumberland the figure was 14,000 tons. By 1937 the North Midland's machine productivity had risen to 24,000 tons, whereas pits in Scotland and Northumberland were cutting less than 17,000 tons per machine.[34]

The North Midlands realized the benefits of a better resource environment as machine mining became more sophisticated. By itself the North Midland's 10 percent seam thickness advantage cannot account for the 50 percent greater machine productivity there compared to

[31] Dintenfass, "Entrepreneurial Failure"; Anthony Slaven, "Earnings and Productivity in the Scottish Coal Industry during the Nineteenth Century," in Peter Payne, *Studies in Scottish Business History* (London, 1967).

[32] Samuel Mavor, *Colliery Guardian* (London, 1924), p. 1510.

[33] K. Bamforth and H. Trist, "Some Social and Psychological Consequences of the Longwall Method of Coal Cutting," *Human Relations*, 4 (1951), pp. 3–38.

[34] Greasley, "Machine Cutting," p. 252.

Scotland or Northumberland in 1937. Other elements in the resource environment favored the North Midlands as well. The man-made underground landscape in the North Midlands collieries allowed machines to work closer to capacity there. A greater output per machine was possible only if the undermined coal could be shifted quickly from face to mineshaft and beyond. Efficient machine mining depended not only on face operations but on the complete mining system. Hence the layout of mines, the effective use of conveyors, an adequate winding capacity, and competent management were all crucial to higher productivity. Modern mines in the North Midlands were favored in a number of respects. First, distances between face and mineshaft were shorter. Derbyshire's mines, for example, had 749 miles of underground roads in 1944 compared with Durham's 2,982 miles, but Durham's output was only twice that of Derbyshire.[35] The underground landscape of the older mining regions, with their legacy of old workings, was also more difficult to convert to modern systems of concentrated longwall machine mining. Moreover, newer pits in the North Midlands also had wider shafts and more effective winding, which lessened the barriers to high throughputs.[36]

The keys to success with longwall machine mining were concentrated workings, a rapidly advancing face, and the speedy removal of undermined coal. Modern mines, less encumbered by an accumulation of old workings, facilitated efficient mining systems. Older fields (Durham especially) with scattered bord-and-pillar workings and meandering underground road networks, gained less from machine systems. Large pits were prevalent in Durham, but unless bigger pits concentrated production spatially, productivity would be adversely affected. Mine size, measured by area, constrained productivity growth. Interestingly, the fields that led the way in the early years of machine cutting, by simply replacing hand hewing in thinner seams, were tardy in adopting mechanical conveyors. Northumberland, Lanarkshire, and West Yorkshire conveyed less than half their output mechanically in 1938. Newer mining regions such as Fife and Nottinghamshire, which trailed with the early use of coal cutters, conveyed over 80 percent of their outputs by machine in 1938. Regional productivity growth disparities in the 1930s did not stem from the numbers of coal cutters used but from the effectiveness with which machines were integrated into a complete mining system. Mechanical cutting and conveying were more readily combined in the newer, more environmentally favored districts—the North Midlands especially—and led to substantial productivity gains.

By the 1930s coal mining verged on becoming a continuous production process. In Britain's newer mining areas, assisted by their favorable resource environments, the discrete elements of the coal-mining cycle

[35] *Fuel and Power Statistical Digest* (P.P. 1944–45, IV, London).

[36] *Report of the Technical Advisory Committee.*

were beginning to be organized as one efficient system. The effect was to raise productivity in the North Midlands to levels well above those elsewhere in Britain. Yet despite progress, the international performance of Britain's coal industry as a whole was no better than average. The secular downward productivity trend in the years before 1914 was reversed, but subsequent progress was held back by the survival of less efficient producers. The effect was to limit productivity growth to rates below those in the Ruhr and Holland. Average productivity growth was lower in Britain not because the best elements of British coal mining were inferior but because output was less ruthlessly concentrated in modern mines. The number of pits in the Ruhr, and working places within pits, was drastically lower.[37] In Holland coal mining was even more concentrated and achieved higher levels and faster growth of O/S than the Ruhr. The Dutch coal industry comprised only 12 mines in 1937, and average output was over one million tons. In contrast, little changed in the structure of the British coal industry between the wars. The North Midlands' contribution to total British coal output rose modestly between 1913 and 1938: up from 26 to 32 percent. Yet between those dates, though British coal output fell 21 percent, 1,870 pits survived, a decrease of only 29 percent from 1913 numbers.[38] Moreover, whereas 43 percent of miners worked for firms employing fewer than 500 men in 1913, this figure had risen to over 50 percent by 1938. The number employed in large undertakings (over 5,000 workers) rose modestly from 14.6 percent in 1913 to 15.9 percent by 1938.

The regional and firm structure of British coal mining was highly inelastic in the half-century before 1939. This was partly owing to the heterogeneity of the product and the ability of weaker collieries to survive so long as they covered their variable costs.[39] But the state was also responsible for the limited restructuring of British coal mining. Clearly, basing quotas on past output (a legacy of the 1930 Coal Mines Act) aided the survival of marginal units and, by promoting regional differences in the utilization of collieries, constrained developments elsewhere.[40] Pits in the North Midlands worked well below capacity by the end of the 1930s. In 1936 pits in Britain averaged 4.86 days of work each week.[41] Coal mines in South Yorkshire, Nottinghamshire, and

[37] The number of working places was reduced from 23,178 in 1926 to 10,005 in 1930 and to 3,749 in 1938. Output per working place increased eight times in the Ruhr between 1926 and 1938. See *Report of the Technical Advisory Committee*.

[38] Supple, *British Coal Industry*, p. 364.

[39] Defensive new investment may also have occurred. See Alexandre Lamfalussy, *Investment and Growth in Mature Economies* (London, 1961).

[40] The workings of this legislation is described by Maurice W. Kirby in "The Control of Competition in the British Coal-Mining Industry in the Thirties," *Economic History Review*, 26 (May 1973).

[41] Days worked are from the *Annual Report of the Secretary for Mines* (Board of Trade, London, 1937).

Derbyshire averaged 4.31, 4.21, and 3.87 days of work per week, respectively, while lower-productivity pits in Northumberland, Durham, and South Wales each worked on the average over 5 days per week. Scottish collieries worked on the average 5.54 days per week in 1936, 30 percent more than pits in Nottinghamshire, the county where the highest-productivity mines were located. The 1930 Coal Mines Act was intended to promote rationalization as well as to control competition. As the legislation singularly failed to force amalgamations, its main effect was to ossify the structure of British coal mining.

CONCLUSIONS

Modernization and structural rigidities coexisted within British coal mining during the 50 years before 1939. Together they shaped the industry's patterns of productivity. Over the half-century British coal mining's productivity record was respectable, whether judged by international standards or by productivity elsewhere in the British economy. Most importantly, the downward productivity trend in the years before 1914 was reversed as modern machine-mining systems were introduced. In the newer mining areas, the North Midlands especially, better technology lifted both labor productivity (O/H) and face multifactor productivity by the end of the 1930s to 50 percent above 1914 levels. Here, at least, the problem of resource depletion had been effectively countered. Other fields fared less well. In consequence the wide productivity variation that characterized British coal mining at the turn of the twentieth century persisted and constrained average productivity in the years up to 1939.

The benefits of mechanization, even in the North Midlands, took a long time to be realized. The availability of compressed air and electric power as flexible power sources meant that machine mining had been practical for 50 years by 1939. Initially machines, as their early use in Scotland shows, did little to improve productivity. Mining in the early years of the twentieth century remained essentially craft oriented, comprising discrete tasks that permitted specialization and disparities in work organization. Regionally distinct patterns of labor specialization, the associated differences in working hours, and a varying resource environment produced substantial productivity diversity within British coal mining. Before 1914 machines did little to decrease that variation, because they simply replaced one discrete element in the mining system. The key to raising productivity was replacing traditional with modern systems of machine mining. Longwall machine mining became the norm within British coal mining by the 1930s. The result was productivity gains throughout the industry. Yet greater uniformity within British coal mining did not produce uniform productivity gains. The integration of coal-cutting machinery into an efficient system of cutting, loading, conveying, and winding was more readily achieved in the newer, more environmentally favored regions (the North Midlands especially), and there led to rapid productivity gains. As other fields benefited less, wide regional productivity disparities persisted into the 1930s. The ability of low-productivity mines to stay in business depressed the average performance of British coal mining, but their survival should not be allowed to obscure the substantial modernization the industry achieved during the 50 years prior to 1939.

Appendix

A. MEASURING LABOR PRODUCTIVITY

Overall O/Y can be measured on an annual basis for all regions, using data from *General Reports and Statistics of Mines and Quarries in the United Kingdom* (P.P. 1903, LXXXII, 1904, CVI, passim, London) and *Statistical Summarys of Output and of Costs of Production Proceeds and Profits of the Coal Mining Industry* (P.P. 1922, XXII, passim, London).

The number of days on which pits wound coal is reported in the *Labour Gazette* (Board of Trade and Ministry of Labour, London) from 1895, though the attendance of miners cannot be gauged before 1921. Hours worked per shift in 1906 were reported by the Eight Hours Committee for hewers, coal getters, machine men, and others who got the mineral, as well as for underground labor generally. Hours for surface workers were not ascertained and are assumed here to equal those of nonface underground labor. The maximum laid down by the 1908 Act excluded winding time, which, according to the evidence of the Chief Inspector of Mines to the *Royal Commission on the Coal Industry* (P.P. 1919, XII, London, questions 5116–9), averaged 30 minutes. Labor hours used here for the years after 1908 are the levels stipulated by the Eight Hours Act and the subsequent changes noted in the *Labour Gazette*. As maximum hours excluded winding time, one average winding time is added to these data. Adjusting labor years for days and hours worked enables the overall O/H to be measured.

Church has recently reported O/H estimates for the years before 1914. These data are for the whole mining operation and show for Britain in general less productivity decline than do my own estimates. This reflects differences in the way hours of work were measured. Church averaged the hours of different classes of miners by assuming that face workers, who worked fewer hours, formed a constant 40 percent of the work force during the period between 1830 and 1913. My own estimates are based on the actual proportions of different classes of underground labor. Because the proportion of face workers was falling, especially in the final prewar decade, miners on the average worked longer hours in 1913 than Church admitted, and his estimates thus overstate productivity. This objection applies to Church's pre-1906 O/H estimates, though the extant hours data for the years prior to 1906 seem too fragmentary to establish precisely the O/H record. John Treble elaborated on the difficulties.[42] Church also reported regional O/H data for the period between 1895 and 1913. The regions are not identical to those used here but do show similar productivity rankings. However, levels of O/H are not the same, because Church adjusted for absenteeism by applying the Durham absentee

[42] John G. Treble, "Sliding Scales and Concilliation Boards: Risk Sharing in the Late Nineteenth Century Coal Industry," *Oxford Economic Papers*, 39 (1987), p. 696.

figures to all regions. Hence Church's O/H levels exceed mine by about 10 percent. Because the Durham and Northumberland absentee figures are strictly for hewers, who comprised a minority of the work force, and the limited data for absenteeism in other fields show wide regional variation—for 1913, for example, estimates of absenteeism range from 6.5 percent in Scotland to 13.8 percent in Yorkshire—Church's adjustments have not been followed.

Constructing consistent indexes of face productivity requires estimates of the proportions of labor employed at the face. *The Report of the Eight Hours Day Committee* (P.P. 1907, XIV, London), Appendix C, tables 1 to 3 detailed by area the employment of hewers (or more strictly hewers, coal getters, machine men, and others who got the mineral) and other face workers in 1906. Finlay Gibson's submission to the *Royal Commission on the Coal Industry* (P.P. 1919, XII, London), Appendix 49 only detailed the regional employment of adult coal getters in 1914. The overall proportion of labor at the face in 1914 is estimated by assuming a constant proportionality between the various classes of face labor for each region in 1906 and 1914. Proportions at the coalface are known for the years after 1921, except for Lancashire and Cheshire, from data in the *Statistical Summarys*. For earlier years, proportions at the face are interpolated between 1906, 1914, and 1921 estimates. Together with the hours data detailed above, these proportions allow $(O/H)_f$ to be measured. However, hours spent at the face by face workers are not measured, as the times required to travel there are included. Travel time was estimated by the Eight Hours Committee to average one hour, though regional variation, especially in Durham and the east of Scotland, with travel times of 79 and 49 minutes, respectively, was found. Because travel time cannot be ascertained for later years, the face productivity data are not adjusted for this influence.

B. MEASURING MULTIFACTOR PRODUCTIVITY

Machine inputs are incorporated into indexes of face productivity using a production function of the form $Q = AL^aM^bC^c$, where Q is coal output; L, face labor hours; M, coal-cutting machine hours; C, face conveyor hours; A, productivity; and a, b, and c, output elasticities with respect to each factor of production. The stocks of coal cutters and face conveyors employed in each region are known from 1902 and 1907, respectively. The sources are Part 2 of *General Reports* and, from 1921, *Annual Reports of the Secretary for Mines* (Board of Trade, London). The basis of collection for the earlier data was inspection districts. Modest adjustments are required to conform these data to the defined regions. For the procedures, see David Greasley, "The Diffusion of a Technology: The Case of Machine Cutting in the British Coal Industry, 1900–38" (Unpublished Ph.D. thesis, University of Liverpool, 1979), pp. 122–44. Machine utilization rates are measured by the number of hours that pits worked. Factor shares, estimated by combining data on factor employment with recently published factor price series, are used to measure the output elasticities for each year.[43] Wage rates can be translated into face labor income using Finlay Gibson's earnings and the labor hours data. For machines, the stock price of a typical rotary coal cutter in 1913 was £315, which, with an annual depreciation rate of 0.25 and a yield on consols of 3.4 percent, produces an annual user cost of £89.46.[44] Annual maintenance and running costs have

[43] See Greasley, "Machine Cutting," pp. 264–66, for the price series.

[44] For machine prices, see Lancashire Records Office, Preston, Box NCBw 4/1. Reports in the technical journals indicate a 3- to 5-year life for rotary machines. See, for example, *Report of the North of England Mining Engineers' Committee on Machine Mining* (Newcastle, 1905).

been estimated roughly to equal the annual interest and depreciation charge.[45] These data, together with those for the user cost and stock of machines, allow the coal cutter's income to be ascertained. Comparable data cannot be constructed for face conveyors, but may be approximated by taking unit costs to be 50 percent of those of a coal cutter, a proportion based on relative machine size as measured by horsepower.[46] The estimates for all districts suggest that labor's share of face income exceeded 99 and 88 percent, respectively, in 1902 and 1938, in all districts. Annual multifactor productivity indexes for the five regions are detailed in Appendix Table 1. A series for Lancashire and Cheshire could not be computed in the absence of face labor data for the interwar period. To allow for changing factor shares, the productivity indexes result from accumulating annual changes. Face conveyors are incorporated from 1907. As the weight of conveyors does not exceed 0.0004 in any district before 1907, their absence before then has no practical significance. The cross-sectional multifactor face productivity indexes also incorporate face conveyors for the years after 1906.

[45] For a discussion see David Greasley, "The Diffusion of a Technology: The Case of Machine Cutting in the British Coal Industry, 1900–38" (Unpublished Ph.D. thesis, University of Liverpool, 1979), p. 230. The data are from the *Mining Engineers' Committee.*

[46] See Greasley, "Diffusion of a Technology," pp. 255–56.

APPENDIX TABLE 1
INDEX OF MULTIFACTOR PRODUCTIVITY AT THE COALFACE
(1902 = 100)

Year	Durham	Northumberland	Scotland	S. Wales	N. Midlands
1902	100.0	100.0	100.0	100.0	100.0
1903	101.6	107.3	100.4	100.9	105.3
1904	104.6	105.9	104.4	102.9	107.0
1905	106.4	109.2	103.8	105.5	111.9
1906	106.1	108.5	105.4	100.9	111.7
1907	104.8	107.0	104.6	100.0	104.6
1908	105.0	105.9	103.3	99.6	104.0
1909	107.6	108.3	108.9[a]	105.3[a]	104.9[a]
1910	100.1	102.0	108.2	103.5	106.3
1911	100.9	108.3	106.9	104.9	107.5
1912	100.6	107.8	106.6	108.4	105.2
1913	97.1	116.1	102.2	108.6	102.2
1914	98.3	116.9	98.1	106.3	99.1
1915	109.5	122.3	103.4	116.6	109.2
1916	104.7	118.6	96.3	111.6	107.3
1917	105.1	123.8	101.3	105.9	106.4
1918	92.2	108.9	93.1	102.1	100.6
1919	75.0	94.5	77.6	84.6	91.2
1920	73.1	93.4	84.8	90.4	102.8
1921[b]	89.3	101.4	99.2	102.0	116.0
1922	99.0	102.9	108.6	113.3	124.7
1923	82.9	89.2	103.3	115.3	122.3
1924	83.6	90.2	109.6	119.5	124.9
1925	93.3	88.4	110.3	120.2	127.3
1926[b]	89.2	94.8	110.8	121.8	130.1
1927	82.6	98.6	112.4	119.6	131.3
1928	81.9	98.9	117.0	119.5	136.5
1929	77.7	101.7	116.4	116.8	135.1
1930	80.8	103.1	115.0	120.4	137.7
1931	84.3	102.7	122.5	121.7	139.4
1932	84.5	105.7	123.7	124.2	145.3
1933	84.2	103.1	123.0	123.6	150.7
1934	81.8	105.2	124.2	127.4	154.0
1935	88.6	104.7	124.9	129.6	156.9
1936	80.5	102.9	120.9	135.5	157.4
1937	78.9	99.5	116.1	128.0	153.6
1938	80.3	99.7	116.4	123.8	155.6

[a] Utilization rates are based on the operation of the Eight Hours Act from July 1.
[b] To avoid the distorting effects of major strikes, inputs and output are measured as the geometric mean of the preceding and subsequent year.
Source: See Appendices A and B.

The Treasury As Developer-Capitalist? British New Town Building in the 1950s

CAROL E. HEIM

In the 1950s the British Treasury made an unusual departure from its traditional effort to minimize government spending, arguing that publicly funded development corporations rather than private developers should build town centers in New Towns so as to reap returns from property development. Often associated with frontier growth, development gain is partly created by the state and can only emerge and be realized with the passage of time and the evolution of expectations. Divisions within the state kept Treasury officials from fully securing a greater public role in New Town center building.

The British Treasury's reputation for fiscal restraint is longstanding. Gladstone's nineteenth-century reforms helped make the Chancellor of the Exchequer responsible for the efficiency and economy of government as a whole. Protecting the interests of the Exchequer frequently was taken to mean spending as little as possible, and the Treasury sought to avoid long-term commitments that would involve the state encroaching upon the private economy. With the advent of Keynesian demand management in the 1940s, a broader conception of the Treasury's role in the economy evolved. But the Treasury remained the primary guardian of fiscal prudence, and intervention was justified primarily on macroeconomic policy grounds, or when salvage operations for ailing firms, industries, or regions were deemed unavoidable.

The mid-1950s brought a limited but interesting reversal of the traditionally restrictive stance. The Labour governments of 1945 to 1951 had embarked on an ambitious program of building New Towns, primarily in the southeast. The aim was to "decant" population and industry from London, which was viewed as overly congested. The Conservatives continued the program, though initially with some reluc-

The Journal of Economic History, Vol. L, No. 4 (Dec. 1990). ISSN 0022-0507.

The author is Associate Professor of Economics, University of Massachusetts, Amherst, MA 01003 and currently a Fellow at the Center for Advanced Study in the Behavioral Sciences, Stanford, CA 94305.

I would like to thank Sir Alec Cairncross, J. B. Cullingworth, Michael Edelstein, Stanley Engerman, Peter Hall, Susan Helper, Jane Humphries, Jane Knodell, Naomi Lamoreaux, Gary Libecap, Philip Mirowski, G. C. Peden, Neil Rollings, Steve Sheppard, Mark Thomas, Ray Thomas, Gavin Wright, anonymous referees for this JOURNAL, and seminar participants at California Institute of Technology, Harvard University, Northwestern University, the University of California at Berkeley, the University of Illinois at Urbana-Champaign, and the University of Massachusetts at Amherst for helpful discussions and comments on earlier drafts. Financial assistance from the Alfred P. Sloan Foundation, the University of Massachusetts, Amherst, and Yale University's Council on West European Studies (Mellon-West European Project) is gratefully acknowledged.

tance, in the early 1950s. The question arose whether private developers should be allowed or encouraged to build the shops, offices, garages, cinemas, and so on in New Town centers. Treasury officials argued that the New Town Development Corporations, whom they supplied with public money, should do this development themselves rather than turning it over to private hands.

The details of this unusual episode are examined in this article to two ends. After sketching the history of the case, the article explores special characteristics of investment in property development. Its central argument is that the existence of development gain and the need for time to elapse before it can be appropriated provide plausible reasons for the Treasury's attitude toward New Town building in the 1950s. Fiscal prudence was not abandoned but rather adapted to the circumstances of developmental investment. The second main theme concerns divisions within the state and their impact on the formulation of government policy. These divisions are explored by examining attitudes of certain state actors who influenced this case: Ministry of Housing and Local Government officials, politicians, and New Town Development Corporations as well as Treasury officials.

TREASURY FINANCE AND THE NEW TOWNS

Treasury control in the 1950s combined traditional roles of overseeing the civil service and the financial operations of the central administration with more recent responsibilities for managing the national economy. The requirement of prior Treasury approval, particularly for increased expenditure by government departments, had antecedents stretching back at least to the 1860s. Consultation between departmental and Treasury officials often preceded formal submission of a scheme to the Treasury for its sanction.[1]

Sir Ivor Jennings's study, *Cabinet Government*, reported in 1951 that "the Treasury is concerned primarily in the almost constant increase in the total of the budget. It will look askance at any proposal which will involve an increase of expenditure, immediately or contingently."[2] This focus was not new. Adherence to the "Treasury view" in the 1920s and 1930s had impeded the adoption of public works programs or other macroeconomic policies to alleviate unemployment, though there were also political and administrative constraints to the adoption of Keynes-

[1] The history of Treasury control and its practice in the 1950s are discussed in Samuel H. Beer, *Treasury Control: The Coordination of Financial and Economic Policy in Great Britain* (2nd edn., Oxford, 1957); Lord Bridges, *The Treasury* (London, 1964); Samuel Brittan, *Steering the Economy: The Role of the Treasury* (rev. edn., Harmondsworth, 1971); Sir Ivor Jennings, *Cabinet Government* (2nd edn., Cambridge, 1951); W. J. M. MacKenzie and J. W. Grove, *Central Administration in Britain* (London, 1957); and Henry Roseveare, *The Treasury: The Evolution of a British Institution* (London, 1969).

[2] Jennings, *Cabinet Government*, p. 141.

ian solutions.[3] While conversion to Keynesian principles did occur, through a process whose exact timing and nature are still being debated, earlier preoccupations persisted. In the late nineteenth century

> the dominant theory of Treasury business was that of "the saving of candle ends"; this theory has gone for ever, but perhaps it tends even now [1957] to swing the mind of the Treasury away from considerations of "planning" to considerations of finance.[4]

Given this institutional history, Treasury officials' desire to undertake town center development in the 1950s is particularly surprising. It also ran counter to the general enthusiasm for the free market that crested after the Conservatives replaced Labour in 1951. The elimination of wartime controls begun under Labour was partially reversed in 1950–51 with rearmament. But by 1954 the last major form of control—the building licensing system—had been removed. Andrew Shonfield argued in 1958 that "perhaps the liberal ideology of the market-place never established quite so firm a grip on any Tory administration before that of 1951–5."[5]

Conservatives of the 1950s did not have as single-minded a commitment to private enterprise as do Thatcherites of the 1980s, and the term "Butskellism" was coined to capture significant continuities in policy between departing Labour Chancellor Hugh Gaitskell and the incoming R. A. Butler.[6] Many also shared with Labour politicians and members of the public an extreme distaste for the unplanned urban sprawl private enterprise had produced in the 1930s. The Conservatives, however, were wary of central (as opposed to local) government initiatives. While supporting the New Towns legislation, they expressed unease over the creation of centrally funded development corporations to carry out its aims and drew a sharp distinction between "control by the Treasury" and "democratic control."[7]

The New Towns were part of the same overall sea-change in policy that led to the introduction of Keynesian ideas under the Coalition and

[3] See Roger Middleton, *Towards the Managed Economy: Keynes, the Treasury and the Fiscal Policy Debate of the 1930s* (London, 1985); G. C. Peden, *Keynes, the Treasury and British Economic Policy* (London, 1988); Jim Tomlinson, *Problems of British Economic Policy, 1870–1945* (London, 1981).

[4] MacKenzie and Grove, *Central Administration in Britain*, p. 317. For a recent contribution to the debate on the "Keynesian revolution" with discussion of earlier work by Booth, Peden, and Tomlinson, see Neil Rollings, "British Budgetary Policy 1945–1954: A 'Keynesian Revolution'?" *Economic History Review*, 42 (May 1988), pp. 283–98.

[5] Andrew Shonfield, *British Economic Policy since the War* (Harmondsworth, 1958), pp. 181–82.

[6] J. C. R. Dow, *The Management of the British Economy, 1945–60* (Cambridge, 1964), pp. 76–77; Nigel Harris, *Competition and the Corporate Society: British Conservatives, the State and Industry, 1945–1964* (London, 1972).

[7] *Hansard* (Commons), 5th ser., vol. 424, 4 July 1946, cols. 2373–86. See also the concerns about central control expressed by Viscount Hinchingbroke, ibid., vol. 422, 8 May 1946, cols. 1154–56. He argued (col. 1151) that a system of regulated private enterprise would suffice to prevent urban sprawl, but other Conservatives disagreed (col. 1170).

Labour governments. While the roots of the New Town idea date back to the turn of the century, with Ebenezer Howard and the Garden Cities movement, the first major public initiative came after World War II. The Labour Government's "New Jerusalem" included among many economic and social welfare programs the idea of "balanced communities" combining employment and residence, a mix of social classes, and access to urban amenities along with proximity to rural life. The New Towns Act of 1946 led to the establishment of a first round of 14 New Towns, 12 in England and Wales and 2 in Scotland. The initial target populations ranged from 10,000 to 60,000.[8]

The New Towns were to be created and run by New Town Development Corporations (NTDCs) modeled after business enterprises but with powers of compulsory land purchase and access to 60-year Treasury finance at the same interest rate as loans from the Public Works Loan Board to local authorities. Public policy controls were limited to "general supervision of the public interest" by the Minister of Town and Country Planning or the Secretary of State for Scotland. Funds were to be obtained entirely from the Ministry of Town and Country Planning (after 1951, the Ministry of Housing and Local Government, or MHLG), subject to the Treasury control described above. The NTDCs had no independent borrowing power.[9]

They were conceived as bodies with specific public purposes and a limited lifetime. The 1946 Act provided for a NTDC to be wound up when the Minister of Town and Country Planning was satisfied that these purposes had been "substantially achieved" and that it would not be expedient on financial grounds to defer the disposal of the undertaking. The assets created (such as housing, sewerage and water systems, roads, and industrial and commercial buildings) were to be turned over to the local authorities in the area.[10] Housing construction, which

[8] *Town and Country Planning, 1943–51*, Cmd. 8204 (*Parliamentary Papers* [henceforth P.P.] 1950–51, xx), pp. 132–35; target populations from annual *Reports of the Development Corporations* (P.P. 1948–49, xviii; 1950–51, xvii; 1951–52, xvii).

[9] Michael Hebbert, "The British New Towns: A Review Article," *Town Planning Review*, 51 (Oct. 1980), pp. 414–20; *Interim Report of the New Towns* [Reith] *Committee*, Cmd. 6759 (P.P. 1945–46, xiv); Nathaniel Lichfield, *Economics of Planned Development* (London, 1956), pp. 242–52; Frank Schaffer, *The New Town Story* (London, 1970). Appropriate methods of Treasury control for this new type of corporation, and the delegation of Treasury financial authority to MHLG, were discussed at various points. See Public Record Office, London [henceforth, PRO], T 227/661, Memo from DJ [Mrs. D. Johnstone] to Mr. Compton, 14.2.51; PRO T 227/326, E. W. Playfair (Treasury) to F. L. Edwards (MHLG), 9.4.52; PRO HLG 90/502, R. W. B. Clarke (Treasury) to F. L. Edwards (MHLG), 19.9.55. Analogies were made with the issues raised by other new public or quasi-public entities such as the civil airways corporations and the BBC. See *First, Third and Fourth Reports from the Committee of Public Accounts* (P.P. 1950, iii), Minutes of Evidence, 4.4.50, pp. 44–58.

[10] Schaffer, *The New Town Story*, p. 215. The Treasury's concurrence was required for disposal. In the late 1950s the Conservative government decided that the assets of new towns should be transferred to a Commission for the New Towns, rather than to local authorities. See J. B.

accounted for about 75 percent of New Town expenditure in the early years, was part of the overall housing drive begun by Labour and intensified under the Conservatives.

The initial authorization for the New Towns program was £50 million, though it was recognized from the outset that further funds would be necessary. Later Acts in 1952 and 1953 brought the total to £150 million, and in 1954 an increase to £250 million was sought, estimated to be sufficient to meet fresh commitments for at least two years. The difficulty of estimating the needs of the half-finished towns, however, meant that the ultimate total expenditure could rise to as much as £300 to 325 million. This sum was approximately 6 percent of annual central government expenditure in 1954.[11]

When the Conservatives took office in October 1951, they were quite concerned about the "alarming commitment" of the New Towns program. Although they continued the politically popular program, they did not designate further New Towns. The Treasury shared the concern about the cost of New Town development. In 1952, with the slackening of economic activity, they sought restrictions on New Towns, preferring town development schemes in which local authorities met some of the costs.[12] Chancellor of the Exchequer Butler, who in 1953 was "anxious not to appear to be raising more money on the market than was strictly necessary," argued that "we must try to find sources of capital finance other than the consolidated fund, and here I have particularly in mind the private developer who may well have a substantial role to play in the future as he has done in the past."[13]

The issue of private investment in the New Town centers began to receive sustained attention after the MHLG received a letter from D. A. Collenette, the Estates Secretary of the Church Commissioners, in December 1953. Collenette reported that "the Church Commissioners have very considerable funds for investment, particularly in land, for which they are seeking outlets wherever sound long-term investment is possible."[14] They were interested in putting in necessary services and leasing plots to industrialists on long-term leases.

Other inquiries followed, and a need apparently was felt to formulate an official policy regarding private development. Economic conditions already were changing, though the boom of 1954 had not yet fully

---

Cullingworth and V. A. Karn, *The Ownership and Management of Housing in the New Towns* (London, 1968), especially pp. 20–33.

[11] *Hansard* (Commons), 5th ser., vol. 535, 10 Dec. 1954, cols. 1291–92; Central Statistical Office, *National Income and Expenditure, 1957* (London, 1957), table 36, p. 33.

[12] J. B. Cullingworth, *Environmental Planning 1939–1969*, Vol. 3, *New Towns Policy* (London, 1979), p. 147.

[13] PRO CAB 134/912, H.A.(53), 9th Meeting, 1.5.53, 12th Meeting, 21.5.53; PRO HLG 90/344, "Ministers' Pronouncements on the role of Private Enterprise in New Towns," [30?].10.54, also quoted in Cullingworth, *New Towns Policy*, p. 123.

[14] PRO HLG 90/344, G. L. Barber (New Towns II, [MHLG]) to Mr. Heady, 7.1.54.

emerged. Many raw material controls, including the general steel allocation, had been eliminated in 1953. The Church Commissioners were not alone in having funds to invest. Insurance companies were interested, and property developers had amassed large fortunes by leveraging wartime acquisitions of properties and taking advantage of the property boom that began to develop in the last 18 months of the war.[15]

In July 1954 letters were sent to New Town General Managers seeking information on approaches by private developers to the NTDCs. Of particular concern were financial arrangements with developers considered by NTDCs (including the possibility of adjustable leases if property values appreciated) and the control that NTDCs would retain over physical development of the sites.[16] Experiences and expectations varied. Most NTDCs, however, anticipated appreciation, and thus sought to retain ownership of property even if, as in Bracknell, they did not consider it possible to ask investors for a clause allowing adjustment on ground rent.

> The investment companies would, of course, prefer a freehold, but the Corporation's policy is a 99 year lease as they consider it essential that their successors should have an opportunity at the end of 99 years of reaping a return on the increased values which by then will certainly have accrued.[17]

A meeting of MHLG officials was held on September 13, 1954, to discuss the replies to M. M. Dobbie's letter. The resulting memorandum recommended that a circular be issued to NTDCs outlining possible methods of involving private capital in New Town centers. For sites, leasehold rather than freehold disposals were to be encouraged in the early years. "Premature freehold disposals will probably not obtain as good a return as would be possible when the Centres are more fully developed whereas leasehold disposals should have a valuable reversionary interest if the Centre is a success."[18] Short, adjustable leases were to be sought, though "substantial traders" would probably require at least a 99-year lease. Specialist buildings such as department stores were to be left to private capital. In cases where the NTDC constructed buildings itself for rack rental or disposal, MHLG reserved the right to obtain details of standards and specifications, to ensure that high costs would not unduly reduce the NTDC's return.

The proposed circular initially received considerable support within MHLG, "but the later papers suggest that the native hue of resolution

[15] Dow, *The Management of the British Economy, 1945–60*, p. 77; Oliver Marriott, *The Property Boom* (London, 1967), pp. 43–65.

[16] PRO HLG 90/344, M. M. Dobbie to General Managers [of NTDCs], 28.7.54.

[17] PRO HLG 90/344, Capt. T. M. Brownrigg, Bracknell Development Corporation, to Dobbie, 9.8.54. Ground rents are returns to land. Rack rents (the term used for rents on, for example, commercial buildings) are divisible into two main parts: return on capital invested and ground rent.

[18] PRO HLG 90/344, "Private Investment in Town Centre Shopping Development," memo by N.T.2, Oct. 1954.

got sicklied o'er with the pale cast of thought," with MHLG officials disagreeing over the extent to which private investment should be encouraged.[19] One group (the New Towns division) supported an earlier agreement in 1953 between Harold Macmillan, then Minister of Housing and Local Government, and Butler, Chancellor of the Exchequer. Both ministers wanted as much investment by private developers in New Towns as possible, to relieve demands on the Exchequer.[20] The other group within MHLG was A.G.D.III, a finance division in the accountant general's department. A.G.D.III sided more closely with Treasury officials in the position they took as consultation processes of Treasury control unfolded during the winter and spring of 1955. This position was diametrically opposed:

> development corporations should put up all the buildings save where there was some special reason for leaving it to private enterprise . . . it would be foolish for the Exchequer to bear the loss involved in unremunerative development and not take its full share of the profitable development.[21]

Henry Roseveare, based on his reading of Samuel Brittan's work, has criticized "the conventional humbug that the departmental policies of the professional Treasury are inseparable from those of the Chancellor of the Exchequer."[22] In this case the Chancellor appears to have acted quite independently. "Apparently official Treasury had not been consulted by the Chancellor at the time, and Mr. Thorley said they knew nothing about it [the earlier agreement between Macmillan and Butler]."[23] Clearly they did not feel bound by the agreement in expressing their position in 1955.

Treasury officials' support for NTDC development of town centers did not imply that they would seek unlimited public spending, even for New Towns. In early 1955 the Treasury was reluctant to support further expansions of London New Towns because of the commitments involved, though a New Town at Cumbernauld ultimately was approved

[19] PRO HLG 90/344, J. Rogerson to Mr. Waddell, 5.4.55.

[20] PRO HLG 90/344, "Private Investment in Town Centres," Note of a meeting held on 3.11.54, n.s.; PRO HLG 90/344, "Ministers' Pronouncements on the role of Private Enterprise in New Towns," [30?].10.54. Macmillan, of course, did not consider it possible to rely entirely on private enterprise, especially for housing. As Minister of Housing and Local Government (1951–1954), he oversaw a major drive to provide public housing, and viewed the New Towns as one aspect of the overall housing program.

[21] PRO HLG 90/344, W. J. Reynolds (A.G.D.III) to Mr. Rogerson, 27.4.55.

[22] Roseveare, *The Treasury*, p. 313.

[23] PRO HLG 90/344, W. J. Reynolds (A.G.D.III) to Mr. Rogerson, 27.4.55. Differences within the Treasury and MHLG, as well as between them and other departments, on New Towns policy underscore the importance of not treating the state as a single-minded, indivisible institution. For an examination of this theme in the case of regional policy, see Carol E. Heim, "Government Research Establishments, State Capacity, and Distribution of Industry Policy in Britain," *Regional Studies*, 22 (Oct. 1988), pp. 375–86.

to meet Glasgow's urgent housing needs.[24] But the Treasury clearly agreed that once a New Town had been created, and funds spent on roads, sewerage, and so on, the best financial results would be secured by rapid spending to complete a viable town center. The Treasury then could reap returns on new commercial and industrial property that would, contemporaries agreed, be significantly higher than returns on housing, with its politically constrained rent levels.[25]

MHLG concerns were expressed in a draft letter to R. W. B. Clarke, head of the Treasury's Social Services Division, in September 1955, noting his "great interest" in the question of whether NTDCs should provide commercial premises themselves for rack renting. The letter explained that

> we would prefer not to press on the corporations too active a policy of development. For one thing, they have for two years been loyally following Mr. Macmillan's request that they should encourage as much private investment as possible . . . this is the sort of engine which cannot be put into reverse quickly.[26]

Some NTDCs were in fact quite critical of what they perceived to be an about-face in policy and sought to continue having a combination of private and NTDC development.[27]

MHLG officials thought that as the financial situation worsened and general restrictions on capital investment were imposed in the summer and autumn of 1955, the Treasury position might change. But despite government measures to curtail local authority borrowing from the Public Works Loan Board in autumn 1955, funding for New Town development simultaneously was allowed to proceed. A Treasury official later explained that even in times of general investment restraint, it had been recognized that "it would be bad for the Exchequer to slow down materially the completion of the new towns because of the amount of capital already sunk in the basic services."[28]

The letter finally sent to the Treasury in January 1956 concluded that the MHLG did not want "to go beyond a simple general statement to the effect that the climate has changed since 1953, and that Corporations

[24] Cullingworth, *New Towns Policy*, 149–51; *Hansard* (Commons), 5th ser., vol. 535, 10 Dec. 1954, col. 1323.

[25] PRO HLG 90/502, "Annual Review of New Towns Policy—1955," Minutes of meeting at Treasury, 8.8.55; PRO T 227/564, P. R. Baldwin to Mr. Fraser, "New Towns: Advances," 1.8.57; on "reasonable" rates of return for housing, commercial, and industrial development see PRO HLG 116/7, AE [A. Sylvester-Evans, MHLG] to W. O. Hart, Hemel Hempstead Development Corporation, 23.1.53.

[26] PRO HLG 90/344, Draft letter [from MHLG] to R. W. B. Clarke (Treasury), n.d., but c. Oct. 1955.

[27] PRO HLG 90/344, T. P. Bennett (Chairman, Crawley Development Corporation) to Sir Thomas Sheepshanks (MHLG), 16.5.55.

[28] PRO HLG 90/502, W. J. Reynolds to Mr. Rogerson, 2.8.55; N. P. Hepworth, *The Finance of Local Government* (rev. edn., London, 1970), p. 204; PRO HLG 90/398, "Restrictions on Capital Investment: Lines to be followed after the Chancellor's Statement" [of 26.10.55]; PRO T 227/564, Minute by FFT [Turnbull, of the Treasury], n.d. but c. 31.7.57.

TABLE 1
PRIVATE INVESTMENT IN NEW TOWN CENTER BUILDING, 1955

Town	Percentage Private Investment	
	Present	Ultimate
Aycliffe	0%	43%
Basildon		83
Bracknell	0	50
Corby	45	30
Crawley	Not quoted	45
Cwmbran	0	Not quoted
Harlow	66	75
Hatfield	100	70
Hemel Hempstead	12	60
Peterlee		25
Stevenage	0	50
Welwyn Garden City	39	31

Source: Public Record Office HLG 90/344, Schedule attached to "Investment in New Town Centres," memo by W. J. Reynolds, A.G.D.III (Ministry of Housing and Local Government), 2.8.55.

can now undertake as much development as they believe to be sound. . . ."[29] The MHLG's hope was that private development would continue to play an important role. Evelyn Sharp, Permanent Secretary to the MHLG and a leading proponent of New Towns, wanted at least half of the industrial and commercial building to be privately owned. She was not sure that the present attractive rents would continue, and explained later that she disliked the mortgage business, preferring that industry and commerce in the New Towns find their own capital. MHLG was sympathetic to the NTDCs' desire to involve private capital, and was reluctant to press an unwelcome policy of public development on NTDCs it did not completely control. With MHLG dragging its heels, Treasury officials were not able fully to indulge their "enthusiasm for rack renting."[30]

Table 1 shows the extent of actual and planned private investment in New Town centers in 1955. General restrictions on capital investment by private investors may have increased the share of NTDC development in early years. The main impression is one of considerable variation, though except for Welwyn Garden City the London New Towns tended to expect higher ultimate percentages of private investment than those in older industrial areas. By 1973, following other ups and downs in the emphasis on private investment in New Towns, "rather over half" of the factories and "rather under half" of the shops

[29] PRO HLG 90/344, F. L. Edwards (MHLG) to F. F. Turnbull (Treasury), 2.1.56.

[30] PRO HLG 90/344, [Sharp] to Mr. Waddell, 22.12.[55]; PRO HLG 116/28, E. A. Sharp to Mr. Waddell and A. G. [Accountant General, MHLG]; PRO HLG 90/344, JHW [Waddell] to Secretary [Sharp], 21.12.[55]. See also Evelyn Sharp, *The Ministry of Housing and Local Government* (London, 1969), pp. 169–70.

and offices built in New Towns had been privately financed, with proportions varying in different towns. In 1986 the total value of private investment in New Towns was unknown but "clearly substantial," with private sources having funded over 50 percent of all investment in Milton Keynes.[31]

PROPERTY DEVELOPMENT AND THE DEVELOPER-CAPITALIST

Why did Treasury officials in the 1950s want NTDCs to do town center development themselves? The answer hinges upon the phenomenon of development gain. Property development is distinctive in yielding two types of return, both of which are taken into account by developer-capitalists in their investment decisions.[32] The first is an ordinary rate of profit on capital invested—for example, in constructing infrastructure or buildings. Over and above this, however, developer-capitalists reap (when successful) a return called "development gain." Development gain is the difference between (1) the ultimate value of the development created and (2) all costs of creating it, *including* the ordinary rate of profit on capital invested.

In their financial calculations, developers in the 1950s included an allowance for "profit on enterprise" that set their minimum necessary return in the form of development gain. Though there was no one accepted procedure, a common allowance was 5 to 20 percent of the total cost of works excluding land, or of the values to be created. If the developed property sold for more than originally anticipated, development gain would exceed this allowance for profit on enterprise. The excess could be considered a profit on the land transaction; the developer could have paid more for the land and still made the appropriate developer's profit on enterprise.[33]

[31] PRO HLG 90/344, R. T. Kennedy (T.P.3) to Mr. Barber, "Private Investment in Town Centre Shopping Areas," 30.10.54; "New Towns in England (NT1)," *Thirteenth Report from the Expenditure Committee (Environment Sub-Committee), New Towns* (P.P. 1974–75, xxiv), in Minutes of Evidence, 10.7.73, p. 9. In Scottish New Towns approximately one-third of the factories, shops, and offices so far built had been privately financed (see "New Towns," *Thirteenth Report*, Appendix 1 to Minutes of Evidence, p. 393.) The 1986 figure is from National Audit Office, Report by the Comptroller and Auditor General, *Department of the Environment: Disposal of New Town Assets*, HC 76 (London, 1986), p. 5.

[32] The term "developer-capitalist" is used by Feagin and others to refer to a distinctive type of capitalist engaged in a variety of economic and political activities associated with property development. See Joe R. Feagin, "Sunbelt Metropolis and Development Capital: Houston in the Era of Late Capitalism," in Larry Sawers and William K. Tabb, eds., *Sunbelt/Snowbelt: Urban Development and Regional Restructuring* (Oxford, 1984), pp. 99–127. While sharing with other capitalists a basic drive toward accumulation, developer-capitalists should be analyzed as a specific institutional form. For further discussion, see Carol E. Heim, "External Spheres and the Theory of Capitalist Development," *Social Concept*, 3 (Dec. 1986), pp. 3–42.

[33] Lichfield, *Economics of Planned Development*, p. 130, 137. In *Housing Policy and Economic Power* (London, 1983), Michael Ball characterizes the development process as a struggle between landowners and housebuilders over the conversion of development gain into land rent or land price.

Development gain thus consists of some mixture of "profit on enterprise," or developer's profit, and a component based on land price. It can include both a surplus-generating aspect and a redistributive aspect. Surplus generation results from the fact that the capitalist economy does not operate within a fixed set of spatial, social, or technological boundaries, but constantly extends or alters them, creating new frontiers as part of a process of accumulation of value. On such frontiers, which may be extensive or intensive (as in urban redevelopment), one sees not simply reallocation through "normal" market processes, with capital and labor flowing into activities with a marginally higher rate of return, but large discontinuous gains—for example, from land speculation, urban promotion, or financial activities. Nineteenth-century cases include the growth of Chicago and other midwestern cities and urban development in the Ruhr, while the twentieth century has seen similar processes in redevelopment of bombed cities after World War II, the growth of U.S. Sunbelt cities, and contemporary gentrification.[34]

With frontier growth the potential exists both to extend the boundaries of the system and to rewrite the "rules of the game." For these reasons development gain should not be conceived simply as an amalgam of standard economic categories of "rent" and "profit." "Rent" generally carries connotations of a return to scarcity. But development gain in the sense of creation of surplus is highest precisely where the boundaries of the system are being extended, whereas Ricardian differential rent, for example, disappears at the frontier. The "profit on enterprise" component might be construed as a return to risk. But property developers often do not accept risk as a given, instead seeking through the political process to transform the "rules of the game" to their advantage. Ex ante risk may be high, but ex post risk may in fact be *lower* in cases of successful property development. Far from simply maximizing subject to constraints, property developers are active economic agents seeking to change the constraints.[35]

Such activities by developers can genuinely increase the surplus of the system as well as merely redistribute it if, for example, viable new

---

The outcome depends upon the contemporary balance of power between landowners and builders, and the planning system is one arena for this struggle. See pp. 115–16, 127–29, 143–55, 232–37.

[34] See Guido di Tella, "The Economics of the Frontier," in Charles Kindleberger and Guido di Tella, eds., *Economics in the Long View: Essays in Honour of W. W. Rostow*, Vol. 1: *Models and Methodology* (New York, 1982); John D. Haeger, *The Investment Frontier: New York Businessmen and the Economic Development of the Old Northwest* (Albany, 1981); Heim, "External Spheres"; Neil Smith and Peter Williams, *Gentrification of the City* (Boston, 1986).

[35] For examples of such active interventions by developers, see Feagin, "Sunbelt Metropolis and Development Capital"; Haeger, *The Investment Frontier*; Gavin Wright, *Old South, New South: Revolutions in the Southern Economy since the Civil War* (New York, 1986); and Sharon Zukin, *Loft Living: Culture and Capital in Urban Change* (Baltimore, 1982). The theoretical issues raised by the concept of development gain go beyond the scope of this article, but I plan to explore them in more detail elsewhere.

cities are added to a system of cities. By contrast, the rent-seeking literature tends to focus on the redistributive aspects of political interventions, without really explaining the origin of the rents to be distributed. But development gain reaped by an individual agent in the system *can* include a component that is purely redistributive, if its capture does not simultaneously increase the system's potential to accumulate. British New Towns in the 1950s do not represent frontier economic development to the same degree as, for example, nineteenth-century U.S. cities (though they were seen as potentially important sites for new export industries in the 1950s). Their "frontier" character was more as a political innovation than an economic process. To this degree the redistributive aspect may have been more dominant in the case of New Towns than in other historical examples of development gain.

Whether development gain results from surplus creation or redistribution, an incentive exists for the state as well as for developers or landowners to appropriate a portion of it. The possibility of doing so at the municipal level was in fact a key element in Howard's original plan for Garden Cities in 1898.[36] Moreover, as a result of public infrastructure investments, planning, and other legislation, the state itself is partly responsible for the existence of development gain. This provides a political rationale for appropriation that is less evident with other types of economic surplus such as profit or interest. There is an extensive history in Britain and elsewhere of efforts to tax development gain, "betterment," or the "unearned increment." It includes Henry George's campaigns, the tangled history of British "compensation and betterment" legislation to address the effects of planning in lowering or raising values, and the successful establishment of site-value taxation systems in Australia, Denmark, New Zealand, and some U.S. cities.[37]

[36] Ebenezer Howard, *Garden Cities of To-morrow* (rev. edn., Eastbourne, 1985). Ray Thomas argues in his Introduction to this edition that Howard saw the new towns as a means of redistributing income and wealth from landlords in old cities to residents of both new towns and old cities.

[37] Henry George, *Progress and Poverty* (New York, 1880), and *The Irish Land Question* (New York, 1881); Elwood P. Lawrence, *Henry George in the British Isles* (East Lansing, 1957); H. Ronald Parker, "The History of Compensation and Betterment since 1900," in Peter Hall, ed., *Land Values* (London, 1965), pp. 53–72; J. B. Cullingworth, *Environmental Planning 1939–1969*, Vol. IV: *Land Values, Compensation and Betterment* (London, 1980); Andrew Cox, *Adversary Politics and Land: The Conflict over Land and Property Policy in Post-War Britain* (Cambridge, 1984); Ball, *Housing Policy and Economic Power*; Paul N. Balchin and Gregory H. Bull, *Regional and Urban Economics* (London, 1987), pp. 205–9.

Particularly when the state is actively involved in its creation, it might be thought that the origin of development gain lies in "positive externalities." But development gain can exist, and be appropriated by developer-capitalists, even when negative externalities result—for example, when private development takes the form of unplanned urban sprawl. It is a share of the economy's value-surplus, which is theoretically significant because its generation and distribution affect the overall accumulation process in a capitalist economy. The standard economic category that comes closer to grasping part of what underlies development gain is rather "external economies" as described by Tibor Scitovsky, "Two Concepts of External Economies," *Journal of Political Economy*, 62 (Apr. 1954), pp. 143–51.

In practice it can prove difficult to determine to what extent increases in property values are due to the initiative and outlay of private owners, as opposed to being created by the community. This was one of the causes of collapse of the 1909–10 Finance Act, whose taxation proposals embodied the Liberals' effort to retain betterment value for the community.[38] But with the New Towns there had been an undeniable public role in providing infrastructure, which bolstered the Treasury's case that collecting development gain was warranted.

Ordinarily, private developer-capitalists remain able to appropriate at least a portion of development gain in their struggle with landowners and the state. If they cannot, private development ceases, as some argue happened in Britain when a 100 percent tax on development gain was imposed by the 1947 Town and Country Planning Act.[39] The importance of development gain—in addition to "ordinary" profits—as an incentive in relation to New Town building was highlighted by the 1974–75 Expenditure Committee report:

> private developers did not feel able to make significant contributions towards the major infrastructure costs because the terms under which land was acquired from Development Corporations eliminated any scope for development as distinct from building profits.[40]

In any case, whoever appropriates development gain must wait for it. In the case of British New Town development, there was awareness from the outset that the values to be created by the development process would only emerge over time and that, if the assets created were to be sold, there would be a time for disposal at which the maximum value could be realized.[41] The hope was that NTDCs would be able to balance their accounts by taking advantage of increased property values through freehold or leasehold sales.

In discussions about the disposal of New Town assets in the mid- and late 1950s, the Treasury was very clear that the manner of disposing of New Town assets would dominate prospects of earning back the Exchequer money invested and that the Treasury, not an occupier,

[38] PRO HLG 81/13, Uthwatt Committee, "Second Statement on Behalf of the Land Agents' Society (Incorporated by Royal Charter)," May 1941.

[39] Cullingworth, *Land Values*, pp. 14–60, 85–138; Cox, *Adversary Politics and Land*, pp. 82–102; Lichfield, *Economics of Planned Development*, p. 314; *Hansard* (Lords), 5th ser., vol. 165, 16 Nov. 1949, cols. 713–66; *Town and Country Planning 1943–51*, pp. 12–13. The 100 percent development charge was repealed by the Conservatives in the 1953 Town and Country Planning Act.

[40] *Thirteenth Report*, Summary of Recommendations, pp. xlv–xlvi. See also *Thirteenth Report*, "New Towns in England (NT1)," pp. 5–6, Minutes of Evidence, 21.11.73, pp. 121–22, and Minutes of Evidence, 21.5.75, p. 795.

[41] PRO HLG 90/344, C. A. C. Turner (Chief Executive, Crawley Development Corporation) to M. M. Dobbie (MHLG), 4.8.54; PRO HLG 90/344, "Investment in new town centres," paper prepared by W. J. Reynolds (A.G.D.III, MHLG), c. August 1955; PRO HLG 116/28, F. F. Turnbull (Treasury) to F. L. Edwards (MHLG), 25.4.58.

must choose the time of sale.[42] In the event the financial position, and ability to continue capital investment, of some NTDCs was significantly improved by the disposal of assets in the 1970s and 1980s. In Basildon and Hatfield capital surpluses from disposals more than offset their accumulated revenue deficits.[43] Contributions of land development activities to the self-financing of investment are evident in other historical contexts as well, including U.S. railroads and urban promotion in the nineteenth century and contemporary development of the London Docklands.

If all actors had complete and accurate expectations about the extent and success of future development, the market would presumably incorporate future development gain into the sale prices of assets, and there would be no advantage in waiting to sell. But

> town centre development has to be started before the bulk of the new population has arrived and before the success of the new town centre can be assured. Prices paid by private enterprise are bound to be affected adversely by this uncertainty.[44]

Similarly, U.S. transcontinental railroads (unlike the midwestern lines) often were build in advance of settlement. Stanley Engerman has observed that the transcontinentals were slower than midwestern railroads to dispose of their land assets. He noted that "the lag is inconsistent with the perfect foresight assumption."[45]

In the crucial role of expectations, property development differs in degree, if not in kind, from nondevelopmental investment. Part of the reason the Conservatives did not immediately dispose of New Town assets (though they did proceed with some denationalization—in steel and parts of road haulage) was that early on there was considerable uncertainty as to whether development gain *would* emerge. Like many Labour initiatives, the New Towns program initially was an experiment justified primarily on social grounds rather than any likelihood of remunerative return. It was in this context that intermediate arrangements—ground leases with building by private developers, rather than disposals of land to private developers, or NTDC construction—frequently were agreed upon.

Expectations about the success of the British New Towns, however,

[42] PRO HLG 90/354, [P. R.] Baldwin (Treasury) to J. Rogerson (MHLG), 28.1.57. See Cullingworth, *New Towns Policy*, pp. 316–40, for a detailed account of the discussions on future ownership of the New Towns.

[43] Meryl Aldridge, *The British New Towns: A Programme without a Policy* (London, 1979), p. 103; Ivan Turok, "Public Investment and Privatisation in the New Towns: A Financial Assessment of Bracknell," *Environment and Planning A* (forthcoming, 1990); National Audit Office, Report by the Comptroller and Auditor General, *Department of the Environment: Financial Reconstruction of New Towns in England*, HC 339 (London, 1987), p. 3.

[44] PRO HLG 90/344, "Investment in new town centres," paper prepared by W. J. Reynolds (A.G.D.III, MHLG), c. August 1955.

[45] Stanley L. Engerman, "Some Economic Issues Relating to Railroad Subsidies and the Evolution of Land Grants," this JOURNAL, 32 (June 1972), p. 457.

became considerably more optimistic by the mid-1950s. As late as 1953 a MHLG/Treasury report concluded that "from a strictly financial point of view there is much more probability of a loss than a profit."[46] But subsequent indirect evidence on matters that might have influenced the Treasury's expectations, assembled below, fits well with the timing of the Treasury position, in 1955, in favor of doing town center development itself through NTDCs. The evidence is consistent with Cullingworth's conclusion that by the mid-1950s it was clear that some of the New Towns were likely to prove highly profitable, and the problem had changed from one of meeting a major investment burden to one of determining how the "profits" should be allocated.

By 1954 Britain was moving from the difficult years of the early 1950s to a full-fledged boom, to be exacerbated by the "serious blunder" of Butler's expansionary 1955 budget. Applications to the Capital Issues Committee for permission to raise capital rose sharply, from a monthly average of 96½ in 1952 to 182 in 1954, and remained at 174 in 1955. A widely cited signal of optimism about New Towns was the *Economist* article of November 1954, "Britain's Boom Towns."[47]

Oliver Marriott has suggested that in late 1953 and early 1954, when the Ravenseft property company became involved, it was by no means clear that building shops in New Towns would be "easy money."[48] But by April 1955 C. G. Thorley of the Treasury

> said that he appreciated that there was some degree of speculation involved but it was fairly clear that the interest now being shown by the investment houses in commercial development in new towns was based on an expectation that the new towns would be a success.[49]

By May 1956 the interest of private developers extended to a proposal for a private enterprise New Town at Allhallows, Kent. The Dolphin Development and Management Company's proposal was, however, rejected by the Kent County Council on grounds of injury to local agricultural interests.[50]

Treasury officials visited the New Towns sometime before June 1955, and by 1954–55 such visits would have provided evidence of considerable progress.[51] Table 2 provides data on new dwellings completed and under construction in the New Towns from 1950 to 1959. The number completed rose from 4,586 by March 1952 to 12,151 by March 1953, 21,897 by March 1954, and 33,324 by March 1955. Planning and

[46] Cullingworth, *New Towns Policy*, p. 121.

[47] Ibid., pp. 147, 316; Brittan, *Steering the Economy*, pp. 200–3; PRO T 266/119, Capital Issues Committee, "Total Number of Applications Considered by Committee and Chairman," table for 1945–55.

[48] Marriott, *The Property Boom*, p. 64.

[49] PRO HLG 90/344, W. J. Reynolds (A.G.D.III, MHLG) to Mr. Rogerson, 27.4.55.

[50] Cullingworth, *New Towns Policy*, pp. 162–63.

[51] PRO HLG 90/344, W. J. Reynolds (A.G.D.III) to A.G., 16.11.55.

TABLE 2
NEW DWELLINGS COMPLETED AND UNDER CONSTRUCTION IN NEW TOWNS

Date	Completed	Under Construction
1950	1,184	
1951	1,183	3,267
1952	4,586	7,013
1953	12,151	9,148
1954	21,897	12,193
1955	33,324	11,034
1956	43,570	14,382
1957	56,158	11,063
1958	66,557	9,602
1959	75,355	9,228

Note: The figure for 1950 includes all dwellings completed and under construction to date. Figures cover all New Towns in England, Wales, and Scotland as of March 31 of each year.
Source: New Towns, *Accounts 1949–50* to *1958–59* (*Parliamentary Papers*, 1950–51, xxi; 1951–52, xix; 1952–53, xviii; 1953–54, xx; 1954–55, viii; 1955–56, xxx; 1956–57, xxi; 1957–58, xix; 1958–59, xx; 1959–60, xxii).

construction of town centers and neighborhood shopping areas were getting under way in all the New Towns; Corby's town center was officially inaugurated in July 1954, Crawley's in December of that year.

For Table 3, I collected data on deficiencies and surpluses on General Revenue Account for the NTDCs. While all showed deficiencies in the early years, surpluses and smaller deficiencies began to appear in the mid-1950s. For many New Towns, in fact, 1954–55 marked an important turning point. The Scottish towns (East Kilbride and Glenrothes) were major exceptions. Very low housing rent levels in Scotland led to persistent large deficiencies. In Basildon there were unusual costs of acquiring and demolishing substandard properties (shacks) in the area. It is important to note that figures throughout Table 3 do not include the large losses on ancillary accounts such as water and sewerage. Treasury officials apparently believed, however, that it would be possible to turn these losses over to local authorities when the NTDCs were wound up (a belief that led one MHLG official to refer to the "cloud cuckooland" the Treasury inhabited).[52]

The only NTDC explicitly to report a rate of return on the cost of development each year was Crawley, and unfortunately it gave few details of its calculations. The rate reported was described as gross income from industry, commercial properties, and housing (including subsidies), divided by the cost at which properties that had fructified and were producing income stood in the Corporation's books. Table 4 shows a reasonable rate of return over the decade, rising especially in the first half. Basildon provided an isolated figure for the year ended

[52] PRO HLG 116/28, F. L. Edwards to Mr. Waddell and Secretary, "New Town Accounts," 26.4.57.

TABLE 3
NEW TOWN DEVELOPMENT CORPORATIONS, GENERAL REVENUE ACCOUNTS

Deficiency (−) or Surplus Carried to Balance Sheet
(in pounds)

Year Ending March 31:	Aycliffe	Basildon	Bracknell	Corby
1948		n.a.	n.a.	n.a.
1949	−£91	n.a.	n.a.	n.a.
1950	−1,999		n.a.	n.a.
1951	−4,105	−£1,112		
1952	−14,269	−17,617	£5,925	£1,419
1953	−12,372	−37,572	−10,619	−10,679
1954	−8,169	−10,953	−28,360	−17,856
1955	4,948	4,004	−24,287	−8,991
1956	2,023	−16,412	−27,952	−7,503
1957	532	−35,318	−49,174	16
1958	496	−87,758	−70,906	−5,615
1959	5,883	−26,318	−17,041	−20,103
1960	2,034	−92,757	18,266	4,281

Year Ending March 31:	Crawley	Cwmbran	Harlow	Hatfield
1948		n.a.		n.a.
1949	−773	n.a.	−1,817	−82
1950	−4,679	n.a.	−3,516	−1,506
1951	−11,999		−8,918	−3,496
1952	−17,739	6,576	−28,375	−7,786
1953	−44,341	−8,278	−25,819	−8,825
1954	−46,075	−17,307	2,649	−6,070
1955	623	−11,861	28,732	127
1956	5,524	−17,298	47,330	2,529
1957	−15,072	−14,505	43,473	18,278
1958	−3,640	−7,511	57,589	−64,353
1959	71,577	−6,912	96,490	24,504
1960	38,441	−10,925	91,978	327

Year Ending March 31:	Hemel Hempstead	Peterlee	Stevenage	Welwyn
1948		n.a.		n.a.
1949	−2,704	−185	−2,856	−122
1950	−4,899	−1,884	−4,670	−9,432
1951	−11,791	−6,610	−7,188	−20,991
1952	−47,205	−11,151	−49,864	−31,065
1953	−45,932	−15,252	−57,773	−27,687
1954	−9,529	−10,775	−72,096	−9,700
1955	2,239	−8,208	−72,388	2,023
1956	5,916	−11,335	−13,699	26,699
1957	20,403	−9,335	13,182	63,324
1958	49,107	−4,032	28,430	49,802
1959	55,976	−17,975	54,013	10,470
1960	93,475	−44,856	272,651	24,977

Year Ending March 31:	East Kilbride	Glenrothes
1948	n.a.	n.a.
1949	−100	n.a.
1950	−1,605	−576
1951	−4,546	−1,264
1952	−28,442	−7,174
1953	−47,110	−15,020

TABLE 3—continued

Year Ending March 31:	Deficiency (−) or Surplus Carried to Balance Sheet (in pounds) East Kilbride	Glenrothes
1954	−91,633	−26,860
1955	−140,724	−35,105
1956	−177,257	−49,506
1957	−242,647	−59,844
1958	−318,959	−66,857
1959	−380,262	−84,678
1960	−369,632	−94,429

n.a. = not available

Note: First available data for each New Town cover periods of less or more than one year (for example, first data for Aycliffe are for 2.7.47 to 1948; first data for Glenrothes are for 25.10.48 to 1950). Accounts from 1952 on are presented in a standardized, more comparable form.

Source: New Towns, *Accounts 1947–48* to *1959–60* (*Parliamentary Papers*, 1948–49, xxii; 1950–51, xxi; 1951–52, xix; 1952–53, xviii; 1953–54, xx; 1954–55, viii; 1955–56, xxx; 1956–57, xxi; 1957–58, xix; 1958–59, xx; 1959–60, xxii; 1960–61, xxii).

March 31, 1954 (5.6 percent) comparable to Crawley's. A rate of return on commercial and industrial development alone cannot readily be calculated from the published accounts, which were specifically designed to rule out such efforts. For purposes of rough comparison the bank rate in 1955 was 3 to 4.5 percent, rising to 5.5 percent in early 1956. Equity or share yields were 6.1 percent in 1953, falling to 4.4 percent in

TABLE 4
CRAWLEY DEVELOPMENT CORPORATION
ANNUAL RATE OF RETURN ON THE COST OF DEVELOPMENT

Date March 31	Fructified Properties in Corporation's Books at: (in pounds)	Rate of Return (percent)
1952	£2,081,500	5.1%
1953	4,444,000	5.1
1954	7,896,000	5.5
1955	12,050,000	5.6
1956	15,050,000	6.0
1957	20,460,000	5.9
1958	25,360,000	6.0
1959	26,350,000	6.1
1960	30,100,000	5.8
1961	31,325,000	5.9
1962	32,170,000	6.2

Note: Rate-of-return figures prior to 1952 are not available. The Crawley Development Corporation's assets were transferred to the Commission for the New Towns on 1.4.62, and the Corporation was dissolved on 5.8.62.

Source: Annual *Reports* of the Crawley Development Corporation (*Parliamentary Papers*, 1952–53, xv; 1953–54, xvii; 1955–56, xxv; 1956–57, xvii; 1957–58, xvi; 1958–59, xviii; 1959–60, xix; 1961–62, xix).

1955, and from 1948 to 1955 prime shop yields were approximately 5.5 percent, prime office yields 6 to 7 percent.[53]

This evidence, while very indirect, is consistent with the idea that by the mid-1950s the Treasury was forming positive expectations about the future financial success of New Towns and seeking to engage in town center development itself through the NTDCs. Possibilities of creating and appropriating development gain (after a sufficient holding period) were becoming increasingly apparent. These arguments might leave one wondering why the state is not *always* active in property development, and why it would ever seek to involve private developers.

Attitudes of the NTDCs and MHLG provide insight on this point. In the 1950s some NTDCs showed more interest in private development than the Treasury, again illustrating divisions within the state. While both Treasury and MHLG officials apparently thought the NTDCs should function as simple extensions of the central state, the NTDCs did not always see their interests as identical. This came out clearly in a running dispute over the terms on which government departments should acquire land from NTDCs, and more importantly over the terms on which NTDCs could borrow from the Treasury. When interest rates rose and NTDCs sought to alter the 60-year rule on borrowing to allow shorter-term loans, the Treasury argued that "the Corporations are, for all financial purposes, only the Government under a different hat. The interests of Exchequer must therefore be uppermost." Added in the margin of the Treasury's note was the comment (probably by Sharp): "Well of course. But the interests of the N.T.C.s *are* the interest of the Treasury."[54]

Where NTDCs showed greater interest in private development, it was partly because they had proved able to capture a part of the development gain by negotiating leases with "escalator clauses" providing for

[53] *Reports of the Development Corporations for the Period Ended 31st March, 1954* (P.P. 1953–54, xvii), p. 52; Sidney Pollard, *The Development of the British Economy: Third Edition, 1914-1980* (London, 1983), p. 410; Hedley Smyth, *Property Companies and the Construction Industry in Britain* (Cambridge, 1985), pp. 135–36. The Wilson Committee, which decided the form of accounts, argued that New Town development should be treated as an integrated whole and that the measure of success should be the total value created. Its immediate aim was to avoid pressure to reduce rents on profitable accounts, instead allowing commercial and industrial development to subsidize housing. See PRO T 227/146, "Report of the Committee on Form of Annual Accounts and other Related Matters [Wilson Report]," 5.10.51; PRO T 233/763, R. H. Wilson to Sir Wilfred Eady (Treasury), 31.1.52; Ray Thomas, "The 1972 Housing Finance Act and the Demise of the New Town and Local Authority Housing Programmes," *Urban Law and Policy*, 5 (June 1982), pp. 107–27.

[54] PRO HLG 90/354, "Capital for New Towns," n.d. but marked "Note handed to me by Sir Herbert Brittain," 6.6.56. See also Crossman's comments on Sharp and the centrally controlled relationship she sought between NTDCs and the Ministry of Housing, in Richard Crossman, *The Diaries of a Cabinet Minister*, vol. 1: *Minister of Housing, 1964–66* (London, 1975), pp. 66, 127, 463–64.

rising rents as development proceeded.[55] A variety of development methods was thought to secure a better "balance" in the towns, and some NTDCs believed that private development would help to bring economic stability. Insurance companies or other developers would be active agents on the demand side as well as the supply side, improving prospects for the town center as a whole. They would

> take all the risks of letting upper floors (no hypothetical problem, as we all know). Indeed, *because* their capital is involved, . . . [they] will see to it that somehow, on some terms, their associates, satellites, professional advisers and others take tenancies under them.[56]

Finally, some clients, such as well-known multiple stores, were unwilling to take NTDC-built premises for rack rents, and in early stages of development the ground-rent option could be an important inducement to private enterprise in general.

The most interesting point, however, concerns the political contradictions of the state acting as a developer-capitalist. Because the state can become an arena for explicit negotiation of the distribution of surplus, it may do better getting its cut of surplus through a mediating institution. The January 1956 letter from MHLG to the Treasury put the point succinctly: "If times turn hard, a tough commercial company will be able to collect its rents more easily than a public corporation which is exposed to political pressure. Here again private investment reduces the risk to public funds."[57] This was also one of the issues in later discussions of transfer of New Town assets to local authorities. Some argued that local authorities would come under strong political pressure to set low rents.

CONCLUSION

Development gain thus helps to explain Treasury officials' enthusiasm in 1955 for New Town center building. The Treasury had not initially sought opportunities to create development gain. In fact, part of what makes this case so striking is that, unlike governments elsewhere, the British state does not have much of a tradition of developmental

[55] PRO HLG 90/344, John H. West (Chief Estates Officer, Basildon Development Corporation) to D. L. Syme (MHLG), 10.8.56.

[56] PRO HLG 90/344, John H. West (Chief Estates Officer, Basildon) to J. Rogerson (MHLG), 17.8.55. Property development may provide unique opportunities for capitalists to create or control the market they then will serve. Marc Weiss, in *The Rise of the Community Builders: The American Real Estate Industry and Urban Land Planning* (New York, 1987), provides a very interesting account of how large developers in the United States actively shaped demand for their product, and sought to maintain its value. Practices they used, such as deed restrictions imposed on lot and home purchasers, later were incorporated into planning legislation. Restrictions sought by private developers included building and yard standards, specification of house paint colors, and non-Caucasian racial exclusion.

[57] PRO HLG 90/344, F. L. Edwards (MHLG) to F. F. Turnbull (Treasury), 2.1.56.

investment, for example in transportation or other infrastructure.[58] But once the original, largely political, decision to create New Towns had been made, the Treasury clearly recognized that it could capture a unique type of surplus through commercial and industrial building, and thereby cover unremunerative spending on infrastructure (an opportunity not equally available to the central state in cases of local authority borrowing from central funds for similar infrastructure in existing towns). The inescapably historical character of development gain, and the role of expectations in property development, meant that reaping this gain required holding the assets long enough for the actual process of settlement and development to proceed. Efforts were made to hasten the process by continuing to fund New Towns despite limitations on other public spending in the fall of 1955.

While Treasury officials wanted to maximize the central government's return by having NTDCs do commercial and industrial building themselves, divisions within the state meant that their wishes could not be unilaterally imposed. NTDCs sought at least some involvement of private capital, and were supported by Sharp and the New Towns division of the MHLG. In sharp contrast to cases where Treasury control could easily be exercised to cut spending, here Treasury officials to some extent were "pushing on a string" and faced resistance from other bodies of government that would be directly responsible for the public investments. The policy outcome—a fluctuating mix of private and public investment in New Town centers—reflects these divisions.

The relationship of development gain to other economic categories such as profit, wages, and rent requires further clarification. Further research is also needed into the institutions that create and appropriate development gain, including private firms, governmental and quasi-governmental bodies, and various forms of "public-private partnership." Even when the state is actively involved in property development, it may not seek to retain most of the development gain. An interesting counterexample is provided by the current London Docklands case. The Thatcher government, while actively intervening in the development process, appears to be seeking to leave as much of the development gain as possible for the private sector—for example, by preparing sites and disposing of them at low prices to developers.

Part of what may account for this difference of the Docklands case from New Town development in the 1950s is the strength and organization of the property industry as a sector of capital. In the 1950s it was still quite new, and perhaps not yet able to use the state for its own ends. By the 1980s the number of property companies had increased dramatically, powerful institutional investors had moved into the field, and

[58] On developmental investment in the U.S. case, see Carter Goodrich, *Government Promotion of American Canals and Railroads, 1800–1890* (New York, 1960).

experience in effectively lobbying the state had been acquired (for example, in the debate in the 1970s over commercial rent control).

The state's own priorities, however, may well be the most important factor. The Thatcher government's desire to limit public involvement in the economy also led to a drive to dispose of remaining New Town assets, which may in some cases have resulted in premature sales and a failure to capture as much development gain as possible for the state.[59] The appropriate conclusion is that the mere existence of development gain does not necessarily ensure that the state will either seek or be able to appropriate it. To know that, one must examine details of history and institutions.

[59] Turok, "Public Investment and Privatisation in the New Towns"; National Audit Office, *Department of the Environment: Disposal of New Town Assets*, p. 8.

The Mule in Southern Agriculture: A Requiem

MARTIN A. GARRETT, JR.

Inquiries into the question of why the use of mules historically dominated that of horses in southern agricultural production have essentially concluded that the southerner preferred the mule while the northerner did not. This notion probably stems from the work of Robert Lamb, whose primary purpose was to document the extent to which the mule was used in the South between 1850 and 1950.[1] From the simple observation that the mule was used more extensively in the South, Lamb concluded: "The use of the mule in the South, eventually to the virtual exclusion of all other draft animals, is an example of cultural preference . . . . another cultural trait that reinforced the identity of the South."[2] Eugene Genovese argued that the antebellum use of the mule and ox instead of the faster horse was another example of retarding technological change in southern agriculture and occurred because they could withstand harsh treatment by slaves better than horses.[3] More recently Jack Kirby stated, "[it is] a wonderful, generations-long mules-versus-horses debate, which reveals so much of southerners' old rural culture and their powerful affection for mules."[4]

Many southerners did have a strong affection for the mule, but it was not this or a cultural trait that resulted in the choice of the mule. A better argument might be that the lack of mules in the North was attributable to the preponderance of farmers from Scandinavian countries who showed a marked preference for the horse.[5] Robert Jones went further in stating that most of the people north of southern portions of Illinois, Indiana, and Ohio had "a contempt for mules as profound as it was unreasoning."[6]

The purpose here is to demonstrate that the use of the mule has an economic explanation resulting from its superior draft abilities in the production of row crops in the South, especially cotton. The formal test of the hypothesis is accomplished with cross-section regression analysis using county data for 19 selected nonsouthern and southern states.

I. DRAFT ABILITIES OF THE HORSE AND MULE: A COMPARISON

Two characteristics of the mule often alluded to—its longevity relative to the horse and its ability to live and work on smaller rations—probably have been overrated. Experiments in Ohio and Illinois demonstrated that under comparable work loads mules

The Journal of Economic History, Vol. L, No. 4 (Dec. 1990). ISSN 0022-0507.

Martin A. Garrett, Jr. is Professor of Economics, College of William and Mary, Williamsburg, VA 23185.

The author wishes to thank Carl Moody for econometric assistance, and a referee and the editor of this JOURNAL for helpful comments and suggestions.

[1] Robert B. Lamb, *The Mule in Southern Agriculture* (Berkeley, 1963).

[2] Ibid., pp. 26, 83.

[3] Eugene Genovese, *The Political Economy of Slavery: Studies in the Economy and Society of the Slave South* (New York, 1963), p. 107.

[4] Jack T. Kirby, *Rural Worlds Lost: the American South, 1920–1960* (Baton Rouge, 1987), p. 198.

[5] See, for example, Fred A. Shannon, *The Farmers Last Frontier: Agriculture, 1860–1897* (New York, 1945), pp. 48–50; and Robert W. Howard, *The Horse in America* (Chicago, 1965), p. 218.

[6] Robert L. Jones, "The Horse and Mule Industry in Ohio to 1865," *Mississippi Valley Historical Review*, 33 (June 1946), p. 83.

and horses need feed in proportion to their weight.[7] It has been stated the mule possesses an "appetite which anything satisfies" and can work with coarser, less expensive rations.[8] However, as G. E. Wentworth rightly observed: "It is probably true that the mule is more cheaply maintained but the mule has not been consulted."[9]

The notion of the longevity of the mule pervades the literature. As editor of *American Farmer*, John Skinner maintained that the probable work life of a mule was 30 years while James Hood suggested that "the life of the mule is twice the life of the horse which is twelve years."[10] Examples of mules living beyond 25 to 30 years have long been reported.[11] D. W. Chittenden reported the average work life of the horse to be roughly 12 to 15 years, while John Moore reported it to be 12 years and that of the mule to be 18 years.[12]

The virtues of horses and mules as draft animals can, however, be enumerated. The horse, always somewhat larger, can pull a heavier load in a short burst, while the mule is agile and its gait more steady in the draft. Although under comparable work conditions the horse and the mule require feed in proportion to their weight, the mule will eat and drink only what it considers necessary. Conversely, the horse will eat and drink until it becomes sick; hence, it must be rationed for continued work. The mule is hardier, less prone to disease, and withstands warm climates better.[13] It takes longer to tire and when fatigued will recover more quickly.[14] It is also less nervous and not as excitable as the horse, hence using less energy under stress and unkind or unskilled handling.[15] The mule is more easily trained to respond to voice commands, making it easier to maneuver in draft work, especially in maintaining the line in row crops. The innate characteristic of the mule to resent injury is a major virtue, although it is probably also responsible for cantankerous acts and may explain the mule's inclination to set the

[7] J. A. Burkhart, "The Reluctant Mule," *Farm Quarterly*, 5 (Sept. 1950), pp. 30–33; and William Johnson, "How to Cope with Mules," *Country Gentlemen*, 87 (Dec. 16, 1922), p. 9.

[8] Alfred G. Smith, "Our Migratory Mules," *Country Gentlemen*, 88 (Feb. 17, 1923), p. 9.

[9] G. E. Wentworth, *Breeders Gazette*, 73 (May 9, 1918), p. 977.

[10] John Skinner, "Address to the Agricultural Society of Maryland," *American Farmer*, 2 (Oct. 20, 1820), p. 239; and James Hood, "The Mule," *American Farmer*, 12 (Apr. 16, 1830), p. 33, quoted in Lamb, *The Mule in Southern Agriculture*, p. 27.

[11] J. L. Jones, "The Mule," U.S. Bureau of Animal Industry, *Annual Report, 8th and 9th, 1891–1892* (Washington, DC, 1893), quoted in "In Praise of Mules," *Living Age*, 291 (Dec. 1916), p. 429.

[12] D. W. Chittenden, "Horses and Mules for Farm Power," *Breeders Gazette*, 84 (June 17, 1923), p. 725; and John H. Moore, *The Emergence of the Cotton Kingdom in the Old Southwest* (Baton Rouge, 1988), pp. 51–52. While the average work life of the mule may have exceeded that of the horse, it has been reported that under a heavy work regime in the Mississippi Delta around the turn of the century, mules worked from six to eight years. Smith, "Our Migratory Mules," p. 9. I am not aware of data on the horse under a heavy work regime.

[13] Although there are no data on the relative incidence of disease between horses and mules in southern agriculture, during World War I the ratio of illness in horses to mules was six to one. See Alexander G. Fraser, "The Draft Mule in the Field in Mexico," *American Veterinary Medical Association Journal*, 52 (Dec. 1917), pp. 357–61. For a discussion of working mule behavior on warm days, see "Marvin Wolfe-Mules," *Loblolly*, 5 (Winter 1977), pp. 49–51. Both of these notions are corroborated by Moore, *The Emergence of the Cotton Kingdom*, pp. 51–52; and John F. Olson, "The Occupational Structure of Plantation Slave Labor in the Late Antebellum Era" (Ph.D. diss., University of Rochester, 1983), p. 70.

[14] Olson, "The Occupational Structure," p. 70.

[15] It may be this characteristic that has led several commentators to conclude that mules were preferred to horses in the slave South because horses could not bear the treatment they received from slaves. There are many similar statements in southern literature. For example, see Frederick Law Olmsted, *A Journey in the Seaboard Slave States in the Years 1853–54, with Remarks on Their Economy* (New York, 1904), p. 51; and Lewis C. Gray, *History of Agriculture in the United States to 1860* (Gloucester, 1958), pp. 851–52.

work pace despite encouragement from the driver.[16] This characteristic becomes especially important in warm climates where the horse will work itself to death for the driver, whereas the mule will slow the work pace during warm days.[17]

There are, however, certain advantages to the horse for draft power. First, it is slightly less expensive to rear. Although the adult mule is less prone to disease, during infancy the mule colt is more susceptible to injury and sickness than the horse, and the mating of the mare and the jack produces a lower fertility rate than does the mare and the stallion. Another advantage is that teamsters showed a marked preference for the horse, which may have been attributable to the belief that the feet of the horse withstood the pounding on the stone pavements of city streets better than the mule's did or that the horse was better suited to stops and starts with heavy loads.[18] It thus provided the northern farmer with a market for the horse.[19]

All things considered, it would appear that the patience, endurance, and work habits of the mule compared with the horse would have made it the preferred draft animal for farm work. The predominant use of the mule in the South was attributable to its virtues in the production of row crops, primarily cotton and tobacco, rather than to a southern cultural preference.

II. EMPIRICAL EVIDENCE

Between 1850 and 1910 mules increased in the border states from 229,000 to 1,042,000, reflecting a 3.5-fold increase, while in the cotton South they increased from 278,000 to 2,242,000, a sevenfold increase.[20] By 1910 horses exceeded mules in all southern states by a ratio of 1.3 to one, but in the states of the cotton South mules exceeded horses by the same ratio.[21] By comparison, in the four midwestern states

[16] J. T. Warder, "Mule Raising," in U.S. Patent Office, *Report of the Commissioner of Agriculture for the Year 1863*, 38th Cong., 1st sess., H. Ex. Doc. 91, serial no. 1196 (Washington, DC, 1864), p. 185; and G. K. Renner, "The Mule in Southern Agriculture 1821–1950," *Missouri Historical Review*, 74 (July 1980), p. 443.

[17] There is an additional economic factor suggesting the mule's superior ability to perform draft work compared with the horse. Although there was some fluctuation over time, the price of a mule was always 10 to 15 percent higher than that of a draft horse in both the North and South. Not unexpectedly, the price of mules varied with cotton prices. John Moore reported that in 1849 plow horses from Kentucky and Tennessee cost $100 while the price of a mule ranged from $120 to $150. Moore, *The Emergence of the Cotton Kingdom*, pp. 51–52. For a comparison of the price of mules from 1860 to 1920, see Gavin Wright, *Old South, New South: Revolutions in the Southern Economy Since the Civil War* (New York, 1986), p. 120; and for a comparison of the price of mules with horses and cotton from 1870 to 1940, see Lamb, *The Mule in Southern Agriculture*, p. 24.

[18] Thomas N. Carver, *Principles of Rural Economics* (Boston, 1932), p. 275.

[19] In southern cities horses outnumbered mules approximately four to one. See U.S. Bureau of the Census, *Thirteenth Census of the United States, 1910*, vols. 6–7, *Agriculture* (Washington, DC, 1912–1914).

[20] Lamb, *The Mule in Southern Agriculture*, tables 2, 3, 4.

[21] Data on the stock of draft animals are available from the *Census of Agriculture, 1910*. This census is especially appropriate: it precedes the introduction of mechanized draft power, and the crop year was typical of southern agricultural production for over a century. Data were obtained for the following states: the cotton South of Alabama, Arkansas, Georgia, Louisiana, Mississippi, North Carolina, Oklahoma, South Carolina, Tennessee, and Texas; and the southern border states of Florida, Kentucky, West Virginia, and Virginia. Missouri is also included because of its importance as a mule-raising state. In addition, data were obtained for four agricultural midwestern states including Illinois, Indiana, Iowa, and Kansas. These states are included in order to have a basis of comparison for the ratio of mules to horses on farms for nonsouthern states. The data included all counties within each state with the exception of those that produced less than $250,000 in agricultural output and those with more mules in cities than on farms. The data include 88

horses on farms exceeded mules by a ratio of nine to one. Mules, however, were not uniformly used as draft animals throughout the South. For example, in counties in Florida and Virginia where cotton or tobacco was not an important crop, horses far exceeded mules. Throughout West Virginia, a state that produced no cotton and only a small quantity of tobacco, in 1910 there were only 8,602 mules compared with 167,117 horses. The draft characteristics of the mule were obviously known to Missouri farmers, yet mules exceeded horses in only four counties in 1910.[22] In two of these, Dunklin and Pemiscost, the value of cotton exceeded that of all other farm products, and a significant amount of cotton was produced in a third, New Madrid County. For the state as a whole, horses on farms exceeded mules three to one.

Throughout the South, however, wherever cotton was the dominant crop, mules on farms usually exceeded horses, suggesting a strong relationship between the use of mules and cotton production.[23] It is also known that mules were used widely in tobacco production, and understandably so. The agility of the mule made it less prone to step on young plants, and since it was easier to train to voice commands, it was easier to keep in line. Moreover, the efficiency of the mule in row cultivation was more important in the production of cotton and tobacco, especially cotton. Cotton was a less land-intensive crop than many other row crops. Prior to the introduction of hybrid corn seed, for example, it was necessary to plant corn rows four feet apart in order for corn ears to fully mature. Cotton rows were only two and one-half to three and one-half feet apart, hence the agility of the mule took on greater significance.[24] These characteristics, especially when combined with the ability of the mule to perform better in warm climates, would cause the mule to be the preferred draft animal in row crop production in the South.

In addition, the ratio of mules to horses should depend upon the ratio of tenant farms to owner-operated farms. Share contracts varied significantly among tenants, but one common element was that the landowner normally furnished the draft power.[25] Since the landowner wanted the tenant to maximize the output of the row crops, it is reasonable to assume that he supplied the most efficient draft animal for that purpose.

---

percent of all counties in the 19 states, and approximately one-half of those excluded are Texas counties that produced less than $250,000 in agricultural output.

[22] By 1890 the mule-raising industry was concentrated in Missouri. Yet, even in the 10 counties in the state that raised the largest number of mules, horses outnumbered mules two to one. It is thus apparent that most Missouri farmers raised mules for cash income, not for draft work. Renner, in "The Mule in Missouri Agriculture 1821–1950," p. 448, estimated that 40 percent of Missouri farmers raised mules solely for cash income.

[23] Although cotton was a major cash crop in the South, the proportion of improved acres devoted to cotton was never very large. For example, in 1910 in the cotton states alone, only 27 percent of the 114.8 million acres of improved farm land was devoted to cotton. Regression analysis, however, clearly suggests the influence of cotton and the ratio of share tenants on the use of mules in the South. John Moore and John Olson have noted the relationship between mules and cotton, and Robert Lamb has demonstrated a correlation between mules and cotton and mules and sharecroppers, although the correlation did not strike him as being important. See Moore, *The Emergence of the Cotton Kingdom*, pp. 51–52; Olson, "The Occupational Structure," pp. 72–73; and Lamb, *The Mule in Southern Agriculture*, pp. 79–80.

[24] It is interesting to note that after the passage of the Agriculture Adjustment Act in the spring of 1933 and farmers were required to plow up a portion of their crop, "It was said that where single-mule plows were used, farmers had a difficult time getting the animals to walk on the row. A *New York Times* editor wrote that mules were being punished 'for refusing to trample down the stalks' which they had been 'taught to revere'." Gilbert C. Fite, *Cotton Fields No More: Southern Agriculture 1865–1980* (Lexington, 1984), p. 130.

[25] For examples of the variety of contracts between landowners and share tenants, see Joseph D. Reid Jr., "Sharecropping As An Undesirable Market Response: The Post-Bellum South," this JOURNAL, 33 (Mar. 1973), pp. 106–30.

If the mule were more efficient in cotton and tobacco production, it would have been the dominant draft animal used on tenant farms. Owner-operated farms also employed mules for draft work but also used horses for transportation and as a consumption good, so they would have a lower ratio of mules to horses. Thus, the lower the share of tenant farms in a county, the lower would be the average ratio of mules to horses.[26]

These hypotheses can be statistically tested using county-level data on the ratio of mules to horses on farms as the dependent variable and as the independent variables: the cotton share of improved farm acres, the tobacco share of improved farm acres, improved acres per farm, and the ratio of share tenants to owner-operated farms. Improved acres per farm is included, in absolute values, to determine the existence of economies of scale. Virtually identical results are obtained if this variable is omitted.

The results presented in Table 1 in log form are for the states normally included in the definition of the South plus Missouri, Oklahoma, and Texas.[27] Missouri was the major mule-raising state in 1910 and cotton was produced in three counties, while Oklahoma and Texas produced significant amounts of cotton.[28] For all southern states plus Missouri, the coefficient for the cotton share of improved acres is positive and highly significant and indicates that a 1 percent increase in the cotton share is associated with a 0.73 percent increase in the ratio of mules to horses. The coefficient for the ratio of tenants to owner-operated farms is also highly significant.[29] In a regression that includes only the cotton states, the coefficient of the cotton acreage share variable is 0.81 while that for the tenant variable is 0.21, and both are highly significant.[30] The results of this analysis are thus consistent with the hypothesis that the two most important factors in determining the use of the mule throughout the South as a draft animal were the proportion of cotton acres per county relative to improved farm land acres and the ratio of tenants to owner-operated farms.[31]

It might be argued that these significantly positive coefficients simply reflect a southern preference for the mule, since cotton and tobacco are predominantly southern

[26] There is an interesting anomaly in the use of the mule by nonsoutherners. By the time of the American Revolution, the Pennsylvania Germans had developed the Conestoga, the only widely known native draft horse produced in America. The breed died out around 1850, which is interesting and of great regret because in some ways it was superior to any of the imported draft animals. See James Westfall Thompson, "A History of Livestock Raising in the U.S.: 1607–1860," U.S. Bureau of Agricultural Economics, *Agricultural History Series*, no. 5 (Nov. 1942), p. 51. It is also interesting that the Amish-Mennonites who developed the breed in eastern Pennsylvania replaced the Conestoga with the mule. By 1910 the proportion of mules to horses on farms in the southeastern Pennsylvania counties with relatively large populations of Amish-Mennonite families ranged between 19 and 33 percent, while in abutting counties with small numbers of families of German descent the proportion ranged from 2.5 to 6.5 percent. Moreover, crop mix within the region could not account for the disparity in the ratios. See John A. Hostetler, *Amish Society* (Baltimore, 1980), p. 131.

[27] The inclusion of all 19 states produces larger coefficients and each coefficient is significant at the 0.0001 level with the correct sign.

[28] The exclusion of these three states from the regression produces almost identical results.

[29] Examination of the regression's residuals indicated the possibility of heteroskedasticity associated with only one variable, the ratio of share tenants to owner-operated farms. Application of generalized least squares to adjust for this yielded results that were essentially the same.

[30] The adjusted R^2 equals 0.6269 with N equal to 1,204. The omitted state dummy is Missouri.

[31] Although it is known that the mule was used widely in tobacco production, the regression analysis does not substantiate the hypothesis. The most probable explanation is that tobacco acreage was always a very small proportion of cultivated acreage on farms, and because horses were used for transportation as well as a consumption good, the proportion of mules to horses on tobacco farms will not be large enough to have a significant sign. In addition, Olson, in "The Occupational Structure," p. 107, found that smaller farming units were less likely to have mules and had fewer mules than horses on average.

TABLE 1
REGRESSION RESULTS

Variable	Coefficient	*T*-Ratio	Probability Value
Intercept	0.0587	0.481	0.6309
Ratio of Share Tenants to Owner-Operated Farms	0.2333	7.354	0.0001
Improved Acres Per Farm	0.0508	1.914	0.0559
Cotton Share of Improved Farm Acres	0.7365	7.366	0.0001
Tobacco Share of Improved Farm Acres	−0.4119	−0.701	0.4834
STATE DUMMY VARIABLES			
Alabama	0.0612	10.213	0.0001
Arkansas	0.0202	3.716	0.0002
Florida	0.0157	2.129	0.0334
Georgia	0.0789	15.521	0.0001
Kentucky	0.1197	2.607	0.0092
Louisiana	0.0963	1.651	0.0991
Mississippi	0.1467	2.512	0.0121
North Carolina	0.4126	7.925	0.0001
Oklahoma	−0.1787	−3.681	0.0002
South Carolina	0.5936	9.007	0.0001
Tennessee	0.2797	5.881	0.0001
Texas	−0.1039	−2.134	0.0331
Virginia	−0.1003	−2.146	0.0320
West Virginia	−0.2453	−4.238	0.0001

Source: U.S. Bureau of the Census, *Thirteenth Census of the United States, 1910*, vols. 6–7, *Agriculture* (Washington, DC, 1912–1914).

crops. That is, they may reflect a spurious correlation between cotton and tobacco production and the use of the mule. Yet, the direction of causality seems clear. Each of the independent variables is exogenous with respect to the ratio of mules to horses on farms. The use of mules did not cause cotton or tobacco to be produced. These crops would have been produced with substitute draft power.

Re-estimating Crop Yields from Probate Inventories: A Comment

MARK OVERTON

Robert C. Allen recently put forward some modifications and extensions to my method of estimating crop yields from probate inventories in early modern England, which was originally published in this JOURNAL some 11 years ago.[1] His developments represent a considerable improvement on my original method and have been incorporated in some re-estimates of grain yields for Norfolk and Suffolk from 1585 to 1735. While I have no quarrel with Allen's general argument, some aspects of his particular application of it to Oxfordshire inventories are open to question. Most importantly, his empirical findings of changes in Oxfordshire yields are based on such slender evidence as to fail to substantiate his conclusion that "most of the yield increase in early modern England occurred in the seventeenth century rather than the eighteenth."[2] The reworking of my material for East Anglia suggests the opposite.

My initial assumption in calculating yields was that inventory appraisers valued standing grain according to its future price and expected yield. Thus

$$v = py \tag{1}$$

where v is the valuation of standing grain per acre; p, its post-harvest price in bushels; and y, yield in bushels per acre.[3]

Allen's first criticism of my method was that I made no allowance for valuations of standing grain based on costs of production rather than on expected prices and yields. In fact, I drew attention to this problem and made every effort to exclude such cost-of-production valuations from my calculations. These are best avoided by using only valuations in inventories from June onward, when appraisers would be able to estimate yields of growing crops.[4] Allen preferred to discard acreage valuations that would produce yields of less than five bushels per acre on the assumption that they represent cost-of-production valuations. This is a dangerous assumption, for yields on some farms in some years could well have sunk to such levels. By excluding them Allen was building an upward bias into his sample of yields.[5]

His second criticism was that inventory appraisers would have deducted the costs of harvesting the grain from their valuations of standing corn and would also have made an allowance for tithes, so that the valuations of standing grain were calculated by them according the formula

$$v = 0.9\,(py - ty - c) - r \tag{2}$$

The Journal of Economic History, Vol. L, No. 4 (Dec. 1990). ISSN 0022-0507.

The author is Lecturer in Geography at the University of Newcastle upon Tyne, Newcastle upon Tyne NE1 7RU, United Kingdom.

I would like to thank Bob Allen, Paul Glennie, and Peter Lindert for the discussions I have had with them on the topic of this comment.

[1] Robert C. Allen, "Inferring Yields from Probate Inventories," this JOURNAL, 48 (Mar. 1988), pp. 117–25; Mark Overton, "Estimating Crop Yields from Probate Inventories: An Example from East Anglia, 1585–1735," this JOURNAL, 39 (June 1979), pp. 363–78. My method has been used by Paul Glennie, "Continuity and Change in Hertfordshire Agriculture, 1550–1700: II—Crop Yields and their Determinants," *Agricultural History Review*, 36 (1988) pp. 145–61.

[2] Allen, "Inferring Yields," p. 117.

[3] This is Allen's notation, which differs from that in my original article.

[4] Overton, "Estimating Crop Yields," pp. 370, 374.

[5] This point is treated in more detail by Paul Glennie, "Measuring Crop Yields in Early Modern England," in Bruce Campbell and Mark Overton, eds., *Land, Labour and Livestock: Historical Studies in European Agricultural Productivity* (Manchester, 1991).

TABLE 1
GROSS YIELDS OF WHEAT, RYE, BARLEY, AND OATS IN NORFOLK AND SUFFOLK
(bushels per acre)

	Wheat		Rye		Barley		Oats	
Years	Yield	Number of Inventories	Yield	Number of Inventories	Yield	Number of Inventories	Yield	Number of Inventories
1587–1599	11.4	42	11.4	31	12.0	73	16.3	22
1628–1640	14.5	37	11.1	18	13.0	69	21.7	24
1660–1679	14.5	40	13.8	13	14.6	55	19.4	4
1680–1709	15.9	26	8.6	5	16.1	33	16.8	10
1710–1735	19.2	70	13.8	13	20.8	75	22.6	33
1660–1699	15.3	54	13.5	14	15.1	70	17.2	5
1700–1735	18.5	82	12.5	17	20.2	93	22.1	42

Source: See the text.

where t is the cost of threshing and dressing the grain; c, carting costs; and r, reaping, binding, and stacking costs. The assumption that these costs were considered by appraisers is probably correct, although they were ignored in my original article.[6] The intention of that article, however, was to indicate the general *trends* in grain yields rather than their absolute levels, which is why graphs of grain yields were published in preference to actual figures. Allen's imaginative extension of my original method has certainly opened the door to more accurate estimates of yields per acre, which may be compared with those of other sources both before and after the period covered by probate inventories. Moreover, Allen's method also improves on mine in allowing individual farm yields to be calculated, thus enabling some of the factors influencing yields to be investigated.[7]

Unfortunately, when he applied his new methods to Oxfordshire inventories Allen was unable to use post-harvest prices derived from the inventories themselves. The alternative is an independent grain price series, and the principal one for the period is based on the prices paid for grain by institutions in southern England. There are two problems in using these prices (aside from questions of accuracy or representativeness). First, allowance should be made for the cost of transporting grain from the farm to the market and from the market to the institutional consumers. Second, not all grain standing in the fields and valued by the appraisers would have been of marketable quality. Appraisers sometimes describe the grain they value, and it is clear that some would not be of sufficient quality to market for human consumption. If this is the case, grains of different quality are being related in the equations. Allen avoided these problems by using estimates of inventory barn prices predicted by a regression equation linking barn prices with wholesale prices. Obviously, when they are available, the actual barn prices are to be preferred.

Whether the actual or predicted prices are used, the allowance for threshing and dressing costs should be dropped from equation 2. Harvested grain stored in barns is never referred to as "dressed" by inventory appraisers, and it is usually unthreshed,

[6] A correction factor for my original estimates that takes account of these costs is in Mark Overton, "Agricultural Productivity in Eighteenth-Century England: Some Further Speculations," *Economic History Review*, 2nd series, 37 (May 1984), p. 250, fn. 37.

[7] This I developed in Mark Overton, "The Determinants of Crop Yields in Early Modern England," in Campbell and Overton, eds., *Land, Labour and Livestock*.

TABLE 2
COSTS USED IN YIELD CALCULATIONS

	Reaping or Mowing, Binding, and Stacking (shillings per acre)			
	Wheat	Rye	Barley	Oats
1587–1599	3.5	3.5	1.6	1.6
1628–1740	5.0	5.0	2.0	2.0

Carting Costs (shillings per acre)	
1587–1599	1.0
1628–1740	1.5

Sources: P. J. Bowden, "Agricultural Prices, Farm Profits, and Rents," in J. Thirsk, ed., *The Agrarian History of England and Wales*. Vol. 4: *1500–1640* (Cambridge, 1967), p. 662; P. J. Bowden, "Agricultural Prices, Wages, Farm Profits and Rents," in J. Thirsk, ed., *The Agrarian History of England and Wales*, Vol. 5 (Cambridge, 1985), pp. 88–89; University of Reading Library Farm Accounts, NORF 14/1 for 1685–98; Paul Brassley, Anthony Lambert, and Philip Saunders, eds., *Accounts of the Reverend John Crakanthorp of Fowlmere 1682–1710*, Cambridgeshire Records Society, Vol. 8 (Cambridge, 1988); G. E. Fussell, ed., *Robert Loder's Farm Accounts 1610–1620*, Camden Society, 3rd series, 53 (1936).

especially if recorded before December. Thus the equation used to re-estimate Norfolk and Suffolk yields is

$$y = \frac{0.9c + r + v}{0.9p_i} \tag{3}$$

where p_i are prices of harvested, unthreshed grain recorded in inventories from October to December.

The estimates for costs depend on wage rates for the particular period and place for which estimates of yields are being made. Allen extrapolated backward from the early nineteenth century to derive his cost estimates (which unfortunately were not reproduced in his article), but it is more satisfactory to use contemporary figures if they survive.

Table 1 gives the new estimates of yields for wheat, rye, barley, and oats for Norfolk and Suffolk. These were calculated using equation 3, excluding inventories with cost-of-production valuations, and with the contemporary estimates of costs shown in Table 2. These results present a rather different picture from Allen's findings for Oxfordshire. Wheat yields rose by 18 percent from the 1590s to the decade before the Civil War, rose by 8 percent for the period from 1660 to 1699, and then jumped by 18 percent in the early eighteenth century. Barley yields rose by only 2 percent from the 1590s to the 1630s; they then climbed by 15 percent for the period from 1660 to 1699, but for the first 35 years of the eighteenth century had grown by 28 percent. It is interesting to note that a comparison of Norfolk yields for the early modern period with a large sample of yields derived from manorial accounts for the period from 1250 to 1450 indicates that early modern yields did not rise significantly above medieval levels until the early eighteenth century.[8] By the turn of the nineteenth century wheat yields for

[8] These figures are reproduced in Bruce M. S. Campbell, "Land, Labour, Livestock and Productivity Trends in English Seignorial Agriculture, 1208–1450," in Campbell and Overton, eds., *Land, Labour and Livestock*, and are the subject of a separate article: Bruce Campbell and Mark Overton, "Five Centuries of Farming: Norfolk Agriculture, 1250–1750," in preparation.

TABLE 3
WHEAT AND BARLEY YIELDS IN NORFOLK AND SUFFOLK
(bushels per acre for runs of complete harvest years for wheat)

	Wheat			Barley		
Years	Yield	Number of Years	Number of Inventories	Yield	Number of Years	Number of Inventories
1587–1593	13.9	7	38	13.9	7	53
1628–1637	14.0	10	35	12.5	10	65
1665–1669	16.3	5	15	12.9	3	10
1672–1678	13.5	7	21	15.6	6	22
1685–1690	17.7	5	11	18.5	4	9
1709–1716	15.3	8	35	16.4	7	44
1721–1725	19.5	5	22	22.3	5	21
1727–1732	20.2	6	13	23.3	5	11

Source: See the text.

Norfolk and Suffolk were estimated at between 20 and 24 bushels per acre and barley yields at between 28 and 32.[9] Wheat yields had already reached 19 bushels per acre by the early 1720s (Table 3), while barley yields were around 22 bushels (Table 4).

It would, however, be unwise to make any comparison between Allen's results for Oxfordshire and these new figures for East Anglia. The Oxfordshire yields have an upward bias in their calculation because they unnecessarily allow for threshing costs (which reduces the denominator in equation 3) and have a cut-off of five bushels per acre in an attempt to avoid cost-of-production valuations. Furthermore, the actual cost estimates used differ, though this may be an accurate reflection of differences in labor costs between the two areas. But even allowing for differences in the method of calculation, the Oxfordshire figures are based on such a tiny sample of yields that they cannot be accepted as reflecting trends in average yields.

Allen's 25-year averages were based on between two and eight observations.[10] Thus for the late sixteenth century we are invited to accept that average yields for the county for a quarter of a century can be represented by the yields on two plots of land for two unspecified years. Even for the early eighteenth century an average for a 28-year period is based on only eight yield figures. Yields vary widely from season to season, from region to region, from farm to farm, and even from field to field on the same farm. At the very least, therefore, average yields for a period should give equal weight to each year. Those for Norfolk and Suffolk in Table 1 weight each harvest year equally and indicate the total number of yield figures on which the mean is based.

Unfortunately, there are still harvest years with no data for some of the period means. Tables 3 and 4 therefore give mean yields for only those runs of harvest years with no gaps. Although the resulting periodization is a little odd, the figures still suggest that it was in the early eighteenth century that yields rose most dramatically, not the seventeenth.

There is no doubt that Allen's contribution has revitalized attempts to estimate grain yields for early modern England. What is now needed is further examination of the basis on which inventory appraisers came to their valuations of standing grain. It is only through more detailed empirical research that the yield equations can be fine-tuned to

[9] Overton, "Estimating Crop Yields," p. 375.
[10] Allen, "Inferring Yields," p. 123, table 3.

TABLE 4
WHEAT AND BARLEY YIELDS IN NORFOLK AND SUFFOLK
(bushels per acre for runs of complete harvest years for barley)

	Wheat			Barley		
Years	Yield	Number of Years	Number of Inventories	Yield	Number of Years	Number of Inventories
1587–1593	13.8	7	38	13.9	7	53
1628–1639	14.5	11	37	13.0	12	69
1661–1664	13.5	2	4	14.5	5	18
1667–1670	17.0	3	12	12.6	4	12
1673–1682	15.4	7	20	15.0	10	31
1708–1711	14.8	3	10	15.3	4	19
1713–1716	15.6	4	24	17.2	4	26
1718–1731	19.5	12	40	23.1	14	42

Source: See the text.

produce even more reliable estimates, but even so they can only be of value when applied to an adequate number of inventories.[11]

[11] Probate inventories, probate accounts, and disputes over probate in the Church courts will be the basis of such further research.

Were Businessmen Afraid of FDR? A Comment on Mayer and Chatterji

ANTHONY PATRICK O'BRIEN

Thomas Mayer and Monojit Chatterji attempted to assess the validity of the political explanation for the retardation of investment spending during the mid-to-late 1930s.[1] They identified six political shocks of the period 1933 to 1938 that might have had a negative impact on investment spending.[2] They ran several autoregressions of the form:

$$X_t = X_{t-1} + X_{t-2} + X_{t-3} + S1 + S2 + S3 + S4 + S5 + S6 \quad (1)$$

where X equals one of six categories of investment spending and the S's are dummy variables representing the periods during which the political shocks were thought to have had their influence.

The test of the importance of the political shocks consisted of examining the t-statistics for the dummy variables. They found that none of the five negative shocks had a statistically significant (at the 1 percent level) effect on any of the six categories of investment spending. The only result consistent with the hypothesis was that the sole positive shock—the 1938 election—had a statistically significant effect on one category of investment spending. Mayer and Chatterji rejected "[t]he hypothesis that political shocks were significant factors in generating the low level of investment in the 1930s."[3]

There are, however, several problems with their analysis. Their formulation of the political explanation for low investment specifies that it resulted from the shock of specific events during the New Deal period. A more common formulation has the low investment resulting more from a general political demoralization. Joseph Schumpeter provided the classic discussion:

> [T]he combined effect of a series of measures unfavorable to investment opportunity can evidently not be evaluated by adding the effects which each of them would have had in the absence of others . . . . The individual measures obviously tend to reinforce each other. "Objectively"—*i.e.*, irrespectively of intentions harbored by any individuals—they amounted to systematic attack on investment opportunity all round . . . [T]he mistake involved in trying to arrive at an estimate of combined effects by that process of addition is not more serious than the mistake of confining attention . . . to the wording of enactments, congressional declarations of policy, and statements of the chief executive . . . . [T]he personnel and methods by which and the spirit in which a measure or set of measures is administered, are much more important than any thing contained in an enactment.[4]

If this characterization is correct, then businessmen might have been sufficiently demoralized by the future prospects under President Franklin Roosevelt to make the

The Journal of Economic History, Vol. L, No. 4 (Dec. 1990). ISSN 0022-0507.

The author is Assistant Professor of Economics at Lehigh University, Bethlehem, PA 18015.

[1] Thomas Mayer and Monojit Chatterji, "Political Shocks and Investment: Some Evidence from the 1930s," this JOURNAL, 45 (Dec. 1985), pp. 913–24.

[2] The six shocks they identified are *S*1—the "events March to June 1933": the United States leaving the gold standard, the passage of the Tennessee Valley Authority bill, the passage of the Agricultural Adjustment Act, and the passage of the bill setting up the National Recovery Administration; *S*2—the 1934 election; *S*3—the "events May to June 1935": the passage of the Wagner Act, a proposal by President Franklin Roosevelt to raise taxes, and Roosevelt's sending to Congress a bill to "phase out public utility holding companies"; *S*4—the 1936 election; *S*5—the sit-in strike at General Motors; and *S*6—the 1938 election.

[3] Mayer and Chatterji, "Political Shocks," p. 924.

[4] Joseph A. Schumpeter, *Business Cycles: A Theoretical, Historical, and Statistical Analysis of the Capitalist Process* (New York, 1939), vol. 2, pp. 1044–45.

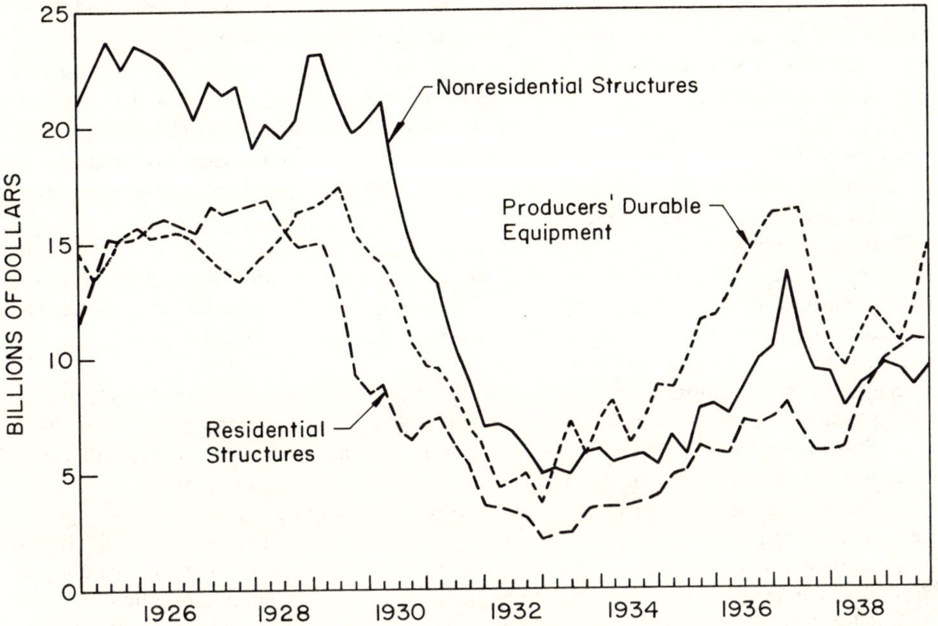

FIGURE 1

COMPONENTS OF REAL INVESTMENT SPENDING
(in billions of 1972 dollars)

Source: Robert J. Gordon, ed., *The American Business Cycle: Continuity and Change* (Chicago, 1986), pp. 810–11, appendix B.

revival of investment spending sluggish, without there necessarily being a statistically significant response to each specific political event.[5]

Another shortcoming is that several of their investment spending categories reflect short-run decisions, not the long-run ones that New Deal policies would have affected. Mayer and Chatterji should have restricted their test to the effect of political shocks on long-term investment projects, such as new business construction.[6] Nonresidential construction spending experienced the largest decline of any category of investment spending after 1929 and had the weakest recovery—scarcely rising above its 1933 low until the fourth quarter of 1935 and ending the decade at about 40 percent of its 1929 peak (see Figure 1). From 1923 through 1928 spending on nonresidential structures had been 40 percent greater than spending on producers' durable equipment, but during the Depression there was a striking reversal in their relative positions: spending on

[5] Even if their procedure of examining the effects of particular episodes is accepted, it is difficult to justify including the second and third quarters of June 1933. They included the period to capture the first spurt of New Deal legislative proposals. However, these months also represent the first two quarters of the recovery. While the recovery is not usually thought of as being investment-led, it would be extraordinary to find a statistically significant *decline* in investment spending during the first two quarters of a recovery.

[6] Robert Aaron Gordon wrote: "Business displayed a notable unwillingness to undertake long-term investment projects, either in new directions or in those lines that had chiefly attracted investment funds in the 1920's. The fact that equipment expenditures made a better showing than business construction suggests that firms were willing to make capital expenditures only as necessary to replace and modernize equipment and to meet relatively minor changes in demand." See Robert Aaron Gordon, *Business Fluctuations* (2nd edn., New York, 1961), p. 436.

producers' durable equipment was greater in every quarter between 1934 and 1939.[7] Mayer and Chatterji's two series on contracts awarded for nonresidential buildings represented long-term decisions, but their other series represented orders for relatively short-lived investment goods and were less useful in a test of the political hypothesis. The demand for such goods was determined largely by short-run factors and not by changes in long-run expectations that political shocks could engender.[8] The proper specification would have confined the test to long-run spending, namely contracts awarded for nonresidential buildings.

A final, larger difficulty arises from Mayer and Chatterji's use of autoregressions, resorted to in order to avoid making debatable assumptions about the structural relationship for investment (see equation 1). Their specification, however, assumes that lagged values of other variables had no effect on current investment beyond that captured by the lagged investment terms.

While this assumption has proven justified in tests of consumption spending, it is not likely to hold for investment spending. In the case of consumption, it has been shown that if the permanent income hypothesis is correct, lagged income terms will not be significant in a regression of current consumption on lagged consumption and lagged income.[9] In the language of intertemporal optimization under uncertainty, the permanent income hypothesis yields Euler equations that severely restrict the projection of consumption on lagged information.[10] If Mayer and Chatterji wish to make an analogous argument for investment spending, they need to provide a similar justification. This would be difficult because no variety of the conventional investment problem yields Euler equations embodying such restrictions. Intuitively, this is because the firm in choosing a time path or sequence for its capital stock relies on forecasts of the future values of variables such as prices, output, and so forth. Since any lagged information that helps to predict these variables is relevant, the Euler equations for the investment problem will not embody the necessary restrictions.

There is no theoretical reason, then, for excluding lagged values of variables ordinarily included in structural investment equations, and since quarterly data on these variables exist for the interwar period they should be included in the autoregression estimations. Table 1 reports the results of regressing two measures of contracts awarded for nonresidential buildings on three lagged values of themselves and on three lagged values of nominal Gross National Product, nominal manufacturing wages, the wholesale

[7] Robert J. Gordon, ed., *The American Business Cycle: Continuity and Change* (Chicago, 1986), appendix B, pp. 810–11.

[8] One of their categories of investment—electric motors—includes motors as small as 1 horsepower, raising the suspicion that consumer demand may have been significant for this product.

[9] Intuitively, this is because forward-looking consumption decisions will have already made use of all of the information contained in previous periods' income values. See Robert E. Hall, "Stochastic Implications of the Life Cycle-Permanent Income Hypothesis: Theory and Evidence," *Journal of Political Economy*, 86 (Dec. 1978), pp. 971–87; and Thomas J. Sargent, *Macroeconomic Theory* (2nd edn., Boston, 1987), esp. chaps. 9, 12, 14.

[10] Under the permanent income hypothesis, the household maximizes the expected value of an intertemporal utility function subject to an intertemporal budget constraint. The Euler equations for this problem embody the result that the marginal utility of consumption follows a univariate first-order Markov process (or a "random walk"). A direct corollary of this result is that consumption itself follows a random walk and that, therefore, no other variable Granger-causes consumption. Variable X is said to Granger-cause variable Y if in a regression of Y on lagged values of X and lagged values of Y, the coefficients of the lagged values of X are not zero. The test is meant to determine if lagged values of X have any contribution to make in explaining Y once the contribution of lagged values of Y is controlled for. See C. W. J. Granger, "Investigating Causal Relations by Econometric Models and Cross-Spectral Methods," *Econometrica*, 37 (July 1969), pp. 424–38.

TABLE 1
ESTIMATES OF THE EFFECTS OF POLITICAL SHOCKS ON INVESTMENT SPENDING

PANEL I	Coefficient	Coefficient as Percentage of the Mean of the Dependent Variable	*t*-statistic	Mayer and Chatterji's Coefficient
*S*1	2,595	5%	0.280	−1,112
*S*2	−5,907	−11	−0.525	853
*S*3	−12,935[a]	−24	−1.652	−549
*S*4	−9,028	−17	−0.880	1,844
*S*5	−17,786[a]	−33	−1.756	501
*S*6	34,106[b]	63	3.391	12,371[b]
Crash	−1,442	−3	−0.142	
Adjusted R^2 = 0.907		Durbin-Watson Statistic = 2.245		
PANEL II				
*S*1	−159	<1%	−0.003	−5,877
*S*2	−35,934	−11	−0.523	4,172
*S*3	−48,363	−14	−1.026	−1,057
*S*4	−65,777	−20	−1.026	9,034
*S*5	−63,508	−19	−1.003	16,276
*S*6	191,935[b]	57	3.132	63,705[b]
Crash	−21,409	−6	−0.344	
Adjusted R^2 = 0.919		Durbin-Watson Statistic = 2.266		

[a] Statistically significant at the 5 percent level.
[b] Statistically significant at the 1 percent level.
Notes: *S*1 equals second and third quarters of 1933. *S*2 equals fourth quarter of 1934. *S*3 equals second and third quarters of 1935. *S*4 equals fourth quarter of 1936. *S*5 equals first quarter of 1937. *S*6 equals fourth quarter of 1938. *Crash* equals fourth quarter of 1929. The dependent variable in both panels is new contracts for nonresidential buildings. In Panel I it is measured in thousands of square feet, in Panel II as thousands of current dollars. An appendix containing the complete autoregressions and the data sources is available from the author.

price index, and the yield on corporate bonds. The regressions were estimated for the time period beginning with the first quarter of 1925 and ending with the fourth quarter of 1939. In addition to the six dummy variables included by Mayer and Chatterji to estimate the effect of political shocks, a dummy variable was included for the fourth quarter of 1929 to estimate the effect of the stock market crash. This was done to determine the ability of the autoregressive procedure to catch the impact of shocks and to compare the results with an estimate of the impact of the stock market crash obtained by Pauline Andrews using a structural investment equation.[11]

The results differ substantially from those of Mayer and Chatterji. In Panel I, where new contracts for nonresidential buildings are measured in real terms, five of the six coefficients on the political shock dummy variables have the expected sign and three are statistically significant.[12] More importantly, five of the six coefficients represent *economically* significant movements of more than 10 percent when measured against the mean of the dependent variable. Mayer and Chatterji's analysis relied entirely on tests

[11] See Pauline Andrews, "Manufacturing Fixed Investment and the Great Depression" (Ph.D. diss., University of California at Berkeley, 1982), esp. chap. 4. Of course, there is not universal agreement that the Oct. 1929 stock market crash represented an important shock to businessmen's long-term expectations.

[12] The only failure is *S*1, the dummy for Mar. to Sept. 1933, which, as argued above, should probably not have been included in the analysis.

of statistical significance and so overlooked valuable information. Their focus impeded an appraisal of substantive significance, and they failed to deal with the problem of interpreting the standard errors in autoregressions.[13] It would have been better to have based their analysis on the size of the estimated coefficients, rather than solely on a comparison of the estimated coefficients to their standard errors. The last column in Table 1 presents the coefficient values from Mayer and Chatterji's autoregressions. In every instance except *S*1 their coefficients were much smaller than mine or were of the wrong sign.[14]

In Panel II, where the dependent variable is measured in nominal terms, only the first of the six political shock coefficients fails to be of economically significant size, although only one is statistically significant. Once again the coefficients from Mayer and Chatterji's autoregressions were much smaller or were of the wrong sign.

The dummy variable representing the impact of the stock market crash fails to be either economically or statistically significant in either regression. This contrasts with Andrews's finding using a structural model. In her regression dummy variables representing the effects of the stock market crash were large and statistically significant. The contrast between her results and mine highlights the sharply differing estimates that can be obtained from structural and autoregression modeling.[15]

Mayer and Chatterji are to be commended for attempting a rigorous test of the common assertion that political factors were responsible for the weak performance of

[13] See Christopher A. Sims, "Macroeconomics and Reality," *Econometrica*, 48 (Jan. 1980), pp. 17–18, esp. fn. 19. For a discussion of the pitfalls of confusing statistical and economic significance, see Donald N. McCloskey, *The Rhetoric of Economics* (Madison, WI, 1985), chap. 9.

[14] In their article Mayer and Chatterji reported only *t*-statistics. Mayer very promptly and graciously provided me with the coefficient values when I requested them.

[15] Andrews's analysis was carried out for a series on contracts awarded for manufacturing buildings rather than for all nonresidential buildings. Conceivably, the different results she obtained could have been due to this difference in the series analyzed, although it seems unlikely that factors affecting the demand for manufacturing buildings would not also have affected the demand for the remainder of nonresidential buildings in a similar way. Andrews attempted to capture the impact of the stock market crash by specifying four dummy variables: one each for the fourth quarter of 1929 and the first and second quarters of 1930 and one for the five quarters beginning with the third quarter of 1930 and ending with the third quarter of 1931. Andrews engaged in a specification search (pp. 181, 185) in arriving at these definitions for her dummy variables. This is a dubious procedure and the result makes the impact of the shock seem implausibly drawn out. I reran the autoregressions with two additional dummy variable specifications of the crash. In the first specification three dummy variables were included: one each for the fourth quarter of 1929 (*Crash*1), the first quarter of 1930 (*Crash*2), and the second of 1930 (*Crash*3). In the second specification one dummy variable was used for the period from the fourth quarter of 1929 through the second quarter of 1930 (*Crash*4). The results, given below, are qualitatively consistent with the results reported in Table 1 and in conflict with the results reported by Andrews. The *t*-statistics are given in parentheses.

	Square Feet	Current Dollars
*Crash*1	−2,931.761	−9,207.941
	(−0.293)	(−0.450)
*Crash*2	−14,838.608	−24,556.984
	(−1.459)	(−1.173)
*Crash*3	9,831.880	26,969.519
	(0.997)	(1.327)
*Crash*4	−1,954.006	−994.820
	(−0.308)	(−0.075)

investment spending in the mid-to-late 1930s. It seems inappropriate, however, to model the antibusiness climate of the 1930s using dummy variables. More importantly, when the analysis is carried out using just the relevant category of long-term investment and employing less restrictive autoregressions, their results are not confirmed. The hypothesis that the negative impact of political events explains the poor performance of investment spending during the 1930s would appear to remain viable.

Reply to O'Brien

THOMAS MAYER AND MONOJIT CHATTERJI

Anthony O'Brien has challenged our conclusion that political shocks are an unlikely explanation of the low level of investment in the 1930s.[1] His first criticism related to our interpretation of the hypothesis that the New Deal frightened business into reducing investment. In his view this hypothesis referred more to the general demoralization of business than to the immediate shocks resulting from specific New Deal measures or from election results that presaged a continuation of the New Deal. In principle, we have no quarrel with his broad interpretation of the hypothesis. We interpreted it in a narrower sense as this is the only way it can be tested; without testing it remains a mere assertion. O'Brien may well claim, however, that we should have stated our results not as a rejection of the broad version of the political demoralization hypothesis, but as a rejection of a testable narrow version. If so, we concede that he is right, but we question the usefulness of the untestable hypothesis.

O'Brien's second comment was that we should not have included the shock of the second and third quarters of 1933, because an extraneous event occurred in these quarters, namely the start of a sharp recovery. But the very fact that this recovery coincided with a negative political shock suggests that political shocks did not have much effect. This is not an entirely convincing argument because, due to lags, the occurrence of a recovery may have been predetermined by the time the political shock occurred. But we did choose our shocks before seeing the results and are a bit uneasy about making ex post changes in our sample.

O'Brien's third point was that the political-shock hypothesis relates more to long-run investment, such as construction, than to short-run investment, such as purchases of machinery. It is not clear, however, why this should be the case. R. A. Gordon's discussion that O'Brien cited reads—in this context—like an attempt to immunize the hypothesis against unfavorable results. As Gordon showed, long-term investment fell more than short-term investment, but there is nothing in the political-demoralization hypothesis that makes it applicable only to long-term investment, though admittedly the more rapid depreciation of machinery than of buildings would cause the percentage decline in machinery investment to be smaller than that in building investment.

O'Brien criticized our reliance on autoregressive equations with dummy variables representing the political shocks. This standard procedure, called "events study," is used extensively in finance literature. It does not imply that nothing "Granger-causes" investment, as O'Brien claimed, but merely that whatever caused investment to be at a certain level in one quarter will cause it to be some multiple (which may be greater or less than unity) of that level in the following quarters. Our procedure determined our objective. We were not interested in "explaining" investment, just in examining whether political shocks had any impact on investment *over and above that of economic variables*. We view our investment equation as being a reduced form.[2] In the light of the uncertainty about the true structural equation for investment, and given our objective, this simple procedure which places few restrictions on a potentially large parameter

The Journal of Economic History, Vol. L, No. 4 (Dec. 1990). ISSN 0022-0507.

Thomas Mayer is Professor of Economics, University of California, Davis, CA 95616. Monojit Chatterji is Bonar Professor of Applied Economics, University of Dundee, Dundee, Scotland, DD1 4HK.

[1] Anthony P. O'Brien, "Were Businessmen Afraid of FDR? A Comment on Mayer and Chatterji," this JOURNAL, 50 (Dec. 1990).

[2] Thomas Mayer and Monojit Chatterji, "Political Shocks and Investment: Some Evidence from the 1930s," this JOURNAL, 45 (Dec. 1985), pp. 913–24. Our view of the investment equation is on p. 917.

space is justifiable. As Christopher Sims has pointed out, "one can obtain macroeconomic models with useful descriptive characteristics within which tests of meaningful hypotheses can be executed without as much of a burden of maintained hypotheses as is usually imposed in such modeling."[3] Our procedure does not require as strong a maintained hypothesis as a structural approach would. Yet our results suggest that we have a reasonable description of investment within which to carry out tests of the political-shock hypothesis.

O'Brien also questioned our reliance on t-values and rightly pointed out that statistical and economic significance are not the same thing. We have much sympathy with this view.[4] We stated that the full results of the regressions were available for readers but did not report them to save space. To be acceptable, however, a hypothesis has to meet two criteria: the strategic coefficients must be large enough to be economically meaningful; *and* their t-values must be large enough, so that these coefficients can be accepted as something more than the accidental result of sampling fluctuations. Failure on either criterion means that the hypothesis is not supported.

O'Brien also raised the point that it is inappropriate to use t-tests in a model with autoregressive terms, the problem being that the t-values of the autoregressive terms may be too low. But our concern was not with the t-values of the autoregressive terms, but with the t-values of the shock terms.

In place of our autoregressive equations, O'Brien presented a model that combines structural and autoregressive elements. We find it unpersuasive. Instead of developing a reduced form of an investment model firmly grounded in valid micro-theory, O'Brien included in his model some variables that do not seem related to any plausible theory of investment. Thus O'Brien used the nominal bond rate, while theory tells us that it is the expected real cost of capital that should be in the investment equation. Since prices were hardly stable in this period, the nominal bond rate is a poor proxy for the expected real cost of capital. Perhaps no better proxy is available, but that does not make it a good proxy. Indeed it suggests that using an autoregressive model instead of a structural one may well be appropriate. Similarly, the accelerator principle tells us that new investment depends on the expected long-run rate of change in GNP. Hence while the level of GNP in the last three quarters, as used by O'Brien, may be an adequate proxy for the demand variables that drive replacement investment, it is a questionable proxy for the variables that determine gross investment.

We have recalculated O'Brien's model for construction, as well as our own autoregressions, because we discovered an anomaly in the data.[5] The construction data prior to 1932 were seasonally adjusted, while the earlier ones were not, a fact that the original source alluded to only briefly in a footnote. We therefore reran his model using seasonal dummies for the period prior to 1932. Table 1 shows the results, for both O'Brien's model and our own autoregressions. Since O'Brien did not include a constant, we present the results both with and without one. While our results differ somewhat from O'Brien's, these differences are not large enough to affect the conclusions. Only one shock is significant at the 5 percent level, and another is almost so. Three others have the right sign, and the disputed (insignificant) 1933 shock has the wrong sign. We believe that these results from O'Brien's structural regression provide at most weak support to the political-shock hypothesis. At the same time, the results from the equipment regressions, as well as from our autoregressions, are unfavorable.

[3] See Christopher A. Sims, "Macroeconomics and Reality," *Econometrica*, 48 (Jan. 1980), pp. 1–49.

[4] See Thomas Mayer, "Economics as an Exact Science: Realistic Goal or Wishful Thinking," *Economic Inquiry*, 18 (Apr. 1980), pp. 165–78.

[5] We also take this opportunity to correct a transcription error. In table 1 of Mayer and Chatterji, "Political Shocks and Investment," the entry for *S5* for machine tools should be 0.32, not 3.19. Our discussion in the text is based on the correct figure.

TABLE 1
T-VALUES OF SHOCK COEFFICIENTS, RESIDENTIAL BUILDING CONTRACTS

	Shock						R^2	Durbin-Watson Statistic
	*S*1	*S*2	*S*3	*S*4	*S*5	*S*6		
O'BRIEN'S STRUCTURAL REGRESSIONS								
With Constant:								
Value	0.89	−0.91	−1.20	−0.84	−0.55	3.07[a]	0.947	1.9
Square Feet	0.92	−0.69	−1.71[a]	−0.65	−1.45	3.39[a]	0.938	1.8
No Constant:								
Value	0.53	−0.92	−1.13	−1.04	−0.72	3.50[a]	0.944	1.9
Square Feet	0.71	−0.76	−1.67[b]	−0.85	−1.56	3.89[a]	0.939	1.9
OUR THIRD-ORDER AUTOREGRESSIONS								
No Cochrane-Orcutt Adjustment:								
Value	0.23	−0.70	0.75	−0.15	0.93	2.92[a]	0.926	1.6
Square Feet	0.15	−0.50	0.54	0.16	0.27	3.62[a]	0.912	1.5
With Cochrane-Orcutt Adjustment:								
Value	0.61	−0.52	−0.46	−1.45	−1.21	3.78[a]	0.942	2.1
Square Feet	0.60	−0.28	−0.74	−1.10	−1.87[a]	5.07[a]	0.939	2.0

[a] Significant at 5 percent level, one-tailed test.
[b] Almost significant at 5 percent level, one-tailed test.
Notes: The Shocks are defined as follow: *S*1 = Events of March to June 1933; *S*2 = 1934 election; *S*3 = Events of May to June 1935; *S*4 = 1936 election; *S*5 = Sit-in strike at General Motors; and *S*6 = 1938 election.
Sources: U.S. Department of Commerce, *Commerce Yearbook* (Washington, DC, 1932); *Survey of Current Business: Supplement* (Washington, DC, 1932, 1936, 1938, 1942); and private communication with Anthony O'Brien.

None of this is intended to denigrate a valuable point that O'Brien made: we tested only a particular empirical implementation of a broad political-shock hypothesis. The failure of the hypothesis on this test *might* be due to the specifics of the empirical implementation, such as focusing on the immediate effects of the shocks.[6] Moreover, if the political-shock hypothesis is interpreted as merely saying that political shocks had *some* effect on investment but not necessarily large enough to show up through the noise of large standard errors, then our data do not reject it. But these are problems that are common to statistical tests. All the same, we agree that we should have stated our results more cautiously, and that O'Brien has done a valuable service by pointing out their limitations.

[6] We did, however, see if lagging the shocks by one quarter makes a difference. It does not.

Editors' Notes

FIFTY-FIRST ANNUAL MEETING

The 1991 Annual Meeting of the Economic History Association will take place in Boulder, Colorado, September 27–29. The 1991 program committee invites submissions of sessions and papers, including—but not limited to—ones relating to the theme of economic and technological leadership. Processes of diffusion, adaptation, and rivalry and associated new forms of business organization exemplify topics evoked by the theme. In composing a program of high scholarly interest, the committee will also seek balance between economic and historical perspectives, among areas and periods, and between emerging and established scholars.

Send two copies of one-page abstracts of papers and proposed sessions (with likely participants) to either co-chair: Professor Alexander J. Field, Department of Economics, Santa Clara University, Santa Clara, CA 95053, or Professor Paul Hohenberg, Department of Economics, Rensselaer Polytechnic Institute, Troy, NY 12180-3590. For full consideration, proposals must be sent before January 25, 1991. Notices of acceptance will be mailed during March.

Persons expecting to receive their Ph.D. in the academic year 1990–1991 are invited to apply to the conveners of the dissertation session: Professor Robert Margo (Department of Economics, Vanderbilt University, Nashville, TN 37235) for North American topics, and Professor Eugene N. White (Department of Economics, Rutgers University, New Brunswick, NJ 08903) for all others. Finalists for the Allen Nevins and Alexander Gerschenkron prizes present summaries at the meeting. Complete dissertations will be due by May 31, 1991; notification will be by July 31, 1991.

AWARDS AT THE 1990 E.H.A. MEETING

At the Fiftieth Anniversary Meeting of the Economic History Association, held in Montreal, September 13–16, the following prizes were awarded:

The Arthur H. Cole Prize for the outstanding article published in the JOURNAL in the September 1989 through June 1990 issues, to Jane Humphries of Cambridge University for her article, "Enclosures, Common Rights, and Women: The Proletarianization of Families in the Late Eighteenth and Early Nineteenth Centuries," which appeared in the March 1990 issue. The Cole Prize recipient is selected each year by the JOURNAL's editorial board.

The Allen Nevins Prize for the outstanding dissertation in United States or Canadian economic history completed during 1989/1990, to Robert Whaples of the University of Wisconsin, Milwaukee, for his "The Shortening of the American Work Week: An Economic and Historical Analysis of Context, Causes, and Consequences," completed at the University of Pennsylvania under the guidance of Claudia Goldin.

The Alexander Gerschenkron Prize for the outstanding dissertation in non-United States or Canadian economic history completed during 1989/1990, to Avner Greif of Stanford University for his "The Organization of Long-Distance Trade: Reputations and Coalitions in the Geniza Documents; Genoa During the Eleventh and Twelfth Centuries," completed at Northwestern University under the guidance of Joel Mokyr.

The recipients of the Nevins Prize and Gerschenkron Prize are selected each year by the conveners of the dissertation session at the annual meeting.

ELEVENTH INTERNATIONAL ECONOMIC HISTORY CONGRESS

Preparations are already under way for the Eleventh Congress of the International Economic History Association, to be held in Milan in September 1994. Those interested in proposing themes or subjects for sessions should submit proposals as soon as possible to M. Joseph Goy, Secrétaire-Général, Association Internationale d'Histoire Economique, Ecole des Hautes-Etudes en Sciences Sociales, 54 Blvd. Raspail, 75007 Paris, with a copy to David Landes, Department of Economics, Harvard University, Cambridge, MA 02138 or Paul Hohenberg, Department of Economics, Rensselaer Polytechnic Institute, Troy, NY 12180-3590.

Please bear in mind that the proposals most likely to be approved are those that deal with topics of an international character and enlist contributions by scholars from different countries. To this end, proposers should submit, along with their theme, the names of likely contributors who have indicated interest.

CALL FOR PAPERS

The 1991 meeting of the History of Economics Society will be held June 15, 16, and 17, 1991, at the University of Maryland, College Park. Papers should be in the field of the history of economic thought and problems of scope and method in economics. Proposals for papers should include the author's name, telephone number, and institutional affiliation; the title of the paper; and an abstract not to exceed 400 words. Those who wish to serve as discussants of a paper should indicate their areas of interest. Proposals must be received by January 15, 1991. Send to Dudley Dillard, Program Chairman, Department of Economics, University of Maryland, College Park, MD 20742. Telephone: (301) 405–3485; FAX (301) 405–3542.

MIDDLE ATLANTIC HISTORICAL ASSOCIATION CONFERENCE

The seventeenth annual conference of the Middle Atlantic Historical Association of Catholic Colleges and Universities will be held March 23, 1991, at the University of Scranton, Scranton, Pennsylvania. Anyone at an institution belonging to the Association or any other interested scholar is invited to participate. Proposals for papers or panels should be sent to Dr. Lee J. Williames, Assistant Provost, University of Scranton, Scranton, PA 18510. Proposals should be received by December 31, 1990.

THE INSTITUTE FOR GREAT LAKES RESEARCH

The Institute for Great Lakes Research, a Division of Libraries and Learning Resources at Bowling Green State University, has recently been awarded a grant from the National Endowment for the Humanities to assist the Institute in processing and making available to scholars, students, and the public significant manuscript and archival collections documenting various aspects of Great Lakes maritime history. For additional information, write Robert W. Graham, Archivist, Institute for Great Lakes Research, 12764 Levis Parkway, Perrysburg, OH 43551, or call (419) 874–3907.

CALL FOR FELLOWS

Scholars Workshop on the Rhetoric of Social History, at the University of Iowa, Sunday, June 21, to Thursday, July 2, 1992. National Endowment for the Humanities Fellows from a variety of disciplines will contribute papers and participate in a two-week workshop examining the ways through which social historians address, cultivate, engage, and seek to persuade their audiences. Paper proposals are due Mar. 1, 1991. Codirectors are Jeffrey Cox, Shelton Stromquist, and Linda K. Kerber of the Department of History, University of Iowa. For a detailed description of the workshop, write to Project on Rhetoric and Inquiry, W700 Seashore Hall, University of Iowa, Iowa City, IA 52242, or call (319) 335–2753.

FORD FOUNDATION POSTDOCTORAL FELLOWSHIPS FOR MINORITIES

The National Research Council plans to award approximately 25 Ford Foundation Postdoctoral Fellowships for Minorities in a program designed to provide opportunities for continued education and experience in research for Native American Indians, Alaskan Natives (Eskimo or Aleut), Black/African Americans, Mexican Americans/ Chicanos, Native Pacific Islanders (Micronesians or Polynesians), and Puerto Ricans. Fellows will be selected from among scientists, engineers, and scholars in the humanities who show greatest promise of future achievement in academic research and scholarship in higher education.

In this national competition sponsored by the Ford Foundation, U.S. citizens who are members of one of the designated minority groups, are preparing for or already engaged in college or university teaching, and hold the Ph.D. or Sc.D. degree may apply for a fellowship award of one year's duration.

Awards in the Ford Foundation Postdoctoral Fellowships for Minorities Program will be made in the behavioral and social sciences, humanities, engineering, mathematics, physical sciences, and biological sciences, or for interdisciplinary programs composed of two or more eligible disciplines. Awards will not be made in professions such as medicine, law, social work, library science, and such areas as business administration and management, communications, health science, home economics, journalism, counseling, personnel and guidance, and education. Tenure of a fellowship provides postdoctoral research experience at an appropriate not-for-profit institution of higher education or research of the fellow's choice. Appropriate institutions include universities, museums, libraries, government or national laboratories, privately sponsored not-for-profit institutes, government chartered not-for-profit research organizations, and centers for advanced study. The deadline for submission of applications will be Jan. 11, 1991. All inquiries concerning application materials and program administration should be addressed to the Fellowship Office, GR420A, National Research Council, 2101 Constitution Ave., Washington, DC 20418.

INSTITUTES AND SEMINARS

The National Endowment for the Humanities will hold a number of Institutes and Seminars across the country and abroad during the summer of 1991. While eligibility differs in each program, successful applicants *will* receive a stipend.

Printed material for both programs may be obtained from NEH 1991 Summer Institutes and Seminars, Room 406, 1100 Pennsylvania Ave., NW, Washington, DC, 20506.

Reviews of Books

MEDIEVAL AND EARLY MODERN

Opera Muliebria: Women and Work in Medieval Europe. By David Herlihy. Philadelphia: Temple University Press, 1990. Pp. xiv, 210. $29.95.

Recent research on women and work in preindustrial Europe has dispelled the notion that women were somehow "better off" before capitalism and industrialization. In a recent review essay Judith Bennett has summarized how the European history of women's oppression as workers goes back to at least the twelfth century (" 'History that Stands Still': Women's Work in the European Past," *Feminist Studies*, 14 [2, 1988], pp. 269–83). So far few historians have studied the preceding centuries due to the challenges of sparse and fragmentary written sources and the difficulties of reading off a sexual division of labor from excavated materials.

In a pioneering synthesis of a millennium of women and work in Europe (500 A.D.–1500 A.D.) David Herlihy addresses this neglected earlier period. Following the organization of his study titled *Medieval Households* (Cambridge, MA, 1985), the author begins by examining women's work in the context of two heritages that shaped early medieval Europe: the late classical Mediterranean and the northern barbarian worlds. Based on early medieval evidence pieced together from saints' lives, royal capitularies, and law codes, broadened to include vernacular romances and Parisian tax rolls, and complemented by his intimate knowledge of the Florentine *catasto* for the later Middle Ages, Herlihy finds that women of early medieval Europe were active and independent participants in economic life. They worked in agrarian, craft, professional, and religious capacities, and their work was valued, on the evidence of literary texts of the period, which often associate women's work with high moral value.

An analysis of women's involvement in textile production is set against this richly conceived setting of women's work. The predominance of women as textile producers in the early medieval period gradually eroded; by the twelfth century male workers had taken over weaving, dyeing, and finishing cloth, leaving to women the various tasks involved in the preparation of yarn. This redefinition of gender and work in textile production did not automatically entail the formation of a European domestic mode of production, a mode in which "women work as part of the family unit and are subject to the authority of its usually male chief" (p. 150). Herlihy regards the high incidence of female heads of households (15 percent, or 2,238) enrolled on the Parisian tax rolls of 1292, among which 39 percent (934) were listed with occupations, as evidence that women were not yet submerged in patriarchal family productive units. By the end of the medieval period women workers had, the author claims, disappeared into such units. Herlihy thus tells a story of a Golden Age of women's work in the early medieval period, followed by a redefinition of some key areas of female productive activity and culminating in the formation of patriarchal family economies.

The findings for the early medieval period are especially intriguing. We could learn much-needed lessons from a time when women led full and rich productive lives and the various aspects of their productive contribution were valued. As much as I long to know about such a world, some contradictions that surfaced in *Opera Muliebria* made me wonder how golden this Golden Age might have been for women workers, especially those involved in textile production. My trouble can be illustrated by the problems of interpreting the women's work place or *gynaeceum*, a "critical institution in the rural organization of textile work" (p. 75).

The limited archaeological evidence for such weaving centers is associated with high-status sites, dating mostly from the troubled economic times of the mid-ninth through tenth centuries. As the author recognizes, there was a strong association of dependent and slave labor with these weaving centers. The early medieval texts cited as evidence of the relations between women's productive activity and their valued status as females also show ambivalence. The texts praise women as weavers but also reveal fears of illicit sexual activities and the need for surveillance of women's workshops. The dependent status of women workers and the ambivalence toward their work places make it difficult to straightforwardly correlate their predominance in early medieval textile production with their valued status as producers (see Penny Schine Gold, *The Lady and the Virgin* [Chicago, 1985] for discussion of the problems of dealing with such ambivalent gendered images in medieval literature). As the early medieval sources are too fragmentary to illuminate how the social reproduction of early medieval households articulated with recruitment into workshops, it is difficult to determine whether early medieval women would have experienced "not working with their natural families" (p. 44) or leaving "their household of origins to take up service" (p. 44) as an autonomous and good activity. The author's positive judgment seems to imply contemporary notions of gendered productive activities in private and public spheres. Nor can we tell whether women experienced the dependent and controlled conditions of the *gynecaea* as preferable to their subsequent exclusion from weaving. The harsh conditions documented for women and children in Mesopotamian *gynecaea*, which have fuller records and where we encounter a comparable configuration of dependent female labor and specialized training, cautions us against idealizing women's work places (see Kazuya Maekawa, "Female Weavers and Their Children in Lagash-, Pre-Sargonic-, and Ur III," *Acta Sumerologia*, 2 [1980], pp. 81–125).

We are indebted to this book for focusing our attention on the profound shift in the gendered organization of medieval textile production. The study opens up the history of gender and work to some crucial questions for future study. We need to learn more about the links between the gendered transmission of knowledge, social identity, and the conception of craft among medieval people. Some of the intriguing sources cited by Herlihy point us in this direction of inquiry (pp. 19, 58). The early medieval stories about women weaving and embroidering "texts," though rooted in classical tropes, nevertheless suggest that training in weaving and needle arts involved not only technique but also the acquisition of a body of lore among women, a kind of "textual" knowledge. Women "wrote" stories and communicated vital information through the medium of textiles. The weaving of such "texts" was possible due to the sequence of the processes involved in textile production in the early Middle Ages. First, dyeing of wool occurred in fleece or on the skein, not after the wool was woven, as happened in the later Middle Ages. Thus women weavers could exercise control over color in original design in a way that was not possible later. In contrast to high-medieval textile production, early medieval cloths were not fulled—that is, subjected to the soaking in urine, fuller's earth, or other compounds that thicken and felt the cloth to enhance its texture (see Frances A. Pritchard, "Late Saxon Textiles from the City of London," *Medieval Archaeology*, 28 [1984], pp. 46–76). The late medieval processes of "finishing" cloths (dyeing, fulling, and shearing) would have erased any "text" that had been produced in the design and weaving stages. Thus, the exclusion of women from textile production in the high Middle Ages becomes not only an economic and technological problem—a question of new loom technologies, mechanizing of finishing processes, access to capital, and so forth—but also a redefinition of signifying practices in medieval material culture. What kind of cultural information would be transmitted through the surfaces of textiles, and how would that transmission be gendered? The question of the redefinition of gender and work in textile production thus becomes a study of gender, knowledge, and power. Herlihy's pioneer study also encourages work on a companion piece that would examine gender and textile production in neighboring medieval Islamic societies, a "textile civilization" of great importance in the same period.

KATHLEEN BIDDICK, *University of Notre Dame*

Money in Sixteenth-Century Florence. By Carlo M. Cipolla. Berkeley: University of California Press, 1989. Pp. xi, 169. $29.95.

Le tre rivoluzioni e altri saggi di storia economica e sociale. By Carlo M. Cipolla. Bologna: Società editrice il Mulino, 1989. Pp. 428. L 42,000.

The tricky nature of money has long been one of Carlo Cipolla's key interests, and *Money in Sixteenth-Century Florence* is another episode in this complex tale. Yet he has never been a narrow specialist. His selected essays, *Le tre rivoluzioni*, range over more than ten centuries and a wealth of topics from medieval castles to plague, the manorial system, economic decline, demographic change, health authorities, poverty, interest rates, wages, prices, technology, autobiography, and California wines. The breadth of his procedures has been no less impressive: some essays are highly focused, technical, with a strong archival basis; others are more discursive "think" pieces.

Money in Sixteenth-Century Florence examines a variety of Florentine coins, their metallic contents, bookkeeping monies (units of account), fluctuations in value (gold versus silver), the Florentine consequences of the flood of silver from the New World, and the city's acute financial crisis of the 1570s and 1580s. The resulting picture is far from simple, not only because of the odd relations between real coins and account monies, but also because of the indeterminable quantities of gold in Florence, the obscure value of wage or workers' money, and the stubborn, if well-intentioned, monetary policies of the grand duke, Francesco de' Medici. Cipolla's findings may be summed up as follows.

Owing to conservative ducal policies and the influx of new silver, Florence lost all initiative in the monetary field. Florentine accountants invented their own bookkeeping monies, but why, exactly, accounts were kept in unreal monies is unclear, unless the practice was imposed by wage money and the double standards of gold and silver. Gold appreciated and silver fell in value, to such an extent that by the late 1580s Florence had all but passed fully over to a silver monometallic system. Ducal efforts to freeze the value of gold made for the flight of gold coins: they were shipped out to seek a higher value in foreign exchange markets. Furthermore in the 1570s and 1580s the financial stranglehold of the Ricci bank—a firm greatly favored by the grand duke—issued in astonishing cash and credit shortages, so that on Saturdays workers often had to go without their pay. In the event, ducal government was forced to lift its restrictions against the circulation of some foreign coins in Florentine Tuscany. We can only puzzle over how the credit noose affected the urban economy and Florentine life at all levels of the population. Luckily for the ruling class, the structure of authoritarian government held fast, all dissent having been extirpated during the middle decades of the century. Eric Cochrane's *Florence in the Forgotten Centuries* (Chicago, 1976) paints the period in too rosy a color.

Omitting only the question of literacy, most of the 29 essays in *Le tre rivoluzioni* treat the many themes that have occupied Cipolla during his long career: metal currencies, long-term economic fluctuations, transformations in land tenure, population changes, short-term crises, the introduction and spread of new technologies, and methodological queries. After about 1970 he took up additional subject matter, including the structure of the professions and the history of plague and epidemic controls. But certain themes and emphases recur in his work, and some of these deserve commentary.

He has rightly held that inflation—hence the continuing devaluation of money—has been a secular trend in Europe for about a millennium. In this *longue durée* but especially after 1300, states tended chronically to spend beyond their means, thereby helping, in this expansion of credit, to devalue money and fuel long-term inflation. Other factors also contributed to the inflationary process, such as increasing populations, rising productivities, and the debasement of metal currencies. But once we raise the question of the state's fiscal impact on inflation, what about its impact on the vicissitudes of the European economies in the late medieval and early modern periods? Moreover, it would be well to have some idea of what portion of all taxes ended in the pockets of the rich—for at Renaissance Genoa, Florence, Venice, and other Italian city-states, they were the great owners or creditors of the public debt. In an early essay, "Prezzi, salari e teoria dei salari in Lombardia alla fine del cinquecento" (pp. 105–16), Cipolla established that wages in sixteenth-century Lombardy were based on a bare subsistence level. The assumption was that workers should be paid just enough to feed themselves. This view, however, was certainly not confined to the Lombard plain. It was also held by fifteenth-century Florentine humanists and seventeenth-century poor-law administrators in England. Indeed, it was a common view in Europe. Knowing this, we can more easily understand Cipolla's opening sentence in a late essay (1981)—"fluttuazioni economiche, pauperismo e intervento pubblico nell'Italia del Cinque e Seicento"—alleging that 75 to 80 percent of preindustrial Europeans were, arguably, mired in poverty. War, crop failures, epidemics, and deficient technologies doubtless contributed to the cycles of haunting poverty, when 20 to 35 percent of the urban populations might suddenly capsize into beggary and dependence on charity. But three other factors also fostered endemic poverty: (1) the payment of mere subsistence wages, with no surplus for future need; (2) the disadvantageous nature of wage money (copper and mixed silver coins) relative to the money used for calculating profits and productivities (gold and large silver pieces); and (3) the state's preeminent reliance on a variety of sales and indirect taxes, which weighed most heavily on poor folk. Production itself was too inelastic, for with their wages workers could never buy back more than a fraction of what they produced. Finally, when it came to putting more wealth into circulation, it was not enough to build numerous grand *palazzi*, if most of the laborers who constructed them were paid a pauper's wage.

LAURO MARTINES, *University of California, Los Angeles*

Trasporti e sviluppo economico: Secoli XIII–XVIII. Edited by Anna Vannini Marx. Florence: Felice le Monnier, 1986. Pp. 375.

The 30 articles that make up this large folio volume were presented at the fifth annual *Settimana di Studio* held in Prato, Italy, in May 1974. This appears to be the fourth volume of Prato papers published to date; as its predecessors have not been reviewed in this JOURNAL, it is worth noting their titles: Vol. I, *La lana come materia prima: I fenomeni della sua produzione e circolazione nei secoli XIII–XVII* (Florence, 1974); Vol. II, *Produzione, commercio e consumo dei panni di lana nei secoli XII–XVIII* (Florence, 1976); Vol. VI, *Domandae consumi: Livelli e strutture nei secoli XIII–XVIII* (Florence, 1978).

The present collection deals with transportation and economic growth in Europe and its surrounding seas, extending from Great Britain to Russia and from the Baltic to the Mediterranean over six centuries. The papers reflect this chronological and spatial breadth, while the subject allows for a variety of approaches from the various contributors. The result is rather heterogeneous fare, with something for just about everyone. In view of the restrictions of a short review, enumerating the contents of the volume seems preferable to commenting on a few articles that catch my medievalist's eye. The volume reproduces the sequence in which the papers were presented at the conference, often with little topical relation among those given on any one day. I will therefore rearrange their order to group them by theme.

Two contributions are relatively general treatments: Jan A. van Houtte's "*Les Grands Itinéraires du commerce (XIIIe–XVIIIe siècles)*," which attempts to provide a historical-geographical background for the other conference papers, and a genial essay by Charles Wilson, "Transport As a Factor in the History of Economic Development."

The sea washes up a bountiful collection. Essays dealing with maritime traffic and technology are Frederick C. Lane's impressive survey of advances in shipping techniques from the end of the Roman Empire to the Industrial Revolution, "Technology and Productivity in Seaborne Transportation"; John E. Dotson's "Stowage Factors in Medieval Shipping"; Jacques Heers's "*Les Nations maritimes et le transport des hommes (guerriers, pèlerins, marchands, esclaves) en Méditerranée de l' an mil à l' an 1500 environ*"; Vilma Borghesi's "*Rotte e tempi di percorrenza nel Mediterraneo tra XV e XVI secolo*"; Gian Carlo Calcagno's "*Rotte e tempi di percorrenza nel Mediterraneo occidentale nel secolo XVII*"; and David W. Waters's "Navigational Developments in the 13th to the 18th Centuries."

Half the presentations, as might be expected, treat aspects of national, regional, or local transportation and economies. These include papers by Natalie Fryde, "The Problems of Transport in Medieval Wales: A Study of an Underdeveloped Society"; Luigi de Rosa, "*Communicazioni terrestri e marittime e depressione economica: Il caso del Regno di Napoli (secoli XIV–XVIII)*"; Victor Rutenburg, "*Le vie commerciali del XV–XVI secolo secondo le cronache italiane*"; Liubov A. Kotelnikova, "*Vie commerciali e alcuni aspeti dello sviluppo economico-sociale della Toscana nei secoli XII–XIV*"; Pierre Ponsot, "*En Andalousie occidentale: Systèms de transports et développement économique (XVIe–XIXe siècles)*"; José Martínez Gijón, "*La comenda y el transporte de mercancías en el derecho español de la baja Edad Media*"; *Philippe Wolff*, "*L' isthme d' Aquitaine: une promesse non tenue*"; Henri Dubois, "*Tecniques et coûts des transports terrestres en France aux XIVe et XVe siècles*"; Alexandre N. Cistozvonov, "*Le corprazioni dei trasporti, le categorie ad esse affini ed il commercio ad Amsterdam (XVI secolo)*"; Teresa Dunin-Wasowics, "*Evoluzione della tecnologia dei trasporti nell' Europa centrale del XIII secolo*"; Jerzy Wyrozumski, "*Les Communications fluviales en Pologne du XIIe au XVIIIe siècles (aspects économiques et techniques)*"; Elena Druzinina, "*Landes- und Wassertransport Sudrusslands im 18. Jahrhundert*"; Morgan A. Rakmatullin, "*La situazione dei trasporti e delle vie di comunicazione nella Russia del XVIII secolo*"; Arkadij Man'kov, "*La regolamentazione legale delle vie commerciali interne nella Russia del XVII*"; and Ondrej R. Halaga, "*La situation des transports commerciaux dans la zone des Carpathes.*"

Five contributions examine commercial and trading connections between specific regions or locales: Eddy Stols's "*Les transports dans le commerce des Pays-Bas méridionaux avec la péninsule ibérique (XIIIe–XVIIIe siècles)*"; Wilfred Brulez's "*Les transports routiers entre les Pays-Bas et l'Italie aux XVIe et XVIIe siècles*"; Wolfgang von Stromer's "*Die Kontinentalsperre Kaiser Sigismunds gegen Venedig 1412–1413, 1418–1433 und die Verlagerung der transkontinentalen Transportwege*"; Hermann Kellenbenz's "*Das Verkehrswesen zwischen den deutschen Nord- und Ostseehäfen und dem Mittel meer im 16. und in der ersten Hälfte des 17 Jahrhunderts*"; and Fritz Glauser's "*Der Gotthardtransit von 1500 bis 1660.*"

The list closes with two articles that deal with the movement of specific commodities (timber and cattle): M. Devese's "*Flottage et transport du bois sur les fleuves européens à l'époque moderne (consequences pour le développement économique)*" and Othmar Pickl's "*Der innereuropäische Schlachtviehhandel vom 15. bis zum 17. Jahrhunderts.*"

It is regrettable that such an excellent group of studies lacks an overarching introductory or closing essay to provide a theoretical framework that might have pulled the individual contributions into a tighter whole. Nevertheless, it is good to have in print the results of this important conference—bringing together each year as it does scholars from East and West. It is to be hoped that other volumes will follow, perhaps in a more timely fashion.

THOMAS W. BLOMQUIST, *Northern Illinois University*

MODERN EUROPE

Da un sistema agricolo a un sistema industriale: Il comasco dal settecento al novecento. Vol. II: *La lunga trasformazione tra due crisi (1814–1880)*. Edited by Sergio Zaninelli. Como: Camera di commercio, industria e agricoltura di Como, 1988. Pp. 715.

This volume, the second of three volumes examining the economic development of the northern Italian province of Como from the eighteenth to the twentieth century, is edited by Sergio Zaninelli, the foremost authority on the modern Lombard economy. The book consists of four long essays exploring the Comascan economy during the years from 1814 to 1880. Until 1859 the region was under Austrian rule, and in 1860 it became a part of independent united Italy. The essays are clearly written and provide a wealth of information on the region's economy. All the essays contain an impressive amount of quantitative data and appendixes of statistical tables as well as a variety of official documents. Overall the contributors argue that the nineteenth century constituted a period of transition in the Comascan economy in which traditional and modern economic elements coexisted. Here Como was no different from many other areas in Europe.

In the first essay, "Agriculture in Search of Equilibrium," Giancarlo Galli concludes that despite certain changes, nineteenth-century Comascan agriculture did not experience substantial structural transformations; rather, it remained very similar to that of the previous century. A good part of the land was uncultivated common land, cultivation methods remained traditional, the use of modern technology and machinery was scarce, and traditional sharecropping contracts persisted. Despite calls for and proposals to introduce changes, the proprietary class resisted contractual reforms that would improve peasants' conditions and was reluctant to invest in the land, while small landowners and sharecroppers lacked the means to invest and introduce major technological improvements. Two changes that did take place were the transfer of church land to secular owners and the expanding cultivation of mulberry trees, an essential product for the Comascan silk industry. Mulberry trees, along with grain and wine, constituted the most important products of the Comascan region.

In the second essay, "The Progressive Success of Industry," Pietro Cafaro explores the incentives that stimulated and the obstacles that hindered textile production and metallurgy, the two primary industries at Como. Silk production, traditionally the most important industry, continued its primacy in nineteenth-century Como. The increasing demand from foreign markets abroad, including France, England, the Hapsburg Empire, and America, spurred the growth of silk-spinning mills, although limited energy sources and raw material and competition from the Far East prevented a faster expansion. Silk weaving lagged behind spinning, yet after 1850 new technology, most notably steam boilers and mechanical looms, was adopted and the number of looms increased from 1,580 in 1835 to 5,557 in the 1870s. The metallurgical industry also suffered from the scarcity and costliness of energy and from foreign competition. Cafaro concludes with a discussion of the poor conditions of industrial workers: low wages, long working hours, and the large number of women and children in the textile industry.

In the third article, "Traditional Routes and Highways of Steam," Aldo Carera describes the development of the land and waterway transportation systems, a highly important network leading from Milan to Switzerland. It is not surprising to learn that Como was the first main city in Lombardy to be connected by railway to Milan (on December 6, 1849). Carera provides a vast amount of information and statistics about road, railway, and navigation quality and conditions; length of routes; costs of construction and maintenance; ticket prices; numbers of passengers; amount of goods shipped; and many other aspects of a transportation network that was among the most developed in Italy. Steamboats traveled in Lake Como, railways were constructed, and in the 1880s the province was fourth among all Italian provinces in road length per square kilometer (p. 392). Yet neither steamboats nor the railway acquired a clear dominance over the old transportation methods. The traditional and the new continued to coexist in the 1880s.

The last essay, "The Lasting Gap Between Resources and Population," by Rosalba Canetta, focuses on social and demographic transformations of the Comascan province. Although agriculture remained the main source of livelihood, an increasing number of people supported themselves in the manufacturing, trade, and service sectors. This, however, did not necessarily improve their material conditions. The period between 1815 and 1880 was, in fact, one of Como's most difficult times (p. 643). Poverty in the country increased, urban workers lived in poor conditions, and insufficient nutrition caused the spread of diseases. A gap between the resources of the province and its rising population (between 1814 and 1881 the population in the Comascan province rose 67 percent) forced many to emigrate.

While the volume provides much useful information, it does not adequately analyze certain questions and topics. Missing is a rigorous examination of the changes in the Comascan area when it became part of united Italy, as well as of the ties between that region and other parts of Lombardy. Also absent is an article on trade and banking. Yet despite these shortcomings, this is a very useful work for anybody interested in the economy of modern Italy. It clearly supplements the more general works by Mario Romani and Kent Roberts Greenfield on the Lombard economy.

ALEXANDER I. GRAB, *University of Maine*

Les villes dans la France moderne: 1740–1840. By Bernard Lepetit. Paris: Editions Albin Michel, 1988. Pp. 490. F 198.

In the last few years urban history studies have veered strongly away from the study of specific cities to the analysis of urbanization and of urban networks, as a growing interest in both demography and geography has encouraged shifts in methods and interpretive frameworks. Where static structures once commanded attention, the interest in process and in interlinkages within a large area now dominates. Because of the methodological influence of the Annales school, even the older style of French urban historians embedded their city histories within regional studies. But more recently French demographers and social historians have shifted their focus to the national level and to systemic links among cities. Bernard Lepetit's work adds substantially to this revision of urban scholarship through his study of the functioning of the French urban hierarchy between 1740 and 1840.

Lepetit's book is bold in its scope as well as novel in its approach. He mixes sophisticated quantitative techniques with a detailed look at the categories and arguments of early modern French urban analysis. Taking seriously contemporary views of towns, he shows how depictions of cities had, by the mid-seventeenth century, acquired a strong sense of urban space and how, by the early eighteenth, the notions of circulation and movement dominated discussions of cities—themes that recurred among engineers and utopian socialist theorists in the early nineteenth century. One of his major points, the limited contemporary conception of urban economic roles, arises from his analysis of writers such as Condillac, Cantillon, and Say and then is reinforced by Lepetit's own view of the limited impact of economic forces in the structuring of the early modern French urban hierarchy. Through his choice of both period and sources, Lepetit deemphasizes urban economies. Indeed, he can trace formal economic institutions, such as chambers of commerce, more effectively than levels of production or labor markets. Lists of fairs, markets, and boutiques allow him to chart interesting regional differences in the forms of commercial activity, but the quantitative importance of each unit is not captured. While tax and *octroi* figures give him some data on levels of economic activity, much is missed. By ending the book before the acceleration of industrial changes and by relying heavily on institutional indicators, Lepetit slants his results toward administrative variables, which are more plentiful and more easily captured.

In both its methods and its message the book emphasizes the political and the social roles of towns. Petit constructs a sample of 309 towns (all with an average of more than 200 baptisms per year) to which he adds information on the presence or absence of about 30 different activities and institutions. With the aid of factoral analysis he ranks towns in terms of their types and numbers of functions. He argues for the importance of an "old regime city" of mixed functions, which he contrasts with those having more specialized roles. Capital cities, whether of regions, departments, or arrondissements, were the most important central places. Lepetit rejects commonly used dualist models of urban functioning, arguing sensibly that in France both a "maritime" and a "continental" model of linkage between towns operated simultaneously. His work shows the substantial overlapping in French towns of all sizes of a variety of administrative and cultural institutions that linked them both to the capital and to one another. His list of cities is subdivided by the complexity of their administrative institutions. He distinguishes among a six-level hierarchy of administrative cities, one that shifted in the middle ranks because of political decisions made during the Revolution and Empire. Hierarchy and scale, therefore, are important elements of his analysis, and he regularly notes the size thresholds that marked different patterns of urban interaction. For example, towns of over 25,000 acquired savings societies at roughly the same rate, whereas smaller ones were less well provided, depending on their size and regional location.

Lepetit rejects the notion of a static French urban system even during a period of stable urbanization levels. He shows clearly that while formal shifts in French urban hierarchies during his period were minimal, changes in the functioning of urban networks took place. He emphasizes the expansion of interurban links, particularly in the north of France. In effect, better road linkages and new institutions drew together into a tightly knit urban system the towns of the northern half of the country; those of the south remained more isolated. Using regional measurements of the dispersion of grain prices, he shows how markets in the south were less responsive to national trends than those in the north. Formally similar structures demonstrated different levels of economic integration. Lepetit's many maps anchor his arguments in a regional framework and give his often abstract arguments a concrete, spatial form.

The novelty of Lepetit's book is threefold. First, he demonstrates the multiplicity of sources that can be used on a national level to distinguish the structural make-up of Old regime cities: lists of learned societies, of building projects, of cafés, and of savings societies (*caisses d'épargne*), to name only a few. Each of these sources helps to distinguish types of sociability and of economic interaction, as well as to trace patterns of diffusion. By moving beyond demographic indicators he develops a sophisticated set of categories for the analysis of urban functions. Second, he presents a dynamic treatment of urban networks, which change over time in their ability to bind settlements into a well-functioning hierarchy. Moreover, he locates pressures to shift interurban links among political decision makers and urban elites, rather than among entrepreneurs. Lepetit's emphasis differs, therefore, from that of many urban historians who give more importance to economic changes rather than political and social ones. A third point of distinction is Lepetit's treatment of Paris, to which he gives no special attention. The resulting picture is of an urban system with regional dynamics, rather than a hierarchy driven by impulses from the center. His revisionist treatment of the French urban system deserves to be widely read and debated.

LYNN HOLLEN LEES, *University of Pennsylvania*

Privilege and Profit: A Business Family in Eighteenth-Century France. By P. W. Bamford. Philadelphia: University of Pennsylvania Press, 1988. Pp. xxv, 347. $45.95.

Like many business histories, this is really the story of a dynasty: a tale of success, but with little hint of rags to riches. And, as is true of so many Old Regime business histories, the state played a big role in this success.

P. W. Bamford's "hero" is the timber merchant and naval armaments manufacturer Pierre Babaud de la Chaussade (c. 1710–1792), but a good third of his book is devoted to the buildup of the family fortunes and activities by his elder brother Jean Babaud (d. 1738) and brother-in-law Jacques Masson (1693–1741).

Each had inherited considerable wealth and experience from ex-Protestant families having ties to the Dutch Netherlands and a history of timber and forge management in central and eastern France at the turn of the century. In the 1720s the pair was heavily involved in large and dubious financial and timber operations for the Duke of Lorraine and the French Navy in eastern France. Masson was a smart but sloppy businessman who kept few records—no doubt deliberately, for he was jailed briefly in 1729 for alleged fraud. On this and other awkward occasions, he relied on the protection of the powerful to see him through. He had links to the Paris brothers, liquidators of John Law's system and financial consultants to the Duke of Lorraine, but his trump card was the support of the navy, in particular of its energetic secretary, Maurepas. Maurepas turned a blind eye to the many fringe profits Masson and associates made on timber deals, such as free *flottage* down the Rhine for their own wood on the navy's timber booms, subsidized shipping, diplomatic coverage, toll exemptions, and the chance to pick up non-navy wood cheaply when moving into an area to cut trees marked for the king. Maurepas gave them extremely generous advances and stifled the qualms of his officials about the quality of the wood delivered. The secretary had a fleet to rebuild and could not afford to be too nice about the means.

Younger brother Pierre Babaud de la Chaussade really represents the next generation of entrepreneurs, which was both established and respectable (Pierre reinforced his noble status by holding the office of *Secrétaire du roi*). His predecessors had diversified into iron in the 1720s and 1730s, buying up forges in the Nivernais. In 1736 Babaud de la Chaussade, by then sole manager of the family firm, got the contract when Maurepas decided to privatize a big forge at Cosne, where the navy had been developing a process for manufacturing high-quality bar anchors using cementation.

Bamford devotes much space to describing Babaud de la Chaussade's management of his forge complex in and near the Nivernais. But in the absence of account books, he cannot really say who was the most important or successful: Babaud the entrepreneur, Babaud the manager, Babaud the forgemaster, Babaud the timber contractor (he re-entered the trade in 1775), Babaud the distributor of subcontracts, or Babaud the seigneur and landlord. It becomes clear that Babaud was a businessman, not an innovator, who concentrated on marketing products of existing processes (though he did have far-seeing plans for the use of structural iron in Paris). He preferred charcoal refining to coal processes for quite rational, economic reasons. Defense contracts evidently gave him enormous advantages, including easy financing. Although he never had a complete monopoly of the navy's anchor supply, he would have been difficult to replace. But such advantages were counterbalanced by the way he, like other government creditors, was transformed into an underwriter of state debt at the end of wars, when the king paid many of his bills with dubious long-term paper. Even the final "nationalization" of Babaud's forges by Necker in 1781 can be seen as a covert device for floating government war debt: much of it was paid in long-term notes, few of which were honored.

How did Babaud make money? Despite the difficulty of collecting from the state, its wars appear to have favored him: he complained that his profits in the Seven Years' War only amounted to the equivalent of simple interest, but at least he lost nothing. Peace may have been kind to him as well. Although he had difficulties with reconversion after the Seven Years' War (his anchors were undersold by Spanish products in the commercial ports), he managed to get a partial monopoly of the anchor trade to the colonies and sold a lot of iron products within France. Moreover, the sheer volume of government wartime business and the influence and help the state gave him—controlling workers, bending tariffs and tolls, and so forth—allowed him to expand his operations to such a scale that he could produce iron goods for peacetime uses at competitive prices.

Babaud fit well into Old Regime society. He was a grand seigneur, landowner, and provincial notable, able to wield influence to gain advantages for his workers such as exemption from militia service. He evidently enjoyed playing the paternal seigneur on his estate and dispensing seigneurial justice. But the coercive elements of the *seigneurie* were hardly essential to his activities; a man of his stature could have leaned on royal tribunals and public authorities to get the same results. *Seigneurie* meant, above all, wood supplies and plant sites; social prestige was an agreeable bonus that Professor Bamford may have exaggerated.

But Babaud did need the state, and the most fascinating aspect of this book is its description of the workings of patronage and client relationships in the Old Regime. Although Maurepas was very kind to Babaud and his relatives while in office, Babaud was by no means his creature: each successive naval secretary, regardless of the faction to which he belonged, supported Babaud through thick and thin. If patronage and favor had built his predecessors' fortunes, Babaud's expertise and plant made him an irreplaceable national asset. There is a lesson here for political and social historians about the practical limits of coercion, privilege, and patronage in the Old Regime. Bamford's careful and extremely detailed study does not lend itself to easy and simple conclusions (his own, characteristically modest and thoughtful, do not get in the way of the evidence), but it will inspire reflection on these and related subjects for many years to come.

T. J. A. Le Goff, *York University, Toronto*

Die Reichsbank und die finanzielle Kriegsvorbereitung 1907 bis 1914. By Reinhold Zilch. Berlin: Akademie-Verlag, 1987. Pp. 239. DM 40.

It is interesting to reflect on how much more exotic this book appears in 1990 than in the summer of 1989.

Then, responding to the inevitable conditioning of all Marxist-Leninist historians, I would have felt impelled to encourage any manifestation of serious empirical scholarship in the GDR that addressed issues of some interest to western historians—if only for the new information it might provide—just as I would have felt inclined to greet positively signs of internal debate within the framework of Marxist-Leninist orthodoxy that showed some tendency to bend rigid categories and circumvent accepted dogmas. One had to assume the existence of unbreachable barriers, but from time to time one could hope to encourage serious research and increase the points of intellectual contact.

Today, with the East German political system in a state of utter collapse, with dogmas discredited and archives open, such efforts have become obsolete, though they will remain a habit for a while. Nevertheless, the question in assessing East German historiography is analogous to that in assessing the entire East German productive apparatus: What is left that can and should be saved? Is it even worth reviewing a study of the Reichsbank and pre-1914 financial mobilization for war that describes mobilization as one of the "roots of the collapse of the gold standard at the outbreak of the First World War, which initiated the permanent crisis of the capitalist currency system lasting to this day as a constituent element of the general crisis of capitalism" (p. 9)?

Happily, as has often been the case with the work of GDR economic historians, there is a good deal more to this book than such apocalyptic liturgy and the usual unenlightening rhetoric about "monopolies" and "imperialists" would suggest. Reinhold Zilch's most important contribution is to take a longer and broader perspective on Germany's financial preparations for war than the narrow concentration on financial mobilization measures and the legislation of August 1914 to be found in the works of both Marxist and non-Marxist historians. Zilch contests neither the limited nature of Germany's financial mobilization nor the inadequacy of those measures to finance a long war without serious inflationary consequences—points that already have been discussed in the literature. Indeed, he provides some important new evidence that Germany's leaders were more conscious of the financial risks they took than has been supposed, and he adds to the evidence for the important role played by diverging economic and bureaucratic interests in undermining the efforts of the Reichsbank and other agencies and interests to prepare more systematically for the war. Thus, using important new materials from the Reichsbank papers in Potsdam, Zilch demonstrates that as late as June 1914 the Reichsbank was unable to implement its plans for the compulsory regulation of the banking industry. It had hoped thereby to reduce competition and increase coverage so it would have sufficient liquidity in the event of a war or economic crisis.

In Zilch's view, however, the failure of such efforts is less significant than the fact that they were made. Not only did those measures prefigure many of the characteristics of the wartime organization of the economy, but they also illustrated how concern for maintaining liquidity was linked "to those ambivalent developments . . . which aimed at a modernization of Germany's monetary and credit system" (p. 90). Here Zilch is at his most suggestive and provides strong support for his thesis. He posits that, especially after the crisis of 1907, two concerns went hand in hand: concern for the Reichsbank's ability to provide liquidity and concern for meeting its coverage requirements, both as the lender of last resort to the banks in times of economic crisis and as the chief source of liquidity in times of war. Both concerns were demonstrated in the attempts to impose greater discipline on the banking system as well as in the promotion of paper money, giro accounts, and other mechanisms aimed at increasing liquidity. There is reason to argue that military urgency grew in importance as war approached, and Zilch shows that the Reichsbank, in collusion with the government, stretched the regulations on paper money issuance because of the international situation.

One point needs more careful analysis than Zilch provides: To what extent was the modernization of the currency system perverted by military demands? More serious attention could also be given to the actual manner in which financial preparation for war undermined the already shaky international gold standard system. Insofar as the Reichsbank had participated in the informal central bank cooperation that some historians feel was essential to maintaining the prewar gold standard, its growing tendency (and that of other central banks) to hoard gold and give priority to mobilization issues certainly may have undermined the gold standard before it collapsed. These matters are worthy of further exploration, and now that Zilch and his colleagues are safely ensconced with the rest of us in the "permanent crisis of the capitalist currency system," one may hope that we can join together in exploring them with renewed vigor.

GERALD D. FELDMAN, *University of California, Berkeley*

The First World War: An Agrarian Interpretation. By Avner Offer. Oxford: Clarendon Press, 1990. Pp. xix, 440. $48.00.

This is a superb piece of historical writing. It is a monograph in the grand tradition: an expansive yet intensively researched argument focused on one specific proposition. Avner Offer's thesis is that German food shortages resulting from the British naval blockade played a more significant role in the defeat of Germany in World War I than has usually been appreciated. Furthermore, he argues, the blockade strategy was an almost inevitable outcome of the tendency of specialized industrial economies to become dependent on external—and especially overseas—food supplies. In developing and backing up his argument Offer ranges prodigiously over a vast amount of research. Consequently, the book deals with far more than its particular thesis would imply.

Offer begins directly enough with a careful examination of the effect of the blockade on Germany. He concludes that the blockade was a very important element in the defeat of Germany: certainly not the sole cause but, in combination with the protracted nature of the war and the battlefront offensive in the late stages, a factor that broke the back of German resistance. It did not actually bring on mass starvation or even the imminent threat of starvation, but the severe shortages of food undermined morale and Germany's willingness to continue the war. There is lots of grist for the economic historian in this account as the author surveys the logistics of wartime food and materials supply.

Offer then turns to the rather extended economic history of Britain's increased reliance on overseas food supplies. This section provides a review of Britain's agricultural policies and the contest between different social orders as well as an examination of agricultural development in the overseas Dominions that contains useful new material. The argument is that the economic benefits of international specialization in foodstuffs were purchased at a cost and sowed the seeds of political instability. The form of Britain's economic development therefore played a greater role in the onset of World War I than has usually been recognized.

In the next section of the book, dealing with military planning, the author makes two main points. One is that national security in regimes heavily reliant on overseas food supplies depended on naval superiority, and naval strength quickly became very expensive. Offer draws an interesting comparison between British and German costs of food: the burden of Germany's grain tariff is balanced against Britain's cheap overseas grain supplies plus the costs of maintaining a navy to protect them. British naval strategists came to worry increasingly about the nation's vulnerability to blockade; this in turn made possible thinking about an offensive blockade. Although Germany was less dependent on overseas grain supplies, she too was vulnerable; blockade could be used effectively to undermine German willingness to wage war. Offer argues persuasively that Britain had actually begun to plan the strategy of naval blockade much earlier than is commonly realized. The legality and morality of a naval blockade were delicate matters; hence, Britain's plans were never made obvious enough to Germany to be effective in forestalling war itself. Offer concludes that "It is a tragedy that the Atlantic orientation was strong enough to win the war but not strong enough to prevent it."

A particularly interesting facet of the argument is that the naval blockade not only helped end the war but also was deliberately used to shape the peace. The blockade was continued well after Germany had capitulated. The screws continued to be tightened as a way of forcing Germany to accept particular terms of the Peace proposal. The role of the overseas Dominions, not just as suppliers of troops and military materiel but also as sources of the agricultural supplies that eventually gave Britain the upper hand, was greatly strengthened in the process. Australia, especially, was thereby able to play a part in the Peace deliberations that far outweighed the status its small population would otherwise have afforded it.

There is so much more to this book than its title suggests, and so much to interest a wide range of readers, that it deserves to be very widely read. Its author must be commended for such a splendid piece of work.

R. M. McInnis, *Queen's University, Canada*

The Robert Hall Diaries, 1947–53. Edited by Alec Cairncross. London: Unwin Hyman, 1989. Pp. 326. $90.00.

It has been known for some years that while Robert Hall (later Lord Robert Hall) was Director of the Economic Section of the U.K. Cabinet Offices, he kept a detailed and revealing diary of the events of his working life that would be of considerable value to economists interested in the policy uses to which their theories are put and to the many economic and political historians studying the early post–World War II years in Britain. The publication of the diary (of which this is the first volume) is therefore very welcome, and it does not disappoint the high expectations of its contents.

Robert Hall was the fourth director of the Section, which had been established in January 1941 under John Jewkes. (The Section had previously been part of the Central Economic Information Service, which was split into the Economic Section and the Central Statistical Office.) The director for most of the war was Lionel Robbins, who returned to the London School of Economics after the end of the war and was succeeded by James Meade. When Meade resigned out of a mixture of frustration and ill health in 1947, Hall was persuaded to abandon his partial postwar return to academic life and move from a part-time position at the Board of Trade, which he had combined with his fellowship at Trinity College, Oxford. By the time Hall took over the Section it had established its permanency in Whitehall, but in spite of Meade's best efforts was still removed from the center of macroeconomic policy action, the Treasury. Under Hall the Section came into its own, becoming the major source of economic policy advice, a position acknowledged in 1953 when it moved into the Treasury. Unlike his two predecessors Hall did not return to academic life. From 1947 to 1961 he was "adviser to a succession of governments. He served under eight Chancellors [of the Exchequer] and exercised more influence on economic policy than perhaps any other official" (p. viii). At such a formative period in the development of the so-called Keynesian policy of aggregate demand management, mainly through the budget, he was uniquely well placed to exert an economist's influence and to observe and comment on the manners and mores of his ministers and colleagues. And his diary records this, as Cairncross justifiably claims, "in a lively and readable way and allows us to trace, week by week, the current preoccupations of the Chancellor's advisers—something difficult to do from the vast mass of official papers in the Public Record Office" (p. viii). As readers of Cairncross's other recent publications—for example, his *Years of Recovery: British Economic Policy 1945–51* (London, 1985)—will know, it provides a good deal of additional information on British economic policy in the late 1940s, most notably on the devaluation of the pound in September 1949, in which Hall played a decisive role.

The diary has been sensibly and unobtrusively edited, with brief explanations and references provided where necessary. There are some slips and inaccuracies, the most surprising of which is apparent in Cairncross's comparison of Hall's diaries with Meade's diary of his stint as director of the Section. He unaccountably claims that

Meade's diary is "limited to three short periods at the end of 1944, the end of 1945 and the middle of 1946" (p. viii), whereas it runs continuously and at considerable length from November 1944 to September 1946 (*The Collected Papers of James Meade, Volume IV: The Cabinet Office Diary 1944–46* [Winchester, MA, 1990]). The occasional errors do not, however, detract from the book's value to scholars, nor from its fascination for anyone interested in the postwar history of Britain or the role of economists in public life.

SUSAN HOWSON, *University of Toronto*

Labour and Business in Modern Britain. Edited by Charles Harvey and John Turner. London: Frank Cass, 1989. Pp. 117.

This brief, informative volume consists of six essays and an introduction by John Turner that seeks "to outline the intellectual context in which they have been written" (p. 1). In the main, the essays attempt to analyze the forces that have shaped British business strategies. Di Drummond looks at management efforts to control labor and labor markets on pre-1914 railways; Alan McKinlay and Jonathan Zeitlin argue that engineering employers did not collectively seek the "deskilling" of their industry during the half-century before World War II; Robert Fitzgerald explores the impetus behind the "welfarist" policies of the Bryant and May matchmaking company following the famous strike of 1888; Gerald Crompton examines the increasingly tense relationship between workers and employers on the railways during the interwar era; Howard Gospel studies the rise and fall of national collective bargaining among flour millers; and Tom Donnelly and David Thoms investigate employer attitudes toward labor relations in Coventry's motor industry from the outbreak of World War II until the mid-1970s.

A common theme unites these efforts. Implicitly, and occasionally explicitly, the contributors argue against the thesis advanced by Harry Braverman 16 years ago in *Labour and Monopoly Capital* (New York, 1974), that under conditions of advanced capitalism employers will fight to control labor by "deskilling" it—that is, by degrading work. The essayists seek to show instead, through their empirical studies, that some British employers at any rate did *not* seek the degradation of labor; that regional or commercial or other situational particularities led employers to implement a variety of strategies, some very different from the one observed and predicted by Braverman; that his argument, in fact, was crudely mechanical.

A second, related thesis also links these essays: that historians who have sought to understand British industrial relations by concentrating on labor and its institutions have grasped only part of the picture. The historians contributing to this volume contend that the specific situation of a business is at least as important as its labor force in determining the policies it will follow and even, sometimes, in establishing the tenor of relations between workers and managers within it.

In sum, this collection shows that product and labor markets, management paternalism, and even the labor process (which is shaped as much by management as by labor—but not by a monolithic management that always shares identical goals), have been the motor force driving the history of industrial relations.

The evidence adduced to support this outlook is certainly convincing. These essays, all of them, are carefully crafted. But are their authors flogging a dead horse? After all, it has been some time since Braverman's thesis was regarded as positing an unproblematic model for *all* advanced capitalist societies. And surely even labor historians no longer insist, if they ever did, that industrial relations history is determined by one single class.

Still, in reminding us to beware all-embracing theories on the one hand and tunnel vision on the other, and in providing empirical case studies that are models of brevity, clarity, and focus, this volume admirably fulfills its purpose as explained by the editor: to combine business history and industrial relations history "to provide a more convincing and lifelike interpretation of the industrial past."

JONATHAN SCHNEER, *Georgia Institute of Technology*

The Origins of Backwardness in Eastern Europe. Edited by Daniel Chirot. Berkeley: University of California Press, 1989. Pp. ix, 260. $40.00.

The recent revolution in eastern Europe guarantees a captive audience for a book of this title. The book definitely deserves to be widely read, especially by western economists and political scientists who are shaping policy in the countries of the former eastern bloc. Both popular discourse and discussions among social scientists in the West still tend to couch current events in post-1945 Cold War terms. Thus, economic backwardness in eastern Europe is almost universally attributed to the failures of socialism. Daniel Chirot's book makes clear what knowledgeable historians already knew: that the economic lag of eastern Europe is deeply rooted in the distant past, not a product of the post-1945 era.

The project that stands behind the book actually predates the revolutionary events of 1989 and makes an important contribution to two branches of scholarship. First, it fills a large gap in the literature of European economic history, in which eastern Europe is greatly underrepresented. Second, it offers a good case study for development theorists who try to understand why growth occurs in some parts of the world but not others.

Certainly one clear aim of the book is to shed light on the longstanding debate about why the whole world is not developed. Is it because Third World countries are trapped in exploitative market relationships with the industrialized world, or because local conditions in the Third World become obstacles to growth-promoting forces? Taken as a whole the individual studies by Robert Brenner, Péter Gunst, Jacek Kochanowicz, Fikret Adanir, John R. Lampe, and Gale Stokes give little support for dependency theory explanations, preferring to emphasize adverse effects of local conditions in peripheral economies. The authors work within a framework that stresses the interaction of politics and economics and of external and internal forces. Between 1500 and 1914, eastern Europe was opened to western trade and political influence. The authors show how western penetration interacted with indigenous social and political structures in eastern Europe to determine a course of relative backwardness.

A short review cannot do justice to the richness of the material, so I will focus on two major themes of the volume. The first is that backwardness in eastern Europe originates far in the past and has domestic roots. Europe was prepared for its "economic miracle" (E. H. Jones) by 1500 apparently because of events in the west, not the east. The authors agree that by 1500 eastern Europe was already backward compared to western Europe. Brenner stresses differences in agrarian systems. Western feudalism began to generate capitalist property relations well before 1500, when eastern Europe still had less flexible, precapitalist property rights systems. Gunst and Lampe point to differences in urban life and population density. In the west, urban centers and their rural hinterlands were highly integrated; in the east, the ebb and flow of urban life was tied to economic and political forces emanating from distant places. In the west, high population density fostered intensive agriculture before 1500; in the east, low population density promoted extensive agriculture long after 1500. When a world market formed in the sixteenth century, eastern Europe developed market ties with the west, serving as a primary producing exporter of foodstuffs and raw materials. The accompanying move toward more coercive forms of labor organization based on serf labor did not result from western penetration but rather from underlying pre-1500 social and political conditions.

The other major theme of the book is the diversity of economic performance *within* eastern Europe. The authors distinguish between the regions in the north—eastern Prussia, Poland, and the territories formerly under Habsburg control—and the Balkan lands to the south that were under Ottoman control. The northern lands were the center of the "second serfdom," where the growth of large manorial estates using coerced labor to produce marketable crops delayed the introduction of capitalist relations. Yet Gunst argues that it was precisely their market orientation toward the west that ultimately placed these estates in the forefront of modernization in the eighteenth and nineteenth centuries. This was especially true for the Bohemian lands and Hungary. As Kochanowicz argues, agriculture became more efficient there than in Poland because the powerful Habsburg state adopted policies that strengthened the peasantry vis-a-vis the nobility.

In the Balkan lands, Ottoman control perpetuated a greater degree of economic backwardness: there, peasant agriculture prevailed. But as Lampe and Adanir show, it suffered under the crushing weight of the centralized Ottoman state, as fiscal and military motives dominated both the *timar* system and the later *çiftlik* system. Commercial agriculture could not flourish because the state siphoned off agricultural surplus to finance military adventures and a bloated bureaucracy. The Balkan territories ceased losing economic ground to western Europe and the more advanced regions of eastern Europe only in the late nineteenth century. Ottoman rule began to crumble and the independent states of Romania, Bulgaria, and Serbia became increasingly integrated into the more powerful economies of the west.

Differential economic performance within eastern Europe had implications for politics in the twentieth century. In the volume's closing essay, Gale Stokes uses Barrington Moore's model of political culture to explain why some areas of pre-1945 eastern Europe (Czechoslovakia) moved toward democracy while others (many Balkan states) tended toward authoritarian regimes.

Chirot's volume does not suffer the normal flaw of most edited works—that is, uneven quality among the individual contributions. Instead the authors used a common approach in producing a uniformly high-quality blend of social science theory and history. Thc volume will aid nonspecialists who want to fill gaps in their knowledge or incorporate material on eastern Europe into their advanced undergraduate and graduate courses in economic history.

David F. Good, *University of Minnesota*

ASIA, AFRICA, AND AUSTRALIA

Brides of the Sea: Port Cities of Asia from the 16th–20th Centuries. Edited by Frank Broeze. Honolulu: University of Hawaii Press, 1989. Pp. xvi, 255. $32.00.

This volume on the port cities of Asia originated in a multidisciplinary conference on Indian Ocean studies, and its focus remains centered in South Asia. Four of its nine papers discuss Indian or Sri Lankan cities or port systems; four others cover port and commercial networks within or tangential to the Indian Ocean, including East Africa and Southeast Asia; only one paper is devoted to the East Asian sphere.

The contributions are selective, reflecting the geographical patchwork of Asian port cities. Jeddah, the "bride of the sea" evoked in the title, is the only West Asian city mentioned; the paper on Shanghai is the single East Asian contribution. Colombo is allowed two papers, but Bombay and Calcutta are neglected altogether. Because the collection sought to identify a new conceptual approach to the study of Asian urbanization, one focusing on the unique nature of the port city, the selection hardly seems to cover Asia, especially considering the omission of Japan.

The book opens with an introduction by Frank Broeze that addresses questions raised in the text. A review article by Broeze, Peter Reeves, and Kenneth McPherson summarizing previous literature follows. The remaining eight papers, termed "case studies," examine three individual cities—Colombo (K. Dharmasena, Michael Roberts), Shanghai (Robert Eng), and Makassar (Heather Sunderland)—or consider port systems more broadly—in precolonial Southeast Asia (Anthony Reid), on the Coromandel coast (S. Arasarantnam), in twentieth-century India (Atiya Habeeb Kidwai). One paper looks at the maritime perspectives of East Africa (B. S. Hoyle). In the concluding paper Rhoads Murphey describes the evolution of the port city.

The studies cover a time span from the sixteenth to the twentieth century. As Reid's paper demonstrates, few Asian port cities began as colonial creations; they were selected by the Dutch or British precisely because they were already important nodes in the precolonial economy. Murphey points out that "port" and "harbor" are not synonymous; many Asian ports, such as Shanghai and Calcutta, are situated on "pitifully poor harbors" while other physically superb harbors go unused. Port cities, according to Broeze, "link together their hinterlands and forelands in dynamic union." Murphey argues that the hinterland connections are by far the most important; the port city is therefore an economic construct before it is a geophysical entity. Only those cities in which maritime activities, including such auxiliary aspects as marine insurance, are still dominant qualify as true port cities. Others, such as twentieth-century Calcutta and Shanghai, have gone beyond the status of port cities to become enormous polyglomerate general cities.

The papers present impressive empirical research, especially the two on Colombo, which serves as a model for the Asian port city. Kidwai (twentieth-century Indian ports) and Eng (Shanghai) emphasize statistical methodology; Hoyle's paper on port systems in East Africa evaluates the effects of changing technology.

Little new theory is offered; the familiar concepts of hinterland and foreland are examined in the Asian context, although the terms *metropolis* and *primate city* could be used with more precision. Implicit in the premise of the book is E. W. Fox's concept of the exogenous international circulation of maritime trade as compared to endogenous inland trading patterns; but Fox's seminal work is never cited. The lack of a theoretical agenda is, however, refreshing: although nearly every paper touches on colonialism, there is no haranguing about "world systems" or "dependency theory."

This handsome volume is well supplied with maps and graphs and 42 superb old etchings and lithographs, courtesy of the Mitchell Library, New South Wales. Unfortunately, this visual essay is supported by no commentary in the text; the plates are often uncoordinated with the chapters they fall among. The European, mainly Dutch, views offer a peculiarly western angle of vision, depicting the "noble savage" (pp. 103, 116) or giving picturesque examples of the exotic (pp. 36, 46, 101) or the technologically backward (pp. 78, 231, 239). Such intriguing illustrations cry out for textual attention.

The text is difficult to read, in part because of small and crowded print, but primarily due to inadequate editing. Jargon, run-on sentences, and dense syntax will deter all but the most committed of readers. Happy exceptions are Dharmasena's paper on Colombo and Murphey's concluding essay, both examples of lucid, compact prose.

Despite shortcomings, the book makes a valuable contribution to an emerging subspecialty that combines urban studies with maritime economic history. Broeze should be congratulated for bringing together Australian, South Asian, U.S., and European scholarship; the new perspectives from Australia are especially welcome.

LINDA COOKE JOHNSON, *Michigan State University*

Between Dayak and the Dutch: The Economic History of Southeast Kalimantan. By J. Thomas Lindblad. Dordrecht: Foris Publications, 1988. Pp. x, 282. Dfl 30.

A quantitative analysis of regional economic history, when the region itself is a part of a larger political entity, is always extremely difficult. In this book J. Thomas Lindblad undertakes the difficult task of writing the history of Southeast Kalimantan (Borneo), even though it represents only a small part of Dutch territories in the Indonesian archipelago and about three-quarters of the Dutch part of the island. However, the colonial administrative structure in Southeast Kalimantan after 1880 became sufficiently consolidated and effective to allow the analysis of the region as a separate entity for the years from 1880 to 1942.

Lindblad subdivides this period into two development stages: the preparatory phase (1880 to 1914) and the era of actual expansion (1914 to 1942). Chapter 1 introduces the region and Chapters 2 and 3 describe the two development stages.

During the preparatory phase various ethnic groups strove "towards monopolization of trade and production." Dutch traders tried to gain control of the region's pepper trade from the early seventeenth century, with little success. By 1810 the colonial power was pushed out of the trade scene and two categories of traders, Bugis and Chinese, filled the vacuum. By 1880 the Malays specialized in riverside and short-distance trade and the Chinese and Europeans in intra-Indonesia and foreign trade. In terms of production, the rice harvest gradually increased over time and new commercial crops—tobacco, coffee, and rubber—were introduced. Lindblad argues that the extraordinarily high risk and high profit encouraged monopolization of activities and created conditions for rapid future expansion.

Defining the era of actual expansion as 1914 to 1942 is somewhat arbitrary. After 1900 the growth rates for almost all sectors of the economy were much higher than before 1900. Production of commercial crops—coal, oil, and forest products—showed a steep upward trend during the latter half of the so-called preparatory phase.

A worldwide increase in rubber demand in 1900 led to the development of large estates at the initial stage. Labor shortages restricted further expansion of the estates, but families found it profitable to learn the technology for operating small-scale gardens. The "Dayaks," the indigenous people, started to cultivate rubber in the late 1920s, when the downturn of the market was already under way. Crude oil output and exports also increased at a rapid rate.

Lindblad argues that two different types of producer behavior supported this expansion of the economy. He argues that the level of production of small-scale producers depended on their "pre-determined" need for cash. This explains the negative relationship observed between prices and output, especially for rubber exports. The second type of behavior is the usual profit-maximization principle of producers. The profit-maximization rule applied to "large-scale capital-intensive production in both oil extraction and refining and modern logging or coal mining" (p. 115). The nature of growth of the economy from 1914 to 1942 does not, however, systematically support this conclusion. Both rubber and oil output expanded even with declining prices in certain specific years.

A negative relationship between output and prices in certain years may not necessarily imply absence of the profit motive. The long gestation period for rubber and the high fixed costs of oil industries with rapidly changing technology can create this type of unexpected result. For the rubber industry, a better indicator of a producer's behavior is the number of trees planted rather than total output or exports at any point in time. In fact, the rapid expansion of rubber planting in the indigenous sector triggered by favorable international prices clearly contradicts the hypothesis that these producers were guided by a predetermined, relatively stable demand for cash.

Chapter 4 describes the system of administration under colonial rule, taxation schemes, tax rates for agricultural and nonagricultural producers, total tax burden by ethnic groups, public expenditures by sectors, and the quality of life of the population in general. Maintenance of the colonial administrative structure alone accounted for more than 40 percent of total public expenditures even during the 1920s and 1930s, long after the end of active rebellion against colonial rule. The high cost of the colonial apparatus kept the resources available for development at a very low level. It is interesting to note that the efforts of the Dutch colonial government to encourage migration from Java to Kalimantan proved as dismaying as the recent costly transmigration program of the Indonesian government.

Chapter 5 analyzes the dynamics of expansion. During the period of expansion the population grew at a much more rapid rate than during the prewar years. Lindblad argues that this population growth is consistent with the hypothesis that better economic conditions allow more mouths to be fed. A closer look at the population growth rates does not support this conclusion. The population grew more in rural areas than in urban areas, though the expansion of rural sectors was much slower (p. 248). Moreover, in all less-developed countries population growth accelerated around this period, with or without economic expansion, due to a rapid decline in mortality. The international movement of population, on the other hand, shows a strong relationship with regional economic expansion.

International trade was the most important engine of growth for the region, and Lindblad examines the terms of trade and the export-import balance using data from colonial documents. He estimates net barter terms of trade and income terms of trade for the years 1900 to 1940. Net barter terms of trade consistently declined from 1.1 during 1915–1919 to 0.34 during 1935–1939. The income terms of trade fluctuated over the years, with no observable trend. In addition to the problems of data quality, equating the import price index with the rice price index makes the estimates highly suspect. Excluding some abnormally low output years, rice accounted for 10 to 20 percent of total imports from 1900 to 1930. After the 1930s rice ceased to be an important import commodity. Therefore, using the rice price will distort the estimates, especially from 1930 to 1940. A change in the ratio of intra-Indonesia trade to international trade, which most likely happened during this period of wildly fluctuating world prices, affects the estimate of income terms of trade significantly, which in turn reduces the intertemporal comparability of the estimates.

The author proposes a macroeconomic model to estimate the system of behavioral equations for the economy. It appears that the equations were estimated directly, without conversion into their reduced forms. Consumption and wage bill equations include endogenous variables on the right-hand side, and the OLS method was used for estimation purposes, which makes the estimates imprecise and biased. The macro model estimated provides no additional useful insight into the working of the economy, and the poor fit of the wage bill equation probably points to errors in the data rather than to a true negative relationship between current output and wage bill.

In many places the book is difficult to follow due to incomplete information on the region's economic structure, sources of data, and definitions of key variables and methods used for calculating the economic aggregates. Moreover, so many crucial points on estimation and test statistics are omitted from the text and reported as notes at the end of the book that a reader must go back and forth quite frequently to understand the results as well as the methods used in the analytical sections. The author does provide data on exports, imports, output, consumption, and investment in the region from 1880 to 1940; the bibliography is also useful.

M. MAHMUD KHAN, *Tulane University*

Economic Growth in Prewar China. By Thomas G. Rawski. Berkeley: University of California Press, 1989. Pp. xxxiii, 448. $49.50.

Nothing is more fundamental to a people's existence than the actions involved in making a living. Far from being solely a technological pursuit, a livelihood implies a myriad of forces defined by a behavioral web of cultural and political mores and rules.

Change the way livings are made and those changes will reverberate throughout society. In *Economic Growth in Prewar China* Thomas Rawski argues for the presence of such fundamental economic changes in early twentieth-century China: "The sustained expansion of output per head became a regular feature of Chinese economic life in the early decades of the present century. This fact, with its momentous economic and social implications, represents the principal finding of my study" (p. 344).

At the outset Rawski makes his research intentions clear: "This study seeks to delineate both the extent and the limits of growth and structural change in China's prewar economy, to investigate the relationship between the modern and the inherited sectors, and to consider the impact of prewar developments on the shape of China's economy in the postwar period of Communist leadership" (p. xix). Quite rightly the author observes that the best pursuit of such an intent is quantitative.

> This offers the most promising avenue for constructing an overall framework that can deepen our knowledge and understanding of issues relating to economic growth and stagnation in prewar China. In a large economy like China's, national or regional trends in output, incomes, investment, prices, taxes, wages and the like are statistical phenomena whose dimensions cannot be inferred from individual testimony or other anecdotal evidence. Reliable generalizations require the statistical foundation that this volume seeks to establish (p. xxxii).

In appendices Rawski provides new and revised series reporting the growth of Chinese manufacturing output between 1912 and 1936, the sectoral composition of that output in 1933, estimates of China's money supply between 1910 and 1936, and the volume of cargo traffic in prewar China. In addition to these series, Rawski also offers revised estimates of most of the other economic sectors' production growth rates during the years 1914–1918 to 1931–1936.

By its construction the book is destined for use as a resource rather than for popular consumption. Much of the text discusses the assumptions and calculations underlying the national income accounting procedures, while analysis of the dynamics underlying the quantitative story is brief. The Introduction and Chapter 1 summarize Rawski's overview of the important characteristics of twentieth-century China's development process, but these insights receive no further elaboration. This is a shame because people may miss the book's importance: it is a painstaking and serious attempt to reconstruct 30 years of China's macroeconomic history and, in the process, to argue for a significantly different interpretation than the one prevailing. By suggesting growth in place of stagnation in early twentieth-century China, Rawski urges China researchers to reexamine their priors before committing their analysis. Such a dramatic shift in the perception of China's aggregate economic performance should almost certainly inspire revised interpretations of individual economic, political, and social interactions. This is not to say, however, there is no room for argument with Rawski's work.

The book presents a national income accounting intended to replace two works by K. C. Yeh and Dwight Perkins. Although all three use many of the same sources, the questionable quality of the data necessitates assumptions regarding missing data, and hence the authors arrive at different conclusions. Both Yeh and Perkins report approximately equal growth rates for aggregate real output and population for the two decades between 1914 and 1936. Rawski revises these estimates and finds that output increased faster than population for the same period.

Rawski revises the Yeh-Perkins estimates in two parts. First he revises their estimates of growth rates in all productive activities outside of agriculture. While he revises upward eight out of ten sectoral growth rates (see Tables 6.1–6.3, p. 280), the impact on aggregate output is not great. Yeh reports an average annual growth rate of 1.1 percent for China's real output as opposed to Rawski's 1.4 percent. Depending on which of two population estimates is used, these figures translate into per-capita growth rates of 0.2 percent or 0.5 percent (Yeh) versus 0.5 percent or 0.8 percent (Rawski). (See Table 6.3.

Yeh's per-capita growth rates are reported to be 0.1 percent and 0.4 percent, but subtracting the population growth rates from the real output growth rates [as was done for all other estimates] yields measures of 0.2 percent and 0.5 percent.)

This raises an obvious question: is a 0.3 percent difference in growth rate estimates significant? Further, should we subscribe to Rawski's statement that ". . . even with generous allowance for possible error, the results in Table 6.3 demonstrate the possibility that prewar China experienced substantial economic growth, both in terms of aggregate and in terms of per capita output" (pp. 279–80)? I suspect 0.3 percent is not a significant difference. I also do not see how the per-capita growth rates of 0.2, 0.5, or 0.8 percent can be described as "substantial." Relative to per-capita real output growth rates registered currently in China, Japan, and other countries as well as historical rates observed in industrializing nations, these rates are small. Further, on an absolute scale, a growth rate of 0.5 percent in real output per capita translates into a doubling of per-capita output only after approximately 150 years (while a growth rate of 0.8 percent for per-capita output would need approximately 100 years for the original amount to double).

The second part of Rawski's revision re-estimates the growth rate of the agricultural sector, by far the dominant sector in the Chinese economy, and incorporates the revised estimates into aggregate output. Here Rawski revises Yeh's estimate of annual agricultural output growth of 0.8 percent to "low," "preferred," and "high" percentages of 1.0–1.3, 1.4–1.7, and 1.8–2.1, respectively. He argues for such revisions using a mix of indirect observations—namely, increasing per-capita consumption of cotton cloth, increasing real wages in agriculture and nonskilled manufacturing occupations using rural labor, and a direct observation, a survey reporting farmers' judged improvements in living conditions in certain farm areas in the 1930s. As Rawski points out, none of these factors on its own can adequately support the conclusion of agricultural growth—all are subject to incalculable sampling biases and errors. (Rawski's discussion of the problems in the surveys is another of the most useful portions of his book.) These estimates, in combination with the revised industrial production growth rates of the first part, produce a "preferred" aggregate real output growth rate of 1.8–2.0 percent for 1914–1918 to 1931–1936 China and a "preferred" per-capita real output growth rate of 1.1 to 1.2 percent for the same period (p. 330).

One needs to adopt the right perspective on this work. This is a book about rates. Further, the temporal scope of these rates is limited to about 20 years. Any reader who has observed contemporary China must reconcile this story of "substantial" economic growth in early twentieth-century China with the observation of current relative poverty. The key to reconciliation, of course, is the short time span of the growth period. At the end of the period, per-capita real product was estimated to be only 60 *yuan*, with personal consumption estimated at 56 *yuan* (p. 25), figures pretty close to subsistence levels. At the suggested growth rates, 20 years would not have a substantial impact on the levels of the economic variables measured.

In general, I believe that Rawski's book enjoys a distinct advantage over Yeh's and Perkins's because he has been able to use material published since their books came out. Indeed, his bibliography offers a good starting point for a review of China's early twentieth-century economic history, especially his extensive citation of the Japanese literature. Yet due to the problems inherent in the data, the combined evidence cannot firmly cement Rawski's claim for economic growth (defined as a sustained increase in per-capita output) in early twentieth-century China. Further, there is even less support for his interpretation of those statistics as "substantial." What the author *has* introduced with these newly constructed numbers is the *possibility* of growth.

Why is this an important finding? The data underlying the works of Rawski, Liu and Yeh, and Perkins are sufficiently imprecise as to preclude one summary view of the early twentieth-century Chinese economy. Yet such has not been the case; ideas of economic stagnation and decline have dominated. Although some researchers such as

Ramon Myers have argued for growth, they sound as lone voices arguing from localized data. Rawski's book directly confronts the evidence on China's early twentieth-century aggregate economic behavior and argues that the data support a hypothesis of growth.

Rawski nowhere suggests that aggregate economic growth brings social complacency. In fact, accepting the possibility of China's growth in the early twentieth century should by no means silence investigations into the social, political, and military foment of the time. What it should do is cast doubt on the oft-cited reason for social protest—increasing economic exploitation (reputed to go hand in hand with economic stagnation or decline). Change, whether detrimental or beneficial, is fundamentally unsettling. When people's routines and methods of earning livelihoods are challenged, there is no predicting how they will react (or who or what they will blame). In fact, one might consider the proposition that social unrest in early twentieth-century China may testify to economic growth rather than stagnation or decline. Such speculation does not prove Rawski's hypothesis, but that is not the point here. What is important is that finally there are at least three different assumptions regarding the general economic climate of early twentieth-century China that researchers can entertain in studying their localized projects.

Economic Growth in Prewar China offers a quantitative study arguing that previously published works suggesting gloomy aggregate economic goings-on in early twentieth-century China need not be correct. On the contrary, economic opportunities may have been expanding during this time, yielding varying consequences for different portions of the population. How and to what extent these changes affected people's individual lives and promoted social, cultural, and political change lies in individual case studies yet to come. For now, however, the author has established the possibility that economic growth began in China not in the immediate decade following 1949, but in the couple of decades prior to it.

BARBARA SANDS, *University of Arizona*

Recovery from the Depression: Australia and the World Economy in the 1930s. Edited by R. G. Gregory and N. G. Butlin. New York: Cambridge University Press, 1988. Pp. x, 378. $49.50.

This useful volume is the product of a conference organized by Noel Butlin and Robert Gregory to analyze the Depression experience in Australia and the worldwide economic recovery process more generally. Six of the thirteen essays focus on the international dimensions of the interwar crisis, with specific reference to Australia, Britain, Canada, Japan, and New Zealand. The remaining papers examine the Australian experience in detail, singling out for investigation the agricultural and manufacturing sectors, the labor market, and fiscal and monetary policy. Butlin and Gregory have succeeded in compiling a fine contribution to the literature on the interwar economic crisis as well as country studies more generally. The sustained examination of what is today called the Pacific Rim is especially welcome.

Gregory's "Overview" essay opens the discussion nicely and sets the stage for Barry Eichengreen's paper on the Australian recovery in an international context. Reframing the findings of his influential 1985 work with Jeffrey Sachs [see this JOURNAL, 45 (Dec. 1985), pp. 925–46], Eichengreen focuses on the impact of devaluation on Australia's international competitiveness, real wages, firm profitability, and interest rates. He finds that depreciation policy stimulated recovery and constituted a net gain for all concerned. His argument is well supported by the essay of Mark Thomas on the Australian manufacturing sector in the mid-thirties. For Thomas, the effect of exchange-rate management on heavy manufacturing and employment explains the recovery process, rather than the impact of import substitution.

Recovery policy in Britain is analyzed by Timothy Hatton, who finds, unlike

Eichengreen, that the data do not unambiguously support an argument that depreciation improved Britain's competitive position. But the general tariff of the early thirties did increase aggregate demand through "expenditure-switching effects" (pp. 75–76). In contrast, Hatton attributes weak employment recovery to cyclical productivity changes rather than substitution effects occasioned by a lower bank rate.

A comparison of economic recovery in Australia and Canada concerns Alan Green and Gordon Sparks. The more robust upturn in Canada is found to be linked to a strong rebound in the United States; Australia lags as a consequence because of Britain's weaker reflation. This essay's main conclusion resonates with much of the work in the book as a whole in underscoring the importance of the impact of the "center" on the recovery experience of the "periphery."

Even so, as Gary Hawke shows in his essay on New Zealand, some smaller trading nations faced profound and often intractable difficulties in their efforts to emerge from the trough. Despite an aggressive and at times quite imaginative policy response, the New Zealand government could not transform a rigidity in the "economy [that] owed more to the limited nature of its non-agricultural resources than to a clear failure of entrepreneurial talent" (p. 134). Dependence on international markets that were quite soft at the time was the inevitable and unfortunate result.

The case of Japan was rather unique, of course, and this fact is brought out vividly by Yasukichi Yasuba. Confirming that the macroeconomic performance of the Japanese economy was better than most during the thirties, Yasuba notes that the aggregate data tend nevertheless to mask the severe rural distress that was also characteristic of the world economy. Yet government consumption made Japan's experience exceptional. From 4 percent of GNE in the early thirties to almost 8 percent by mid-decade, much of the public purchase of goods and services was linked to military procurement and planning for war.

Thomas Valentine's outstanding counterfactual essay opens the second part of the volume concerning the Australian interwar experience. By constructing a model of the interwar Australian economy Valentine is able to assess the "battle of the plans" determining government policy. Counterfactual simulations allow for a systematic comparison of Keynesian, monetarist, and exchange-rate approaches to the Australian slump. Regression results then enable Valentine to propose his own "Hindsight Plan": a combination of loose monetary, aggressive fiscal, and currency measures that would have worked "best." The major virtues of Valentine's exercise owe less to an understanding of actual events down under during the thirties than to an appreciation of the continuing serviceability of Keynesian, as distinct from the so-called New Macro-economic, approaches to understanding the trade cycle.

Australian budgetary policies were actually constrained, argues Jonathan Pincus, by the limited availability of domestic and foreign credit for public capital formation. Along with such obstructions to Keynesian solutions to the crisis, traditional views of the need for conservative monetary measures enervated government's role, as Matthew Butlin and Patricia Boyce show in their paper.

Australian unemployment data for the interwar period fail to confirm the legitimacy of job-search modeling of idleness, argue Robert Gregory, Vivian Ho, and Laura McDermott. Noting relatively stable real wages and productivity levels, these coauthors claim that "the long duration of unemployment . . . rule[s] out any labour market supply-side explanation of the [Australian] depression" (p. 244). Colin Forster takes a more disaggregated view of the labor statistics and finds an extremely uneven recovery in employment by the mid-thirties. Skilled and semiskilled workers did remarkably well by that time; other members of the work force did not. "A solution to the unemployment problem," writes Forster, "required a transformation of . . . industrial structure and the labour market. A quick solution . . . required a war" (p. 310).

Whether relief employment aided or hindered recovery occupies Graeme Snooks in his most interesting essay on Australian fiscal policy. Government efforts, he argues, had little effect either way because aid "programmes resulted in a shift of workers from full-time public works to part-time relief projects, [and so] the unemployed were given relief only at the expense of creating further unemployment" (p. 312). His paper stands as an important reminder that expenditure policies cannot be examined by historians in aggregate terms alone; their institutional contours must also be assessed.

Bruce Davidson and Ian McLean author two of the volume's most intriguing offerings. Davidson ponders the anomaly of Australian agriculture during the Depression. Despite the fact that farm prices fell more than manufacturing prices and general wages, real farm output actually rose during the thirties. The 1932 Ottawa Agreement, granting preferential tariff treatment to members of the British Empire (in exchange for which British exports were treated leniently by the Dominions), explains some of this remarkable turn of events. Davidson also finds that lower labor costs (and lower prices for some manufactured farming inputs) were a significant factor. Faced with high unemployment in nonfarm alternatives, and given the fact that farm incomes still managed to exceed the dole, rural producers stayed in their fields rather than participate in an exodus from the land.

The distributional aspects of the slump concern McLean, who here presents another part of the extremely important work he has been doing on interwar income distribution. Greater inequality generated by the downturn was ultimately ameliorated by an increase in the Australian government's share of national income by the end of the Depression decade. That rise was clearly due to the beginning of war in the Pacific and elsewhere, and its leveling effects serve (in McLean's mind) to lend support to the arguments of Kuznets and Williamson and Lindert concerning the general twentieth-century experience of industrialized nations.

This fine anthology does not disappoint. But I do have one quibble with it. While repeatedly speaking of the "recovery" process, the authors actually discuss the turning point rather than the reacquisition of precrash levels of output and employment. The point is not simply one of semantics. Investigations of the trough, as important and interesting as they are, do not—because they cannot—address questions of *trend* rates of change in major economic variables. Such long-run structural matters deserve continued attention from macroeconomists. Although this collection of essays adds a great deal to our knowledge of the international economic crisis of the interwar years, it leaves unaddressed those questions of secular growth and stagnation with which some economists and economic historians have, for more than a half-century, been preoccupied.

MICHAEL A. BERNSTEIN, *University of California, San Diego*

LATIN AMERICA

Real hacienda y economía en Hispanoamérica, 1541–1820. By B. H. Slicher van Bath. Amsterdam: CEDLA (Center for Latin American Research and Documentation), 1989. Pp. x, 182. $17.50.

This book takes on a huge and significant topic: the aggregate performance and nature of the Royal Treasury in Spanish America during nearly three centuries of colonial rule. It is not for the number-shy historian. In 182 pages, the reader encounters no less than 68 tables, 34 graphs, and 37 pages of statistical appendices; and much of the intervening text explicates these sometimes numbing numbers.

B. H. Slicher van Bath's is among the first attempts to produce global statistics from the monumental multivolume data set of Spanish American treasuries worked up and recently published by historians John TePaske and Herbert Klein. These complex regional data, still in largely unprocessed form, constitute one of the most remarkable continuous fiscal series in the Western world. They promise to transform thinking about Latin America's colonial government, economy, and society.

This book, then, is clearly a welcome and challenging exercise. Slicher van Bath's computer has organized, simplified, and analyzed revenues and expenditures from 44 of the known *Cajas* (regional treasuries), covering more than 39,000 monthly accounts. The information is rearranged into 20-year cycles and 9 major comparative regions. The book seeks simple correlations between regional fiscal trends. Separate chapters probe revenue transfers (a valiant clarifying task), taxation, military expenditures, and relationships—if any—to other existing long-range economic indicators such as prices. Discerning historians will find many of these numbers suggestive—particularly those revealing subtle regional shifts and changing patterns of revenue from commerce, mining, tribute, and consumption.

Yet *Real hacienda* remains a largely descriptive technical study with several peculiarities. First, Slicher van Bath glosses over troublesome questions about the suitability and reliability of aggregates based on the local TePaske-Klein accounts. An invaluable effort, his should be a more critical one. The work does not show, for example, how its statistics relate to other estimates of colonial finance. Second, the book is abstracted from the vast historical literature on colonial fiscality and from broader economic and social theory about fiscal development. It is conspicuously silent about the work of earlier economic historians. This creates several problems. General readers will have no idea whether its findings dispel or support existing historiography (concerning, for example, the seventeenth-century depression or the growing late-colonial fiscal pressures and regional differentiation). In general, the book is lacking in interpretation. Indeed, at times the multiplication of tables, charts, and calculations (sometimes poorly explained) leaves the impression of a wandering "SPSS history." Third, even as pure quantification it has oversimplifications and flaws. For example, the indexed series use each preceding subperiod as base years—not the clearest way to communicate long-term developments.

In short, this book serves as a useful first glimpse at the larger colonial fiscal system in the Americas. But others will have to decipher these numbers' veracity—and meanings.

PAUL GOOTENBERG, *SUNY–Stony Brook*

Essays on the Price History of Eighteenth-Century Latin America. Edited by Lyman L. Johnson and Enrique Tandeter. Albuquerque, NM: University of New Mexico Press, 1990. Pp. xiii, 419. $49.50, cloth; $17.95, paper.

For over two decades, historians have known that administrative changes in the Spanish and Portuguese empires of the eighteenth century had important economic consequences. Yet their measure has been hard to take. By providing much new evidence and analysis the essays at hand offer one way of approaching the task, and in so doing make an important contribution to the economic historiography of Latin America.

Several of the papers show, for instance, that changes in Spanish commercial policy greatly reduced the price of imports (especially of cloth and paper) in Upper and Lower Peru, in New Spain, and in Santiago de Chile. Demand was apparently quite elastic, for expenditure on imports of cloth and their share of consumption rose rapidly enough to displace long-established domestic producers. However, this shift was noted mainly in the silver-mining colonies or in their hinterlands such as wheat-exporting Chile. There, the fall in import prices essentially implied an improvement in the terms of trade and was generally associated with a certain ambivalence toward independence—or at least with substantial loyalist sentiments. Of course, royalism demanded more than improving terms of trade or a falling cost of living, and the Argentine case is at once more complex and ambiguous. Perhaps the inclusion of an essay on Cuba, the "ever-faithful isle," would have been instructive. Yet what Roberto Cortés Conde called "the first stages of modernization" were clearly incipient under the Bourbons.

The papers by Lyman Johnson on Buenos Aires and by Richard Garner on New Spain have the denouement of empire as an implicit subtext. Garner speculates that real (agricultural) growth stalled toward the century's end, while Johnson identifies a pattern of deteriorating real wages after 1800. Still there is much controversy over the link between living standards, dearth, and political rebellion. The editors might well have charged John Coatsworth with examining the matter in his introductory essay. As it is, the colonial revolution that swept the Spanish empire after 1808 is too little in evidence.

The individual studies will be useful to specialists in national historiographies, though few serve economic and historical sensibilities in equal measure. The papers by Dauril Alden (Salvador de Bahia), Kendall Brown (Arequipa), Javier Cuenca-Esteban (export prices), Lyman Johnson (Buenos Aires), and Enrique Tandeter and Nathan Wachtel (Potosí and Charcas) are amply researched and well executed.

RICHARD J. SALVUCCI, *Trinity University*

The Demography of Inequality in Brazil. By Charles H. Wood and José Alberto Magno de Carvalho. New York: Cambridge University Press, 1988. Pp. xii, 303. $42.50.

A demographic approach to Latin American studies is a well-practiced subdiscipline among social and economic historians of colonial Mexico and Peru. In contrast to some similar earlier approaches, however, Charles Wood (a sociologist) and José Alberto de Carvalho (an economist) have produced a highly readable and serious book on Brazilian population and development. Because the field of development economics was heavily shaped by Keynesian principles, as the popularity—or more importantly the relevancy—of the Keynesian ideas diminished in the early 1980s so did the field. It failed to produce exciting theories or new ideas. Wood and Carvalho propose a demographic approach to reanimate this once-most-popular field of economics. Their book offers insights into the controversial history of Brazil's economic development during the past three decades and suggests new directions for future research.

The book is divided into twelve chapters. Chapters 1 through 3 offer an excellent historical overview of demographic studies, particularly those relating to the analysis of Brazil's economic development and growth. Chapters 4 and 5 delve into wage and income trends. Chapters 6 and 7 analyze birth and mortality rates and their implications for race and class. Chapter 8 examines the interrelationship between demographic growth and income distribution. Chapters 9 and 10 relate population changes to agrarian growth in general, particularly in the Amazon development. And Chapters 11 and 12 offer insightful concluding observations on the larger ramifications of regional and class inequalities and propose an array of interesting but controversial perspectives on Brazil's past and present growth and development paths.

Wood and Carvalho link the country's demographic organization to social, economic, and political forces lying outside Brazil and within the context of "a larger world system" (p. 21). The authors consider demographic dynamics an integral part of the larger societal infrastructure and contend that no studies on Third World economic growth and development are complete if they do not consider population phenomena (p. 48). The authors reveal new perspectives on the country's overall changes, especially under the military authoritarian rule (1964 to 1985) whose positive and negative contributions scholars, politicians, and journalists are just beginning to scrutinize.

Hence this book is a very timely addition to the current debate on the withdrawal of the military from the locus of power and the return of civilian democracies.

Birth and mortality rates and rural-to-urban migration make up the centerpiece of the book. Traditional beliefs and attitudes, coupled with the economic value attached to children (labor) contributed in the past to high birth rates. The economic transformations from the import-substituting industrialization of 1950 to 1964 to the rise of an export economy since the mid-sixties led to a decline in birth rates. This inverse relationship has been well documented. Between 1940 and 1970 the average live birth rate per woman declined 11 percent, from 6.5 (1940) to 6.3 (1950) and then to 5.8 (1970). An additional drop to 4.5 children per woman occurred by 1980 (pp. 155, 255). Other factors contributing to the decline of fertility among the poor include self-imposed birth control, an increasingly politicized struggle for better living conditions, the general awareness of the high cost of quality child rearing, and superior survival rates of infants since the second half of the 1970s thanks to better health care for mothers and infants, food subsidies, potable water, and better sanitation.

Death rates also have been affected by economic and social changes. Between 1930 and 1940 the average life expectancy of Brazilians was 41 years. This steadily improved to 43.6 years by 1950, 53.4 years by 1970, and 62 by 1980, an increase of 20.4 years over a half a century (p. 87). But regional discrepancies in life expectancy sharpened: the lowest life expectancy was registered in the poorest region (the northeast, with 42.8 years in 1970), while the highest was found in the richest (the southeast, with 66.9 years). The industrial southeast, which includes São Paulo, the heartland of Brazil's modern economy, represented 42.7 percent of the total population but claimed 64.5 percent of national income (pp. 73, 94). The quality of life, the authors assert, has improved but has been distributed unevenly, resulting in spatial inequality through the country. This is the crux of modern Brazil's dilemma and the challenge for the new democratic civilian regimes of José Sarney and Fernando Collor de Mello.

Not entirely neglecting the traditional pull-and-push factors but avoiding rigid economism, Wood and Carvalho cogently argue that the spatial (and therefore income?) inequality of Brazil led to regional differences in fertility, mortality, and migration. During the first half of the military rule (1964 to 1985), the authors claim, the suppression of wage raises among the poor had the effect of increasing infant mortality, whereas during the second half of the rule the purchasing power of wages rose and the mortality rate fell. They point out that a factor not to be discounted was the state's role in improving public health conditions for the poor (p. 253).

The concentration of land in the hands of a few, the increasing commercialization and mechanization of agricultural enterprises (to meet the demands of the world system and to expand Brazil's exports), not to mention the state's deliberate policies of sectoral modernization, set off migration from the rural to the urban regions of Brazil: during the import-substituting decade 13.8 million people moved from rural to urban areas, while 17.3 million left the backlands for the cities during the export economy consolidation phase (p. 256). This enormous migration has reshaped Brazil's economy, its demographics, and its infrastructure. The authors' assertion that Brazil's economic, political, and population changes are closely tied to and regulated by forces in the global economy is well borne out and can be substantiated by future research.

Several studies on the income inequities of the 1970s have provided fuel for criticizing the military regime. This book, though persuasively focusing on the spatial and income inequalities of many Brazils, does not lend itself to criticism of the military. In fact, the authors credit the state with improving the quality of life in the 1960s and 1970s, a view that is certainly controversial. The book is well written, analytical, and ideologically balanced.

EUL-SOO PANG, *Colorado School of Mines*

UNITED STATES AND CANADA

Americans and Their Forests: A Historical Geography. By Michael Williams. New York: Cambridge University Press, 1989. Pp. xxii, 599. $49.50.

Michael Williams's *Americans and Their Forests* is an effort to bring within one volume a comprehensive history of what may be the most important natural resource in the history of the U.S. economy. Williams concentrates primarily on the technology of timber harvesting and use; for the role of the forest in American culture, the best source is still Roderick Nash's *Wilderness and the American Mind* (New Haven, 1973), while those interested in the political economy of timber use are better served by J. Willard Hurst's study of the Wisconsin lumber industry, *Law and Economic Growth* (Madison, 1984), or William Robbins's *Lumberjacks and Legislators* (College Station, TX, 1982). Still, in terms of sheer scope and encyclopedic coverage, Williams's study is an unprecedented and, on the whole, very useful survey.

The book is a very large one, appropriately so for the epic scale of its subject: "the clearing of the forest from pre-European times to the present and . . . its subsequent regrowth since the middle years of this century" (p. xvii). The sheer numbers involved are staggering: aboriginally, commercially useful timber covered some 850 million acres, or about 45 percent of what would become the continental United States. By 1920 only 138 million acres of original forest remained, the rest taken for construction, for fuel, or simply cleared and burned to make way for new farms. Americans burned almost 900 million cords (more than twelve *billion* cubic yards) of fuelwood during the 1850s; peak consumption for all purposes came in 1906 at 45 billion board-feet. Consumption has declined since 1920 or so, both in absolute and per capita terms, from 82 cubic feet per person in the peak year of 1906 to about 30 in 1970. It is very clear, as Williams shows, that the forest played a crucial role in the development of the U.S. economy, although its importance has diminished in recent decades.

Williams divides the history of the forests according to Lewis Mumford's tripartite system, in terms of the technology used to harvest and process the timber resource. The "eotechnic" period encompassed both the pre-Contact and European settlement eras until the end of the eighteenth century; European colonists generally relied on Indian agricultural methods because they conserved scarce labor resources and required no help from draft animals or heavy equipment. Williams makes the by-now uncontroversial point that aboriginal Americans made careful, deliberate use of fire as a tool of land management. What may be new to many readers is the extent of their impact on the forest: it is now believed that repeated firing by nomadic hunting cultures led to a significant expansion of the Midwestern grassland at the expense of forest. North American bison, for example, apparently crossed the Mississippi River eastward about A.D. 1000, entered the South by the fifteenth century, and reached as far east as Pennsylvania and Massachusetts by the seventeenth (p. 46). European settlement may have actually prompted an extension of the forest cover at first, as the extirpation of Indian economies let areas where timber growth had previously been controlled by Indian burning go back to woods (p. 49).

Williams is at his best in his discussion of the "paleotechnic" period, which covers the nineteenth century and occupies most of the book's space. The second half of this period, roughly from 1860 to 1920, saw the industry advance first into the Great Lakes region, then the South, and finally the Pacific Coast. End uses of timber—fuel first, followed by waste incidental to clearing for agriculture, and then sawtimber—changed relatively little during this period, although the scale and thoroughness of exploitation increased dramatically. Systematic clear-cutting of large areas of land replaced the selective harvesting of individual trees. Large-scale ownership of standing timber became as important to economic success in the industry as improvements in production and distribution. As this period progressed, an increasing number of concerned observers pointed to the country's profligate use of timber and began laying the groundwork for a more rational, sustainable approach to its harvest in the twentieth century.

Again, while Williams offers brief sketches of George Perkins Marsh, John Muir, Franklin Hough, Gifford Pinchot, and other significant personalities in the history of American forests, the politics of timber conservation and management are better treated elsewhere. The key influence of public lands policy on the structure and development of the timber industry, likewise, gets only brief mention here. The book does, however, contain excellent descriptions of the technology of lumbering and a number of downstream industries, particularly iron making. Williams also does a good job of showing how important railroads were to the industry, in terms of both delivering timber to distant markets and moving logs from the site of cutting to the sawmills. The book contains a great wealth of maps, charts, tables, and photographs to illustrate the technology of the industry and its relative growth by state and by region over time.

The book is at its weakest in its treatment of the "neotechnic" period, which Williams marks with the introduction of electricity and gasoline as power sources in logging and milling in the early twentieth century. In this period public policy for forest management took center stage in the industry's affairs, and the conflicts that began in the 1890s have only begun to be resolved in the last decade or so. Save for a brief epilogue, however, the book itself leaves off during the New Deal era. There is some discussion of the politics of multiple-use management in the national forests and of fire control, but these are cursory and disappointing.

Williams' sympathies clearly follow the political line maintained by the U.S. Forest Service in favor of multiple use, intensive management, and cooperation with private industry. This is by no means unusual among historical works on the American forests, but a more critical treatment might have made the book more useful as a historical study. There is very little treatment of the forest as an ecosystem, save for a brief discussion of the ecology of Indian burning. The book is wonderful for what it does; it is a marvelous reference work on the American forest and its economic use over the greater part of three centuries. Ultimately, however, it treats the forest primarily as the lumber industry and the Forest Service have historically treated it: as a stock of standing sawtimber. A comprehensive study of the American forest in ecological, cultural, and economic contexts remains to be written. When it is, however, Williams's book will be an invaluable resource for it.

ARTHUR F. MCEVOY, *Northwestern University*

The Formation of a Planter Elite: Jonathan Bryan and the Southern Colonial Frontier. By Alan Gallay. Athens: University of Georgia Press, 1989. Pp. xx, 282. $35.00.

This admirably written and thoroughly researched case study of a southern planter expands our understanding of South Carolina and Georgia politics and society. Jonathan Bryan (1708–1788) was the son of an immigrant English planter and Indian trader who had arrived in South Carolina in the 1690s. Bryan grew up in the Port Royal district, where he gained an intimate knowledge of the southern frontier from military expeditions into Florida, negotiations with the Indians, and aid to the early settlers of Georgia. He also gained a sense of the disadvantage of living in an undeveloped and insecure section of a colony controlled by the wealthier Charleston-based planters and merchants. Alan Gallay considers Bryan's experience on the frontier, an arena of European imperial rivalries and of substantial cultural and economic exchanges among Europeans, Africans, and Indians, critical in the development of his ambitions and methods of dealing with people, as well as of southern Anglo-American systems of thought, social organization, technology, and culture in general. Bryan's transformation "from frontiersman to pillar of a slaveholding community" (p. xx) typified the rising planter elite.

Jonathan and his brothers improved their fortunes in the 1730s and 1740s through government contracts, diversified entrepreneurial activities (especially during downturns in the local economy), land speculation, and service in public office, and they gained influence through friendship with James Oglethorpe. The family jeopardized their social position when they converted to evangelical religion in the 1740s and became closely associated with George Whitefield's program for reforming society and improving the condition of slaves by actively attempting to convert them to Christianity. South Carolina officials soon curtailed these efforts, and the evangelicals abandoned confrontation for an agenda of converting their own slaves (essential to "their self-images as Christian slaveholders" [p. 53]), and of attempting to reform society by personal example. Bryan came to believe "his political, social, and religious objectives could only be satisfied in the context of his ownership of large plantations worked by slave laborers" (p. 64).

Alienated by the South Carolina government's failure to aid the Port Royal district in the depressed 1740s, and outside the inner circles of power, Bryan moved to Georgia once slavery was legalized there in 1750. There a paucity of qualified leaders enabled him to rise to the colony's council and to place other family members in positions of power in the third quarter of the eighteenth century.

The new colony offered unparalleled opportunities to extend his estate and endow his children. Bryan "interpreted his Christian duty as providing him the right to accumulate land, wealth, and power for use in promoting the well-being of his fellow man," especially that of "family, friends, and self" (p. 105). He used his high political office as a vehicle for advancing his own and his family's interests, as well as those of a local constituency. He amassed over 32,000 acres by government grant and by purchase, selecting choice tracts that he developed either into rice and indigo plantations or cowpens (he usually had five farms in operation at any given time worked by up to 250 slaves) or else traded in unimproved land. Bryan tested several areas and sold holdings in places like the Altamaha basin that failed to prosper, eventually concentrating his holdings along the Savannah River. When his most expansive speculations were thwarted by colonial and British officials and finding a shortage of quality rice land in Georgia, in 1773 Bryan secured a 99-year lease of 4 to 5 million acres in Florida from the Creek Indians with whom he maintained good relations. There he hoped to settle a new colony independent of British control. Bryan's operations upset imperial plans and ended in temporary expulsion from the Georgia Assembly.

Unlike most Georgia council members, after a period of fence sitting, Bryan cast his lot with the patriots and became an active member of the Council of Safety. Captured by the British in 1778, he spent 22 months on a prison ship off Long Island. Bryan retired from office in 1782, retaining political influence through his sons, and devoted his final years to religious activities and to renewing his plantations.

Unfortunately for readers of this JOURNAL, Gallay uncovered little about Bryan's economic activities. Like most other documentary sources for eighteenth-century Georgia, the Bryan family papers supplied almost no information on plantation operations, Bryan's division of attention between rice and indigo, the scale of crop production, or his relations with local and English merchants. Thus it is unclear how much plantation agriculture contributed to Bryan's rise vis-à-vis land speculation and other entrepreneurial activities, or how his dealings with British merchants may have affected political choices. Bryan's methods of slave management are also undocumented, and Gallay's assertion that Bryan's bondspeople "worked efficiently" because they were relatively "well treated" (p. 98) strikes me as naive.

Finally, while Bryan's use of political position and family connections to further his ambitions and his success in land speculations are common factors in the rise of the southern gentry, readers could better judge his typicality had Gallay provided comparative data on the land and slaveholdings and religious affiliations of other members of the Georgia elite.

LORENA S. WALSH, *Colonial Williamsburg Foundation*

A Union of Interests: Political and Economic Thought in Revolutionary America. By Cathy D. Matson and Peter S. Onuf. Lawrence: University Press of Kansas, 1990. Pp. x, 237. $25.00.

Potential readers of this book should be advised that its subtitle promises more than the contents deliver. This inaugural volume of a series on American Political Thought does not provide a comprehensive survey of political and economic thought in Revolutionary America. Its central concern instead is to examine the relation between notions of group, state, and regional economic interest on the one hand, and the ideas and institutions of revolutionary federalism on the other. After an opening chapter summarizing such familiar elements of eighteenth-century political economy as republicanism, mercantilism, and free trade, and a second, too brief chapter surveying state economic policy after 1776, Cathy Matson and Peter Onuf quickly focus on the consequences of state economic rivalries and the countervailing efforts to imagine and explain how a reconstituted national government could truly pursue a union of interests. Not surprisingly, the debates over the framing and adoption of the Federal Constitution frame the narrative climax of the analysis.

When Matson and Onuf describe political thought, they mean ideas about the utility of federalism rather than the development of American thinking about such other crucial topics as representation, the enhancement of judicial and executive power, or the definition of rights. Their description of economic thought is similarly confined to issues where national policy was most clearly implicated—notably the development of the West and the regulation of Atlantic trade—rather than other matters (for example, the chartering of banks) where the states continued to play more active roles.

In many ways, the story Matson and Onuf tell follows a predictable line. Reformers who favored strengthening the national government had to struggle to explain how an effective union could advance the admittedly disparate interests that an extended republic would embrace. The very reality of regional conflict and political paralysis under the Articles of Confederation at once demonstrated why radical changes were necessary while reinforcing doubts as to whether constitutional reform would overcome deeper differences. For reform to succeed, Matson and Onuf argue, Americans had to accept new teachings about the benefits of economic development and especially the meliorating effects of commerce. At the same time, the political leaders who gathered at Philadelphia had to craft the specific compromises that would originally illuminate how interests could be reconciled. The fact that the optimism of the reformers (later Federalists) overcame the arguments of their opponents does not mean that the latter's doubts were somehow less sound; it merely illuminates how the political challenges of the 1780s attracted the former to new and more hopeful notions of economics and politics alike.

Within the brief compass of this work, Matson and Onuf frogmarch the reader through an astonishing amount of material, richly documented in the endnotes. Still, their absorption with federalism, western lands, and the dilemmas of regional and other rivalries has some drawbacks, *if* one can assume that the subtitle promises more than the book delivers. Especially disappointing, in my view, is the relative neglect of the response of the states to all the questions of economic policy the Revolution generated. For a work whose avowed topic is the political economy of the Revolutionary era, it is surprising how little attention is paid to asking what Americans learned from frustrating years of trying to control their wartime economies. On a host of issues—not just the familiar problem of paper money, but such other matters as the control of markets, the value of subsidies and embargoes, efforts to use the positive legislative power of the state to inspire suitable private activities—the mobilization of resources during the war was, by eighteenth-century standards, probably as sweeping in its impact as the more extensively studied transformations in political economy that have accompanied recent wars. This was the single most intense experience in economic regulation, broadly defined, that Americans had ever known, and it is difficult to believe that it did not contribute to the postwar positions the authors so ably analyze. (This defect is, however, less the fault of the authors than a reflection of gaps in the scholarly literature. For the sole examplary study that cuts against this complaint, see Richard Buel, Jr., *Dear Liberty: Connecticut's Mobilization for the Revolutionary War* [Middletown, CT, 1980].)

As is so often the case in the writing of American history, then, too great a fascination with events at the national level may obscure a more important if less tractable story to be told about the states. But that would require another book—or rather, a different series of books—which would be nice of our authors, having succeeded so well here, to undertake.

JACK N. RAKOVE, *Stanford University*

Cultivating Gentlemen: The Meaning of Country Life among the Boston Elite, 1785–1860. By Tamara Plakins Thornton. New Haven: Yale University Press, 1989. Pp. xii, 244. $29.95.

This carefully crafted, gracefully written, and richly illustrated book brings the Boston Brahmins down to earth, quite literally. While the story of these socially prominent, economically innovative, and politically powerful people has often been told, Tamara Plakins Thornton sheds new light on their cultural values by analyzing their behavior in previously neglected contexts: on their country estates and in the agricultural and horticultural societies they founded and controlled before the Civil War. The Brahmins' engagement in rural pursuits, she reveals, was more than a curious affectation; it was central to their sense of character as individuals and as a social class.

Thornton takes a generational approach to her subject. She portrays elite Bostonians in the post-Revolutionary era as men of commerce who took up experimental farming on country estates in search of personal fulfillment. Modeling themselves mainly on the English gentry, whom they regarded as less decadent than the titled aristocracy yet more refined than the common sort, they aspired to lead private lives of civilized leisure while pursuing public lives of civic virtue and statesmanship. In 1792 they formed the Massachusetts Society for Promoting Agriculture, in part to demonstrate their avowedly disinterested concern for the general welfare. In both their private and public endeavors, Thornton argues, they sought to prove themselves a legitimate elite in a republican society where status was supposed to be earned, not acquired as a privilege at birth.

The generation that came of age after the War of 1812 faced new challenges. The Federalist party was dead as a national political force, and as the population growth of Massachusetts failed to keep pace with that of New York and other states, elite Bostonians feared the further erosion of their influence. According to Thornton, they turned to rural pursuits for a remedy. In the past they had claimed no special expertise in agricultural matters and had pleaded with common farmers to share their practical knowledge. Now, as merchants and men of wealth with access to the wider world, elite Bostonians claimed cosmopolitan superiority over the yeomanry and waged a campaign for agricultural reform. During the 1820s the Massachusetts Society for Promoting Agriculture sponsored cattle shows and urged Massachusetts farmers to adopt the intensive techniques of English cultivators rather than migrate west. Likewise, reformers emphasized the utility of fruits and vegetables as crops suitable to the regional environment and market.

Such efforts yielded meager results, however. As the more innovative members of the Boston elite recognized early, the future of the Massachusetts economy lay in manufacturing, not agriculture. Yet the men who headed the Massachusetts Society for Promoting Agriculture and the similarly oriented Massachusetts Horticultural Society—founded in 1829—felt little enthusiasm for the industrial way of life that their investments, or at least those of their friends and relatives, helped to create. As the Boston elite grew more closed and caste-like after 1830, Thornton argues, its members also grew more committed to the values and trappings of aristocracy. Distrust of luxury gave way to disdain for utility. Elite Bostonians sought ever harder to prove themselves above the crass materialism of ordinary folks. At mid-century they more frequently did so by means of elaborate gardens and other forms of ornamental display than by the old-fashioned means of public service. While they still preached the gospel of hard work for others, they acted on the premise of inherited privilege, not practicality, in their own lives.

Thornton interprets the evolution of the Boston elite's rural activities as evidence of a gradual repudiation of entrepreneurial values in favor of a more thoroughly aristocratic world view, one that put the Brahmins at odds with the mass of Americans. On the whole her analysis meshes well with those of Peter Dobkin Hall, Frederic Cople Jahrer, and Ronald Story, who have focused their scholarly attention on the Boston elite's urban activities. Yet Thornton may exaggerate the extent of ideological transformation within the Boston elite between the Revolution and the Civil War. By her own account, the post-Revolutionary generation of proper Bostonians had decidedly aristocratic cultural aspirations even if their wealth derived mainly from mercantile economic foundations. They would not have settled on country estates if they had found the values of bourgeois life compelling. Moreover, as Richard Bushman has shown, the ideal of cultivation had been embraced by American elites long before the Revolution. Although the Revolution converted Americans at all levels of society to republican political ideas, it did not force a halt to the cultural process of anglicization at the apex of the social order—especially in Boston and its vicinity. Examined from this perspective, Thornton's evidence suggests that the Boston Brahmins of the mid-nineteenth century fulfilled, rather than betrayed, the hopes of their eighteenth-century forebears.

Although economic historians looking for detailed consideration of the Boston elite's business strategies between the Revolution and the Civil War would do better to turn to Robert F. Dalzell, Jr.'s *Enterprising Elite: The Boston Associates and the World They Made* (Cambridge, MA, 1987), readers interested in the changing cultural landscape of New England during this era should find Thornton's volume quite valuable. *Cultivating Gentlemen* is fruitful scholarship.

GARY J. KORNBLITH, *Oberlin College*

Another Civil War: Labor, Capital, and the State in the Anthracite Regions of Pennsylvania, 1840–68. By Grace Palladino. Urbana: University of Illinois Press, 1990. Pp. xii, 195. $26.50.

"[O]rganized capital," Grace Palladino writes, "relied on the state to cripple working-class opposition to the revolutionary extension of corporate power . . . . The combined power of organized capital and the state . . . so clearly illustrated during the Civil War, significantly constrained organized labor's ability to muster its forces. But if this combination subverted both the structure and the promise of a producer's republic, it could not destroy the ideal" (p. 173). This is the major premise of this well-written and challenging work, which joins two other fine studies of the interrelationship between industrialization and the Civil War in the North by Iver Bernstein, *The New York City Draft Riots* (New York, 1989), and J. Matthew Gallman, *Mastering Wartime* (New York, 1990).

The focus of Palladino's work is more on industrializing than on war—the first 94 pages of this 175-page volume deal with prewar conditions. In those pages she describes how the emerging coal-mining industry in Pennsylvania developed two options. One, dominant in the Lehigh district, found full control of mining, selling, and transporting in the hands of one company, the Lehigh Coal and Navigation Company. In the Schuylkill district different companies operated the three branches of the business, and miners leased land from owners. Law forbade landowners and shippers from selling or mining. Operators in the latter area condemned the "despotism and tyranny" over "the liberties of the people" that they saw in Lehigh. But rhetoric fell to reality. Larger combinations meant better profits even in the Schuylkill region where the Hecksher family worked around the law and built a large and powerful company with help from New York financiers and politicians like Salmon Chase and Simon Cameron.

These increasing aggregations of power did little to end commitment to individualism. Some independent operators refused to join with others in setting prices or production, thus leaving the companies at the mercy of stronger market forces. It put independent owners in the position also of finding ways to cut costs to remain competitive—and "labor costs and mine maintenance seemed to be the only variables in the individual operator's control" as "miners and laborers who produced the coal, and their families, shouldered the heaviest burdens of this anarchistic trade" (p. 37). Among the burdens were wages paid in credit at company stores where prices were inflated.

When miners struck in the early 1840s, they destroyed an earlier order that placed owners and workers side by side as independent "republican workers." Owners still proclaimed harmony of interest between the two, but unstable prices, expansion of the laboring population, the need to dig in more dangerous ways to get coal, and increasing competition all combined to undercut the ideal. By the time of the strike of 1842, the local militia were available to sustain the owner's position and local newspapers agreed. The problem was that miners combined and struck rather than dealing with grievances on an individual basis. Supporters of the owners refused to believe that economic inequities were really the source of problems. They conjured visions of lazy and ignorant Irishmen influenced by Democratic demagogues to believe that conspiracy and not disciplined work was the way to improve conditions.

When war came little changed in the divided workplace. Miners were often able to use the need for coal in the conflict to strike successfully. But owners trumped miner protest by using the wartime emergency as an excuse to bring in soldiers to put down strikes which owners linked to draft dodging as well as to obstructing wartime production. The army was consistently on the owners' side. "Obviously miners in Schuylkill County were held to much higher standards of patriotism than operators and dealers were" (p. 160).

Palladino's work is essentially an apology for the miners who suffered under the changes that industrialization brought. She explains away the nativism of miners, justifies their antidraft rioting, and avoids the term "Molly Maguires" whenever possible. At the same time she makes a strong case that the mine owners and their friends have a lot of explaining to do about their use of the military in wartime emergencies to "save managerial prerogative" (p. 135).

Still one would like to see attention to larger contexts. Just what were the circumstances that shaped the decisions of mine owners during the war? Palladino admits that business was competitive, but what was the nature of that competition? This is essentially a local study, but the judgments that she makes about patriotism and the war effort call for some discussion on her part of what the war situation was while miners and owners clashed. There is a strong case to be made that the economically powerful enhanced their power under the cover of war. The provost marshal, empowered to enforce the draft in Schuylkill County, was a large investor in the coal industry. Palladino does describe contrary views between miners and owners as to what the best economy might be, but she does not note how the war built shared values that allowed a persuasive argument to be made by owners. She especially fails to consider the power of the "free labor" ideal in the midst of a war against its nemesis the "Slave Power."

"Wartime outrages [by which Palladino means the clashes between miners and mine owners]—and especially their resolution—have more to tell us about the development of the industrial capitalist system, its relation to class conflict, and the process of building a national state than they do about disloyalty" (p. 8). The sentence summarizes the strength and weakness of this book. Palladino has described well how industrialization shaped the lives of miners during the war era. She has told us very little about how those changes fit into the nation's most complex and important war.

PHILLIP S. PALUDAN, *University of Kansas*

Conflict and Compromise: The Political Economy of Slavery, Emancipation, and the American Civil War. By Roger L. Ransom. New York: Cambridge University Press, 1989. Pp. xv, 317. $39.50, cloth; $12.95, paper.

As Roger Ransom explains with grace and charm in the preface, this book is a result of his transformation from an economist to a "Civil War historian." This book is a product of the methodology, perspectives, and insights that an economic historian brings to the most traumatic political event, the bloodiest war, and the most revolutionary social transformation in American history. It is, in short, an examination of the political economy of the Civil War. Written for students and nonspecialists, it synthesizes existing research rather than breaks new ground. But it can be read with profit by the economist for its history and by the historian for its economics.

Ransom places the sectional conflict in the economic context not of plantation agriculture versus industrial capitalism (as did Charles Beard), but of a society and economic system based on slave labor versus one based on free labor. Each system generated an ideology and a dynamic expansionism that clashed with the other in the contest over control of the territories. This contest by the 1850s concerned the future of the United States: would the country remain a "house divided" between slavery and freedom, or would one system be placed on the road to "ultimate extinction"? Both systems were economically viable; both helped fuel the extraordinary growth of the American economy in the nineteenth century; but the northern free-soil majority became increasingly convinced that slavery was an immoral and obsolete institution that had no place in the future of a "free" country. For Ransom the sectional conflict really was irrepressible: "the presence of slavery in the United States represented a contradiction that eventually could only be removed by an armed conflict between the slave South and the nonslave North" (p. 15). With a wealth of data presented in tables and graphs, he outlines the economic infrastructure of the intensifying ideological and political controversies that finally exploded into armed conflict in 1861.

"Slavery not only 'caused' the war," Ransom argues, it also "undermined the Confederacy's war effort by creating a divisiveness that crippled the mobilization effort" (p. 16). The South's plantation-agrarian economy proved unable to organize and finance the resources necessary to wage the kind of total war that the Civil War became. The more mature and diversified market economy of the North, by contrast, produced both guns and butter without the disastrous inflation and economic breakdowns that plagued the Confederacy. In one of his most important insights, Ransom maintains that "the production decisions involving the North's military effort were effectively *decen-*

tralized through the market process," while "because markets in the South were far less developed, the mobilization effort was forced to rely on *centralized* decisions made by the government in Richmond . . . a decision-making apparatus that became overcentralized and was ultimately unable to meet either military or civilian needs" (pp. 203–4). In another provocative suggestion, Ransom argues that the Confederacy could not pursue a military strategy of trading space for time, as George Washington had done with such success in the Revolution, because "to do so would undermine the very foundation of the southern cause: the defense of slavery. Southern commanders had to protect territory from invasion because of the need to protect slave property" (p. 178).

Union armies nevertheless penetrated deeply into Confederate territory. Wherever they did so, the most negative effect of slavery on the southern war effort manifested itself: the slaves voted with their feet for freedom. By the thousands they made their way into Union lines, viewing Abraham Lincoln's soldiers as an army of liberation before Lincoln and the army itself did. Indeed, these "contrabands" helped prod the Lincoln administration into a policy of emancipation as a means of both winning the war by siphoning off the Confederacy's labor force and securing future peace by abolishing the divisive institution that had brought on the war.

Ransom considers emancipation "the one great accomplishment of the Civil War" (p. 16). In measuring its impact on the South, he reiterates the points that he and Richard Sutch laid out in *One Kind of Freedom* (New York, 1977): emancipation produced a large transfer of capital and income from masters to freedmen; the freed slaves reduced the hours they worked by one-third from the level of slavery; sharecropping was a compromise between the former masters' preference for gang labor and the freed people's preference for independent status as farm owners; the promise of prosperity and equal rights inherent in free labor and the Reconstruction amendments was betrayed by racism, reaction, and the crop lien system that fastened its tentacles on the credit-starved postwar South. Nevertheless, concludes Ransom, the Civil War was a Second American Revolution of the scope portrayed more than 60 years ago by Charles and Mary Beard, for it destroyed the labor system and political power of the planter class and replaced them with the ethos and dynamism of free-labor industrial capitalism.

With regret I must offer one caveat about this otherwise valuable study. It is marred by numerous factual errors. With respect to the historian's concern for accuracy in facts, events, and dates, Ransom seems not to have experienced the zeal of a convert. Some of the errors are of the trivial sort that creep into any book and are not worth mentioning. But the cumulative impact of many others in a book aimed at the nonspecialist does merit mention. The author and his publisher have been guilty of carelessness toward the nuts and bolts of history: wrong dates for the abolition of the African slave trade (pp. 33, 45, 57); the Dred Scott decision (p. 147); Lincoln's first try for the Senate (pp. 159–60); his inauguration as president (p. 165); the firing on Fort Sumter (p. 166); both the Confederate and Union conscription laws (p. 196); the first Union confiscation act (p. 206); Lincoln's appointment of Ulysses Grant as *general* in chief (not *commander* in chief, which is the president's designation under the Constitution [p. 210]); and the defeat of Thaddeus Stevens's bid for election to the Senate (p. 250). The number of killed and wounded at Gettysburg was not 50,000 (p. 2); the Republicans did not capture control of Congress in the elections of 1860—only southern secession enabled them to do so (p. 7); the Confederate law passed in March 1865 to enlist slaves as soldiers did not provide for their freedom (pp. 14, 213); Mexico claimed the Nueces River as its border with Texas (not the Sabine, which forms the Texas-Louisiana border) (p. 93); *three* slave states (including Florida) came into the Union after 1821 (p. 109); the author of the crucial compromise proposal in 1860–1861 was John J. Crittenden, not John C. Breckinridge (p. 165); the table on p. 156 and the text on p. 164 reverse Breckinridge's and Bell's popular vote totals in 1860; the most "radical" Northerners *had* been urging equal citizenship for blacks for many years (p. 173); Grant moved *up* not down the Tennessee River (p. 181) to Shiloh, which was a church not a courthouse (p. 182); it was Henry Heth's division not Jubal Early's that launched the attack starting the battle of Gettysburg (p. 194); the Confederate government did *not* take over the Tredegar (not Treadegar) Ironworks (p. 200); the Panic of 1857 put a rather large dent in "the bustling prosperity [of] the last years of the antebellum decade" (p. 253); most Jacksonians were *not* advocates of "easy money"—just the opposite (p. 276); the crucial word in the first section of the Fourteenth Amendment, subject to extensive litigation concerning corporate regulation, was "person" not "individual," a word that does not appear in that amendment (p. 282).

Finally, on a matter of interpretation more than of fact, I would take exception to Ransom's assertions that the "one unequivocal result" of the Civil War was the abolition of slavery and that by 1877 "the victorious North let much of what had been gained through four years of hard fighting slip through its fingers" (pp. 11, 14). The North fought to preserve the existence of the United States as one country. Its success was unequivocal, for no state or region has tried to secede since 1865. This "result" of the war perhaps is so obvious that it is taken for granted and its enormous importance overlooked. The war generation did not overlook its importance, nor should we. If the United States had separated into two countries, with a precedent thereby established for further divisions, there would have been a vast difference in the political economy as well as in every other aspect of the history of North America—and perhaps of the world—since 1865. And while it is true that the Reconstruction experiment in racial equality was buried by the Compromise of 1877, this experiment was not what the North had fought for; it was a product of postwar political battles. None of what the North "gained through four years of hard fighting" was lost in 1877: the United States remained one nation and the freed slaves remained free. These facts are worth remembering as unequivocal results of the Civil War.

JAMES M. MCPHERSON, *Princeton University*

Soldiers and Settlers: Military Supply in the Southwest, 1861–1885. By Darlis A. Miller. Albuquerque: University of New Mexico Press, 1989. Pp. xviii, 506. $45.00.

In *Soldiers and Settlers* Darlis Miller puts forward a powerful argument for continuity in the economic patterns of the American Southwest. In the nineteenth century as well as twentieth century, federal money was a mainstay—and, often enough, *the* mainstay—of the local economy. In the nineteenth century a network of forts in New Mexico, Arizona, western Texas, and southern Colorado provided a range of economic opportunities for local civilians. The army needed food, forage, freighting services, and skilled labor; filling those needs gave residents a valuable source of income and investment capital. Military contracting, moreover, directly reshaped economic activity; farmers planted larger crops and entrepreneurs launched flour mills and other businesses in direct response to the needs of quartermasters and subsistence officers. The southwestern military presence functioned as both the armed protection and the market stimulant for local producers.

Robert W. Frazer's *Forts and Supplies: The Role of the Army in the Economy of the Southwest, 1846–1861* (Albuquerque, 1983) explored the topic of regional military contracting up to 1861; Miller's study begins with the Civil War and ends in 1885. By that year the arrival of railroads had transformed the whole picture of military supply and regional economic development.

Before the railroad, the vast spaces, aridity, and comparative treelessness of this region doubled the standard headaches of building and supplying forts and posts. An added burden came with the chronic stinginess of the post–Civil War Congress, making the obligation to economize part of every supply officer's duty. A congressional eagerness to meet—and even anticipate—the "needs" of the military establishment did not characterize the nineteenth century.

Stingy allocations or not, the releasing of federal funds into the southwestern economy was a major force for economic development. This was not, by anyone's intention, regionally targeted charity at work; to the military, purchasing supplies locally seemed the logical way to avoid higher prices from transportation costs. Most commonly, merchants seized the opportunity to contract with local farmers or ranchers for grain, forage, or cattle. Like other western enterprises, this one carried the risks of uncooperative weather, crop failure, Indian attacks on supply trains, or the contingencies of changing prices, which could transform an anticipated profit into an actual loss.

In a number of ways *Soldiers and Settlers* is as interesting for its hints and glimpses of regional economic life as it is for its direct and explicit discussion of military supplying. The picture of Navajos working for wages in the construction of forts, or of Hispanic farmers supplying grain to Army posts, shows the relation between conqueror and conquered as something much deeper than simple opposition. In addition, the following "side issues" carry considerable significance in their own right: the early and comparatively widespread practice of irrigation in New Mexico; the role of scouts and interpreters as paid civilian agents of conquest; the frequent abandonment and generally transitory status of western posts and forts; the need for civilian clerks to keep up with what was already a "prodigious amount of paperwork" (p. 265); and the disheartening living conditions of enlisted men, conditions which were often a direct result of congressional parsimony.

At its bedrock, *Soldiers and Settlers* is an archival *tour de force*. Miller's determination in tracking contracts and correspondence through local and national archives borders on the heroic. The assembly of this avalanche of documentation into orderly chapters is an equally impressive achievement. Following a brief preface and a chapter on the supply situation during the Civil War, Miller's chapters take up grain production, forage provision, milling services, cattle supplying, fort construction, and freighting. The final chapter looks briefly at the problem of fraud and theft.

Opening and concluding sections of each chapter record the general patterns in the data. Between those sections of summation, the reader can feel unmoored in a sea of numbers, prices, and not-easily-recognized proper names. While this full inclusion of detail conveys a gritty sense of the day-to-day reality of the contracting business, it can also induce a certain amount of fatigue in the reader. While no arbiter has set a universal standard for the proper proportions of detail and analysis in a historical monograph, the hard labor that produced the data for this book gave the author a broader license for interpretation than she chose to exercise. One wishes for a concluding chapter of analysis and reflection on the many important and interesting issues raised by this book. Nonetheless, this study is wonderfully free of the entrapping conventions of older varieties of western American history. By focusing on the complicated economic relations of conquest and by refusing to refight any of the stale old battles of Turnerian frontier historiography, this book makes a direct approach to historical reality. Centering on the proposition that "the military was the cornerstone of the economy" (p. 352), *Soldiers and Settlers* provides an essential case study in the vital topic of the American West's dependence on federal money.

PATRICIA NELSON LIMERICK, *University of Colorado, Boulder*

Economic Law and Economic Growth: Antitrust, Regulation, and the American Growth System. By George E. Garvey and Gerald J. Garvey. New York: Greenwood Press, 1990. Pp. xv, 168. $45.00, cloth; $14.95, paper.

This book studies the historical relationship between public economic law in the United States, principally antitrust law and utility regulation, and U.S. economic policy—primarily a policy of sustaining economic growth. The book features graphical applications of elementary microeconomic theory and is directed toward scholars and students in history, government, and public policy. It is extensively documented so that readers can pursue particular topics of interest in the academic literature of law and economics.

The discussion covers the following periods: the pre–Civil War era; the age of industrialization; and the years after World War II. In each period the authors identify a "virtuous cycle" of factors that sustained economic growth and show how contemporary economic law contributed to this process. However, these surveys are very broad; for example, the Great Depression is reviewed in only two paragraphs, with no consideration of monetary forces (p. 50). The discussion of modern economic law covers the neopopulism of the Warren Supreme Court, the neoclassical views of the Chicago School of antitrust analysis, and the application of contestability theory to natural monopolies. This treatment is accurate and balanced but is again lacking in detail.

The book concludes with a proposal to tailor antitrust and regulatory law more closely to a national policy of sustaining economic growth. The authors assert that the United States needs major capital investments in its industrial base to improve productivity and compete more effectively in an increasingly competitive global economy. They claim that neither neopopulism nor neoclassicism is an appropriate legal doctrine to support reindustrialization. The reason is that neopopulism tolerated production inefficiency by enforcing atomistic market structures and favoring small business units; likewise, neoclassicism is deficient because its focus on consumer welfare, and especially low prices, may prevent competitive industries with strong growth prospects from obtaining sufficient capital for expansion. So the authors propose an alternative legal doctrine that would tend to unify antitrust law and utility regulation into a body of public law whose express goal is to restore and maintain economic growth as the "overarching criterion of policy choice" (p. 145). They call this doctrine the "administered resource transfer approach" (p. 137). It would be a body of public law implemented by a new administrative agency of the federal government and is intended to supplement the capital financing of firms and industries with strong growth prospects. While the authors give few specifics, they do envision that a doctrine of administrative resource transfers would allow some industries to increase profits, for investment purposes only, at the expense of consumers through cartelization (p. 146). This doctrine also would allow more joint ventures between competitors and impose entry restrictions on some nonutility industries (p. 150). Managers of firms that benefited from administered resource transfers would acquire additional fiduciary duties to ensure that the capital received from charging higher prices to consumers was invested in ways that contribute to national economic growth. The book concludes by briefly considering objections to administered resource transfers, including doubts about the substitution of public for private judgments regarding business investment and the capture of independent regulatory agencies by the firms they regulate. The authors' best argument for their transfer proposal is that the United States already has the equivalent of a national economic policy—albeit a very ad-hoc, haphazard, and uncoordinated one—for politically powerful industries.

This book may find a wide audience in graduate and advanced undergraduate courses in political science and public policy. It is certainly refreshing to see economic modeling applied explicitly in these fields. The discussion may also be of interest to legal scholars and government officials. However, it probably will not prove useful to economic historians and economists generally, because the analysis is very elementary and lacks interesting historical detail. The discussion is clear and well written except for one annoying quirk. Prospective readers should be warned: keep a dictionary handy! This book will needlessly enlarge your vocabulary. Among the obscure new words I learned are fundament, revivify, genera, farrago, discombobulation, and recrudescence. I hope to forget them very soon.

MALCOLM R. BURNS, *University of Kansas*

Fertility Change on the American Frontier: Adaptation and Innovation. By Lee L. Bean, Geraldine P. Mineau, and Douglas L. Anderton. Berkeley: University of California Press, 1990. Pp. xiv, 295. $40.00.

To explain the fertility transition experienced by most of the developed countries in the nineteenth century has been an objective of several generations of social scientists. Scholars have employed the paradigms of a number of disciplines to address the many questions posed by the precipitous decline of human fertility. In *Fertility Change on the American Frontier* Lee Bean, Geraldine Mineau, and Douglas Anderton employ data from the Mormon Historical Demographic Project (MHDP) to analyze the frontier fertility behavior and subsequent fertility transition of the (predominantly Mormon) population in and around nineteenth- and early twentieth-century Utah.

At the beginning of the chapter describing the collection, organization, and quality of the data, the authors invite readers for whom the results are paramount to skip ahead, but it is the richness of the data that makes this a fascinating volume, and most readers will not want to accept the invitation to pass over this chapter. Many of the results would be difficult if not impossible to extract from less complete data. Still, for all their advantages, it is worth keeping in mind that even these data are limited in the questions they can answer.

The authors describe their analysis as "theoretically driven" because they test whether the fertility transition represented "innovation," the adoption of new social norms, or "adaptation," a response to a change in relative prices. They derive three propositions from the literature on the European fertility transition that describe the transition as a process of innovation and diffusion: pretransition fertility was not parity dependent; early fertility limitation was due to truncation not spacing; and fertility control begins with some identifiable subset and then spreads to other groups. The MHDP population was analyzed to see if it displayed the European pattern.

Once the transition began, the pattern of broad-based decline in age-specific fertility rates for subsequent birth cohorts is contrary to the innovation-diffusion view that fertility limitation would have started with older women. The birth cohorts are broken down by ethnicity, arrival date, religious commitment, and urbanization. The early cohorts of the American-born women had higher fertility than European-born women, but from the 1860s on, the differences declined. Those who arrived on the frontier as youngsters or early in their childbearing years had higher fertility than others. Families that displayed a relatively strong religious commitment had higher fertility than those with less commitment to the church. Mobile or noncentral geographic families had higher fertility than stable centrally located ones. Despite these differences in fertility levels, all of the groups experienced the fertility transition at roughly the same time. Furthermore, there was little change in the interbirth intervals for given completed family sizes throughout the fertility transition. In other words, the fertility decline experienced by this population was caused by a shift in the proportion of families that desired fewer children, and they obtained fewer children by extending the birth interval at all parities. Based on these and other findings, such as the initial rise in frontier fertility, the authors reject the innovation-diffusion hypothesis as an explanation of the fertility transition experienced by the MHDP population.

Economists may be disappointed by the theoretical foundation of these arguments for three reasons. First, a major contribution of economics is to analyze responses to relative price changes when other factors such as tastes and cultural norms are held constant, and the debate among economists in recent decades has principally been how, not whether, relative price changes caused the fertility transition. Second, there is no single adaptation argument, and recent work on theories of strategic bequests and child default is omitted. Third, the analysis does not include measures of income or wealth; therefore, any tests of economic hypotheses are indirect at best. For this reason, even though lacking in other aspects, matched samples from the decennial censuses, such as the one constructed by Fred Bateman and James Foust, remain a potentially more valuable tool for many fertility transition questions. In fairness, it should be noted that the authors are aware of this shortcoming and provide opportunities for matching this sample with those that contain measures of wealth.

In addition, historians may wish for more narrative on the social and economic lives of this population, but to say that those in some disciplines will take exception to the paradigms of others is expected from a topic that commands the attention of so many different disciplines. The demographic analysis of the MHDP population is an important contribution to historical demography, and every student of the field, regardless of discipline, will want to be familiar with these results.

LEE A. CRAIG, *North Carolina State University*

The Butte Irish: Class and Ethnicity in an American Mining Town, 1875–1925. By David M. Emmons. Champaign: University of Illinois Press, 1989. Pp. xiii, 443. $25.95.

The publication of *The Butte Irish* brings a new level of sophistication to the field of American history. David Emmons has written an elegant account of a remarkable western community, and one of the most impressive studies of the postfamine Irish.

American historians have largely ignored the late nineteenth-century emigration of the Irish, preferring to concentrate upon the dynamic decade following the famine of 1845. Yet Emmons points out that the 81,000 Irish immigrants who came to America in 1883 represented a greater percentage of the Irish population than those who departed in 1846. As late as 1905, 53,000 Irish arrived in the United States.

Butte, Montana, seems like an unlikely place to find a large Irish enclave. Indeed, the closest Hibernian enclave existed 350 miles away. Yet one had to search even further to find an ethnic group so in control of its destiny. By 1900 several thousand Irish had clustered in Butte, but the history of that city's Irish involved more than numbers, or economic function, or copper. In Butte the Irish bore the primary responsibility for ensuring the social order of the community. Economically, skilled miners bolstered by steady work, exclusive unions, and unending streams of immigrants stabilized Butte's Irish ranks.

The Butte Irish dominated the cadres of skilled miners and achieved impressive success in preserving their group status. Perhaps more remarkably, the miners did not strike during the period 1878 to 1914, an era of fierce class struggle in the West. Curiously, these conservative miners eagerly supported Irish nationalism in their homeland. Emmons explains this seeming paradox, elaborating upon and refining an earlier study of Irish nationalism by Thomas Brown, by suggesting that the miners' conservatism and ethnicity resulted from a cold calculation of how they—as miners and Irishmen—could best survive the turbulent times and dangerous mines. Radicalism was blunted; workers acutely conscious of their class instead found alternate expressions and passions.

Emmons has written an engaging book which should reach a wide range of readers interested in immigration, and western and labor history. Copious notes underscore the exhaustive research. Rigorously researched and deftly written, *The Butte Irish* deserves a wide audience. It stands next to Kerby Miller's *Emigrants and Exiles* (New York, 1985) as the best works dealing with the Irish-American experience.

GARY R. MORMINO, *University of South Florida*

Eisenhower Versus 'The Spenders': The Eisenhower Administration, the Democrats and the Budget, 1953–60. By Iwan W. Morgan. New York: St. Martin's Press, 1990. Pp. xii, 223. $35.00.

The 1950s have often been characterized as a period outstanding only for its banality, when the head of state "preferred golf to government" (p. 1). Historians have reconstructed Dwight Eisenhower's leadership style but have given scant attention to the evolution of economic policy during the 1950s and to his role in fiscal policy formation. Iwan Morgan's *Eisenhower Versus 'The Spenders'* goes far in filling this void and provides an insightful, interesting discussion of fiscal policy formation during the Eisenhower years.

For many economic historians, the 1950s seems to have been a nonevent sandwiched between the New Deal–Fair Deal and the New Frontier—a period of general prosperity punctuated by a few inventory recessions, or in current vernacular, slowdowns. Neither depression, war, nor rapid inflation occupied center stage. For Morgan, however, the 1950s represents a compelling decade when the contours of the debate over the proper scope of fiscal policy in the postwar years emerged.

Shaping this debate were external factors such as the return of the presidency to Republican leadership, the advent of the cold war, and the continued development of the corporate welfare state. Internally, the debate over fiscal policy took shape in a highly partisan environment when such irascible characters as Arthur Burns, George Humphrey, Lyndon Johnson, and Richard Nixon all, in varying degrees, influenced policy.

As Morgan points out, Eisenhower was the first Republican president since Herbert Hoover and was sensitive, especially in his first term, to charges of Republican economic mismanagement. Despite his renowned concern over the budget, Eisenhower made no attempts to offset the reduction in revenue associated with the recession of 1953–1954. While not a prescriptive Keynesian willingly engaging in active countercyclical policies, Eisenhower allowed automatic stabilizers to soften the downturn and even managed to authorize a speed-up of government expenditures "intended to generate jobs in the areas where Republican electoral prospects would benefit" (p. 64).

Whereas Eisenhower's "determination to rescue Republicanism from the crippling image of Hooverism" (p. 61) waned in his second term, the cold war overshadowed much of political life throughout the 1950s. According to Morgan: "Defense expenditure was the subject of the longest running partisan dispute over the budget during the Eisenhower era" (p. 34). From the cut in defense expenditures following the Korean involvement to the Soviet launching of Sputnik in 1957 to the "missile gap" rhetoric of the John Kennedy campaign, Democrats criticized Eisenhower for, in Kennedy's words, his "willingness to place fiscal security ahead of national security" (p. 35). Not to appear soft on communism, congressional Democrats sought to increase defense expenditures in every year except 1957, when the Democrats made a brief attempt to out-Eisenhower Eisenhower on the subject of economy in government.

According to Morgan, "Eisenhower's conduct of national security policy was guided by a sense of the economic limits of American military power" (p. 51). This posture led, of course, to the desire to achieve "effectiveness with economy" or, more crudely, "more bang for the buck" and eventually led Democrats to criticize the structure of the budget rather than its size. For Democrats, the danger in criticizing the level of defense spending lay in appearing fiscally irresponsible. The 1960 election demonstrates the dilemma facing both parties when trying to appear fiscally frugal and tough on communism at the same time. As Morgan points out, both Nixon and Kennedy ran as fiscal conservatives while calling for expansion in both domestic and defense expenditures.

Funding the continuation of the corporate welfare state exerted additional pressure on fiscal policy in the 1950s. Eisenhower's fiscal conservatism did not prevent him from supporting federal programs such as the Interstate Highway Act that would benefit business by strengthening the nation's infrastructure. Yet, the president's devotion to balancing the budget made him inflexible on some issues. The debate over tax reduction carried on by the Republican right and, periodically, the Democrats was one such issue. In 1954, when the economy slid into recession, Johnson criticized Eisenhower's policies as promoting "that state of affairs in which the rich get richer and the poor are expected to balance the budget" (p. 38). While supply-side arguments which had been around since the 1920s surfaced again in the 1950s, Eisenhower was never convinced and chose to forgo major tax reductions in lieu of a balanced budget.

There are many things to like about this book. For those interested in presidential politics, it is delightful. For politicians hoping to learn from the past, it is instructive. And for understanding the debate over military spending, the budget, and inflation in the postwar period, it is essential. In short, Morgan's contribution to our understanding of policy formation in the 1950s and beyond is substantial.

ANN MARI MAY, *University of Nebraska, Lincoln*

Evolution of United States Budgeting: Changing Fiscal and Financial Concepts. By Annette E. Meyer. Westport: Greenwood Press Inc., 1989. Pp. xiv, 179. $39.95.

Annette Meyer's study provides us with a useful survey of the economic research of the last two decades on the budget process of the U.S. government. The book is divided into four parts. The first briefly traces the development of concepts of fiscal policy and public finance, especially since World War II, with the primary emphasis on the 1960s and 1970s. The second part describes the institutions shaping the budget process, beginning with the Budget and Accounting Act of 1921. In this section Meyer emphasizes the growth of congressional power since the Congressional Budget Act of 1974. The third part surveys the trends in spending, revenue, lending, and deficit finance and describes the introduction of the "unified budget" in fiscal year 1969. The fourth part discusses a set of topics under the rubric of "budget reporting and control"—budget authority, capital budgets, tax expenditures, off-budget spending, and deficit finance.

Meyer's central assessment and policy prescriptions are compelling. She finds that the reporting of both fiscal policy and federal financial activity is seriously inadequate. She points to the need for "independent verification of the accuracy of budget revenues and outlays over time" (p. 90). She ends with a call for "restructuring budget authority and clarifying the relationship to budget outlays, introducing overall assessment of budget outcomes, improving financial management and government-wide accounting systems, and reinstating the audit and review phase of the budgeting process" (p. 163). Perhaps most importantly, she argues for greater sophistication in the reporting of the financial activities of the federal government.

The primary value of Meyer's book is its concise survey of the vast body of recent economic literature on federal public finance. Setting her study firmly in the context of this contemporary literature, however, means accepting its limitations. Most important, Meyer does not tell us how the budget system and process developed prior to 1960, or what have been the sources of institutional change. Taxation receives short shrift, even in the discussion of the recent past. For example, Meyer does not mention, or discuss the implications of, the fact that the Gramm-Rudman-Hollings Act left taxation outside the sequestration process. And the Tax Reform Act of 1986 receives only two brief mentions. More generally, she omits any substantial discussion of how policy makers think about taxation issues, and how this affects the budget process.

Despite its limitations, this is a helpful and timely book. Students of public policy would do well to recognize the validity of the statement with which Meyer begins her study: "The foremost expression of the economic policy of the U.S. government is contained in the federal budget" (p. xiv). Both economists and historians need more historical study of the federal budget process, and for those who would undertake it, Meyer's work is required reading.

W. ELLIOT BROWNLEE, *University of California, Santa Barbara*

Wrong Number: The Breakup of AT&T. By Alan Stone. New York: Basic Books, Inc., 1989. Pp. xi, 381. $21.95.

Since 1985 there has developed a cottage industry in the production of histories on the demise of the Bell Telephone System. These histories, with rare exception, weigh heavily against the rationale of the federal government's antitrust case against American Telephone and Telegraph (AT&T). In *Wrong Number* Alan Stone adds his voice to the clamor. He blames not just the political cynicism and economic shortsightedness of the Department of Justice, but also the ineptitude of the Federal Communications Commission (FCC) for what, he implies, was a travesty of national industrial policy.

As a critique of public policy in action, *Wrong Number* is a thoughtful and clearly written treatise in political economy. As a work of scholarly history, the book is less detailed, more limited in its sources, and more argumentative than the most ambitious of the Bell break-up books, Peter Temin's *The Fall of the Bell System* (New York, 1987), with which, nonetheless, Stone's work merits favorable comparison. Unlike Temin, who focused primarily on the interaction of AT&T and the Justice Department, concluding that AT&T's Bell System was a victim of a changing ideological climate, Stone casts his story in a wider net of complex political forces. In his version of the story, changing ideologies are subsumed by a more fundamental shift in the balance of power between telephony's dominant network manager, AT&T, and its unproven upstart rivals, such as MCI, who emerged to "skim the cream" on the peripheries of technological and market change.

Stone argues that since early in the century, AT&T's vertically integrated monopoly was efficiently organized, innovative, and generally responsive to the demands of the marketplace. It managed a system that allocated resources and set prices in accordance with the broad public interest. Though huge and powerful, AT&T was a responsible corporate citizen; it did not try, for example, to use its market power to extract monopoly profits. Though he does not really prove these points beyond assertion and description, Stone is in good company with far more rigorous analyses of the economic history of the telephone.

It then follows that the Bell System was not an appropriate target for deregulation, and certainly not for destruction. That it *was* destroyed Stone attributes largely to the fact that the FCC, which had primary responsibility for regulating the industry at the federal level, failed to recognize that case-by-case exceptions it began to make on questions of market entry at the peripheries of the Bell System had fundamental implications for overall policy until it was too late.

Ultimately the FCC lost its ability to control telecommunications policy altogether, as power shifted to the courts and the legislature. Once that shift was complete, AT&T became helpless to defend itself against aggressive rivals who could cloak themselves as defenders of the public interest against monopoly power in whatever venue suited them at a time when "deregulation" and "competition" were increasingly in vogue in government circles. Yet, with the fall of the Bell System, we have not dispensed with regulation. Instead, we have gained a more complex industry structure in which an even wider array of contending forces and agencies is engaged in the setting of telecommunications policy. If nothing else, *Wrong Number* serves as a useful reminder that any analysis of industrial policy cannot rely solely on rational economic precepts.

The book is divided into three parts: the first, a pre–World War II history of the evolution of the public policy regime of telecommunications that established AT&T as the regulated network manager for the nation's telephone service; the second, a close examination of the process by which that regime was attacked in various hearings and proceedings from the 1950s to 1970s, as new technologies, shifts in demand for new services, and a changing political and ideological climate combined to weaken the legitimacy of AT&T's claim as network manager; the third, an account of the Department of Justice's second antitrust case against the Bell System, which resulted in the settlement, in 1981, that led to the splintered (and not really competitive) industry structure of the present day. Within a larger chronology, the story is organized topically—some topics dealing with key episodes, others with institutions or issues—providing convenient and well-organized reference points for students of this complex subject.

The story, and Stone's telling of it, is far more complicated than it is possible to convey in this space. Suffice it to say that he has given us a useful study of the muddled workings of American industrial policy. His observations on the often-conflicting roles of regulatory agencies, Congress, and the courts are very instructive. There are also nicely capsulized histories of such important and changing concepts as the "public interest" and "natural monopoly." Nowhere have I read a more succinct presentation on the inconsistency between the principles of antitrust and public service, both of which have endured in uneasy juxtaposition as cornerstones of public policy toward business since the late nineteenth century.

On the other hand, the illogical fate of the Bell System makes me yearn for yet another book, one that would offer an overarching historical framework that can embrace the fragmented, contentious, and often contradictory structure of American industrial policy. Perhaps no such framework can credibly be said to exist, but it strikes me that the apparent inconsistencies of policy have well-defined roots that extend back to the formative years of the Republic—roots which might help make some historical sense out of events that otherwise seem so politically crass and economically dubious.

GEORGE DAVID SMITH, *New York University*

Canadian Papers in Rural History. Volume VII. Edited by Donald H. Akenson. Gananoque, Ontario: Langdale Press, 1990. Pp. 406. $35.00.

For scholars interested in the new rural history, this multivolume series introduces them to the work that Canadian scholars are doing in the field and contains several articles of interest to economic historians in general. The strength of the series as a whole is its multidisciplinary nature. In volume seven, like the others, the editor presents a diversity of topics, viewpoints, and methods and provides a short, useful introduction identifying themes and comparing approaches. Many of the articles either challenge conventional views or explore previously neglected topics.

The catholicity of this volume is demonstrated by the inclusion of topics ranging from political history to demography, all unified under the rubric of rural. For example, Ian Clarke examines the Social Credit's failed attempt to intervene in depression-hit Alberta; Wendy Cameron discusses how the Trent-Severn Waterway took shape under its first engineer; and William Marr provides a detailed statistical analysis of the 1851 Ontario census for evidence on family-size limitation. Marr's article will interest economists as he builds upon Marvin McInnis's work on land availability and fertility. One wonders, however, if Marr's questions might be more satisfactorily answered by using family reconstitution. Three articles deal with non-Canadian topics. Ruth-Ann Harris studies seasonal migration between Ireland and England prior to the Famine, and Donald Akenson rejects Kirby Miller's interpretation of the Irish in the New World through a textual analysis of immigrant letters. Finally, Colin Duncan, in a fascinating and controversial review of the literature on the English Agricultural Revolution, argues that we should stop assuming that modernization leads us away from an agrarian to an industrial society and learn to say the words "modern" and "agrarian" in the same breath. It is time to envision, he propounds, a thoroughly modern agrarian society, one that is not just a prologue to industry or subordinate to it.

Economic historians will be particularly interested in the articles that examine rural crafts prior to industrial capitalism and the rise of controlled marketing in the early twentieth century. Although William Wylie focuses on the material culture of the blacksmith in early nineteenth-century Ontario, he gives a fascinating account of how the blacksmith fitted into the larger industrial and commercial economy. Wylie argues that this was not a golden age of independence for the blacksmith, as he was limited by a commercial system dominated by wholesale merchants and government administrators. By placing the blacksmith within the social milieux of Upper Canada, the artisanal traditions of the Old World, and the secondary literature on labor organization, Wylie argues that the blacksmith was a precapitalist or transitional craftsman. Profit and loss were less important than a comfortable lifestyle that included time for leisure and education, while still affording property ownership. Woven into the growing international literature on proto-industrialization is Janine Roelen and Kris Inwood's examination of cloth production at home in eastern Canada, in particular, Leeds County, Ontario. Using an economist's model of household labor allocation in conjunction with a sample of 100 families who were weaving at home in 1870, they found that cloth production was common, and that weavers were usually women, particularly the foreign-born, the middle-aged, and those living in a marginal agricultural situation. Even though they claim that Leeds seems to have been an exception in Ontario, their work suggests that eastern Canada may have experienced a proto-industrialized era similar to the British Isles about which so much has been written. Certainly much more work is necessary to determine the extent and significance of domestic production in the nineteenth century.

Also of interest to economic historians are two articles dealing with agricultural marketing in the early twentieth century. Ian MacPherson draws our attention to the importance of British Colombian fruit growers and dairymen in being some of the most ardent proponents of controlled marketing in Canada and possibly the world. Their struggle, resulting in legislation in the early 1930s, was quickly imitated elsewhere and brought stability to agriculture but not prosperous security. Charles Johnston examines rural capitalism in Ontario and how farmers emulated urban business techniques in their search for organized agricultural marketing. Both MacPherson and Johnston identify two layers of farmers, those who "played the market" and those who merely survived. This diversity made a unified political front on agricultural issues difficult to achieve.

The articles in this volume vary greatly in their quality and significance. Overall, however, the authors probe a wide range of issues central to understanding rural life.

CATHARINE ANNE WILSON, *University of Guelph*

ECONOMIC THOUGHT

Historians, Economists and Economic History. By Alon Kadish. New York: Routledge, 1989. Pp. xii, 297. $65.00.

At the outset Alon Kadish describes his book accurately, but somewhat uninvitingly, as "a blow-by-blow account of the emergence of economic history as an academic discipline in England" (p. ix) from about 1875 to the early twentieth century. It is, indeed, somewhat heavy in detail, as indicated by the 1200 or so footnotes, many of which refer to original manuscript or obscure secondary sources, and this is testimony to the author's thoroughness and skill in uncovering significant new or neglected evidence. The citation of modern secondary sources is, incidentally, far less comprehensive; there is no bibliography.

As Kadish notes, much of the groundwork for his study has already been laid, not least by his own two valuable earlier books *The Oxford Economists of the Late Nineteenth Century* (New York, 1982) and *Apostle Arnold: The Life and Death of Arnold Toynbee, 1852–1883* (Durham, 1986); this latest contribution is designed to explain "the creation of a new institutional scientific discipline" (p. ix). To this end he surveys in Part I the views of a series of Oxford historians—professors, tutors, and their students—and the educational objectives and curricular arrangements under which they worked. In Part II he examines the somewhat more familiar subject of Cambridge economics in the same period. Cambridge history appears too, but less prominently than its Oxford counterpart in earlier chapters. A review of the state of affairs in 1885, when Marshall first occupied the chair, is followed by chapters on "Tinkering with the Triposes" and "The Liberation of Economics" (that is, from the Moral Science and History Boards). Part III deals with economic history and with the contraction of economics as the twentieth-century specialties appear.

As a reviewer familiar with Kadish's earlier works and with those of contemporary toilers in the same or closely related historical vineyards, I have constantly been impressed by Kadish's ability to add to existing knowledge and fill missing gaps in the story. Most historians of economics and economic historians will be surprised by the extent to which history, rather than economics, provided the context from which academic economic history emerged. Methodological, doctrinal, and policy disagreements among economists, and between them and the pioneering economic historians, have hitherto attracted disproportionate attention. Kadish's work is thus more than a gentle trot (hardly a canter, let alone a gallop) through familiar, well-tended pastures. It repays careful reading by all who are interested in the interrelationships between the three I's: ideas, individuals, and institutions—academic structures and educational management systems, in this instance.

Some reservations remain, however. For example, despite the author's initial emphasis on explanation, his primary interest and ability is in narrative—almost "thick description" perhaps—and he is overcautious when it comes to generalization or speculation, for he heavily emphasizes intellectual biography. The rich sociology of science literature—for example, on the emergence of new disciplines—could have provided some fruitful hypotheses or conjectures; and the geographical focus is largely, indeed almost exclusively, on Oxbridge. There were in fact other university institutions, even in England, and certainly elsewhere in the United Kingdom.

Nevertheless, within its fairly severe limits, this is a very scholarly and instructive addition to our knowledge.

A. W. Coats, *Duke University*

The Spread of Economic Ideas. Edited by David Colander and A. W. Coats. New York: Cambridge University Press, 1989. Pp. xvi, 262. $34.50.

The Annual Middlebury College Conference on Economic Issues was the original setting for these 18 papers. Often such collections are uneven and the papers ill suited to one another: these are not. Whatever rough edges may have existed have been smoothed out nicely by the editors, and the engaging style of the contributions makes for enjoyable, provocative reading. The central subject of economic ideas allows the contributors, who come both from within and without the academy, to draw on their own particular areas of expertise. The result is an eclectic volume that should appeal to a wide audience.

The transmission of economic ideas is discussed under four headings: within the profession, to the lay public, to the policy maker, and funding. In the first essay Robert Clower addresses whether there *are* any valuable ideas rather than *how* economic ideas are disseminated. His experience from journal editing leads him to lament "[w]hat was remarkable was the absolute dullness, the lack of any kind of new idea, that predominated in the selection of papers. . . ." (p. 27). Next, in a theme he revisits in Part IV, Colander argues furiously that new ideas are impeded by the "internal dynamics of the profession: who is allowed to become a member, who gets promoted, who gets paid what, [and] who gets the laurels. . . ." (p. 32). The dialogue, though polite, heats up with the next piece, by Robert Solow, who disagrees with the conclusions reached by the previous authors and asserts that so do "most of the functioning economists" he knows. Charles Kindleberger suggests that with the proliferation of journals it has become virtually impossible to remain current in the discipline. Using examples drawn from international economics, he proposes five life profiles of economic ideas. Colin Day, representing university publishing, differentiates readers by a knowledge line and argues that books may serve to communicate ideas better than journals, which face greater space constraints.

Robert Solow, in Part II, posits that if ideas are communicated to the public, they are turned to "mush" in the process. Mind you, says Solow, that is not all bad: "the World Out There believes that the economist's case for the market is stronger that it really is . . . . without that illusion the World Out There would not appreciate how strong the case really is" (p. 78). David Warsh, an economic columnist for the *Boston Globe*, examines the vastly different methods that led to the forging of a strategic trade policy. To understand the diffusion of ideas, he suggests, we should look at the degree of skepticism involved in each of those methods. In a critical essay Donald Lamm, chair of W. W. Norton, argues that very few economic books are written for the common reader primarily because "economists insist on placing the highest value on exchanges with other economists. . . ." (p. 105).

A. W. Coats begins Part III by identifying the particular skills and abilities needed to communicate and persuade others of economic ideas. Few economists, he says, are inclined toward those attributes. William Barber finds scant evidence that the world is ruled by little else than our ideas, despite the ever-increasing number of economists in the government. Those economists who return to the academy from a stint of government service, however, are equipped to "speak with some authority about what is relevant in public debate" (p. 126). James Galbraith, an economist at the Lyndon B. Johnson School of Public Affairs, analyzes the institutional restraints within Congress to surmise that the spread of ideas may be seen as an "exchange of favors for commitments, between those with political capital to spare and those without" (p. 131). Although it is in vogue in our profession to call for policy rules, he argues that such simplifications subvert the means by which ideas may be translated into law. In Joseph Minarik's essay the passage of the Tax Reform Act of 1986 unfolds like a Spielberg movie. He observes that once economists stopped urging a comprehensive income tax it was adopted by policy makers: the implication being, he suggests cautiously, that the "way to spread an economic idea is to abandon it" (p. 148).

Part IV begins with Craufurd Goodwin's examination of the inherent tension between the underlying principles of the Ford Foundation and the economics profession. This tension has resulted in reduced funding for economists, which may lead "economics to join the humanities in genteel poverty. . . ." (p. 159). James Smith examines the role and structure of think tanks, which he views as pivotal in the new politics of ideas. The director of the National Science Foundation's Economics Program, Daniel Newlon, provides a vigorous defense of the NSF's funding process and argues that it has been instrumental in the purveyance of economic ideas. In the final essay Gordon Tullock argues that adoption of a patent system of ideas would increase incentives and swell the production and funding of economic ideas.

I cannot imagine a reader who could not find something of interest in this volume. Some might take exception to the casual and informal style but that, of course, is consistent with the editors' sociological approach. This does pose something of a dilemma for Colander, in particular, who argues that only formal models are accepted within the profession: if the book is well received by economists, it may mean he needs to re-examine his thesis.

KATE J. STIRLING, *University of Puget Sound*

GENERAL AND MISCELLANEOUS

Homework: Historical and Contemporary Perspectives on Paid Labor at Home. Edited by Eileen Boris and Cynthia R. Daniels. Champaign: University of Illinois Press, 1989. Pp. x, 299. $32.50, cloth; $12.95, paper.

Our image of homework has been based more on the polemics of policy advocates than the painstaking reconstructions of social scientists. This superb collection of essays moves us beyond the conventional, one-dimensional stereotypes of, on the one hand, immigrant women and children sweating away their lives in cramped tenements surrounded by piles of unstitched garments or, on the other, "middle-class women handcrafting while their toddlers play by the fire" (p. 247). Through a series of well-chosen and nuanced case studies, homeworkers emerge in all their variety: from the privileged script-writer, unionized newspaper reporter, or skilled professional starting up a home business, to the "artisanal" Vermont handknitter and the self-employed black laundress, to the marginal and beleaguered insurance claim processor bleary-eyed from unremitting doses of full-time child care and piecework.

Yet paradoxically, as the social reality of homework emerges, the category itself begins to dissolve. Whether a particular homeworker achieves a living wage, flexibility and autonomy at work, or enhanced power in the domestic sphere, a sense of workplace community and a feeling of productive accomplishment appears to depend more on the bargaining leverage of the individual than the site at which the work takes place. Indeed, for those few homeworkers who are male or unionized, the problems often described as inherent to homework—low pay, insecurity of income, invisibility of work, and social isolation—disappear. In short, as many of the authors make clear, the policy issues concerning homework have as much to do with correcting persistent sexual inequalities in both the public and private sphere as with the location of waged work within the home.

The editors are to be commended for their insightful introductory chapter which carefully pinpoints the themes that are then echoed and complicated in the ensuing essays. In part because of their thoughtful editing, the volume has unusual coherence and cumulative power. The essays are also consistently well written, theoretically sophisticated, and empirically grounded. In fact, as opposed to many edited collections, this volume succeeds in being greater than the sum of its parts.

In addition to providing a complex portrait of the economics of homework and the meaning(s) of homework to those so employed, the essays offer a fascinating account of historical and contemporary attempts to formulate public policy in regard to homework. Most authors agree that no single approach is adequate given the variety of homework, but certain proposals do surface repeatedly. The miscategorization of homeworkers as independent contractors (thus removing them from wage and hour protections under the Fair Labor Standards Act and denying them unemployment insurance, workers' compensation, and social security payments) should be corrected; better child care support is also essential if homework is to be a "humane alternative to a labor market alien to the needs of working parents" (p. 6) rather than a "choice" forced upon homebound women who lack other real options.

No clear concensus emerges, however, on the efficacy of either regulating or banning homework. One author concludes that the "exploited labor, meager wages, and excessive hours" of homework theoretically could be regulated, but "no evidence suggests that the state could do so adequately in the future when it so consistently has failed in the past" (p. 250). Another essay appears to agree with the conclusion of the International Ladies' Garment Workers' Union that given the unorganizable character of industrial homework and the impossibility of state regulation, the only viable policy in many cases may be a ban. Yet, Sheila Allen's account of the British unions' choice to join the "National Group on Homeworking," a group dedicated to improving the conditions of homeworkers through self-organization and regulatory statutes, raises questions about conclusions based solely on an analysis of the U.S. experience.

This volume thus opens up significant new areas for research while simultaneously making important contributions to those research projects. For example, only one of the essays attempts a systematic portrait of the number of homeworkers nationally, how they are distributed occupationally, and how that has changed in the last decades. Clearly, more data on homeworkers must be gathered and analyzed in order to test the numerous provocative hypotheses put forward in this volume. More comparative work would also be illuminating, especially for those concerned with creating better policy options and ensuring that the "better face of homework" emerges.

DOROTHY SUE COBBLE, *Rutgers University*

Racism, Sexism, and the World-System. Edited by Joan Smith, Jane Collins, Terence K. Hopkins, and Akbar Muhammad. New York: Greenwood Press, 1988. Pp. xii, 221. $45.00.

The point of departure for the essays in this volume is the premise that "racism and sexism should no longer exist" (p. ix). Published under the advisory editorship of Immanuel Wallerstein, these essays embrace his World-System view that global capital accumulation is the most fundamental force shaping economic, social, and political developments within and among nation-states. Capitalism's "ideological legitimation of universalism" therefore seem at odds with the "continuing reality of racism and sexism" (p. 3).

In one of the introductory essays Wallerstein suggests a resolution to this tension: both are "needed." "We know what happens when racism goes to far . . . We can imagine what happens when universalism goes too far . . . What we see therefore is a system that operates by a tense link between the right dosage of universalism and racism-sexism" (p. 9). In the second introductory essay June Nash summarizes ethnographic evidence on changes in the household economy, work place, and informal economy during the expansion of capitalism to illustrate this "tense link."

The four essays in the second section focus on the impact of global capital accumulation on race and gender. Martha Gemenez calls attention to distortions and injustices that result when the oppressed are identified in terms of ethnicity, whereas laborers of *many* classes move across international boundaries. Nancy Lutz documents similarities in the image of docility applied to female textile workers across countries and historical periods. Peter Bell points out the effect of global capital accumulation on gender relations in the Third World and the development of a contradictory relationship between women in the core and on the periphery. Kathie Kasaba describes the historical processes and social relationships that made male Russian Jewish garment workers in New York about the turn of the century just as economically vulnerable as native-born white females.

The six essays in the third section examine the impact of race and gender on global capital accumulation. Ann Forsythe and Roberto Korzeniewicz draw examples from textile production in Argentina, England, France, and Germany in the late nineteenth and early twentieth centuries. John Horton and Eun-Jin Lee look at the semiconductor industry in the twentieth century. Terry Boswell and David Jorjani review evidence on the migration of blacks, Chinese, and Mexicans to the United States. All three essays emphasize the ways in which race and gender differentiation prior to the advent of capitalism shaped the development of the market for paid labor.

Kathryn Ward describes the Igbo Women's War of 1929 as an example of the effects of global capital accumulation in reducing women's status and acting as a spur to their collective behavior. Richard Williams takes issue with the ethnic small-business literature for the United States, which blames blacks' social immobility on their reluctance or inability to take advantage of small-business opportunities. Ethnics who successfully used small businesses to advance may not have been poor, Williams suggests. James Geschwender and Rita Carroll-Seguin discuss Asian-American "exceptionalism." They argue that "much of the apparent affluence of Asian-Americans is the simple consequence of a much higher rate of female participation in the labor force" (p. 204).

These essays develop no new evidence and say little that will surprise readers of this JOURNAL. They are probably best thought of as efforts to retell familiar stories in ways that emphasize the power of capitalists, patriarchs, and nation-states and downplay the role of competition, efficiency, and choice.

SUSAN B. CARTER, *Smith College*

Index to Volume L

ARTICLES

BARSKY, ROBERT B. AND J. BRADFORD DE LONG, *Bull and Bear Markets in the Twentieth Century* 265
BERNSTEIN, MICHAEL A., *American Economic Expertise from the Great War to the Cold War: Some Initial Observations* 407
BLACK, ROBERT A. AND CLAIRE G. GILMORE, *Crowding Out during Britain's Industrial Revolution* 109
BRANDT, LOREN AND BARBARA SANDS, *Beyond Malthus and Ricardo: Economic Growth, Land Concentration, and Income Distribution in Early Twentieth-Century Rural China* 807
BROWN, JOHN C., *The Condition of England and the Standard of Living: Cotton Textiles in the Northwest, 1806–1850* 591
CALOMIRIS, CHARLES W., *Is Deposit Insurance Necessary? A Historical Perspective* 283
CARLOS, ANN M. AND STEPHEN NICHOLAS, *Agency Problems in Early Chartered Companies: The Case of the Hudson's Bay Company* 853
CARTER, SUSAN B. AND ELIZABETH SAVOCA, *Labor Mobility and Lengthy Jobs in Nineteenth-Century America* 1
COWAN, ROBIN, *Nuclear Power Reactors: A Study in Technological Lock-in* ... 541
DAVIS, GEORGE K. AND GARY M. PECQUET, *Interest Rates in the Civil War South* 133
DE LONG, J. BRADFORD (See Barsky, Robert B.)
DUPRÉ, RUTH, *Regulating the Quebec Dairy Industry, 1905–1921: Peeling Off the Joseph Label* 339
ELTIS, DAVID, *Welfare Trends among the Yoruba in the Early Nineteenth Century: The Anthropometric Evidence* 521
GILMORE, CLAIRE G. (See Black, Robert A.)
GREASLEY, DAVID, *Fifty Years of Coal-mining Productivity: The Record of the British Coal Industry before 1939* 877
GROSS, NACHUM T., *Israeli Economic Policies, 1948–1951: Problems of Evaluation* 67
HARRISON, MARK, *The Volume of Soviet Munitions Output, 1937–1945: A Reevaluation* 569
HEIM, CAROL E., *The Treasury As Developer-Capitalist? British New Town Building in the 1950s* 903
HUMPHRIES, JANE, *Enclosures, Common Rights, and Women: The Proletarianization of Families in the Late Eighteenth and Early Nineteenth Centuries* ... 17
HUNT, EDWIN S., *A New Look at the Dealings of the Bardi and Peruzzi with Edward III* 149
KHAN, B. ZORINA (See Sokoloff, Kenneth L.)
LA CROIX, SUMNER J. AND JAMES ROUMASSET, *The Evolution of Private Property in Nineteenth-Century Hawaii* 829
MAY, ANN MARI, *President Eisenhower, Economic Policy, and the 1960 Presidential Election* 417
MIRON, JEFFREY A. AND CHRISTINA D. ROMER, *A New Monthly Index of Industrial Production, 1884–1940* 321
NICHOLAS, STEPHEN (See Carlos, Ann M.)
NOVAK, STEVEN J., *The Real Takeover of the BIA: The Preferential Hiring of Indians* 639
PECQUET, GARY M. (See Davis, George K.)
REDISH, ANGELA, *The Evolution of the Gold Standard in England* 789

ROMER, CHRISTINA D. (See Miron, Jeffrey A.)
ROSENBLOOM, JOSHUA L., *One Market or Many? Labor Market Integration in the Late Nineteenth-Century United States* 85
ROSENTHAL, JEAN-LAURENT, *The Development of Irrigation in Provence, 1700–1860: The French Revolution and Economic Growth* 615
ROUMASSET, JAMES (See La Croix, Sumner J.)
SANDS, BARBARA (See Brandt, Loren)
SAVOCA, ELIZABETH (See Carter, Susan B.)
SHIELLS, MARTHA ELLEN, *Collective Choice of Working Conditions: Hours in British and U.S. Iron and Steel, 1890–1923* 379
SOKOLOFF, KENNETH L. AND B. ZORINA KHAN, *The Democratization of Invention During Early Industrialization: Evidence from the United States, 1790–1846* 363
SULLIVAN, RICHARD J., *The Revolution of Ideas: Widespread Patenting and Invention During the English Industrial Revolution* 349
SUNDSTROM, WILLIAM A., *Was There a Golden Age of Flexible Wages? Evidence from Ohio Manufacturing, 1892–1910* 309
TEMIN, PETER, *Socialism and Wages in the Recovery from the Great Depression in the United States and Germany* 297
WHAPLES, ROBERT, *Winning the Eight-Hour Day, 1909–1919* 393
WHATLEY, WARREN C., *Getting a Foot in the Door: "Learning," State Dependence, and the Racial Integration of Firms* 43

NOTES, DISCUSSIONS, DISSERTATION SUMMARIES, AND REVIEW ARTICLES

ADELMAN, IRMA AND CYNTHIA TAFT MORRIS, *A Note of Technical Correction* . 262
BARBEZAT, DANIEL, *International Cooperation and Domestic Cartel Control: The International Steel Cartel, 1926–1938* 436
BOGUE, ALLAN G., *Fogel's Journey through the Slave States* 699
CAMPA, JOSÉ MANUEL, *Exchange Rates and Economic Recovery in the 1930s: An Extension to Latin America* 677
CARRUTHERS, BRUCE G., *Politics, Popery, and Property: A Comment on North and Weingast* 693
CHATTERJI, MONOJIT (See Mayer, Thomas)
COSGEL, METIN M., *Scattering and Contracts in Medieval Agriculture: Challenges Ahead* 663
CRAIG, LEE A., *Farm Output, Productivity, and Fertility Decline in the Antebellum Northern United States* 432
GARRETT, MARTIN A., JR., *The Mule in Southern Agriculture: A Requiem* 925
HETHERINGTON, BRUCE W., *Bank Entry and the Low Issue of National Bank Notes: A Re-examination* 669
HOOD, ADRIENNE D., *Organization and Extent of Textile Manufacture in Eighteenth-Century Rural Pennsylvania: A Case Study of Chester County* 434
HUBERMAN, MICHAEL, *Vertical Disintegration in Lancashire: A Comment on Temin* 683
MAYER, THOMAS AND MONOJIT CHATTERJI, *Reply to O'Brien* 942
MITCH, DAVID, *The Role of the Textbook in Undergraduate Economic History Courses: Indispensable Tool or Superficial Convenience?* 428
MOKYR, JOEL AND JOHN V. C. NYE, *La Grande Quantification* 172
MORRIS, CYNTHIA TAFT (See Adelman, Irma)
NYE, JOHN V. C. (See Mokyr, Joel)
O'BRIEN, ANTHONY PATRICK, *Were Businessmen Afraid of FDR? A Comment on Mayer and Chatterji* 936

OVERTON, MARK, *Re-estimating Crop Yields from Probate Inventories: A Comment* ... 931
PATTERSON, MARGARET AND DAVID REIFFEN, *The Effect of the Bubble Act on the Market for Joint Stock Shares* ... 163
REIFFEN, DAVID (See Patterson, Margaret)
ROSENBLOOM, JOSHUA L., *Labor Market Institutions and the Geographic Integration of Labor Markets in the Late Nineteenth-Century United States* ... 440
ROSENTHAL, JEAN-LAURENT, *The Fruits of Revolution: Property Rights, Litigation, and French Agriculture, 1700–1860* ... 438
TEMIN, PETER, *Product Quality and Vertical Integration in the Early Cotton Textile Industry: A Reply* ... 691
THORNTON, M. K. AND R. L. THORNTON, *The Financial Crisis of A.D. 33: A Keynesian Depression?* ... 655
THORNTON, R. L. (See Thornton, M. K.)
WOLCOTT, SUSAN, *Keynes vs. Churchill: British Unemployment in the Twenties* . 442

REVIEWS OF BOOKS

ABRAMOVITZ, MOSES, *Thinking About Growth and Other Essays on Economic Growth and Welfare* ... 506
ABU-LUGHOD, JANET L., *Before European Hegemony: The World System A.D. 1250–1350* ... 455
ACCAMPO, ELINOR, *Industrialization, Family Life, and Class Relations: Saint-Chamond, 1815–1914* ... 199
AKENSON, DONALD H., Ed., *Canadian Papers in Rural History*. Volume VII .. 992
ADAS, MICHAEL, *Machines as the Measure of Men: Science, Technology, and Idealogies of Western Dominance* ... 510
ALBERT, PETER J. (See Kaufman, Stuart B.)
ALTER, GEORGE, *Family and the Female Life Course: The Women of Verviers, Belgium, 1849–1880* ... 202
ANDERSON, DALE G. (See Felton, John Richard)
ANDERSON, TERRY L. AND PETER J. HILL, *The Birth of a Transfer Society* 766
ANDERTON, DOUGLAS L. (See Bean, Lee L.)
BACKHOUSE, ROGER, *Economists and the Economy: The Evolution of Economic Ideas, 1600 to the Present Day* ... 241
BAILEY, MARK, *A Marginal Economy? East Anglian Brackland in the Later Middle Ages* ... 456
BAMFORD, P. W., *Privilege and Profit: A Business Family in Eighteenth-Century France* ... 956
BASKERVILLE, PETER, Ed., *Canadian Papers in Business History*. Vol. I 772
BEAN, LEE L., GERALDINE P. MINEAU, AND DOUGLAS L. ANDERTON, *Fertility Change on the American Frontier: Adaptation and Innovation* ... 987
BECNEL, THOMAS A., *The Barrow Family and the Barataria and Lafourche Canal: The Transportation Revolution in Louisiana, 1829–1925* ... 490
BERESFORD, MAURICE, *East End, West End: The Face of Leeds During Urbanisation, 1684–1842* ... 197
BERGIER, JEAN-FRANÇOIS, Ed., *Montagnes, fleuves, fôrets dans l'histoire: Barrières ou lignes de convergence?* ... 713
BIDDICK, KATHLEEN, *The Other Economy: Pastoral Husbandry on a Medieval Estate* ... 184
BLANCHARD, IAN, *Russia's "Age of Sliver": Precious-Metal Production and Economic Growth in the Eighteenth Century* ... 477
BOLINO, AUGUST C., *A Century of Human Capital by Education and Training* . 511

BORDO, MICHAEL D., Ed., *Money, History, and International Finance: Essays in Honor of Anna J. Schwartz* 259
BORGES, WILLIAM (See Fabritius, M. Manfred)
BORIS, EILEEN AND CYNTHIA R. DANIELS, Eds., *Homework: Historical and Contemporary Perspectives on Paid Labor at Home* 996
BOTHWELL, ROBERT, IAN DRUMMOND, AND JOHN ENGLISH, *Canada, 1900–1945* 501
BOWMAN, JOHN R., *Capitalist Collective Action: Competition, Cooperation and Conflict in the Coal Industry* 492
BROEZE, FRANK, Ed., *Brides of the Sea: Port Cities of Asia from the 16th–20th Centuries* 963
BROWN, BRENDAN, *The Flight of International Capital: A Contemporary History* 258
BROWN, HENRY PHELPS, *Egalitarianism and the Generation of Inequality* 254
BRULAND, KRISTINE, *British Technology and European Industrialization: The Norwegian Textile Industry in the Mid Nineteenth Century* 194
BRYANT, KEITH L., JR., Ed., *Encyclopedia of American Business History and Biography: Railroads in the Age of Regulation, 1900–1980* 222
BUCHANAN, R. A., *The Engineers: A History of the Engineering Profession in Britain, 1750–1914* 470
BUCKLEY, KEN AND TED WHEELWRIGHT, *No Paradise for Workers: Capitalism and the Common People in Australia, 1788–1914* 209
BUTLIN, N. G. (See Gregory, R. G.)
CAIRNCROSS, ALEC, Ed., *The Robert Hall Diaries, 1947–53* 960
CAIRNCROSS, ALEC AND NITA WATTS, *The Economic Section, 1939–1961: A Study in Economic Advising* 730
CAMPBELL, JOAN, *Joy in Work, German Work: The National Debate, 1800–1945* 472
CAMPBELL, RANDOLPH B., *An Empire for Slavery: The Peculiar Institution in Texas, 1821–1865* 488
CAMPORESI, PIERO, *Bread of Dreams: Food and Fantasy in Early Modern Europe* 718
CARELESS, J. M. S., *Frontier and Metropolis: Regions, Cities, and Identities in Canada Before 1914* 499
CARR, LOIS GREEN, PHILIP D. MORGAN, AND JEAN B. RUSSO, Eds., *Colonial Chesapeake Society* 751
CARVALHO, JOSE ALBERT MAGNO DE (See Wood, Charles H.)
CHALKLIN, C. W. AND J. R. WORDIE, Eds., *Town and Countryside: The English Landowner in the National Economy, 1660–1860* 726
CHIROT, DANIEL, Ed., *The Origins of Backwardness in Eastern Europe* 962
CIPOLLA, CARLO M., *Le tre rivoluzioni e altri saggi di storia economica e sociale* 950
CIPOLLA, CARLO M., *Money in Sixteenth-Century Florence* 950
CLARK, GORDON L., *Unions and Communities Under Siege: American Communities and the Crisis of Organized Labor* 770
CLARKE, PETER, *The Keynesian Revolution in the Making, 1924–1936* 243
CLARKE, SIMON, *Keynesianism, Monetarism and the Crisis of the State* 504
CLEARY, M. C., *Peasants, Politicians and Producers: The Organisation of Agriculture in France Since 1918* 471
CLINGERMAN, HAROLD BENNETT, *Field Man: The Chronicle of a Bank Farm Manager in the 1940s* 232
COATS, A. W. (See Colander, David)
COLANDER, DAVID AND A. W. COATS, Eds., *The Spread of Economic Ideas* ... 995
COLLINS, JAMES B., *Fiscal Limits of Absolutism: Direct Taxation in Early Seventeenth-Century France* 191
CURRIE, DAVID AND DAVID VINES, Eds., *Macroeconomic Interactions between North and South* 260

CURTIN, PHILIP D., *Death by Migration: Europe's Encounter with the Tropical World in the Nineteenth Century* 724
DANIELS, CYNTHIA R. (See Boris, Eileen)
DARITY, WILLIAM, JR., Ed., *Race, Radicalism, and Reform: Selected Papers of Abram L. Harris* 227
DASGUPTA, AJIT K., *Growth, Development and Welfare: An Essay on Levels of Living* 515
DAVENPORT-HINES, R. T. P. AND JONATHAN LIEBENAU, Eds., *Business in the Age of Reason* 467
DAVIES, R. W., *The Soviet Economy in Turmoil, 1929–1930* 744
DEANE, PHYLLIS, *The State and the Economic System: An Introduction to the History of Political Economy* 240
DE LEÓN, ARNOLDO AND KENNETH STEWART, *Tejanos and the Numbers Game: A Socio-Historical Interpretation from the Federal Censuses, 1850–1900* 762
DICKMAN, HOWARD (See Paul, Ellen Frankel)
DON, YEHUDA AND VICTOR KARADY, Eds., *A Social and Economic History of Central European Jewry* 741
DRUMMOND, IAN (See Bothwell, Robert)
DUBOFF, RICHARD B., *Accumulation and Power: An Economic History of the United States* 496
DUPUY, ALEX, *Haiti in the World Economy: Class, Race, and Underdevelopment Since 1700* 747
DUPUY, GABRIEL (See Tarr, Joel A.)
EDELMAN, ROBERT, *Proletarian Peasants: The Revolution of 1905 in Russia's Southwest* 743
EICHENGREEN, BARRY AND PETER H. LINDERT, Eds., *The International Debt Crisis in Historical Perspective* 782
EICHLER, NED, *The Thrift Debacle* 237
EMMONS, DAVID M., *The Butte Irish: Class and Ethnicity in an American Mining Town, 1875–1925* 988
ENGERMAN, STANLEY L. (See Solow, Barbara L.)
ENGLISH, JOHN (See Bothwell, Robert)
FABRITIUS, M. MANFRED AND WILLIAM BORGES, *Saving the Savings and Loan: The U.S. Thrift Industry and the Texas Experience, 1950–1988* 237
FELTON, JOHN RICHARD AND DALE G. ANDERSON, Eds., *Regulation and Deregulation of the Motor Carrier Industry* 228
FERRIS, WILLIAM (See Wilson, Charles Reagan)
FINK, LEON AND BRIAN GREENBERG, *Upheaval in the Quiet Zone: A History of Hospital Workers' Union, Local 1199* 233
FISHER, STEPHEN, Ed., *Innovation in Shipping and Trade* 784
FITZGERALD, SHIRLEY, *Rising Damp: Sydney, 1870–90* 208
FLANDERS, M. JUNE, *International Monetary Economics, 1870–1960: Between the Classical and the New Classical* 779
FOX-GENOVESE, ELIZABETH, *Within the Plantation Household: Black and White Women of the Old South* 759
GALLAY, ALAN, *The Formation of a Planter Elite: Jonathan Bryan and the Southern Colonial Frontier* 976
GALLOWAY, J. H., *The Sugar Cane Industry: An Historical Geography from its Origins to 1914* 517
GARVEY, GEORGE E. AND GERALD J. GARVEY, *Economic Law and Economic Growth: Antitrust, Regulation, and the American Growth System* 985

GARVEY, GERALD J. (See Garvey, George E.)
GESELOWITZ, MICHAEL N. (See Gibson, D. Blair)
GIBSON, D. BLAIR AND MICHAEL N. GESELOWITZ, Eds., *Tribe and Polity in Late Prehistoric Europe: Demography, Production and Exchange in the Evolution of Complex Social Systems* 182
GOLDBERG, DAVID J., *A Tale of Three Cities: Labor Organization and Protest in Paterson, Passaic, and Lawrence, 1916–1921* 225
GOODMAN, JORDAN AND KATRINA HONEYMAN, *Gainful Pursuits: The Making of Industrial Europe, 1600–1914* 194
GOODSTEIN, ANITA SHAFER, *Nashville, 1780–1860: From Frontier to City* 752
GOOTENBERG, PAUL, *Between Silver and Guano: Commercial Policy and the State in Postindependence Peru* 748
GREENBERG, BRIAN (See Fink, Leon)
GREGORY, R. G. AND N. G. BUTLIN, Eds., *Recovery from the Depression: Australia and the World Economy in the 1930s* 969
GROSSMAN, JAMES R., *Land of Hope: Chicago, Black Southerners, and the Great Migration* 768
GUTIÉRREZ BROCKINGTON, LOLITA, *The Leverage of Labor: Managing the Cortés Haciendas in Tehuantepec, 1588–1688* 211
HABER, STEPHEN H., *Industry and Underdevelopment: The Industrialization of Mexico, 1890–1940* 213
HAIMSON, LEOPOLD AND CHARLES TILLY, Eds., *Strikes, Wars, and Revolutions in an International Perspective: Strike Waves in the Late Nineteenth and Early Twentieth Centuries* 466
HALLAM, H. E., Ed., *The Agrarian History of England and Wales*. Vol. 2: *1046–1350* 714
HART, GILLIAN, ANDREW TURTON, AND BENJAMIN WHITE, Eds., *Agrarian Transformations: Local Processes and the State in Southeast Asia* 483
HARVEY, CHARLES AND JOHN TURNER, Eds., *Labour and Business in Modern Britain* 961
HAYWARD, KEITH, *The British Aircraft Industry* 732
HERLIHY, DAVID, *Opera Muliebria: Women and Work in Medieval Europe* 948
HILL, PETER J. (See Anderson, Terry L.)
HOCH, CHARLES AND ROBERT A. SLAYTON, *New Homeless and Old: Community and Skid Row Hotel* 518
HOCH, STEVEN L., *Serfdom and Social Control in Russia: Petrovskoe, a Village in Tambov* 477
HONEYMAN, KATRINA (See Goodman, Jordan)
HOUNSHELL, DAVID A. AND JOHN KENLY SMITH JR., *Science and Corporate Strategy: Du Pont Research and Development, 1902–1980* 223
HOWARD, M. C. AND J. E. KING, *A History of Marxian Economics*. Vol 1: *1883–1929* 503
HUDSON, PAT, Ed., *Regions and Industries: A Perspective on the Industrial Revolution in Britain* 729
HUGHES, THOMAS P. (See Mayntz, Renate)
HYBEL, NILS, *Crisis or Change: The Concept of Crisis in the Light of Agrarian Structural Reorganization in Late Medieval England* 717
ILIFFE, JOHN, *The African Poor: A History* 204
ISRAEL, JONATHAN I., *Dutch Primacy in World Trade, 1585–1740* 462
ISRAEL, JONATHAN I., *European Jewry in the Age of Mercantilism, 1550–1750* . 192
JOHNSON, LYMAN L. AND ENRIQUE TANDETER, Eds., *Essays on the Price History of Eighteenth-Century Latin America* 972
JONES, STEPHANIE, *Trade and Shipping, Lord Inchcape, 1852–1932* 198

KADISH, ALON, *Historians, Economists and Economic History* 994
KARADY, VICTOR (See Don, Yehuda)
KAUFMAN, STUART B. AND PETER J. ALBERT, Eds., *The Samuel Gompers Papers*. Vol. 3: *Unrest and Depression, 1891–94* 494
KELLENBENZ, HERMANN AND PAOLO PRODI, Eds., *Fisco religione Stato nell'età confessionale* 187
KESSLER-HARRIS, ALICE (See Moody, Carroll)
KIMELDORF, HOWARD, *Reds or Rackets? The Making of Radical and Conservative Unions on the Waterfront* 231
KINDLEBERGER, CHARLES P., *The German Economy, 1945–1947: Charles P. Kindleberger's Letters From the Field* 203
KINDLEBERGER, CHARLES P., *Spenders and Hoarders: The World Distribution of Spanish American Silver, 1550–1750* 721
KING, J. E. (See Howard, M. C.)
KLEINBERG, S. J., *The Shadow of the Mills: Working-Class Families in Pittsburgh, 1870–1907* 765
KUZNETS, SIMON, *Economic Development, the Family, and Income Distribution: Selected Essays* 787
LAL, DEEPAK, *The Hindu Equilibrium*. Vol. 1: *Cultural Stability and Economic Stagnation*. Vol. 2: *Aspects of Indian Labour* 206
LAWRENCE, ROBERT Z. (See Litan, Robert E.)
LAXER, GORDON, *Open For Business: The Roots of Foreign Ownership in Canada*. 771
LEBOUTTE, RENÉ, *Reconversions de la main-d'oeuvre et transition démographique: Les bassins industriels en aval de Liège XVIIe–XXe siècles* 739
L'Électricité et ses consommateurs 200
LEPETIT, BERNARD, *Les villes dans la France moderne: 1740–1840* 954
LEVY-LEBOYER, MAURICE (See Teichova, Alice)
LIEBENAU, JONATHAN (See Davenport-Hines, R. T. P.)
LINDBLAD, J. THOMAS, *Between Dayak and the Dutch: The Economic History of Southeast Kalimantan* 964
LINDER, MARC, *The Employment Relationship in Anglo-American Law: A Historical Perspective* 513
LINDERT, PETER H. (See Eichengreen, Barry)
LITAN, ROBERT E., ROBERT Z. LAWRENCE, AND CHARLES L. SCHULTZE, Eds., *American Living Standards: Threats and Challenges* 236
LOCKE, ROBERT R., *Management and Higher Education Since 1940: The Influence of America and Japan on West Germany, Great Britain and France* 785
LUTTRELL, CLIFTON B., *The High Cost of Farm Welfare* 226
MARGAIRAZ, DOMINIQUE, *Foires et marchés dans la France préindustrielle* 463
MASON, ROGER S., *Robert Giffen and the Giffen Paradox* 502
MATHIAS, PETER AND SIDNEY POLLARD, Eds., *The Cambridge Economic History of Europe*. Vol. 8: *The Industrial Economies: The Development of Economic and Social Policies* 459
MATOSSIAN, MARY KILBOURNE, *Poisons of the Past: Molds, Epidemics, and History* 718
MATSON, CATHY D. AND PETER S. ONUF, *A Union of Interests: Political and Economic Thought in Revolutionary America* 978
MAYNTZ, RENATE AND THOMAS P. HUGHES, Eds., *The Development of Large Technical Systems* 252
MCCRAW, THOMAS K., Ed., *The Essential Alfred Chandler: Essays Toward a Historical Theory of Big Business* 250
MELTZER, ALLAN H., *Keynes's Monetary Theory: A Different Interpretation* 244

MEYER, ANNETTE E., *Evolution of United States Budgeting: Changing Fiscal and Financial Concepts* 990
MILLER, DARLIS A., *Soldiers and Settlers: Military Supply in the Southwest, 1861–1885* 984
MINEAU, GERALDINE P. (See Bean, Lee L.)
MIROWSKI, PHILIP, *Against Mechanism: Protecting Economics from Science* .. 247
MOODY, CARROLL AND ALICE KESSLER-HARRIS, Eds., *Perspectives on American Labor History: The Problems of Synthesis* 761
MORGAN, IWAN W., *Eisenhower Versus 'The Spenders': The Eisenhower Administration, the Democrats and the Budget, 1953–60* 989
MORGAN, PHILIP D. (See Carr, Lois Green)
MORI, GIORGIO, Ed., *Prato: Storia di una città*. Vol. 3, Parts 1 and 2: *Il tempo dell'industria (1815–1943)* 740
MORONE, JOSEPH G. AND EDWARD J. WOODHOUSE, *The Demise of Nuclear Power? Lessons for Democratic Control of Technology* 234
NEUFELDT, LEONARD N., *The Economist: Henry Thoreau and Enterprise* 242
NICHOLAS, STEPHEN, Ed., *Convict Workers: Reinterpreting Australia's Past* ... 745
NIEHANS, JÜRG, *A History of Economic Theory: Classic Contributions, 1720–1980* 773
NUMBERS, RONALD L. AND TODD L. SAVITT, Eds., *Science and Medicine in the Old South* 486
NUSSBAUM, HELGA (See Teichova, Alice)
OFFER, AVNER, *The First World War: An Agrarian Interpretation* 959
OLLERENSHAW, PHILLIP, *Banking in Nineteenth Century Ireland: The Belfast Banks, 1825–1914* 734
ONUF, PETER S. (See Matson, Cathy D.)
ORSER, CHARLES E., JR., *The Material Basis of the Postbellum Tenant Plantation: Historical Archaeology in the South Carolina Piedmont* 219
PALLADINO, GRACE, *Another Civil War: Labor, Capital, and the State in the Anthracite Regions of Pennsylvania, 1840–68* 980
PAUL, ELLEN FRANKEL AND HOWARD DICKMAN, Eds., *Liberty, Property, and Government: Constitutional Interpretation Before the New Deal* 498
PHELAN, CRAIG, *William Green: A Biography of a Labor Leader* 229
PHILLIPS, ANNE, *The Enigma of Colonialism: British Policy in West Africa* 481
POHL, HANS, Ed., *Die Bedeutung der Kommunikation für Wirtschafts und Gesellschaft* 785
POHL, HANS AND WILHELM TREUE, Eds., *The Concentration Process in the Entrepreneurial Economy Since the Late Nineteenth Century* 257
POLLARD, SIDNEY (See Mathias, Peter)
POMFRET, RICHARD, *Unequal Trade: The Economics of Discriminatory International Trade Policies* 507
PRESS, JON, *The Footwear Industry in Ireland, 1922–1973* 736
PRODI, PAOLO (See Kellenbenz, Hermann)
PRYOR, JOHN H., *Geography, Technology, and War: Studies in the Maritime History of the Mediterranean, 649–1571* 186
RANSOM, ROGER L., *Conflict and Compromise: The Political Economy of Slavery, Emancipation, and the American Civil War* 982
RAPPAPORT, STEVE, *Worlds Within Worlds: Structures of Life in Sixteenth-Century London* 457
RASMUSSEN, WAYNE D., *Taking the University to the People: Seventy-five Years of Cooperative Extension* 220
RAWSKI, THOMAS G., *Economic Growth in Prewar China* 966
REINHARDT, NOLA, *Our Daily Bread: The Peasant Question and Family Farming in the Colombian Andes* 485

RIESS, STEVEN A., *City Games: The Evolution of American Urban Society and the Rise of Sports* 487
RODGER, RICHARD, *Housing in Urban Britain, 1780–1914: Class, Capitalism and Construction* 468
ROGOWSKI, RONALD, *Commerce and Coalitions: How Trade Affects Domestic Political Alignments* 509
ROSEN, HARVEY S., Ed., *Fiscal Federalism: Quantitative Studies* 261
ROY, SUBROTO, *Philosophy of Economics: On the Scope of Reason in Economic Inquiry* 775
RUSSO, JEAN B., *Free Workers in a Plantation Economy: Talbot County, Maryland, 1690–1759* 749
RUSSO, JEAN B. (See Carr, Lois Green)
SAVITT, TODD L. (See Numbers, Ronald L.)
SCHOFIELD, ROGER (See Walter, John)
SCHULTZ, STANLEY K., *Constructing Urban Culture: American Cities and City Planning, 1800–1920* 757
SCHULTZE, CHARLES L. (See Litan, Robert E.)
SCHUMPETER, JOSEPH A., *Essays and Entrepreneurs: Innovations, Business Cycles and the Evolution of Capitalism* 246
SCHWARTZ, HERMAN M., *In the Dominions of Debt: Historical Perspectives on Dependent Development* 514
SHAFIR, GERSHON, *Land, Labor and the Origins of the Israeli-Palestinian Conflict, 1882–1914* 480
SHATZMILLER, JOSEPH, *Shylock Reconsidered: Jews, Moneylending, and Medieval Society* 715
SHAW, G. K., *Keynesian Economics: The Permanent Revolution* 777
SLAYTON, ROBERT A. (See Hoch, Charles)
SLICHER VAN BATH, B. H., *Real hacienda y economía en Hispanoamérica, 1541–1820* 971
SMITH, JOAN ET AL., Eds., *Racism, Sexism, and the World-System* 997
SMITH, JOHN KENLY, JR. (See Hounshell, David A.)
SNOWDEN, FRANK M., *Violence and Great Estates in the South of Italy: Apulia, 1900–1922* 743
SOLOW, BARBARA L. AND STANLEY L. ENGERMAN, Eds., *British Capitalism and Caribbean Slavery: The Legacy of Eric Williams* 212
SPANN, EDWARD K., *Brotherly Tomorrows: Movements for a Cooperative Society in America, 1820–1920* 217
SPURLOCK, JOHN C., *Free Love: Marriage and Middle-Class Radicalism in America, 1825–1860* 489
STEEDMAN, IAN, *From Exploitation to Altruism* 777
STEEL, EDWARD M., Ed., *The Speeches and Writings of Mother Jones* 221
STEWART, KENNETH (See De León, Arnoldo)
STONE, ALAN, *Wrong Number: The Breakup of AT&T* 991
SWAIN, JOHN T., *Industry before the Industrial Revolution: North-East Lancashire, c. 1500–1640* 189
TANDETER, ENRIQUE (See Johnson, Lyman L.)
TARR, JOEL A. AND GABRIEL DUPUY, Eds., *Technology and the Rise of the Networked City in Europe and America* 255
TEICHOVA, ALICE, *Wirtschaftsgeschichte der Tschechoslowakei, 1918–1980* 475
TEICHOVA, ALICE, MAURICE LEVY-LEBOYER, AND HELGA NUSSBAUM, Eds., *Historical Studies in International Corporate Business* 781
THORNTON, TAMARA PLAKINS, *Cultivating Gentlemen: The Meaning of Country Life among the Boston Elite, 1785–1860* 979

TILLY, CHARLES (See Haimson, Leopold)
TOLLIDAY, STEVEN AND JONATHAN ZEITLIN, Eds., *The Automobile Industry and its Workers: Between Fordism and Flexibility* 495
TRACY, MICHAEL, *Government and Agriculture in Western Europe, 1880–1988* . 464
TREUE, WILHELM (See Pohl, Hans)
TRUXES, THOMAS M., *Irish-American Trade, 1660–1783* 214
TURNER, JOHN (See Harvey, Charles)
TURTON, ANDREW (See Hart, Gillian)
URIARTE AYO, RAFAEL, *Estructura, desarrollo y crisis de la siderurgia tradicional vizcaína (1700–1840)* 479
VAN DER WEE, HERMAN, Ed., *The Rise and Decline of Urban Industries in Italy and in the Low Countries (Late Middle Ages–Early Modern Times)* 720
VANNINI MARX, ANNA, Ed., *Trasporti e sviluppo economico: Secoli XIII–XVIII* 951
VINES, DAVID (See Currie, David)
WALTER, JOHN AND ROGER SCHOFIELD, Eds., *Famine, Disease and the Social Order in Early Modern Society* 183
WARD, DAVID, *Poverty, Ethnicity, and the American City, 1840–1925: Changing Conceptions of the Slum and the Ghetto* 491
WARREN, KENNETH, *The American Steel Industry, 1850–1970* 764
WATTS, NITA (See Cairncross, Alec)
WEATHERILL, LORNA, *Consumer Behavior and Material Culture in Britain, 1660–1760* 727
WEBB, STEVEN B., *Hyperinflation and Stabilization in the Weimar Republic* ... 473
WEISSBACH, LEE SHAI, *Child Labor Reform in Nineteenth-Century France: Assuring the Future Harvest* 737
WHEELWRIGHT, TED (See Buckley, Ken)
WHITE, BENJAMIN (See Hart, Gillian)
WILKINS, MIRA, *The History of Foreign Investment in the United States to 1914* 754
WILLIAMS, MICHAEL, *Americans and Their Forests: A Historical Geography* .. 975
WILSON, CHARLES REAGAN AND WILLIAM FERRIS, Eds., *Encyclopedia of Southern Culture* 215
WOOD, CHARLES H. AND JOSÉ ALBERTO MAGNO DE CARVALHO, *The Demography of Inequality in Brazil* 973
WOOD, OLIVER, *West Cumberland Coal, 1600–1982/3* 196
WOODHOUSE, EDWARD J. (See Morone, Joseph G.)
WORDIE, J. R. (See Chalklin, C. W.)
YOUNG, JAMES HARVEY, *Pure Food: Securing the Federal Food and Drugs Act of 1906* 767
ZANINELLI, SERGIO, Ed., *Da un sistema agricolo a un sistema industriale. Il comasco dal settecento al novecento.* Vol. II: *La lunga trasformazione tra due crisi (1814–1880)* 953
ZEITLIN, JONATHAN (See Tolliday, Steven)
ZILCH, REINHOLD, *Die Reichsbank und die finanzielle Kriegsvorbereitung 1907 bis 1914* 957

Contributors

Articles are marked (a); notes, discussions, review articles, and dissertation summaries are marked (b); and reviews of books are marked (c).

Accampo, E., 739(c)
Adelman, I., 262(c)
Alston, L. J., 219(c)
Anderson, J., 515(c)
Babson, S., 495(c)
Bandera, V. N., 781(c)
Barbezat, D., 436(b)
Barsky, R. B., 265(a)
Becker, N., 507(c)
Berger, R. M., 457(c)
Berkowitz, E. D., 766(c)
Bernstein, M. A., 407(a), 969(c)
Biddick, K., 948(c)
Black, R. A., 109(a)
Blomquist, T. W., 951(c)
Bogue, A. G., 699(b)
Brandt, L., 807(a)
Brown, J. C., 208(c), 255(c), 591(a)
Brownlee, W. E., 990(c)
Buell, L., 242(c)
Burns, M. R., 985(c)
Cain, L., 757(c)
Calomiris, C. W., 283(a)
Campa, J. M., 677(b)
Campos, J. E. L., 483(c)
Capie, F., 258(c)
Carlos, A. M., 853(a)
Carruthers, B. G., 693(b)
Carter, S. B., 1(a), 997(c)
Chatterji, M., 942(b)
Childs, W. R., 228(c)
Clifton, J. M., 488(c)
Coats, A. W., 994(c)
Cobble, D. S., 996(c)
Cohen, A. J., 240(c)
Colander, D., 241(c)
Cookingham, M. E., 227(c)
Cosgel, M. M., 663(b)
Cowan, R., 234(c), 541(a)
Craig, L. A., 432(b), 987(c)
Crisp, J. E., 762(c)
Cudd, A., 775(c)
Cumbler, J. T., 765(c)
Curtin, P. D., 481(c)
Davis, G. K., 133(a)
De Long, J. B., 265(a)
DeWindt, E. B., 717(c)
Dillard, D., 243(c)
Dotson, J. E., 186(c)
Doucet, M. J., 491(c)
Duggan, E. P., 233(c)
Dupré, R., 339(a), 772(c)
Eichengreen, B., 259(c)
Eltis, D., 521(a), 724(c)
Engerman, S. L., 487(c), 745(c)
Feldman, G. D., 957(c)
Field, A. J., 247(c), 459(c)
Fischbaum, M., 486(c)
Fishman, R., 197(c)
Fitch, N., 202(c)
Flynn, D. O., 721(c)
Freudenberger, H., 194(c)
Friedman, G., 466(c), 761(c)
Friedrichs, C. R., 192(c)
Frost, R. L., 200(c)
Galassi, F. L., 740(c)
Gang, I. N., 494(c)
Garner, R. L., 485(c)
Garrett, M. A., 925(b)
Gilmore, C. G., 109(a)
Gitelman, H. M., 225(c)
Gonzales, M. J., 748(c)
Good, D. F., 475(c), 962(c)
Goodman, A. H., 182(c)
Gootenberg, P., 971(c)
Grab, A. I., 953(c)
Graddy, D., 237(c)
Graham, R. C., 220(c)
Grandy, C., 496(c)
Grantham, G., 463(c), 471(c), 718(c)
Greasley, D., 877(a)
Green, A. G., 501(c)
Green, R. D., 752(c)
Gregory, P. R., 744(c)
Greif, A., 455(c)
Grodin, J. R., 513(c)
Gross, N. T., 67(a)
Haines, M. R., 787(c)
Hamilton, J. S., 456(c)
Hanson, J. R., 260(c)
Harley, C. K., 784(c)
Harrison, M., 569(a)
Hébert, R. F., 502(c)
Heim, C. E., 730(c), 903(a)

Heitman, J. A., 223(c)
Hetherington, B. W., 669(b)
Hiltpold, P., 479(c)
Hoffman, P. T., 444(b)
Holt, M. P., 191(c)
Hood, A. D., 434(b)
Howell, M., 720(c)
Howland, F. M., 226(c)
Howson, S., 960(c)
Huberman, M., 198(c), 683(b)
Hughes, M. L., 473(c)
Humphries, J., 17(a), 729(c)
Hunt, E. S., 149(a)
Irwin, D. A., 509(c)
Isserman, M., 231(c)
Jacoby, D., 511(c)
Jensen, H. E., 504(c)
Johnson, L. C., 963(c)
Kamien, M. I., 246(c)
Kelly, W. J., 743(c)
Khan, B. Z., 363(a)
Khan, M. M., 964(c)
Kindleberger, C. P., 782(c)
Knight, F. W., 747(c)
Kooij, P., 713(c)
Kornblith, G. J., 979(c)
Kussmaul, A., 726(c)
La Croix, S. J., 829(a)
Lambert, R., 232(c)
Langdon, J. L., 714(c)
Langmuir, G. I., 715(c)
Lebergott, S., 254(c)
Lees, L. H., 954(c)
Legler, J. B., 261(c)
Le Goff, T. J. A., 956(c)
Lehning, J. R., 199(c)
Leiby, J., 518(c)
Lepovitz, H. W., 472(c)
Levine, D., 196(c)
Lewis, F. D., 209(c)
Liebowitz, J. J., 464(c)
Libecap, G. D., 767(c)
Limerick, P. N., 984(c)
Lipartito, K., 252(c)
Lorenz, E. H., 732(c)
Lyons, J. S., 189(c)
MacDonald, J. M., 257(c)
Mancall, P. C., 749(c)
Manning, P., 204(c)
Martines, L., 950(c)
Matossian, M. K., 183(c)
May, A. M., 417(a), 989(c)
Mayer, T., 942(b)
McClelland, C. E., 741(c)
McCook, S., 510(c)
McCraw, T. K., 492(c)
McEvoy, A. F., 975(c)
McInnis, R. M., 959(c)
McPherson, J. M., 982(c)
Melton, E., 477(c)
Menard, R. R., 212(c)
Meyer, D. R., 764(c)
Miller, N., 490(c)
Milward, A. S., 203(c)
Miron, J. A., 321(a)
Mitch, D., 428(b)
Mokyr, J., 172(b)
Molho, A., 187(c)
Mongiovi, G., 773(c)
Mormino, G. R., 988(c)
Morris, C. T., 262(b)
Moss, D. J., 734(c)
Mott, T., 777(c)
Nelson, D., 770(c)
Nicholas, S., 853(a)
Niemi, A. W., 785(c)
Novak, S. J., 639(a)
Nye, J. V. C., 172(b), 194(c)
O'Brien, A. P., 936(b)
Officer, L. H., 779(c)
O'Rourke, K., 736(c)
Overton, M., 931(b)
Owen, T. C., 477(c)
Paludan, P. S., 980(c)
Pang, E.-S., 973(c)
Patterson, M., 163(b)
Pecquet, G. M., 133(a)
Perkins, E. J., 214(c)
Platt, H. L., 498(c)
Price, J. M., 462(c)
Radford, G., 468(c)
Rakove, J. N., 978(c)
Ransom, R. L., 444(b)
Redish, A., 789(a)
Reiffen, D., 163(b)
Resnick, S., 503(c)
Roberts, B., 777(c)
Robinson, E., 470(c)
Rock, D., 514(c)
Romer, C. D., 321(a)
Rosen, G., 206(c)
Rosenbloom, J. L., 85(a), 440(b)
Rosenthal, J.-L., 438(b), 615(a)
Rosseger, G., 785(c)
Roumasset, J., 829(a)
Rubin, B. A., 229(c)

Sacks, D. H., 727(c)
Salvucci, R. J., 972(c)
Sands, B., 807(a), 966(c)
Savoca, E., 1(a)
Schiming, R. C., 244(c)
Schneer, J., 961(c)
Schofield, A., 221(c)
Schubert, E. S., 467(c)
Schwaller, J. F., 211(c)
Shiells, M. E., 379(a)
Smith, G. D., 991(c)
Smolensky, E., 236(c)
Snow, M. S., 217(c)
Sokoloff, K. L., 363(a)
Stacey, R. C., 184(c)
Stirling, K. J., 995(c)
Sullivan, R. J., 349(a)
Sundstrom, W. A., 309(a)
Szostak, R., 499(c)
Temin, P., 297(a), 691(b)
Thornton, M. K., 655(b)
Thornton, R. L., 655(b)
Topik, S., 213(c)
Tuma, E. H., 480(c)
Tuttle, C., 737(c)
Ulen, T. S., 222(c)
Urquhart, M. C., 506(c)
Walsh, L. S., 976(c)
Wandersee, W. D., 489(c)
Weiman, D. F., 759(c)
Wetherell, C., 751(c)
Whaples, R., 393(a)
Whatley, W. C., 43(a), 768(c)
Whitten, D. O., 517(c)
Wilson, C. A., 992(c)
Wolcott, S., 442(b)
Wright, G., 215(c)
Wylie, P., 771(c)
Yeager, M., 250(c), 754(c)

STATEMENT OF OWNERSHIP, MANAGEMENT AND CIRCULATION (Required by 39 U.S.C. 3685). 1A. Title of publication: Journal of Economic History (The). 1B. Publication no. 279-580. 2. Date of filing: 9/25/90. 3. Frequency of issue: Quarterly. 3A. No. of issues published annually: Four (4). 3B. Annual subscription price: $60.00. 4. Complete mailing address of known Office of Publication: Cambridge University Press--American Branch, 40 West 20th Street, New York City, New York County, NY 10011. County, NY 10011. 5. Complete mailing address of the headquarters of general business offices of the publisher: Cambridge University Press, Edinburgh Bldg., Staftesbury Rd., Cambridge, CB2 2RU, England. 6. Full names and complete mailing address of publisher, editor and managing editor. Publisher: Cambridge University Press--American Branch, 40 West 20th Street, New York, NY 10011. Editor: Professor Paul Hohenberg, Dept. of Economics, Rensselaer Polytechnic Institute, Troy, NY 12181. Managing Editor: James Alexander, Cambridge University Press--American Branch, 40 West 20th Street, New York, NY 10011. 7. Owner: The Economic History Association, Dept. of History, George Washington University, Washington, DC 20052 (A nonprofit organization). 8. Known bondholders, mortgagees, and other security holders owning or holding 1 percent or more of total amount of bonds, mortgages or other securities: None. 9. Not applicable. or other securities: None. 9. Not applicable. 10. Extent and nature of circulation. Average no. of copies each issue during preceding 12 months: A. Total no. of copies (Net press run): 4172. B. Paid and/or requested circulation: 1. Sales through dealers and carriers, street vendors and counter sales: 0. 2. Mail subscription (Paid and/or requested): 2258 C. Total paid and/or requested circulation: 2258. D. Free distribution by mail, carrier or other means. Samples, complimentary, and other free copies: 19. E. Total distribution: 2277. F. Copies not distributed: 1. Office use, left over, unaccounted, spoiled after printing: 1895. 2. Return from news agents: 0. G. Total 4172. Actual no. of copies of single issue published nearest to filing date: A. Total no. of copies (Net press run): 4218. B. Paid and/or requested circulation: 1. Sales through dealers and carriers, street vendors and counter sales: 0. carriers, street vendors and counter sales: 0. 2. Mail subscription (Paid and/or requested): 2273. C. Total paid and/or requested circulation: 2273. and/or requested circulation: 2273. D. Free distribution by mail, carrier or other means. Samples, complimentary, and other free copies: 19. E. Total distribution: 2292. F. Copies not distributed: 1. Office use, left over, unaccounted, spoiled after printing: 1926. 2. Return from news agents: 0. G. Total 4218. 11. I certify that the statements made by me above are correct and complete. Signature and title: Lynda DiCaprio, Journals Fulfillment Manager, Cambridge University Press.

QUESTIONNAIRE FOR POTENTIAL REVIEWERS

Insofar as possible the Editors will select reviewers from among readers of the JOURNAL. If you are willing to write reviews please fill out and return this form to Thomas Weiss, JOURNAL OF ECONOMIC HISTORY, 211 Watkins Home, Hall Center for the Humanities, the University of Kansas, Lawrence, KS 66045.

Name (last name first): ________________________

Address: ________________________

____

____

____

____

Institutional affiliation (if not in address) and academic status: ________

____

____

____

____

Areas of reviewing competence in economic history (specify country and place): ________________________

____

____

____

____

____

____

Languages other than English in which you have a reading proficiency: ________________________

____

____

____

____

Representative recent publications (maximum of five):

____

____

____

____

____